Praise for *Freedom Betrayed*

"Finally, after waiting for close to half a century, we now have Hoover's massive and impassioned account of American foreign policy from 1933 to the early 1950s. Thanks to the efforts of George H. Nash, there exists an unparalleled picture of Hoover's world view, one long shared by many conservatives. Nash's thorough and perceptive introduction shows why he remains America's leading Hoover scholar."

— JUSTUS D. DOENECKE, author of *Storm on the Horizon: The Challenge to American Intervention, 1939–1941*

"A forcefully argued and well documented alternative to, and critique of, the conventional liberal historical narrative of America's road to war and its war aims. Even readers comfortable with the established account will find themselves thinking that on some points the accepted history should be reconsidered and perhaps revised."

— JOHN EARL HAYNES, author of *Spies: The Rise and Fall of the KGB in America*

"*Freedom Betrayed* offers vivid proof of William Faulkner's famous dictum that "The past is never dead. It's not even past." For those who might think that history has settled the mantle of consensus around the events of the World War II era, Hoover's iconoclastic narrative will come as an unsettling reminder that much controversy remains. By turns quirky and astute, in prose that is often acerbic and unfailingly provocative, Hoover opens some old wounds and inflicts a few new ones of his own, while assembling a passionate case for the tragic errors of Franklin Roosevelt's diplomacy. Not all readers will be convinced, but *Freedom Betrayed* is must-read for anyone interested in the most consequential upheaval of the twentieth century."

— DAVID M. KENNEDY is professor of history emeritus at Stanford University and the author of *Freedom from Fear: The American People in Depression and War, 1929–1945.*

"Herbert Hoover's *Freedom Betrayed* is a bracing work of historical revisionism that takes aim at U.S. foreign policy under President Franklin Delano Roosevelt. Part memoir and part diplomatic history, Hoover's magnum opus seeks to expose the 'lost statesmanship' that, in Hoover's eyes, needlessly drew the United States into the Second World War and, in the aftermath, facilitated the rise to global power of its ideological rival, the Soviet Union. *Freedom Betrayed,* as George Nash asserts in his astute and authoritative introduction, resembles a prosecutor's brief against Roosevelt — and against Winston Churchill as well — at the bar of history. Thanks to Nash's impressive feat of reconstruction, Hoover's 'thunderbolt' now strikes — nearly a half-century after it was readied. The former president's interpretation of the conduct and consequences of the Second World War will not entirely persuade most readers. Yet, as Nash testifies, like the best kind of revisionist history, *Freedom Betrayed* "challenges us to think afresh about our past."

— BERTRAND M. PATENAUDE, author of *A Wealth of Ideas: Revelations from the Hoover Institution Archives*

"What an amazing historical find! Historian George H. Nash, the dean of Herbert Hoover studies, has brought forth a very rare manuscript in *Freedom Betrayed*. Here is Hoover unplugged, delineating on everything from the 'lost statesmanship' of FDR to the Korean War. A truly invaluable work of presidential history. Highly recommended."

> —DOUGLAS BRINKLEY is professor of history at Rice University and editor of
> *The Reagan Diaries.*

"Nearly fifty years after his death, Herbert Hoover returns as the ultimate revisionist historian, prosecuting his heavily documented indictment of US foreign policy before, during, and after the Second World War. Brilliantly edited by George Nash, *Freedom Betrayed* is as passionate as it is provocative. Many no doubt will dispute Hoover's strategic vision. But few can dispute the historical significance of this unique volume, published even as Americans of the twenty-first century debate their moral and military obligations."

> —RICHARD NORTON SMITH is a presidential historian and author, former
> director of several presidential libraries, and current scholar-in-residence at
> George Mason University.

Freedom Betrayed

Herbert Hoover (1874–1964)

Freedom Betrayed

Herbert Hoover's Secret History
of the Second World War
and Its Aftermath

Edited with an Introduction by
George H. Nash

HOOVER INSTITUTION PRESS
Stanford University • Stanford, California

www.hoover.org

Hoover Institution Press Publication No. 598

Hoover Institution at Leland Stanford Junior University,
  Stanford, California, 94305-6010

First printing 2011
18 17 16 15 14 13 12   8 7 6 5 4 3

Manufactured in the United States of America

♾ The paper used in this publication meets the minimum Requirements of the American National Standard for Information Sciences—Permanence of Paper for Printed Library Materials, ANSI/NISO Z39.48-1992.

Library of Congress Cataloging-in-Publication Data
Hoover, Herbert, 1874–1964, author.
Freedom betrayed : Herbert Hoover's secret history of the Second World War and its aftermath / edited with an introduction by George H. Nash.
    p. cm. — (Hoover Institution Press publication ; No. 598)
Includes bibliographical references and index.
ISBN 978-0-8179-1234-5 (cloth : alk. paper) —
ISBN 978-0-8179-1236-9 (e-book)
1. World War, 1939–1945—United States. 2. United States—Foreign relations—1933–1945. 3. United States—Foreign relations—1945–1953.
4. United States—Politics and government—1933–1953. 5. Cold War.
I. Nash, George H., 1945– editor. II. Title. III. Series: Hoover Institution Press publication ; 598.
D769.H68 2011
940.53'73—dc23   2011036861

CONTENTS

[*Illustrations follow pages 54, 526, and 582*]

EDITOR'S ACKNOWLEDGMENTS

IT IS A PLEASURE TO ACKNOWLEDGE and thank the Herbert Hoover Foundation for its support of the *Freedom Betrayed* publication project, including grant support to the Hoover Institution on War, Revolution and Peace for my work as editor. At the Hoover Institution itself, where the bulk of Hoover's Magnum Opus files now reside, the director, John Raisian, and his colleagues Stephen Langlois and Richard Sousa have been unfailingly supportive. At the Hoover Institution Archives, where I spent part of the summer of 2009 as a visiting fellow, I benefited greatly from the expertise and unstinting helpfulness of Linda Bernard and her colleagues, particularly Lyalya Kharitonova, Carol Leadenham, and Nicholas Siekerski—assistance that continued, via telephone and e-mail, until this undertaking was completed. During my weeks in residence at the Hoover Institution, Deborah Ventura and Celeste Szeto efficiently handled the paperwork and arranged for my use of the academic resources of Stanford University.

Although Charles Palm is now retired as director of the Hoover Institution Archives, he and his wife, Miriam, continue to live nearby and to welcome this traveling scholar whenever I visit the neighborhood. I am grateful to Charles for generously sharing his large store of knowledge about Herbert Hoover and for facilitating my work on this project in many ways.

At the Herbert Hoover Presidential Library in Iowa, where a small but valuable cache of Magnum Opus–related material is held, the director, Timothy Walch, and his team have also been enthusiastically supportive. My thanks go particularly to Matt Schaefer for his informative and rapid responses to many queries, and to his colleagues Jim Detlefsen, Spencer Howard, Lynn Smith, and Craig Wright for their help as well. I much appreciate also the information provided by two of the library's interns: Wesley Beck and Mary Kate Schroeder.

My thanks to Bob Clark and Alycia Vivona for locating an interesting document for me at the Franklin D. Roosevelt Library and to Sam Rushay for similar services at the Harry S. Truman Library.

Closer to home, the dedicated reference librarians of Mount Holyoke College helped me locate obscure sources on several occasions. The nearby Five College Library Depository was also useful. The indefatigable interlibrary loan officer at the South Hadley Public Library, Robert Williford, and his able successor, Desirée Smelcer, tracked down several items that I needed to examine.

All this underscores a point that historians understand: archivists and librarians are the unsung facilitators of modern scholarship. Again, my thanks to each individual whose name I have mentioned here.

Research and writing, of course, are only a part of the publishing process. In shepherding Herbert Hoover's Magnum Opus to publication, I have been pleased to work with several individuals at the Hoover Institution Press and the Hoover Institution's media relations office: Jennifer Presley, Marshall Blanchard, Barbara Arellano, Sarah Farber, Shana Farley, Jennifer Navarrette, Julie Ruggiero, Eryn Witcher, and Ann Wood—dedicated professionals all. For proofreading assistance I am grateful to Laurie Gibson and Jennifer Holloway. My thanks to Marci Freeman for preparing the index.

I am grateful to Rebeckah Allgood and the Herbert Hoover Presidential Library Association for permission to quote from several oral histories to which the association holds copyright. I thank Timothy Walch of the Herbert Hoover Presidential Library for permission to quote from the diary of Edgar Rickard in the library's holdings.

Herbert Hoover commenced what became his Magnum Opus more than sixty-five years ago. It seems appropriate to record, in alphabetical order, at least a partial list of those members of his staff, and those of the Hoover Institution staff, who in one way or another assisted him in his arduous labors years ago: Suda L. Bane, Loretta F. Camp, Rita R. Campbell, W. Glenn Campbell, M. Elizabeth Dempsey, Joan Dydo, Julius Epstein, Diana Hirsh, Arthur Kemp, Crone Kernke, Bernice Miller, Hazel Lyman Nickel, Madeline Kelly O'Donnell, Marie Louise W. Pratt, Mary Lou Scanlon, Kay Stalcup, Cynthia Wilder, and Naomi Yeager.

It is also particularly fitting to acknowledge here the late Herbert Hoover III, known to all as "Pete," who passed away several months before this volume went to press. Pete Hoover's interest in his grandfather's legacy—including the Magnum Opus—was keen and unflagging.

During the past year-and-a-half and more, as I worked my way through the myriad complexities of this project, my sister Nancy, a writer herself, was always encouraging.

Finally, and with great pleasure, I thank Jennifer Holloway, who cheerfully and expertly typed virtually every word of the volume before you and helped with other technical tasks as well. It became a magnum opus of her own, well done.

EDITOR'S INTRODUCTION

Herbert Hoover's
Mysterious Magnum Opus

The Blunders of Statesmen

IN NOVEMBER 1951, a public relations executive named John W. Hill met Herbert Hoover at a dinner in New York City. It was an unhappy time in the United States, especially for conservative Republicans. Abroad, the Korean War had turned into a bloody stalemate that President Harry Truman's administration seemed unable to end. Earlier in the year, the president had abruptly dismissed General Douglas MacArthur, a conservative hero, from America's Far Eastern military command, to the consternation of Hoover and millions of others. At home, Truman's liberal Democratic administration was under furious assault from conservative critics of its policies toward communist regimes overseas and communist subversion within our borders.

How quickly the world had changed since the close of the Second World War a few years earlier. Then the future had seemed bright with promise. Nazi Germany and imperial Japan had been crushed; fascism as an ideology had been discredited; the birth of the United Nations had appeared to presage an era of global peace. Now, a mere six years later, in Asia and along the Iron Curtain in Europe, a third world war—this time against communist Russia and China—seemed a distinct possibility.

"Mr. Hoover," said Hill that November evening, "the world is in one hell of a mess, isn't it?"

"It certainly is," Hoover replied.

"It has always occurred to me," Hill continued, "that we are in this mess because of the mistakes of statesmen. Somebody ought to write a book [on the subject] like [E. S. Creasy's] 'Fifteen Decisive Battles of the World'; I think it would be a classic."

"You are absolutely right," Hoover responded. "That should be done, and I am going to tell you what should be the first chapter."

"What is that?" asked Hill.

"When Roosevelt put America in to help Russia as Hitler invaded Russia in June, 1941. We should have let those two bastards annihilate themselves."

Hill was delighted. "That would be a great book. Why don't you write it, Mr. Hoover?"

"I haven't the time," Hoover countered. "Why don't you write it?"[1]

What Hill did not know—and what Hoover, that evening, did not tell him—was that for several years Hoover had been at work on a book with a similar theme: a comprehensive, critical history of American diplomacy between the late 1930s and 1945, with emphasis on the misguided policies of President Roosevelt. It was a volume in which the Roosevelt administration's wartime alliance with the Soviet Union would be subject to withering scrutiny.

Twenty years later, in 1971, in a conversation with an interviewer, Hill lamented that no one had ever written the book he had once proposed to Hoover on "The Fifteen Decisive Blunders of Statesmen." "I have always wished somebody would do it," he added. "It would be controversial because every one of the decisions the author stated would cause trouble, would cause somebody to come up and defend it, and the book would sell like hotcakes."[2]

What Hill did not realize was that nearly eight years earlier Hoover had completed his own book of diplomatic blunders. Unlike the scattershot collection of essays that Hill had envisaged, Hoover's tome was tightly focused. Originally conceived as the section of his memoirs that would cover his life during World War II, the "War Book" (as he called it) had morphed into something far more ambitious: an unabashed, revisionist reexamination of the entire war—and a sweeping indictment of the "lost statesmanship" of Franklin Roosevelt.

Hoover ultimately entitled his manuscript *Freedom Betrayed.* More informally, and with a touch of humor, he and his staff came to refer to it as the Magnum Opus. The label was apt. For nearly two decades, beginning in 1944, the former president labored over his massive manuscript, producing draft after draft, "edition" after "edition." He finished the final version (save for some minor editing and additional fact-checking) in September 1963 and prepared in the ensuing months for the book's publication. Death came first, on October 20, 1964. A little over two months earlier, he had turned ninety years old.

After Hoover's passing, his heirs decided not to publish his Magnum Opus. Since then, for nearly half a century, it has remained in storage, unavailable for examination.

This volume, *Freedom Betrayed*—in its final, author-approved edition of 1963–64—is the book that is now in your hands. It is published here—and its contents thereby made available to scholars—for the first time.

To the handful of historians who have written about it (sight unseen) since the 1960s, Hoover's Magnum Opus has long been a source of mystery. The manuscript's inaccessibility has only heightened their puzzlement. Why, at age seventy, did Hoover undertake this daunting project? Why did he pursue it with such tenacity and zeal? How did he conceptualize his work and conduct his research? On whom did he rely for assistance and advice? Why, toward the end of his life, did he refer to his manuscript as "top secret"? Why, in short, was it so supremely important to him, and why was it not published immediately after his death?

Above all, what did the mysterious Magnum Opus actually say—about Franklin Roosevelt, about World War II, about Hoover himself?

The answer to this last question is now easy: it is contained in the text of the volume before you. The answers to the other questions are not so easy and are provided later on in this introduction.

The Background: Franklin Roosevelt's "Lost Statesmanship"

To understand the history of Hoover's Magnum Opus project, we need to know its prehistory: the context out of which the text eventually emerged.

When Herbert Hoover left the White House on March 4, 1933, he did not, like most ex-presidents before him, fade away. After a period of self-imposed quiescence at his home in California, he burst back into the political arena in the autumn of 1934 with a best-selling book entitled *The Challenge to Liberty*. It was a forceful, philosophical critique of the ascendant statist ideologies of the 1930s: Nazism, fascism, communism, socialism, and "regimentation"—his term for Franklin Roosevelt's New Deal.[3] To Hoover, FDR's policies were no mere grab bag of moderate measures designed to reform and "save capitalism" but rather a dangerous, collectivist assault on the traditional American system of ordered liberty. "The impending battle in this country," Hoover told a friend in 1933, would be between "a properly regulated individualism" and "sheer socialism."[4] For the rest of his life, he resisted without stint the lurch to the Left initiated by his successor.

Hoover soon became Roosevelt's most formidable critic from the political Right. Once upon a time, the former president had actually thought of himself—and had been perceived by many others—as a Progressive Republican in the tradition of Theodore Roosevelt, not Calvin Coolidge. In the tempestuous political atmosphere of the mid-1930s, as the nation's political center of gravity veered leftward, Hoover found that his point d'appui had changed. Increasingly, he termed his political philosophy "historic liberalism" and lambasted the regimenting "false liberalism" of the New Deal. "The New Deal," he said in 1937, "having corrupted the label of liberalism for collectivism, coercion, [and] concentration of political power, it seems 'Historic Liberalism' must be conservatism in contrast."[5] The onetime Bull Moose Progressive had become a man of the Right.

Although Hoover himself would never publicly admit it, from 1934 (if not sooner) he hankered for a rematch against Roosevelt at the polls.[6] Denied this opportunity in 1936, the former president persisted in firing verbal fusillades at New Deal liberalism and its perpetrators in an endless string of public addresses from coast to coast.[7]

Early in 1938 the ex-president's crusade against the New Deal began to shift focus. In Europe, Nazi Germany under Adolf Hitler and fascist Italy under Benito Mussolini were ominously restless. Farther east, the Soviet Union under Joseph Stalin was purging the highest echelons of Communist Party officialdom and sending millions of ordinary citizens to slave labor camps. In Spain, the Nationalists under General Francisco Franco, backed by Italy and Germany, were slowly winning a civil war against a leftist government dominated by Moscow. From afar, Europe had begun to look like a pressure cooker whose cover might fly off at any time.

Hoover had never been a conventional isolationist. Hailed as the Great Humanitarian for his prodigious relief work during and after World War I—labors that had saved literally tens of millions of people from privation and death—in 1920 he had favored America's ratifying the Treaty of Versailles and joining the League of Nations. It was a necessary step, he contended, toward restoring shattered Europe to prosperity and political stability. A decade later, as president of the United States from 1929 to 1933, he had vigorously promoted international disarmament conferences and multilateral initiatives to end the Great Depression. But Hoover had spent too much time in Europe before and during the Great War to believe that the United States could redeem the Old World from its age-old rivalries and hatreds. As war clouds began to form over Europe in 1938, he deliberately pulled back from that seething cauldron—just as, to his growing dismay, the current occupant of the White House moved in the opposite direction.

In a nationally broadcast speech on January 15, 1938, Hoover outlined a set of U.S. "policies for peace" for the years ahead. Americans, he declared, must "fight for our independence to the last shred of our material and physical strength" and must be prepared to defend ourselves against attack. This was our "greatest assurance from aggression against us." Americans should, however, "limit our arms solely to repel aggression against the Western Hemisphere" and otherwise "preserve our neutrality." We must not "engage ourselves to use military force in endeavor to prevent or end other people's wars." Nor should we "join any economic sanctions or embargoes or boycotts to prevent or end other people's wars." Instead, Americans should energetically "cooperate" with other nations in efforts to promote the world's "economic and social welfare." We should also cooperate, "by every device and on every opportunity," to "exert moral force" and "build pacific agencies" for the preservation of peace and resolution of conflicts in the world.[8]

Hoover's speech was not, in the most literal sense, isolationist—a label he seemed anxious to avoid. (Isolation, he told his audience, was an "illusion.") Nor, despite his Quaker religious background and upbringing, was his "policy for peace" categorically pacifistic. What it was—and would resolutely remain until December 7, 1941—was anti-interventionist. We Americans, he had just declaimed, should go to war *solely* to defeat aggression against us in our self-proclaimed zone of safety, the Western Hemisphere. Otherwise, we must refrain from military embroilment in foreign disputes.

Hoover's aversion to overseas military entanglements had many sources: in his perception—going back to his pre-1914 mining engineering days based in London—that the Old World and the New had developed radically different civilizations "that had grown 300 years apart"[9]; in his glimpses of the horrific Battle of the Somme on the western front in World War I, while he was administering relief to German-occupied Belgium; in his disillusioning encounters with European "power politics" throughout and after that terrible war; in his fear that contemporary Europe was sinking into a morass of illiberalism; and in his carefully distilled political philosophy of American exceptionalism, articulated in his 1922 book *American Individualism.* Hoover's anti-interventionism was also rooted in what he perceived as the baneful, *domestic* lessons from the recent Great War. One such lesson, he told his radio audience, was that "the victors suffer almost equally with the vanquished" in economic misery and "spiritual degradation." Indeed, he prophesied, if the United States, with its current level of national debt, should have to finance another great war, the result would be inflation so virulent that it "would confiscate the savings of all of their present holders."[10]

Perhaps "the most important of all these lessons," Hoover added, was that "democratic government now, and for many years to come, probably could not stand the shock of another great war and survive as a democracy." Before long he would assert that any war fought by America against fascism would require fascistic methods. At the beginning of 1938, he put it only slightly less starkly: "Those who would have us again go to war to save democracy might give a little thought to the likelihood that we would come out of any such struggle a despotism ourselves."[11]

Less than a month after uttering these admonitions, Hoover sailed to Europe for his first visit there since 1919. For the next several weeks, citizens and governments in western and central Europe showered him with honors for his unparalleled humanitarian achievements during and after the Great War. He received so many honorary degrees and medals that he lost count.[12] Ostensibly Hoover was traveling in response to formal invitations from Belgium and other countries eager to express their gratitude and affection. In fact, he had been angling for such a journey for some time, not for the accolades (although he surely enjoyed them) but for the opportunity such a tour would give him to observe European social and political conditions. It is also possible that, with political ambition still burning unquenched inside him, he saw his fact-finding trip as a way to burnish his credentials as a statesman. In any case, by the time he was done in late March, he had conversed with the rulers and governing elites of a dozen nations and had received audiences with Adolf Hitler and Neville Chamberlain.

Hoover's nearly seven-week European sojourn—during which Nazi Germany annexed Austria—loomed large in his eventual Magnum Opus, in which he described the experience in copious detail. Particularly revealing for insight into his developing geopolitical vision was his interview with Prime Minister Neville Chamberlain of Great Britain on March 22. According to Hoover's later account of this meeting to a close friend, he told the British leader bluntly that another world war would probably destroy the British empire and that war must be avoided if at all possible. To accomplish this objective (he advised), the expansionist urges of Nazi Germany must be accommodated to some extent. Germany was a "virile nation" (he told Chamberlain), which felt itself to be "in a cage" encircled by France and its allies. In the opinion of the American ex-president, Germany would remain a "menace" so long as this "cage" existed.

Hoover was convinced, however, that, if "given a certain freedom," Germany would not cause trouble in western Europe. He did not believe that Germany intended to attack in the West. Just back from his conversations with Hitler and other European leaders, Hoover opined that Germany was now looking eastward, toward the Ukraine, and that its pressure in that direction should not concern the British. According to Hoover, Neville Chamberlain concurred.[13]

If anything, Hoover had been even more emphatic. According to what he later claimed were his contemporary notes of his conversation with Chamberlain, he told the prime minister that the Germans were "the most virile people in the Continent"—a "land people" (not a "sea people") whose "face" had now "turned east." An explosion involving Germany was bound to happen "somewhere," Hoover asserted. He had a "hunch" that "another Armageddon is coming, and my hope is that if it comes it will be on the Plains of Russia, not on the Frontiers of France." "Western Civilization," he added, "will be infinitely better off if the Germans fight in the east instead of the west. It would be a disaster if the western Democracies were dragged down by a war the end result of which would be to save the cruel Russian despotism." According to Hoover, Chamberlain agreed completely with his guest's "hunch."[14]

Privately, then—or so he later asserted in his Magnum Opus—by March 1938 Hoover was convinced that a major European war was now certain, although not, he thought, for at least another eighteen months.[15] Publicly he seemed somewhat more sanguine. "I do not believe a widespread war is at all probable in the near future," he informed the London press on March 18.[16] Arriving back in New York City some days later, he professed to see "no immediate prospect of war."[17] "The spirit abroad is one of defense, not of offense," he said; there was "always a chance to avoid war despite the preparations."[18]

Hoover's cautiously worded optimism could not conceal his apprehension. In a public address on radio across the United States on March 31, 1938, he painted a disturbing portrait of the "forces now in motion" in Europe: "the rise of dictatorships" with "so-called Planned Economies"; a "feverishly" growing arms race; "increased governmental debts and deficits"; economic protectionism; a League of Nations "in a coma"; and more. Fear was omnipresent, he reported, and along with it growing "brutality," "terrorism," "[c]oncentration camps, persecution of Jews, political trials," and other marks of "an underlying failure of morals." Hoover took special note of the illiberal ideology of fascism as he had just experienced it in Nazi Germany: a "gigantic spartanism" embracing "a sort of mysticism based on theories of racialism and nationalism." Although Hoover had "no doubt that fascism will fail sometime" ("just as Marxian socialism has failed already"), he also had no doubt that this time was far off. "[L]et no one believe," he warned, that fascism "is about to collapse."

What, then, should Americans do about this "maze of forces" now ensnaring the Old World? Hoover's answer was unequivocal: Americans should "harden our resolves" to "keep out of other people's wars," and we should convince Europe "that this is our policy." We must not pursue "collective action" with the European democracies—something Franklin Roosevelt had recently hinted at in a speech calling for "quarantining" aggressive nations. A U.S. alliance with Great Britain and France against Germany and Italy, said Hoover, not only would embroil us in British "imperial problems" and France's alliance with Communist Russia but would foster "the worst thing that can happen to civilization": "the building up of a war between government faiths or ideologies," with the attendant "hideous elements" of wars of religion.

"We should have none of it," Hoover thundered. "If the world is to keep the peace, then we must keep peace with dictatorships as well as with popular governments. The forms of government which other people pass through in working out their destinies is not our business. We can never herd the world into the paths of righteousness with the dogs of war."

Instead of throwing our military and economic might behind schemes for "preserving peace by making war," Hoover proposed that Americans mobilize "the collective moral forces to prevent war." The "greatest force for peace is still the public opinion of the world," he averred. And the "national mission" of the United States at the present time was plain. In a world where fascistic zealots and "planned economies" were extinguishing individual liberty, America must "keep alight the lamp of true liberalism" at home. The "greatest service that this nation can give to the future of humanity," he concluded, was to "revitalize" and purify our own democracy, "insist upon intellectual honesty," and "keep out of war."[19]

One of Hoover's purposes in making this address, he confided to a friend, was to bring "our people to a realization that we must live with other nations."[20] In the months ahead, he found repeated occasions to drive home his message. On April 8, 1938, he asked an audience in San Francisco to imagine what it would be like if California were living under current "conditions on the Continent" of Europe. Imagine that "500,000 troops and 2,000 aeroplanes" were "looking at us hatefully from over the Oregon line." Imagine "another 400,000 men and 2,000 planes ready to march over the Nevada line" and several hundred thousand more being drilled in Arizona and "ready to pounce upon us." Imagine having to pay taxes "for about 400,000 men in our own State to make faces at these sister States." Imagine if every Californian were required to own a gas mask. Imagine—if the Golden State were "an up-to-date authoritarian state"—the presence on its soil of concentration camps and other forms of repression. "Altogether," Hoover concluded, "I am glad Europe is still 7,200 miles from California."[21]

Although Hoover was cognizant of "the dangers to free men" inherent in the new racialism stirring in Europe, he insisted that America itself had nothing militarily to fear. "There is not the remotest chance that our national independence will be challenged from abroad," he told his California listeners.[22] What did disturb him was the *intellectual* and *economic* turn toward collectivism in Europe—and signs that this "new philosophy of government and life" had begun to penetrate the United States. Hoover had alluded to this in his speech on March 31: "If our own so-called planned economy is not an infection from the original stream of fascism it is at least a remarkable coincidence."[23] A week later, in San Francisco, he returned to this theme. At least a dozen other nations in Europe, he declared, together containing nearly 300,000,000 people, had abandoned liberty and "popular government" for authoritarian rule. In every case, he claimed, they had done so after compromising "true liberalism" with socialism or "government dictation" of the private sector. In every case, they had "tried various breeds of Planned Economy." The ensuing "fear," loss of "confidence," sapping of private "initiative," "depressions," and "panics" had led to "chaos" and a willingness by the populace to surrender "all liberty to the State to save themselves." For Hoover, the lesson of recent European history was clear. "Western civilization," he lectured, "does not turn to socialism or communism [in such circumstances]. They [*sic*] turn invariably to fascism."

Could such a denouement be on the horizon here? In the early months of 1938, the struggling U.S. economy unexpectedly slid back into a deep recession. Unemployment, already high, soared to levels unseen since 1933. To an anxious Hoover, there appeared to be an "uncanny parallel" between the measures Franklin Roosevelt was taking in the name of a planned economy and the "steps . . . which had bred the sort of chaos in Europe from which Fascism sprang."

> I do not say that our economic system has been brought to this dangerous point where Fascism is its destination. But with all the solemnity I can command I do say that the direction that we are going in today is precisely that which in the end creates the demoralization from which Fascism invariably springs.[24]

The former president was determined to thwart such a calamity with every fiber of his being. During the next seven months, as America's midterm elections drew nearer, he unleashed a blistering barrage of criticism of the administration in Washington. He charged that America was suffering "a moral recession in government"—a direct result, he said, of the Roosevelt administration's flagrant misuse of patronage, budgetary trickery, propaganda, and "repulsive" demonization of the New Deal's opponents—to the point that our very system of self-government was in danger.[25] He asserted that America was on the path of "creeping collectivism," a direction inimical to "liberty itself." In just nineteen years, he said, more than a dozen nations of Europe had taken that treacherous course. "They all undertook New Deals under some title" and step by step had given up their liberty. These "great human laboratories" in Europe—democratic no longer—had proven once again "that economic and political freedom are organically connected."[26] He accused the New Dealers of advocating "the very gospel of dictatorship": the evil notion that the ends justify the means—"That is, if you can get away with it."[27]

On November 8, 1938, Hoover's philippics, and those of his allies, bore fruit at the polls: the Republican Party scored sweeping election victories. Meanwhile, that autumn, Europe had narrowly averted an appointment with catastrophe. Like most other Americans—including, briefly, Franklin Roosevelt[28]—Hoover appeared to approve the peaceful outcome of the Munich conference on September 29–30, 1938, at which the British and French governments agreed to Hitler's seizure of the German-speaking Sudetenland from Czechoslovakia.[29] In return, Hitler signed a brief communiqué (prepared by Neville Chamberlain) affirming Germany and Britain's "desire . . . never to go to war with one another again." On arriving back in London, a jubilant Neville Chamberlain held the paper aloft as signifying "peace for our time."

Initially, Herbert Hoover was not so sure.[30] But in an address in New York City on October 26, he declared that, whatever the Munich agreement's flaws, "we can at least conclude that some immediate strains have been appeased, and that war is today more remote." There were still "forces of peace in Europe," he said, and one was "of superlative value": "The democratic statesmen of Europe are determined to give the healing processes of peace a chance."

But if war between the western European democracies and "the despotisms" should nevertheless come, Hoover added, the United States should not join in. "Free economic life is not built on war," he asserted; mobilization for a "major war" would turn our country into "practically a Fascist government" with restraints on "personal liberty" that might not be lifted "for generations." Furthermore, American intervention in such a conflict would ultimately be futile: "We can make war but we do not and cannot make peace in Europe"—a continent plagued with "mixed populations," contested borders, and animosities stretching back a thousand years. Nor was there any "clear call of liberty from Europe" in its present balance of forces. If America were to ally itself with France, for instance, it would willy-nilly find itself on the side of France's unsavory ally, "dictatorial Russia." For all these reasons (and more), Hoover concluded that America would best "serve the world" and "liberty itself" by staying aloof from European wars.

If it did, he reassured his listeners, it had nothing to fear. The totalitarian regimes of Germany, Italy, and Japan did not "threaten our safety." Protected by the "frontier fortifications" of the Atlantic and Pacific Oceans, America was dominant in the Western Hemisphere and could expect to remain so. More subtly, Hoover perceived in the behavior of the European fascist states not simply ideological "aggressiveness" but assertiveness of another sort: an economic drive for relief for their people from "shortages of food and materials"— a drive that could not be sated by waging war on Britain and France. For the first time in public, Hoover advanced the pivotal geopolitical argument that he had made to Neville Chamberlain several months before: that the "faces" of Germany and its allies were directed toward expansion in eastern Europe. "Certainly it is my belief," said Hoover on October 26, 1938, "that neither Germany nor the Fascist states want war with the Western democracies unless these democracies interfere with their spread eastward."

To Hoover the "lines of least resistance" for the totalitarian nations of Europe were "not westward," which for him was part of the significance of the conference at Munich. What had transpired there was not just the cession of the Sudetenland to Hitler's Reich but the "removal of impediments to the eastward movement." It was a development that Hoover seemed to view with equanimity.[31]

The former president was therefore taken aback when, just a few months later, the government of Neville Chamberlain abruptly reversed itself and tried to block Hitler's Drang nach Osten. On March 15, 1939, the armies of Nazi Germany invaded what remained of Czechoslovakia after the German seizure of the Sudetenland region the previous October. The stunned and weakened Czechs did not resist. In the United States, Hoover publicly expressed his "indignation" at the Germans' "shameless" and immoral action and predicted that this "wrong" would someday be righted. The Czech "race," he said, "will emerge again from bondage."[32]

Until the spring of 1939, Adolf Hitler's ambitions on the continent had arguably been focused on incorporating nearby Germanic populations into the Fatherland and on rectifying the "injustice" of the Treaty of Versailles. His brazen conquest and dismemberment of Czechoslovakia—a non-Germanic state—exposed the falsity of that analysis. Intoxicated with his latest triumph, Hitler ratcheted up the pressure on neighboring Poland over the status of the so-called Polish Corridor (separating Germany from East Prussia) and of the German-dominated Free City of Danzig (mostly surrounded by Polish territory). Almost as quickly, and far more unexpectedly, the British and French governments now decided to rein him in. On March 31, 1939, Prime Minister Neville Chamberlain solemnly informed the House of Commons that during the present round of diplomatic consultations, "in the event of any action which clearly threatened Polish independence and which the Polish Government accordingly considered it vital to resist with their national forces, His Majesty's Government would feel themselves bound at once to lend the Polish Government all support in their power."[33] France concurred. In plain English, the British and French governments had pledged to go to war against Germany if Germany attacked Poland.

To Hoover, the Anglo-French volte-face was "utterly astonishing"—"a complete reversal" of their previous policy "to let Hitler go east if he wants to." "They cannot in any circumstance protect Poland from invasion by Hitler," he told a friend. "It is simply throwing the body of Western Civilization in front of Hitler's steam-roller which is on its way to Russia."[34]

Hoover now feared that a European "debacle" was in the offing, although he "naturally hope[d]" that Chamberlain would succeed in his "new undertaking."[35] Probably "the only thing that will keep us out of war is the British," he remarked privately in mid-April. "They have sanity. They do not want to go to war. And they are today the only outstandingly skillful group of world diplomats."[36] But Hoover never overcame his initial feeling that, by issuing its fateful guarantee to Poland, the British had committed a "gigantic blunder"—the greatest in their history.[37] They had gotten in the way of "the inevitable war between Hitler and Stalin."[38] This was where Neville Chamberlain went wrong, Hoover later told friends.[39] The perceived folly of the Polish guarantee was one of the intellectual linchpins of his Magnum Opus.[40]

The problems with Neville Chamberlain's diplomacy, then—in Hoover's eyes—was not that the British prime minister had tried to appease Germany but that he had stopped. Before long Hoover would argue that, far from deterring Adolf Hitler's aggressive tendencies, the Polish guarantee had goaded Hitler into turning west, against the democracies—a direction that Hoover believed the Nazi dictator had never intended to go.[41]

But why had Chamberlain so precipitously reversed course? According to Hoover, in a private letter at the end of March, there were only three possible "rational" explanations: "first, Chamberlain is trying to prove he is not an appeaser; second, Britain and France are bluffing; or third, they are depending upon American help."[42]

The third hypothesis provided the key to the next phase of Hoover's anti-interventionism. Up to the end of 1938, his addresses on world affairs had been heartfelt but largely hypothetical, concentrating on why America should stay out of a foreign war if one should erupt. Early in 1939 his pronouncements on foreign policy acquired a new and sharper edge. Increasingly, the former president sensed a threat to America's peace and well-being not in Berlin but in Washington, in the devious, meddlesome diplomacy of Franklin Roosevelt.

In his State of the Union message to Congress on January 4, 1939, President Roosevelt bluntly discussed the "storm signals" now flaring "from across the seas." Amid a stirring summons to national unity and robust rearmament, Roosevelt injected a warning signal of his own. The "God-fearing democracies of the world," he declared, "cannot forever let pass, without effective protest, acts of aggression against sister nations—acts which automatically undermine all of us."

> Words may be futile, but war is not the only means of commanding a decent respect for the opinions of mankind. There are many methods short of war, but stronger and more effective than mere words, of bringing home to aggressor governments the aggregate sentiments of our own people.
>
> At the very least, we can and should avoid any action, or any lack of action, which will encourage, assist or build up an aggressor.[43]

Reading these words, Herbert Hoover scented trouble. In a nationwide radio broadcast on February 1, 1939, he accused Roosevelt of announcing a portentous "new departure" from the nation's traditional approach to foreign affairs. "He says we must use methods stronger than words and short of war," said Hoover. It was a "new policy" of direct or indirect "coercion" that could lead us straight to war. "Our foreign policies in these major dimensions must be determined by the American people and the Congress, not by the President alone," he pronounced, and he asked:

1. Shall we reverse our traditional policies at this time?
2. Shall we set ourselves up to determine who the aggressor is in the world?

3. Shall we engage in embargoes, boycotts, economic sanctions against aggressor nations?
4. Shall we do this where the Western Hemisphere is not attacked?
5. Shall we provide an armament greater than that necessary to protect the Western Hemisphere from military invasion?
6. Shall we take collective action with other nations to make these more-than-words-and-short-of-war policies effective?
7. Are we to be the policeman of the world?

To Hoover the answer to each of these questions was "an emphatic no."

The ex-president denied that the United States faced any "imminent dangers," either ideological or military, from "aggressive nations." "Ideas cannot be cured with battleships or airplanes," he asserted; "I am confident that if the lamp of liberty can be kept alight [at home] these ideologies will yet die of their own falsity." Nor need America fear military attack from overseas. The "faces" of the totalitarian states were turned in other directions, and every one of these states suffered "grave internal weakness." To think that Germany, Italy, Russia, or Japan "or all of them together" had "the remotest idea" of attacking the Western Hemisphere was, in Hoover's words, "sheer hysteria."[44]

What was not fanciful to Hoover was the rising specter that America's own president, by imprudent acts or—even worse—by design, might take the nation into the bloody morass of a European war. At first Hoover was inclined to believe that Roosevelt was whipping up a war scare to distract Americans from the "total domestic failure" of his administration.[45] But as the months passed, Hoover's suspicions grew darker. He became convinced that Roosevelt and his diplomatic henchmen (especially Ambassador William C. Bullitt) were secretly encouraging Great Britain, France, and Poland to stand up to Germany and possibly promising to come to their rescue if war broke out. It was a theme he later developed, with supporting evidence, in his Magnum Opus. "I do not believe for one moment that these democracies are in any danger of attack from Germany or Italy," Hoover confided to a friend on July 18, 1939. "I am convinced it is Roosevelt's action which has stirred public opinion in France and England into the abandonment of the appeasement policy and into aggressive lines." By doing so, Roosevelt had "measurably advanced the possibilities of war in the world, and the end of that war to save democracy will be that there will be no democracy in the world."[46]

What Roosevelt should have done, Hoover had intimated to friends a few months earlier, was to have stayed away from the European imbroglios and readied himself to enter the world stage "at the proper moment" as a mediator, breaking the European "stalemate" "around a council table." That would have been a great "contribution to peace in this generation." If only Roosevelt "had maintained at least the tone of Chamberlain in this situation, he might have been able to be of great service to the world."[47]

Instead, on April 15, 1939, Roosevelt had sent Adolf Hitler a sensational cable, released in Washington before its delivery, asking Hitler to pledge to refrain from attacking thirty specified nations for the next ten years at least. If Hitler agreed, Roosevelt promised that the United States would seek "reciprocal assurances" toward Germany from these thirty countries and would promote speedy diplomatic "discussions" leading toward disarmament and the opening up of international trade on an equitable basis.[48] Hitler did not agree. In a lengthy diatribe to the Reichstag on April 28, he scathingly mocked Roosevelt's appeal.[49]

To Hoover, writing a week before Hitler's public rebuff of FDR, the president's appeal was "a publicity stunt at best," intended to "create propaganda among the dictator states." If Roosevelt had truly wanted to "effect a result," Hoover grumbled, "he should not have insulted the people whom he addressed." His gesture was "not very conducive to their accepting of the President of the United States as a mediator in so desperate a situation as this."[50]

Day by day it was becoming more apparent to Hoover—and a source of growing bitterness—that the man in the White House wanted "to join in the mess" in Europe.[51] "In my view, the greatest contribution that can be made today is to convince these people [the Europeans] that we are not going to help the making of war," Hoover remarked in late July.[52] Determined to block FDR if he could, Hoover urged Congress in early April to act to prevent our "engaging in European power politics" or in "warlike acts of the economic type" without congressional approval.[53] A week later, writing in *Liberty* magazine, he charged Roosevelt by name with launching a "radical departure" in American foreign policy and warned that "[a]ny such change should be frankly submitted to and confirmed by the American people."[54] In foreign policy as well as domestic, Hoover now saw a challenge to liberty arising from unconstrained executive power.

In the August issue of *American Magazine* the former president intensified his attack. In an article provocatively entitled "Should We Send Our Youth to War?" he now alleged that the "dangers of our being dragged into war" came from three directions: "foreign propaganda" inflaming our emotions and minds; "preachments of our mistaken officials and citizens" in support of this propaganda; and "[s]teps taken by our own government which, while denying that they are intended to take us into war, yet entangle us with these very controversies, the end of which may be war." Pleading with his fellow Americans to avoid the thicket of European discord, Hoover openly accused Roosevelt of leaping right in. "He has joined the chessboard of Europe," Hoover asserted. "He lines us up in the balance of power"—a condition fraught with mortal peril.

"We as a people can keep out of war in Europe," Hoover claimed, "if we have the resolute will to do so." Unfortunately, our will could be "insidiously undermined by sitting in the game of European power politics."

> The first thing required is a vigorous, definite statement from all who have responsibility [including Roosevelt], that we are not going to war with anybody in Europe unless they attack the Western Hemisphere. The second thing is not to sit in the game of power politics.
>
> These are the American policies that will make sure that we do not send our youth to Europe for war.[55]

Yet if Hoover for a host of reasons rejected American military intervention in the Old World, he was not indifferent to the humanitarian tragedy that was already beginning to unfold. Like nearly all Americans, he was appalled by the anti-Jewish pogrom known as "Kristallnacht" that erupted in Nazi Germany during November 9–10, 1938. In that night and day of terror, organized Nazi mobs smashed Jewish property across the Reich. Scores of Jews were killed; thirty thousand more were arrested and sent to concentration camps; more than seven thousand Jewish-owned businesses and two hundred synagogues were damaged or destroyed. The western world recoiled in shock and horror. A few days later, Herbert Hoover joined five other prominent Americans in a special nationwide radio broadcast condemning what Hoover called "this outrage"—"an outbreak of intolerance which has no parallel in human history."[56] A week later, he termed it "the most hideous persecution of the Jews since the expulsion from Spain in the Middle Ages."[57]

Nor did Hoover stop at merely verbal denunciation. Early in 1939 he helped the president of Harvard University raise money to place German-Jewish refugee scholars in American academic institutions.[58] He warmly endorsed the Wagner-Rogers bill, which would waive America's immigration quota vis-à-vis Germany and permit the admission of 20,000 German (Jewish) refugee children to the United States.[59] He listened avidly that spring to word from friends that the Roosevelt administration was trying to effect an international plan to settle European Jewish refugees in British east Africa—and that Roosevelt considered Hoover the best man to administer the colonization project. Hoover was receptive; "I add my entire collection of fingers and toes to those that are to be crossed," he told his intimate friend Lewis Strauss.[60] Unfortunately, World War II soon intervened, and the scheme came to naught.[61]

Meanwhile, in July, the Great Humanitarian announced a "concrete proposal" for "constructive action" to "mitigate the barbarities" of a future war. The man who had fed millions of Europeans between 1914 and the early 1920s now proposed that all nations "willing to do so" should agree not to attack food ships in wartime and not to bomb civilian populations. Food vessels, he declared, "should go freely," and bombing should target only armies, navies, and munitions works. To enforce the agreement, Hoover would have neutral nations serve as "referees" whose "good will" (he argued) would be eagerly sought by belligerents. Drawing on his experience feeding German-occupied Belgium in World War I, Hoover urged that a commission of neutral nations manage the delivery of food to any blockaded country. Similarly, "neutral observers" should be stationed in belligerent countries to "determine the facts of any killing of civilians from the air."[62]

Hoover's suggestions had little discernible impact on world leaders.[63] Nor did his growing revulsion at fascist and communist totalitarianism shake his convictions on how best to deal with them. "My sympathies are with the democracies," he declared in July 1939. "But the democracies of Western Europe have the resources to defend themselves." Even if they should fall (which he did not believe would happen), "the exhaustion of the dictators" would compel them to "leave us alone for a quarter of a century at least." Moreover, the "whole totalitarian structure "under the dictator states was "weakening." Their very brutality and repression of liberty were giving rise to opposition within their borders. The "vicious persecution of Jews and other religious groups" had "raised the hate of the world" against them. The Nazi, fascist, and communist regimes were "failing to produce the standards of living they have promised." Oppressive government, Hoover seemed to say, could not endure forever: "People who have known liberty will yet regain it for themselves."[64]

And always, through the gathering gloom, Hoover clung to his conception of America as a redeemer nation—peaceful, humane, and politically neutral—holding the "light of liberty" and "standards of decency" in the world. A nation devoted to law, economic cooperation, moral influence, reduction of armament, and relief for victims of persecution: a nation that could be "of service to the world." All this, he feared, would be jeopardized if America became a belligerent, turned itself into a "totalitarian state" to "fight effectively," and thereby sacrificed its own liberty "for generations."[65]

On August 22, 1939, Nazi Germany and the Soviet Union—hitherto the bitterest of ideological enemies—shocked the world by signing a nonaggression pact (whose secret clauses carved up Eastern Europe between them). With his eastern flank secure, Hitler was now free to turn on Great Britain and France if they dared interfere with his designs on Poland. In the last days of August, Hoover, in California, searched anxiously for signs that the European democracies might yet come to terms with Hitler over his latest demands. Hitler seemed willing to "hold to a compromise" on Danzig "to which I think the world would concede," said Hoover, and to "some connection across the Polish Corridor." To Hoover the Nazi dictator's "demands" on these points "would not seem to be impossible of solution if it were not for the background of [Germany's] seizure of Prague [Czechoslovakia] which leaves the whole world without any confidence." In fact, Hoover contended, "divested of the Prague background, this is no issue for Europe to go to war about."[66]

By now, of course, the "Prague background"—not to mention the Anglo-French promise to support Poland if it were attacked—was too conspicuous for anyone in Europe to ignore. And Adolf Hitler's ambitions far transcended such comparative trivialities as the status of Danzig. On September 1, 1939, Hitler's armies invaded neighboring Poland without warning. Two days later, Great Britain and France declared war on Nazi Germany. On September 17, the armies of Soviet Russia invaded Poland from the east. By the end of the month, the Polish state was no more.

On the evening of September 1 (before Great Britain and France had become belligerents), Hoover took to the airwaves from San Francisco to announce that "America must keep out of this war." It would be a long war, he predicted—"a war of slow attrition"—and probably "the most barbarous war that we have ever known." It would mean "another quarter century of impoverishment" for the entire world. Hoover expected that the American people (to whom "the whole Nazi system is repugnant") would mostly sympathize with the democracies (as did Hoover himself). "But whatever our sympathies are," he added, "we cannot solve the problems of Europe." The United States could do more for that continent and for humanity by remaining outside the fray and preserving America's "vitality and strength" for "use in the period of peace which must sometime come."[67]

In the autumn of 1939 the former president threw himself into his anti-interventionist crusade. "We need to keep cool," he admonished his compatriots in early October; the British and French cannot be defeated. They "can and will control the seven seas" and "can sit there until their enemies are exhausted." At worst, the European war might turn into a "stalemate."[68] As Congress, under President Roosevelt's prodding, debated repealing the arms and munitions embargo provisions of the Neutrality Act (thereby permitting weapons sales to nations at war), Hoover worked to minimize the revisions in the law. He did not object to permitting Great Britain and France to buy arms in the United States on a cash-and-carry basis. Indeed, he thought that permitting them to do so "would give an emotional outlet to the American people" that might ease domestic pressure to join in the war.[69] But he did oppose, on humanitarian grounds, the sale of any weapons that might make the waging of war more terrible and indiscriminate. In mid October, after consulting Charles Lindbergh, among others, Hoover proposed that the embargo be only *partially* lifted so as to authorize sale of "defensive" weapons (such as antiaircraft guns and pursuit planes). The sale of "offensive" weapons (such as bombers and submarines), as well as any weapons that could terrorize civilians, should be totally prohibited.[70]

Hoover's search for a humane middle ground between "repeal" and "no repeal" of the arms embargo soon foundered. On October 26, his compromise plan was defeated, fifty-six to thirty-six, in the U.S. Senate.[71] A few days later, Congress easily approved changes in the Neutrality Act largely desired by President Roosevelt, including authority for unlimited arms and munitions sales to belligerent countries. Immediately Britain and France made plans for massive weapons purchases in the United States.

To Hoover it was now apparent that American nonparticipation in the conflict would depend not on the provisions of law but on "will"—the will of the American people and of Franklin Roosevelt.[72] "For two years [Roosevelt] has been moving step by step into power politics," Hoover complained privately in September.[73] To friends such as Lindbergh he shared his conviction that the president wanted to get the United States into the war eventually.[74]

To forestall him—and to buttress American anti-interventionist sentiment—Hoover escalated his own war of words. In the *Saturday Evening Post* on October 27, he depicted Europe as a continent of "26 races" beset by "a hell's brew of malign spirits." Invoking what he called "the voice of experience" (including his own) in World War I, he warned that America could never bring enduring "peace" or reconstruction to Europe. "The social regeneration of nations," declared Hoover, "must come from within." Do not let your "indignation" overcome your "reason," he pleaded.[75] In the months ahead, in the *Post* and elsewhere, he implored his fellow citizens to eschew wartime "hate" and to wait for the healing tasks that America could perform *after* the war, at the peace settlement.[76]

For Hoover himself this opportunity came almost instantly and from a totally unexpected source. On September 11 an emissary named Myron Taylor called on Hoover in New York City with an invitation from President Roosevelt: Would Hoover come to the White House two days hence to confer with Roosevelt on creating an American relief organization to assist the victims of the war in Europe? The inspiration for this overture, at least in part, came from Roosevelt's wife, Eleanor, who was eager to launch the women and children's side of the effort with a special White House conference, if Hoover agreed to lead the relief undertaking.[77]

Hoover immediately declined. An appropriate relief agency was already in place, he countered: the American Red Cross. If the Red Cross appointed "some capable administrator" to head its European division, the agency could start work "on an hour's notice." When Taylor disclosed that Roosevelt wished to keep the Red Cross within its limited sphere as "an adjunct to military activities," Hoover retorted that the agency had "long since" outgrown this "narrow field." Moreover, to create a "parallel" and "equal" "mechanism" at this juncture would be onerous and time consuming.

According to his memoranda of this conversation, Hoover made it plain that he had no interest in the president's offer. Although willing (he said) to advise Roosevelt further on this matter (if Roosevelt "would address any question to me"), he also bluntly told his visitor that "I wished to devote my whole energies to keeping the United States out of this war." To go to the White House in person, he said, "would only create speculation and unnecessary discussion in the country." He asked Taylor to tell Roosevelt that Hoover "had some responsibility to the Republican Party" and that Hoover was certain that his party would support Roosevelt on a policy of staying out of the European conflict.[78]

Hoover's rebuff and counterproposal did not sit well with the White House. After conferring with the chairman of the American Red Cross, Norman H. Davis, President Roosevelt dispatched a second emissary—Davis himself—to Hoover on September 14 with the message that Roosevelt wanted Hoover to assume the leadership of the entire American relief effort for Europe.[79] Hoover again demurred. The Red Cross, he insisted, along with its European affiliates, possessed the requisite prestige, personnel, and resources to handle war-torn Europe's civilian distress, including the most immediate area of need: Poland.[80] To Davis he evidently intimated a second reason (beyond his antiwar commitment) for refusing to set up an independent relief mechanism: in 1940 "he might be directing a political campaign."[81]

After talking at length with Davis on the fourteenth, Hoover agreed to put his counterproposal in writing, for Davis to submit to the Red Cross's executive committee. This Hoover did the next day in a formal letter to Davis urging a Red Cross takeover of European relief work and a national fund-raising drive.[82] Hoover also agreed to attend the executive committee's next meeting (September 18) in Washington and even join the committee, but he continued to decline any contact with Roosevelt.[83]

Davis had scarcely returned to Washington when Hoover began to develop cold feet. He asked Davis to release his formal letter to Davis to the press before the meeting, so as to "avoid useless speculation" and "clear the public mind" about the purpose of his visit. Davis objected that he could not very well publicize Hoover's letter before the executive committee had even had a chance to learn about and ponder its remarkable proposition. Whereupon — to Davis's and his colleagues' annoyance — Hoover decided not to travel to Washington.[84]

On September 18 the American Red Cross's executive committee met and declined to accept Hoover's plan. The committee decided that the agency must "draw a line" between its traditional "emergency relief" work, which it had always conducted with private contributions, and the long-term, government-financed "mass feeding" operations that Hoover had administered in war-torn Europe a quarter of a century before. Moreover, the situation in Europe was still too murky for the committee to determine what it might attempt to do for civilian victims of the war. It must "wait for developments," Davis informed Hoover. Another reason for caution was bureaucratic: many Red Cross chapters were cool to the idea of initiating a relief campaign for Europe when there was still so much unemployment and destitution at home.[85]

Over the next few days, by telephone and correspondence, Davis and Hoover engaged in a fruitless "exchange of views." By now, Hoover suspected that Roosevelt, through Davis, was trying to divert the Republican ex-president into European relief work and place "a very unpopular" American fund-raising appeal on his shoulders.[86] Hoover was also miffed that Roosevelt had not approached him directly, preferring to sound him out through intermediaries.[87] Nor, it seems, was he pleased to learn that Eleanor Roosevelt was trying through a mutual friend to persuade him to take sole charge of the problem.[88] He did not know that the whole idea seems to have been Eleanor's in the first place.

For her part, Mrs. Roosevelt seemed to feel that she and her husband had been snubbed. "Mr. Hoover turned us down," she told a friend in late

September. "He refused to call on the President."[89] FDR evinced his displeasure in a different way. On September 20 he held a "national unity conference" with fourteen Democratic and Republican leaders to discuss how to keep America neutral and at peace. The Republican presidential candidate in 1936, Alf M. Landon, received an invitation; Herbert Hoover conspicuously did not.[90] Meanwhile, at the Red Cross, even some Republican members of its central committee were complaining that Hoover was impossible to work with—that "he gave orders instead of advice."[91]

Certainly Hoover's fear of causing "useless speculation" seemed like an odd excuse for failing to make his case in person to the Red Cross. Why, twice in one week, had he spurned invitations (including one from FDR himself) to visit Washington? One reason was something no one could have guessed. On March 4, 1933, in his last moments as president, Hoover, fearing assassination, had asked through an aide for Secret Service protection to accompany him to New York City, once he left the inaugural ceremony. As a soon-to-be-private citizen, he had no legal right (under the law at the time) to such protection, and the head of the Secret Service turned down his request. Ever afterward, Hoover believed that the incoming president, Franklin Roosevelt, had ordered the Secret Service that day to deny his plea. It was, for Hoover, an unforgivable act. For the next six-and-a-half years he refrained (with one exception) from setting foot in Washington when Roosevelt was in town, lest the former president be obliged to pay a courtesy call on his successor.[92]

In mid September 1939, Hoover apparently divulged his grievance to Myron Taylor or Norman H. Davis, who promptly shared this news with FDR. From Davis came back word that Roosevelt did not understand why Hoover was unfriendly to him and that FDR had never heard of the withdrawal of Secret Service protection for Hoover on the day of FDR's inaugural. Hoover seemed disinclined to believe him.[93]

But if personal animosity toward Roosevelt made Hoover loath to venture to the nation's capital, his larger apprehension lay in his current sense of priorities. If he permitted himself to head up a nebular relief program for Europe at Roosevelt's request, he would be drawn into an entangling alliance with his archrival. Worse yet, he would forfeit his cherished political independence, at a moment when high politics—the politics of war and peace, and the election of 1940—was uppermost in his mind.

Still, the Great Humanitarian could not ignore the pleas of Polish Americans and others begging him to assist their hapless brethren in Europe. In late September Davis informed him that the American Red Cross was sending a delegation to Europe to survey and report on the relief problem. For Hoover it was too little and too late.[94] Disgusted by the Red Cross's hesitancy to step forward, on September 25 he and a group of close associates in past relief enterprises formed the Commission for Polish Relief (CPR) with himself as honorary chairman and behind-the-scenes wirepuller. During the next several months, the CPR raised several hundred thousand dollars and successfully supplied more than 4,600,000 pounds of food mainly to Polish refugees in Romania, Hungary, and Lithuania.[95]

Nor was Hoover unresponsive to another appeal for help in December—this time from Finland. On November 30 the armies of Bolshevik Russia brutally attacked little Finland, the only European nation that had made steady payments on its World War I debt to the United States. Hoover, a fierce anti-Communist, who at that moment was in California, immediately condemned the invasion as a "new low" in civilization. We are "back," he said, "to the morals and the butchery of Genghis Khan."[96] He was therefore receptive when, on December 3, his friend Lewis Strauss telephoned him from New York with a startling message. The Finnish minister to the United States, Hjalmar Procopé, an old friend of Strauss's, had telephoned him that morning in despair. Everywhere he went in Washington, the diplomat said, he was receiving sympathy but no commitments to help—not even from the Red Cross. Strauss, who had been Hoover's secretary in 1917–19, had an idea: Herbert Hoover should lead a relief mission for Finland similar to his Commission for Relief in Belgium (CRB) in World War I. The Finns could use the money saved on food to buy war materiel to fight the Russian invaders.

Either before or after Procopé came to see him late on December 3, Strauss telephoned Hoover in California with his proposal. "The Chief" (as Hoover's intimates called him) immediately assented and authorized Strauss to incorporate the Finnish Relief Fund.[97]

The next day Hoover, still in California, began to assemble "my old colleagues in Belgian Relief" to manage the nascent organization.[98] He also prepared to make a dramatic fund-raising appeal to the American people.[99] He was doing all this, he later confessed (in a document prepared for his Magnum Opus), "not only for the intrinsic effect for Finland" but for two other reasons: to create favorable "public opinion" in America for governmental loans to Finland ("the real financial aid") and "to bring home to the American people the meaning of Communism" and "the character of the Russian Government." The Soviet Union, he wrote, was a "monster" that had committed an "unprovoked" and "most unspeakable" "assault" upon "a little and frail democracy."[100]

With "various sporadic bodies" (as he termed them) already "in motion" for Finnish relief, Hoover was anxious to move quickly.[101] But before he went public, he wanted to be certain that the Finnish government approved.[102] On December 5, in a long-distance telephone call to Minister Procopé, Hoover received the assurances that he sought. That same evening, he announced to the nation's press that he was undertaking to create an organization to raise money for the succor of homeless people in Finland.[103]

The next day, December 6, the Finnish Relief Fund was duly incorporated. Two days later it held its founding meeting in New York City and elected Hoover chairman. In a signal of official Finnish support, Procopé became honorary chairman.[104]

But now a shadow appeared on the horizon. In his eagerness to establish the Finnish Relief Fund, Hoover had made no effort to consult or coordinate with the American Red Cross, of which he was vice president. Late on December 5, he learned from Strauss that the Red Cross would be launching its own appeal for Finland in the press the next morning—despite having told Procopé, the week before, that it had no such plan. Clearly worried that the Red Cross would get the jump on him, Hoover released his "preliminary hint of our undertaking" to the press that very evening.[105]

His gambit worked. The next day, December 6, on the front page of the *New York Times,* right next to the Red Cross's plea for money to "alleviate the suffering" of the Finns, was the report of Hoover's plan to set up *his* organization to do the same thing.[106]

The Red Cross's unexpected initiative put Hoover in a quandary. Back in September, he had lauded the Red Cross lavishly as the sole agency equipped to undertake European relief programs—until, in his opinion, it had started dithering over Poland. But now Norman Davis's Red Cross apparatus showed sudden signs of taking charge. Already it had allocated $25,000 for Finnish relief measures and had delivered $10,000 to London to purchase medicine for its Finnish affiliate.[107] On December 7, therefore, Hoover telephoned Davis and asked him outright: Was the Red Cross planning to undertake "general relief work" in Finland? If so, and if it intended a fund-raising campaign for this purpose, Hoover said that he would gladly "back it up." According to Hoover, Davis explained that the Red Cross could not undertake such a broad responsibility. Then how about a joint "fifty-fifty" drive? Hoover asked. Davis replied that his agency could not participate in joint efforts. Finally (according to Hoover), he and the Red Cross chairman agreed that Hoover would insert into his forthcoming public appeal for general relief a supportive reference to the Red Cross's call for funds for its traditional specialties: medicines, hospital supplies, and garments. Hoover also pledged to "cooperate fully" with Davis's agency.[108]

Satisfied (or so he later claimed) that the Red Cross had no intention of organizing the kind of large-scale effort he contemplated, on December 9 Hoover announced the formation of the Finnish Relief Fund and asked the American people to help it alleviate the "hideous suffering of the Finnish people."[109] In a masterful public relations stroke (but one that inevitably undercut the Red Cross), he asked the nation's newspapers to serve as collection agencies in order to curtail administrative expenses. More than 1,200 daily newspapers agreed to do so.[110] In the coming weeks the nation's press reported almost daily on the avalanche of mass meetings, concerts, theatrical events, radio addresses, and other devices that Hoover tirelessly employed to raise awareness and money.

At first the financial contributions—though numerous—were disappointingly small. Toward the end of December, Hoover was obliged to pledge $100,000 of his own money as a guarantee against overdrafts of the fund's account at the Chase National Bank.[111] But as Finland, to the world's amazement, continued to hold out against the Soviet behemoth, the plight of the gallant little nation became an American cause célèbre. Politicians, clergymen, athletes, and film stars flocked to assist the Finnish Relief Fund's efforts. Greta Garbo sent a check for five thousand dollars.[112] By the time its drive ended in 1940, the fund had pulled in around $3,500,000.[113]

Behind the scenes, however, Hoover's spectacular campaign had aroused resentment. Although the Red Cross, with its three thousand chapters and seven thousand branches, eventually raised more than $2,300,000 for medicine and related supplies for the suffering Finns,[114] its lackluster publicity was no match for Hoover's. Publicly, Hoover claimed that the two organizations were cooperating fully and was careful to note their division of labor. But privately Davis admonished him on December 14 that this was not true—they were *not* cooperating on "the raising of funds"—and that this was causing confusion and friction.[115] But Davis had to concede that despite its appeal for Finland his agency was not planning a concerted *drive* for Finland. And Hoover promised that if and when the Red Cross initiated a drive for a general war relief fund, he would discontinue his efforts and support the Red Cross. The outcome of their tense conversation was that the two competitors for charitable money continued to perform their tasks as before.[116]

To Hoover it was evident that the Red Cross leadership was not happy with his encroachment on its domain.[117] To Hoover's archrival in the White House, however, the problem was more than a bureaucratic turf war. As enthusiasm for Finnish relief soared across the nation, so, too, did acclaim for its most visible impresario. For the first time in a decade, Herbert Hoover was in the news in a favorable light — at the very moment that the 1940 presidential campaign season was impending. To Franklin Roosevelt and his entourage — already convinced that Hoover was a presidential candidate[118] — it looked like the former chief executive was brazenly hijacking Finnish relief to promote his political comeback. More worrisome still, the ubiquitous Hoover was stirring the nation's conscience at a time when the Roosevelt administration — navigating treacherous diplomatic waters — was offering the embattled Finns encouraging words but little else.[119] What if Hoover should convince Finnish (and Polish) Americans (and perhaps others) that he cared more about their relatives in the "old country" than Roosevelt did?

Furious at Hoover's return to the limelight in this fashion, and at Norman Davis for letting Hoover "get away with this," Roosevelt and his team took countermeasures.[120] In mid December a number of Roosevelt's journalistic allies — almost certainly with his knowledge and connivance — attempted to knock "Herbie the Hooter" off his pedestal.[121] First, the pro–New Deal columnist Doris Fleeson accused Hoover of grabbing "the Finnish relief football" from Davis's team while the Red Cross's "dignified masterminds" twiddled their thumbs on the sidelines "in helpless agony."[122] Other reporters and observers pointed out that the Red Cross had already been assisting Finland when Hoover stepped in, that Red Cross officials considered his intervention unnecessary, and that he had not consulted the Red Cross before creating his own organization.[123]

Most dangerous of all, between December 13 and 15 newspapers in Washington, D.C., and New York City buzzed with a sensational revelation that almost certainly emanated from Roosevelt (and possibly Davis): that, just three months earlier, Roosevelt had asked Hoover to take over a "coordinated relief effort" for Europe in the United States and that Hoover had refused for political reasons.[124]

As the media assault on Hoover got under way, Roosevelt, at a press conference on December 12, blandly denied that there was any friction between the Red Cross and Hoover's Finnish Relief Fund.[125] But just two days later, FDR's own press secretary, Stephen T. Early, confirmed to the White House press corps the story sweeping through the capital: yes, Roosevelt *had* asked Hoover, through Davis, to become a "sort of 'General Manager of Relief'" in Europe around the outbreak of the war but that Hoover apparently "did not accept the offer."[126]

The fat was now in the fire. If the press reports from Washington were true, the Great Humanitarian had acted from less than altruistic motives in September and might well be acting from similar motives now. If this perception took hold, it could tarnish his humanitarian halo and derail his presidential hopes.

Yet what could he say in rebuttal? He could not deny that Roosevelt had asked him to form an American war relief organization for Europe in early September and that he had refused, preferring to let the Red Cross take charge; his own memos of his conversations with Taylor and Davis confirmed this. Nor could he deny that he had refused partly because he had political ambitions for 1940: he had said as much to Davis in mid September.[127] Nor could he readily disclose his other reason for rejecting Roosevelt's offer: his desire to pour his entire energies into keeping the United States out of the war. If that were the case, why was he working now at full throttle to raise money to help Finland?

At a news conference in New York City on December 14—shortly before Stephen T. Early's explosive press briefing at the White House—reporters confronted Hoover with the story that he had spurned Roosevelt's invitation to make him "general director of all American relief efforts for Europe" because Hoover "wished to take part in the 1940 election campaign and did not want to be identified with the New Deal." Hoover was outraged. "There is not a word of truth in the whole story," he fumed. The press should expose such "malicious stuff"; its "only purpose is to poison the wells of human misery." He also emphatically denied that there was any friction between his Finnish Relief Fund and the American Red Cross.[128]

The press reports to which Hoover reacted so vehemently contained a number of factual inaccuracies, making it easier for him to brush them aside. One account claimed that Hoover had been asked to displace Norman Davis as chairman of the Red Cross—a charge Hoover properly denied.[129] Less refutable, however, was Stephen T. Early's disclosure that day to the White House press corps. But Early, in his briefing to reporters, seemed to imply that Roosevelt had approached Hoover shortly *before* the European war broke out on September 1 (rather than shortly after). This chronological misstep enabled Hoover and his secretary Lawrence Richey (in a formal press release) to sidestep Early's factual claims and suggest that Roosevelt's press secretary was confused: he must have been referring to other discussions that Hoover had had with various parties about a resettlement scheme for European political refugees *before* the war.[130]

Incensed by the orchestrated attack on him by Roosevelt's allies, and aware of the danger it posed to his reputation, Hoover swiftly dispatched Richey to Washington with a carefully prepared, self-exculpatory dossier of documents (including his September correspondence with Davis) to show to various reporters and columnists.[131] The counterattack seemed to stop what Hoover called "the mud flow."[132] With a boost from his journalist friends, he managed to fend off his enemies' "smear" and ride out the storm.[133]

Convinced that Norman Davis was the source of the disparaging press leaks, Hoover immediately resorted to a defensive measure. For the next several months he secretly recorded Davis's telephone calls to him from Washington.[134] (The transcripts are in Hoover's papers.)[135] But eventually the angry ex-president concluded that the real culprit had been none other than the man in the Oval Office.[136] A few years later, in an early draft of his "War Book," Hoover asserted that, in the course of his fund drive for Finland, "Mr. Roosevelt gave an order to his officials to impede it in every way possible." Hoover added that this was "a personal affront to me" and was "not directed at the Finns."[137] Whether or not FDR ever gave such an order, Hoover's belief that he did further poisoned the wells of their relationship. The "mud flow" of December 1939 became part of the emotional impetus for Hoover's Magnum Opus.

But there was one thing on which the two rivals did agree: beleaguered Finland needed much more than private charity. In the first weeks of the Russo-Finnish war, the Roosevelt administration, acting through the Reconstruction Finance Corporation, loaned the Finnish government $10,000,000 with which to buy nonmilitary supplies in the United States. (Hoover's protégé Lewis Strauss helped instigate this transaction.)[138]

Then, in January 1940, President Roosevelt asked Congress to extend more credits for Finland for still more nonmilitary purchases.[139] Hoover immediately endorsed Roosevelt's request.[140] A few weeks later, Congress passed legislation permitting $20,000,000 in additional U.S. government loans to the Finnish government, again for the purchase solely of civilian supplies.[141] The next day, Hoover claimed credit for this outcome, telling his representative in Helsinki that "it was largely the public sentiment which we have created" that enabled Roosevelt's measure to sail through Congress.[142]

Certainly Hoover and his team had done more than anyone to keep Finland's travails in the headlines and thereby provide an outlet for material support by private citizens. It is certainly possible that the Roosevelt administration and Congress would have done far less for Finland had it not been for the mass indignation Hoover so effectively mobilized. Unfortunately for the Finns, the U.S. government's loan credits of March 1940 came too late to affect Finland's struggle against the Russian hordes. Overwhelmed by the invading armies, the Finns were forced to sue for peace in early March.[143]

Although Hoover kept the Finnish Relief Fund alive and sent additional money to Helsinki for assistance to the war's refugees,[144] the end of hostilities and the U.S. government's fresh loan to Finland freed him to concentrate again on other things. Contrary to the insinuations by Roosevelt's "Fifth Columnists" (as Hoover later dubbed them),[145] there is little evidence that he had reentered the relief field in the autumn of 1939 specifically to further his political aspirations. But as Roosevelt and his savvy associates accurately foresaw, the net effect of Hoover's reentry was to enhance his public stature—and at a most propitious time, as Hoover himself surely understood. Once his Finnish relief campaign abated in the spring of 1940, the humanitarian dynamo was ready to resume his pursuit of political vindication.[146]

His strategy was simple: disclaim all ambition, build up his reputation—through writings and speeches—as the Republican party's most experienced statesman and intellectual leader, and work for a convention deadlock among the lesser lights. Then, through a mighty speech to the assembled convention delegates, position himself as the manifestly superior alternative. It was all for naught. At the convention in June, the party did indeed reject its more prosaic presidential aspirants—for a charismatic newcomer named Wendell Willkie.

But not before Hoover had made one last supreme attempt to win the prize. In a stemwinding address to the Republican national convention on June 25, 1940, he excoriated the Roosevelt administration and the "totalitarian 'liberals'" who sustained it. For eight years, he charged, Americans had witnessed "a steady sapping of our system of liberty" and "the mismanagement of government." The weakening of liberty at home was part of "a war of hostile ideas, philosophies and systems of government"—a war that had already been fought and virtually lost in the Old World. In "every single case" in Europe since 1919, liberty had been subverted by "economic planners" before the final plunge into dictatorship:

> Each of these nations had an era of starry-eyed men who believed that they could plan and force the economic life of the people. . . . They exalted the state as the solvent of all economic problems.
>
> These men thought they were liberals. But they also thought they could have economic dictatorship by bureaucracy and at the same time preserve

free speech, orderly justice and free government. They can be called the totalitarian 'liberals.' They were the spiritual fathers of the New Deal.

As for the war now sweeping across western Europe, Hoover exhorted his listeners not to abandon "the ground of realism" by entering it.

> The first policy of calm realism is not to exaggerate our immediate dangers. Every whale that spouts is not a submarine. The 3000 miles of ocean is still a protection. . . .

> . . . The first responsibility of the President of the United States is to abate war, not to stimulate it. It is not the province of the President of the United States to create hate.[147]

Hoover had hoped that his biting oration would stampede the convention. Instead, a large number of delegates in the hall were unable to hear him, and the demonstration when he finished was relatively muted. Hoover and his associates came to believe—and probably rightly—that the microphone had been tampered with at the instigation of the chairman of the arrangements committee, a Willkie supporter. The Hooverites also suspected that this same party official had packed the galleries with Willkie supporters using duplicate tickets.[148]

Hoover's failure to win the 1940 presidential nomination was a bitter disappointment. With his sixty-sixth birthday only weeks away, he knew that he would never get another chance to redeem himself at the polls. As the convention dispersed, he seemed to sense that an era in his life was over. To a number of friends he mentioned having reached a "turning-point."[149] "I am going fishing," he told reporters after leaving the convention. "I want to get politics off my mind."[150]

On June 28, Hoover wrote a poignant letter to some of his closest associates:

> There are things in the world that cannot be brought about. There are mistakes that cannot be repaired. But there is one thing sure—that loyalty and friendship are the most precious possessions a man can have. You have given it to me unreservedly, but it is my wealth and you make it.[151]

Less than four weeks later, he started in earnest to write his memoirs.[152]

Yet the world would not leave him alone (or vice versa). A few weeks earlier, the German army had unleashed a terrible onslaught in western Europe. By late June, Norway, Denmark, Belgium, Holland, and most of France had fallen under the Nazi heel. Only Great Britain, led by its new prime minister, Winston Churchill, was holding out, but for how long?

Throughout the awful summer of 1940, Hoover (as he later admitted) was on pins and needles as "the Battle of Britain" raged. But he never lost his faith that the British would withstand the German assault from the air.[153] When they eventually did, the former president had a new argument for his anti-interventionist arsenal: If Hitler could not convey his armies a handful of miles across the English Channel, why should America fear that he could reach the Western Hemisphere?[154]

In the autumn of 1940, despite growing frustration with the chaotic campaign of Wendell Willkie, Hoover threw himself into the battle to prevent Franklin Roosevelt from winning a third term. "This Administration is steadily developing the same growth of personal power that has swept the world into nazism and fascism," Hoover charged; this administration "is taking this country steadily towards war."[155] In a scathing speech in Lincoln, Nebraska, on October 31, he ripped into Roosevelt's claim to be the indispensable man to conduct American foreign policy in the present crisis. In seven years as President, Roosevelt—said Hoover—had contributed "hardly one act" conducive to "our peace with the world" and "hundreds of acts" tending to drag America into the current war. He accused Roosevelt of "dabbling in foreign power politics" and "continuously sticking pins into tigers all over the world." "History alone," Hoover asserted, "will tell how much our playing of power politics may have created unjustified hopes or influenced action in Europe." He blasted Roosevelt for extending diplomatic recognition to the Soviet Union in 1933—a disastrous error that had permitted the Communists' "revolutionary conspiracies" to "run riot in the United States" for the past six years, "despite their pledged word." He accused Roosevelt of bombast and "billingsgate" and of fanning a "war psychosis" and "hysteria" at home. He warned that if America did enter the European conflict, it would be no quick, eighteen-month affair but "more likely . . . another Thirty Years War." America should arm "to the teeth" and stay out of it, while furnishing Britain all possible support "within the law."[156]

A week later the American people reelected Roosevelt to a third term by a comfortable margin. Hoover was tremendously disappointed.[157] But he could take consolation from one development. The night before he spoke in Nebraska, Roosevelt—campaigning in Boston—had made a public pledge:

And while I am talking to you mothers and fathers, I give you one more assurance.

I have said this before, but I shall say it again and again and again:
Your boys are not going to be sent into any foreign wars.[158]

If Willkie had become president, Hoover intended to move to Washington, where he and his wife, Lou, still owned a home at 2300 S Street, in which they had lived while he was secretary of commerce in the 1920s. Now, with FDR securely back in the White House, Hoover decided to make New York City his permanent center of operations. On December 3, 1940, he and Lou moved into Suite 31-A in the Waldorf Towers of the Waldorf-Astoria Hotel, where he principally resided for the remainder of his life.[159] Here he would write most of his Magnum Opus and much else.

The election setback of 1940 did nothing to dampen Hoover's aversion to Roosevelt's foreign policy. In fact, it soon led to a new front in their personal war. For a number of months Hoover had been looking for ways to augment the humanitarian work he had undertaken for Poland the year before, if possible with appropriations from the Polish government in exile and other foreign governments.[160] On February 29 he had actually testified before Congress (while Roosevelt was out of town) on behalf of a $20,000,000 governmental appropriation for aid to the suffering Poles.[161] As the European war spread in the spring and summer of 1940, so did the breadth of Hoover's design. In mid May, as the Belgian army was reeling before the German invasion, he created the Commission for Relief in Belgium, a namesake of the organization that had catapulted him to fame in 1914.[162] Two weeks later he joined representatives of eleven other private American relief agencies in establishing the Allied Relief Fund to raise money for "civilian relief in Europe." The parties agreed that the money they raised would be funneled solely to an "American Relief Administration," chaired by Hoover, which would immediately set up "an organization for distribution in Europe."[163]

Meanwhile—and perhaps not entirely by coincidence—Franklin Roosevelt and the American Red Cross were swinging into action. On May 10 the Red Cross ("our official national volunteer relief agency") appealed to the American people to contribute at least $10,000,000 for a European war relief fund; the drive eventually collected twice that amount.[164] Although Hoover dutifully supported this drive (as he had earlier promised), privately he suspected the worst. From an informant he heard that Franklin and Eleanor Roosevelt had met with Norman Davis and decided to prevent Hoover from leading the European relief effort. Instead, they supposedly intended to send Eleanor to France to take charge.[165]

A few weeks later, as the war zone in Europe became flooded with hapless refugees, President Roosevelt asked Congress to appropriate $50,000,000 in taxpayer money to assist the Red Cross in coping with destitution "in other lands."[166] Congress obliged.[167] When an admirer of Hoover's suggested that FDR select Hoover to handle such a fund, Roosevelt promised to give it "very careful consideration."[168] But when it came time in July to set up administrative procedures for the appropriated money, the president ordered two members of his Cabinet to work with the Red Cross.[169]

A week later Hoover glumly confessed to a friend that "Mr. Roosevelt does not intend to allow us to have any hand in it [European relief] if he can help it, even though people starve."[170] Hoover was probably referring not to Roosevelt's favoritism for the Red Cross but to his attitude toward the larger scheme Hoover now had in mind. In the summer of 1940, Hoover (and many other seasoned observers) believed that much of war-torn Europe faced the likelihood of a terrible famine in which millions of adults and children might die.[171] To avert it, Hoover dispatched his friend Hugh Gibson and another representative to London and Berlin, respectively, to explore establishing an American-led, neutral relief mission acceptable to the warring British and Germans. The mission would import and distribute food to the civilian populations of German-occupied Poland, Norway, the Netherlands, and Belgium, where, he said, there were 18,000,000 persons "who are going to die unless food is gotten to them at once."[172]

His proposal—modeled on his successful experience in Belgium in World War I—was straightforward. The Germans must promise not to seize any imported food or any domestic produce of the four conquered nations. They must permit the neutral relief agency to control food distribution and to verify that the Germans were complying with their guarantees. The British must permit food cargoes to pass unmolested through their naval blockade of enemy-held territory. The governments in exile of the four countries must furnish the money for the undertaking: a sum Hoover reckoned at twenty to forty million dollars a month.[173]

In mid August, after a leak in the British press, Hoover publicly floated his proposal.[174] From the outset the portents were not good. Although the Germans seemed amenable, the British government under Winston Churchill plainly loathed to permit any weakening of their best weapon: their naval blockade. The conquered populations were the Germans' responsibility, the British contended, and the Germans had food enough to meet it if they desired. Even if the Germans kept their hands off any imported cargoes, massive imports would reduce the economic pressure on them.[175] In a speech before Parliament on August 20, Prime Minister Churchill categorically refused to permit food to pass through the blockade to the "subjugated peoples." It would only "prolong the agony" and benefit the Nazis.[176]

Hoover was fit to be tied. Years later he publicly accused Churchill of willfully misrepresenting the terms of his proposal and of ignoring the careful conditions that Hoover had attached to ensure German compliance.[177] Privately he suspected that Churchill's unyielding attitude had been "either approved or coached on by Washington." From Gibson in London he learned that success there was "impossible" unless Hoover secured "the prior approval" of the Roosevelt administration—something he had no reason to expect.[178] Roosevelt and the Red Cross were sabotaging his every move, he complained to a friend in mid August.[179] "The New Dealers would rather see the people of Central Europe starve than to see the opposition have anything to do with any kind of constructive or humanitarian action."[180]

Stymied in London, Hoover decided to hold his fire until after the election. Then, if the Republicans won, he would "make short and swift work of these attitudes in Washington."[181] "I cannot let the fate of these 30 millions of people rest where it is," he confided to Hugh Gibson in October; "I shall break loose as soon as the election is over."[182]

Roosevelt's reelection did not deter him in the least. On November 15, 1940, in an address at Vassar College, Hoover appealed for a massive international relief program for the "five little nations" of Finland, Norway, the Netherlands, Belgium, and Central Poland: 37,000,000 people, "of whom about 15 million are children." Four of these five nations were under German occupation. To achieve his objective, he explained, the Germans must agree to certain controls and outside supervision, and the British must allow food ships to pass through their blockade.[183] That same day he published a powerful article in *Collier's* entitled "Feed Hungry Europe."[184] The great Hooverian publicity blitz had begun.

In Washington, Franklin Roosevelt was worried. Although most Americans strongly sympathized with the British in their war with Nazi Germany, many Americans were uneasy about a possibly imminent famine in the German-held "little democracies."[185] If American public opinion should blame the British blockade for such a catastrophe, it could harm the British cause and greatly complicate Roosevelt's pro-British foreign policy. On November 28 the president conferred about Hoover's initiatives with Norman Davis and Thomas W. Lamont of the J. P. Morgan Company, who had recently met with Hoover. Lamont promised to do what he could to keep Hoover under control.[186]

On December 7, 1940, Hoover officially launched the National Committee on Food for the Five Small Democracies, with himself as honorary chairman and his team of past relief associates in key positions. The committee's stated purpose was simple: to give "expression" to American "feeling" that something be done to save the people of the five German-occupied small democracies from impending starvation. Specifically, it proposed to "raise a voice on behalf of these people" so that the German and British governments would enact agreements with a "neutral organization" that would implement a feeding program.[187] Put more plainly, Hoover proposed (as he said privately) "to break down the barriers against food to the five small democracies."[188] Because the biggest barrier by far was the recalcitrant British government, Hoover's coming propaganda campaign would be directed almost entirely at London.

It did not take long for London to respond. Three days later, on December 10, the British ambassador to the United States formally announced that His Majesty's Government would not grant permission for the passage of food through its naval blockade. Any such "scheme" as Hoover's, he said, "under present conditions" would be "of material assistance to Germany's war effort" and "thereby postpone the day of liberation" of the subject peoples. The "risk of starvation" on the continent, he added, had been "greatly exaggerated."[189]

Now commenced a protracted struggle by Hoover to open the door that Churchill's government had just slammed shut. Try as he might to overcome various objections, the former president got nowhere. The British—backed to the hilt by the Roosevelt administration—refused to yield.[190] In the winter of 1941 Roosevelt's undersecretary of state, Sumner Welles, hinted to the press that Hoover might be subject to punishment under the Logan Act for negotiating with foreign governments on his food plan.[191] Roosevelt himself evidently told diplomats from the "five small democracies" that they might get food relief more easily if Hoover were not involved in the matter.[192]

Roosevelt's opposition to Hoover's crusade could be expected. Harder to take were the increasingly hostile attacks by some of the nation's most vocal pro-British citizens, who denounced his plan repeatedly in public forums. It would weaken Britain, they said, and strengthen Britain's enemy.[193] In some circles he was accused of spreading anti-British propaganda and even of being an Anglophobe.[194]

Despite the opposition, Hoover mustered considerable support for his humanitarian crusade, particularly among the nation's religious leaders.[195] Many Americans agreed with him that a way must be found to rescue millions of innocents from privation and pestilence.[196] Hoover himself could not bear "to stand still and witness the useless and preventable starvation" of ten to twenty million people.[197] But the winds of war were blowing against his transnational project. To win out, he must either pressure the British to relent (out of fear of antagonizing American public opinion) or compel Roosevelt to put pressure on the British (for the same reason). It was a tough sell, made all the more so by what he considered hysterical attacks, misrepresentations, and smears.

It is unnecessary to recount here the innumerable maneuvers and machinations that marked this yearlong battle (Hoover eventually told much of the story himself).[198] What is most noteworthy, in the present context, is the residue of indignation that the tempest left in his soul. Some years later, in his published account of this episode, the Quaker-born humanitarian described Churchill as "a militarist of the extreme school who held that the incidental starvation of women and children was justified if it contributed to the earlier ending of the war by victory."[199] For Roosevelt—who had done so much to undercut him—Hoover's anger found expression in another place: his Magnum Opus.[200]

While Hoover was attempting in vain to re-create on a grander scale his Belgian relief commission of World War I, he was also striving to stop what he saw as Roosevelt's march toward war. In January 1941 FDR asked Congress to approve a gigantic military assistance plan for Great Britain and its allies known as Lend-Lease. In the words of the *New York Times,* the proposed legislation would confer on the president "practically unlimited power to place American war equipment, new and old, at the disposal of foreign nations in the interest of the defense of the United States."[201] Hoover strenuously objected—not to military assistance per se (which he endorsed) but to the extraordinary discretionary powers that the legislation would give the president. This bill, Hoover charged, "would abolish the Congress for all practical purposes."[202] It would surrender to the president "the power to make war," reduce Congress to a "rubber stamp," and empower him "to drive the country still further toward a national socialist state." It would enable him to become the "real dictator of opposition policies to the Axis." In truth, he lamented to a friend, it was "a war bill, yet 95 per cent of the people think it is only aid to Britain."[203]

As signed into law on March 11, the Lend-Lease Act was a remarkable piece of legislation. It authorized the president, "in the interest of national defense," to order the head of any agency of the federal government to manufacture "or otherwise procure" any "defense article" for "the government of any country whose defense the President deems vital to the defense of the United States."

The act further authorized the commander in chief to sell, lease, lend, or otherwise dispose of such "defense articles" on any terms he deemed satisfactory, to a value of up to $1,300,000,000.[204] Winston Churchill later acclaimed the enormous aid package as "without question the most unsordid act in the whole of recorded history."[205] Hoover, although content with the aid itself, saw something far more sinister: a congressional abdication of power of incredible magnitude.

In the aftermath of the Lend-Lease debate, Hoover became increasingly discouraged. The bill, he predicted on March 9, "will further channel the public mind into the rapids which lead inevitably to military war"—a war which would probably last twenty years.[206] Convinced that the United States was now in the midst of a "war psychosis," he expected the country to be in "active war within 90 days."[207] He remarked, with gallows humor, that he might not be taking a fishing trip next summer because "I may be in a concentration camp by that time."[208]

Early in April, in reply to a journalist's query, Hoover attempted to prophesy what would happen in the war during the next six months. The American people, he wrote, "do not realize that they have been pulled into a war without any constitutional or democratic process—but they will realize it before six months are over." He predicted that the United States would begin convoying ships to Great Britain, with resultant hostile engagements with German submarines and the loss of American lives. He predicted that "the combined policies and propaganda from Washington, the unrestricted British propaganda, the steady impact of the New York intellectuals, the killing of Americans, [and] the further outrages which will be committed by Hitler will cause a steady rise in war psychosis that cannot be stemmed." Of his eighteen predictions, the final one was the most arresting: "Western civilization has consecrated itself to making the world safe for Stalin."[209]

Wariness toward the Soviet Union and detestation of its ideology were nothing new for Hoover, of course. In the spring of 1940, after Russia's aggression against Finland, he had published a magazine article condemning Roosevelt's recognition of Soviet Russia as "a gigantic political and moral mistake." It had given "the mark of respectability" to the Bolshevik regime and had opened the door to its penetration and "poisoning" of American political and cultural life. The New Deal was not Communist, said Hoover, but "it has neither refused [the Communists'] aid nor properly exorcised them from New Deal support."[210]

It was not communist subversion at home, however, that was disturbing Hoover in the spring of 1941 as much as what the world would look like if the war did not end soon. On February 28, 1941, he visited Secretary of State Cordell Hull on relief business. During their conversation Hull briefed him on the war and divulged some surprising information: the Germans had massed 1,250,000 soldiers on the Russian frontier, and the Russians were "scared to death."[211]

Although Hull believed that Germany would ultimately move against Russia, he also told Hoover that Germany would attack Britain ferociously very soon.[212] The Germans wanted to conquer the world, Hull exclaimed. If Britain fell, the Germans would immediately lure South America into their orbit and then attack the United States.

Hoover emphatically disagreed. He had, he said, "entirely another thesis": that the Germans had "no intention" of attacking the Western Hemisphere, "at least for a very long time." Once they "had settled with the British," he prophesied, they would try "to dominate Russia." The Germans were "a soldier people not a sea people." Russia "could be had with two Army Corps, while the Western Hemisphere would require gigantic sea equipment." To Hoover the Germans' objective in the current war was to free themselves from "eastern encirclement." If the British and French had not opposed German expansion in the south and east, Germany would have attacked there instead of in the west. What they would have done to France and Britain afterward, he added, no one could say. But he was certain that there would have been no war against the western allies until Germany could have consolidated its "eastern acquisitions."[213]

Hull's assertion that a German invasion of Britain was imminent was one of a number of factors that increased Hoover's anxieties in the spring of 1941. From America's former ambassador to Great Britain, Joseph P. Kennedy, he heard a prediction in April that Britain would give in within ninety days.[214] From Kennedy and Colonel Truman Smith of the U.S. Army's Military Intelligence staff, he heard assertions that the British would make peace quickly (or would have done so long ago) if it were not for their hope for a bailout by Roosevelt.[215] Great Britain "cannot win" the war, Hoover remarked to Charles Lindbergh on May 31.[216] As Hoover monitored rumors that Britain and Germany were engaged in talks for a negotiated peace agreement, he almost seemed to be hoping for such an outcome.[217] Then, presumably, Hitler could resume his Drang nach Osten.

Hitler, it turned out, decided not to wait. On June 22, 1941, the Nazi dictator hurled his legions against communist Russia. Instantly Winston Churchill offered to aid the Russians in a common struggle against the "bloodthirsty guttersnipe" in Berlin.[218] Nearly as quickly, the Roosevelt administration signaled its willingness to consider opening the spigots of Lend-Lease to the Russians if they held out.[219]

To Hoover the stunning turn of events in Eastern Europe radically transformed the nature of the war and provided new impetus for America to stay out. For one thing, he told the press on June 23, the German attack in the East greatly relieved the pressure on the British.[220]

As it happened, Hoover had been planning another major address on the war to the American people. He now saw an opportunity to change the course of world history. To his confidant John C. O'Laughlin he wrote on June 26:

> I am convinced Germany will defeat Russia and dispose of that infecting center of Communism. And I am convinced that at the end of the campaign, which I think will move rapidly, that Hitler will propose terms to the British that they will accept. I am hoping for this speech only that it may help stay our hands from the trigger until these events arrive.[221]

It was a remarkable disclosure. If Hoover's geopolitical scenario played out as he expected, Nazi Germany would soon be the unchallenged master of continental Europe, Great Britain would be forced into a modus vivendi, and the war would end—before (he hoped) the United States could intervene.

Three nights later, Hoover spoke to the American people on national radio. For the rest of his days, he considered this speech the most important one of his life. In the course of rebutting seven arguments for America's entering the war, he exhorted his fellow citizens not to make an alliance with the Soviet Union—"one of the bloodiest tyrannies and terrors ever erected in history." Why should we hasten to the rescue of Stalin's "militant Communist conspiracy against the whole democratic ideals of the world"? To collaborate now with the Soviets would make "the whole argument of our joining the war to bring the four freedoms to mankind a gargantuan jest." When we promised a few days earlier to help Russia, he added, the "ideological war to bring the four freedoms to the world died spiritually." Moreover, if the United States now entered the war and won, we would have "won for Stalin the grip of Communism on Russia" and new opportunities for it to expand after the war. "Joining in a war alongside Stalin to impose freedom is a travesty."[222]

Several years later, in his Magnum Opus, Hoover ridiculed many American observers who had expected the Germans swiftly to conquer the Soviet Union.[223] At the time, though, he shared this expectation and was unperturbed.[224] Even if the Germans won in the East, he argued, they would still pose no military threat to the United States, "arm[ed] to the teeth" and impregnable in the Western Hemisphere. "Evil ideas contain the germs of their own defeat," he asserted. Hitler might prove victorious on the European continent, but he would then be saddled with tens of millions of rebellious subjects filled with "undying hate." When peace came, Hoover prophesied, the Nazi system would "begin to go to pieces." The once-free, conquered nationalities of Europe would never accept "a new order based on slavery. . . . Conquest always dies of indigestion."[225]

No longer was the world conflict an unambiguous struggle "between tyranny and freedom," Hoover declared in August. The alliance of the British with the Russians against Germany had destroyed "that illusion."[226] Instead, he was quite content to let the two evil dictators—Hitler and Stalin—fight it out on their own. Be patient, he urged Americans in mid September; Hitler was "on his way to be crushed by the vicious forces within his own regime." The danger of "ultimate totalitarian success" was "very much less than even ten weeks ago." The "fratricidal war" between Hitler and Stalin was weakening both of them every day.[227]

Once again, in terms he later saw as prophetic, he solemnly warned his countrymen "to take a long look now before we leap." Russia was "rightly defending herself against Nazi aggression," but Russia was also "an aggressor nation against democracies." What will happen, he asked, "to the millions of enslaved people of Russia and to all Europe and to our own freedoms if we shall send our sons to win this war for Communism?"[228]

Often that summer it seemed to him that the country had succumbed to a "war psychosis" as Roosevelt nudged the United States into an undeclared war. On June 20 Hoover dedicated the towering building at Stanford University that would now be the home of the archives and library known as the Hoover Institution on War, Revolution and Peace. "The purpose of this institution is to promote peace," he declared. "Its records stand as a challenge to those who promote war." He called special attention to its remarkable collection of propaganda literature from World War I. "As war sanctifies murder," he declaimed, "so it sanctifies the lesser immoralities of lies." These files at the Institution are "a silent challenge to the intellectual honesty of all governments when they go to war." Today, he pointedly observed, "belligerent governments" were flooding America with similar propaganda in an attempt "to mislead and becloud American thinking."[229]

Stanford's most distinguished alumnus was therefore not amused when, only a few weeks later, 176 members of his alma mater's faculty signed a petition asking Americans to give President Roosevelt, as commander in chief, "unified support" in the current "national emergency." The professors also demanded "a more dynamic policy of action" against "the totalitarian menace."[230] Hoover exploded in dismay:

> The confusion of mind in American intellectuals over the United States supporting Communism is almost beyond belief. And that is what these Stanford professors are doing. I wonder if it ever occurred to them what would happen to the world if we entered the war and brought victory to Russia.[231]

Meanwhile, Hoover had become alarmed by developments in the Far East. As early as the summer of 1940 he had privately criticized Roosevelt's decision to curb American exports of scrap iron and aviation fuel to Japan. It was "only sticking pins in a rattlesnake," he charged. "Either we should leave this thing alone or we will be drawn into real trouble."[232] In the summer and fall of 1941, as President Roosevelt's Far Eastern policy became more confrontational, Hoover's fears intensified. The administration's "handling of the Japanese situation is appalling to me," he informed a close friend in August; it was "based upon bluffing." If only America had "kept still these last three years," the Japanese "would have gone to pieces internally."[233] By September he was convinced that FDR and his associates were "certainly doing everything they can to get us into war through the Japanese back door."[234] (Japan was a treaty partner of Germany and Italy in the Axis alliance.) The "logical thing" for Japan to do, Hoover mused, was "to take Eastern Siberia on the inevitable break-up of Russia." That would be in America's interest, he contended; unfortunately, our de facto alliance with Russia seemed to foreclose such a Japanese move.[235]

By mid autumn 1941, Hoover was deeply disheartened by what he saw as Roosevelt's devious maneuvers to bring America into war via Japan.[236] On November 1 he told a friend that war was now inevitable and might flare up in the Pacific within days.[237] Increasingly that fall, a mood of fatalism gripped him. Only a "negotiated peace" in Europe, he thought, could restrain the United States from entering the war. He thought a settlement might well happen once Germany's "Russian campaign" was over.[238]

The indefatigable noninterventionist pressed on. In November he published a three-part series in the *Saturday Evening Post* that he soon published as a book called *America's First Crusade,* a memoir (written, he said, in 1934–35) of his experiences at the Versailles peace conference of 1919. It was a doleful tale of naïve American idealism thwarted and betrayed by European wickedness (the obvious moral: it could happen again).[239] On November 19 he took to the airwaves, arguing that the war in Europe had reached a stalemate and that it would be a "futile waste of American life" to send an expeditionary force overseas.[240] Hoover also struggled, unsuccessfully, to stop Roosevelt and Congress from weakening what was left of the Neutrality Act.[241] Just days before Pearl Harbor, he helped a New York attorney representing the Japanese embassy get in touch (through Bernard Baruch) with President Roosevelt, in a desperate, last-ditch attempt to achieve a modus vivendi between Japan and the United States.[242]

Convinced by mid November that war was imminent, Hoover and his diplomat-friend Hugh Gibson began working on a book about what the ultimate peace should be when the coming war was over.[243] Hoover's frustration was on full display in a letter to Alf M. Landon on November 29:

> I have felt that what we stand for in this mess is a *limited objective,* i.e., preparedness and aid to the democracies. Any enlargement of this objective is wicked for four consequences: to attempt a military ending of the war by our friends is a futility and a gigantic waste of life and resources; if we won the war, the result in a lasting peace is a futility; we shall have created some sort of collective system in the United States; aid to Russia may sound practical now but we and the world will pay dearly for this debauchery of the ideals of freedom.[244]

Just over a week later, Japanese bombs at Pearl Harbor put an end to Hoover's ordeal. Since 1938 he had crusaded unremittingly for three objectives: his election as president in 1940, providing sustenance to millions of war-numbed and hungry Europeans, and keeping America out of overseas military conflicts. He had lost, and lost decisively, on every front. Immediately and patriotically, Hoover pledged his support of the nation's war against Japan. "The President took the only line of action open to any patriotic American," he announced on December 8. "He will and must have the full support of the entire country. We have only one job to do now and that is to defeat Japan."[245] Among close friends, though, he remained "unreconstructed." "You and I know" (he said to one of them the day after Pearl Harbor) "that this continuous putting pins in rattlesnakes finally got this country bitten."[246] To another he wrote, "The day will come when this war will be put into the scales of judgment, and when this time comes you and I will be found to have been right."[247]

Despite his public contribution to national unity, Hoover was certain that the White House would never ask for his services during the war.[248] Nevertheless, on at least two occasions he tried. Early in 1942 he put out a feeler to the

White House through the publisher John C. O'Laughlin, only to discover, to his surprise, that FDR held some kind of grievance against him. Neither Hoover nor O'Laughlin ever wrote down what it was.[249] For his part, Hoover could not forget that throughout Roosevelt's presidency the White House had been "the source of direct and indirect personal attacks"—something "unique," so far as Hoover knew, "in the history of the White House."[250]

A little later in the war, as manpower problems caused dislocations on the home front, Hoover again signaled his availability for service, this time via his friend Bernard Baruch. But when the financier touted Hoover's name at the White House, Roosevelt refused. "Well, I'm not a Jesus Christ," he said. "I'm not going to raise him from the dead."[251]

And so Hoover was condemned to "four years of frustration."[252] To be sure, the years between Pearl Harbor and V-J day were not unproductive. As always, the Chief kept busy. With Hugh Gibson he wrote a best-selling book, *The Problems of Lasting Peace,* which evoked much discussion and probably steered the Republican Party toward a nonisolationist posture in the postwar world.[253] He strove to strengthen the already magnificent archives of his Hoover Institution at Stanford University. He remained active in the Republican Party and endeavored to curb the influence in it of Wendell Willkie, whose liberal "one worldism" he despised. He spoke frequently on food production problems and other domestic issues, often to the irritation of President Roosevelt. From time to time he tried in vain to revive his proposal for a neutral relief program for the German-occupied small democracies. He watched with disappointment in 1942 when Roosevelt appointed Herbert Lehman, the Democratic governor of New York, to lead the new United Nations Relief and Rehabilitation Administration (UNRRA), an analogue of the American Relief Administration (ARA) that Hoover had led with great success in 1919. Hoover met Lehman, proffered advice, and returned to the sidelines where he remained, largely ignored. In late 1944, as the end of fighting in Europe loomed, Hoover remarked sadly: "This Administration will not let us within a mile of relief this time. We will have to sit by and see them mess it up."[254]

And always he kept his eye on the war. As late as July 1942 he expected that Soviet Russia would collapse under the Nazi onslaught and that the ultimate peace would at least be "more lasting with that center of a furnace of revolution in other countries eliminated."[255] But as the war raged on and Russia did not collapse, his apprehensions mounted. By mid 1944 he was gloomily convinced that "the Stalin form of Communism" was inevitable for Poland, Yugoslavia, five other East European states, and possibly Germany as well.[256]

That autumn found Hoover in near despair. "[T]here is no island of safety in the world," he lamented.[257] "The whole world is rapidly moving toward Collectivism in some form."[258]

Perhaps, in retrospect, it might have been better for Roosevelt if he had given his rival some constructive part to play in the war effort. It might have kept Hoover occupied and away from his role as FDR's foremost antagonist. As it happened, in the four years after Pearl Harbor the former president— for all his other activities—found abundant time on his hands: time to start work on his memoirs, including the chunk that became his Magnum Opus.

The crusader-prophet against Roosevelt's foreign policy was about to become a crusader-historian.

"The biggest subject I have ever undertaken"

In a sense, the Magnum Opus was born on December 7, 1941. Hoover was convinced that the Roosevelt administration, by its "trade restrictions" against Japan and other "provocations," had driven the Japanese government into a corner, from which, like a rattlesnake, it had struck back at Pearl Harbor. The very next day, Hoover asked his intimate friend William R. Castle Jr., who had served as his undersecretary of state, to "preserve every record and every recollection" bearing on the background of the war with Japan that had just begun (see appendix, Document 1). He told Castle and Edgar Rickard that he intended to write a book on the diplomatic negotiations leading up to Pearl Harbor. He was positive that he could demonstrate that the war in the Pacific could have been averted.[259]

By March 1942 Hoover was busy collecting documents on America's relations with Japan since 1930.[260] He had even begun to write the opening chapters of his volume (see appendix, Document 3).[261] As part of his preparation, early in 1942 he compiled the first handwritten drafts of a sprawling "diary" for 1938–41.[262] It was not a true diary (composed at the time of the events it describes) but a retroactively created desk calendar of world happenings during those years. In later versions the "diary" incorporated copies of some of his most relevant correspondence, citations to his speeches, and his pithy comments on the events listed in his chronology.[263] In its final form, the compendium comprised nearly 1,400 typewritten pages.[264]

Hoover seems to have intended this document to serve as an aide-mémoire. In due course it became a building block and research tool for his narrative memoir/history of World War II.

While constructing his diary outline, Hoover persisted in other habits that were to serve him well as a memoirist and historian. Throughout the Second World War, a number of distinguished and well-connected Americans called on Hoover from time to time at his quarters in the Waldorf-Astoria in New York City and shared "inside" news about President Roosevelt's conduct of the war. These visitors included former Ambassador Joseph P. Kennedy, Colonel Truman Smith of U.S. Army Intelligence, Ambassador Patrick Hurley, Bernard Baruch, James A. Farley, and the journalists Constantine Brown and H. V. Kaltenborn. Their briefings and revelations whetted Hoover's determination to set the historical record straight. After these meetings, he routinely prepared memoranda of the conversations for his files: source material for his eventual Magnum Opus.[265] (In the appendix, Documents 2 and 7 are examples.)

During the war the former president also received, on a more-or-less weekly basis, lengthy, single-spaced, typewritten letters on events in Washington from his longtime confidant Colonel John C. O'Laughlin, publisher of the *Army and Navy Journal*.[266] O'Laughlin was on intimate terms with the U.S. Army's leadership, including General George C. Marshall, and was able to supply Hoover with a wealth of information and gossip that kept the Chief au courant. Some of this data eventually found its way into the Magnum Opus.

Hoover appears soon to have abandoned his projected book on U.S.-Japan relations before Pearl Harbor—though not his intense curiosity about the subject. Roosevelt's "lost statesmanship" toward Japan, in fact, became one of the dominant themes of the volume in your hands. But in 1942 Hoover was not yet ready for an intellectual assault on FDR's Far Eastern foreign policy. Now nearing seventy, the ex-president had other fish to fry first: notably his memoirs.

In July 1940, as mentioned earlier, Hoover began to compose his memoirs in earnest.[267] By December the early portion (apparently covering his life before 1914) was complete.[268] In the summer of 1942 he commenced what eventually became volume II.[269] In 1943–44 he turned to drafting volume III.[270] In the spring of 1944 he revised volume I; later in the year he turned back to volume II.[271]

In these as well as other book projects to come, his practice was invariant. First, he wrote a section of his manuscript in longhand; one of his staff of secretaries then typed it. Then, using his ever-present pencil, he corrected and revised the typescript, which was then retyped and returned to him for further revisions, a back-and-forth process that might go on for some time. All the while, Hoover would be composing and revising other segments of his manuscript in the same manner. When Hoover considered the revisionary process well advanced, he would send out a large batch of typescript pages to a printer, who would convert them into page proofs, in order (it seems) to give Hoover a sense of how his manuscript would look in print. Then he would proceed to edit and revise the printer's handiwork. In due time, it might go back to the printer for resetting. It was a laborious process as well as a costly one: the charge for preparing page proofs must have been substantial. But Hoover liked his books done this way and never wavered from his procedure until the invention of xeroxing.[272]

To assist him, he employed several secretaries headed by Bernice "Bunny" Miller, who joined him at the end of 1940 and remained until the early 1960s. One of his staff, Loretta F. Camp, arrived late in 1941 and stayed until his death; in time she became the principal office manager of the Magnum Opus.[273] In the spring of 1943 Hoover hired a young Yale instructor in economics named Arthur Kemp to assist him in preparing speeches and writings on agricultural issues. Kemp worked only a few weeks before entering the U.S. Army Air Force, but the experience had been mutually agreeable. Soon after the war he returned to Hoover's employ in an enhanced role.[274]

On January 7, 1944, Hoover's beloved wife, Lou, died suddenly at their home in the Waldorf–Astoria, less than three months short of her seventieth birthday. As Hoover strove to cope with his loss, he poured his energies into preparing his burgeoning memoirs. By June he had completed a bound page proof edition covering most of his life from his birth in 1874 to 1921 (the eventual volume I). By November, he had assembled bound page proof editions for his years as secretary of commerce (volume II) and as President (volume III): in all, more than nine hundred printed pages.[275]

Up to this point, most of Hoover's as yet unpublished memoirs had focused on himself and his extraordinary achievements—in mining engineering, humanitarian work, and government service. But what would he write next, about the still-unfolding phase of his life *after* 1932—after his rejection at the polls by the American people?

More than any other former president in American history (with the possible exceptions of Richard Nixon and Jimmy Carter), Hoover in his later years was a man driven by an unceasing quest for vindication. And more than most of the individuals who have made it to the White House, he was animated by a deeply held political and social philosophy and by a vision of America as a "lamp of liberty" among nations. These facts—and his deepening alarm at the New Deal's challenge to his philosophy and vision—drove him into the next, and most contentious, phase of his memoirs project. If he could not win political redemption for himself at the polls, he might at least gain an ideological victory in print by documenting his unbending resistance to America's wrong turning since 1933. For Hoover, then, the latter part of his memoirs would be the continuation of his war on Rooseveltian liberalism by other means.

Hoover's writing now developed along two tracks. In the autumn of 1944 he began to compose what was in effect the fourth volume of his projected memoirs. He entitled it *Twelve Years 1932–1944*; eventually he renamed it *Collectivism Comes to America.*[276] Its subject was his crusade in the 1930s against "the creeping collectivism of the New Deal."[277]

That same autumn, he wrote out the first rough chapters of a parallel volume devoted to World War II and his fight to keep America out of it. He referred to the manuscript informally as the "War Book." An early table of contents bore the title "Volume V: World War II."[278] It was the embryo of what became the Magnum Opus.

In an early chapter completed (after several revisions) on December 13, Hoover offered a précis of his argument (appendix, Document 6). Of Franklin Roosevelt he wrote:

> It is my conviction that during the year 1938 until some time after the beginning of the war (September, 1939) Roosevelt did not wish to go to war, but his interventionism was simply the time-honored red herring to divert public attention from the failure of the New Deal, to restore employment by playing up dangers from abroad and engaging in power politics. This thesis of statesmanship was as old as Machiavelli.
>
> But after the war began (September, 1939) Roosevelt pushed the country, step by step, toward war, and every step was portrayed as "to keep us out of war" or "short of war," with scores of the most solemn assurances of his devotion to peace and that American boys would never be sent into the fight on foreign land or water.
>
> After the election in 1940, however, the tone changed; there was no more "short of war" or promises to keep out. On the contrary, soon in 1941 there began a series of provocations and actions by the administration which amounted to an undeclared war upon Germany, and a few months later upon Japan.[279]

Clearly the course of events since Pearl Harbor had not shaken Hoover's convictions about the correctness of his prewar stance.[280] And clearly the

"War Book" was to be no ordinary memoir. In the very first paragraph of his précis chapter, he made a remarkable vow:

> Not until the inner history of the events leading up to our entry into World War II are [sic] brought into the daylight can the final history of how we got into it be written. And if I live long enough I propose to write that history.[281]

In the ensuing months—soon to be years and then decades—the Chief was as good as his word. Early in 1945 his friend Edgar Rickard recorded in his diary that Hoover was "preparing a careful treatise on events leading up to the War, and I read much of material, which accuses F. D. R. of deliberately forcing us in, while publicly proclaiming he will not send our boys overseas."[282] During 1945, in fact—the year of the Allied victory—Hoover labored at the first drafts of his critical history-cum-memoir, introducing themes that became integral to his revisionist interpretation: for example, that the Tehran summit conference of December 1943—not the Yalta conference of February 1945—had been the truly catastrophic turning point for the postwar settlement. "It was here," Hoover charged in late 1945, "that Churchill and Roosevelt acquiesced in Russian annexation of the Baltic States, Western Finland, Western [Eastern] Poland, Bessarabia and various other unilateral actions."[283]

In one draft, dated November 15, 1945, Hoover wrote scathingly of the contrast between President Roosevelt's idealistic "Four Freedoms" proclamation of 1941 and the actual condition of the postwar world. Roosevelt had defined the first freedom as "freedom of speech and expression—everywhere in the world." "Yet," Hoover rejoined, "150 million people of nations in Europe have far less of it, if any at all, than before the war." In 1941 Roosevelt had acclaimed his vision as "a definite basis for the kind of world attainable in our own time and generation." To which Hoover, in 1945, retorted: "Did any man or woman of the remotest thought or understanding believe a word of this? It was soapbox oratory from a man who knew better—and it stirred the emotions of the ignorant to acquiesce in their Golgotha."[284]

Initially Hoover intended to include in volume V an account of his unsuccessful crusade for food relief for civilians in Nazi-occupied Europe during World War II—the effort that Roosevelt and Churchill had blocked.[285] Before long, however, the ex-president decided to tell this story separately, in a sixth volume of his memoirs. Thus the "War Book" or Magnum Opus proper became exclusively focused on the (mis)conduct and baleful consequences of the Second World War.

Early in 1946, Arthur Kemp—freshly discharged from the United States military—returned to Hoover's entourage in New York City. The thirty-year-old academic took a position as an assistant professor of economics (while working toward his doctorate) at New York University. He also became Hoover's research assistant, an essentially half-time job that he filled for the next seven years.[286]

As a trained economist (and unabashed conservative), Kemp helped Hoover research and revise his third volume of memoirs, which analyzed the Great Depression and defended Hoover's record.[287] But the young professor's principal responsibility was to work with the Chief on the "War Book." In part this entailed meticulous fact-checking and suggesting possible changes in Hoover's drafts.[288] But mostly Hoover relied on Kemp to scout out and appraise the growing array of memoirs, monographs, government publications, and other historical source material on the war that was making its way, year by year, into print: sources like the Congressional Pearl Harbor hearings, the transcripts of the Nuremburg war crimes trials, the documentary compendia in the U.S. State Department's *Foreign Relations* series, and Winston S. Churchill's multivolume history of the Second World War. After perusing a relevant work, Kemp usually prepared a brief book report for Hoover and identified excerpts from the work for his secretaries to copy and for Hoover to use if desired. Between 1946 and 1953 Kemp spent innumerable hours as Hoover's designated reader.[289]

With Kemp's return in early 1946, work on the "War Book" shifted into even higher gear. In a memorandum to the new research assistant in mid February (Document 8), Hoover instructed him to examine the entire manuscript for grammar, diction, vocabulary, and "any doubtful points" and to "[b]ear in mind the 12 theses." Among them:

a. War between Russia and Germany was inevitable.

b. Hitler's attack on Western Democracies was only to brush them out of his way.

c. There would have been no involvement of Western Democracies had they not gotten in his (Hitler's) way by guaranteeing Poland (March, 1939).

d. Without prior agreement with Stalin this constituted the greatest blunder of British diplomatic history. . . .

f. The United States or the Western Hemisphere were never in danger of invasion by Hitler.

h [*sic*]. This was even less so when Hitler determined to attack Stalin.

i. Roosevelt, knowing this about November, 1940, had no remote warranty for putting the United States in war to "save Britain" and/or saving the United States from invasion.

j. The use of the Navy for undeclared war on Germany was unconstitutional. . . .

l. The Japanese war was deliberately provoked. . . . [290]

Here, obviously, was no gentle memoir or detached scholarly study in the making. Hoover knew what he believed. What he needed — and what he was sure existed — was the incontrovertible evidence to sustain his astounding claims.

Always he was on the lookout for fresh data and fresh corroboration of his "theses." In a conversation with General Douglas MacArthur in Tokyo in May 1946 (Document 9), Hoover asserted that "the whole Japanese war was a madman's desire to get into war" — an unmistakable allusion to Franklin Roosevelt. MacArthur agreed and further concurred with Hoover that the Roosevelt administration's imposition of economic sanctions on Japan in July 1941 had been "provocative" — so much so that it had made war nearly certain. MacArthur also seconded another of Hoover's favorite theses: that Roosevelt could have come to terms with the peace-minded Japanese prime minister, Prince Konoye, in the early autumn of 1941, when Konoye had sought a rapprochement with the United States in the Far East. Roosevelt's response to Konoye's initiative was to play prominently in the drama of the Magnum Opus.

Meanwhile, as the founder/benefactor of the Hoover Institution on War, Revolution and Peace, the Chief redoubled his efforts to acquire unique and invaluable historical documentation from around the world concerning the recent global cataclysm and its aftermath. Even before the war was over, he had obtained the files of the America First Committee and had secured about $235,000 in gifts and pledges for postwar collecting activities. On a trip to Europe in 1946, he acquired portions of the diary of Nazi Germany's deceased propaganda minister, Joseph Goebbels, as well as the files of the wartime Polish underground.[291] Soon the Hoover Institution would be a home for a number of exiled, anticommunist, European scholars as well as a trove of historical treasure on which Hoover relied for his own research.

As if all this were not enough to occupy him, in 1946 Hoover — at President Truman's request — conducted a worldwide survey of food and famine conditions on five continents. The former president visited thirty-eight countries and traveled more than fifty thousand miles. The following year he returned to Germany and Austria to reappraise conditions there.[292] More than a decade later, his experiences were to shape the final portion of his Magnum Opus.

Despite these interruptions, the preparation of his memoirs continued. By mid 1947 the production of the "War Book" had advanced to the page proof stage. It was now arranged strictly chronologically, with a chapter for each year between 1938 and 1946. "Chapter," though, is perhaps a misnomer; the section for 1941 contained 240 pages. As returned from the printer in install-ments that spring and summer, the manuscript (now labeled the "4th" or "5th" edition) encompassed 1,099 printed pages.[293] It was but one of six volumes of memoirs now in preparation.

Despite its gargantuan size and abundant detail, the latest version of vol-ume V packed a considerable wallop, as the excerpts reprinted in the appen-dix of this volume attest (Documents 12 and 13). With neither hesitation nor apology, Hoover castigated the "lost statesmanship" of President Roosevelt and declared flatly that "Mr. Roosevelt wanted war." Although Hoover labeled his work in progress a memoir, it increasingly resembled a prosecutor's brief, condemning Roosevelt—and Churchill, too—at the bar of history.

In mid 1947 Roosevelt's successor, Harry Truman, invited Hoover to chair a newly created federal agency: the prestigious Commission on the Organiza-tion of the Executive Branch of the Government. Almost at once it became known as the Hoover Commission. For the next year and a half, he directed its deliberations at a pace that would have exhausted people half his age. Even he had to slow down for a spell after contracting a case of shingles.[294]

Nevertheless, in 1948 he somehow found time to revise parts of what be-came volumes II and III of his memoirs.[295] And the "War Book" was never distant from his thoughts. By the end of 1949 he had generated another proof version, even longer than the 1947 one.[296] As always, he was hungry for more. In 1949 he asked his diplomat-friend William R. Castle Jr.—a fellow noninter-ventionist—for extracts from his diary pertaining to Japanese American rela-tions before the war.[297] He asked the conservative columnist George Sokolsky for help in compiling a list of known Communists and fellow travelers in the Roosevelt administration in every year between 1933 and 1945 (Document 15). It was a sign of an important new interest of Hoover's in the aftermath of the Alger Hiss case of 1948: the scope and significance of communist penetration of the U.S. government during the Roosevelt-Truman years—indeed, the in-fluence of "left wingers" generally in formulating American foreign policy in this period, especially toward China. In 1950 Hoover hired a secretary to col-lect the names of such persons from congressional hearings on communist subversion and similar sources and to keep her lists in a card file in his quarters.[298] Some of this data soon made its way into the Magnum Opus.

Hoover also took careful note of the rival "magnum opus" that Winston Churchill was publishing under the title *The Second World War.* Hoover admired the literary excellence of Churchill's work but not its substance and criticized it severely in essay notes for his "War Book" (Documents 14 and 16). Eventually (for reasons we shall mention later), he decided to remove these adverse commentaries from his manuscript.

For all its magnitude, Hoover's "War Book" remained only one component of his postpresidential memoirs. Early in 1950 he sent to the printer a two-volume manuscript entitled *Collectivism Comes to America,* covering Franklin Roosevelt's first and second presidential terms. As set up in page proofs, it totaled 538 pages.[299] In the preface to this tome (in effect, volume IV of his *Memoirs* as they took shape), Hoover succinctly gave its raison d'être:

> I have prepared these memoirs for several purposes. First, to prove the follies of our departure from the American system we have steadily built over 300 years. Second, to strip polluted history of its falsehoods. That is necessary if a people are to be guided by experience and truth. Third, to give the views I held on these questions at the time.

He explained that he was dividing his postpresidential memoirs into three series. The first he called *The Crusade against Collectivism in America* (another name for the volume whose preface he was writing). The second he entitled *Memoirs upon the Foreign Policies of the United States, 1933–1947* (embracing "my crusade to keep America out of World War II and an analysis of Roosevelt's foreign policies from 1933 to 1945 and their consequences"). This, of course, was the Magnum Opus. This crusade, he remarked, had "failed at Pearl Harbor through Roosevelt's provocative and unconstitutional actions." The third series he labeled *Food and Economics in the Second World War.*[300] (Elsewhere he labeled it *The Four Horsemen in World War II.*) [301]

All this was only a segment of the even more immense autobiographical undertaking in which he had been immersed, on and off, for nearly a decade. On May 21, 1950, he informed Lewis Strauss that his memoirs had reached "an advanced stage" covering no fewer than eight different topics:

1. 1874–1914 — Private Life (which you have)
2. 1914–1919 — Food and Reconstruction in World War I (which you have)

3. 1919–1929 — Reconstruction in the United States (being my eight years in the Department of Commerce)
4. 1929–1933 — Policies, Development and Reform (in one volume)
5. 1929–1933 — The Great Depression and the Campaign of 1932 (in one volume)
6. 1933–1940 — Collectivism comes to the United States (in two volumes)
7. 1938–1947 — Foreign Policies of the United States (in three volumes)
8. Food and Relief in World War II (or The Four Horsemen in World War II) (in one volume.)[302]

The accumulated page proofs probably exceeded three thousand printed pages.

By now even Hoover seemed a bit uncertain about the dimensions of his oeuvre. He told Strauss that item number 7 (the Magnum Opus) consisted of three volumes and embraced the years 1938–47. Ten days later he informed Strauss that it contained two volumes covering 1938–50. He also disclosed that he had "almost completed" it, along with the *Collectivism Comes to America* memoir and the *Four Horsemen* volume.[303]

If Hoover seemed momentarily confused about what he had wrought, one can imagine the state of mind, at times, of his secretaries as they typed, re-typed, and proofread his multitudinous drafts. Years later Arthur Kemp observed: "I often thought we were trying to write eight, ten, twelve volumes all at once. This is the way he worked."[304]

Late in 1950 Hoover initiated the publication of his autobiography. He se-lected the Macmillan Company to be his publisher and *Collier's* magazine for serialization. The chief articles editor at *Collier's*, Diana Hirsh, so impressed him that he eventually hired her to edit a number of his other writings.[305]

In 1951–52 Macmillan published three volumes of *The Memoirs of Herbert Hoover*. The first, subtitled *Years of Adventure, 1874–1920*, incorporated items one and two on the May 1950 list he had sent to Lewis Strauss. The second, subtitled *The Cabinet and the Presidency, 1920–1933*, embraced items three and four. The third volume, subtitled *The Great Depression, 1929–1941*, in-cluded item five and a portion of six.

Hoover's conceptualization of his third volume was especially revealing, both in itself and as a clue to the concurrent shaping of the Magnum Opus. Es-chewing the pleas of the historian Allan Nevins (who read the manuscript),[306]

Hoover insisted on including in volume III not only an elaborate defense of his anti-Depression policies as president but also a caustic critique of his successor's policies as well. Thus the final section of volume III (called "The Aftermath") drew heavily on the first half of his *Collectivism Comes to America* manuscript and included titles such as "Fascism Comes to America" and "Collectivism by Thought Control and Smear." Hoover's polemical intent was further underscored by his choice of subtitle, suggesting that Roosevelt and the New Deal had not ended the Great Depression but that World War II had. Thus the third installment of Hoover's published *Memoirs* turned out to be a hybrid: part memoir and apologia and part indictment of "the spectacle of Fascist dictation" that the New Deal had brought to American economic life.[307] Not for the last time, Hoover the crusading historian had eclipsed Hoover the memoirist.[308]

At this point the publication of Hoover's *Memoirs* stopped. In May 1950 he had confided to a friend that his "Collectivism" book, "War Book," and "Four Horsemen" book "should not be issued for some years"[309]—presumably because of their explosive character and perhaps for fear of offending living persons. This did not, however, prevent him from pressing forward with his historical inquest. Sometime in 1950 he gave his "War Book" a new name— *Lost Statesmanship*—another token of his didactic and prosecutorial intent.[310] Arthur Kemp continued to provide him reports on the latest publications,[311] and Hoover himself continued to edit and revise. No longer was the volume's cutoff date 1945 or even 1947; by the early 1950s its new terminus was the fall of China to the Communists in 1949.

Not long after the election of 1952—which sent a Republican to the White House for the first time in twenty years—Hoover completed another updating of *Lost Statesmanship*. As returned from the printer in early 1953, the proofs comprised eighty-nine chapters in 1,001 printed pages.[312] To some in his entourage who examined its contents, it contained Hoover's finest writing ever. One reader at the Hoover Institution exclaimed that it was "the most *electric* history" she had ever read.[313] (Excerpts are reprinted in the appendix, Documents 17 and 18.) Fearlessly, lucidly, unsparingly, he laid out his indictment of America's wartime diplomatic follies and their terrible consequences.

> The grip of Communism has spread from 200,000,000 of Russian people to an Asiatic horde of over 900,000,000. Today it threatens all civilization. And we have no peace.
>
> I have shown in this memoir the road down which Roosevelt and Churchill took mankind. I need not again repeat their acquiescences and their

appeasements or their agreements with the greatest enemy of mankind. Their declarations and secret agreements at Moscow in November, 1943, at Teheran in December the same year, at Yalta in February, 1945. Truman, at Potsdam in August, and his policies in China from 1945 to 1951 are the inscriptions on tombstones which marked the betrayal of mankind. These peoples wallowing in human slavery in their nightmarish dreams, may sometimes have recollected these Roosevelt promises—but only to awaken in a police state.

And Communism was still on the march threatening the rest of the world.[314]

In a stirring, climactic chapter Hoover listed nineteen "gigantic errors" that American and British policy makers had committed since 1933, including Roosevelt's recognition of Soviet Russia in 1933; the Anglo-French guarantee of Poland in 1939; Roosevelt's "undeclared war" of 1941 before Pearl Harbor; the "tacit American alliance" with Russia after Hitler's invasion in June 1941 ("the greatest loss of statesmanship in all American history"); Roosevelt's "total economic sanctions" against Japan in the summer of 1941; his "contemptuous refusal" of Japanese prime minister Konoye's peace proposals that September; the headline-seeking "unconditional surrender" policy enunciated at the Casablanca conference in 1943; the appeasing "sacrifice" of the Baltic states and other parts of Europe to Stalin at the Moscow and Tehran conferences in 1943; Roosevelt's "hideous secret agreement as to China at Yalta which gave Mongolia and, in effect, Manchuria to Russia"; President Harry Truman's "immoral order to drop the atomic bomb" on Japan when the Japanese had already begun to sue for peace; and Truman's sacrifice of "all China" to the Communists "by insistence of his left-wing advisors and his appointment of General Marshall to execute their will." As for Hoover's own stance in these years, the ex-president was unrepentant. "I was opposed to the war and every step in it," he wrote. "I have no apologies, no regrets."[315]

Some years later Arthur Kemp suggested that if Hoover had published *Lost Statesmanship* more or less in this form, and at this juncture, its "emotional impact" would have been "tremendous."[316] Appearing during the Korean War and the ascendancy of Senator Joseph McCarthy, amid clamorous debates over Roosevelt's conduct at Yalta and the question of "who lost China," such a book might indeed have electrified the nation. Surprisingly—considering the intensity of his convictions—Hoover continued to hold back. He had already indicated privately in 1950 and 1951 that his Magnum Opus would not be published "for some years,"[317] a remark he repeated to Lewis Strauss on February 4, 1953.[318] Instead, then, of racing to publish his sizzling manuscript while the political iron was hot, just six days later (February 10) he farmed it out to Diana Hirsh—not for serialization by *Collier's* but for still more editing and feedback.[319] During the next several months (and perhaps longer), she carefully corrected his manuscript and made suggestions for improvement.[320] Hoover paid her $2,500 (a not insubstantial sum in those days) for her assistance.[321]

Meanwhile his hefty parallel volume—*Collectivism Comes to America*—was undergoing its own growing pains. In the spring of 1951 he decided to convert it into a book entitled *The Years as Crusader,* encompassing his "crusade against collectivism" on the home front since 1933 as well as other subjects.[322] By the spring of 1953 it had evolved into a book of forty-six chapters (all in page proofs) renamed *The Crusade Years,* focusing on four topics: his private life since leaving the White House; his crusade for "benevolent institutions" (such as the Boys Clubs movement, which he headed); his "crusade" for relief in Europe in World War II; and his anticollectivist "crusade" in domestic politics in the 1930s and 1940s.[323] Hoover plainly savored the fighting word *crusade,* with its connotations of dynamism and idealism, as a description of his public activity during the Roosevelt-Truman era. But, as with his *Lost Statesmanship* manuscript, he seemed unready to release his *Crusade* volume promptly, probably because of its unvarnished candor about Harry Truman and certain other living politicians.[324]

So the cycle of research, revision, editing, fact-checking, and more revision resumed for the Magnum Opus. In 1953, after teaching seven years (and earning his doctorate) at NYU, Arthur Kemp accepted a professorship at Claremont Men's College in California.[325] Although Hoover had now lost the steady services of his capable research assistant, Kemp continued to send in book reports, to identify fresh historical source material for analysis, and to edit the latest versions of Hoover's manuscript when given the chance, particularly during the summers of 1954 and 1955.[326] Still, between 1953 and 1955 the pace of production on the Magnum Opus slowed.

It was not that Hoover was in danger of lapsing into lethargy; quite the contrary. In the summer of 1953 Congress voted to create another Commission on Organization of the Executive Branch of the Government, and President Eisenhower promptly invited Hoover to chair it. To the aging Republican and foe of nearly all things Rooseveltian, it was an opportunity for vindication on a new and heroic scale: a chance to devise and implement an agenda to curtail the federal bureaucracy, reduce federal expenditures, check "creeping Socialism," and "help clean up the mess which General Eisenhower inherited."[327] It was a chance to rebuild the endangered foundations of the American economic system and whack at the jungle growth of the New Deal. During the next two years, the Chief devoted himself to the work of what was informally known as the Second Hoover Commission and gained new accolades from much of the public. It did not seem to faze him that on August 10, 1954, in the midst of these grueling exertions, he turned eighty years old.

In 1955, after completing this latest service to the nation, the chairman of the Hoover Commission refocused on his private affairs, including an increasingly nagging question: What to do about the remainder of his *Memoirs*? One idea seems to have been to break down the massive *Crusade Years* manuscript of 1953 into smaller components and turn them into separate publications. Thus late in 1955 section IV of *The Crusade Years* went off to the printer (in somewhat revised form) as *The Crusade against Collectivism in American Life*. It returned in a clean, page-proof version numbering 282 pages.[328] But no sooner did Hoover venture in this direction than he evidently changed his mind. For reasons that remain unclear, he put aside this entire latest variant of volume IV—a candid account of twenty years of his life in Republican politics—and never published it.

One reason may have been that a new publishing project had begun to absorb his thoughts. Sometime in 1955 or early 1956 Hoover conceived the idea of writing a detailed chronicle of his Commission for Relief in Belgium in World War I and of his gigantic food distribution efforts in Europe during and after that war. In June 1956 he hired a graduate student named Walter R. Livingston to assist him for three months; Livingston ended up staying two and a half years. Originally Hoover intended to write two volumes, but they soon became three and ultimately four: a comprehensive history of American "enterprises of compassion" (primarily *his* enterprises) that had saved literally millions of lives from famine and disease during and after World Wars I and II. By the time Livingston left the Chief's employ at the end of 1958, Hoover and his staff were working on all four volumes simultaneously.[329]

In 1958 and 1959 Hoover retained Diana Hirsh to edit at least three of these volumes, to which at one point he gave the title *Forty-four Years*.[330] Other friends and staffers contributed as well. Between 1959 and 1964 he published the series under a much better title: *An American Epic*.[331] Nearly two thousand printed pages in toto, it was his tribute to a monumental record of American generosity, "compassion and conscience"—a stupendous achievement of which few of his countrymen seemed to have any knowledge.

By now it was plain that Hoover the historian rarely proceeded in a straight line. Early in 1957, while working on part of the *American Epic* series, he had another idea: Why not take the chapter he was then writing about the Paris peace conference of 1919 and expand it into a book about Woodrow Wilson's "crucifixion" at that conclave?[332] Instantly Walter Livingston and other members of Hoover's staff dropped other tasks and hastened to supply him with the requisite documentation.[333] Diana Hirsh, among others, was called in to help edit his rapidly developing manuscript.[334] Part personal memoir and part historical narrative, *The Ordeal of Woodrow Wilson* appeared on April 28, 1958.[335] It was the first book ever written by a former president about another president, and it proved to be one of Hoover's most admired publications.[336]

By the mid 1950s, Suite 31-A in the Waldorf Towers seemed more like a writing factory than a residence. On June 8, 1956, Hoover informed the director of the Stanford University Press that he was preparing at least six more volumes for publication in the same format as his three volumes of memoirs already released by Macmillan.[337] A young secretary who worked for him in 1955–56 recalled some years later that the Chief was immersed in something like seven book projects simultaneously.[338] The Magnum Opus, or "Roosevelt book," was only one of them.

Added to all these endeavors were the daily demands of life as an elder statesman. Between January 1946 (when the Magnum Opus project accelerated) and April 1959, Hoover delivered 185 major speeches and published seven books.[339] Between June 1957 and July 31, 1958 (according to his staff's statistics), he regularly worked seven days a week. He received 1,620 invitations to speak and accepted thirty of them. He published one book, visited Belgium as President Eisenhower's representative to the Brussels World's Fair, and employed four secretaries and a research assistant. More than 55,000 letters were sent out under his name, not counting routine acknowledgments of birthday and Christmas greetings.[340]

Hoover's staff was amazed by his efficiency, phenomenal memory, and remarkable capacity for work. Now in his eighties, he arose daily around 5:30 A.M. and was at his desk by six. Around 7:00 or 7:30 A.M. he stopped for a cup of coffee. After an early breakfast—usually with scheduled guests—he devoted his mornings to writing at his desk. Until his final months of life, he wore a suit and necktie. After a short lunch (he was a very fast eater), he retreated with a sheaf of papers to his bedroom, although his staff suspected that he merely sat in bed and worked rather than napped. In midafternoon came an extended coffee break with his secretaries and visitors, after which he usually returned to his desk until six or seven o'clock.

Hoover did not write in the evenings; he told a secretary that the work product he generated after 6 or 7 P.M. was not worth the effort. Instead, he partook of a catered dinner in his suite, almost invariably with guests, followed by a game of canasta. At 10 P.M. he went off to bed.

But not for long. Often, in his last years, he arose around 2 A.M., warmed up a can of soup, perhaps, in the kitchen, and spent the next hour or more at his desk writing letters and laboring over his manuscripts. Whereupon he went back to bed. When his secretaries arrived in the morning, they had plenty of fresh scribbling awaiting them.[341]

Even on vacation his pace of work did not completely subside. Beginning in the late 1940s Hoover routinely spent part of the winter after the holidays at the Key Largo Anglers Club in Florida, where he had a houseboat named the *Captiva*. Although there he enjoyed many blissful hours bonefishing, his manuscripts, such as *The Ordeal of Woodrow Wilson*, were always nearby, along with documents sent from the Hoover Institution and the Waldorf-Astoria. Even in nominal repose, he took time to write and rewrite.[342]

Not even a serious illness could hold him down for long. On April 19, 1958, he underwent gall bladder surgery in New York City. Friends feared that he might not survive. Two weeks later he returned to his suite at the Waldorf, declaring that he would "get back into public service somewhere in another two weeks."[343]

The evolving structure of *An American Epic* solved one problem for Hoover: how to disclose the story of his "crusade against famine" during World War II. For the fourth volume of the *Epic* series, he revised, condensed, and in some places toned down the sometimes acerbic text of the *Four Horsemen* volume that he had completed in 1950 and 1951.[344] In effect, volume IV of the *Epic* filled the niche of volume VI of the *Memoirs* as he had earlier conceived them. With the domestic installment of his postpresidential memoirs (*The Crusade against Collectivism in American Life*) now in indefinite limbo, one huge gap remained: the "War Book," *Lost Statesmanship*.

At some point in the 1950s, General Bonner Fellers, a former aide to General Douglas MacArthur, visited Hoover at Suite 31-A. The Chief was scribbling furiously. "What are you doing, Mr. President?" the general asked. "I'm making my book on Roosevelt more pungent," Hoover replied.[345]

In fact, as early as 1954 he had begun to do just the opposite. On May 1 of that year he sent Arthur Kemp a memorandum (Document 19) with instructions for summer work on the Magnum Opus. Among other things, Hoover asked Kemp to note pages in the manuscript "where there are acid remarks about Churchill and Roosevelt. We may want to consider some of them again." He also asked Kemp to consider whether they should replace the title *Lost Statesmanship* with something "more effective and more objective." The manuscript now consisted of two volumes, Hoover noted, divided at December 7, 1941. He wondered whether they should be entitled "*Memoirs of Herbert Hoover—Foreign Relations of the United States from 1933 to Pearl Harbor* (Volume I), and *Foreign Relations of the United States from Pearl Harbor to 1953* (Volume II)."[346]

Although Hoover had previously shown some hesitation about publishing his "War Book" in the near future, his concern about "acid remarks" and objectivity was something new. It signaled the beginning of a slow but discernible change in the texture of his Magnum Opus. Particularly after 1959, the manuscript became less accusatory and more understated in tone. Meanwhile the footnote citations gradually became more numerous and precise. Although Hoover continued to call his work in progress a memoir, bit by bit it took on the appearance of a doctoral dissertation.

Thus, for example, his reproachful footnotes about Winston Churchill (Documents 14 and 16) disappeared, and a new preface prepared for *Lost Statesmanship* in 1957 (Document 20) contained a list of more than fifty separate historical works pertinent to his research—a subtle sign that he had read and mastered the relevant literature.

Hoover did not conceal the fact that he was preparing a "critical assessment" of "lost statesmanship" since 1938.[347] His determination to call Roosevelt and Churchill to judgment had by no means vanished. But his strategy, to a considerable degree, had shifted. Instead of driving his lessons home in a hard-hitting way to his "jury" (as he had done in the climactic pages of his 1953 draft), he seemed increasingly to guide his readers toward the correct conclusion more unobtrusively, by the sheer, unstoppable weight of his evidence. Ultimately he would claim (in his introduction to the book before you) that he had omitted his own views entirely from his work and would "demonstrate the truth from the words and actions of world leaders themselves" (as well as from other documentation).

Why this modulation of the tenor of his book? Unfortunately, the record is silent, and we can only speculate. Hoover's elevation in 1953 to the chairmanship of the second Hoover Commission, and the acclaim he received on the occasion of his eightieth birthday, may have had something to do with it. For many Americans he had become an elder statesman, and men of such status are expected to remain above the political fray. The departure from New York City in 1953 of Arthur Kemp—an outspoken conservative—may have removed a daily influence for a more aggressive statement of Hoover's theses. The editorial feedback of Diana Hirsh and other readers may have softened some of the sharper expressions of Hoover's views. In the mid 1950s Neil MacNeil, a retired assistant night managing editor of the *New York Times*, joined Hoover's inner circle and became one of his literary advisers,[348] after serving as editorial director of the second Hoover Commission.[349] MacNeil (as we shall see) was among those who later counseled Hoover to tone down his manuscript.

The new strategy carried certain risks. Hoover could no longer simply assert his "theses" and prosecute his enemies (as in a memoir). He must now *prove* his case using the most convincing evidence, and the weight of such evidence might feel heavy for nonscholars. Moreover, the reservoir of pertinent evidence was steadily expanding. In 1955, for instance, the State Department published its long-awaited compilation of documents pertaining to the Yalta conference—another indispensable trove that he had to scrutinize. As Hoover strained to keep up with the latest source materials, he was obliged to revise his text and update his footnotes further, thereby tilting his manuscript still more in a scholarly direction.

In another small sign of mellowing, in 1958 Hoover prepared a brief introductory memoir for *Lost Statesmanship* entitled "My Personal Relations with Mr. Roosevelt." Here he confirmed what he had long been reluctant to admit publicly: he and Franklin Roosevelt had been "good friends" in World War I and the 1920s. In his essay Hoover related how their friendship had frayed in the election campaign of 1928 when Roosevelt sent out political letters critical of Hoover and his advisers: appeals that Hoover considered "less than fair play." He also revealed that he had "offered my services" to President Roosevelt after Pearl Harbor but that the president had "made no reply." "Despite the urging of such mutual friends" as Bernard Baruch and Secretary of War Henry L. Stimson, "he frigidly declined any association with me." Then, in an unusual acknowledgment that Hoover's polemics against Roosevelt might have contributed to this rebuff, Hoover added, "I did not blame him for this attitude as my speeches in opposition to his foreign activities were probably hard for him to bear."[350]

Hoover eventually dropped his mini-memoir of Roosevelt from the Magnum Opus (it has since been published elsewhere).[351] And his new tone did not supplant his urge to expose error. In 1958 he retitled his manuscript *Lost Statesmanship: The Ordeal of the American People*.[352] As returned from the printer in January 1959, the latest version was more than eight hundred pages long for the pre–Pearl Harbor volume alone. Despite some apparent gestures toward greater objectivity, it was every bit as judgmental as the version of 1953.[353]

History will ask [Hoover concluded] some stern questions of Mr. Roosevelt's statesmanship. It will list his promises to keep out of war; the deceptions in

Lend-Lease; his undeclared wars on Germany and Japan; his alliance with Communist Russia; his refusal of repeated opportunity for peace in the Pacific; his campaign of a dozen fictions of frightfulness; and finally it will ask questions of his good faith with regard to the Constitutional processes of our Republic. They will not be answered by a single reference to the Japanese attack at Pearl Harbor.[354]

The Magnum Opus now began to move in a new direction that changed the shape of the final product. Ever since the late 1940s Hoover had been deeply interested in revelations of communist infiltration of American institutions during the Roosevelt/Truman period. He carefully monitored the sensational investigation of communist subversion by the House Un-American Activities Committee and other congressional bodies. Like many others on the Right, he grew alarmed at mounting evidence that Communists, fellow travelers, and befuddled liberals had disastrously influenced American foreign policy toward China during its civil war in the mid 1940s: a conflict that had ended in the Communists' triumph in 1949. Hardline anticommunists such as Richard Nixon and the journalists George Sokolsky and Eugene Lyons were among his friends.[355] One token of Hoover's interest was his inclusion in the Magnum Opus, as early as 1954, of a chapter on "Communist forces in motion" in American life (including the federal government) in the 1930s and afterward.[356] By 1957 the chapter, drawing on the extensive data assembled for his card files, was thirty-four printed pages long (Document 21).

To Hoover and other conservative Republicans in the mid 1950s, the overwhelming evidence of communist penetration of our national government in the 1930s and 1940s was no antiquarian concern. The militantly anticommunist former president was convinced that it was Franklin Roosevelt, with his "leftish leanings," who had "opened the door" to the communist plague at home. More important, Hoover believed, as he wrote in 1959, that this infiltration had had "potent effects upon peace and war" and had helped to inflict "great disasters upon the American people." The communist "web of subversion" (to borrow James Burnham's term) had *not* been "of little consequence"[357] but was part of the chain of causation that historians of the period must comprehend.

As of January 1959, Hoover's elaborately documented account of "The Communist Infiltration into the United States" was now seventy-two printed pages long and constituted chapter 16 in his manuscript.[358] Not long afterward he decided to divide it in half and move both parts to the front of his volume, where they became chapters 4 and 5. To these he now added three more chapters on communist principles and methods, the U.S. recognition of Soviet Russia in 1933, and the Kremlin's subsequent "onslaught" against the American people. To this new section—the opening section of the Magnum Opus—he gave the title "A Great Intellectual and Moral Plague Comes to Free Men."

Logically there seemed no reason for Hoover to start his book with a tutorial on the theory and practice of communism, followed by a systematic disclosure of those who had been its adherents and agents in the United States. Hitherto his drafts had begun with world events in 1938 or (in more recent revisions) 1933. But Hoover, with his didactic motives, seemed determined to place his chapters on communism at the beginning of his text, and there they remained to the end. The rearrangement reflected a developing feature of his thinking about his Magnum Opus in his final years. To him it was no longer just an inquest into the diplomatic fatuities of the Second World War and the men responsible for them. It was a history as well of the origins of "this greatest calamity in our national life" (Document 22): the Third World War now under way with the Communists.[359] More and more, the Cold War weighed on his mind—the Cold War and the need to explain to Americans the reasons for their peril.

On August 10, 1959, Hoover turned eighty-five. The day before his birthday, he appeared on the television program *Meet the Press,* where he was asked about his health. "I feel physically perfect," he answered. "About 68 I should think."[360] Certainly he acted like sixty-eight—or, more accurately, like thirty-four. In the next twelve months he delivered five major speeches, attended thirty-five public functions, dedicated four Boys Clubs, answered 21,195 letters, and traveled more than fourteen thousand miles.[361]

Still he persevered with the Magnum Opus. Sometime in 1959 or 1960 he concluded that his colossal manuscript was too long and must be condensed. How he arrived at this fateful judgment is unknown. But by the summer of 1961 he had completed a condensed version ("Edition No. 5") to which he gave the working title *The Ordeal of the American People.*[362]

Now commenced still another episode in the saga of the Magnum Opus. Sometime in the early 1960s (the precise date is uncertain) Hoover designated three close friends—Neil MacNeil, the radio broadcaster H. V. Kaltenborn, and Frank Mason, a retired NBC vice president—to serve as a committee of literary advisers (chaired by MacNeil) as he steered his work toward publication.[363] Early in 1961, he showed them his manuscript and asked for comments and suggestions.[364] He also solicited again the editorial services of Diana Hirsh.[365] With an eye on security, he sent two copies of the *Ordeal* to an attorney in California for safekeeping.[366] Anxious to wrap up the enormous undertaking as quickly as possible, in August 1961 he asked Arthur Kemp to leave Claremont Men's College for a few months and return to New York City to "assist me in finishing this book" on "the biggest subject I have ever undertaken." "I will . . . make it worthwhile," he promised.[367] But Kemp had pressing obligations and regretfully declined.[368]

Undaunted, Hoover soldiered on. By early 1962 he had produced another "edition" (No. 6).[369] That is, he had worked his way, pencil in hand, through Edition No. 5 and had returned it to his secretaries for retyping and photocopying—at which point it became Edition No. 6. (With the advent of the Xerox machine, he had abandoned his costly practice of putting each edition into page proofs.) Once the clean copy came back from "the photostat man," he dispatched it to his trusted advisers for additional feedback.[370]

In March 1962 Hoover's intimate friend Lewis Strauss visited the Chief in Key Largo and found him working on the Magnum Opus, for which he had now chosen a new title (and, as it happened, the final one): *Freedom Betrayed.*[371] Hoover believed that he could finish his project within two years. As Strauss listened, it was apparent that the effort was keeping the old man alive. Before they parted, Hoover disclosed that he was seriously ill and that his doctors had given him one year, possibly two, to live. He asked Strauss to divulge this to no one, not even to Hoover's two sons.[372]

Burdened though he now was by the knowledge of his approaching demise, he was heartened by most of the feedback that he received. Kaltenborn was especially enthusiastic; he called the work Hoover's "crowning achievement" and urged him to publish it as speedily as possible.[373] MacNeil also was strongly supportive, though he cautioned Hoover against referring to Hitler and Stalin as Satan and Lucifer in the text. To MacNeil it was important that Hoover not vitiate the "feeling of objectivity" that his documentation conveyed.[374] The strength of Hoover's book, he asserted, would lie largely in its "objectivity"—its condemnation of his subjects "out of their own words." On the copy of the manuscript that MacNeil returned to the Chief, he altered the passages where, as he put it, Hoover had allowed his "personal feelings" to show.[375] It was the very antithesis of the approach Hoover had taken a decade earlier.

Frank Mason also was initially impressed by the contents of Hoover's manuscript (in its *Lost Statesmanship* version) at the beginning of 1961.[376] But at some point in the next year or two, he evidently turned critical, and, in a couple of heated conversations, he let the Chief know it. He even counseled against publishing the book in Hoover's lifetime—advice which the elderly author evidently did not appreciate. Although Hoover sought Mason's comments in late 1962, after that he evidently no longer sent Mason drafts to read.[377]

On August 20, 1962, Hoover—now eighty-eight years old—entered a hospital in New York City for what he thought would be a routine annual checkup. Eight days later he underwent surgery to remove what turned out to be a malignant tumor in his colon. The good news was that the doctors did not expect the cancer to return.[378]

After nearly a month in the hospital, Hoover returned to his home on the thirty-first floor of the Waldorf-Astoria. His recovery was remarkably rapid; even while recuperating in his hospital bed, he worked a little on what the press vaguely described as a book with "a historical background."[379] His bout with cancer appeared not to slow him down. In November he completed the *tenth* edition of volume I of *Freedom Betrayed* and duly sent it off to Kaltenborn, Mason, and MacNeil.[380]

Here Hoover finally drew the line. After correcting Edition No. 10, he renamed it Edition Z—significantly, the last letter of the alphabet.[381] Even then he could not resist making still more changes. The altered edition became known as Z+H.[382]

In November 1962 the Chief informed his staff of another decision (Document 24): henceforth the Magnum Opus would consist of three volumes, not two. For more than a year he had been preparing a series of "tragic case histories" of four nations—China, Germany, Korea, and Poland—that had fallen into chaos or communism in the years immediately after World War II. Initially he intended to include these studies in volume II, which dealt with the period after Pearl Harbor. He now decided that they would constitute volume III. Well into 1963 he endeavored to put its projected components into final shape. Although he never produced a unified typescript with that label, it has been possible to construct one from the drafts he left behind. Volume III, then, appears here in the full text and sequence that he intended.[383]

By now a question or two may have occurred to readers: Why did Hoover feel compelled to rewrite his Magnum Opus? Why could he not bring himself to stop? The never-ending flood of new source material was one reason, but the problem went deeper. Hoover had long been a perfectionist about his principal writings, even down to the placement of commas and other minutiae.[384] Abjuring ghostwriters, as president of the United States he had laboriously drafted and redrafted his addresses and campaign speeches. His 1931

State of the Union message had gone through twenty-two such editions.[385] On one occasion in later years, he composed and recomposed a radio talk twenty-nine times.[386]

In the case of the Magnum Opus, Hoover's perfectionism was compounded by his knowledge that he was writing a relentlessly revisionist history of Franklin Roosevelt's foreign policy and that he could expect to be attacked by the targets of his criticism. His very title, *Freedom Betrayed,* hinted at gross misjudgments, even perfidy, in high places. He told a friend, "There is not a word or sentence or date that I dare to put in this book without checking, without knowing I have proof."[387] He wanted his volumes to be irrefutable in every respect.

Hoover's incessant tampering with his text may also have reflected a lingering feeling of insecurity as a writer. His struggle with the English composition requirement had nearly prevented his graduating from Stanford University.[388] All his life his spelling was irregular (in the Magnum Opus he routinely spelled Joseph Stalin's name "Stallin"). Although his prose was often robust and expressive, he seemed to feel the need for constant editing by his friends. The more he sought, the more he got, and it delayed him from wrapping up his project.

Toward the end of 1962, the former president launched a new effort to reach the finish line. In a memorandum to his staff of six full-time secretaries and one accountant (Document 24), he defined their responsibilities for the months ahead and instructed them to turn "our maximum energies to completing the books we have in the mill before starting anything new." This meant, primarily, the Magnum Opus and the fourth volume of *An American Epic.* Although each secretary worked a conventional five-day week, he asked that "some one of the six secretaries" henceforth be with him "every day of the week." "In my situation," as he put it (apparently alluding to his uncertain health), he needed their assistance constantly.

In the spring and summer of 1963 Hoover sent out copies of volume I (Z+H edition) for comment to a small circle of conservative friends, including General Douglas MacArthur, General Albert Wedemeyer, Lewis Strauss, William C. Mullendore, Raymond Henle, Albert Cole of the *Reader's Digest,* and Richard Berlin of the Hearst publications empire, among others (Document 26). Hoover had always been guarded about his manuscript; to some of these friends he labeled it "top secret"—no doubt to forestall "leaks" that might embarrass him. He also asked for advice on when the book should be published. From his "focus group" came back words of high praise and suggestions that he publish the book expeditiously. It was, they all seemed to agree, a tremendous achievement.[389]

As much as anything now, a sense of duty was driving Hoover on: a conviction that he especially—with his extraordinary life experiences and peerless collection of historical records—was equipped to lay before the American people the whole truth about the "betrayals of freedom" in the past thirty years.[390] He regarded his onerous task as a solemn calling—the one thing he wished to complete before his death.[391] He told a friend in early 1963 that he hoped to leave behind his three-volume opus "as a sort of 'will and testament' before I finally vanish" (Document 25). "I have not got far to go," he confided to his principal secretaries in June 1963, "and this is the most important job of my remaining years" (Document 27).

Yet after all his prodigious exertions in recent months, he still seemed hesitant to take the final plunge. "My own view" (about publication), he told friends, was "not yet."[392] The problem, as he saw it, was that the manuscript still needed two more years of work (Document 25). To facilitate "production," in June 1963 he proposed a shift in responsibilities in his New York office (Document 28). He also relied increasingly on the archival staff of the Hoover Institution on points of fact.[393]

In mid June 1963 the press reported that Hoover was again seriously ill, this time with "anemia, secondary to bleeding from the gastro-intestinal tract."[394] Although the public did not know it, his illness (apparently a bleeding ulcer) nearly proved fatal. At one point one of his sons telephoned President Kennedy that death was imminent.[395] But in the coming days, the bleeding stopped and Hoover gradually recovered; his team of physicians termed it "almost miraculous."[396] During the emergency Hoover had told his two sons not to worry: he was going to "pull through," he said; he still had "a great deal of work to do."[397] For much of the summer he remained bedridden and enfeebled. But on the occasion of his eighty-ninth birthday, on August 10, the *New York Times* reported that he was again working for short spells at his desk and was "impatient" to finish a book "he considers his 'Magnum Opus,' a history of the last 30 years."[398]

On September 26, 1963, Hoover wrote to his friend George Mardikian:

Generally, I am making slow progress, but my major job, the case history of the Second World War and its betrayal of freedom is now completed except my staff overhaul to check every sentence for its accuracy. The staff can complete it in about another year.[399]

Even now he could not resist another round of editing. Between September 1963 and the spring of 1964, he tinkered one last time with the text of volume II of his Z+H edition. With few exceptions, his revisions were small. To all intents and purposes, he completed volumes I and II of his Magnum Opus (except his staff's fact-checking) in September 1963. His work on the four "case histories" had stopped some months earlier.[400]

Volumes I and II of the Magnum Opus now comprised about eight hundred typewritten pages—substantially condensed from the versions of the 1940s and 1950s but still a formidable work. While Hoover waited for his staff to "overhaul" it, he began to consider possible publishing arrangements. At Albert Cole's suggestion, he sent a copy of volume I to *Reader's Digest* for possible condensation.[401] The senior editors and management seemed highly enthusiastic; for a time Hoover believed that the monthly magazine would publish a condensed version in 1964.[402] But the *Digest* evidently felt handicapped by the absence of a final version to condense, and the effort died on the vine.[403]

Meanwhile other publishing opportunities loomed on the horizon. The militantly anticommunist *Chicago Tribune* and Richard Berlin of the Hearst Corporation both expressed interest in serializing the work.[404] In 1964 the Chicago publisher Henry Regnery, who was bringing out *An American Epic* and whose father had helped to bankroll the America First Committee, asked to publish Hoover's study.[405]

But as the first rays of light seemed to shine at the end of the publishing tunnel, Hoover appeared to feel the tug of conflicting emotions: his burning desire to tell the historical truth and his yearning for esteem in the eyes of the American people. Could he reconcile his self-appointed role as crusader-prophet with his growing prestige as an avuncular elder statesman?

It was not that Hoover's deepest feelings about the past had dissipated. Years later, two secretaries who worked for him in his final years recalled his fierce antipathy to Winston Churchill. On one occasion he turned red in the face when he discovered that a member of his staff had visited an exhibit of Churchill's art at the Metropolitan Art Museum. Why, Hoover asked her, had she wasted her time looking at the works of *that* man?[406] To DeWitt Wallace, founder of the *Reader's Digest,* Hoover wrote in 1963: "I am determined to tell this gigantic betrayal of freedom out of these men's own mouths; otherwise, nobody would believe such a betrayal was possible."[407] The *method* of his indictment had changed but not his fundamental objective. He told Neil MacNeil that he wanted the Magnum Opus published without regard to costs or consequences.[408]

Yet Hoover dreaded the "mud volcanoes" of vituperation that he was certain would "arise from the Left" when the opus appeared.[409] He was also sensitive about the pain that his book's title might cause Harry Truman, with whom he had been friendly for several years. In November 1963 he therefore notified Truman (through MacNeil) of the Magnum Opus's existence and explained that the title *Freedom Betrayed* referred to *Communist* duplicity, not to the words or deeds of America's leaders. On behalf of Hoover, MacNeil asserted that the work was mainly "documentary" and nonpolitical, that Hoover esteemed Truman highly, and that Hoover would never intentionally give Truman offense. From Truman came back a warm assurance that nothing Hoover could do "would cause me to lose my admiration of him."[410]

Hoover's oral message was somewhat disingenuous. Earlier drafts of his Magnum Opus had severely criticized Truman's foreign policy (see Document 18). And the "betrayals of freedom" about which Hoover had been writing was scarcely limited to those of communist leaders. But it is fair to say that Truman himself, for whom Hoover developed considerable respect, was not the intended object of his indictment.

As Hoover waited for his staff to slog through its "overhaul," he could look with satisfaction on all the other products that his "factory" had turned out in the previous five years. In 1959 and 1960 came volumes I and II of *An American Epic*. In 1961, volume III of the *Epic* and the seventh installment in his series of *Addresses Upon the American Road*. In 1962, a delightful collection of his letters to children entitled *On Growing Up*, edited by his friend William Nichols. In 1963, his whimsical book *Fishing for Fun—And to Wash Your Soul*. In mid-1964, the fourth and final volume of *An American Epic*. It was an amazing feat: seven books, published between the ages of eighty-five and ninety.

But not yet the Magnum Opus, the one that mattered most. Early in 1964, apparently displeased by the pace of the "overhaul" effort in his New York office, Hoover was persuaded to send a copy of volumes I and II to the Hoover Institution, for a research associate named Julius Epstein to check.[411] Epstein set to work immediately and reported in mid August that he hoped to complete the task in about three months.[412] With the burden of clean-up and fact-checking now transferred to California, Hoover seemed to take a new lease on life. On April 18 he announced to Bonner Fellers that he was working on a *new* book, covering "recent history I didn't touch on [in] my previous volumes." It appeared to have something to do with the dismissal of General MacArthur from his command during the Korean War.[413]

But the curtain was beginning to fall on the former president. He had not ventured out of his "comfortable monastery" (as he called Suite 31-A) since

May 22, 1963; he would not do so again until his death.[414] In February 1964 he was stricken with a bleeding kidney and a pulmonary infection.[415] Although he survived, he grew increasingly feeble. By the time of his ninetieth birthday in August, he had more nurses attending him than staff: he had just two secretaries now, it was reported, instead of the seven he had employed a year before.[416] Still, the *New York Times* disclosed that the former president was at work on his thirty-third book: something "he calls his magnum opus, a study that traces the 'betrayal of the West by Soviet Russia' since President Roosevelt accorded it diplomatic recognition in 1933."[417] It was the closest he had ever come to publicly heralding the thunderbolt he hoped soon to unleash.

In the final weeks of his life, in the opinion of a good friend who was permitted to visit him, the Chief seemed discouraged about his Magnum Opus—a startling change in attitude.[418] Perhaps he sensed that he would never see it in print. In mid October, massive internal hemorrhaging set in. On October 20, 1964, Hoover died in the Waldorf Towers at the age of ninety years, two months, and ten days.

Under the terms of Hoover's will, ownership of his "memorabilia, documents, personal papers and books" was bequeathed to an entity known as the Hoover Foundation, Inc., of New York, which he had created in 1959.[419] The directors of this foundation included his sons Herbert Jr. and Allan and a few other family members and friends.[420] As the custodian of the Magnum Opus, the Hoover Foundation superseded the advisory committee of Kaltenborn, MacNeil, and Mason. It would be up to the foundation to decide what course to follow.

The first step was to complete the review of Hoover's Z+H volumes, which had been undergoing scrutiny at the Hoover Institution. Well into 1965 the process continued, as first Epstein and then a few other resident scholars examined the text and offered suggestions.[421]

Meanwhile, Neil MacNeil, living in Florida, spent part of 1965 (on behalf of the foundation) reediting Epstein's copy of volume I, which MacNeil had edited before Epstein received it.[422] Late in the summer, MacNeil received an edited copy of volume II from the Hoover Institution (via the Hoover Foundation) and proceeded to reedit the Magnum Opus from scratch, for what was now, for him, the fourth time. He wished to have a single, unified manuscript for the Hoover Foundation to consider. Early in 1966 the seventy-five-year-old retired newspaper editor finished the task.[424] In May 1966 he delivered his edited version of *Freedom Betrayed* to the foundation with the recommendation that it offer the two-volume set to the world "as an unfinished work" on which Hoover had labored "until his final illness." (The work was "unfin-ished," MacNeil asserted, because it lacked volume III.)[425]

Allan Hoover now circulated MacNeil's handiwork to various members of the Hoover Foundation as a prelude to deciding its fate.[426] Here for a time the matter rested.[427] As 1966 slipped into 1967, with no word of a formal deci-sion in New York, interviewees for Raymond Henle's Herbert Hoover Oral History Program speculated about the reasons for the delay.[428] The hesitation seemed to revolve around two questions: Was the manuscript good enough to be published, and—more worrisomely—would it kick up bitter contro-versy and retaliation by Hoover's political foes?

Hoover himself, in a memo to his son Allan sometime between 1962 and 1964, remarked that he and his political principles had long been vilified by "smear and misrepresentation of myself personally" to a degree "probably unequalled in American public life." He expected these attacks, which had recently "abated," to resume once he published *Freedom Betrayed,* and he seemed inclined to hold off until "some of the mud volcanoes have passed on."[429] Now that Hoover himself was gone, would publication of his "will and testament" to the American people reopen old wounds and reignite the fires of controversy that he had managed to transcend in his final years?

In the end the Hoover Foundation did not proceed to publication, and the Magnum Opus remained out of view. Since Herbert Hoover Jr. (1903–69), Allan Hoover (1907–93), and their key associates at the time are now deceased, one cannot say for certain, on the basis of available evidence, what tipped the scales. Most likely it boiled down to apprehension about the re-sponse that publication might generate, especially so soon after Hoover's dig-nified burial in 1964.

Whatever the concerns, the passage of nearly half a century has removed them. Time heals all wounds, it is said, and (as Edwin M. Stanton remarked in 1865 of Abraham Lincoln), Herbert Hoover now "belongs to the ages." His writings are part of the patrimony of American civilization. In 2009 the Hoover Institution invited me to edit *Freedom Betrayed* for publication. The result is the book you now hold.

Concluding Observations

Freedom Betrayed was the culmination of an extraordinary literary project that Hoover launched during World War II. As indicated earlier, it originated as a volume of his memoirs, a book initially focused on his battle against President

Roosevelt's foreign policies before Pearl Harbor. As time went on, Hoover widened his scope to include Roosevelt's foreign policies during the war, as well as the war's consequences: the terrible expansion of the Soviet empire at war's end and the eruption of the Cold War against the Communists. As a historian of these events, he became interested not only in the diplomatic blunders of the Roosevelt administration vis-à-vis Stalin but in the influence on it of advisers who proved to be Communists or their willing accomplices. To Hoover the "calamity" of the Cold War was the direct result of misjudgments by American leaders between 1933 and 1953—failures that enormously strengthened our postwar enemy, the Soviet Union. To prove this thesis became the intent of the Magnum Opus.

In its final form, *Freedom Betrayed* is part memoir and part diplomatic history. Although Hoover in his last years deliberately removed himself from the foreground of his Magnum Opus, he never ceased to call it a memoir, and more than a dozen chapters are of this character. At the same time—and, increasingly, after he shifted his rhetorical strategy—he strove to write a work that conformed to the canons of scholarship. He wanted, that is, to compose not only a memoir—full of personal comment and polemical verve—but also a history, meticulously footnoted and dispassionate in tone. The result was a hybrid that partakes of both genres.

Here it helps to recall the historian's distinction between a primary source, in which the author is a direct witness to, or participant in, the events he narrates, and a secondary source, in which the author writes *about* the events but does not experience them firsthand. *Freedom Betrayed* is thus both a primary source and a secondary source simultaneously.

Keep this distinction in mind as you weigh the significance of Hoover's book. Considered strictly as a work of historical scholarship—that is, as a secondary source—*Freedom Betrayed* has certain limitations. Completed nearly fifty years ago, it rests not on traditional archival research (most of the pertinent archives were not yet open)[430] but almost entirely on published materials available to Hoover and other historians at the time—documents (such as memoirs of war leaders) that are only a fraction of the evidentiary database available to later scholars. Although readers will discover some tantalizing nuggets, Hoover's book contains relatively few revelations that are not already familiar to historians of World War II and its aftermath.

Nevertheless, *Freedom Betrayed* deserves our attention for two reasons. First, as historians of American foreign relations will recognize, Hoover's opus is one of the best examples of a genre of scholarship and polemic that flourished for a decade and more after World War II: revisionist, conservative historiography on American diplomacy during that war.[431] Indeed, the Magnum Opus is probably the most ambitious and systematic work of World War II revisionism ever attempted, and its author none other than a former president of the United States.

On issue after issue, Hoover raises crucial questions that continue to be debated to this day. Did Neville Chamberlain err in his guarantee to Poland in March 1939? Did Franklin Roosevelt deceitfully maneuver the United States into an undeclared and unconstitutional naval war with Germany in 1941? Did the United States government ignore or even willfully sabotage a chance for a modus vivendi with Japan in the autumn of 1941? Did Roosevelt make a gigantic mistake in effecting an alliance with the Soviet Union in 1941–42? Did he unnecessarily appease Joseph Stalin at the pivotal Tehran conference in 1943? Was Tehran (not Yalta) the occasion for a great betrayal of the Atlantic Charter and the ideals for which America fought? Was Roosevelt's wartime policy of "unconditional surrender" a blunder? Should the Allies have invaded the Balkans instead of southern France in 1944? Was Chiang Kai-shek's Nationalist government in China grievously undermined by Roosevelt at Yalta? Was the use of the atomic bomb on Japan a necessity? Did communist agents and sympathizers in the White House, Department of State, and Department of the Treasury play a malign role in some of America's wartime decisions? Did a cabal of left-wing advisers steer President Truman's policy toward China in a direction that undermined Chiang Kai-shek and paved the way for the fall of China to the Communists?

On these and other controversies *Freedom Betrayed* takes its stand. Hoover's work reflects the foreign policy thinking not just of himself but of many American opinion makers during his lifetime and beyond. As such, it is a document with which historians should be acquainted.

Nor are all of Hoover's concerns hoary chestnuts. The startling Venona disclosures and other revelations of recent years about the extent of Soviet espionage in wartime Washington are prompting a reappraisal of communist infiltration of the United States government in the 1940s.[432] In this respect parts of *Freedom Betrayed* are especially pertinent.

Despite the passage of time, then, the intrinsic interest of Hoover's book remains strong, in part because it insistently raises issues—in some cases *moral* issues—with whose consequences we live even now. One cannot, for example, read the "tragic case histories" in volume III of *Freedom Betrayed* without reflecting anew about some of America's foreign policy initiatives during and after the Second World War. Hoover reminds us that history is made by *people* and that the great decisions of World War II were made by a handful of men whose statesmanship, "lost" or otherwise, had life-and-death implications for the world. His Magnum Opus should be read not so much as a monograph but, more importantly, as an argument that challenges us to think afresh about our past. Whether or not one ultimately accepts his argument, the exercise of confronting it will be worthwhile.

Second, *Freedom Betrayed* merits study because of its extraordinary and enduring value as a *primary* source: as a window on the mind and worldview of one of the twentieth century's preeminent leaders. For two decades Hoover devoted phenomenal energy to preparing this tome; it had a commanding place in his thoughts. He considered it one of the great undertakings of his life and the most important of all his writings. From a biographical perspective one cannot fully understand Hoover's postpresidential career without reading his Magnum Opus. Its publication, one hopes, will serve future studies of this remarkable man.

Nearly seventy years ago, during World War II, Hoover began to scribble the first words of this work. He did so in the shadow of three great disappointments: his inability to win the Republican presidential nomination in 1940; his failed crusade to keep the United States out of World War II; and his frustrated bid to become the Great Humanitarian in Europe for a second time. Yet he fought back, on the printed page and elsewhere. In 1964 he was buried where he was born, in West Branch, Iowa, after a career extraordinarily rich in achievement and honors.

Only one accomplishment eluded him at the end: publication of *Freedom Betrayed*. But history, someone has said, is "a conversation without end." Nearly fifty years after he completed work on his Magnum Opus, it seems fitting to welcome Mr. Hoover back to the conversation.

George H. Nash
South Hadley, Massachusetts
October 2010

NOTES

1. John W. Hill oral history (1971), pp. 5, 6, copies in the Hoover Institution Archives (hereinafter HIA) at Stanford University and in the Herbert Hoover Presidential Library (hereinafter HHPL), West Branch, Iowa. According to the Herbert Hoover Calendar at HHPL, Hill met Hoover for the first time on November 19, 1951.

2. Hill oral history, pp. 5, 17.

3. Herbert Hoover, *The Challenge to Liberty* (New York: Charles Scribner's Sons, 1934).

4. Hoover to Edward Eyre Hunt, September 14, 1933, Post-Presidential Individual File (hereinafter PPI), Herbert Hoover Papers, HHPL.

5. Hoover to William Allen White, May 11, 1937, PPI, Hoover Papers, HHPL.

6. The evidence on this point is overwhelming. One of the best contemporary sources on Hoover's maneuvering is the diary of his longtime friend and confidant Edgar Rickard, at HHPL. For excellent accounts of Hoover's political activities in the 1930s, see Gary Dean Best, *Herbert Hoover: The Post-Presidential Years* (Stanford, CA: Hoover Institution Press, 1983), and Richard Norton Smith, *An Uncommon Man: The Triumph of Herbert Hoover* (New York: Simon and Schuster, 1984).

7. Most of Hoover's principal writings and speeches during this period were collected in Herbert Hoover, *Addresses upon the American Road, 1933–1938* (New York: Charles Scribner's Sons, 1938).

8. Ibid., pp. 300–308; *New York Times*, January 16, 1938, pp. 1, 4.

9. Herbert Hoover, *America's First Crusade* (New York: Charles Scribner's Sons, 1942), p. 76.

10. Hoover, *Addresses ... 1933–1938*, p. 301.

11. Ibid., pp. 301–2.

12. He told reporters that he had received "seven or eight honorary degrees, I can't remember the exact figure, and 15 or 18 medals." *Palo Alto Times*, March 29, 1938, Clippings File, HHPL.

13. William R. Castle Jr. diary, March 7, 1939, HHPL, quoting verbatim Hoover's account to him that day of Hoover's conversation with Neville Chamberlain the year before. Hoover told Castle that this was the first time he had repeated the conversation to anyone.

14. Hoover, notes of his interview with Neville Chamberlain, March 22, 1938, as printed in "An Examination of Europe," pp. 43–44, in the 1947 page proof edition of the 1938 section of his Magnum Opus, in Herbert C. Hoover Papers, Box 3, "M. O. 6" envelope, HIA. Hoover's original notes have not been found. A condensed version of them appears in the final version of the Magnum Opus in this volume.

15. According to his interview notes cited in the preceding footnote, Hoover told Chamberlain that the Germans needed another eighteen months to complete "their plans"; after that, Hoover said, anything was possible.

16. *New York Times*, March 19, 1938, p. 3.

17. *Palo Alto Times*, March 29, 1938; *San Francisco News*, March 29, 1938; *New York Herald Tribune*, March 29, 1938; copies of all in Clippings File, HHPL. See also *New York Times*, March 29, 1938, p. 10.

18. *New York Herald Tribune*, March 29, 1938.

19. *New York Times*, April 1, 1938, pp. 1, 4, 5; also in Hoover, *Addresses ... 1933–1938*, pp. 309–24.

20. Hoover to Hugh R. Wilson, April 25, 1938, "Hoover, Herbert," Hugh R. Wilson Papers, HHPL.

21. Hoover, *Addresses ... 1933–1938*, pp. 325–36 (full text of speech: pp. 325–34).

22. Ibid., pp. 327, 329.

23. *New York Times*, April 1, 1938, p. 5; Hoover, *Addresses . . . 1933–1938*, p. 323.

24. *New York Times*, April 9, 1938, p. 1; Hoover, *Addresses . . . 1933–1938*, pp. 332–33.

25. *New York Times*, April 26, 1938, p. 4; Hoover, *Addresses . . . 1933–1938*, pp. 335–42.

26. *New York Times*, May 6, 1938, pp. 1, 19; Hoover, *Addresses . . . 1933–1938*, pp. 343–54.

27. *New York Times*, September 29, 1938, p. 22; Hoover, *Further Addresses upon the American Road, 1938–1940* (New York: Charles Scribner's Sons, 1940), p. 4 (pp. 3–20 for full text).

28. Frederick W. Marks, *Wind over Sand: The Diplomacy of Franklin Roosevelt* (Athens, GA: University of Georgia Press, 1988), p. 146; Robert E. Hertzstein, *Roosevelt & Hitler: Prelude to War* (New York: Paragon House, 1989), p. 216. After the Munich agreement, Roosevelt told Neville Chamberlain: "We in the United States rejoice with you and with the world at large."

29. See appendix, Document 18.

30. On October 3 Hoover wrote to a friend: "I do not think the world has anything to congratulate itself about at any point over the whole European episode, and of course my impression is that it is only a portend [*sic*] of worse to come. I would like to persuade myself otherwise." Hoover to Walter Lichtenstein, October 3, 1938, PPI, Hoover Papers, HHPL.

31. *New York Times*, October 27, 1938, pp. 1, 15; Hoover, *Further Addresses . . . 1938–1940*, pp. 85–92.

32. Hoover statement on the seizure of Czechoslovakia, March 27, 1939, Public Statements File, Hoover Papers, HHPL.

33. *New York Times*, April 1, 1939, pp. 1, 3.

34. Hoover letter to his close friend Ray Lyman Wilbur, dated March 30, 1939, as printed on pages 42–43 of the 1947 page proof edition of the 1939 section of his Magnum Opus, in Herbert C. Hoover Papers, Box 3, "M. O. 6" envelope, HIA.

Despite intensive searching, the original of this letter has not been found. Hoover did not use it in the final version of *Freedom Betrayed* published here. The date of the letter (March 30) is almost certainly erroneous, because Neville Chamberlain did not announce his change of policy in the House of Commons until March 31, although word of the impending change leaked out of London late on March 30 and appeared the next morning (March 31) in the American press. (See *New York Times*, March 31, 1939, p. 1.) Despite the ambiguity about the date, Hoover's letter to Wilbur appears to be an accurate reflection of his feelings about the Polish guarantee at the time, feelings that he expressed to various friends several years before he composed his Magnum Opus.

35. Hoover to William R. Castle Jr., April 10, 1939, PPI, Hoover Papers, HHPL.

36. Hoover to John C. O'Laughlin, April 14, 1939, Herbert Hoover Subject Collection, Box 320, HIA.

37. See appendix, Documents 8 and 14.

38. See appendix, Document 18.

39. Raymond Moley diary, June 11, 1940, Raymond Moley Papers, Box 1, HIA; Payson J. Treat notes of a talk with Hoover, August 25, 1940, Payson J. Treat Papers, Box 45, HIA;

Hoover "diary," November 10, 1940, Arthur Kemp Papers, Box 23, HIA. In this "diary" entry Hoover wrote: "*November 10 . . .* Chamberlain died. He went wrong over Poland." For more on this "diary" (actually a chronology or aide-mémoire compiled some time after the fact), see my discussion later in the Introduction.

Hoover was not alone in thinking that the Anglo-French guarantee to Poland had been a terrible blunder. His close friend William R. Castle Jr., who had been undersecretary of state in the latter part of Hoover's presidential administration, thought so, too. Castle diary, February 28, 1941.

40. See appendix, Document 18.

41. In a speech in Chicago on February 1, 1939, Hoover again asserted: "The face of Germany is turned more east than toward Western Europe." *New York Times*, February 2, 1939, p. 6; Hoover, *Further Addresses . . . 1938–1940*, p. 100.

42. Hoover to Wilbur, March 30 (?), 1939.

43. *New York Times*, January 5, 1939, p. 12.

44. Ibid., February 2, 1939, p. 6; Hoover, *Further Addresses . . . 1938–1940*, pp. 93–103.

45. Hoover to Ashmun Brown, April 3, 1939, PPI, Hoover Papers, HHPL. See also Hoover to John C. O'Laughlin, February 8, 1938, Herbert Hoover Subject Collection, Box 320, HIA.

46. Hoover to John C. O'Laughlin, July 18, 1939, Herbert Hoover Subject Collection, Box 320, HIA.

47. Hoover to William R. Castle Jr., April 10, 1939, PPI, Hoover Papers, HHPL; Hoover to John C. O'Laughlin, April 14, 1939, Herbert Hoover Subject Collection, Box 320, HIA.

48. *New York Times*, April 16, 1939, pp. 1, 41.

49. Ibid., April 28, 1939, pp. 1, 8.

50. Hoover to John C. O'Laughlin, April 21, 1939, Herbert Hoover Subject Collection, Box 320, HIA.

51. Hoover to O'Laughlin, July 18, 1939.

52. Hoover to O'Laughlin, July 25, 1939, Herbert Hoover Subject Collection, Box 320, HIA.

53. *New York Times*, April 8, 1939, p. 6.

54. Herbert Hoover, "President Roosevelt's Foreign Policy," *Liberty*, April 15, 1939, pp. 5–8; reprinted in Hoover, *Further Addresses . . . 1938–1940*, pp. 104–15.

55. Herbert Hoover, "Shall We Send Our Youth to War?" *American Magazine* 128 (August 1939): 12–13, 137–39, reprinted in Hoover, *Further Addresses . . . 1938–1940*, pp. 116–28. The reprint version mistakenly dates the articles as appearing on July 15. The issue of *American Magazine* carrying Hoover's article was actually released on July 4 (*New York Times*, July 5, 1939, p. 4). Hoover read part of the article on a nationwide radio hookup on July 5 (*New York Times*, July 6, 1939, p. 9).

56. Hoover broadcast protesting persecution of German Jews, November 14, 1938, Public Statements File, Hoover Papers, HHPL; *New York Times*, November 15, 1938, pp. 1, 4.

57. *New York Times*, November 23, 1938, p. 7.

58. Smith, *An Uncommon Man*, p. 268.

59. *New York Times*, April 23, 1939, p. 1.

60. Lewis L. Strauss to Hoover, March 14 and 15, 1939, PPI, Hoover Papers, HHPL; Hoover to Strauss, March 25, 1939, "Hoover, Herbert: General, 1938–39," Name and Subject File I, Lewis L. Strauss Papers, HHPL. Bernard Baruch, in particular, brought Hoover's name to President Roosevelt's attention. Hoover's correspondence with Lewis L. Strauss in the spring and summer of 1939 revealed Hoover's continuing interest in the idea. See also Hoover memorandum concerning possible area of settlements of Jewish refugees, June 9, 1939, Public Statements File, Hoover Papers, HHPL.

61. Smith, *An Uncommon Man,* pp. 268–69.

62. *New York Times,* July 7, 1939, pp. 1, 6; Hoover, *Further Addresses . . . 1938–1940,* pp. 129–38.

63. But his proposal of a neutral fact-finding commission elicited some positive feedback in the American and European press, according to Hoover a few weeks later. *New York Times,* September 16, 1939, p. 9.

64. Hoover, *Further Addresses . . . 1938–1940,* pp. 125, 127. On April 15, 1939 Hoover had said of the "destructive ideologies" of Germany and Russia: "It is my belief that they have reached their high point." Ibid., p. 111.

65. Ibid., p. 127. See also ibid., pp. 114–15.

66. Hoover to O'Laughlin, August 28, 1939, Herbert Hoover Subject Collection, Box 320, HIA.

67. *New York Herald Tribune,* September 2, 1939, Clippings File, Hoover Papers, HHPL; *Vital Speeches* 5 (September 15, 1939): 736. Two days before the war's outbreak, Hoover wrote a friend: "I am one who wants the democracies to win, but wants the United States to stay out for many and urgent reasons" (Hoover to Frank Kent, August 30, 1939, PPI, Hoover Papers, HHPL). In a radio speech several weeks later (after the war had begun), he declared: "My sympathies are with the Allies. Nevertheless, my deepest conviction is that America must keep out of this war, and it is in the interest of the whole world if we are to be of any help to rebuild this civilization when the war is over. The most difficult job we have in these months before us is to remain at peace" (*New York Times,* October 21, 1939, p. 6).

68. *New York Times,* October 4, 1939, p. 12; *New York Herald Tribune,* October 4, 1939, Clippings File, Hoover Papers, HHPL.

69. Hoover to O'Laughlin, September 4, 1939, Herbert Hoover Subject Collection, Box 320, HIA.

70. Edgar Rickard diary, September 12, 1939, HHPL; Charles A. Lindbergh, *The Wartime Journals of Charles A. Lindbergh* (New York: Harcourt Brace Jovanovich, 1970), p. 270; *New York Times,* October 11, 1939, pp. 1, 16.

71. Edgar Rickard diary, October 26, 1939.

72. "We will keep out if we have the resolute national will to do so" (Hoover speech, September 1, 1939, cited in note 67).

73. Hoover to O'Laughlin, September 24, 1939, Herbert Hoover Subject Collection, Box 320, HIA.

74. Lindbergh, *Wartime Journals,* p. 260 (entry for September 21, 1939) and p. 272 (entry for October 7, 1939).

75. *New York Times*, September 25, 1939, p. 10; Hoover, "We Must Keep Out," *Saturday Evening Post* 212 (October 28, 1939): 8–9,74,76–78, reprinted in Hoover, *Further Addresses . . . 1938–1940*, pp. 139–57.

76. For example, ibid; *New York Times*, September 26, 1939, p. 12; ibid., February 3, 1940, p. 1.

77. Franklin D. Roosevelt calendar, September 6, 1939 (meeting with Myron Taylor), Franklin D. Roosevelt Library, Hyde Park, New York (hereinafter FDRL); Eleanor Roosevelt to Bernard Baruch, September 10, 1939, Eleanor Roosevelt Papers, Series 100, FDRL; Eleanor Roosevelt to Marie Meloney, September 10, 1939, Eleanor Roosevelt Papers, Series 100; Hoover memorandum of conversation with Myron Taylor, September 11, 1939, PPI, Hoover Papers, HHPL. Taylor was former chairman of U.S. Steel.

78. Hoover memorandum of conversation with Taylor, September 11, 1939; Hoover memoranda, September 18, 1939, of his conversation with Taylor on September 11, "Roosevelt, Franklin D.—Drafts re FDR," Post-Presidential Subject File, Hoover Papers, HHPL; Hoover memorandum, n.d., of his September 11, 1939, meeting with Taylor, in National Committee on Food for the Small Democracies (hereinafter NCFSD) Records, Box 61, HIA. In his various drafts on September 18 of his conversation with Taylor on September 11, Hoover toned down his first draft of that day. His original statement, that he wished "to devote my whole energies to keeping the United States out of this war," became "I stated that I felt that my greater service would be to devote my whole energies to keeping the United States out of this war." There are indications that Hoover was drafting and redrafting his memorandum with an eye toward publishing it.

79. Stephen T. Early diary, September 12 and 13, 1939, Stephen T. Early Papers, FDRL; Rickard diary, September 14, 1939.

80. Hoover to Norman H. Davis, September 15, 1939, RG 200—American Red Cross, Group 3 (1935–46), File Class 900.02: Finnish Relief Fund, Box 1316, National Archives and Records Administration, Washington, D.C. A copy is in the Norman H. Davis file, PPI, Hoover Papers, HHPL.

81. The quoted words are Eleanor Roosevelt's in a letter to Marie Meloney, September 17, 1939 (Eleanor Roosevelt Papers, Series 100). Mrs. Roosevelt probably heard this from Franklin Roosevelt, who probably heard it directly from Norman Davis, who conferred with President Roosevelt on September 16 (Early diary, September 16, 1939).

82. Hoover to Davis, September 15, 1939 (cited in note 80).

83. Ibid.; Rickard diary, September 14, 1939; Davis to Hoover, September 22, 1939 (first file cited in note 80).

84. Norman H. Davis memorandum of telephone conversation with Hoover, September 19, 1939 (first file cited in note 80); Davis to Hoover, September 22, 1939; Hoover to Davis, September 24, 1939 (first file cited in note 80). Davis claimed that Hoover had first agreed to come but then said he could not come unless his letter to Davis was made public by Davis before the meeting. Hoover claimed that he had only *suggested* releasing the letter but had readily withdrawn his "suggestion" when Davis declined to do so. He had "understood" that Davis was to submit Hoover's letter to the Red Cross executive

committee members and was "to await their conclusions." If they accepted Hoover's plan, he would "sit with the Committee in carrying it out." Whatever the source of the misunderstanding, Hoover did not come to Washington and the Red Cross officials were not pleased. Neither, it appears, was Franklin Roosevelt, with ultimately severe consequences for Herbert Hoover's role in World War II.

85. Davis memorandum of telephone conversation with Hoover, September 19, 1939; Hoover "diary" for September 20, 1939, Herbert C. Hoover Papers, Box 145, HIA (for more on this document, see below); Davis to Hoover, September 22, 1939.

86. Rickard diary, September 19, 1939; Hoover "diary" for September 20, 1939. In the latter source, Hoover commented that the unpopularity of such a relief appeal "seemed to explain why Roosevelt wanted me to do it."

87. This feeling of annoyance surfaced in one of Hoover's drafts on September 18 of his meeting on September 11 with Myron Taylor. He wrote: "I assume that if the President wished me to call upon him I would receive a phone or letter directly from the White House" (version in NCFSD Records, Box 61). A few weeks later Eleanor Roosevelt remarked that she had heard "that Mr. Hoover felt a little hurt that Franklin had not talked to him himself. I think he has a right to feel that way because I think Franklin should have talked to him, but many of the men around Franklin felt it was wiser to sound Mr. Hoover out first" (Eleanor Roosevelt to Marie Meloney, October 8, 1939, Eleanor Roosevelt Papers, Series 100).

88. Rickard diary, September 19, 1939.

89. Eleanor Roosevelt to Martha Gellhorn, September 27, 1939, Eleanor Roosevelt Papers, Series 100.

90. *New York Times*, September 21, 1939, pp. 1, 16.

91. Harold Ickes diary, September 23, 1939, Harold Ickes Papers, Library of Congress.

92. Various accounts of the Secret Service incident appear in a number of the oral histories at HHPL and HIA. See also Edmund W. Starling, *Starling of the White House* (New York: Simon and Schuster, 1946), p. 306. It is noteworthy that between 1933 and 1940 Hoover visited Washington, D.C., only twice. On the first occasion (December 11, 1936), President Roosevelt was out of town. On the second occasion (December 9, 1938), Roosevelt was at the White House but Hoover did not call on him—a fact noted by the *New York Times* (December 10, 1938, p. 11). On this occasion, Hoover arrived early in the morning by train, had breakfast with several friends, and attended the annual meeting of the Carnegie Institution, of which he was a trustee. He then returned to New York City after only six hours in the capital.

Hoover's next brief trip to Washington occurred at the end of February 1940, when he came to testify briefly before a congressional hearing. According to a newspaper columnist at the time, Hoover did so only after learning that Roosevelt would be out of the city, on vacation. According to the columnist, Hoover "always had insisted that he'd never visit Washington, for any purpose, while you're there [i.e., Roosevelt]—because he wanted to avoid a White House call." See Leonard Lyons, "The Lyons Den," *New York Post*, April 14, 1940, copy in "Finnish Relief Fund, Inc.: Printed Material Clippings 1940," Post-Presidential Subject File, Hoover Papers, HHPL. Hoover seemed to be under the impression that as a former president he was under an obligation to visit the current president during any trip to the nation's capital.

93. Rickard diary, September 14, 1939.

94. Davis to Hoover, September 27, 1939, in the first file cited in note 80.

95. For accounts of the work of the Commission for Polish Relief, see Herbert Hoover, *An American Epic*, vol. IV (Chicago: Henry Regnery Company, 1964), pp. 4–9; Hal Elliott Wert, "Flight and Survival: American and British Aid to Polish Refugees in the Fall of 1939," *Polish Review* 34, no. 3 (1989): 227–48; Hal Elliott Wert, "U.S. Aid to Poles Under Nazi Domination, 1939–1940," *Historian* 59 (Spring 1995): 511–24. Hoover himself remarked in November 1939 that "after the Red Cross backed and filled so much, I took it upon myself to push the [Polish relief] organization work ahead" (Hoover to Rufus Jones, November 25, 1939, NCFSD Records, Box 61).

96. *New York Times*, December 1, 1939, p. 8.

97. For Strauss's explanation of the origins of the Finnish Relief Fund, see Lewis L. Strauss, draft letter (unsent) to Arthur Krock, December [15?], 1939, "Hoover, Herbert: General, 1938–39," Name and Subject File I, Strauss Papers; Strauss to Rudolf Holsti, December 18, 1939, "Finnish Relief Fund, Inc.: Correspondence, 1939," Name and Subject File II, Strauss Papers; Strauss to Bernice Miller, March 21, 1946, Strauss file, PPI, Hoover Papers, HHPL; Strauss, *Men and Decisions* (Garden City, NY: Doubleday & Company, 1962), p. 66. In three of the accounts Strauss indicated that he telephoned Hoover *after* meeting Procopé. In one of the accounts (the 1946 letter to Hoover's secretary, Bernice Miller) Strauss said that he telephoned Hoover with his suggestion—and that Hoover agreed to it—*before* Procopé arrived. This point is of interest because some observers and enemies of Hoover implied that Hoover had leapt into his Finnish relief project before seeking the approval of the Finnish government or its diplomatic representative in Washington. The implication, of course, was that Hoover had done so for less than purely altruistic reasons. See, for example, Arthur Krock's column in the *New York Times*, December 15, 1939, p. 24.

98. Hoover, night letter to Edgar Rickard, December 4, 1939, NCFSD Papers, Box 61.

99. Ibid.; Strauss, *Men and Decisions*, pp. 66–67.

100. Hoover "diary" for December 5–6, 1939, Herbert C. Hoover Papers, Box 145, HIA. As mentioned in note 39, this was not a true diary but a chronology or aide-mémoire created by Hoover more than two years later.

101. Hoover night letter to Edgar Rickard, December 5, 1939, Rickard file, PPI, Hoover Papers, HHPL; Rickard diary, December 4, 1939.

102. Hoover night letter to Rickard, December 4, 1939.

103. Strauss draft letter to Krock, December [15?], 1939; Hoover night letter to Rickard, December 5, 1939; *New York Times*, December 6, 1939, p. 1; *Los Angeles Times*, December 6, 1939, p. 1; "Hammering Hoover," *Newsweek* 14 (December 25, 1939): 12–13.

104. Finnish Relief Fund, Publicity Division, press release, December 8, 1939, NCFSD Records, Box 61; *New York Times*, December 9, 1939, pp. 1, 5.

105. Hoover night letter to Rickard, December 5, 1939; Rickard diary, December 5, 1939.

106. *New York Times*, December 6, 1939, p. 1.

107. Ibid.

108. "Finnish Relief Fund" (unsigned memo) in Norman Davis file, PPI, Hoover Papers, HHPL; "Finnish Relief Fund" (unsigned memo), "American Red Cross: Correspondence, 1933–44," Post-Presidential Subject File, Hoover Papers, HHPL; Hoover "diary," December 7, 1939, Herbert C. Hoover Papers, Box 145, HIA; Breckinridge Long diary, December 7, 1939, Breckinridge Long Papers, Box 5, Library of Congress.

109. *New York Times,* December 9, 1939, pp. 1, 5; Norman H. Davis memorandum, December 14, 1939, of conversations with Hoover on December 12 and 14, first file cited in note 80 above. According to Davis, Hoover said on December 14 that he was making a fund drive because Davis had told him that the Red Cross would not be making one.

110. *New York Times,* December 9, 1939, p. 5; ibid., December 12, 1939, p. 16.

111. Hoover to Chase National Bank, December 26, 1939, NCFSD Papers, Box 61.

112. Newspaper coverage of the campaign was extensive. See Clippings File for December 1939–March 1940, HHPL.

113. Hoover, *An American Epic,* vol. IV, p. 12 (where the figure given is $3,546,526.11). According to the *New York Times,* October 15, 1940, p. 9, the figure as of that time was $3,430,000. This was more than half of worldwide contributions to the Finnish relief cause.

114. Hal Elliott Wert, "Hoover, Roosevelt and the Politics of American Aid to Finland, 1939–1940," in Robert W. Hoeffner, ed., *World War II: A Fifty Year Perspective on 1939* (Albany, NY: Siena College Research Institute Press, 1992), p. 102.

115. Davis memorandum, December 14, 1939.

116. Ibid.

117. Hoover "diary," December 7, 1939.

118. Harold Ickes diary, November 26, 1939; Breckinridge Long diary, December 7, 1939; Wert, "U.S. Aid to Poles Under Nazi Domination, 1939–1940," p. 519.

119. The Roosevelt administration, through its Reconstruction Finance Corporation, did authorize a loan of $10,000,000 to the Finns on December 10 (*New York Times,* December 11, 1939, pp. 1, 5). The loan could be used to purchase "agricultural surpluses and other civilian supplies" in the United States. Although Roosevelt spoke of aiding Finland in every way possible, this did not include military assistance, which the Finns needed most urgently.

120. Harold Ickes diary, December 24, 1939, printed in *The Secret Diary of Harold Ickes,* vol. III (New York: Simon and Schuster, 1955), pp. 95–96.

121. When the liberal *St. Louis Post-Dispatch* suggested on December 20, 1939, that Hoover might be playing "presidential politics" with his "emotional appeals" for Finland, a member of the White House staff sent a copy of the editorial to Roosevelt with the notation, "Ain't this a sock in the puss for Herbie the Hooter" (Wert, "Hoover, Roosevelt and the Politics of American Aid to Finland, 1939–1940," p. 98).

122. Doris Fleeson column in Washington *Times-Herald,* December 11, 1939, copy in Raymond Clapper Papers, Box 151, Herbert Hoover folder, Library of Congress.

123. Doris Fleeson/Fred Pasley article in Washington *Times-Herald,* December 12, 1939, p. 8, copy in Clapper Papers, Box 151, Hoover folder; Raymond Clapper column in *New York World-Telegram,* December 13, 1939, copy in Misrepresentations File, Chronological

File Series, December 1939 folder, Hoover Papers, HHPL; Arthur Krock column in *New York Times,* November 15, 1939, p. 24; "Hammering Hoover: The New Deal Tries to Link His Finnish Aid to Politics," *Newsweek* 14 (December 25, 1939): 12–13.

124. Clapper column, December 13, 1939; *New York Journal-American,* December 14, 1939, copy in Misrepresentations File, Chronological File Series, December 1939 folder, Hoover Papers, HHPL; *New York Daily News* (?) clipping (United Press story), December 14, 1939, Clippings File, HHPL; *Christian Science Monitor,* December 15 (?), 1939, Misrepresentations File, December 1939 folder; *Los Angeles Times,* December 15, 1939, p. 7; *New York Times,* December 15, 1939, pp. 13, 24; Doris Fleeson column, *New York World-Telegram,* December 15, 1939, Clippings File, HHPL.

125. *New York Times,* December 13, 1939, p. 1.

126. Stephen T. Early diary, December 14, 1939; *New York Journal-American,* December 14, 1939; *Los Angeles Times,* December 15, 1939, p. 7; *New York Times,* December 15, 1939, p. 13.

127. See Eleanor Roosevelt to Marie Meloney, September 17, 1939, cited in note 81.

128. Hoover press statement on Red Cross controversy, December 14, 1939, Public Statements File, Hoover Papers, HHPL; *New York Journal-American,* December 14, 1939; *New York Daily News* (?) clipping, December 14, 1939; *Los Angeles Times,* December 15, 1939, p. 7; *New York Times,* December 15, 1939, p. 13.

129. *New York Journal-American,* December 14, 1939.

130. Hoover draft press release ("All of this discussion seems to hinge on matters under discussion before the war broke out in Europe"), December 14, 1939; Lawrence Richey press release, December 14, 1939; both in NCFSD Records, Box 61. See also *Los Angeles Times,* December 15, 1939, p. 7; *New York Times,* December 15, 1939, p. 13. Hoover and Richey claimed that Early must have been referring to the abortive negotiations to establish a home for European refugees in Africa—discussions in which Hoover said he had participated.

131. Edgar Rickard diary, December 15, 1939; transcript of Hoover telephone conversation with Norman Davis, December 19, 1939, Misrepresentations File, December 1939 folder, Hoover Papers, HHPL. Lewis Strauss, for his part, protested to *New York Times* columnist Arthur Krock but won only a limited correction of Krock's column of December 15. See Strauss letter (unsent) to Krock, December 15, 1949 (and cover memo), "Hoover, Herbert: General, 1938–39," Name and Subject File I, Strauss Papers, *New York Times,* December 19, 1939, p. 22.

132. Transcript of Hoover conversation with Davis, December 19, 1939.

133. Ashmun Brown column in *Providence Journal,* December 17, 1939, copy in Clippings File, HHPL; *Chicago Herald-American* editorial, December 19, 1939, copy in Misrepresentations File, December 1939 folder, Hoover Papers, HHPL; John C. O'Laughlin to Hoover, December 23, 1939, Herbert Hoover Subject Collection, Box 320, HIA; Frank R. Kent column, December 28, 1939, Kent file, PPI, Hoover Papers, HHPL.

134. Edgar Rickard diary, December 15 and 16, 1939.

135. In addition to the transcript cited in note 131, see the Davis file, PPI, Hoover Papers, HHPL.

136. Hoover was so informed by one of his most trusted scouts in Washington, John C. O'Laughlin. See O'Laughlin to Hoover, December 16, 1939, Herbert Hoover Subject Collection, Box 320, HIA.

137. Hoover, 1947 page proof edition of his Magnum Opus, 1939 section, p. 128, in Herbert C. Hoover Papers, Box 3, "M. O. 6" envelope, HIA. In the December 8, 1939, entry for his 1939 "diary" (actually compiled in 1942), Hoover stated that the American "enthusiasm" for Finland "affected the Roosevelt administration in three ways: first, the non-Communists in the Administration wanted to get politically astride the popularity of the cause; the Communists in the Administration hated it; and both groups united in hating me about it" (Herbert C. Hoover Papers, Box 145).

138. Strauss, *Men and Decisions*, p. 66.

139. *New York Times*, January 16, 1940, pp. 1, 10.

140. Ibid., January 18, 1940, p. 4.

141. Ibid., March 1, 1940, p. 4, and October 15, 1940, p. 9.

142. Hoover to Robert Maverick, March 1, 1940, NCFSD Records, Box 61.

143. Hoover declared that the harsh terms imposed on the Finns marked "another sad day for civilization" (*New York Times*, March 14, 1940, p. 2).

144. Ibid.; ibid.: March 15, 1940, p. 8; October 15, 1940, p. 9; October 27, 1940, p. 26; Hoover, *An American Epic*, vol. IV, p. 13.

145. Hoover "diary," December 16, 1939, Herbert C. Hoover Papers, Box 145, HIA.

146. For details of his presidential quest in the spring of 1940, see note 6.

147. For the full text of Hoover's convention address, see *New York Times*, June 26, 1940, p. 17, and Hoover, *Addresses upon the American Road, 1940–1941* (New York: Charles Scribner's Sons, 1941), pp. 205–23.

148. Rickard diary, June 28, 1940; ibid., review of 1940; Hoover "diary" for June 25, 1940, Herbert C. Hoover Papers, Box 145, HIA; Best, *Herbert Hoover: The Postpresidential Years*, pp. 162–163; Smith, *An Uncommon Man*, pp. 284–85; Allan Hoover to Thomas T. Thalken, March 23, 1978 (copy in my possession).

149. Hoover to William Starr Myers, Larry Sullivan, and John Spargo, June 29, 1940 (separate letters), PPI, Hoover Papers, HHPL.

150. *New York Times*, June 30, 1940, section I, p. 2.

151. For example, see Hoover to Arthur M. Hyde and Mark Sullivan, June 28, 1940 (separate letters), PPI, Hoover Papers, HHPL.

152. Edgar Rickard diary, review of 1940.

153. Hoover to O'Laughlin, August 15, 1940, Herbert Hoover Subject Collection, Box 321, HIA; Payson J. Treat notes of a conversation with Hoover, August 25, 1940, Payson J. Treat Papers, Box 45, HIA; Hoover, *Addresses . . . 1940–1941*, p. 45.

154. For example, see Hoover, *Addresses . . . 1940–1941*, p. 45.

155. Hoover's remarks on war trend of the Roosevelt administration, October 22, 1940, Public Statements File, Hoover Papers, HHPL.

156. For the full text of this address, see Hoover, *Addresses . . . 1940–1941*, pp. 34–51.

157. Rickard diary, November 6, 1940.

158. Samuel I. Rosenman, comp., *The Public Papers and Addresses of Franklin D. Roosevelt,* 1940 volume (New York, 1941), p. 517.

159. Rickard diary, November 30 and December 4, 1940. Hoover and his wife kept their home on the Stanford University campus and visited it often, especially in the summertime.

160. Hoover to Roy W. Howard, March 1, 1940, PPI, Hoover Papers, HHPL; Breckinridge Long diary, April 4 and 30, 1940; William R. Castle Jr. diary, April 20 and 26, 1940.

161. *New York Times,* March 1, 1940, pp. 1, 5.

162. Ibid., May 16, 1940, p. 11; Castle diary, May 16, 1940; Rickard diary, May 18, 1940.

163. Hoover to Rufus Jones, May 31, 1940 (plus enclosed memorandum), NCFSD Records, Box 62.

164. *New York Times,* May 11, 1940, pp. 1, 8; ibid., September 12, 1940, p. 7.

165. Hoover telegram to Norman H. Davis, May 12, 1940, NCFSD Records, Box 62; Rickard diary, May 18, 1940.

166. *New York Times,* June 12, 1940, p. 25.

167. Ibid., June 21, 1940, p. 19.

168. Senator Francis Maloney to Franklin D. Roosevelt, June 14, 1940 (plus enclosure); Roosevelt to Maloney, June 17, 1940; both in President's Personal File 2279, Franklin D. Roosevelt Papers, FDRL.

169. *New York Times,* July 28, 1940, pp. 1, 5.

170. Hoover to Edgar Rickard, August 5, 1940, NCFSD Records, Box 62.

171. See, for example, *New York Times,* July 6, 1940, p. 4; ibid., August 7, 1940, pp. 1, 3. A Red Cross official in Europe estimated that at least 35,000,000 Europeans would be on near-starvation rations by mid autumn. The U.S. ambassador to Belgium predicted that 8,000,000 Belgians would be enduring a near-famine by winter.

172. *New York Times,* August 11, 1940, section I, p. 1.

173. Ibid., August 12, 1940, p. 8.

174. Ibid.; ibid., August 11, 1940, section I, p. 8; Hoover cable to Edgar Rickard, August 14, 1940, NCFSD Records, Box 62.

175. *New York Times,* August 12, 1940, pp. 1, 8.

176. Great Britain, Parliament, House of Commons, *Parliamentary Debates,* 5th Series, vol. 364, p. 1162; *New York Times,* August 21, 1940, p. 4.

177. Hoover, *An American Epic,* vol. IV, p. 20.

178. Hoover to William R. Castle Jr., August 21, 1940, PPI, Hoover Papers, HHPL.

179. Rickard diary, August 13 and 19, 1940.

180. Hoover to Castle, August 21, 1940.

181. Ibid.

182. Hoover to Hugh Gibson, October 4, 1940, Hugh Gibson Papers, HIA.

183. *New York Times,* November 16, 1940, pp. 1, 7; Hoover, *Addresses . . . 1940– 1941,* pp. 121–31.

184. Hoover, "Feed Hungry Europe," *Collier's* 106 (November 23, 1940): 12, 69–72. This issue of *Collier's* appeared on the newsstands on November 15.

185. "Food for Conquered?" *Newsweek* 16 (December 16, 1940): 17–18.

186. *New York Times,* November 29, 1940, pp. 1, 17; *Secret Diary of Harold Ickes,* p. 385.

187. *New York Times,* December 8, 1940, section 1, p. 44; Hoover to David Lawrence, December 9, 1940 (plus enclosure), David Lawrence Papers, Box 57, Princeton University. The Committee later dropped the word "Five" from its masthead.

188. Hoover to R. Douglas Stuart Jr., December 6, 1940, "America First Committee: 1940–46," Post-Presidential Subject File, Hoover Papers, HHPL.

189. *New York Times,* December 11, 1940, pp. 1, 20.

190. Ibid., March 11, 1941, pp. 1, 6. According to Hoover's confidential informant John C. O'Laughlin, Roosevelt and Sumner Welles of the State Department were "the most virulent in opposition to your work. They are encouraging the British in their refusal to open the blockade" (O'Laughlin to Hoover, February 24, 1941, Herbert Hoover Subject Collection, Box 321, HIA).

191. *New York Times,* February 18, 1941, p. 7; Castle diary, March 5, 1941.

192. Castle diary, March 5, 1941.

193. See, for example, *New York Times,* February 18, 1941, p. 7.

194. Castle diary, March 29, 1941. The Washington, D.C., political gossip columnists Drew Pearson and Robert Allen accused Hoover of Anglophobia and "seething bitterness" against the British because they were resisting his food plan (Pearson and Allen column, December 1, 1940, copy in Thomas W. Lamont Papers, Box 98, Baker Library, Harvard Business School).

195. *New York Times,* March 17, 1941, p. 8.

196. The National Committee on Food for the Small Democracies won hundreds of distinguished sponsors, including General John J. Pershing, various college and university presidents, and several noted authors and retired diplomats. See *New York Times,* January 13, 1941, p. 6, for a partial list.

197. Hoover to Walter Lippmann, April 11, 1941, PPI, Hoover Papers, HHPL.

198. Hoover, *An American Epic,* vol. IV, pp. 29–73.

199. Ibid., p. 17.

200. Roosevelt's sabotaging of Hoover's efforts was a theme in the diaries of Hoover's close friends William R. Castle Jr. and Edgar Rickard. In his diary entry of March 5, 1941, Castle wrote that he had confirmed from "independent sources" that Roosevelt had told diplomats from the five small democracies that it might be easier for them to receive food "if Hoover were out of the picture." Hoover later accused the Roosevelt administration and Churchill's government of pressuring the governments in exile of the small democracies to withdraw their official support of Hoover's committee—which some of them did (Hoover, *An American Epic,* vol. IV, pp. 68–73).

201. *New York Times,* January 11, 1941, p. 1.

202. Ibid., p. 4; ibid., January 17, 1941, pp. 1, 7.

203. Hoover to Castle, March 1, 1941, PPI, Hoover Papers, HHPL.

204. Lend-Lease Act as approved, March 11, 1941. *United States Statutes at Large,* vol. 55 (Washington, 1942), pp. 31–33.

205. *New York Times,* November 11, 1941, p. 4.

206. Hoover to O'Laughlin, March 9, 1941, Herbert Hoover Subject Collection, Box 321, HIA.

207. *New York Times,* March 29, 1941, p. 4; Hoover to Ben S. Allen, April 2, 1941, PPI, Hoover Papers, HHPL; Rickard diary, April 9, 1941.

208. Hoover to Arthur M. Hyde, April 5, 1941, PPI, Hoover Papers, HHPL.

209. Hoover to William J. Gross, April 7, 1941, PPI, Hoover Papers, HHPL.

210. Hoover, "Russian Misadventure," *Collier's* 105 (April 27, 1940): 21–22, 75–77, reprinted in Hoover, *Further Addresses . . . 1938–1940,* pp. 158–71.

211. Hoover memorandum of conversation with Cordell Hull, February 28, 1941, PPI, Hoover Papers, HHPL.

212. Castle diary, February 28, 1941. Oddly, Hoover did not include Hull's prediction of a German attack on Great Britain in the memorandum cited in the previous footnote. But Hoover saw his friend Castle that same day after seeing Hull. Castle then recorded in his diary what Hoover told him.

213. Hoover memorandum of conversation with Hull, February 28, 1941.

214. Rickard diary, April 17, 1941.

215. Ibid.; Hoover memorandum of a conversation with Colonel Truman Smith, June 1, 1941, PPI, Hoover Papers, HHPL.

216. *Wartime Journals of Charles A. Lindbergh,* p. 498.

217. Ibid.; Sumner Welles to Franklin Roosevelt, June 24, 1941 (plus enclosure), President's Secretary's File, Departmental File, Box 77, "State: Welles, Sumner," Roosevelt Papers, FDRL. Welles's enclosure was a memorandum of a conversation that day with Lord Halifax, the British ambassador to the United States. Halifax reported that Hoover was circulating rumors that the Germans had sent peace offers to the British government and that leaders of Churchill's Conservative Party threatened to desert his coalition unless he agreed to discuss the German peace proposals. Lord Halifax stated that the reports (which Hoover insisted were correct) were completely untrue.

218. *New York Times,* June 23, 1941, pp. 1, 8.

219. Ibid., June 25, 1941, p. 1.

220. Ibid., June 23, 1941, p. 1.

221. Hoover to O'Laughlin, June 26, 1941, Herbert Hoover Subject Collection, Box 321, HIA.

222. For the text of Hoover's speech, see *Congressional Record* 87 (June 30, 1941): A3178–81, and Hoover, *Addresses . . . 1940–1941,* pp. 87–102.

223. See chapter 35 in this volume.

224. Hoover to O'Laughlin, June 26, 1941, July 7, 1941, and August 3, 1941; all in Herbert Hoover Subject Collection, Box 321, HIA. On July 7, Hoover wrote: "These Russians will be promptly mopped up." But this did not appear to disturb him: "However, when Hitler wins, he will need one million men to garrison the place against the conspiracies of the OGPU [Soviet secret police], then driven underground. And he will find it an empty shell except for wheat and oil." On August 3 he predicted that Hitler would win in Russia "eventually."

225. Hoover, *Addresses . . . 1940–1941,* pp. 91–92, 96, 101.

226. Joint statement by Hoover et al., August 5, 1941, printed in *New York Times,* August 6, 1941, p. 6.

227. *New York Times,* September 17, 1941, pp. 1, 12; Hoover, *Addresses ... 1940–1941,* pp. 103–14 (for the full text of his speech).

228. Hoover, *Addresses ... 1940–1941,* p. 111.

229. Ibid., pp. 196–98.

230. George H. Nash, *Herbert Hoover and Stanford University* (Stanford, CA: Hoover Institution Press, 1988), p. 114.

231. Ibid., pp. 114–15.

232. Hoover to O'Laughlin, August 5, 1940, Herbert Hoover Subject Collection, Box 321, HIA.

233. Hoover to O'Laughlin, August 3, 1941, Herbert Hoover Subject Collection, Box 321, HIA.

234. Hoover to Castle, September 4, 1941, PPI, Hoover Papers, HHPL.

235. Hoover to O'Laughlin, September 6, 1941, Herbert Hoover Subject Collection, Box 321, HIA.

236. Rickard diary, October 10, 1941.

237. Julius Klein to Hoover, June 20, 1942, enclosing an account of his conversation with Hoover on November 1, 1941, Julius Klein Papers, Box 3, HIA.

238. Castle diary, October 11, 1941.

239. The three-part series appeared in the November 1, 8, and 15, 1941, issues of the *Saturday Evening Post.*

240. Hoover address in Chicago, November 19, 1941, Public Statements File, Hoover Papers, HHPL; *New York Times,* November 20, 1941, pp. 1, 20.

241. Hoover to Wallace H. White Jr., November 5, 1941; Hoover to Robert E. Wood, November 12, 1941; both in PPI, Hoover Papers, HHPL. See also Hoover telegram to Representative Ritter, November 13, 1941, Public Statements File, Hoover Papers, HHPL.

242. Best, *Herbert Hoover: The Postpresidential Years,* pp. 200–202; Smith, *An Uncommon Man,* pp. 304–6.

243. Castle diary, November 20, 1941.

244. Hoover to Alf M. Landon, November 29, 1941, PPI, Hoover Papers, HHPL.

245. *New York Times,* December 9, 1941, p. 44.

246. Hoover to Castle, December 8, 1941, PPI, Hoover Papers, HHPL.

247. Hoover to Boake Carter, December 11, 1941, PPI, Hoover Papers, HHPL.

248. He had said this to Julius Klein on November 1. Klein to Hoover, June 20, 1942. See also Hoover to William Hyde Irwin Jr., December 18, 1941, PPI, Hoover Papers, HHPL.

249. O'Laughlin to Hoover, February 21, 1942; Hoover to O'Laughlin, February 24, 1942; O'Laughlin to Hoover, February 25, 1942; all in Herbert Hoover Subject Collection, Box 322, HIA. In an early draft of the Magnum Opus, Hoover wrote: "I sent word to Mr. Roosevelt through Mr. Baruch and again through Colonel O'Laughlin that I would be glad to aid in any way possible. There was no response." Hoover, 1947 page proof version

of Magnum Opus, 1941 section, p. 232, in Herbert C. Hoover Papers, Box 37, "M. O. 7" envelope, HIA.

250. Hoover to O'Laughlin, February 24, 1942.

251. Alonzo Fields oral history (1970), p. 18, copies at HIA and HHPL; Smith, *An Uncommon Man*, p. 309.

252. Hoover used this phrase to describe his travails in his relief efforts between 1939 and 1943 (*An American Epic*, vol. IV, pp. xvii, 15, 81). The term seems equally applicable to his experiences between 1941 and 1945.

253. Herbert Hoover and Hugh Gibson, *The Problems of Lasting Peace* (Garden City, NY: Doubleday, Doran and Company, 1942).

254. Hoover to George Barr Baker, September 2, 1944, George Barr Baker Papers, Box 3, HIA.

255. Hoover to O'Laughlin, July 14, 1942, PPI, Hoover Papers, HHPL.

256. Hoover to William E. Barrett, August 4, 1944, PPI, Hoover Papers, HHPL.

257. Hoover to Homer E. Mann, November 20, 1944, PPI, Hoover Papers, HHPL.

258. Hoover to Francis W. Hirst, December 3, 1944, PPI, Hoover Papers, HHPL.

259. Rickard diary, February 22, 1942; Castle diary, March 5, 1942.

260. Castle diary, March 5, 1942; Rickard diary, March 9, 1942.

261. In addition to the document cited printed in the appendix, Document 3, see Hoover, "Going to War with Japan" (typescript dated 3/17/42), Arthur Kemp Papers, Box 4, Envelope 40, HIA.

262. Copies of Hoover's "diary" can be found in the Herbert C. Hoover Papers, Box 145, HIA, and in the Arthur Kemp Papers, Boxes 4 and 23, HIA.

263. Thus some of Hoover's daily "diary" entries for 1938–41 contained observations that look like a standard diary entry but were actually inserted some time later.

264. The ribbon copy of the "diary" is in the Herbert C. Hoover Papers, Box 145, HIA.

265. A number of these memoranda are scattered throughout his Magnum Opus file (the Herbert C. Hoover Papers at HIA) as well as in various PPI files at HHPL. In the course of research on Hoover over many years, I have heard a story that Hoover systematically filed these memoranda of conversations in as many as twenty black books or binders that looked like photo albums. These volumes did not turn up during the editing of *Freedom Betrayed*, and I do not know of their current whereabouts—if, indeed, they still exist. Nor, to the best of my knowledge, has any archivist ever seen them.

266. O'Laughlin's voluminous correspondence with Hoover between 1933 and 1949 can be found in these places: the Herbert Hoover Subject Collection at HIA; the O'Laughlin folders in the PPI file at HHPL; and the John C. O'Laughlin Papers, Library of Congress.

267. The earliest known drafts of volume I of Hoover's *Memoirs* date from July 1940. They are in the *Memoirs of Herbert Hoover* Book Manuscript File, Box 1, HHPL.

268. Rickard diary, review for 1940. In 1951, when Hoover published volume I of his *Memoirs*, he asserted in his introduction that he wrote the first part of it "at odd times during 1915–1916" and the rest of it "at various times from 1920 to 1924." No such early

drafts have been found. The extant files on his *Memoirs* at HHPL show clearly that he commenced the writing of his *Memoirs* in the summer of 1940.

In 1952 Hoover made a similar claim about his composition of the next two published volumes of his *Memoirs*. He asserted that parts of volume II were written in 1925 or 1926, parts between 1933 and 1936, and parts in 1942 and 1943. He stated that most of volume III was written "less than three years after I left the White House," and the final portion between 1942 and 1944. Again, no drafts from the pre-1940 period have been found.

Although Hoover may well have written fragments (or more) of his *Memoirs* before 1940, the available evidence in the *Memoirs of Herbert Hoover* Book Manuscript File strongly indicates that the systematic preparation of his *Memoirs* was a project of his World War II years. And as already noted, his confidant Edgar Rickard recorded at the end of his 1940 diary that Hoover began to write his autobiography that year.

269. See drafts in *Memoirs of Herbert Hoover* Book Manuscript File.

270. Ibid.

271. Ibid.

272. Loretta F. Camp to Rita R. Campbell, August 8, 1964, Hoover Institution Records, Box 2800, Magnum Opus folder, HIA.

273. Rickard diary, review of 1940; Loretta F. Camp oral history (1969), pp. 1–4, copies at HIA and HHPL.

274. Arthur Kemp oral history (1968), pp. 1–8, copies at HIA and HHPL.

275. These are in the *Memoirs of Herbert Hoover* Book Manuscript File, HHPL.

276. See drafts of "Twelve Years 1932–1944," chapter 1 (dated 12/19/44 and Dec. 24–28, 1944) in "The Aftermath: Twelve Years 1932–1944 Edition, Incomplete Drafts, December 1944," *Memoirs of Herbert Hoover* Book Manuscript File, Box 13, HHPL.

277. Hoover, "Twelve Years 1932–1944: Chapter 1," p. 21 (page proof version), in "The Aftermath: Twelve Years 1932–1944 Edition Undated," *Memoirs of Herbert Hoover* Book Manuscript File, Box 13.

278. Hoover, table of contents of "Volume V: World War II," June 4, 1945, in "Magnum Opus: 1932–44, Vol. V (1)," Magnum Opus Materials, Box 5, HHPL.

279. Hoover, "Twelve Years 1932–1944" (typescript dated December 13, 1944), in "Magnum Opus: Vol. 5 (2)," Magnum Opus Materials, HHPL.

280. Ibid. There he wrote: "I was not always right in the details of these appraisals of the forces in motion, but history will record that their major conclusions were correct."

281. Ibid.

282. Rickard diary, March 23, 1945.

283. Hoover, "Roosevelt's Foreign Polices in World War II" (typescript, November 16, 1945), in Arthur Kemp Papers, Box 23, Envelope 50, HIA.

284. Hoover essay on Roosevelt's "Four Freedoms" proclamation, November 15, 1945, Kemp Papers, Box 23, Envelope 50, HIA.

285. See table of contents of "Volume V: World War II" (cited in note 278).

286. Kemp oral history, pp. 5–8.

287. Ibid., pp. 14–15, 17.

288. Ibid., pp. 12–13, 15.

289. Ibid., pp. 25, 37. The Kemp Papers and Herbert C. Hoover Papers at HIA contain many of Kemp's book reports. See, for example, Kemp's review (March 1, 1949) of J. F. C. Fuller's *The Second World War,* in the Kemp Papers, Box 28.

290. Hoover memorandum to Kemp, February 11, 1946, Kemp Papers, Box 37, Envelope 12, HIA.

291. Nash, *Herbert Hoover and Stanford University,* pp. 118–19; Bertrand M. Patenaude, *A Wealth of Ideas: Revelations from the Hoover Institution Archives* (Stanford, CA: Stanford University Press, 2006), p. 140.

292. Hoover described this mission at length in volume IV of his series *An American Epic* (1964), which we revisit below.

293. This version of the Magnum Opus is found in the Herbert C. Hoover Papers, Box 3, HIA.

294. Best, *Herbert Hoover: The Postpresidential Years,* pp. 302–3, 312, 327–30.

295. See *Memoirs of Herbert Hoover* Book Manuscript File, Boxes 7, 9, and 11.

296. This version (some of which was returned from the printer in early 1950) is in the Herbert C. Hoover Papers, Boxes 9 and 10, HIA.

297. William R. Castle Jr. to Hoover, October 19 and November 2, 1949, PPI, Hoover Papers, HHPL. Hoover also asked Castle to read and correct his "preliminary galleys" (page proofs) pertaining to Japan—which Castle did. Hoover to Castle, November 23, 1949, PPI, HHPL; Castle's notes in "Notes on Magnum Opus from W. R. Castle 1949," Magnum Opus Materials, Box 4, HHPL.

298. Her name was Madeline Kelly (later Madeline Kelly O'Donnell). See her oral history (1969), at HIA and HHPL; Marie Pratt oral history (1970), pp. 23–24, also at HI and HHPL; Arthur Kemp to Hoover, August 26, 1954, Kemp Papers, Box 26, HIA. Some time after 1955 (when she left to get married), Mrs. O'Donnell again collected biographical data for Hoover's file. See [Madeline O'Donnell] to Hoover, April 25, 1961, and Bernice Miller to Madeline O'Donnell, May 23, 1961, both in Herbert C. Hoover Papers, Box 123, HIA.

299. The first page of the proofs for volume I ("Roosevelt's First Term, 1933–1936") (pp. 1–283) is labeled in pencil "Fifth Printing" and "ret'd from printer 4/7/50." A copy of this volume is in the *Memoirs of Herbert Hoover* Book Manuscript File, Box 13. A copy of the table of contents of volume II ("Roosevelt's Second Term, 1936–1940") (pp. 284–538) is in the Kemp Papers, Box 47, folder 63, HIA.

300. Preface to *Collectivism Comes to America,* pp. 1–2.

301. Hoover, page proofs of *The Four Horsemen in World War II* (215 pages, dated May 2, 1951), in Herbert C. Hoover Papers, Box 19, Envelope "M. O. 19," HIA.

302. Hoover to Lewis Strauss, May 21, 1950, PPI, Hoover Papers, HHPL.

303. Hoover to Strauss, May 31, 1950, PPI, Hoover Papers, HHPL.

304. Kemp oral history, p. 16.

305. Chronological notes, n.d. (post–January 10, 1952) concerning Hoover's dealings on his *Memoirs* with *Collier's* magazine and Diana Hirsh, Herbert C. Hoover Papers, Box 142, HIA; Diana Hirsh correspondence file, PPI, Hoover Papers, HHPL; *New York Times,* November 21, 1992, p. 48.

306. Allan Nevins to M. S. Latham, June 20, 1951, PPI, Hoover Papers, HHPL.

307. Hoover, *The Memoirs of Herbert Hoover*, vol. III: *The Great Depression 1929–1941* (New York: The Macmillan Company, 1952), p. 408; Kemp oral history, pp. 14–15.

308. Arthur Kemp later remarked of volume III: "It was not really Mr. Hoover's personal memoirs. It was an effort on our part to indict the New Deal. I think we did a pretty good job of it" (Kemp oral history, p. 17).

309. Hoover to Strauss, May 21, 1950.

310. Bernice Miller to Hazel Lyman Nickel, September 23, 1953, Magnum Opus Materials, Box 4, folder 2, HHPL.

311. See, for example, Kemp's book review (January 2, 1952) of William L. Langer and S. Everett Gleason, *The Challenge to Isolation, 1937–1940*, in Kemp Papers, Box 28, HIA, and Kemp's book review (October 20, 1952) of George Racey Jordan, *From Major Jordan's Diaries*, in Kemp Papers, Box 24, HIA.

312. Many of the page proofs for this version are in the Herbert C. Hoover Papers, Box 11, HIA.

313. Hazel Lyman Nickel to Bernice Miller, May 22, 1952, Magnum Opus Materials, Box 2, folder 2, HHPL.

314. Hoover, *Lost Statesmanship* page proofs (April–May 1953 version), p. 804, Herbert C. Hoover Papers, Box 11, "M. O. 21" envelope, HIA.

315. See appendix, Document 18, for the full text.

316. Kemp oral history, pp. 24, 26.

317. Hoover to Strauss, May 21, 1950; Hoover, introduction to *The Years as Crusader*, April 26, 1951, in Herbert C. Hoover Papers, Box 10, "M. O. 19" envelope: "*The Years as Crusader* as of 4/26/51," HIA.

318. Hoover to Strauss, February 4, 1953, PPI, Hoover Papers, HHPL.

319. Loretta F. Camp to Diana Hirsh, February, 10, 1953, Herbert C. Hoover Papers, Box 142, Envelope 19b, HIA.

320. Diana Hirsh comments and suggestions on draft of *Lost Statesmanship*, n.d.; Arthur Kemp to Hoover, April 17, 1953; Kemp to Hirsh, April 23, 1953 (attached to an undated handwritten note by Hoover). All in Kemp Papers, Box 25, HIA. See also Kemp to Hirsh (plus attachment), April 23, 1953, Herbert C. Hoover Papers, Box 142, Envelope 19b, HIA; Hirsh to Hoover, June 15, 1953, PPI, Hoover Papers, HHPL; Hoover to Hirsh, June 28, 1953, PPI, Hoover Papers, HHPL.

321. Hirsh to Hoover, June 20, 1957, PPI, Hoover Papers, HHPL.

322. The page proofs of *The Years as Crusader* are in the Herbert C. Hoover Papers, Box 10, "M. O. 19" envelope, HIA. The manuscript is 280 pages.

323. Hoover, "Introduction" to *The Crusade Years* (page proof edition as returned from the printer, May 29, 1953), in Herbert C. Hoover Papers, Box 13, "M. O. 23" envelope, HIA.

324. In his 1953 *Crusade Years* page proofs (ibid., p. 340), Hoover described Truman as "a dual personality. On the one hand he was a man of amiability and good-will, without malice or vindictiveness, with much loyalty to his friends. He was at heart more a right-winger than a left-winger, but in fact had little ideological knowledge or instinct.

"His other personality was a Pendergast inheritance—Votes at any price, whether collectivism or freedom with the boys participating, in the good fruits of office."

As one who was now friendly with Truman, Hoover probably did not want to publish his ambivalent assessment at that time.

325. Kemp curriculum vitae attached to his 1968 oral history.

326. For example, Kemp report to Hoover, October 12, 1953, on William L. Langer and S. Everett Gleason, *The Undeclared War, 1940–1941*, in Herbert C. Hoover Papers, Box 142, Envelope 19b, HIA; Kemp report to Hoover, October 19, 1953, on Herbert Feis, *The China Tangle*, in Kemp Papers, Box 28, HIA; Kemp note to Hoover on *Lost Statesmanship* manuscript, August 26, 1954, Kemp Papers, Box 26, HIA; Kemp to Bernice Miller, July 25, 1955, and Miller to Kemp, August 2, 1955, "Hoover, Herbert," Arthur Kemp Papers, Box 3, HHPL. (Note: The latter is a separate collection from the Kemp Papers at HIA cited earlier in this footnote and in previous footnotes.)

327. Hoover remarks at the Bohemian Grove Encampment, August 1, 1953, Public Statements File, Hoover Papers.

328. This document is in the Herbert C. Hoover Papers, Box 17, "M. O. 33" envelope, HIA. It was returned from the printer between November 25 and December 20, 1955. Around this time, Hoover began to write a few chapters of yet another volume, to which he gave the title *My Crusade against Collectivism*. It was returned from the printer on December 23, 1955. It is different from the "Crusade Against Collectivism" section of *The Crusade Years* manuscript (1953). A memo on his typescript draft says: "12/1/55. New collectivism." Hoover evidently soon abandoned this spin-off project. The manuscript is in the Herbert C. Hoover Papers, Box 19, "M. O. 36" envelope, HIA.

According to Loretta F. Camp some years later, in 1955 Hoover broke his *Crusade Years* manuscript into eight components, all with the word "Crusade" in their title, including: *The Crusade against Collectivism in American Life, Crusade against Waste in the Federal Government, Crusade Book—Family Life*, and five others. He seems never to have published any of them, except, perhaps, parts of *Crusade against Famine*. Camp to Bernice Miller, August 8, 1964.

329. Leon E. Seltzer memorandum, June 8, 1956, attached to Seltzer to Dare Stark McMullin, June 8, 1956, from Charles Palm's files as director of the Hoover Institution Archives (hereinafter cited as Palm files); Walter R. Livingston oral history (1969), pp. 3–6, copies in HIA and HHPL. Livingston went to work for Hoover on June 10, 1956. Hoover's phrase "enterprises in compassion" appears in the first volume of his relief history series: *An American Epic*, vol. I (Chicago: Henry Regnery Company, 1959), p. xiii.

330. Hirsh to Bernice Miller, May 16, 1958, December 30, 1958; Hirsh to Hoover, July 8, 1959; undated memo ("Diana Hirsh has finished working on Manuscript"). All in Hirsh file, PPI, Hoover Papers, HHPL.

The title *Forty-four Years* presumably referred to the years between 1914 (when Hoover's Belgian relief work started) and 1958. It appears from Hirsh's file that Hoover's original manuscript covered his relief work in the United States during his presidency. At some point he dropped that material (which Hirsh had edited) from his multivolume history.

331. The conservative Chicago publisher Henry Regnery published all four volumes. Regnery's father had been an active noninterventionist before Pearl Harbor; Henry was well known for bringing out critical studies of American foreign policy after

World War II. Regnery's papers are now among the holdings of the Hoover Institution Archives.

332. Hoover to J. Reuben Clark, March 4, 1957, PPI, Hoover Papers, HHPL; Livingston oral history, pp. 6–7; Neil MacNeil oral history (1967), p. 30, copies at HIA and HHPL. MacNeil stated that it was he who gave Hoover the idea of writing a separate book about his experiences with Woodrow Wilson.

333. Livingston oral history, pp. 6–7.

334. Hirsh to Hoover, June 20, 1957; Hoover to Hirsh, June 23, 1957; Bernice Miller to Hirsh, June 24, 1957, and August 1, 1957. All in Hirsh file, PPI, Hoover Papers, HHPL.

335. McGraw-Hill Book Company press release, April 27, 1958, "Books by Hoover: *Ordeal of Woodrow Wilson*, Correspondence, 1958, March–April," Post-Presidential Subject File, Hoover Papers, HHPL.

336. For an excellent account of the making of *The Ordeal of Woodrow Wilson*, see Timothy Walch, "The Ordeal of a Biographer: Herbert Hoover Writes about Woodrow Wilson," *Prologue* 40 (Fall 2008): 12–19.

337. Leon E. Seltzer memorandum, June 8, 1956.

338. Marie Pratt oral history, pp. 1, 21.

339. "Resumé of Mr. Hoover's Activities, January 1946–April 1959," in "Hoover's Statistics: 1946–1964," Post-Presidential Subject File, Hoover Papers, HHPL.

340. "Statistics, June 1957–July 31, 1958," in "Hoover's Statistics: 1946–1964."

341. This outline of a typical Hoover day in his last decade or so is drawn from many sources, including the MacNeil, O'Donnell, and Pratt interviews cited earlier and my conversations with several people who worked for Hoover in Suite 31-A in his final years.

342. Hal Elliott Wert, *Hoover The Fishing President* (Mechanicsburg, PA: Stackpole Books, 2005), p. 334.

343. Ibid., p. 332; *New York Times*, April 20, 1958, p. 1; ibid., May 4, 1958, p. 1.

344. This conclusion comes from comparing the text of volume IV of *An American Epic* with the May 2, 1951, page proofs of *The Four Horsemen of World War II* (cited in note 301).

345. Bonner Fellers oral history (1967), p. 28, copies at HIA and HHPL.

346. Hoover to Kemp, May 1, 1954 (plus attached memorandum), PPI, Hoover Papers, HHPL.

347. Hoover, Introduction, p. 21, to *Lost Statesmanship* (July 1, 1957, page proof version), in Herbert C. Hoover Papers, Box 19, "M. O. 39" envelope, HIA.

348. Frank E. Mason oral history (1966), p. 53, copies at HIA and HHPL.

349. *New York Times*, December 31, 1969, p. 25.

350. Hoover, "My Personal Relations with Mr. Roosevelt" (typescript, September 26, 1958), copies in Herbert C. Hoover Papers, Box 21, "M. O. 42" envelope, HIA, and in "Roosevelt, Franklin D.: Drafts re FDR," Post-Presidential Subject File, Hoover Papers, HHPL.

351. Timothy Walch and Dwight M. Miller, eds., *Herbert Hoover and Franklin D. Roosevelt: A Documentary History* (Westport, CT: Greenwood Press, 1998), 209–11.

352. As returned from the printer, January 8, 1959. A partial typewritten draft is in Herbert C. Hoover Papers, Box 24, "M. O. 49" envelope, HIA. Page proofs are in ibid., Box 26, "M. O. 51" envelope.

353. The 1959 version emphasizes the vast documentary resources available to him, including "the greatest collection of them all" in the Hoover Institution on War, Revolution and Peace that he founded ("Introduction," p. ix). But the final chapter (70) of volume I unflinchingly lists seven instances of "lost statesmanship" by President Roosevelt before Pearl Harbor.

354. Hoover, *Lost Statesmanship: The Ordeal of the American People*, vol. I (1959 page proof edition), part XII, chapter 70, pp. 300–301, Herbert C. Hoover Papers, Box 26, "M. O. 51" envelope, HIA.

355. Lyons wrote two biographies of Hoover: *Our Unknown Ex-President* (Garden City, NY: Doubleday & Company, 1948) and *Herbert Hoover: A Biography* (Garden City, NY: Doubleday & Company, 1964).

356. A copy is filed in the Herbert C. Hoover Papers, Box 19, "M. O. 39" envelope.

357. Hoover, *Lost Statesmanship: The Ordeal of the American People*, vol. I (1959 page proof version), part III, chapter 5, p. 5. See also the appendix, Document 23, of this volume.

358. Ibid., vol. I, chapter 16. Hoover continued to collect information on this subject. See note 298.

359. See his Introduction in this volume.

360. Herbert Hoover, *Addresses upon the American Road, 1955–1960* (Caldwell, ID: The Caxton Printers, 1961), p. 75.

361. "Statistics, August 7, 1959–August 10, 1960," in "Hoover's Statistics: 1946–1964."

362. Copies of "Edition No. 5" of *The Ordeal of the American People* are in the Herbert C. Hoover Papers, Boxes 41 and 42, HIA, and in the Magnum Opus Materials, Boxes 3 and 6, HHPL. There are some variations among them.

It is unclear when Hoover began counting new drafts or "editions." Because some sections of the "War Book" had reached the fifth and even sixth editions in the late 1940s and early 1950s, it would appear that Hoover began to renumber his editions from scratch when he started to condense his 1959 manuscript (then entitled *Lost Statesmanship*).

According to Neil MacNeil, who was familiar with the project in its last years, there were eleven or twelve versions of Hoover's Magnum Opus. But MacNeil seems only to have been counting the editions of the manuscript under the titles *The Ordeal of the American People* and *Freedom Betrayed*.

Before Edition No. 5 of the *Ordeal* manuscript, there was Edition No. 4. Parts of it, as returned from the Xerox company on July 1, 1961, are in the Herbert C. Hoover Papers, Box 33, "M. O. 64" envelope, HIA. In the months prior to July 1961, Hoover had been hard at work on this version (see Boxes 30–33).

363. Hoover to Kaltenborn, October 21, 1963, PPI, Hoover Papers, HHPL (in which Hoover explicitly mentioned his "committee of advisors"); MacNeil oral history, p. 49. In his oral history MacNeil did not provide a date for Hoover's appointment of his literary advisory committee. The biographical note for MacNeil's papers at HHPL states that this occurred in 1964, but Hoover's letter to Kaltenborn suggests that this is incorrect.

364. Frank E. Mason diary, January 17, 19, 1961, Frank E. Mason Papers, Box 29, HHPL; Hoover to MacNeil, March 23, 1961, Neil MacNeil Papers, Box 1, HHPL; Kaltenborn to

Hoover, May 3, 1961, PPI, Hoover Papers, HHPL. In his letter to MacNeil, Hoover referred to the manuscript as "my new *magnum opus*" and "a condensation of a greater one."

365. Kay Stalcup to Diana Hirsh, March 23, 1961, PPI, Hoover Papers, HHPL.

366. The attorney, Ira Lillick, was an old friend and fellow trustee of Stanford University. The two copies were returned to the Hoover family after Lillick's death and are now filed among the Magnum Opus Materials at HHPL.

367. Hoover telegram to Kemp, August 7, 1961, "Hoover, Herbert," Kemp Papers, HHPL.

368. Kemp to Hoover, August 8, 1961, ibid.

369. Hoover to Kaltenborn, March 11, 1962; Loretta F. Camp to Kaltenborn, March 14 and April 6, 1962; all in Kaltenborn file, PPI, Hoover Papers, HHPL.

370. Hoover to Kaltenborn, March 11, 1962; Camp to Kaltenborn, April 6, 1962; Hoover to MacNeil, June 21, 1962, MacNeil Papers, Box 1.

371. Lewis Strauss memorandum for his files, March 27, 1962, "Hoover, Herbert: 1962," Name and Subject File II, Strauss Papers; MacNeil oral history, p. 44. MacNeil said that Hoover himself selected the title *Freedom Betrayed*.

372. Strauss memorandum for his files, March 27, 1962.

373. Kaltenborn to Hoover, May 3, 1961, April 21, 1962, and April 24, 1962; all in PPI, Hoover Papers, HHPL.

374. MacNeil to Hoover, May 1, 1961, MacNeil Papers, Box 1.

375. MacNeil to Hoover, November 11, 1961, copies in MacNeil Papers, Box 1, and in Herbert C. Hoover Papers, Box 115, vertical file folder, HIA.

376. Mason diary, January 17, 1961. In 1954 Mason had read an earlier version of *Lost Statesmanship*—probably the most polemical one—and had praised it highly. He urged Hoover to publish it in time to influence the 1954 congressional elections. Mason, undated note (ca. 1954) to Hoover, "Hoover Books: Magnum Opus," Mason Papers.

377. MacNeil oral history, p. 55; Mason to MacNeil, February 11, 1966, "MacNeil, Neil: 1966–68," Mason Papers. Mason did receive a copy of a corrected version (Edition No. 10) after its completion near the end of 1962 (note on "M. O. 120" envelope in Herbert C. Hoover Papers, Box 56, HIA).

378. The *New York Times* reported frequently on Hoover's medical condition between August 28 and September 17, 1962.

379. Ibid., September 6, 1962, p. 20.

380. Hoover to Kaltenborn, December 3, 1962; Hoover to MacNeil, December 3, 1962, both in PPI, Hoover Papers, HHPL. See also Hoover to Mason, December 3, 1962, "Hoover Books: Magnum Opus," Mason Papers. Hoover signed this letter "Affectionately, Herbert." Either he had forgiven Mason or their heated arguments occurred after this.

Around December 1962 Hoover sent copies of the latest edition of *Freedom Betrayed* to two other persons to read: the journalist William L. White and Dr. Rudolph N. Schullinger (one of Hoover's physicians). Both were impressed. See White to Hoover, December 18, 1962; Schullinger to Hoover, December 19, 1962; both in Herbert C. Hoover Papers, Box 115, vertical file folder, HIA.

381. A note on the "M. O. 120" envelope in Box 56 of the Herbert C. Hoover Papers at HIA says of its contents (Edition No. 10 of volume I): "This edition #10 corrected and later became Edition Z."

In a letter to Kaltenborn in early 1963, Hoover said he was incorporating Kaltenborn's suggestions (which he had made on a copy of Edition No. 10) into "Edition Z—which is to be final as far as I am concerned! I hope to get it done within a few months" (Hoover to Kaltenborn, January 20, 1963, PPI, Hoover Papers, HHPL.)

382. Occasionally in his correspondence, Hoover called it the Z+HH edition. See, for example, Hoover to MacNeil, March 28, 1963, PPI, Hoover Papers, HHPL.

383. For more details about this, see my "Editor's Note on Sources and Editing Methods" and my editorial comments in volume III.

384. Many of those who worked with him noted this trait, as well as his resistance to altering his phraseology and grammar. See Kemp oral history, p. 13, Livingston oral history, pp. 7, 11–14. Hoover was very much in command of his "product." On the other hand, he sought and often accepted suggestions he deemed wise.

385. Theodore J. Joslin diary, December 6, 1931, Theodore J. Joslin Papers, HHPL.

386. Frank E. Mason to Michael Horacek, n.d. (probably ca. September 1976), "Magnum Opus: 1976–77," Mason Papers.

387. Perry M. Shoemaker oral history (1970), p. 21, copies in HIA and HHPL.

388. Nash, *Herbert Hoover and Stanford University*, pp. 17–18.

389. Most of this correspondence is collected in the Herbert C. Hoover Papers, Box 115, vertical file folder, HIA. Some of it can also be found in the relevant PPI files at HHPL.

390. MacNeil oral history, p. 53; Shoemaker oral history, p. 22; Strauss memorandum for his files, March 27, 1962. When Strauss told Hoover in 1962 that he had a duty to publish his Magnum Opus, the Chief appeared pleased by this advice.

391. Walter Trohan oral history (1966), p. 31, copies at HIA and HHPL.

392. Hoover to MacNeil, March 28, 1963, PPI, Hoover Papers, HHPL; Hoover to Kaltenborn, March 28, 1963, Herbert C. Hoover Papers, Box 115, vertical file folder, HIA; Hoover to William C. Mullendore, March 28, 1963, ibid.

393. See, for example: Rita R. Campbell (Archivist, Hoover Institution) to Elizabeth Dempsey, July 11, 1963; Loretta F. Camp to Campbell, July 15, 1963; both in Herbert C. Hoover Papers, Box 66, envelope #10, HIA; Mary Lou Scanlon to Campbell, July 18, 1963, Palm files; Campbell to Scanlon, July 29, 1963, Palm files; Campbell to Scanlon, August 5, 1963, Herbert C. Hoover Papers, Box 115, vertical file folder, HIA. There were many such exchanges in 1963–64 between Hoover's New York office staff and the archivist of the Hoover Institution.

394. *New York Times*, June 15, 1963, p. 24. The newspaper carried many updates on Hoover's illness in the ensuing days.

395. Mason oral history, pp. 10–11.

396. *New York Times*, June 21, 1963, p. 6.

397. Mason oral history, p. 10.

398. *New York Times*, August 10, 1963, p. 20.

399. Hoover to George Mardikian, September 26, 1963, PPI, Hoover Papers, HHPL.

400. For more details, see my "Editor's Note on Sources and Editing Methods."

401. Hoover to DeWitt Wallace, October 2, 1963, copies in "Hoover Books: Magnum Opus," Mason Papers, and in Magnum Opus Materials, Box 4, HHPL.

402. DeWitt Wallace to Hoover, September 24, 1963, "Hoover Books: Magnum Opus," Mason Papers; MacNeil to William L. White, November 4, 1963, February 15, 1964, MacNeil Papers, Box 1; Hoover to Clarence Budington Kelland, November 6, 1963, PPI, Hoover Papers, HHPL; MacNeil to Hobart Lewis, March 16, 1964, MacNeil Papers, Box 1 and MacNeil file, PPI, Hoover Papers, HHPL.

In March 1964 Hoover's son sent a copy of both volumes of the *Freedom Betrayed* manuscript to the vice president of the *Reader's Digest* (Allan Hoover to Hobart Lewis, March 18, 1964, copy in MacNeil file, PPI, Hoover Papers, HHPL). Apparently Hoover thought the *Digest* was still interested.

403. Undated draft letter from an unnamed *Reader's Digest* executive to "Al" (Albert Cole?), ca. 1963–1964, copy in "Hoover Books: Magnum Opus," Mason Papers; Charles Edison to Hoover, December 14, 1963, Magnum Opus Materials, Box 4, folder 3, HHPL. Frank Mason later claimed that one of the *Reader's Digest*'s senior officers told Hoover that the *Digest* would publish the Magnum Opus but did not really mean it. Mason note on a letter to him from Michael Horacek, September 7, 1976, in "Magnum Opus: 1976–77," Mason Papers.

404. MacNeil oral history, p. 48. This may have happened after Hoover's death. MacNeil's account is not clear on the date.

405. Henry Regnery to W. Glenn Campbell, August 11, 1964, Hoover Institution Records, Box 2800, Magnum Opus folder.

406. Editor's interviews with Joan Dydo (April 6, 1989) and Cynthia Wilder (April 7, 1989), in New York City.

407. Hoover to Wallace, October 2, 1963.

408. MacNeil oral history, p. 53.

409. Hoover to Kelland, November 6, 1963; Hoover memorandum to his son Allan, n.d. (but sometime between early 1962 and 1964), in "*Freedom Betrayed* Manuscript: Memos to Staff and Letter Regarding Hoover Foundation, n/d," Loretta Camp Frey Papers, HHPL.

410. MacNeil to Allan Hoover, November 13, 1963, Magnum Opus Materials, Box 4, folder 3, HHPL; MacNeil to Herbert Hoover, n.d. (late November 1963), ibid.; F. Clifton Daniel to Harry S. Truman, November 13, 1963, and Truman to Daniel, November 18, 1963, both in "Hoover, Herbert C.," Secretary's Office File, Post-Presidential Papers, Harry S. Truman Papers, Harry S. Truman Presidential Library, Independence, Missouri; MacNeil oral history, pp. 24–25.

411. Bernice Miller to W. Glenn Campbell, March 30, 1964; Julius Epstein to Bernice Miller, March 31, 1964; both in Herbert C. Hoover Papers, Box 115, vertical file folder, HIA.

412. Julius Epstein to Loretta F. Camp, August 11, 1964, copies in ibid. and in Julius Epstein Papers, Box 181, HIA.

413. Hoover to Bonner Fellers, April 18, 1964, PPI, Hoover Papers, HHPL.

414. *New York Times,* August 10, 1964, p. 49.

415. Ibid., February 26, 1964, p. 71; ibid., February 28, 1964, p. 10.

416. Ibid., August 10, 1964, p. 49.

417. Ibid., p. 33.

418. Shoemaker oral history, p. 25. According to the Hoover Calendar at HHPL, Shoemaker last saw Hoover on August 5, 1964.

419. A copy of Hoover's will is printed in Herbert R. Collins, *Wills of the U.S. Presidents* (New York: Communication Channels, 1976), pp. 190–94.

420. Mason to MacNeil, February 11, 1966, "MacNeil, Neil: 1966–1968," Mason Papers.

421. Epstein to the Department of the Treasury, December 6, 1964, Epstein Papers, Box 181; Rita R. Campbell to Allan Hoover, April 20, 1965, Palm files; Allan Hoover to Rita Campbell, April 26, 1965, Palm files; Rita R. Campbell to W. Glenn Campbell, May 6, 1965 (plus attachment), Palm files; Allan Hoover to Frank E. Mason, June 15, 1965, "Hoover, Allan: 1965–67," Mason Papers.

422. MacNeil to Mason, March 27, June 8, and July 29, 1965, "MacNeil, Neil: 1964–65," HHPL.

423. MacNeil to Mason, August 18 and 28, 1965, ibid.

424. MacNeil to Mason, February 2 and 18, 1966, ibid; MacNeil to Allan Hoover, March 4, 1966, MacNeil Papers, Box 1.

425. MacNeil to Allan Hoover, March 4, 1966; MacNeil to Mason, "MacNeil, Neil: 1966–1968," Mason Papers.

426. Allan Hoover to MacNeil, May 31, 1966, MacNeil Papers, Box 1.

427. The foundation had evidently made no decision as of October 1966. MacNeil to Mason, October 15, 1966, "MacNeil, Neil: 1966–1968," Mason Papers.

428. For example, Graham Stuart oral history (1967), pp. 16–17; John K. Stewart oral history (1967), p. 53; William S. Nichols oral history (1968), pp. 19–20. All at HIA and HHPL.

429. Hoover memo to his son Allan, n.d. (cited in note 409).

430. The British government's Cabinet Office records on World War II were not opened to scholars until several years after Hoover's death.

431. An excellent monograph on this subject is Justus D. Doenecke, *Not to the Swift: The Old Isolationists in the Cold War Era* (Lewisburg, PA: Buckell University Press, 1979).

432. John Earl Haynes and Harvey Klehr, *Venona: Decoding Soviet Espionage in America* (New Haven and London: Yale University Press, 1999); John Earl Haynes, Harvey Klehr, and Alexander Vassiliev, *Spies: The Rise and Fall of the KGB in America* (New Haven and London: Yale University Press, 2009).

EDITOR'S NOTE ON
SOURCES AND EDITING METHODS

Sources

Between the early 1940s and 1964, Herbert Hoover labored over what he and his staff came to call his Magnum Opus. Originally intended to be a single volume (focused on World War II) in a multivolume set of his memoirs, the "War Book" (as he initially referred to it) grew and grew, until, by 1963, it had itself become a multivolume manuscript, with two volumes essentially complete and a third under construction.

During these twenty-odd years, Hoover appears to have produced at least ten distinct "editions" of his Magnum Opus, under at least four working titles culminating in *Freedom Betrayed*. Finally, in early 1963, as intimations of his mortality became stronger, Hoover corrected Edition No. 10 of *Freedom Betrayed* and renamed it Edition Z—significantly, the last letter of the alphabet. Whereupon, a perfectionist always, he proceeded to revise it still further into what came to be known as Edition Z+H.

With such a plethora of drafts (filling literally dozens of boxes) to work with, the question arises: Which of the many variants of Hoover's Magnum Opus should be published today? The answer, for me, seems plain: it is the version that Hoover himself wished to publish, the Z+H edition (volumes I and II), on which he completed work, for all practical purposes, in September 1963. Except for some later, mostly minor, emendations (discussed below), the Z+H edition was Hoover's final draft. In addition to this, I have selected for publication the most advanced drafts of four "case histories" that he intended to place in a projected volume III.

The basic, working text of volumes I and II of *Freedom Betrayed*—the Z+H edition of September 1963—is contained in four bound, typescript volumes in the Herbert C. Hoover Papers, Box 70, Hoover Institution Archives, at Stanford University. A duplicate set is filed among the Magnum Opus Materials in the Herbert Hoover Presidential Library, West Branch, Iowa. The first two typed volumes—constituting volume I of *Freedom Betrayed*—contain an annotation labeling this the Z+H✓ edition. The check mark (✓) appears to signify that someone—probably Hoover himself—had examined and finished correcting this text. The other two typed volumes—comprising volume II of *Freedom Betrayed*—carry only the marking Z+H, without the check mark, indicating that Hoover had not yet "signed off" on this portion of his last edition. Indeed, the latter two bound volumes at the Hoover Institution bear the handwritten inscription "Uncorrected 1964" on their cover.

After the summer of 1963, Hoover no longer worked systematically on his Magnum Opus. Yet in the ensuing months, as members of his secretarial staff methodically fact-checked every line of his second volume, he could not refrain from another round of editing. Between September 1963 and the spring of 1964, he managed to tinker one last time with volume II of his Z+H edition.

Two boxes in the Herbert C. Hoover Papers hold the fruit of this final exertion. Box 63, Envelope 6, and Box 64, Envelope 7, contain unbound copies of volume II of the Z+H edition, in two forms: a "research copy" (on which his fact-checkers worked) and a copy marked as belonging to Mr. Hoover. This material encompasses sections XI–XVIII (chapters 43–85) of *Freedom Betrayed*. On several dozen of these pages, there are penciled revisions (mostly minor) in Hoover's own hand.

None of these alterations appears in the Z+H set in Box 70. Indeed, notes by one or two of Hoover's secretaries (found in Box 64) indicate that as of March 30, 1964, Hoover's penciled changes in Sections XIV through XVIII (chapters 61–85) had not yet been made on a "clean set." Nevertheless, these late alterations do reflect his last known wishes for the wording of his Magnum Opus. In recognition of his manifest intent, I have incorporated these scattered revisions into the text printed here.

Some of the revisionary materials in Boxes 63 and 64 are more problematic. On a number of research copy pages there are changes, *not* in Hoover's hand, which were then transferred to his personal copy around January 1964. Hoover's fact-checker for these chapters was one of his senior secretaries, Loretta Camp, who had worked for him for more than twenty years. It seems unlikely that she entered these revisions onto Hoover's copy of the manuscript without his knowledge and approval. I have therefore accepted most of these (usually quite small) alterations as in all likelihood indicative of Hoover's intent.

A few pages in the research and Hoover copies contain mysterious handwritten alterations (such as inserted words) that seem not to have come from Mrs. Camp and that someone else may have added later on. Also, in a couple of instances Mrs. Camp proposed to move certain passages in Hoover's manuscript from one chapter to another one and inserted notes to this effect at the relevant points in his copy. It is not certain that Hoover agreed to her recommendations.

Unless otherwise indicated in the footnotes, I have resolved these ambiguities and perplexities by rejecting those changes and reverting to the unedited language of the Z+H edition in Box 70 of the Herbert C. Hoover Papers. In other words, I have accepted the revisions in Boxes 63 and 64, only if (a) the changes are in Hoover's own handwriting, or (b) they appear likely to have been recorded on his personal copy of his manuscript with his consent. (For the only significant exception, see chapter 53, note 4, and chapter 55, note 2.)

Hoover's final burst of editing nearly always entailed small adjustments in his manuscript (a new word or phrase here, a revised sentence there)—not any drastic or substantial rewriting. To all intents and purposes, he completed volumes I and II of the Magnum Opus (except his staff's fact-checking) in September 1963.

My approach to Hoover's final revisions has also governed my treatment of the Z+H edition mentioned earlier. The basic text in Box 70 of Hoover's papers turns out to contain a few inked-in alterations, including inserted cards and notes, offered by someone—probably a friend—who read the manuscript at some point and proposed to change it in places. This person appears to have been Hoover's friend and literary adviser Neil MacNeil. Because these revisions are not in Hoover's handwriting, and because there is no evidence that he ever saw and approved of them, I have ignored them in preparing the manuscript for publication.

In short, the first two volumes in this book consist of the Z+H edition of September 1963, plus certain revisions that Hoover is known to have made (or is believed to have authorized) between that date and the end of March 1964.

Determining the proper text for Volume III has proven more complicated. Around 1961, as Hoover reshaped his manuscript into what became known as *Freedom Betrayed*, he began to prepare a series of "tragic case histories" of five nations that had descended into chaos or communism in the years just after World War II. According to a note in Box 77 of his papers, these countries were Poland, China, Korea, Japan, and Germany. Each of them Hoover had visited (at the request of President Truman) in 1946 and (in the case of Germany) in 1947 also.

Initially Hoover planned to include these case histories in the latter part of volume II of the Magnum Opus. But sometime in 1962 he changed his mind and decided to place them together, in a separate, third volume of his still-evolving manuscript.

As far as can be ascertained from his extant research files, Hoover soon dropped Japan from his list. In a memorandum to his staff late in 1962 (see appendix, Document 24), he announced that volume III of the Magnum Opus would consist of case histories for four countries only: Poland, China, Korea, and Germany, in that order.

Hoover did not leave behind a polished, typewritten copy of volume III. But we know what it was meant to contain, and, as it happens, Hoover's Magnum Opus papers hold extensive files for his case histories. On each of them he labored diligently between 1961 and 1963. In every instance, he produced multiple drafts. For Poland and China especially, his studies went through repeated editions and meticulous editing.

It has therefore been possible to identify publishable texts for each one of Hoover's quartet of case histories. As with volumes I and II, for volume III I have sought out the latest typewritten drafts of each case study in Hoover's files. To these texts I have added any subsequent, handwritten revisions that he demonstrably desired to make. In this way, I have been able to assemble the four components of volume III in their approximately final, intended form— or at least the form to which Hoover had brought them, after sustained effort, before he stopped working on them in 1963.

Volume III, then, as printed in this book, contains the full text of this last installment of the Magnum Opus, as Hoover ultimately conceived it. The location of the individual essays is given in my editorial notes in volume III.

Finally, I have included in this book a collection of documents relating to the origins, evolution, and purposes of Hoover's Magnum Opus. This selection is entirely my own. These items are printed, and their provenance explained, in the Appendix.

Editing Methods

We turn now from the documentary sources for *Freedom Betrayed* to some further remarks about editorial methods.

In editing the Hoover manuscripts identified above, I have tried to bear in mind that his Magnum Opus is, first and foremost, a primary source, the "will and testament" (as he called it) of a noted twentieth-century statesman. Moreover, its author is not here to ratify or nullify editorial suggestions. I have therefore endeavored to reproduce the text as nearly as possible as Hoover composed it, nearly half a century ago.

This book at hand is not, however, a mere photostat of Hoover's final work product. From time to time, I have made minor grammatical or typographical corrections in his text—such as adding or deleting commas, lowercasing words, or adding accent marks—in the interest of elementary correctness or clarity. Such changes fall into the category of what Hoover, in directives to his staff, called "clean up"—or, as we might say, copyediting. In no case, however, have I knowingly altered his meaning or tried to rewrite his text. On the few occasions when it has seemed advisable to modify or clarify his narrative by inserting a word or a phrase, I have done so in brackets with the attached abbreviation "ed." I have also streamlined the formatting of Hoover's table of contents and chapter titles and have removed the subtables of contents that he had prepared for each of the eighteen sections of volumes I and II.

I have not attempted to verify every one of Hoover's thousands of factual claims and hundreds of footnote citations—a monumental task that his staff strained to perform for him in 1963 and 1964. In the course of editing and proofreading his text and attendant footnotes, however, I have consulted most of the sources that he cited and have carefully checked these against his quotations from them in his manuscript. In a number of instances, I have discovered typographical and transcription errors in Hoover's version. Where such mistakes have been detected, I have corrected them and have made due note of this within brackets or in footnotes.

Every effort, then, has been made to reproduce Hoover's text, in the final form in which he left it, subject only to the imperatives of factual accuracy and "clean up."

With Hoover's footnotes, however (as distinguished from the regular text above them), I have felt compelled to take a somewhat different approach. As one might expect of a sprawling manuscript that was repeatedly annotated and revised over a period of twenty years, the footnote form in the final edition of the Magnum Opus was inconsistent. Hoover followed no manual of style. His citation procedure, for example, at times varied from chapter to chapter—and sometimes even within a chapter. Now and then he repeated a complete citation for a source in the same chapter. Sometimes he did so in the very next footnote. Only rarely did he use the word *ibid*.

These and other idiosyncrasies raise an editorial problem for which there is no perfect solution. One option was to present Hoover's footnotes exactly as he wrote them, at the price of distracting and at times confusing the reader. A second option was to rewrite his footnotes from scratch in compliance with modern canons of scholarship, at the price of anachronism and of sacrificing Hoover's distinctive, authorial voice.

On reflection, I have chosen a middle course. One purpose of a footnote citation is to enable a reader to find the cited source. Invoking this principle as my guide, I have decided to retain Hoover's overall footnote style but to insert, where needed, within brackets, additional information (such as date and place of publication) that will permit a curious reader to track down the source being cited. Readers interested in the quality and flavor of Hoover's citations will therefore be able to see most footnotes in their original, as well as amplified, forms.

I have modified this approach, however, in places where it has seemed only sensible to do so. Throughout the footnotes I have regularly deleted needless redundancies (such as duplicate citations of the same source in the same chapter). Wherever possible, I have inserted the useful word *ibid.* Where Hoover cites the *New York Times,* I have omitted the superfluous *the,* which he routinely placed in front of it. I have also renumbered his footnotes when required. In a few instances, usually involving citation of U.S. government documents, I have felt obliged to reorganize a footnote in order to convey the needed information in a more coherent way.

None of this copyediting affects the substance of Hoover's narrative or his supporting evidence. Nor, in my judgment, does it significantly alter the feel of his scholarly apparatus. Again, the aim of my limited editorial adjustments has been to provide the reader important additional data while remaining faithful to the general texture of Hoover's footnotes.

Herbert Hoover was not a professional scholar. But he *was* a prolific writer, an amateur historian, and the author of more than thirty separate books. With *Freedom Betrayed*—the most ambitious of all his writing projects—I have tried to let him speak to us as he wished, in his own words, with a minimum of editorial filtering.

Freedom Betrayed

by

Herbert Hoover

VOLUME I

INTRODUCTION

THE PILGRIMS LANDED ON THIS CONTINENT bringing with them the vital spark of American life—freedom. Since then, there have been four times when freedom has been dangerously near the tragedy of defeat:

The War of the Revolution
The War between the States
The Second World War
The Cold War.[1]

Statesmanship brought expanded liberty from the Revolution and the Civil War. The Nation grew to strength and to prosperity unknown in all human history.

In the Second World War, we, with our Allies, crushed militarily the forces of Nazism and Fascism. But we have no peace. During the war one of our Allies, Stalin, expanded the Communist dictatorship and empire of Russia to endanger freedom in the whole world. We are now deeply involved in the "Cold War" which imperils our very existence.

To protect our own freedom—in this, in reality a third world war—we must carry the major burden of defending the free nations of the world. This burden itself imperils our future.

The purpose of this memoir is to analyze step-by-step when, where, how, and by whom we were plunged into the Second and Third World Wars, with the resulting betrayals of freedom. I will likewise record those who warned against and opposed these ominous decisions which led to this turning-point in civilization.

---

1. Some might list the Spanish-American War and the First World War as having endangered that vital spark of American life. The Spanish-American War expanded liberty in the world as did also the First World War, which brought freedom to many nations. In neither was there danger of defeat nor the reduction of freedom in the United States.

In this memoir I will omit views of my own as to what took place. I will demonstrate the truth from the words and actions of world leaders themselves, and the documentation which has come to light.

From a true record of human experience alone may come the understanding which can guide our future.

Even today important segments of the American people and American leadership are not fully aware of the menace to freedom which lies in socialism and other forms of centralized government.

◆ ◆ ◆

Search for the truth on the events and the commitments of world leaders which brought us to this calamity has been fraught with great difficulties. The records are strewn not only with the natural misunderstandings between men and women and different civilizations, but with deliberate suppression and destruction of vital documents. Secret verbal commitments which resulted in the betrayal of freedom often must be proved by subsequent actions and events. Other suppressions can be proved by scrutinizing the texts of governmental publications. Vital suppressions have been from time to time exposed by the press and by historians. At times notations of top-level meetings of leaders state: "No official minutes of this meeting found or made."

For instance, the papers of the important Third Washington Conference of Messrs. Roosevelt and Churchill during the Second World War are a glaring example of suppression. Complete publication of these papers was promised, but to date this has not been done. Other exhibits are the published papers of the Tehran and Yalta Conferences.[2] In the second volume of this work I shall give the written statement of a former State Department official who was directed to destroy and omit many important documents. He did so.

On the other hand, an invaluable aid to the historian in uncovering the truth comes from the speeches, autobiographies and books by the secondary participants in high level conferences.

◆ ◆ ◆

At the outset of this work I wish the reader to be under no misapprehension as to my position upon America's joining the Second World War. I had

---

2. The official title of the "Tehran Papers" is [U.S. Department of State], *Foreign Relations of the United States, Diplomatic Papers, The Conferences at Cairo and Tehran, 1943* (United States Government Printing Office, Washington: 1961). The official title of the "Yalta Papers" is [U.S. Department of State,] *Foreign Relations of the United States, Diplomatic Papers, The Conferences at Malta and Yalta, 1945* (United States Government Printing Office, Washington: 1955).

supported our entry into the First World War. When American alliance with Russia in the Second World War loomed up at the time of Hitler's attack upon Stalin, I stated in a nation-wide address on June 29, 1941:

We know ... Hitler's hideous record of brutality, of aggression and as a destroyer of democracies. Truly Poland, Norway, Holland, Belgium, Denmark, France ... are dreadful monuments. But I am talking of Stalin at this moment. ...

... now we find ourselves promising aid to Stalin and his militant Communist conspiracy against the whole democratic ideals of the world. ... it makes the whole argument of our joining the war to bring the four freedoms to mankind a gargantuan jest. ...

If we go further and join the war and we win, then we have won for Stalin the grip of Communism on Russia and more opportunity for it to extend in the world. ...

... These two dictators—Stalin and Hitler—are in deadly combat. One of these two hideous ideologists will disappear in this fratricidal war. In any event both will be weakened.

Statesmanship demands that the United States stand aside in watchful waiting, armed to the teeth, while these men exhaust themselves.

Then the most powerful and potent nation in the world can talk to mankind with a voice that will be heard. If we get involved in this struggle we, too, will be exhausted and feeble.

To align American ideals alongside Stalin will be as great a violation of everything American as to align ourselves with Hitler.[3]

◆　◆　◆

It is proper for me to review my experience for undertaking the preparation of these three volumes. For more than sixty years, I have had opportunities available to few other living men to observe the political and economic forces in motion in almost every important nation in the world. I have lived and worked in forty-five countries, in some of them several times. They include all the great nations which control the fate of mankind—Great Britain, France, Germany, Russia, China, India, Italy, and Japan, as well as the leading nations of Latin America and a host of smaller nations.

I have worked in countries under kings and dictators, and under both Fascists and Communists. I was associated with the statesmen of many free

---

3. I give the full text of this address later in Section IX of these memoirs. [*Editor's note:* See chapter 34 and p. 582, note 9.]

nations and their spiritual leaders. Even before the First World War I saw the squalor of Asia and the frozen class barriers of Europe. One of my never-to-be suppressed memories was in Czarist Russia where I witnessed groups of intelligent men and women chained together awaiting their journey to Siberia.

I have served at different times in positions in our own Government, which involved our relations with foreign governments and their leaders, for a total of about twenty years. At those periods I served in two score special missions to overseas peoples.

I have directed the relief from famine and pestilence in the aftermath of the two world wars in which over fifty nations were involved. I have witnessed the full depth of human suffering. I have seen the agonies of mass starvation among millions of people. I have seen cities where the children ceased to play in the streets. I have seen tens of thousands of refugees trudging along the highways, with their backs loaded with children and their last belongings. Many dropped by the wayside.

I have had special experience in dealing with Communism and Communist conspiracies. After Nikolai Lenin came to power in Russia in November 1917, the Communists lost no time in launching conspiracies to take over the governments of most of Europe's newly liberated states. In these conspiracies, the Communists had the advantage of trained agents from the Third International, the Czar's gold reserves which they had seized, and nation-wide hunger. At one time or another during the Armistice after the First World War, they gained control of a dozen cities, some whole provinces, and one entire nation. In my job I had to deal with these activities. Snuffing out these conspiracies was not accomplished by military action. Relief of hunger and sickness was far more powerful than machine guns. The rising hope of freedom was much more effective than the preachments of Karl Marx. Our government did not preach the Christian faith as the answer to materialism and agnosticism. We practiced it.

During this period I sought to inform myself on the philosophy, methods and purposes of Communism. I studied most of the writings of Karl Marx, the father of modern Communism, and all of the statements obtainable in English of Lenin, its fanatic new leader.[4] I collected the proceedings of the "Third International" which undertook the planning of the world Communist Revolution.

---

4. A literary curio in my library is one of the three known surviving originals of the *Communist Manifesto* by Karl Marx and Friedrich Engels, issued in 1848.

An occasion for the better understanding of Communism in practice arose in 1921, when an appeal came to the United States from Lenin and other top Soviet officials for help to combat the devastating famine which had befallen Russia. From Washington, where I was then Secretary of Commerce, I organized and directed the relief of this famine on behalf of the American people—the only source from which relief could come. The Soviet leaders themselves confirmed that we Americans had saved more than 20,000,000 lives, and attested in writing that the Soviet government would never forget—which it did promptly and callously.[5]

◆ ◆ ◆

My work in preparation of these memoirs has been aided by the unique documentation at my disposal. Early in the First World War, I started what became the library of the Hoover Institution on War, Revolution and Peace at Stanford University. This library now contains some 25,000,000 documents, speeches, books, diaries, pamphlets, the press of many countries and records of negotiations and treaties of critical periods and in many languages. These collections have been enriched by the papers of hundreds of important persons from all over the world. Most of this confidential material has been made available to me by the depositors.

Work upon this memoir for more than twenty years has required the scrutiny of literally thousands of such records in many languages. A number of these required translation. The task would have been insuperable but for a preliminary weeding out of less important materials by my friends, by my own staff, and by the staff of the Hoover Institution.

◆ ◆ ◆

The text is divided into sections chronologically arranged, and covering longer or shorter periods beginning and ending with some major event or action which changed the shape of things to come. Within each section, I have usually treated subjects topically rather than chronologically.

The immense documentation of enemy countries seized after the war could not have been known to leaders of the free nations at the time of their own

---

5. I have published the details of these activities in both World Wars and their aftermaths in four volumes entitled *An American Epic,* wherein an account is given of the American charitable agencies which saved the lives of more than one billion human beings. (Henry Regnery Company, Chicago: 1959, 1960, 1961 and 1964). See also [Herbert Hoover], *The Ordeal of Woodrow Wilson* (McGraw-Hill Book Company, Inc., New York: 1958).

actions or decisions. Justice to these leaders requires that such disclosures not be used in the appraisal of their statesmanship at the actual time they made these decisions. To make this clear, I have presented such *ex post facto* information in footnotes or, in one or two cases, in chapters so indicated.

◆ ◆ ◆

When meetings of leaders were held where important commitments were made, I review briefly the military situation of the time in order to clarify the background. But this memoir is not a detailed military history.

I believe that throughout this period the fate of mankind has been determined less by military action than by the decisions of political leaders.

A Great Intellectual and Moral Plague Comes to Free Men

CHAPTER 1

The Creators, Leaders, Principles, and Methods of Communism

BEFORE DEALING WITH what Communism really is, a short resumé of the origin and rise of the most disastrous plague which has come to free men may be helpful to readers not already familiar with it.

While Communism was not unknown in ancient history, it was enunciated as a complete economic and social system by two German economic and social theorists, Karl Marx and Friedrich Engels, in their *Communist Manifesto* (*Manifest der Kommunistischen Partei*) published in 1848. It is a cynical fact that Marx earned part of his living as a London correspondent for Horace Greeley's *New York Tribune*.

The *Manifesto's* twentieth-century great apostle was Nikolai Lenin (Vladimir Ilyich Ulyanov), a Russian expatriate who had taken part in the organization of the Communist Third International. In April 1917, Lenin was secretly smuggled back into Russia by the Germans to stir up revolution against the newly established Kerensky democratic regime. Leon Trotsky, a leading Russian Communist then in the United States, joined him.

In the early meetings of the Communists in Russia, they split into two groups: the Bolsheviks, who favored revolution by violence, and the Mensheviks, who advocated less violent measures. The Bolsheviks under Lenin's leadership prevailed. He and his associates seized the government by violence in November, 1917. Most of the Mensheviks joined or were liquidated.

Under the title of Chairman of the Council of People's Commissars, Lenin established himself as dictator of Russia, so continuing until his death in January, 1924. Lenin was succeeded by Joseph Stalin, who remained dictator until his death in March, 1953, when his body was enshrined in Lenin's tomb. Stalin was succeeded by a shaky triumvirate which included Lavrenti P. Beria, Georgi M. Malenkov, and Vyacheslav M. Molotov. This trio was followed by

Nicolai A. Bulganin. Then in 1958, Nikita S. Khrushchev came into power, renouncing Stalin and all his works. The culmination of Stalin's repudiation came on October 30, 1961, when the Communists at their 22nd Congress decreed the eviction of his body from its resting place alongside Lenin.

All of these succeeding dictators repeatedly affirmed their devotion to the doctrines of Karl Marx and Lenin, and their pictures are displayed in every public place in Russia. Annually, at the November celebration of the Revolution in Red Square in Moscow, the Russian hierarchs renew their vows of their fidelity to Marx and Lenin.

The Principles and Methods of Communism

I should say at the outset that Communism is a fiery spirit infecting men's minds. Its great parallels in history are the Christian and Mohammedan religions. Communism is a crusading spirit, ruthless of all opposition, and over the years it has evolved beliefs, methods and organization. Within it is a vehement demand for expansion and a suppression of all such human emotions as piety. It is sadistic and cruel.

The principles and methods can best be described from the speeches and statements of its own leaders, and for the convenience of the reader, I present these according to major theme. There are differences in translation into English, and that one most generally accepted is given here.

On Dictatorship

Lenin stated:

> ... The scientific concept 'dictatorship' means nothing more nor less than unrestricted power, absolutely unimpeded by laws or regulations and resting directly upon force. *This* is the meaning of the concept 'dictatorship' *and nothing else. ...*[1]

Stalin elaborated on Lenin's theory in 1924:

> ... Lenin's theory of the dictatorship of the proletariat is not a purely "Russian" theory, but a theory which necessarily applies to all countries.

---

1. V. I. Lenin, *Selected Works*, Volume VII, *After the Seizure of Power (1917–18)*, (International Publishers, New York [1943]), "A Contribution to the History of the Question of Dictatorship," October 20, 1920, p. 254.

Bolshevism is not only a Russian phenomenon. "Bolshevism," says Lenin, is *"a model of tactics for all." . . .*[2]

On Religion and Morals

Lenin echoed the atheism of Karl Marx, stating:

> . . . Religion is the opium of the people. Religion is a kind of spiritual gin in which the slaves of capital drown their human shape and their claims to any decent human life.[3]

These words of Lenin, "Religion is the opium of the people," were inscribed on the wall of a government building near the Red Square.[4]

On International Relations

On March 8, 1918, Lenin said:

> . . . In war you must never tie your hands with considerations of formality. It is ridiculous not to know the history of war, not to know that a treaty is a means of gaining strength; . . . the history of war shows as clearly as clear can be that the signing of a treaty after defeat is a means of gaining strength . . .[5]

As early as 1913, Stalin manifested his lack of faith in international agreements. He stated:

> . . . A diplomat's words *must* contradict his deeds—otherwise, what sort of a diplomat is he? Words are one thing—deeds something entirely different. Fine words are a mask to cover shady deeds. A sincere diplomat is like dry water, or wooden iron.[6]

---

2. J. V. Stalin, *Works,* Volume VI, *1924* (Foreign Languages Publishing House, Moscow: 1953), "The October Revolution and the Tactics of the Russian Communists," p. 382. The reference is to the English version of Lenin's *Selected Works,* Volume VII, *After the Seizure of Power (1917–1918)* (International Publishers, New York [1943]), "The Proletarian Revolution and the Renegade Kautsky," p. 183. See also Joseph Stalin, *Selected Writings* (International Publishers, New York: 1942), p. 14.

3. V. I. Lenin, *Selected Works,* Volume XI (International Publishers, New York [1943]), "Socialism and Religion," p. 658.

4. H. V. Kaltenborn, *Fifty Fabulous Years* (G. P. Putnam's Sons, New York: 1950), p. 131.

5. V. I. Lenin, *Selected Works,* Volume VII, *After the Seizure of Power (1917–1918),* "Speech in Reply to the Debate on the Report of War and Peace," March 8, 1918, p. 309.

6. J. V. Stalin, *Works,* Volume II, *1907–1913* (Foreign Languages Publishing House, Moscow: 1953), "The Elections in St. Petersburg," January 12 (25), 1913, p. 285.

The Method of Communist Revolutions is by Violence

Lenin stated:

Great questions in the life of nations are settled only by force. . . .[7]

. . . the victory of socialism is possible, first in a few or even in one single capitalist country. The victorious proletariat of that country, having expropriated the capitalists and organized its own socialist production, would *confront* the rest of the capitalist world, attract to itself the oppressed classes of other countries, raise revolts among them against the capitalists, and, in the event of necessity, come out even with armed force against the exploiting classes and their states. . . .[8]

Stalin wrote in 1924:

While it is true that the *final* victory of Socialism in the first country to emancipate itself is impossible without the combined efforts of the proletarians of several countries, it is equally true that the development of the world revolution will be the more rapid and thorough, the more effective the assistance rendered by the first Socialist country to the workers . . . of all other countries.

In what should this assistance be expressed?

Stalin answers his own question by repeating words of Lenin:

It should be expressed, first, in the victorious country achieving the "utmost possible in one country *for* the development, support and awakening of the revolution *in all countries.*" (Lenin, *Selected Works,* Vol. VII, p. 182.)

Second, it should be expressed in that the "victorious proletariat" of one country, "having expropriated the capitalists and organized its own Socialist production, would *stand up* against the rest of the world, the capitalist world, attracting to its cause the oppressed classes of other countries, raising revolts in those countries against the capitalists, and in the event of necessity coming out even with armed force against the exploiting classes and their states. (Lenin, *Selected Works,* Vol. V, p. 141.)[9]

---

7. V. I. Lenin, *Selected Works,* Volume III, *The Revolution of 1905–07* (International Publishers, New York [1943]), "The Two Tactics of Social-Democracy in the Democratic Revolution," p. 126.

8. V. I. Lenin, *Selected Works,* Volume V, *Imperialism and Imperialist War (1914–1917)* (International Publishers, New York [1943]), "The United States of Europe Slogan," August 23, 1915, p. 141.

9. J. Stalin, *Problems of Leninism* (Foreign Languages Publishing House, Moscow: 1940), pp. 115–116.

In a speech on March 10, 1939, Stalin stressed the need for trained revolutionaries:

The training and molding of our young cadres usually proceeds in some particular branch of science or technology, along the line of specialization. . . . But there is one branch of science which Bolsheviks in all branches of science are in duty bound to know, and that is the Marxist-Leninist science of society, of the laws of social development, of the laws of development of the proletarian revolution, of the laws of development of socialist construction, and of the victory of communism. . . .[10]

On Subversion of Labor Unions and Strikes

In April, 1920, Lenin thus counseled his followers:

. . . It is necessary to be able to withstand all this, to agree to any and every sacrifice, and even—if need be—to resort to all sorts of stratagems, manoeuvers and illegal methods, to evasion and subterfuges in order to penetrate the trade unions, to remain in them, and to carry on Communist work in them at all costs. . . .[11]

Stalin, in 1925, stated:

. . . the support of our revolution by the workers of all countries, and still more the victory of the workers in at least several countries, is a necessary condition for fully guaranteeing the first victorious country against attempts at intervention and restoration, a necessary condition for the final victory of socialism.[12]

A resolution passed at the Sixth World Congress of the Communist International (July–August, 1928) declared:

. . . the Communists in capitalist countries must reject the phrase "Reply to war by general strike," and have no illusions whatever about the efficacy of such phrases, nevertheless, in the event of war against the Soviet Union

---

10. Joseph Stalin, *Selected Writings,* "Report on the Work of the Central Committee to the Eighteenth Congress of the Communist Party of the Soviet Union," March 10, 1939, pp. 466–467.
11. V. I. Lenin, *Selected Works,* Volume X (International Publishers, New York: 1943), "'Left-Wing' Communism, an Infantile Disorder," April 27, 1920, p. 95.
12. J. V. Stalin, *Works,* Volume VII, *1925* (Foreign Languages Publishing House, Moscow: 1954), "The Results of the Work of the Fourteenth Conference of the R.C.P. (B.)," May 9, 1925, p. 120.

becoming imminent, they must take into consideration the increased opportunities for employing the weapon of mass strikes and the general strike, prior to the outbreak of war and during the mobilization . . .[13]

On Subversion of Legislative Bodies

Lenin said:

. . . The party of the revolutionary proletariat must take part in bourgeois parliamentarism in order to enlighten the masses . . .[14]

And again Lenin said:

. . . As long as you are unable to disperse the bourgeois parliament and every other type of reactionary institution, you *must* work inside them, *precisely* because in them there are still workers who are stupefied by the priests and by the dreariness of village life; otherwise you run the risk of becoming mere babblers.[15]

In June 1920, Lenin said:

. . . the Communist International must enter into a temporary alliance with bourgeois democracy in colonial and backward countries, but must not merge with it, and must unconditionally preserve the independence of the proletarian movement even in its most rudimentary form. . . .[16]

In 1935, when the Seventh Congress of the Communist International met in Moscow, speech after speech dwelt on the determination to bore from within in every nation. The Secretary-General, "Comrade" Georgi Dimitrov of Bulgaria, recalled the Trojan horse technique and advised its general use.[17]

---

13. *The Struggle Against Imperialist War and the Tasks of the Communists* (Workers Library Publishers, New York City: March, 1932), pp. 28–29.

14. V. I. Lenin, *The Constituent Assembly Elections and the Dictatorship of the Proletariat* (Foreign Languages Publishing House: Moscow: 1954) p. 36.

15. V. I. Lenin, *Selected Works*, Volume X, "'Left-Wing' Communism, An Infantile Disorder," April 27, 1920, p. 100.

16. V. I. Lenin, *Selected Works*, Volume X (International Publishers, New York: 1943), "Preliminary Draft of Theses on the National and Colonial Questions," June 1920, p. 237.

17. United States Department of State, *Foreign Relations of the United States: Diplomatic Papers, The Soviet Union, 1933–1939* ([Government Printing Office,] Washington: 1952), pp. 228–244. See also 76th Cong., 1st sess., House Report No. 2, *Investigation of Un-American Activities and Propaganda*, Report of the Special Committee on Un-American Activities pursuant to H. Res. 282 (75th Congress) January 3, 1939, p. 27.

In 1940, Congressman Martin Dies published an account of the use of this tactic in the United States.[18]

On Stirring Up Strife Between Nations and Groups

In November 1920, Lenin stated:

> The fundamental thing in the matter of concessions . . . we must take advantage of the antagonisms and contradictions between two capitalisms . . . inciting one against the other. . . .
>
> . . . can we, as Communists, remain indifferent and merely say: "We shall carry on propaganda for Communism in these countries." That is true, but that is not all. The practical task of Communist policy is to take advantage of this hostility and to incite one against the other. . . .[19]

In 1921, at the Tenth Congress of the Russian Communist Party, Stalin, in criticizing articles written by the then Commissar of Foreign Affairs, said:

> . . . Chicherin . . . under-estimates, the internal contradictions among the imperialist groups and states. . . . But these contradictions do exist, and the activities of the People's Commissariat of Foreign Affairs are based on them.
>
> . . . It is precisely the function of the People's Commissariat of Foreign Affairs to take all these contradictions into account, to base itself on them, to manoeuver within the framework of these contradictions. . . .[20]

Again in 1921, Stalin wrote in *Pravda*:

> The Party's tasks . . . are:
>
> 1) to utilise all the contradictions and conflicts among the capitalist groups and governments which surround our country, with the object of disintegrating imperialism.[21]

In 1924, Stalin said:

---

18. Martin Dies, *The Trojan Horse in America* (Dodd, Mead & Company, New York: 1940).

19. V. I. Lenin, *Selected Works*, Volume VIII, *The Period of War Communism (1918–1920)* (International Publishers, New York [1943]), "Speech Delivered at a meeting of Nuclei Secretaries of the Moscow Organization of the Russian Communist Party (Bolsheviks)," November 26, 1920, pp. 279, 284.

20. J. V. Stalin, *Works*, Volume V, *1921–1923* (Foreign Languages Publishing House, Moscow: 1953), "The Tenth Congress of the R.C.P. (B.)," March 10, 1921, p. [41–] 42.

21. J. V. Stalin, *Works*, Volume V, *1921–1923*, "The Party Before and After Taking Power," August 28, 1921, p. 113. See also David J. Dallin, *Russia & Postwar Europe* (Yale University Press, New Haven: 1943), p. 74.

... The reserves of the revolution can be ... contradictions, conflicts and wars ... among the bourgeois states hostile to the proletarian state. ... [22]

On There Can Be No Peace

Lenin said:

... If war is waged by the proletariat after it has conquered the bourgeoisie in its own country, and is waged with the object of strengthening and extending socialism, such a war is legitimate and "holy." [23]

Again Lenin said:

... If we are obliged to tolerate such scoundrels as the capitalist thieves, each of whom is preparing to plunge a knife into us, it is our direct duty to make them turn their knives against each other. ...

... As long as capitalism and socialism exist, we cannot live in peace: in the end, one or the other will triumph—a funeral dirge will be sung either over the Soviet Republic or over world capitalism. ... [24]

In a speech on June 23, 1938, Commissar of Foreign Affairs, Maxim Litvinov, noted the tendency to forget that:

... "with the preservation of the capitalist system a long and enduring peace is impossible." ... [25]

On December 21, 1939, in response to a birthday greeting, Stalin said:

Do not doubt, my comrades, that I am ready to devote all my efforts and ability and, if necessary, all my blood, drop by drop, to the cause of the working class proletarian revolution and world communism. [26]

In the course of the alliance with the Americans and British during the Second World War, Stalin issued a number of glowing statements on the virtues of freedom and democracy. In 1942, and repeatedly thereafter, the Soviet

---

22. J. V. Stalin, *Works*, Volume VI, *1924*, "The Foundations of Leninism," p. 161. See also David J. Dallin, *Russia & Postwar Europe*, p. 74.

23. V. I. Lenin, *Selected Works*, Volume VII, *After the Seizure of Power (1917–18)*, "'Left-wing' Childishness and Petty Bourgeois Mentality," May 1918, p. 357.

24. V. I. Lenin, *Selected Works*, Volume VII, *The Period of War Communism (1918–1920)*, "Organization of the Russian Communist Party (Bolsheviks)," November 26, 1920, pp. 288, 297.

25. Department of State, *Foreign Relations of the United States: Diplomatic Papers—The Soviet Union, 1933–1939*, pp. [587–588–ed].

26. *New York Times*, December 22, 1939.

Union and Stalin himself accepted the terms of the Atlantic Charter. These acts neatly fitted into the category of "dodges and tricks" prescribed by Lenin, as later chapters on the Second World War will show.

If any one believes these statements I have quoted from Lenin and Stalin are mere revolutionary bombast, he may turn to the present leader of the Communist world. In September 1955, Nikita Khrushchev, at a dinner at the Kremlin for the visiting East German Communist delegation, declared:

> They often say in the West when speaking of Soviet leaders, that something has changed since the Geneva conference [of the Big Four Powers]. They are starting to smile but have not changed their line of conduct. . . .
>
> But if anyone believes that our smiles involve abandonment of the teaching of Marx, Engels and Lenin he deceives himself poorly. Those who wait for that must wait until a shrimp learns to whistle.[27]

On November 17, 1956, Khrushchev made this statement to Western diplomats at a reception in Moscow:

> . . . Whether you like it or not, history is on our side. We will bury you.[28]

Khrushchev said on November 22, 1957:

> . . . We, Communists, the Soviet politicians, are atheists.[29]

Khrushchev said in January 1959:

> We have always followed, and will also follow in the future, the great international teachings of Marx, Engels, and Lenin. Figuratively speaking our Communist Party regards itself as one of the leading detachments of the worldwide communist movement, a detachment which is the first to scale the heights of communism. On the way to these heights we shall not be stopped by avalanches or landslides. No one shall forcibly deflect us from the path of the movement toward communism. . . . We regard it as imperative to strengthen by every means the might of the socialist camp, to consolidate still further the unity of the international communist movement. . . .[30]

---

27. *New York Times,* September 18, 1955.

28. *Time* Magazine, November 26, 1956.

29. Interview with William Randolph Hearst, Jr., November 22, 1957; *Pravda,* November 29, 1957. Quoted in [U.S.] Department of State, *Soviet World Outlook* [Department of State Publication 6836] (Washington: 1959), p. 47.

30. Speech at the Twenty-first Congress of the Communist Party of the Soviet Union, January 27, 1959; Moscow radio broadcast, January 28, 1959. Quoted in Department of State, *Soviet World Outlook,* p. 67.

On September 4, 1959, in a comment on the eventual victory of communism over capitalism, Khrushchev said Soviet bloc economic conditions were improving and "we have no reason not to be patient." Capitalists, he said, were digging their own graves and "I am not going to labor to dig their graves."[31]

At a Kremlin reception on the occasion of the 43rd Anniversary of the Bolshevist Revolution, Khrushchev said:

> We are working toward communism, but war will not help us reach our goal—it will spoil it.
>
> We shall win only through the minds of men.

He continued:

> We must rest on the position of [peaceful] coexistence and nonintervention. It is not necessary to whip people along this road . . . but communism eventually will be in force all over the earth.[32]

On April 14, 1961, Khrushchev said:

> We proclaim . . . that after successfully carrying out the building of socialism, begun in 1917 by the October Revolution, we are advancing surely and boldly along the path indicated by the great Lenin to the building of communism. We say that there is no force in the world capable of turning us off this path.[33]

Khrushchev could well justify this statement. Communism has spread from about 5% or 6% of the world's population in Lenin's time to over 30%. And its conspiracies continue in every free nation in the world.

The Communist dedication to the victory of Communism over other ideologies is evidenced in some of Khrushchev's more recent statements.

At a Moscow reception held February 15, 1963, he said to the Red Chinese Ambassador Pan Tzu Li:

> . . . I promise you that when we throw a last shovel on the grave of capitalism, we will do it with China.[34]

On April 20, 1963, in an interview with an Italian newspaper Editor (Italo Pietra) Khrushchev said:

---

31. *New York Times,* September 5, 1959.

32. Ibid., November 8, 1960.

33. Ibid., April 15, 1961.

34. Ibid., Western Edition, February 16, 1963. See also *Life* Magazine, March 1, 1963.

. . . peaceful coexistence of states with different social regimes does not imply a peaceful coexistence in the field of ideology. . . .

. . . we Communists never have accepted and never will accept the idea of peaceful coexistence of ideology. On this ground there cannot be compromises. . . .

. . . In the hard fight of the two antagonistic ideologies . . . we are and will be on the offensive. We will affirm Communist ideals. . . .[35]

---

35. *New York Times*, April 22, 1963.

CHAPTER 2

The Recognition of Soviet Russia in November 1933

PRESIDENT WILSON SOON AFTER the First World War stated the United States policy of no recognition of the Communist government of Russia. His views on recognition were expressed in an authorized statement by Secretary of State Bainbridge Colby to the Italian Ambassador in Washington, Baron Avezzana, on August 20, 1920:

> ... the Bolsheviki ... an inconsiderable minority of the people by force and cunning seized the powers and machinery of government and have continued to use them with savage oppression. ...

> ... responsible spokesmen ... have declared ... that the very existence of Bolshevism in Russia ... must ... depend upon ... revolutions in all other great civilized nations, including the United States. ...

> ... the Third Internationale ... heavily subsidized by the Bolshevist Government ... has for its openly avowed aim the promotion of Bolshevist revolutions throughout the world. ...

> ... There can be no mutual confidence ... if pledges are to be given ... with a cynical repudiation ... already in the mind of one of the parties. We cannot recognize ... a government which is determined and bound to conspire against our institutions. ...[1]

Mr. Wilson had abundant confirmation for his views. He had before him the public declarations of Lenin and his own experience with Communist conspiracies during the Paris Peace Conference in 1919. Throughout this

---

1. U.S. Department of State, *Papers Relating to the Foreign Relations of the United States, 1920*, Volume III (Washington: 1936), pp. 463–468. See also Herbert Hoover, *The Ordeal of Woodrow Wilson* (McGraw-Hill Book Company, Inc., New York: 1958), p. 150.

period the Communists seized control of the governments of many large cities and even of one whole nation—Hungary. The Supreme Council of which
Mr. Wilson was a member had the task of dealing with these conspiracies,
and in a number of cases I was assigned the duty of snuffing them out.[2] Our
method was not by military force, but by placing the distribution of food supplies in the hands of the democratic elements of these countries.

With this experience, Presidents Harding and Coolidge resisted all pressures for recognition. From my personal experience I was naturally opposed
to opening the doors of the United States to these conspiracies against free
men. Thus, four Presidents and their six Secretaries of State for over a decade
and a half held to this resolve.

When Mr. Roosevelt came to the Presidency, he had knowledge of two
current glaring examples of Communist conspiracy specifically directed
against the United States. These were the so-called "Bonus March" of 1932
and the flooding of the world with counterfeit American money printed in
Moscow and used for Communist purposes.

Without at this point going into the details of the "Bonus March" on Washington, which was mostly made up of veterans asking Congress for relief, I
may say that our Army and Navy Intelligence services determined at that
time that the "march" had been largely engineered by Communists with the
fantastic idea that they would exploit the veterans to overthrow the United
States Government. At the time of the march, I publicly pointed out its Communist inspiration. That this was no figment of the imagination was amply
confirmed. At the Seventh Congress of the Communist International in Moscow three years later in 1935, the Communists openly claimed credit for the
march.[3] Subsequent disclosures by repentant Communists added proof that
it had been directed from the Kremlin. A former General Secretary of the
American Communist Party, Benjamin Gitlow, revealed:

---

2. Herbert Hoover, *The Ordeal of Woodrow Wilson*, Chapter 10; Herbert Hoover, *An American
Epic*, Volume III [Henry Regnery Company, Chicago: 1961], Chapters 13, 35 passim. Nor was there
lack of confirmation of the hideous brutality of the Communist regime. An eye-witness, George
Vernadsky, one-time Professor of Russian History at Yale University, wrote in 1931: "If the number
of people killed at the direct instigation of Lenin be taken into account—disregarding those killed
in the 'regular' civil war—and also the number of people who died from famine in consequence of
his economic policy, the result is a staggering figure. . . . If judgment is to be based on the number
of human lives destroyed by the government of Lenin, then it is impossible not to list Lenin among
the most fearful tyrants history has known." (*Lenin, Red Dictator*, New Haven, Yale University Press:
1931, p. 320.)

3. U.S. Department of State, *Foreign Relations of the United States: Diplomatic Papers—The Soviet
Union, 1933–1939* [Government Printing Office, Washington: 1952], p. 229.

... On May 19 [1932] the communist Worker Ex-Servicemen's League formed a Provisional Bonus March Committee. . . . The Communist party members of the provisional committee met daily with the special rep of the Comintern and the national leaders of the Communist party to formulate plans and work out strategy and policies.[4]

Another ex-Communist, John T. Pace, later a deputy sheriff in Tennessee, stated:

I led the left wing or Communist section of the bonus march.
I was ordered by my Red superiors to provoke riots.
I was told to use every trick to bring about bloodshed. . . .
The Communists didn't care how many veterans were killed. . . .[5]

Before Mr. Roosevelt took office, I informed him of the details of the Moscow counterfeiting of millions of dollars in American currency. These fake notes were circulated intermittently from 1928 to 1932 over Europe, China and the Middle East. Our Federal Reserve Banks issued many warnings on the subject to the public both here and abroad.

On January 3, 1933, two months prior to Mr. Roosevelt's inauguration, our Secret Service arrested a German named Hans Dechow on his arrival in the United States with a large quantity of these counterfeit bills. The next day, in New York they arrested a Russian Communist, Dr. Valentine Gregory Burtan, for passing such bills. He was subsequently convicted on Dechow's evidence as to previous deliveries and sentenced to prison.

On February 24, 1933, just before Mr. Roosevelt's inauguration, the *New York Times* exposed the fact that the counterfeits were of Soviet government origin.[6]

---

4. Benjamin Gitlow, *The Whole of Their Lives* (Charles Scribner's Sons, New York: 1948), pp. 226–227.

5. *New York Journal-American*, August 28, 1949. See *Congressional Record*, Senate, 81st Cong., 1st sess. Vol. 95, Pt. 9, August 31, 1949, pp. 12529–12531. See *Communist Tactics Among Veterans' Groups* (Testimony of John T. Pace), Hearing Before Committee on Un-American Activities—House of Representatives, 82nd Cong., 1st sess., July 13, 1951, pp. 1925–1964. Mr. Pace's testimony was suppressed until 1951. See also Chicago *Daily Tribune*, June 1, 1951.

6. The *New York Times* account was subsequently confirmed by Walter G. Krivitsky, a former Russian intelligence officer, in an article in the *Saturday Evening Post* of September 30, 1939, entitled "Counterfeit Dollars." Krivitsky stated that during the years 1928 to 1932 Stalin undertook a gigantic counterfeiting scheme, that a Russian agent had procured the proper paper in the United States, and that $10,000,000 worth of bills were printed by the Russian government's engraving establishment. See also W[alter] G. Krivitsky, *In Stalin's Secret Service* (New York: Harper & Brothers Publishers, 1939), pp. 116–138.

The Recognition Negotiations

On October 10, 1933, eight months after taking office, Mr. Roosevelt dispatched a message to President Kalinin of the Soviet All-Union Central Executive Committee suggesting that Russia send a representative to Washington to negotiate recognition. Seven days later, the Soviet government replied that they were sending their People's Commissar for Foreign Affairs, Mr. Maxim Litvinov.[7]

The Soviet policy as stated and signed by Litvinov on November 16, 1933, included the following:

> . . . it will be the fixed policy of the Government of the Union of Soviet Socialist Republics:
>
> . . . to refrain from interfering in any manner in the internal affairs of the United States. . . .
>
> To refrain, and to restrain all persons . . . under its direct or indirect control . . . from any act . . . liable in any way whatsoever to injure the tranquility, prosperity, order, or security . . . or any agitation or propaganda having as an aim, the violation of the territorial integrity of the United States . . . or the bringing about by force of a change in the political or social order of the whole or any part of the United States, its territories or possessions.
>
> . . . Not to permit the formation . . . of any organization or group . . . which has as an aim the overthrow of . . . the political or social order of . . . the United States. . . .[8]

There were also Soviet assurances of Russia's peaceful intentions throughout the world.[9]

Secretary of State Cordell Hull promptly issued a glowing eulogy of the agreement.[10]

In the course of the discussions with Litvinov, Mr. Roosevelt proposed that the Soviet government repay, over a long period of years, the loans which the United States had made to Russia during World War I. The curious method of repayment he suggested was that the United States would lend Russia

---

7. U.S. Department of State, *Foreign Relations of the United States: Diplomatic Papers, The Soviet Union, 1933–1939*, pp. 17–18.

8. Ibid., pp. 28–29.

9. James A. Farley gives sidelights on this part of the transaction. *Jim Farley's Story: The Roosevelt Years* (McGraw-Hill Book Company, Inc., New York: 1948), pp. 43–44.

10. U.S. Department of State, *Foreign Relations of the United States: Diplomatic Papers — The Soviet Union, 1933–1939*, p. 39.

additional credits at a high rate of interest, and the excessive portion of the interest rate on these would be applied as installments on our wartime advances to Russia. The amount of the existing Soviet debt to the United States was to be negotiated as being between $75,000,000 and $150,000,000.[11] The loan was not consummated. Litvinov declared in October 1934 that he would not have accepted the terms of the recognition agreement had he not expected fulfillment of the promised loan.[12] Finally, on January 31, 1935, Secretary Hull issued a statement to the effect that the deal was off.[13]

No sooner had they won recognition than the Communists began violating their pledge not to conspire for the overthrow of the American Government. The day recognition was granted, Litvinov brought the good news directly from the White House to three top Communists. In 1939, one of them, D. H. Dubrowsky, former director of the Soviet Red Cross, gave an account of this meeting to the Un-American Activities Committee:

> ... Litvinoff came in all smiles and stated and said "Well, it is all in the bag; we have it. . . . they wanted us to recognize the debts that we owed them and I promised we were going to negotiate.
>
> ... but they did not know we were going to negotiate until doomsday." . . .[14]

Within forty-eight hours after the signing of the agreement, the American Communists issued a statement reaffirming their determination to follow their revolutionary principles.[15] Benjamin Gitlow, who had been high in the American Communist Party councils, relates in his book that Litvinov met with the American Communist leaders in New York and explained to them that the agreement did not bind the American Communists, who were part of the Third International; that it bound only the Soviet government.

Gitlow states that Litvinov told the Communists as to the agreement:

> ... Don't worry about the letter. It is a scrap of paper which will soon be forgotten in the realities of Soviet-American relations.[16]

---

11. Ibid., pp. 26–27, 63–165.

12. Ibid., p. 160.

13. Ibid., pp. 172–173.

14. [U.S. Congress, House of Representatives, Special Committee on Un-American Activities,] *Investigation of Un-American Propaganda Activities in the United States,* 76th Congress, 1st Session, pp. 5148–5149.

15. *New York Times,* November 19, 1933.

16. Benjamin Gitlow, *The Whole of Their Lives,* p. 265.

At a November 17, 1933 press conference, Litvinov was asked how recognition would affect the propaganda of the Communist Party of the United States. Litvinov answered:

> The Communist Party of Russia doesn't concern America and the Communist Party of the United States doesn't concern Russia. . . .

When questioned about how the propaganda agreement would affect the Third International, Litvinov replied:

> The Third International is not mentioned in this [the recognition] document . . . You must not read more into the document than was intended.[17]

The recognition of Russia by the United States gave the Soviet government a stamp of respectability before all the world. Other nations followed our lead, thus opening their gates to conspiracies which plague them to this day.

---

17. *Daily Worker,* November 20, 1933.

CHAPTER 3

The Kremlin Onslaught against the American People

THE RECOGNITION OF RUSSIA touched off an era of uninhibited growth and activity for the Communists in the United States. According to the Federal Bureau of Investigation, membership of the American Communist Party grew from about 13,000 prior to the Litvinov agreement to over 80,000 by mid-1938.[1]

In 1936, the American Ambassador in Moscow, William C. Bullitt, cabled Washington.

We should not cherish for a moment the illusion that it is possible to establish really friendly relations with the Soviet Government or with any communist party or communist individual.[2]

The first *official* exposure of the infiltration of Communists into important positions in the Federal government began in 1938, with the appointment of a special House Committee on Un-American Activities under the chairmanship of Representative Martin Dies. Dies served as Chairman until he left Congress on January 3, 1945, because of ill health. The Committee has been continued by the House up to this writing, under vigorous chairmanship.[3]

---

1. Information provided by the Federal Bureau of Investigation.
2. [U.S. Department of State,] *Foreign Relations of the United States: Diplomatic Papers—The Soviet Union 1933–1939*, (a collection of Department of State documents not made public until 1952), p. 294.
3. Some of the outstanding House Committee reports on the subject of Communist activity are:

Excerpts from Hearings Regarding Investigation of Communist Activities in Connection with the Atom Bomb, Eightieth Congress, Second Session, September 1948.
Hearings Regarding Communist Infiltration of Radiation Laboratory and Atomic Bomb Project at the University of California, Berkeley, Calif. – Vol. I, 1949; Vol. II, 1948 and 1949, Eighty-first Congress, First Session.
Guide to Subversive Organizations and Publications by the Committee on Un-American Activities, U.S. House of Representatives, December 1, 1961.

The Senate, in 1950, established the Internal Security Subcommittee of the Committee on the Judiciary to undertake similar inquiries. It, too, has continued up to this writing.[4]

These committees disclosed a long list of treacheries and conspiracies to overthrow our government, naming the participants. Soon after the recognition, American members of the Communist Party began filtering into the most important government departments, thus gaining access to matters of national security, and the opportunity to influence or even to make major policies.[5] They also infiltrated labor unions, stirring up class hatred and strikes. They infiltrated college campuses, sowing seeds of doubt in the minds of youth as to our basic principles and institutions. They created subversive fronts to mold public opinion. They stole the secrets of the atomic bomb.

Enticement of the intellectuals to join the party was far more important to them than rallying the "common man," although the latter could be of use in their deliberately staged riots and disturbances.

Much of the Communist "apparatus" in the United States was financed with Soviet gold.[6] Agents were sent from Moscow to supervise the Communist movement here. The entry and exit of these agents through our immigration barriers were effected by systematic passport frauds. By 1939, the State Department's Passport Division reported that there was a

> ... widespread conspiracy to violate the passport laws of the United States and to promote the interests of the Soviet Union and to work against the foreign policy of the United States Government. . . .[7]

---

4. Important Senate Committee reports on the subject of Communist activity are:

U.S. Senate Permanent Subcommittee on Investigations of the Committee on Government Operations, Hearings, 83d Congress, 1st Session, *Communist Infiltration in the Army*, 1953; also, Hearings, 83d Congress, 1st and 2d Session, *Army Signal Corps-Subversion and Espionage*, Part 1–10, 1953–1954; also Hearings, 83d Congress, 1st Session, *Security-United Nations*, Parts 1–2, 1953.

U.S. Senate Internal Security Subcommittee, 84th Congress, 2d Session, *Report for the Year 1956*, Section IV, 1957; also, its Hearings, 82d Congress, 1st and 2d Session, *Institute of Pacific Relations*, Part 1–15, 1951–1953.

U.S. Senate Internal Security Subcommittee Hearings, 83rd and 84th Congress, *Interlocking Subversion in Government Departments*, Part 1–30, 1953–1955.

Ibid., 83rd Congress, 1st and 2d Session, *Activities of United States Citizens Employed by the United Nations*, Part 1–6, 1952–1954.

5. Proof of such influence will be presented in later chapters.

6. Benjamin Gitlow, *The Whole of Their Lives* (Charles Scribner's Sons, New York: 1948), pp. 117, 119, 123, states instances of such remittances, and a House of Representatives' Committee exposed others.

7. [U.S. Congress, Senate, Committee on the Judiciary, *Internal Security Annual Report for 1956:*] *Report of the . . . Subcommittee to Investigate the Administration of the Internal Security Act and Other*

The House Committee on Un-American Activities declared that the Communist Party of the United States was under Moscow's direct control.[8]

For further aid and comfort, American Communists could look to a number of Soviet agencies openly established within the United States. The Russian Embassy in Washington, cloaked in diplomatic immunity, became a headquarters for espionage.[9] The official news service of the Soviet government, *Tass*, placed press representatives at White House and Capitol Hill press conferences.[10] Trading companies and cultural organizations set up by the Soviets after 1933 operated as centers and outlets for propaganda and spy activities.

A clue to Mr. Roosevelt's attitude toward exposure of the Communist conspiracies may be gleaned from a statement by Congressman Dies concerning two conversations he had at the White House during his tenure as Chairman of the House Committee on Un-American Activities.

Dies records:

> ... I opened hearings on the CIO in August, the 8th or 10th [1938] and I got a telephone call from the White House to come. I went to the White House and Senator Sheppard was there. He had been talking to the President before I went in. ...
>
> ... The President turned to Senator Sheppard and said, "Senator, what are we going to do about Martin?" The Senator said, "What do you mean?" "Well," the President said, "You know, all this business about investigating Communists is a serious mistake. ... "
>
> ... He stated, in effect, to me that he didn't want Communism investigated. He wanted me to confine my efforts to Nazism. ... [11]

In December, 1941, just before Pearl Harbor, Dies received another call to come to the White House:

Internal Security Laws to the Committee on the Judiciary, United States Senate, Eighty-fifth Congress, First Session, Section XII (United States Government Printing Office, Washington: 1957), pp. 214–215. See also Benjamin Gitlow, *The Whole of Their Lives*, p. 114.

8. U.S. Congress, House Special Committee on Un-American Activites, *Investigation of Un-American Propaganda Activities in the United States*, House of Representatives, 76th Congress, 3d Session, Report No. 1476, January 3, 1940, p. 4.

9. *Report of the ... Subcommittee to Investigate the Administration of the Internal Security Act and Other Internal Security Laws* to the Committee on the Judiciary, United States Senate, Eighty-fifth Congress, First Session, Section II.

10. Ibid., Section VIII.

11. Interview in the *U.S. News and World Report*, August 20, 1954, pp. 57ff. (Congressman Dies and Senator Sheppard called at the White House on August 15, 1938.)

When I went into Roosevelt's office, he had a reporter there to take down the whole conversation. . . . "You can get a copy of it," the President said.

We spent then over an hour and I told him exactly what was going on inside his Government. I told him the Communists were using those 2,000 persons inside this Government and that they were stealing everything in the world that they wanted and had access to.

We talked the whole thing over, and he told me, I remember distinctly, "You must see a Red under your bed every night."[12]

Under the bed or not, the Communists were just about everywhere else, as will be seen from the next two chapters, devoted respectively to the extent of their infiltration into the Federal government and into other vital areas of our nation.

---

12. Ibid., p. 58.

CHAPTER 4

Infiltration of Members of the Communist Party into the Federal Government

IT IS NOT LIKELY that we shall ever accurately know the full extent of infiltration of American Communists into our government. Discovery of the people involved often came only after they had been in the government for years.

That the reader may realize that this infiltration was no fantasy of emotional persons, this chapter will cite specific examples of American Communists in our government who were cooperating with the Kremlin by furnishing information on our national policies and scientific secrets in our defense.[1] It

---

1. Throughout this chapter, I refer to numerous Congressional Investigations. These references include:

House Committee on Un-American Activities (referred to hereafter as HUAC):
Hearings, methods of Communist infiltration in the United States Government (referred to here as *Infiltration*) 1952 et al.
Hearings, regarding Communist espionage in the United States Government (referred to here as *Espionage*) 1948.
Hearings, Communist methods of infiltration (Education) (referred to here as *Education*) 1953.
Hearings regarding Communist infiltration of Radiation Laboratory and atomic bomb project at the University of California, Berkeley, California, 1948–1950, Vols. I–III (referred to here as *Radiation Laboratory*).
Hearings, Investigation of Communist Infiltration of Government (referred to here as *Government*) 1955–1956.

The Subcommittee to Investigate the Administration of the Internal Security Act and other Internal Security Laws of the Committee on the Judiciary, United States Senate (referred to here as SISS):
Hearings, Subversive Influence in the Educational Process 1952 and 1953 (referred to here as *Educational*).
Hearings, Interlocking Subversion in Government Departments (referred to here as *Interlocking Subversion*).
Hearings, Activities of United States Citizens Employed by the United Nations (referred to here as *United Nations*).
Hearings, Institute of Pacific Relations (referred to here as *IPR*) 1951–1952.

will be seen that these Communist informers gained strategic positions in the armed services, in almost every civil department, on the staffs of some Congressional committees and even had access to the White House. They were employed on missions sent to Russia, Germany, France, Italy, Britain, Latin America, China and elsewhere. It may be observed that they became advisors and secretaries at many important conferences of Allied leaders in the Second World War.

In its onslaught against us, the Kremlin used two different methods of organization. Their initial method was to set up "cells," composed exclusively of party members among government employees. They organized such cells in intellectual circles, in industrial and labor organizations, and in newspaper and publishing concerns.

The second method was to set up "fronts," where persons not necessarily Communists themselves but sympathetic to Communist aims were enlisted under the leadership of party members. These "fronts" aided in conspiracy, propaganda and the collection of money.

The case history of one early Communist cell in the Federal government became known years after its inception through the confession of a repentant Soviet agent, Whittaker Chambers. He reported that his cell, wholly made up of party members, was established in the Department of Agriculture in 1933, soon after the recognition of Russia. The cell was originally under the direction of Harold Ware, then a departmental advisor. He was succeeded by Nathan Witt (who in 1934 was appointed by President Roosevelt to the National Labor Relations Board) and later was followed by John Abt.[2] In all, this cell comprised seven or more employees who held influential posts in the Department. From 1934 to 1937, Chambers served as the cell's "transmission belt" to Russian officials stationed in the United States.

Other confessed former Communist agents shed light on additional government cells. Elizabeth Bentley revealed that from 1941 to 1945 she was the "transmission belt" for two cells of top-level government employees who supplied information for transmission to the Kremlin agents. She also collected information and dues from individuals not associated with these cells. During her testimony before the Senate Internal Security Subcommittee in 1953,

Hearings Before the Permanent Subcommittee on Investigations of the Committee on Government Operations, United States Senate (referred to here as PSI):
  Hearings, Army Signal Corps—Subversion and Espionage (referred to here as *Army Signal Corps*) 1953–1954.
  Hearings, Security—Government Printing Office (referred to here as *GPO*) 1953.

2. HUAC Hearings, 80th Cong., 2d sess., *Espionage*, July 31–September 9, 1948, pp. 565ff.

Miss Bentley stated that she was aware of the existence of two other cells in Washington, but had no specific knowledge of them.[3]

Testimony by Herbert Fuchs, Mortimer Riemer, and James E. Gorham, themselves Federal employees and self-confessed Communist Party members, described the Communist activities of individuals in various government departments between 1934 and 1946. They had no knowledge of the top-level apparatus with which Whittaker Chambers and Miss Bentley were connected, but they did know and gave testimony about leaders of cells to which they had belonged.[4]

As the Second World War drew near, American Communists moved into every phase of our defense effort, including intelligence, research, industry, and atomic energy. With the war's close, they set up cells among United States citizens working in the United Nations. Their activities continued in many cases over several years.

In order that there can be no doubt in the reader's mind as to the scope of the Kremlin's subterranean war against our official institutions, I give the following sample list of 37 Federal employees, together with dates and official positions. I have selected only those persons who at one time or another confessed their Communist Party membership. This list is but a minor fragment of the total roll, but is given here as an indication of the widespread Communist activity in our government. It was compiled from the records of Congressional investigations, grand juries, and other sources of authoritative information.

Barry G. Albaum, Ph.D.	1950–1952	Research for United States Air Force	Self-confessed Communist Party member 1944–1945.[5]
Isadore Amdur, Ph.D.	1943–1944	Office of Scientific Research and Development. Also, Ordnance Bureau, Department of the Navy	Self-confessed Communist Party member 1938–1944.[6]
Dr. Lewis Balamuth, Professor	1943–1944	Atomic Energy Commission Manhattan Project (A-bomb)	Self-confessed Communist Party member 1936–1941.[7]

---

3. SISS Hearings, 83d Cong., 1st sess., *Interlocking Subversion—Report,* July 30, 1953, pp. 2–3.

4. HUAC Hearings, 84th Cong., 1st sess., *Government,* December 13, 1955, testimony of Herbert Fuchs, Part 1, pp. 2957–3019; December 14, 1955, testimony of Mortimer Reimer, Part 2, pp. 3022–3043; 84th Cong., 2d sess., February 14, 1956, testimony of James E. Gorham, Part 3, pp. 3111–3136.

5. SISS, Hearings, *Educational,* 82d Cong., 2d sess., September 25, 1952, pp. 209–222, 224–228.

6. HUAC, Hearings, *Education,* Part 3, 83d Cong., 1st sess., April 22, 1953, pp. 1047–1050.

7. SISS, Hearings, *Educational,* Part 10, 83d Cong., 1st sess., May 13, 1953, pp. 951–964.

Whittaker Chambers	1937	Works Progress Administration (National Research Project)	Self-confessed Communist Party member 1924–1937.[8]
James Charnow, A.B.	1942–1947	U.S. Government employee United Nations	Self-confessed Communist Party member 1938.[9]
Harriman H. Dash	1947–1950	Army Signal Corps (Federal Telecommunications Laboratories in Nutley, N.J.)	Self-confessed Communist Party member 1933–1939 and 1947–1950.[10]
Robert R. Davis, Ph.D.	1942	Radiation Laboratory at Berkeley, California	Self-confessed Communist Party member 1943.[11]
	1943–1948	Atomic Energy Commission Los Alamos Bomb Project	
Kenneth Eckert	1944–1945	United States Army	Self-confessed Communist Party member, 1948. Trained in Lenin School, Moscow 1931–1932.[12]
Max Elitcher, B.S.	1938–1948	Naval Bureau of Ordnance	Self-confessed Communist Party member.[13]
Stephen M. Fischer	1944	United States Army Information & Education Division	Self-confessed Communist Party member.[14]
Herbert Fuchs, Professor of Law	1936–1937	Staff Senate Committee investigating railroad holding companies and related matters	Self-confessed Communist Party member 1934–1946.[15]
	1937–1942	National Labor Relations Board	
	1942–1945	National War Labor Board	
	1946–1948	National Labor Relations Board	
Klaus Fuchs, Ph.D.	1944–1946	Atomic Energy Commission Los Alamos Bomb Project	Self-confessed Communist. Convicted of espionage in Britain in 1950 by British Courts and served a sentence in British prisons.[16]

8. HUAC, Hearings, *Espionage*, 80th Cong., 2d sess., 1948, pp. 564–565, 1286.

9. SISS, Hearings, *United Nations*, 82d Cong., 2d sess., December 11, 1952, pp. 321–324.

10. PSI, Hearings, *Army Signal Corps*, Part 10, 83d Cong., 1st sess., 1954, p. 431.

11. HUAC, Hearings, *Radiation Laboratory*, v. 1, 81st Cong., 1st sess., April 22, 1949, pp. 279ff; *New York Times*, June 11, 1949.

12. SISS, Hearings, *Union Officials*, 82d Cong., 2d sess., 1952, pp. 41ff.

13. *New York Times*, March 9, 1951, p. 12:3.

14. SISS, Hearings, *Interlocking Subversion*, Part 20, 83d Cong., 2d sess., July 6, 1954, p. 1501.

15. HUAC, Hearings, *Government*, Part 1, 84th Cong., 1st sess., Dec. 13, 1955, pp. 2957ff; *New York Times*, March 15, 1956, March 23, 1956.

16. Joint Committee on Atomic Energy, Hearings, *Soviet Atomic Espionage*, 82d Cong., 1st sess., April, 1951, p. 1.

Wendell H. Furry, Associate Professor of Physics	1943–1945	Radar research at MIT	Self-confessed Communist Party member 1938–1951.[17]
Irving Goldman, Ph.D.	1942–1943	Coordinator of Inter-American Affairs	Self-confessed Communist Party member 1936–1942.[18]
	1943–1945	United States Army and Office of Strategic Services	
	1946– June 1947	Department of State	
James Edgar Gorham, B.A.	1934–1935	Railroad Retirement Board	Self-confessed Communist Party member 1934–1942.[19]
	1935	Works Progress Administration	
	1936–1938	Staff Senate Subcommittee investigating railroad holding companies	
	1938	Brotherhood of Railroad Trainmen	
	1938–1942	Securities and Exchange Commission	
	1942–1947	Office of Price Administration	
	1947–1956	Civil Aeronautics Board	
Peter A. Gragis	1936–1945	Ford Instrument and other defense plants	Self-confessed Communist Party member 1934 or 1935–1951.[20]
	1945–1950	Army Signal Corps	
David Greenglass, B.S.	1943–1944	United States Army	Self-confessed Communist at Rosenberg trial. Convicted by Federal Court.[21]
	1944–1946	Atomic Energy Commission Projects	
David Hawkins, Ph.D.	1943–1945	Atomic Energy Commission Historian, Los Alamos Project Access to all its files	Self-confessed Communist Party member from 1938–1943.[22]
Donald Horton, Ph.D.	1943–1944	War Department consultant	Self-confessed Communist Party member 1935 or 1936–1944.[23]
Felix A. Inslerman, University graduate	1946–1949	Army Defense work	Self-confessed Communist Party member.[24]
Leon J. Kamin, M.A.		Government Radar Research	Self-confessed Communist Party member 1945–1946 and 1947–1950.[25]

---

17. *New York Times,* January 16, 1954, p. 6:3–4.

18. SISS, Hearings, *Educational,* Part 6, 83d Cong., 1st sess., April 1, 1953, pp. 721ff.

19. HUAC, Hearings, *Government,* Part 3, 84th Cong., 2d sess., February 14, 1956, pp. 3113–3115.

20. PSI, Hearings, *Army Signal Corps,* Part 9, 83d Cong., 2d sess., 1954, p. 377.

21. Joint Committee on Atomic Energy, *Soviet Atomic Espionage,* 82d Cong., 1st sess., April 1951, pp. 3 and 60–144.

22. SISS, Hearings, *Educational,* Part 9, 83d Cong., 1st sess., May 8, 1953, pp. 931ff.

23. Ibid., Part 12, 83d Cong., 1st sess., June 8, 1953, pp. 1083–1086.

24. PSI, Hearings, *Subversion and Espionage in Defense Establishments and Industry,* Part 2, 83d Cong., 2d sess., February 20, 1954, pp. 97ff.

25. PSI, Hearings, *Subversion and Espionage in Defense,* Part 9, 84th Cong., 1st sess., January 15, 1954, p. 361.

Fred J. Kitty, Engineer	1942–1945	Army Signal Corps Evans Signal Laboratory	Self-confessed Communist Party member 1938–1941.[26]
	1945–1952	Army classified work Bendix	
John Lautner	1942–1945	United States Army Intelligence	Self-confessed Communist party member 1930–1950.[27]
William T. Martin, Ph.D.	1943 or 1944	United States Army	Self-confessed Communist Party member 1938–1946.[28]
	1944 or 1945	War Labor Board	
James McNamara	1942–1953	Federal Mediation Board Commissioner of Conciliation at Cincinnati	Self-confessed Communist Party member.[29]
Philip Morrison, Ph.D.	1942–1946	Atomic Energy Commission research in Los Alamos; "as a representative of the Secretary of War" on a mission to Japan to study A-bomb effects. Was leader in *American Peace Crusade* cited as subversive by the Attorney General.	Self-confessed Communist Party member.[30]
Frank F. Oppenheimer, B.S.	1941–1947	Research Associate at Radiation Laboratory at University of California. Atomic Energy Commission research at Oak Ridge and Los Alamos.	Self-confessed Communist Party member 1937–1941.[31]
Doris W. Powell		Army Quartermaster Corps	Self-confessed Communist Party member.[32]
Lee Pressman, Ll.B.	1933–1935	Assistant General Counsel Department of Agriculture, Agricultural Adjustment Administration	Self-confessed Communist Group affiliate in 1934; Elizabeth Bentley, Whittaker Chambers, and Nathaniel Weyl stated in sworn testimony that Pressman was a member of the Ware Communist cell in the Department of Agriculture. In 1948 HUAC Hearings, Pressman refused to testify regarding
	1935	General counsel for Federal Employment Relief Administration; later, Works Progress Administration	

---

26. PSI, Hearings, *Army Signal Corps*, 83d Cong., 1st sess., Part 1, December 1953, pp. 62–66.

27. SISS, Hearings, *Educational*, 82d Cong., 2d sess., October 1952, pp. 244–255.

28. HUAC, Hearings, *Education*, Part 3, 83d Cong., 1st sess., April 22, 1953, p. 1015.

29. HUAC, Hearings, *Government-Labor*, Part 3, 83d Cong., 1st sess., September 15, 1953, pp. 3028ff.

30. SISS, Hearings, *Educational*, Part 9, 83d Cong., 1st sess., May 7, 1953, pp. 899ff.

31. HUAC, Hearings, *Radiation Laboratory*, Vol. 1, 81st Cong., 1st sess., June 14, 1949, pp. 356ff.

32. PSI, Hearings, *Army Civilian Workers*, 1954, p. 16. See also, *New York Times*, March 12, 1954, [p.] 11:1.

			Communist Party activities under the 5th Amendment. Hearings, 1950, admitted Communist activity.[33]
Mortimer Riemer	1940–1947	Trial examiner, National Labor Relations Board	Self-confessed Communist Party member, 1935 or 1936–1943.[34]
Sidney Rubinstein	1953–1954	United States Army	Self-confessed Communist Party member, 1947.[35]
John Saunders	1945–1954	Army Signal Corps Federal Telecommunications Laboratory	Self-confessed Communist Party member, 1947–1949.[36]
Nathan Sussman	1940–1942	Government Inspector, Department of Navy	Self-confessed Communist Party member, 1935–1940 and 1942–45.[37]
	1942–1947	Defense Contracts, Western Electric Company	
Evelyn Thaler (Stern)	1946–	United Nations	Self-confessed Communist Party member 1942–45.[38]
Nathaniel Weyl, B.S.	1933	Agricultural Adjustment Administration	Self-confessed Communist Party member winter 1932–1933. Member of Ware's cell in the Department of Agriculture. Broke with Communist Party in 1939; went to F.B.I. in 1950 with story.[39]
Frank C. White	1936	Tennessee Valley Administration	Self-confessed Communist Party member 1937.[40]
	1937	Federal Housing Administration	
	1946	Department of State	
	1946–	United Nations	

33. HUAC, Hearings, *Communism in the United States Government*, Part II, 81st Cong., 2nd sess., August 28, 1950, pp. 2844–2901; HUAC, Hearings, *Espionage*, 80th Cong., 1948, pp. 1021–29. See also New York Times, August 4 and August 21, 1948, and August 28, 1950. See SISS, Hearings, *Educational*, Part 6, 83d Cong., 1st sess., March 30, 1953, testimony of Nathaniel Weyl, p. 712. See also James Burnham, *The Web of Subversion* [The John Day Company, New York: 1954] pp. 36–37.

34. HUAC, Hearings, *Communist Infiltration of Government*, 84th Cong., 1st sess., Part 2, December 14, 1955, pp. 3023ff.

35. PSI, Hearings, *Army Signal Corps*, Part 9, 83d Cong., 2d sess., March 1, 1954, pp. 369ff.

36. PSI, Hearings, *Army Signal Corps*, 83d Cong., 2d sess., March 1954, Part 10, pp. 462ff.

37. PSI, Hearings, *Army Signal Corps*, Part 1, 83d Cong., 1st sess., December 8, 1953, pp. 57ff.

38. SISS, Hearings, *United Nations*, 82d Cong., 2d sess., 1952, pp. 324–326. See also *New York Times*, January 2, 1953, [p.] 1:2.

39. SISS, Hearings, *Educational*, 83d Cong., 1st sess., 1953, Part 6, pp. 710ff.

40. HUAC, Hearings, *Propaganda Activities*, 76th Cong., 3d sess., vol. II, Part 2, 1940. [*Editor's note:* Hoover is referring here to U.S. Congress, House of Representatives, Special Committee on Un-

Marshall J. Wolfe, A.B.	1942–1945 1946 1946–	United States Army Department of State United Nations	Self-confessed Communist Party member, 1938.[41]

To the above listing of self-confessed Communists may be added these Federal employees, whose connections with Communist activity were subject to court action:

Dr. Horst Baerensprung	1953	Office of Strategic Services	See Dr. Hans Hirschfeld.
Abraham Brothman	1953	Technician in defense work— Radar plant at Port Jervis, New York	Convicted by U.S. Court in 1950 for conspiracy to obstruct justice during espionage investigation (see Harry Gold trial). Served 2 years in prison.[42]
Judith Coplon, A.B.	1943–1949	Department of Justice	Arrested by F.B.I. in act of delivering information to Communist agent but escaped conviction on a technicality.[43]
Robert W. Dorey	1952–1953	United States Army	Convicted of espionage by U.S. Army Court martial in 1953.[44]
Hans Freistadt, B.S.	1944–1946 1949	Army Signal Corps Atomic Energy Fellowship	Army Signal Corps Hearings. Not cleared for security 1944– 1946.[45]
Dr. Hans Hirschfeld	1943	Office of Strategic Services	A German employed by United States in

American Activities, *Investigation of Un-American Propaganda Activities in the United States,* Executive Hearings, vol. II, 76th Congress, 3d Session, 1940, pp. 656–660.]

41. SISS, Hearings, *United Nations,* vol. I, 82d Cong., 2d sess., October 24, 1952, pp. 171–182. See also *New York Times,* January 2, 1953.

42. *New York Times,* November 5, 1953, p. 21:3.

43. Ibid., March 6, 1949.

44. Ibid., November 1, 1953.

45. Ibid., May 13, 1949, p. 1:6–7; p. 15:5. [*Editor's note:* Hoover's description of the Freistadt case appears to be partially in error. In 1949 Freistadt—an avowed Communist and a graduate student in physics at the University of North Carolina—was discovered to be holding a fellowship from the Atomic Energy Commission for advanced study in nuclear physics. The disclosure generated a storm of controversy in Congress. Freistadt soon testified before a Congressional committee and appeared on *Meet the Press.* After he declined to sign a non-Communist affidavit newly required of federal fellowship recipients by Congress and the AEC, his fellowship was revoked. But there appears to be no evidence that he was ever subject to court action, either in connection with his U.S. Army service (1944–46) or his later activities as a publicly professed Communist. His name did not come up in the Congressional hearings on Communist activities in the Army Signal Corps in 1953–54.]

			Washington. Sworn testimony before Federal Grand Jury of Mrs. Johanna Koenen Beker, courier for Russian spy ring, said he and Dr. Baerensprung supplied her regularly with OSS reports to give to Dr. Robert A. Soblen for transmission to Russia.[46]
Alger Hiss, A.B., Ll.B.	1933	Agricultural Adjustment Administration	Convicted of perjury as to his Communist connections [in–*ed.*] 1950 and sentenced to five years in prison.[47]
	1934–	Legal counsel for Senate Committee Investigating the Munitions Industry	
	1934–1936	Office of Solicitor General	
	1936–1947	Department of State, Director of Office of Special Political Affairs	
	1945	Advisor to the President at the Yalta Conference with Stalin	
	1945	Secretary of the United Nations Conference which produced the United Nations Charter	
Aldo Icardi	1941–1945	Office of Strategic Services	Convicted in absentia in Italian Court to life imprisonment for ordering murder of OSS Major William V. Holohan for Communists. Never returned to Italy. Sentence not carried out.[48]
Emmanuel S. Larsen, University graduate	1935–1944	Office of Naval Intelligence Analyst China and Far East	Pleaded "nolo contendere" in AMERASIA case and fined $500 by U.S. Court for aiding
	1944–1945	Department of State Specialist	

---

46. Ibid., July 11, 1961, p. 14:1.

47. HUAC, Hearings, *Espionage*, 80th Cong., 2d sess., 1948, pp. 642ff. and p. 1163. See also *New York Times,* January 26, 1950.

48. *New York Times,* November 7, 1953, p. 1:5–6. [*Editor's note:* After denying before a Congressional committee that he had plotted Major William Holohan's murder while on an OSS mission in wartime Italy in 1944, Aldo Icardi was indicted for perjury. He maintained his innocence. In a brief trial in 1956, his attorney, Edward Bennett Williams, persuaded the judge to render a directed verdict of acquittal on the grounds that Icardi's Congressional hearing had been a perjury trap and had served no valid legislative purpose. According to Williams, Italian Communist partisans had murdered the strongly anti-Communist Major Holohan, whom they perceived as a threat to their interests, and neither Icardi nor his American OSS associate, Carl LoDolce, had been involved in the crime. See *New York Times,* April 15, 17, 18, and 20, 1956, and Edward Bennett Williams, *One Man's Freedom* (Atheneum, New York: 1962), pp. 30–58.]

			removal of government records.[49]
Carl G. LoDolce	1941–1945	Office of Strategic Services	Convicted in Italian Court to 17 years' imprisonment for the murder of OSS Major William V. Holohan. Never returned to Italy. Sentence not carried out.[50]
Carl Aldo Marzani, B.A.	1939 1942	Works Progress Administration Office of Coordinator of Information	Convicted in 1947 by U.S. Court and sentenced [to–ed.] two and one-half years
	1942–1945 1945	Office of Strategic Services Department of State	for withholding information on Communist affiliations.[51]
Dr. William Perl	19– – 1939–1946	Department of Navy U.S. Government employee on air research	Convicted of perjury by [before a–ed.] Federal Grand Jury on June 5, 1953. (See Rosenberg case.)[52]
Kurt Ponger (See Otto Verber)	19– –	U.S. War Crimes Commission in Germany	Convicted of espionage on June 8, 1953.[53]
William Walter Remington, M.A.	1936–1937 1940–1941	Tennessee Valley Authority National Resources Planning Board	E. Bentley in sworn testimony before HUAC, 1948, stated that Remington
	1941–1942 1942–1944 1944–1945	Office of Price Administration War Production Board United States Navy, Russian translator	furnished her with information for Russians. He denied this activity. January
	1945	London, Economic Affairs Mission	1953 Federal Grand Jury indicted him for
	1945	Office of War Mobilization and Reconversion	perjury in espionage trial.[54]
	1945	Office of the President	
	1950	Department of Commerce— approving licenses for exports to Russia and satellites	
Julius Rosenberg	1940s	Army Signal Corps, Inspector Atomic Energy Commission	Indicted with his wife by Federal Grand Jury on espionage charges. Tried, convicted, and

---

49. [U.S. Congress, Senate, Committee on Foreign Relations,] *State Department Employee Loyalty Investigation* [*Hearings Before a Subcommittee ... Pursuant to S. Res. 231*], 81st Cong., 2d sess., [1950] Part 2, [Appendix,] pp. 1937–1939.

50. *New York Times*, November 7, 1953. [*Editor's note:* see note 48.]

51. Ibid., May 23, 1947; SISS, Hearings, *Interlocking Subversion*, June 1953, Part 12, p. 802.

52. *Exposé of Soviet Espionage, May 1960*, prepared by FBI, Department of Justice, transmitted by direction of Attorney General for use of SISS, 86th Cong., 2nd sess., July 2, 1960. Senate Document No. 114.

53. Ibid. See also HUAC Report, *Patterns of Communist Espionage*, January 1959, p. 40.

54. *New York Times*, January 28, 1953.

			in 1953, executed. David Greenglass, his business associate, stated in sworn testimony before Grand Jury that he passed information on the Atom bomb to Rosenberg for transmission to Russia; also that Rosenberg told him he had stolen an Army Signal Corps proximity fuse and given it to the Russians.
Morton Sobell	1938–1941 (approximately)	Bureau of Naval Ordnance	Convicted by Federal Court with Rosenbergs in 1951 for espionage.[55]
Wallace H. Spradling	1940s	U.S. Army Reserve Major Bureau of Naval Ordnance	Sentenced to five years in Federal prison on January 5, 1953, for having falsely denied that he was ever a Communist when he applied for a Navy job in 1951.[56]
Alfred K. Stern Martha Dodd Stern			Indicted for espionage by Federal Grand Jury September 8, 1957. They fled to Czechoslovakia and did not stand trial in the United States.[57]
Otto Verber (See Kurt Ponger)		Army Intelligence United States Army and War Crimes Commission in Germany	Convicted of espionage in 1953.[58]
Henry Julian Wadleigh— Oxford University	1930 1932 1936 1943 1944 1946	Federal Farm Board Department of Agriculture Department of State Foreign Economic Administration Department of Agriculture United Nations Relief and	Wadleigh refused under the Fifth Amendment to testify about Communist affiliations.[59] Admitted in 1949 that he had delivered "hundreds of docu-

---

55. Ibid., March 30, 1951.
56. Ibid., January 6, 1953.
57. Ibid., September 10, 1957, p. 21: 1–3; October 15, 1957, p. 15:6.
58. *Exposé of Soviet Espionage, May 1960.* See also HUAC Report, *Patterns of Communist Espionage,* January 1959, p. 40.
59. HUAC, Hearings, *Espionage,* 80th Cong., Part 2, December 1948, pp. 1429–1449.

		Reconstruction Administration	ments" to Whittaker Chambers.[60]
George Shaw Wheeler	1934–1938	National Labor Relations Board	In 1944 Civil Service
	1938–1942	Department of Labor	Commission's Loyalty
	1942–1943	War Production Board	Board found Wheeler
	1943–1945	Foreign Economic Administration	"unfit for Government service" due to
	1945–1947	War Department, European Chief De-nazification branch of manpower Division of the Military Government in Germany	Communist Party activities. President Truman had him re-instated. He is now behind the iron curtain.[61]
Jane Foster Zlatovski		Office of Strategic Services	Indicted on July 8, 1957, by Federal Grand Jury for conspiracy with Russians. Refused to return to the United States to stand trial.[62]
George Zlatovski	1943–1948	U.S. Army Office of Strategic Services	Indicted on July 8, 1957, by Federal Grand Jury for conspiracy with Russians. Refused to return to the United States to stand trial.[63]

From the nature of the sources of information as to these individuals (American Communists), the details of different statements regarding them vary. That they were members of the Communist Party engaged in subversive purposes, however, cannot be denied. [64]

In addition to the above, the following were also actively engaged in subversive activities:

George Blake Charney (also known as George Blake)	World War II— United States Army in the Pacific	Served Communist Party since 1933 as its trade union secretary and an organizer, and as acting state

60. *U. S. News & World Report,* November 27, 1953, p. 23.

61. (need evidence of Civil Service Commission Loyalty Board findings.) See [Senator Joseph R.] McCarthy speech in *New York Herald Tribune,* November 25, 1953. [*Editor's note:* See also *New York Times,* November 25, 1953 for discussion of the Wheeler case.]

62. *New York Times,* July 9, 1957.

63. Ibid., July 9, 1957.

64. [*Editor's note:* Hoover provided no further substantiation for this claim. It is not certain that all the individuals he listed in the preceding pages were actual Communist Party members and/or engaged in subversive purposes. See notes 45, 48, and 50.]

			chairman. Convicted July 31, 1956, in Federal Court in New York of violating Smith Act by teaching and advocating overthrow of U.S. Government by force. Sentenced to prison for two years.[65]
Morris U. Cohen, Ph.D.	1942	Technical Research Laboratories, Montclair, New Jersey	Refused to testify whether Communist.[66]
	1943–1945	Gussack Machine Products Company, Long Island City, New York, under contract for Armed Forces	
Harold Ware	1934	Department of Agriculture	Active in organizing the "Ware group." Died in 1935.[67]
Nathan S. Witt, Ll. B.	1933–1934	Agricultural Adjustment Administration	Refused to testify whether Communist.[68]
	1934–1940	National Labor Relations Board	

There are other categories of Federal employees engaged in Communist activities which merit examples, but for space reasons are not included here. One category covered those who invoked the Fifth Amendment when asked about their Communist affiliations by authorized officials. They occupied positions in practically every agency of the government. Such persons were entitled to refuse to give information, if it would incriminate them, but in view of the dangers involved for our country, they could at least be considered "bad risks."

Another category consisted of Federal employees who, in sworn testimony before official bodies, were charged with having some connection with the Communist conspiracy against our government.

I will not cumber this text with these lengthy listings. These can be found at Washington sources.

In July 1947, Arthur S. Flemming, then Chairman of the Civil Service Commission, testified before an Appropriations Committee of the House of

---

65. *New York Times,* August 1, 1956. See also *New York Times* for April 16 and September 18, 1956.

66. SISS, Hearings, *Educational,* 83d Cong., 1st sess., Part 10, May 1953, pp. 995–999.

67. HUAC, Hearings, regarding *Communism in the United States Government,* Part 2, 81st Cong., 2d sess., August 28, 1950, pp. 2853 and 2996. See also James Burnham, *The Web of Subversion,* pp. 69–70. See also HUAC, Hearings, *Espionage,* 80th Cong., 2d sess., 1948.

68. HUAC, Hearings, *Espionage,* 80th Cong., 2d sess., August 20, 1948, pp. 1029, 1033.

Representatives that 1,300 government workers had been discharged as disloyal. He added that if a loyalty investigation were held, "derogatory information" would be collected on some 29,000 Federal employees. Derogatory information was not always concerned with Communism—it included other items, but scarcely warranted retention in Federal employment.

In 1949 the House Committee on Un-American Activities published a report stating that 3,000 government employees were Communist Party members.

In 1953, over 2,000 persons were discharged from the Government as "bad risks"; their names were withheld.

On September 28, 1955, Philip D. Young, Chairman of the Civil Service Commission, reported to a Senate Subcommittee that from May 28, 1953 to June 20, 1955, 20,720 government workers were discharged or allowed to resign "under the security program." On November 28, 1955, Chairman Young reported that in the four months—between May 28, 1953 and September 30, 1953—3,685 government employees were discharged on security grounds and that 5,920 others resigned with adverse security information in their files.

The specific experience of the Atomic Energy Commission in such problems was revealed by Admiral Lewis L. Strauss, former Chairman of the Commission, in his book, *Men and Decisions,*[69] in which he states that in the first seven years of the Commission 494 persons were denied clearance and that nearly four thousand others resigned.

As this narrative proceeds it will be found that these persons influenced our foreign policies and stole our defense secrets, thereby requiring us to spend billions of dollars to protect ourselves from the Russians, to whom these secrets were given.

---

69. Lewis L. Strauss, *Men and Decisions* (Doubleday & Company, Inc., Garden City, New York: 1962), p. 261.

CHAPTER 5

The Communist Fronts

COMMUNIST CONSPIRATORS PENETRATED most phases of American life through a multitude of subversive "fronts."

The House Committee on Un-American Activities defined a "Communist front" as:

> ... an organization or publication created or captured by the Communists to do the party's work in areas where an openly Communist project would be unwelcome. Because subterfuge often makes it difficult to recognize its true nature, the Communist front has become the greatest weapon of communism in this country. . . .[1]

The usual method of organizing a front was to establish a more or less hidden core of Communists and surround it with a host of "liberal" sympathizers, or persons innocent of guile, or those who just wanted to join something.

J. Edgar Hoover testified before the House Committee on Un-American Activities:

> The first requisite for front organizations is an idealistic sounding title. . . .[2]

This sort of organization was part of the original Lenin apparatus called "transmission belts." As Lenin described it:

> ... the dictatorship of the proletariat cannot be effected by organisations that embrace the whole of the proletariat. It is impossible to effect the dictatorship without having a number of "transmission belts" from the vanguard [the

---

1. Committee on Un-American Activities, U.S. House of Representatives, *Guide to Subversive Organizations and Publications* (revised and published as of January 2, 1957), pp. 1–2.
2. Committee on Un-American Activities, U.S. House of Representatives, *Guide to Subversive Organizations and Publications* [82d Congress, 1st Session, House Document No. 137] May 14, 1951, p. 6.

Communist Party] to the masses of the advanced class [meaning the "intellectuals"], and from the latter to the masses of the toilers. . . .[3]

Most of the American "fronts" were organized after the recognition of Russia in November, 1933. They were able to operate freely under the protection of the Bill of Rights except in cases of overt acts to overthrow the government by violence. They were careful to avoid this. However, the end purpose was to establish a Communist government of the United States.

Prior to December 1, 1961, more than one thousand of these groups were publicly exposed and officially denounced as subversive by legislative committees and/or by Federal or State Attorney-Generals, or by other official agencies.[4] To indicate the vast scope of their activities I have broken them down into categories.[5]

There were sixty-one fronts or committees engaged in political activity under such labels as "Communist Party, USA," "Communist Political Association," "United Communist Party," and "American Workers Party."

At least sixteen of these activities were set up to influence legislation, such as the "Conference for Social Legislation" with various state committees for specific legislative objectives.

Forty-seven were concerned with civil rights, such as the "Civil Rights Federation," "Emergency Civil Liberties Committee," "National Civil Rights Federation," and "Civil Rights Congress." (The latter was organized into many local branches.)

There were numerous fronts or committees for "freedom and democracy" operating under such names as the "American Committee for Democracy and Intellectual Freedom," and the "Conference for Democratic Action" (with branches).

Fronts or committees were at work in forty-seven colleges, universities and schools; in twenty-four bookstores and book distributing agencies; in fifty-one news services, newspapers, periodicals and publications; and in eleven camps—a total of one-hundred thirty-three subversive organizations in these fields alone.

Thirty were active among the arts, sciences, letters and professions, such as the "World Federation of Scientific Workers," "Revolutionary Writers

---

3. V. I. Lenin, *Selected Works,* Volume IX (International Publishers, New York: 1943), p. 6.

4. Committee on Un-American Activities, U.S. House of Representatives, *Guide to Subversive Organizations and Publications,* May 14, 1951, January 2, 1957, and December 1, 1961.

5. The full study of these fronts, giving some detail as to their operations, is available for inspection at the Hoover Institution on War, Revolution and Peace at Stanford University, California.

Federation," "United American Artists," "National Council of the Arts, Sciences, and Professions," and "National Institute of Arts and Letters."

Five worked among religious societies, such as the "Methodist Federation for Social Action" and "People's Institute of Applied Religion."

Six were specifically directed at women, such as the "Congress of American Women," "International Congress of Women," "Wives and Sweethearts of Servicemen," and "Women's International Democratic Federation."

Thirteen were active among war veterans: "The Council of United States Veterans," "Unions of Progressive Veterans," "United States Veterans Council," "United Veterans for Equality," and "American League of Ex-Servicemen."

Many fronts concentrated on foreign relations. They bore such names as the "Greek-American Council," "Free Italy Society," "American Committee for Free Yugoslavia (The)," "Committee for a Democratic Far Eastern Policy," "Friends of Chinese Democracy," and "American Committee for a Korean People's Party."

Numerous committees and fronts operated among foreign-language groups. Among some twenty-six nationalities represented, there were, for example, nineteen fronts for Yugoslavia, four for Poles, four for Italians, four for Hungarians, two for Rumanians, five for Finns, three for Estonians, five for Lithuanians, and two for Czechs.

Among the minority groups, there were seven Jewish fronts or committees, such as "Chicago Jewish Committee for Protection of Foreign Born," and "Jewish Blackbook Committee of Los Angeles."

Fifty-one were engaged in the furtherance of "understanding" Communist Russia, including the "American Russian Institute," "American Council on Soviet Relations," and "International Red Aid."

Several were concerned with African affairs, such as "Council on African Affairs" and "International Committee on African Affairs."

One hundred ten asserted an interest in the broad issues of war or peace, under such titles as the "National Labor Conference for Peace" (with local branches), "Yanks Are Not Coming Committee," "Cultural and Scientific Conference for World Peace," "United States Congress Against War," "World Committee Against War," and "World Peace Council."

Thirty-two supported the Communists in the Spanish Civil War, including the "Abraham Lincoln Brigade," "American Committee for Spanish Freedom," "Emergency Committee to Aid Spain," "Social Workers Committee to Aid Spanish Democracy," "United Spanish Aid Committee," and "Veterans of the Abraham Lincoln Brigade."

At least forty-eight organizations operated among students and youth councils (with local branches), under such titles as the "Socialist Youth League," "Student Rights Association," "Teenage Art Club," "Young Communist League," "Young Progressive Citizen's Committee," "Young Workers League," "American Youth Congress," "American Youth for Democracy," "International Union of Students," and "East Bay Youth Cultural Center."

Sixty-nine focused on labor, under such titles as the "Independent Communist Labor League of America," "Joint Committee for Trade Union Rights," "National Unemployment Councils," "Trade Union Advisory Committee," and "United Toilers."

Four worked among farmers, such as the "United Farmers League," "Western Council for Progressive Labor in Agriculture," and "Farm Research."

Four were organized for consumers, such as the "Consumers' National Federation," and "Consumers Union."

Five concentrated on the legal profession, such as the "National Lawyers' Guild" and the "International Association of Democratic Lawyers."

Forty-three operated in the entertainment field—television, radio, stage, actors, etc., under such labels as "Group Theatre," "Hollywood Theatre Alliance," "League of Workers Theatres," "Motion Picture Artists' Committee," "New Theatre League," "People's Orchestra," "People's Songs," "Trade Union Theatre," "Film and Photo League," and "Artists and Writers Guild."

Twenty-three worked among American Negroes, including the "League of Struggle for Negro Rights," "National Negro Congress," "National Negro Labor Congress," "Negro Cultural Committee," and the "Scottsboro Defense Committee."

Thirty-nine were general organizations to defend or obtain clemency for convicted Communist spies or other persons indicted for inciting violence. In addition, a total of sixty-two groups were set up to propagandize on behalf of specific individuals involved in court actions: six committees for Harry Bridges, five for Earl R. Browder, two for Gerhard Eisler, five for Tom Mooney, forty-four for Morton Sobell, and Julius and Ethel Rosenberg.

Many cannot be classified according to their names, but included committees on the unemployment problem, such as the "Workers International Relief," "League for Mutual Aid," "Down River Citizens Committee," "American Investors Union, Inc." and "Committee of One Thousand."

Public demonstrations were organized by such committees as the "Zero Hour Parade" and "United May Day Committee." All these organizations were declared subversive by authorized agencies.

The Case History of a Group in Action

The Communists made a major advance toward their goal of control of the labor unions when John L. Lewis, President of the United Mine Workers of America, created the Committee for Industrial Organization (C.I.O.) in 1935 and 1936. He employed known Communists to assist him. Lewis himself was far from a Communist, but in his labor organization battles, he used any weapon available.

The C.I.O. plunged into the political arena from its start. In 1943, it welded its unions into the Political Action Committee called the "P.A.C." The purpose of this group in turn was to defeat Congressional and Presidential candidates hostile to its program.

When the House Un-American Activities Committee scrutinized this operation, it stated:

> The C.I.O. executive board which established the Political Action Committee is composed of 49 members among whom there are at least 18 whose records indicate that they follow the "line" of the Communist Party with undeviating loyalty. . . .[6]

The head of the Political Action Committee was Sidney Hillman, who was high in the Roosevelt Administration's councils, both as "labor advisor" to the President and labor representative in the wartime Office of Production Management. Born in Russia and a participant in early revolutionary activities there, Hillman had come to the United States in 1907 and worked as a labor organizer, rising in 1914 to the presidency of the powerful Amalgamated Clothing Workers of America. According to sworn testimony before a Senate Committee,[7] he was in 1922 a member of the Communist Party. In that year he visited Moscow. He also wrote articles in support of Communist Russia. A long listing of his association with Communist activities was published by the House Committee.

One of Hillman's principal assistants was the lawyer for the Political Action Committee, Lee Pressman. Pressman was a Communist Party member in 1934, and from 1934 to 1935 held high positions in the Federal Govern-

---

6. U.S. House Special Committee on Un-American Activities, 78th Congress, 2d Session, *Investigation of Un-American Propaganda Activities in the United States . . . Report on the C.I.O. Political Action Committee, 1944* (House Report No. 1311), p. 4.

7. U.S. Senate Committee on the Judiciary, 81st Congress, 1st Session, *Hearings before the Subcommittee on Immigration and Naturalization,* on S. 1832, September 14, 1949, pp. 785, 800.

ment. He publicly confessed his one-time Communist Party membership on
August 27, 1950.[3]

The Political Action Committee instituted a compulsory assessment upon
members of many of the C.I.O. unions, thus creating a political fund estimated at $2,000,000 per annum. Hillman refused to submit the Political Ac-
tion Committee's books to the Congressional Committee.

The C.I.O., from the first, and later the Political Action Committee, systematically and in highly organized fashion listed, for the benefit of their
members, the names of the candidates who were to be opposed. Practically
the same lists were issued by the Communist party itself.

Sidney Hillman became so politically powerful that at the 1944 Democratic National Convention, Mr. Roosevelt, when the question of the choice
of Vice President arose, issued his famous order to "Clear it with Sidney."

A number of important American Federation of Labor unions also fell
under Communist domination. This Communist take-over was certainly not
deterred by the National Labor Relations Board whose chairman and attorney were themselves party members.[9]

---

8. *New York Times,* August 28, 1950.

9. See Chapter 4. [*Editor's note:* In chapter 4 Hoover listed four known or suspected Communists
who held positions at one time or another at the National Labor Relations Board (NLRB). One of
these served as the Board's assistant general counsel and then as its secretary (chief administrative
officer) for a time. It is to these individuals that Hoover was evidently alluding here. But none of
these individuals served as the Board's actual chairman or general counsel. For more on Communist
activity at the NLRB in the 1930s and 1940s, see James Burnham, *The Web of Subversion* (The John
Day Company, New York: 1954), pp. 101–107, a source cited by Hoover in chapter 4.]

Herbert Hoover meets Adolf Hitler. Berlin, Germany, March 8, 1938.
[*Left to right:* Hoover, Hitler, Dr. Paul Schmidt (German Foreign Office translator), and Hugh Wilson (U.S. Ambassador to Germany)]

Following page, top: Herbert Hoover and President Wilhelm Miklas of Austria. Vienna, Austria, March 4, 1938.

Following page, bottom: Herbert Hoover (*right*) meets President Ignatz Moscicki of Poland. Warsaw, Poland, March 12, 1938.

President Kyösti Kallio of Finland and Herbert Hoover. Helsinki, Finland, March 15, 1938.

Advertisement for a Finnish Relief mass meeting. New York City, December 1939.

Herbert Hoover appeals for relief for suffering Poland.
Pulaski Memorial Day, New York City, October 11, 1939.

Facing page, top: Herbert Hoover and the actress Gertrude Lawrence at an art auction to raise money for Finland during the Russo-Finnish War of 1939–40. New York City, January 4, 1940.

Facing page, bottom: Herbert Hoover receives a contribution to the Finnish Relief Fund from "Popeye the Sailor." New York City, Winter 1940.

Celebrities for Finnish Relief: (*left to right*) Tallulah Bankhead, Herbert Hoover, Helen Hayes, and Katharine Hepburn at a luncheon given by the Stage and Screen Division of the Finnish Relief Fund. New York City, January 12, 1940.

Facing page: In 1942, Hoover co-authored a bestselling book about war and peace. Shown is an advertisement for the book that appeared in the *New York Times*, June 30, 1942, page 38.

© New York Times

Nationwide Praise for a Great American Book

THE PROBLEMS OF LASTING PEACE
by HERBERT HOOVER and HUGH GIBSON

THE PROBLEMS OF Lasting Peace BY HERBERT HOOVER AND HUGH GIBSON

"The purpose of this war, the most terrible of three centuries, is to make a lasting peace. We must first win the war. But we will not win lasting peace unless we prepare for it, and we can prepare only by full and free public discussion of the world surgery of analysis."

5th large printing

THE PROBLEMS OF LASTING PEACE is a big, clothbound book of 300 pages. It gives complete analyses of every major problem in the widest distribution of the volume in American sins and events everywhere.

$2

DOUBLEDAY, DORAN.

Herbert Hoover testifies before a subcommittee of the Senate Foreign Relations Committee in support of sending food relief to civilians in German-occupied Europe. Washington, D.C., November 4, 1943.

I Make an Appraisal of the Forces Moving among Nations in 1938

INTRODUCTION

IN 1936 AND 1937 the great expansion of military strength of Stalin and Hitler, together with their aggressive attitudes, created many forebodings in my mind of an oncoming war and the possibility that it would bring great dangers to the United States. Both of these powerful dictators were threatening violence not only to each other but conquest of parts of Europe and Asia.

As noted earlier, over the years I had received invitations from officials of many institutions and governments in Europe to visit them so that they might express appreciation for my services in the First World War and its aftermath.[1] I resolved to take advantage of these invitations to make an examination on the spot, in order that I might be of service to the American people in advising them as to the nature of and dangers from these rising forces.

On this journey I visited Belgium, Holland, France, Britain, Germany, Poland, Czechoslovakia, Austria, Switzerland, Latvia, Estonia, Finland, Sweden, and Norway, and made a special trip to the League of Nations in Geneva.

I was accompanied by Perrin Galpin and Paul Smith, who devotedly set up and managed our appointments and travel arrangements and were present at many of my discussions with European officials. We left New York on February 9, 1938 on the U.S.S. *Washington* and returned on March 28 on the *Normandie.*

In this section I include a brief narrative of the forces moving in Italy, Russia, and China and Japan. Although I did not visit these countries on this journey, my former residence in them and my prior services abroad helped me to understand the major forces in motion within them.

In each country visited I was able to discuss the economic and political situation with its leaders. Some of the men with whom I talked were old friends,

---

1. An account of these activities may be found in Volumes I, II, and III of [Herbert Hoover,] *An American Epic,* published by Henry Regnery Company, Chicago: 1959, 1960 and 1961.

and others were usually frank and outspoken but naturally expressed themselves in confidence. However, I feel that at this writing, twenty-five years later, there can be no embarrassment caused by repeating statements of those who have passed on.

On this journey, I had over three hundred interviews with officials and other important persons, many meetings with university faculties and received honorary degrees. Also I attended numerous receptions given by municipal and civic bodies. In order to refresh my memory, I usually jotted down notes of important statements when I returned to my hotel. In the presentation of these conversations, I have utilized these notes in the chapters of this section.[2]

The account of this survey perhaps has additional interest because of a second on-the-ground appraisal I was able to make of the forces in motion in these same countries eight years later (1946), after the Second World War had been fought.[3]

At the time of the peace treaty of Versailles following the First World War, every country in Europe except Russia—twenty-three in all—already possessed or had adopted representative government in parliamentary form. By the time of this visit in 1938—nineteen years later—the face of Europe had changed. Revolutions in ten of these countries, whose combined populations exceeded 240,000,000, had established Fascist governments. Only thirteen free governments remained: Britain, Belgium, France, Holland, Denmark, Finland, Estonia, Latvia, Lithuania, Sweden, Norway, Switzerland, and Czechoslovakia,[4] whose aggregate populations amounted to 140,000,000.

---

2. Personal notes of my trip of 1938.

3. Chapter [85–ed.]

4. It may relieve the somber account which follows to mention a lighter note of my 1938 journey. Soon after the First World War, the astronomical observatory at Vienna had named a planet for me. The Brussels Observatory gave me another one. Some nomenclature committee within the profession protested that planets should not be named after living persons; they preferred Greek gods. I was temporarily banished from the sky. But the Vienna and Brussels astronomers were not to be deterred, and by their adding a Greek suffix to my name I was restored to planetary immortality.

In passing, I may add a further note on the uncertainties of efforts to immortalize public men of the day. Streets and parks in several Belgian, northern French, Austrian, Czech, and Polish cities had been renamed for me during and after the First World War. I also stood in a Polish park in the form of a statue. But with the Second World War, the Germans and Russians renamed the Hoover streets and avenues in their annexed territories in honor of their own heroes. In these changing fortunes, the greatest suffering I endured was to have the head of my image in a Warsaw public park blown off by a Mills bomb at the hands of the Nazis. On a visit there in 1946, I found that I was still headless. (I elaborated on this subject in an article in *This Week* Magazine of February 18, 1962, apropos of the banishment of Stalin's body from the tomb of Lenin.)

[*Editor's note:* The two minor planets or asteroids that were named after Herbert Hoover are "932 Hooveria" and "1363 Herberta."]

CHAPTER 6

Belgium and France

Belgium

My first visit in 1938 was to Belgium. I had served with Belgian leaders during five years of the First World War. Moreover, Belgium for centuries had a tenuous and dangerous existence among conflicting European forces, and for its self defense was, and is, one of the best politically informed centers on the Continent. I had the opportunity of intimate discussions of the European situation with King Leopold III, Prime Minister Paul Janson and other Cabinet members, the leaders of the opposition parties, the rectors and professors of the universities, prominent businessmen and labor leaders—and especially our own able Ambassador, Hugh Gibson.

King Leopold had shown great moral strength and understanding of European problems. Among other things, he said:

> Of course Hitler and his national socialism with its racialism and aggressiveness are a constant menace. But the French are an equal liability to the peace of Europe.
>
> France is so torn by internal dissension, there is such degeneration in its leadership and in political life, that the French are a menace through weakness. A strong France and a strong Britain would be an assurance that Hitler would at least leave the Western Democracies alone, but the Germans have no fear of France.[1]

I asked for his views as to why Britain has been so complacent in the face of Hitler's repudiation of the Versailles Treaty and the Locarno Pact, his rearmament, his occupation of the Rhineland, and the formation of the Berlin-Tokyo Axis. He replied:

---

1. Personal notes of my trip of 1938. See Section II, Introduction. [*Editor's note:* Hoover's conversation with King Leopold III took place on February 18, 1938.]

Britain is fearful of the growth of Russia's military power, has lost faith in France. She is engaged in her traditional practice of "balance of power."[2]

I asked him how he accounted for the degeneration in France. He said:

Probably the primary cause is the depletion of the race for a generation as the consequence of being bled white in the last war, but the immediate cause is the disintegrating influence of the Communists and Communistic ideas which reached alarming proportions under Prime Minister Blum.[3]

Léon Blum's ministry had fallen some months before, to be succeeded by the ministry of Camille Chautemps.

The King explained that their recent termination of the Franco-Belgian military alliance was due to Belgium's fear that France, with its weakness and its alliance with Russia, might involve the Belgians.

The Belgian Prime Minister gave me the same impressions. I asked his opinion as to what motivating forces had led many democracies in Europe into Fascist dictatorships. His reply was inclusive:

Misery; socialists; Communists, aided by liberals who believed they could have totalitarian economics and maintain personal liberty; spenders; demagogues; too many political parties; weak compromise governments.

The movement away from democracy in each country was gradual at the start, but created its own accelerations by frightening business and thus increased disorganization of the economic system and increased unemployment.[4]

The possible conflict of Hitler and Stalin was causing the Belgian leaders great anxiety as any war between great powers endangered them.

From several Cabinet members, I heard for the first time on my journey a new note as to the United States. I was to hear it again and again from leaders in the smaller countries. It came in response to an inquiry of mine designed to provoke discussion. "What do you think the relation of the United States to Europe should be?" The replies were, in summary:

If war comes again, the United States should keep out. First, because you must maintain at least one great center of social stability, of moral and economic power, around which the world can rally after a war is over; and second, your

2. Ibid.
3. Ibid.
4. Ibid.

American insistence on racial independence and freedom are not fitted to the European scene. Your ideas introduce cross currents, fan conflicts which can only delay those settlements which Europe must find for itself. If general war comes again, European civilization will be near death; it can only revive if you have preserved it in America from the moral and physical destructions which would come from war.

When I asked from which direction war might come, the Belgians, and others subsequently, had one constant reply:

The ultimate and inevitable conflict in Europe is between Germany and Russia, both for ideological and economic and political reasons. The Germans are land people; their military strength is on land; they want land; they will sooner or later clash with Russia for Russia alone has the opportunities they want. And the Germans want to remove what they consider as their greatest menace, Communism. Russia would have no objection to Germany at war with Britain and western Europe as that would weaken both the Democracies and Germany. The greatest folly of all history would be for the western Democracies to cultivate war with Germany. The western powers should not be drawn into conflict with her. It would only demoralize them and aid Russia and the spread of Communism in the end.

When I asked *when* war might come, the answer in summary was:

Who knows? Perhaps a year, perhaps two years, perhaps never. The very fear of its coming stirs every peace-anxious statesman to action. But the whole structure of Europe was left unstable by the Treaty of Versailles and the explosives which it laid.[5]

France

I visited France first at Lille, en route from Belgium to Paris. Lille had been a center of our relief operations in the First World War. My old French associates had prepared various demonstrations of appreciation. On these occasions and others, I had the opportunity to discuss the French situation with the provincial and university authorities, business and labor leaders. I was also met at Lille by two former associates of war days—Edmond Labbé and Louis Chevrillon—both of whom were men of important influence. Robert D. Murphy of the American Embassy also joined us there. Murphy, Labbé,

---

5. Ibid.

Chevrillon, and I motored together to Paris and thus had ample time to canvass the political situation in France and in Europe, generally.

In Paris, Foreign Minister Georges Bonnet called upon me and escorted me to call on President Albert Lebrun. I met with Premier Camille Chautemps and the President of the Bank of France, the Chancellor of the Sorbonne, six high-ranking members of the permanent civil service, two senators, four deputies, two former French Ambassadors to the United States, six mayors, two engineers, two editors, two leading economists, two labor leaders, seven educators, one poet, six American correspondents and three American Embassy officials—in all, forty-eight particularly well-informed persons. It is unnecessary to quote their views at length as they were in agreement with the summations already given in Belgium.

The opinion of these men was that the dominant influence in French foreign policies was fear of the rising strength of Germany. As Labbé, who was Chancellor of the University of Liège and President of the World Exposition then being held in Paris, phrased it:

> The French people within our own resources cannot defend ourselves against Hitler. For security since the First World War, we have formed military alliances with Great Britain, Poland, Czechoslovakia and, in 1935, with Soviet Russia. Aside from these military alliances, France must rely for defense upon our infantry, artillery, and our impregnable fortification the Maginot Line.[6]

Chevrillon was not so confident. He, on one occasion, informed me:

> Both the Nazis and the Communists have infected the army. Beyond that, a great sickness had come over France. Not only had she been bled white during the First World War, but there had not been time to develop a new generation of vigorous leadership. The stamina which France had so nobly demonstrated in the First World War has not been revived.[7]

The French parliament was plagued with a multitude of weak political parties. From Versailles in 1919 to my visit in mid-1938, France had forty-one ministries—an average life of under six months. Léon Blum had become Premier in June, 1936, by support of the combined left-wing and Communist members of the French assembly. He had organized a "popular front" government of radical complexion. He had introduced Mr. Roosevelt's "New Deal"

6. Ibid.
7. Ibid.

into France, using that phrase. The result was to frighten the commercial and industrial community. Production slackened. Exports dropped and imports increased. There was a flight of capital. Exchange difficulties developed, with a drain on French gold reserves. In the defense field, Blum had not maintained French military strength. Production of planes dropped from 50 to 17 per month, compared to the 300 to 400 per month which Germany was turning out. All but 84 of the existing 700 French tanks, it was reported to me, were obsolete; Germany had thousands of new planes and tanks.

The Blum regime fell in June, 1937. At the time of my visit in 1938 Prime Minister Chautemps had not been able to remedy the situation. I came away greatly depressed by the plight of France.

CHAPTER 7

Germany and Italy

A Visit with Hitler

Hitler had been in power for five years. I had long since been aware, from his speeches, statements and actions, that he had three *idées fixes*: to unify Germany from its fragmentation by the Treaty of Versailles; to expand its physical resources by moving into Russia or the Balkan States—a drive for "Lebensraum," living space; and to destroy the Russian Communist government. These objectives were compounded by Hitler's boundless egoism. It was obvious that he had the support of the German people, who still bitterly recollected the humiliations of defeat, dismemberment, and disarmament, their sufferings from the continued blockade after their surrender in the war, from the famine which was its aftermath, and from the brutalities of the Communist uprisings in German cities during the Armistice period.

We had motored to Berlin from Czechoslovakia, as I wished to have a glimpse at some of the new German housing developments. When we arrived on March 7, 1938, I received an invitation from Hitler to call upon him. His emissary stated that der Fuehrer wished to express the appreciation of the German people for my part in their relief from starvation and pestilence during the Armistice, and for the rehabilitation of the German children afterwards, as well as for the service I had rendered to his nation as President during the world-wide financial crisis of 1930.

I accepted his invitation as I hoped at least partly to explore the furniture in his mind. I was accompanied by Hugh Wilson, who had just been appointed our Ambassador to Germany. Although the visit [at noon on March 8, 1938—ed.] was scheduled to last for fifteen minutes, Hitler held us much longer. He noted that I had toured the housing developments, and gave a most lucid and informative statement regarding these improvements. I found him well-informed, and with an accurate memory, at least on the non-political matters we discussed. I came away with the conviction that the earlier books and press reports which had pictured him as the dummy front man for some group of Nazis were false. He was unquestionably the boss.

Two incidents during the conversation convinced me that he was also a dangerous fanatic. He seemed to have trigger spots in his mind which, when touched, set him off like a man in furious anger. The Ambassador made some reference to Communist Russia, whereupon Hitler erupted into a verbal explosion. There was a milder but similar explosion when the Ambassador, commenting on a statement of mine about the world economic situation, used the term "democracy." Hitler certainly did not favor either form of government.

My major sources of information in Germany were old friends, such as the Minister of Interior during the First World War, Theodor Lewald, who had given the Belgian Relief strong support. He was strongly anti-Nazi. I also had a long conversation with various leaders including Hjalmar Schacht whom I had met before the war and since. He, however, was carefully reserved in his comments on the Nazi political regime but communicative on the economic situation.

My best appraisals of the German situation took place at the American Embassy from Americans in Berlin, particularly Louis Lochner, a long-time representative of the Associated Press; Douglas Miller, our commercial attaché, who had served under me when I was Secretary of Commerce; and our able military attaché, Colonel Truman Smith.

Lochner and Miller described life under the Nazis. It has been fully stated in many books and needs no repetition here. In any event, my interests were peace and war. Miller stated that the whole German agriculture and industry were being tuned to war. I asked him when he thought their plans would be complete; his reply was "about eighteen months." Colonel Smith gave me a lucid account of the build-up of the German armies; he said that they were manufacturing military planes at the rate of 4,800 a year. His conclusion was that it would take eighteen months to complete their military program to the point where they could initially launch 2,000,000 men on a battle front.

Hitler had defied the Versailles Treaty by building up the German army. He had also violated it by his military occupation of the Rhineland. He had torn Germany's signature from the Locarno Pact. On my inquiry, wherever I could discreetly make it, as to how he was able to get away with these violations, I met invariably with an answer to the effect that the British had raised no opposition, and were willing to see him build up a balance of power against Communist Russia, and that the French were too weak to present him with any opposition except words.

The American Ambassador confirmed that Hitler, in his determination to unify the Germans in Europe, might precipitate annexations of the Sudeten Germans in Czechoslovakia and Austria.

Hitler's Attitude Toward Stalin

As these two dictators overshadowed all other dangers in Europe I was naturally interested in how implacable Hitler was in his attitude toward Stalin. The indications were that there could be no healing of Hitler's antagonisms to Communist Russia.

On March 7, 1936, Hitler said:

> Soviet Russia, however, is the constitutionally organized exponent of the revolutionary philosophy of life. Its State creed is its confession in favor of world revolution.[1]

In a speech at Nuremberg, September 12, 1936, he said:

> If I had the Ural Mountains with their incalculable store of treasures in raw materials, Siberia with its vast forests, and the Ukraine with its tremendous wheat fields, Germany and the National Socialist leadership would swim in plenty![2]

Again in a speech at Nuremberg on September 14, 1936, he said:

> These are only some of the grounds for the antagonisms which separate us from communism. I confess: these antagonisms cannot be bridged. Here are really two worlds which do but grow further apart from each other and can never unite.[3]

There had been many other speeches of this temperament.

On October 24, 1936, the Berlin-Rome Axis was formed as a result of a visit of Count Ciano, Italian Foreign Minister, to Berlin. This agreement strengthened the position of both Germany and Italy with respect to France and Great Britain. As published it provided for cooperation for joint action "to defend European civilization against grave danger threatening its social and cultural structure." One month later the idea was developed further in the

---

1. Adolf Hitler, *My New Order* (edited by Raoul de Roussy de Sales, Reynal & Hitchcock, New York: 1941), p. 378. R. de Sales italics deleted.
2. Ibid, p. 400. [R. de Sales' italics deleted by Hoover—*ed.*]
3. Ibid, p. 403. [R. de Sales' italics deleted by Hoover—*ed.*]

Anti-Comintern Pact signed with Japan (November 25, 1936). The same Pact was signed by Italy on November 6, 1937. The Pact said:

> The government of the German Reich and the Imperial Japanese Government, recognizing that the aim of the Communist International, known as the Comintern, is to disintegrate and subdue existing States by all the means at its command; convinced that the toleration of interference by the Communist International in the internal affairs of the nations not only endangers their internal peace and social well-being, but is also a menace to the peace of the world; desirous of co-operating in the defence against Communist subversive activities; have agreed as follows:
>
> ... to inform one another of the activities of the Communist International, to consult with one another on the necessary preventive measures, and to carry these through in close collaboration.
>
> ... [to] jointly invite third States whose internal peace is threatened by the subversive activities of the Communist International to adopt defensive measures in the spirit of this agreement or to take part in the present agreement. . . .[4]

The reaction of the Soviet Government to these pacts was instantaneous. On November 27, the *New York Times* reported:

> The Congress of Soviets at today's session became the Bolsheviki's deliberate answer to the Nazi party's Nuremberg congress. To the hymns of hate sung by Chancellor Adolf Hitler and his aides Soviet speakers replied in kind.

To Hitler's speculation on how enriched Germany would be if she had the Ukraine they said: "Only let Germany try and she will be beaten back on her own soil."[5]

On November 28, Foreign Commissar Maxim Litvinov said:

> The German-Japanese anti-Communist agreement is a mask for military action against the Soviet Union. That Japan so understood it is evidenced by two attacks on our soil in the Far East in the past forty-eight hours.
>
> We have exact information that Italy, wishing at any cost to follow in the footsteps of her new mentor, Germany, has asked Japan to conclude an agreement analogous to the published portion of the Japanese-German agreement.[6]

---

4. *Documents on International Affairs, 1936* (Royal Institute of International Affairs, London), pp. 297–298.

5. *New York Times*, November 27, 1936, p. 1:8.

6. Ibid., November 29, 1936.

An Associated Press dispatch from Moscow, on November 26 (1936) reported *Pravda* as saying "that Soviet Russia had documentary evidence to support its declaration that Japan and Germany had a military pact against Russia."[7]

The indication at the time of my visit was that there could be no healing of Hitler's antagonism to Stalin.

A Visit with the No. 2 Nazi

Further insight into the character of Nazidom's top echelon was afforded by a session with Hitler's right-hand man, Field Marshal Hermann Goering. When Goering sent word that he would like me to lunch with him, I accepted it as an opportunity also to explore the furniture in his mind. Our Ambassador urged my acceptance, as he had never met the No. 2 Nazi personally.

The luncheon took place some distance outside Berlin, at "Karinhall," Goering's huge hunting lodge.[8] Before lunch, he invited me into his study, where we were alone except for his interpreter. He had a memorandum, provided by some functionary, containing various questions to ask me. He began the conversation by stating that all Germans appreciated the help I had given during the Armistice and its aftermath. He declared that Germany would never have another famine, as they had developed agriculture to the point where they were self-supporting within their own boundaries. I did not believe this, but the assertion itself struck me as a portent of war.

Goering asked several economic questions and some particulars as to the standardization of industrial parts, which had largely been inaugurated by the Department of Commerce while I was Secretary. In my reply I mentioned that our standards required the voluntary approval of those concerned, to which he replied that national socialism had no bothers like that: "If I am

---

7. Ibid., November 27, 1936.

8. When our cars entered the courtyard we were stopped, for no apparent reason, by a sentry. In a few moments fourteen or sixteen men, dressed as huntsmen and armed with French horns, emerged from side doors and played the Huntsman's Call from *Siegfried* more beautifully than I had ever heard it before.

This over, we pulled up at the entrance, and the atmosphere changed again. Many years before I had seen a play on the American stage called "Beggar on Horseback." Its chief impression on my memory was twelve butlers, each with twelve footmen. They were all present here. Perhaps part of the contingent were secret service men in livery, posted to prevent visitors from doing bodily harm to our host. In any event, some of them were always within reach.

"Karinhall" was an immense structure, with rooms that seemed as large as a Waldorf-Astoria dining-room. They were crammed with hundreds of thousands of dollars' worth of furniture, paintings, and *objets d'art,* including two or three busts of Napoleon. Goering came from an impecunious military family and had never legitimately enjoyed more than a general's salary.

given such a rationalization in the morning it is in effect by noon." He had been informed of my engineering practice in Russia before World War I, and asked many questions as to her mineral resources. But my information was long out of date and limited to facts already well known.

He then pushed a button and an illuminated map of Europe appeared on the wall, with different brilliant colors for Germany's various neighbors. He pointed to Czechoslovakia and asked, "What does the shape of that country remind you of?" Nothing apropos occurred to me so he continued, "That is a spearhead. It is a spearhead plunged into the German body."

My net impressions of Goering were that he was a more agreeable person than Hitler and had an adroit mind; but his bulldog neck and tough face indicated a ruthless and probably utterly cruel person.

The Nazi regime, with its destruction of personal liberty, its materialistic and militaristic aspects, and its persecution of the Jews, has been fully described elsewhere. My visitors who called at my hotel rooms all seemed reserved as if there might be microphones in the room. There were on the streets more people in some kind of uniform than I saw anywhere else in Europe. From it all I experienced a sort of indescribable sense of oppression and dread while in Germany. This impression is perhaps indicated by the great lift of spirit that came over me the moment we passed over the frontier into Poland.

Italy

I did not visit Italy on this journey, but from many sources it was clear that Mussolini was still nursing grievances over the Treaty of Versailles. Italy had joined the war in 1915 under a secret treaty with the British and French by which she was to have acquired concrete territorial gains for her participation on the Allied side. With the peacemaking, the Italians had suffered a rude jolt. Their claims were largely ignored.[9]

In 1938 Benito Mussolini, acknowledged founder of Fascism, was at the peak of his dictatorial glory. He had, beginning in 1922, introduced great reforms into Italy. He had reorganized the government and the army; established

---

9. Italy's grievances were heightened by the system of "mandates" set up under the Treaty of Versailles, because through this device the British enlarged their empire by 1,607,053 square miles of territory and 35,000,000 inhabitants; the French by 402,392 square miles and 4,000,000 inhabitants; the Japanese by 833 square miles of Pacific islands and 133,000 inhabitants, together with China's Shantung province and its 20,000,000 inhabitants; the Belgians by about 18,000 square miles and about 4,000,000 inhabitants. Italy received small consideration acquiring only a very few million people.

integrity in public officials and efficiency in the railways and public utilities; encouraged industry and agriculture. Because of these measures Italy had gained in prosperity. Due to failures in the parliamentary form of government, Mussolini's system had been adopted by a large part of Europe, including Germany. Few Americans observed that the economic part of Fascism was simply the adoption of the measures applied in the United States, Britain and other democracies when combatants in the First World War.

In May 1936 Italy had seized Ethiopia, and as a result economic sanctions had been imposed on her by the League of Nations, but they were short-lived.

Mussolini was in 1938 making common cause with Hitler against Communism. He was a founding partner of the Anti-Comintern Pact, and jointly, he and Hitler had successfully backed General Francisco Franco in the defeat of the Russian-supported Communist revolution in Spain.

The British and French, anxious to woo Mussolini from his alliance with Hitler, had made several concessions to Italian colonial desires in Africa, including recognition of the Italian conquest of Ethiopia. On January 2, 1937, the British and Italian governments signed a declaration of assurances with respect to the Meditteranean.[10]

An abortive attempt at British appeasement of Italy early in 1938 led to Anthony Eden's resignation as British Minister of Foreign Affairs. However, the British government resumed its negotiations with the Italians and an extensive agreement was signed on April 16, 1938. But none of these succeeded in winning Il Duce away from der Fuehrer.[11]

---

10. *New York Times,* January 3, 1937; Great Britain, Foreign Office, *Italy No. 1 (1937). DECLARATION by His Majesty's Government in the United Kingdom and the Italian Government regarding the MEDITERRANEAN [With an Exchange of Notes regarding the status quo in the Western Mediterranean dated December 31, 1936] Rome, January 2, 1937. Presented by the Secretary of State for Foreign Affairs to Parliament by Command of His Majesty.* London: H. M. Stationery Office, 1937. 4 p (Cmd. 5348).

11. To those who seek some gleam of humor in power politics, I commend a statement made by Mussolini at a reception given him by Hitler in Berlin on September 26, 1937. The Italian leader proclaimed: "The greatest and most genuine democracies that the world knows today are Germany and Italy." (As quoted in Dr. Paul Schmidt's *Hitler's Interpreter,* The Macmillan Company, New York: 1951, p. 73.)

CHAPTER 8

Austria, Czechoslovakia, and Poland

Austria

Although Austria had been trimmed down to six million people by the Treaty of St. Germain, the city of Vienna was still one of the great intellectual centers of Europe. But it had an overshadowing national problem which was Hitler's threat of annexation.

Chancellor Kurt Schuschnigg, in our conversations, told me of his brutal treatment by Hitler during an interview at Berchtesgaden a few days before and of Hitler's demand for Austria's annexation to Germany. He said that he would never consent to Hitler's demands. He had just made a courageous and eloquent address to the Austrian Parliament defying Hitler. His stand was of no avail. Ten days after my visit the Germans moved in and took over.

I formed the impression that Chancellor Schuschnigg was perhaps less than a great statesman, but a person of great nobility of character; a student rather than a man of action, with tremendous moral courage and integrity.

I asked him what he thought America's role in Europe should be. He exclaimed:

Keep out of European power politics and wars! Your people do not understand the forces reigning in Europe. You make things worse; your great part is to preserve a sanctuary where civilization can live.

In a dinner discussion with Finance Minister Rudolf Neumayer, President Victor Kienböck of the Austrian National Bank and two economic professors, I asked their views as to the underlying causes of the European economic collapse in 1931, which had been touched off from Vienna. I was certainly interested because the most disastrous of the woes of my administration, the Great Depression, had its greatest impulse from the financial collapse of Austria. His statement was as follows:

There were several primary and a number of secondary causes. The primary causes were:

First, the weakening of the economic structure of every nation in Europe by the war.

Second, the economic consequences of the Treaty of Versailles which had divided the Danube Valley among five states on a racial basis, most of which had set up trade barriers by the tariffs, discriminatory rail rates, import quotas, etc., and thus weakened and impoverished the productivity of that whole great area. This had especially impoverished the great financial and trade center of Vienna with its skills and financial resources.

Third, the set up of reparations and intergovernmental war debts which were impossible of payment, and in trying to meet these obligations had distorted all finance and exchange and, through such pressures, had forced the export of goods into unnatural channels.

Fourth, the economic isolation of Russia by Communist destruction of her productivity, thus stopped the flow of food and raw materials from her into Europe and closing a large part of the market in Russia for European manufactured goods.

Fifth, immediately after the Treaty and despite the League, military alliances and power politics had steadily increased armaments with their inevitable unbalanced budgets.

Sixth, the rise of the school of totalitarian liberals who believed governments could produce employment and increase productivity by bureaucratic control with the consequent fright to business. From this followed hesitation and increasing unemployment.

Seventh, the attempts of governments to meet this unemployment by public works drove budgets into further deficits with a train of foreign and domestic borrowing, kiting of trade bills and disguised inflation.

From all this flowed government controls of imports and exports in an effort to protect currencies and gold reserves, which created more unemployment.

The whole process was an aftermath of the World War and the Treaty of Versailles. If there had been no war, there would have been no world depression.

The crack started at its weakest point, that is, in Austria, and was widened when the French demanded payment of short-term bills as a pressure measure to prevent the proposed economic union with Germany in 1931.

Czechoslovakia

During our visit to Czechoslovakia, I stayed with our American minister, Wilbur J. Carr. He arranged opportunities for discussions with over fifty officials and civic leaders. They included President Eduard Benes; the Prime Minister, Dr. Milan Hodza; the Minister of Foreign Affairs, Dr. Kamil Krofta; and Dr. Emil Franke, the Minister of Education.

I had known President Benes during and after the First World War. He told me that peace could be preserved only if the Western democracies were firm enough with the Germans. He blamed the British for the rebuilding of German military might. Aside from military preparedness to protect his country against Germany, he relied upon a long-standing military alliance with France and a recent alliance with Communist Russia. President Benes gave me no hint of internal tensions, but his Prime Minister spoke bitterly of the ferment of independence being fanned by Hitler among the Sudeten Germans.

To understand the effectiveness of these agitations, it should be borne in mind that instead of organizing the Czech state on the cantonal basis stipulated at St. Germain, by which the 2,500,000 Sudeten Germans and 2,000,000 Slovaks would have had a large degree of local self-government, the Czechs had set up a centralized state in which they were in control of all important matters. Naturally, the Czechs had a bitter recollection of 150 years of oppression by their neighbors, and were not disposed to trust the Sudeten Germans or the Slovaks. The League of Nations had at one time taken them to task for their treatment of these minorities.

Both the Prime Minister and President Benes referred to their great military strength. They said that they had a standing army of 500,000 men and 1,000,000 efficiently equipped first reserves. I made a mental note that in proportion to the population, this would be the equivalent of a standing military force for the United States of about 4,500,000 men with 9,000,000 more in reserves. It did not look much like the expectation of peace.

The Czech military alliances with France and Russia, intended to encircle Germany, seemed to me weak, because with Russia there would be little fidelity, and with France there was no strength. The Americans in Prague were a great deal less than confident of the durability of the Czech state.

The people of Czechoslovakia were making steady economic progress. Art, music, education and industry had flowered beautifully under their independence and with Presidents Masaryk and Benes. The people compelled admiration for their courage, morale, character and industry. But I could not feel at all optimistic for the political future of Czechoslovakia, caught as it was between Hitler and Stalin.

Poland

Upon entering Poland on March 10, 1938, we were met at the frontier by Michael Kwapiszewski of the Polish Foreign Office, who accompanied us throughout our journey. He informed me that the Poles had prepared a great program of hospitality to evidence their appreciation of services rendered during four years after the First World War. They had arranged a journey by special train to Posnan, Krakow, and thence to Warsaw. In the first two cities I had opportunities at banquets and receptions to discuss the problems of the times with the local authorities and the chancellors and the professors of the universities. The sum of their opinions was (1) that freedom was disappearing in Poland; (2) that she was in a "nutcracker" held by Hitler and Stalin.

Eighteen years before this visit to Warsaw, the democratic Polish regime under Ignace Paderewski had been overthrown by the dictator-minded Chief of State, Jozef Pilsudski, and a half-Fascist regime had been installed. He was succeeded by a group of his supporters (the "Colonels") who were in effective control of Poland at the time of my visit.

I had extensive conversations with President Ignace Moscicki, Premier Felician Slawoj Skladowski, Vice Minister of Foreign Affairs Count Szembek, the Minister of Education Waclaw Jedrzejewicz, and Marshal Edward Smigly-Rydz, the "Marshal of Poland" and real power behind the throne. Altogether, I had the opportunity to converse with over one hundred officials, prominent in university, business and labor life, and our old leaders in the post-war relief.

I asked such independent-minded persons as I properly could why Poland had turned half-way toward Fascism and dictatorship. The universal answer was that the Communists and Socialists were boring from within; that the multiplicity of parties in the Parliament made constructive government impossible; that "strong government was necessary to save Poland from Communism." The President, the Prime Minister, and the Vice Minister of Foreign Affairs spoke at length of the dangerous situation in which they were placed—caught between Hitler's Germany and Stalin's Russia. They were gloomy at the prospect that the conflict between the two might result once more in the loss of Poland's independence by possible partition. The Prime Minister asserted that the Western powers were too weak to stop either Hitler or Stalin.

At this time, the Poles were obviously endeavoring to keep up good relations with both of them. At the same time, they had organized a great army, hoping they could hold both enemies at bay.

Despite the authoritarian trend of the regime, the Poles in 1938 had more freedom than the Germans. There were no concentration camps or liquidations, and there appeared to be a fairly free press.

The most cheerful aspect of Poland was the astonishing cultural and economic expansion under the sunlight of independence given her at Versailles. On the other hand, the entire political structure of the country at this time seemed to me very weak.

CHAPTER 9

Latvia, Estonia, Finland, Sweden

Latvia

One of my most illuminating discussions on this journey in 1938 was in Riga with President Karlis Ulmanis of Latvia.

Born in Latvia in 1877, Ulmanis emigrated to Nebraska in 1905. He graduated from the University of Nebraska in 1909. Soon thereafter he returned to Latvia. After the First World War he led in establishing Latvia's independence and constitutional government. At that time I was directing Allied relief operations, and had many transactions with him. He proved most cooperative.

Ulmanis spoke English in the American idiom which was a great advantage in terms and meaning when discussing political and economic matters. Such is not always the case when interpreters are employed.

By now, Latvia had a Fascist government. In citing the steps by which this had come about, Ulmanis told me that parliamentary government had broken down because of a multiplicity of parties.

He said that when the country had fallen into "complete chaos" from weakness and Communist conspiracies, he, together with the commander of Latvia's little army, had dissolved Parliament and abolished the supreme court. He had conducted the government ever since.

Ulmanis frankly described his regime as an adaptation of Italian Fascism and his own role as that of a dictator. But he declared this only a passing phase, and that later he would be able to restore a representative government and constitutional guarantees.

I asked him to trace the pattern of Fascist revolution away from constitutional government in Europe generally. As amplified from my short notes, his reply was:

There were two roots to Fascist revolution and several fertilizers. The main root was that few Continental people are adapted to parliamentary democracy. That form of liberalism conceives at least one majority party. When there are half a dozen, it is unworkable. Ministries are then formed by compromise, they are founded mostly on negative action—they cannot last or give strong constructive government.

The second root of revolution was the slow recovery from the impoverishment of war. The financial debacle of 1931, originating in Central Europe, was simply an accumulation of war aftermaths, of which government spending for armament, unemployment, unbalanced budgets, inflation, dislocation of trade channels by the Treaty of Versailles with its dissolution of the economic unit of the Danube Valley, and especially the Communist economic isolation of Russia from the economy of Europe were a part.

The fertilizers were the fifth column operators of the Russian Communists boring into labor groups and with the intellectuals who believed in personal liberty but who thought you could have economic totalitarianism and maintain the personal freedoms. This stage with its "managed economy" at once curtailed and frightened business, thereby increasing unemployment and government spending. Finally there was chaos.

He indicated that the United States was on the road to chaos because we had established a "managed economy."

I commented that, if all this were to be the destiny of the United States, I would like to know what chaos looked like when it was approaching. He took me over to the window overlooking the square, and said:

When you see armed mobs of men in green shirts, red shirts [Communists] and white shirts [Fascists] coming down different streets, converging into the square, fighting with clubs and firearms, mobs of women and children crowding in and demanding bread, then you know chaos has come.

When with the head of the Army I took possession, I thought I could preserve personal liberty by mere restoration of public order, but I quickly discovered that the fundamental cause of chaos was fear—fear in businessmen, fear in workmen, fear in farmers, fear of [for–*ed.*] the stability of the currency, fear of the government, all paralyzing economic and moral life. The only way to dissolve fear is more fear. I had to tell men and groups exactly what they had to do and put them in fear of the concentration camps if and when they wouldn't do it; fix prices; fix wages; order employees to start the factories, working men to work and order farmers to bring their products to market; issue new currency, and order people to take it and lock people up if they wouldn't. By and by, the system began to function again; confidence returned and the worst was over. Don't let anyone tell you that personal liberty can survive in a so-called managed economy nor ever stop short of collectivism. Today, Latvia has full employment, remunerative wages and prices and the currency has a sound gold reserve.

Ulmanis had said earlier that he hoped to restore representative government and personal liberties. I asked him how he proposed to do it. He replied:

The British parliamentary form of democracy based upon territorial representation is a failure. We must establish a fixed executive for a term as in the American form, but our legislative body must be based upon vocational representation. We must realistically accept the fact that we are no longer dealing with a civilization in which individuals are competing with each other for advancement but one in which the real competition is between classes and groups.

He was of the opinion that territorial representation had already failed in the United States because our representatives were actually chosen by groups or group pressures and that the members of our legislative bodies no longer acted on their own independent judgment. He mentioned that 500 different groups had offices around our Capitol in Washington to watch their representatives perform. He asserted that it would be better if, for instance, the farmers elected their own representatives. I opined that I did not agree that America had sunk so deeply into this sort of political quicksand but that it would be a valuable experiment for the world if he would try out his plan. He replied:

America with its "Managed Economy" is well on the road to chaos and the eclipse of democracy; I have been through it and am on the way out.

And he went on:

America may need expert advice later on and I will come home—I mean come back—and help.

This slip into the word "home" echoed in my mind for days, for that is the grip America takes on men's souls.[1]

---

1. I may add here the ultimate fate of Ulmanis, as described in a letter of April 2, 1962, to me from Osvalds Akmentins, Secretary of the Latvian Press Society in America. I mention only those paragraphs relating to his death:
   "After 20 years of silence the Soviet publications for the first time announced that Karlis Ulmanis, the last President of the Latvian Republic, died in 1942. The acknowledgment of his death was learned through the book, "Literarais Mantojums" [Heritage of Literature] published in Latvian

The American Chargé d'Affaires, Earl L. Parker, arranged an interview at our legation with Vilhelms Munters, the Minister of Foreign Affairs, and Ludwig Elkins, the Minister of Finance. Both expressed great fear that the Communist longing for outlets on the Baltic and the contrast of Russian poverty with the prosperity on this side of the border, might lead to the Soviet invasion of their homeland.

Estonia

Two officials from the Estonian Foreign Office, Edgar V. Körver and Albert Tattar, came to Riga to accompany us to their country by train. Both had recently served in the Estonian Legation in Moscow, and we talked far into the night about the possibility of conflict between Russia and Germany, and the conditions in Russia which I describe elsewhere.

When we arrived at Tallinn, we were met by the Estonian Minister of Foreign Affairs, Dr. Friedrich Akel, and the American Minister, Walter E. Leonard. I was unable to meet with the President as he was ill, but I received an excellent briefing on their situation from other officials.

The government was mostly fascist, patterned upon that of Latvia. The country was prosperous, but the people were haunted by fear of the Communists.

I found in Estonia, as in all the Baltic States, an astonishing degree of social, economic and cultural progress since their independence in 1919. As a matter of fact, the standard of living in the Baltic States was at the time of my visit as high as that in any other country in Europe. The people's looks, their

---

by the Academy of Soviet Science in Riga, Latvia. The book "Literarais Mantojums" Vol. 2 contains the works of poet Janis Rainis, one time Education Minister of the Latvian government. Karlis Ulmanis' death was not mentioned as a subject, but only in the bibliography of that book. The news of his death was not printed in any newspaper behind the Iron Curtain and Ulmanis' death was kept in secret.

"Even now after so long a time, . . . the Soviet authorities will not give any more details about Ulmanis' life in Russian exile and the circumstances how, where, he died and where his body is buried.

". . . He left Riga in a railway car with drawn curtains. He was seen getting off the train in Moscow under heavy escort. He was not brought before any court or other tribunal in the Soviet Union, and no announcement has ever been made by Soviet authorities with regard to his fate. . . .

". . . [P]ublic opinion in the world has never agitated to ascertain whatever happened to him. He was an honorable man and . . . a courageous statesman. His people in Latvia under Soviet occupation still remember him and usually say: 'Ulmanis' time was the best time for the country.' In 1954 Latvian people in U.S.A. and Canada erected a memorial plaque for Ulmanis at the University of Nebraska. . . ."

clothing, their shop windows, their markets displaying tropical products, and even their jewelry stores proclaimed prosperity.

Finland

Prime Minister Aimo Kaarlo Cajander, Minister of Foreign Affairs Rudolph Holsti, the staff of the American Legation, and a vociferous crowd of 30,000 citizens met us at the dock in Helsinki.

I had discussions with President Kyösti Kallio; the Prime Minister; the Minister of Foreign Affairs; Harold Tanner of the Administrative Bureau of the Foreign Office; the Governor of the Bank of Finland, Risto Ryti, and two former Presidents; Väinö Hakkila, the President of the House of Representatives; Hugo Suolahti, the Chancellor of the University of Helsinki; several professors; and the publishers of the leading Finnish newspapers. The dominant and recurrent theme of all our conversation was twofold: the conditions of life then prevailing in Russia, and Finnish fears of Communist invasion.

Under freedom, the Finns, like the other Baltic peoples, had achieved a remarkable advance in culture and economic well-being. They were, likewise, furiously anti-Communist. But beyond that, they were also anti-Russian, an attitude ingrained from a hundred years of Russian oppression prior to the Finns' liberation in 1918. They needed no lessons against Communism than the contrast between their own country, flowing in milk, honey, meat and white bread, and Soviet Russia with all its misery and hunger, only a few miles away. But, as in Latvia and Estonia, this contrast was a serious threat to Finland's future.

The Finns, an exception to the rule in Central Europe and the other Baltic States, were successfully maintaining parliamentary government. When I asked what the differences were that enabled Finland to hold to this fundamental, they said that Finland, except for the century of Russian oppression, had had some form of representative government and a tradition of personal freedom for three hundred years. The other Baltic States had no background of such experience.

Sweden

At Stockholm I spent an hour with Rickard Sandler, the Minister of Foreign Affairs, and, in the absence of King Gustav, had lunch with Crown Prince

Rudolf. Fred Morris Dearing, the American Minister, who was one of my old associates, gave a dinner where the Minister of Foreign Affairs, together with Dr. Börje Brilioth, a leading editor in Sweden, and two economists—Professor Bertil Ohlin of Stockholm Commercial College and Professor Gunnar Myrdal of Stockholm University—were present. Their conclusions on the dangers posed in case of war between the Germans and Russians were much the same as those that had been reported to me elsewhere.

CHAPTER 10

Russia

I DID NOT VISIT RUSSIA in 1938. I had no doubt that I was *persona non grata* because of my service to the Allies in extinguishing the Communist outbreaks during the Armistice period in 1919. Although I had organized the relief of the great famine in Russia in 1921–1923 and had received from them a gorgeous scroll stating my goodness, my expressions as to Communism generally during twenty years hardly commended me to them. However, having visited Russia professionally before the First World War and having dealt with their post-war conspiracies had given me considerable background information.

On this journey I received illuminating information as to the situation in Russia from officials in five of the independent border nations—Czechoslovakia, Poland, Latvia, Estonia, and Finland. The diplomatic officers of these countries came and went across the Russian frontiers, as did thousands of engineers and mechanics employed by the Soviet Union in its feverish arms build-up.

Impelled on the one hand by the internal urge for expansion of Communism, and on the other by fear of Germany, Stalin was vigorously strengthening his armies and war-support industries. To secure the needed time, he had signed non-aggression pacts with all of his border states. He had joined the League of Nations, signed the Kellogg Pact, and entered into alliances with France and Czechoslovakia. By the end of 1938, the Soviet Union was to put its signature to such peace pacts a total of thirty-seven times. Five of these agreements had been signed during the Lenin regime and thirty-two by Stalin.

The Soviet government had much to fear: Hitler's violent antagonism; his expressed determination to seek more living space; the spread of Fascism; and the Anti-Comintern Pact between Germany and Italy, later to be joined by Japan, were obvious threats.

But, in turn, the Communists were making progress in three directions: First, in the build-up of their armies and the war-industry plants to support them. Second, in establishing substantial Communist parties and the usual conspiracy apparatus throughout the countries of the free world, including the United States. Only in the Fascist states were these conspiracies inoperative. Third, in the development of a steady production of gold in Siberia. This resource was a substantial replacement of the Czarist gold reserve, which the Communists had long since put into use for subversion in many nations.

Soviet Relations with the United States up to Mid-1938

William C. Bullitt, a most able man, had been appointed our first Ambassador to Moscow on November 17, 1933 at the time of American recognition of the Russian regime. Hopeful for happy relations with the Communists, he was destined to become sadly disillusioned.

On July 13, 1935, he reported to our Secretary of State Cordell Hull that Maxim Litvinov, who had negotiated the recognition agreement in Washington in 1933, had informed him that he had made no promise to President Roosevelt that the Communist Third International would cease its activities in the United States.[1] Those promises only pledged the Soviet Government.

A week later, on July 19, Bullitt reported to the Secretary of State, this time giving his conclusions as to Communist objectives:

> ... Diplomatic relations with friendly states are not regarded by the Soviet Government as normal friendly relations but "armistice" relations ... [which] can not possibly be ended by a definitive peace but only by a renewal of battle. The Soviet Union genuinely desires peace on all fronts at the present time but this peace is looked upon merely as a happy respite in which future wars may be prepared.
>
> ... It is the primary object of the Soviet Foreign Office to maintain peace everywhere until the strength of the Soviet Union has been built up to such a point that it is entirely impregnable to attack and ready, if Stalin should desire, to intervene abroad.
>
> ... War in Europe is regarded as inevitable and ultimately desirable from the Communist point of view. ...
>
> It is, of course, the heartiest hope of the Soviet Government that the United States will become involved in war with Japan. ...

---

1. U.S. Department of State, *Foreign Relations of the United States: Diplomatic Papers, The Soviet Union, 1933–1939* [Government Printing Office, Washington: 1952], p. 223.

... To maintain peace for the present, to keep the nations of Europe divided, to foster enmity between Japan and the United States, and to gain the blind devotion and obedience of the communists of all countries so that they will act against their own governments at the behest of the Communist Pope in the Kremlin, is the sum of Stalin's policy.[2]

Few more accurate summations of Communist intentions have ever been made.

In July, 1935, the Seventh Communist International Congress met in Moscow. It was attended by Soviet leaders, including Stalin, and among the American Communists present were Earl Russell Browder, Secretary-General of the Communist Party of the United States; William Z. Foster, its Chairman; Gil Green (Gilbert Greenberg), Secretary of the Young Communist League; and Sam Darcy (Samuel Adams Dardeck), District Organizer of the San Francisco District of the Communist Party. Speeches were made by Browder, Darcy, and Green, as well as by Wilhelm Pieck, a German, putting forth great claims of Communist expansion in the United States. They boasted that the Communists had penetrated many labor unions and that they had fomented the bonus march of 1932, as well as a seamen's strike at San Francisco.[3] Mr. Bullitt sent Washington the details of this meeting on August 2 and 21, 1935. Noting that the proceedings were managed by the Kremlin he pointed out that they were proof of gross violation of the United States-Russian recognition agreement.[4]

Secretary of State Hull sent a formal protest to the Soviet government on August 25, 1935.[5] In a press release six days later (August 31) he declared:

... it is not possible for the Soviet Government to disclaim its obligation to prevent activities ... directed toward overthrowing the political or social order in the United States. ... [6]

Moscow, in reply, denied responsibility for the activities of the Communist International, and Secretary Hull let the matter die.

Loy Henderson, our Chargé d'Affaires in Moscow, advising Secretary Hull of the Soviet government's military activities, reported on January 15, 1936, that the Russian military budget had increased from 8.2 billion rubles in 1935

2. Ibid., pp. 224–227.
3. Ibid., pp. 228–332.
4. Ibid., pp. 233–235, 244.
5. Ibid., pp. 250–251.
6. Ibid., p. 259.

to 14.8 billion rubles in 1936, and that this sum enabled them to maintain a standing army of 1,300,000 men.[7] On August 18, 1936, Henderson further advised Secretary Hull that the expanded Soviet army would number between 1,500,000 and 2,000,000 men.[8]

Mr. Bullitt returned to the United States in early June, 1936, resigned his post, and on November 16, 1936, was replaced by Joseph E. Davies, a wealthy Washington lawyer without diplomatic experience. Mr. Davies arrived in Moscow on January 19, 1937, and soon became an extoller of Soviet virtues.[9]

In a general summation of his views, Ambassador Davies advised the State Department on June 6, 1938:

> . . . there is no doubt of the present sincerity of this regime in its desire to maintain Peace. . . .
>
> There are no conflicts of physical interests between the United States and the U.S.S.R. There is nothing that either has which is desired by or could be taken by the other. . . .
>
> There is one situation, where a very serious issue might develop. That is the possible intrusion of the U.S.S.R. through the Comintern into the local affairs of the United States. Fortunately that has been measurably eliminated by the agreement entered into between President Roosevelt and Commissar Litvinov in 1934 [1933]. . . .
>
> A common ground between the United States and the U.S.S.R., and one that will obtain for a long period of time, in my opinion, lies in the fact that both are sincere advocates of World Peace.
>
> In my opinion, there is no danger from communism here, so far as the United States is concerned. . . . [10]

Mr. Davies should have awakened when Litvinov, on June 23, 1938, less than two weeks after the above dispatch, delivered a vigorous speech in which he said that there was a tendency to forget that

> . . . with the preservation of the capitalist system a long and enduring peace is impossible.[11]

---

7. Ibid., pp. 285–287.

8. Ibid., p. 300.

9. See Joseph E. Davies, *Mission to Moscow* (Garden City Publishing, Co., Inc., New York: 1943).

10. *Foreign Relations of the United States: Diplomatic Papers, The Soviet Union, 1933–1939*, pp. 555–557.

11. Ibid., pp. 587–589.

Stalin's Attitude toward Hitler

Stalin's attitude toward Hitler was an important aspect of the European scene of 1938. Despite Hitler's avowed enmity, Stalin consistently attempted conciliation while he built up his armies and fifth columns and fostered quarrels between Hitler and other powers. The theme of conciliation of Germany was touched on by Stalin's top lieutenants, Litvinov, Molotov, and Kaganovitch, time and again in speeches from 1935 to 1938. Hitler was not at the time responsive to these overtures, and Communist alarm at his attitude was abundantly evidenced in speeches made by Molotov in January, 1935, and by Litvinov in November 10, 1936.[12]

They had reason to be alarmed by Hitler's Anti-Comintern Pact of November, 1936. Some indications of the true relations between Russia and Germany in this era were disclosed during the Moscow trials and purges of Stalin's opponents between 1936 and 1938. These men were found guilty of conspiracy with

> the Fascist forces of Germany and Japan in fomenting war against the Soviet Union . . . and planning dismemberment of the U.S.S.R. according to which the Ukraine was to be given to the Germans and the Maritime Provinces to the Japanese.[13]

Stalin continued to pursue conciliatory tactics toward Hitler.[14]

Life in Communist Russia

It is pertinent to note here some of the information as to life in Russia as of 1938 which I collected while visiting Czechoslovakia, Poland, Estonia, Latvia, and Finland.

---

12. Reported in the *New York Times,* of January 29, 1935, and November 11, 1936.

13. *New York Times,* November 27, 1936.

14. General Walter G. Krivitsky, long the principal Soviet agent in Germany, in an article: "Stalin's international policy during the last six years has been a series of maneuvers designed to place him in a favorable position for a deal with Hitler. When he joined the League of Nations, when he proposed the system of collective security, when he sought the hand of France, flirted with Poland, courted Great Britain, intervened in Spain, he calculated his every move with an eye upon Berlin, in the hope that Hitler would find it advantageous to meet his advances. . . .

"The record of Stalin's policy of appeasement of Hitler—both the open and the secret record—reveals that the more aggressive Hitler grew both at home and abroad, the more Stalin pressed his courtship. And the more strenuous became Stalin's wooing, the greater was Hitler's appetite. . . .

"Stalin's outstretched hand was ignored in Berlin. Hitler had other ideas on the subject. But Stalin would not be discouraged." *The Saturday Evening Post,* April 29, 1939, pp. 13, 84.

My informants emphatically denied that Russia was "turning toward capitalism"—an idea then being peddled by some of the foreign press. I was told that although Russian workmen were now paid differential and incentive wages, they could not choose their callings; they could not leave their jobs and had no right to strike; that their wages were fixed by the state; and that if they left their jobs, they could not take their ration cards with them.

Russian farmers were compelled to work on collective farms and were allotted no more than two free acres (usually less) for their own truck gardens; they could not leave the collective farms; if they did, they could get no food.

No real property or inheritance rights existed; therefore any savings from wages could be invested only in government bonds, and thus were reabsorbed by the state. My informants stated that they had never heard of the bonds being paid off.

My informants all agreed that the top Commissars had adopted the pomp and circumstance of the Czarist regime; that the leaders of the Communist Party comprised a sort of middle class, who enjoyed the privileges of substantial incomes, access to clothing and food, and luxuries not available to the masses, but that among the plain people, by Western standards of living, Russia was a land of poverty.

They said further that the purported restoration of freedom of worship by the Communists was an illusion, because the churches had been steadily destroyed or put to other uses. Their number had decreased from 46,000 to under 5,000 and their gold and silver icons had long since been confiscated.

I was told that the people were constantly terrorized by the secret police; that "liquidation" was commonplace; that there were millions of people in Siberian work-camps. The number of political convicts in Siberia under the Czars probably never had exceeded 200,000. My informants insisted that Stalin had swelled the number to over 5,000,000, and that in the camps they were dying at the rate of 500,000 every year.[15]

However, the huge population of political prisoners was at least proof that the spirit of resistance to Communism survived among the Russian people.

I remarked to the President of a neighboring country that Stalin seemed to me to be a reincarnation not only of the policies of Lenin, but also of Ivan the Terrible. He replied that you could add to that a little of Peter the Great and a large amount of Genghis Khan and you had him.

---

15. These facts have long since been corroborated from many sources which may be found in the Hoover Institution on War, Revolution and Peace at Stanford University, Stanford, California.

CHAPTER 11

China in 1938

I DID NOT VISIT THE FAR EAST on my journey in 1938. However the infiltration of Communism into China and the strivings of the Chinese people to be free were a vital part of the whole world struggle of freedom.

I had considerable background knowledge of China, having lived there in the practice of my profession as engineer at the turn of the century. The struggle of the Chinese for liberation from the tyranny of the Manchu dynasty and for freedom from foreign encroachment had begun even before that time.

A young Emperor, Kuang Hsü, at four years of age, had ascended the throne in 1875. He was not permitted to use his imperial powers until 1889. Then he had inaugurated a number of reforms with the aid of an able minister, K'ang Yu-wei. The old Empress Dowager, who was opposed to reforms in general, dethroned and imprisoned the Emperor in 1898. K'ang Yu-wei escaped with his life.

Among K'ang Yu-wei's reforms was the establishment of a Department of Mines.[1] Chang Yen-Mao, the Director-General of the Department, having some supporters among the Manchus around the Empress Dowager, was able to continue this agency under her regime. I was engaged to come from Australia to be the Chief Engineer of the Department. With Chang Yen-Mao's authority, I employed a staff of six American and British engineers, and opened headquarters in both Peking and Tientsin.

The great mineral need of China at that time was to discover sources of iron, other base metals, and metallurgical coal. The Director-General collected information from Chinese sources as to occurrences of the base metals,

---

1. *The Memoirs of Herbert Hoover,* Volume I [The Macmillan Company, New York: 1951], pp. 35–72.

and during our first two years on the job my colleagues and I made long journeys to track down these prospects. I thus traveled in the Hopeh, Shensi, Shansi, Shantung, and Jehol provinces, as well as in Mongolia, Manchuria, and the Gobi Desert areas. On these journeys I was accompanied by one of my engineering assistants, and also had the aid of an accomplished Chinese scholar (a "Mandarin") and a capable Chinese interpreter.

Chinese officials made little distinction between the engineering specialists, and on one occasion, despite my protest that I was not that variety of engineer, at the insistence of Viceroy Li Hung-chang, I inspected parts of the interior canal system and the flood-control works of the Yellow River, where I found Chinese engineers centuries before had demonstrated great ingenuity and my conclusions were to expand their works. On another occasion, I supervised the building of a small ice-free harbor at Chinwangtao on the Gulf of Chihli.

Our engineering activities were brought to an end by the Boxer movement, directed against foreigners and all their works. We hurried from the interior to Tientsin, where we and other foreigners were besieged by the "Boxers" and a foreign-trained Chinese army under orders of the Empress Dowager. My staff and I took part in the defense of the settlement.

Although the Boxer movement was largely mystic and senseless, it did represent a protest of foreign encroachment in China. The foreign settlement in Tientsin, and the similarly besieged foreign legations in Peking, were relieved by military and naval units sent by eleven foreign nations.[2] Afterward I was employed by these Allies to reconstruct the railways and by the bondholders of extensive coal mines of North China. I retired from China early in 1902.[3]

From all this experience I became aware of the deep yearnings of the Chinese for a new era in government. Over the years prior to the Boxer disturbances, many young Chinese had sought education abroad. The number of such students was greatly augmented by the assignment of the American indemnities from the Boxer war to scholarships in technical schools of the United States. The returning students gave leadership to the aspirations of the Chinese people.

It was not until eleven years after the Boxer outbreak that the ferments of freedom reached their explosive point. Under the leadership of Sun Yat-sen the Manchu dynasty was overthrown and the Republic of China was created.

2. For a description of the Boxer movement and the activities of the foreign governments in China at that period, see my *Memoirs*, Volume I, p. 47.

3. I visited Manchuria again in 1910 [1909–*ed.*]. I also visited Chiang Kai-shek at Nanking on an American Government mission in 1946.

In the course of Sun's revolutionary activities he set up a political organization called the Kuomintang, which was to have a profound part in China's evolution. This organization was not made up of elected membership but was an oligarchy of selected men devoted to reform and progress.

It is not the purpose of this chapter to narrate Sun Yat-sen's internal reforms in China, but rather to emphasize China's struggles with encroachments from abroad.

Sun Yat-sen's government joined the Allies in the First World War and sent a delegation to the Peace Conference at Versailles in 1919. Unfortunately the Conference awarded the German-occupied Chinese province of Shantung to Japan. But in 1922, at the Washington Naval Conference, Secretary of State Charles Evans Hughes secured three treaties of high importance to China: (a) the Nine-Power Treaty, which pledged respect for China's sovereignty, independence, territorial and administrative integrity; (b) a treaty to maintain the "open door" policy established by Secretary of State John Hay after the Boxer disturbances; and (c) a Sino-Japanese treaty which promised the evacuation of Japanese from Shantung and the restoration to China of all former German interests in that province.

Meantime, however, the Communist infiltration of China had begun. In 1920, only three years after their seizure of power at home, the Russian Communists sent agents to traffic with the war lords in North China, and at the same time organized a Communist party with headquarters in Shanghai. In 1923, Sun, enlisting the offices of a Russian ambassador passing through Shanghai, requested that the Soviet government send him advisers.[4] In October, 1923, Michael Borodin and General V. Blucher arrived with staffs. They wrote a constitution for the Kuomintang, making Sun Yat-sen President of China for life. They undertook the organization of an army for Sun and arranged that military supplies be furnished from Russia. They established an academy for training army officers at Whampoa near Canton. An indication of Sun's leanings was his declaration at one point that the purposes of the Kuomintang were identical with those of the Russian Communists.

Also in 1923, Leo Karakhan, who was appointed Soviet Ambassador to China, came to Peking to negotiate with the North China war lords. In 1924, an agreement was signed with them, mainly directed toward establishing

---

4. The most penetrating and understanding book that has been published on these subjects is George E. Sokolsky's *The Tinder Box of Asia* (Doubleday, Doran, & Co., Inc., Garden City, New York: 1932). Also, an important narrative is given by George Creel, *Russia's Race for Asia* (The Bobbs-Merrill Company, Inc., Indianapolis, 1949).

friendly relations. Thus, the Kremlin was supporting the northern war lords on one hand and the Kuomintang on the other.

In the meantime two future leaders of the Chinese people had emerged. They were Chiang Kai-shek, a military officer, who was made Director of the Military Academy in 1924, and Chu Teh, a graduate of the Hunan Provincial First Normal School, where he embraced Communism. Chu Teh was later succeeded by Mao Tse-tung, as leader of the Communist party.

Sun Yat-sen died in March 1925, and Chiang Kai-shek, with the cadets of the Military Academy, seized control of the Kuomintang with the approval of the Russians. In late 1926, Chiang broke with the Russians and occupied Shanghai with his military forces in April 1927 and established an anti-Communist regime, with his capital at Nanking.

The Communists, under Borodin's inspiration, staged an insurrection in Hankow and Canton. Chiang suppressed this movement. Borodin was driven from the country, but Mao Tse-tung, with the remnants of this army, was able to build a stronghold in Kiangsi Province, which he was to defend against Chiang's attacks from 1930 to 1934. At that time, Chiang with his Kuomintang Nationalist forces finally drove Mao and his followers onto their "long march" of some 6,000 miles to Yenan in the Shensi Province. Mao there organized the "Chinese Soviet Republic," with military and financial aid from Moscow.

During this same period, Chiang was to meet another great trial. In 1931, the Japanese invaded Manchuria and other parts of North China. The League of Nations declared Japan an aggressor, but failed in its efforts to secure Japanese withdrawal.

In 1937, the Japanese waged an all-out war against China. They ultimately occupied all North and Central China, including the whole Pacific seaboard. In November of that year, Chiang was compelled to move his capital inland to Chungking in Szechwan Province. Some supply routes were still open to him through Hong Kong and Indo-China.

Chiang Kai-shek and the Kuomintang Nationalists, fighting against Japan for a free China, made a temporary truce with the Mao Tse-tung Communists in North China in 1937. However, this "united front" weakened in the latter part of 1938. The Nationalists charged the Communists with violating their pledge and expanding their political control. The Communists accused Chiang of assuming dictatorial powers.[5]

---

5. United States Department of State, *United States Relations with China* [Department of State Publication 3573] (1949), pp. 45–53. See also Don Lohbeck, *Patrick J. Hurley* (Henry Regnery Company, Chicago: 1956), pp. 250–252.

CHAPTER 12

Japan

ANOTHER IMPORTANT COUNTRY I did not visit on this journey was Japan, but I introduce a short description of her situation as it affected the international scene in mid-1938.

Japan was a constitutional monarchy headed by the Emperor, who was also the religious head of the State. The government for the most part was carried on by a parliament (the Diet). The Prime Minister and his Cabinet, being nominally appointed by the Emperor (usually approved by the elder statesmen), were responsible to and subject to the confirmation of the Imperial Diet. The ministry, however, had one peculiarity hitherto unknown in constitutional governments. The army and navy appointed their own members of the ministry.

There were in Japan an able group of leaders, referred to by foreigners as "liberals," who were opposed to military aggression. At times they had dominated the government, as in 1922 when Japan signed the treaties proposed by Secretary of State Charles Evans Hughes on naval reduction, and on the return to China of Shantung Province, which under the terms of the Treaty of Versailles had been conceded to Japan. The life of the liberals was, however, precarious. These men had opposed the "war lords" with courage and at great cost to themselves. Many of them had been assassinated by army extremists. Despite the occasional dominance of the "liberals," Japan was the center of aggressive militarism in the Far East. As I have already stated, in 1931 Japan attacked China, and in effect annexed Manchuria. She rejected the intervention of the League of Nations with which the United States cooperated. In 1937, she started an all-out invasion of China which had resulted in the occupation of northern and central China and the whole of the Pacific seaboard.

Although restraints upon Japanese expansion in China and aid to the Chinese government had been under discussion in Washington prior to mid-1938, none of the American views had been actually adopted at this time.

CHAPTER 13

The Decline and Fall
of the League of Nations

IN THE COURSES OF MY European travels I went to Geneva in February 1938 to ascertain from old friends just what was happening to the League of Nations. By this time, the League was almost twenty years old; it was visibly in its decline and near its fall.

The League had been the offspring of governments of free men. Woodrow Wilson's vision that it should never be polluted by the admission of dictator governments had been abandoned by the inclusion in its membership of Russia, Germany, and some smaller dictator states. Moreover, Prime Minister Chamberlain, some weeks previous to my visit, had announced that the League was "mutilated." He had given a sort of notice that the British did not consider themselves bound by League action such as economic or military sanctions except insofar as the British might agree upon the merits of each case. This straw would have broken the League's back as to collective security, if it had not already been badly injured.

I had discussions with Joseph Avenol, the Frenchman who was the League's Secretary-General, with six other League officials, and with members of our legation in Geneva. The men in the political section of the League seemed utterly discouraged, and Avenol had no realistic suggestion as to how the peace of Europe could be preserved. He blamed Communist conspiracies for the rise of Fascism. He blamed Britain for the rise of Hitler and said that Europe was [witnessing–*ed.*] the full return of the balance-of-power theory of peace—which, he said, "was the negation of collective security."

If the revival of the dictators and balance of power were not enough to kill the League, the network of military alliances and non-aggression pacts outside the League was steadily sapping its vitality. I concluded that as a peace agency it was dead.

However, when these officials blamed the United States for the condition of Europe because of American failure to join the League, it was more than my amiability could take. In reply to such assertions, I asked questions. My notes of them were:

> Do you think that the dragon's teeth sown by the Treaty of Versailles over Mr. Wilson's protest have not contributed to the European situation? Did he not state that the League of Nations could only survive if confined to Free Nations?
>
> Do you think the United States could have after the war compelled Continental states to stop their riotous spending, their unbalanced budgets and their inflation? Or the succession states setting up a maze of trade barriers against each other; or prevented this maze of military alliances; or the incompetence of multiple political parties in their Parliaments which produced chaos in their governmental action; and the rise of Fascism.
>
> Did we not take full part in the League's attempt at land disarmament and did not the nations on the Continent defeat our proposals; did we not bring about the limitations on naval arms after the League had failed; and did we not cooperate in the League's effort to stop Japanese attack on China?

I also pointed out that what they were arguing was that the United States should have undertaken interference in the domestic affairs of a dozen nations on the Continent, which would have required military force. Our discussions wandered about amid abstract phrases and nebulous ideas, always coming back to the failure of the United States to join the League as the cause of Europe's self-made bankruptcy of freedom.

To the League's credit there was due the settlement of a number of disputes between the smaller nations and it provided a forum for debate between larger powers. But in the international political field it was nearly impotent. Its greatest field of success had been the cooperation between nations in the economic, social and health measures. Strong organizations were functioning in all these spheres to the great advantage of the whole world. The League's ally, the International Labor Organization, was establishing standards and methods of great value to economic life. Its other ally, the World Court, was functioning with many member nations adhering to its basic aims and decisions. In fact the efforts at Versailles to organize a lasting peace had been an advance over the previous efforts of five hundred years.

CHAPTER 14

Great Britain

FOLLOWING MY TOUR of the Continent I visited Great Britain. At that time the British were faced with many difficulties, among which was the spread of Communism particularly in their Asian possessions. Because of the low Asian standard of living the people in that part of the Empire were easy prey to Communist promises to divide the wealth of the small percent of "haves" among the huge percent of "have-nots."

British troubles with the Russian regime had begun within a year after the end of the First World War. The Communists in 1920 organized a "Congress of The Peoples of the East" which included representatives from British possessions.

On March 16, 1921, at the time of the signing of the Trade Agreement between Great Britain and Soviet Russia, Cabinet Minister Sir Robert Horne, President of the British Trade Board, in a letter to M. Krassin, the Russian representative in the trade negotiations, complained of the anti-British activities of the Soviet government.[1] He accused the Soviets of seeking to overthrow British rule in India, engaging in various other hostile acts, conspiracies, and furnishing arms for revolutionary purposes.

Despite these early portents, however, the British Ministry in 1924 tried to get along with the Soviet regime by recognition and the exchange of ambassadors. The House of Commons refused to ratify the recognition because of the discovery of a plan to organize Communist cells in the British army and navy. Between May and November, 1926, the Kremlin subscribed over a million dollars to a coal miners' strike in Great Britain. The British government published a White Paper disclosing this interference in its internal affairs.

---

1. *The Times* (London), March 17, 1921.

In 1930, the British made a trade agreement with Russia but terminated the agreement in October, 1932. In March, 1933, some employees of the British Vickers Company, which had been hired by the Soviet government to erect an arms factory, were jailed on charges of sabotage. The British demanded their release and, to give emphasis to their demands, prohibited the importation of most Soviet goods to Britain. The Russians countered with a ban on imports from Britain. On July 1, 1933, the prisoners were released and the embargoes removed. In March, 1934, a new Anglo-Soviet trade agreement was signed.

The British Return from Collective Security to Balance of Power

That Britain was deliberately building up Hitler as a "balance of power" against Stalin and Communist Russia was widely believed on the Continent, and so expressed to me by several leaders whom I interviewed. Their conclusion was based on several arguments: The fostering of a so-called "balance of power" was an old and effective defensive measure for England, with its small population and its widespread possessions in a world of counter-empire building. It was pointed out that Britain had been catholic in her attitude as to when and through whom the balance was to be brought about, and often was compelled to shift her support or opposition to any single nation anywhere that could upset the power balance and thus jeopardize the Empire.

But more pertinent arguments were: (a) that the British Asian empire was being endangered by Communist conspiracies; (b) that the British had acquiesced in Hitler's occupation of the Ruhr; (c) that they had raised no real protest at Hitler's violation of the Versailles Treaty's limitation of 100,000 men under arms while he was building up the German armed forces to 2,000,000 men.

As imperial statecraft was not usually conducted for the benefit of the press or other forms of literature, no open pronouncement on this aspect of British policy could be expected. But if Britain was engaged in these measures, they were in my view amply justified as Britain was the only strong pillar of peace in the crumbling pillars of the European temple of peace.

A Talk with Chamberlain

During my stay in England, Prime Minister Neville Chamberlain invited me to call upon him. After some generalities, he abruptly asked my views on the political situation on the Continent. I replied that no doubt the British were much better informed than I could possibly be, and that I had mostly "hunches" about the political future. He laughed and said that he had plenty of information, and would like a hunch. What I told him was of course not news. However, on returning to my hotel, I made a memorandum of my recollections on the interview. It was in fact my appraisal of the whole continental situation up to that time.

In the course of our conversation I said:

> Prior to the outbreak of war in 1914, the dominant spiritual note of the Continent was hope, confidence, progress and expanding human liberty. The note now, 24 years after, is fear, even despair, and widespread restrictions of personal liberty—excepting a few minor nations. The explosive centers are of course Russia and Germany.
>
> The Russians are arming for defense against Germany. I doubt if the Russians will start anything except conspiracies for the present at least.
>
> Now the face of Germany is turned east. They are a land people; they demand more space and natural resources to exploit with their expanding people.
>
> Being land hungry, the only great land expanses open to them are in Russia and the Balkans.
>
> Add to all this an underlying desire for revenge, a revival of German unification, dictatorship, growing armies, the urge to destroy Communism, and Hitler's unstable character. These are bound to explode sometime.
>
> My hunch is that another Armageddon is coming. My hope is that if it comes it will be on the Plains of Russia, not on the Frontiers of France.
>
> My information is that it will take the Germans another eighteen months to complete their plans. After that anything can happen.[2]

Mr. Chamberlain stated that he was in agreement with my hunch, and added:

---

2. Although I was of course unaware of it at that time, Hitler had made a long secret speech to the top Nazi leaders on November 5, 1937—four months before my visit to Germany—in which he outlined Nazi policies to gain "living space." Hitler discussed three alternatives: (1) "autarchy," which he found wanting for lack of raw materials; (2) participation in a world economy, which he considered blocked by other sea powers for many years; and (3) a rapid expansion eastward to annex Austria and Czechoslovakia and dominate Poland. He discounted the possibility of dangerous interference from France and Great Britain, and therefore favored the third alternative. In stating the problem, Hitler said, "The question for Germany is where the greatest possible conquest could be made at lowest cost." (Office of United States Chief of Counsel for Prosecution of Axis Criminality, *Nazi Conspiracy and Aggression* [Documents from International Military Tribunal at Nurnberg, Germany], U.S. Government Printing Office, Washington: 1946), Vol. III, pp. 295ff.)

The weakness of the democratic powers is France. You have seen it; they are now in alliance with Russia. In consequence, Hitler may think he had better polish off the weakest first.

If from this interview I had been called upon to describe Mr. Chamberlain, I would have said he was a man of peace, integrity, devotion to principles and to duty as he envisioned them, together with all the pleasing attributes of what the British call "a gentleman."

Another prominent Briton with whom I exchanged views during my stay in London was Lord Lothian, who came to breakfast with me. I had known him well as Philip Kerr, secretary to Prime Minister Lloyd George during the First World War. He had called upon me in Palo Alto some time before my journey to discuss American attitudes toward the European scene. At this breakfast in London, I summarized to him the "hunch" I had expressed to Prime Minister Chamberlain, with which he said he was in full agreement. At this time Lord Lothian was an isolationist on the question of possible British military operations on the Continent. After this conversation he sent me a copy of a speech he had made in the House of Lords a year before (March 2, 1937) stating his view.

Some paragraphs were profoundly prophetic:

> ... This new alliance system, now ennobled by the phrase "collective security," began with the military alliances between France and the Little Entente and Poland. It has now been extended to Russia by the Treaty of Mutual Assistance between France and Russia, a Treaty which has its duplicate or its parallel in the Treaty between Czechoslovakia and Russia. That is one side of the alliance system. Inevitably, as has always happened in the past ... that system has begun to produce an alliance system on the other side. It produced what is called the Rome-Berlin axis, it produced the Anti-Comintern Agreement between Germany and Japan.
>
> ... Collective security is supported by three groups of people. First, there are the genuine believers in peace ... who believe ... that if there is agreement between Russia and France and ourselves then we shall have in some way exorcised the spectre of war. It does not do anything of the kind. It produces a counter-alliance, and in the end we go from one crisis to another ... until finally we get to a state of tension in a world knit by alliances, so that by accident a fool or a knave presses the button which lets off a world war. . . .
>
> The second group consists of those who frankly want an Anti-Fascist Alliance, people who are much more preoccupied with the dangers of Fascism than the dangers of Communism. . . . I see myself no fundamental difference

between the two systems of government. They are both wholly unfriendly to and completely contradictory of the institutions in which we ourselves believe. . . .

Finally, there are those people whose ideas are based upon fear of Germany. . . .

. . . the Franco-Russian Treaty of Mutual Assistance has the inevitable effect that, if a war breaks out, it tends to make certain that the war shall be in the West and directed at the West and will not be concerned in the first instance with Eastern Europe. . . .

. . . the only possible cause we could be fighting for would be to insist on the maintenance of the anarchy of Europe. . . . I venture to think that that is not a cause for which it is worth while laying down the lives of British men. . . .[3]

Other British Problems

Internally no less than externally, Great Britain was confronted with grave difficulties. The First World War had wiped out much of the flower of her youth. At the start of the war the British had raised the first million of their army from volunteers and thus among the best they had; they were mostly exterminated, and further fearful losses followed as the war went on.

The British had also been weakened economically by shifts in world production and trade. Before 1914, Britain had obtained raw materials cheaply as the return cargo for her coal exports, and had functioned as the "corner grocery store" of Europe. But the increased use of oil and electricity had disturbed the raw-material cycle.

Worse still, the British had turned to cartels and trusts rather than to reliance on a more vigorous competitive system. Because of these trusts or cartels, the attitude of industrialists was to gain profits through price fixing and controlled distribution, rather than through decreasing costs by plant improvement, as under our American system, where trusts or cartels are prohibited.

A Parliamentary inquiry had been made into Britain's industrial problems. An old acquaintance and member of this inquiry, Lord Phillimore, gave me a table of unit output per man in different industries, compared with that

---

3. [Great Britain, Parliament,] *The Parliamentary Debates,* Fifth Series, Volume CIV, House of Lords, Second Volume of Session 1936–37 (London: Printed and published by His Majesty's Stationery Office, 1937), pp. 391–399 [403–*ed.*]

of the United States. It showed that from 1¼ to 4 times as many men were required to secure the same output as in the United States. The average over-all ratio showed that one American workman produced as much as 2.12 English workmen.

There were, however, some certainties about the British. Knowing them as I did, having lived and worked both in England and the Commonwealth, I had no doubt that Britain would come back. With a people of rugged character, deep religious faith, devotion to freedom, and with a virile oncoming generation, no decline and fall was in prospect for this nation—if it were not drawn into another war.

CHAPTER 15

My Report to the American People on the Forces of Motion in Europe

WHILE WAITING IN LONDON for the departure home on the fog-bound *Normandie*, and during the voyage, I put together my impressions of my European visit for an address to the American people, for which I had received insistent invitations by cable.

I found myself under some limitations. In stating my conclusions, I could not use as confirmation any quotations from the European leaders who had given me their confidences so freely. There was a further limitation. I was convinced that a second world war was inevitable from the clash of Communism under Stalin and German Fascism under Hitler. Yet hundreds of devoted men in Europe were desperately trying to save the peace, and it would have been wrong for me to minimize or discourage their efforts by predicting that their efforts would be doomed to failure.

I delivered three nation-wide broadcasts. The first of these was from New York on March 31, 1938; the second from San Francisco on April 8; and the third from Oklahoma City on May 5.[1]

A few paragraphs will indicate the tenor of these speeches, all of which were directed to warning the American people of the rising dangers in Europe.[2]

My Address from New York

It seems unnecessary to state to an American audience that we are not isolated from the fateful forces that sweep through Europe. . . . While we cannot wholly protect ourselves against these intellectual, economic, or political

---

1. For the full text, see [Herbert Hoover] *Addresses Upon the American Road, 1933–1938* [Charles Scribner's Sons, New York: 1938], pp. 309–324, 325–334, 343–354.

2. When I used the word "democracy" in this speech 25 years ago it covered the then current meaning of this term — representative government. In the intervening twenty-five years, the word

forces, it is imperative that we understand them. Through understanding, we can avoid some mistakes. We must abate some of their violence.

. . . I am not here tonight to tell governments or nations abroad what they should do. It is not the right of any American to advise foreign peoples as to their policies. But it is our duty to consider for ourselves the forces outside our borders which inevitably affect us. . . .

. . . the rise of dictatorships . . . [has] certainly not diminished in nineteen years. At one moment (if we include the Kerensky regime in Russia) over 500,000,000 people in Europe embraced the forms of . . . [representative government].

Today, if we apply the very simple tests of free speech, free press, free worship and . . . protections to individuals and minorities, then liberty has been eclipsed amongst about 370,000,000 of these people. . . .

The . . . movement today . . . is the race to arms. Every nation in Europe . . . is now building for war or defense more feverishly than ever before in its history. . . . Europe today is a rumbling war machine, without the men yet in the trenches. . . .

. . . There is a brighter side. Their recovery from the depression has been better than ours. They have little unemployment. . . . I do not believe general war is in immediate prospect. War preparations are not complete. The spirit is yet one of defense. . . . New balances of power emerge to neutralize each other. . . . groups are constantly working for peace and appeasement of the strains. . . . Many of their statesmen have skill and great devotion in guiding the frail craft of peace around the rocks in the rapids. But the world cannot go on forever building up for war and increasing fear and hate. Yet, so long as there is peace, there is hope. . . .

There sounds constantly through this labyrinth the shrill note of new philosophies of government and the echoes of old orders of society. . . .

And these movements contain . . . many dangers for the American people. . . .

. . . Fourteen nations in Europe, with 240,000,000 people, have adopted these notions of Fascism. . . . [Russia, with 140,000,000 people had long since adopted Communism.]

Let no man mistake that we in America have avoided the infection of these European systems. . . .

"democracy" has been so corrupted as to be meaningless—both the Communists and the Fascists have claimed it. To avoid confusion for the reader I have used the term "representative government" in this text.

My Address from San Francisco

In my second address I tried to describe what free California would be like if located in Europe amid the totalitarian governments. I said:

If we [in California] had 500,000 troops and 2,000 aeroplanes looking at us hatefully from over the Oregon line, another 400,000 men and 2,000 planes ready to march over the Nevada line, and another few hundred thousand being drilled in Arizona ready to pounce upon us, this would be a less comfortable place. And if we had to pay taxes for about 400,000 men in our own State to make faces at these sister States, then it would be still more uncomfortable. And if we had to continue all sorts of shifting alliances with our neighbors to balance off their powers for evil, it would be a still more anxious place to live. . . .

If we had an up-to-date authoritarian state, there are still other possibilities of discomfort. Then your soul belongs generally to the state. If you carry over the old idea that perhaps it belongs to you, then you go to a concentration camp to rest your nerves. If you are a farmer you plant what the agricultural policeman tells you to plant. And you raise the pigs and cows . . . [the dictator] thinks are good for the state. If you are a worker you work where you are told. And you get the wages you are told. Your trade union having been dissolved you can belong to a government recreation project. You will also be taught to sing cheerful songs in the recreation hours and to march all about. You have social security if you conform. If you do not conform you get security in [a] concentration camp. . . . So as not to have your doubts raised and your feelings harried by critics of this more redundant life . . . [you] are just put away in the same concentration camps. Your freedom of speech is a sort of one-way street. You do gain something by saving half the public speeches in the country by doing away with all those of the opposition. . . .

But let no man underestimate the dangers to free men [from either Communism or Fascism]. . . . [They] not only . . . represent . . . ruthless economic organization at the sacrifice of all personal liberty. . . . [They] represent the extinction of pity and mercy which Christianity gave the world. . . . [They] represent] an upsurge of abhorrent brutality. . . .

One long-held conviction has been greatly hardened [during this journey]. That is that we have grown a long way from Europe in our century and a half of national life. A new race with its own soul has grown on this continent. The life-stream of this nation is the generations of millions of human particles acting under impulses of freedom and advancing ideas gathered from a thousand native springs. These springs and rills have gathered into streams which have nurtured and fertilized the spirit of this great people over centuries.

. . . Of one thing we may be sure. When a great race has been refreshed over centuries with the waters of liberty, those living waters will not be denied it.

My Address from Oklahoma City

I referred as follows to the rising Communism or Fascism of many European states:

> Not one of those 14 totalitarian nations started with the intention to surrender liberty. They started by adopting panaceas to cure slumps or overcome economic difficulties. They all undertook . . . [change] under some title, usually Planned Economy. In variable doses they undertook credit and currency manipulation, price fixing, pump priming, and spending with huge deficits and huge taxes. Step by step they sapped the vitality of free enterprise by government experiments in dictation and socialistic competition. They had the illusion that . . . [there was] a middle road between Fascism on the right and Socialism on the left . . .
>
> Every succeeding step was egged on by politicians fanning class hate, exaggerating every abuse and besmirching every protesting voice. Every step was accompanied by greater corruption of the electorate, increasing intellectual and moral dishonesty in government. . . .
>
> These forces finally jammed the mainspring by which private enterprise is moved to production. . . .
>
> Let there be no mistake; a new way of life is rising in the world. It directly challenges all our American concepts of free men. And let me tell you that upon my recent journey over and over again men of responsibility breathed to me one prayer. They did not seek military alliances with us. They did not seek loans. What they prayed was that we hold the fort of liberty in America. For that is the hope of the world.

A Note on Revolutions

During my 1938 journey, I had some opportunity to observe the workings of deep-seated revolutions. In such revolutions, of necessity, new regimes of men with great ambitions come into authority. By propaganda the people are pressured into a fever pitch of self-sacrifice; they become imbued with a sense of new purpose and new glory. Their constant impulse is to new adventures and new demonstrations of national power. Sooner or later these dynamisms take the form of a demand for national expansion and military conquest.

That was the history of the French Revolution. The American Revolution, too, gave birth to such spirit and such an urge to expand. Fortunately, its dynamism spent itself in the conquest of an almost vacant hinterland and not in war with other nations.

To me, as the result of my journey, only one conclusion was possible: that the two revolutions of Fascism and Communism were bound to clash and produce a world explosion, and that our problem was to keep the United States from being involved.

A Revolution in American Foreign Policies

CHAPTER 16
President Roosevelt Abandons Isolationism and Enters Foreign Politics

IN HIS FIRST FOUR YEARS in office, President Roosevelt had made speeches and statements on public affairs totaling more than 400,000 words. Of these, fewer than 3,000—the equivalent of one speech—concerned our foreign relations. The recurrent theme was one of extreme isolationism, as reflected in his frequent reiteration of George Washington's famous pronouncement of no foreign entanglements.[1]

There were other indications of Mr. Roosevelt's isolationist attitude. Although in those early years, as throughout his Presidency, he commanded an overwhelming Senate majority, yet he made no real effort to secure passage of even American adherence to the World Court. Woodrow Wilson was one of the creators. Mr. Harding and Mr. Coolidge had urged its adoption. I urged it and I had secured through Elihu Root such amendments to our adherence as would meet the Senate criticism of it.

Despite the growing danger from aggressive dictators in Germany, Japan, and Russia, he reduced defense expenditures by about twenty-five percent from those of my Administration. And in 1935, 1936 and 1937, he secured passage of Neutrality Acts, which effectively prevented the United States from supplying arms even to nations struggling for freedom, thus providing an advantage to the aggressor nations which had their own facilities for arms manufacture.

On October 5, 1937, a great change came to Mr. Roosevelt. On this day he made a dramatic reversal of his previous attitude in an address at Chicago

---

1. President Roosevelt used the words "entanglements" or "unentangled" in public statements on August 31, October 2, 17, and 23, 1935; and on June 12 and August 18, 1936.

which became known as the "quarantine" speech.[2] Although missing from the advance press release, the following paragraphs were given in the speech as delivered:

> ... The peace, the freedom and the security of ninety percent of the population of the world is being jeopardized by the remaining ten percent who are threatening a breakdown of all international order and law. Surely the ninety percent who want to live in peace under law and in accordance with moral standards that have received almost universal acceptance through the centuries, can and must find some way to make their will prevail ...
>
> It seems to be unfortunately true that the epidemic of world lawlessness is spreading.
>
> When an epidemic of physical disease starts to spread, the community approves and joins in a quarantine of the patients in order to protect the health of the community against the spread of the disease.[3]

While I agreed with the President's statement of the situation, I did not agree with the implication that the United States should engage in intervention in foreign nations. Incidentally, it soon developed that Stalin was not included among the objectionable dictators.

Secretary of State Hull, who until this time had been a vigorous supporter of isolationism, was greatly surprised and grieved at the implication of this statement. He later wrote that his efforts for peace were set back six months.[4]

The President himself somewhat retreated from the implications of his Chicago pronouncement in a press conference the next day, as may be seen from a portion of the transcript:

> **Q.** ... you were speaking ... of something more than moral indignation. ....
> Is anything contemplated? Have you moved?
>
> **The President:** No; just the speech itself.

Questioned on how he reconciled this with the Neutrality Act and whether it would mean economic sanctions, the President replied:

---

2. W. L. Langer and S. E. Gleason, in their book *The Challenge to Isolation, 1937–1940* (Harper & Brothers Publishers, New York: 1952), pp. 18ff., make much of this speech to "prove" Mr. Roosevelt's anti-isolationism. But the book ignores his consistent role throughout the previous four years.

3. [Samuel I. Rosenman, comp.] *The Public Papers and Addresses of Franklin D. Roosevelt, 1937* [volume] [The Macmillan Company, New York, 1941], p. 410.

4. *The Memoirs of Cordell Hull* (The Macmillan Company, New York: 1948), Vol. I, p. 545.

No, not necessarily. . . . "sanctions" is a terrible word to use. They are out of the window. . . .

Q. Is there a likelihood that there will be a conference of the peace-loving nations?

The President: No; conferences are out of the window. You never get anywhere with a conference.

Q. Foreign papers put it as an attitude without a program.

The President: That was the London *Times*. . . .

Q. Wouldn't it be almost inevitable if any program is reached, that our present Neutrality Act will have to be overhauled?

The President: Not necessarily. . . .[5]

Whatever the impression such qualifications were intended to give, this speech marked the end of the President's isolationism. It was quickly followed by American entry into foreign power politics. Three months later in January 1938, Mr. Roosevelt sought British opinion of a Presidential appeal to the nations of the world for international cooperation. Prime Minister Chamberlain's initial response was negative, although he reconsidered and sent a message of approval two weeks later. Mr. Roosevelt's appeal was never made.[6]

The Prime Minister, on January 14, informed the President that he proposed to recognize the Italian conquest of Ethiopia. Mr. Roosevelt protested this move. However, after the British granted this recognition on April 16, 1938, the President approved the British action as a product of peaceful negotiation, but noted that we adhered to the policy of non-recognition of the results of aggression.[7] This policy declaration had been made during my Administration and had been applied to Japanese conquests in China.[8]

---

5. *The Public Papers and Addresses of Franklin D. Roosevelt*, 1937 [volume], pp. 423–424. For a more detailed account of the "quarantine" speech and subsequent confusion over it, see Charles A. Beard, *American Foreign Policy in the Making, 1932–1940* (Yale University Press, New Haven: 1946), pp. 186–222.

6. Sumner Welles, *The Time for Decision* (Harper and Brothers Publishers, New York: 1944), pp. 65ff.; Keith Feiling, *The Life of Neville Chamberlain* (Macmillan & Co., Ltd., London: 1946), pp. 336ff.; part of Chamberlain's letter to Roosevelt (unpublished) appears in Charles C. Tansill, *Back Door to War* (Henry Regnery Company, Chicago: 1952), pp. 368ff.; *The Memoirs of Anthony Eden, Earl of Avon: Facing the Dictators* (Houghton Mifflin Company, Boston: 1962), pp. 622–645.

7. [Samuel I. Rosenman, comp.] *The Public Papers and Addresses of Franklin D. Roosevelt*, 1938 [volume] (The Macmillan Company, New York: 1941), pp. 248–249.

8. *The Memoirs of Herbert Hoover, 1920–1933, The Cabinet and the Presidency* (The Macmillan Company, New York: 1952), pp. 372ff.

CHAPTER 17

Actions Stronger than Words

ON JANUARY 4, 1939, in an address to the Congress, the President projected the United States into a more definite role of action in foreign affairs, saying:

> ... There are many methods short of war, but stronger and more effective than mere words, of bringing home to aggressor governments the aggregate sentiments of our own people.[1]

It was not long before action began. The same day, in a conference with Secretary of War Woodring and the General Staff, Mr. Roosevelt proposed the immediate manufacture of 40,000 planes which he wished to place at the disposal of the British and French. The General Staff finally convinced him that this would take years, and induced him to agree to a program of 6,000 planes.[2]

About a month later, on January 31, 1939, at a secret conference with the Senate Military Affairs Committee at the White House, Mr. Roosevelt told the Senators: "Our frontiers are somewhere in France"; that he was working closely with Britain and France and that he meant his statement of "action more effective than mere words; that ... the United States must get into the fight against dictators."[3] As the meeting was "confidential," the half dozen Senators, as was inevitable, promptly relayed details of it to their friends. The White House violently denied this latter statement, but newspaper

---

1. [Samuel I. Rosenman, comp.,] *The Public Papers and Addresses of Franklin D. Roosevelt,* 1939 [volume] (The Macmillan Company, New York: 1941), p. 3.
2. Information to me personally from Secretary Woodring.
3. These statements were reported to me separately by Senators Nye, Bridges, and Holman, all members of the Committee. I received indirect corroboration from Senators Sheppard, Clark, and Johnson (Colorado) who were also present. They all agreed that Mr. Roosevelt had said these things.

correspondents reported it as authentic.[4] On the floor of the Senate the President was denounced for secretly trying to commit us to war.[5]

In consequence of the President's proposal of action "more than words," I made a nation-wide broadcast from Chicago a month later, on February 1, 1939. I analyzed possible kinds of action in international life that would be "short of war":

> I have no need to recite the malevolent forces rampant in the world. In twenty nations desperate peoples have surrendered personal liberty for some form of authoritarian government. They are placing their trust in dictatorship clothed in new ideologies of Utopia. Some of them are making war or are aggressively threatening other nations. The world is taut with fear. Five times more men are under arms than before the Great War.
>
> We in America are indignant at the brutalities of these systems and their cruel wrongs to minorities. We are fearful of the penetration of their ideologies. We are alarmed at their military preparations and their aggressiveness....
>
> We have need to strip emotion from these questions as much as we can. They are questions of life or death not only to men but also to nations.
>
> We have need to appraise coolly these dangers. We have need of sober, analytical debate upon the policies of government toward them. We must do so without partisanship....
>
> Mr. Roosevelt ... says we must use methods stronger than words and short of war. He asks for armament to back his extensions....
>
> ... The only known effective methods short of war and more than words are that we either support one side with supplies of food, raw materials, finance and munitions, or that we deny these to the other side by embargoes, boycotts or other economic sanctions....
>
> ... These proposals to use some sort of coercion against nations are of course a complete departure from neutrality in other peoples' wars. It is the method of coercion, not persuasion. It is in direct violation of Secretary Hull's reaffirmation, on which the ink is but sixty days dry, of an old Amer-

---

4. *The Public Papers and Addresses of Franklin D. Roosevelt,* 1939 [volume]. pp. 110–115. See also [Samuel I. Rosenman, comp.,] *The Public Papers and Addresses of Franklin D. Roosevelt,* 1940 [volume] [The Macmillan Company, New York: 1941], pp. 323–324.

5. *New York Times,* February 2, 1939; U.S. Congress, *Congressional Record:* proceedings and debates, 76th Congress, 3d Session, Volume 86, Part 12, Senate, October 28, 31, 1940, pp. 13598ff., 13604ff.

ican policy that "the intervention of any state in the internal and external affairs of another is inadmissible. . . . "

. . . Such policies are provocative of reprisals and must be backed by armament far beyond that required for defense of the Western Hemisphere. If we are to provoke we must be prepared to enforce.

. . . Economic pressures inevitably run into pressures upon civil populations. Civil populations are mostly women and children. The morals of starvation by force rank no higher than killing from the air. . . .

Let me say at once than any form of direct or indirect coercion of nations is force and is the straight path to war itself. No husky nation will stand such pressures without bloody resistance.

Those who think in terms of economic sanctions should also think in terms of war.

It will be said that these measures will preserve peace; that if nations know we will throw our weight into the balance they will not transgress on others. That is world-wide power politics. That is the exact theory of joining in the balance of power throughout the world. That setting has in the long and tragic history of Europe inevitably exploded in war.

All this becomes the most momentous change in American policies of peace and war since we entered the Great War.

Moreover the European democracies have accepted it as a complete change of national policy by the United States. If it is not a proposal to change radically our policies then they are under a misapprehension.

But to determine the issue, let me propose some questions that the American people deserve to have answered.

1. Shall we reverse our traditional policies at this time?
2. Shall we set ourselves up to determine who the aggressor is in the world?
3. Shall we engage in embargoes, boycotts, economic sanctions against aggressor nations?
4. Shall we do this where the Western Hemisphere is not attacked?
5. Shall we provide an armament greater than that necessary to protect the Western Hemisphere from military invasion?
6. Shall we take collective action with other nations to make these more than words and short of war policies effective?
7. Are we to be the policeman of the world?

Certainly it is due to Mr. Roosevelt, to the Congress, and to the American people that we know exactly what all this means. The Congress should have this adventure clarified before we go blindly into great increases in armament.

The Dangers of the Western Hemisphere

Before we answer these questions and before we venture into these paths of force and conflict, even short of war, we should realistically examine how serious the so-called imminent dangers are from aggressive nations.

Our dangers are obviously in two forms—the penetration of their ideologies, which would destroy democracies, and their military aggressiveness.

And their military aggressiveness has to be appraised in two aspects. First, the direct dangers to the Western Hemisphere, and second, our further concern in the dangers to our sister democracies in Europe and Asia.

Penetration of Ideologies

The first segment of this danger is the ideologies. The penetration of these ideologies, whether it be the Communism of Russia, the National Socialism of Germany, or the Fascism of Italy, is an internal problem for each country where they penetrate. Ideas cannot be cured with battleships or aeroplanes. I say this as I do not assume that we intend to attack dictators or extirpate ideologies in their home sources. That would lead the world to worse destruction than the religious wars of the Middle Ages.

Our job of defense against these un-American ideologies is to eliminate Communist, Socialist and Fascist ideas and persons from our own institutions. It is to maintain the ideals of free men, which make this unprofitable soil for such alien seed.

I am confident that if the lamp of liberty can be kept alight these ideologies will yet die of their own falsity. They spring not from moral and spiritual inspirations but from the cupidity of men. In any event no additional appropriations for arms will settle those problems.

The Military Dangers

The second segment of danger is that of military attack of the dictatorships upon democracies.

And we may first explore the imminent dangers of military attack upon the Western democracies. And again we should consider it in the light of realism rather than the irritating words that emanate from world capitals.

Our people must realize that even if there were no dictators present, the blunders in the peace treaties, the pressures of population, the impoverishment of peoples will create periodic European crises. That has been the history of Europe since long before America was born.

As terrifying as these crises look in the morning paper, there are more realistic pressures for peaceful adjustments than for war.

Since the Great War land fortifications for defense have increased in power faster than offensive land weapons. The dictatorships know that if they were to attack the Western democracies they would probably find their land and sea defenses impregnable. Attack from the air offers hideous destruction, but it also brings sobering reprisals. It stiffens resolution and it does not capture capital cities. It is my belief that the Western democracies of Europe can amply defend themselves against military attack.

And in this connection we must not close our eyes to one condition under which the American people, disregarding all other questions, might join in European war. We are a humane people, and our humanity can be overstrained by brutality. That was one of the causes of our entry into the last war. For instance, if wholesale attack were made upon women and children by the deliberate destruction of cities from the air, then the indignation of the American people might not be restrained from action.

I do not believe officials of any nation have become so foolish or dare the depth of barbarism of such an undertaking. The indignation in the United States today at such killings in Spain and China, where it is excused as the accident of attempt to demoralize munitions supply, should be warning of the temper which would be raised.

There are other realistic forces which weigh against military attack by the dictatorships on the democracies. Despite so-called "demands" the dictatorships are in reality mainly interested elsewhere. The face of Germany is turned more East than toward Western Europe. The face of Japan is turned West into Asia. The Russians are amply engaged at home. The Italians claim grievances with England and France arising out of the treaties under which they came into the Great War, but these are not impossible of solution.

Beyond all this, every one of the totalitarian states has its own grave internal weaknesses.

Above all, the common people in no country in Europe want war. They are terrified of it.

Do not think I believe the situation is not dangerous in Europe. Far from it. But it is not so imminent as the speeches abroad might make it appear. And what is not imminent is often preventable.

Obviously our dangers are much less than those of the overseas democracies. The Western Hemisphere is still protected by a moat of 3000 miles of ocean on the East and 6000 miles on the West. No aeroplane has yet been built that can come one-third the way across the Atlantic and one-fifth of the way across the Pacific with destructive bombs and fly home again. In any event, these dictatorships have nothing to gain by coming 3000 miles or 6000 miles to attack the Western Hemisphere. So long as our defenses are maintained they have everything to lose.

That any of these dictatorships, whether Japan, Germany, Italy, or Russia, or all of them together, have the remotest idea of military attack upon the Western Hemisphere is sheer hysteria.

It will be said that we must be prepared to go across the seas and enforce lawful rights for American trade by military action. I do not agree with that thesis. There always comes a time, with patience, when such ends can be accomplished by the processes of peace.

Some Ultimate Possible Consequences

There are other factors that we need to consider also before we decide to use force beyond protection of the Western Hemisphere. We must not refuse to look at the possible ultimates before we start down these paths.

If we join with force in Europe or Asia, even though it be short of war, we must consider its consequences should it lead to war. For that is the most probable result. The call to join is based upon the preservation of human liberty in the world. Our first purpose is to maintain liberty in America. If civilization based on liberty fails in the United States it is gone from the earth. We must safeguard that, not only in our own interest but in the interest of the world. . . .

This world can never reach peace by threats and force. If this is to be the blind leadership of men, nothing can save the world from a catastrophe to civilization.

No nation has alone built this civilization. We all live by heritages which have been enriched by every nation and every century. And to save this civilization there must be a changed attitude of men. Our country standing apart can make a contribution of transcendent service in holding aloft the banner of moral relationships.

If we are to hold that banner of morals aloft the people of America should express unhesitatingly their indignation against wrong and persecution. They should extend aid to the suffering.

We should not be isolationists in promoting peace by the methods of peace. We should not be isolationists in proposals to join in the most healing of all processes of peace—economic cooperation to restore prosperity.

But surely all reason, all history, all our own experience show that wrongs cannot be righted and durable peace cannot be imposed on nations by force, threats, economic pressures, or war. I want America to stand against that principle if it is the last nation under that banner. I want it to stand there because it is the only hope of preserving liberty on this continent.

That is America's greatest service to mankind.[6]

---

6. Herbert Hoover, *Further Addresses upon the American Road, 1938–1940* [Charles Scribner's Sons, New York: 1940], 93–103.

1939: In Europe, a Year of Monstrous Evils for Mankind

CHAPTER 18

The Rape of Czechoslovakia

HITLER, HAVING PROVED the soft attitude of the British and French to-ward his absorption of bordering German peoples by the occupation of the Rhineland and Austria, now moved to take some three million Sudeten Germans from Czechoslovakia.[1] Thereby he would again be on the way to carry out one of his *idées fixes*—German racial unity.

For clarity as to what happened to Czechoslovakia in 1939, it is necessary to reach into the background.

The Czechs had failed to carry out the terms of the treaty they had signed with the Allies at Saint-Germain-en-Laye on September 10, 1919 to fashion their government on the model of Switzerland where different nationalities enjoyed a large amount of autonomy and a minimum of centralized authority. Because of this failure discontent had grown steadily over the years among the different nationality groups, particularly the Sudeten Germans.

On May 16, 1935, Czechoslovakia made a military alliance with Communist Russia. It was probably unpalatable to Hitler.

On May 19, 1935, there was a general election in Czechoslovakia in which the Sudeten Germans won forty-four out of seventy-two seats in the Czech Parliament. (There were three hundred seats in all.)

In 1937, the Sudetens made repeated demands upon the Czech government in Prague for greater local autonomy.

In February, 1938, Hitler announced that he would interest himself in their protection.

On April 24, 1938, Konrad Henlein, the Sudeten leader, presiding over a mass meeting at Carlsbad, made eight specific demands relating to more

---

1. In Section II, Chapter 8, I have given other details of the background of the Czech situation prior to 1937.

autonomy. The government refused the demands. Hitler invited Henlein to visit him and sent some troops to the Czech border "for maneuvers." Benes responded by calling up certain army reserves.

On May 21, Benes declared his determination to "let nothing destroy Czechoslovakia's democracy." He described the draft of the nationalities statute, and he emphasized the government's wish to negotiate with all minority groups in an effort to achieve domestic unity.[2]

On June 8, 1938, not satisfied, the Sudeten German party presented to Premier Hodza a memorandum that went even beyond Henlein's previous demands.

On July 26, 1938, the Benes ministry offered to compromise and introduced a bill in the Parliament that would have established full cantonal government. It was too late. The Sudeten Germans' demands had by now advanced to separation from the Czech state and joining Hitler's Germany.

The situation was becoming dangerous to the general peace. In early August, Prime Minister Chamberlain sent Lord Runciman, a member of the British Cabinet, to Prague with instructions "to conciliate, advise and report." Runciman concluded that the only solution was a plebiscite in the Sudeten German districts to determine which of these wished to remain in Czechoslovakia or to join Germany.

On September 8, 1938, the Czech dilemma was compounded by a mass meeting of all racial minority representatives at which each bloc demanded greater autonomy for itself.

Hitler fed the fire by a violent speech on September 12, demanding the "right of self-determination" for the Sudetens. The Benes ministry replied by declaring martial law in the Sudeten districts and issuing a warrant for the arrest of Henlein for treason.

On September 13, 1938, Prime Minister Chamberlain swallowed a thousand years of British pride and telegraphed Hitler offering to go to Germany for a conference. The meeting took place at Berchtesgaden on September 15, 1938. The Prime Minister urged the Runciman plan as providing for an orderly transfer of Sudeten districts to Germany. Hitler was belligerent but indicated that this new idea might be acceptable and agreed to undertake no hostilities while Chamberlain consulted the French and Czech governments.

On September 19, the Czech government announced that it would consent neither to the Runciman plebiscite nor to the Anglo-French Plan of Septem-

---

2. *New York Times,* May 22, 1938.

ber 18 which called for the cession of the Sudeten districts to Germany. Hitler now mobilized thirty divisions on the Czech frontier.

On September 21, 1938, the Czech government agreed to accept the Runciman plan.

On September 22, Chamberlain again journeyed to Germany, this time to Godesberg, only to find that Hitler had increased his demands and had set the time of the German invasion of Czechoslovakia a few days hence.

On September 23, with their minds made up that war was inevitable, the British and French governments notified the Czechs that they could not now advise them to accept the German terms. The Czechs mobilized the same day.

On September 24, the French ordered a partial mobilization of their army.

On September 27, the British ordered their fleet mobilized.

On September 28, Prime Minister Chamberlain was in the act of describing the situation to the House of Commons as war. In the midst of his address, he was handed an invitation from Hitler to meet at Munich with Premier Daladier and Mussolini.[3] It appears that this meeting was proposed to Mussolini by Daladier and that it was urged upon Hitler by the Italian dictator. The question of who was responsible for Hitler's change in direction at the critical moment is the subject of a large amount of historical speculation. At this distance, it would seem that the war preparations of the Western Powers, plus Mussolini's intervention, were the major factors in his change.

Munich

An agreement dated September 29, 1938, was signed by Hitler, Chamberlain, Daladier, and Mussolini at Munich. It provided for the transfer of the majority of Sudeten districts to Germany under the supervision of an international commission and a pact by the signatories including Hitler, guaranteeing the independence of the remaining Czech state.[4]

---

3. President Roosevelt also added his urgings to those of Mussolini, but they arrived after the meeting had been agreed upon. His colleagues in Washington credited the President with having brought about the Munich conference, but subsequent British disclosures show that Chamberlain, among the Western statesmen, had played the major role in this regard. I shall comment on Roosevelt's participation later.

4. The utter dishonesty of Hitler's signature is sufficiently indicated by the Nurnberg documents which show that he had prepared to invade Czechoslovakia months before. [Office of United States Chief of Counsel for Prosecution of Axis Criminality,] *Nazi Conspiracy and Aggression* (United States Government Printing Office, Washington: 1946), Vol. I, pp. 515ff.

On September 29, 1938, the Polish government added to the confusion by demanding that the Czechs transfer to Poland the district of Teschen, in which there was a large Polish population.

Chamberlain returned to England with his famous announcement that there would be "peace for our time." Daladier, like Chamberlain, received a tumultuous welcome from the people for having aided in preserving peace.

On October 11, 1938, President Roosevelt wrote Prime Minister Mackenzie King [of Canada—*ed.*]:

> . . . I can assure you that we in the United States rejoice with you, and the world at large, that the outbreak of war was averted.[5]

But the word "Munich" was to become a world-wide synonym for appeasement. Attacks on Prime Minister Chamberlain for his "policy of general appeasement" grew to a fever pitch. British officials led the denunciation. Alfred Duff Cooper, First Lord of the Admiralty, resigned October 3, 1938, in protest against the government's action. Anthony Eden raised a bitter outcry. Lloyd George declared ". . . a bad peace is no peace at all."[6] The most eminent of the critics was Winston Churchill who charged that the country was "without adequate defence or effective international security."[7] He further decried the "errors of judgment" in foreign policy.[8] Lord Lloyd criticized the "weak and supine leadership."[9]

The Disintegration of Czechoslovakia

The Czech state, already weakened by Munich, was next faced with a declaration of independence by its Slovak area.

On March 10, 1939, President Hácha ousted the Slovak Prime Minister, Josef Tiso, and his cabinet, and dispatched troops to occupy Bratislava, the capital of the Slovak government. Tiso turned to Hitler.

On March 15, 1939, Hitler launched his invasion of Czechoslovakia in absolute violation of his solemn guarantee of the integrity of Czechoslovakia given at Munich. The bleeding remains of the Czech state could put up no adequate

---

5. *F.D.R.: His Personal Letters,* [*1928–1945*], ed. Elliot Roosevelt (Duell, Sloan and Pearce, New York: 1950), Vol. II, p. 816.

6. *The Times* (London), October 27, 1938.

7. Great Britain, House of Commons, *Parliamentary Debates,* Official Report (Hansard), 5th Series, vol. 339 [Twelfth volume of Session 1937–38], pp. 366–367.

8. *The Times* (London), December 10, 1938.

9. Ibid., November 15, 1938.

resistance and the Czechs surrendered. Polish and Hungarian armies at once marched in to snatch from the dying republic the areas of their nationals. Hitler promptly began the barbaric execution of anti-Nazi Czech leaders and condemned thousands of Czechs to concentration camps. On March 23, 1939, he added still more fuel to the fire of European fears by occupying Memel, a predominantly German city in Lithuania.

The Reaction in the United States

On March 17, 1939, Acting Secretary of State Sumner Welles, on behalf of President Roosevelt, issued a denunciation of these flagrant aggressions.[10] However, these events had stimulated no perceptible desire on the part of the American public to join in a European war. After the fall of Czechoslovakia, the informal polls showed that 85 percent of the American people were opposed to American involvement in the turmoil abroad.

The Reaction in Britain

Prime Minister Chamberlain's opposition seized upon Hitler's aggression in an effort to drive the Prime Minister from office. In a speech on March 14, 1939, Winston Churchill fired every gun in his arsenal at the Prime Minister, saying in part:

> . . . I pointed out that a disaster [Munich Agreement] of the first magnitude had befallen France and England. Is that not so . . . It is because in the destruction of Czechoslovakia the entire balance of Europe was changed. . . .
>
> Many people at the time of the September crisis [Munich] thought they were only giving away the interests of Czechoslovakia, but with every month that passes you will see that they were also giving away the interests of Britain, and the interests of peace and justice. . . .[11]

On March 15, 1939, the following day, in the House of Commons, Mr. Chamberlain expressed himself bitterly over Hitler's actions but reaffirmed his determination not to go to war. He seemed to dismiss Hitler's action on the two grounds that the Slovak National Assembly had declared its independence

---

10. [Samuel I. Rosenman, comp.,] *The Public Papers and Addresses of Franklin D. Roosevelt*, 1939 [volume] (The Macmillan Company, New York: 1941), pp. 165–166.
11. Winston S. Churchill, *Blood, Sweat, and Tears* (G. P. Putnam's Sons, New York: 1941), "The Fruits of Munich," pp. 95–97. See also *The Times* (London), March 15, 1939.

from Czechoslovakia, and that the Czech government had directed its people not to resist Hitler. He also announced that the Munich Pact no longer held, attributing this to Slovakia's declaration of independence, saying:

> ... The effect of this declaration [by Slovakia] put an end by internal disruption to the State whose frontiers we had proposed to guarantee ... and His Majesty's Government cannot accordingly hold themselves any longer bound by this obligation.[12]

On March 17, 1939, speaking at Birmingham, the Prime Minister with a fervor born of great indignation again denounced Hitler's flagrant breach of faith.

On March 10, 1939, five days before Hitler's march into Czechoslovakia, Stalin made an important speech in Moscow. Despite Hitler's long years of persecution of the Communists in Germany, and his frequent threats to obtain his living space from Russia, in this speech Stalin extended an olive branch to him, saying:

> ... It looks as if the object of this suspicious hullabaloo was to incense the Soviet Union against Germany, to poison the atmosphere and to provoke a conflict with Germany without any visible grounds.

Stalin charged that the Western Democracies were building up Hitler against him. He asserted that their failure to intervene to save Austria and Czechoslovakia from Hitler was an encouragement to Hitler to invade Russia. The speech was long and at times so rambling that it was difficult to follow, but some paragraphs indicate Stalin's strong feelings and his policies:

> Even more characteristic is the fact that certain European and American politicians and newspapermen, having lost patience waiting for "the march on the Soviet Ukraine," are themselves beginning to disclose what is really behind the policy of non-intervention. They are saying quite openly, putting it down in black and white, that the Germans have cruelly "disappointed" them, for instead of marching farther east, against the Soviet Union, they have turned, you see, to the west and are demanding colonies. One might think that the districts of Czechoslovakia were yielded to Germany as the price of an undertaking to launch war on the Soviet Union, but that now the Germans are refusing to meet their bills and are sending them to Hades.

---

12. Great Britain, Parliament, House of Commons, *Parliamentary Debates,* Official Report (Hansard), 5th Series, vol. 345 [Fifth volume of Session 1938–39], p. 437.

... It must be remarked, however, that the big and dangerous political game started by the supporters of the policy of non-intervention may end in a serious fiasco for them.

Such is the true face of the prevailing policy of non-intervention.

Such is the political situation in the capitalist countries.

Stalin threw out this general defiance to the world:

[We intend] . . . not [to] allow our country to be drawn into conflicts by war-mongers who are accustomed to have others pull the chestnuts out of the fire for them.

To strengthen the might of our Red Army and Red Navy to the utmost.[13]

---

13. Joseph Stalin, *Selected Writings* (International Publishers, New York: 1942), pp. 441, 442, 444. See also *New York Times,* March 11 and 12, 1939.

CHAPTER 19

Hitler Moves on Poland

HITLER NOW HAD A SUM of huge gains, with scarcely the loss of a single soldier. He had occupied the Rhineland with a population of 14,000,000, and he had annexed Austria with a population of 7,000,000 and all this with no more opposition than mere words. With his conquest of Czechoslovakia and its 15,000,000 people, he had increased the population of the Reich by 36,000,000 people. He had also added thousands of square miles of territory, with its industries, food resources and potential military strength. It might be added that he had opened a road to Russia through Czechoslovakia.

He now turned his attention to Poland. On March 21, 1939, less than a week after his armies had rolled into Prague, he made a demand upon Poland for the annexation of Danzig, the return of other Germans in Polish territory, and restrictions of the Polish Corridor to the Baltic.

On March 25, the Polish Government replied, denying Hitler's claims and refusing any consequential concessions. Three days later, Foreign Minister Beck of Poland warned H. A. von Moltke, the German Ambassador in Warsaw, against any German action involving Danzig.[1]

The British and French Guarantee the Independence of Poland

On March 31, alarmed at Hitler's expanding aggression, Prime Minister Chamberlain suddenly announced in the House of Commons that Great Britain would support Poland against Germany. Chamberlain first stated that

---

1. [Republic of] Poland, Ministerstwo spraw zagranicznych [Ministry for Foreign Affairs], *Official documents concerning Polish-German and Polish-Soviet Relations, 1933–1939: The Polish White Book* (Hutchinson & Co., London: 1939) pp. 61–69.

the British Government had urged the Poles to settle their differences with Germany by direct negotiations, and that he saw no occasion for threats. He then declared:

> ... I now have to inform the House that during that period, in the event of any action which clearly threatened Polish independence, and which the Polish Government accordingly considered it vital to resist with their national forces, His Majesty's Government would feel themselves bound at once to lend the Polish Government all support in their power. They have given the Polish Government an assurance to this effect.
>
> I may add that the French Government have authorised me to make it plain that they stand in the same position in this matter as do His Majesty's Government.[2]

There was a momentary spasm of rejoicing in Britain that appeasement of Hitler was ended.

Thirteen days later the British and French guarantees were also extended to Rumania, presumably to protect them from aggression by both Germany and Italy.

The problem of militarily making good on the guarantees soon arose through a question put by Lloyd George in the House of Commons. Churchill also referred to this matter in a speech in the House on May 19, 1939, saying:

> ... His Majesty's Government have given a guarantee to Poland. I was astounded when I heard them give this guarantee. I support it, but I was astounded by it, because nothing that had happened before led one to suppose that such a step would be taken.... the question posed by ... [Mr. Lloyd George] ten days ago, and repeated today has not been answered. The question was whether the General Staff was consulted before this guarantee was given as to whether it was safe and practical to give it, and whether there were any means of implementing it. The whole country knows that the question has been asked, and it has not been answered. ... [3]

Mr. Roosevelt brought into action his policies of "Action stronger than words and less than war." A question involved was whether the British were influenced by Mr. Roosevelt to make the guarantees.

---

2. Great Britain, *Parliamentary Debates*, Fifth Series, Volume 345, House of Commons, Official Report, p. 2415 [March 31, 1939].
3. Ibid., Vol. 347, House of Commons, Official Report, p. 1846 [May 19, 1939].

Ambassador Joseph P. Kennedy later informed me that he was instructed to "put a poker up Chamberlain's back and to make him stand up."

In confirmation is a passage from the diary of James Forrestal, then Under Secretary of the Navy, as follows:

> . . . I asked him [Kennedy] about his conversations with Roosevelt and Neville Chamberlain from 1938 on. He said Chamberlain's position in 1938 was that England had nothing with which to fight and that she could not risk going to war with Hitler. Kennedy's view: That Hitler would have fought Russia without any later conflict with England if it had not been for Bullitt's . . . urging on Roosevelt in the summer of 1939 that the Germans must be faced down about Poland; neither the French nor the British would have made Poland a cause of war if it had not been for the constant needling from Washington. Bullitt, he said, kept telling Roosevelt that the Germans wouldn't fight, Kennedy that they would, and that they would overrun Europe. . . . In his telephone conversation with Roosevelt in the summer of 1939 the President kept telling him to put some iron up Chamberlain's backside. Kennedy's response always was the putting iron up his backside did no good unless the British had some iron with which to fight, and they did not. . . .

> What Kennedy told me in this conversation jibes substantially with the remarks Clarence Dillon had made to me already, to the general effect that Roosevelt had asked him in some manner to communicate privately with the British to the end that Chamberlain should have greater firmness in his dealings with Germany. Dillon told me that at Roosevelt's request he had talked with Lord Lothian in the same general sense as Kennedy reported Roosevelt having urged him to do with Chamberlain. Lothian presumably was to communicate to Chamberlain the gist of his conversation with Dillon.[4]

(Forrestal was slightly wrong in his dates as the Polish guarantee was at the end of March 1939, not in "the summer of 1939.")

On the same day (March 17, 1939) that Acting Secretary of State Sumner Welles, in accordance with the President's policies, issued the statement denouncing lawlessness and aggression,[5] some restrictions were placed by the United States on German trade. On March 22 the President made a state-

---

4. *The Forrestal Diaries,* edited by Walter Millis (The Viking Press, New York: 1951), pp. 121–122.
5. The full text is given in [U.S. Department of State,] *Peace and War, United States Foreign Policy, 1931–1941* (United States Government Printing Office, Washington: 1943), pp. 454–455. See also *New York Times,* March 18, 1939.

ment to the Italian Ambassador, Prince Colonna, in Washington, that in case of war

... the United States would [give] ... such assistance as this country could render [to the Democracies]. . . . [6]

On March 24, 1939, seven days prior to the guarantees, Lord Halifax records a conversation with Ambassador to Britain Joseph P. Kennedy, in which Mr. Kennedy asked "whether His Majesty's Government and France really meant business."[7]

The German Embassy in London had earlier reported Kennedy's activities by informing the German government on March 20, 1939, that:

... Kennedy, the United States Ambassador here, is playing a leading part. He is said to be in personal contact with the Missions of all the States involved, and to be attempting to encourage them to adopt a firm attitude by promising that the United States . . . would support them by all means ("short of war").[8]

Another action by Mr. Roosevelt was his influence upon the Poles not to negotiate the question of Danzig.

The adamant attitude of the Poles against negotiations received support from the Washington Administration.

The separation of the German city of Danzig from Germany, and the size of the Corridor at the time of the Treaty of Versailles had long been a cause of agitation by the Germans. Both were a part of vengeance and there was merit in the German claims. I had stated at one time that they should be corrected.[9] The Poles at this time were fearful that any compromise with Hitler was of no use.

After the Germans had invaded Poland on September 1, 1939, and seized the Polish Foreign Office records, they released a mass of documents which certainly indicated that the American Ambassador to France, William C. Bullitt, who could act only on Mr. Roosevelt's authority, in January, 1939, had

---

6. William L. Langer and S. Everett Gleason, *The Challenge to Isolation, 1937–1940* (Harper & Brothers, New York: 1952), p. 78.

7. Great Britain, Foreign Office, *Documents on British Foreign Policy 1919–1939* (London, H.M. Stationery Office: 1951), Third Services, Vol. IV, 1939, p. 499.

8. *Documents on German Foreign Policy, 1918–1945*, Series D (1937–1945), Volume VI: *The Last Months of Peace, March-August 1939* [Her Majesty's Stationery Office, London: 1956], p. 51.

9. During my Administration in Washington Prime Minister Laval of France visited the United States. He stated to me that the city should be returned to Germany and the Corridor narrowed.

made a profusion of oral assurances to officials of Poland and France which they could only interpret as a promise of assistance of some kind of force from the United States. These statements by Bullitt were contained in numerous dispatches from Polish Ambassadors abroad to their Foreign Ministers in Warsaw.[10]

When published, these documents were denounced as fabrications by Ambassador Bullitt, the Polish Ambassador to Washington, Count Jerzy Potocki, and by our State Department. But subsequently, the Polish Ambassador in Washington informed me that the documents were genuine and that he had denied their authenticity at the request of the State Department.

However, more convincing than these denials are the files of the Polish Embassy in Washington which were given to the Hoover Institution at Stanford University. A new translation showed only minor differences from the German publication. There were many of these documents—too long to reproduce here. A typical paragraph in one of Polish Ambassador Potocki's dispatches to the Polish Foreign Office, dated January 16, 1939, nearly two months before the guarantees, but after Hitler's demands, reads:

> ... In talking with Bullitt I had the impression that he had received from President Roosevelt a very detailed definition of the attitude taken by the United States towards the present European crisis. He will present this material at the Quai d'Orsay and will make use of it in discussions with European statesmen. The contents of these directions, as Bullitt explained them to me in the course of a conversation, lasting half an hour, were:
>
> 1.–The vitalizing foreign policy, under the leadership of President Roosevelt, severely and unambiguously condemns totalitarian countries.
> 2.–The United States preparation for war on sea, land and air which will be carried out at an accelerated speed and will consume the colossal sum of 1, 250 million dollars.
> 3.–It is the decided opinion of the President that France and Britain must put end to any sort of compromise with the totalitarian countries. They

---

10. For comment by German officials in the United States, see *Documents on German Foreign Policy, 1918–1945*, Series D, Volume IX: *The War Years, March 18, 1940–June 22, 1940* (United States Department of State, Washington: 1956), pp. 45, 48, 225, 281, 624. See also The German White Book, No. 3. [*Editor's note:* The latter source was probably the *German White Book: Documents Concerning the Last Phase of the German-Polish Crisis* (German Library of Information, New York: 1939), a reprint (with a prefatory note) of the German White Book of the same title published by the German Foreign Office in Berlin in 1939, after the German invasion of Poland.]

must not let themselves in for any discussions aiming at any kind of territorial changes.

4.–They have the moral assurance that the United States will leave the policy of isolation and be prepared to intervene actively on the side of Britain and France in case of war. America is ready to place its whole wealth of money and raw materials at their disposal.[11]

Another of the documents, a dispatch from Polish Ambassador Jules Lukasiewicz in Paris addressed to the Polish Foreign Minister in Warsaw, dated Paris, February 1939, about two months before the guarantees, states:

> . . . if war should break out between Britain and France on the one hand and Germany and Italy on the other, and Britain and France should be defeated, the Germans would become dangerous to the realistic interests of the United States on the American continent. For this reason, one can foresee right from the beginning the participation of the United States in the war on the side of France and Britain, naturally after some time had elapsed after the beginning of the war. Ambassador Bullitt expressed this as follows:
>
> "Should war break out we shall certainly not take part in it at the beginning, but we shall end it." . . .
>
> For the time being, I should like to refrain from formulating my own opinion of Ambassador Bullitt's statements. . . . One thing, however, seems certain to me, namely, that the policy of President Roosevelt will henceforth take the course of supporting France's resistance, to check German-Italian pressure, and to weaken British compromise tendencies.[12]

The documentation of our State Department on these matters is as yet undisclosed.

The Swinging Balance of Power

In the wake of Hitler's demands on Poland and of the countering Anglo-French guarantees of her independence, ominous lightning at once flashed from every capital in the world. Once again the balance of power had shifted, and in a way more precarious than ever to the peace of mankind. We may well

---

11. Germany, Auswärtiges Amt, *The German White Paper* (New York: Howell, Soskin, & Co., 1940), Seventh Document, pp. 32–33, issued by the Berlin Foreign Office.
12. Ibid., Ninth Document, pp. 43–45, issued by the Berlin Foreign Office.

examine the forces in motion at this moment in the three great centers of aggression—Nazi Germany, Communist Russia and Militarist Japan.

Hitler's Situation

The balance of power in Europe had swung toward Hitler as a result of his racial expansions and the acquiescence of Britain and France in these activities. But now the Anglo-French guarantees of Poland introduced new weights in this balance. If Hitler attempted to enforce his demands on Poland, the British and French might attack him on his Western Front. And with Stalin's ample knowledge of Hitler's *idée fixe* against Russia, the Russians might join the Western powers to extinguish him. Loath as he might be to engage himself, Hitler's only secure course to fend off this twofold danger would be an agreement with Stalin which would protect his Eastern Front.

Stalin's Situation

Never in their history had the Russian Communists been placed in such a key position to advance their purposes.

Since the time of Peter the Great, Russia, with its vast land mass, had been constantly pressing for outlets to the Baltic Sea. As a result of the First World War, the historic Russian "window on the Baltic" had been reduced to a narrow peephole at Leningrad, which, because of the ice-blocked Gulf of Finland, was open only in the summer. A conflict between the Western Democracies and Hitler might afford Stalin an opportunity to recover the Baltic outlets.

Moreover, if Hitler became involved with the Democracies, the Anti-Comintern Pact might fall apart, and the danger to Stalin of a squeeze attack from Germany and Japan would be lessened.

Japan's Situation

The Russian dangers from Japan were very real. The great Russian fortress of Vladivostok, with its armies and especially its air force, posed a constant threat to the inflammable paper and wood buildings of Tokyo. In their invasion of China, the Japanese had penetrated along a thousand miles of the Siberian frontier. Clashes were frequent along these borders, but tempting as an invasion of Siberia might be to the Japanese, they had to reason that the

United States, in her sympathies with China, might join China and Russia to check further Japanese expansion.

In short, of the three great aggressor nations, the Communists were in the best position at this time. They could advance their objective of expanding their ideology world-wide by giving their favor either to the Western Democracies, or alternatively to Hitler—for a consideration and without war on their own part.

At this moment, therefore, the balance of power definitely lay in Stalin's hands.

CHAPTER 20

Shall We Send Our Youth to War?

IN THE MIDST OF THESE FORCES and contentions I spoke my mind, hoping to aid my countrymen to understand the direction to which European forces were leading us. In this period I prepared two magazine articles: one for the *Liberty* Magazine of April 15, 1939; the second was published in the August 1939 issue of the *American Magazine*.

The *Liberty* Magazine article was an analysis of the rising dangerous ideologies of Hitler and Stalin, saying in part:

> . . . Most of us intensely dislike every color of Nazism, Fascism, Socialism, and Communism. They are the negation of every ideal that we hold. They are the suppression of all liberty. In Germany the persecution of the Jews. . . . in Russia the wholesale executions, the destruction of . . . worship . . . all of them outrage our every sense of justice. . . . we resent the . . . taking advantage of our liberties of free speech and free assembly to . . . destroy those very liberties.[1]

The *American Magazine* article was entitled "Shall We Send Our Youth to War?" I hoped that it would help the American people to understand the realities of war. I give here some excerpts:

> The American people are today tense with anxiety lest they be led into another great war.
>
> . . . Truly many years have already gone by since we ceased to feed boys to the cannon. It seems difficult to believe that only about one third of the living American people are old enough to remember the World War well.

---

1. Herbert Hoover, ["Foreign Policies Today,"] *Liberty* Magazine, April 15, 1939, pp. 5–8. Also see Herbert Hoover, *Further Addresses Upon the American Road, 1938–1940* [Charles Scribner's Sons, New York: 1940], p. 107.

We have urgent need today to recall the realities of modern war. . . .

I am perhaps one of the few living Americans who had full opportunity to see intimately the moving tragedy of the World War from its beginnings down through the long years which have not yet ended. I saw it not only in its visible ghastliness, but I lived with the invisible forces which moved in its causes and its consequences. I am perhaps justified in recalling that experience.

Before the War I knew Europe—Russia, Germany, France, Italy, and England—fairly intimately, not as a tourist but as part of their workaday life. . . .

What War Really Is

First, let me say something from this experience of what war really is. Those who lived in it, and our American boys who fought in it, dislike to recall its terribleness. We dwell today upon its glories—the courage, the heroism, the greatness of spirit in men. I, myself, should like to forget all else. But today, with the world driving recklessly into it again, there is much we must not forget. Amid the afterglow of glory and legend we forget the filth, the stench, the death, of the trenches. We forget the dumb grief of mothers, wives, and children. We forget the unending blight cast upon the world by the sacrifice of the flower of every race.

I was one of but few civilians who saw something of the Battle of the Somme.[2] In the distant view were the unending trenches filled with a million and a half men. Here and there, like ants, they advanced under the thunder and belching volcanoes of 10,000 guns. Their lives were thrown away until half a million had died. Passing close by were unending lines of men plodding along the right side of the road to the front, not with drums and bands, but with saddened resignation. Down the left side came the unending lines of wounded men, staggering among unending stretchers and ambulances. Do you think one can forget that? And it was but one battle of a hundred.

Ten million men died or were maimed for life in that war. There were millions who died unknown and unmarked. Yet there are miles of unending crosses in a thousand cemeteries. The great monument to the dead at Ypres carries the names of 150,000 Englishmen who died on but a small segment

---

2. While engaged in some negotiations with the German General Staff concerning the Belgian Relief, I accepted their invitation to take me to one of their observation posts overlooking the Battle of the Somme. See Volume I, *Memoirs of Herbert Hoover* [The Macmillan Company, New York: 1951], p. 193.

of the front. Theirs was an inspiring heroism for all time. But how much greater a world it would be today if that heroism and that character could have lived.

And there was another side no less dreadful. I hesitate to recall even to my own mind the nightmares of roads filled for long miles with old men, young women, and little children dropping of fatigue and hunger as they fled in terror from burning villages and oncoming armies. And over Europe these were not just a few thousands, but over the long years that scene was enacted in millions.

And there was the ruthless killing of civilians, executed by firing squads who justified their acts, not by processes of justice, but on mere suspicion of transgression of the laws of war. Still worse was the killing of men, women, and even children to project terror and cringing submission. To the winds went every sense of justice. To the winds went every sense of decency. To the winds went every sense of tolerance. To the winds went every sense of mercy. The purpose of every army is to win. They are not put together for afternoon teas. They are made up of men sent out to kill or be killed. . . .

And there were the terrors of the air. In a score of air raids I saw the terror of women and children flocking to the cellars, frantically, to escape from an unseen enemy.

In another even more dreadful sense I saw inhuman policies of war. That was the determination on both sides to bring subjection by starvation. The food blockade by the Allied Governments on one side, and the ruthless submarine warfare by the Central Powers on the other, had this as its major purpose. Both sides professed that it was not their purpose to starve women and children . . . it is an idiot who thinks soldiers ever starve. It was women and children who died of starvation. It was they who died of the disease which came from short food supplies, not in hundreds of thousands, but in millions.

And after the Armistice came famine and pestilence, in which millions perished and other millions grew up stunted in mind and body. That is war. Let us not forget.

We were actually at the front in this war for only a few months, but it cost us the lives of 130,000 men. It has placed 470,000 persons on the national pension list already. It has cost us 40 billions of dollars. And that represents more than just dollars. Today we have a quarter to a third of the American people below a decent standard of living. If that 40 billions of wealth had remained in America, these people would not be in this plight. A large segment of our people have already been impoverished for a quarter of a century. And the end is not yet.

We may need to go to war again. But that war should be on this hemisphere alone and in the defense of our firesides or our honor. For that alone should we pay the price. . . .

. . . I reluctantly joined in the almost unanimous view of our countrymen that America must go into that war. We had been directly attacked. . . . I believed that with our singleness of purpose we could impose an enlightened peace; that we could make it a war to end war. I believed we could make the world safe for the spread of human liberty. If experience has any value to nations, there are in the wrecking of these hopes a thousand reasons why we should never attempt it again. . . .

I then briefly recounted President Wilson's magnificent record:

. . . He helped some nations to freedom. He hoped that, with time for hate and avarice to cool, the League of Nations could reconstruct the failures of the treaty.

Americans will yet be proud of that [great] American who fought a fight for righteousness although he partially lost. But he proved that American idealism and American ignorance of the invisible forces in Europe can only confuse the grim necessities of European peace.

What is happening today? Europe is suffering repeated earthquake shocks from the fault of the Treaty of Versailles.

But beyond all of this which is obvious, something else is moving. Europe is again engaged in a hideous conflict of power. Stripped to its bones, today the quarrel is much the same. Dictators in Germany and Italy rise to power on opposition to Communism, launched into their peoples by the Dictator of Russia. . . . Again France, a democracy, ties herself to the dictatorship in Russia. England becomes endangered should the dictators of Germany and Italy overwhelm France. And thus again begins this dreadful treadmill. . . .

I stated:

The second danger of war comes from the policies of our own government. President Roosevelt has taken a seat at the table where power politics is being played. . . . He lines us up in the balance of power. It is said we can do this without joining in war.

It is said we will do something more than words and less than war. . . .

If the dictators believe we will stop short of war they will credit us with having small chips in this game. Their chips are soldiers and guns. If our partners [the Allies] believe our chips of more than words and less than war are valuable, it is because they believe that when we have exhausted these chips we will put our soldiers and guns into the game. . . .

And right before our eyes the game shifts. We were originally going to quarantine dictators and again save democracy. Today we have two or three dictators on our team. . . .

. . . we can hold the light of liberty alight on this continent. That is the greatest service we can give to civilization. . . .

. . . The first thing required is a vigorous, definite statement from all who have responsibility, both publicly and privately, that we are not going to war with anybody in Europe unless they attack the Western Hemisphere. The second thing is not to sit in this game of power politics.[3]

---

3. Herbert Hoover, "Shall We Send Our Youth to War?" *American Magazine*, August, 1939, pp. 12–13, 137–139. Also see Herbert Hoover, *Further Addresses Upon the American Road, 1938–1940*, pp. 116–128.

CHAPTER 21

The Allies and Hitler Each Bid for an Alliance with Stalin

The Allied Bid

Two weeks after they had announced their guarantee to Poland, the British, as a protection against Hitler, sought an alliance with Stalin.[1] The French negotiated separately as, presumably, they had a more favorable relationship with Stalin [than–ed.] did the British, because of their military alliance with Russia.[2]

The dismissal of Soviet Foreign Commissar Maxim M. Litvinov on May 3, 1939, was a bad omen for the Allies. He was succeeded by Vyacheslav Molotov. Litvinov had been generally favorable to a policy of amicable relations with the Western Democracies. Molotov was a fanatical Communist, brutal, cunning, and fully representative of the Communist determination to conquer the free world.

Stalin's asking price for an alliance with the Allies gradually emerged from Prime Minister Chamberlain's statements before the House of Commons on May 10, May 19, and June 7, 1939.[3] The price was British agreement to the annexation by the Soviet Union of Finland, Estonia, Latvia, Lithuania, East Poland, Bessarabia, and Bukovina, which had been a part of the Russian Empire prior to the First World War. The Baltic States, anxiously watching the negotiations, themselves confirmed the price sought by their public protests.

In London, Churchill, Lloyd George, and Eden continued their violent attacks on Prime Minister Chamberlain's policy. On May 19, 1939, Lloyd George, in the House of Commons, asked how Poland could be defended

---

1. The details of these negotiations can be found in [Great Britain, Foreign Office,] *Documents on British Foreign Policy, 1919–1939*, 3rd Series, Vols. V and VI (Her Majesty's Stationery Office, London: 1952, 1953). Therefore I do not cite the authority for each incident discussed.

2. Ibid., Vol. V, p. 273.

3. Great Britain, *Parliamentary Debates* [Fifth Series], House of Commons, Vol. 347 [Seventh volume of Session 1938–9], pp. 453–456, 1828–1840; Vol. 348, pp. 400–402.

without the help of Russia. Churchill demanded that the Russian terms be accepted. In this, he was supported by Eden and others.[4]

With the Prime Minister's moral scruples against selling the freedom of peoples, he had nothing to offer Stalin except the assurance that, by an alliance with the West, he would be more safe from attack by Hitler. The last of the British and French missions which had arrived in Moscow on August 11 to negotiate with the Russians returned home empty-handed after the announcement of the German-Soviet Pact of August 23, 1939.

Hitler's Bid

For the detailed facts as to Hitler's bid for an alliance with Stalin, we draw on documents seized by the Allies after the German defeat in 1945. It is clear that Stalin initiated the negotiation. In May, 1939, the Russians suggested negotiations for a Nazi-Soviet commercial agreement. The talks were to be carried on by Molotov and the German Ambassador to Moscow, Count Friedrich von der Schulenburg. Seemingly unwilling to give up his *idée fixe* of destroying the Communist government of Russia and his *idée fixe* of expansion of his "living space" in that area, Hitler, through his Foreign Minister, Joachim von Ribbentrop, had instructed his Ambassador in Moscow "to maintain extreme caution."[5] On May 30, however, he reversed himself and directed the Ambassador to renew negotiations. But he soon suspended them again. On June 5, von der Schulenburg reported that Molotov "almost invited political discussions."[6] Some further negotiations ensued, but on June 30, von Ribbentrop again instructed the Ambassador not to continue negotiations.

Hitler's hesitation apparently was due partly to his uncertainty as to whether the Allies would fight if he invaded Poland, and partly to Chamberlain's proposals to him for further British-German negotiations, which will be discussed later. Paul Schmidt, Hitler's official interpreter, recorded that Hitler's main theme at a meeting with his staff members on August 12 was:

... The democracies are not as powerful as Germany and will not fight. ...[7]

Also, according to Schmidt, Hitler told Count Galeazzo Ciano, the Italian Foreign Minister:

---

4. Ibid., Vol. 347, pp. 1815–[1820], 1840–1847 [1848], 1854–1860.
5. [U.S. Department of State,] *Nazi-Soviet Relations, 1939–1941* [U.S. Government Printing Office, Washington: 1948], p. 8.
6. Ibid., p. 19.
7. Paul Schmidt, *Hitler's Interpreter* [The Macmillan Company, New York: 1951], p. 132.

I am unshakably convinced that neither England nor France will embark upon a general war.[8]

Suddenly, however, on August 14, Hitler seemingly became alarmed at Allied attitudes, and instructed von der Schulenburg to push negotiations with Stalin, giving him elaborate instructions.[9] Negotiations proceeded, but Hitler wanted greater haste, and on August 20 sent a personal telegram to Stalin accepting the Russian terms and suggesting that Foreign Minister von Ribbentrop go to Moscow at once for the final formalities.[10]

On August 23 Moscow announced to the world that a German-Soviet non-aggression pact had been signed by von Ribbentrop and Molotov. Its significance was alarming enough to the Democracies, but its full import was not clear until a little later. The actions of Hitler and Stalin were to confirm that a much more menacing agreement had been made. This agreement was as follows:

The German Reich Government and the Union of Soviet Socialist Republics, moved by a desire to strengthen the state of peace between Germany and the U.S.S.R. and in the spirit of the provisions of the neutrality treaty of April, 1926, between Germany and the U.S.S.R., decided the following:

---

8. Ibid.

9. For further evidence of Hitler's vacillations see *Nazi-Soviet Relations*, pp. 15, 60, 66, 67, et. seq.

10. On August 22, two days after his acceptance of the Russian terms, Hitler made a ferocious speech to his military commanders regarding his real intentions. Thanks to the German habit of taking shorthand notes, we have this record of his speech:

"Our strength is in our quickness and our brutality. Ghengis Khan had millions of women and children killed by his own will and with a gay heart. History sees only in him a great state builder. What weak Western European civilization thinks about me does not matter. . . . I have sent to the East only my 'Death's Head Units' with the order to kill without pity or mercy all men, women, and children of Polish race or language. Only in such a way will we win the vital space that we need. Who still talks nowadays of the extermination of the Armenians?

". . . Poland will be depopulated and colonized with Germans. My pact with Poland was only meant to stall for time. And besides, gentlemen, in Russia will happen just what I have practiced with Poland. After Stalin's death (he is seriously ill), we shall crush the Soviet Union. . . .

"The occasion is favorable now as it has ever been. I have only one fear and that is that Chamberlain or such another dirty swine comes to me with propositions or a change of mind. He will be thrown downstairs. . . .

"No, for this it is too late. The invasion and the extermination of Poland begins on Saturday morning. I will have a few companies in Polish uniform attack in Upper Silesia or in the Protectorate. Whether the world believes it doesn't mean a damn to me. The world believes only in success.

"Glory and honor are beckoning to you. . . . Be hard. Be without mercy. Act quicker and more brutally than others. The citizens of Western Europe must quiver in horror. That is the most human warfare for it scares them off . . . "([Office of United States Chief of Counsel for Prosecution of Axis Criminality,] *Nazi Conspiracy and Aggression* [United States Government Printing Office, Washington: 1946], Volume VII, pp. 753–754).

Article I

The two contracting parties obligate themselves to refrain from every act of force, every aggressive action and every attack against one another, including any single action or that taken in conjunction with other powers.

Article II

In case one of the parties of this treaty should become the object of war-like acts by a third power, the other party will in no way support this third power.

Article III

The governments of the two contracting parties in the future will constantly remain in consultation with one another in order to inform each other regarding questions of common interest.

Article IV

Neither of the high contracting parties will associate itself with any other grouping of powers which directly or indirectly is aimed at the other party.

Article V

In the event of a conflict between the contracting parties concerning any question, the two parties will adjust this difference or conflict exclusively by friendly exchange of opinions or, if necessary, by an arbitration commission.

Article VI

The present treaty will extend for a period of ten years with the condition that if neither of the contracting parties announces its abrogation within one year of expiration of this period, it will continue in force automatically for another period of five years.

Article VII

The present treaty shall be ratified within the shortest possible time. The exchange of ratification documents shall take place in Berlin. The treaty becomes effective immediately upon signature.

Drawn up in two languages, German and Russian.
Moscow, 23d of August, 1939.

For the German Government:
Ribbentrop.

In the name of the Government of the U.S.S.R.:
Molotoff [Molotov–*ed.*].[11]

By another protocol, a joint German-Russian invasion of Poland was to be undertaken. Stalin was to have Estonia, Latvia, Finland, and the return from Rumania of Bessarabia and a part of Lithuania. Hitler was to have a free hand in the conquest of Western Europe.[12] Thus the independence of Poland and the Baltic States which they had enjoyed for twenty years was to be snuffed out.

Hitler had an explanation to make to Mussolini as to this cracking up of the Berlin-Rome-Tokyo Axis. On August 25 he addressed a long letter to Mussolini. The Italian dictator replied amiably but declared that he was in no state of preparedness to join in a war.

By the Stalin-Hitler alliance, Hitler also in effect violated the Berlin-Tokyo Axis. It came as a great shock to Japan. The Hiranuma Ministry, then in power, fell.

The British Attempt Negotiations with Hitler

In the midst of the competitive Allied-Nazi bidding for alliances with Stalin, the British, anxious to avoid war, attempted to reach an understanding directly with Hitler. During May, June, and July of 1939 second-string British and German officials met a number of times and tried to work out some accord. Finally, on August 22, Chamberlain addressed a letter directly to Hitler. The Prime Minister, probably at this moment unaware of the terms of the

---

11. *New York Times,* August 24, 1939.

12. The actual signed paper became public when the Allies seized the German Foreign Office documents at the time of the German surrender in May, 1945.

I saw the original in Berlin in April, 1946. A month later, at the Nurnberg trials, it was offered in evidence by the Germans but on Russian objection it was disallowed. However, on October 19, the contents of the document were published in London. In 1948, the American Government officially released the text.

The probable explanation of the Soviet objection at Nurnberg is that the Russians, having joined at Nurnberg in establishing *ex post facto* Nazi crimes by which aggression became punishable by death, did not wish so obvious a conviction of themselves to be placed on record. See the *New York Times,* January 2, 1948, p. 19:3.

Stalin-Hitler alliance, suggested a truce, a simple guarantee by all the powers of Poland's independence, a consideration of German claims, and of German wishes for colonial outlets. He continued:

At this moment I confess I can see no other way to avoid a catastrophe that will involve Europe in war.[13]

Hitler's reply on August 23 (the day his pact was signed with Stalin) was scarcely encouraging.

On August 25, Hitler apparently again changed his mind and sent for the British Ambassador in Berlin, Sir Nevile Henderson, and indicated that he would be satisfied by the annexation of Danzig and a settlement of the Polish Corridor question. He declared that he did not want war with Britain. The old Hitler demand for restoration of the ex-German colonies was not too emphatic; he suggested negotiation of that issue.

That same day a mutual assistance agreement was signed by Poland and Britain.[14] Ten days later France signed a mutual assistance pact with Poland.[15]

A letter, dated August 26, from Premier Daladier notified Hitler that the French would fight if Poland were invaded.[16] So again Hitler momentarily postponed his attack.[17]

On August 28, the British replied to Hitler's proposals as outlined to Ambassador Henderson. They accepted the idea of negotiating British-German colonial questions, urged direct settlement between Germany and Poland as a necessary preliminary step, and indicated that British interest in that settlement was only to assure the independence of the Poland state, thus implying

---

13. [Great Britain, Foreign Office,] *Documents on British Foreign Policy, 1919–1939*, Third Series, Volume VII (Her Majesty's Stationery Office, London: 1954), p. 171. See also *Documents on German Foreign Policy, 1918–1945*, Series D, Volume VII: *The Last Days of Peace* [*August 9–September 3*], 1939 (United States Government Printing Office, Washington: 1956), Doc. No. 200, p. 216.

14. The text of this treaty was not published by the British until six years later—April 5, 1945. See *Polish White Book*, pp. 100–102; *New York Times*, April 6, 1945.

15. The *Polish White Book*; official documents . . . 1933–1939, p. 137ff. [*Editor's note:* See Chapter 19, note 1, for the full citation.]

16. International Military Trials, Nurnberg, [Office of United States Chief of Counsel for Prosecution of Axis Criminality,] *Nazi Conspiracy and Aggression*, Vol. VIII, pp. 529–530; Schmidt, *Hitler's Interpreter*, pp. 141–148.

17. This is confirmed in German documents captured after the war. See *Nazi Conspiracy and Aggression*, Vol. III [Vol. VIII—*ed.*], pp. 534, 535, 536. Goering, in his testimony at Nurnberg, stated: ". . . the Fuehrer called me on the telephone and told me that he had stopped the planned invasion of Poland. I asked him then whether this was just temporary or for good. He said, "No, I will have to see whether we can eliminate British intervention." So then I asked him, "Do you think that it will be any different within four or five days?"

that they were no longer interested in the limited problems of Danzig and the Corridor.

On August 29, Hitler handed the British Ambassador in Berlin a long but generally amiable note, stating that the Germans would put their conditions in writing.

On August 30, the British replied, accepting Hitler's proposals regarding German negotiations with Poland.[18] The Poles consented to negotiate on the questions of the Corridor and Danzig, subject to the condition that no troops cross their borders pending the negotiation.

Foreign Minister von Ribbentrop informed the British Ambassador in Berlin that Germany had asked the Polish government to send an authorized negotiator to Berlin at once. The Polish government instructed their Ambassador in Berlin, M. Lipski, to contact von Ribbentrop, which he did. On August 31, von Ribbentrop stated that the terms he was prepared to offer the Poles included the provisions that Danzig go to the Reich, and that a plebiscite be held in the Corridor for its division, with communications guaranteed for both Poles and Germans across the Corridor, and exchange of minority nationals. If these terms were accepted the armies were to be demobilized.

Later, the German Foreign Ministry explained that although the Polish Ambassador had indeed come, the Ambassador was without authority to sign any agreement, and therefore the promised Polish "negotiator" had not arrived, although the Germans waited "two days in vain."

The Leaders of Nations Explain

One of the indispensable facts of history which stands out in these discussions was the utter dishonesty of Hitler's immediate pre-war negotiations with Chamberlain, particularly after August 22. He had already pledged himself to Stalin, and his agreement to deal with the Poles was sheer camouflage.

Chamberlain and Daladier had every right to righteous indignation. On September 1, as the German armies rolled into Poland, Chamberlain spoke in the House of Commons as follows:

> . . . To begin with let me say that the text of these proposals has never been communicated by Germany to Poland at all. . . .

---

18. *Documents on British Foreign Policy, 1919–1939*, 3rd Series, Vol. VII, Doc. 543, p. 413–414. [*Editor's note:* The British reply, cited by Hoover, noted that Hitler's government had accepted the *British* proposal and that the Germans were prepared to negotiate directly with the Poles.]

... Germany claims to treat Poland as in the wrong because she had not by Wednesday night [August 30, 1939] entered upon discussions with Germany about a set of proposals of which she had never heard.

... On that Wednesday night, ... Herr von Ribbentrop produced a lengthy document which he read out in German, aloud, at top speed. Naturally, after this reading our Ambassador asked for a copy of the document, but the reply was that it was now too late, as the Polish representative had not arrived in Berlin by midnight. ... [19]

Addressing the French Chamber of Deputies the next day, Premier Daladier added more details of the final German perfidy. Giving a considerably different account of the meeting on August 31 between von Ribbentrop and the Polish Ambassador to Berlin, he reported that Hitler had agreed that day, August 31, to hold direct negotiations with Poland; that at one o'clock that afternoon the Polish Ambassador to Germany had requested a meeting with von Ribbentrop, but that he was not received until 7:45 P.M., and that von Ribbentrop had refused to give him the German proposals on the pretext that the Ambassador did not have power to direct negotiations.

Daladier continued:

At 9 P.M. the German wireless was communicating the nature and the full extent of these claims; it added that Poland had rejected them. That is a lie. That is a lie, since Poland did not even know them.

And at dawn on September 1 the Führer gave his troops the order to attack. Never was aggression more unmistakable and less warranted. ... [20]

The American Attitude

President Roosevelt's attitude toward Stalin, during the malign days when the Communist dictator was auctioning off his support to either the Allies or Hitler, remains shrouded in mystery. William L. Langer, a historian who had access to many documents of the time which were not available to the general public, has stated that there is little record of any discussions or communications between American officials in Moscow and in Washington at this time.

---

19. Great Britain, *Parliamentary Debates* (Commons), 5th Series, Vol. 351 [Eleventh volume of Session 1938–9], pp. 128–129.

20. [France, Ministère des affaires étrangères,] *The French Yellow Book, Diplomatic Documents (1938–1939)* (Reynal & Hitchcock, New York: 1940), p. 385. See also the *New York Times,* September 3, 1939.

Early in the fateful August of 1939, Mr. Roosevelt, in conversation with Constantine Oumansky, the Russian Ambassador in Washington, spoke of the futility of the situation and proposed that a general agreement against "aggression" be drawn up by the European powers.[21]

On August 11, twelve days before the unholy alliance of Russia and Germany, Laurence A. Steinhardt, the newly-appointed American Ambassador to Moscow, presented his credentials at the Kremlin. Mr. Roosevelt had directed him to give Soviet Foreign Minister Molotov a message of similar import to the one he had given Oumansky. After his arrival in Moscow, Steinhardt was kept informed of Stalin's bargaining with Hitler by the (secretly anti-Nazi) German Ambassador.[22] Dispatches on this subject are noticeably lacking in the published records of the State Department.

On August 24, the day after the secret Stalin-Hitler alliance was signed, the President, probably ignorant of this fact, sent messages to King Victor Emmanuel of Italy, to Hitler, and to President Ignace Moszicki of Poland, urging arbitration of the Polish-German differences.[23]

On August 25, Mr. Roosevelt reported the acceptance by the Polish Government of his suggestion, and urged Hitler also to accept.[24] But the fate of many nations was already sealed by the Stalin-Hitler alliance.

21. [William L.] Langer and [S. Everett] Gleason, *The Challenge to Isolation, 1937–1940* (Harper & Brothers, New York: 1952), p. 161. See also *The Memoirs of Cordell Hull*, Volume I (New York: The Macmillan Company, 1948), pp. 656–657.

22. Langer and Gleason, *The Challenge to Isolation, 1937–1940*, pp. 124–125.

23. [Samuel I. Rosenman, comp.], *The Public Papers and Addresses of Franklin D. Roosevelt*, 1939 [volume] [The Macmillan Company, New York: 1941], pp. 444ff.

24. Ibid., pp. 449–450.

CHAPTER 22

A Tragedy to All Mankind without End

WITHIN ALL THE URGENT dispatches by heads of state, prime ministers, the running about of ambassadors, and all the hurried high-level conferences, there was being enacted on the world stage in the month of August one of history's most terrible tragedies. Hell itself could not have conceived a more frightful drama. Its title could have been *Doom*.

The audience was all the nations in the world—two billion terrified human beings. The leading parts were acted by Hitler, a consummate egoist, the incarnation of the hates of a defeated nation, cunning, intent on conquest, without conscience or compassion; and Stalin, intent on spreading Communism over the world, a ruffian, cold, calculating, an Ivan the Terrible and Genghis Khan reborn. Boiling with hatred of each other, and despising the free nations, they were united only in a determination to destroy the free men—and then each other.

All about them were the malevolent spirits of imperialism, of wicked ideologies, of lust for personal power.

Wandering about the stage were the figures of Chamberlain—aristocratic, uncertain, swayed hither and yon by the cries of his critical countrymen, but a man of moral stature; and Daladier—a politician, well-intentioned, but vain and terrified.

There were other actors in the wings: Mussolini, crying "Me too"; Polish Foreign Minister Beck, trying to play both sides; Roosevelt, now and again appearing on stage, alternately urging Chamberlain and Daladier to "Stand up to them!" and crying "Peace, peace!", then vanishing from the stage again; Churchill, prodding the British leaders to unmoral agreements.

In the audience, frozen with fear, helplessly awaiting execution, were the little peoples—the Poles, Finns, Estonians, Latvians, Lithuanians, Bessarabians, Bukovinians, Bulgarians, Serbians, Rumanians, Czechs, Greeks, Belgians, Dutch, and Norwegians.

The last act was Stalin's sale of his alliance. If Chamberlain signed it, there would be handed to the Communists the free peoples of eastern Europe. But his British integrity and conscience would not permit him to sign. If Hitler signed with Stalin, these small nations were destined to be ravaged, and then Communism would gain such power that it would spread over the world.

Had there been a Greek chorus to this tragedy, its chant would have been "Doom, doom—scores of free nations will perish. Hundreds of millions will become slaves."

I had been too close an observer of the action on the world stage over twenty-five years not to watch these scenes with dread.

Out of it all would again march forth the Four Horsemen of the Apocalypse—War, Death, Famine and Pestilence—with a fifth Horseman bearing propaganda loaded with lies and hate, and a sixth Horseman bringing airplanes and submarines to kill men and innocent women and children. A seventh Horseman, even more sinister, would be Revolution, in which men betrayed and killed their own blood and kin.

The foul treachery dealt to civilization by Stalin and Hitler spread fear and panic everywhere. Telephone and telegraph messages, ambassadors and messengers sped over the earth. Millions of anxious human beings, with the horrors of the First World War still fresh in their minds, hung upon the press and radio. In despair they awaited the Second World War.

The guns began to bark on September 1, 1939.

The Communist-Nazi
Conquest of Europe

CHAPTER 23

Communist and Nazi Conquest of Poland and the Baltic States

THE COMBINED GERMAN and Russian armies completed the conquest of Poland in less than a month. The vaunted Polish military machine of 600,000 men proved to be made up of brave men with inferior equipment and incompetent generals. It is doubtful if the Germans and Russians lost more than 30,000 men in the extinguishment of this free people.

Stalin promptly deported some 250,000 military captives to Siberian work camps. He also deported 1,500,000 Polish civilians to Siberia.[1] Hitler seized several hundred thousand military prisoners and civilians for his work camps, and began the systematic extermination of the great Jewish community in Poland.

The Polish Ministry escaped via Rumania, carrying with them the gold reserve of their National Bank, totaling some $40,000,000, but the burden was too great and they were compelled to leave about $3,000,000 in Bucharest. They eventually set up a government-in-exile in London.

Many Polish civilians escaped through Rumania and Hungary and were organized by their exile leaders into an army to assist the Allies. The Poles in Poland, supported by the exiled group, organized a vigorous underground to keep up opposition to the German and Russian invaders.

At the request of the Polish Exiled Government in London, my colleagues and I organized The Commission for Polish Relief. We received a contribution of a million dollars from the Exiled Government itself and a large response from the American people. The Exiled Government assigned to us the gold left at Bucharest, but the Bank of Rumania refused to hand it over to us.

---

1. Stanislaw Mikolaczyk, *The Rape of Poland* (McGraw-Hill Book Company, Inc., New York: 1948), p. 14. Also see Lt. Gen. W[ladyslaw] Anders, *Hitler's Defeat in Russia* (Henry Regnery Company, Chicago: 1953), pp. 243–244.

We garnisheed the balances of that bank in New York and received a favorable judgment. However, the war intervened and we were unable to collect the judgment. In a compromise settlement after the war we received an amount covering the Commission's outstanding liabilities.

We carried on extensive relief in Poland until the British imposed the blockade upon such activities.[2]

Stalin lost little time in occupying Estonia and Latvia. Within sixty days after his alliance with Hitler, on a pretense of mutual assistance, he placed Communist garrisons in their cities, and in June, 1940, the total Soviet occupation began. In the same month, also under the title of mutual assistance, he seized Bessarabia and Bukovina from Rumania.

Finland

The Finns alone defied Stalin's demands. He launched an attack upon them on November 30, 1939. On that day the Finns made their valiant stand:

> We will die on our feet rather than on our knees.

In a speech I gave that night, I said:

> Civilization struck a new low with the Communists' attack on peaceful Finland. It is a sad day to every decent and righteous man and woman in the world. We are back to the morals and butchery of Ghengis Khan. . . .
>
> Greatness lies in the industry, the courage, the character of people. It lies in the intelligence, the education, the moral and spiritual standards of a people. It lies in their love of peace and freedom. All these measures of greatness can be expressed in one word—Finland.
>
> They will make a brave fight. They may be overwhelmed by the hordes whose morals are the morals of Communism. . . . Even if Finland falls, the day will come when it will rise again—for the forces of righteousness are not dead in the world.[3]

The next day, December 1, 1939, President Roosevelt issued a very effective statement.

> The news of the Soviet naval and military bombings within Finnish territory has come as a profound shock to the Government and people of the United

---

2. See Herbert Hoover, *An American Epic*, Vol. IV (Henry Regnery Company, Chicago: 1964).
3. *San Francisco Chronicle*, December 1, 1939.

States. Despite efforts made to solve the dispute by peaceful methods . . . one power has chosen to resort to force of arms. . . . All peace-loving peoples in those nations that are still hoping for the continuance of relations throughout the world on the basis of law and order will unanimously condemn this new resort to military force as the arbiter of international differences.[4]

And on January 20, 1940, Prime Minister Churchill eloquently declared:

Only Finland—superb, nay, sublime—in the jaws of peril—Finland shows what free men can do. The service rendered by Finland to mankind is magnificent.[5]

In early December 1939, the Finnish Minister to the United States, Hjalmar Procopé, appealed to me to organize charitable support for Finland. This appeal was followed by a request from Prime Minister Risto Ryti. With the magnificent assistance of the American press, my colleagues and I organized the Finnish Relief Fund. We collected about $4,000,000, and during our collection campaign the Congress made a $20,000,000 contribution directly to Finland.

On December 14, 1939, Russia was expelled from the League of Nations as an "aggressor."[6]

Minister Procopé informed me that his countrymen were receiving arms not only from Britain and Sweden, but from *Italy* and *Germany*. This latter source of support for the Finns was, to say the least, peculiar in view of the alliance between Hitler and Stalin. This odd state of affairs, however, is confirmed by an entry of December 8, 1939, in the diary of Count Galeazzo Ciano, son-in-law of Mussolini and at that time Foreign Minister of Italy:

The [Finnish] Minister . . . confides to me that Germany herself has supplied arms to Finland, turning over to her certain stocks especially from the Polish war booty. . . . [7]

Procopé freely voiced the suspicion to me that Hitler had already begun to doublecross Stalin.

---

4. United States Department of State, *Foreign Relations of the United States: Diplomatic Papers— The Soviet Union, 1933–1939* (U.S. Government Printing Office, Washington: 1952), pp. 799–800.
5. Winston S. Churchill, *Blood, Sweat, and Tears* (New York: G.P. Putnam's Sons, 1941), p. 215.
6. League of Nations, *Official Journal*, 20th Year, Part II (November–December, 1939), pp. 505–508.
7. Ciano, Count Galeazzo, *The Ciano Diaries, 1939–1943* (Doubleday & Company, Inc., Garden City, New York: 1946), p. 177.

On March 7, 1940, the Finns, unable to cope with the huge Communist armies, asked for peace terms through Sweden. Five days later they obtained them—but at a terrible price. They lost one-quarter of their farm land, and four hundred and fifty thousand of their people were driven from their homes onto the charity of their countrymen. They were subjected to indemnities and were compelled to accept Russian garrisons in their midst.

The Finns had certainly put up a resistance at great cost to the Russian invaders, for Commissar Molotov reported to the Supreme Soviet of the U.S.S.R. on March 29, 1940, that Russian casualties in the war with Finland came to 49,000 killed and 159,000 wounded—a total equal to about three-quarters of the whole Finnish Army.

The Conflagration of Treaties

With the Stalin-Hitler alliance, the start of war and its subsequent development, a multitude of treaties and non-aggression pacts were consigned to flames.

Communist Russia had joined the League of Nations, had put its signature to the Kellogg Pact, and had made a number of special non-aggression or peace pacts with her neighbors. The following are some of the treaties violated by the Communists.

With Poland:

a) Peace Treaty signed at Riga March 18, 1921.
b) Treaty of non-aggression signed July 25, 1932.
c) May 5, 1934 Protocol extending the validity of the non-aggression Treaty until December 31, 1945. The Soviet government had reconfirmed the validity of the non-aggression treaty in a note on September 10, 1934, and in a joint statement with the Polish government on November 26, 1938.
d) Treaty concerning conciliation procedures, signed November 23, 1932.

With Finland:

a) Peace Treaty signed at Tartu October 14, 1920.
b) January 21, 1932 Treaty concerning non-aggression and peaceful settlement of disputes.
c) Convention concerning conciliation procedures, signed April 22, 1932.
d) April 7, 1934 Protocol extending the validity of the non-aggression Treaty until December 31, 1945.

I may mention here that in its note to Finland of November 28, 1939, the Soviet Government denounced the non-aggression Treaty in 1932. The denunciation itself was done in a manner which violated the Treaty.

With Lithuania:

a) Peace Treaty signed at Moscow July 12, 1920.
b) September 28, 1926 Treaty of non-aggression signed at Moscow.
c) May 6, 1931 Protocol extending the validity of the non-aggression treaty for five years.
d) May 4, 1934 Protocol extending the validity of the non-aggression Treaty until December 31, 1945.
e) Treaty of Mutual Assistance of October 10, 1939, reaffirming the validity of the non-aggression Treaty.

With Estonia:

a) Peace Treaty signed at Tartu February 2, 1920.
b) May 4, 1932 Treaty of non-aggression and peaceful settlement of disputes.
c) June 16, 1932 Convention concerning conciliation procedures.
d) April 4, 1934 Treaty extending the validity of the non-aggression Treaty until December 31, 1945.
e) September 28, 1939 Pact of Mutual Assistance reconfirming the validity of the non-aggression Treaty.

With Latvia:

a) Peace Treaty signed at Riga, August 11, 1920.
b) February 5, 1932 Treaty of non-aggression.
c) June 18, 1932 Convention concerning conciliation procedures.
d) April 4, 1934 Protocol extending the validity of the Treaty of non-aggression until December 31, 1945.
e) October 5, 1939 Pact of Mutual Assistance reconfirming the non-aggression Treaty.

A bilateral agreement, June 29, 1934, with Rumania on non-interference in each others affairs was violated by Russia.

At the outbreak of war, Nazi Germany, like Communist Russia, defiled her pledges in a number of treaties. By his alliance with Stalin, Hitler made a mockery of German signatures on peace or non-aggression pacts with Finland, Poland, Estonia, Latvia, Lithuania, and Rumania. He had long since violated the Treaty of Versailles and the Locarno Pact, but was forehanded enough previous to the war's outbreak to denounce them, along with the German membership in the League of Nations. Hitler apparently had forgotten, however, that Germany was still a signatory of the Kellogg Pact.

Mussolini, by his acquiescence in the Hitler-Stalin alliance, violated treaties he had made with Latvia, Lithuania, Estonia, Poland and Rumania.

Altogether, more than fifty solemn agreements pledging non-aggression and respect for sovereignty went up in this conflagration of sacred obligations between nations.

At this moment in history, Hitler could count his new acquisitions as some 15,000,000 people from Poland, including 5,000,000 Jews in Poland and Lithuania. But Stalin's gains were greater. He had annexed six nations totaling about 35,000,000 people, who ultimately were reduced from freedom to Communism.

CHAPTER 24

The Surrender of Western Europe

ON SEPTEMBER 3, 1939, two days after Hitler's and Stalin's attack on Poland,[1] Britain and France declared war on Germany. The French mobilized their full armed strength; the British recruited and landed large forces in France. A tight naval blockade was established on Germany.

Denmark, unable to oppose Hitler's armies, was occupied by consent on April 9, 1940. On the same day, Hitler invaded southern Norway. The British later made a landing in northern Norway, but had to withdraw.

Some seven months went by with little military action in the West. Then, as soon as the winter mud had dried sufficiently, Hitler on May 10, 1940 launched his armies along the entire front of Holland, Belgium and France.

Eight months before these onslaughts, according to Mr. Churchill,[2] the Germans had about 42 divisions on the Western front. By the time of the attack, they had brought up the number to 126 regular divisions and 10 heavily armored Panzer divisions of combined infantry tanks and air coverage. The total Allied divisions on the Western front were 135 divisions, of which 94 were French, 22 Belgian, 10 Dutch, and 9 British. The French General Maurice Gustave Gamelin was placed in chief command.

The Dutch and Belgians could not believe that Hitler would violate his neutrality agreements with them, and delayed accepting British and French support until after the attack began. The Dutch surrendered on May 14, 1940. Meanwhile the Germans had killed 15,000 civilians in an air assault on the unprotected city of Rotterdam.

---

1. [*Editor's note:* The Soviet Union's attack on Poland did not commence until September 17, 1939.]

2. Winston S. Churchill, *Their Finest Hour* [Houghton Mifflin Company, Boston: 1949], pp. 28–30.

Using their new formation of Panzer divisions, the Germans broke through the Belgian and French lines from Liège to Sedan, dispersing one French northern army and advanced to Abbeville near the coast. Thus the Germans separated the Belgian army and the northern contingents of the British and French armies from those in the south of France.

After failing in an attempt to cut this German corridor, the British and Allies abandoned their arms and retreated to Dunkirk. From there, fleets of boats ferried these remnants across the Channel. Miraculously about 240,000 British and Allied troops were landed from Dunkirk and approximately 99,000 from the beaches.[3] Hitler made little attack on these fleeing troops. With the British withdrawal, the helpless Belgian army surrendered to the Germans on May 28.

Political Confusion

Parallel with the military confusion, confusion also arose at the top of the Allied governments. In the French Assembly Premier Edouard Daladier was replaced by Paul Reynaud on March 21, 1940. The Chamberlain Ministry fell on May 10, and Mr. Winston Churchill became Prime Minister. Despite several cabinet changes Premier Reynaud was forced to resign and on June 16 Marshal Henri Philippe Pétain, who had been Vice Premier since May 18, took over the reins of the government.

On May 19 the French Ministry removed General Gamelin from command of the Allied forces and appointed General Maxime Weygand in his place. But the German Panzer divisions thundered through France, occupying Paris on June 13. France surrendered nine days later—on June 22, 1940.

In the meantime, Prime Minster Churchill and Premier Reynaud made several attempts to reorganize their armies remaining in southern France. They made agonizing appeals to President Roosevelt for America to join in the war to save France. But the President, certain that he could get no declaration of war from the Congress and having no great army at his disposal, could only promise supplies if the French held out.

Prior to the French surrender, the British evacuated from the Normandy Brittany area in France their remaining forces of about 136,000 men along with a contingent of about 20,000 Polish troops.[4]

---

3. Ibid., p. 115.
4. Ibid., pp. 193–194.

After the French surrender, the Germans permitted certain French leaders to organize the interior districts of the country under a French-conducted but German-controlled government with its capital at Vichy. General Pétain became President and Pierre Laval Premier.

Hitler's invasion of Western Europe precipitated the problem of food supplies for Norway, Holland, and Belgium, all of which were dependent upon overseas imports of food. These nations—each of them—appealed to me to revive the measures of the First World War on their behalf. The British, however, refused to permit supplies to go through the blockade under neutral protection. My colleagues and I created a *National Committee on Food for the Small Democracies* to present the cause of the helpless women and children and destitute of these ravaged countries.[5]

The defeat of France was one of the great catastrophes to befall our civilization. But the French tragedy did not date from Hitler's attack on France; it dated from the decadence of the Blum regime and its Communist infiltration.[6]

---

5. [*Editor's note:* Hoover's organization initially called itself "the National Committee on Food for the Five Small Democracies." The word "Five" was later dropped.]

6. See Section II, Chapter 6.

CHAPTER 25

A Great Trial for
but No Defeat of Britain

HITLER, WITH STALIN GUARDING his eastern flank, now occupied every nation in Western Europe except the smaller states of Switzerland, Sweden, Spain, Portugal, and that of his ally Italy. He had at his disposal the manufactures and food supplies of the occupied nations. He had accomplished these military triumphs with a loss of probably only 200,000 men—a handicap overcome by a single new draft. From a military point of view, at this moment Hitler could justifiably consider himself as great as Napoleon.

His greatest remaining problem in Western Europe was the British. He had driven their armies from the Continent, but he had underestimated their courage and recuperative powers. And he did not realize the ability of the British navy to prevent his men from crossing the great British moat—the English Channel. The Germans organized a huge flotilla for this purpose but, after much hesitation, concluded that the British would have to be paralyzed by a great air blitz before a cross-channel landing could be made.[1]

The Battle of Britain

The Germans launched their air blitz on England with a daylight attack in early August 1940. Its impact was terrific, but the British put up one of the most heroic defenses in all history. The whole of America was spellbound by their courage, and anxious about the outcome. By radio, Prime Minister Chur-

---

1. German records captured after the war show the vacillation of the German staff over the idea of a frontal invasion of England by water. In July, 1940, Hitler gave orders to prepare Operation "Seeloewe" (Sea Lion); but despite staff differences of opinion, it was decided to await the achievement of air supremacy. (*Documents on German Foreign Policy, 1918–1945*, Series D, Vol. X [United States Department of State, Washington: 1957], pp. 226–229, 390–391.)

chill's superb oratory again and again poured accounts of the great drama into our sympathetic ears.

So successful was the British air resistance that the daylight battles in the skies were mostly over by mid-September. So confident was Prime Minister Churchill that there would be no attempt at a land invasion of Britain that he dispatched troops from England to support the British forces in Egypt.[2]

Late in September, the Germans switched their air strategy from daylight attacks to sporadic night bombing raids on Britain's industrial centers. The British put the city lights out, and thus the attacks did little harm to production plants scattered around the darkened cities, but inflicted a terrible toll on civilian life in the populous districts. These ferocious attacks on Birmingham, Liverpool, Leeds, Glasgow, Manchester, and London failed to break either British arms production or the spirit of the people.

The Germans pressed their attacks on British shipping, not only with submarines but also, at intervals, by the use of surface raiders, such as the cruiser *Hipper*. The total tonnage losses in merchant ships—British, Allied and neutrals—from all causes during the six months from June 1 to November 30, 1940, including normal sea losses, amounted to less than 3,000,000 tons. These figures do not represent a serious depletion of the 30,000,000 to 40,000,000 tons of Allied and neutral shipping available to the British at the outset of the war.

Despite all their losses and sufferings, the British remained to be Hitler's nemesis.

Demobilization of the French Navy

Before its surrender the French Government had given verbal assurances to the British that it would not allow its navy to be used against the British. The French armistice terms with the Germans stipulated that the fleet would remain in French ports. This arrangement, even if carried out, did not protect the British from attack by French naval units in foreign ports, since the Germans were in control of the Vichy government, which could command those units. On July 3, 1940, the British seized those French ships which were in British ports, and delivered an ultimatum to the French fleet at Oran to surrender. When the French admiral in command refused, the British opened fire and put most of the ships out of commission, killing about 1,000 French

2. William L. Langer and S. Everett Gleason, *The Challenge to Isolation, 1937–1940* (Harper & Brothers Publishers, New York: 1952), p. 666.

sailors. Also the British put out of action the French battleships *Jean Bart* and *Richelieu* by an air attack. An aircraft carrier and two light cruisers took refuge at the French port of Martinique in the West Indies and were protected by the American government.

Prime Minister Churchill quickly organized the forces which had taken refuge in Britain into the "Free French" under General Charles de Gaulle.

In August, British and Free French forces made an attack on Dakar in French West Africa. However, on September 25, the Vichy government forces repulsed the attack with considerable losses to the British and Free French.

The Italian Attacks on the British Colonies

Benito Mussolini had declared Italian neutrality at the time of the Stalin-Hitler alliance, but at the fall of France in June, 1940, he decided to join Hitler in the war. On August 6, the Italians started an invasion of the British crown colony of Somaliland. The British were ultimately forced to evacuate the country. On September 13, the Italians began operations in North Africa in order to drive the British from their hold on the one-thousand mile road from Tripoli to the Egyptian frontier. The British slowly withdrew. The Italians finally arrived at the Egyptian frontier with 70,000 to 80,000 men. On December 9, 1940, the British counter-attacked with a mixed force of British, Indians, Australians, and New Zealanders. By December 15, the Italians were driven back. The British announced that the Italians had lost 38,000 prisoners, and that their own casualties were less than 500.

More American Action—Stronger Than Words—but Less Than War

CHAPTER 26

Revision of the Neutrality Laws

PRESIDENT ROOSEVELT HAD SECURED the passage of rigid neutrality laws in the years 1935, 1936 and 1937.[1] I had opposed these laws because by their prevention of, or restriction on, shipment of arms from the United States, they would in effect favor aggressor nations. The dictator nations had established great munitions factories. The peace-loving nations had little or certainly fewer of them.[2]

With these laws in action it was impossible for the President to direct the exports of arms from the United States to the purpose of "more than words and less than war." For this or other reasons Mr. Roosevelt, on March 7, 1939, pointed out the failures of the neutrality legislation.[3]

Four months later, July 14, 1939, in a message to Congress, he urged modification of the Acts, appending a statement by Secretary Hull, supporting the amendments. However, the Secretary also warned:

... this nation should at all times avoid entangling alliances or involvements with other nations.

... in the event of foreign wars this nation should maintain a status of strict neutrality ... to keep this country from being drawn into war.[4]

On July 18, 1939, the Senate leaders, aware of opposition to Mr. Roosevelt's "actions more than words," announced that no action on the President's request to amend the Neutrality Acts would be taken at this time.[5]

---

1. See Section III, Chapter 16.

2. Herbert Hoover, *Further Addresses Upon the American Road, 1938–1940* (Charles Scribner's Sons, New York: 1940), p. 95.

3. [Samuel I. Rosenman, comp.], *The Public Papers and Addresses of Franklin D. Roosevelt,* 1939 [volume] (The Macmillan Company, New York: 1941), pp. 154–157.

4. Ibid., p. 382.

5. Ibid., pp. 387–388.

Inasmuch as the neutrality laws themselves were *un-neutral,* I urged the Republican members of Congress to support the amendments, and for the most part, they did.

On July 21, 1939, at a press conference, the President stated that he had been advised by leaders of both parties in the Congress that the amendments could not be passed in that session and therefore the subject must go over to the January 1940 meeting of Congress. In the meantime, the Second World War had begun in September 1939, by the Hitler-Stalin invasion of Poland.

As required by law, the President, on September 5, 1939, four days after the war began, formally declared the neutrality of the United States and issued a proclamation declaring it to be unlawful, under the Neutrality Act of 1937, to export any arms or munitions to belligerent nations.[6]

The day before, on September 4, 1939, I wrote to Colonel John Callan O'Laughlin in Washington:[7]

> ... Americans rightly are 97% against Hitler. [They ought to have been equally against Stalin.] At the moment, they are 97% against joining in a war. This makes a critical emotional situation which can be turned at any moment. ...
>
> If the allies could obtain arms in this country, it would give an emotional outlet to the American people. To refuse to sell arms will only dam up the tide which will break loose in a demand for participation.

Three weeks later, on September 24, 1949, I wrote to Colonel O'Laughlin again on the neutrality amendments, saying:

> It becomes clearer day by day that the crux of this situation [amendment of the Neutrality Act] is the profound public distrust of the President. For two years he has been moving step by step into power politics. ... these steps if continued will lead us into war or at least great embarrassment. ... I am convinced if any other one of our 31 presidents had made the address which he made Thursday to the Congress on the Neutrality Bill it would be passed immediately.

---

6. Ibid., p. 473.

7. Colonel O'Laughlin had been a highly respected newspaper correspondent in Washington for more than thirty years. He was at this time publisher of the influential *Army and Navy Journal.* For many years he advised me weekly of behind-the-scenes war and peace activities in Washington.

Efforts to Persuade Dictators

On April 14, 1939, about four months before the Hitler-Stalin alliance, the President made an address to the Pan-American Union, in which he said:

> ... Do we really have to assume that nations can find no better methods of realizing their destinies than those *which were used by the Huns and the Vandals fifteen hundred years ago?*[8]

The President was probably not intentionally giving Hitler and Mussolini these violent names. However, the German and Italian press gave it the objectionable interpretation.[9]

The day of this speech, Mr. Roosevelt addressed a strong note to Hitler (and to Mussolini). After listing Hitler's various acts of aggression, he continued:

> You have repeatedly asserted that you and the German people have no desire for war. If this is true there need be no war....
>
> It is therefore no answer to the plea for peaceful discussion for one side to plead that unless they receive assurances beforehand that the verdict will be theirs, they will not lay aside their arms. In conference rooms ... it is customary and necessary that they leave their arms outside the room where they confer.

The President asked:

> Are you willing to give assurance that your armed forces will not attack or invade the territory or possessions of the following independent nations: Finland, Estonia, Latvia, Lithuania, Sweden, Norway, Denmark, The Netherlands, Belgium, Great Britain and Ireland, France, Portugal, Spain, Switzerland, Liechtenstein, Luxemburg, Poland, Hungary, Rumania, Yugoslavia, Russia, Bulgaria, Greece, Turkey, Iraq, the Arabias, Syria, Palestine, Egypt and Iran.
>
> Such an assurance clearly must apply not only to the present day but also the future sufficiently long to give every opportunity to work by peaceful methods for a more permanent peace. I therefore suggest that you construe the word "future" to apply to a minimum period of assured non-aggression— ten years at the least—a quarter of a century, if we dare look that far ahead.[10]

---

8. *The Public Papers and Addresses of Franklin D. Roosevelt,* 1939 [volume], p. 198. Italics mine.
9. *New York Times,* April 15, 1939.
10. *The Public Papers and Addresses of Franklin D. Roosevelt,* 1939 [volume], pp. 202–204.

If his suggestions were accepted, the President proposed United States' participation in international negotiations that would begin the reduction of armaments. The suggestions in the message naturally did not appeal to either Hitler or Mussolini, and on April 20 and 28, they issued statements jeering at the proposal.

On April 25, 1939, Secretary Hull made an address urging peace for mankind. He described his purpose in his memoirs:

> I sought to dissuade the nations from the dangerous extremes of isolationism and aggrandizement. . . . [11]

Hull very properly was trying to use the moral influence of his position to bring Hitler, Mussolini, and the Japanese war lords to repent of their evil ways. Also, through diplomatic channels, these efforts were followed on May 17, 1939, by a warning of more than words. The Italian Minister for Foreign Affairs, Count Galeazzo Ciano, in his diary, noted:

> The American Ambassador [William Phillips] . . . stressed one point, namely, that the American people, who originated in Europe, intend unanimously to concern themselves in European affairs, and it would be folly to think that they would remain aloof in the event of a conflict. . . . [12]

---

11. *The Memoirs of Cordell Hull*, Vol. I (The Macmillan Co., New York: 1948), p. 622.

12. *The Ciano Diaries, 1939–1943* (Doubleday & Company, Inc., Garden City, New York: 1946), p. 83.

CHAPTER 27

Military Preparedness

IN THE SPRING OF 1940, the Congress was conducting an investigation of the security and management of our defense. They exposed some very disagreeable facts.[1]

On May 26, President Roosevelt made an extensive speech defending his position from the Congressional exposures. At the same time he blamed my Administration, which had ended seven years previously, for the weakness now being exposed. I replied in a national broadcast the following day. Both addresses have some interest as they reflect the American relations to the rest of the world as well as the vital question of the proper defense establishment and its administration in the United States.

Mr. Roosevelt said in part:

> . . . It is a known fact, however, that in 1933, when this Administration came into office, the United States Navy had fallen in standing among the navies of the world, in power of ships and in efficiency, to a relatively low ebb. The relative fighting power of the Navy had been greatly diminished by failure to replace ships and equipment. . . .
>
> But between 1933 and this year, 1940—seven fiscal years—your Government will have spent one billion four hundred eighty-seven million dollars more than it spent on the Navy during the seven years that preceded 1933. . . .
>
> The fighting personnel . . . [has risen] from 79,000 to 145,000.

---

1. General Douglas MacArthur was Chief of Staff and Admiral William V. Pratt Chief of Naval Operations in my Administration, which ended in 1933. The Congress had never lodged a complaint of our conduct of the forces.

During this period 215 ships . . . have been laid down or commissioned, practically seven times the number in the preceding seven-year period. . . .

. . . in 1933 we had 1,127 useful aircraft [Navy] and today we have 2,892 on hand *and on order.* . . .

The Army . . . in 1933 consisted of 122,000 enlisted men. Now, in 1940, that number has been practically doubled. The Army of 1933 had been given few new implements of war since 1919. . . .

We are calling on men now engaged in private industry to help us in carrying out this program [later termed the "Council of National Defense"]. . . .

. . . The functions of the business men whose assistance we are calling upon will be to coordinate this program—to see to it that all of the plants continue to operate at maximum speed and efficiency.[2]

The speech contained many misrepresentations. Also, it contained many misleading implications. It ignored the most essential facts in world armament.

It ignored the fact that serious aggressive militarism had been absent from the world for fourteen years following the First World War until the time of Mr. Roosevelt's election. It was not his fault that Hitler, Stalin and the Japanese war lords had become threatening. They came into aggressive power a few months prior to his election.

His speech ignored the fact that in both the Coolidge Administration and in mine, we had secured agreements for a great reduction in the world's powerful navies, including British, French, and Japanese, and we were bound by these agreements to reduce our own.

And above all it ignored the fact that Mr. Roosevelt had been in power for seven years during the rise of aggression in the world since my administration had ended, during which time he had taken little substantial action.

Despite the growth of these dangers, Mr. Roosevelt, on the contrary, in the early years of his Administration, reduced the level of military expenditures of my Administration by about $100,000,000 a year. It was not until four and one-half years after he came into office that the levels of my defense expenditures had been restored.

The President had the authority, under the National Defense Act of 1920, to increase the Army to 298,000 men (including officers). Nevertheless, in the face of increasing world danger, he had held it at less than 180,000 for the

---

2. [Samuel I. Rosenman, comp.,] *The Public Papers and Addresses of Franklin D. Roosevelt, 1940* [volume] [The Macmillan Company, New York: 1941], pp. 232–233, 236. Italics mine.

first six years of his Administration. Despite the expenditure by Mr. Roosevelt's seven years of $3,439,000,000 on the Navy, the number of fighting ships had been increased by only 260,000 tons more than at the end of my Administration.

In my address on May 27, 1940, I said:

> The increasing dangers in the world make it imperative that we be better prepared. But equally the time has come when the American people must insist that adequate organization be set up within the government which will produce this defense. It must be an organization directed by men of outstanding experience in production, management and labor unhampered by partisan politics.

Speaking of the rise of militarism and the alliance of Stalin and Hitler, I continued:

> Today we are onlookers at the most tremendous human tragedy of centuries. We are horrified at each gigantic scene. Scene after scene is so great and so terrible that even across three thousand miles of ocean our people are filled with sympathy, with indignation, with hopes and with fear. Our people are justly alarmed for our own safety. . . .
>
> . . . Whatever the outcome in Europe may be or whatever the intentions of European war-makers may be, that is not the problem I wish to discuss. What America must have is such defenses that no European nation will even think about crossing this three thousand miles of ocean at all. We must make sure that no such dangerous thoughts will be generated in their minds. We want a sign of "Keep Off the Grass" with a fierce dog plainly in sight.
>
> I was born and raised in that religious atmosphere which for three hundred years has never varied in its extreme devotion to peace. Yet I know that peace comes in the modern world only to those nations which are adequately prepared to defend themselves. The European Allies are now paying in blood and disaster for their failure to heed plain warnings. With adequate preparedness they might have escaped attack.
>
> The anxiety and alarm which in recent days have gripped our people have not been all due to the rise of a new system of government in Europe which does not hesitate to overrun innocent neutrals. It is not all due to the new character of mechanized armies. It is not all due to the barbaric use of these weapons against peaceful people and against women and children. It is also due to alarm and shock over the disclosure of the inadequacy of our preparedness plans and our defense.

The Congress has hugely increased appropriations for national defense, steadily for the past five years. The expenditures upon the Army and Navy have more than doubled from about 550 million in 1934 to over one billion three hundred thousand this year. Now the Chief of Staff tells the Congress that we are not organized to wage modern war—that our arsenals are not equipped to produce the guns we should have; that it will take until June, 1942, to obtain the necessary new rifles for our present force; that we are woefully behind in anti-tank guns; in anti-aircraft guns; in coast defense; and in tanks.

Congress was told that we could only put 75,000 men into the field as a mobile force at the present time, and that these would not be fully equipped. Further, that it would take 18 months at least to equip our present army and reserves of 450,000 men. We are told we do not even have sufficient clothing for this army.

And the Chief of the Air Corps comes before the Congress and says that none of the Army's airplanes can be regarded as modern. Asked how many of our 2700 military airplanes "can be modernized," the Air Corps Chief replied: "Offhand, I should say a half dozen." And perhaps most disheartening of all was his statement that the whole production of military airplanes even under the impulse of Allied orders is only about 340 per month. And this contrasts with a sudden statement that we need 4000 per month.

President Roosevelt in his address last evening implied that previous administrations had been derelict in providing national defense. . . . I could challenge the implications of Mr. Roosevelt's figures. For instance, despite the number of warships commissioned or not commissioned, the Statistical Abstract, published by Mr. Roosevelt's Administration, shows we had available fighting ships to a total of about 1,100,000 tons when he took office, against about 1,350,000 tons today.

Of far more importance, however, national defense is a relative thing. It is relative to the military menace in the rest of the world. No government has the right to impose unnecessary burdens on all those who toil.

For fourteen years after the Great War, and up to the end of the last Administration, the face of the civilized world was kept turned toward peace. All major nations were in agreement limiting their navies and these agreements were being observed. Germany was limited by the Treaty of Versailles to 100,000 men and not much navy. Agreement to limit land armament among other nations was making progress. Methods for settlement of disputes by peaceful means were becoming stronger. During this time we in the United States spent about $700 million a year on our Army and Navy.

President Roosevelt considered the outlook throughout the world for peace and disarmament was so promising that he in 1934 himself reduced this rate of expenditure by about $100,000,000.

The peaceful democratic government of Germany collapsed into dictatorship under Hitler two months after Mr. Roosevelt was elected. It was in Mr. Roosevelt's Administration that Europe began to rumble with aggression and armament. The German Army grew to 2,500,000 men. Their navy expanded. Great Britain, France, Russia and Japan and all others at once expanded their expenditures 400 percent. The total of sixty nations increased expenditures from 4 billion in 1932 to 17 billion in 1938. The suggestion that we should have armed against menaces that had not been born seems overdone. . . .

What we are interested in now is not recrimination. What we want is to be prepared.

The first step in adequate preparedness must be made right in Washington. Our governmental machinery must be made capable of producing preparedness. . . .

The Congressional exposures and the growing world menace had made reorganization of our whole defense mandatory. Therefore, I made some recommendations:

This experience of the whole world leads to certain definite and specific conclusions as to organization of preparedness in industry when governments are under strain.

First and foremost: This is a business requiring expert knowledge of manufacturing, industry, labor and transportation and agriculture. . . .

. . . such operations cannot be controlled by boards or councils or conferences.

They must be controlled by a singlehanded trusted and experienced man. . . .

Therefore . . . essentials of this organization . . . [require]:

1. That a Munitions Administration be created in Washington.
2. That it should have a singleheaded Administrator. . . .

I concluded:

Human liberty may need take refuge upon this continent. We must efficiently be prepared to defend it as the last hope of the world.[3]

---

3. Herbert Hoover, *Addresses Upon the American Road, 1940–1941* (Charles Scribner's Sons, New York: 1941), pp. 4–13.

My address was answered not by fact and argument but by a bitter attack upon me by Assistant Secretary of War Louis Johnson, on May 28, 1940. The next day (May 29), I replied to Secretary Johnson as follows:

> In view of the crisis we face and all the exposures of the past month, the country will be disappointed that President Roosevelt has chosen to set up another advisory committee instead of reorganizing the War and Navy Departments and appointing somebody from industry for the production of munitions. There are three or four good men on this committee, and the country will gain confidence if it boldly insists that these things be done at once.
>
> Certainly, Assistant Secretary of War Louis Johnson last night demonstrated that his capabilities at political smearing exceed the capacities he has shown in past years in production of airplanes and guns.
>
> We need action now and not advisory reports for the files.[4]

Two months later, Secretary Johnson, having resigned his position, apologized to me for his speech and informed me that it had been written in the White House and that he had been ordered to deliver it. He also stated that my radio address had contributed to a general shake-up in the military administration. Within a month after my address the President appointed Henry L. Stimson, Secretary of War, and Frank Knox, Secretary of the Navy. Stimson had been Secretary of State during my Administration, and Knox had been the Republican Vice Presidential candidate in 1936. They were able men. I may mention here that Secretary Johnson has become my devoted friend.

Our Domestic Communists Go into Action against Preparedness

With the starting of the European war in 1939, the Communists undertook sabotage and the stimulation of strikes in our industries supplying England and France with munitions. The Attorney General—Frank Murphy—denounced them roundly and publicly.[5] However, none of the Communists in Mr. Roosevelt's official family were expelled.[6]

---

4. *New York Times,* May 30, 1940.
5. Ibid., October 15, 1939 and November 1, 1939.
6. It was not until Hitler's invasion of Russia on June 22, 1941, that the American left-wing saw the war in a new light. At that point the Communist party line instantly switched and began demanding American participation in what now overnight had "become a people's war."

CHAPTER 28

More Than Words in the Balkans

THE PRESIDENT AND SECRETARY HULL dispatched an able New York attorney—Colonel William J. Donovan—to the Balkans to stir up action against Hitler, or to prevent the absorption of these states into the German orbit.

Secretary Hull records in his memoirs that our Minister to Yugoslavia, Arthur Bliss Lane, on January 24 and 25, 1941, cabled that he and Colonel Donovan had secured an assurance from the Regent—Prince Paul—and the Prime Minister—Dragisha Cvetkovic—that

> . . . Yugoslavia would not permit troops or war materials to pass [to the Germans]. . . . [1]

However, under German threats, Yugoslavia about two months later (March 25, 1941) signed up as a member of the Axis. But a dissenting group under General Dusan Simovitch overthrew the Regent Prince Paul and the Prime Minister, and installed young King Peter II on the throne by a *coup d'etat* two days later, on March 27. That same day, Mr. Churchill added a mite of cheer to the new Yugoslav government in a speech to the Central Council of the National Union of Conservative and Unionist Associations in London:

> . . . I have great news for you and the whole country. Early this morning the Yugoslav nation found its soul. A revolution has place in Belgrade. . . .
>
> We may therefore cherish the hope . . . that a Yugoslav Government will be formed worthy to defend the freedom and integrity of their country. Such a government in its brave endeavour will receive from the British Empire, and, I doubt not, in its own way from the United States, all possible aid and

---

1. *The Memoirs of Cordell Hull*, Vol. II (The Macmillan Company, New York: 1948), p. 928.

succour. The British Empire and its Allies will make common cause with the Yugoslav nation, and we shall continue to march and strive together until complete victory is won.[2]

Mr. Roosevelt, on March 28, cabled congratulations.[3]

The Germans, ten days later (April 6, 1941), invaded Yugoslavia. On April 13, 1941, I wrote Colonel O'Laughlin:

> I was dismayed by the President's cable to Jugoslavia, assuring those people of our assistance. These are a simple minded people and they will be looking for American planes and American soldiers within a week. Roosevelt knows perfectly well that we cannot deliver any such assistance. And to their ultimate defeat will be added bitterness towards the United States.

The Yugoslavs surrendered to the Germans four days later, on April 17.[4]

Nor was this the whole story. The German attack was accompanied by the butchery of bombing unprotected Belgrade and by the subsequent execution of civilians. The press reported that 30,000 civilians were killed.

Greece

The Italian Army invaded Greece on October 28, 1940. The Greeks put up a noble defense and on December 3, 1940, King George II of Greece appealed to President Roosevelt for help. Two days later (on December 5), Mr. Roosevelt replied:

> As Your Majesty knows, it is the settled policy of the United States Government to extend aid to those governments and peoples who defend themselves against aggression. I assure Your Majesty that steps are being take to extend such aid to Greece which is defending itself so valiantly.[5]

There was no aid from the United States but three months later (March 13–14, 1941) the British diverted troops, naval and air strength from Egypt to assist the Greeks. The Germans quickly invaded Greece (April 6, 1941) in support of the Italians. Two weeks later (April 23) the major Greek armies surrendered

---

2. [Winston S.] Churchill, *The Unrelenting Struggle* (Little, Brown and Company, Boston: 1942), pp. 69–70.

3. *New York Times,* March 29, 1941.

4. Some years later Ambassador Lane confirmed to me the pressures which had been applied upon Hull's instructions.

5. [Samuel I. Rosenman, comp.,] *The Public Papers and Addresses of Franklin D. Roosevelt, 1940* [volume] (The Macmillan Company, New York: 1941), p. 599.

to the Germans. Within a week, the British withdrew to Crete with losses of some 12,000 of their troops and extensive materiel. The Germans attacked the British fleet from Greek air bases on May 20, and from the air imposed one of the great British naval disasters of the war. Two cruisers and four destroyers were sunk; two battleships and several cruisers were damaged.

There were still other tragedies as a result of the British action in Greece.

The British had driven the Italians out of Egypt at the end of 1940, and had advanced west along the North African coast as far as Benghazi. But they had fatally depleted their North African forces for the expedition to Greece. On April 3, 1941, the British were forced by the Italians to retreat to their Egyptian base with considerable losses.

At the end of May, 1941, I received a letter from Colonel O'Laughlin giving more confirmation of American activities in Yugoslav and Greek affairs. He said:

> Some absolutely reliable information, which I got this week, throws a flood of light upon the attitude of the President. . . . Mr. Roosevelt was entirely and solely responsible for the unsuccessful British expedition in Greece. He had been so committed by his promises to Yugo-Slavia and Greece, promises which caused the overthrow of the Paul Government at Belgrade, and the organization of the new Government which repudiated the Paul-von Ribbentrop agreement, that he felt it was imperative to make a show of military assistance to those countries. He discussed the matter at length with Secretary Knox and Bill Donovan, and they advised that action of this kind must be taken, first, in the hope that another front could be established against Germany and Italy, and, second, because of the stimulating effect it would have upon the conquered peoples of Europe. Mr. Roosevelt discussed the proposal with Secretary Stimson and General Marshall. Both strongly opposed it. It was the conviction of General Marshall, as well as of Stimson, that the [British] expeditionary force would be unable to resist the onslaught of the Germans, and they pointed out the effect of the depletion of General Wavell's force in North Africa, from which the expeditionary force for Greece would have to be drawn. The strategic dispositions of German Armies they regarded as assuring the early conquest of Greece and Yugo-Slavia, and they forecasted that the reinforced Axis troops in Tripoli would instantly take advantage of Wavell's [the British] weakness, and advance toward Alexandria and the Suez Canal.

> The President preferred to listen to Knox and Donovan, instead of the General Staff. He felt he was forced to do so in order to fulfill his commitments

to the Balkan States. It had been by his instruction that our Minister to Yugo-Slavia, Arthur Bliss Lane, had given pledges to the Yugo-Slavs which they regarded as a guarantee that the United States would preserve their country from German occupation. Equally direct representations were made to the Greek Government by our Minister at Athens. As interpreted by the two Governments, the statements of our representatives constituted official assurances of all out aid. And all out aid in their view, meant arms, armies and ships. Poor, misguided patriots, they did not know how unable we were to do any of the things promised them.

As the President felt that under all the circumstances he could not let the Yugo-Slavs and Greeks down, and as we could not supply either men or equipment, he communicated with Mr. Churchill, and urged him to send an expeditionary force to support the Balkan States. Mr. Churchill offered strenuous opposition. He declared it was a military mistake to attempt an operation which was bound to fail, and which offered prospects of grave repercussions. In the end he was obligated to yield to the President's insistence, and the consequences followed which he had anticipated, and which Secretary Stimson and General Marshall had foreseen. The Germans, who might not have advanced in the Mediterranean area by sea, now are picking up Island after Island so as to have a water borne route to the Levant, along which they will march toward the Suez Canal. Simultaneously they drove General Wavell's army back into Egypt. . . .

. . . Hitler had given them [the "conquered peoples"–*ed.*] an object lesson which impressed them, and which they will not soon forget. Consequently, they are more under his heel than they have ever been.

Actions Stronger Than Words in the Far East 1938–1940

As early as July 1, 1938, in an effort to restrain Japan's wholly immoral attacks on China, Mr. Roosevelt imposed embargoes on specific munitions to Japan by Administration requests to American firms to stop such shipments.[6]

On July 10, 1939, Secretary Hull delivered a vigorous protest to Japanese Ambassador Kensuke Horinouchi in Washington on the subject of their international relations.[7] Ten days later, he delivered another lecture to the Ambassador on the subject of international sin in general.[8]

---

6. [U.S.] Department of State, *Peace and War, United States Foreign Policy, 1931–1941* [United States Government Printing Office, Washington: 1943], Document 109, p. 422.

7. *The Memoirs of Cordell Hull*, Vol. I, pp. 632ff.

8. Ibid., p. 634.

On July 21, 1939, alarmed at British attempts at an amicable settlement of their frictions with Japan in order not to add to their war dangers now rising in Europe, the Secretary sent a dispatch to our chargé d'affaires in Tokyo, Eugene H. Dooman, expressing the hope that no agreement would be made by Britain with Japan.[9] However, the British went ahead with their negotiations and three days later announced a compromise formula which amounted to acceptance of the Japanese situation in Asia.

Two days later, on July 26, 1939, Secretary Hull took "action stronger than words." He gave Japan six months' notice of our intention to abrogate our commercial treaty of 1911. The Secretary stated in his memoirs:

> In addition to the psychological factor, we had a practical consideration in mind as well. This involved embargoes on the shipment of certain materials to Japan. We already had applied a moral embargo . . . against the shipment of airplanes to Japan. . . . [10]

American Ambassador to Japan Joseph C. Grew stated at the time:

> . . . In both my talks with the President I brought out clearly my views that if we once start sanctions against Japan we must see them through to the end, and the end may conceivably be war. . . . [11]

The Japanese inquired as to the purpose of our abrogation of the commercial treaty. Secretary Hull's reaction, as noted in his memoirs, was:

> . . . I felt that our best tactic was to keep them guessing. . . . [12]

The Secretary of State, however, was probably worried over this action since about 3,500 words in his memoirs are devoted to an explanation.

On August 26, 1939, the Secretary delivered another statement to the Japanese Ambassador concerning American-Japanese relations.[13]

The Burma Road

The Burma Road, extending several hundred miles from northern Burma to Yunnan Province, China, had been built by the Chinese. They were largely

---

9. Ibid., Vol. I, p. 635.
10. Ibid., p. 636.
11. Joseph C. Grew, *The Turbulent Era* (Houghton Mifflin Company, Boston: 1952), Vol. II, p. 1211.
12. *The Memoirs of Cordell Hull*, Vol. I, p. 638.
13. Ibid., pp. 630–640.

dependent upon it for military supplies, all other routes having been closed by the Japanese invaders. In the summer of 1940 the Japanese pressed Britain to close this supply route for China. The British, by this time locked in a life-and-death struggle with Hitler, had no desire to take on Japan as well.

Secretary Hull records in his memoirs that on June 27, 1940, the British Ambassador, Lord Lothian, came in to see him and handed him an *aide-mémoire* which proposed a settlement of the China problem, as follows:

> Britain . . . believed there were only two courses open. One was for the United States to increase pressure on Japan either by imposing a full embargo on exports to Japan or by sending warships to Singapore, fully realizing that these steps might result in war. The second was to negotiate a full settlement with Japan.
>
> Britain wanted to know if we would adopt the first course, saying she would cooperate. If not, would we join with Britain in making proposals for a Far Eastern settlement? Such proposals might embrace: joint assistance in bringing about a peace with China that would leave China independent; Japan to remain neutral in the European War and to respect the integrity of Occidental possessions in the Orient; the United States and Britain to give Japan financial and economic assistance; the Allied Governments to be guaranteed against reexports to enemy countries; status of foreign settlements and concessions in China to be settled after restoration of peace in Europe and China.
>
> After I had listened to Lothian's reading of this *aide-mémoire,* I said that my Government for manifest reasons would not be in position to send the Navy as far away as Singapore, even assuming that it might desire to do so, which I was not assuming. I promised to let him know later my reaction to his second proposal.[14]

The next day, Hull turned down the Lothian proposals but stated that the United States would have no objection to the British and Australians trying to bring peace between Japan and China. However, he said that the United States must make two points in this connection:

> . . . First, the principles underlying Japan's application of her "new order in East Asia" would need negativing or at least serious modifying. Second, no properties or interests of China should be offered to Japan by Britain or the United States. In other words, we do not make peace with Japan at the

---

14. Ibid., p. 897.

expense of China or of the principles I set forth in July, 1937, when Japan invaded China.

Hull adds:

Finally I suggested that, in addition to the two courses of action proposed by Britain, there might be a third choice. "Many impairments of the rights and interests of Britain and the United States have occurred in the Far East," I said. "In combating them, however, the various Governments concerned have not resorted to either of the methods you suggest. We all have had to acquiesce in various of them. Acquiescence may be a matter of necessity. Giving of assent, however, is quite another matter. If a process of bargaining is engaged in, that which may be conceded or given by those powers now on the defensive will become irrevocable. And the future performance of Japan, in return for them, still remains problematical."[15]

Two weeks later (July 12, 1940), the British informed Hull that the Japanese might declare war on Britain at any time unless they closed the Burma Road. Ambassador Lothian stated that his government was going to adopt one of two alternatives:

... One was to close the road for three months to any larger volume of freight than existed the previous year. This period was during the rainy season when the flow of goods to China over the highway was very limited. The other was to suspend the transport of all war materials for three months, and devote this period to an effort at a general settlement of the Sino-Japanese War.[16]

On July 15 and 18 the British pressed Hull further. In September, they again suggested that American naval forces be sent to Singapore.[17]

On October 4, Churchill notified Roosevelt that the British would reopen the Burma Road on October 17,[18] and again asked that an "American squadron, the bigger the better," be sent to Singapore.

The squadron was not sent and in the end the British closed the road and all transport to China depended upon an airlift protected by the "American Volunteer Group" (Flying Tigers).

---

15. Ibid., pp. 898–899.
16. Ibid., p. 900.
17. Ibid., p. 911.
18. [Winston S.] Churchill, *Their Finest Hour* [Houghton Mifflin Company, Boston: 1949], pp. 497–498.

SECTION VII

Brainwashing the American People

CHAPTER 29

"Hitler's Coming!"

THE FIRST WORLD WAR marked the first time in our history that our government organized all the powerful agencies of publicity and manipulation of news without moral restraint under the genius of skilled men, to get America into war.

Being alarmed that again we might be drawn into a European war, I published an article in the August, 1939, issue of *The American Magazine.*[1] I included the following observations upon what we politely called "propaganda" in the First World War. I said in part:

> ... There were built up a skill and a technique in front of which every citizen was helpless to know the truth. And since that time the radio has become an additional weapon....
>
> From the beginning of the Great War I saw the development of the propaganda directed at the United States from both ... [combatants]. I was so impressed that I collected this material for years. The War Library at Stanford University holds stack after stack of this emanation from every government at war. And, in the light of what we now know ... it comprises the greatest collection of past lies on the face of the earth....
>
> We are told that we must join in war or democracy will disappear from the earth....

It has been rightly said that truth is the first fatality of war. But truth in modern war had its first fatality in propaganda.

Continuously from the outbreak of the Second World War, the American people were again brainwashed by a deluge of propaganda which in its mildest

---

1. See Section IV, Chapter 20.

form was greatly diluted truth. Moreover, this brainwashing was not confined to words but included elaborate activities.

It came from three sources: (a) the officials of our government; (b) our citizens organizations; (c) from European countries and their agents in the United States.

Our Domestic Campaign of Fright That "Hitler Is Coming!"

A major effort in brainwashing was the portrayal of horrors that would happen to the American people when Hitler invaded our shores. This gruesome picture was often described in detail as to his preparations and his route, and what the Nazis would do as occupational troops in our country.

During the Presidential campaign of 1940, the President repeated this fright in speeches on May 10, 16, and 26. Administration speakers joined in with horrifying tales of Hitler's arrival in the United States. Among these speakers were Secretaries Hull, Stimson, Knox, Ickes, and Perkins. Also adding heat to the fire of terror were Vice President Henry A. Wallace, Ambassador to France William C. Bullitt, and John G. Winant, our Ambassador to Britain.

As examples: Secretary Hull contributed a bit on July 22, 1940, by warning the Nazis to keep their hands off the Western Hemisphere.[2] Ambassador Bullitt, on August 18, 1940 (then at the White House daily), said:

America is in danger.

It is my conviction, drawn from my own experience and from the information in the hands of our government in Washington, that the United States is in as great peril today as was France a year ago. And I believe that unless we act now, decisively, to meet the threat we shall be too late. . . .

What stands today between the Americas and the unleashed dictatorships? The British Fleet and the courage of the British people. How long will the British Fleet be able to hold the exits from Europe to the Atlantic? I cannot answer that question nor can any man. . . .

Do we want to see Hitler in Independence Hall making fun of the Liberty Bell?[3]

In a "fireside chat" on December 29, 1940, the President envisaged a new crisis for America. He said:

---

2. *The Memoirs of Cordell Hull* [The Macmillan Company, New York: 1948], Vol. I, p. 823.
3. *New York Times,* August 19, 1940.

Never before since Jamestown and Plymouth Rock has our American civilization been in such danger as now. . . .

The Nazi masters of Germany have made it clear that they intend not only to dominate all life and thought in their own country, but also to enslave the whole of Europe, and then to use the resources of Europe to dominate the rest of the world. . . .

There are those who say that the Axis powers would never have any desire to attack the Western Hemisphere. That is the same dangerous form of wishful thinking which has destroyed the powers of resistance of so many conquered peoples. The plain facts are that the Nazis have proclaimed, time and again, that all other races are their inferiors and therefore subject to their orders. And most important of all, the vast resources and wealth of this American hemisphere constitute the most tempting loot in all of the round world.

Let us no longer blind ourselves to the undeniable fact that the evil forces which have crushed and undermined and corrupted so many others are already within our gates. . . .[4]

Nor did this "fright campaign" of Hitler's invading the Western Hemisphere cease when official Washington knew positively that he was turning his armies to the east and was about to invade Russia.[5]

In Mr. Roosevelt's speech of March 15, 1941, after the passage of the Lend-Lease Act on March 11, he envisaged the Nazi invasion of the United States, saying:

Nazi forces are not seeking mere modifications in colonial maps or in minor European boundaries. They openly seek the destruction of all elective systems of government on every continent—including our own; they seek to establish systems of government based on the regimentation of all human beings by a handful of individual rulers who have seized power by force.[6]

On May 27, 1941, the President said in a nation–wide broadcast:

---

4. Ibid., December 30, 1940.
5. See Chapter [33–ed.].
6. [Samuel I. Rosenman, comp.,] *The Public Papers and Addresses of Franklin D. Roosevelt, 1941* [volume] (Harper & Brothers, Publishers, New York: 1950), p. 62. See also the *Memoirs of Cordell Hull* (The Macmillan Company, New York: 1948), Vol. II, pp. 967–973. Secretary Hull shows that American officials knew that Hitler was moving on Russia.

The first and fundamental fact is that what started as a European war has developed, as the Nazis always intended it should develop, into a war for world domination.

Adolf Hitler never considered the domination of Europe as an end in itself. European conquest was but a step toward ultimate goals in all the other continents. It is unmistakably apparent to all of us that unless the advance of Hitlerism is forcibly checked now, the Western Hemisphere will be within range of the Nazi weapons of destruction. . . .

Your government knows what terms Hitler, if victorious, would impose. They are, indeed, the only terms on which he would accept a so-called "negotiated" peace.

And, under those terms Germany would literally parcel out the world—hoisting the swastika itself over vast territories and populations, and setting up puppet governments of its own choosing, wholly subject to the will and the policy of a conqueror. . . .

. . . they [dictatorships] are even now organizing—to build a naval and air force intended to gain and hold and be master of the Atlantic and the Pacific as well.

They would fasten an economic strangle–hold upon our several Nations. . . .

. . . I am not speculating about all this. I merely repeat what is already in the Nazi book of world conquest. . . . They plan . . . to strangle the United States of America and the Dominion of Canada. . . .

. . . our right to worship would be threatened. . . .

They . . . have the armed power at any moment to occupy Spain and Portugal; and that threat extends . . . also to the Atlantic fortress of Dakar, and to . . . the Azores and Cape Verde Islands.

[Yes, these] Cape Verde Islands are only seven hours' distance from Brazil by bomber or troop-carrying planes. . . .

The War is approaching the brink of the Western Hemisphere itself. It is coming very close to home.

Control or occupation by Nazi forces of any of . . . the Atlantic would jeopardize the immediate safety of portions of North and South America. . . .[7]

On August 15, 1941, a little more than seven weeks after Hitler had actually attacked Russia, Secretary of War Stimson delivered this terrorizing statement:

---

7. *New York Times,* May 28, 1941. See also *The Public Papers and Addresses of Franklin D. Roosevelt, 1941* [volume], p. 181ff.

... The bombing airplane already has a range of several thousand miles. . . . these hostile weapons may easily become an instrument for the invasion of this hemisphere. . . .

At Dakar, which is held by Vichy forces, now friendly with Germany, the great western bulge of the African coast narrows the South Atlantic Ocean until the distance from Dakar to the easternmost point of Brazil can be easily traversed either by air or sea. . . .

If, by combining an air attack with a fifth-column revolution, an Axis power should succeed in making a lodgment upon the coast of South America . . . it would not be difficult for any enemy lodged there to get within easy bombing distance of the Panama Canal. . . .

Then, indeed, we would be face to face with a danger which even our isolationists would recognize as the danger of invasion. Such an attack would be no playboy affair. . . . The Germans have a trained army of over seven million men and an air force of over half a million men. Japan has today under arms over two million men. . . .[8]

This particular contribution of fright was founded upon too many "ifs": if the Germans could cross the desert to Dakar; if, after arrival, they had a naval force which could overcome the American Navy in the crossing to Brazil; if, on arriving at Brazil, they could establish air bases against American opposition; and, if they had bombers which could reach the United States, etc., etc. And it might be observed that Hitler was deeply engaged in Russia at this moment and needed all his men and air equipment in that task.

In an address on September 11, 1941, when Hitler was already deep in Russia, the President again returned to his "fright" campaign, saying:

No tender whisperings of appeasers that Hitler is not interested in the Western Hemisphere, no soporific lullabies that a wide ocean protects us from him—can long have any effect on the hard-headed, far-sighted, and realistic American people.

He added:

. . . when you see a rattlesnake poised to strike, you do not wait until he has struck before you crush him. . . .

. . . From now on, if German or Italian vessels of war enter the waters, the protection of which is necessary for American defense, they do so at their own peril.

8. *New York Times,* August 16, 1941.

The orders which I have given as Commander in Chief of the United States Army and Navy are to carry out that policy—at once.[9]

In an address on October 27, 1941, when Hitler was already stuck in the Russian morass with all of his military equipment, the President again envisaged more "fright," saying:

> ... I have in my possession a secret map made in Germany by Hitler's Government—by the planners of the new world order. It is a map of South America and a part of Central America, as Hitler proposes to reorganize it. Today in this area there are fourteen separate countries. But the geographical experts of Berlin have ruthlessly obliterated all existing boundary lines; they have divided South America into five vassal states, bringing the whole continent under their domination. And they have also so arranged it that the territory of one of these new puppet states includes the Republic of Panama and our great life line—the Panama Canal. ...
>
> This map, my friends, makes clear the Nazi design not only against South America but against the United States as well.
>
> Your Government has in its possession another document, made in Germany by Hitler's Government. It is a detailed plan, which, for obvious reasons, the Nazis did not wish and do not wish to publicize just yet, but which they are ready to impose, a little later, on a dominated world—if Hitler wins. It is a plan to abolish all existing religions—Catholic, Protestant, Mohammedan, Hindu, Buddhist, and Jewish alike. The property of all churches will be seized by the Reich and its puppets. The cross and all other symbols of religion are to be forbidden. The clergy are to be forever liquidated, silenced under penalty of the concentration camps, where even now so many fearless men are being tortured because they have placed God above Hitler.
>
> In the place of the churches of our civilization, there is to be set up an International Nazi Church—a church which will be served by orators sent out by the Nazi Government. And in the place of the Bible, the words of *Mein Kampf* will be imposed and enforced as Holy Writ. And in the place of the cross of Christ will be put two symbols—the swastika and the naked sword. ...[10]

---

9. *The Public Papers and Addresses of Franklin D. Roosevelt*, 1941 [volume], pp. 389–391.
10. Ibid., pp. 439–440.

Where Mr. Roosevelt got this apparition has not been disclosed.[11]

Weary of this frightfulness campaign and its threatened horrors, I sought the opinion of Retired Admiral William V. Pratt, who in years past had been the Chief of Naval Operations of the United States. I made the following note of what the Admiral said:

The British-Dutch fleet consists of about 1,600,000 tons of combat ships. The German-Italian fleet is now about 520,000 tons. A land operation against Britain would require that they cross the Channel and establish beachheads. They could not hold these beachheads without at least 300,000 men and a million tons of equipment and supplies carried in a huge armada of merchant ships. They would need follow it with at least 1,000,000 more men. In the meantime, the British Fleet would be in action.

This idea of invasion across the Channel is nonsense, and without it the British cannot be defeated. All this stuff about the British surrendering their fleet to the Germans at once falls to the ground, as the British cannot be defeated.

That the British Fleet protects the United States from Hitler's invading the Western Hemisphere is also nonsense. If Hitler cannot cross the Channel, he cannot cross 3,000 miles of the Atlantic. Even supposing that Hitler overcame the British and undertook the 3,000 mile expedition to the United States, he must prepare two million men and an armada of at least 10,000,000 tons of merchant ships to keep them supplied. Hitler's air fleet could give this armada protection for only the first 500 miles. Then they would meet the American Navy with its 1,300,000 tons of fighting ships, including our submarines in mid-Atlantic. When Hitler got his remnants within 500 miles of our shores, our American air fleet would go into action. From our air fleet we would know where Hitler was going to land. And when he got within ten miles of those spots, he would have to meet every big Coast Guard gun we possess. While he was coming we could have ample time to get them into action. If he landed his remnant forces on our beaches, he would have to meet

---

11. Four years later, after the German surrender, I was in Germany. The American Army authorities informed me they had been instructed to search for these plans. Our officials informed me there were no such plans in the captured German files. Not only did the captured German records and the severe interrogations of their generals and political leaders show no such plans or intentions, but a search of our own departmental documents disclosed not an atom of such information. It is worthy of note that in all the detailed stenographic record of the Molotov-Hitler conference of November, 1940, about dividing Europe and Asia (see page [228–ed.]) there was not one word of reference to the occupation of the Western Hemisphere.

every fighting man in the United States. The German generals and admirals know that such an expedition is sheer nonsense.

Admiral Pratt insisted that even should a Hitler Quisling get possession of England, he would not control Canada and Australia, and that the British Navy had a sense of responsibility to their brothers in the Commonwealth. The Admiral added that any idea that Hitler would make such an attack on the United States via South America was still greater nonsense. Hitler's ships would be twice as long at sea over the South American route and would be exposed to American submarines and battleship action for twice as long a time. He summed up these propaganda stories about Hitler landing on the Western Hemisphere as either fabrications or hysteria.

The Admiral was also emphatic that unless we provoked a war the Japanese would not attack the United States, as their objectives were elsewhere.

General Albert C. Wedemeyer was an important member of the War Plans Division of the American Army during this period. In his book, *Wedemeyer Reports!*, the General describes the scene at this time:

> ... President Roosevelt tried to curdle our blood by talking about Nazi plans to invade South America from Dakar in Africa, when in fact there never was any such menace. Hitler had neither threatened nor planned to attack the Western Hemisphere. . . .[12]

The General says:

> Any military man, or anyone versed in military science, would recognize at once that such an advance by the Germans was preposterous. . . .[13]

On December 30, 1953, Stetson Conn, an official United States Army historian, delivered a paper before the American Historical Association in which he reported upon his exhaustive research into German documents on the subject of a possible attack on the Western Hemisphere. Conn said:

> So far as is known, Nazi Germany never had any explicit territorial ambitions in either North or South America.[14]

Our Army Intelligence knew and informed me at that time that there was no possibility of invasion of the Western Hemisphere.

---

12. A. C. Wedemeyer, *Wedemeyer Reports!* (Henry Holt and Company, New York: 1958), pp. 17–18.
13. Ibid., p. 19.
14. *New York Times*, December 30, 1953. See also the *American Historical Review*, Vol. LIX, No. 3, April 1954, p. 789.

Major-General J. F. C. Fuller, an eminent British military historian, says:

... From the captured German archives there is no evidence to support the President's claims that Hitler contemplated an offensive against the western hemisphere. . . .[15]

In General George C. Marshall's Report to the Secretary of War dated September 1, 1945, he said:

As evaluated by the War Department General Staff, the interrogations of the captured German commanders disclose the following: . . . .

No evidence has yet been found that the German High Command had any over-all strategic plan. . . .[16]

Our Domestic Brainwashers

Dozens of citizen committees sprang up demanding various degrees of intervention in the war.[17] Practically all of them originated in New York. The most important was the "Committee to Defend America by Aiding the Allies," which was under the chairmanship of William Allen White, editor of *The Emporia Gazette* of Kansas.

Among the other organizations were the "Social Democratic Federation," "Fight for Freedom Committee" (later Freedom House), "Council for Democracy," "Citizens for Victory: To Win the War To Win the Peace," "Committee for National Morale," "Associated Leagues for a Declared War," "Coordinating Committee for Democratic Action," "Defenders of Freedom," and the "Women's Action Committee." All these organizations engaged in "frightfulness" propaganda of Hitler's coming.

There was an amazing interlocking of officers and members among these organizations. A published list showed that ten persons who were officials in the William Allen White Committee were also officials of eight similar organizations, while another ten persons were directors of six more committees.

---

15. Major-General J. F. C. Fuller, *A Military History of the Western World* (Funk & Wagnalls Company, New York: 1956), Volume 3, p. 629.

16. *The Winning of the War in Europe and the Pacific* (Biennial Report of the Chief of Staff of the United States Army, July 1, 1943 to June 30, 1945, to the Secretary of War), p. 1. Also reported in the *New York Times,* October 10, 1945.

17. Fortunately for history, the "insiders" in such movements, always proud of their handiwork, are anxious (at least temporarily) to leave posterity accounts of their feats. Such an historian was Professor Walter Johnson of the University of Chicago (*The Battle Against Isolation,* University of Chicago Press, Chicago: 1944). Some of the details I give concerning the William Allen White Committee are taken from this book.

A partial count shows that in 1940, between July and the Presidential election in November alone, more than one hundred statements and advertisements were issued by these groups or committees favoring our intervention in the war. These committees collected more than $1,000,000 in public contributions for their propaganda.

Conscientious William Allen White found himself in increasing difficulty with his colleagues. Some of them persisted in urging the United States to join in the war. He wrote a letter to a friend, in which he declared, "The only reason in God's world I am in this organization is to keep this country out of war. . . ." He asserted that if he were making slogans, the real slogan of his committee would be "The Yanks Are Not Coming."[18]

On December 26, 1940, White resigned. He wrote in an editorial about his resignation in *The Emporia Gazette* on January 3, 1941:

> . . . I had a definite sense that the war fever was rising and I didn't like it. All my life I have been devoted to peace, to the belief that War is futile. . . .[19]

The Christian Century on January 8, 1941, editorially declared that:

> . . . the eastern interventionist end of the William Allen White Committee to Defend America by Aiding the Allies might be taking its honored chairman for a ride. . . ."[20]

The Saturday Evening Post of February 1, 1941, stated that:

> . . . the and-America strategists who controlled the war propaganda knew better than to name their objectives in the beginning. . . .
>
> It was perfect strategy . . . A time would come when it would be necessary to introduce a trestle phrase by which to pass from the false premise to the true one. It would have to be a phrase strong enough to bear not only the engine but a long train of cars in which many innocents were riding in good faith. . . .[21]

The Non-Interventionists

Those who opposed American entry into the war were likewise active. There were some local organizations but the most important was the "America First Committee." It was launched from Chicago in September, 1940, under the

---

18. Walter Johnson, *The Battle Against Isolation*, pp. 181–182.
19. *The Emporia* (Kansas) *Daily Gazette*, January 3, 1941.
20. *The Christian Century*, January 8, 1941, p. 44.
21. *The Saturday Evening Post* [vol. 213], February 1, 1941, p. 26.

chairmanship of General Robert E. Wood. Its membership comprised a great number of substantial citizens from every calling and occupation. There was a large attendance at the meetings held by the Committee in nearly every town and city. Funds were raised mostly from collections at these meetings, and amounted to several hundred thousand dollars. Among the Committee's speakers was Colonel Charles A. Lindbergh, on whom the interventionists concentrated an attack of almost unbelievable smear and vilification.

I did not join any group. I believed that [by–*ed.*] not being committed to statements of others, I could carry more weight. I made many addresses in opposition to our intervention in the war. I spoke in New York City on October 26, 1938; in Chicago on February 1, 1939; in Lincoln, Nebraska on October 31, 1940; in New Haven on March 28, 1941; again in New York City on May 11, 1941; and in Chicago on June 29 and September 16, 1941. All these addresses were broadcast nation-wide. I published articles opposing intervention in magazines on April 15, 1939; July 15, 1939; October 27, 1939; April 27, 1940; and June 5, 1940.[22]

One of the saddest products of these years of our national debate on peace or war was the passions aroused among our people. There were sincere persons on both sides, but emotion everywhere clouded reason.

Smear and character assassination were too often the fuel in the fiery furnace of propaganda. Intolerance and impatience brought barrages and counterbarrages of the poison gas of name-calling. Those poured on the opposition by the President of the United States in his speeches included such terms as "isolationist," "defeatists," "appeasers," "ostrich," "armchair strategists," "amateurs," "turtle," and "copperheads." Those opposed to war never quite achieved the same effectiveness with their slogans of "warmongers" and "blood mad."

I did not like the stirring up of hatred between my own countrymen by use of such terms. Therefore, I used only the stodgy words "intervention" and "non-intervention," with the "lists" attached. These labels, I hoped, implied some degree of personal respect.

Brainwashing from Abroad

From the recognition of Russia in 1933, the American people were continuously brainwashed by both Russian and American Communists. I have, in

---

22. All these statements are given in full in the volumes, *Addresses Upon the American Road,* 1938–1940 and 1940–1941. If the reader will refer to these addresses I am confident that he will agree that they were accurate in statement of fact and forecasts.

Chapters 3, 4, and 5, given a description of this elaborate apparatus for corrupting the American mind.

The British, with their backs to the wall, were naturally active in brainwashing the American people for the purpose of securing our aid in the war. By far the most eminent propagandist was Prime Minister Churchill. His urgent need and hope was to get the United States into the war. The greatest orator of our time, he inspired a nation fighting for its very life. He had only one goal: to save the Empire from the Hitlerian danger. He took little public notice of the dangers from Stalin, who as Hitler's ally had made the Nazi attack on Britain possible. Churchill's magnificent orations were transmitted by radio into American homes, and listened to by a sympathetic and emotional people. His address to the House of Commons on May 13, 1940, soon after his accession to office, is one of the great orations in our times. One passage in particular appealed to American hearts:

> . . . I would say to the House, as I said to those who have joined this Government: "I have nothing to offer but blood, toil, tears, and sweat."
>
> We have before us an ordeal of the most grievous kind. We have before us many, many long months of struggle and of suffering. You ask, What is our policy? I will say: "It is to wage war, by sea, land and air, with all our might and with all the strength that God can give us: to wage war against a monstrous tyranny, never surpassed in the dark, lamentable catalogue of human crime. That is our policy." You ask, What is our aim? I can answer in one word: Victory—victory at all costs, victory in spite of all terror, victory however long and hard the road may be; for without victory there is no survival. Let that be realized; no survival for the British Empire; no survival for all the British Empire has stood for; no survival for the urge and impulse of the ages, that mankind will move forward towards its goal. . . .[23]

Lord Lothian, British Ambassador to the United States, busied himself speaking before colleges and other groups whom he thought in need of enlightenment. British consular and other officials daily delivered speeches to American groups. Lord Halifax, who succeeded Lord Lothian, was unceasing in his propaganda activities. He began as early as January 27, 1941, in a press conference, followed by addresses on March 25, April 15 and April 25, May 22, June 3 and June 18. The speeches, although diplomatically phrased, were certainly not directed to keeping us out of war.

---

23. Winston Churchill, *Blood, Sweat, and Tears* [G. P. Putnam's Sons, New York: 1941], p. 276.

The British created the "British Information Services" in New York City. This agency turned out magazine articles, pamphlets and press releases, imported speakers and scheduled them for meetings and public dinners. From England came such popular personalities as Sir George Paish, H. G. Wells, and Noel Coward.

The British propaganda was not restrained by adherence to the exact truth. Probably the most notable of their propagandist accomplishments was establishing in American minds that the British might be compelled to surrender, in which case the British fleet would be taken by the Germans and the American naval protection lost.

That this brainwashing "fright" was deliberate can be found in the record of the negotiations with respect to a request of the British in the summer of 1940 for fifty destroyers from the American navy. Our Government was in favor of giving them to the British but lacked the authority to do this without some *quid pro quo*. Secretary Hull found the legal solution by making the swap of the destroyers for leases on some British military bases in the West Indian Islands and Canada.

Also, there arose some question of giving away the destroyers if the British navy by any chance should go the Germans. In the negotiations, Mr. Roosevelt sought an outright undertaking from Mr. Churchill that, in case of a Nazi invasion of Britain, the British fleet would be sent to Commonwealth ports. The following correspondence vividly illuminates Mr. Churchill's expertness in brainwashing techniques.

On June 28, 1940, the Prime Minister sent this message to his Ambassador in Washington:

> . . . Never cease to impress on President and others that, if this country were successfully invaded and largely occupied after heavy fighting, some Quisling Government would be formed to make peace on the basis of our becoming a German Protectorate. In this case the British Fleet would be the solid contribution with which this . . . Government would buy terms. . . . We have really not had any help worth speaking of from the United States so far. . . .[24]

On July 5/6, 1940, Ambassador Lothian warned Churchill that this "fright blitz" might boomerang. Churchill records:

> He [Lord Lothian] said . . . It would, however, be extremely difficult to get American public opinion to consider letting us have American destroyers

---

24. Churchill, *Their Finest Hour* [Houghton Mifflin Company, Boston: 1949], pp. 228–29.

unless it could be assured that in the event of the United States entering the war the British Fleet or such of it as was afloat would cross the Atlantic if Great Britain were overrun.[25]

On August 3, Mr. Churchill cabled Lord Lothian that if the United States requested the lease of air bases in exchange, it would be agreed to.[26]

But Mr. Roosevelt continued to insist on his demand for an undertaking as to the disposition of the British fleet if we gave the fifty destroyers.

Mr. Churchill states in his book:

> ... On August 6, Lothian cabled that the President was anxious for an immediate reply about the future of the Fleet. He wished to be assured that if Britain were overrun, the Fleet would continue to fight for the Empire overseas and would not either be surrendered or sunk. This was, it was said, the argument which would have the most effect on Congress in the question of destroyers. ...[27]

Churchill cabled Lothian on August 7, saying:

> ... I have repeatedly warned you in my secret telegrams and those to the President of the dangers United States would run if Great Britain were successfully invaded and a British Quisling Government came into office to make the best terms possible for the surviving inhabitants. I am very glad to find that these dangers are regarded as serious, and you should in no way minimise them. We have no intention of relieving United States from any well-grounded anxieties on this point. ... I have already several weeks ago told you that there is no warrant for discussing any question of the transference of the Fleet to American or Canadian shores. ... Pray make it clear at once that we could never agree to the slightest compromising of our full liberty of action. ...
>
> ... in my speech of June 4 I thought it well to open up to German eyes the prospects of indefinite oceanic war. ... Of course, if the United States entered the war and became an ally, we should conduct the war with them in common. ... You foresaw this yourself in your first conversation with the President, when you said you were quite sure that we should never send any part of our Fleet across the Atlantic except in the case of an actual war alliance.[28]

---

25. Ibid., p. 401.
26. Ibid., pp. 402–403.
27. Ibid., p. 404.
28. Ibid., pp. 405–406.

Two months earlier, Mr. Churchill had warned the Canadian Prime Minister Mackenzie King:

> We must be careful not to let Americans view too complacently prospect of a British collapse, out of which they would get the British Fleet and the guardianship of the British Empire, minus Great Britain. . . .[29]

On August 15, Churchill telegraphed the President, again pressing for the destroyers but weakening on the question of the fleet surrender:

> . . . As regards an assurance about the British Fleet, I am, of course, ready to reiterate to you what I told Parliament on June 4. We intend to fight this out here to the end, and none of us would ever buy peace by surrendering or scuttling the Fleet. . . .[30]

On August 27, in reply to a telegram from Roosevelt asking if Churchill's June 4, 1940 statement that the " . . . British Fleet would in no event be surrendered or sunk, but would be sent overseas for the defense of other parts of the Empire"[31] was settled policy of the British Government, Churchill replied:

> You ask, Mr. President, whether my statement in Parliament on June 4, 1940, about Great Britain never surrendering or scuttling her Fleet "represents the settled policy of His Majesty's Government." It certainly does. . . .[32]

However, on January 9, 1941, Mr. Churchill conveyed a renewed hint that his country might make a compromise peace if we did not come through, saying:

> If the co-operation between the United States and the British Empire in the task of extirpating the spirit and regime of totalitarian intolerance . . . *were to fail,* the British Empire, rugged and embattled, might indeed hew its way through and preserve the life and strength of our own country and our own Empire for the inevitable renewal of the conflict on worse terms, *after an uneasy truce.*[33]

It must be borne in mind by Americans that Mr. Churchill was fighting with his back to the wall to save England and the British Empire. He was making a magnificent fight.

---

29. Ibid., p. 145.
30. Ibid., p. 406.
31. Ibid., p. 414.
32. Ibid.
33. Winston Churchill, *Blood, Sweat and Tears*, p. 447. Italics mine.

The American Attitude

Despite the deluge of brainwashing, the American people were little persuaded that they ought to go to war. This is evidenced by the popular polls of the times, which gave the following indications:

In answer to the question: "Do you think the United States should declare war on Germany and send our Army and Navy abroad to fight?"

	Yes	No
September, 1939 (outbreak of war)	6%	94%
October, 1939	5%	95%
December, 1939	3.5%	96.5%
April, 1940 (after invasion of Norway)	3.7%	96.3%
May 29, 1940 (after invasion of France)	7%	93%

And later, in answer to the question: "If you were asked to vote to-day on the question of the United States entering the war against Germany and Italy, how would you vote?

	Go In	Stay Out
July 7, 1940 (after French surrender)	14%	86%
July 15, 1940	15%	85%
October 13, 1940	17%	83%
December 29, 1940	12%	88%
February 1, 1941	15%	85%
May 16, 1941	21%	79%
July 9, 1941 (after Hitler's invasion of Russia)	21%	79%

The Revolution in American Foreign Policies Continued

CHAPTER 30

The Presidential Election of 1940

THE REPUBLICAN CONVENTION nominated Wendell Willkie on June 28, 1940. The Democratic Convention renominated President Roosevelt for a third term twenty days later on July 18.[1]

The President's foreign policy of "actions more than words, but less than war" played little part in the campaign debates. These debates settled down to mostly a competition of promises that the United States would never join in the war at all. During the campaign Mr. Roosevelt made eleven such promises to which may be added the five he had made before the campaign began. Mr. Willkie during the campaign made eight promises to keep the United States out of the war.

Mr. Willkie gave his strongest assurance on this subject on October 17, two weeks before the election, saying:

> . . . We do not want to send our boys over there again. And we do not intend to send them over there again. And if you elect me President we won't.
>
> . . . if you re-elect the third-term candidate they will be sent. We cannot and we must not undertake to maintain by arms the peace of Europe.[2]

Just before the election, on October 30, Mr. Roosevelt made his strongest assurance, saying:

> And while I am talking to you mothers and fathers, I give you one more assurance.

---

1. For an account of this convention, see *Jim Farley's Story — The Roosevelt Years,* by James A. Farley (Whittlesey House, McGraw-Hill Book Company, Inc., New York: 1948), pp. 271–306.
2. *New York Times,* October 18, 1940.

I have said this before, but I shall say it again and again and again:

Your boys are not going to be sent into any foreign wars.[3]

It was significant that during the campaign Mr. Roosevelt, while often denouncing Hitler, made no mention of Stalin's partnership with Hitler.

In an address at Lincoln, Nebraska, on October 31, 1940, I sought to cover these omissions in Mr. Roosevelt's speeches. I stated:

Now we may examine a sample of policies which bear upon preserving our domestic tranquility, peace abroad and appeasement of dictators all at one time.

Over a period of fifteen years, four Presidents, including myself, and six Secretaries of State, both Democratic and Republican, refused to recognize the Communist government of Russia or to have anything to do with it.

President Wilson's administration used such words as these about the Communists: "by force and cunning seized the government," "murderous tyranny," "terror," "bloodshed, murder." "They declare their existence depends on revolution in all other great civilizations including the United States." "They use the public revenues of Russia to promote this revolution in other countries." There can be "no confidence in pledges given with cynical repudiation already in their mind." "We cannot recognize a government . . . determined and bound to conspire against our institutions."

Republican Presidents and Secretaries of State held to these views of President Wilson.

Recognition of new governments is more than an establishment of legalistic or trade relations.

When our neighbors choose to live a life of disrepute, we do not go to war or shoot them up. But we can hold up the moral and social standards in the world just a little better if we do not associate with them. Moreover we do not invite them to come into our homes and corrupt our family life.

However, in November, 1933, Mr. Roosevelt recognized the Soviet government. He made an agreement on a piece of paper that they would not conspire among the American people. He announced that the principal purpose was to "co-operate for the preservation of the peace of the world."

For six years their revolutionary conspiracies were allowed to run riot in the United States despite their pledged word. Hundreds of thousands of Americans were brazenly enlisted as their fellow travelers. The Communists

---

3. [Samuel I. Rosenman, comp.,] *The Public Papers and Addresses of Franklin D. Roosevelt, 1940* [volume] (The Macmillan Company, New York: 1941), p. 517.

supported Mr. Roosevelt in elections. Their vote was the deciding factor in the defeat of Mr. Dewey for Governor of New York.

On January 3, 1940, after six years of it, the unanimous report of the Dies Committee, consisting of Democrats and Republicans, a committee by the way that Mr. Roosevelt tried to discredit, said this:

"... The Communist party is a foreign conspiracy masked as a political party ... The party's activities constitute a violation of the Treaty of Recognition.

"... The Communist party under instruction from the Comintern (Moscow) has from time to time pursued policies in direct violation of the laws of the United States ... Moscow has from the very beginning of the Communist party in the United States supplied the party here with funds for its subversive activities." [... –ed.]

Now let us look at the Russian government "co-operating ... for the preservation of the peace of the world." How about the unprovoked attacks upon Poland, upon Finland, upon Latvia, upon Estonia, upon Lithuania, upon Bessarabia? Most of these were democratic states. Today they are slaves to Communism. It is true Mr. Roosevelt expressed our moral disapproval of these actions. But within the last two months, perhaps the last two weeks, we seek to appease Russia with machine tools which we badly need ourselves, and airplane gasoline. I presume this will stimulate some more of the same kind of "co-operation for the peace of the world."[4]

Mr. Roosevelt's economic and naval pressures on Japan brought an important incident during the campaign.

At the end of September, 1940, the Berlin-Rome-Tokyo Axis was transformed into a complete military alliance. The essential provisions of the alliance were: recognition of the leadership of Germany and Italy in the establishment of a new order in Europe, and for Japan the foundation of a "new order in greater East Asia." The members of the alliance agreed to assist each other with "political, economic and military means" if any of them was attacked by a power not involved in the present European War or in the Chinese-Japanese conflict.[5] The United States was the only consequential power not involved in the war.

---

4. Herbert Hoover, *Addresses Upon the American Road, 1940–1941* (Charles Scribner's Sons, New York: 1941), pp. 38–40.

5. [U.S. Department of State,] [*Papers Relating to the*] *Foreign Relations of the United States, Japan: 1931–1941* [United States Government Printing Office, Washington: 1943], Vol. II, pp. 165ff. It is stated that the Japanese reserved the right to interpret this provision. See the *New York Times*,

Portentous as was the alliance, Mr. Roosevelt made no significant public reference to it during the campaign. On October 2, Wendell Willkie paraphrased and used parts of a suggestion which I had made to him on this alliance, saying:

> It is clear enough . . . that Germany, Italy and Japan are thinking of the United States in terms of war. . . . Either they have aggressive designs against us or else they suspect us of having aggressive designs against them . . .
>
> . . . Where are we? How did we get into this position? What have we done, overtly or secretly, to cause the most ruthless States in the world to make this aggressive declaration?[6]

In my Lincoln, Nebraska, speech I remarked on this subject:

> Thus for the first time in our history we are faced with a military alliance directed to bring pressure upon us.
>
> It is directed against us not on one flank but on both flanks. By way of military statesmanship, a high corporal in the army knows better than to invite attack upon his front and his flank at the same time.[7]

Another Sudden Revolution in American Foreign Policies

The day Mr. Roosevelt was elected to a third term his *Mothers' and Fathers' Speech* was still ringing in American ears. But promises to keep America out of war were heard no more.

Day by day the attitudes of Mr. Roosevelt's principal advisers became more warlike. Such were the implications in a memorandum of Admiral Harold R. Stark in mid-November, 1940;[8] such was a speech of Secretary of War Knox a few days after the election;[9] and an entry in Secretary Stimson's diary on December 16.[10]

November 10, 1941, and H. L. Trefousse, *Germany and American Neutrality, 1939–1941* (Bookman Associates, New York: 1951), p. 71.

6. *New York Times,* October 3, 1940.

7. Herbert Hoover, *Addresses Upon the American Road, 1940–1941,* pp. 43–44.

8. [Robert E.] Sherwood, *Roosevelt and Hopkins* [Harper & Brothers, New York: 1948], pp. 271–272.

9. *New York Times,* November 15, 1940.

10. [Henry L.] Stimson and [McGeorge] Bundy, *On Active Service in Peace and War* [Harper & Brothers, New York: 1948], p. 366.

CHAPTER 31

The Lend-Lease Law
[and] The ABC-1 Agreement

THE PROBLEMS OF AID to Britain by war supplies had been postponed until after the election.

On December 8, 1940, Prime Minister Churchill addressed a long letter to Mr. Roosevelt.[1] He urged a program of joint actions in the war, and outlined in detail the munitions, supplies, ships and finance that the British needed immediately. He also described certain calamities that would result from Mr. Roosevelt's inaction. However, he stated that the British did not want American manpower.

The final paragraph of his letter was:

> ... If, as I believe, you are convinced, Mr. President, that the defeat of the Nazi and Fascist tyranny is a matter of high consequence to the people of the United States and to the Western Hemisphere, you will regard this letter not as an appeal for aid, but as a statement of the minimum action necessary to achieve our common purpose.[2]

On December 13, Mr. Churchill sent another urgent dispatch to Mr. Roosevelt, reviewing the serious shortage of North Atlantic shipping as a result of U-boat and air attacks.[3]

At a White House press conference on December 17, 1940, the President proposed a plan of "Lend-Lease" supplies, by which the United States would lend military and other supplies—these supplies or their equivalent values to be returned later. He said:

---

1. [Winston S.] Churchill, *Their Finest Hour* [Houghton Mifflin Company, Boston: 1949], pp. 558–567.
2. Ibid., p. 567.
3. Ibid., pp. 606–607.

. . . we would enter into some kind of arrangement . . . with the understanding that when the show was over, we would get repaid sometime in kind,
thereby leaving out the dollar mark in the form of a dollar debt and substitut-
ing for it a gentleman's obligation to repay in kind. . . .[4]

The question involved was how or when the supplies could be paid for, if
ever. I had lived through this same problem, representing our government in
World War I. That experience amply proved, except for a trivial percentage,
that such supplies for mutual economic reasons, could never be paid for.[5]

It seemed to me that in the end this would be the case in the Second World
War. I believed we should give supplies to Britain. I therefore favored Mr. Roosevelt's proposal with the full belief that there would be no repayment; that
some method was required which, in the end, would dispose of the question
of substantial repayment.

But when the legislation was introduced into Congress on January 10, 1941,
it was far from a simple provision to lend supplies to the British. It contained
provisions which might be construed to use our naval forces in the delivery
of these supplies. And it even contained language which might be construed
as taking away from the Congress the power to make war and vesting it in the
President.

Immediately after reading the bill, I issued a statement to the press:

> The first thing Congress has to consider is the suggestion of enormous surren-
> der of its responsibilities. No such powers were granted in the last war. . . .
>
> We all wish our industry tuned up to maximum output for our defense
> and to aid other countries to defend their independence. But . . . this legisla-
> tion is something else. . . .[6]

One of America's greatest constitutional authorities—John Bassett
Moore—confirmed my views. In a letter to the House Foreign Affairs Committee he gave his opinion on the provisions in the bill:

> There can be no doubt that, under the guise of certain phraseology, the
> pending bill assumes to transfer the war making power from the Congress, in
> which the Constitution lodges it, to the Executive. . . .

---

4. [Samuel I. Rosenman, comp.,] *The Public Papers and Addresses of Franklin D. Roosevelt, 1940*
[volume] [The Macmillan Company, New York: 1941], p. 608.

5. I discuss this experience and the resultant conclusion at length in the Appendix to Volume III
of *An American Epic* [Henry Regnery Company, Chicago: 1961].

6. *New York Times,* January 11, 1941. See also [Herbert Hoover,] *Addresses Upon the American
Road, 1940–1941* [Charles Scribner's Sons, New York: 1941], p. 63.

... the tide of totalitarianism in government which has swept over many other lands has not only reached our shores but has gone far to destroy constitutional barriers which, once broken down, are not likely to be restored.[7]

The Minority Report of the House Committee stated:

... we cannot repeal war; we cannot repeal bankruptcy; and we cannot repeal dictatorship. [Under this bill–ed.] ... [t]he oldest and last constitutional democracy surrenders its freedom under the pretext of avoiding war, with the probable result that the newest dictatorship will soon go to war.[8]

Governor Thomas E. Dewey, then District Attorney of New York, who agreed with me, issued a statement to the same effect. Various Senators and Congressmen expressed similar views.

Almost every important official of the Administration appeared before the congressional committees to urge the passage of the bill, and most of them predicted great dangers to the United States from Hitler if the bill was not enacted.

On January 21, in reply to press questions, Mr. Roosevelt asserted that he would never dream of using the powers granted him under the bill to order United States convoying of foreign ships. He said that such action, or the sale of war vessels, would mean war, and described reports to this effect as "cow-jump-over-the-moon, Old Mother Hubbard stuff. . . ."[9]

The outstanding feature of the Congressional debate was that a very large majority of both the Senate and the House favored aid to Britain. However, questions were raised regarding war powers given to the President and other provisions in the bill, which might be interpreted to authorize the carrying of supplies in American ships or naval convoys into the war zones. Amendments were passed which the Congress believed prevented any such interpretations.

As to delivery of the supplies, the Congress amended the bill by stating:

... Nothing in this Act shall be construed to authorize or to permit the authorization of convoying vessels by naval vessels of the United States.

---

7. *New York Times,* January 18, 1941.

8. 77th Congress, 1st Session, House of Representatives Report No. 18: *To Promote the Defense of the United States,* Part 2, *Minority Views (to accompany H.R. 1776),* p. 2.

9. *New York Times,* January 22, 1941. A similar phrase was also used in the press conference of January 17 (*New York Times,* January 18, 1941). Both of these are omitted from the 1941 volume of Mr. Roosevelt's *Public Papers and Addresses.*

... Nothing in this Act shall be construed to authorize or to permit the authorization of the entry of any American vessel into a combat area in violation of section 3 of the Neutrality Act of 1939.[10]

The legislation was purported in both Houses of Congress to be a peace measure—a law that would prevent the United States from becoming involved in the war, and that it gave no authorities involving the constitutional expansion of the war powers of the President.

This interpretation was supported by such leaders as John W. McCormack (D) of Massachusetts; John D. Dingell (D) of Michigan; William R. Poage (D) of Texas; and in the Senate by Senator Walter F. George (D) of Georgia; Senator Alben W. Barkley (D) of Kentucky, the Majority leader in the Senate; Senator Tom Connally (D) of Texas; Senator Claude Pepper (D) of Florida; Senator Albert B. Chandler (D) of Kentucky; Senator James E. Murray (D) of Montana; Senator Morris Sheppard (D) of Texas.

The bill was denounced as involving us in the war by such leaders of the House as Thomas A. Jenkins (R) of Ohio; Bartel J. Jonkman (R) of Michigan; Usher L. Burdick (R) of North Dakota; Hugh Peterson (D) of Georgia; Dewey Short (R) of Missouri; James F. O'Connor (D) of Montana; and in the Senate by Senator Guy M. Gillette (D) of Iowa; Senator Arthur H. Vandenberg (R) of Michigan; Senator John A. Danaher (R) of Connecticut; Senator David I. Walsh (D) of Massachusetts; Senator D. Worth Clark (D) of Idaho; Senator Robert A. Taft (R) of Ohio, Senator Alexander Wiley (R) of Wisconsin; Senator George D. Aiken (R) of Vermont.

The majority report on the bill of the Senate Committee on Foreign Relations declared [the bill to be–*ed.*]:

... not a war measure but a practical safeguard aimed at keeping us out of war.[11]

The report of the minority of the Senate Committee stated:

1. It is successful only in concealing its purpose. It is not a bill for aiding Britain nor a bill for the national defense of our own country.
2. If read realistically, it grants extraordinary powers to the President, such as have never before been granted to a Chief Executive.

---

10. 77th Congress, 1st Session, H.R. 1776. *United States Statutes at Large 1941–1942*, Volume 55, Part 1, p. 32.

11. 77th Congress, 1st Session, Senate Report No. 45: *Promoting the Defense of the United States*, p. 2.

3. It makes of the Chief Executive a dictator and worse, a dictator with power to take us into war.
4. It transfers the war-making power from the Congress to the President.
5. It leaves to the President (a) the determination of aggressor nations, and (b) what punishment shall be meted out to them.
6. It commits the American people permanently to support the course he takes, for once embarked on a course it will be necessary for the people to follow through.[12]

The House passed the bill on February 8 by a vote of 260 to 165. 135 Republicans and 25 Democrats were among those who opposed the measure.

On March 1, I wrote to former Assistant Secretary of State William R. Castle:

The American people have been so fooled as to the purpose and character of this bill that there remains no hope of adequately amending it. It is a war bill, yet 95 percent of the people think it is only aid to Britain.

The bill . . . surrenders to the President the power to make war, any subsequent action by Congress will be rubber stamp work. . . . [It] empowers the President to become real dictator. . . . He can determine who, in what way and how much aid any nation may receive from the United States. . . .

How the President uses these powers remains to be seen. Whether it is the beginning of our military participation in the war or not it substantially projects the American people further out into the emotional rapids which lead to the cataract of war. . . .

. . . Already the real interest of America and the long-view interest of the world are being drowned by foreign propaganda, the suppression of truth, the beating down of every warning voice. . . . For instance, soon after the bill passes we shall hear the cry, "Why provide all this material and have it sunk in the Atlantic? We should convoy it with our navy!" Then we will have American boys torpedoed and war is on. . . .

All that we can hope to do is to use our energies and influence to keep down emotions and to hold the President to his promises not to spill American blood. So long as we do not enter armed conflict we are not in a technical state of war. So long as we are not in a technical state of war, we still have a chance. . . .

---

12. Ibid., Part 2, p. 6.

The Senate passed the bill on March 8 by a vote of 60 to 31. The vote in opposition was 13 Democrats, 17 Republicans, and 1 Progressive.

On March 9, the day after the Senate vote, I wrote Colonel O'Laughlin:

> The carrying out of the Lend-Lease Bill, aside from its direct purpose, will further channel the public mind into the rapids which lead inevitably to military war. The British propaganda, our natural sympathies, our indignations and fears over the Nazi regime have already conditioned thought to a readiness for that definite action.
>
> I hope still that we will not get to that depth of action. In full war we cannot pull out without military victory. There can be no negotiated peace in modern war when civilian hate always rises to a point where no statesman can propose the necessary compromises that negotiated peace requires. It is likely to be a twenty years war, for it can only be ended by exhaustion and revolution.[13]

The ABC-1 Agreement

On March 27, 1941, just a few weeks after passage of the Lend-Lease Act, the so-called ABC-1 (American British Command Agreement) was signed in Washington with the British.

Robert E. Sherwood, an Administration aide, thus describes the discussions on this agreement:

> . . . The opening sessions were addressed by [Army Chief of Staff] Marshall and [Chief of Naval Operations] Stark, who urged that utmost secrecy surround these conferences, since any publicity might provide ammunition for the opponents of Lend Lease and produce other consequences which "might well be disastrous."
>
> The members of the British delegation wore civilian clothes and disguised themselves as "technical advisers to the British Purchasing Commission." . . .
>
> The staff talks . . . produced a plan, known as ABC-1, which suggested the grand strategy for the war. . . .[14]

---

13. Six years later as Secretary of State, on February 22, 1947, at Princeton University, General Marshall declared: ". . . The war years were critical . . . but I think that the present period is in many respects even more critical. . . . We have had a cessation of hostilities . . . but we have no genuine peace . . ." (*New York Times*, February 23, 1947).

14. [Robert E.] Sherwood, *Roosevelt and Hopkins* [Harper & Brothers, New York: 1948], pp. 272–273.

Another account by Admiral Ernest J. King, then in command of our Atlantic Fleet, makes clear the spirit of the agreement:

... The "ABC-1 Staff Agreement" had indicated that, in the event of United States entry into the war, the protection of shipping and sea communication in the Atlantic would be the principal naval task of the United States, but that, without declaration of war, the United States Navy would assume the responsibility for protecting transatlantic merchant convoys at the earliest practicable date. . . .[15]

One of the statements in this agreement was certainly warlike:

... The High Command of the United States and United Kingdom will collaborate continuously in the formulation and execution of strategical policies and plans which shall govern the conduct of the war. . . .
... The broad strategic objective . . . of the Associated Powers will be the defeat of Germany and her Allies.[16]

The agreement contained provisions with regard to Japan. These were extended at a conference in Singapore—April 21 to 27, 1941—and again at the Atlantic Charter Conference on August 10, 1941. I deal with them more fully in Section X of this book.

The Singapore version was not pacific in tone, saying:

... *Our object* is to defeat Germany and her allies, and hence in the Far East to maintain the position of the Associated Powers against Japanese attack, in order to sustain a long-term economic pressure against Japan until we are in a position to take the offensive.[17]

The text of the agreement was only disclosed years later in a report of the Pearl Harbor investigation.

According to Admiral King's record, in anticipation of the ABC-1 agreement:

... Admiral Stark on 15 February had ordered the creation . . . of a Support Force, to be formed around three destroyer squadrons and four squadrons

---

15. Ernest J. King and Walter Muir Whitehill, *Fleet Admiral King: A Naval Record* (W. W. Norton & Company, Inc., New York: 1952), p. 338.

16. [United States Congress, Joint Committee on the Investigation of the Pearl Harbor Attack, 79th Congress, 1st Session,] *Pearl Harbor Attack* [*Hearings Before the Joint Committee on the Investigation of the Pearl Harbor Attack,* United States Government Printing Office, Washington: 1946], Part 15, p. 1489.

17. Ibid., Exhibit No. 50, p. 1558.

of patrol planes ... A base for these destroyers at Londonderry, Northern Ireland, was turned over by the Royal Navy and developed with lend-lease funds. . . .[18]

Mr. Churchill's memoirs show that ABC-1 was no mere piece of paper. He states:

... In March, 1941, American officers visited Great Britain to select bases for their naval escorts and air forces. Work on these was at once begun. . . .[19]

At the Pearl Harbor investigation, it was disclosed that Admiral Stark, on April 3, 1941, had referred to the agreement as follows:

... The question as to our entry into the war now seems to be *when,* and not *whether.* . . .[20]

The ABC-1 Agreement was submitted neither to the Congress nor to the Congressional Committees concerned. The Constitutional authority of Congress was ignored.

---

18. King and Whitehill, *Fleet Admiral King: A Naval Record,* pp. 338–339.
19. [Winston S.] Churchill, *The Grand Alliance* [Houghton Mifflin Company, Boston: 1950], p. 138.
20. *Pearl Harbor Attack,* Part 17, p. 2463.

CHAPTER 32
There Were to Be No Convoys

THERE WERE NO "CONVOYS" but there were "patrols." The Navy, however, did not always conform to the right word. For instance, in a memorandum attached to a letter from Admiral H. R. Stark to Admiral H. E. Kimmel on April 4, 1941, it says:

> To keep present flow of traffic moving, 2 to 3 convoys a week, 7 escort units are necessary.[1]

After the Lend-Lease Act (March 11, 1941) and the ABC-1 Agreement (March 27, 1941), events moved rapidly in the Atlantic. On April 9, Danish Minister Henrik de Kauffmann signed an agreement placing Greenland under United States jurisdiction and authorizing the construction of American military bases there.[2] On April 24, the President authorized the construction of American bases in Scotland and Northern Ireland.[3]

During April, some question arose that Hitler was about to invade Spain and Portugal, taking Gibraltar and the Azores, thus closing the Mediterranean. On April 24, Mr. Churchill cabled Mr. Roosevelt:

> . . . the moment Spain gives way . . . we shall dispatch two expeditions which we have long been holding in readiness, one from Britain to one of the islands in the Azores . . . and the second expedition to . . . the Cape Verdes. . . . It would be a very great advantage if you could send an American squadron for a friendly cruise in these regions at the earliest moment. . . .[4]

---

1. *Pearl Harbor Attack, Hearings before the Joint Committee on the Investigation of the Pearl Harbor Attack,* Congress of the United States, Seventy-ninth Congress, Part 16, p. 2162 (United States Government Printing Office, Washington: 1946).
2. *The Memoirs of Cordell Hull* (The Macmillan Company, New York: 1948), Vol. II, p. 936.
3. [*Editor's note:* Hoover supplied no citation for this footnote.]
4. Winston S. Churchill, *The Grand Alliance* (Houghton Mifflin Company, Boston: 1950), p. 145.

We have not been able to find Mr. Roosevelt's reply in the public records, but Churchill cabled him the same day:

Greatly cheered by the news. . . .[5]

On April 27, 1941, Mr. Churchill, in a radio broadcast to the British people, observed progress toward American convoys, saying:

It was . . . with indescribable relief that I learned of the tremendous decisions lately taken by the President. . . . I could not believe that they would allow the high purposes to which they have set themselves to be frustrated and the products of their skill and labour sunk to the bottom of the sea. . . . When I said ten weeks ago: "Give us the tools and we will finish the job," I meant *give* them to us: put them within our reach. . . .[6]

On June 11, at a press conference, Secretary Knox denounced the publication of reports that an American destroyer had dumped depth bombs on a German submarine. At a press conference on July 2 the Secretary emphatically denied that American naval units were engaged in convoying ships at sea or participating in encounters with German craft.[7]

However, navy officers arriving in Boston reported that depth bombs were being used. Later, it was confirmed by a Senate inquiry that American depth bombs had been used.

On July 19, Admiral King, apparently not troubled about restrictions in the Lend-Lease law, noted in an operational plan:

On July 19 he [Admiral King] issued a further operation plan organizing a task force "to escort convoys of United States and Iceland flag shipping, including shipping of any nationality which may join such United States or Iceland flag convoys. . . ."[8]

---

5. Ibid.

6. Winston S. Churchill, *The Unrelenting Struggle* (Little, Brown and Company, Boston: 1942), pp. 98–99.

7. *New York Times*, July 3, 1941.

8. Ernest J. King and Walter Muir Whitehill, *Fleet Admiral King—A Naval Record* (W. W. Norton & Company, Inc., New York: 1952), p. 343.

The Opportunity to Make Lasting Peace Comes to Franklin Roosevelt

CHAPTER 33

Hitler Turns His Might against Communist Russia

WITH HIS CONQUEST of most of western Europe completed by the surrender of France in June 1940, Hitler was free to revive one of his foremost ambitions: the destruction of the Communist government of Russia and the annexation of "living space," *Lebensraum,* from Russia and the Balkans. Observers like myself had long believed that this was inevitable.[1]

At this time, Hitler was under no immediate danger from the surviving democracies. The British armies had abandoned most all of their equipment in their escape from France. American public opinion, while favoring the sending of arms and supplies to the British, showed in every popular poll that over eighty percent of the people were against joining the war and the Congress was overwhelmingly against it.

Signs that Hitler was about to violate his alliance with Stalin and attack Russia began to reach the American Government immediately after his conquest of France.

Colonel Truman Smith, our able military attaché in Germany, predicted to the War Department on June 20, 1940, that if Hitler's campaign in the west succeeded Germany would attack the Soviet Union.[2] One month after the fall of France, on July 24, he relayed word of German troop movements toward Russia. On October 11, he reported that "the probability of a land attack on the British Isles during the present year was decreasing rapidly. . . ."

Other portents were reported in the American press. Hitler had put pressure on Hungary, Rumania, and Bulgaria to join the Axis. Hungary finally yielded on November 20, 1940, and Rumania three days later. Bulgaria also

---

1. See Section II where I mention my conclusions from a visit to Germany in 1938.
2. The reports of the Army Intelligence officials have been generously furnished to me for this memoir.

came in after King Boris himself went to Berlin on November 18 to plead in vain for some consideration of his embarrassment with Russia which such an action could produce for his country.

On December 11, 1940, Colonel Smith, then on a visit to Washington, reported that sixty-five percent of the Germany army was concentrated in the East—"in Germany, Poland and Southeast Europe." A few days later he reported that any units in the West which might conceivably be used for an invasion of England had been withdrawn. At about this time our military attaché in Moscow reported the constant movement of Russian troops toward Germany.

In the latter half of January, 1941, Under Secretary of State Sumner Welles informed the Russian Ambassador in Washington, Constantine Oumansky, that Germany was preparing an attack on Russia late that spring. Welles did not in any way qualify his warning to Oumansky.[3] The State Department record shows that on January 21 he also informed the Russian Ambassador:

> *Following our recent conversations,* I am happy to inform you that the Government of the United States of America has decided that the policies set forth in the statement issued to the press by the President on December 2, 1939, and generally referred to as the "moral embargo," are no longer applicable to the Union of Soviet Socialist Republics.[4]

The moral embargo on the shipment of munitions to Russia had been in force for fourteen months—since the Soviet attack on Finland.

The background of Welles' warning to Ambassador Oumansky is given in Secretary Hull's *Memoirs.* Hull states:

> . . . In January, 1941, there came to me a confidential report from Sam E. Woods, our commercial attaché in Berlin. Woods had a German friend who, though an enemy of the Nazis, was closely connected with the Reichs ministries, the Reichsbank and high Party members. As early as August,

---

3. Confirmation of this fact appeared in an article by Forrest Davis and E. K. Lindley in the *Ladies Home Journal* (July, 1942) p. 107. They wrote: "Midway of January, 1941, Sumner Welles warned Constantine Oumansky that Hitler had marked Russia for slaughter in the following June." I asked Mr. Davis the source of this information. He replied: "Under Secretary Welles." [William L.] Langer and [S. Everett] Gleason, in *The Undeclared War* [Harper & Brothers, New York, 1953], p. 342, put the date of Welles' warning at March 1, but aside from the above, it is unlikely that he held this information up for that length of time. Cf. Sumner Welles, *The Time for Decision* (Harper & Brothers, New York: 1944), pp. 170–171.

4. U.S. *Department of State Bulletin,* Vol. IV, No. 83, January 25, 1941, p. 107, italics mine. Cf. *The Memoirs of Cordell Hull* [The Macmillan Company, New York; 1948], Vol. II, p. 969.

1940, this friend informed Woods that conferences were then taking place at Hitler's headquarters concerning preparations for war against Russia. . . .

Woods used to meet this friend in a Berlin motion-picture house. By buying reserved seats from an agency and sending a ticket to Woods, the friend managed to sit alongside him and in the semidarkness slipped notes into Woods's coat pocket.

The information from Woods was in marked contrast to the considerable evidence that Hitler was planning an invasion of Britain, but the contacts of Woods's friend said that the air raids against England served as a blind for Hitler's real and well calculated plans and preparations for a sudden, devastating attack on Russia.

Later Woods's friend informed him that an organization of the Wehrmacht for the old twenty-one Russian Czarist regional governments had been formed, and that the economic staffs for these territories had been appointed. Bales of banknotes in rubles had been printed. . . .

When Woods's report embracing all this information came to me it was so circumstantial that, at first, I believed it a German "plant." I turned it over to J. Edgar Hoover, Chief of the Federal Bureau of Investigation, for his comment. Hoover thought it authentic. Woods having told us of a method of confirming the standing and contacts of the source by checking with a prominent German exile in the United States, I asked Assistant Secretary of State Breckinridge Long to see him and obtain this confirmation, which he did. I also talked over the report with the President.

. . . I requested Welles . . . to call this information to the [Russian] Ambassador's attention. This Welles did.

When further information from the same source came to me, I again turned it over to Welles, requesting him to communicate it to Oumansky. This he did on March 20.

Oumansky no doubt forwarded this information to his Government. . . .[5]

On February 3, 1941, Colonel Smith reported that 500,000 or 600,000 German troops were concentrated on the Russian frontier in Rumania.

I met with Secretary Hull in Washington during February, 1941, to discuss relief matters, subsequent to which we had a general conversation. In reply to my query as to what the Germans were doing against Russia, Hull told me that they had concentrated 1,250,000 troops along their eastern frontiers, and at least 300,000 additional troops on the Bulgarian frontier. He also told me

---

5. *The Memoirs of Cordell Hull*, pp. 967–8.

that the Russians were "scared to death." I observed that it was obvious from many signs that a Hitler attack upon Stalin was coming, that Britain would be safe, and that our Government should at once stop all warlike action and wait for the Great Dictators to destroy each other. And I said our officials should cease stating that Hitler was going to invade the Western Hemisphere. Mr. Hull made no comment on this advice.

All of this vital information of the coming attack of Hitler on Stalin and its implications were suppressed from the American people during the debate and action upon the Lend-Lease bill. Had this information as to the diversion of Hitler's armies to Russia been known to Congress, much of the oratorical pressure that Britain and the United States were in any danger of invasion by Hitler would have been demonstratively false.

Further evidence of Hitler's intentions accumulated rapidly. In mid-March 1941, Colonel Truman Smith reported to Washington that "it was difficult to judge whether the Germans really meant to attack the British Isles or not, although he thought they probably did not." On March 17 he reported a further large movement of German troops from the west to the Russian frontier.

On April 8, the American military attaché in Moscow, Major Ivan D. Yeaton, further warned Washington of the coming attack by Hitler. On April 9, Mr. Churchill, in a public address, predicted that this event was impending:

> . . . At the present time he [Hitler] is driving south and south-east through the Balkans. . . . But there are many signs which point to a Nazi attempt to secure the granary of the Ukraine, and the oilfields of the Caucasus . . .[6]

On April 15, our military attaché in Berlin confirmed that a German attack on Russia was certain. On May 5, the British government broadcasting system mentioned the oncoming attack of Hitler on Russia. On May 13, our military attaché in Berlin again reported to Washington that the German-Russian situation had reached a critical stage, and that there were large German troop concentrations on the Russian border.

Mr. Churchill remarked to Mr. Jock Colville, his private secretary:

> . . . I have only one purpose, the destruction of Hitler, and my life is much simplified thereby. If Hitler invaded Hell I would make at least a favourable reference to the Devil in the House of Commons.[7]

---

6. Churchill, *The Unrelenting Struggle* (Little, Brown and Company, Boston: 1942), p. 86.
7. Winston S. Churchill, *The Grand Alliance* (Houghton Mifflin Company, Boston: 1950), p. 370.

Hitler was master of about 280,000,000 people at this time. His armies were at peak strength and he could secure fifty more divisions of troops from his allies in the Balkans and Italy.

Stalin's Defense Preparations

Over the years Stalin had been neither idle nor without guile. There was ample information that he was straining Russia's every resource to strengthen his army and provide it arms. I give an account of his huge efforts at armament in an earlier chapter[8] and the size of his armies in a later chapter.[9]

Hitler's easy conquest of the West must have been a shock to Stalin. Not a single editorial article on the war appeared in *Pravda* or *Izvestia*, the official Russian newspapers, for a month after the fall of France. However, the daily communiqués disclosed pro-German sympathies. Stalin had been handing out supplies and olive branches to Hitler up to the moment of the attack on Russia.[10]

Moreover, he attempted to stem Hitler's diplomatic advance and succeeded in effecting a neutrality pact with Turkey on March 25, 1941, and a reversal of the Japanese commitment to the Rome-Berlin-Tokyo Axis by a non-aggression pact with them on April 13, 1941.

The Attack Begins and Hitler Explains

On June 22, 1941, Hitler and his armies of over 2,000,000 men attacked along the Russian border over a front of 2,500 miles.[11] As in ancient Chinese wars where all battles were heralded by violent verbal volleys, Hitler, in his proclamation on the day of the invasion, emphasized that he had been reluctant to enter the alliance with Stalin two years before, in August 1939, saying:

> *"It was . . . only with extreme difficulty that I brought myself . . . to send my foreign minister to Moscow. . . ."*[12]

He claimed four violations by Stalin of their agreement: (1) Russian annexations of the Baltic States (although Hitler had previously agreed to

---

8. See Section II, Chapter 10.
9. See Chapter 35.
10. See Section IV, Chapter 18.
11. Adolf Hitler, *My New Order* [edited with commentary by Raoul de Roussy de Sales] (Reynal & Hitchcock, New York: 1941), p. 976.
12. Ibid., p. 979. Editor's italics.

these); (2) Russian attempts to overthrow the Rumanian and Bulgarian governments friendly to Germany; (3) Russian desire to control the Dardanelles; and (4) Russia's move into Bukovina.[13]

The Russians Complain

Upon Hitler's attack, Soviet Foreign Minister Vyacheslav M. Molotov complained that Russia was a peace-loving nation without the slightest intention of harming anyone. He did not, of course, refer to the forced annexations of the Baltic nations and other states which Stalin had exacted as the price for his alliance with Hitler in August, 1939.[14]

Molotov said on June 22, 1941:

This unheard of attack upon our country is perfidy unparalleled in the history of civilized nations. . . .

That attack . . . was perpetrated despite the fact that . . . the German Government could not find grounds for a single complaint . . . as regards observance of this treaty.[15]

Stalin, in a speech on July 3, protested great surprise at the attack, saying:

. . . Fascist Germany suddenly and treacherously violated the non-aggression pact she concluded in 1939 with the U.S.S.R. . . . Naturally, our peace-loving country, not wishing to take the initiative of breaking the pact, could not resort to perfidy. . . .

Non-aggression pacts are pacts of peace between two States. It was such a pact that Germany proposed to us in 1939. . . . not a single peace-loving State could decline a peace treaty with a neighboring State even though the latter was headed by . . . Hitler and Ribbentrop. . . .

What did we gain. . . . We secured for our country peace for a year and a half and the opportunity of preparing its forces to repulse Fascist Germany. . . .

[The enemy] . . . is out . . . to restore Czarism, to destroy national culture and the national State existence of Russians, Ukrainians, Byelo-Russians,

---

13. Ibid., pp. 980–986.

14. From the postwar records it would appear that Molotov probably had another cause for grief. He had visited Berlin in November, 1940, about eight months before Hitler's attack. He had been received with great pomp and circumstance. In his long discussions with Foreign Minister Ribbentrop they had ranged over what would they do to all nations on earth, but mostly to the British Empire after the British had been defeated—which Hitler assured Molotov was a certainty. The visit was hailed in both Moscow and Berlin as a great success in confirming German-Russian friendship.

15. *New York Times,* June 23, 1941.

Lithuanians, Letts, Estonians, Uzbeks, Tartars, Moldavians, Georgians, Armenians, Azerbaijanians, and the other free peoples of the Soviet Union, to Germanize them, to convert them into the slaves of German princes and barons.[16]

Stalin's assertion of the sanctity of non-aggression pacts seemed a little hollow,[17] though his claim of treachery was correct. He was no doubt grieved that his purpose of mutually exhausting Hitler and the Western democracies had misfired by Hitler's conquest of most of western Europe with so little loss.

The attack by Hitler was no surprise to Stalin or to Molotov. Russia had been informed of the impending attack both by our State Department and by Churchill. Moreover, it is unbelievable that the Communists were without an intelligence service in Germany.[18]

Stalin himself certainly showed potential infidelity when he justified having made the alliance with Germany solely on the ground that it had given Russia time to prepare. All which indicated neither surprise at the attack, unpreparedness, nor an affection for Hitler.

---

16. Ibid., July 3, 1941.

17. See Section V, Chapter 23, "Communist and Nazi Conquest of Poland and the Baltic States."

18. *Survey of International Affairs, 1939–1946: America, Britain, & Russia; Their Co-operation and Conflict, 1941–1946* by William Hardy McNeill (Oxford University Press, London, New York, Toronto: 1953), p. 72, fn. 1: "Kalinov [...] says that the intelligence services of the Red Army foresaw German attack, but were overruled by the M.V.D. [i.e. the Ministry for Internal Affairs, at that time called N.K.V.D.—i.e. People's Commissariat of Internal Affairs], whose foreign intelligence branch believed that German troop concentrations on the Russian borders were only a bluff intended to wring greater economic concessions from the Russians."

CHAPTER 34

My Appeal that the United States Stay on the Side Lines until the Great Dictators Exhaust Each Other

TO MR. ROOSEVELT NOW came the greatest opportunity to make lasting peace in the world that ever knocked at the door of one man. The two dictators of the world's two great aggressor nations were locked in a death struggle. If left alone, these evil spirits were destined, sooner or later, to exhaust each other.

But twenty-four hours after Germany's attack on Russia, on June 23, 1941, Sumner Welles, Under Secretary of State, implied at a press conference that the United States would give material aid to Russia.[19]

At a press conference on June 24, two days after Hitler's attack, the President stated that "the United States would give all possible aid to Soviet Russia." He announced that the Treasury, acting on his orders, had released $40,000,000 in Soviet credits, frozen June 14.[20] Welles, at another press conference on June 25, stated that the President would not invoke the Neutrality Act against Russia. This would enable American merchant ships to carry war supplies from the United States to Russian ports.[21]

The promised supplies were furnished the Communists under the Lend-Lease law—a possible action never disclosed to the Congress during the Lend-Lease debate.

Alarmed by this American association with the Communists in war, I decided to speak to my countrymen in what seemed to me to be the most important address of my life. I secured radio time for a nationwide broadcast on the evening of June 29, 1941—five days after the President's announcement.

The reader should bear in mind the world background of this address. By Hitler's diversion of his armies to Russia, the British had not only been made

---

19. *New York Times,* June 24, 1941.
20. Ibid., June 25, 1941. [*Editor's note:* The quoted words are those of the *New York Times* reporter.]
21. Ibid., June 26, 1941.

doubly safe from defeat, but could now even look toward the prospect of victory by Hitler's exhaustion in his attack on Russia. Seven days previously, President Roosevelt had made an appeal to American youth to support his "four freedoms."

I released the text of my address to the press two days before its delivery in Chicago. But events were moving so rapidly that I found it necessary to introduce new material, delete parts, and rearrange the order, so that the broadcast text as given differed somewhat in wording from that of the press release.[22] The essential parts of the address were:

Six weeks ago I made a statement to the American people upon the relations of the United States to this war. . . .

I shall speak again without betraying the emotion that arises within me when the whole destiny of my country is imperiled. I can hope to appeal only to reasoning people. And it is cold reason, not eloquence, that America needs today. . . .

. . . The Constitution of the United States provides that Congress has the sole authority to declare war. It is equally their responsibility to see that this country does not go to war until they have authorized it.

The only reason for not submitting the matter to the Congress would be that Congress could not be trusted to do their bidding. . . . No president in a democracy should take that responsibility. . . .

. . . The constant question is what we should do now . . . there are certain eternal principles to which we must adhere. There are certain consequences to America and civilization which we must ever keep before our eyes.

In the last seven days that call to sacrifice American boys for an ideal has been made as a sounding brass and a tinkling cymbal. For now we find ourselves promising aid to Stalin and his militant Communist conspiracy against the whole democratic ideals of the world.

. . . it makes the whole argument of our joining the war to bring the four freedoms to mankind a gargantuan jest.

We should refresh our memories a little.

Four American Presidents and . . . [six] Secretaries of State, beginning with Woodrow Wilson, refused to have anything to do with Soviet Russia

---

22. The revised version was published in a book entitled [Herbert Hoover], *40 Key Questions About Our Foreign Policy,* prepared by Dr. Arthur Kemp (published by the Updegraff Press, Ltd., Scarsdale, New York: 1952.) The final script of the address is in the possession of Herbert Hoover, Jr. [*Editor's note:* Hoover published the unrevised version in his *Addresses upon the American Road, 1940–1941* (Charles Scribner's Sons, New York: 1941), pp. 87–102. Neither text precisely matched the speech as delivered. See pp. 581–82, notes 8–9.]

on the ground of morals and democratic ideals. They . . . refused diplomatic recognition. They did so because here is one of the bloodiest tyrannies and terrors ever erected in history. It destroyed every semblance of human rights and human liberty; it is a militant destroyer of the worship of God. It brutally executes millions of innocent people without the semblance of justice. It has enslaved the rest. Moreover, it has violated every international covenant, it has carried on a world conspiracy against all democracies, including the United States.

When Russia was recognized by the United States in 1933, the Soviets entered into a solemn agreement that they would refrain from any propaganda, any organization, or from injuring in any way whatsoever the tranquility, prosperity, order or security in any part of the United States.

Seven years later, the Dies Committee reported unanimously and specifically that the Communist Party in the United States is a Moscow conspiracy, masked as a political party; that its activities constitute a violation of the Treaty of Recognition; that under instructions from Moscow the Communists had violated the laws of the United States; that throughout the entire time they had been supplied with funds from Moscow for activities against the American people and the American Government. The Dies Committee only confirmed what most Americans already know. Is the word of Stalin any better than the word of Hitler?

In these last weeks it is declared not only by public officials but by labor leaders themselves that the strikes which hamstring the defense of the United States have been Communist conspiracies. Thus Russia has continued her mission of destroying our democracy down to last week.

Less than two years ago, Stalin entered into an agreement with Hitler through which there should be joint onslaught on the democracies of the world. Nine days later Stalin attacked the Poles jointly with Hitler and destroyed the freedom of a great and democratic people. Fourteen days later Stalin destroyed the independence of democratic Latvia, Lithuania and Estonia. Ninety days later on came the unprovoked attack by Russia on democratic Finland. Is that not aggression and is not every case a hideous violation of treaties and international law?

Stalin has taken advantage of the very freedoms of democracy to destroy them with the most potent fifth column in all history. He contributed to the destruction of France. He has daily implanted class hate in America and a stealthy war against our institutions.

We know also Hitler's hideous record of brutality, of aggression and as a destroyer of democracies. Truly, Poland, Norway, Holland, Belgium,

Denmark, France and the others are dreadful monuments. But I am talking of Stalin at this moment.

One of the real compensations America received for our enormous sacrifices in the last war was from the large part we played in establishing the democracies of Finland, Poland, Estonia, Latvia and Lithuania. We nursed them in their infancy. We spent hundreds of millions to help them grow to manhood. Does America feel quite right about aiding Stalin to hold his enslavement of them? That is where power politics will carry us. No doubt we will promise to aid Russia. But the war to bring the four freedoms to the world will die spiritually when we make that promise.

If we go further and join the war and we win, then we have won for Stalin the grip of communism on Russia, the enslavement of nations, and more opportunity for it to extend in the world. We should at least cease to tell our sons that they would be giving their lives to restore democracy and freedom to the world.

Practical statesmanship leads in the same path as moral statesmanship. These two dictators—Stalin and Hitler—are in deadly combat. One of these two hideous ideologists will disappear in this fratricidal war. In any event both will be weakened.

Statesmanship demands that the United States stand aside in watchful waiting, armed to the teeth, while these men exhaust themselves.

Then the most powerful and potent nation in the world can talk to mankind with a voice that will be heard. If we get involved in this struggle we, too, will be exhausted and feeble.

To align American ideals alongside Stalin will be as great a violation of everything American as to align ourselves with Hitler.

Can the American people debauch their sense of moral values and the very essence of their freedom by even a tacit alliance with Soviet Russia? Such an alliance will bring sad retributions to our people.

If we go into this war we will aid Stalin to hold his aggression against the four little democracies. We will help him to survive and continue his terror and his conspiracies against all democracies. We should stop the chant about leading the world to liberalism and freedom.

Again I say, if we join the war and Stalin wins, we have aided him to impose more communism on Europe and the world. At least we could not with such a bedfellow say to our sons that by making the supreme sacrifice, they are restoring freedom to the world. War alongside Stalin to impose freedom is more than a travesty. It is a tragedy. . . .

We cannot slay an idea or an ideology with machine guns. Ideas live in men's minds in spite of military defeat. They live until they have proved themselves right or wrong. These ideas are evil. And evil ideas contain the germs of their own defeat. . . .

. . . Whatever that future may be, only one defeat can come to America. We have no need to fear military defeat if we are prepared. Our only defeat would be if we lost our own freedoms and our potency for good in the world. . . .

There is no course we can pursue amid these stupendous dangers that is perfect, or without risks, or that may not require change. But let me propose for reasoning people a course for us at this time which avoids the most destructive forces and holds fast to the most constructive forces. And that program is neither defeatist, nor isolationist, nor interventionist.

We should give every aid we can to Britain and China within the law, but do not put the American flag or American boys in the zone of war. Arm to the teeth for defense of the Western Hemisphere, and cease to talk and to provoke war. Uphold Congress steadily in assuming the responsibility to determine peace or war. Stop this notion of ideological war to impose the four freedoms on other nations by military force and against their will. Devote ourselves to improving the four freedoms within our borders that the light of their success may stir the peoples of the world to their adoption.

The day will come when these nations are sufficiently exhausted to listen to the military, economic and moral powers of the United States. And with these reserves unexhausted, at that moment, and that moment only, can the United States promote a just and permanent peace. . . .

Here in America today is the only remaining sanctuary of freedom, the last oasis of civilization and the last reserve of moral and economic strength. It we are wise, these values can be made to serve all mankind.

My countrymen, we have marched into the twilight of a world war. Should we not stop here and build our defense while we can still see? Shall we stumble on into the night of chaos?[23]

In other parts of this address I made an appraisal of the world's military and American defense situation as it manifested itself at that time. And I discussed preparedness and the economic and social penalties upon the American people by participation in another war. I also discussed the difficulties of the world making peace after involvement in the war.

---

23. [*Editor's note*: Italics Hoover's. These italics do not appear in either of the published versions cited in note 4. Evidently Hoover decided to italicize these passages for this volume.]

CHAPTER 35

The Reactions in the Western World

THE CATACLYSMIC SHIFT of power weights by Hitler's attack on Russia brought many reactions in the British and American governments.

The British naturally rejoiced at this gigantic diversion of danger. Prime Minister Churchill at once promised aid to Russia by way of supplies and coordinated military action against Hitler. Britain needed no further aid from the United States except that of financing her supplies.

The Prime Minister found no difficulty in getting into bed with Stalin, even though he had at one time been most articulate about the characteristics of Communism. His comments on them had abounded in such expressions as:

> ... Of all tyrannies in history the Bolshevist tyranny is the worst, the most destructive, and the most degrading. . . .
>
> ... that foul combination of criminality and animalism . . .[1]
>
> ... Everyone can see how Communism rots the soul of a nation; how it makes it abject and hungry in peace, and proves it base and abominable in war. . . .[2]

This latter remark had been made in the course of an eloquent tribute to the heroism of Finland in its defense against the Communists.

However, Mr. Churchill displayed his honesty with his countrymen by making no apologies for his former views of communism when, on June 22, 1941, he said:

> ... The past with its crimes, its follies and its tragedies, flashes away. I see the Russian soldiers standing on the threshold of their native land, guarding

---

1. *The Times*, London, April 12, 1919.
2. [Winston S.] Churchill, *Blood, Sweat, and Tears* (New York: G. P. Putnam's Sons, 1941), p. 215.

the fields which their fathers have tilled from time immemorial. I see them guarding their homes where mothers and wives pray—ah yes, for there are times when all pray—for the safety of their loved ones, the return of the breadwinner, of their champion, of their protector. . . .

. . . Any man or state who fights on against Nazidom will have our aid. Any man or state who marches with Hitler is our foe. . . .[3]

On July 12, Britain and Russia signed a mutual assistance pact by which they agreed to make no peace except by mutual consent. The pact read:

. . . The two governments mutually undertake to render each other assistance and support of all kinds in the present war against Hitlerite Germany.

They further undertake that during this war they will neither negotiate nor conclude an armistice or treaty of peace except by mutual agreement. . . .[4]

Reaction of the Washington Administration

Mr. Roosevelt's Cabinet and his advisers, who had already urged American entry into the war, at once became even more pressing. They employed reasons of urgency which to anyone familiar with Russia or Russian history would be unbelievable were it not for the documentary evidence.

Robert Sherwood, who sat in the high councils of the Roosevelt Administration and who wrote from government documentary sources one of the most important histories of the Second World War,[5] records the following memorandum which Secretary of War Henry L. Stimson sent to the President thirty hours after the Hitler attack on Stalin:

For the past thirty hours I have done little but reflect upon the German-Russian war and its effect upon our immediate policy. To clarify my own views I have spent today in conference with the Chief of Staff [Marshall] and the men in the War Plans Division of the General Staff. I am glad to say that I find substantial unanimity upon the fundamental policy which they think should be followed by us. I am even more relieved that their views coincide so entirely with my own.

First: Here is their estimate of controlling facts:

---

3. [Winston S.] Churchill, *The Unrelenting Struggle* (Boston: Little, Brown and Company, 1942), pp. 171–172.

4. *New York Times,* July 14, 1941.

5. [Robert E.] Sherwood, *Roosevelt and Hopkins* (Harper & Brothers, Publishers, New York: 1948).

1. Germany will be thoroughly occupied in beating Russia for a minimum of one month and a possible maximum of three months.

2. During this period Germany must give up or slack up on
   a. Any invasion on the British Isles.
   b. Any attempt to attack herself or prevent us from occupying Iceland.
   c. Her pressure on West Africa, Dakar and South America.
   d. Any attempt to envelop the British right flank in Egypt by way of Iraq, Syria or Persia.
   e. Probably her pressure in Libya and the Mediterranean.

Second: They were unanimously of the belief that this precious and unforeseen period of respite should be used to push with the utmost vigor our movements in the Atlantic theater of operations. They were unanimously of the feeling that such pressure on our part was the right way to help Britain, to discourage Germany, and to strengthen our own position of defense against our most imminent danger.

As you know, Marshall and I have been troubled by the fear lest we be prematurely dragged into two major operations in the Atlantic, one in the northeast and the other in Brazil. . . . By getting into this war with Russia Germany has much relieved our anxiety, provided we act promptly and get the initial dangers over before Germany gets her legs disentangled from the Russian mire. . . .[6]

The only explanation of this amazing statement that Hitler would be victorious over Russia in a minimum of thirty days, or a maximum of ninety days, is that it was an opinion of men who:

(a) ignored or were ignorant of Russian history. The experience of Napoleon in his attack on Russia was given in the textbooks of most American schools. Someone's memory of Tchaikovsky's "1812" overture might well have recalled Napoleon's ignorance of Russian powers of defense.

(b) ignored Russian geography and climate. Her military strength was not Russia's only defense. Napoleon had been defeated by many "generals" other than generals of the Russian army. There were General Endless Distances over endless plains, General Endless Expendable Men, and General Scorched Earth Tactics as practiced by the retreating Russian armies. And above all, there were General Autumn Rain and General Winter, who would come into action within a few months.

---

6. Ibid., pp. 303–304.

(c) ignored dispatches sent to the State Department by our own Ambassador to Russia, and our military intelligence dispatches from Moscow to the War Department. In Section II in the chapter devoted to Russia, I give an account of these dispatches during the years 1935 to 1938. They estimated that Stalin's army numbered more than 1,300,000 equipped men in January 1936, and increased to between 1,500,000 to 2,000,000 in August 1936.

In July, 1937, they told of an increase in the Soviet military budget by twenty times that of six years earlier. On October 31, 1938, our representative had reported further increases in Soviet armament.

Stalin's speech of March 10, 1939, had contained a flat notice that he was expanding still further the fighting power of the Red Army.[7]

In July, 1940, our military attaché in Moscow advised that there were even greater increases in the army and in the industrial support for it.

Accurate information from Russia on July 1, 1941, showed that at least in numbers the Russian army and its major items of equipment actually exceeded those of the German army.

The only rational explanation of the Marshall-Stimson prophecy of a Hitler victory in ninety days is that these men were bent on rushing the President into war.

Stimson's authorized biography states as to his attitude of mind:

> ... During this period [from April 1941] it was ... [Stimson's] strong belief that the situation required more energetic and explicit leadership than President Roosevelt considered wise. . . . [Stimson] was convinced that if the policy of sustaining Great Britain was to succeed, America must throw the major part of her naval strength into the Atlantic battle. . . .
>
> ... in a letter of May 24 [1941] to the President ... [Stimson] had suggested that the President ask Congress for power "to use naval, air, and military forces of the United States" in the Atlantic battle.
>
> ... As Stimson constantly pointed out at the time, only the President could take the lead in a warlike policy. . . .[8]

Also of interest is the following note in Stimson's diary on June 17, 1941, five days before Hitler's attack on Stalin:

---

7. For the authority of these items, see Chapters 10 and 18, [in] Sections II and IV.

8. Henry L. Stimson and McGeorge Bundy, *On Active Service in Peace and War* (Harper & Brothers, New York: 1948), pp. 366, 371, 375.

... At present, from all the despatches, it seems nip and tuck whether Russia will fight or surrender. Of course, I think the chances are she will surrender.[9]

Varied Reactions

The immediate Congressional reaction to the war varied greatly. Harry S. Truman, then Democratic Senator from Missouri, discussing the Nazi invasion of Russia, on June 23, 1941, said:

> If we see that Germany is winning we ought to help Russia and if Russia is winning we ought to help Germany and that way let them kill as many as possible, although I don't want to see Hitler victorious under any circumstances. Neither of them think anything of their pledged word.[10]

Senator Bennett C. Clark, Democrat from Missouri, on June 23, 1941, said:

> It's a case of dog eat dog. Stalin is as bloody-handed as Hitler. I don't think we should help either one. We should tend to our own business. . . .[11]
>
> If the United States should accept Josef Stalin as a virtual ally we can do not less than take Communism to our bosom and release Earl Browder from the penitentiary and make him an honored guest at the White House.[12]

Also on June 23, 1941, Senator Robert M. La Follette, Jr. of Wisconsin said:

> In the next few weeks the American people will witness the greatest whitewash act in all history. They will be told to forget the purges in Russia by the OGPU, the persecution of religion, the confiscation of property, the invasion of Finland and the vulture role Stalin played in seizing half of prostrate Poland, all of Latvia, Estonia and Lithuania. These will be made to seem the acts of a "democracy" preparing to fight Nazism. The interventionists will scream that now is the time for us to go to war.[13]

Senator Robert A. Taft, on June 25, 1941, said that

> ... the victory of communism in the world would be far more dangerous to the United States than the victory of fascism. . . .[14]

---

9. [William L.] Langer and [S. Everett] Gleason, *The Undeclared War* (Harper & Brothers, Publishers, New York: 1953), p. 528.

10. *New York Times,* June 24, 1941.

11. Ibid.

12. *New York Herald Tribune,* June 24, 1941.

13. Ibid.

14. *New York Times,* June 26, 1941.

In a June 28 radio address, Senator Claude Pepper, Democrat of Florida, envisioned the results of a Hitler victory over Russia:

"If Russia falls, if the Nazis march across this ancient land," he said, "they will have thwarted British ships, British planes, British sentinels; they will have broken out of Europe; they will have reached us in spite of all the heroic Poles, British and French and Greeks and Yugoslavians have done to hold them back.

"If Russia falls you and I know there would not be anybody else between Hitler and Alaska, and with Alaska taken only Canada, a nation the size that Belgium was, will stand between Hitler and us here in the continental United States."[15]

In the House of Representatives on June 24, 1941, Congressman Frank C. Osmers, Jr., Republican of New Jersey, exhorted:

... Let us make no ill-considered promise to send nonexistent war material on nonexistent ships to a nation whose whole concept of life is repugnant to us. Let us, rather, use this precious time to aid Great Britain and to arm ourselves.[16]

However, on the same day, Congressman Estes Kefauver, Democrat from Tennessee, declared:

Communism has been a challenge to us, but in a different sort of way. It is not and never has been an armed challenge. We can deal with the communistic challenge by improving our democratic processes and by cleaning out the communistic agitators. If need be, this can be done later, but today is our chance to deal with Hitler.[17]

Representative Robert F. Rich, Republican from Pennsylvania, stated on the floor of the House on June 26, 1941:

Those people who want us to get into this war on the side of Russia want us to get into bed with a rattlesnake and a skunk.[18]

On July 1, at a press conference, the President revised his formula for "keeping our of war."

---

15. Ibid., June 29, 1941.
16. *Congressional Record,* 77th Congress, First Session, Vol. 87, p. 5460.
17. Ibid., p. 5484.
18. Ibid., p. 5553.

"Mr. President, back when the war first started, it was a popular question to ask you if you thought we could keep out of war," a reporter said. "You always said that we could."

The President answered that he had not said so. He had stated that he hoped we could. . . .

The President insisted, however, that the matter of wording had not changed his position. He had been giving the same answer to the question of whether this country could keep out of war since Sept. 1, 1939, when hostilities started in Europe.[19]

There had been no mention of the qualifying word "hope" in his "mothers and fathers" speech or in at least fourteen of his other promises prior to the election, now only eight months past.

After the Hitler attack on Russia, Stimson, on July 3, 1941, wrote the President enclosing a memorandum suggesting points to be made in Mr. Roosevelt's forthcoming address to Congress, saying in part:

> . . . The effort to avoid the use of force is proving ineffective. . . . It has now become abundantly clear that, unless we add our every effort, physical and spiritual as well as material, to the efforts of those free nations who are still fighting . . . we shall ourselves . . . be fighting alone. . . .[20]

Stalin's Real Military Strength

President Roosevelt dispatched Harry Hopkins to Russia as his personal representative to Stalin. Hopkins arrived in Moscow on July 30, 1941. In his report to the President of July 31, 1941,[21] Hopkins said that:

> . . . Mr. Stalin outlined the situation as follows:
>
> He stated that in his opinion the German Army had 175 divisions on Russia's western front at the outbreak of the war, and that since the outbreak of the war, this had been increased to 232 divisions; he believes that Germany can mobilize 300 divisions.
>
> He stated that Russia had 180 divisions at the outbreak of the war, but many of these were well back of the line of combat, and could not be quickly

---

19. *New York Times,* July 2, 1941; see also [Samuel I. Rosenman, comp.,] *The Public Papers and Addresses of Franklin D. Roosevelt,* 1939 [volume] [The Macmillan Company, New York: 1941], p. 457.

20. Stimson and Bundy, *On Active Service in Peace and War,* pp. 372–373.

21. Sherwood, *Roosevelt and Hopkins,* pp. 333–334.

mobilized, so that when the Germans struck it was impossible to offer adequate resistance. The line which is now held is a far more propitious one than the more advanced line which they might have taken up had their divisions been prepared. Since war began, however, divisions have been placed in their appropriate positions, and at the present time he believes that Russia has a few more divisions than Germany, and places the number of Russian divisions at 240 in the front, with 20 in reserve. Stalin said that about one third of these divisions had not as yet been under fire.

Mr. Stalin stated that he can mobilize 350 divisions and will have that many divisions under arms by the time the spring campaign begins in May 1942.

Stalin also informed Hopkins that the Germans already had shown a weakness in attack due to the numbers of men required to guard their extended communication lines. He said that German attacks had lessened in strength in the past ten days.

Stalin's statement of his strength should have been a shock to those who asserted that Hitler could conquer Russia in a maximum of ninety days.

Even the *New York Times,* a staunch supporter of the President, expressed doubts as to the consequences of extending aid to Stalin, saying editorially on August 6, 1941:

> . . . It is more than a little too bad that Mr. Oumansky's Government is just now discovering the community of interest of the freedom-loving nations. Where was Stalin in the Summer . . . when the war began, if not playing ball with Hitler? . . .
>
> . . . Stalin is on our side today. Where will he be tomorrow? In the light of his record, no one can say that he will not switch sides again, make a sudden treacherous peace with Germany and become, in effect, Hitler's *Gauleiter* in the East. We should be in a fine state of affairs if we succeeded in landing a hundred bombers on Russian soil just in time for this reconciliation.

Hanson W. Baldwin, military analyst of the *New York Times,* says in his book *Great Mistakes of the War:*

> There is no doubt whatsoever that it would have been to the interest of Britain, the United States, and the world to have allowed—and indeed, to have encouraged—the world's two great dictatorships to fight each other to a frazzle. Such a struggle, with its resultant weakening of both Communism and Nazism, could not but have aided in the establishment of a more stable peace; it would have placed the democracies in supreme power in the

world, instead of elevating one totalitarianism at the expense of another and *of the democracies*. The great opportunity of the democracies for establishing a stable peace came on June 22, 1941, when Germany invaded Russia, but we muffed the chance. . . .[22]

On July 30, after the commitment of aid to Stalin had been made, I wrote the following memorandum to Secretary Stimson:

My dear Mr. Secretary:

We need agreements with Stalin making conditions on Lend-Lease and at once before we begin. We must not fool ourselves. You and I know that agreements have no binding quality in Communist philosophy. We need no better exhibit than the cruel aggression on Finland, Latvia, Estonia, Lithuania and Eastern Poland in violation of the thrice-enacted non-aggression pacts made at Stalin's initiative in the past 15 years. The independence and very life of these peoples have been crushed. The Stalin-Hitler alliance of 1939 not only provided for these annexations and a violation of his [Stalin's] own alliance agreement with France, but also it precipitated this world war.

Now that Hitler is attacking Stalin we are about to give . . . [Stalin] Lend-Lease. Despite all Russian history we should make agreements with him now to restore the independence of these many despoiled peoples as a condition of our assistance. Such agreements may be no good as agreements, but they are possibly enforceable if we make continuance of Lend-Lease conditional upon stipulated performance in specific periods. In any event, they would establish standards of conduct for all the world to see.

I fear the Administration will not approach this situation in the light of grim reality but in the glow of our left-wing lamps.

Do impress the situation upon your colleagues. In it lies the only hope of real peace for the world. . . .

Yours faithfully,
/s/ Herbert Hoover

It was not from lack of urging that Mr. Roosevelt failed to take action along this line. The former Washington envoys of Estonia, Latvia, Lithuania, and Poland—all of them familiar with Russian methods and diplomacy—at once informed me that they had pressed the President to act to secure agreement for the freedom of their nations.

---

22. Hanson W. Baldwin, *Great Mistakes of the War* (Harper & Brothers, New York: 1950), p. 10.

Cold Comfort for the Vatican

Catholic leaders were greatly disturbed over American support of Stalin, the arch foe of religious faith. Both the American and British Governments submitted comforting notes to the Vatican on July 6.

Also, Mr. Roosevelt, in a personal letter to His Holiness Pope Pius XII, on September 3, 1941, asserted that the churches in Russia were still open and that the survival of Russia was less dangerous to religion than the continuation of the German dictatorship.[23] The Vatican was no doubt aware that Hitler, as evil as he was, had not suppressed the Catholic places of worship and that the Communists had closed and plundered eighty percent of the churches in Russia.

23. Delivered by Myron C. Taylor, Personal Representative of the President to the Vatican, September 9; quoted at length by Langer and Gleason in *The Undeclared War*, p. 795; quoted in full in [Elliott Roosevelt, ed.,] *F.D.R.*[,] *His Personal Letters*, [1928–1945,] Vol. II (Duell, Sloan and Pearce, New York: 1950), pp. 1204–1205.

The Road to War

CHAPTER 36

Via Germany

WITH THE AMERICAN PEOPLE and the Congress greatly opposed to entering the war, our participation appeared unlikely unless some overt act against us was made either by Germany or Japan which would reverse this tide. Certain elements in the Washington Administration seemed to hold this view and undertook measures to bring about such an attack.

A Joint Army and Navy Basic War Plan drawn up during April and May 1941, and approved by Secretary of the Navy Knox on May 28 and by Secretary of War Stimson on June 2, 1941, originally emphasized the defeat of the Axis Powers.

Vice Admiral Richmond K. Turner, War Plans Officer for the Chief of Naval Operations, described it:

> The plan contemplated a major effort on the part of both the principal associated Powers against Germany, initially. It was felt in the Navy Department, that there might be a possibility of war with Japan without the involvement of Germany, but at some length and over a considerable period, this matter was discussed and it was determined that in such a case the United States would, if possible, initiate efforts to bring Germany into the war against us in order that we would be enabled to give strong support to the United Kingdom in Europe. We felt that it was encumbent on our side to defeat Germany, to launch our principal efforts against Germany first, and to conduct a limited offensive in the Central Pacific, and a strictly defensive effort in the Asiatic.[1]

---

1. *Pearl Harbor Attack,* testimony of Vice Admiral Richmond K. Turner, USN, April 3, 1944, Part 26 [*Proceedings of Hart Inquiry*], p. 265, question 10. See also testimony of Rear Admiral Husband E. Kimmel, USN (ret.), *Pearl Harbor Attack* hearings, Part 6, p. 2502. [*Editor's note:* See Chapter 31, note 16, for the full citation of this Congressional document.]

There followed a series of activities in the Atlantic that the German military mind must have observed.

The President on July 7, 1941, informed Congress of the landing of American troops in Iceland, Trinidad, and British Guiana, saying:

> ... forces of the United States Navy have today arrived in Iceland in order to supplement, and eventually to replace, the British forces. . . .
>
> The United States cannot permit the occupation by Germany of strategic outposts in the Atlantic to be used as air or naval bases for eventual attack against the Western Hemisphere. We have no desire to see any change in the present sovereignty of those regions.[2]

Mr. Roosevelt revealed a message from the Prime Minister of Iceland approving this action.

The British originally had intended to withdraw their garrison from Iceland but they changed their mind about withdrawing. Mr. Churchill stated in a speech to the House of Commons on July 9, 1941:

> ... We still propose to retain our Army in Iceland, and, as British and United States Forces will both have the same object in view, namely, the defence of Iceland, it seems very likely they will co-operate closely and effectively in resistance of any attempt by Hitler to gain a footing. . . .[3]

The idea that bases in Iceland or the West Indies could be occupied by Germans seems a little remote inasmuch as Hitler had not even been able to cross the 21 mile-wide English Channel and his air force seemed likely to be fairly busy in Russia for some time.

However, the arrival of the United States troops in Iceland set the stage for further United States naval operations. Prime Minister Churchill recalls:

> ... Thereafter American convoys escorted by American warships ran regularly to Reykjavik, and although the United States were still not at war they admitted foreign ships to the protection of their convoys.[4]

Senator Robert A. Taft protested the occupation:

---

2. *New York Times,* July 8, 1941. See also [Samuel I. Rosenman, comp.,] *The Public Papers and Addresses of Franklin D. Roosevelt,* 1941 [volume] [Harper & Brothers Publishers, 1950], pp. 255ff.

3. Great Britain, House of Commons, *Parliamentary Debates,* Official Report (Hansard), 5th Series, Vol. 373, p. 182. See also Winston S. Churchill, *The Unrelenting Struggle* (Little, Brown and Company, Boston: 1942), p. 176.

4. Winston S. Churchill, *The Grand Alliance* (Houghton Mifflin Company, Boston: 1950), p. 150.

I think the President has grossly exceeded his constitutional authority.[5]

On July 9, Navy Secretary Knox implied that orders to attack German submarines had been given.[6]

On July 11, the Senate Naval Affairs Committee summoned Secretary Knox and Admiral Stark, Chief of Naval Operations, to a closed session where Secretary Knox reportedly admitted that depth bombs had been dropped against a German submarine by an American destroyer attached to the Atlantic patrol.[7]

Also on July 11, Nelson A. Rockefeller, then a member of Mr. Roosevelt's Administration, announced the black-listing of about 2,000 Latin-American firms and individuals having connections with the Axis.[8] We were not yet at war.

On August 5, I joined in a declaration against the current warlike actions. The signers of this declaration were, among others, former Vice-President Charles G. Dawes, former Under Secretaries of State J. Reuben Clark and Henry P. Fletcher, President Felix Morley of Haverford College, President Ray Lyman Wilbur of Stanford University, writers Clarence Budington Kelland and Irvin S. Cobb, and operatic star Geraldine Farrar.

The statement read as follows:

> The American people should insistently demand that Congress put a stop to step-by-step projection of the United States into undeclared war. Congress has not only the sole power to declare war but also the power and responsibility to keep the country out of war unless and until both Houses have otherwise decided.
>
> Exceeding its expressed purpose, the lease-lend bill has been followed by naval action, by military occupation of bases outside the Western Hemisphere, by promise of unauthorized aid to Russia and by other belligerent moves.
>
> Such warlike steps, in no case sanctioned by Congress, undermine its constitutional powers and the fundamental principles of democratic government. The representatives of the people, in passing the lease-lend bill, expressed the national conviction that preservation of the British Empire and China is desirable for us and for civilization.

---

5. *New York Times,* July 8, 1941.
6. Ibid., July 10, 1941.
7. Ibid., July 12, 1941.
8. Ibid.

We hold that view but the intent of Congress was that lease-lend material should be transferred to belligerent ownership in the United States and utilized only to protect the independence of democracies.

We hold that in giving generous aid to these democracies at our seaboard we have gone as far as is consistent either with law, with sentiment or with security. Recent events raise doubts that this war is a clear-cut issue of liberty and democracy. It is not purely a world conflict between tyranny and freedom. The Anglo-Russian alliance has dissipated that illusion.

In so far as this is a war of power-politics, the American people want no part in it. American participation is far more likely to destroy democracy in this country and thus in the Western Hemisphere than to establish it in Europe. The hope of civilization now rests primarily upon the preservation of freedom and democracy in the United States.

That will be lost for a generation if we join in this war. We maintain that American lives should be sacrificed only for American independence or to prevent the invasion of the Western Hemisphere.

Few people honestly believe that the Axis is now, or will in the future be in a position to threaten the independence of any part of this hemisphere if our defenses are properly prepared.

Energies of this country should be concentrated on the defense of our own liberties. Freedom in America does not depend on the outcome of struggles for material power between other nations.[9]

The Atlantic Charter

On August 9, 1941, President Roosevelt and Prime Minister Churchill, together with their staffs, met on warships off the coast of Newfoundland.[10] On August 14, 1941, they issued the following statement which was destined to play a large part in the future of mankind:

---

9. Ibid., August 6, 1941.

10. Those who attended the conference were:

For the United States: President Franklin D. Roosevelt, W. Averell Harriman, Sumner Welles, Harry L. Hopkins, Admiral Ernest J. King, Admiral Harold R. Stark, General George C. Marshall, Major General Henry H. Arnold, Rear Admiral Richmond K. Turner, Commander Forrest P. Sherman, Rear Admiral Ross T. McIntire, Major General Edwin M. Watson, Captain John R. Beardall.

For Great Britain: Prime Minister Winston S. Churchill, Sir Alexander Cadogan, Lord Beaverbrook, Lord Cherwell, Admiral of the Fleet Sir Dudley Pound, General Sir John Dill, Air Chief Marshal Sir Wilfred Freeman, Colonel L.C. Hollis, Commander Charles Thompson, J.M. Martin.

References for the above names: [U.S. Department of State,] *Foreign Relations of the United States*, [*Diplomatic Papers*], *1941* [United States Government Printing Office, Washington: 1958],

The President of the United States and the Prime Minister, Mr. Churchill, representing His Majesty's Government in the United Kingdom, have met at sea.

They have been accompanied by officials of their two Governments, including high ranking officers of their military, naval, and air services.

The whole problem of the supply of munitions of war, as provided by the Lease-Lend Act, for the armed forces of the United States and for those countries actively engaged in resisting aggression has been further examined.

Lord Beaverbrook, the Minister of Supply of the British Government, has joined in these conferences. He is going to proceed to Washington to discuss further details with appropriate officials of the United States Government. These conferences will also cover the supply problems of the Soviet Union.

The President and the Prime Minister have had several conferences. They have considered the dangers to world civilization arising from the policies of military domination by conquest upon which the Hitlerite government of Germany and other governments associated therewith have embarked, and have made clear the steps which their countries are respectively taking for their safety in the face of these dangers.

They have agreed upon the following joint declaration:

The President of the United States of America and the Prime Minister, Mr. Churchill, representing His Majesty's Government in the United Kingdom, being met together, deem it right to make known certain common principles in the national policies of their respective countries on which they base their hopes for a better future for the world.

FIRST, their countries seek no aggrandizement, territorial or other;

SECOND, they desire to see no territorial changes that do not accord with the freely expressed wishes of the peoples concerned;

THIRD, they respect the right of all peoples to choose the form of government under which they will live; and they wish to see sovereign rights and self-government restored to those who have been forcibly deprived of them;

FOURTH, they will endeavor, with due respect for their existing obligations, to further the enjoyment by all states, great or small, victor or vanquished, of access, on equal terms, to the trade and to the raw materials of the world which are needed for their economic prosperity;

Vol. I, pp. 341ff.; [Robert E. Sherwood,] *Roosevelt and Hopkins* [Harper & Brothers Publishers, New York: 1948], pp. 349, 353, 363; [Ernest J. King and Walter Muir Whitehill,] *Fleet Admiral King* [W. W. Norton & Company, Inc., New York: 1952], pp. 331–335.

FIFTH, they desire to bring about the fullest collaboration between all nations in the economic field with the object of securing, for all, improved labor standards, economic adjustment and social security;

SIXTH, after the final destruction of the Nazi tyranny, they hope to see established a peace which will afford to all nations the means of dwelling in safety within their own boundaries, and which will afford assurance that all the men in all the lands may live out their lives in freedom from fear and want;

SEVENTH, such a peace should enable all men to traverse the high seas and oceans without hindrance;

EIGHTH, they believe that all of the nations of the world, for realistic as well as spiritual reasons, must come to the abandonment of the use of force. Since no future peace can be maintained if land, sea, or air armaments continue to be employed by nations which threaten, or may threaten, aggression outside of their frontiers, they believe, pending the establishment of a wider and permanent system of general security, that the disarmament of such nations is essential. They will likewise aid and encourage all other practicable measures which will lighten for peace-loving peoples the crushing burden of armaments.[11]

The declaration which became known as the "Atlantic Charter" was well published by an elaborate propaganda campaign. It was read over the radio repeatedly. It was emblazoned in bold type headlines by the press. It was printed at government expense in large type for display in schools and public places.

The Charter covered many of the same ideas as Woodrow Wilson's "Fourteen Points and Subsequent Addresses." The Atlantic Charter, like Mr. Wilson's declaration, became a beacon of hope to a score of nations which had been deprived of sovereign rights and self-government by Stalin and Hitler.

As I have stated, the tenor of the Congress was adverse to "war-like" action. A few days earlier the Army service extension bill was passed in the House by only one vote. This narrow margin was interpreted by several leaders of both parties to indicate that any attempt to secure a declaration of war against Germany would be defeated by a large majority.[12]

---

11. *New York Times,* August 15, 1941. See also *The Public Papers and Addresses of Franklin D. Roosevelt,* 1941, pp. 314–315.

12. *New York Times,* August 13–14, 1941; cf. C[arlisle] Barge[r]on, *Confusion on the Potomac* [Wilfred Funk, New York: 1941], p. 218ff.

On August 14, the joint statement of Mr. Roosevelt and Mr. Churchill was discussed in the Senate. Senator Pat McCarran called it "tantamount to a declaration of war by this country." Senator David I. Walsh said that it "goes far beyond the Constitutional powers of the President." Senators D. Worth Clark and Robert R. Reynolds also expressed their disapproval.

Other members of the Senate commended the action. Senator Alben Barkley expressed the view that the joint statement "will find an enthusiastic response in the hearts of all peoples everywhere who believe in freedom and democracy." Senator Claude Pepper declared the statement "magnificent" and "the nearest thing to a declaration of world independence I have ever heard." Among the others who approved were Senators Tom Connally, Elbert D. Thomas, and W. Lee O'Daniel.[13]

The members of Congress, however, were not aware of the many military and political agreements made at this Atlantic meeting which were outside the Charter and were not disclosed until long after.[14]

Prime Minister Churchill on August 24, in a broadcast, proclaimed that President Roosevelt had agreed to join in the war, saying:

> . . . the President of the United States and the British representative in . . . the Atlantic Charter have jointly pledged their countries to the final destruction of the Nazi tyranny. That is a solemn and grave undertaking. It must be made good. It will be made good. . . . many practical arrangements to fulfill that purpose have been and are being organized and set in motion.[15]

In describing the "Atlantic meeting," Prime Minister Churchill later wrote:

> Continuous conferences also took place between the naval and military chiefs, and a wide measure *of agreement* was reached between them. . . . [16]

The most authoritative account of the Conference was Under Secretary Sumner Welles' memoranda which were revealed to the public years later at

---

13. *New York Times*, August 15, 1941.

14. Comprehensive information about the meeting is contained in the *Pearl Harbor Attack*, published in 1946; Sherwood's *Roosevelt and Hopkins*, published in 1948; *Foreign Relations of the United States, 1941*, Vol. I, published in 1958; and Churchill's account, *The Grand Alliance*, published in 1950. The military discussions are described in the Army Department's *United States Army in World War II: The War Department, Chief of Staff: Prewar Plans and Preparations,* by Mark Skinner Watson published [by the Historical Division, Department of the Army, Washington, D.C.] in 1950.

15. *New York Times*, August 25, 1941. See also Winston S. Churchill, *The Unrelenting Struggle*, p. 237.

16. Winston S. Churchill, *The Grand Alliance*, p. 437. Italics mine.

the Pearl Harbor hearings.[17] Welles confirmed one of the military agreements made, saying:

> ... Mr. Churchill stated that the British Government would be in a position to occupy the Cape Verde Islands with the understanding that it would later turn over the protection of those islands to the United States at such time as the United States was in a position to take those measures. . . . [18]

The constitutional questions raised by the Charter had been circumvented by the device of using such words as "they desire," "they will endeavor," "they hope," and "they believe" instead of the words "agreed" or "agreement."

17. *Pearl Harbor Attack,* Part 4, pp. 1783–1792.
18. Ibid., p. 1786.

CHAPTER 37

Via Germany (Continued)

HAD HITLER, AT THIS TIME, been so inclined he might have taken umbrage at the words in the Atlantic Charter "after the final destruction of the Nazi tyranny."

On August 19, the *Chicago Tribune* asserted that at a conference with Congressional leaders the previous day, President Roosevelt had revealed Atlantic Conference agreements which would require an American expeditionary force to Europe. Senator Alben W. Barkley, Majority Leader of the Senate, called the reports a "deliberate falsehood."[1]

In an address to workers in a Bethlehem, Pennsylvania, steel plant a week earlier, Rear Admiral Clark H. Woodward, U.S.N. (retired), naval representative on the Federal Board of Civilian Defense, expressed his belief that the United States "will be actively engaged in the war in a short time."

The *New York Herald Tribune* reported the Admiral as saying:

As a matter of fact, we already are at war, so there is no use trying to fool ourselves about it.

The report continued that the Admiral:

. . . urged "all possible assistance" to Great Britain and China to ensure the defeat of Germany and Japan, "these unscrupulous war-makers."

"This means . . . the manufacture and safe delivery of war materials to them, which in turn involves the protection of convoys and may result in shooting. We may or may not become involved in active conflict. Personally, I believe we will be actively engaged in the war in a short time."[2]

---

1. *Chicago Tribune,* August 19–20, 1941. See also *New York Times,* August 20, 1941.
2. *New York Herald Tribune,* August 13, 1941.

Prime Minister Churchill, always frank in his declarations to the British people, also said in his August 24 broadcast to the world:

The question has been asked: "How near is the United States to war?" There is certainly one man who knows the answer to that question. If Hitler has not yet declared war upon the United States it is surely not out of his love for American institutions. It is certainly not because he could not find a pretext. He has murdered half a dozen countries for far less. Fear, fear of immediately redoubling the tremendous energies now being employed against him is no doubt the restraining influence. But the real reason is . . . to be found in the method to which he has so faithfully adhered and by which he has gained so much.

What is that method? It is a very simple method. One by one—that is his plan. That is his guiding rule. That is the trick by which he has enslaved so large a portion of the world.[3]

On September 1, Mr. Churchill asked Mr. Roosevelt to assign American ships to transport two Commonwealth divisions to the Middle East.[4] This was done, and the 40,000 men duly landed.

On September 4, the Navy announced that the U.S. destroyer *Greer*, en route to Iceland with the mail, had been attacked by torpedoes from a submarine, and that the *Greer* had counterattacked with depth charges. At a press conference the next day the President described it as an attack.[5]

The President, on September 11, 1941, reviewed various incidents as overt acts of the Germans by attacks on American shipping. Referring to an incident of the American ship, the *Greer*, he said:

. . . It was not the first nor the last act of piracy which the Nazi government has committed against the American flag in this war, for attack has followed attack.

He commented on another American ship, the *Robin Moor*:

A few months ago an American flag merchant ship, the *Robin Moor*, was sunk by a Nazi submarine in the middle of the South Atlantic, under circumstances

---

3. *New York Times*, August 25, 1941. See also Churchill, *The Unrelenting Struggle* [Little, Brown and Company, Boston: 1942], pp. 237–238.

4. Churchill, *The Grand Alliance* [Houghton Mifflin Company, Boston, 1950], pp. 491–493.

5. *New York Times*, September 6, 1941. See also [Samuel I. Rosenman, comp.,] *The Public Papers and Addresses of Franklin D. Roosevelt*, 1941 [volume] [Harper & Brothers Publishers, New York: 1950], p. 374.

violating long-established international law and violating every principle of humanity. . . .

The ship had been carrying contraband, and the passengers and crew were allowed to leave the ship.

The President further reported:

In July, 1941 . . . an American battleship in North American waters was followed by a submarine which for a long time sought to maneuver itself into a position of attack upon the battleship. The periscope of the submarine was clearly seen. . . .

No submarine at that time could attain the speed of a battleship. Mr. Roosevelt next recounted that:

Five days ago a United States Navy ship on patrol picked up three survivors of an American-owned ship operating under the flag of our sister republic of Panama, the S.S. *Sessa.* . . .

The *Sessa* was carrying supplies and was not flying the American flag. Mr. Roosevelt added further:

Five days ago another United States merchant ship, the *Steel Seafarer,* was sunk by a German aircraft in the Red Sea 220 miles south of Suez. . . . [6]

The *Steel Seafarer,* flying the American flag, was carrying contraband arms to the British army in Egypt. The crew were all saved.

The Senate demanded to see the log of the *Greer.* Instead the Senate Naval Affairs Committee received a statement from Admiral Stark which told the story. It developed that a British plane had advised the *Greer* of the location of a German submarine. The *Greer* had searched for the submarine, located it, and trailed it for three and one-half hours until it turned around and fired a torpedo. Having been thus "attacked," the *Greer* used depth charges until it lost contact. [7]

I Speak Again

Although there was but a faint hope that we would be allowed to avoid being plunged into a second world war, I felt it my duty to again raise the

6. *New York Times,* September 12, 1941. See also *The Public Papers and Addresses of Franklin D. Roosevelt,* 1941 [volume], pp. 384–392.

7. *New York Times,* October 15, 1941. See also *Congressional Record,* Seventy-Seventh Congress, First Session, Vol. 87, Part 8, pp. 8314–8315.

policy of watching the dictators weaken and destroy each other before we took action.

I spoke from Chicago over a nation-wide broadcast on September 16, 1941:

... I wish again to speak to my countrymen upon America's relation to this war. I shall speak analytically and dispassionately, for cool thinking is needed now as never before. ...

Since ten weeks ago the military scene in the world has enormously shifted. ...

No one will deny that if we keep up this step-by-step policy it will lead inevitably to sending our sons into this war. ... It is the ultimate end of this road that must be looked at. And that I propose to discuss tonight. ...

If we would preserve the very spirit of free institutions American boys must not be sent to death without the specific declaration by the Congress. ...

I hold, and 99 percent of Americans hold, that totalitarianism, whether Nazism or Communism, is abominable. Both forms are unmoral because they deny religion, and there is no sanctity of agreement with them. They are abhorrent because of their unspeakable cruelty and their callous slaughter of millions of human beings. I abhor any American compromise or alliance with either of them.

A cold survey of this world situation will show that the dangers of ultimate totalitarian success are very much less than even ten weeks ago. The fratricidal war between Hitler and Stalin is daily weakening both dictators. ...

... Hitler cannot cross the English Channel with his armies. And England is even more impregnable because of this breathing spell for production of more planes, tanks and ships and our increasing aid in war tools. Her loss of ships and supplies at sea has greatly decreased. ...

Thoughtful men agree that the revolution in weapons makes the Western Hemisphere impregnable from invasion by Hitler if we are prepared. A statement of mine on this some time ago was challenged. But it has been more than confirmed by Colonel Phillips of our United States Army General Staff, who recently wrote:

"The bomber has made the American coast impregnable to invasion.

"And this still would be true if our Navy were inferior to that of any invading power.

"It makes it possible for this country to insure not only its own continental territory ... but ... to insure the impregnability of all North and South America."

And I may add that if Hitler had all the shipyards in Europe he could not in five years build an armada big enough even to start across the Atlantic. . . .

Under any American policy, whether interventionist or non-interventionist, in either Europe or Japan, if we have common sense we will concentrate upon the building up of our own production, give Britain her tools and await the development of all these forces, both East and West. . . .

. . . the President's policy of edging our warships into danger zones, of sending American merchant ships with contraband raises the most critical of all questions. These steps to war are unapproved and undeclared by the Congress. . . .

Here, my countrymen, you should listen to the stern voice of American experience.

Before the last world war we were indignant as we are now at aggression by dictator governments. Our sense of compassion and justice was aroused on behalf of the victims. We believed the New World could bring to the Old World a new order of justice, right and freedom. We would make the world safe for democracy. We would fight a war to end all war.

I advocated joining in that war. I occupied highly responsible positions in the war, and in the peace and its aftermaths. I was part of these events. I can speak from facts, from record, from personal knowledge. . . .

The victorious Allies in Europe were impoverished. They had suffered dreadful butcheries and wrongs. They demanded revenge, punishment, colonies, and money. Their statesmen, representing their peoples, were not free agents to make peace upon President Wilson's basis. A thousand years of history, fear and hate demanded and obtained seats at that peace table. They will sit at the next peace table of Europe. And America will be just as much foreign to that table as it was before. . . .

The stern voice of experience says that America cannot impose its freedoms and ideals upon the twenty-six races of Europe or the world. We should not again sacrifice our sons for that proved will-o'-the-wisp. . . .

Russia is rightly defending herself against aggression. But when it comes to sending our sons into this war we are confronted with something else. We need to take a long look now before we leap. Russia is also an aggressor nation against democracies. And what happens to the millions of enslaved people of Russia and to all Europe and to our own freedoms if we shall send our sons to win this war for Communism? . . .

To send our sons into this war must also be weighted in the scales of future America. Should we not weigh in this scale the dead and maimed? Should we not weigh the one-third of underfed, undernourished, underhoused, undereducated Americans for another generation that will be inevitable? Should we not weigh the loss of our own freedoms? . . .

What is the constructive policy for America? Is it isolation? Is it intervention? Neither is possible, and neither is wisdom.

We must have impregnable defense. This defense must include the other twenty nations in the Western Hemisphere. That is not isolation.

We must give the tools of defense to the democracies. That is not isolation.

We should reserve our strength that unexhausted we may give real aid to reconstruction and stabilizing of peace when Hitler collapses of his own overreaching. That is neither isolation nor intervention.

We can do our greatest service to civilization by strengthening here in the Western Hemisphere free institutions and free men and women. That is not isolation. It is a service to all mankind.

But to send our boys out to kill and be killed, that is intervention. . . .

Let us never forget we came over the ocean to this oasis of liberty. We extended this oasis greatly by mighty streams of freedom. They were dug and builded by the toil of our fathers and defended with their blood. Are we now to march out into the desert of European war and see the wells of freedom dried up behind us?[8]

On September 30, Mr. Churchill was less than helpful to American propagandists for entry into the war by telling the House of Commons that British, Allied and neutral shipping losses for the third quarter of 1941 had only been one-third of those for the second quarter.[9]

On October 17, the destroyer *Kearny,* 350 miles southwest of Iceland and 1,500 miles from the United States, was convoying ships carrying munitions to England. She attacked a German submarine with depth bombs. The submarine counterattacked. The *Kearny* reached port—eleven men on board had been killed. The facts were admitted to a Senate Committee by Admiral Stark a few days later and were publicly admitted by Navy Secretary Knox on October 29. It might be recalled that the Lend-Lease law had prohibited convoying by the American navy.

On October 22, General Robert E. Wood of the America First Committee issued a challenge to the President that he go before Congress and ask for a positive vote on peace and war. The President did not make the test.

---

8. Herbert Hoover, *Addresses upon the American Road, 1940–1941* (Charles Scribner's Sons, New York: 1941), pp. 103–114. See also the *New York Times,* September 17, 1941.

9. *New York Times,* October 1, 1941. See also Churchill, *The Unrelenting Struggle,* p. 265.

On October 27, the President delivered another address, asserting "the shooting has started," and ending:

... we Americans have cleared our decks and taken our battle stations. . . . [10]

An effective answer to Mr. Roosevelt's repeated charges of German overt acts against us came from an unexpected quarter. On November 5, Arthur Krock, the intellectually honest and able head of the Washington Bureau of the *New York Times,* addressed the Association of the Alumni of Columbia College and gave an analysis of President Roosevelt's speeches about German attacks on our shipping. Mr. Krock said:

... in my opinion, Hitler can throw at us both the dictionary and the facts when he says we "attacked" him. Why should the American Government ever have attempted to obscure it? . . .
Yet our Government did attempt to obscure it, as the record shows. . . . [11]

During the Pearl Harbor Investigation Admiral Stark testified that on November 7, 1941 he wrote Admiral Hart:

... The Navy is already in the war of the Atlantic, but the country doesn't seem to realize it. . . . Whether the country knows it or not, *we are at war.*[12]

Later during the same investigation, Representative Bertrand W. Gearhart asked the Admiral:

It was because of action which the President was directing from day to day against the Germans—the ... exchange of fire with German submarines which resulted—that caused you to state that we were at war in the Atlantic before Pearl Harbor?

Stark replied:

That is correct. . . .
... it commenced about the time of the shooting order, along after the President talked ... in September—that is, his talk to the Nation. And the actual shooting orders we gave in October. . . .

---

10. *New York Times,* October 28, 1941. See also *The Public Papers and Addresses of Franklin D. Roosevelt, 1941* [volume], pp. 438–444.
11. *New York Times,* November 6, 1941.
12. *Pearl Harbor Attack,* Part 5, p. 2121. [*Editor's note:* See Chapter 31, note 16, for the full citation of this document.]

Technically . . . we were not at war . . . because war had not been declared, but actually, so far as the forces operating under Admiral King in certain areas, it was war against any German craft that came inside that area.[13]

On November 7, 1941, Mr. Churchill, in a speech at Hull, England, said that the English were "now once again masters of our own destiny." New York newspapers reported the speech under the optimistic headlines—"Churchill Asserts Worst is Over," "Peril Over—Churchill," and "Churchill Asserts Darkest Peril Is Passed."[14]

The sum of all this was that the Congress did not respond to the President's insistence that there had been an overt act against the United States.

Hugh Gibson and I lunched with Bernard Baruch on November 9, 1941. He repeated to us a remark of Mr. Roosevelt's that "You can spit in Hitler's eye and he will take it."

13. Ibid., Part 5, p. 2310.
14. *New York Herald Tribune*, November 8, 1941; New York *Journal-American*, November 7, 1941; New York *Sun*, November 7, 1941.

CHAPTER 38

Via Japan—the Total Economic Sanctions on Japan and Japanese Proposals of Peace

IT IS NOT THE PURPOSE of this memoir to go into the full story of our relations with Japan during the years prior to mid-1941. But as Japan was the direct route by which the United States entered the war it is necessary to examine the major actions during this period which brought about the Japanese attack upon Pearl Harbor. This is the more necessary since not only were the actions of our government not disclosed to the American people at the time, but a generation of school children have grown up who never knew the truth of these actions.

About mid-1941 there was a definite shift in international forces. Hitler, by his attack upon Communist Russia in June 1941, abandoned the Berlin-Rome-Tokyo Axis and thus deprived Japan of some security against Russian attack. The mounting American economic and naval pressures on Japan to aid China had added to Japan's jeopardies. Through her aggressive wars in China, Japan's armies had occupied all the central seaboard of China, but they were now bogged down by their inability to complete this conquest. One consequence of Japan's difficulties was to seek peace with the United States and Britain—the Anglo-Saxons.

President Roosevelt had, since 1940, been imposing progressive economic pressures on the Japanese in an effort to relieve China. As an additional pressure, Washington had moved the American Pacific naval forces from their headquarters on the Pacific Coast to Pearl Harbor in Hawaii.

The center of Japanese militarist aggression had long been in their Army and War Department. The Japanese navy was aligned with the liberal elements headed by Prince Fumimaro Konoye, the Prime Minister, who was seeking to end the current tensions, in particular, with the United States and Britain—"the Anglo-Saxons."

Official Japanese proposals for better relations in the Pacific had been made to Washington in May, 1941, through Admiral Kichisaburo Nomura, a strong pro-American, who was sent by Prime Minister Konoye as Ambassador to the United States. But any success for Nomura's negotiations was hindered in Tokyo by the bitterly anti-American Foreign Minister Yosuke Matsuoka. On July 18, 1941, Prime Minister Konoye formed a new cabinet, excluding Matsuoka and replacing him with Admiral Teijiro Toyoda, who was pro Anglo-Saxon. Toyoda's appointment should have been a signal to both President Roosevelt and Secretary Hull that the liberal elements in Japan had now come into the ascendancy,[1] and that the atmosphere was much more favorable for ending Japanese aggression and restoring freedom to China. In September 1940, Ambassador Grew sent Washington his "green light" telegram recommending that the embargoes be put into effect. However, his later communications (particularly in 1941) urged that peace was possible and repeatedly warned that economic sanctions were dangerous.

The Total Economic Sanctions

However, on July 25, 1941, a month after Hitler's attack upon Stalin, President Roosevelt, suddenly ignoring the Japanese proposals, announced further economic sanctions upon them.[2] All American imports from and exports to Japan were put under the control of the government and all Japanese assets in the United States were frozen. Similar action was taken by the British Empire and by the Government of the Netherlands Indies.

The sanctions presented Japan with a choice of one of three alternatives: (1) invade the nations southward and thus obtain her urgent needs of food and oil from captured countries, such as Thailand, Malaya and the Dutch East Indies; (2) attack the United States, the leader in the economic blockade; or (3) attempt again to make peace with the "Anglo-Saxons."

On August 4th Prince Konoye conferred with both the Navy and War Ministers, and announced his plan to seek a meeting with President Roosevelt. Konoye's resolution to make a renewed effort for peace despite the sanctions, received the complete support of the Navy and also the consent of the

---

1. Joseph C. Grew, *Ten Years in Japan* (Simon and Schuster, New York: 1944), pp. 406ff. See also Joseph C. Grew, *Turbulent Era* (Houghton Mifflin Company, Boston: 1952), Vol. II, p. 1295.
2. *New York Times*, July 26, 1941.

Army. The Emperor directed Konoye to meet with the President as soon as possible.[3]

On August 8, 1941, Ambassador Nomura, on instructions from Tokyo, formally proposed to Secretary Hull a meeting of Prime Minister Konoye with President Roosevelt at some place on the American side of the Pacific. Secretary of War Stimson was against the meeting. He noted in his diary, August 9:

> The invitation to the President is merely a blind to try to keep us from taking definite action.[4]

With the information from Japan in their hands, Mr. Churchill and Mr. Roosevelt at the Atlantic Charter meeting (August 9 to 14, 1941) determined on certain further steps as to Japan. Ignoring the proposed meeting with Konoye, they agreed that a stern warning should be sent to the Japanese. Churchill was doubtful if the President would be sufficiently vigorous. On August 12, he telegraphed the Lord Privy Seal, saying:

> . . . We have laid special stress on the warning to Japan which constitutes the teeth of the President's communication. One would always fear State Department trying to tone it down; but President has promised definitely to use the hard language.[5]

Nevertheless, Mr. Churchill had anxieties over what might happen to the British if the Japanese should turn to military action to secure food and other supplies from Britain's possessions in the Far East.

Apparently to assuage Churchill's anxiety, Mr. Roosevelt undertook to extend negotiations with the Japanese in order to fend off any precipitate action from them.

---

3. *Pearl Harbor Attack,* Part 20, pp. 3999–4001. [*Editor's note:* See Chapter 31, note 16, for the full citation of this source.] After the war, records disclosed that the Japanese Navy had urged peace. In the latter part of July, Admiral Osami Nagano, Chief of Naval General Staff, advised the Emperor that the Japanese must try hard to make peace with the United States, even abandoning the alliance with Germany if necessary. The Admiral recommended that strong efforts be made to avert war. When the Emperor asked if they could achieve a decisive victory as in the Russo-Japanese War, Nagano replied that it was doubtful if Japan could win at all. (*International Military Tribunal for the Far East,* Record, p. 10185—from the entry of 31 July '41, Kido Diary.) [*Editor's note:* Hoover's reference is to the stenographic *Record of Proceedings of the International Military Tribunal for the Far East:* Tokyo, 1946–1948.]

4. Unpublished diary of Henry L. Stimson quoted by Herbert Feis, *The Road to Pearl Harbor* (Princeton University Press, Princeton, New Jersey: 1950), p. 259.

5. Churchill, *The Grand Alliance* [Houghton Mifflin Company, Boston: 1950], p. 446.

Forrest Davis and Ernest Lindley, in their book *How War Came*, relate that at this Atlantic meeting, Roosevelt asked Churchill:

"Wouldn't we be better off in three months?" . . . Churchill agreed, still doubting, however, that the respite would be forthcoming without immediate concerted action.

"Leave that to me," said the President. "I think I can baby them along for three months."[6]

I later asked Mr. Davis where this information came from. He said, "From Under Secretary Welles, who was present."

Upon his return from the Atlantic meeting, Mr. Roosevelt met with Nomura on August 17. At this meeting, the President presented Nomura with a statement which Mr. Churchill and he had drafted at the Atlantic Conference. However, the State Department had made some revisions in the original text, dividing the message into what Hull terms "a warning" and "an olive branch."[7] The "warning" was worded:

Such being the case, this Government now finds it necessary to say to the Government of Japan that if the Japanese Government takes any further steps in pursuance of a policy or program of military domination by force or threat of force of neighboring countries, the Government of the United States will be compelled to take immediately any and all steps which it may deem necessary toward safeguarding the legitimate rights and interests of the United States and American nationals and toward insuring the safety and security of the United States.[8]

The "olive branch" section concluded with the words:

. . . it would be helpful if the Japanese Government would be so good as to furnish a clearer statement than has yet been furnished as to its present attitude and plans, just as this Government has repeatedly outlined to the Japanese Government its attitude and plans.[9]

At the same meeting, Nomura delivered the already-known text of Konoye's proposal for a personal meeting and assured Roosevelt of Konoye's

---

6. Forrest Davis and Ernest Lindley, *How War Came* (Simon & Schuster, New York: 1942), p. 10.
7. *The Memoirs of Cordell Hull* [The Macmillan Company, New York, 1948], Vol. II, p. 1018. See also [Robert E.] Sherwood, *Roosevelt and Hopkins* [Harper & Brothers, New York: 1948], pp. 356–357.
8. *The Memoirs of Cordell Hull*, Vol. II, p. 1018.
9. Ibid., p. 1020.

belief that they could come to a successful agreement.[10] Such a meeting involved great personal risk for Prime Minister Konoye. If it failed, it would mean his political extinction.[11]

Roosevelt told Nomura that he was not averse to the meeting with Konoye and suggested Alaska as the place.[12]

Ambassador Grew's Reports

An entry in Ambassador Grew's diary (a copy of which was sent monthly to Dr. Stanley K. Hornbeck in the State Department) dated August 18, 1941, summarized a long discussion between Ambassador Grew and Foreign Minister Toyoda. As to Konoye's visit, Toyoda commented that:

> ... the Premier's going abroad would have no precedent in Japanese history. Nevertheless, the Prime Minister, Prince Konoye, has firmly resolved to meet the President. . . . This determination of Prince Konoye is nothing but the expression of his strongest desire to save the civilization of the world from ruin as well as to maintain peace in the Pacific by making every effort in his power. . . . [13]

On August 18, Grew telegraphed Washington his recommendation:

> ... The Ambassador urges . . . with all the force at his command, for the sake of avoiding the obviously growing possibility of an utterly futile war between Japan and the United States, that his Japanese proposal not be turned aside without very prayerful consideration. . . . The good which may flow from a meeting between Prince Konoye and President Roosevelt is incalculable. The opportunity is here presented . . . for an act of the highest statesmanship . . .

---

10. Joseph C. Grew, *Turbulent Era*, Vol. II, pp. 1301ff; [Joseph C. Grew,] *Ten Years in Japan*, pp. 416–421.

11. Postwar documents (particularly the memoirs of Konoye and Kido's Diary, which confirm each other) in the Hoover Institution at Stanford University, show clearly that Konoye had commitments from the Emperor and the Navy that they would back him in any terms he might make to get peace, even to defiance of the Army. Konoye, in an Associated Press interview three months previous to his suicide on December 16, 1945, said: "I felt confident that if I had been able to see Mr. Roosevelt I could have established a basis for intervention of the Imperial House in the rising war tide within Japan at that time." *New York Times,* September 14, 1945. Cf. Pearl Harbor Investigation [i.e., *Pearl Harbor Attack*], Part 20, pp. 3999–4000. [*Editor's note:* See Chapter 31, note 16, for the full citation of the latter source.]

12. *Pearl Harbor Attack*, Part 17, p. 2753; Part 20, p. 4001. Nomura's telegrams were intercepted by *Magic* and therefore most probably known to Roosevelt.

13. Joseph C. Grew, *Ten Years in Japan*, p. 420. (Toyoda's remarks are paraphrased by Mr. Grew.)

with the possible overcoming thereby of apparently insurmountable obstacles to peace hereafter in the Pacific.[14]

During this period Grew repudiated the entire thesis that Japan could be
brought to her knees by the economic sanctions. On August 19 Grew apprised
Washington:

> It is possible . . . that the Japanese Government has been forced to take this
> unprecedented step [proposal of Konoye-Roosevelt meeting] by virtue of
> the fact that Japan is economically nearing the end of her strength and is not
> in a position to live through a war with the United States. Conversely, even if
> Japan were faced with an economic catastrophe of the first magnitude, there
> is no reason whatever to doubt that the Government however reluctantly
> would with resolution confront such a catastrophe rather than yield to pres-
> sure from a foreign country.[15]

Grew warned against the illusion in some sectors of the Washington Administration that Japan would not fight. He did so throughout 1941 in messages to the State Department on February 7, May 27, July 17 and July 22. After
the sanctions, he repeated this warning, as in the August 19 communication
quoted above and again in his messages of August 27, September 5 and 29 and
November 3.[16]

A State Department telegram of August 27, replying to a·complaint from
Japan about the hostile tone of the American press, stated that this attitude
was due to Japanese intransigence, and expressed the belief that "*some positive
action on the part of the Japanese Government*" could influence American public
opinion.[17] Eleven years later Grew commented that this telegram revealed
Washington's uncompromising stand. He wrote in his book, *Turbulent Era*:

> The foregoing telegram, in conjunction with the fact that no action was taken
> on the important recommendation presented in my telegram of August 30,
> 6 P.M., rendered it clear that the Administration expected "positive action"
> on the part of the Japanese Government while withholding any helpful step
> by the United States of a nature to assist Prince Konoye in his efforts to create
> a situation where such "positive action" by Japan could eventually be brought

---

14. [U.S. Department of State, *Papers Relating to the*] *Foreign Relations* [*of the United States*],
Japan: 1931–1941 [United States Government Printing Office, Washington: 1943], Vol. II, p. 565.
15. Joseph C. Grew, *Turbulent Era*, Vol. II, p. 1311.
16. Ibid., pp. 1282–1289.
17. Ibid., p. 1339.

about without wrecking his Government. When the Prime Minister offered to come to confer with the President of the United States, while at the same time assuring us that at such a conference Japan would meet the desires of the United States in a way to give full satisfaction, the rebuff implied in the unhelpful attitude of the American Government as revealed in the foregoing telegram and in the virtual stagnation of the Washington conversations, as well as in the failure of our Government to accept Prince Konoye's proposal to come to the United States to meet the President, led logically to the fall of Prince Konoye.[18]

On August 28, Nomura presented a personal letter from Prime Minister Konoye to President Roosevelt, dated August 27. This communication again urged the President to agree to a meeting, saying:

> The present deterioration of the Japanese-American relations is largely due, I feel, to a lack of understanding which has led to mutual suspicious and misapprehensions, and also encouraged the machinations and maneuvers of Third Powers.
>
> ... This is why I wish to meet Your Excellency personally for a frank exchange of views. . . .
>
> I consider it, therefore, of urgent necessity that the two heads of the Governments should meet first to discuss from a broad standpoint all important problems between Japan and America covering the entire Pacific area, and to explore the possibility of saving the situation. Adjustment of minor items may, if necessary, be left to negotiations between competent officials of the two countries, following the meeting.[19]

Hull's attitude is well illustrated by passages in his *Memoirs*, giving his reactions to this message from Konoye:

> It was difficult to believe that the Konoye Government would dare to agree to proposals we could accept. Konoye, Toyoda, and Nomura were insisting that their suggestion for the meeting be kept strictly secret, for the reason that, if premature publicity occurred, the elements in Japan hostile to any such move would defeat it. . . .
>
> We had no real assurance that Konoye himself would desire to carry out an agreement that would turn Japan into the paths of real peace. . . .

---

18. Ibid., p. 1340.

19. *Foreign Relations* [. . .], *Japan: 1931–1941*, Vol. II, pp. 572–573. See also Grew, *Turbulent Era*, Vol. II, p. 1305.

During the next few weeks we received numerous appeals from Tokyo to hasten the Roosevelt-Konoye conference. Ambassador Grew recommended it. But Grew, who had an admirable understanding of the Japanese situation, could not estimate the over-all world situation as we could in Washington.[20]

At this time, an incident involved a serious question as to the conduct of our State Department. As shown above, Prince Konoye had asked that his proposal of a meeting with Mr. Roosevelt be kept secret, so as not to embarrass him in Japan. It was reported in the *New York Herald Tribune* on September 3. The information was probably leaked by American officials, since no one outside these ranks knew of the negotiations. On September 3, a press statement from White House Press Secretary Stephen T. Early denied that Konoye *had proposed a meeting with Roosevelt in the Pacific*. Early's statement read:

1. The President has no invitation.
2. If the Herald Tribune had seen fit to check with the White House . . . I would have told them that.[21]

In a further effort to achieve a meeting with Mr. Roosevelt, Prince Konoye arranged a secret meeting with Ambassador Grew. On September 5, the day preceding this meeting with Konoye, Mr. Grew advised Washington:

> . . . If an adjustment of relations is to be achieved some risk must be run, but the risk [of a Konoye-Roosevelt Conference] . . . would appear to be relatively less serious than the risk of armed conflict entailed in the progressive application of economic sanctions which would result from a refusal to accept these proposals.[22]

After their meeting on September 6, Grew informed the Japanese Prime Minister that his report to the President on this conversation would be the most important cable of his diplomatic career.[23] Grew then sent a memorandum to Washington in which he reported:

> This evening the Prime Minister invited me to dine at a private house of a friend. . . . The conversation lasted for three hours and we presented with entire frankness the fundamental views of our two countries. The Prime Minister requested that his statements be transmitted personally to the President.

20. *The Memoirs of Cordell Hull*, Vol. II, pp. 1024–1025.
21. *New York Times*, September 4, 1941.
22. *Foreign Relations . . . Japan: 1931–1941*, Vol. II, p. 603.
23. *New York Times*, December 28, 1945. See also *Pearl Harbor Attack*, Part 20, p. 4006.

... Prince Konoye, and consequently the Government of Japan, conclusively and wholeheartedly agree with the four principles enunciated by the Secretary of State as a basis for the rehabilitation of relations between the United States and Japan.

Grew further reported to Hull on this conversation with Konoye:

... only he [Konoye] can cause the desired rehabilitation to come about. In the event of a failure on his part no succeeding Prime Minister, at least during his own lifetime, could achieve the results desired. Prince Konoye is therefore determined to spare no effort, despite all elements and factors opposing him, to crown his present endeavors with success. ...

... [The Prime Minister] expressed the earnest hope that in view of the present internal situation in Japan the projected meeting with the President could be arranged with the least possible delay. Prince Konoye feels confident that all problems and questions at issue can be disposed of to our mutual satisfaction during the meeting with the President, and he ended our conversation with the statement that he is determined to bring to a successful conclusion the proposed reconstruction of relations with the United States regardless of cost or personal risk.[24]

In his reply of September 9, Secretary Hull found the "assurances of the Japanese Prime Minister ... very gratifying ... " but maintained that a "solution ... must await some further initiative on the part of the Japanese Government."[25]

On September 22, Grew wrote a personal letter to the President filled with urgent and convincing statements that peace could be had with honor to both sides.[26]

A Prayer to the President

On September 29 a dispatch arrived for President Roosevelt and Secretary Hull from Ambassador Grew. It was supported by one from British Ambassador Craigie in Japan. These messages constituted a sort of prayer for peace from two Ambassadors of lifelong experience in many parts of the world.

---

24. *Foreign Relations ... Japan: 1931–1941*, Vol. II, pp. 604–606. See also Joseph C. Grew, *Ten Years in Japan*, pp. 425–428.

25. [U.S. Department of State,] *Foreign Relations [of the United States, Diplomatic* Papers], 1941, Volume IV, *The Far East* [United States Government Printing Office, Washington: 1956], pp. 432–434.

26. Joseph C. Grew, *Turbulent Era*, Vol. II, pp. 1315f. There is no mention of this letter in Joseph C. Grew, *Ten Years in Japan*, which was published eight years earlier in 1944. The historian is certainly entitled to ask: "Why?"

Grew said:

... I earnestly hope that we shall not allow this favorable period to pass. . . .

... Japan ... is now endeavoring to get out of a very dangerous position in which it has enmeshed itself by pure miscalculation. The impact of foreign developments, as I have pointed out to our Government, inevitably reacts on the foreign policies of Japan and I have indicated that the liberal elements in this country might well be brought to the top through the trend of events abroad. This situation has now come and I believe that there is a favorable chance that *under these new conditions*[27] Japan may be induced to fall into line. . . . the impact upon Japan of developments abroad, has rendered the political soil of this country hospitable to the sowing of new seeds. If these seeds are now carefully planted and fostered, the anticipated regeneration of thought in Japan and a complete readjustment of the relations between our two countries may be brought about.

... There has been advanced from certain quarters ... the belief that an American-Japanese understanding at this particular moment would merely afford Japan a breathing spell and that ... she would use this opportunity to recuperate and strengthen her military forces in order to continue, at the next favorable moment, her program of aggressive expansion. That thought cannot with certainty be gainsaid. This school of thought also maintains that if the United States, Great Britain and the Netherlands now follow a policy of progressively intensifying their economic sanctions against Japan, this country will be obliged to give up her program of expansion owing to the deterioration of her domestic economy and the danger of social, economic and financial disaster. If all this is true, our Government has been faced with the dilemma of choosing between two methods of approach to obtain our desiderata, on the one hand the method of strangling Japan through progressive economic measures and on the other hand the methods of constructive conciliation which is quite different from so-called appeasement. . . . From the point of view of far-sighted statesmanship it would appear that the wisdom of our choice could not be questioned. If either now or subsequently this method of constructive conciliation should fail we would always be in a position to enforce the other method of economic pressure. . . .

Grew then expressed the opinion that even with peace in the Pacific, the United States must remain armed due to dangers elsewhere, and continued:

---

27. Grew's italics.

... Whatever course we may pursue in dealing with Japan must admittedly and inevitably involve certain risks, but I firmly believe ... that if our exploratory conversations can be brought to a head by the proposed meeting between the President and the Prime Minister, substantial hope will be held out ... of preventing the Far Eastern situation from moving from bad to worse. . . . I firmly believe that the opportunity is now presented ... without war or the immediate risk of war, and that we shall be confronted with the greatly augmented risk of war if the present opportunity fails us. . . .

[. . .–ed.] Japanese psychology is basically different from the psychology of any nations in the West; we cannot gauge Japanese actions by any Western measuring rod ... and I feel that it is most important for us to understand that psychology in connection with the present problem. . . .

. . . If we expect and wait for Japan to undertake in the exploratory conversations such clear-cut commitments as would be satisfactory to the United States in point both of principle and concrete detail, there is grave risk that ... the conclusion will be reached ... by those elements which support the Government in aiming at an understanding with the United States that ... we are merely playing for time. . . . such a contingency might and probably would bring about a serious reaction ... discrediting of the Konoye Cabinet. *Such a situation might well bring about irrational acts ... in which it would be very difficult to avoid war. In such a contingency the fall of the present Government and the coming into power of a military dictatorship which would have neither the disposition nor the temperament to avoid a clash with the United States would be the logical result. . . .* [28]

After reciting Japan's various difficulties he said:

... We are informed ... that in the proposed direct negotiations Prince Konoye is in a position to offer to the President far-reaching assurances which could not fail to satisfy us. . . . It therefore seems quite possible that at the proposed meetings with the President Prince Konoye might be in a position to undertake commitments more satisfactory and explicit than those already undertaken in the exploratory conversations.

... Unless we are ready to impose a reasonable degree of confidence in the sincerity of intention and the professed good faith of the Prime Minister and his supporters ... I do not believe that we shall be successful in creating a new turn of thought ... which will justify the hope of ... avoidance of

28. Italics mine.

eventual war in the Pacific. . . . I believe that it is in accordance with the highest traditions of statesmanship and wisdom that we bring our present efforts to a head before the force of their initial impetus shall be lost and before the opposition, which we believe will steadily and inevitably increase in Japan, may intervene and overcome those efforts.[29]

The British Ambassador to Japan, Sir Robert Craigie, added his voice to Grew's as he sent warnings to the British Government.[30]

On September 29–30, 1941, Ambassador Craigie sent a message to Foreign Secretary Eden and Ambassador Halifax pointing out that "The present moment is the best chance of settling [the] Far Eastern question." The Ambassador stated:

> . . . With his [former Foreign Minister Matsuoka's] departure, a very considerable . . . change has occurred in the political situation here, and there exists a more real prospect . . . of setting in motion a steady swing away from the Axis and towards more moderate policies.
>
> . . . The main difficulty appears to be that, while the Japanese want speed and cannot yet afford to go beyond generalizations, the Americans seem to be playing for time and to demand the utmost precision in definition before agreeing to any contract for a step of rapprochement. . . . (?There is) [sic–ed.]reason to believe that the American requirement undoubtedly makes little account of Japanese psychology or of the internal situation here, which brooks of no delay. If persisted in, it bids fair to wreck the best chance of bringing about a just settlement of Far Eastern issues, which has occurred since my arrival in Japan.
>
> . . . My United States colleague and I consider that Prince KONOYE is . . . sincere in his desire to avert the dangers towards which he now sees the Tripartite Pact and the Axis connection (for which he naturally accepts his share of responsibility) are rapidly leading Japan. But the strength of the opposition to his new policy . . . leads the Japanese Government to feel that they can only retain a sufficient body of supporters for this policy and face . . . wrath of their Axis partners, if some overt and striking sign of progress in the discussions can be given at an early date. The Prime Minister has staked his political

---

29. Ambassador Grew later explained to me his term "progressive economic measures" meant *continuing* the sanctions as they were already complete. The complete paraphrase of Ambassador Grew's dispatch of September 29 can be found in *Turbulent Era*, Vol. II, pp. 1316–1323. See also the substance of this telegram in *Foreign Relations* [. . .] *Japan: 1931–1941*, Vol. II, pp. 645–650.

30. Sir Robert Craigie, *Behind the Japanese Mask* (Hutchinson & Co., Ltd., London: 1945), p. 133.

future on this move. . . . Despite the Emperor's strong backing, I doubt if he and his Government . . . survive if the discussions prove abortive or drag on unduly.

. . . my United States colleague and I are firmly of the opinion that on balance this is a chance which it would be . . . folly to let slip. Caution must be exercised, but an excessive cynicism brings stagnation.

. . . it goes without saying that we should maintain the full vigour of our economic reprisal until such time as concrete evidence of a change of Japanese policy is forthcoming. . . . [31]

On September 30, Grew reported:

. . . Prince Konoye's warship is ready waiting to take him to Honolulu or Alaska or any other place designated by the President, and his staff of the highest military, naval, and civil officers is chosen and rarin' to go.[32]

Reduced to the bare bones, what these two statesmen of world-wide experience in settlement of world conflicts were saying was: (a) you cannot force surrender of Japan by the economic sanctions or threats; (b) they will commit hara-kiri before they submit to such humiliation; (c) they are prepared, and Konoye is authorized, to concede any reasonable terms at conference in the Pacific staged as a meeting of equals; and (d) this is the last chance.

On October 2, a memorandum[33] constituting a lecture on international morals was made by Hull and handed to Ambassador Nomura.

This memorandum created confusion in Tokyo.

On October 7, Eugene Dooman, the American Embassy's Counselor in Tokyo, was informed by Konoye's private secretary, Tomohiko Ushiba, that:

. . . Prince Konoye was at a loss to know what further he could do, the opposition had now something concrete to use in their attacks on the Cabinet, and the future looked dark. . . .

---

31. Craigie to Anthony Eden, *International Military Tribunal for the Far East*, Record, 25848–25852. The Japanese Government, cognizant of Craigie's message through "unimpeachable sources," cabled the "gist of Craigie's opinions" to Admiral Nomura in Washington on October 3, 1941. Our Naval Intelligence intercepted, decoded, translated and made these Japanese communications available to the Washington officials concerned by October 4, 1941. See *Pearl Harbor Attack*, Part 12, pp. 50–51.

32. Joseph C. Grew, *Ten Years in Japan*, pp. 444–445.

33. *Foreign Relations* [. . .] *Japan: 1931–1941*, Vol. II, pp. 656–661.

... [It looks as if] the United States never had any intention of coming to any agreement with Japan. ... [34]

Ushiba was right.

Stimson's handwritten notation on his copy of a War Department memorandum was indicative of his opinion:

> ... while I approve of stringing out negotiations ... they should not be allowed to ripen into personal conference between the President and P.M. [Prime Minister]. I greatly fear that such a conference if actually held would produce concessions which would be highly dangerous to our vitally important relations with China.[35]

On October 10, the Japanese Minister of Foreign Affairs told Grew he could not get the point of the memorandum of October 2. Toyoda also said that on October 3 he had instructed Nomura to ask Hull:

> ... whether the United States Government would set forth in precise terms the obligations which the United States Government wished the Japanese Government to undertake. ... [36]

The Minister further informed Grew that on October 6, when no word from Nomura had been received, Toyoda again instructed the Japanese Ambassador to place this inquiry before Hull.

Toyoda also advised Grew that on October 9 Nomura notified Tokyo that he could not secure any statement as to further American views on the Japanese proposals. Toyoda now asked Grew to intercede and gave Grew the following statement:

> ... Will the American Government now set forth to the Japanese Government for its consideration the undertakings to be assumed by the Japanese Government which would be satisfactory to the American Government?[37]

Hull, in his *Memoirs,* gives only a meager account of these extensive communications and dismisses the entire negotiation with the following:

> The conversations of the previous six months, and the limited commitments that Konoye and his Government were willing to make, showed clearly that

---

34. Ibid., p. 662.
35. *Pearl Harbor Attack,* Part 5, p. 2092. See also *Pearl Harbor Attack,* Part 14, p. 1388.
36. *Foreign Relations [...] Japan: 1931–1941,* pp. 677–678.
37. Ibid., Vol. II, p. 678.

Japan was not prepared to make a general renunciation of aggression. She was adamant in refusing to withdraw her troops from northern China and Inner Mongolia, because the presence of her armed forces in those territories gave her control over them. And she was equally adamant in refusing to state that she would not declare war on us if we became engaged in war with Germany as a result of our measures of self-defense. She was also insistent on qualifications and interpretations that would continue to give her a preferred economic position in the Far East.[38]

This statement was scarcely the truth in the face of the record of Konoye's proposals, Grew's and Craigie's dispatches, and the world situation. In any event no harm could come to the United States by exploring their proposals.

The Fall of Konoye

As Grew had warned, Konoye was risking his whole public position, as failure to make peace with the "Anglo-Saxons" would result in his downfall. On October 16, Grew wrote:

> The Konoye cabinet fell . . . this afternoon. . . . I knew that the failure of progress in the American-Japanese conversations would almost certainly bring about Konoye's fall. . . . I had not looked for it so soon.[39]

The fall of Konoye marked one of the tragedies of the twentieth century. His eulogy should record that he had continually striven to hold the Japanese militarists in check; that he was a man dedicated to peace, at any personal sacrifice.[40]

Grew's Conclusions on the Konoye Negotiations

On October 19, three days after the fall of Konoye, Grew's diary has this entry:

---

38. *The Memoirs of Cordell Hull*, Vol. II, p. 1035.
39. Joseph C. Grew, *Ten Years in Japan*, p. 456.
40. Konoye's subsequent life was a confirmation of this. He refused to take part in the war but did agree to undertake a special mission to Moscow in an effort to seek peace. The mission (scheduled for July, 1945) never left Japan due to Russia's reaction to the proposal. After the war Konoye offered his services in the problems of reconstruction. But he was accused of being part of the war conspiracy. He committed suicide rather than bear the humiliation of a trial as a war criminal.

Why on earth should we rush headlong into war? When Hitler is defeated, as he eventually will be, the Japanese problem will solve itself.[41]

Churchill's Attitude

Churchill, in his history of this period, ignores these dispatches. It cannot be believed that the British Foreign Office, having received Craigie's message indicating that the way was open to peace in the Pacific, could have failed to call Churchill's attention to this. It is, therefore, desirable to review Churchill's attitude toward Roosevelt's Japanese policies during this period.

At the Atlantic Charter meeting in August, 1941, Churchill had expressed his anxieties about the Japanese situation when he impressed upon Sumner Welles, his belief that:

> . . . some declaration of the kind he had drafted with respect to Japan was in his opinion in the highest degree important, and that he did not think that there was much hope left unless the United States made such a clear-cut declaration of preventing Japan from expanding further to the south, in which event the prevention of war between Great Britain and Japan appeared to be hopeless. He said in the most emphatic manner that if war did break out between Great Britain and Japan, Japan immediately would be in a position through the use of her large number of cruisers to seize or destroy all of the British merchant shipping in the Indian Ocean and in the Pacific, and to cut the lifelines between the British Dominions and the British Isles unless the United States herself entered the war. He pled with me [Welles] that a declaration of this character participated in by the United States, Great Britain, the Dominions, the Netherlands and possibly the Soviet Union would definitely restrain Japan. If this were not done, the blow to the British Government might be almost decisive.[42]

However, Churchill did not believe that the Japanese would fight. He says:

> . . . The State Department at Washington believed, as I did, that Japan would probably recoil before the ultimately overwhelming might of the United States.

But if they did fight, even that would be satisfactory to him:

---

41. Joseph C. Grew, *Turbulent Era,* Vol. II, p. 1286.
42. *Pearl Harbor Attack,* Part 4, p. 1785. The Atlantic Charter meeting with Churchill was no secret to the Japanese. Nomura reported it to Tokyo on August 7 (*Pearl Harbor Attack,* Part 12, p. 14).

... I confess that in my mind the whole Japanese menace lay in a sinister twilight, compared with our other needs. My feeling was that if Japan attacked us the United States would come in. If the United States did not come in, we had no means of defending the Dutch East Indies, or indeed our own Empire in the East. *If, on the other hand, Japanese aggression drew in America I would be content to have it....* [43]

Churchill had joined fully in the complete economic sanctions of July 26, 1941. But after that act, he appears at times to have become concerned over what he had done, for he says:

As time passed and I realised the formidable effect of the embargoes which President Roosevelt had declared on July 26, and in which we and the Dutch had joined, I became increasingly anxious to confront Japan with the greatest possible display of British and American naval forces in the Pacific and Indian Oceans.... [44]

On August 29, Mr. Churchill sent a note to the First Sea Lord:

... I must add that I cannot feel that Japan will face the combination now forming against her of the United States, Great Britain, and Russia, while already preoccupied in China. It is very likely she will negotiate with the United States for at least three months without making any further aggressive move or joining the Axis actively.... [45]

Grew's Subsequent Summations on this Period

In 1952 Ambassador Grew reviewed the situation which existed in late summer 1941. These subsequent reflections are worthy of note:

During this critical period the Embassy ... made clear in repeated telegrams to Washington the following considerations: the political soil in Japan was for the first time in ten years ripe for the sowing of new seeds which should be planted with constructive wisdom; we believed that Prince Konoye was in a position to carry the country with him in a program of peace.... [46]

---

43. Churchill, *The Grand Alliance*, p. 587. Italics mine.
44. Ibid., p. 588. Mr. Churchill was referring to a proposal to re-enforce Singapore with American warships.
45. Ibid., p. 859.
46. Joseph C. Grew, *Turbulent Era*, Vol. II, pp. 1263–1264.

However, Mr. Grew recalled:

> ... Our telegrams ... seldom brought response; they were rarely even re-
> ferred to, and reporting to our Government was like throwing pebbles into a
> lake at night; we were not permitted to see even the ripples. For all we knew,
> our telegrams had not in any degree carried conviction. Obviously I could
> only assume that our recommendations were not welcome, yet we continued
> to express our carefully considered judgment on the developing situation.[47]

Grew frequently expressed his complete frustration at the actions of Roo-
sevelt and Hull.[48] He states that after the memorandum on October 2, 1941,
Hull did not answer any of his or the Japanese inquiries or proposals until
November 26—long after the fall of the Konoye Cabinet.[49]

Again in a review of these negotiations, Grew states:

> ... Yet when successive Japanese Governments pleaded for the assistance
> of the United States in the creation of conditions which would supply the
> necessary incentive to a complete reorientation of policy and an undoing of
> her international misdeeds ... such assistance was coldly withheld. Thus two
> of Japan's foremost statesmen, Baron Hiranuma in 1939 and Prince Konoye in
> 1941, were tacitly rebuffed in their far-sighted efforts to turn their country into
> new channels in which good relations with the United States and the other
> democracies could, for them, become practicable. .... was this ... attitude of
> the United States one of far-seeing and constructive statesmanship?[50]

No word of all these negotiations or cables from Grew or Craigie was revealed to the Congress or the American people—until years later.

---

47. Ibid., p. 1273. See also Herbert Feis, *The Road to Pearl Harbor*, p. 298ff.
48. Joseph C. Grew, *Turbulent Era*, Vol. II, pp. 1272, 1273, 1333, 1334, 1342, 1343, 1347.
49. Ibid., p. 1338.
50. Ibid., pp. 1348–1349.

CHAPTER 39

Via Japan—yet Again Comes
a Chance for Peace in the Pacific

WITH THE FALL OF KONOYE, there came into power on October 18, 1941, a ministry with General Hideki Tojo as Prime Minister. It was composed, with one exception, of militarists. The exception was Foreign Minister Shigenori Togo (not to be confused with Prime Minister Tojo). Foreign Minister Togo belonged to the group which opposed war with "the Anglo Saxons."

On October 25, Grew reported to the State Department that he had been informed that the Emperor had again intervened and in

> ... a conference of the leading members of the Privy Council and of the Japanese armed forces ... the Emperor ... inquired if they were prepared to pursue a policy which would guarantee that there would be no war with the United States. The representatives of the Army and Navy who attended this conference did not reply to the Emperor's questions, whereupon the latter, with a reference to the ... policy pursued by the Emperor Meiji, his grandfather, in an unprecedented action ordered the armed forces to obey his wishes. . . . [1]

At this time (the end of October, 1941), the Japanese were confronted with a new difficulty because of the failure of their ally, Hitler, to realize his expectations of a quick conquest of the key objectives—Leningrad and Moscow. The Japanese were no doubt fully informed by their Ambassador and their military attaché in Moscow.

The Russians, in battling with Hitler, had followed the traditional "defense in depth" strategy which defeated Napoleon. The strategy had worked again

---

1. Joseph C. Grew, *Ten Years in Japan* [Simon and Schuster, New York: 1944], p. 462. All of which was confirmed by the Japanese records seized after the war and the fact that Foreign Minister Togo was supported by Navy Minister Shimada and the "Elder Statesmen."

as it brought the new Napoleon to at least a temporary stop. The Germans were making contact with Generals Red Army, Space, Rain, Winter, Scorched Earth, and Destroyed Roads and Railways.[2] In north Russia, they reached as far as the outskirts of Leningrad on September 24. In mid-Russia, by October 16, they were only a few miles from Moscow. In south Russia, they reached as far as Odessa on October 16 and Kharkov on October 24.

However, the director of the Soviet Information Bureau on October 5 announced in the press that German losses were 3,000,000 men killed, wounded and prisoners, 11,000 tanks, 13,000 cannon, and 9,000 airplanes destroyed or captured. Their statement required considerable discount as it amounted to the destruction of almost half of the German army. Certainly it justified Soviet confidence in Hitler's failure.[3]

By the end of October, the actual German advance was stopped by the weather. Although the Germans made some sporadic attacks late in November, they were obliged to dig in for the winter. Hitler had possibly learned more about Napoleon's disastrous Russian campaign. Certainly Hitler's Russian stalemate was not good news for Japan, Hitler's Axis partner.

British Anxieties Again

Churchill was again becoming worried. The United States had not come into the war. On November 5, in a message to Roosevelt, he said:

> ... The Japanese have as yet taken no final decision, and the Emperor appears to be exercising restraint. When we talked about this at Placentia [Atlantic Charter meeting], you spoke of gaining time, and this policy has been brilliantly successful so far. But our joint embargo is steadily forcing the Japanese to decisions for peace or war.[4]

A week later (November 12), the British were continuing to worry. Ambassador to Washington Lord Halifax visited Welles and presented a report of a conversation between their Ambassador to Japan, Sir Robert Craigie, and Foreign Minister Togo, in which Togo had explained his difficulties and ex-

---

2. J. F. C. Fuller, *The Second World War* (Duell, Sloan and Pearce, New York: 1949), pp. 122ff.; W[ladyslaw] Anders, *Hitler's Defeat in Russia* (Henry Regnery Company, Chicago: 1953), p. 59; Vice Admiral Kurt Assmann, "The Battle for Moscow, Turning Point of the War," *Foreign Affairs* (January, 1950), pp. 320–323.

3. *New York Times,* October 6, 1941.

4. *Pearl Harbor Attack,* Part 19, p. 3467. [*Editor's note:* See chapter 31, note 16, for the full citation of this source.]

pressed his surprise that the British did not take part in matters so vital to them. The memorandum reported:

> ... The Minister [Togo] said he had a strong impression that, for reasons best known to themselves, the United States Government were deliberately dragging out the negotiations. If this were so it would of course be impossible for the Japanese Government to continue them.[5]

Churchill did not agree with Hull's insistence on a specific disavowal by the Japanese of their alliance with Hitler and Mussolini. In a letter to his Foreign Secretary on November 23, 1941, he said:

> ... The formal denunciation of the Axis Pact by Japan is not, in my opinion, necessary. Their ... [stepping] out of the war is in itself a great disappointment and injury to the Germans. . . . [6]

Churchill's mind was at this time no doubt centered upon his struggle with Hitler as his voluminous history of this period,[7] written years afterwards, is very scanty in regard to Japan. His historical work of several hundred thousand words, is a mass of minute detail and documents on other phases of the war, but only about 5,000 words are devoted to Japanese matters, and these mostly on side issues. The dangerous consequences of the total economic sanctions are referred to but little. The Konoye peace proposals get only a bare mention.

The Japanese Propose a Truce

Foreign Minister Togo, in accord with the Emperor's directive, had undertaken renewed negotiations with the United States.

On November 3, Ambassador Grew, being aware that a proposal was coming from the Japanese, cabled Washington, repeating his previous warnings that the Japanese would not collapse from the sanctions. The substance of this message was:

> ... The Embassy in Japan has never been convinced by the theory that Japan's collapse as a militaristic power would shortly result from the depletion and

---

5. *Ibid.*, p. 3479.
6. [Winston S.] Churchill, *The Grand Alliance* [Houghton Mifflin Company, Boston: 1950], p. 595.
7. [Winston S.] Churchill, *The Second World War*, 6 v[olumes].

the eventual exhaustion of Japan's financial and economic resources, as propounded by many leading American economists. . . .

[. . .–*ed.*] If the fiber and temper of the Japanese people are kept in mind, the view that war probably would be averted . . . by . . . imposing drastic economic measures is an uncertain and dangerous hypothesis. . . . War would not be averted by such a course. . . .

. . . The Ambassador's purpose is only to ensure against the United States becoming involved in war with Japan because of any possible misconception of Japan's capacity to rush headlong into a suicidal struggle with the United States. While national sanity dictates against such action, Japanese sanity cannot be measured by American standards of logic. . . . [8]

On November 4, Mr. Grew recorded in his diary:

. . . If war should occur, I hope that history will not overlook that telegram . . . the statement that if our peace efforts should fail, Japan may go all-out in a do-or-die effort to render herself invulnerable to foreign economic pressure, even to the extent of committing national hara-kiri, and that those of us who are in direct touch with the atmosphere from day to day realize that this is not only possible *but probable* . . . [9]

Mr. Grew stated on the same day that:

Kase came at 12:10 with a message from the Foreign Minister that he wanted to send Kurusu to Washington to help Admiral Nomura with the conversations. . . . [10]

Ambassador Saburo Kurusu, former Japanese Ambassador to Germany, arrived in Washington on November 15.

Secretary of State Hull requested advice on the American position on a possible Japanese offensive against Kunming and the Burma Road. As a result, on November 5, Chief of Staff General Marshall and Chief of Naval Operations Admiral Stark, apparently worried over the Japanese situation, sent a memorandum to President Roosevelt, endeavoring to exert a restraining hand. The pertinent paragraphs are:

---

8. [U.S. Department of State, *Papers Relating to the*] *Foreign Relations* [*of the United* States], *Japan: 1931–1941* [United States Government Printing Office, Washington: 1943], Vol. II, pp. 702–704. See also Grew, *Ten Years in Japan*, pp. 468–469.

9. Grew, *Ten Years in Japan*, p. 470.

10. Ibid.

The question . . . is whether or not the United States is justified in undertaking offensive military operations with U.S. forces against Japan. . . . They [Marshall and Stark] consider that such operations, however well-disguised, would lead to war. . . .

. . . War between the United States and Japan should be avoided while building up defensive forces in the Far East. . . . Military action against Japan should be undertaken only in one or more of the following contingencies:

(1) A direct act of war by Japanese armed forces against . . . the United States, the British Commonwealth, or the Netherlands East Indies;

(2) The movement of Japanese forces into Thailand to the west of 100° East or South of 10° North; or into Portuguese Timor, New Caledonia, or the Loyalty Islands. . . .

It is of historic significance that our military leaders ended this memorandum to the Administration with the specific recommendation:

That no ultimatum be delivered to Japan.[11]

On November 4 and 5, Washington intercepted secret dispatches from Tokyo to Ambassador Nomura proposing new terms to avoid war. These intercepted proposals were in two parts. In case Proposal "A" was not accepted, Proposal "B" was to be presented.[12]

The Congress and the American people were not allowed for several years to know one word of these proposals.

The substance of Proposal "A" was:

1. Japan recognized the principle of non-discrimination in trade to be applied to all Asia if it were also applied to the rest of the world.
2. The Japanese agreed to act toward their partners in the Axis alliance in accordance with Japan's own interpretation of the meaning of the pact—not that of Germany or Italy.
3. Upon peace with China, all Japanese troops in China were to be withdrawn within two years except for garrisons in North China, on the Mongolian border regions, and on the Island of Hainan. Japanese troops were to be withdrawn from Indo-China when peace with China was established.

---

11. *Pearl Harbor Attack,* Part 14, pp. 1061–1062. Italics mine.
12. Ibid., Part 12, pp. 94ff.

On November 7, according to the following memorandum made by Secretary Stimson, the President canvassed his Cabinet's opinions about the situation:

> ... he [Roosevelt] started to have what he said was the first general poll of his Cabinet and it was on the question of the Far East—whether the people would back us up in case we struck at Japan down there [England in Malaya or the Dutch in the East Indies] and what the tactics should be. ... He went around the table ... and it was unanimous in feeling the country would support us. ... [13]

On the evening of November 7, Ambassador Nomura expounded the scope of Proposal "A" to Secretary Hull, and expressed his "desire to meet with the President at the earliest possible moment."[14]

On November 10, an intercepted message showed that Nomura reported to Tokyo that the President said to him:

> ... we will endeavor immediately to continue the parleys. ... What the United States most desires is (1) to prevent the expansion of the war, and (2) to bring about a lasting peace.[15]

Ambassador Nomura stated to his Government that the President agreed to study the proposal. However, Hull, as indicated in his *Memoirs*, regarded Proposal "A" to be unsatisfactory.

On November 15, in reply to Nomura, Hull criticized the "A" proposals. However, he suggested that the proposals as to trade be broadened to include reciprocal tariffs and the lowering of trade barriers, and to exclude monopolistic rights of trade in China.

Colonel O'Laughlin had informed me of the truce terms proposed by the Japanese which had been given to him by Ambassador Nomura. I wrote O'Laughlin on November 16, saying:

> ... There is no sense in having a war with Japan. ... [The Administration is] so anxious to get into the war somewhere that they will project it. They know there will be less public resistance to this than to expeditionary forces to Europe.

---

13. An entry in Secretary Stimson's diary, which was published in *Pearl Harbor Attack*, Part 11, p. 5432.
14. *Pearl Harbor Attack*, Part 12, p. 104.
15. Ibid., p. 112.

According to Hull's *Memoirs,* on November 18, he gave Nomura and Kurusu a lecture on the unrighteousness of the Japanese tripartite alliance with
Germany and Italy.[16]

On November 20, upon instructions from Tokyo, Ambassador Nomura
formally presented Proposal "B" to Secretary Hull.[17] In diplomatic terms it
was a proposal of a temporary *modus vivendi*—in popular words—a "truce."
It was of course already known to the State Department through interception
and deciphering of the Japanese coded messages.

The Proposal "B"—the truce—covered the following points:

1. Both the Governments of Japan and the United States undertake not
   to make any armed advancement into any of the regions in the South-
   eastern Asia and the Southern Pacific area excepting the part of French
   Indo-China where the Japanese troops are stationed at present.

2. The Japanese Government undertakes to withdraw its troops now
   stationed in French Indo-China upon either the restoration of peace
   between Japan and China or the establishment of an equitable peace in
   the Pacific area.

   In the meantime the Government of Japan declares that it is prepared
   to remove its troops now stationed in the southern part of French Indo-
   China to the northern part of the said territory upon the conclusion
   of the present arrangement which shall later be embodied in the final
   agreement.

3. The Government of Japan and the United States shall cooperate with a
   view to securing the acquisition of those goods and commodities which
   the two countries need in Netherlands East Indies.

4. The Government of Japan and the United States mutually undertake
   to restore their commercial relations to those prevailing prior to the
   freezing of the assets.

   The Government of the United States shall supply Japan a required
   quantity of oil.

5. The Government of the United States [during the truce] undertakes
   to refrain from such measures and actions as will be prejudicial to the
   endeavors for the restoration of general peace between Japan and China.[18]

---

16. *The Memoirs of Cordell Hull,* Vol. II, pp. 1064ff.

17. *Pearl Harbor Attack,* Part 12, p. 161.

18. *Foreign Relations ... Japan, 1931–1941,* Vol. II, pp. 755–756; Herbert Feis, *The Road to Pearl
Harbor* (Princeton University Press, Princeton, New Jersey: 1950), p. 309.

Hull states in his *Memoirs* that the truce proposals were wholly un-acceptable.[19]

On November 22, Secretary Hull called a meeting of the British and Chinese Ambassadors and the Netherlands and Australian Ministers to discuss the Japanese proposals of November 20 and a substitute *modus vivendi* (truce proposal) prepared by our State Department. An "outline of a ten-point peace settlement to accompany this *modus vivendi*" had also been drafted by the State Department. The Chinese Ambassador, Dr. Hu Shih, was the only representative to express any dissatisfaction.

Hull states:

> I made it clear that there was probably not one chance in three that Japanese would accept our modus vivendi. . . .[20]

On November 24 Hull held another meeting of the Allied representatives in Washington to discuss the latest draft of our truce proposal. Only the Netherlands Minister had instructions from his government relative to the truce proposal. The Secretary expressed his strong disappointment in the "lack of interest and lack of disposition to cooperate" shown by the British, Chinese and Australian representatives and their governments.[21]

On November 25, China again registered its opposition to the truce proposal. That same day the President held a meeting of the War Council. Secretary Hull, Secretary Stimson, Secretary Knox, the Army Chief of Staff General Marshall, and the Chief of Naval Operations Admiral Stark were present. Secretary Stimson's notes of the meeting submitted to the Pearl Harbor inquiry state:

> . . . The question was *how we should maneuver them into the position of firing the first shot without allowing too much danger to ourselves.* . . .[22]

It is indeed difficult to interpret any such attitude of the United States toward any nation.[23]

---

19. *The Memoirs of Cordell Hull,* Vol. II, p. 1069.
20. Ibid., p. 1074.
21. *Pearl Harbor* [*Attack*–ed.], Part 14, pp. 1143–1146.
22. Ibid., Part 11, p. 5433. Italics mine.
23. At the *Pearl Harbor Attack* Hearings, Admiral J. O. Richardson, who was commander in chief of United States Fleet from 1940 to 1941, testified that on October 8, 1940 ". . . I asked the President if we were going to enter the war. He replied that . . . they [the Japanese] could not always avoid making mistakes and that as the war continued and the area of operations expanded sooner or later they would make a mistake and we would enter the war." (*Pearl Harbor Attack,* Part 1, p. 266.)

That night Prime Minister Churchill cabled Washington his sympathy for the Chinese position.

Hull records:

> After talking this [the Chinese protest and Churchill's cable] over again with the Far Eastern experts of the State Department, I came to the conclusion that we should cancel out the modus vivendi. Instead, we should present to the Japanese solely the ten-point proposal for a general settlement to which originally the modus vivendi would have been in the nature of an introduction.[24]

The Communists Enter the Scene

At this point I inject an incident which I doubt had important influence on the forces in motion but which indicated the activities of the American Communists in our government. The Moscow line was naturally opposed to American peace with Japan. Such a peace would free Chiang Kai-shek to extinguish the Mao Tse-tung Communist government in North China. Owen Lattimore was at this time in Chungking as the President's personal representative. Lattimore sent the following cable to Lauchlin Currie,[25] an administrative assistant to President Roosevelt in the White House:

> . . . I feel you should urgently advise the President of the Generalissimo's very strong reaction. . . . Any "Modus Vivendi" now arrived at with China [Japan?] would be disastrous to Chinese belief in America. . . . It is doubtful whether either past assistance or increasing aid could compensate for the feeling of being deserted. . . . I must warn you that even the Generalissimo questions his ability to hold the situation together if the Chinese national

---

24. *The Memoirs of Cordell Hull,* Vol. II, p. 1081.

25. See Chapter 4. Currie was proven to be very close to the Communist Party, and migrated to Bolivia. [*Editor's note:* It was Colombia. Between 1939 and 1945 Currie was a senior administrative assistant to President Franklin Roosevelt, who twice sent him on special missions to China as Roosevelt's personal representative. After the Second World War, Currie was accused of having secretly worked for Soviet intelligence during the war. Despite his repeated denials, it has now been established that he did indeed pass secret U.S. government information to the Soviet intelligence agency through its spy network in Washington, D.C., and was formally recruited by this same agency in 1945. Never prosecuted, he emigrated to Colombia a few years after the war. See John Earl Haynes, Harvey Klehr, and Alexander Vassiliev, *Spies: The Rise and Fall of the KGB in America* (Yale University Press, New York and London: 2009), pp. 262–267.]

trust in America is undermined by reports of Japan's escaping military defeat by diplomatic victory.[26]

Secretary Hull records the receipt of a protesting note from the Chinese Foreign Minister on November 25, accusing the United States of wishing "to appease Japan at the expense of China."[27] Stimson and Knox also received the Lattimore-inspired messages of protest of November 25 from Chiang.[28]

---

26. *Pearl Harbor Attack,* Part 20, p. 4473.
27. *The Memoirs of Cordell Hull,* Vol. II, p. 1077. For telegram's text, see *Pearl Harbor Attack,* Part 14, p. 1170.
28. *Pearl Harbor Attack,* Part 14, p. 1161.

CHAPTER 40

Via Japan—the Ultimatum

On November 26, Secretary Hull delivered his ten-point proposal[1] to the Japanese Ambassador in Washington. The text was not released to the American public at that time.

The text was in two sections. Section I was an offer of a mutual declaration of policy to include prohibitions against territorial or aggressive designs and interference in internal affairs of other nations. It proposed to guarantee inviolability of territorial integrity, independent sovereignty to all nations, equality of commercial opportunity, reliance upon international cooperation and conciliation of differences, abolition of excessive trade restrictions, non-discriminatory access to raw materials, and the establishment of international finance to aid essential enterprise and development.

Section II was:

Steps to be taken by the government of the United States and by the government of Japan.

The government of the United States and the government of Japan propose to take steps as follows:

1. The government of the United States and the government of Japan will endeavor to conclude a multilateral non-aggression pact among the British Empire, China, Japan, the Netherlands, the Soviet Union, Thailand and the United States.
2. Both governments will endeavor to conclude among the American, British, Chinese, Japanese, the Netherland and Thai governments an agreement where-under each of the governments would pledge itself

---

1. See p. [288–*ed.*], Chapter 39.

to respect the territorial integrity of Indo-China and, in the event that there should develop a threat to the territorial integrity of Indo-China, to enter into immediate consultation with a view to taking such measures as may be deemed necessary and advisable to meet the threat in question. Such agreement would provide also that each of the governments party to the agreement would not seek or accept preferential treatment in its trade or economic relations with Indo-China and would use its influence to obtain for each of the signatories equality of treatment in trade and commerce with French Indo-China.

3. The government of Japan will withdraw all military, naval, air and police forces from China and from Indo-China.

4. The government of the United States and the government of Japan will not support—militarily, politically, economically—any government or regime in China other than the national government of the Republic of China with capital temporarily at Chungking.

5. Both governments will give up all extra-territorial rights in China, including rights and interests in and with regard to international settlements and concessions, and rights under the Boxer protocol of 1901.

    Both governments will endeavor to obtain the agreement of the British and other governments to give up extraterritorial rights in China, including rights in international settlements and in concessions and under the Boxer Protocol of 1901.

6. The government of the United States and the government of Japan will enter into negotiations for the conclusion between the United States and Japan of a trade agreement, based upon reciprocal most-favored-nation treatment and a reduction of trade barriers by both countries, including an undertaking by the United States to bind raw silk on the free list.

7. The government of the United States and the government of Japan will, respectively, remove the freezing restrictions on Japanese funds in the United States and on American funds in Japan.

8. Both governments will agree upon a plan for the stabilization of the dollar-yen rate, with the allocation of funds adequate for this purpose, half to be supplied by Japan and half by the United States.

9. Both governments will agree that no agreement which either has concluded with any third power or powers shall be interpreted by it in such a way as to conflict with the fundamental purpose of this

agreement, the establishment and preservation of peace throughout the Pacific area.

10. Both governments will use their influence to cause other governments to adhere to and to give practical application to the basic political and economic principles set forth in this agreement.[2]

On November 27, our military leaders again voiced their views and warned that "If the current negotiations end without agreement, Japan may attack. . . ." Secretary Hull states in his *Memoirs:*

General Marshall and Admiral Stark sent a memorandum to the President . . . with a copy to me, in which they pleaded for more time, particularly because of the reenforcements en route or destined for the Philippines. They recommended meantime that military counter-action be considered only if Japan attacked or directly threatened United States, British, or Dutch territory. . . .[3]

Hull recalls the November 28 meeting of the War Council where he reviewed the ten-point proposal which he had presented to the Japanese on November 26:

"There is practically no possibility of an agreement being achieved with Japan," I said.[4]

On December 7, 1945, during the Pearl Harbor Investigation, General Marshall was asked:

. . . Were you kept fully advised as to diplomatic developments all through the latter part of November and on up to the first part of December?

General MARSHALL. I, of course, did not know all of the matters, but I would say that I was kept very fully advised; and so far as Mr. Hull personally is concerned, I remember hearing him say with considerable emphasis

---

2. *New York Times,* December 8, 1941. See also U.S. *Department of State Bulletin* [Vol. V,] December 13, 1941, pp. 462–464. Also [U.S. Department of State, *Papers Relating to the*] *Foreign Relations* [*of the United States*], *Japan, 1931–1941* [United States Government Printing Office, Washington: 1943], [Vol. II], pp. 768–770.

3. *The Memoirs of Cordell Hull* [The Macmillan Company, New York: 1948], Vol. II, p. 1087. See also *Pearl Harbor* [*Attack*], Part 14, p. 1083. [*Editor's note:* See Chapter 31, note 16, for the full citation of this source.]

4. *The Memoirs of Cordell Hull,* p. 1087.

in those last days apropos of his discussions with the Japanese envoys, "These fellows mean to fight and you will have to watch out."[5]

Also at the Pearl Harbor investigation, General Marshall testified to the possibility that if the war could have been delayed for even a month, the Japanese, in face of the defeats of Hitler in Russia, might never have attacked the United States.[6]

In his examination before the Pearl Harbor Investigation in 1946, General George C. Marshall gave this testimony:

> **Senator BREWSTER.** . . . You and Admiral Stark had both concurred in hoping that decision [of the Japanese to attack] might be deferred for at least 2 or 3 months.
>
> **General MARSHALL.** That was our great desire.
>
> **Senator BREWSTER.** Yes. That was the occasion of the discussion of the modus vivendi?
>
> **General MARSHALL.** That is correct.[7]

On November 28, in a press conference, the President, for the first time since the announcement of the sanctions four months before, on July 25, 1941, publicly discussed the negotiations with Japan. He did not mention the peace offers of Konoye, or of Togo, or Mr. Hull's ten points given Japan two days before. The press obviously had some information about the Togo truce proposals, as they asked:

> **Q.** Mr. President, would this mean that we are working for the status quo? . . .
>
> **THE PRESIDENT:** (*interposing*) Wait a minute. I wouldn't say working for the status quo, because we—
>
> **Q.** (*interposing*) Temporary status quo?
>
> **THE PRESIDENT:** You have got to leave China out of the status quo. We are certainly not working for the status quo in China.
>
> **Q.** (*interjecting*) That's right.
>
> **THE PRESIDENT:** (*continuing*) Or Indo-China, for that matter.
>
> **Q.** Against further aggression?

---

5. *Pearl Harbor Attack*, Part 3, p. 1148.
6. Ibid., p. 1149.
7. Ibid., Part 11, p. 5177.

THE PRESIDENT: Against further aggression. We are working to remove the present aggression. . . .

Q. That Chinese situation is absolutely solid and set, is it not?

THE PRESIDENT: Absolutely.

Q. No chance of compromise?

THE PRESIDENT: No. . . .[8]

On November 29, it was reported from Tokyo that the Japanese press denounced Hull's proposal as an ultimatum. Obviously, our American military leaders considered it an ultimatum or they would not have protested its issuance, or General Marshall would not have notified his area commanders on November 27 that the Japanese negotiations "appear to be terminated."[9] Secretary Hull recalls:

Australian Minister Casey also came to me on November 29 and suggested that Australia would be glad to act as mediator between the United States and Japan. *I answered that the diplomatic stage was over, and that nothing would come of a move of that kind.*[10]

Some of our Washington officials believed the Japanese would not fight or that war with them could last but a few months. I have seen a personal letter from Navy Secretary Knox written at this time which said:

We can wipe the Japanese off the map in three months.

Former Governor Huntley N. Spaulding of New Hampshire, an intimate friend of Secretary Knox, informed me that Secretary Knox had stated to him that "the Japanese cannot fight longer than two months."

Stanley K. Hornbeck, one of Hull's leading advisers, was among those who did not believe the Japanese would fight.[11]

---

8. [Samuel I. Rosenman, comp.,] *The Public Papers and Addresses of Franklin D. Roosevelt, 1941* [volume] [Harper & Brothers, New York: 1950], p. 502.

9. *Pearl Harbor Attack*, Part 14, pp. 1328–1329.

10. *The Memoirs of Cordell Hull*, Vol. II, p. 1089. Italics mine. See also Lord Casey, *Personal Experiences, 1939–1946* (David McKay Company, Inc., New York: 1962) pp. 54–58.

11. *Pearl Harbor Attack*, Part 5, pp. 2089–2090: Memo by Hornbeck, November 27, 1941: "Problem of Far Eastern Relations — Estimate of Situation and Certain Probabilities" [:] ". . . The Japanese Government does not desire or intend or expect to have *forthwith* armed conflict with the United States." Dr. Hornbeck said that he "would give odds of five to one that the United States and Japan will not be at 'war' on or before December 15, . . . would wager three to one that the United States and Japan will not be at 'war' on or before the 15th of January . . . would wager even money that the

James A. Farley, a member of Mr. Roosevelt's Cabinet from 1933 to 1940, subsequently informed me:

Hull and Roosevelt never believed that the Japanese would fight.

On December 2, a week after the ultimatum had been sent, the President, at a press conference, gave a review of Japanese relations and discussed an episode concerning Indo-China. However, he made no reference to the truce that the Japanese had proposed, nor did he refer to Hull's final dispatch.[12]

On December 5, Hull recorded:

... I wirelessed instructions to our diplomatic representatives in Tokyo and other points in the Far East concerning the destruction of codes, secret archives, passports, and the like, the closing of offices, and the severance of local employees, in the event of a sudden emergency cutting off communications with the Department.[13]

It would seem that at this time Hull must have believed that his document would provoke war or he would not have made his remark to the War Council on November 28, nor his remark to the Australian Minister, Richard Casey, on November 29, nor given the instructions to the American diplomatic posts on how to close the offices and destroy the records.[14]

Rear-Admiral Clark Howell Woodward, U.S.N., Ret. reviewed the situation in the press. After telling of the superior strength of the Allied fleets, he said:

A Far Eastern war would be fought principally in Japanese waters or neighboring areas. The Japanese fleet would have to remain close to its home

---

United States and Japan will not be at 'war' on or before March 1.... Stated briefly, the undersigned does not believe that this country is now on the immediate verge of 'war' in the Pacific."

12. *The Public Papers and Addresses of Franklin D. Roosevelt,* 1941 [volume], pp. 508–510.

13. *The Memoirs of Cordell Hull,* Vol. II, p. 1093.

14. On December 4, 1941, just before Pearl Harbor, the *Chicago Daily Tribune* and the Washington *Times-Herald* published a sensational story of the war preparations being completed in the War Plans Division of the Army, implying that the United States would take the initiative. The account was an accurate disclosure of the plans. The leak created a great sensation in the War Department and the Congress, and supported the conviction held by some that the President's intention was to get into the war. An extensive account of the incident may be found in General Albert C. Wedemeyer's *Wedemeyer Reports!* [Henry Holt & Company, New York: 1958], pp. 15ff. General Wedemeyer states: "... it became all too clear that the Chicago *Tribune* correspondent had published an exact reproduction of the most important parts of the Victory Program.... Dramatically described by correspondent Manly as 'an astounding document which represents decisions and commitments affecting the destinies of peoples throughout the civilized world,' the Administration's secret war plan was now revealed to the world."

bases, for should it move any distance to the southward it would be cut off by American and British naval forces.[15]

On December 6, President Roosevelt sent a telegram to the Emperor asking for peace.[16] Hull commented in drafting the President's message that "its sending will be of doubtful efficacy, except for the purpose of making a record."[17]

15. *New York Journal-American,* December 7, 1941.
16. *New York Herald Tribune,* December 8, 1941.
17. *Pearl Harbor Attack,* Part 14, p. 1202.

CHAPTER 41

Via Japan—Pearl Harbor

AMBASSADOR GREW'S REPEATED WARNING that the Japanese would commit hara-kiri rather than submit to American dictation or starvation came true. They struck at Pearl Harbor on December 7, 1941.

President Roosevelt, addressing the Congress on December 8, asked for a declaration of war with the Japanese Empire. And on December 11, the President asked for declarations of war on Germany and Italy. We were in the Second World War with Communist Russia and the British Empire as our major allies.

Secretary of War Henry L. Stimson, who had long been striving to push the United States into war somewhere, noted in his diary on December 7:

> When the news first came that Japan had attacked us, my first feeling was of relief that the indecision was over and that a crisis had come in a way which would unite all our people. . . .[1]

The Naval Consequences

The Japanese attack resulted in about 3,500 American casualties, with over 2,300 service dead. Eight of our battleships were sunk or disabled for months. In addition, two cruisers and three destroyers were lost or badly damaged, and almost 200 planes were destroyed. So far as is known, an estimated 68 men were lost by the Japanese.[2]

On December 10, three days after Pearl Harbor, two British capital ships were sunk off the Malay Peninsula. Under that date, General Sir Alan F. Brooke,

---

1. *Pearl Harbor Attack,* Part 11 (April–May 1946), p. 5438. [*Editor's note:* See Chapter 31, note 16, for the full citation of this source.]

2. Ibid., Part 1, pp. 58–9, 188.

the newly appointed Chief of the British Imperial General Staff, wrote in his diary:

> ... that from Africa eastwards to America through the Indian Ocean and Pacific we have lost command of the sea.[3]

American, British, and Dutch naval vessels put out of action in the first seven months of the war (to July 1942) were: 15 battleships, 5 aircraft carriers, more than 15 cruisers, and 20 destroyers. At the low point, Allied fighting craft capable of immediate action had been reduced from 2,200,000 tons to 1,400,000 tons. The enemy lost comparatively little fighting tonnage in this period and was in control of far more of the Seven Seas than even General Sir Alan Brooke had indicated. Japanese submarines appeared within sight of the United States on the Pacific Coast and German submarines carried on their destruction along our Atlantic Coast.

On land, the Japanese forces within the seven months after Pearl Harbor occupied the Philippines, Thailand, Guam, Wake Island, Attu and Kiska of the Alaskan Aleutian Islands, Hong Kong, Malaya, Singapore, the Andaman Islands in the Bay of Bengal, the Netherlands East Indies, a number of British islands in the southwest Pacific, and most of Burma. From Malaya, the Dutch Indies, Burma, and Thailand, the Japanese were able to secure necessary supplies to carry on the war for years.

The loss of naval protection was at once reflected in the appalling destruction of Allied merchant shipping. The Navy Department later furnished me with data showing that prior to Pearl Harbor, the Allies had some 25 million tons of merchant shipping of their own and available from neutral charters. After the enemy got into full action in February, 1942, the sinkings in the subsequent year totaled 8,100,000 tons. Thousands of merchant seamen were lost. The rate of construction of new ships was not half that of the losses.

It required two years to re-establish a merchant fleet large enough to carry the full war needs—at a cost to the Allies of billions of dollars.

The effectiveness of the remaining American and British naval fleets was reduced by the necessity of protecting Hawaii, the Pacific Coast, and India, as well as by the need to convoy merchant ships carrying vital supplies. That even this protection was inadequate is indicated by the heavy loss of munitions and supplies at sea. In April, May, and June of 1942, over 250,000 tons of munitions were sunk by the enemy en route. Diversion of naval vessels

---

3. Arthur Bryant, *The Turn of the Tide* [Doubleday & Company, Inc., Garden City, N.Y.: 1957], p. 226.

to convoying by the remnant British navy in the Mediterranean permitted the Germans and Italians to restore their transport of troops across to North Africa. This contributed to the defeat of British forces by Marshal Rommel in June, 1942.

The loss of the British, Dutch, and American land possessions in southeast Asia cut off two-thirds of the supplies to the United States and Britain of vegetable oils, of rice, rubber and hemp. It reduced the sugar supply be one-quarter. It cost one-quarter of the petroleum, three-quarters of the tin, and large amounts of lead, zinc, tungsten, and practically all of the quinine.

Food, gasoline, rubber, tin and other supplies had to be drastically rationed in the United States, the British Commonwealth and other Allied countries. Further, to secure raw materials, the United States had to spend billions of dollars to build plants and equipment for the manufacture of substitutes for rubber, tin and hemp. We had to spend additional billions to create production from un-economic mineral deposits.

Victory over Japan came three and one-half years after Pearl Harbor.[4] But we are still in an unending war.

---

4. There are unending books of analyses on who, what, when, and where lay the responsibility of war with Japan and the events at Pearl Harbor. Space limits review of them to but a few paragraphs. [*Editor's note:* See Chapter 42.]

CHAPTER 42
Via Japan—Finding Someone to Blame

FROM THE INTERCEPTED Japanese dispatches the Administration in Washington knew that an attack was coming upon some Allied country. What happened in these few hours has been the subject of a vast amount of writing, speculation and investigation, some of it generous in spirit and some of it bitter criticism. The public had not been allowed to know of Grew's warnings. No American that I know of had believed any nation was capable of deliberate suicide. Any normal thinking would be that the attack would be directed to the Dutch East Indies or the Philippines from which Japan could obtain supplies to mitigate the Allied sanctions from which the Japanese were suffering so greatly. And they needed more oil to support their navy which could only come from the Dutch East Indies.

A statement from a critical viewpoint is that of General Albert C. Wedemeyer who at that time was a major in the War Plans Division of the Army and stationed in Washington. In his book, *Wedemeyer Reports!* he states an illuminating detail:

> When, on December 6, our intercepts told us that the Japanese were going to strike somewhere the very next day, whether in the Central Pacific or to the south in the Philippines and Dutch East Indies, the President of the United States, as Commander in Chief of our military forces . . . could have gone on the radio and broadcast to the wide world that he had irrefutable evidence of an immediate Japanese intention to strike. This would have alerted everybody from Singapore to Pearl Harbor. Even though inadequate in some cases to defend effectively, nevertheless our forces would have been able to take a toll which would have blunted the Japanese attack. In Hawaii, the capital ships might have been moved out of the congested harbor to sea, where Admiral Kimmel had at least had the foresight to keep the far more vital aircraft

carriers. Furthermore, our carrier task force in the mid-Pacific might have attacked the Japanese task force when its planes were aloft. There are many possibilities which would have given our men at least a fighting chance.

Captain L. F. Safford, U.S. Navy, in charge of the Communications Security Section of Naval Communications in Washington . . . testified before the Admiral Hart Board that "On December 4, 1941, we received definite information from two independent sources that Japan would attack the United States and Britain but would maintain peace with Russia." At 9:00 P.M. Washington time, December 6, 1941, we received positive information that Japan would declare war against the United States at a time to be specified thereafter. This information, so Safford testified, was positive and unmistakable and was made available to Military Intelligence virtually at the moment of its decoding. Finally, at 10:15 A.M. Washington time, December 7, 1941, we received positive information from the Signal Intelligence Service, War Department, that the Japanese declaration of war would be presented to the Secretary of State at 1:00 P.M. Washington time that date; when it was 1:00 P.M. in Washington it would be daybreak in Hawaii and approximately midnight in the Philippines, which indicated a surprise air raid on Pearl Harbor in about three hours. According to Safford, Lieutenant Kramer of the Navy appended a note to this effect to the paper sent over from Secret Intelligence Service before presenting it to the Secretary of the Navy.

President Roosevelt had ample time to broadcast a warning. Conjecturally, such a warning might even have caused the Japanese to call off their surprise attack. In any event, we would not have permitted 3,500 Americans to die at Hawaii without an opportunity to fight back. . . .[1]

Faced by the worst defeat in all our military history, Secretary Knox made an immediate flight to Hawaii. On December 15, he reported to the nation that:

. . . The United States services were not on the alert against the surprise air attack on Hawaii. This fact calls for a formal investigation, which will be initiated immediately by the President. . . .[2]

Secretary Knox also submitted a secret report to the President in which he admitted:

---

1. General A. C. Wedemeyer, *Wedemeyer Reports!* [Henry Holt & Company, New York: 1958], pp. 429–430.
2. *New York Times,* December 16, 1941.

... the best means of defense against air attack consists of fighter planes. Lack of an adequate number of [fighter planes at Pearl Harbor] ... is due to the diversion of this type ... to the British, the Chinese, the Dutch and the Russians.

The next best weapon against air attack is ... anti-aircraft artillery. There is a dangerous shortage of guns of this type on the Island. This is through no fault of the Army Commander who has pressed consistently for these guns.[3]

On December 16 Admiral Kimmel and General Short were notified by wire that they were relieved of their commands at Hawaii. At the same time the President named a Commission of Inquiry under Supreme Court Associate Justice Owen J. Roberts. The report of the *Roberts Commission* condemned the Army and Navy Commanders in Hawaii—General Short and Admiral Kimmel—for not having been prepared and on the alert.[4]

Secretary Knox sanctioned this condemnation with the comment:

The report speaks for itself.[5]

The American people were not satisfied with the Washington explanations of the disaster. Less than three years later demands from various quarters produced a Naval inquiry under Admiral Hart in February to June 1944. An Army inquiry was conducted from July to October of that same year. This *Army Pearl Harbor Board* condemned negligence by General Marshall and other officers for having knowledge of the attack from the "intercepts" and for not having alerted Short. Dissatisfied with this report, Secretary of War Stimson ordered Lt. Colonel Henry C. Clausen to conduct a supplemental investigation. The *Clausen Investigation* took place from November 1944 to September 1945. Another Army inquiry—the *Clarke Investigation*—was conducted in September 1944 and from July to August 1945. This investigation examined the way top communications had been handled. The *Naval Court of Inquiry* took place from July to October 1944. This inquiry cleared Admiral Kimmel and criticized Admiral Stark. A further inquiry was held by the Navy—the *Hewitt Inquiry* of May to July 1945. The reports of the *Naval Court of Inquiry* and the *Army Pearl Harbor Board* were not released to the public until August 29, 1945.

---

3. *Pearl Harbor Attack*, Part 5, p. 2342. [*Editor's note:* See Chapter 31, note 16, for the full citation of this source.]

4. Ibid., Part 39, pp. 1–21.

5. *New York Times*, January 25, 1942.

When the Army report was released, Secretary Stimson took issue with the criticism of General Marshall. Stimson defended the Chief of Staff and attributed the responsibility for the Army disaster to General Short.[6]

However, Arthur Krock commented in the *New York Times:*

> ... The reports stop discreetly on the threshold of the White House, though that was the clearing-point in those days of all the military and diplomatic activities of the Government and President Roosevelt was publicly stressing his responsibility as Commander in Chief of the armed forces.[7]

Although public pressures forced these seven investigations by the Army and Navy, no court martial proceedings were allowed where Kimmel and Short could divulge their account and defend themselves.

The Congressional Pearl Harbor Investigation

The Congress was apparently not satisfied with these investigations and reports.

The most important of the Pearl Harbor inquiries was the Congressional Pearl Harbor investigation established in 1945.[8] It pursued its inquiry from November 1945 to May 1946. This was after the war was over and four years after the attack. The record of this and the earlier investigations has been published in the *Pearl Harbor Attack,* which consists of 11 volumes of evidence and 10 volumes of exhibits of the Congressional investigation and 18 volumes of the records of the preceding investigations.

The Congressional investigation, however, had a political complexion, for administration supporters made up the majority of this Joint Committee.

Among the conclusions announced in the majority report were:

1. The December 7, 1941, attack on Pearl Harbor was an unprovoked act of aggression by the Empire of Japan. . . .
2. The ultimate responsibility for the attack and its results rests upon Japan. . . .
3. The diplomatic policies and actions of the United States provided no justifiable provocation whatever for the attack by Japan on this

---

6. *New York Times,* August 30, 1945.
7. Ibid., September 4, 1945.
8. [*Investigation of the Pearl Harbor Attack:*] *Report of the Joint Committee on the Investigation of the Pearl Harbor Attack,* 79th Congress, 2d Session, Senate Document No. 244 [United States Government Printing Office, Washington: 1946].

Nation. The Secretary of State fully informed both the War and Navy Departments of diplomatic developments and, in a timely and forceful manner, clearly pointed out to these Departments that relations between the United States and Japan had passed beyond the stage of diplomacy and were in the hands of the military.

4. The committee has found no evidence to support the charges, made before and during the hearings, that the President, the Secretary of State, the Secretary of War, or the Secretary of Navy tricked, provoked, incited, cajoled, or coerced Japan into attacking this Nation in order that a declaration of war might be more easily obtained from the Congress. On the contrary, all evidence conclusively points to the fact that they discharged their responsibilities with distinction, ability, and foresight and in keeping with the highest traditions of our fundamental foreign policy.

5. The President, the Secretary of State, and high Government officials made every possible effort, without sacrificing our national honor and endangering our security, to avert war with Japan.

6. The disaster of Pearl Harbor was the failure . . . of the Army and the Navy to institute measures designed to detect an approaching hostile force. . . .

7. Virtually everyone was surprised that Japan struck the Fleet at Pearl Harbor at the time that she did. Yet, officers both in Washington and Hawaii, were fully conscious of the danger from air attack; they realized this form of attack on Pearl Harbor by Japan was at least a possibility; and they were adequately informed of the imminence of war.

8. . . . the Hawaiian commands failed— . . . To discharge their responsibilities in the light of the warnings received from Washington. . . . [9]

Senators Alben W. Barkley (D) of Kentucky, Walter F. George (D) of Georgia, and Scott W. Lucas (D) of Illinois signed this majority report as did Congressman Jere Cooper (D) of Tennessee, J. Bayard Clark (D) of North Carolina, John W. Murphy (D) of Pennsylvania, Bertrand W. Gearhart (R) of California and Frank B. Keefe (R) of Wisconsin.

The question arises whether the majority members of this Committee, even though politically biased, could have read and understood the Grew, Hull, and Craigie-Eden correspondence during the period of the total economic sanctions and still have reached these conclusions.

---

9. Ibid., pp. 251–252.

Representative Keefe also filed additional views. Here are some quotes from his report:

> ... I find myself in agreement with most of these conclusions and recommendations [of the majority report]. ...
>
> ... Throughout the long and arduous sessions of the committee in the preparation of the committee report, I continuously insisted that whatever "yardstick" was agreed upon as a basis for determining responsibilities in Hawaii should be applied to the high command at Washington. ... I feel that facts have been martialed, perhaps unintentionally, with the idea of conferring blame upon Hawaii and minimizing the blame that should properly be assessed at Washington. ...
>
> ... I cannot suppress the feeling that the committee report endeavors to throw as soft a light as possible on the Washington scene.[10]

The minority report of the Committee was filed by Senators Homer Ferguson (R) of Michigan and Owen Brewster (R) of Maine. This minority report stated:

> It is extremely unfortunate that the Roberts Commission Report was so hasty, inconclusive, and incomplete. Some witnesses were examined under oath; others were not. Much testimony was not even recorded. ...
>
> ... By one way or another, control over papers, records, and other information remained in the hands of the majority party members. ...
>
> ... permission to search files and other records was denied by majority vote to individual members *even when accompanied by Committee counsel.* Rightly or wrongly it was inferred from this that there was a deliberate design to block the search for the truth. ...
>
> Permission was asked to conduct exploration for certain missing records. Vigorous and public denial was made—presumably on Executive authority—that any records were missing. Subsequently it developed that several records were missing and most inadequate explanations were supplied. ...
>
> ... Through the Army and Navy Intelligence Services extensive information was secured respecting Japanese war plans and designs, by intercepted and decoded Japanese secret messages, which indicated the growing danger of war and increasingly after November 26 the imminence of a Japanese attack.
>
> ... Army and Navy information which indicated growing imminence of war was delivered to the highest authorities in charge of national preparedness

---

10. Ibid., pp. 266–266A.

for meeting an attack, among others, the President, the Secretaries of State, War, and Navy, and the Chief of Staff and the Chief of Naval Operations. . . .

In the diplomatic documents, exhibits, and testimony before the Committee there is a wealth of evidence which underwrites the statement that the tactics of maneuvering the Japanese into "the position of firing the first shot" were followed by high authorities in Washington after November 25, 1941. Examples of such tactics are. . . .

. . . The rejection of appeals made to President Roosevelt by General Marshall and Admiral Stark on November 5 and also later on November 27, 1941, for a delay in bringing about a breach with Japan—appeals based on their belief that the Army and Navy were not then ready for a war with Japan. . . .

The fleet was stationed at Pearl Harbor in a large measure, if not entirely, for the purpose of exercising a deterring effect on the aggressive propensities of the Japanese Government during the diplomatic negotiations and of making the Government more likely to yield to the diplomatic representations of the United States in matters of policy. This was done contrary to the advice of the Commander in Chief of the U.S. Fleet, Admiral Richardson (who was removed because of protest on that issue), and with which Admiral William D. Leahy, former Chief of Naval Operations agreed. . . .

Testimony and documents before the Committee lend support to . . . the Sixteenth Conclusion of the President's [Roberts] Commission which found:

> "The *opinion* prevalent in diplomatic, military, and naval circles, and in the public press," was "that any immediate attack by Japan would be in the Far East." [Italics supplied] . . .

> The fatal error of Washington in . . . [the lack of material at Pearl Harbor] was to undertake a world campaign and world responsibilities without first making provision for the security of the United States, which was their prime constitutional obligation.

. . . High Washington authorities did not communicate to Admiral Kimmel and General Short adequate information of diplomatic negotiations and of intercepted diplomatic intelligence which, if communicated to them, would have informed them of the imminent menace of a Japanese attack in time for them to fully alert and prepare the defense of Pearl Harbor. . . .

Wholly apart from the merits or demerits . . . in the Japanese proposal of November 20, here was an opportunity at least to prolong "the breathing spell" for which General Marshall and Admiral Stark were pleading in their efforts to strengthen the armed forces of the United States for war. . . .

The failure to perform the responsibilities indispensably essential to the defense of Pearl Harbor rests upon the following civil and military authorities:

Franklin D. Roosevelt . . .
Henry L. Stimson . . .
Frank Knox . . .
George C. Marshall . . .
Harold R. Stark . . .
Leonard T. Gerow. . . .

The failure to perform the responsibilities in Hawaii rests upon the military commanders:

Walter C. Short . . .
Husband E. Kimmell. . . . [11]

Admiral Robert A. Theobald, who commanded the Destroyer Division at Pearl Harbor, in a careful review of the facts, says:

Diplomatically, President Roosevelt's strategy of forcing Japan to war by unremitting and ever-increasing diplomatic-economic pressure, and by simultaneously holding our Fleet in Hawaii as an invitation to a surprise attack, was a complete success. . . . One is forced to conclude that the anxiety to have Japan, beyond all possibility of dispute, commit the first act of war, caused the President and his civilian advisers to disregard the military advice which would somewhat have cushioned the blow. . . . [12]

Twelve years after the report of the first Commission of Inquiry, headed by Owen J. Roberts, Admiral William H. Standley, a member of the Roberts Commission, wrote his story of that Commission's proceedings. He narrated the injustice to Short and to Kimmel, and concluded:

---

11. Ibid., pp. 497–573. Percy L. Greaves, Jr. acted as research expert for the minority members of this Joint Congressional Committee. Mr. Greaves observes: "The investigations of the Pearl Harbor attack have been many and varied. The complete facts will never be known. Most of the so-called investigations have been attempts to suppress, mislead, or confuse those who seek the truth. From the beginning to the end, facts and files have been withheld so as to reveal only those items of information which benefit the administration under investigation. Those seeking the truth are told that other facts or documents cannot be revealed because they are intermingled in personal diaries, pertain to our relations with foreign countries, or are sworn to contain no information of value." Percy L. Greaves, Jr., "The Pearl Harbor Investigations," [in] Perpetual War for Perpetual Peace, edited by Harry Elmer Barnes (The Caxton Printers, Ltd., Caldwell, Idaho: 1953), p. 409.

12. Rear Admiral Robert A. Theobald, U.S.N. (ret), The Final Secret of Pearl Harbor (The Devin-Adair Company, New York: 1954), p. 5.

... these two officers [Short and Kimmel] were martyred.... if they had been brought to trial, both would have been cleared of the charge of neglect of duty....

The "incident" which certain high officials in Washington had sought so assiduously in order to condition the American public for war with the Axis powers had been found.... [13]

A mass of literature has grown up around the "Pearl Harbor incident." *Pearl Harbor: The Story of the Secret War,* an exhaustive study of the Pearl Harbor attack by George Morgenstern, was published in 1947. In Morgenstern's judgment:

... given the benefit of every doubt ... all of these men [the high authorities in Washington] still must answer for much. With absolute knowledge of war, they refused to communicate that knowledge, clearly, unequivocally, and in time, to the men in the field upon whom the blow would fall....

Pearl Harbor provided the American war party with the means of escaping dependence on a hesitant Congress in taking a reluctant people into war....

Pearl Harbor was the first action of the acknowledged war, and the last battle of a secret war upon which the administration had long since embarked. The secret war was waged against nations which the leadership of this country had chosen as enemies months before they became formal enemies by a declaration of war. It was waged also, but psychological means, by propaganda, and deception against the American people.... The people were told that acts which were equivalent to war were intended to keep the nation out of war. Constitutional processes existed only to be circumvented, until finally, the war-making power of Congress was reduced to the act of ratifying an accomplished fact.[14]

In *America's Second Crusade,* William Henry Chamberlin concludes:

It is scarcely possible, in the light of this [Admiral Stark's testimony regarding President Roosevelt's October 8, 1941 order to American warships in the Atlantic to fire on German ships] and many other known facts, to avoid the conclusion that the Roosevelt Administration sought the war which began

---

13. Admiral W[illia]m. H. Standley, U.S.N., Ret., "More About Pearl Harbor," in *U.S. News and World Report,* April 16, 1954.

14. George Morgenstern, *Pearl Harbor: The Story of the Secret War* (The Devin-Adair Company, New York: 1947), pp. 328–330.

at Pearl Harbor. The steps which made armed conflict inevitable were taken months before the conflict broke out.[15]

George F. Kennan, a lifelong and distinguished member of the American diplomatic corps and a recognized authority on Russian culture and history, has given this summary:

> ... a policy carefully and realistically aimed at the avoidance of a war with Japan ... would certainly have produced a line of action considerably different from that which we actually pursued and would presumably have led to quite different results.[16]

An objective British historian, Captain Russell Grenfell, in his great study of the war, concludes:

> No reasonably informed person can now believe that Japan made a villainous, unexpected attack on the United States. An attack was not only fully expected but was actually desired. It is beyond doubt that President Roosevelt wanted to get his country into the war, but for political reasons was most anxious to ensure that the first act of hostility came from the other side; for which reason he caused increasing pressure to be put on the Japanese, to a point that no self-respecting nation could endure without resort to arms. Japan was meant by the American President to attack the United States. As Mr. Oliver Lyttelton, then British Minister of Production, said in 1944, "Japan was provoked into attacking America at Pearl Harbour. It is a travesty of history to say that America was forced into the war."[17]

It is, at this writing, over thirty years since the beginning of the events and actions which have led to the calamity which today embraces all mankind. The aims of this memoir will be fulfilled if historical truth is better established, and if the lessons to be learned from the millions who died because of lost statesmanship are not forgotten. As Santayana said:

> Those who do not remember the past are condemned to relive it.[18]

---

15. William Henry Chamberlin, *America's Second Crusade* (Henry Regnery Company, Chicago: 1950), p. 353.

16. George F. Kennan, *American Diplomacy, 1900–1950* (The University of Chicago Press, Chicago: 1951), p. 82.

17. Captain Russell Grenfell, R. N., *Main Fleet to Singapore* (The Macmillan Company, New York: 1952), pp. 107–108.

18. [*Editor's note:* The precise wording of George Santayana's oft-quoted aphorism is: "Those who cannot remember the past are condemned to repeat it."]

VOLUME II

SECTION XI

The March of Conferences

Introduction

I HAVE OUTLINED IN VOLUME I the action and forces by which the United States became involved in the Second World War.

The alignment of nations were Communist Russia, Great Britain, the United States and China, and a group of smaller nations calling themselves the "United Nations." The major enemies were Germany under Hitler's dictatorship, Italy under Mussolini, and Japan under its militarist warlords—generally referred to as the Berlin-Rome-Tokyo Axis, and embraced a number of small nations in Southeast Europe.

Periodic conferences of the leaders of the major members of the United Nations were held to determine military action and political policies. Although many questions of military strategy were resolved at these conferences, it was from the political agreements and understandings that these leaders determined the fate of billions of people in the world.

Whenever Prime Minister Churchill, President Roosevelt, Marshal Stalin, or Generalissimo Chiang Kai-shek was present, each was accompanied by a large staff. The names of both the civilian and military members of each conference are given in footnotes. When the leaders of the major powers could not attend, the agreements were relayed to them. There was naturally no publication of conclusions regarding military tactics or strategy available at the time of these conferences. However, the victories, defeats, advances, and retreats of the fighting forces on both sides were revealed daily by the press whose representatives accompanied the armies. Thus the general military situation at any particular time was a matter of public knowledge.

After United Nations' conferences where political policies or actions were determined, a communiqué was usually issued to the public. Naturally, these communiqués were not very informative, and were chiefly notable as an affirmation of purpose to win the war. Usually these statements also contained expressions of fidelity to the Atlantic Charter. In the latter stages of the war some of the United Nations' conference declarations, intended to influence the Axis states, were made public. However, most political agreements and plans were kept secret; many of these, affecting the United States, did not come to light until years after the war. The extensive publications by the State Department proved to have many omissions or suppressions which have seriously obstructed the work of the historian. Nevertheless, by checking and cross-checking data from various sources, it is possible to present the facts in this memoir. Especially useful are the scores of books published by many of the men who participated in these conferences; also, certain information has been gained from observing the events which followed the political meetings.

Usually each of the conferences and each major military operation were given a name—in the case of political conferences, there were such names as TRIDENT and QUADRANT. The military operations were given such names as TORCH and OVERLORD. These names were for purposes of secrecy at the time and also for brevity in dispatches and memoranda. There were more than fifty such terms. To use them in this text would confuse the reader by requiring constant reference to an explanatory index. Therefore, to simplify description of political conferences, I have given them under the name of the place at which they were held. When more than one conference was held in the same place, I use the terms "First," "Second" or "Third." When I speak of a military operation, I usually follow the military term and in addition give the place, date or purpose.

For better understanding of the actions taken at each conference, I include a short summary of the military situation at the time of the conference as, obviously, the conclusions reached at the conferences were affected by the progress of the war.

For the convenience of the reader, I give the following list of the political conferences at which decisions of important took place.

They were:

1. *The Atlantic Conference:* August 9–12, 1941, between President Roosevelt and Prime Minister Churchill.
2. *The First Washington Conference:* December 22, 1941–January 14, 1942, between President Roosevelt and Prime Minister Churchill.
3. *The Atlantic Charter Ratification Meeting:* Representatives of twenty-six nations met in Washington on January 1, 1942.

4. *The Second Washington Conference:* June 18–25, 1942, between President Roosevelt and Prime Minister Churchill.

5. *The Casablanca Conference:* January 14–24, 1943, comprising President Roosevelt, Prime Minister Churchill, and General Charles de Gaulle, representing the Free French.

6. *The Third Washington Conference:* May 12–25, 1943, comprising President Roosevelt, Prime Minister Churchill, and T. V. Soong, representing Chiang Kai-shek.

7. *The First Quebec Conference:* August 11–24, 1943, comprising President Roosevelt, Prime Minister Churchill, Prime Minister of Canada MacKenzie King, and T. V. Soong, representing Chiang Kai-shek.

8. *The First Moscow Conference:* October 19–30, 1943. This was primarily a conference of Foreign Ministers, and present were Secretary of State Cordell Hull, Minister of Foreign Affairs Anthony Eden, Russian Minister of Foreign Affairs Vyacheslav M. Molotov, and Dr. Foo Ping-Sheung, representing Chiang Kai-shek.

9. *The First Cairo Conference:* November 22–26, 1943, comprising President Roosevelt, Prime Minister Churchill, and Generalissimo Chiang Kai-shek.

10. *The Tehran Conference:* November 27–December 1, 1943, comprising President Roosevelt, Prime Minister Churchill, and Marshal Stalin.

11. *The Second Cairo Conference:* December 2–7, 1943, between President Roosevelt and Prime Minister Churchill.

12. *The Dumbarton Oaks Conference:* August 21–October 7, 1944, comprising representatives of the United States, Great Britain, the Soviet Union, the Chinese Government, and others of the United Nations. The purpose was to make a preliminary draft of a world organization to preserve peace.

13. *The Second Quebec Conference:* September 11–16, 1944, comprising President Roosevelt, Prime Minister Churchill, and Prime Minister MacKenzie King of Canada.

14. *The Second Moscow Conference:* October 9–20, 1944, comprising Marshal Stalin, Prime Minister Churchill, British Minister of Foreign Affairs Anthony Eden, and the American Ambassador at Moscow, W. Averell Harriman, representing the United States.

15. *The Malta Conference:* January 30–February 2, 1945, between Prime Minister Churchill and United States representatives. (Mr. Roosevelt arrived for the session on February 2.)

16. *The Yalta Conference in the Crimea:* February 4–11, 1945, comprising President Roosevelt, Prime Minister Churchill, and Marshal Stalin.
17. *The United Nations Charter Conference* in San Francisco: April 25– June 26, 1945, comprising representatives of each of the nations allied in the war to prepare for the adoption of a Charter for the preservation of peace.
18. *The Potsdam Conference* at Berlin: July 17–August 2, 1945. It was attended by President Truman, Marshal Stalin, and Prime Minister Clement A. Attlee, who had defeated Prime Minister Churchill in the intervening election. Attlee replaced Churchill at the Conference on July 28, 1945.

There had been conferences at which agreements were entered into among the Allies against the Axis before the United States came into the war. The most important were the British and Russian conferences in respect to establishing a second front in France, and a conference of all the then United Nations at St. James's Palace in London on September 24, 1941.

The Second Front

Stalin repeatedly urged the British to make an attack on Germany by a cross-Channel landing in France. This would divide the German forces and relieve the pressure upon Russia. He made such demands prior to Pearl Harbor on July 18, 1941,[1] and on September 3, 1941.[2] Great Britain was already in a precarious situation, and Churchill replied on September 4, refusing.[3]

Stalin answered him:

. . . I can only repeat that its absence is playing into the hands of our common enemies.[4]

The Meeting at St. James's Palace

The meeting at St. James's Palace in London on September 24, 1941, was called by Prime Minister Churchill and was mostly to reaffirm the Atlantic Charter.

---

1. [U.S.S.R., Ministry of Foreign Affairs,] *Stalin's Correspondence with Churchill, Attlee, Roosevelt and Truman, 1941–45* [Lawrence & Wishart, London: 1958], Vol. I, p. 13.
2. Ibid., p. 21.
3. Ibid., p. 22.
4. Ibid., p. 24.

The United States not being at war sent no representative. Polish Ambassador to the United States Jan Ciechanowski stated:

... representatives of all the Allies took part in it.... the Soviet Union was represented by Mr. Maisky, its Ambassador to the Court of St. James's, and by Mr. Bogomolov, Soviet Ambassador to Poland....

Ambassador Maisky in an inspiring speech declared, on behalf of the Soviet Union, that it "was, and is, guided in its foreign policy by the principle of self-determination of nations.

"Accordingly," he continued, "the Soviet Union defends the right of every nation to the independence and territorial integrity of its country, and its right to establish such a social order and to choose such a form of government as it deems opportune and necessary for the better promotion of its economic and cultural prosperity."

Maisky went on denouncing "all and any attempts of aggressive Powers to impose their will upon other peoples," and stressed the fact that the Soviet Union has been and still is "striving for a radical solution of the problem of safeguarding freedom-loving peoples against all the dangers they encounter from aggressors."

After which Maisky solemnly declared the acceptance of, and adherence to, the Atlantic Charter in the following words:

"In accordance with a policy inspired by the above principles ... the Soviet Government proclaims its agreement with the fundamental principles of the declaration of Mr. Roosevelt, President of the United States, and of Mr. Churchill, Prime Minister of Great Britain—principles which are so important in the present international circumstances."

Mr. Eden then put the following resolution ... [:]

The Governments of Belgium, Czechoslovakia, Greece, Luxemburg, the Netherlands, Norway, Poland, Union of Soviet Socialist Republics, and Yugoslavia, and the representatives of General de Gaulle, leader of free Frenchmen,

Having taken note of the Declaration recently drawn up by the President of the United States and by the Prime Minister, Mr. Churchill....

Now make known their adherence to the common principles of policy set forth in that Declaration and their intention to cooperate to the best of their ability in giving effect to them.

Through this conveniently forgotten document ... at that meeting at St James's Palace, Soviet Russia's formal adherence to the Atlantic Charter was officially declared.[5]

Getting a Meeting with Stalin

During the first two years of the war, one of the problems was to secure the attendance of Marshal Stalin at conferences. President Roosevelt believed that a meeting with Stalin could be more easily arranged if Mr. Churchill was not present. The President wrote to Prime Minister Churchill three months after Pearl Harbor (March 18, 1942) saying:

> ... I know you will not mind my being brutally frank when I tell you that I think I can personally handle Stalin better than either your Foreign Office or my State Department. Stalin hates the guts of all your top people. He thinks he likes me better, and I hope he will continue to do so.[6]

About three weeks later Secretary Hull reported that Mr. Roosevelt invited Stalin to meet him in the neighborhood of Alaska the following summer. Stalin did not accept the invitation.[7]

Although Stalin had twice refused to come to meetings[8] before the Casablanca Conference (in January, 1943), the two Western leaders apparently hoped that he would attend this conference. However, Stalin refused saying he could not leave the critical military situation in Russia.

Major-General John R. Deane, who was Chief of the United States Military Mission to the Soviet Union, wrote:

> At ... the Casablanca Conference, President Roosevelt was anxious to have General Marshall go to Moscow. ... Stalin could not see that a visit by General Marshall ... would serve any useful purpose. This slight to our Chief of Staff was keenly felt by all Americans who knew about it. ... The Russian leaders could see only another American effort to pry into their affairs. ...[9]

---

5. [Jan] Ciechanowski, *Defeat in Victory* [Doubleday & Company, Garden City, N.Y.: 1947], pp. 50–51. [*Editor's note:* The italics are Ciechanowski's.]

6. [Winston S.] Churchill, *The Hinge of Fate* [Houghton Mifflin Company, Boston: 1950], p. 201.

7. *The Memoirs of Cordell Hull* [The Macmillan Company, New York: 1948], Vol. II, p. 1249.

8. [Robert E.] Sherwood, *Roosevelt and Hopkins* [Harper & Brothers, New York: 1948], p. 671.

9. [John R.] Deane, *The Strange Alliance* [The Viking Press, New York: 1947], p. 144.

Jan Ciechanowski, the Polish Ambassador in Washington, reports that in April, 1943, Mr. Roosevelt commented to him:

> I have made five attempts to see this man . . . but he has always eluded me.[10]

Sometime in May, 1943, the President again developed the idea that Stalin might be willing to meet him alone without Churchill. It was decided to send former Ambassador Joseph E. Davies to Moscow to present the matter to Stalin. In a letter dated May 5, 1943, carried personally by Davies, Roosevelt said:

> I want to get away from the . . . red tape of diplomatic conversations. Therefore, the simplest and most practical method . . . would be an informal and completely simple visit for a few days between you and me. . . .
>
> . . . I do not believe that any official agreements or declarations are in the least bit necessary.[11]

Stalin, in a letter to Roosevelt, gave a qualified approval of a meeting with the President, to be held in July or August.[12] Prime Minister Churchill was in Washington for the Third Washington Conference—May 11–May 26, 1943—when Davies was en route to, or in Moscow, but apparently Mr. Roosevelt did not wish to mention his plan to the Prime Minister at this time. A month later, on June 30, he dispatched Ambassador Averell Harriman to London to inform the Prime Minister. Mr. Churchill's reaction was hardly one of pleasure, and this private meeting of Stalin and Roosevelt was called off.[13]

An effort was also made to attract Stalin to the First Quebec Conference, which was held in August, 1943.[14]

Having failed to get Stalin to a conference, Mr. Churchill and Mr. Roosevelt proposed to him that their four Foreign Ministers should have a conference in Moscow. Stalin assented, and fixed the date for October, 1943 (The First Moscow Conference). Among other instructions, Secretary Hull and Foreign Minister Eden were directed, if possible, to get Stalin to come somewhere to a meeting. The Foreign Ministers succeeded, and the meeting was set to take

---

10. Jan Ciechanowski, *Defeat in Victory,* p. 153.

11. [Elliott Roosevelt, ed.,] *F.D.R., His Personal Letters,* [*1928–1945,*] Vol. II [Duell, Sloan and Pearce, New York: 1950], pp. 1422–1423.

12. *Stalin's Correspondence with Churchill, Attlee, Roosevelt and Truman,* Vol. II, p. 66.

13. Sherwood, *Roosevelt and Hopkins,* pp. 737–739.

14. *The Memoirs of Cordell Hull,* Vol. II, p. 1252.

place at Tehran, Iran, a month later,[15] a short journey for Stalin but a long one for Messrs. Roosevelt and Churchill.

Stalin also attended the Yalta Conference in February, 1945, with Messrs. Churchill and Roosevelt, and the Potsdam Conference in July-August, 1945, with Mr. Truman and initially with Mr. Churchill. Owing to Mr. Churchill's defeat in the British elections, he was succeeded by Prime Minister Clement Attlee in the midst of that conference. The three principal leaders met only three times during the entire war, and Messrs. Churchill and Roosevelt, with or without the other leaders, twelve times.

---

15. Ibid., pp. 1252, 1254, 1292–1296, 1313.

CHAPTER 43

The First Washington Conference

December 22, 1941 to January 14, 1942

THE PRINCIPALS AT the First Washington Conference were President Roosevelt and Prime Minister Churchill.[1]

The military situation at the time of this conference was indeed discouraging and perilous. The only bright military spots were Stalin's temporary halt of Hitler's invasion of Russia the previous November, and the British armies in Africa holding their own against the German and Italian attacks.

The First Washington Conference accomplished two vitally important arrangements: The first was the establishment of the combined American and British Chiefs of Staff Committee in Washington, the British being represented by high officers stationed permanently in that city. This committee reviewed all military plans; devised unifying military strategy; sought efficient allocation of manpower and munitions; and coordinated communications.[2]

---

1. The military staff membership of the First Washington Conference:

For the United States: General George C. Marshall, Chief of Staff of the United States Army; Admiral Harold R. Stark, Chief of Naval Operations; Admiral Ernest J. King, Commander in Chief, United States Fleet; Rear Admiral W. R. Sexton, President of the General Board; Rear Admiral Frederick J. Horne, Assistant Chief of Naval Operations; Rear Admiral John H. Towers, Chief of the Bureau of Aeronautics; Rear Admiral Richmond K. Turner, of the War Plans Division of the Office of Naval Operations; General Thomas Holcomb, the Commandant of the Marine Corps; Major General Henry H. Arnold, of the Army Air Corps; Major General L. T. Gerow, Chief of the War Plans Division.

For Great Britain: Admiral of the Fleet Sir Dudley Pound; Field Marshal Sir John Dill; Air Chief Marshal Sir Charles Portal; six British military and naval representatives.

2. Mr. Churchill, in his book, *The Grand Alliance,* gave some account of this establishment, saying in part: "It may well be thought by future historians that the most valuable and lasting result of our first Washington Conference . . . was the setting up of the now famous 'Combined Chiefs of Staff Committee.' Its headquarters were in Washington, but since the British Chiefs of Staff had to live close to their own Government they were represented by high officers stationed there permanently. These representatives were in daily, indeed hourly, touch with London, and were thus able to state and explain the views of the British Chiefs of Staff to their United States colleagues on any and every war problem at any time of the day or night. . . . [There were] two hundred formal meetings held by

As a matter of fact the United States had agreed with Britain as to the grand strategy of the war in the ABC agreement in February, 1941, ten months before Pearl Harbor. The basis of this plan was that in the event of the United States and Great Britain fighting a war with Germany and Japan, the concentration of force should be against Germany.[3]

This strategy, however, was still tentative at the time of the First Washington Conference, and the British feared that the events in the Pacific might bring a reversal in strategy to an all-out American effort against Japan. Their fears quickly disappeared when General Marshall and Admiral Stark presented a memorandum to the conference which stated:

> . . . notwithstanding the entry of Japan into the War, our view remains that Germany is still the prime enemy and her defeat is the key to victory. Once Germany is defeated, the collapse of Italy and the defeat of Japan must follow.[4]

The second major accomplishment of the conference was the signing of the United Nations Pact. Through this pact all the nations at war with the Axis pledged fidelity to the principles of the Atlantic Charter and pledged their resources and cooperation in the war. A declaration was issued, which reads as follows:

The Governments signatory hereto,

Having subscribed to a common program of purposes and principles embodied in the Joint Declaration of the President of the United States of America and the Prime Minister of the United Kingdom of Great Britain and Northern Ireland dated August 14, 1941, known as the Atlantic Charter.

Being convinced that complete victory over their enemies is essential to defend life, liberty, independence and religious freedom, and to preserve human rights and justice in their own lands as well as in other lands, and that they are now engaged in a common struggle against savage and brutal forces seeking to subjugate the world, *declare:*

(1) Each Government pledges itself to employ its full resources, military or economic, against those members of the Tripartite Pact, and its adherents with which such government is at war.

---

the Combined Chiefs of Staff Committee during the war. . . ." (Winston S. Churchill, *The Grand Alliance,* Houghton Mifflin Company, Boston: 1950, pp. 686–687.)

3. Robert E. Sherwood, *Roosevelt and Hopkins* (New York: Harper & Brothers, 1948), p. 273.
4. Ibid., p. 445.

(2) Each Government pledges itself to cooperate with the Governments signatory hereto and not to make a separate armistice or peace with the enemies.

The foregoing declaration may be adhered to by other nations which are, or which may be, rendering material assistance and contributions in the struggle for victory over Hitlerism.

Done at Washington January First, 1942.[5]

Initially, there were twenty-six signatories; twenty-one signed later, making a total of forty-seven.

The original signatories were:

Australia	India
Belgium	Luxembourg
Canada	Netherlands
China	New Zealand
Costa Rica	Nicaragua
Cuba	Norway
Czecho-Slovakia	Panama
Dominican Republic	Poland
El Salvador	Union of South Africa
Greece	Union of Soviet Socialist Republics
Guatemala	United Kingdom of Great Britain and Northern Ireland
Haiti	United States of America
Honduras	Yugoslavia

Of these, the following nations were at this time occupied by Hitler's armies and their signatories were representatives of their exiled governments. And to them came this special assurance of independence and freedom.

Belgium	Netherlands
Czecho-Slovakia	Norway
Greece	Poland
Luxembourg	Yugoslavia

The declaration was signed on January 1, 1942.

---

5. *Review of the United Nations Charter, A Collection of Documents,* Document No. 87, [United States] Senate [Committee on Foreign Relations,] Subcommittee on the United Nations Charter, 83d Congress, [1st Session,] (United States Government Printing Office, Washington: 1954), pp. 38–39.

CHAPTER 44

The Second Washington Conference

June 18 to June 25, 1942

PRIME MINISTER CHURCHILL, President Roosevelt, and their staffs constituted the Second Washington Conference.[1]

The Military Situation

By the time of this conference the Allies had lost control of the seven seas except for the areas near their shores and convoys of merchant ships. The loss of merchant ships rose to 800,000 tons per annum or twice the rate of new construction.

With the German and Italian navies free to operate in the Mediterranean, these two nations reinforced their armies in North Africa, and compelled the British to retreat toward Egypt.

Hitler's armies in Russia, which had been stalled in November, 1941, had resumed their invasion, and at the time of this conference had driven deeply into Russia as far as Sevastopol.

The American army in the Philippines had surrendered in May, a month before the conference.

On the more cheerful side, huge armies were in training in the United States. A great expansion of ship repair and building was in progress. The munition output was increasing in both Britain and the United States.

---

1. *The British staff members were:* General Sir Alan Brooke, Chief of the British Imperial Staff; Major General Sir Hastings Ismay, Secretary of the Imperial Defense Council; Brigadier General G. M. Stewart, Director of Plans at the War Office. *The American military representatives were not officially named but presumably they were:* General George C. Marshall, Army Chief of Staff; Admiral Ernest J. King, Commander in Chief of the United States Fleet; Lieutenant General Henry H. Arnold, Chief of the Army Air Force.

The Second Front

The subject of the Second Front became an important matter at this conference. Previously, on February 26, 1942, Maxim Litvinov, the Soviet Ambassador to the United States, in an address before the Overseas Press Club in New York, urged the United Nations to launch simultaneous offensives against the Axis on two or more widely separated fronts.[2]

Some American forces had been landed in England and on April 3, 1942, the President sent General Marshall, Lieutenant Colonel Albert C. Wedemeyer, and Harry Hopkins to London to secure British approval of the joint second front. They returned to Washington with an agreement to proceed on that basis.[3]

On May 29, 1942, over two weeks before the Second Washington Conference, Molotov had arrived in Washington, having stopped in London en route. One of the objects of his mission was to press for the second front.

Sherwood, from Hopkins' notes, says that as the result of Molotov's urging:

> The President then put to General Marshall the query whether developments were clear enough so that we could say to Mr. Stalin that we are preparing a second front. "Yes," replied the General. The President then authorized Mr. Molotov to inform Mr. Stalin that we expect the formation of a second front this year [1942].[4]

This promise was repeated by Mr. Roosevelt a few days later[5] (June 11) in a statement released from the White House about Molotov's visit.

> ... This visit ... afforded an opportunity for a friendly exchange of views. ...
>
> In the course of the conversations full understanding was reached with regard to the urgent tasks of creating a second front in Europe in 1942. ...[6]

Churchill left the Second Washington Conference on June 25, having given limited approval to the President's second front commitment. However, fifteen days earlier, on June 10, when Molotov had stopped in London

---

2. *New York Times,* February 27, 1942. Address to Overseas Press Club in New York City.

3. General Albert C. Wedemeyer in his book *Wedemeyer Reports!* [Henry Holt & Company, 1948] gives a detailed account of these negotiations on pp. 97, 105, 112, 114–134.

4. [Robert E.] Sherwood, *Roosevelt and Hopkins* [New York: Harper & Brothers,: 1948], p. 563.

5. Ibid., p. 574.

6. [Samuel I. Rosenman, comp.,] *The Public Papers and Addresses of Franklin D. Roosevelt,* 1942 [volume] [Harper & Brothers Publishers, New York: 1950], pp. 268–269.

on his return journey to Moscow, he had been given a carefully worded *aide-mémoire* from Mr. Churchill which stated the British position in a somewhat different light. It said in part:

> We are making preparations for a landing on the Continent in August or September, 1942. . . . Clearly however it would not further either the Russian cause or that of the Allies as a whole if, for the sake of action at any price, we embarked on some operation which ended in disaster. . . . It is impossible to say in advance whether the situation will be such as to make this operation feasible when the time comes. *We can therefore give no promise in the matter. . . .*[7]

On July 16, General Marshall, Admiral King, and Harry Hopkins flew to London at President Roosevelt's request,[8] but they failed to secure a change in the Prime Minister's mind. Finally, the decision was made to postpone the second front until 1943.

On July 18, Stalin was sent a message from Churchill which outlined present and future naval operations but did not mention the proposed "second front." Marshal Stalin replied to Churchill on July 23, 1942, saying:

> I gather from the message . . . that despite the agreed Anglo-Soviet Communiqué on the adoption of urgent measures to open a second front in 1942, the British Government is putting off the operation till 1943. . . .
>
> As to . . . opening a second front in Europe, I fear the matter is taking an improper turn. In view of the situation on the Soviet-German front, I state most emphatically that the Soviet Government cannot tolerate the second front in Europe being postponed till 1943.[9]

Churchill and Harriman flew to Moscow on August 12 to explain the decision to Stalin that there would be no second front in 1942. Harriman reported to Washington the following day that Stalin was almost insulting, saying:

> Last night the Prime Minister and I had an extended meeting with Stalin. Also present were Molotov, Voroshilov and the British Ambassador. British

---

7. [Winston S.] Churchill, *The Hinge of Fate* [Houghton Mifflin Company, Boston: 1950], p. 342. Also quoted in Sherwood, *Roosevelt and Hopkins*, p. 577. See also Chester Wilmot, *The Struggle for Europe* [Harper & Brothers, New York: 1952], p. 105.

8. [Ernest J.] King and [Walter Muir] Whitehill, *Fleet Admiral King* [W. W. Norton & Company, Inc., New York: 1952], pp. 400–401. See also Sherwood, *Roosevelt and Hopkins*, p. 606.

9. [U.S.S.R., Ministry of Foreign Affairs,] *Stalin's Correspondence* [*With Churchill, Attlee, Roosevelt and Truman, 1941–1945*] [Lawrence & Wishart, London: 1950], Vol. I, p. 56.

and American strategic plans for the rest of 1942 and 1943 and their effect on the Russian military situation formed the center of the discussion.

It is my belief that, considering all the circumstances, the discussion could not have been better developed nor more satisfactory conclusions reached. Churchill explained the various possibilities of SLEDGEHAMMER [the second front] and the reasons for its postponement in full detail and told of the plans for and proposed strength of the major trans-Channel operation.

At every point Stalin took issue with a degree of bluntness almost amounting to insult. He made such remarks as—that you cannot win wars if you are afraid of the Germans and unwilling to take risks. . . .[10]

At this meeting in the Kremlin on August 13, Stalin handed copies of an *aide-mémoire* to Churchill and Harriman which again insisted on a second front in 1942.

Sherwood states that:

From that point on, the visitors from the West encountered "very rough sledding," as Harriman put it. . . . It was at this point that Stalin made the observation that if the British infantry would only fight the Germans as the Russians had done—and indeed as the R.A.F. had done—it would not be so frightened of them. Churchill said, "I pardon that remark only on account of the bravery of the Russian troops."[11]

Despite all this acrimony regarding the second front, it went over until 1943. Lt. General Anders, who commanded the Polish armies in Russia and later on the Italian front, makes the following comment on the Russian situation at this time in his book:

. . . Russian losses in killed, wounded, and prisoners of war were so great that on January 1, 1942 the Red Army had no more than 2,300,000 men. . . . Perhaps even greater were her losses in equipment and war matériel; for to the losses on the battle fields should be added the losses caused by the fall of large industrial areas into German hands. . . . In this respect, the Soviet Union was aided by her Western Allies, whose gigantic supplies enabled her to pass through the critical period until the transplanted industries behind the Ural were in position to function again. How feeble the Red Army

---

10. Sherwood, *Roosevelt and Hopkins,* p. 617.
11. Ibid., p. 620.

had become is best shown by the fact that until [near] the end of 1942 the initiative remained in German hands.[12]

The Atomic Bomb

After the formal Second Washington Conference, June 18 to 25, President Roosevelt and Prime Minister Churchill continued their talks at Hyde Park, where they discussed the atomic bomb.

In his book, *Roosevelt and Hopkins,* Sherwood states:

> One subject that came up during their first talks at Hyde Park was not mentioned in this press release nor in any other public statement until four months after Roosevelt's death [April, 1945]: the progress of experiments on the fission of uranium. "This difficult and novel project," as Churchill then called it, was known by the British code name of "Tube Alloys" and the American designation of "S-one." Churchill later cabled Hopkins concerning the discussions at this time, "My whole understanding was that everything was on the basis of fully sharing the results as equal partners. I have no record, but I shall be much surprised if the President's recollection does not square with this."[13]

The Prime Minister's views of the origin of research for the bomb do not agree with the American historians, but the fact that the possibility of the bomb was discussed in June, 1942, at Hyde Park is of historic interest, as is also Churchill's claim of the pledge to pool the results of research and production.

Churchill states in his book:

> We had reached this point when I joined the President at Hyde Park. I had my papers with me, but the discussion was postponed till the next day, the 20th, as the President needed more information from Washington. . . .
>
> I told the President in general terms of the great progress we had made, and that our scientists were now definitely convinced that results might be reached before the end of the present war. . . . We both felt painfully the dangers of doing nothing. We knew what efforts the Germans were making to procure supplies of "heavy water"—a sinister term, eerie, unnatural, which began to creep into our secret papers. . . .

---

12. [Wladyslaw] Anders, *Hitler's Defeat in Russia* (Henry Regnery Company, Chicago: 1953), p. 80.
13. Sherwood, *Roosevelt and Hopkins,* p. 593.

I strongly urged that we should at once pool all our information, work together on equal terms, and share the results, if any, equally between us. The question then arose as to where the research plant was to be set up. . . . We therefore took this decision jointly, and settled a basis of agreement. . . . I have no doubt that it was the progress that we had made in Britain and the confidence of our scientists in ultimate success, imparted to the President, that led him to his grave and fateful decision.[14]

A Major Shift in Strategy

At this conference the Prime Minister proposed consideration of a shift in strategy to an attack upon French North Africa which later was named TORCH. I give an account of this development and action upon this idea in Chapter 45.

The communiqué issued after the conference:

WASHINGTON, June 27—The text of the joint statement by President Roosevelt and Prime Minister Churchill today follows:

The week of conferences between the President and the Prime Minister covered very fully all of the major problems of the war which is conducted by the United Nations on every continent and in every sea.

We have taken full cognizance of our disadvantages as well as our advantages. We do not underrate the task.

We have conducted our conferences with the full knowledge of the power and resourcefulness of our enemies.

In the matter of the production of munitions of all kinds, the survey gives, on the whole, an optimistic picture. The previously planned monthly output has not reached the maximum but is fast approaching it on schedule.

Because of the wide extension of the war to all parts of the world, transportation of the fighting forces, together with the transportation of munitions of war and supplies still constitutes the major problem of the United Nations.

While submarine warfare on the part of the Axis continues to take heavy toll of cargo ships, the actual production of new tonnage is greatly increasing month by month. It is hoped that as a result of the steps planned at this conference the respective navies will further reduce the toll of merchant shipping.

14. Churchill, *The Hinge of Fate,* pp. 379–381.

The United Nations have never been in such hearty and detailed agreement on plans for winning the war as they are today.

We recognize and applaud the Russian resistance to the main attack being made by Germany and we rejoice in the magnificent resistance of the Chinese Army. Detailed discussions were held with our military advisers on methods to be adopted against Japan and the relief of China.

While exact plans, for obvious reasons, cannot be disclosed, it can be said that the coming operations which were discussed in detail at our Washington conferences, between ourselves and our respective military advisers, will divert German strength form the attack on Russia.

The Prime Minister and the President have met twice before, first in August, 1941, and again in December, 1941. There is no doubt in their minds that the over-all picture is more favorable to victory than it was either in August or December of last year.[15]

---

15. *New York Times,* June 28, 1942.

CHAPTER 45

The Development of TORCH (the North African Campaign)

THE BASIC STRATEGY of the war in Europe was at all times the second front in France. For that purpose American forces were poured into England as rapidly as possible. In the meantime, there was insufficient strength to make the grand attack on the Germans across the Channel.

At the Second Washington Conference Prime Minister Churchill pressed for the attack on French North Africa (named TORCH). He proposed that the forces be supported by the British and American naval and air strength.[1]

There was considerable doubt as to the wisdom of TORCH. General Wedemeyer says:

> All of us felt with Marshall that the decision to invade North Africa was a radical change, practically a repudiation of the over-all strategy that had been agreed to earlier by the British. . . .
>
> TORCH was a wasteful side show. But it was, tactically speaking, a grand success.[2]

General Mark Clark says in his book that Prime Minister Churchill was determined to block the cross-Channel invasion favored by the American military. He says:

> Both Ike and I felt that direct action was the best idea and that it was necessary to carry the war to the European continent as directly and as quickly as possible. . . . we felt that . . . [TORCH] would detract from whatever hope

---

1. The planning and execution of TORCH was one of the most brilliant operations in the war, and credit for its success was due to Generals Dwight D. Eisenhower, Albert C. Wedemeyer, Mark W. Clark, George S. Patton, Jr., and James Doolittle. The British Generals Sir Bernard Montgomery, Sir Harold Alexander, Sir Alan Brooke, and Air Marshal Sir Charles Portal deserve equal credit.

2. General Albert C. Wedemeyer, *Wedemeyer Reports!*, pp. 163–170. [*Editor's note:* For a full citation, see footnote 4.]

there was of striking directly at Europe with a limited invasion program in 1942, or of mounting a large-scale invasion operation in 1943.[3]

Nevertheless, Mr. Churchill got his way.

The French North African provinces were controlled by the German dominated Vichy Government. It was hoped that such French naval vessels as had taken refuge in these provinces and their army of about 150,000 men could be induced to join the Allies as part of the whole program of French liberation.

The French North African possessions included about 600 miles of the Atlantic coast and about 800 miles along the Mediterranean (and encircled about 200 miles more of the Mediterranean coast in Spanish Morocco). The German and Italian and French North African armies, under General Rommel, were in possession of about 1,000 miles of the Mediterranean coast eastward to the British armies in Egypt, which were under the command of General Sir Bernard Montgomery.

The British were badly out of favor with the French because of their attacks on Dakar and on French naval units outside of France. It was, therefore, concluded that if Americans should direct the operation, it would probably be more acceptable to the French in North Africa.

General Dwight D. Eisenhower, then in charge of the American forces in England, was made Allied Commander-in-Chief of the operation. He appointed General Mark W. Clark as his deputy and placed General George S. Patton, Jr., in command of the American landing forces that would make the attack.[4]

The American Consul General in Algiers, Robert D. Murphy, had been instructed to undertake negotiations with the French military leaders.

Good fortune came to the Allies in the midst of these operations when in October, 1942, the British Eighth Army in Egypt, under General Montgomery, launched an attack upon General Rommel's German, Italian and local French forces at El Alamein and inflicted a great defeat upon them. Arthur Bryant, in his book, *The Turn of the Tide*, gives the following details of the victory:

---

3. General Mark W. Clark, *Calculated Risk*, p. 28. [*Editor's note:* For a full citation, see footnote 4.]

4. I have dealt with the operation in North Africa only so far as it related to the whole world struggle. I have omitted the long and tedious details of negotiations with the French officials in North Africa as these do not concern the purpose of this memoir. Detailed accounts are to be found in General Eisenhower's book, *Crusade in Europe* (Doubleday and Company, New York: 1948); Prime Minister Churchill's account, *The Hinge of Fate* (Houghton Mifflin Company, Boston: 1950); General Mark Clark's book *Calculated Risk* (Harper and Brothers, New York: 1950); also, General Albert Wedemeyer's book, *Wedemeyer Reports!* (Henry Holt and Company, New York: 1958).

... 30,000 prisoners, 350 tanks and 400 guns had been taken in the Western Desert. Rommel and the remnants of the Afrika Korps were in full retreat, four German and eight Italian divisions had ceased to exist. . . .[5]

An American landing in French Morocco was made on November 8, 1942, by an expeditionary force directly from the United States. It met with some opposition, especially from the French navy, but it nevertheless quickly occupied Morocco. Landings of General Eisenhower's American forces from England were made at points in Algiers from November 8 to November 12. Some opposition arose, but on November 11 Admiral Jean François Darlan, the French Governor-General of Algiers, signed a cease-fire agreement with General Mark Clark. General Clark also persuaded Pierre Boisson, Governor-General of French West Africa, to surrender that province. Admiral Darlan was assassinated by a fanatic on December 24 and was succeeded by General Henri H. Giraud, who was approved by the Allies.

A general conference of Allied leaders was called to be held at Casablanca on January 14, 1943.

5. Arthur Bryant, *The Turn of the Tide* (Doubleday and Company, Inc., Garden City, New York: 1957), p. 422.

CHAPTER **46**

The Casablanca Conference

January 14 to January 24, 1943

THE CONFERENCE BEGAN on January 14, 1943. The principals present were President Roosevelt and Prime Minister Churchill.[1] Marshal Stalin was unable to come.

The Military Situation

In North Africa the Allies were still fighting General Rommel's armies to the east at the time of the Conference.

In Russia, the Germans had been defeated at Stalingrad in November 1942 and the remainder of their troops in that sector had been surrendered to the Russians.

General Anders said of it:

---

1. *The United States staff members were:* Harry Hopkins, Chairman of the British-American Munitions Assignments Board; W. Averell Harriman, United States Defense Expediter in England; Robert Murphy, United States Minister to French North Africa; General George C. Marshall, Chief of Staff of the United States Army; Admiral Ernest J. King, Commander in Chief of the United States Navy; Lieutenant General Henry H. Arnold, commanding the United States Army Air Forces; Lieutenant General B. B. Somervell, Commanding General of the Services of Supply, United States Army; Lieutenant General Dwight D. Eisenhower, Commander in Chief of the Allied Expeditionary Force in North Africa; Lieutenant General Mark W. Clark, United States Army [Commander of the United States Fifth Army in Tunisia]; Lieutenant General F. M. Andrews, United States Army; Major General Carl Spaatz, Air Commander of the Allied Expeditionary Force in North Africa.

The British staff members were: Lord Leathers, British Minister of War Transport; Admiral of the Fleet Sir Dudley Pound, First Sea Lord; General Sir Alan Brooke, Chief of the Imperial General Staff; Air Chief Marshal Sir Charles Portal, Chief of the Air Staff; Field Marshal Sir John Dill, head of the British Joint Staff Mission in Washington; Vice Admiral Lord Louis Mountbatten, Chief of Combined Operations; Lt. Gen. Sir Hastings Ismay, Chief of Staff to the Office of the Minister of Defense; Harold Macmillan, British Resident Minister for Allied Headquarters in North Africa; Admiral of the Fleet Sir Andrew Cunningham, Naval Commander of the Allied Expeditionary Force in North Africa; General Sir Harold Alexander; Air Chief Marshal Sir Arthur Tedder.

The battle of Stalingrad was the turning point of the German-Soviet war; its consequences were tremendous, especially in the military, psychological, and political fields. For Germany it was a blow from which she never recovered....[2]

In the Pacific the forces under General Douglas MacArthur had achieved success in New Guinea and the Solomon Islands, notably at Guadalcanal.

At the time of Casablanca, the Japanese were in occupation of northern and central China and all the Pacific seaboard of China. The Chinese Nationalist Government under Chiang Kai-shek had been compelled to retreat to Chungking in Szechwan Province where they established their headquarters. The Chinese Communists under Mao Tse-tung, with their headquarters in north China at Yenan, were systematically extending their area in China. The Nationalists were thus fighting on two fronts—Japanese and Communist.

The Allied Merchant Marine continued to suffer great losses from attacks by enemy submarines and surface raiders. Fortunately, ship construction facilities were increasing.

Military Plans at Casablanca

It was decided at the conference that:

The defeat of the U-boat must remain a first charge on the resources of the United Nations....[3]

It was also determined that the next military operation would be an invasion of Italy, beginning with an attack on Sicily.

---

2. General Wladyslaw Anders, *Hitler's Defeat in Russia* (Chicago: Henry Regnery Company, 1953), p. 153. General Anders also quotes (pp. 47–48) from the diary of General Halder of the German army. It indicates that the German situation was not entirely comfortable at this time. General Halder said: "The whole situation makes it increasingly plain that we have underestimated the Russian colossus, who consistently prepared for war with that utterly ruthless determination so characteristic of totalitarian States. This applies to organisational and economic resources, as well as the communication system, and most of all to the strictly military potential. At the outset of the war we reckoned with about 200 enemy divisions. Now we have already counted 360. These divisions indeed are not armed and equipped according to our standards and their tactical leadership is often poor. But there they are, and if we smash a dozen of them, the Russians simply put up another dozen.... And so our troops, sprawled over an immense frontline, without any depth, are subjected to the incessant attacks of the enemy. Sometimes those are successful, because too many gaps must be left open in these enormous spaces." ([Franz Halder], The Halder Diaries, VII, 36).

3. Winston S. Churchill, *The Hinge of Fate* [Houghton Mifflin Company, Boston: 1950], p. 692. See pp. 692–693 for a summary of the main decisions of the Chiefs of Staff and a letter attached by the President and Prime Minister. See also Arthur Bryant, *The Turn of the Tide* [Doubleday & Company, Inc., Garden City, N.Y.: 1957], pp. 457–459.

Regarding the second front, the Casablanca plans called for only a limited offensive in August 1943, *if practicable;* in the meantime gathering forces in England to invade the continent whenever German strength should be sufficiently weakened.[4]

After Casablanca Churchill, explaining that he was authorized to speak for Roosevelt as well, telegraphed Stalin on February 9, 1943:

> . . . We are . . . pushing preparations to the limit of our resources for a cross-Channel operation in August, in which British and United States units would participate. Here . . . shipping and assault-landing craft will be the limiting factors. If the operation is delayed by the weather or other reasons, it will be prepared with stronger forces for September. The timing of this attack must, of course, be dependent upon the condition of German defensive possibilities across the Channel at that time.[5]

Stalin was not satisfied with this vague promise of August or September as the date for the cross-Channel operation. In messages to the President and Prime Minister, he expressed impatience for a "blow from the West . . . in spring or early summer"[6] of 1943 to relieve the pressure on the Russian front.

As an aid to China it was proposed to attack the Japanese armies in Burma which had cut off the supply load from India to Chiang Kai-shek. This attack was to be made by the British army from India, an amphibious landing on the coast of Burma, and a simultaneous attack by the Chinese armies, supported by American air forces. The timing for this attack went over until the succeeding Third Washington Conference.

The Casablanca Communiqué

The official communiqué from the Casablanca Conference was released to the press on January 26, 1943. After listing the names of the persons attending the conference, the communiqué continued:

> For ten days the combined staffs have been in constant session, meeting two or three times a day and recording progress at intervals to the President and Prime Minister.

---

4. Winston S. Churchill, *The Hinge of Fate,* p. 693.

5. [U.S.S.R., Ministry of Foreign Affairs,] *Stalin's Correspondence with Churchill, Attlee, Roosevelt and Truman, 1941–1945* [Lawrence & Wishart, London: 1958], Vol. II, pp. 54–55.

6. Ibid., p. 56.

The entire field of the war was surveyed theatre by theatre throughout the world, and all resources were marshaled for a more intense prosecution of the war by sea, land, and air.

Nothing like this prolonged discussion between two allies has ever taken place before. Complete agreement was reached between the leaders of the two countries and their respective staffs upon war plans and enterprises to be undertaken during the campaigns of 1943 against Germany, Italy and Japan with a view to drawing the utmost advantage from the markedly favorable turn of events at the close of 1942.

Premier Stalin was cordially invited to meet the President and Prime Minister, in which case the meeting would have been held very much farther to the east. He was unable to leave Russia at this time on account of the great offensive which he himself, as Commander in Chief, is directing.

The President and Prime Minister realized up to the full the enormous weight of the war which Russia is successfully bearing along her whole land front, and their prime object has been to draw as much weight as possible off the Russian armies by engaging the enemy as heavily as possible at the best selected points.

Premier Stalin has been fully informed of the military proposals.

The President and Prime Minister have been in communication with Generalissimo Chiang Kai-shek. They have apprised him of the measures which they are undertaking to assist him in China's magnificent and unrelaxing struggle for the common cause.

The occasion of the meeting between the President and Prime Minister made it opportune to invite General Giraud [General Henri Honoré Giraud, High Commissioner of French Africa] to confer with the Combined Chiefs of Staff and to arrange for a meeting between him and General de Gaulle. . . . The two generals have been in close consultation.

The President and Prime Minister and their combined staffs, having completed their plans for the offensive campaigns of 1943, have now separated in order to put them into active and concerted execution.[7]

The documentation of the conference has not yet been published by the State Department, although it was held almost twenty years ago. However, what took place can be gleaned from the military records, the press releases and from statements of participants in the Conference.[8]

---

7. *New York Times,* January 27, 1943.
8. The official [U.S. Department of State] volume of documents on the Cairo and Tehran Conferences of 1943, released June 17, 1961, p. 434n, reports that "The records of the Casablanca

The Declaration of Unconditional Surrender

The Casablanca Conference was primarily concerned with military affairs. However, out of this conference came the historic demand of Unconditional Surrender.

On January 24, at the close of the official meetings, President Roosevelt and Prime Minister Churchill held a press conference. At the end of the conference President Roosevelt added informally that there was another matter he wished to discuss. He said that he and Prime Minister Churchill

> were determined to accept nothing less than the unconditional surrender of Germany, Japan and Italy. . . .[9]

Churchill says:

> It was with some feeling of surprise that I heard the President say at the Press Conference on January 24 that we would enforce "unconditional surrender" upon all our enemies. . . . General Ismay . . . was also surprised. In my speech which followed the President's I of course supported him and concurred in what he had said. . . .[10]

Churchill quotes Harry Hopkins who reported that the President said to him:

> . . . then suddenly the Press Conference was on, and Winston and I had had no time to prepare for it, and the thought popped into my mind that they had called Grant "Old Unconditional Surrender," and the next thing I knew I had said it.[11]

Sherwood, basing his statement on the notes of Hopkins (who was present), says:

> Roosevelt himself absolved Churchill from all responsibility for the statement. Indeed, he suggested that it was an unpremeditated one on his own part. . . .[12]

Conference of January 1943 are scheduled to be published subsequently in another volume of the *Foreign Relations* series."

9. [Robert E.] Sherwood, *Roosevelt and Hopkins* [Harper & Brothers, New York: 1948], pp. 693–4.

10. Winston S. Churchill *The Hinge of Fate*, pp. 686–687.

11. Ibid., p. 687. Also, see Robert E. Sherwood's *Roosevelt and Hopkins*, p. 696.

12. Robert E. Sherwood, *Roosevelt and Hopkins*, p. 696.

The Chiefs of Staff were apparently not consulted. Admiral William D. Leahy, in his book, says:

> . . . As far as I could learn, this policy had not been discussed with the Combined Chiefs and, from a military viewpoint, its execution might add to our difficulties in succeeding campaigns because it would mean that we would have to destroy the enemy. . . . Before the war was over, there were occasions when it might have been advantageous to accept conditional surrender in some areas, but we were not permitted to do it.[13]

It would appear from these quotations that Mr. Roosevelt was the sole author. However, Mr. Churchill, in another statement, says he had authorized Mr. Roosevelt to make the statement on his behalf:

> It was only after full and cold, sober and mature consideration . . . that the President, with my full concurrence as agent of the War Cabinet, decided that the note of the Casablanca Conference should be the unconditional surrender of all our foes. Our inflexible insistence upon unconditional surrender does not mean that we shall stain our victorious arms by any cruel treatment of whole populations. . . .[14]

On February 12, 1943, Mr. Roosevelt repeated his slogan of "unconditional surrender" in an address to the White House Correspondents' Association.[15]

Some Consequences of the "Unconditional Surrender" Ultimatum

The "unconditional surrender" slogan continued to echo throughout the war. I may well complete the subject here rather than to constantly interrupt the text to relate incidents which flowed from it.

General Albert C. Wedemeyer, who at the time of Casablanca was in the War Plans Division of the General Staff of the United States Army, states in his book that he said at the time of Mr. Roosevelt's statement:

> . . . that unconditional surrender would unquestionably compel the Germans to fight to the very last. This worried me, for I was confident that there were

---

13. William D. Leahy, *I Was There* [McGraw-Hill Book Company, Inc., New York: 1950], p. 145.

14. Winston S. Churchill, *Onwards to Victory* [Little, Brown and Company, Boston: 1944], p. 25.

15. [Samuel I. Rosenman, comp.,] *The Public Papers and Addresses of Franklin D. Roosevelt,* 1943 [volume] [Harper & Brothers Publishers, New York: 1950], p. 80.

many people in Germany—more than we were permitted to realize because of anti-German as distinct from anti-Nazi propaganda—who wanted to get rid of Hitler. Our demand for unconditional surrender would only weld all of the Germans together. . . .[16]

Sherwood relates that seven months after the Casablanca Conference (August 1943) Hopkins took a memorandum from top military levels in Washington to the First Quebec Conference. The memorandum stated that the result of the "unconditional surrender" policy would be to destroy Germany and thus Russia would dominate Europe after the end of the war.[17]

Mr. Roosevelt, also, seems to have become fearful of the effects of his pronouncement. He made the following statement in August, 1943:

> The people of Axis-controlled areas may be assured that when they agree to unconditional surrender they will not be trading Axis despotism for ruin under the United Nations. The goal of the United Nations is to permit liberated peoples to create a free political life of their own choosing and to attain economic security. These are two of the great objectives of the Atlantic Charter.[18]

Stalin, who had not been consulted on unconditional surrender, protested it. At Tehran, ten months after Casablanca, a memorandum of his views said in part:

> As a war time measure Marshal Stalin questioned the advisability of the unconditional surrender principle with no definition of the exact terms which would be imposed upon Germany. He felt that to leave the principle of unconditional surrender unclarified merely served to unite the German people, whereas to draw up specific terms, no matter how harsh, and tell the German people that this was what they would have to accept, would, in his opinion, hasten the day of German capitulation.[19]

Hull states[20] that following Tehran, on December 17, 1943, he received a cable from a member of General Eisenhower's staff which said that they

---

16. [Albert C. Wedemeyer,] *Wedemeyer Reports!* (Henry Holt and Company, New York: 1958), p. 186.

17. Robert E. Sherwood, *Roosevelt and Hopkins*, pp. 748–749. See Chapter ___. [*Editor's note:* Hoover did not fill in this cross-reference.]

18. *New York Times*, August 26, 1943.

19. Sherwood, *Roosevelt and Hopkins*, pp. 782–783.

20. *The Memoirs of Cordell Hull* [The Macmillan Company, New York: 1948], Vol. II, pp. 1571–1572.

understood that at Tehran, Stalin and Churchill had objected to the principle of "unconditional surrender." Roosevelt told Hull that we would not revise the term.[21]

Hull apparently raised the question again with Mr. Roosevelt in the middle of January, 1944, proposing "conversations to define the term." The President in a reply dated January 17 refused.[22]

On February 22, 1944, in a speech in the House of Commons, Churchill sought to soften the German reaction to Roosevelt's pronouncement:

> Here I may point out that the term "unconditional surrender" does not mean that the German people will be enslaved or destroyed. . . .[23]

Public Criticism

Hanson W. Baldwin, military editor of the *New York Times,* gives us his view as follows:

> . . . [Unconditional surrender] was perhaps the biggest political mistake of the war. In the First World War Wilson took care to distinguish between the Kaiser and the militaristic Junkers class and the German people; in the Second, Stalin drew a clear line between Hitler and the Nazis, and the German people, and even the German Army. The opportunity of driving a wedge between rulers and ruled, so clearly seized by Wilson and by Stalin, was muffed by Roosevelt and Churchill. Unconditional surrender was an open invitation to unconditional resistance; it discouraged opposition to Hitler, probably lengthened the war, cost us lives, and helped to lead to the present abortive peace. . . .
>
> Unconditional surrender was a policy of political bankruptcy, which delayed our military objective—victory—and confirmed our lack of a reasoned program for peace. It cost us dearly in lives and time, and its essentially negative concept has handicapped the development of a positive peace program.
>
> By endorsing the policy, we abandoned any pragmatic political aims; victory, as defined in these terms, could not possibly mean a more stable peace, for "unconditional surrender" meant, as Liddell Hart has noted, the "complete disappearance of any European balance. . . ."

---

21. Ibid., pp. 1576–1577.
22. [Elliott Roosevelt, ed.,] *F.D.R., His Personal Letters,* [*1928–1945,*] Vol. II [Duell, Sloan and Pearce, New York: 1950], p. 1485.
23. *New York Herald Tribune,* February 23, 1944.

Unconditional surrender could only mean unlimited war, and unlimited war has never meant—save in the days when Rome sowed the fields of Carthage with salt and destroyed her rival with fire and sword—a more stable peace.

This political policy, coupled with a military policy of promiscuous destruction by strategic bombing, could not help but sow the dragon's teeth of future trouble.[24]

B. H. Liddell Hart, a British military writer, stated that in his postwar interviews with German generals

All to whom I talked dwelt on the effect of the Allies' "unconditional surrender" policy in prolonging the war. They told me that but for this they and their troops—the factor that was more important—would have been ready to surrender sooner, separately or collectively. . . .[25]

The German underground opposed to Hitler, as noted by Albrecht von Kessel in his diary, felt that the unconditional surrender formula greatly handicapped their efforts. Kessel writes:

. . . our slogan made it most difficult to drive a wedge between Hitler and the German people. . . .[26]

The effect of "Unconditional Surrender" upon the Allied invasion of Italy is given by Lord Hankey, a member of the British War Cabinet, as follows:

While these interminable delays, due largely to Unconditional Surrender were taking place, and while the Allied politicians were continuing to harass, by their meticulous insistence on a barren formula, the man [Badoglio] who had risked his life in carrying out their own advice, the very man from whom they had most to expect, the Germans were pouring divisions into Italy and building up step by step the defence that caused such terrible losses to the Allies and such dreadful destruction to the fairest land in Europe. What had been called the "soft" underbelly was thus turned by Unconditional Surrender into fortified positions. The time lost was to cost us dear.

---

24. Hanson W. Baldwin, *Great Mistakes of the War* [Harper & Brothers, New York: 1950], pp. 14, 24–25.

25. B. H. Liddell Hart, *The German Generals Talk* (William Morrow & Co., New York: 1948), pp. 292–293.

26. Albrecht von Kessel, in the German Foreign Office, "was on the fringes" of the anti-Hitler conspiracy in Germany. His diary was quoted in *Germany's Underground* by Allen W. Dulles (The Macmillan Company, New York: 1947), p. 132. [*Editor's note:* The quoted words in the text are actually those of Dulles, commenting on Kessel's viewpoint.]

Of Germany, he said:

> ... this unfortunate phrase prolonged the war for the German people to the last extremity of human endurance. Not one of the German leaders was willing to sign such humiliating terms as unconditional surrender. . . .

He summarized the results of the declaration:

> ... lengthening and embittering the war, bleeding our country needlessly and making it impossible to conclude a real and lasting peace.[27]

Early in 1943 Count Francisco Gomez Jordana y Souza, Spanish Foreign Minister, sent a memorandum to the British Ambassador, Sir Samuel Hoare, which contained the following prophetic words:

> ... If events develop in the future as they have up to now, it would be Russia which will penetrate deeply into German territory. And we ask the question: if this should occur, which is the greater danger not only for the continent but for England herself, a Germany not totally defeated and with sufficient strength to serve as a rampart against Communism, a Germany hated by all her neighbours, which would deprive her of authority though she remained intact, or a Sovietized Germany which would certainly furnish Russia with the added strength of her war preparations, her engineers, her specialised workmen and technicians, which would enable Russia to extend herself with an empire without precedent from the Atlantic to the Pacific? . . . And we ask a second question: is there anybody in the centre of Europe, in that mosaic of countries without consistency or unity, bled moreover by war and foreign domination, who could contain the ambitions of Stalin: There is certainly no one. . . .[28]

Allen W. Dulles, who represented the United States in Europe in charge of war propaganda and underground contacts, wrote:

> ... Goebbels quickly twisted it [unconditional surrender] into the formula "total slavery," and very largely succeeded in making the German people believe that was what unconditional surrender meant.

---

27. The Right Hon. Lord Hankey, *Politics, Trials and Errors* (Henry Regnery Company, Chicago: 1950), pp. 45, 50.

28. Rt. Hon. Sir Samuel Hoare, *Complacent Dictator* (Alfred A. Knopf, New York: 1947), pp. 183–184.

... the Goebbelses and Bormanns were able to use "unconditional surrender" to prolong a totally hopeless war for many months. . . .[29]

Edward C. W. von Selzam, a former member of the German foreign service, in a letter to the *New York Times,* in 1949, points out that the

> . . . declaration of "unconditional surrender" . . . drove most of the vacillating generals away from the opposition, and attached them for "better or worse" to Hitler, thus weakening detrimentally the cause of the opposition and strengthening considerably Hitler's power of resistance. In this, I contend, the real tragedy of the Casablanca Declaration is to be found.[30]

Lord Beaverbrook, a member of the British Cabinet, in an address at Toronto in mid-November, 1949, denounced "Unconditional Surrender" as the greatest blunder of the war and declared that it destroyed all prospects for peace and recovery.

General John R. Deane wrote:

> President Roosevelt's "Unconditional Surrender" slogan. . . . strengthened the propaganda statements of enemy leaders that they must continue the war to the bitter end as their only chance of survival. . . .[31]

---

29. Allen W. Dulles, *Germany's Underground,* pp. 132–133.
30. *New York Times,* July 31, 1949.
31. John R. Deane, *The Strange Alliance* (The Viking Press, New York: 1947), p. 162.

SECTION XII

The March of Conferences

CHAPTER 47

The Third Washington Conference
May 12 to May 25, 1943

AT THE THIRD Washington Conference (called TRIDENT), the principals were President Roosevelt and Prime Minister Churchill. When the conference dealt with Chinese matters, the Chinese Foreign Minister, T. V. Soong, was at times consulted.[1]

Information

The only official information given to the public relative to the proceedings of the conference was a statement by President Roosevelt on May 27, 1943:

> The conference of the Combined Staffs in Washington has ended in complete agreement on future operations in all theatres of the war.[2]

It was promised that the official records of the conference would be published, but up to this writing the proceedings have not been made public, although twenty years have passed. Vital political questions were dealt with at this conference; therefore, what took place must be gleaned from other sources.[3] Happily, Hopkins, Harriman, King, Leahy, Stilwell, and Chennault

---

1. The American staff present included: Harry L. Hopkins, W. Averell Harriman, General George C. Marshall, Admiral Ernest J. King, Admiral William D. Leahy, Lieut. Gen. Joseph W. Stilwell, Major Gen. Claire L. Chennault, Lieut. Gen. Joseph T. McNarney, General Henry H. Arnold.

The British staff included: General Sir Hastings L. Ismay, Admiral Sir Dudley Pound, General Sir Alan F. Brooke, Air Chief Marshal Sir Charles F. A. Portal, Admiral Sir James Somerville, Air Marshal Sir Richard Peirse, Lord Beaverbrook, Lord Cherwell, Lord Leathers.

2. *New York Times,* May 28, 1943.

3. It is stated in the *Cairo and Tehran Papers* that "The records of the Third Washington Conference of Roosevelt and Churchill, May 12–25, 1943, are scheduled to be published subsequently in another volume of the *Foreign Relations* series." ([U.S. Department of State,] *Foreign Relations of the United States, Diplomatic Papers, The Conferences at Cairo and Tehran, 1943,* United States Government Printing Office, Washington: 1961, p. 4.)

have written books in which each gives details of the conference from his own point of view.

The Military Situation

In the four months after the Casablanca Conference (January 1943), there was further improvement in the Allied situation. As to the submarine war, Chester Wilmot, in his book *The Struggle for Europe,* records that:

> A week after Casablanca, Hitler indicated his determination to intensify the attack on Allied shipping. . . . This . . . opened a new phase in the Battle of the Atlantic and, in a review of the situation in February, the [British] Admiralty wrote: "Never before has the enemy displayed such singleness of purpose in utilising his strength against one objective—the interruption of supplies from America to Great Britain. . . ."[4]

But Mr. Wilmot places the peak of the submarine struggle in March, 1943, when the initiative began to pass to the Allies, and states:

> . . . June 1943, as Churchill told the House of Commons, "was the best month from every point of view we have ever known in the whole forty-six months of the war [at sea]." At the time he could not disclose the figures which justified his confidence, but in fact the number of merchantmen sunk in the Atlantic had fallen from ninety in March, to forty in May, and to six in June.[5]

On the Russian front, a second Russian winter offensive against the Germans, following Stalingrad, was under way. In three months of fighting—from January to March, 1943—the losses of the Germans and their allies, in killed and captured, exceeded 500,000.[6] Despite this, the Germans opened a spring drive which temporarily checked the Russian tide.

On the Chinese front the major change was the expansion of the Mao Tse-tung Chinese Communist Republic of North China. At this time, it embraced about 60,000,000 people with an army of about 400,000 men. Meantime Chiang Kai-shek was losing ground fighting the Japanese. With the Burma

---

4. Chester Wilmot, *The Struggle for Europe* (Harper & Brothers Publishers, New York: 1952), p. 125.

5. Ibid., p. 127.

6. William L. Langer, *An Encyclopedia of World History* (Houghton Mifflin Company, Boston: 1948), p. 1153.

Road closed by the Japanese occupying Burma, Chiang was dependent for supplies on the American airlift—a most difficult operation.[7]

At this Third Washington Conference, the question of the time and place for opening the cross-channel second front arose again. It was decided that the attack should once more be postponed—from the spring of 1943 until May, 1944.[8] Stalin did not react favorably to this further postponement.[9] Robert Sherwood reported that:

> ... Stalin received copies of the full plans drawn up at the TRIDENT conference [as to the Second Front] and he was evidently not impressed. In the latter part of June—I do not know the exact date—he sent Churchill a cable in which he reviewed at length all the assurances that had been given during the past thirteen months relative to the opening of a Second Front, and concluded with words which could be interpreted only as charges of deliberate bad faith by the Western Allies.
>
> Churchill usually consulted Roosevelt on the text of any important cable that he was sending to Stalin and there was often ... discussion back and forth ... on the precise choice of words. But now Churchill was evidently so angry that he sent off a scorching cable to which Roosevelt would never have agreed had he been given a chance to read it in advance. During this period of tension, Stalin recalled Litvinov from Washington, and Maisky from London....[10]

Sherwood's statement is confirmed in the book, *Stalin's Correspondence with Churchill, Attlee, Roosevelt and Truman, 1941–45,* which gives the actual message to Churchill on June 24, 1943, from Stalin. It reminded Churchill and Roosevelt of their previous assurances about opening the second front in 1943, and concluded:

> ... I must tell you that the point here is not just the disappointment of the Soviet Government, but the preservation of its confidence in its Allies, a confidence which is being subjected to severe stress. One should not forget

---

7. Many American airmen died in the loss of 468 transports, but they delivered over 730,000 tons of supplies before the end of the war in 1945. See Lin Yutang, *The Vigil of a Nation* ([The John Day Company], New York: 1945), p. 119; Claire L. Chennault, *Way of a Fighter* (G. P. Putnam's Sons, New York: 1949), p. 234.

8. Fleet Admiral William D. Leahy, *I Was There* (Whittlesey House, New York: 1950), p. 161.

9. [U.S.S.R., Ministry of Foreign Affairs,] *Stalin's Correspondence with Churchill, Attlee, Roosevelt and Truman, 1941–1945,* Vol. I (E. P. Dutton & Co., Inc., New York: 1958), pp. 131–132.

10. Robert E. Sherwood, *Roosevelt and Hopkins* (Harper & Brothers, New York: 1948), p. 734.

that it is a question of . . . reducing the enormous sacrifices of the Soviet armies, compared with which the sacrifices of the Anglo-American armies are insignificant.[11]

Churchill replied to Stalin on June 27, 1943, reviewing the problems confronting the Western Allies, and said:

. . . I am satisfied that I have done everything in human power to help you. Therefore the reproaches which you now cast upon your Western Allies leave me unmoved. Nor, apart from the damage to our military interests, should I have any difficulty in presenting my case to the British Parliament and the nation.[12]

China

The China situation was one of the major problems of this and subsequent conferences, and in them two American personalities—General Joseph W. Stilwell and General Claire L. Chennault—played leading roles.

General Joseph W. Stilwell

At Generalissimo Chiang Kai-shek's request, President Roosevelt on January 20, 1942, less than two months after American entry into the war, had appointed General Joseph W. Stilwell to be Chiang's military adviser. General Stilwell had many years before served as military attaché to the American Embassy in Peking. He spoke Chinese and had a store of information about China. He was a special protégé of the Chief of Staff, General George C. Marshall. General Stilwell was a well trained soldier of stormy temperament. By the time of this Conference he had developed a bitter antagonism toward Chiang Kai-shek, indications of which appear repeatedly in his diary.[13]

---

11. *Stalin's Correspondence with Churchill, Attlee, Roosevelt and Truman, 1941–45*, Vol. I, p. 138. Churchill's retort is also given therein on pp. 140–141. See also Vol. II, pp. 73–76. The recall of the Ambassadors recorded by Sherwood is confirmed in the book, *Admiral Ambassador to Russia* by William H. Standley and Arthur A. Ageton (Henry Regnery Company, Chicago: 1955), pp. 467–468 and 472.

12. *Stalin's Correspondence with Churchill, Attlee, Roosevelt and Truman, 1941–45*, Vol. I, pp. 140–141.

13. In 1948, after Stilwell's death, Mrs. Stilwell published a volume of passages from his diary and letters entitled *The Stilwell Papers* (William Sloane Associates, Inc., New York) [edited by Theodore H. White].

The conference adopted a proposal by Chennault to enlarge his air forces for attack on the Japanese and to expand the program of airlifting supplies from India. Stilwell opposed Chennault's projects as interfering with his proposed Burma campaign. Stimson, in his memoir, says:

> ... In spite of all opposition Chennault's view was approved. ... [14]

A presidential directive was issued ordering that Chennault's plans be carried out. General Chennault published his memoirs in 1949 and in them he describes Stilwell's refusal to carry out the President's directive.[15]

As an indication of Stilwell's attitude toward Chiang, in an entry in his diary referring to Chiang, Stilwell wrote:

> ... This insect, this stink in the nostrils, superciliously inquires what we will do, who are breaking our backs to help him, supplying everything—troops, equipment, planes, medical, signal, motor services, setting up his goddam SOS, training his lousy troops, bucking his bastardly chief of staff, and general staff, and he the Jovian Dictator, who starves his troops and who is the world's greatest ignoramus, picks flaws in our preparations. ... [16]

General Stilwell had been provided with five advisers by Secretary of State Cordell Hull—John Stewart Service, Raymond P. Ludden, Owen Lattimore, George Atcheson, and Lauchlin Currie.[17]

General Stilwell and these advisers developed the idea that there should be a political coalition of the Nationalists under Chiang Kai-shek and the Communists under Mao Tse-tung which, they claimed, would bring a unification of Chinese military might against Japan. Their proposed first step was that Chiang Kai-shek should accept two members in his cabinet appointed by Mao Tse-tung.

Stilwell's group was supported in these ideas by the American Ambassador at Chungking, Clarence E. Gauss. In pursuit of this coalition, Stilwell dispatched John P. Davies, an American Embassy official, to Mao Tse-tung's headquarters in Yenan to negotiate with him. Desperate and dependent on American support, Chiang raised no objection to this mission but he resolutely refused to accept Communist representatives into his Cabinet.

---

14. Henry L. Stimson and McGeorge Bundy, *On Active Service in Peace and War* (Harper & Brothers, New York: 1948), p. 534.

15. Claire Lee Chennault, *Way of A Fighter*, pp. 220–221, 224.

16. *The Stilwell Papers*, p. 210.

17. The Communist leanings or activities of these men is given in Chapter 4 of this memoir.

Stilwell and his advisers, consciously or unconsciously, became a political pressure group—a sort of cabal of more than military objectives. As shown later, they began a campaign of denunciation of Chiang as a corrupt reactionary and lauded Mao Tse-tung as an agrarian reformer.

General Claire L. Chennault

Captain Claire L. Chennault, a U.S. Army Air Corps officer, retired from the army early in 1937, and in the same year went to China. He became Chiang Kai-shek's aviation adviser and in 1941 founded the American volunteer air group in the Chinese army who later became known as the "Flying Tigers." They performed brilliant service and when the United States entered the war four years later Chennault was reinstated in the American army and by the time of this conference had been promoted to the rank of Major-General and was in command of all the Chinese Air Force. Chennault was an ardent supporter of Chiang Kai-shek.

General Albert C. Wedemeyer was a witness to Stilwell's and Chennault's attitudes. He states in his book:

> ... General Marshall allowed me to sit in his office while Stilwell discussed the problems of his theater. ... My notes confirm how he castigated the Chinese President as coolie class, arrogant, untrustworthy, and absolutely impossible to get along with.
>
> ... Chennault, whom I had met for the first time during my brief visit to China in 1943, looked the part of a fighter—a man of stocky build, leathery skin, piercing brown eyes, and a protruding chin that announced grit and extreme determination. He was, however, soft-spoken and amenable in his manner. ...
>
> When I asked Chennault about the Generalissimo his reaction was poles apart from Stilwell's. In his estimation the Generalissimo was a great democratic leader, a devout Christian, and a man of absolute integrity, a real patriot. When I mentioned the Generalissimo's threat to stop fighting unless he received the support he had demanded when I was in Chungking earlier in the spring, Chennault said that Chiang would go on fighting in any event.[18]

---

18. Albert C. Wedemeyer, *Wedemeyer Reports!* (Henry Holt & Company, New York: 1958), pp. 202, 203.

After the Conference

A memorandum from John P. Davies, Jr., of the Chungking legation to the State Department, dated June 24, 1943, a month after the Trident Conference, fully disclosed the attitude of the Stilwell group:

> As the Chinese Communists moved away from world revolution to nationalism they also moved in the direction of more moderate internal political and economic policy. Whether these other moves were in compliance with Comintern dictates is less material than that they were historically and evolutionarily sound. . . .
>
> . . . the Communists, with the popular support which they enjoy and their reputation for administrative reform and honesty, represent a challenge to the Central [Nationalist] Government and its spoils system. . . .
>
> The Communists, on the other hand, dare not accept the Central Government's invitation that they disband their armies and be absorbed in the national body politic. To do so would be to invite extinction. . . .[19]

The Russians now protested in Washington, London, and Chungking at Chiang's attitude toward Mao Tse-tung and began a persistent propaganda attack on him.[20] The State Department continued pressures on Chiang, and on September 13, 1943, Chiang issued a statement exposing Communist violations of their previous pledges. He added an olive branch, however, saying:

> If the Chinese Communist Party can prove its good faith by making good its promises the Central Government, taking note of its sincerity and loyalty in carrying on our war of resistance [to the Japanese], will once more treat it with sympathy and consideration so that we may accomplish hand in hand the great task of resistance and reconstruction.[21]

George Creel, who visited China, says of this period in his book:

> Naturally news of the conference [Trident] reached Chiang and combined with other things to incite his anger. As proved by the *Papers*, General Stilwell's headquarters in Chungking had become a Cave of Adullam where

---

19. [U.S. Department of State,] *Foreign Relations of the United States* [*Diplomatic Papers*], *1943, China* (United States Government Printing Office, Washington: 1957), pp. 260, 262, 263.

20. Herbert Feis, *The China Tangle* (Princeton University Press, Princeton: 1953), pp. 86–87.

21. [U.S. Department of State,] *United States Relations with China* (Department of State Publication 3573, Washington: 1949), p. 531. [*Editor's note:* This eventually became known as *The China White Paper.*]

the American left-wing contingent—authors, correspondents and minor State Department officials—listened eagerly to his diatribes against the Chinese Government and persuaded him of the superior patriotism of the Communists. All of these happenings, put together, determined Chiang Kai-shek to ask for the general's recall, and only the pleading of Madame Chiang and her sister, Madame King, induced him to change his mind.[22]

---

22. George Creel, *Russia's Race for Asia* (The Bobbs-Merrill Company, Inc., New York: 1949), p. 97.

CHAPTER 48

The First Quebec Conference
August 11 to August 24, 1943

THE PRINCIPALS AT the First Quebec Conference were Prime Minister Churchill, President Roosevelt, and Prime Minister of Canada Mackenzie King.[1] The Chinese Foreign Minister, T. V. Soong, represented Chiang Kai-shek at some of the meetings.

The Military Situation

In the Pacific, the forces under General MacArthur had made further progress by driving the Japanese from Guadalcanal in the Solomon Islands on February 8, 1943, and from Attu Island in the Aleutians about May 30. General MacArthur began a concerted offensive in the South Pacific on July 1 and captured Rendova Island on July 2 and the Japanese base at Munda on New Georgia Island on August 7, four days before the conference.

In the Mediterranean, the American and British armies had completed the conquest of French North Africa with the capitulation of the German-Italian armies three months before the conference (May, 1943). The Allies occupied the Italian island of Pantelleria on June 11, and on July 10, they invaded Sicily. These events so undermined Italian confidence in Mussolini that he was deposed as premier on July 25, 1943, several weeks before the conference. At

---

1. The American staff present included: Secretary of State Cordell Hull, Secretary of War Henry L. Stimson (for one day), Secretary of Navy Frank Knox, Admiral William D. Leahy, General George C. Marshall, Admiral Ernest J. King, General Henry H. Arnold, Harry Hopkins, Stephen T. Early, Lt. General Brehon B. Somervell, Rear Admiral Wilson Brown, Brig. Gen. Thomas T. Handy.

The British staff included: Foreign Minister Anthony Eden, General Sir Alan F. Brooke, Lord President of the Council Sir John Anderson, Admiral Sir Dudley Pound, Air Chief Marshal Sir Charles F. A. Portal, Field Marshal Sir John Dill, Vice Admiral Lord Louis Mountbatten, Major-General Sir Hastings L. Ismay.

this time the total American force in the Mediterranean area "was close to 400,000, which included well over 200,000 ground troops, 80,000 in the Air Force, and the remainder in service personnel."[2]

In Russia, on July 5, 1943, Hitler had launched his fourth major offensive on the Russian front, but the Russian army had stopped their [his–*ed.*] drive and developed a massive counterattack, which had crushed the German strongholds of Orel and Belgorod by August 5, six days before the conference.

War against the U-boats had reduced merchant shipping losses to 187,000 tons in the month of May.[3]

Information

The official papers of this conference have never been published. However, the publications of participants in after years disclose the major activities.

Churchill's Proposal for an Attack on the "Soft Underbelly" of Europe

Secretary Hull states:

> ... Prior to my arrival [at Quebec] President Roosevelt and Prime Minister Churchill had engaged in some days of intensive military discussions.
>
> They had decided that an Anglo-American invasion of northern France should be made in the spring of 1944. Mr. Churchill had argued—and continued to argue up to the Tehran Conference—that the invasion of Europe by the Western Allies should be through the Balkans, the "soft underbelly of Europe." ... He also felt than an Anglo-American entry into the Balkans and southern Europe would prevent a Soviet rush into that area which would permanently establish the authority of the Soviet Union there, to the detriment of Britain and incidentally of the United States.[4]

General Wedemeyer states:

> On August 10, just before leaving for the QUADRANT [Quebec] conference, the Joint Chiefs of Staff met with the President at the White House. ... The President told the Joint Chiefs of Staff that Mr. Churchill was still looking

---

2. Albert C. Wedemeyer, *Wedemeyer Reports!* [Henry Holt and Company, New York: 1958], p. 214.

3. Chester Wilmot, *The Struggle for Europe* [Harper & Brothers Publishers, New York: 1952], p. 126.

4. *The Memoirs of Cordell Hull* [The Macmillan Company, New York: 1948], Vol. II, p. 1231.

toward operations in the Balkans. Mr. Stimson modified the President's remark to the effect that the Prime Minister wanted to give aid to the guerrillas in the Balkans in order to bring about uprisings. . . .

. . . The President added the curious statement that he did not understand the British viewpoint in this connection, for he, Roosevelt did not believe that the Soviets wanted to take over the Balkan states but wished only to establish "kinship with other slavic peoples." . . .[5]

Trusteeship of Backward Nations

America's passion of anti-colonialism broke out again at this conference.

Secretary Hull states in his memoirs[6] that at this conference he discussed with Foreign Secretary Eden the question of international supervision of dependent peoples, and that he furnished Eden a tentative draft of an agreement providing for an International Trusteeship Administration. Eden pointed out that there were varying degrees of self-government; that the word "independence" could never satisfactorily mean what various governments might have in mind by it. As to this, Hull says:

> I believed the subject was too important for the long-range advancement of the world to let it drop. Digging my toes in for a lengthy struggle, I brought it up again and again with the British in the months that followed. . . . [7]

The Secretary had apparently forgotten Mr. Churchill's memorable statement of the previous year that he had "not become the King's First Minister in order to preside over the liquidation of the British Empire."[8]

The Atomic Bomb

As I have stated in Chapter [44–*ed.*], Messrs. Churchill and Roosevelt had had some discussion of the atomic bomb—code name "Tube Alloys"—at the Hyde Park meeting during the Second Washington Conference of June, 1942.[9] Considerable progress was now being made in the development of this weapon.

---

5. Albert C. Wedemeyer, *Wedemeyer Reports!*, pp. 241–242.
6. *The Memoirs of Cordell Hull*, Vol. II, pp. 1234–1238.
7. Ibid., p. 1238.
8. [Winston S.] Churchill, *The End of the Beginning* (Little, Brown and Company, Boston: 1943), p. 268.
9. [Winston S.] Churchill, *The Hinge of Fate* (Houghton Mifflin Company, Boston: 1950), p. 378ff.

The Prime Minister records a telegram he sent from the conference to the Deputy Prime Minister on August 25, 1943:

> Everything here has gone off well. We have secured a settlement of a number of hitherto untractable questions, e.g., the Southeast Asia Command, "Tube Alloys," and French Committee recognition. . . .[10]

A secret agreement of the utmost importance as to the atomic bomb was made between Mr. Roosevelt and Mr. Churchill at this conference. This agreement was not disclosed to the public until eleven years later (April 5, 1954) by Prime Minister Churchill in an address to the House of Commons. Mr. Churchill's disclosure stemmed from a bill pending in the Congress in which there was a prohibition against sharing nuclear information. Questions had been raised in the House of Commons, and Mr. Churchill in his address of April 5, 1954, said:

> I feel that it will be in the national interest, and can do nothing but good on both sides of the Atlantic, if I now make public for the first time the agreement which I made in 1943 with President Roosevelt, which was signed by both of us at Quebec. President Eisenhower has informed me that he is content that I should do so. The House will find this document in the Vote Office when I sit down. I thought it right to lay the facsimile before the House, but here are the salient facts. I wrote them out myself those many years ago.
>
> "It is agreed between us
>
> "First, that we will never use this agency against each other. [. . . –ed.]
>
> "Secondly, that we will not use it against third parties without each other's consent.
>
> "Thirdly, that we will not either of us communicate any information about Tube Alloys"— ["to third parties except by mutual consent."–ed.]
>
> "Fourthly, that in view of the heavy burden of production falling upon the United States as a result of a wise division of war effort, the British Government recognize that any postwar advantages of an industrial or commercial character shall be dealt with as between the United States and Great Britain on terms to be specified by the President of the United States to the Prime Minister of Great Britain. The Prime Minister expressly disclaims any interest in these industrial and commercial aspects beyond what may be consid-

---

10. [Winston S.] Churchill, *Closing the Ring* (Houghton Mifflin Company, Boston: 1951), p. 93.

ered by the President of the United States to be fair and just and in harmony with the economic welfare of the world."[11]

This agreement which involved the foreign relations of the United States was not submitted to or ratified by the Senate. There was subsequent debate on the subject but nothing came of it.

---

11. [Great Britain,] *Parliamentary Debates* (Hansard), Fifth Series, Vol. 526, House of Commons, 3rd sess., 40th Parl. of U.K., 1953–54, April [5], 1954, [p. 50]. Mr. George Crocker in his book, *Roosevelt's Road to Russia* (Henry Regnery Company, Chicago: 1959) calls attention to this secret agreement on page 194.

CHAPTER 49

The First Moscow Conference
October 19 to October 30, 1943

THE FIRST MOSCOW CONFERENCE comprised the Foreign Secretaries or Ministers of the four nations. The United States was represented by Mr. Cordell Hull; the United Kingdom by Mr. Anthony Eden; and the Soviet Union by Mr. Vyacheslav M. Molotov. Chiang Kai-shek was represented by the Chinese Ambassador in Moscow, Dr. Foo Ping-Sheung.[1]

I discuss the military situation at this time in the chapter on the Cairo and Tehran conferences which took place a month later.

The Foreign Secretaries issued a communiqué to the press on November 1, 1943, of which the following are the essential paragraphs:[2]

> ... this is the first time that the foreign secretaries of the three governments have been able to meet together in conference.
>
> ... there were frank and exhaustive discussions of the measures to be taken to shorten the war against Germany and her satellites in Europe. Advantage was taken of the presence of military advisers representing the respective chiefs of staff in order to discuss definite military operations. ...

There followed a declaration of agreement to continue close cooperation until the end of the war. The communiqué continued:

---

1. In addition to the Foreign Secretaries, the following staff took part in the conference: *For the United States:* Mr. W. Averell Harriman, Ambassador of the United States, Major General John R. Deane; United States Lend-Lease representative in Moscow; Mr. Green H. Hackworth; Mr. James C. Dunn.

For the United Kingdom: Sir Archibald Clark Kerr, His Majesty's Ambassador; Mr. William Strang; Lieutenant General Sir Hastings Ismay.

For the Soviet Union: Marshal K. E. Voroshilov; Mr. A. Y. Vyshinski and Mr. M. M. Litvinov, Deputy People's Commissars for Foreign Trade; Major-General A. A. Gryzlov, of the General Staff; Mr. G. F. Saskin, Senior Official for People's Commissariat for Foreign Affairs. All three delegations were accompanied by technical experts.

2. *New York Herald Tribune,* November 2, 1943.

... [the conference] decided to establish in London a European advisory commission to study these questions and to make joint recommendations to the three Governments. ...

The conference also agreed to establish an advisory council for matters relating to Italy. ... This council will deal with day-to-day questions other than military preparations and will make recommendations designed to co-ordinate allied policy with regard to Italy. ...

The three Foreign Secretaries declared it to be the purpose of their governments to restore the independence of Austria. At the same time they reminded Austria that in the final settlement, account will be taken of efforts that Austria may make towards its own liberation. ...

A declaration was made by the Foreign Secretaries again pledging adherence to the Atlantic Charter, mutual consultation, unconditional surrender, unity of action on the terms of German surrender and the creation of an international organization to maintain peace. It further provided:

... That they will confer and cooperate with one another and with other members of the United Nations to bring about a practicable general agreement with respect to the regulation of armaments in the post-war period.[3]

Marshal Stalin approved this declaration.

Secretary Hull says:

I was truly thrilled as I saw the signatures affixed. Now there was no longer any doubt that an international organization to keep the peace, by force if necessary, would be set up after the war. ...[4]

Punishment for German Atrocities

This conference was made the occasion for the issuance of a Joint Declaration by Marshal Stalin, Prime Minister Churchill, and President Roosevelt as to punishment for German atrocities. The essential paragraphs were:

... the recoiling Hitlerites and Huns are redoubling their ruthless cruelties. This is now evidenced with particular clearness by monstrous crimes on the territory of the Soviet Union which is being liberated from Hitlerites and on French and Italian territory.

---

3. Ibid.
4. *The Memoirs of Cordell Hull* [The Macmillan Company, New York: 1948], Vol. II, p. 1307.

Accordingly, the aforesaid three Allied powers, speaking in the interests of the thirty-two United Nations, hereby . . . declare and give full warning . . . as follows:

At the time of granting of any armistice to any government which may be set up in Germany, those German officers and men and members of the Nazi party who have been responsible for or have taken a consenting part in the above atrocities, massacres and executions will be sent back to the countries in which their abominable deeds were done in order that they may be judged and punished according to the laws of these liberated countries. . . .

The above declaration is without prejudice to the case of German criminals, whose offenses have no particular geographical localization and who will be punished by joint decision of the governments of the Allies.[5]

One of the purposes of the conference, not mentioned in public statements, was to arrange a meeting of Churchill and Roosevelt with Stalin—a meeting which they had not been able to bring about in the past two years. This conference was set to be held in Tehran, Iran, for November 28, 1943.

A Mystery from the Conference of the Four Foreign Ministers

Upon the Secretary's return to Washington on November 18, he addressed the Congress concerning his accomplishments at Moscow, saying among other things:

As the provisions of the four-nation declaration are carried in effect, there will no longer be need for spheres of influence, for alliances, for balance of power or any other of the special arrangements through which, in the unhappy past, the nations strove to safeguard their security or to promote their interests.[6]

The Secretary states in his memoirs that there was agreement on a proposal by Eden, which he described as follows:

. . . another proposal on the agenda . . . [was] that the three Governments state their opinion in favor of joint responsibility for Europe as against separate areas of responsibility.

---

5. *New York Herald Tribune,* November 2, 1943.
6. Ibid., November 19, 1943.

On this point I said that my Government very much hoped that no decision would be taken at this conference in favor of separate areas of responsibility or zones of influence. . . .

Molotov said he knew of no reason to believe that the Soviet Government would be interested in separate zones or spheres of influence, and he could guarantee that there was no disposition on the part of his Government to divide Europe into such separate zones.[7]

However, there is no mention of this agreement, as represented by Hull, in any of the lengthy statements issued by the conference. That there had been such an agreement became an *idée fixe* in Hull's mind, although it had no influence on the actions of the four leaders of mankind.

7. *The Memoirs of Cordell Hull,* Vol. II, p. 1298.

CHAPTER 50

The Supplementary Purposes of Roosevelt, Churchill, Stalin, and Chiang Kai-Shek

BEFORE DEALING WITH the conferences at Cairo and Tehran in November and December 1943, it is desirable to sum up some of the background which had now developed and illuminated these critical conferences.

Aside from the defeat of Germany and Japan, the four leaders—Roosevelt, Churchill, Stalin, and Chiang Kai-shek—had certain supplementary, and divergent, personal policies and purposes.

Mr. Roosevelt's De-Empiring

Mr. Roosevelt's supplementary activity was the de-empiring of empires. His targets were not just the German, Italian, and Japanese, but also the empires of Britain, France, and the Netherlands. The one exception from this program involved his actions or acquiescence which resulted in a gigantic and aggressive empire—that of the Soviet Union.

Mr. Roosevelt had begun his de-empiring activities as early as the Atlantic Charter meeting in August, 1941.[1]

---

1. Chester Wilmot, in his book, *The Struggle for Europe* [Harper & Brothers Publishers, New York: 1952], on pages 633 and 634 notes that:

"Roosevelt's 'assault' upon the colonial concept began with the Atlantic Charter. . . . Reporting to the House of Commons on September 9th, 1941 the Prime Minister said: 'At the Atlantic meeting we had in mind the restoration of the sovereignty . . . of the states . . . now under the Nazi yoke.' This, he insisted, was 'quite a separate problem from the progressive evolution of self-governing institutions in the regions and peoples that owe allegiance to the British Crown.'

"The President, on the other hand, had no such limited view. During the 'Atlantic Charter Conference' he told Churchill: 'I can't believe that we can fight a war against fascist slavery, and at the same time not work to free people all over the world from a backward colonial policy.'. . . Thus, when he added to Churchill's draft the statement that he and

Mr. Roosevelt continued his de-empiring of Britain in the Lend-Lease negotiations.[2] Within sixty days after Pearl Harbor, in an exchange of communications with Churchill, beginning on March 10, 1942, Roosevelt applied more pressures.[3]

Early in April, 1942, Mr. Roosevelt dispatched Louis A. Johnson, and later William Phillips, to India to stir up the Nationalist demands for independence. Louis A. Johnson's activities were the subject of protest by the Governor General of India.[4] William Phillips wrote a book in which he described his activities.[5]

Apropos the visit of the Soviet Commissar of Foreign Affairs Molotov to Washington in June 1942, Sherwood, from the State Department's records, notes that the President said to Molotov:

... there were, all over the world, many islands and colonial possessions which ought, for our own safety, to be taken away from weak nations. He suggested that Mr. Stalin might profitably consider the establishment of some form of international trusteeship over these islands and possessions.

In reply Mr. Molotov declared [after reviewing other items]. . . . He had no doubt that the President's trusteeship principle would be equally well received in Moscow.

The President then pointed out that the acceptance of this principle would mean the abandonment of the mandate system. . . . [6]

A part of the colonial system were the mandates created by the Treaty of Versailles. Britain had received mandates covering an area of 863,000 square miles with a population of about 8,000,000 people. The French had received

---

the Prime Minister wished to 'see sovereign rights and self-government restored to those who have been forcibly deprived of them,' Roosevelt was thinking not only of the occupied countries of Europe but also of colonial peoples throughout the world. Furthermore, when he inserted an article declaring that they would endeavour 'without discrimination to further the enjoyment by all states, great or small, victor or vanquished, of access, on equal terms, to the trade and to the raw materials of the world,' the President was avowedly aiming at the Ottawa Agreements, the foundation of Imperial Preference. Appreciating this, Churchill demanded that the words 'without discrimination' should be replaced by the phrase 'with due respect to their existing obligations,' but this gained him only a brief respite from American pressure."

2. [Robert E.] Sherwood, *Roosevelt and Hopkins* [Harper & Brothers Publishers, New York: 1948], pp. 506–508.

3. [Winston S.] Churchill, *The Hinge of Fate* [Houghton Mifflin Company, Boston: 1950], p. 218.

4. Sherwood, *Roosevelt and Hopkins*, pp. 524–525.

5. William Phillips, *Ventures in Diplomacy* (The Beacon Press, Boston: 1952), pp. 342–396.

6. Robert E. Sherwood, *Roosevelt and Hopkins*, pp. 572–573.

248,000 square miles with about 5,500,000 population. The Belgians had also received large mandates in Africa.[7] Over the years since Versailles these areas had been welded into the colonial systems. No challenge to these titles could have been made short of war.

Sherwood, from Hopkins' notes, gives this further information of an interview of the President with Molotov:

> Turning to the question of colonial possessions, the President took as examples Indo-China, Siam, and the Malay States, or even the Dutch East Indies. The last-mentioned would some day be ready for self-government, and the Dutch know it. Each of these areas would require a different lapse of time before achieving readiness for self-government, but a palpable surge toward independence was there just the same, and the white nations thus could not hope to hold these areas as colonies in the long run. . . .
>
> The Commissar expressed the opinion that this problem deserves serious allied attention. . . . Mr. Molotov expressed his conviction that the President's proposals could be effectively worked out. The President said he expected no difficulties once peace was achieved.[8]

President Roosevelt's son, Elliott, records in his book the following statement made by Mr. Roosevelt at the time of the Casablanca Conference (January, 1943):

> It's all part of the British colonial question. . . . Burma—that affects India, and French Indo-China, and Indonesia—they're all interrelated. If one gets its freedom, the others will get ideas. That's why Winston is so anxious to keep de Gaulle in his corner. De Gaulle isn't any more interested in seeing a colonial empire disappear than Churchill is. . . .
>
> . . . I've tried to make it clear to Winston—and the others—that while we're their allies, and in it to victory by their side, they must never get the idea that we're in it just to help them hang on to the archaic, medieval Empire ideas. . . .
>
> Great Britain signed the Atlantic Charter. I hope they realize the United States government means to make them live up to it.[9]

---

7. Herbert Hoover, *The Ordeal of Woodrow Wilson* [McGraw-Hill Book Company, Inc., New York: 1958], p. 228.

8. Sherwood, *Roosevelt and Hopkins*, pp. 573–574.

9. Elliott Roosevelt, *As He Saw It* (Duell, Sloan and Pearce, New York: 1946), pp. 72, 121–122.

Sherwood records Hopkins' statement to him that when British Foreign Minister Anthony Eden visited Washington (March 12–30, 1943):

> I suggested to Eden, in the light of this evening's conversation . . . that we not explore anything beyond the European situation tonight and that we give two more evenings—one to the problems of the Southwest Pacific and the Far East and a third evening to Africa. . . . it was clear that in these latter two areas there were bound to be conflicts of opinion but, nevertheless, I thought that we should exchange, with complete frankness, our points of view about such ticklish subjects, as HONG KONG, MALAYAN STRAITS, INDIA.[10]

Hull recalls that just prior to his departure for the Moscow Conference, on October 6, 1943:

> . . . Mr. Roosevelt had said we ought to lay great stress on the possibilities of the trusteeship idea and apply it widely to all sorts of situations. The areas he mentioned ranged from the Baltic to Ascension Island in the South Atlantic and to Hong Kong. . . .[11]

Prime Minister Churchill's undeviating purpose second only to winning the war was to hold the British Empire intact and to expand it where possible. His statement that he had not been chosen Prime Minister to liquidate the British Empire was meant to focus on this subject.

As to the Prime Minister's intent to expand the British Empire or its sphere of influence I may cite an agreement made at the Second Moscow Conference on October 9, 1944 (full details of which are given in Chapter 58), where he and Stalin agreed that Russia and Great Britain would divide their interests in the Balkans as follows:

Rumania
    Russia   90%
    The others   10%
Greece
    Great Britain   90%
    (in accord with U.S.A.)
    Russia   10%
Yugoslavia   50–50%

---

10. Robert E. Sherwood, *Roosevelt and Hopkins*, p. 712.
11. *The Memoirs of Cordell Hull*, Vol. II, pp. 1304–5.

Hungary	50–50%
Bulgaria	
Russia	75%
The others	25%[12]

Marshal Stalin's Supplementary Purpose

Dictator Stalin never departed from the fundamental Communist purpose of communizing the world. This narrative will show his huge success.

Chiang Kai-shek's Supplementary Purpose

Chiang Kai-shek had a triple purpose: to save China from Communism by the defeat of Mao Tse-tung; to save her independence by the defeat of Japan; and to recover for China the encroachments by foreign nations during the past hundred years.[13]

---

12. Winston S. Churchill, *Triumph and Tragedy* [Houghton Mifflin Company, Boston: 1953], p. 227.

13. It might be observed that by the end of the war Britain lost all of the division of states agreed upon with Stalin, and the bonds of the British Commonwealth were so weakened as to make India and South Africa practically independent states. Stalin secured for his empire fifteen states in Europe, all of the Chinese Empire except Formosa, and one-half of Korea. The French, although defeated, held most of their empire. The Dutch ultimately lost [*Editor's note:* The sentence is incomplete. Hoover was presumably referring to the Dutch empire in Asia.]

SECTION XIII

The March of Conferences

The Tehran-Cairo Conferences
November–December 1943

CHAPTER 51

The Conferences at Cairo and Tehran
November 22 to December 7, 1943

Organization, Military Situation, Public Information

The three conferences—the First Cairo Conference, the Tehran Conference, and the Second Cairo Conference extended over a period from November 22 to December 7, 1943.

Of the leaders of the Allied world, Prime Minister Churchill and President Roosevelt attended all three conferences. Marshal Stalin attended only the Tehran Conference and Generalissimo Chiang Kai-shek attended only the First Cairo Conference.[1]

---

1. The American staff included: Harry L. Hopkins, Admiral William D. Leahy, General George C. Marshall, Admiral Ernest J. King, General Henry H. Arnold, Lieutenant General Joseph W. Stilwell, Lieutenant General Brehon B. Somervell, Major General Raymond A. Wheeler, Major General George E. Stratemeyer, Major General Claire L. Chennault, Major General Albert C. Wedemeyer, Major General John R. Deane, Major General Thomas T. Handy, Major General Muir S. Fairchild, Vice Admiral Russell Willson, Rear Admiral Charles M. Cooke, Jr., Rear Admiral Bernhard H. Bieri, Rear Admiral Oscar C. Badger, Rear Admiral Wilson Brown, Rear Admiral Ross T. McIntire, Rear Admiral Clarence E. Olsen, Major General Edwin M. Watson, Major General Rickard K. Sutherland, Brigadier General Frank D. Merrill, Brigadier General Haywood S. Hansell, Jr., Brigadier General Laurence S. Kuter, Brigadier General Patrick H. Tansey, Brigadier General Frank N. Roberts, Captain Austin K. Doyle, Captain Forrest B. Royal, Captain Edmund W. Burrough, Captain William L. Freseman, Colonel Emmett O'Donnell, Jr., Colonel Claude B. Ferenbaugh, Colonel Thomas T. Timberman, Colonel Joseph Smith, Colonel William W. Bessell, Jr., Colonel Thomas W. Hammond, Colonel Walter E. Todd, Colonel Reuben E. Jenkins, Colonel Andrew J. McFarland, Colonel Elliott Roosevelt, Commander Victor D. Long, Lieutenant Colonel Frank McCarthy, Lieutenant Commander George A. Fox, Major William W. Chapman, Major John Boettiger, Major De Witt Greer, Major George H. E. Durno, Major John Henry, Captain G. E. F. Rogers, Captain Henry H. Ware. General Dwight D. Eisenhower attended a staff meeting at Cairo.

At one time or another President Roosevelt also had the following civilians attend these conferences: Ambassador John G. Winant (United Kingdom), Ambassador W. Averell Harriman (Soviet Union), Ambassador Patrick J. Hurley (Roving), Ambassador Laurence A. Steinhardt (Turkey), Alexander C. Kirk (Minister in Egypt), John J. McCloy (Assistant Secretary of War), Advisors James M. Landis and Foreign Service Officer Charles E. Bohlen, Lewis W. Douglas (Deputy Administrator, War Shipping Administration).

The Military Situation at the Time of the
Cairo and Tehran Conferences

The tide of the war had turned toward the Allis about twelve months before the Cairo-Tehran Conferences.

On the Russian front, Generals Space, Scorched Earth, Winter and Red Army had cast the shadow of Napoleon's fate over Hitler. After his defeat at Stalingrad and the surrender of his forces there January 31 and February 2, 1943, he renewed his attack in the spring of 1943 driving in the Caucasus. The Russians launched a counter offensive, and by September 1943, two months before the First Cairo Conference, Hitler had begun his final retreat from Russia. And in his rage over the failures of his armies, he at various times dismissed his seasoned generals—Halder, von Brauchitsch, von Bock, von Rundstedt, Guderian, Hoepner, von Leeb and von Sponeck.

One month before the Cairo-Tehran Conferences, Stalin stated in a public address:

> In the battles on the Soviet-German front during the past year the German fascist army lost more than 4,000,000 officers and men, including not less

---

The United Kingdom staff included: Foreign Secretary Anthony Eden, General Sir Alan Brooke, Air Chief Marshall Sir Charles Portal, Admiral of the Fleet Sir Andrew Cunningham, Field Marshal Sir John Dill, Admiral Lord Louis Mountbatten, Lord Leathers (Frederick James), Sir Alexander Cadogan, Sir Archibald Clark Kerr, Brigadier Harold Redman, Commander Richard R. Coleridge, Lieutenant General Sir Hastings Ismay, Lieutenant General A. Carton de Wiart, General Sir Thomas Riddell-Webster, Captain Charles Edward Lambe, Lieutenant General Geffard Le Quesne Martel, Brigadier Cecil Stanway Sugden, Brigadier Anton Head, Brigadier E. H. W. Cobb, Brigadier John Kirkland McNair, Brigadier Leslie Chasemore Hollis, Air Commodore William Elliott, Colonel J. H. Lascelles, Major General Robert E. Laycock, Major Arthur H. Birse, Captain Hugh A. Lunghi, Lieutenant Colonel W. A. C. H. Dobson.

The Chinese staff attending the First Cairo Conference included: Madame Chiang Kai-shek, General Shang Chen, Lieutenant General Lin Wei, Vice Admiral Yang Hsuan-ch'eng, Lieutenant General Chou Chih-jou, Major General Chu Shih-ming, Major General Tsai Wen-chih, Dr. Wang Chung-hui.

The Russian staff which attended at Tehran included: Commissar Vyacheslav Molotov; Valentin Mikhailovich Berezhkov, Soviet Interpreter; Kliment Efremovich Voroshilov, Marshal of the Soviet Union, Military Advisor to Marshal Stalin; Mikhail Alexeyevich Maximov, Soviet Chargé d'Affaires in Iran; Vladimir Nikolayevich Pavlov, Personal Secretary and Interpreter to Marshal Stalin.

Others who attended the Second Cairo Conference included: Field Marshal Jan Christian Smuts, Prime Minister of the Union of South Africa; President Ismet Inönü of Turkey; Sükrü Saracoglu, Prime Minister of Turkey; Numan Menemencioglu, Turkish Minister of Foreign Affairs; George II, King of the Hellenes; Peter II, King of Yugoslavia; Prince Mohamed Ali, Heir Presumptive to the throne of Egypt.

Others who attended the Tehran Conferences included: Shah Mohammad Reza Pahlavi, Shah of Iran; Ali Soheili, Prime Minister of Iran; Mohammed Sa'ed-Maragheh'i, Minister of Foreign Affairs of Iran; Hosein Ala, Minister of the Iranian Imperial Court.

than 1,800,000 killed. During this year the Germans lost also more than 14,000 aircraft, over 25,000 tanks, and not less than 40,000 guns.[2]

(This was an overstatement as the Germans did not have this many men in Russia altogether.)

In the Pacific the forces under General Douglas MacArthur by taking New Guinea and the Solomon Islands had protected Australia from Japanese attack. The army under his command and the navy under Admiral Nimitz at this time had established an air and naval superiority that held the Japanese navy near to the shores of Asia. The Japanese had abandoned their occupation of the Aleutian Islands off the coast of Alaska. But the Japanese armies still held the East China Pacific and a large section of the Chinese mainland, having driven the Chinese government to Chungking in the Szechwan Province.

On the seas, through repairs and new construction, Allied naval strength in battleships, carriers, cruisers and destroyers had increased from the low point of about 2,000,000 tons in mid-1942 to more than 3,300,000 tons at the time of the Cairo-Tehran Conferences. Combined enemy naval strength had decreased to about 1,200,000 tons.

The Allies were now in command of all the seven seas except for a fringe along the Asiatic coast. Occasional forays of enemy submarines and surface raiders still continued. But losses of Allied merchant shipping had decreased from over 600,000 tons per month in 1942, to less than 200,000 tons by the time of the Cairo Conference. New shipbuilding now exceeded the monthly losses.

The Allied armies had completely occupied North Africa and had advanced in Italy to a position just south of Naples, at Salerno. The Italian government had surrendered only part of its army, and was still supporting the Germans on the Rome front. The Italians had withdrawn their armies from Yugoslavia.

Sources of Information

Search for the truth as to political agreements or commitments at these conferences presents the historian with many obstacles.

The communiqués, press statements, and public declarations during the conferences were necessarily restricted.

---

2. Joseph Stalin, *The Great Patriotic War of the Soviet Union* (International Publishers, New York: 1945), p. 93. See also *New York Times*, November 7, 1943.

In after years the truth was revealed only slowly. Some information was disclosed from the speeches of Churchill and Roosevelt following the conferences. Most of it has emerged from books and statements of the participants at the conferences; from the works of writers privileged to inspect the State Department archives; and from deductions which can be drawn from circumstantial evidence and events which came to light in later months.[3]

It was not until June 1961 that the State Department issued a publication entitled *Foreign Relations of the United States—The Conferences at Cairo and Tehran, 1943*. To simplify the State Department title I shall refer to it as "The Cairo-Tehran Papers." This publication was issued by the State Department eighteen years after the date of the conferences and was withheld for six years after the publication of the papers on the Yalta Conference which took place subsequent to Cairo and Tehran.

The Cairo-Tehran Papers comprise more than 270,000 words. From descriptions by participants and circumstantial evidence of what took place, it is obvious that this publication does not give the whole story, and the suspicion naturally arises as to whether there were deletions and suppression of

---

3. I may well mention the more important of these publications although many of them have been previously noted.

Churchill's volumes on the war give much information as to what happened at Tehran: *The Hinge of Fate* (Houghton Mifflin Company, Boston: 1950); *Closing the Ring* (Houghton Mifflin Company, Boston: 1951); *Triumph and Tragedy* (Houghton Mifflin Company, Boston: 1953).

Admiral William D. Leahy published a book, *I Was There* (McGraw-Hill Book Company, Inc., New York: 1950).

Robert Sherwood published the diary and correspondence of Harry L. Hopkins in his book *Roosevelt and Hopkins* (Harper and Brothers, New York: 1948).

Admiral Ernest J. King and Walter Muir Whitehill published a book entitled *Fleet Admiral King— A Naval Record* (W. W. Norton & Company, Inc., New York: 1952). Admiral William H. Standley with Admiral Arthur A. Ageton wrote *Admiral Ambassador to Russia* (Henry Regnery Company, Chicago: 1955).

Secretary of State Hull published two volumes entitled *The Memoirs of Cordell Hull* (The Macmillan Company, New York: 1948).

Dwight D. Eisenhower, *Crusade in Europe* (Doubleday & Company, Inc., Garden City, New York: 1948).

James F. Byrnes, *Speaking Frankly* (Harper & Brothers, New York: 1947).

John R. Deane, *The Strange Alliance* (The Viking Press, New York: 1947).

Edward R. Stettinius, Jr., *Roosevelt and the Russians: The Yalta Conference* (Doubleday & Company, New York: 1949).

Henry L. Stimson and McGeorge Bundy, *On Active Service In Peace and War* (Harper & Brothers, New York: 1948).

William C. Bullitt, *The Great Globe Itself* (Charles Scribner's Sons, New York: 1946).

Mark W. Clark, *Calculated Risk* (Harper & Brothers Publishers, New York: 1950).

Arthur Bliss Lane, *I Saw Poland Betrayed* (The Bobbs-Merrill Company, New York: 1948).

Jan Ciechanowski, *Defeat in Victory* (Doubleday & Company, Inc., New York: 1947).

Albert C. Wedemeyer, *Wedemeyer Reports!* (Henry Holt & Company, New York: 1958).

documents. As a minor indication, the State Department publication shows five meetings between Roosevelt and Churchill, and three meetings between Roosevelt and Chiang at the First Cairo Conference in which, with minor variations, the statement "no record can be found," appears.

At once I may say that the minutes of the military meetings carry conviction of scrupulously complete records. Also, the notes of Charles E. Bohlen, of the State Department who was the United States interpreter of Russian, are obviously conscientious so far as published.

The account of the Second Cairo Conference in the "Cairo-Tehran Papers" shows that no record of four meetings between Roosevelt and Churchill "could be found" and no record "could be found" of three meetings of Roosevelt, Churchill, President Inönü of Turkey, and Mr. Sergei Vinogradov, Soviet Ambassador in Turkey. What commitments may have been made are therefore not clear.

In a search for the truth as to the Cairo-Tehran papers, I made contact with Professor Donald M. Dozer, who had been a member of the State Department historical staff and had a part in the preparation of the Cairo-Tehran papers for publication. Professor Dozer informed me that he had been "released" from the State Department in July 1954, eleven years after the Conference, because of his protests at the suppression and destruction of parts of the Cairo-Tehran papers. Upon his appeal to the Civil Service Commission his status was restored but he was released again in 1956. Professor Dozer confirmed his verbal statements to me in a letter which he has given me permission to publish. The pertinent paragraphs are:

August 15, 1961

Dear President Hoover:

I am glad to confirm to you in writing the points that I discussed with you in our conference two weeks ago dealing with United States diplomacy during World War II and particularly the summit conferences at Cairo and Tehran in November-December 1943.

As the original compiler of the diplomatic papers of the Cairo-Tehran conferences in the Historical Division of the State Department I know that the compilation as published by the Department a few weeks ago does not represent the complete documentation of the conferences. When I began in October 1953 to prepare this compilation I was shocked to discover how few reports on the conferences could be found in the State Department archives. The preparations for the Roosevelt-Churchill-Stalin-Chiang Kai-shek conferences, as you know, were made not by the State Department but by the White

House, representatives of the State Department as such were not included in the conferences, and very few memoranda of decisions reached at the conferences found their way into the files of the Department.

When I was assigned the task of compiling these records the efforts that were made by responsible officials of the Historical Division to gain access to records in the Pentagon, in the Stettinius Papers, the Morgenthau Papers, the Hopkins Papers, and even the Roosevelt Papers at Hyde Park were deplorably inadequate and unproductive. Despite the public commitment made by the Department in May 1953 to publish the records of the summit conferences of World War II responsible officials were patently averse to the publication of these records, not, so far as I could ascertain from any fear of compromising national security, for this was only a very incidental factor, but rather from a desire to protect the political and historical reputations of the individual involved. By dint of considerable personal research and prodding I succeeded in bringing together substantially all the documents included in the present publication. A few of them I had not seen before the present volume was published, as for example, Roosevelt's letter to Congressman Mruk dated March 6, 1944, printed on page 877, which is unmitigated falsehood.

When I left the State Department in January 1956 the Cairo-Tehran records had not yet been put in galleys. My comments to you on them as now published are based only on my recollection of the documents that I compiled, for, of course, I could not bring away with me either a check list or any documents with which to compare the printed edition. On this basis I may mention the following omissions:

1. Before and during the Moscow Conference of Hull, Eden, and Molotov in October 1943 various officials of the State Department prepared position papers, some twenty-two or twenty-five in number as I remember, analyzing foreign policy problems all around the world. Since these formed an essential background to an understanding of the problems which were discussed at Cairo and Tehran, I urged that they be included, but, though many Moscow Conference documents are included in the present volume, only two of the State Department's position papers are reproduced in it. One of these, printed on pages 162–164, concerns oil concessions in the Middle East, the other, printed on pages 168–171, concerns the ownership of islands in the Central Pacific. But others dealing, as I remember, with such important matters as the postwar status of Germany, relations with Soviet Russia, the Polish problem, Yugoslavia, aid to China, and a host of other Far Eastern Problems prepared by Joseph Ballantine, Alger Hiss, George Hubbard Blakeslee, and

other officials were eliminated from my compilation by the chief of the Historical Division, G. Bernard Noble, over my protests.

2. At my insistence, continued over a period of some six months, we finally obtained the 22– or 23–page diary notes of the Cairo Conference made by John Paton Davies, Jr., and after we obtained them they were eliminated from my compilation by Mr. Noble on the ground that they were not dignified. They are referred to in several footnotes in the published compilation but are not printed even in partial form. And yet they contain, among other significant items, a report of a highly important conference in Cairo on December 5 or 6 between Roosevelt and Stilwell in which Roosevelt showed that he had been persuaded after his conference with Stalin at Tehran to abandon Chiang Kai-shek and thus retreat from the commitments which he had made to Chiang in person just a few days before at Cairo. The full consequence of this policy reversal, of course, became apparent in the Communist conquest of China in 1949.

3. It appears to me that some omissions have been made in the documentation dealing with (a) Roosevelt's offers of assistance to Chiang Kai-shek at his meetings with him in Cairo on November 22–26 having to do with *Buccaneer, Tarzan,* and, financial assistance, and (b) Roosevelt's offer of ⅓ of the Italian fleet to Stalin. These offers were quite specific, and their omission seems to render plausible the questions that were subsequently raised about them.

4. A serious omission is the cablegram that Roosevelt sent to Churchill dated, I think October 23, 24, or 25, 1943, in which he proposed to Churchill that the United States and England admit Soviet representatives to the Combined Chiefs of Staff, that they share all their logistical and strategic information with the Russians, and that they should not ask from them any information in return. This proposal was approved by Marshall, Leahy, Arnold, and King, as well as by Roosevelt. It is paraphrased in Leahy's *I Was There* and is alluded to vaguely in the Churchill volume covering this period. Some of the documents printed in the present volume refer to it, but this key document itself is missing. The reasons for the omission, I think, can easily be deduced.

The above are the most egregious omissions that I can spot. But a criticism of a more general nature that needs to be made concerns the mutilation of the documents that are here printed. Any reader should be suspicious of the frequent deletions, indicated by rows of dots across the page, that occur in a great number of these documents. These are too numerous to list here but occur on almost every page. As a result the reader gets decidedly less than the full story and can only guess at what has been deleted and why it has been deleted. This procedure is tantalizing to the historian and presents an unfair picture to the American public, who are entitled, I am convinced, to a full report of the diplomatic record of their presidents. . . .

s/ Donald M. Dozer

I do not speculate here as to whose reputations were being protected by these doings.

CHAPTER 52

The First Cairo Conference
November 22 to November 26, 1943

PRIME MINISTER CHURCHILL, President Roosevelt, and Generalissimo Chiang Kai-shek were the principals at the First Cairo Conference. Marshal Stalin did not attend.

The records show that there were twenty-four meetings of various civilian and military groups during the five days of this Conference. One of the important purposes of this conference was a review of the military situation over the world and the making of future military plans.[1]

There were three meetings in which all three—Messrs. Roosevelt, Churchill, and Chiang—participated. There were three meetings of Messrs. Roosevelt and Chiang without Churchill. There were three meetings of American military and civil officials with Chiang.

The most important action at the Cairo Conference in respect to China was the consideration of the tentative proposal made at the Casablanca Conference to recover Burma from the Japanese by (a) an Anglo-American land attack from India's northeast provinces; (b) a large-scale invasion by the Chinese armies from the north, with (c) simultaneous British amphibious landings on the Andaman Islands in the Bay of Bengal and on the Burmese mainland near Rangoon.

President Roosevelt promised Generalissimo Chiang Kai-shek that this operation would be carried out in full scale and that American support would be provided. There is only a vague reference to this promise in the published papers of the Cairo Conference. Reporting a meeting between Roosevelt and Chiang at Cairo on November 25, 1943, the editors of the Cairo-Tehran Papers noted that:

---

1. Messrs. Roosevelt and Churchill participated in three of the military conferences. Eleven of these meetings were between the British and American military staffs.

No official record of the substance of this meeting has been found. . . .

It was probably at this meeting that Roosevelt gave Chiang the promise (referred to in Churchill [*Closing the Ring*], p. 328) "of a considerable amphibious operation across the Bay of Bengal within the next few months." . . .[2]

Two other practical matters were discussed during this First Cairo Conference: the question of bringing Russia into the war with Japan and the possibility of bringing Turkey into the war, the discussion of which was continued in the Second Cairo Conference.

As to this question of Russia joining the war against Japan, the minutes of a meeting of the Joint Chiefs of Staff at Cairo record:

> Ambassador Harriman thought that the Soviets had every intention of joining the U.S. and the British in the war against Japan *as soon as Germany had capitulated*. They fear, however, a premature break with Japan and placed great value on the substantial amount of supplies which they are now receiving through Vladivostok. He reiterated that the pressure on the Soviet Government to end the war could not be over-emphasized.[3]

This proposed attack on the Japanese in Burma was taken up again at the Tehran Conference.

A communiqué was issued from the First Cairo Conference on December 1, 1943, as follows:

> The several military missions have agreed upon future military operations against Japan. The three great Allies [United States, United Kingdom and China] expressed their resolve to bring unrelenting pressure against their brutal enemies by sea, land and air. This pressure is already rising.
>
> The three great Allies are fighting this war to restrain and punish the aggression of Japan. They covet no gain for themselves and have no thought of territorial expansion. It is their purpose that Japan shall be stripped of all the islands in the Pacific which she has seized or occupied since the beginning of the first World War in 1914, and that all territories Japan has stolen from the Chinese, such as Manchuria, Formosa, and the Pescadores, shall be restored to the Republic of China. Japan will also be expelled from all other territories which she has taken by violence and greed. The aforesaid three [United

---

2. [U.S. Department of State,] *Foreign Relations of the United States,* [*Diplomatic Papers,*] *The Conferences at Cairo and Tehran, 1943* [United States Government Printing Office, Washington: 1961], pp. 349–350.

3. Ibid., p. 328. Italics mine.

States, United Kingdom and China] great powers, mindful of the enslavement of the people of Korea, are determined that in due course Korea shall become free and independent.

With these objects in view the three Allies, in harmony with those of the United Nations at war with Japan, will continue to persevere in the serious and prolonged operations necessary to procure the unconditional surrender of Japan.[4]

---

4. Ibid., pp. 448–449.

CHAPTER 53

The Tehran Conference
November 27 to December 1, 1943

Organization, Information, Military Matters

Organization

The Tehran Conference was the first meeting of President Roosevelt and Prime Minister Churchill jointly with Marshal Stalin—almost two years after Pearl Harbor.[1] Tehran was less than a day's flight for Stalin, but it required an exhausting journey of several days for Churchill and Roosevelt. Major General John R. Deane, who was present at Tehran, sums up a phase of the matter:

> ... No single event of the war irritated me more than seeing the President of the United States lifted from wheel chair to automobile, to ship, to shore, and to aircraft, in order to go halfway around the world as the only possible means of meeting J. V. Stalin.[2]

Information

In Chapter 51 I have already discussed the information, the lack of information, and the suppression of information as to what took place at Tehran. The official communiqué issued by the Conference was as follows:

---

1. There were twenty-two meetings at the Conference. Of these, five were among subordinate officials.

President Roosevelt attended seventeen meetings. Five of them were of President Roosevelt with Marshal Stalin or Russian officials where Prime Minister Churchill was not present.

The three leaders jointly participated in ten meetings. Prime Minister Churchill was present at ten meetings and Marshal Stalin at thirteen meetings. No doubt both attended meetings of their own staffs which are not recorded in the Cairo-Tehran papers.

Over one-half of the text of 82,000 words as to Tehran were devoted to the military situation at the time.

(Compiled from [U.S. Department of State,] *Foreign Relations of the United States,* [*Diplomatic Papers,*] *Conferences at Cairo and Tehran, 1943* [United States Government Printing Office, Washington: 1961].)

2. John R. Deane, *The Strange Alliance* (The Viking Press, New York: 1947), p. 160.

Declaration of the Three Powers

We—the President of the United States, The Prime Minister of Great Britain, and the Premier of the Soviet Union, have met these four days past in this, the capital of our ally, Iran, and have shaped and confirmed our common policy.

We express our determination that our nations shall work together in war and in the peace that will follow.

As to war—Our military staffs have joined in our round table discussions, and we have concerted our plans for the destruction of the German forces. We have reached complete agreement as to the scope and timing of the operations which will be undertaken from the East, West and South.

The common understanding which we have here reached guarantees that victory will be ours.

As to peace—we are sure that our concord will make it an enduring peace. We recognize fully the supreme responsibility resting upon us and all the United Nations, to make peace which will command the good will of the overwhelming mass of the peoples of the world, and banish the scourge and terror of war for many generations.

With our diplomatic advisers we have surveyed the problems of the future. We shall seek the cooperation and the active participation of all nations, large and small, whose peoples in heart and mind are dedicated, as are our own peoples, to the elimination of tyranny and slavery, oppression and intolerance. We will welcome them, as they may choose to come, into a world family of democratic nations.

No power on earth can prevent our destroying the German armies by land, their U-boats by sea, and their war plants from the air.

Our attack will be relentless and increasing.

Emerging from these friendly conferences we look with confidence to the day when all peoples of the world may live free lives, untouched by tyranny, and according to their varying desires and their own consciences.

We came here with hope and determination. We leave here, friends in fact, in spirit and in purpose.

Signed at Teheran, December 1, 1943.

F. D. Roosevelt

J. Stalin

W. Churchill[3]

---

3. *Foreign Relations of the United States, [Diplomatic Papers, The] Conferences at Cairo and Tehran, 1943*, pp. 640–641.

The Tehran Conference dealt with several important military operations. The only written military agreement signed at the conference was naturally kept secret. It was as follows:

Military Conclusions of the Tehran Conference

The Conference:-

(1) Agreed that the Partisans in Yugoslavia should be supported by supplies and equipment to the greatest possible extent, and also by commando operations:

(2) Agreed that, from the military point of view, it was most desirable that Turkey should come into the war on the side of the Allies before the end of the year:

(3) Took note of Marshal Stalin's statement that if Turkey found herself at war with Germany, and as a result Bulgaria declared war on Turkey or attacked her, the Soviet would immediately be at war with Bulgaria. The Conference took further note that this fact could be explicitly stated in the forthcoming negotiations to bring Turkey into the war:

(4) Took note that Operation OVERLORD [the Second Front in France] would be launched during May 1944, in conjunction with an operation against Southern France. The latter operation would be undertaken in as great a strength as availability of landing-craft permitted. The Conference further took note of Marshal Stalin's statement that the Soviet forces would launch an offensive at about the same time with the object of preventing the German forces from transferring from the Eastern to the Western Front:

(5) Agreed that the military staffs of the three Powers should henceforward keep in close touch with each other in regard to the impending operations in Europe. In particular it was agreed that a cover plan to mystify and mislead the enemy as regards these operations should be concerted between the staffs concerned.

F. D. R.

И. С.

Teheran, December 1, 1943.   W S C[4]

---

4. Ibid., p. 652. [*Editor's note:* The initials of the second signatory are those of Joseph Stalin in Cyrillic.]

The Cross Channel Attack by American and British Forces

The details of this operation (OVERLORD) had been settled prior to the Tehran Conference, and General Dwight D. Eisenhower had been placed in command. The attack, which had been promised Stalin on sequent occasions in 1942 and 1943, was now to be made in May 1944, and it was decided to move a part of the army in Italy under General Mark W. Clark to the south of France (Operation ANVIL).

Rome and the Po Valley

It was also decided that General Mark Clark should continue his attack until he had occupied Rome and the Po Valley.

The Soft Underbelly of Europe

Prime Minister Churchill, at the First Quebec Conference—August 11–24, 1943—prior to Tehran, had urged an operation which came to be called an attack on the "soft underbelly of Europe." The concept was that in addition to operations on the Italian mainland, and across the Channel to France, an attack should proceed northward from either the head of the Adriatic or Aegean Sea. Churchill's purpose in this operation was to create an Allied wall against Communist occupation of Yugoslavia, Austria, Czechoslovakia, and Hungary which otherwise would likely occur with the German retreat. The Prime Minister's project was supported by General Sir Alan Brooke, the British Chief of Staff, who pointed out that prior to the cross-Channel attack on the Germans in France there would be "five or six months during which something must be done to keep the German divisions engaged."[5] Prime Minister Churchill repeatedly urged his strategy. In a meeting of the Combined Chiefs of Staff at Tehran on November 28, 1943, he stated that:

> . . . he dreaded the six months' idleness between the capture of Rome and the mounting of OVERLORD [the second front in France]. Hence, he believed

---

At this point in his Z+H edition, Hoover had a section captioned "The Projected Attack Upon the Japanese Armies Occupying Burma." He subsequently deleted a sentence of it, probably because it contained a factual error. In early 1964, one of Hoover's fact-checking secretaries, Loretta Camp, urged him to move this entire section to Chapter 55, where it properly belonged chronologically. That is where it is now printed. See Chapter 55, note 2.]

5. *Foreign Relations of the United States,* [*Diplomatic Papers, The*] *Conferences at Cairo and Tehran, 1943,* pp. 515–517.

that secondary operations should be considered in order to deploy forces available.

... He wished to go on record as saying that it would be difficult and impossible to sacrifice all activity in the Mediterranean in order to keep an exact date for OVERLORD. There would be 20 divisions which could not be moved out of the Mediterranean because of a lack of shipping. These should be used to stretch Germany to the utmost. He expressed the hope that careful and earnest consideration should be given to making certain that operations in the Mediterranean were not injured solely for the purpose of keeping the May date for OVERLORD. . . .[6]

As to the urgency of the Prime Minister, Major General John R. Deane, who was present at this meeting, states:

Churchill used every trick in his oratorical bag, assisted by illustrative and emphasizing gestures, to put over his point. At times he was smooth and suave, pleasant and humorous, and then he would clamp down on his cigar, growl, and complain. . . .

... Stalin's refutation of Churchill's argument consisted of a few very terse comments which can be summed up in his insistence that Overlord should be the primary operation and that nothing should be undertaken which would delay it. . . .[7]

An account of this Conference in Sherwood's *Roosevelt and Hopkins* confirms Deane's statement from Hopkins' notes:

... Churchill employed all the debater's arts, the brilliant locutions and circumlocutions, of which he was a master, and Stalin wielded his bludgeon with relentless indifference to all the dodges and feints of his practiced adversary. . . .[8]

General Mark Clark who was not present at Tehran, but at that time in command of the Allied Armies in Italy, strongly supported the Prime Minister's strategy as is shown by the following statements from his book, *Calculated Risk:*

... A campaign that might have changed the whole history of relations between the Western world and Soviet Russia was permitted to fade away, not

---

6. Ibid., pp. 506–507.
7. Deane, *The Strange Alliance*, p. 42.
8. [Robert E.] Sherwood, *Roosevelt and Hopkins* [Harper & Brothers, New York: 1948], p. 789.

into nothing, but into much less than it could have been. These were decisions made at a high level and for reasons beyond my field and my knowledge; but I do not think that it is outside my bailiwick to discuss, from a military viewpoint, what might have been achieved had the Fifth Army been kept together and strengthened in the coming months instead of being torn apart.

... Not alone in my opinion, but in the opinion of a number of experts who were close to the problem, the weakening of the campaign in Italy in order to invade southern France and instead of pushing on into the Balkans was one of the outstanding political mistakes of the war.

... Stalin, it was evident, throughout the Big Three meeting ... knew exactly what he wanted in a political as well as a military way; and the thing that he wanted most was to keep us out of the Balkans, which he had staked out for the Red Army. If we switched our strength from Italy to France, it was obvious to Stalin ... that we would be turning away from central Europe.... It was easy to see, therefore, why Stalin favored ANVIL at Teheran and why he kept right on pushing for it; but I never could understand why ... the United States and Britain failed to ... take another look at the overall picture....

... After the fall of Rome, Kesselring's [the German] army could have been destroyed—if we had been able to shoot the works in a final offensive. And across the Adriatic was Yugoslavia ... and beyond Yugoslavia were Vienna, Budapest and Prague....

The circumstances and viewpoints outlined above developed rather slowly over a period of weeks or months, as far as I was concerned; ... the net result was that after the fall of Rome we "ran for the wrong goal," both from a political and a strategical standpoint....

... I later came to understand, in Austria, the tremendous advantages that we had lost by our failure to press on into the Balkans.... Had we been there before the Red Army, not only would the collapse of Germany have come sooner, but the influence of Soviet Russia would have been drastically reduced.

... the decision to steer clear of the Balkans was one that puzzled the German High Command for many weeks....[9]

The Prime Minister, in an argument with Stalin on his "soft underbelly" plan, was at a disadvantage. He could not explain that his objective was to stop the spread of Communism in Central Europe.

---

9. Mark Clark, *Calculated Risk* [Harper & Brothers, New York: 1950], pp. 368, 370, 371, 372.

Churchill again returned to his plan ten months later, in September 1944. He stated:

> Another matter lay heavy on my mind, I was very anxious to forestall the Russians in certain areas of Central Europe. . . .[10]

On the 13th of that month, at the Second Quebec Conference, he presented his views on the war. In his book he stated the following:

> . . . Our objective should be Vienna. . . . Another reason for this right-handed movement [from Italy] was the rapid encroachment of the Russians into the Balkan peninsula and the dangerous spread of Soviet influence there.[11]

After the war, Churchill summed up the consequences of failure to adopt his strategy.

> . . . The army which we had landed on the Riviera at such painful cost to our operations in Italy arrived too late to help Eisenhower's first main struggle in the north. . . . Italy was not to be wholly free for another eight months; the right-handed drive to Vienna was denied to us; and, except in Greece, our military power to influence the liberation of Southeastern Europe was gone.[12]

Churchill's comment on President Roosevelt's attitude toward the "soft underbelly" was:

> . . . the President was oppressed by the prejudices of his military advisers, and drifted to and fro in the argument, with the result that the whole of these subsidiary but gleaming opportunities were cast aside. . . .[13]

---

10. [Winston S.] Churchill, *Triumph and Tragedy* [Houghton Mifflin Company, Boston: 1953], p. 148.
11. Ibid., p. 151.
12. Ibid., p. 126.
13. Churchill, *Closing the Ring*, p. 346.

CHAPTER 54
Other Conclusions at Tehran

THE COMMUNIQUÉ FROM the First Cairo Conference of December 1, 1943 had promised the restoration to the Republic of China of "all [the–*ed.*] territories Japan has stolen from the Chinese," including Manchuria, Formosa, and the Pescadores Islands. The record of the Tehran Conference states:

> ... THE PRIME MINISTER asked Marshal Stalin whether he had read the proposed communiqué on the Far East of the Cairo conference.
>
> MARSHAL STALIN replied that he had and that although he could make no commitments he thoroughly approved the communiqué and all its contents. He said it was right that Korea should be independent, and that Manchuria, Formosa and the Pescadores Islands should be returned to China. . . .
>
> THE PRIME MINISTER and THE PRESIDENT expressed agreement with Marshal Stalin's views.[1]

Prime Minister Churchill raised the subject of an ice-free port for Russia in the Pacific. Marshal Stalin observed:

> ... that there was no port in the Far East that was not closed off, since Vladivostok was only partly ice-free, and besides covered by Japanese controlled Straits.
>
> THE PRESIDENT said he thought the idea of a free port might be applied to the Far East besides, and mentioned Dairen as a possibility.
>
> MARSHAL STALIN said he did not think that the Chinese would like such a scheme.

---

1. [U.S. Department of State,] *Foreign Relations of the United States,* [*Diplomatic Papers, The*] *Conferences at Cairo and Tehran, 1943* [United States Government Printing Office, Washington: 1961], p. 566.

To which THE PRESIDENT replied that he thought they would like the idea of a free port under international guaranty.[2]

Iran

During the Conference certain agreements were reached with respect to Iran. Iran had been occupied by Allied forces to protect the supply railroad to Russia. A declaration signed by Roosevelt, Churchill, and Stalin assured the independence, sovereignty, and territorial integrity of Iran and also in its text affirmed the Atlantic Charter. It stated:

> ... They [the Allied Powers] count upon the participation of Iran, together with all other peace-loving nations, in the establishment of international peace, security and prosperity after the war, in accordance with the principles of the Atlantic Charter, to which all four Governments have subscribed.[3]

This was about the sixth Soviet affirmation of the Charter.

The Treatment of Germany

There were extensive discussions at Tehran on the treatment of Germany after her surrender. It was agreed that Germany should be disarmed and dismembered. There was also some discussion as to the elimination of the Nazi concept from the German mind.

Stalin's views expressed during the evening of November 28, 1943 are given by Charles E. Bohlen in a memorandum which he prepared at the Tehran Conference:

> In regard to Germany, Marshal Stalin appeared to regard all measures proposed by either the President or Churchill for the subjugation and for the control of Germany as inadequate. He on various occasions sought to induce the President or the Prime Minister to go further in expressing their views as to the stringency of the measures which should be applied to Germany. He appeared to have no faith in the possibility of the reform of the German

---

2. Ibid., p. 567.

3. *New York Herald Tribune*, December 7, 1943. Also see *Foreign Relations of the United States*, [*Diplomatic Papers, The*] *Conferences at Cairo and Tehran, 1943*, p. 647. [*Editor's note:* In early 1964 Hoover and/or his staff changed the final words of this quotation to read: "have continued to subscribe." I have retained the wording printed here, as it appears in the *Foreign Relations* volume cited in this footnote.]

people and spoke bitterly of the attitude of the German workers in the war against the Soviet Union. . . .[4]

The Treatment of Turkey

There were long discussions at Tehran as to how and when Turkey could be brought into the war. The record shows that:

THE PRIME MINISTER said that one of the greatest things under consideration was the matter of bringing Turkey into the war, persuading her in, and opening the communications into the Dardanelles, Bosphorus and the Black Sea. Such operation would make possible an attack on Rhodes and other islands in the Aegean. The above would have a very important effect in that it would be possible for convoys to supply the U.S.S.R. through that route and these convoys could be maintained continuously. . . .[5]

It was proposed that President Roosevelt and Prime Minister Churchill meet with the President of Turkey—M. Ismet İnönü. Meetings took place at the Second Cairo Conference on December 4, 5 and 6. I give further information on this subject in the chapter on the Second Cairo Conference.

Air Bases in Siberia

President Roosevelt wrote a note to Marshal Stalin at Tehran on November 29 asking that he arrange for the use of air bases in Siberia for the landing of American bombers engaged in the war against Japan.[6] Stalin promised to study the proposal, but these bases were never acquired.

The European Advisory Commission[7]

The creation of this commission had been agreed upon at the First Moscow Conference in October of 1943. Upon his return from that Conference, Hull,

---

4. Ibid., p. 513.
5. Ibid., p. 503.
6. Ibid., p. 618.
7. [*Editor's note:* Markings on the January 1964 research copy of Section XIII, chapter 54 of Hoover's manuscript (in the Herbert C. Hoover Papers, Box 63, Envelope 6) suggest that Hoover may have planned to delete (or move elsewhere) his paragraphs in the text on the European Advisory Commission. A cut copy of these is filed with Hoover's personal copy of Section XIII, chapter 54 (in the same box). A marking on the cut copy ("p. 70a") suggests that he or his secretary may have intended to move the passage to the end of chapter 49. But Hoover's final disposition of this matter

in a speech to Congress on November 18, described the functions of the Commission as follows:

> ... The Conference [First Moscow] ... decided to set up a European Advisory Commission with its seat in London. This Commission will not of itself have executive powers. Its sole function will be to advise the Governments of the United States, Great Britain, and the Soviet Union. It is to deal with nonmilitary problems relating to enemy territories and with such other problems as may be referred to it by the participating governments. It will provide a useful instrument for continuing study and formulation of recommendations concerning questions connected with the termination of hostilities.[8]

The establishment of this Commission was formally agreed at Tehran.[9]

An Agreement Opposing Territorial Aggrandizement

THE PRIME MINISTER then said it was important that the nations who would govern the world after the war, and who would be entrusted with the direction of the world after the war, should be satisfied and have no territorial or other ambitions. If that question could be settled in a manner agreeable to the great powers, he felt then that the world might indeed remain at peace. He said that hungry nations and ambitious nations are dangerous, and he would like to see the leading nations of the world in the position of rich, happy men.

THE PRESIDENT and MARSHAL STALIN agreed.[10]

But this happy solution for mankind seemed to disappear suddenly and so far as I can discover, without comment.

---

is uncertain. I have therefore retained the paragraphs here, where they appear in the September 1963 "Z+H" typescript edition.]

8. *International Conciliation*, No. 396, January, 1944, p. 115.—"Report on the Moscow Conference," Address by C. Hull before the Congress, November 18, 1943.

9. [*Editor's note:* The January 1964 research copy says "Cairo." In fact, the decision to create the European Advisory Commission had already been made. The two Cairo conferences worked out the details.]

10. *Foreign Relations of the United States*, [*Diplomatic Papers, The*] *Conferences at Cairo and Tehran, 1943*, p. 568.

The Organization to Preserve Peace

At a meeting with Marshal Stalin on November 29, President Roosevelt spoke at length on his ideas of a world organization to preserve peace. The record shows:

> THE PRESIDENT then outlined the following general plan:
>
> (1) There would be a large organization composed of some 35 members of the United Nations which would meet periodically at different places, discuss and make recommendations to a smaller body.
>
> MARSHAL STALIN inquired whether this organization was to be world wide or European, to which the President replied, world-wide.
>
> THE PRESIDENT continued that there would be set up an executive committee composed of the Soviet Union, the United States, United Kingdom and China, together with two additional European states, one South American, one Near East, one Far Eastern country, and one British Dominion. He mentioned that Mr. Churchill did not like this proposal for the reason that the British Empire only had two votes. This Executive Committee would deal with all non-military questions such as agriculture, food, health, and economic questions, as well as the setting up of an International Committee. This Committee would likewise meet in various places.
>
> MARSHAL STALIN inquired whether this body would have the right to make decisions binding on the nations of the world.
>
> THE PRESIDENT replied, yes and no. It could make recommendations for settling disputes with the hope that the nations concerned would be guided thereby, but that, for example, he did not believe the Congress of the United States would accept as binding a decision of such a body. THE PRESIDENT then turned to the third organization which he termed "The Four Policemen," namely, the Soviet Union, United States, Great Britain, and China. This organization would have the power to deal immediately with any threat to the peace and any sudden emergency which requires this action . . .[11]

In the discussion Marshal Stalin suggested regional committees of such an organization and raised the question of whether or not United States forces would be sent to Europe to enforce decisions.

---

11. Ibid., p. 530.

THE PRESIDENT pointed out that he had only envisaged the sending of American planes and ships to Europe, and that England and the Soviet Union would have to handle the land armies in the event of any future threat to peace. . . . THE PRESIDENT added that he saw two methods of dealing with possible threats to the peace. In one case if the threat arose from a revolution or developments in a small country, it might be possible to apply the quarantine method, closing the frontiers of the countries in question and imposing embargoes. In the second case, if the threat was more serious, the four powers, acting as policemen, would send an ultimatum to the nation in question and if refused, [it] would result in the immediate bombardment and possible invasion of that country.[12]

Stalin's remarks indicated acceptance of this organization to preserve peace.[13]

---

12. Ibid., pp. 531–532.
13. Ibid., p. 531.

CHAPTER 55

The Second Cairo Conference
December 2 to December 7, 1943

THE PRINCIPAL PARTICIPANTS in the conference were President Roosevelt and Prime Minister Churchill. Chiang Kai-shek had returned to China. The American and British civilian and military staffs were those of the First Cairo Conference.[1]

Persuading Turkey to Join the War

President Roosevelt had prolonged conferences with Prime Minister Churchill and President Inönü of Turkey during the Second Cairo Conference. There is an extensive record of these discussions in the Cairo-Tehran Papers but as the meeting had no important results, I merely outline what happened.

President Inönü, being pro-ally and having a long-standing military alliance with the British, was anxious to cooperate with them against the Germans. However, he had a military situation which made any action impossible at this time. He stressed that his armies were unprepared, that the German armies were on his frontiers, that any action toward preparedness would subject his country at once to German invasion, and that the Allies could give him no military aid in time to prevent it.

Despite the strong urging of Messrs. Roosevelt and Churchill, he declined to join in the war at this time. He did join the Allies after the German retreat from the borders of Turkey on February 25, 1945, fifteen months later and three months prior to the German surrender.

---

1. There were 28 meetings during the six days of the conference. Of these, seven were of the military staffs. Eight were between Churchill and Roosevelt, with or without staff members.

The Projected Attack upon the Japanese Armies Occupying Burma[2]

I have already stated that this project had been agreed upon by Roosevelt, Churchill, and Chiang Kai-shek at the First Cairo Conference.[3] Chiang Kai-shek had left that conference with Roosevelt's assurance that it would be carried out. As shown previously, there is only a vague reference to this promise of Roosevelt's in the Cairo-Tehran Papers. But that the promise had been made was evident by its withdrawal following the Tehran discussions.[4]

Admiral William D. Leahy, President Roosevelt's personal Chief of Staff, states that at Cairo:

> . . . [Churchill] was well aware that at staff talks beginning the next day [December 2] his representatives were to resist stubbornly any attempt to carry out a promise made to our Far East ally—the promise Roosevelt had made to Generalissimo Chiang Kai-shek to carry out a vigorous campaign to recapture Burma with land operations in the north coordinated with an amphibious attack on the Andaman Islands in the Bay of Bengal in the south.[5]

Admiral Leahy records that Mr. Roosevelt joined in the repudiation of this commitment. He stated:

> When the American Chiefs met with Roosevelt at 5 o'clock, [on December 6, 1943] he informed us that in order to bring the discussions to an end, he had reluctantly agree[d] to abandon the Andaman plan and would propose some substitute to Chiang. He was the Commander-in-Chief and that ended the argument. It must have been a sad disappointment to Chiang. The Chinese leader had every right to feel that we had failed to keep a promise.[6]

---

2. [*Editor's note:* Hoover originally included this section in chapter 53. (See chapter 53, note 4.) Early in 1964 one of his fact-checking secretaries, Loretta Camp, recommended that he move this section to chapter 55, where, she pointed out, it seemed to belong. She also placed a typed copy of this portion of chapter 53 in chapter 55 of Hoover's copy of Section XIII of his manuscript.

Whether Hoover approved of Mrs. Camp's proposed change is uncertain. But she was factually correct, and I have printed the passage here in its proper context.]

3. See chapter 52.

4. [U.S. Department of State,] *Foreign Relations of the United States,* [*Diplomatic Papers, The*] *Conferences at Cairo and Tehran, 1943* [United States Government Printing Office, Washington: 1961], pp. 479, 484, 488, 498, and 587. See also [William D.] Leahy, *I Was There* [McGraw-Hill Book Company, Inc., New York: 1950], p. 212, and [Winston S.] Churchill, *Closing the Ring* [Houghton Mifflin Company, Boston: 1951], p. 376.

5. Leahy, *I Was There,* p. 212.

6. Ibid., p. 213.

In his authorized biography Admiral King states:

> ... This broken promise to China, which greatly distressed King, was the one instance during the war in which he felt that the President had gone against the advice of his Joint Chiefs of Staff. Hindsight is futile, but in the light of subsequent events it is permissible to speculate as to what might have occurred in postwar years had the promise to the Chinese not been broken. . . .[7]

China at the Second Cairo Conference

During this conference, President Roosevelt sent a telegram to Generalissimo Chiang Kai-shek on December 5, 1943, regarding the joint British-American-Chinese attack upon the Japanese forces in Burma, saying:

> Conference with Stalin involves us in combined grand operations on European continent in late spring giving fair prospect of terminating war with Germany by end of summer of 1944. These operations impose so large a requirement of heavy landing craft as to make it impracticable to devote a sufficient number to the amphibious operation in Bay of Bengal simultaneously with launching of TARZAN [a proposed attack by Chiang on the Japanese in Burma] to insure success of operation.
>
> This being the case: Would you be prepared go ahead with TARZAN as now planned, including commitment to maintain naval control of Bay of Bengal coupled with naval carrier and commando amphibious raiding operations simultaneous with launching of TARZAN? Also there is the prospect of B-29 bombing of railroad and port Bangkok.
>
> If not, would you prefer to have TARZAN delayed until November to include heavy amphibious operation. Meanwhile concentrating all air transport on carrying supplies over the hump to air and ground forces in China.
>
> I am influenced in this matter by the tremendous advantage to be received by China and the Pacific through the early termination of the war with Germany.[8]

---

7. [Ernest J.] King and [Walter Muir] Whitehill, *Fleet Admiral King—A Naval Record* [W. W. Norton & Company, Inc., New York: 1952], pp. 525–526.

8. *Foreign Relations of the United States,* [*Diplomatic Papers, The*] *Conferences at Cairo and Tehran, 1943,* pp. 803–804.

The Generalissimo's reply reached the President on December 9, while he was still in Cairo:

I have received your telegram of December Sixth. Upon my return I asked Madame Chiang to inform you of the gratifying effect the communiqué of the Cairo Conference has had on the Chinese army and people in uplifting their morale to continue active resistance against Japan. This letter is on the way and is being brought to you by the pilot, Captain Shelton.

First, prior to the Cairo Conference there had been disturbing elements voicing their discontent and uncertainty of America and Great Britain's attitude in waging a global war and at the same time leaving China to shift as best she could against our common enemy. At one stroke the Cairo communiqué decisively swept away this suspicion in that we three had jointly and publicly pledged to launch a joint all-out offensive in the Pacific.

Second, if it should now be known to the Chinese army and people that a radical change of policy and strategy is being contemplated, the repercussions would be so disheartening that I fear of the consequences of China's inability to hold out much longer.

Third, I am aware and appreciate your being influenced by the probable tremendous advantages to be reaped by China as well as by the United Nations as a whole in speedily defeating Germany first. For the victory of one theater of war necessarily affects all other theaters; on the other hand, the collapse of the China theater would have equally grave consequences on the global war. I have therefore come to this conclusion that in order to save this grave situation, I am inclined to accept your recommendation. You will doubtless realize that in so doing my task in rallying the nation to continue resistance is being made infinitely more difficult.

... Because the danger to the China theater lies not only in the inferiority of our military strength, but also, and more especially, in our critical economic condition which may seriously affect the morale of the army and people, and cause at any moment a sudden collapse of the entire front. Judging from the present critical situation, military as well as economic, it would be impossible for us to hold on for six months, and *a fortiori* to wait till November 1944. . . .

From the declaration of the Teheran Conference Japan will rightly deduce that practically the entire weight of the United Nations' forces will be applied to the European front thus abandoning the China theater to the mercy of Japan's mechanized air and land forces. It would be strategic on Japan's part to . . . liquidate the China Affair during the coming year. It may therefore be expected that the Japanese will before long launch an all-out offensive against China so as to remove the threat to their rear, and thus re-capture the militarists' waning popularity and bolster their fighting morale in the Pacific. This is the problem which I have to face. Knowing that you are a realist, and as your loyal colleague, I feel constrained to acquaint you with the above facts. Awaiting an early reply.[9]

---

9. *United States Army in World War II, China-Burma-India Theater, Stilwell's Command Problems,* by Charles F. Romanus and Riley Sunderland, Office of the Chief of Military History, Department of the Army, Washington, D.C., 1956, pp. 74–75.

CHAPTER 56

The Two Great Commitments at Tehran Which Destroyed Freedom in Fifteen Nations[1]

I HAVE DELAYED the narrative of the two vital commitments at Tehran until less important matters have been dealt with. These two commitments or understandings between Roosevelt, Churchill, and Stalin were the greatest blows to human freedom in this century.

They were not explicit, signed documents. They are only slightly indicated in the published Cairo-Tehran papers. They are overwhelmingly proved by subsequent statements of Roosevelt, Hull, and Churchill. They are confirmed by Stalin's immediate activities following these commitments.

The first of these understandings or commitments was that the Soviet Union should be allowed to annex, either wholly or in part, seven peoples which had been under Russian rule prior to the First World War and had been freed as a result of that war and so agreed by Russia.

The second of these commitments was an agreement that Communist Russia should have a periphery of "friendly border states" which in reality meant that these states were condemned to have Communist domination.

Thus, by acquiescence or by secret understandings or commitments, fifteen nations were engulfed in Communism and the independent life and freedom they had enjoyed were snuffed out.

---

1. [*Editor's note:* The January 1964 research copy of chapters 56–59 contains a few handwritten, stylistic changes of unknown authorship. The handwriting is not Hoover's, and one cannot be sure that it was that of his fact-checker, Mrs. Camp. (There is evidence that a Mr. Epstein—probably Julius Epstein, a scholar at the Hoover Institution—reviewed some of this material at some point.) I have therefore not incorporated these possibly unauthorized alterations into the text, unless they involve a clearly factual or obviously typographical correction, or unless there is other evidence—such as a notation in the margin—that the change was Hoover's. Revisions in Hoover's own handwriting have, of course, been incorporated.]

In subsequent text I refer to these actions as the "two great commitments" made at Tehran.

The Seven Annexed Peoples

The seven peoples or areas to be annexed by the Soviet Union immediately upon German retreat were Estonia, Latvia, Lithuania, Bessarabia, Bukovina, a part of Finland and a part of Poland. It is appropriate to recall here the recent backgrounds of these peoples.

After the establishment of their independence from Russia during or after the First World War (1918–1919) Finland, Estonia, Latvia, and Lithuania had been invaded by the Communists but had held their independence after bitter fighting with practically untrained peasants. The then defeated Communists had recognized their independence and signed peace pacts with them. During twenty years in the sunlight of freedom, they had grown in every avenue of well being.[2]

After June 1941, when Hitler turned against Stalin, the Germans occupied all of these states with their armies. Hitler's forces were still in occupation at the time of the Cairo-Tehran Conferences.

Hope for independence and freedom had risen in every heart among these peoples from the promises of the Atlantic Charter in August, 1941, and again when twenty-six nations, including Russia, declared their adherence to the Charter in January, 1942.

It may be recalled that when Stalin, in 1939, had offered his alliance to the highest bidder, the price was approval of his annexation of these states. Prime Minister Chamberlain refused the price on moral grounds. Mr. Churchill, then a member of the House of Commons, had urged the acceptance of the Soviet price. Apparently Mr. Churchill was little interested in the freedom of these states. Three months after the United States entered the war at Pearl Harbor, on March 7, 1942, he wrote to Mr. Roosevelt:

> ... The increasing gravity of the war has led me to feel that the principles of the Atlantic Charter ought not to be construed as to deny Russia the fron-

---

2. See Herbert Hoover, *An American Epic*, Volumes II and III, Henry Regnery Company, Chicago: 1959. [*Editor's note:* Hoover's citation is incorrect. These volumes were published in 1960 and 1961, respectively.]

tiers she occupied when Germany attacked her. . . . I hope therefore that you will be able to give us a free hand to sign the treaty. . . .[3]

Two days later, on March 9, Mr. Churchill informed Stalin of his letter to Mr. Roosevelt.

Harry Hopkins, who was one of the eyewitnesses present when this question was discussed at Tehran, writes:

> . . . The President then said he would be interested in the question of assuring the approaches to the Baltic Sea and had in mind some form of trusteeship with perhaps an international state in the vicinity of the Kiel Canal. . . . Due to some error of the Soviet translator Marshal Stalin apparently thought that the President was referring to . . . the Baltic States. On the basis of this understanding, he replied categorically that the Baltic States by an expression of the will of the people voted to join the Soviet Union and that this question was not therefore one for discussion. . . .[4]

We have been unable to find any record of such a free vote. However, Stalin's statement sealed any hope of freedom for these states if and when Hitler was defeated. There was no recorded protest by Roosevelt or Churchill to Stalin's pronouncement. After the German retreat, Stalin annexed these states to the Soviet Union.

Finland had joined Germany in the war and at the time of the Tehran Conference the Finns were still fighting the Allies. There were discussions at Tehran on the terms which might be given to Finland after the German defeat. The record states that:

> THE PRIME MINISTER said that the British Government desired first of all to see the Soviet Government satisfied with the border in the west, and secondly would like to see Finland remain independent. . . .

Stalin outlined the Soviet terms as follows:

1. The restoration of the Treaty of 1940 [with Finland] with the possible exchange of Petsamo for Hango. However, whereas Hango had been leased, Petsamo would be taken as a permanent possession.
2. Compensation for 50% of the damage done to the Soviet Union by the Finns, the exact amount to be discussed.

3. [Winston S.] Churchill, *The Hinge of Fate* [Houghton Mifflin Company, Boston: 1950], p. 327.
4. [Robert E.] Sherwood, *Roosevelt and Hopkins* [Harper & Brothers, New York: 1948], p. 782.

3. Break with Germany, and the expulsion of Germans from Finland.
4. Reorganization of the [Finnish] army.[5]

However, when peace terms were put into effect after the German retreat, the Soviet Union annexed huge areas of east and north Finland which embraced great natural resources, including the nickel mines and the forests. By this annexation, the Soviets established a boundary reaching to northern Norway.

Roosevelt and Churchill raised no objection to these terms as far as we can ascertain.

Poland

The future of Poland was also raised at Tehran. The following excerpt is from the transcript of the discussion on November 28, 1943 given in the Cairo-Tehran Papers:

MR. CHURCHILL then inquired whether it would be possible this evening to discuss the question of Poland. He said that Great Britain had gone to war with Germany because of the latter's invasion of Poland in 1939 and that the British Government was committed to the reestablishment of a strong and independent Poland but not to any specific Polish frontiers. . . .

MARSHAL STALIN said that he had not yet felt the necessity nor the desirability of discussing the Polish question. . . .

MR. CHURCHILL said that he personally had no attachment to any specific frontier between Poland and the Soviet Union; that he felt that the consideration of Soviet security on their western frontiers was a governing factor. He repeated, however, that the British Government considered themselves committed to the reestablishment of an independent and strong Poland which he felt a necessary instrument in the European orchestra.

MR. EDEN then inquired if he had understood the Marshal correctly at dinner when the latter said that the Soviet Union favored the Polish western frontier on the Oder. [In Germany]

MARSHAL STALIN replied emphatically that he did favor such a frontier for Poland and repeated that the Russians were prepared to help the Poles achieve it.

---

5. [U.S. Department of State,] *Foreign Relations of the United States*, [*Diplomatic Papers, The*] *Conferences at Cairo and Tehran, 1943* [United States Government Printing Office, Washington: 1961], p. 592.

MR. CHURCHILL then remarked that it would be very valuable if here in Teheran the representatives of the three governments could work out some agreed understanding on the question of the Polish frontiers which could then be taken up with the Polish Government in London. He said that, as far as he was concerned, he would like to see Poland moved westward in the same manner as soldiers at drill. . . .[6]

At the Tehran meeting of Roosevelt, Churchill, and Stalin three days later on December 1, the subject of the frontiers of Poland was further discussed. Stalin insisted that the boundary of East Poland which was to be annexed to Russia should be the "Curzon Line" (a boundary for Poland's eastern frontier laid down at Versailles on December 8, 1919). It was proposed that Poland should be compensated with a segment of Germany.[7]

The Exiled Polish Government, learning of this agreement, at once protested vigorously. I deal extensively with Poland's reactions later on in a separate section of this memoir, "The Case History of Poland."

An Episode in Bringing Freedom to the World

On the subject of the "two great understandings" of Tehran as to annexations and "friendly border states," Sherwood, on the authority of Hopkins, states that on the afternoon of December 1:

> . . . Roosevelt had a private talk with Stalin and Molotov for the purposes of putting them in possession of certain essential facts concerning American politics. . . .
>
> Roosevelt felt it necessary to explain to Stalin that there were six or seven million Americans of Polish extraction, and others of Lithuanian, Latvian and Estonian origin who had the same rights and the same votes as anyone else and whose opinions must be respected. Stalin said that he understood this, but he subsequently suggested that some "propaganda work" should be done among these people.[8]

Charles Bohlen, the interpreter, confirms the Sherwood statement as follows:

---

6. Ibid., p. 512. Italics mine. [*Editor's note:* None of this quotation is italicized in Hoover's manuscript.]

7. Ibid., pp. 597–599.

8. Sherwood, *Roosevelt and Hopkins*, p. 796.

THE PRESIDENT said he had asked Marshal Stalin to come to see him as he wished to discuss a matter briefly and frankly. He said it referred to internal American politics.

He said that we had an election in 1944 and that while personally he did not wish to run again, if the war was still in progress, he might have to.

He added that there were in the United States from six to seven million Americans of Polish extraction, and as a practical man, he did not wish to lose their vote. He said personally he agreed with the views of Marshal Stalin as to the necessity of the restoration of a Polish state but would like to see the Eastern border moved further to the west and Western border moved even to the River Oder. He hoped, however, that the Marshal would understand that for political reasons outlined above, he could not participate in any decision here in Tehran or even next winter on this subject and that he could not publicly take part in any such arrangement at the present time.

MARSHAL STALIN replied that now the President explained, he had understood.

THE PRESIDENT went on to say that there were a number of persons of Lithuanian, Latvian, and Estonian origin, in that order, in the United States. He said that he fully realized the three Baltic Republics had in history and again more recently been a part of Russia and added jokingly that when the Soviet armies re-occupied these area, he did not intend to go to war with the Soviet Union on this point.[9]

Thus did Mr. Roosevelt acquiesce in the annexations of the seven peoples. His approval of the doctrine of friendly border states will appear later.

It is interesting at this point to note the opinion of George F. Kennan, a great student of European agreements. He says:

. . . At the Tehran Conference in November 1943 both Churchill and Roosevelt urged upon Stalin the device that was eventually to be adopted: namely, that of moving Poland bodily several hundred miles to the west, thus making way for the satisfaction of Russian demands in the east and letting the Germans pay the bill by turning over to Poland extensive territories, going even as far as the Oder, from which many millions of German inhabitants would have to be displaced. It is hard for me now to understand—and it was hard at that time—how anyone could fail to recognize that a Poland with

---

9. *Foreign Relations of the United States,* [*Diplomatic Papers, The*] *Conferences at Cairo and Tehran, 1943,* p. 594.

borders so artificial, ones which involved so staggering a dislocation of population, would inevitably be dependent for its security on Soviet protection. To put Poland in such borders was to make it perforce a Russian protectorate, whether its own government was Communist or not. Whether Churchill or Roosevelt realized this, I cannot say. In any case, this proposal for moving Poland westward, with its utter lack of regard for the future political stability of eastern Europe and with its flagrant defiance of the principles of the Atlantic Charter of which Roosevelt and Churchill were themselves the authors, came—I am sorry to say—primarily from them rather than from Stalin.[10]

The Commitment to "Friendly Border States"

There is no record of a specific written agreement on this subject at Tehran except [that–*ed.*] at the meeting on December 1, Prime Minister Churchill is recorded as saying:

> ... that the British Government was first of all interested in seeing absolute security for the Western frontiers of the Soviet Union against any surprise assault in the future from Germany.[11]

This second great commitment to "friendly border states" was amply confirmed by statements of Churchill, Roosevelt, Hull, and the immediate action of Stalin in preparing Communist ministries for those states ready for the German retreat. It soon developed that the friendly border states were to be West Poland, East Germany, Czechoslovakia, Hungary, Albania, Bulgaria, Yugoslavia, and Rumania. By common world designation they became "Russian satellite" or "Communist puppet" states.

In subsequent chapters I describe the process of engulfment of each of these peoples and the stamping out of their independence and freedoms.

---

10. George F. Kennan, *Russia and The West Under Lenin and Stalin*, Little Brown and Company, [Boston: 1961], pp. 360–61.

11. *Foreign Relations of the United States*, [*Diplomatic Papers*,] *The Conferences at Cairo and Tehran, 1943*, p. 598.

CHAPTER 57

President Roosevelt's Statements as to the Decisions at Cairo and Tehran

ON DECEMBER 24, 1943, upon his return from the Cairo and Tehran Conferences, Mr. Roosevelt delivered a radio broadcast address.

The pertinent paragraphs were:

The Cairo and Tehran conferences, however, gave me my first opportunity to meet the Generalissimo, Chiang Kai-shek, and Marshal Stalin—and to sit down at the table with these unconquerable men and talk with them face to face. We had planned to talk to each other across the table at Cairo and Teheran; but we soon found that we were all on the same side of the table. . . .

Regarding Chiang Kai-shek, he said they were able:

. . . not only to settle upon definite military strategy but also to discuss certain long-range principles which we believe can assure peace in the Far East for many generations to come.

Of Stalin, he said:

. . . We talked with complete frankness on every conceivable subject connected with the winning of the war and the establishment of a durable peace after the war. . . .

. . . we were concerned with basic principles—principles which involve the security and the welfare and the standard of living of human beings in countries large and small.

To use an American and somewhat ungrammatical colloquialism, I may say that "I got along fine" with Marshal Stalin. . . . I believe that we are going to get along very well with him, and the Russian people—very well indeed. . . .

... The rights of every nation, large or small, must be respected and guarded as jealously as are the rights of every individual within our own republic.

The doctrine that the strong shall dominate the weak is the doctrine of our enemies—and we reject it. . . .

It has been our steady policy—and it is certainly a common-sense policy—that the right of each nation to freedom must be measured by the willingness of that nation to fight for freedom. And today we salute our unseen allies in occupied countries. . . .

This address also included the following statement:

Within the past year—within the past few weeks—history has been made, and it is far better history for the whole human race than any that we have known, or even dared to hope for. . . .

At Cairo and Teheran we devoted ourselves not only to military matters; we devoted ourselves also to consideration of the future, to plans for the kind of world which alone can justify all the sacrifices of this war.[1]

In his message to Congress on January 11, 1944, which was a further report on Tehran, Mr. Roosevelt said:

And right here I want to address a word or two to some suspicious souls who are fearful that Mr. Hull or I have made "commitments" for the future which might pledge this nation to secret treaties, or to enacting the role of Santa Claus.

To such suspicious souls—using a polite terminology—I wish to say that Mr. Churchill and Marshal Stalin and Generalissimo Chiang Kai-shek are all thoroughly conversant with the provisions of our Constitution. And so is Mr. Hull. And so am I.

Of course, we made some commitments. We most certainly committed ourselves to very large and very specific military plans which require the use of all Allied forces to bring about the defeat of our enemies at the earliest possible time.

But there were no secret treaties or political or financial commitments.[2]

Secretary Hull states in his memoirs that on February 7, 1944 (two months after Tehran), he cabled Ambassador Harriman

---

1. *New York Times,* December 25, 1943.
2. Ibid., January 12, 1944.

... a message from the President to Stalin, which we had prepared in the State Department. Mr. Roosevelt said to Stalin that, in communicating with him on the basis of the conversations they had had at Tehran, he wanted to make it plain that he neither desired nor intended to suggest, much less to advise him in any way, where Russia's interests lay with regard to Poland, since he fully realized that Russia's future security was rightly Stalin's primary concern. . . .[3]

This would seem to be an abandonment of any interest in the fate of Poland by the United States and to give Stalin a free hand.

Disclosure in February 1944, three months after Tehran, by Prime Minister Churchill that there were secret agreements made at Tehran as to Poland apparently stirred Congressman Mruk to make an inquiry of President Roosevelt, who replied as follows on March 6, 1944:

I am afraid I cannot make any further comments except what I have written to you before—*there were no secret commitments made by me at Teheran and I am quite sure that other members of my party made none either.* This, of course, does not include military plans which, however, had nothing to do with Poland.[4]

On October 21, 1944, Mr. Roosevelt again repeated there were no secret commitments, saying:

After my return from Teheran, I stated officially that no secret commitments had been made. The issue then is between my veracity and the continuing assertions of those who have no responsibility in the foreign field—or, perhaps I should say, a field foreign to them.[5]

Prime Minister Churchill Discloses the Two Great Commitments at Tehran

On February 22, 1944, a month after Mr. Roosevelt's return home address, Mr. Churchill addressed the House of Commons. He implied that an agreement had been made at Tehran as to the border states, saying:

---

3. *The Memoirs of Cordell Hull* [The Macmillan Company, New York: 1948], Vol. II, p. 1439.

4. [Elliott Roosevelt, ed.,] *F.D.R., His Personal Letters,* [1928–1945] [Duell, Sloan and Pearce, New York: 1950], Vol. II, p. 1498. Italics mine.

5. *New York Times,* October 23, 1944. Italics mine. [*Editor's note:* After this quotation, Hoover made the following comments in his Z+H edition: "In view of Mr. Roosevelt's explanation of 'American politics' to Mr. Stalin, I am disposed to believe this statement is technically correct. It would take

. . . Russia has the right of reassurance against future attacks from the West, and we are going all the way with her to see that she gets it, not only by the might of her arms but by the approval and assent of the United Nations. . . . I cannot feel that the Russian demand for a reassurance about her Western frontiers goes beyond the limits of what is reasonable or just. . . .[6]

In a speech in the House of Commons more than five months later (August 2, 1944) Mr. Churchill said in respect to the doctrine of "friendly border states":

. . . They ask that there should be a Poland friendly to Russia. This seems to me very reasonable. . . .

It seems to me that Rumania must primarily make its terms with Russia. . . . The same applies to Bulgaria. . . .[7]

Less than two months later, on September 28, 1944, in another speech to the House of Commons, Mr. Churchill again supported the doctrine of the "friendly border states," saying:

I cannot conceive that it is not possible to make a good solution whereby Russia gets the security which she is entitled to have, and which I have resolved that we will do our utmost to secure for her, on her Western Frontier. . . .[8]

On January 18, 1945, Mr. Churchill again addressed the House of Commons and confirmed another segment of the secret agreements with regard to Stalin's control of the "border states," saying:

Recently Bulgaria and Rumania have passed under the control of the Soviet military authorities, and Russian-controlled armies are in direct contact with Yugoslavia. As we feared that there might be misunderstandings and contrary policies between us and the Soviet Government about Yugoslavia, which can easily arise when armies enter a country which is in great disorder, the Foreign Secretary and I reached at Moscow an understanding with Marshal Stalin by which our two countries pursue a joint policy in these regions, after constant discussions. This agreement raised no question of divisions of territory or spheres of interest after the war. It was aimed only at the avoidance,

---

too much space to discuss the moral problems involved." Hoover later deleted these sentences. See the January 1964 research copy (and Hoover's personal copy) of chapter 57.]

6. [Winston S.] Churchill, *The Dawn of Liberation* [Little, Brown and Company, Boston: 1945], pp. 25–26.

7. Ibid., pp. 208, 209–210.

8. Ibid., p. 253.

during these critical days, of friction between the great Allies. In practice I exchange telegrams on behalf of His Majesty's Government personally with Marshal Stalin about the difficulties which arise, and about what is the best thing to do. We keep President Roosevelt informed constantly.

In pursuance of our joint policy, we encouraged the making of an agreement between the Tito Government, which, with Russian assistance, has now installed itself in Belgrade, and the Royal Government of Yugoslavia, which is seated in London, and recognized by us, as, I believe, by all the Powers of the United Nations. . . . We believe that the arrangements of the Tito-Subasitch agreement are the best that can be made for the immediate future of Yugoslavia. . . .[9]

An Article in "The Saturday Evening Post"

There was confusion and doubt in some American minds as to commitments at the Cairo-Tehran Conferences.

Then Mr. Roosevelt did an extraordinary thing. He called in one of the writers of *The Saturday Evening Post,* the very capable Forrest Davis, and gave him an account of accomplishments and objectives at Tehran, all to be written on Davis' own responsibility. When Davis' manuscript was completed, he submitted it to Mr. Roosevelt, who revised it in his own handwriting. Mr. Davis told me that this revised copy with Mr. Roosevelt's handwriting has been preserved. Davis' story was published in two issues of *The Saturday Evening Post*—May 13 and 20, 1944.

According to the account given to Davis, Mr. Roosevelt had discovered a "great design" for peace. A part of the "great design" was appeasement (Roosevelt's own interpolated word) in order to include Stalin in this peace project.

At this point I may point out that the records of the Cairo-Tehran Conference show that Stalin had tacitly agreed during the Tehran Conference to Mr. Roosevelt's proposal for a world organization to preserve peace, and apparently no inducement was necessary. The proposal, as shown in Chapter [54–*ed.*], was a four-nation policing of the world.[10]

These magazine articles have importance because they confirm other disclosures with regard to what actually happened at Tehran. Such pertinent paragraphs are:

---

9. [Winston S.] Churchill, [*Onwards to*] *Victory* [Little, Brown and Company, Boston: 1944], p. 7.
10. [U.S. Department of State,] *Foreign Relations of the United States,* [*Diplomatic Papers, The*] *Conferences at Cairo and Tehran, 1943* [United States Government Printing Office, Washington: 1961], p. 531.

. . . the President's objective, as he sees it, calls for finesse, a skillful state-craft that cannot always be exposed to view. In the interest of his objective, Mr. Roosevelt has avoided the slightest cause of offense to the Kremlin. Pursuing a soft policy instead of the firm line urged by certain advisers, he has followed the Biblical injunction to walk the second mile.

Mr. Davis continues:

The core of his policy has been the reassurance of Stalin. That was so, as we have seen, at Teheran. It has been so throughout the difficult diplomacy since Stalingrad. Our failure to renew our offer of good offices in the Russo-Polish controversies must be read in that light. Likewise our support, seconding Britain, of Tito, the Croatian Communist partisan leader in Jugoslavia. So it is also with the President's immediate and generous response to Stalin's demand for a share in the surrendered Italian fleet or its equivalent. Our bluntly reiterated advice to the Finns to quit the war at once without reference to Soviet terms falls under the same tactical heading. . . .

Suppose that Stalin, in spite of all concessions, should prove *unappeasable* [note that this word was approved by Roosevelt], determined to pursue his own policy regardless of the west? What assurance does the Roosevelt approach hold that he may not capture all Poland, Finland, the Balkans and even Germany from within, as was the case with the Baltic states, once his armies occupy those countries and he can recognize his own Moscow-dominated undergrounds? A Europe dominated by the hammer and sickle, with the Baltic and Black seas Russian ponds, the Danube basin a Russian protectorate, and Soviet power on the Rhine, might suit this country's vital interests even less than the torn and distracted Europe of 1939. . . .

Mr. Roosevelt, gambling for stakes as enormous as any statesman ever played for, has been betting that the Soviet Union needs peace and is willing to pay for it by collaborating with the west. . . .[11]

As to personal relations among the Big Three, Mr. Davis (text as approved by Mr. Roosevelt), said:

. . . Mr. Stalin thawed only slowly under the sun of Mr. Roosevelt's justly celebrated charm. . . . Stalin, too, is noted for joviality. . . .

His edged wit, aimed at Winston Churchill, subsequently was to affect the amenities among the Big Three. Churchill . . . was easily nettled and retorted

---

11. Forrest Davis, "What Really Happened at Teheran," *The Saturday Evening Post,* [vol. 216,] May 13, 1944, p. 37. Italics mine.

to Stalin in kind. It thereupon became Roosevelt's self-appointed chore to moderate the asperities before they drew blood. . . . throughout the four days of the meeting, Stalin, while frequently rawhiding Churchill, treated Roosevelt with a consideration approaching deference. . . .

. . . The prime minister, a scion of dukes, and the Georgian ex-revolutionary are powerful, opinionated and free-spoken individuals. . . . They tangled, no doubt inevitably, at Teheran. . . .

Over the sharp exchanges at Teheran, Mr. Roosevelt played his own lighthearted colloquial humor. . . .

So it went at Teheran. The President quipped and yarned, relieving tension, suggesting bridges of compromise between the Briton and the Russian. . . .[12]

The editors of *The Saturday Evening Post* put one of their other writers— Demaree Bess—on the job to write "The Cost of Roosevelt's 'Great Design'" in their next issue. The essential parts of this article were:

We know now that Marshal Stalin exacted a down payment from us at Teheran. He insisted that Russia is entitled to make its own territorial adjustments in Eastern Europe, without regard to the "no territorial aggrandizement" pledge of the Atlantic Charter or the glowing promises of the Four Freedoms. . . .

. . . How far have those compromises already gone? So far as Britain is concerned, we have tacitly undertaken to support the British and Western European colonial systems. So far as Russia is concerned, we have tacitly conceded all the claims she has presented concerning Eastern Europe.

. . . on paper, Mr. Roosevelt conceded nothing at Teheran. . . .

. . . so that Secretary of State Cordell Hull can correctly declare, as he did in April, "Neither the President nor I have made or will make any secret agreement or commitment, political or financial."

Nevertheless, Teheran actually changed everything, because of the tactics employed by President Roosevelt at that conference. In his eagerness to win Stalin's confidence, our President quickly passed over any question which the Soviet premier did not care to discuss. This amicable attitude of Mr. Roosevelt's was interpreted as a tacit understanding, and Stalin's subsequent actions have demonstrated his reliance upon that understanding.

When Mr. Roosevelt did not challenge Russia's claims in Eastern Europe, when he did not protest Stalin's interpretation of the Atlantic Charter as

---

12. Ibid., pp. 11, 39, 41.

applied to Russia's border regions, the settlement in Eastern Europe—so far as the United States is concerned—went by default.

Not only did the President's tactics decide the question of the Baltic states in Russia's favor but they also assented to her recovery of those portions of Poland and Rumania which she annexed in 1939 and 1940 by agreement with Germany. . . .

Encouraged by Mr. Roosevelt's sympathetic attitude, Stalin began to make his aggressive diplomacy felt in Jugoslavia and Greece, in Czechoslovakia and Poland, in Turkey and Bulgaria, and even in Italy and France. . . .

Because Mr. Roosevelt sided with Stalin, the British Prime Minister was compelled to alter his own policy at Teheran, and in the end he went even farther than the President did in conciliating the Russians. . . . It becomes increasingly apparent that Russia and Britain have entered into an understanding which has the effect of dividing Europe into spheres of influence.[13]

I Speak My Mind

I concluded that I must raise my voice regarding what had been done at Tehran. I, of course, did not know all that had taken place, but Major General Patrick J. Hurley, who was present at the Tehran Conference, told me that Messrs. Churchill, Roosevelt, and Stalin had reached an understanding at Tehran that Russia should have the "annexation" states and the domination of "friendly border states."

General Hurley had been Secretary of War in my Administration and at this period was roving Ambassador for Mr. Roosevelt. The General also gave me a sidelight on the attitude of the Russians toward Americans. He stated that he was very doubtful if, after the war, any agreement of Stalin with the Western Democracies would be of much consequence in the preservation of peace. He said Stalin and all the generals with whom he had come in contact were more bitterly opposed to the Western Democracies than they had been to the Nazis.

In my address before the Republican Convention in Chicago on June 27, 1944, broadcast to the public, I said:

> . . . It is obvious the American people have but one purpose in this war. We want to live in peace. We do not want these horrors again. We want no territory except some Pacific island bases that will protect the United States. We

---

13. Demaree Bess, "The Cost of Roosevelt's 'Great Design,'" *The Saturday Evening Post,* [vol. 216,] May 27, 1944, pp. 17, 90.

want no domination over any nation. We want no indemnities. We want no special privileges.

But we do want the freedom of nations from the domination of others, call it by whatever name we will—liberation of peoples, self government or just restored sovereignty. We want it both in the cause of freedom and we want it because we know that there can be no lasting peace if enslaved peoples must ceaselessly strive and fight for freedom.

There are constants in the relations between nations that are more nearly to be found in their history, their surroundings, their ideals, their hearts, than in the declarations of their officials. Foreign relations are not sudden things created by books or speeches or banquets. The history of nations is more important than their oratory.

The ideal of freedom for other peoples lies deep in American history and the American heart. It did not arise from Woodrow Wilson's 14 Points nor from the Atlantic Charter. It was embedded in the hearts of the American people by the suffering and sacrifice with which they won their own independence. It was in response to the cry for liberation and freedom of peoples that we established the Monroe Doctrine, that we fought the Mexican War, the Spanish War, and the first World War. And now, after twenty years, we again sacrifice the sons of America to the call of freedom.

Without this spiritual impulse of freedom for others we would not have engaged in a single one of these wars. Had we not been concerned with the freedom of China, we would not have been attacked at Pearl Harbor. Only because freedom was in jeopardy in all Europe are we making this gigantic effort.

Therefore, the American people are not likely to welcome any settlements which do not include the independence of Poland as well as every other country which desires to be free from alien domination. Americans do not want this war to end in the restriction of freedom among nations. It is obvious that the United States will emerge from this war the strongest military, and thus political, power in the world. Our power to bring freedom to the world must not be frittered away.

I then referred to the disclosures of Mr. Roosevelt's "Great Design" in *The Saturday Evening Post:*

We are told Mr. Roosevelt had this Great Design in mind during his recent conference at Teheran.

So far as these published descriptions go this method is power politics and balance-of-power diplomacy. That is not the diplomacy of freedom. . . .

The basis of lasting peace for America must be friendship of nations not brokerage of power politics.

There may have been no political commitments at Teheran. But certainly since that Conference we have seen a series of independent actions by Russia which seem to be the negative of restored sovereignty to certain peoples. Certainly the Atlantic Charter has been sent to the hospital for major amputations of freedom among nations. The American people deserve a much fuller exposition of this Great Design.

And the Teheran Conference raises another question. Under our form of government the President cannot speak either for the Congress or the conclusions of American public opinion. The only way for America to succeed in foreign relations is by open declaration of policies. They must first have seasoned consideration and public understanding. These do not come by secret diplomacy. America cannot successfully bluff, intrigue or play the sordid game of power politics. . . .

President Wilson also had a "great design" most of which was lost by the blandishments and pressures of personal negotiation. Every thinking American views with great apprehension a repetition of 1919. America needs a change in administration to get out of personal power diplomacy.[14]

I was under a misapprehension in this speech. I did not then know that the Atlantic Charter had been secretly buried at Tehran. I thought it had only been sent to the hospital for amputations.

The Forrestal Diaries

Secretary of the Navy, James Forrestal, apparently irked by appeasement of Stalin, wrote on September 2, 1944, to a friend:

I find that whenever any American suggests that we act in accordance with the needs of our security he is apt to be called a god-damned fascist or imperialist, while if Uncle Joe suggests that he needs the Baltic Provinces, half of Poland, all of Bessarabia and access to the Mediterranean, all hands agree that he is a fine, frank, candid and generally delightful fellow who is very easy to deal with because he is so explicit in what he wants.[15]

---

14. [Herbert Hoover,] *Addresses upon the American Road, 1941–1945* [D. Van Nostrand Company, New York: 1946], pp. 251, 252, 253, 254. [Italics added by Hoover.]

15. *The Forrestal Diaries.* Edited by Walter Millis with the collaboration of E. S. Duffield (The Viking Press, New York, 1951), p. 14.

CHAPTER 58

Stalin by Action Proves the Two Secret Undertakings

THESE "TWO GREAT COMMITMENTS" were the instrument by which fifteen peoples fell under the control of the Communists. The complete confirmation that these commitments were made at Tehran is evidenced by Stalin's immediate action. He began to move even before the German retreat from eastern Europe. There is no recorded protest from Messrs. Roosevelt or Churchill.

Finland

In February 1944, when Germany started to weaken, Finland began negotiations with Russia for peace. I have already given the terms which Stalin announced at Tehran that would be imposed upon her. An indemnity of $800,000,000 at pre-war exchange rates was required by Stalin.[1] This was in proportion to her resources, the equivalent of a levy of about 250 billion dollars on the United States. Mr. Roosevelt issued appeals to the Finns to accept the Russian demands and Hull breathed intimidations.[2] On March 21, 1944, the Finnish Parliament unanimously rejected the Russian terms.[3] Mr. Roosevelt expelled the Finnish Minister from Washington and a little later broke off diplomatic relations.[4]

On August 4, 1944, the Finnish Parliament elected Field Marshal Carl Gustav Mannerheim President. He demanded that the Germans leave

---

1. Hugh Shearman, *Finland* (London Institute of World Affairs [London: 1950]), passim.
2. [Samuel I. Rosenman, comp.,] *The Public Papers and Addresses of Franklin D. Roosevelt* (1944 [volume]) [Harper & Brothers Publishers, 1950], p. 103; *The Memoirs of Cordell Hull* [The Macmillan Company, New York: 1948], Vol. II, pp. 1449–1450.
3. *New York Times,* March 22, 1944.
4. *The Memoirs of Cordell Hull,* Vol. II, p. 1450.

Finland. As the Germans needed their troops elsewhere they retreated but wantonly destroyed all Finnish homes in their path.

On September 4, President Mannerheim asked for peace with Russia, which was consummated on September 19. This treaty was practically the same as Stalin had proposed at Tehran, but in addition to the indemnity, it required the Finns to arrest and bring to trial as war criminals their leaders whose crime was fighting for freedom. They [i.e., the Finns–ed.] were also required to set up a Cabinet satisfactory to Stalin.

The Baltic States

Any hope of independence and freedom for the Baltic States died at Tehran. However, during the year after Tehran urgent appeals for President Roosevelt's intervention came to him from the exiled former officials of these states in the name of the Atlantic Charter. Such appeals on September 12 and October 17, 1944 were answered by the State Department:

> The . . . questions growing out of the situation . . . are receiving the constant attention of the appropriate officials. . . .[5]

In each Baltic state an "underground" had sprung up which collected names, dates and places of Communist atrocities.

Their records showed:

> From Estonia alone 60,910 people of all classes were deported to Russia, 7,129 of whom had first been sentenced to ten to twenty-five years' hard labor. 1,800 Estonians were killed; 32,187 men were mobilized into the Red Army.
>
> In Latvia, more than 60,000 people disappeared, including 20,000 women and 9,000 children (the International Red Cross at Geneva listed in 1943 the names of 35,000 who have been traced). 1,700 people were killed.
>
> In Lithuania it was estimated that at least 50,000 civilians were deported to Russia . . . and 3,000 persons killed by NKVD. The head of the family was invariably separated from . . . children who were put in training camps for young Communists. . . .

---

5. This quotation is taken from the Lithuanian American Information Center pamphlet, *Supplement To The Appeal To Fellow Americans On Behalf of the Baltic States by United Organizations of Americans of Lithuanian, Latvian and Estonian Descent*, New York, November 1944, pp. 8, 15–18.

The deportees were piled into locked cattle trucks without water or any sanitary arrangements whatever, in which condition they traveled for weeks to Siberia and Asiatic Russia. . . .[6]

Bukovina and Bessarabia

When the Germans retreated from Rumania in late August, 1944, Stalin at once occupied these peoples and annexed them to the Soviet Union.

Poland

If anything more were needed to confirm the "two secret agreements" it was the fate of Poland. The descent of Poland into a Communist state is so much an historic example of Communist methods and the weakness of the leaders of free nations at this time that I deal with it in detail in a separate section entitled, "The Case History of Poland."

I may say here that East Poland up to the so-called Curzon Line was promptly occupied and annexed by Stalin upon the German retreat. With regard to West Poland: Stalin, on February 12, 1944, three months after Tehran, began preparing a Communist Ministry to be installed at the German retreat. This Ministry, comprising [comprised–ed.] about twenty men of whom twelve were seasoned Communists and the others, "liberal" representatives. This Ministry was ultimately set up at Lublin.

Czechoslovakia

President Benes was quick to realize the import of Tehran. These signs led him at once to Moscow. Within a month after Tehran, he reached an agreement with Stalin (on December 12, 1943) the meaning of which, together with subsequent understandings, was that immediately upon liberation from the Germans, Czechoslovakia would accept Communist representation in its provisional government and adhere to Communist Russia as a "friendly state."[7]

Five months later (May, 1944), with the German retreat, President Benes duly formed a Ministry with a large Communist representation in its membership.

---

6. "The Baltic States," *The New Leader,* [vol. 28], April 14, 1945, p. 12.
7. Statement made to me by Benes in 1946.

Albania

The Germans retreated from Albania late in 1944. With the support of the Russian Communists and General Tito of Yugoslavia, the Albanian Communists seized control of the Government. By December, 1944 [1945–*ed.*], opposition parties had been eliminated and the usual single-ticket Communist election was held, establishing a Communist, Enver Hoxha, as Premier.[8]

Hungary

With his usual technique, soon after Tehran, Stalin set up in Moscow a Communist Ministry for Hungary, under Janos Gyonygosy. A year later, after the German retreat, Soviet troops occupied Hungary (November 1944) and Stalin's ministry was installed in December 1944. The real governing powers were the Soviet military commander, Marshal Voroshilov, and the leader of the Communist Party in Hungary, Matyas Rakosi.

Bulgaria

With the approaching retreat of the Germans, the democratic elements in the country on September 2, 1944, overthrew the German puppet government and established a provisional government under Prime Minister Konstatin Muraviev. The Russians, three days later, declared war upon them, and on September 9, 1944, Bulgaria surrendered. She was immediately occupied by the Red Army, the democratic government was ousted and the Prime Minister imprisoned. The Russians created a Ministry of approved Communists under the leadership of a veteran of their faith—Georgi Dimitrov.[9] Dimitrov liquidated some 2,000 of the democratic leaders.[10] Leon Dennen, an American news correspondent, reported on April 14, 1945 [December 30, 1944–*ed.*]:

> The people of the United States are not being told the truth. They were never informed of the fact that Soviet Russia ruthlessly suppressed a genu-

---

8. E[rnest] O. Hauser, "[The] Red Rape of Albania," *The Saturday Evening Post,* [vol. 222,] November 26, 1949, p. 26. See also Andrew Gyorgy, *Governments of Danubian Europe* ([Rinehart & Company, Inc.,] New York: 1949).

9. [World Peace Foundation,] *Documents on American Foreign Relations,* Vol. III, [July] 1944– [June] 1945 [Princeton University Press: 1947], pp. 239–243; *New York Times,* September 6, 1944.

10. Leon Dennen, *The New Leader,* April 14, 1945; Hal Lehrman, *Russia's Europe* ([D. Appleton-Century Company, Inc.,] New York: 1947), pp. 258–277.

ine democratic revolution in Bulgaria, that Russian tanks and bayonets and American lend-lease material have imposed on Bulgaria a . . . Communist government, [and–*ed.*] that all pro-Americans have been shot or jailed by [Russian] General Tolbukhin.[11]

Yugoslavia

In Chapter [53–*ed.*] I have given the text of the secret agreement signed at Tehran on December 1, 1943, by Roosevelt, Churchill, and Stalin, which recognized Tito and his Communists as dominant in Yugoslavia.

At that time there were two underground forces in Yugoslavia. One, under the anti-Communist General Draja Mikhailovic, had fought the Germans from their first invasion of the country in 1941. The other, under Josip Broz Tito, had come upon the scene in 1942 and organized a rival underground which was wholly Communist. Tito was a Communist agent of Stalin of twenty years' standing. He had taken part in the Communists' revolution in Spain against the Franco forces. Yugoslavia's descent into a Communist satellite state can be dated from the installation of Tito.

From Hopkins' memorandum account of the Tehran Conference which he attended, it seems that the proposal to install Tito has come from Mr. Roosevelt. Hopkins writes:

> . . . Roosevelt said he wished to lend Stalin a report from a U.S. Army officer who had been with Tito in Yugoslavia and had the highest respect for the work being done there by the Partisan forces. . . .[12]

This report was prepared by the American Office of Strategic Services. It complained that:

> [. . .–*ed.*] Mihailovitch made the fatal mistake of allowing his political beliefs and his plans for the future to overcome his better judgment. He feared Communism more than he feared the common enemy. . . .[13]

---

11. [Leon Dennen, "A Guide Through Balkan Chaos,"] *The New Leader,* December 30, 1944. [*Editor's note:* Hoover's original citation date was inaccurate. I have corrected the error.]

12. [Robert E.] Sherwood, *Roosevelt and Hopkins* [Harper & Brothers, New York: 1948], p. 784. This report favorable to Tito is given in [U.S. Department of State,] *Foreign Relations of the United States,* [*Diplomatic Papers,*] *The Conferences at Cairo and Tehran, 1943* [United States Government Printing Office, Washington: 1961], pp. 606–615.

13. *Foreign Relations of the United States,* [*Diplomatic Papers,*] *The Conferences at Cairo and Tehran, 1943,* p. 608.

Exiled King Peter II of Yugoslavia visited Mr. Roosevelt during the Cairo Conference.[14] No record of their conversations is given in the Cairo-Tehran papers but King Peter, in his book *A King's Heritage*,[15] says the subject discussed was the reconciling of Mikhailovic and Tito.

General Eisenhower, at the meeting of the Joint Chiefs of Staff at Tehran on November 26, 1943, expressed the opinion that:

> ... all possible equipment should be sent to Tito since Mikhailovitch's ... forces were of relatively little value.[16]

Whatever the reasons were, it is certain that at Tehran Mikhailovic was abandoned. It was a tragic betrayal of freedom.

On December 4, 1943, while Roosevelt and Churchill were still at the Second Cairo Conference, Tito set up a provisional government in Yugoslavia called the "Yugoslav Committee of National Liberation," composed of communists.

King Peter tried to get an appointment with Roosevelt after he and Churchill came back from Tehran. He reports the result of this attempt as follows:

> I asked to see Mr. Roosevelt on his return from Teheran, but was told that he was very ill and not receiving anybody.[17]

Churchill, in a speech to the House of Commons on February 22, 1944, two months after Tehran, described the Tito arrangement at Tehran, saying:

> ... in Yugoslavia we give our aid to Marshal Tito. . . .
>
> ... two main forces are in the field. First, the guerrilla bands under General Mihailovitch. These were the first to take the field, and represent, to a certain extent, the forces of old Serbia. For some time after the defeat of the Yugoslav army [by Germany], these forces maintained a guerilla [organization]. . . .
>
> However, a new and far more formidable champion appeared on the scene. In the autumn of 1941, Marshal Tito's Partisans[18] began a wild and furious war for existence against the Germans. . . . Soon they began to inflict heavy injury upon the Germans and became masters of wide regions. Led

---

14. Ibid., p. 345.

15. King Peter II of Yugoslavia, *A King's Heritage* (G.P. Putnam's Sons, New York: 1954), pp. 195–196.

16. *Foreign Relations of the United States,* [*Diplomatic Papers,*] *The Conferences at Cairo and Tehran, 1943,* p. 361.

17. King Peter II of Yugoslavia, *A King's Heritage*, p. 199.

18. The frequent use of "Partisan" for communists may be noted as a method for camouflaging the truth.

with great skill, organized on the guerilla principle, they were at once elusive and deadly. . . . The Partisan movement soon outstripped in numbers the forces of General Mihailovitch. . . .

. . . In Marshal Tito, the Partisans have found an outstanding leader, *glorious in the fight for freedom.* Unhappily, perhaps inevitably, these new forces came into collision with those under General Mihailovitch. . . . At the present time, the followers of Marshal Tito outnumber many times those of General Mihailovitch, who acts in the name of the Royal Yugoslav Government. . . .

For a long time past, I have taken a particular interest in Marshal Tito's movement, and have tried, and am trying, by every available means, to bring him help. . . .[19]

Mikhailovic, ultimately captured by Tito, was "tried" by a Communist court and executed.

I have been unable to find in the record that a single official protest was made by the American Government at whose insistence Mikhailovic had initiated the first revolt against the Germans in 1941; nor was there protest from the British even though Mikhailovic had bravely sabotaged the German-controlled railways through Serbia and thereby saved the remnants of the British Army in Greece.

Many books and articles have been written on the service of Mikhailovic (including one by Ruth Mitchell, sister of U.S Attorney General William Mitchell),[20] and the abandonment of him. A thousand excuses have been offered for the Mikhailovic tragedy. His fake trial as a "traitor" and his execution have filled many columns in the press.

On May 24, 1944, Churchill again returned to the subject of Mikhailovic and Tito in a speech to the House of Commons, this time indicating that Tito had reformed from Communism:

It must be remembered, however, that this question does not turn on Mihailovitch alone; there is also a very large body, amounting to perhaps 200,000 of Serbian peasant proprietors who are anti-German but strongly Serbian, and who naturally hold the views of a peasant-owner community in regard to property, and are less enthusiastic in regard to communism than some of

---

19. [Winston S.] Churchill, *The Dawn of Liberation* [Little, Brown and Company, Boston: 1945], pp. 17, 20, 21. Italics mine. [*Editor's note:* Churchill and Hoover used different spellings of the Serbian general's name. The most common spellings today are Mihailovic and Mihailovich.]

20. [*Editor's note:* Hoover's identification of Ruth Mitchell's brother is inaccurate. She was the sister of the military aviation pioneer, Brigadier General William ("Billy") Mitchell. For her obituary, see *New York Times*, October 26, 1969, p. 82.]

those in Croatia or Slovenia. Marshal Tito has largely sunk his communist aspect in his character as a Yugoslav patriot leader. He repeatedly proclaims that he has no intention of reversing the property and social systems which prevail in Serbia. . . .[21]

At this time, a Yugoslav government-in-exile in London represented the "democratic elements," under the leadership of King Peter and Prime Minister Dr. Ivan Subasic. As a result of the pressure from the British and Americans, they signed an agreement with Tito's "Yugoslav Committee of National Liberation" on June 16, 1944, six months after Tehran, by which Tito was to head the state but "democratic elements" were to be incorporated in the Provisional Government.[22]

Churchill met with Tito and Subasic two months later (August, 1944) and endeavored to get them into agreement. At this time Tito assured Mr. Churchill that he would not impose Communism on Yugoslavia. However, when Churchill invited Tito to make the statement in public, Tito refused.[23]

When the Germans retreated from Yugoslavia in October, 1944, Tito at once installed his Provisional Government, with a Ministry of fifteen Communists and fellow-travelers. On November 1, he admitted Dr. Subasic and one other non-Communist into his Ministry. However, he gave them inactive ministries.

The result of all this in terms of human freedom is indicated by the report of *A Committee of American Serbs,* headed by Bishop Dionisije who on December 1, 1944—a year after Tehran—declared:

> More than 40,000 leading persons, officers and soldiers and members of the families of men in exile, whether in government service, military service or imprisoned in Germany, have been arrested in Belgrade and Serbia. This has been accompanied with a threat that unless those in exile submit to dictator Tito's edicts, they shall be held as hostages in concentration camps and eventually executed. Up to December 1st [1944] 245 leading citizens of Belgrade have been arrested and executed by dictator Tito's forces under direct orders of the supposed liberators of Belgrade.[24]

---

21. Churchill, *The Dawn of Liberation,* p. 122.

22. *Documents on American Foreign Relations,* Vol. VII, [July] 1944–[June] 1945, p. 907.

23. [Winston S.] Churchill, *Triumph and Tragedy* [Houghton Mifflin Company, Boston: 1953], p. 90.

24. The ultimate descent of Yugoslavia to a Communist state will appear in later chapters.

Rumania

At the time of the Tehran Conference Rumania was still fighting with the Germans against the Allies. At the conference British Foreign Minister Eden stated that the Allies would discuss peace with the Rumanians only on the basis of unconditional surrender.[25]

Mr. Churchill, in an address to the House of Commons on May 24, 1944, gave assurances as to the future of Rumania:

> ... The terms offered by Russia to Rumania make no suggestion of altering the standards of society in that country, and are in many respects, if not in all, remarkably generous. . . .[26]

I have in Chapter [59–ed.] described President Roosevelt's agreement, and Secretary Hull's reluctance, to Russia's conducting all negotiations with Rumania.

With the retreat of the German armies, Rumania made a military surrender to Russia on August 24, 1944. Young King Michael, by a peaceful *coup d'etat* immediately after the German retreat, eliminated the pro-German government of General Ion Antonescu and appointed General Constantin Sanatescu as Prime Minister. However, he was compelled to accept the representation of Communists in the Ministry and the Russian terms for an armistice. By these terms the Soviet government was to receive an indemnity from Rumania. From September 1, 1944 to December 31, 1945, it covered the following:

Cattle	317,000	head
Sheep	365,000	head
Hogs	135,000	head
Horses	120,000	head
Cereals	608,000	tons
Fodder	94,000	tons
Oil Products	3,611,000	tons
Lumber	557,000	cubic meters.[27]

---

25. *Foreign Relations of the United States,* [*Diplomatic Papers,*] *The Conferences at Cairo and Tehran, 1943,* p. 166.

26. Churchill, *The Dawn of Liberation,* p. 127.

27. Secret enclosure from United States Mission to Bucharest, May 8, 1946. [*Editor's note:* Hoover provided no further information about this source.]

Churchill's Confirmation to Stalin on the Fate of the Balkan States

The Prime Minister journeyed to Moscow in October, 1944, for a conference with Marshal Stalin (the Second Moscow Conference). A further account is given in Chapter 61. Mr. Churchill's account of his meeting with Stalin on October 9 where there was great expansion of their empires is as follows:

... At ten o'clock that night we held our first important meeting in the Kremlin. There were only Stalin, Molotov, Eden, Harriman, and I, with Major Birse and Pavlov as interpreters. ...

The moment was apt for business, so I said, "Let us settle about our affairs in the Balkans. Your armies are in Rumania and Bulgaria. We have interests, missions, and agents there. Don't let us get at cross-purposes in small ways. So far as Britain and Russia are concerned, how would it do for you to have ninety per cent predominance in Rumania, for us to have ninety per cent of the say in Greece, and go fifty-fifty about Yugoslavia?" While this was being translated I wrote out on a half-sheet of paper:

Rumania	
Russia	90%
The others	10%
Greece	
Great Britain (in accord with U.S.A.)	90%
Russia	10%
Yugoslavia	50–50%
Hungary	50–50%
Bulgaria	
Russia	75%
The others	25%

I pushed this across to Stalin, who had by then heard the translation. There was a slight pause. Then he took his blue pencil and made a large tick upon it, and passed it back to us. It was all settled in no more time than it takes to set down. ...

After this there was a long silence. The pencilled paper lay in the centre of the table. At length I said, "Might it not be thought rather cynical if it seemed we had disposed of these issues, so fateful to millions of people, in such an offhand manner? Let us burn the paper." "No, you keep it," said Stalin.[28]

---

28. Churchill, *Triumph and Tragedy,* pp. 226, 227–228.

Here again was confirmation of the second secret commitment for "friendly border states" made at Tehran. With Marshal Stalin's Communist ministries already set up for Hungary, Bulgaria, Yugoslavia, and Rumania, the percentages for "The others" had slim chance.[29]

Mr. Churchill's report to the House of Commons on October 27, 1944, about two weeks after this agreement, was:

> Upon the tangled question of the Balkans, where there are Black Sea interests and Mediterranean interests to be considered, we were able to reach complete agreement. I do not feel that there is any immediate danger of our combined war effort being weakened by divergencies of policy or of doctrine in Greece, Rumania, Bulgaria, Yugoslavia, and, beyond the Balkans, Hungary. We have reached a very good working agreement about all these countries, singly and in combination, with the object of concentrating all their efforts, and concerting them with ours against the common foe, and of providing, as far as possible, for a peaceful settlement after the war is over. We are, in fact, acting jointly, Russia and Britain, in our relations with both the Royal Yugoslav Government headed by Dr. Subasic and with Marshal Tito, and we have invited them to come together for the common cause, as they had already agreed to do at the conference which I held with them both at Naples. . . .
>
>   . . . All these discussions were part of the process of carrying out and following up the great decisions taken nearly a year ago at Teheran. . . .[30]

This last sentence would seem confirmation of an undisclosed agreement at Tehran which fixed the fate of eight nations.

I have described in Chapter [58–*ed.*] an agreement between Churchill and Stalin by which Greece was "90%" assigned to the British sphere in the Mediterranean after the German retreat.

This agreement with Stalin apparently did not preclude internal Communist conspiracies to seize the government. Mr. Churchill records the events in 1944:

> As the Germans fled, a Greek government in formal relations with the Allies had been brought back to Athens. This operation was undertaken with the full approval of President Roosevelt. The King . . . and his brother naturally wished to return at the head of this small expedition. However, British policy . . . had been to seek a plebiscite on the Monarchist issue. . . . In this way I

---

29. [*Editor's note:* Hoover did not fill in this footnote.]
30. Churchill, *The Dawn of Liberation,* pp. 285, 286–287.

hoped to convince leftist sections of American opinion that British policy on Greece was based upon the freely expressed will of the Greek people. . . .

In early December [1944] the Communist buccaneers made their bold bid to capture Athens. . . . British troops, in small parties, advanced and fired upon the attacking Communists . . . who fell back a little at this check and gave time for what was left of the Greek Government to pull itself together. . . .

. . . Eventually Athens and the Greek nation were saved from becoming a Communist totalitarian state. . . .[31]

Mr. Churchill, in an address to the House of Commons on December 5, 1944, said:

. . . Greece is faced with . . . civil war which we are trying to stop. . . . The main burden falls on us. The responsibility is within our Allied military sphere— that is, our military sphere agreed upon with our principal allies.[32]

Some outcries appeared in the American press directed at the British rough action in putting down the Communists.[33]

Mr. Roosevelt, in a telegram to Mr. Churchill of December 13, 1944, refused to publicly support the Prime Minister. Whereupon Mr. Churchill, on December 17, reminded the President:

. . . We embarked upon it [the occupation] with your full consent. . . .[34]

The Communists developed a real war. The British Army under Lieutenant General Scobie finally put down the conspiracy.

With this defeat of the Communists, a sort of agreement and armistice was reached with them on February 12, 1945, in which the Communists agreed to surrender their arms in return for legalization as a political party, the holding of elections and a plebiscite on the monarchy within a year.

---

31. Churchill, "What Really Happened in Greece," *Reader's Digest,* July, 1947, pp. 110–113. See also Churchill's *Triumph and Tragedy,* pp. 283–325.

32. *New York Times,* December 6, 1944. [*Editor's note:* Hoover's quotation from Churchill, as rendered in Hoover's manuscript, contains several transcription errors which I have corrected.]

33. Ibid.

34. Churchill, *Triumph and Tragedy,* p. 304.

CHAPTER 59

Secretary Cordell Hull's
Bewilderment

SECRETARY HULL WAS SLOW to understand the "two great commitments" made at Tehran. He had not attended the conference. I give his confusions at some length because they are a record which contributes proof of the existence of the two great commitments.

The Secretary's bewilderment stemmed from his belief that he had, at the First Moscow Conference (a month before Tehran), secured an agreement from the British and the Russians that there were to be no "spheres of influence" nor "domination of peoples." He had glowingly reported this agreement to Congress on November 18, 1943, nine days before Tehran, saying:

> As the provisions of the Four-Nation Declaration [of the Moscow Conference] are carried into effect, there will no longer be need for spheres of influence, for alliances, for balance of power, or any other of the special arrangements through which, in the unhappy past, the nations strove to safeguard their security or to promote their interests.[1]

There can be no doubt of the probity of Secretary Hull.

On January 2, 1944, thirty days after Tehran, Wendell Willkie's suspicions seem to have been aroused as he said:

> One of the most pressing questions in everybody's mind is what Russia intends to do about the political integrity of small states around her borders— Finland, Poland, and the Baltic and Balkan states.[2]

---

1. *The Memoirs of Cordell Hull* [The Macmillan Company, New York: 1948], Vol. II, pp. 1314–1315.
2. *New York Times Magazine,* January 2, 1944.

The Russian press replied to Willkie on January 5, 1944, indicating that no one had a right even to mention this already settled matter. All of which alarmed Secretary Hull, for he says:

... The Soviet newspaper *Pravda* had published a bitter reply to an article by Wendell Willkie dealing in part with Russia's supposed intentions concerning the political integrity of states around her borders, Finland, Poland, the Baltic and Balkan countries. This reply ... had had far-reaching effect on public opinion here because it was interpreted as an indication that the Soviet Government proposed to follow a course of unilateral action. ...[3]

The Secretary was soon to suffer further surprises. In his memoirs, he states:

... British Ambassador Halifax inquired of me on May 30, 1944, how this Government would feel about an arrangement between the British and Russians whereby Russia would have a controlling influence in Rumania, and Britain a controlling influence in Greece. He said that difficulties had risen between Russia and Britain over the Balkans, especially with regard to Rumania.[4]

There followed further bewilderments from the British adherence to the "friendly nations agreement," about which Hull had apparently never been informed. The British, pressed by the Russians for formal agreements as to the "friendly border states," in turn pressed Mr. Roosevelt who, as far as the record goes, had avoided putting anything in writing. He turned the British communications over to Mr. Hull who held staunchly to his belief that there were to be "no spheres of influence."

However, in October, 1944, Hull's fears regarding "spheres of influence" were confirmed at the Second Moscow Conference. He states in his Memoirs:

Events fully justified the apprehensions we entertained over this Anglo-Russian arrangement, which duly entered into effect following the President's acquiescence. When Prime Minister Churchill and Foreign Secretary Eden went to Moscow in October, 1944, to see Stalin and Molotov, they extended the arrangement still further, even reducing to percentages the relative degree of influence which Britain and Russia individually should have

---

3. *The Memoirs of Cordell Hull*, Vol. II, p. 1437.
4. Ibid., p. 1451.

in specified Balkan countries. . . . Later the Russians took it for granted that by the agreement of June, 1944, Britain and the United States had assigned them a certain portion of the Balkans including Rumania and Bulgaria, as their sphere of influence. This assumption had its untoward effect at the Yalta Conference in February, 1945.[5]

Hull['s–*ed.*] confusion is partially explained by a statement of Arthur Bliss Lane, Ambassador to Poland (formerly Minister to Yugoslavia) and at this time on duty in the State Department. He says in his book:

> . . . A special means of communication had been established between the White House and our Embassy in Moscow, through the use of the United States Navy facilities, thus rendering it possible for the President—or Harry Hopkins—to telegraph directly to Harriman without having recourse to the Department of State—the channel normally used by a President of the United States when desiring to communicate with any American ambassador abroad. Thus the Department of State often was unaware of messages exchanged between the White House and the Embassy at Moscow. . . .[6]

A further evidence of Mr. Roosevelt's two great commitments at Tehran is given by Ambassador Lane who records that at a meeting with the President on November 20, 1944:

> Mr. Roosevelt said that he thought Stalin's idea of having a *cordon sanitaire*, in the shape of a Poland under Russian influence, as a bulwark to protect the Soviet Union against further aggression was understandable; Stalin himself had pointed out to the President that after World War I the Allies had formed a cordon sanitaire to the east to protect them from the threat of Bolshevism and now he claimed a corresponding right to protect himself from the west.[7]

Ambassador Lane also records of this meeting:

> I said that in my opinion it was very important that we insist with the Soviet Government that the independence of Poland be maintained, and I added that if we were not going to be strong at a time when we had the largest Army,

---

5. Ibid., p. 1458.
6. [Arthur Bliss] Lane, *I Saw Poland Betrayed* [The Bobbs-Merrill Company, Indianapolis and New York: 1948], p. 68.
7. Ibid., p. 67.

Navy and Air Forces in the world and at a time when the President had just received another mandate from the American people [his re-election in November], I did not see when we ever would be strong.

The President asked rather sharply and with a note of sarcasm, "Do you want me to go to war with Russia?"

I replied that there was no thought on my part that we would have to go to war, but that if we would take a strong line and not deviate from it, I felt confident we would accomplish our objectives. I observed, however, that the Soviet view of an independent Poland was quite different from our conception.

The President stated that he had entire confidence in Stalin's word and he felt sure that he would not go back on it. . . .

I said that I regretted I could not agree with him, as Stalin's previous actions had shown him not to be dependable. . . .[8]

An Epitaph for Tehran

The leaders of mankind had loosed dreadful evils at Tehran.

I could take no satisfaction in the fact even though I had warned the American people two and one-half years before, in my speech of June 29, 1941, that:

> . . . now we find ourselves promising aid to Stalin and his militant Communist conspiracy against the whole democratic ideals of the world. Collaboration between Britain and Russia will bring them military values, but it makes the whole argument of our joining the war to bring the four freedoms to mankind a gargantuan jest. . . .
>
> If we go further and join the war and we win, then we have won for Stalin the grip of Communism on Russia and more opportunity for it to extend in the world. We should at least cease to tell our sons that they would be giving their lives to restore democracy and freedom to the world. . . .[9]

---

8. Ibid., p. 66.
9. See Chapter [34–*ed.*]

SECTION XIV

The March of Conferences

CHAPTER 60

The Second Quebec Conference
September 11 to September 16, 1944

Organization

The Second Quebec Conference opened September 11, 1944 and comprised President Roosevelt, Prime Minister Churchill, and Prime Minister Mackenzie King of Canada, with their staffs.[1]

Information

The communiqué issued at the conference read as follows:

> The President and the Prime Minister and the Combined Chiefs of Staff held a series of meetings, during which they discussed all aspects of the war against Germany and Japan. In a very short space of time they reached decisions on all points both with regard to the completion of the war in Europe, now approaching its final stages, and the destruction of the barbarians of the Pacific.
>
> The most serious difficulty with which the Quebec conference has been confronted has been to find room and opportunity for marshaling against Japan the massive forces which each and all of the nations concerned are ardent to engage against the enemy.[2]

---

1. The American staff included: Secretary of the Treasury Henry Morgenthau; Admiral William D. Leahy; General George C. Marshall; Admiral Ernest J. King; General Henry H. Arnold; Lieutenant General Brehon B. Somervell; Vice Admiral Emory S. Land; Vice Admiral Russell Willson; Rear Admiral Charles M. Cooke, Jr.; Rear Admiral L. D. McCormick; Major General Thomas T. Handy; Major General Muir S. Fairchild; Major General Laurence S. Kuter; Stephen Early, the President's secretary.

   The British staff included: Foreign Minister Anthony Eden; Lord Cherwell; Lord Moran; Lord Leathers; Field Marshal Sir Alan Brooke; Air Chief Marshal Sir Charles Portal; Admiral of the Fleet Sir Andrew Cunningham; Field Marshal Sir John Dill; General Sir Hastings Ismay; Admiral Sir Percy Noble; Lieutenant General G. N. Macready; Air Marshal Sir William Welsh; Major General R. E. Laycock.

2. *New York Times*, September 17, 1944.

The records of the conference have never been published but the actions taken are clear from the statements and books by the participants.

The Morgenthau Plan for Pastoralization of Germany

There was a secret agreement at this Quebec meeting which was to have an evil influence on the entire world. That was Secretary of the Treasury Henry Morgenthau's plan for "the pastoralization of Germany" after the war. Germany was to be reduced to an agricultural state with some minor production of consumer goods.

The text of the agreement was:

"At a conference between the President and the Prime Minister upon the best measures to prevent renewed rearmament by Germany, it was felt that an essential feature was the future disposition of the Ruhr and the Saar.

"The ease with which the metallurgical, chemical, and electric industries in Germany can be converted from peace to war has already been impressed upon us by bitter experience. It must also be remembered that the Germans have devastated a large portion of the industries of Russia and of other neighboring Allies, and it is only in accordance with justice that these injured countries should be entitled to remove the machinery they require in order to repair the losses they have suffered. The industries referred to in the Ruhr and in the Saar would therefore be necessarily put out of action and closed down. It was felt that the two districts should be put under some body under the world organization which would supervise the dismantling of these industries and make sure that they were not started up again by some subterfuge.

"This programme for eliminating the war-making industries in the Ruhr and in the Saar is looking forward to converting Germany into a country primarily agricultural and pastoral in its character.

"The Prime Minister and the President were in agreement upon this programme.

O.K.

F.D.R.

W.S.C.

"September 16, 1944"   15 9.[3]

---

3. [*Editor's note:* Hoover's manuscript does not have a citation for this document. It is printed in its entirety in U.S. Department of State, *Foreign Relations of the United States, The Conference at Quebec, 1944* (United States Government Printing Office, Washington: 1972), pp. 466–467.]

A week after the Conference, the plan leaked in *The Wall Street Journal*,[4] which gave an extensive report of its essentials. A few days later, I saw Secretary Henry L. Stimson on other matters. During our visit I inquired what he knew about the plan reported in the newspaper.

The Secretary related to me that late in August 1944, Secretary Morgenthau had laid this plan before the Cabinet. He stated that the idea was at once denounced by Secretary Hull and himself; that Mr. Roosevelt then appointed Hull, himself and Morgenthau as a committee to consider the plan.

Secretary Stimson drew from his portfolio and showed to me the full text of the agreement at Quebec, together with his considered and prophetically-written denunciation of the whole idea—in which Secretary Hull concurred. Stimson stated that neither Secretary Hull nor he had been invited to the Quebec Conference, although Prime Minister Churchill was accompanied by officials of their rank.

According to a State Department memorandum on the Quebec meeting, British Minister of Foreign Affairs Anthony Eden opposed the "plan."[5] Prime Minister Churchill, in his account of the Quebec Conference, states:

> ... At first I violently opposed this idea. But the President, with Mr. Morgenthau—from whom we had much to ask—were so insistent that in the end we agreed to consider it.
>
> ... All this was of course subject to the full consideration of the War Cabinet, and in the event, with my full accord, the idea of "pastoralizing" Germany did not survive.[6]

However, it did survive as this narrative will show. George Sokolsky, two years and eight months later, in his column of May 21, 1947, published a slightly different text of the plan. He stated a reader of his column had made inquiry as to the plan at the State Department and was informed:

> "... This Government has never adopted any so-called 'Morgenthau Plan' for the treatment of Germany. ..."[7]

This statement was somewhat short of the whole truth, as evidenced by the text and the initials on the agreement.

---

4. *Wall Street Journal*, September 23, 1944.

5. [U.S. Department of State,] *Foreign Relations of the United States*, [*Diplomatic Papers*,] *The Conferences at Malta and Yalta, 1945* (United States Government Printing Office, Washington: 1955), p. 135.

6. [Winston S.] Churchill, *Triumph and Tragedy* [Houghton Mifflin Company, Boston: 1953], pp. 156–157.

7. *New York Sun*, May 21, 1947.

Influence of American Communists in the Morgenthau Plan

One of the strong influences upon Morgenthau in the formulation of these ideas was that of Under Secretary of the Treasury Harry Dexter White. On September 2, 1944, nine days before the Quebec Conference, a group of State, War and Treasury officials met to discuss postwar policy.

According to the State Department memorandum:

> It was at this meeting that Dr. White produced the Treasury plan [Morgenthau Plan] for Germany and gave a lengthy interpretation of this plan which, in its general tenor, was more extreme than the memorandum itself. . . .[8]

White testified before the House Committee on Un-American Activities[9] that he had participated in a major way in the formulation of the plan. Morgenthau subsequently confirmed this saying: "White worked as a labor of love on my book." A memorandum by H. Freeman Matthews of the State Department, dated September 20, 1944 (four days after the Quebec Conference), states that White went to Quebec and helped Morgenthau convince the British.[10]

White, in 1945, was denounced by Elizabeth Bentley and Whittaker Chambers, repentant Communist agents, to the Federal Bureau of Investigation. In consequence of this and other evidence, the Federal Bureau of Investigation on November 8, 1945, reported to the White House that White was a spy. The report was suppressed. The entire story was exposed nine years later by the Attorney General and the Subcommittee of the Senate Judiciary [Committee–ed.] in November, 1953.[11] White had been furnishing documents to the Soviet government. Providentially for him, Harry Dexter White died before his misdeeds caught up with him.

---

8. *Foreign Relations of the United States,* [*Diplomatic Papers,*] *The Conferences at Malta and Yalta, 1945,* p. 160.

9. August 13, 1948. HUAC [House Un-American Activities Committee], *Hearings Regarding Communist Espionage in the United States Government* [80th Congress, 2d Session] [Part 1], July–August–September, 1948, p. 904. Also see statement by Attorney General [Herbert Brownell, Jr.] to the press, November 6, 1963 [1953–*ed.*]. It is interesting to note that Morgenthau does not acknowledge White in the book, *Germany is Our Problem.* [*Editor's note:* See footnote 12 for the citation.]

10. *Foreign Relations of the United States,* [*Diplomatic Papers,*] *The Conferences at Malta and Yalta, 1945,* p. 134.

11.[U.S. Congress,] Senate [Committee on the Judiciary, Subcommittee to Investigate the Administration of the Internal Security Act and Other Internal Security Laws, 83d Congress, 1st Session,] Hearings, *Interlocking Subversion in Government Departments,* Part 16 (November–December, 1953), pp. 1110–1142.

Fortunately for history, Mr. Morgenthau, in October 1945, about one year after the Quebec Conference, published a book on his plan. In this book he gives his full plan, which went far beyond the Quebec Agreement.[12]

His full plan called for the complete demobilization of German military forces; the destruction of the armament production facilities; the liquidation of all coal mines and industry in the Ruhr either by destruction or removal to Allied countries; reparations to be paid by the removal of all plant and equipment within the International Zone to Allied countries, by forced German labor outside of Germany, and by all transferable assets of any kind; the elimination of aviation in Germany and prevention of its revival in the future. Morgenthau also proposed East Prussia be divided between the Soviet Union and Poland; that Germany be divided into two parts; and that France should annex the Saar. He proposed cleansing the German mind by control of education and the press.

Later chapters will show the evil influence of the Morgenthau plan on postwar reconstruction of Europe.[13]

Italy

After the Quebec Conference, Mr. Churchill met with President Roosevelt at Hyde Park on September 18 and 19. At these meetings they made important decisions and plans which they described in the following joint communiqué issued on September 26:

> The President and the Prime Minister held further discussions Monday and Tuesday, Sept. 18 and 19, at Hyde Park, on subjects dealing with post-war policies in Europe. The result of these discussions cannot be disclosed at this time for strategic military reasons, and pending their consideration by our other Allies.
>
> The present problems in Italy also came under discussion, and on this subject the President and the Prime Minister issued the following statement:
>
> "The Italian people, freed of their Fascist and Nazi overlordship, have in these last twelve months demonstrated their will to be free, to fight on the

---

12. Henry Morgenthau, *Germany is Our Problem* (Harper & Brothers, New York: 1945). Some supplementary material is contained in a series of newspaper articles by Mr. Morgenthau entitled "Our Policy Toward Germany," *New York Post,* November 24–29, 1947.

13. Two and one-half years after the adoption of the Morgenthau idea at Quebec, I was appointed by President Truman to report to him upon the economic debacle in Germany and its consequences to the United States and to Europe. My reports of this mission, published in February and March of 1947, note the influence of the Morgenthau plan upon recovery of the world.

side of the democracies, and to take a place among the United Nations devoted to principles of peace and justice.

"We believe we should give encouragement to those Italians who are standing for a political rebirth in Italy, and are completing the destruction of the evil Fascist system. We wish to afford the Italians a greater opportunity to aid in the defeat of our common enemies.

"The American and the British people are of course horrified by the recent mob action in Rome, but feel that a greater responsibility placed on the Italian people and on their own Government will most readily prevent a recurrence of such acts.

"An increasing measure of control will be gradually handed over to the Italian Administration, subject of course to that Administration's proving that it can maintain law and order and the regular administration of justice. To mark this change the Allied Control Commission will be renamed 'the Allied Commission.'

"The British High Commissioner in Italy will assume the additional title of Ambassador. The United States representative in Rome already holds that rank. The Italian Government will be invited to appoint direct representatives to Washington and London.

"First and immediate considerations in Italy are the relief of hunger and sickness and fear. To this end we instructed our representatives at the UNRRA [United Nations Relief and Rehabilitation Administration] conference to declare for the sending of medical aids and other essential supplies to Italy. We are happy to know that this view commended itself to other members of the UNRRA Council.

"At the same time, first steps should be taken toward the reconstruction of an Italian economy—an economy laid low under the years of the misrule of Mussolini and ravished by the German policy of vengeful destruction.

"These steps should be taken primarily as military aims to put the full resources of Italy and the Italian people into the struggle to defeat Germany and Japan. For military reasons we should assist the Italians in the restoration of such power systems, their railways, motor transport, roads and other communications as enter into the war situation, and for a short time send engineers, technicians and industrial experts into Italy to help them in their own rehabilitation.

"The application to Italy of the Trading With the Enemy Acts should be modified so as to enable business contacts between Italy and the outside world to be resumed for the benefit of the Italian people.

"We all wish to speed the day when the last vestiges of fascism in Italy will have been wiped out, and when the last German will have left Italian soil, and when there will be no need of any Allied troops to remain—the day when free elections can be held throughout Italy, and when Italy can earn her proper place in the great family of free nations."[14]

---

14. *New York Times*, September 27, 1944.

CHAPTER 61

The Second Moscow Conference
October 9 to October 20, 1944

THE SECOND MOSCOW CONFERENCE comprised Prime Minister Churchill, Marshal Stalin, and Foreign Minister Eden. They were joined by Ambassador W. Averell Harriman as an "observer."

The military background at this time was: On the Russian front the Germans had retreated from Russia and most of the intermediate states. Russian armies were following them up and had entered Germany at East Prussia. The Italian government had surrendered and joined the Allies. German armies were holding out in northern Italy, but they were moving out and had evacuated the city of Florence.

The American and British forces, four months before this conference, had started the liberation of France by OVERLORD and ANVIL. By mid-September the Battle [of–*ed.*] France had been won. American troops crossed the boundary into German territory on September 12, 1944—a month before the Second Moscow Conference started. The Russians had occupied Finland, most of Estonia, Latvia, Lithuania, and Poland as far as the Vistula, and were advancing into Hungary and Yugoslavia.

President Roosevelt was apparently worried about this conference of Churchill and Stalin alone. On October 3, the President sent the following telegram to Marshal Stalin, through Ambassador Harriman:

> It had been my hope that no important meeting would be held until you and Mr. Churchill and I could get together but I understand the Prime Minister's wish to confer with you now. There is in this global war literally no question, either military or political, in which the United States is not interested. You will naturally understand this. It is my firm conviction that the solution to still unsolved questions can be found only by the three of us together. Therefore, while I appreciate the necessity for the present meeting, I choose to

consider your forthcoming talks with Mr. Churchill merely as preliminary to a conference of the three of us which can take place, so far as I am concerned, any time after our national election.

Therefore, I am suggesting that Mr. Harriman be present at your forthcoming meetings with Mr. Churchill as an observer for me, if you and Mr. Churchill approve. Of course Mr. Harriman could not commit this government relative to any important matters which, very naturally, may be discussed by you and the Prime Minister.

I wish to reiterate to you my complete acceptance of the assurances that we have received from you relative to the war against Japan. You will have received by now from General Deane the statement of the position taken by our Combined Chiefs of Staff on this. The war against Germany is being successfully waged by our three great countries and surely we shall have no less success joined together in crushing a nation which, I feel sure in my heart, is as great an enemy of the Soviet Union as she is of the United States.[1]

Despite the President's warning, Mr. Churchill raised and settled several important questions with Marshal Stalin.

The Division of Control of the Balkan States between Churchill and Stalin

In order to complete the evidence of the existence of the two secret agreements, I have already, in Chapter 58, given the division of influences in the Balkan States by percentages between Mr. Churchill and Marshal Stalin, by which both empires would be greatly expanded.

Mr. Churchill, in a report to the House of Commons on October 27, 1944, a week after the Conference, said:

Upon the tangled question of the Balkans, where there are Black Sea interests and Mediterranean interests to be considered, we were able to reach complete agreement. I do not feel that there is any immediate danger of our combined war effort being weakened by divergencies of policy or of doctrine in Greece, Rumania, Bulgaria, Yugoslavia, and, beyond the Balkans, Hungary. We have reached a very good working agreement about all these countries, singly and in combination, with the object of concentrating all their efforts, and concerting them with ours against the common foe, and of providing, as

---

1. [Robert E.] Sherwood, *Roosevelt and Hopkins* [Harper & Brothers, New York: 1948], p. 834.

far as possible, for a peaceful settlement after the war is over. We are, in fact, acting jointly, Russia and Britain, in our relations with both the Royal Yugoslav Government headed by Dr. Subasic and with Marshal Tito, and we have invited them to come together for the common cause, as they had already agreed to do at the conference which I held with them both at Naples. . . .

 . . . *All these discussions were part of the process of carrying out and following up the great decisions taken nearly a year ago at Teheran. . . .*[2]

Poland

The purpose of and the discussion at this conference related to the desperate situation facing Poland because of a revolt by the Poles against the Germans in Warsaw at Russia's request. I have given a description of these tragic and poignant incidents during this conference in *The Case History of Poland*.[3] The Russian armies were across the river from Warsaw but refused to help the Poles. Prime Minister Mikolajczyk of the London exiled Polish Government was present at this conference in Moscow, but his pleadings to Stalin were of no avail. In the course of the meeting Molotov declared to the Polish Prime Minister that President Roosevelt at Tehran had agreed to the division of Poland, the annexation of East Poland by Russia and the setting up of a puppet government for West Poland. Mikolajczyk demanded of Churchill and Harriman if this were true. Churchill confirmed it, and Harriman said he must consult the President before replying.

Russia and the Japanese War

The entry of Russia into the war against Japan was again discussed at this conference. General John R. Deane, who took part in this discussion, has described it at great length.[4] However, Stalin did not budge from the formula he had given at Tehran: that Russia would come into the war against Japan after victory over Germany. He stipulated that in the meantime supplies and equipment from American lend-lease and British sources should be built up in Siberia for such an attack.

---

2. [Winston S.] Churchill, *The Dawn of Liberation* [Little Brown and Company, Boston: 1945], pp. 285, 286–287. [*Editor's note:* italics added by Hoover.]

3. See Section ___. [*Editor's note:* Hoover's "Case History" of Poland is printed below, in Volume III.]

4. [*Editor's note:* Hoover left this footnote blank. In all likelihood he was referring to John R. Deane, *The Strange Alliance* (The Viking Press, New York: 1949), pp. 244–249.]

As a matter of fact, the Russians did not join in the war against Japan until August 8, 1945—ninety-three days after Hitler's surrender of Germany.

Churchill and Stalin issued the following communiqué on October 21:

> Meetings were held at Moscow from Oct. 9 to 18 between Mr. Churchill and Mr. Eden, representing the United Kingdom, and Marshall Stalin and Mr. Molotoff, assisted by their political and military advisors.
>
> The unfolding of military plans agreed upon at Teheran was comprehensively reviewed in the light of recent events and conclusions of the Quebec conference on the war in western Europe. Utmost confidence was expressed in the future progress of Allied operations on all fronts.
>
> Free and intimate exchange of views took place on many political questions of common interest. Important progress was made toward solution of the Polish question, which was closely discussed between the Soviet and British Governments.
>
> They held consultations both with the Prime Minister and Minister for Foreign Affairs of the Polish Government and with the president of the National Council and chairman of the Committee of National Liberation at Lublin.
>
> These discussions have notably narrowed differences and dispelled misconceptions. Conversations are continuing on outstanding points.
>
> The march of events in southeast Europe was fully considered and agreement was reached on main points in the Bulgarian armistice terms.
>
> The two Governments agreed to pursue a joint policy in Yugoslavia designed to concentrate all energies against the retreating Germans and bring about a solution of Yugoslav internal difficulties by a union between the Royal Yugoslav Government and the National Liberation movement.
>
> The right of the Yugoslav people to settle their future Constitution for themselves after the war is of course recognized as inalienable.
>
> The meeting took place with the knowledge and approval of the United States Government, which was represented at the conversations by the United States Ambassador at Moscow, Mr. Averell Harriman, acting in the capacity of observer.[5]

---

5. *New York Times*, October 21, 1944.

CHAPTER 62

Getting Along with Stalin

Operations Lend-Lease

Stalin and his subordinates were far from cooperative with the American and British representatives in Moscow. The British, with their own needs, were unable to furnish much war material to Russia, so that the burden fell mainly upon the United States. Many of the American difficulties are given in detail in the books of Admiral William H. Standley[1] and General John R. Deane.[2]

Admiral Standley was appointed our Ambassador to Russia on February 9, 1942. The Admiral was a blunt sailor who lost patience with Communist behavior, and finally exploded to the press on March 8, 1943, eight months before the Tehran Conference, saying:

> Ever since I have been here, I have been carefully looking for recognition by the Russian press of the fact that they are getting material help through America, not only through lend-lease but through the Red Cross and Russian-American Relief. And I have yet failed to find any acknowledgement of that.
>
> They seem to be trying to create the impression at home as well as abroad that they are fighting the war alone.[3]

The Admiral had to contend with arrogant refusals of Russia officials to supply needed information as to military matters. They would not allow our officials to visit any important sector of the front. They refused requests for data to justify their lend-lease requests, and withheld information even on

---

1. William H. Standley and Arthur A. Ageton, *Admiral Ambassador to Russia* ([Henry Regnery Company,] Chicago: 1955).

2. John R. Deane, *The Strange Alliance* ([The Viking Press,] New York: 1947). Specif. pp. 289–304.

3. *New York Times,* March 9, 1943.

minor matters. They were unnecessarily slow in complying with the most insignificant requests.[4]

Stalin further troubled the Admiral by receiving American visitors in Moscow without their being accompanied by the Ambassador.

The Admiral also had grievances at his own government. An Associated Press dispatch states:

> Since Admiral Standley has been Ambassador there have been several prominent visiting firemen such as Wendell Willkie, Patrick Hurley, W. Averell Harriman and, most lately, Joseph E. Davies.
>
> In more than one case the first news the United States Ambassador to the Soviet Union got of these gentlemen was when he heard it over the British Broadcasting System. In one case he cabled to ask what it was all about and in at least one case he never did get a reply.
>
> . . . when Mr. Davies went to see Premier Stalin to present a letter from President Roosevelt . . . The United States Ambassador went along to present Mr. Davies to the Premier, but he did not sit in on the conversation. He was told to go home, and he did.[5]

The Admiral resigned on October 1, 1943, and W. Averell Harriman was appointed the new American Ambassador.[6] Major-General John R. Deane succeeded General Faymonville, in charge of the Moscow end of lend-lease. Deane's book[7] shows that he was no more successful in securing cooperation than his predecessors. He says:

> . . . There were many times when I had the greatest desire to recommend that our flow of supplies to Russia be shut off until the Soviet Union showed some more tangible evidence of the co-operation it had promised. . . .[8]

As an explanation of Russian non-cooperation during the war, Deane offers the following:

> . . . The long-range objectives of the Communist leaders were clear, and it was logical to them to take for granted that Capitalist leaders had equal vision. They suspected that Allied probing for closer contacts with Russia was

---

4. For instances of the frustrating experiences suffered by an Ambassador, see William H. Standley and Arthur A. Ageton, *Admiral Ambassador to Russia*.

5. *New York Times*, June 8, 1943.

6. Three years later I listened to an off-the-record address by Harriman bitterly attacking the whole system—and Stalin.

7. John R. Deane, *The Strange Alliance*.

8. Ibid., p. 254.

for the purpose of obtaining intelligence that would be useful in the struggle between ideologies that would eventually come. . . .[9]

General Deane made a pungent statement on Communism in general:

. . . there can no longer be any doubt that Soviet leadership has always been motivated by the belief that Communism and Capitalism cannot coexist. Nor is there any doubt in my mind that present-day Soviet leaders have determined upon a program pointed toward imposing Communism on those countries under their control, and elsewhere, creating conditions favorable to the triumph of Communism in the war against Capitalism which they consider to be inevitable. . . .

. . . I believe that their strategic aim is world Communism to be directed from Moscow. . . . If the end can be reached without resort to force, so much the better; if not, force will be used when it is safe to do so. . . .[10]

Deane stated that the Russians were cooperative in one respect—giving banquets for American officials. His description is:

. . . Each person high in public life proposes a toast a little sweeter than the preceding one on Soviet–British–American friendship. It is amazing how these toasts go down past the tongues in the cheeks. After the banquets we send the Soviets another thousand airplanes, and they approve a visa that has been hanging fire for months. We then scratch our heads to see what other gifts we can send, and they scratch theirs to see what else they can ask for.[11]

Deane comments on Mr. Roosevelt's policies:

. . . [Roosevelt] wished all material promised to the Soviet Union . . . to be released for shipment and shipped at the earliest possible date regardless of the effect of these shipments on any other part of the war program.

. . . it was the beginning of a policy of appeasement of Russia from which we have never fully recovered and from which we are still suffering.[12]

When Secretary Hull arrived in Russia for the First Moscow Conference of Foreign Ministers in October 1943, General Deane presented to him certain requests for military cooperation. These embraced a request for landing fields to enable shuttle bombing of German industrial centers by British

---

9. Ibid., p. 295.
10. Ibid., pp. 319–322.
11. Ibid., p. 84.
12. Ibid., p. 89.

and American aircraft; a request for a more effective mutual interchange of weather information, and a request that communication facilities and air communication between the two countries be improved. Hull took up these matters and secured from Molotov an agreement "in principle" to them.[13]

Deane's general observation on the Russians at this moment was:

> ... I learned two important lessons for my future dealings with Soviet officials. The first was that no subordinate official in Russia may make a decision on matters in which foreigners are involved without consulting higher authority. . . . In most cases subordinate officials will not even discuss proposals made by foreigners for fear of expressing opinions that would not be down the party line. . . .
>
> The second lesson was that an "approval in principle" by the Soviet Government means exactly nothing. . . .[14]

While discussing the problems of supplies to Russia I may well review the whole lend-lease operations with the Soviet Union.

Consequential lend-lease shipments from the United States had not begun until after the Russians had stopped Hitler in front of Moscow and Leningrad in October and November of 1941. But thereafter they rapidly increased. The total lend-lease supplies which we furnished Russia in round numbers amounted to 16,523,000 tons, worth $10,670,000,000. Among other items, there were included 375,000 trucks, about 52,000 jeeps, 7,000 tanks, some 6,300 other combat vehicles, 2,300 artillery vehicles, 35,000 motorcycles, 14,700 aircraft, 8,200 anti-aircraft guns, 1,900 steam locomotives, 66 Diesel locomotives, 11,000 railway cars of various types, 415,000 telephones, 3,786,000 automobile and truck tires, 2,670,000 tons of oil products, 4,478,000 tons of foodstuffs, 15 million pairs of army boots, 6 oil refineries, and a factory for the production of motors, tires, etc. Total British deliveries ran to a value of £312,000,000 (the equivalent of $1,248,000,000) bringing the joint worth of American and British aid, not counting Canadian help, to $11,918,000,000.[15]

---

13. *The Memoirs of Cordell Hull* [The Macmillan Company, New York: 1948], Vol. II, p. 1302.

14. John R. Deane, *The Strange Alliance*, p. 20.

15. The Polish General, Wladyslaw Anders, who made an exhaustive study of the Russian side of the war says: "Towards the end of the war, Soviet Russia . . . demanded more and more machine tools and industrial equipment. This raised numerous objections in the United States . . . [that she was trying] to build up her post-war military potential. Moreover, it came to light during the war that the Soviets were selling part of the military equipment received from the West to Japan, with whom the Western Powers were engaged in a life and death struggle. This applied particularly to British tanks. . . . Even at this occasion, Stalin did not miss the opportunity to cheat his Allies. . . . this should not surprise anyone, for had Stalin not done so, he would not have been himself." (*Hitler's Defeat in Russia* [Henry Regnery Company, Chicago: 1953], p. 225.)

The March of Conferences

The Yalta Conference
February 4–11, 1945

CHAPTER **63**

The Conference at Malta
Prelude to Yalta from January 30 to February 2, 1945

A CONFERENCE OF Prime Minister Churchill, President Roosevelt and their staffs was held at Malta en route to the forthcoming conference at Yalta in Russian Crimea.[1]

The purpose of the Malta conference apparently was to coordinate American and British views before meeting the Russians at Yalta.

Sherwood notes that:

> ... relations between the White House and Downing Street were more strained than they had ever been before. Hopkins received plenty of information to indicate that his honored friend, the Prime Minister, was in an extremely dangerous and explosive mood which might make plenty of trouble at the forthcoming Big Three Conference which was now in prospect for the end of January. . . .[2]

Mr. Churchill was at Malta for the full conference but Mr. Roosevelt did not arrive until the last day.[3] In the early meetings, Secretary of State Edward R. Stettinius, Jr. and Ambassador W. Averell Harriman represented the United States.

There were important decisions taken by the British and American military staffs, mainly upon European strategic matters.

---

1. The staff members are given in the next chapter on Yalta.

2. [Robert E.] Sherwood, *Roosevelt and Hopkins* [Harper & Brothers, New York: 1948], p. 839.

3. President Roosevelt had stayed in the United States in order to be sworn in for the fourth term. His doctors had advised him not to fly over the mountains to Yalta so he went by ship to Malta and flew from there.

Prime Minister Churchill again propounded his strategy of attack upon "the soft under-belly of Europe" but got nowhere.[4]

There were meetings between the British Minister of Foreign Affairs Anthony Eden and Secretary of State Stettinius, in which other civilian staff members participated. On the American side, Alger Hiss and Harry Hopkins attended. As to this meeting, an editorial note in the State Department papers on the Conferences at Yalta and Malta states: "No record of the substance of this meeting has been found."

At a further meeting of Secretary Stettinius and Minister Eden held on the same day it is recorded that, among other things, they planned American-British strategy as to the zones of occupation in Germany and Austria, and discussed the Polish problem. It was agreed that the Communist Lublin government should not be recognized. It was also agreed that the independence of Iran should be sustained and that it was important to try to get the Russians to agree (a) to the principle of gradual *pari passu* withdrawal from Iran, and (b) that the Iranian government was "entitled to decline to negotiate oil concessions as long as foreign troops were in occupation of their territory."[5]

The question of warm water ports for Russia in China was raised. The possible unification of the Mao Tse-tung Communists and the Chiang Kai-shek Nationalist government was discussed. Stettinius urged that "the British, Soviet and American Governments make every effort to bring about agreement between Chiang Kai-shek and the Communists."[6]

The conferees discussed the work of the Dumbarton Oaks Conference, the Polish-German frontier, and the Austro-Yugoslav frontier. Allied Control Commissions had been established in Rumania, Bulgaria, and Hungary. Russian behavior was the subject of strong complaint because they were frequently taking action in the name of the Control Commissions without prior consultation with the Americans and the British.

---

4. [U.S. Department of State,] *Foreign Relations of the United States,* [*Diplomatic Papers,*] *The Conferences at Malta and Yalta, 1945* [United States Government Printing Office, Washington: 1955], p. 543.

5. Ibid., p. 501.

6. Ibid., p. 502.

CHAPTER 64

Organization, the Military Situation, Sources of Information

THE PRINCIPALS AT the Yalta Conference were President Roosevelt, Prime Minister Churchill, and Marshal Stalin.[1]

---

1. The staffs were:

For the United States: Edward R. Stettinius, Jr., Secretary of State; Fleet Admiral William D. Leahy, U.S.N., Chief of Staff to the President; Harry L. Hopkins, Special Assistant to the President; Justice James F. Byrnes, Director, Office of War Mobilization and Reconversion; General of the Army George C. Marshall, U.S.A., Chief of Staff, United States Army; Fleet Admiral Ernest J. King, U.S.N., Commander in Chief, United States Fleet, and Chief of Naval Operations; Lieutenant General Brehon B. Somervell, U.S.A. Commanding General, Army Service Forces; Vice Admiral Emory S. Land, U.S.N. (retired), War Shipping Administrator, Chairman of the United States Maritime Commission, and United States member of the Combined Shipping Adjustment Board; Major General Laurence S. Kuter, U.S.A., Assistant Chief of Staff for Plans, United States Army Air Forces, at the Malta and Yalta Conferences represented General of the Army Henry H. Arnold, U.S.A., who was ill; W. Averell Harriman, American Ambassador to the Soviet Union; H. Freeman Matthews, Director, Office of European Affairs, Department of State; Alger Hiss, Deputy Director, Office of Special Political Affairs, Department of State; Charles E. Bohlen, Assistant to the Secretary of State, interpreter to President Roosevelt at the Yalta Conference; Vice Admiral Charles M. Cooke, Jr., U.S.N., Chief of Staff and Aide to the Commander in Chief, United States Fleet; Rear Admiral Lynde D. McCormick, U.S.N., Assistant Chief of Naval Operations for Logistic Plans and member of the Joint Logistics Committee of the Joint Chiefs of Staff; Major General John R. Deane, U.S.A., Commanding General, United States Military Mission to the Soviet Union; Major General Harold R. Bull, U.S.A., Assistant Chief of Staff for Operations (G-3), Supreme Headquarters, Allied Expeditionary Force; Major General Frederick L. Anderson, U.S.A., Deputy Commanding General of the United States Strategic Air Forces in Europe, in Charge of Operations; Major General John E. Hull, U.S.A., Assistant Chief of Staff, Operations Division, War Department General Staff; Wilder Foote, Assistant to the Secretary of State; and other military and diplomatic advisors.

For the United Kingdom: Anthony Eden, Secretary of State for Foreign Affairs; Lord Frederick James Leathers, Minister of War Transport; Sir Archibald Clark Kerr, British Ambassador to the Soviet Union; Sir Alexander Cadogan, Permanent Under-Secretary of State for Foreign Affairs; Sir Edward Bridges, Secretary of the War Cabinet; Field Marshal Sir Alan Brooke, Chief of the Imperial General Staff; Marshal of the Royal Air Force Sir Charles Portal, Chief of Air Staff; Admiral of the Fleet Sir Andrew Cunningham, Bart., R.N., First Sea Lord and Chief of Naval Staff; General Sir Hastings Lionel Ismay, Chief of Staff to the Minister of Defence and Deputy Secretary (Military) to the War Cabinet; Field Marshal Sir Harold Alexander, Supreme Allied Commander, Mediterranean Theater; Field Marshal Sir Henry Maitland Wilson, Head of the British Joint Staff Mission in

The Military Situation at the Opening of the Yalta Conference

The Yalta Conference opened about a year and two months after the Tehran Conference. France, Belgium, and Holland had been liberated by the American and British armies. Italy had withdrawn from the war in September 1943, and had made peace with the Allies. Mussolini had gone into exile in the extreme north of Italy at Rocca delle Caminante, closely guarded by a special detachment.

Hitler's armies had retreated to within the borders of Germany. More than one half of their military strength was exhausted. Russian troops had advanced across the Oder to within a hundred miles from Berlin.

There had been steadily increasing strategic bombing of the Reich by the Anglo-American air forces. According to Lieutenant General Wladyslaw Anders:

> That the strategic bombing almost completely paralyzed the German war machine is confirmed by Dr. Speer [German Minister of Armament and Production for War]. When he was asked whether bombing alone would have forced the Germans to end the war, he answered in the affirmative, and stated that the destruction of the German synthetic fuel industry alone would have brought such a result.[2]

Washington; Admiral Sir James Somerville, R.N., Head of the Admiralty Delegation, British Joint Staff Mission in Washington; Rear Admiral Ernest Russell Archer, R.N., Head of the British Military Mission to the Soviet Union; Major General Robert Edward Laycock, British Chief of Combined Operations; Major General Noel Galway Holmes, Deputy Quarter-Master General of the War Office; Major Arthur Birse, Second Secretary, British Embassy, Moscow, Interpreter to Prime Minister Churchill; and other military and diplomatic advisors.

For the Soviet Union: Vyacheslav Mikhailovich Molotov, People's Commissar for Foreign Affairs of the Soviet Union; Fleet Admiral Nikolay Gerasimovich Kuznetsov, People's Commissar of the Soviet Navy; General of the Army Alexey Innokentyevich Antonov, First Deputy Chief of Staff of the Soviet Army; Andrey Yanuaryevich Vyshinsky, First Deputy People's Commissar for Foreign Affairs of the Soviet Union; Ivan Mikhailovich Maisky, Deputy Commissar for Foreign Affairs of the Soviet Union; Marshal of Aviation Sergey Vladimirovich Khudyakov, Deputy Chief of the Soviet Air Staff; Fedor Tarasovich Gusev, Soviet Ambassador to the United Kingdom and representative on the European Advisory Commission; Andrey Andreyevich Gromyko, Soviet Ambassador to the United States; Lieutenant General Anatoly Alekseyevich Gryzlov, Assistant to the Deputy Chief of Staff of the Soviet Army; Vice Admiral Stepan Grigoryevich Kucherov, Deputy Chief of Staff of the Soviet Navy; Vladimir Nikolayevich Pavlov, Personal Secretary and Interpreter to Marshal Stalin; and other military and diplomatic advisors. Lavrenty Pavlovich Beriya, Deputy Chairman of the Council of People's Commissars of the Soviet Union, member of the State Defense Committee, and People's Commissar for Internal Affairs (NKVD), was also in Yalta at the time of the Conference.

([U.S. Department of State,] *Foreign Relations of the United States, [Diplomatic Papers,] The Conferences at Malta and Yalta, 1945* (United States Government Printing Office, Washington: 1955), Department of State Publication 6199.)

2. Lt. Gen. W[ladyslaw] Anders, *Hitler's Defeat in Russia* [Henry Regnery Company, Chicago: 1953], p. 228. Field Marshal Gerd von Rundstedt, German Commander in Chief in the West, stated

Hitler's desperate last-ditch counterattack through the Belgian Ardennes in December 1944 (two months before the Conference) had failed, the German army being without adequate military forces to follow through their initial success.

General Douglas MacArthur's forces in the Pacific had paralyzed any major action by the Japanese navy, but Japanese armies were still holding on to their occupied areas in China and southward.

Mao Tse-tung's North China Communist Republic had steadily increased its armies and extended its area. Thus Chiang Kai-shek was still fighting on two fronts: the Japanese and Mao Tse-tung.

Sources of Information Regarding What Happened at the Yalta Conference

Vital agreements and understandings affecting the fate of the world were entered into at the Yalta Conference. Some of the agreements and declaration were issued to the press during the conference, but the major agreements were kept secret.

It is worthy of note that in the documents issued to the press during the conference the words "democratic," "peace," "peace-loving," "freedom," "security," "safeguard," "rights," "right to choose its own government," "liberation," and "liberated," occur about thirty times. The ghost of the Atlantic Charter was twice invoked from its grave and appeared in the conference.

Two years after the conference some of the Yalta secret agreements were issued to the press (March 17, 1947). Other commitments and agreements gradually leaked from statements and publications by participants and Congressional investigations. It was not until March 1955, ten years after the conference, that the State Department issued its book on the Yalta Conference under the title "The Conferences at Malta and Yalta." I refer to this publication as the "Yalta Papers."

In spite of over 400,000 words in the State Department "Yalta Papers," there are many grave omissions and suppressions.

Senator Knowland on March 18, 1953 in the Senate stated that Mr. Roosevelt's address to the Congress on March 1, 1945 reporting on the Yalta Conference was misleading as it stated that the conference:

---

later to Allied interrogators: "As far as I was concerned . . . the war was ended in September [1944]." (Quoted in William L. Shirer, *The Rise and Fall of the Third Reich* [Simon and Schuster, New York: 1960], p. 1086.)

. . . concerned itself only with the European war and with the political problems of Europe, and not with the Pacific war."[3]

Senator Knowland further stated:

I can thoroughly understand, in war-time, the necessity of not making certain documents available for general public use. I can understand an expression wherein a President of the United States, reporting to a coequal branch of the Government, might say that in the national interest it was not well to discuss certain matters in public. I can understand, under certain circumstances, his making no mention of the situation at all in a public session. But I think—and I say it reluctantly—that that report comes near to being what, in the Army, we called a "false official report" to a coequal branch of the Government of the United States.[4]

The "Yalta Papers" were issued in March 1955. The first extensive exposure of the omissions and suppression was made by the *Chicago Tribune* on November 6, 1955, in a dispatch from their Washington office under the title "50,000 Words Suppressed in Yalta Report." Upon my inquiring as to the source of their information, they stated that it was an indignant employee in the State Department Historical Division.

The *Tribune* article gives important suppressions or omissions.

. . . Several folders of notes by Alger Hiss, later revealed as a soviet informant, which disclose that he played a much larger role at the conference than hitherto reported. . . .

Noble[5] has been accused by two ousted state department historians as the man responsible for the suppression of important papers in the Yalta records. Donald M. Dozer and Bryton Barron, both historians of standing for year[s], declared they were penalized because they fought "a partial and distorted compilation."

In a sworn statement, appealing his dismissal to the civil service commission, Dozer charged that Noble and other appointees in the state department deleted important documents from the Yalta record because their publication would embarrass the Democratic . . . administration of Roosevelt.[6]

---

3. *Congressional Record* [vol. 101], March 18, 1955, p. 3137.

4. Ibid.

5. [*Editor's note:* Dr. George B. Noble, Chief of the Historical Division of the Department of State.]

6. [*Editor's note:* Hoover's transcription here is incorrect. The clause in the *Chicago Tribune's* story reads: "because their publication would embarrass the Democratic regimes of Roosevelt and Truman."]

At least three additional folders of Hiss notes were suppressed. In this material was found two original documents from Russian sources which indicated that Hiss was in touch with soviet representatives, including Molotov. Additional papers showed Hiss' interest in the subject of reparations, outside the scope of his activities.

The official role of Hiss at Yalta was supposedly confined to preparations for the forthcoming United Nations drafting conference at San Francisco. The published Yalta papers would indicate he was a somewhat minor figure. The censored material reveals him as an important participant.

In this connection, Dozer has charged that data was suppressed which showed that Mr. Roosevelt personally insisted upon taking Hiss with him to the conference.

A letter which I received from Professor Donald M. Dozer, substantiating some of the material in the *Tribune* article, is given in Chapter [51–*ed.*] in this memoir.[7] I also consulted Professor Bryton Barron who corroborated to me much of the *Tribune* statement.

The official in charge of compiling the Yalta documents, Bryton Barron, wrote:

> . . . Much information is missing. I, for instance, was repeatedly refused permission to go to the Roosevelt Library in Hyde Park to see papers which are housed there, despite the fact that these papers are under custody of an official of this government, and despite the fact that I had reason to believe that there were papers housed there which were relevant to the Yalta story but which were never included in the compilation. The Department also failed to obtain access to the personal notes taken by Governor Byrnes at Yalta, to the papers of Secretary of State Stettinius and the papers of Ambassador Harriman (Ambassador to the Soviet Union at the time), who played a leading role in the negotiation of the agreement which made many concessions to Russia in the Far East.[8]

7. See page[s 377–80–*ed.*].
8. "The Historical Blackout in the State Department," *National Review*, [vol. 1,] March 14, 1 956, p. 20.

CHAPTER 65

The Declarations on Liberated Europe and Poland

The Declaration on Liberated Europe

A declaration [at Yalta–*ed.*] from President Roosevelt, Prime Minister Churchill and Marshal Stalin contained an inspiring paragraph.

> By this declaration we reaffirm our faith in the principles of the Atlantic Charter, our pledge in the Declaration by the United Nations, and our determination to build in cooperation with other peace-loving nations a world order under law, dedicated to peace, security, freedom and the general well-being of all mankind.[1]

It must have brought renewed hope of independence and freedom among those fifteen peoples delivered over to Communist domination under the two secret commitments made at Tehran by President Roosevelt, Prime Minister Churchill and Marshal Stalin. These states and the dates of their submergence into Communism prior to the Yalta Conference were:

Annexed

East Finland	September 1944
Latvia	September 1943
Lithuania	September 1943
Estonia	September 1943
Bessarabia	September 1943
Bukovina	September 1943
East Poland	September 1943[2]

---

1. [U.S. Department of State,] *Foreign Relations of the United States*, [*Diplomatic Papers*,] *The Conferences at Malta and Yalta, 1945* [United States Government Printing Office, Washington: 1955], p. 972.

2. [*Editor's note:* The 1943 dates here are apparently a typographical error in Hoover's manuscript. Presumably he meant September 1944.]

Fitted with Communist Ministries

West Poland	June 1944
Yugoslavia	October 1944
Rumania	November 1944
Bulgaria	September 1944
Czechoslovakia	May 1944
Hungary	December 1944
Albania	December 1944

Communist representation in the Ministry of West Finland had been imposed in September 1944.

The reader will probably conclude that none of these peoples would live to witness that inspiring paragraph come into action.

The complete text of the Declaration on Liberated Europe was:[3]

The Premier of the Union of Soviet Socialist Republics, the Prime Minister of the United Kingdom, and the President of the United States of America have consulted with each other in the common interests of the peoples of their countries and of those of liberated Europe. They jointly declare their mutual agreement to concert during the temporary period of instability in liberated Europe the policies of their three Governments in assisting the peoples liberated from the domination of Nazi Germany and the peoples of the former Axis satellite states of Europe to solve by democratic means their pressing political and economic problems.

The establishment of order in Europe and the rebuilding of national economic life must be achieved by processes which will enable the liberated peoples to destroy the last vestiges of Nazism and fascism and to create democratic institutions of their own choice. This is a principle of the Atlantic Charter—the right of all peoples to choose the form of government under which they will live—the restoration of sovereign rights and self-government to those peoples who have been forcibly deprived of them by the aggressor nations.

To foster the conditions in which the liberated peoples may exercise these rights, the three governments will jointly assist the people in any European liberated state or former Axis satellite state in Europe where in their judgment conditions require (a) to establish conditions of internal peace; (b) to carry out emergency measures for the relief of distressed people;

---

3. *New York Times*, February 13, 1945. See also *Foreign Relations of the United States,* [*Diplomatic Papers,*] *The Conferences at Malta and Yalta, 1945,* p. 972.

(c) to form interim governmental authorities broadly representative of all democratic elements in the population and pledged to the earliest possible establishment through free elections of governments responsive to the will of the people; and (d) to facilitate where necessary the holding of such elections.

The three governments will consult the other United Nations and provisional authorities or other governments in Europe when matters of direct interest to them are under consideration.

When, in the opinion of the three governments, conditions in any European liberated state or any former Axis satellite state in Europe make such action necessary, they will immediately consult together on the measures necessary to discharge the joint responsibilities set forth in this declaration.

By this declaration we reaffirm our faith in the principles of the Atlantic Charter, our pledge in the Declaration by the United Nations, and our determination to build in cooperation with other peace-loving nations a world order under law, dedicated to peace, security, freedom and the general well-being of all mankind.

The declaration, in stating that it applied to the peoples "liberated from the domination of Nazi Germany and the peoples of the former Axis satellite states of Europe," certainly covered all of the fifteen peoples, as they had all been occupied by the German armies.

The declaration was no doubt an effort by Prime Minister Churchill and President Roosevelt to rescue some degree of independence and freedom for the fifteen nations which had been sacrificed at Tehran.

These "Freedom Rescue Operations" may well be recapitulated for reference purposes as each of them arises time and again over future years.

"Freedom Rescue Operations":

No. 1. To establish internal peace.

No. 2. Relief of distressed peoples.

No. 3. To form interim governments broadly representative of all democratic elements.

No. 4. Free elections and secret ballot at the earliest possible time.

No. 5. To facilitate, where necessary, the holding of such elections.

No. 6. (later on) No recognition of these governments until these actions were completed.

One of the astonishing actions at Yalta bearing upon these "Freedom Rescue Operations" was the addition of four words not in the original Atlantic

Charter which changed the whole import of the Charter from its original text. This was the paragraph in the original Charter which says:

> Third, they respect the right of all peoples to choose the form of government under which they will live; and they wish to see sovereign rights and self-government restored to those who have been forcibly deprived of them;[4]

To this four words were added, "by the aggressor nations."

The Soviet Union in all documents and statements was now referred to as a "peace-loving nation." Thus, not being an "aggressor nation" the Atlantic Charter did not apply to any act by Russia but only to those of the enemy. Some stickler for truth might contend that this subsequent rewording scarcely removed the stigma of violation of the Charter by Communist prior action as to the fifteen peoples.

Also the concept that Soviet Russia was not an aggressor nation was somewhat cynical in view of her expulsion from the League of Nations on December 14, 1939, as an "aggressor" for her attack on Finland. And it was the more cynical in view of the public denunciation by Roosevelt and Churchill at that time for her aggression.[5]

The Prime Minister also took a hand in amending the Atlantic Charter. This is shown in the next chapter where it [the Charter–*ed.*] was revised not to include the British Colonies in its proposals of freedom.

The Declaration on Poland

The conference issued to the press the following declarations as to Poland:

> A new situation has been created in Poland as a result of her complete liberation by the Red Army. This calls for the establishment of a Polish Provisional Government which can be more broadly based than was possible before the recent liberation of western Poland. The Provisional Government which is now functioning in Poland should therefore be reorganized on a broader democratic basis with the inclusion of democratic leaders from Poland itself and from Poles abroad. This new government should then be called the Polish Provisional Government of National Unity.
>
> M. Molotoff, Mr. Harriman and Sir A. Clark Kerr are authorized as a commission to consult in the first instance in Moscow with members of the

---

4. [U.S. Congress,] House Document No. 358 [August 21, 1941,] 77th Congress, 1st Session.

5. [*Editor's note:* Here Hoover placed a footnote referring readers to Volume I, Section V, Chapter 23, page 4 of his manuscript. See — in the book as now printed — pp. 156–57.]

present Provisional Government and with other Polish democratic leaders from within Poland and from abroad, with a view to the reorganization of the present Government along the above lines. This Polish Provisional Government of National Unity shall be pledged to the holding of free and unfettered elections as soon as possible on the basis of universal suffrage and secret ballot. In these elections all democratic and anti-Nazi parties shall have the right to take part and to put forward candidates.

When a Polish Provisional Government of National Unity has been properly formed in conformity with the above, the Government of the U.S.S.R., which now maintains diplomatic relations with the present Provisional Government of Poland, and the Government of the United Kingdom and the Government of the United States of America will establish diplomatic relations with the new Polish Provisional Government of National Unity, and will exchange Ambassadors, by whose reports the respective Governments will be kept informed about the situation in Poland.

The three heads of Government consider that the eastern frontier of Poland should follow the Curzon Line, with digressions from it in some regions of five to eight kilometres in favor of Poland. They recognize that Poland must receive substantial accessions of territory in the north and west. They feel that the opinion of the new Polish Provisional Government of National Unity should be sought in due course on the extent of these accessions and that the final delimitation of the western frontier of Poland should thereafter await the peace conference.[6]

Admiral Leahy comments on this declaration:

... British Foreign Minister Eden ... [read] a compromise report on the new Polish Government agreed upon by the Foreign Ministers. Roosevelt handed me a copy. . . . I felt strongly that it was so susceptible to different interpretations as to promise little toward the establishment of a government in which all the major Polish political parties would be represented. I handed the paper back to Roosevelt and said, "Mr. President, this is so elastic that the Russians can stretch it all the way from Yalta to Washington without ever technically breaking it." The President replied, "I know, Bill—I know it. But it's the best I can do for Poland at this time." The compromise report was approved.[7]

---

6. *New York Times,* February 14, 1945. See also *Foreign Relations of the United States,* [*Diplomatic Papers,*] *The Conferences at Malta and Yalta, 1945,* pp. 898 and 905.

7. [William D.] Leahy, *I Was There* [McGraw-Hill Book Company, Inc. New York: 1950], pp. 315–316.

How the "Freedom Rescue Operation" Worked in Poland

None of the "freedom rescue operations" were deemed to apply to East Poland which was annexed by Russia. As to the elections in West Poland, Arthur Bliss Lane, later Ambassador to Poland, observed:

> ... no provision was made for the supervision of the elections by the three Allies. It was merely provided that the ambassadors to be appointed would inform their respective governments about the situation in Poland. And how could elections be free as long as Red Army forces and the NKVD remained to enforce the will of the Kremlin. . . .[8]

Some light is thrown upon this arrangement as to Poland by a letter from Mr. Roosevelt to Marshal Stalin dated February 6, 1945, shortly prior to the Conference at Yalta, in which Mr. Roosevelt stated:

> ... I am determined that there shall be no breach between ourselves and the Soviet Union. Surely there is a way to reconcile our differences. . . .
>
> I hope I do not have to assure you that the United States will never lend its support in any way to any provisional government in Poland that would be inimical to your interests.[9]

The hideous tragedy of Poland can be comprehended only from the special section I give later on in this Memoir, "The Case History of Poland."[10]

---

8. Arthur Bliss Lane, *I Saw Poland Betrayed* [The Bobbs-Merrill Company, Indianapolis and New York: 1948], pp. 81–82.

9. *Foreign Relations of the United States, [Diplomatic Papers,] The Conferences at Malta and Yalta, 1945,* pp. 727–728.

10. [*Editor's note:* See Volume III.]

CHAPTER 66

Declarations and Agreements
as to Germany

THE PROGRAM FOR Germany's future, decided at Tehran, was further elaborated at Yalta. Certain of the agreements were kept secret for two years. In order to distinguish between those agreements made public during the conference and those kept secret, I give the secret agreements in italics.

On February 13, 1945, at the close of the conference, the following statement was released to the press regarding Germany:

The Defeat of Germany

We have considered and determined the military plans of the three Allied powers for the final defeat of the common enemy. The military staffs of the three Allied nations have met in daily meetings throughout the conference. These meetings have been most satisfactory from every point of view and have resulted in closer coordination of the military effort of the three Allies than ever before. The fullest information has been interchanged. The timing, scope and coordination of new and even more powerful blows to be launched by our armies and air forces into the heart of Germany from the east, west, north and south have been fully agreed and planned in detail.

Our combined military plans will be made known only as we execute them, but we believe that the very close-working partnership among the three staffs attained at this conference will result in shortening the war. Meetings of the three staffs will be continued in the future whenever the need arises.

Nazi Germany is doomed. The German people will only make the cost of their defeat heavier to themselves by attempting to continue a hopeless resistance.

The Occupation and Control of Germany

We have agreed on common politics and plans for enforcing the unconditional surrender terms which we shall impose together on Nazi Germany after German armed resistance has been finally crushed. These terms will not be made known until the final defeat of Germany has been accomplished. Under the agreed plan, the forces of the three powers will each occupy a separate zone of Germany. Coordinated administration and control have been provided for under the plan through a central control commission consisting of the Supreme Commanders of the three powers with headquarters in Berlin. It has been agreed that France should be invited by the three powers, if she should so desire, to take over a zone of occupation and to participate as a fourth member of the control commission. The limits of the French zone will be agreed by the four Governments concerned through their representatives on the European Advisory Commission.

It is our inflexible purpose to destroy German militarism and Nazism and to insure that Germany will never again be able to disturb the peace of the world. We are determined to disarm and disband all German armed forces; break up for all time the German General Staff that has repeatedly contrived the resurgence of German militarism; remove or destroy all German military equipment; eliminate or control all German industry that could be used for military production; bring all war criminals to just and swift punishment and exact reparation in kind for the destruction wrought by the Germans; wipe out the Nazi party, Nazi laws, organizations and institutions; remove all Nazi and militarist influences from public office and from the cultural and economic life of the German people; and take in harmony such other measures in Germany as may be necessary to the future peace and safety of the world. It is not our purpose to destroy the people of Germany, but only when nazism and militarism have been extirpated will there be hope for a decent life for Germans, and a place for them in the comity of nations.

Reparation by Germany

We have considered the question of the damage caused by Germany to the Allied Nations in this war and recognized it as just that Germany be obliged to make compensation for this damage in kind to the greatest extent possible. A commission for the compensation of damage will be established. The commission will be instructed to consider the question of the extent and methods for compensating damage caused by Germany and the Allied countries. The commission will work in Moscow.[1]

On March 24, 1947, about two years after the Yalta conference, the Department of State released to the press the secret agreements made at the Yalta Conference regarding Germany. This release was divided into two sections, giving (a) the agreements signed by Roosevelt, Stalin, and Churchill, and (b) the agreements signed by Stettinius, Molotov, and Eden. As there is some repetition in (a) and (b), I give only that part of (b) which does not appear in (a).

DISMEMBERMENT OF GERMANY

It was agreed that Article 12(a) of the Surrender Terms for Germany should be amended to read as follows:

"The United Kingdom, the United States of America and the Union of Soviet Socialist Republics shall possess supreme authority with respect to Germany. In the exercise of such authority they will take such steps, including the complete disarmament, demilitarization and the dismemberment of Germany as they deem requisite for future peace and security."

The study of the procedure for the dismemberment of Germany was referred to a Committee, consisting of Mr. Eden (Chairman), Mr. Winant and Mr. Gusev. This body would consider the desirability of associating with it a French representative.

ZONE OF OCCUPATION FOR THE FRENCH AND CONTROL COUNCIL

It was agreed that a zone in Germany, to be occupied by the French Forces, should be allocated to France. This zone would be formed out of the British and American zones and its extent would be settled by the British and Americans in consultation with the French Provisional Government.

It was also agreed that the French Provisional Government should be invited to become a member of the Allied Control Council for Germany.

[. . . . .–ed.]

---

1. *New York Times,* February 13, 1945.

PROTOCOL

ON THE TALKS BETWEEN THE HEADS OF THE THREE GOVERNMENTS AT THE CRIMEAN CONFERENCE ON THE QUESTION OF THE GERMAN REPARATIONS IN KIND

The Heads of the three governments agreed as follows:

1. *Germany must pay in kind for the losses caused by her to the Allied nations in the course of the war. Reparations are to be received in the first instance by those countries which have borne the main burden of the war, have suffered the heaviest losses and have organised victory over the enemy.*

2. *Reparation in kind are [sic–ed.] to be exacted from Germany in three following forms:*
   a) *Removals within 2 years from the surrender of Germany or the cessation of organized resistance from the national wealth of Germany located on the territory of Germany herself as well as outside her territory (equipment, machine-tools, ships, rolling stock, German investments abroad, shares of industrial, transport and other enterprises in Germany etc.), these removals to be carried out chiefly for purpose of destroying the war potential of Germany.*
   b) *Annual deliveries of goods from current production for a period to be fixed.*
   c) *Use of German labour.*

3. *For the working out on the above principles of a detailed plan for exaction of reparation from Germany an Allied Reparation Commission will be set up in Moscow. It will consist of three representatives—one from the Union of Soviet Socialist Republics, one from the United Kingdom and one from the United States of America.*

4. *With regard to the fixing of the total sum of the reparation as well as the distribution of it among the countries which suffered from the German aggression the Soviet and American delegations agreed as follows:*

"The Moscow reparation commission should take in its initial studies as a basis for discussion the suggestion of the Soviet Government that the total sum of the reparation in accordance with the points (a) and (b) of the paragraph 2 should be 20 billion dollars and that 50 percent of it should go to the Union of Soviet Socialist Republics."

The British delegation was of the opinion that pending consideration of the reparation question by the Moscow reparation commission, no figures of reparation should be mentioned.

*The above Soviet-American proposal has been passed to the Moscow repara-
tion commission as one of the proposals to be considered by the commission.*

WINSTON S. CHURCHILL

FRANKLIN D. ROOSEVELT

J. STALIN[2]

February 11, 1945

The Use of Prisoners for Labor After the War

This secret agreement providing for the "use of German labour" in the Protocol above was a return, after centuries, to the use of military prisoners of war
as slave labor. During the war, prisoners were provided with some protection by the previous Geneva Convention, signed by most civilized nations,
and also by fear of reprisals. Now these civilized considerations were to be
abandoned.

The American State Department favored the use of forced labor of German prisoners, as shown by the "Briefing Book" taken to Yalta by the American delegation which contained such a recommendation.[3]

Expulsion of Germans from West Poland

Under "The Treatment of Germany," dated January 12, 1945, the State Department recommended:

> . . . That Poland acquire East Prussia (except for the Koenigsberg area), the
> former Free City of Danzig, German Upper Silesia, and the eastern portion
> of Pomerania possessing an area of approximately 6,812 square miles. . . .
>
> The cessions to Poland recommended above would bring under Polish
> sovereignty approximately 3,400,000 Germans in addition to more than
> 700,000 resident there before the present war. Both the Polish Government-
> in-exile and the Lublin Committee have expressed the desire to expel this
> German population. In addition the Government-in-exile of Czechoslovakia
> wishes to remove more than 1,500,000 Sudeten Germans.[4]

---

2. [U.S. Department of State,] *Foreign Relations of the United States,* [*Diplomatic Papers,*] *The
Conferences at Malta and Yalta, 1945* [United States Government Printing Office, Washington: 1955],
pp. 978, 982, and 983. Italics here indicate secret agreement. [*Editor's note:* Although Hoover's footnote indicates that he planned to italicize this document, it is not italicized in his manuscript. I have
italicized it here in accordance with his intent. I have also corrected a few typographical errors in his
transcription from the source cited.]

3. Ibid., p. 193.

4. Ibid., p. 189.

A letter from Ambassador Harriman to Secretary of State Stettinius, dated December 19, 1944, a month prior to Yalta, stated:

> Both the Lublin Poles and Mikolajczyk indicated in the October talks that they did not wish any German population to remain within Polish territory. . . . Churchill in his recent speech mentions the transfer of six million Germans out of territory to be given to the Poles. The new suggested boundary to the Neisse would evidently necessitate the transfer of several million more Germans.
>
> Stalin also agreed with Benes in December 1943 that some if not all of the Sudeten Germans should be transferred.[5]

Admiral Leahy commented:

> I felt sorry for the German people. We were planning . . . to obliterate a once mighty nation. . . .
>
> . . . the proposed peace seemed to me a frightening "sowing of dragon's teeth" that carried germs of an appalling war of revenge at some time in the distant future. . . .
>
> There was another compelling factor that kept me from sharing in the feeling of great hope, almost exultation, that prevailed in our American delegation as we left Yalta, as to the practicability of maintaining world peace through the United Nations Organization. The essential agreement to destroy German militarism accepted at the conference would make Russia the dominant power in Europe. . . .[6]

When I visited Prague in 1946, I asked President Benes if all of the Sudetens had been expelled from Czechoslovakia. He replied that all but a few thousands had been expelled in a "humane" way. The "humane" manner was expulsion with only the goods they could carry on their backs and the backs of their children. Had it not been for the benevolent action of the American army, then in occupation of Germany, in providing for the refugees, tens of thousands would have perished.

It might be pointed out that these expulsions were not only a violation of human decency, they were a violation of the Atlantic Charter provision that "they desire to see no territorial changes that do not accord with the freely expressed wishes of the peoples concerned."

---

5. Ibid., p. 220.
6. [William D.] Leahy, *I Was There* [McGraw-Hill Book Company, Inc., New York: 1950], pp. 322–323.

CHAPTER 67

Sundry Agreements

As previously stated, the agreements or declarations at Yalta which were published during the Conference are given in full type, those held secret at that time are given in italics.

An agreement about Italo-Yugoslav and Italo-Austria frontiers read:

Notes on these subjects were put in by the British delegation and the American and Soviet delegations agreed to consider them and give their views later.[1]

There was also the following note on Yugoslav-Bulgarian relations:

There was an exchange of views between the Foreign Secretaries on the question of the desirability of a Yugoslav-Bulgarian pact of alliance. The question at issue was whether a state still under an armistice regime could be allowed to enter into a treaty with another state. Mr. Eden suggested that the Bulgarian and Yugoslav Governments should be informed that this could not be approved. Mr. Stettinius suggested that the British and American Ambassadors should discuss the matter further with M. Molotov in Moscow. M. Molotov agreed with the proposal of Mr. Stettinius.[2]

Among the actions at Yalta was one referring to Bulgarian and Rumanian oil:

The British Delegation put in notes for the consideration of their colleagues on the following subjects:

---

1. [U.S. Department of State,] *Foreign Relations of the United States,* [*Diplomatic Papers,*] *The Conferences at Malta and Yalta, 1945* [United States Government Printing Office, Washington: 1955], p. 981. Italics here indicate secret agreement.

2. Ibid. Italics here indicate secret agreement.

(a) the Control Commission in Bulgaria

(b) Greek claims upon Bulgaria, more particularly with reference to reparations.

(c) Oil equipment in Roumania.[3]

At Yalta an agreement was made implying change in the control of the Dardanelles.

> It was agreed that at the next meeting of the three Foreign Secretaries to be held in London, they should consider proposals which it was understood the Soviet Government would put forward in relation to the Montreux Convention and report to their Governments. The Turkish Government should be informed at the appropriate moment.
>
> The foregoing Protocol was approved and signed by the three Foreign Secretaries at the Crimean Conference, February 11, 1945.[4]

The existing control of the Dardanelles had been set up by the Montreux Convention which was signed on July 20, 1936 by Bulgaria, France, Great Britain, Greece, Japan, Rumania, Turkey, the USSR and Yugoslavia.

The Council of Foreign Ministers

This Council was suggested at Tehran and was agreed to at Yalta. The communiqué issued to the press defining its duties said:

> ... the conference agreed that permanent machinery should be set up for regular consultation between the three Foreign Secretaries. They will, therefore, meet as often as may be necessary, probably about every three or four months. These meetings will be held in rotation in the three capitals, the first meeting being held in London, after the United Nations' conference on world organization.[5]

This Council was confirmed at the Potsdam Conference and its duties further defined.

---

3. Ibid. Italics here indicate secret agreement.
4. Ibid., p. 982. Italics here indicate secret agreement.
5. *New York Times*, February 13, 1945.

The Secret Proposal of Loans from the United States to Russia for Reconstruction

Assurances had been given the Russians prior to Yalta that they would receive large loans from the United States after the war. Stettinius says that Molotov had:

> ... expressed the hope that the Soviet Union would receive long-term credits from the United States.[6]

He further states:

> Secretary of the Treasury Morgenthau ... sent a letter to the President on January 1, 1945, stating that he had discussed Soviet credits several times with Harriman. "We are not thinking of more Lend-Lease or any form of relief but rather of an arrangement that will have definite and long-range benefits for the United States as well as for Russia. . . . I am convinced that if we were to come forward now and present to the Russians a concrete plan to aid them in the reconstruction period it would contribute a great deal towards ironing out many of the difficulties we have been having with respect to their problems and policies."[7]

A month before Yalta, on January 6, 1945, Ambassador Harriman, from Moscow, cabled the State Department:

> ... we should do everything we can to assist the Soviet Union through credits in developing a sound economy. I feel strongly that the sooner the Soviet Union can develop a decent life for its people the more tolerant they will become. . . . I am satisfied that the great urge of Stalin and his associates is to provide a better physical life for the Russian people, although they will retain a substantial military establishment.[8]

Secretary of State Stettinius conveyed a hint of these glad tidings to Molotov at Yalta, saying:

> I immediately stated that my government had studied the question of Soviet credits and that I personally was ready to discuss the matter either here or later in Moscow or Washington. Molotov expressed the opinion that, now

---

6. [Edward R.] Stettinius [Jr.], *Roosevelt and the Russians* [Doubleday & Company, Inc., Garden City, N.Y.: 1949], p. 119.

7. Ibid., p. 120.

8. *Foreign Relations of the United States,* [*Diplomatic Papers,*] *The Conferences at Malta and Yalta,* 1945, p. 314.

that the end of the war was in sight, it was most important for agreement to be reached on these economic questions.

The State Department had actually been devoting considerable study to the question of a loan to the Soviet Union. . . .[9]

There was evidence that the State Department was inclined to be less generous than the Treasury. Morgenthau wanted to give the Soviets $10 billion at two percent, but the State Department opposed this amount.[10]

An Agreement as to Palestine

Early in the war, the Jewish community in the United States had started a renewed and determined drive to force Britain to reverse her policies of restricted immigration of Jews to Palestine. In the Congress majorities of the Foreign Relations Committee of the House were supporting pleas for a Jewish homeland.

The British, greatly concerned over their relations with the Arab states, wanted no such statement of American policy. Secretary of War Henry L. Stimson wrote to the Chairmen of the Senate Foreign Relations and the House Foreign Affairs Committees that favorable action on the pending resolutions "would be prejudicial to the successful prosecution of the war."[11]

The Jewish community was disappointed. President Roosevelt gave his private backing (through New York's Senator Wagner) to a plank in the Democratic platform desired by the American Zionist leaders, which read:

We favor the opening of Palestine to unrestricted Jewish immigration and colonization and such a policy as to result in the establishment there of a free and democratic Jewish commonwealth.[12]

When it had been incorporated into the platform, Mr. Roosevelt addressed a letter to Senator Wagner, expressing his satisfaction with this action:

Dear Bob:
Please express my satisfaction that, in accord with the traditional Democratic policy and in keeping with the spirit of the "four freedoms," the

---

9. Stettinius, *Roosevelt and the Russians*, pp. 119–120.
10. *Foreign Relations of the United States*, [*Diplomatic Papers,*] *The Conferences at Malta and Yalta*, *1945*, pp. 315–323.
11. The documentation of this incident was collected and published in the *Congressional Record* [vol. 91] (October 24, 1945), pp. A4475–7, by Congressman Vursell of Illinois.
12. *Congressional Record*, [vol. 91,] October 24, 1945, p. A4476.

Democratic Party, at its convention, included the following plank in its platform. . . .

The President then quoted the above plank and continued:

If elected, I shall help to bring about its realization.[13]

The Zionist leaders were not yet satisfied and the original Palestine resolutions were brought up again before the Committees in Congress. Secretary Stimson withdrew his objection.

This raised to the skies the hopes of American Zionists, but it also again awakened the strong British fears concerning the attitude of the Arab states if the United States were to carry out such a pledge. Mr. Roosevelt had to choose between the dangers to Britain and carrying out a campaign promise. A month after his election, the President instructed Secretary of State Stettinius to tell the Committees of the Senate and House that "passage of the Palestine resolution at the present time would be unwise from the standpoint of the general international situation."[14]

The Secret Agreement with Ibn Saud, King of Saudi Arabia

The situation of the Zionists was uncertain enough but on February 13, 1945, the President, on his way back from Yalta, met with King Ibn Saud of Saudi Arabia, then a leader in the Arab world, and made some pledges to him. Ibn Saud apparently believed in having matters in writing. On March 10, 1945, he addressed a letter to President Roosevelt, setting forth the Arab position on the rights of the Arabs in Palestine and protesting vigorously against the whole Zionist movement.

To this Mr. Roosevelt replied on April 5, 1945, and after acknowledging Ibn Saud's letter, continued:

> . . . I am also mindful of the memorable conversation which we had not so long ago and in the course of which I had an opportunity to obtain so vivid an impression of Your Majesty's sentiments on this question.
>
> Your Majesty will recall that on previous occasions I communicated to you the attitude of the American Government toward Palestine and made clear our desire that no decision be taken with respect to the basic situation in that country without full consultation with both Arabs and Jews.

---

13. Ibid., p. A4477.
14. Ibid.

Your Majesty will also doubtless recall that during our recent conversation I assured you that I would take no action, in my capacity as Chief of the Executive Branch of this Government, which might prove hostile to the Arab people.

It gives me pleasure to renew to Your Majesty the assurances which you have previously received regarding the attitude of my Government and my own, as Chief Executive, with regard to the question of Palestine and to inform you that the policy of this Government in this respect is unchanged.[15]

This secret agreement was not communicated to the Zionists until it was published by Secretary of State Byrnes on October 18, 1945[16]—eight months after the meeting between President Roosevelt and the King of Saudi Arabia. Where the Zionists stood at this moment is a little difficult to determine. However, despite the implications of this understanding between the President and Ibn Saud, the devoted persistence of the Zionists ultimately won for them their homeland of refuge.

---

15. *New York Times*, October 19, 1945.
16. Ibid.

CHAPTER **68**

The Secret Far Eastern Agreement

I HAVE DELAYED the narrative of the most important and most fatal agreement made at Yalta until after the European undertakings were described.

This secret agreement was in writing. It gave enormous concessions to Stalin at the expense of Free China. The stated reasons were to induce Soviet Russia to join in the war against Japan. Stalin had repeatedly agreed to do this as soon as the Germans were defeated. He gave such an assurance to Ambassador W. Averell Harriman in 1942,[1] to Ambassador Major General Patrick J. Hurley in April 1943,[2] and to Secretary of State Hull in October 1943.[3] At Tehran in December 1943 he again agreed to join in war against Japan after the Germans were defeated.

On October 10, 1944, about four months before Yalta, Ambassador Harriman cabled President Roosevelt from Moscow:

> ... We now have a full agreement from Stalin not only to participate in the Pacific war but to enter the war with full effort. ... .[4]

Five days later, however, on October 15, 1944, British Minister of Foreign Affairs Anthony Eden, and American Ambassador Harriman, met with Stalin. Marshal Stalin now began to make further conditions. At this time his formula was:

---

1. [John R.] Deane, *The Strange Alliance* [The Viking Press, New York: 1947], p. 226.
2. [William D.] Leahy, *I Was There* [Whittlesey House, McGraw Hill Book Company, Inc., New York: 1950], p. 147.
3. *The Memoirs of Cordell Hull* [The Macmillan Company, New York: 1948], Vol. II, p. 1309.
4. [U.S. Department of State,] *Foreign Relations of the United States,* [*Diplomatic Papers,*] *The Conferences at Malta and Yalta, 1945* [United States Government Printing Office, Washington: 1955], p. 362.

... the Soviet Union would take the offensive against Japan three months after Germany's defeat provided the United States would assist in building up the necessary reserve supplies and provided the political aspects of Russia's participation had been clarified. . . .[5]

These "political aspects" to be clarified were indicated in a telegram of December 15, 1944—about two months before Yalta—from Harriman to Roosevelt, saying:

In my talk with Stalin last night I said that you were anxious to know what political questions he had indicated in October should be clarified in connection with Russia's entry in the war against Japan. . . . He said that the Kurile Islands and the lower Sakhalin should be returned to Russia. He explained that the Japanese now controlled the approaches to Vladivostok, that we considered that the Russians were entitled to protection for their communications to this important port and that "all outlets to the Pacific were now held or blocked by the enemy." He drew a line around the southern part of the Liaotung Peninsula including Port Arthur and Dairen saying that the Russians wished again to lease these ports and the surrounding area.

I said that I recalled that you and he had discussed this question at Teheran and that, if my memory was correct, you had in fact initiated yourself the question of the need for Russia to have access to a warm water port in the Pacific but that on the other hand I thought you had in mind an international free port rather than the lease of this area by the Russians; that this method, you felt, would give the Soviets the needed protection and was more in the line with present day concepts of how international questions of this kind could best be dealt with. He said "This can be discussed." Stalin said further that he wished to lease the Chinese-Eastern Railway. I asked him to define the exact lines in Manchuria in which he was interested and he pointed out the lines from Dairen to Harbin thence northwest to Manchuli and east to Vladivostok. He answered affirmatively when I asked if these were the only railroad lines in Manchuria in which he was interested. In answer to my question he specifically reaffirmed that he did not intend to interfere with the sovereignty of China in Manchuria. There is of course no doubt that with control of the railroad operations and with the probability of Russian troops to protect the railroad Soviet influence will be great. He said the only consideration he had not mentioned at Teheran was the recognition of the

---

5. Deane, *The Strange Alliance*, p. 247.

status quo in Outer Mongolia—the maintenance of the Republic of Outer Mongolia as an independent identity. . . .[6]

What Stalin's demands were and what was agreed by Roosevelt and Churchill can be given best by the agreement itself which was as follows:[7]

The leaders of the three Great Powers—the Soviet Union, the United States of America and Great Britain—have agreed that in two or three months after Germany has surrendered and the war in Europe has terminated the Soviet Union shall enter in the war against Japan on the side of the Allies on condition that:

   1. *The status quo in Outer-Mongolia (The Mongolian People's Republic) shall be preserved;*

   2. *The former rights of Russia violated by the treacherous attack of Japan in 1904 shall be restored, viz:*

     (a) the southern part of Sakhalin as well as all the islands adjacent to it shall be returned to the Soviet Union,

     (b) the commercial port of Dairen shall be internationalized, the preeminent interests of the Soviet Union in this port being safeguarded and the lease of Port Arthur as a naval base of the USSR restored,

     (c) the Chinese-Eastern Railroad and the South-Manchurian Railroad which provides an outlet to Dairen shall be jointly operated by the establishment of a joint Soviet-Chinese Company it being understood that the preeminent interests of the Soviet Union shall be safeguarded and that China shall retain full sovereignty in Manchuria;

   3. *The Kuril islands shall be handed over to the Soviet Union.*

It is understood, that the agreement concerning Outer-Mongolia and the ports and railroads referred to above will require concurrence of Generalissimo Chiang Kai-shek. The President will take measures in order to obtain this concurrence on advice from Marshal Stalin.

The Heads of the three Great Powers have agreed that these claims of the Soviet Union shall be unquestionably fulfilled after Japan has been defeated.

For its part the Soviet Union expresses its readiness to conclude with the National Government of China a pact of friendship and alliance between the USSR

---

6. *Foreign Relations of the United States, The Conferences at Malta and Yalta, 1945,* pp. 378–379. See also [Herbert] Feis, *The China Tangle* [Princeton University Press, Princeton, N.J.: 1953], p. 233.

7. [*Editor's note:* This was Hoover's handwritten insertion, probably made in early 1964. The sentence which this one replaced reads: "The secret Far Eastern agreement, giving all Stalin's major demands was as follows:".]

and China in order to render assistance to China with its armed forces for the purpose of liberating China from the Japanese yoke.

J. STALIN
FRANKLIN D. ROOSEVELT
WINSTON S. CHURCHILL[8]

February 11, 1945

Despite all the awards and gifts to Stalin in this Far Eastern Agreement, he did not join in the war against Japan until after she was in fact defeated by the use of the atomic bomb. However, he held on to all the concessions in the Far Eastern Agreement.

The text of this agreement was not furnished to Chiang Kai-shek for some months, nor to all the members of the Yalta Conference, nor was it given to the American people until February 11, 1946, a year after the Agreement was signed.

---

8. *Foreign Relations of the United States,* [*Diplomatic Papers,*] *The Conferences at Malta and Yalta, 1945,* p. 984. Italics here indicate secret agreement. [*Editor's note:* Hoover intended to italicize this passage but did not do so in his manuscript. I have supplied the italics in accordance with his intent.]

CHAPTER 69

Were These Sacrifices Necessary to Defeat Germany?

IT IS THE DUTY of an historian to review and appraise the consequences of the actions of men and the alternative courses they could have taken.

It will occur to some students that three months after Germany was defeated the combined strength of the United States and Great Britain, now free from the European war, added to the strength of China, needed no help to bring about defeat of Japan or to bring the Japanese to accept defeat as inevitable.

However, the questions rightly can be asked: "If Roosevelt and Churchill had refused to agree to the Far Eastern Agreement at Yalta, would Stalin have quit the war?" And, "if so, what then?" If he quit he would have needed to make some sort of peace with his implacable enemy Hitler and, in such case, the Allies would not stop their war on Hitler and where would Russia be after their victory?

Mr. Roosevelt at the First Cairo Conference in November 1943 had promised Chiang Kai-shek, according to the official record:

> President Roosevelt proposed that, after the war, China and the United States should effect certain arrangements under which the two countries could come to each other's assistance in the event of foreign aggression and that the United States should maintain adequate military forces on various bases in the Pacific in order that it could effectively share the responsibility of preventing aggression. . . . President Roosevelt, on his part, proposed that China and the United States should consult with each other before any decision was to be reached on matters concerning Asia. The Generalissimo indicated agreement.[1]

---

1. [U.S. Department of State,] *Foreign Relations of the United States, [Diplomatic Papers, The] Conferences at Cairo and Tehran, 1943* [United States Government Printing Office, Washington: 1961], p. 324.

The secret Far Eastern Agreement would hardly seem consistent with this undertaking.

The Communist Influences Around President Roosevelt

It is essential that there should be some reference to the influences of American Communism around President Roosevelt.

I have described in Chapters [4–ed.] and [5–ed.] the numbers of American Communists in the Roosevelt Administration, and the even larger horde of subversive groups—the "fronts." I have given the facts as to the cabal in the legation at Chungking and the State Department in Washington, who were steadily undermining Chiang Kai-shek and at least giving moral support to Communist Chinese leader Mao Tse-tung.[2]

An important adviser to the President at Yalta was Alger Hiss. Subsequent to the Yalta Conference, the House Un-American Activities Committee exposed that Hiss had been furnishing confidential material to Soviet agencies long before Yalta.[3] And Lauchlin Currie, one of Mr. Roosevelt's personal assistants with his office in the White House, was also furnishing information to the Communists.

Ralph de Toledano and Victor Lasky in their book, *Seeds of Treason,* review the subject of Hiss at Yalta:

> How important was Hiss' role at Yalta? He himself testified that "I think it is an accurate and not an immodest statement to say that I [helped formulate the Yalta Agreement] to some extent." There is also the mute testimony of the phone directory published for the American delegation in the Crimea. At a meeting so star-studded with the biggest figures in our political, military, and diplomatic worlds—figures such as General Marshall, Admiral King, Stettinius, Hopkins—protocol was important. President Roosevelt's number was "1." Alger Hiss's was "4." Yet in the monumental *Roosevelt and Hopkins,* Robert E. Sherwood gives not one single mention to Hiss.[4]

The Sherwood book was published three years after Yalta.

---

2. Chapter [47–ed.].

3. Chapter [Editor's note: Hoover did not complete this footnote. There are references to Hiss in chapters 4 and 64.]

4. Ralph de Toledano and Victor Lasky, *Seeds of Treason,* p. 108. Funk & Wagnalls Company, New York: 1950. [Editor's note: In his final corrections of his manuscript, Hoover removed the brackets around the words "helped to formulate the Yalta Agreement" in this quotation. Since the brackets are in the book cited, I have retained them here.]

Mr. Roosevelt's Admiration for Stalin

Apparently one of the influences on Mr. Roosevelt was his admiration for and confidence in Stalin. In a speech after the conference at Tehran, on December 24, 1943, he said of Stalin:

> He is a man who combines a tremendous relentless determination with a stalwart good humor. I believe he is truly representative of the heart and soul of Russia; and I believe that we are going to get along very well with him and the Russian people—very well indeed.[5]

General Albert C. Wedemeyer states:

> ... Franklin Roosevelt declared, on March 8, 1944, [three months after Tehran] "I think the Russians are perfectly friendly. They aren't trying to gobble up all the rest of Europe. They haven't got any ideas of conquest. These fears that have been expressed by a lot of people here that the Russians are going to try and dominate Europe, I personally don't think there is anything in it." ....[6]

Sherwood makes the following statement from the notes of Harry Hopkins:

> *Mr. Hopkins* said that on the trip home from Yalta the President had frequently reviewed with him the results of the Crimea Conference and that he had come away from that Conference with renewed confidence that the United States and the Soviet Union could work together in peace as they had in war. President Roosevelt on the trip home had frequently spoken of the respect and admiration he had for Marshal Stalin and he was looking forward to their next meeting which the President hoped would be in Berlin.[7]

Samuel I. Rosenman, the President's special speech writer, joined the President en route home from Yalta. He says:

> The President made it clear, not only when we were working alone on the speech, but in luncheon and dinner conversation, that he was certain that the Yalta Conference had paved the way for the kind of world that he had been dreaming, planning, and talking about. He felt that he understood Stalin and

---

5. *New York Times,* December 25, 1943.
6. Albert C. Wedemeyer, *Wedemeyer Reports!* [Henry Holt & Company, New York: 1958], p. 430.
7. [Robert E.] Sherwood, *Roosevelt and Hopkins* [Harper & Brothers, New York: 1948], p. 888.

that Stalin understood him. He believed that Stalin had a sincere desire to build constructively on the foundations that had been laid at Yalta; that Stalin was interested in maintaining peace in the world. . . .[8]

That the President wanted no criticism of Stalin is indicated by an episode concerning former Governor George H. Earle of Pennsylvania, who had been Mr. Roosevelt's special Ambassador to the Balkans. According to Earle, in a statement he made in the *New York Times* in December, 1947, he wrote a letter to Mr. Roosevelt after Roosevelt's return from Yalta warning him of trickery and saying in part:

> . . . "Russia is a greater menace than Germany" . . . "while they are posing as allies they are tearing the democracies to pieces."
>
> . . . "I have seen this with my own eyes" and "unless I hear from you within a week I will make a statement to the American people."[9]

Mr. Roosevelt's reply (received on March 24, 1945, a month after Yalta) read:

> Dear George:
>
> . . . I have noted with concern your plan to publicize your unfavorable opinion of one of our allies at the very time when such a publication from a former emissary of mine might do irreparable harm to our war effort. . . .
>
> You say you will publish unless you are told before March 28 that I do not wish you to do so. I not only do not wish it, but I specifically forbid you to publish any information or opinion about an ally that you have acquired while in office or in the service of the United States Navy.
>
> . . . I shall withdraw any previous understanding that you are serving as an emissary of mine and I shall direct the Navy Department to continue your employment wherever they can make use of your services. . . .
>
> Franklin Roosevelt[10]

A short time thereafter, Earle was ordered to Samoa, in the South Pacific.

Years later, Earle testified before a Congressional Committee that he had received proof (in the form of affidavits and pictures) of Russian guilt in the Katyn Forest massacre. He stated that when he presented the evidence to Mr. Roosevelt, he was told that it was all a German plot. Roosevelt said:

---

8. [Samuel I.] Rosenman, *Working with Roosevelt* [Harper & Brothers, New York: 1952], p. 526.
9. *New York Times*, December 9, 1947.
10. Ibid.

I am absolutely certain the Russians didn't do this.

Earle further testified:

The love, respect and belief in the Russians in the White House and other places in Washington was simply unbelievable.[11]

---

11. *New York Times*, November 14, 1952.

CHAPTER 70

The Claim That Mr. Roosevelt Signed the Far Eastern Agreement Because of Military Pressures

A MAJOR EXCUSE given by Mr. Roosevelt's colleagues for his signing the Far Eastern Agreement (the ruin of China) was that he had been pressed into so doing by his military advisers in order to induce Stalin to join the war against Japan.

For instance, Secretary of State Stettinius, who was present at Yalta, says in his book:

> I knew at Yalta . . . *of the immense pressure put on the President by our military leaders to bring Russia into the Far Eastern war.* . . .
>
> Soon after the President arrived at Yalta he had top-level conferences with the Marshal [Stalin] over the question of Russia's entrance into the Japanese war. . . . Approximately halfway through the Yalta Conference, Harriman and Hopkins told me that the President had asked them to advise me that discussions were taking place between the President and the Marshal [Stalin] on this question.
>
> I was told . . . that Stalin had said that . . . certain concessions desired in the Far East . . . were essential for Russian entry into the war against Japan. . . .
>
> . . . I asked the President . . . whether or not there was anything in connection with this matter that he wished the State Department delegation to pursue. The President stated that, *since it was primarily a military matter . . . he thought it had best remain on a purely military level.*
>
> Military considerations of the highest order dictated the President's signing of the Far Eastern agreement. The *military insisted* that the Soviet Union had to be brought into the Japanese war. . . .

Even as late as the Potsdam Conference, after the first atomic bomb had exploded at Los Alamos on July 16, the military insisted that the Soviet Union had to be brought into the Far Eastern war. . . .[1]

James F. Byrnes who was present at Yalta succeeded Stettinius as Secretary of State. On September 4, 1945, at a press conference, Byrnes stated in reply to a question as to concessions to Stalin:

> . . . the matter had been first broached to this government at the Yalta conference . . . but that no "agreement" had been reached or even attempted. . . .[2]

In a press interview five months later, on January 29, 1946, Secretary Byrnes said:

> . . . [the Far Eastern] agreement had been reached with full knowledge of the nation's military leaders.[3]

Who Were the Military Leaders Who Did or Did Not Advise Mr. Roosevelt to Make the Far Eastern Agreement?

It is important in the interest of truth to examine who of the military leaders advised Mr. Roosevelt to make the Far Eastern Agreement and, equally important, which of them opposed or disapproved of it.

The important military officials present at Yalta were Chief of Staff General George C. Marshall, Admiral William D. Leahy, Mr. Roosevelt's personal Chief of Staff, and Admiral Ernest J. King, Chief of Naval Operations.

Obviously the other military leaders most competent to advise on questions raised by the Far Eastern Agreement were General Douglas MacArthur, in command of the forces operating against Japan, with Admiral Chester W. Nimitz in command of the naval support; General Emmett O'Donnell in command of General MacArthur's air forces; and Major General Curtis LeMay, who directed the air attacks on Japan. General Dwight D. Eisenhower and General Mark W. Clark also loomed large in our military leadership.

In the spring of 1951 a long Senate inquiry endeavored to discover who was responsible for the Far Eastern Agreement.

Senator William F. Knowland queried Admiral King as to his part in the matter. The Admiral said:

---

1. E. R. Stettinius, *Roosevelt and the Russians* [Doubleday & Company, Inc., Garden City, N.Y.: 1949], pp. 90, 92, 96, 98. Italics mine.
2. *New York Times*, September 5, 1945.
3. *New York Herald Tribune*, January 30, 1946.

When the late President Roosevelt asked me about making concessions to Premier Stalin in order to get him to "play ball," I replied that I would concede him only the southern half of the island of Sakhalin and that as a "sop."[4]

Later recorded in his authorized book, published in 1952, Admiral King recalled that:

... the Joint Chiefs of Staff did not agree with the President's ideas of "sweetening" Stalin in order to obtain his help against the Japanese, for it seemed to King and his military colleagues that the price asked was far too high. The Russians wished to take over the railroad in Manchukuo, ice-free ports in Manchuria, the Japanese-held southern half of Sakhalin, and all of the Kurile Islands. The Joint Chiefs felt that the southern part of Sakhalin would have been quite enough, but as the Joint Chiefs did not make political policy, their views did not prevail. . . .[5]

Admiral Leahy stated his views on the secret Far Eastern Agreement in his book, *I Was There*, published in 1950. He wrote:

... I was of the firm opinion that our war against Japan had progressed to the point where her defeat was only a matter of time and attrition. Therefore, we did not need Stalin's help to defeat our enemy in the Pacific. . . .[6]

As for General MacArthur, in a debate in the Senate on March 22, 1955, Senator Herbert H. Lehman asserted that General MacArthur "urgently recommended that Soviet Russia be involved in the war against Japan."[7]
General MacArthur issued a statement the following day, saying:

Neither directly nor indirectly did I have the slightest connection with the Yalta conference. My views on the advisability of Soviet Russia entering the war at that late date were never solicited. Neither I nor any member of my command was present at the Yalta Conference and I personally did not even know it was being held.

---

4. [King letter to Senator Knowland, June 21, 1951, printed in U.S. Congress, Senate,] *Military Situation in the Far East, Hearings Before the Committee on Armed Services and the Committee on Foreign Relations,* 82nd Congress, 1st Session, (hereafter cited as Senate Hearings, 1951) Part 4, [p. 3055–] p. 3056; Ernest J. King and Walter Muir Whitehill, *Fleet Admiral King—A Naval Record* [W. W. Norton & Company, New York: 1952], pp. 591–592.

5. Ernest J. King and Walter Muir Whitehill, *Fleet Admiral King—A Naval Record*, p. 591.

6. Fleet Admiral William D. Leahy, *I Was There*, p. 293, Whittlesey House, McGraw-Hill Book Company, New York: 1950.

7. *Congressional Record*, March 22, 1955, Vol. 101, Part 3, pp. 3351, 3352.

The imminent collapse of Japan was clearly apparent several months before Yalta when we seized the Philippines. All of my dispatches and reports clearly enunciated this viewpoint. For instance as early as September 21, 1944, I stated that the campaign was "entering its decisive phase" and that Japan had "neither the imagination nor the foresighted ability to continue total war" and that "defeat now stares her in the face."

One month later, on Oct. 20, 1944, I further reported:

"The strategic result of capturing the Philippines will be decisive. The enemy's so-called Greater East Asia co-prosperity sphere will be cut in two. His conquered empire to the south, comprising the Dutch East Indies and the British possessions of Borneo, Malaya and Burma will be severed from Japan proper.

"The great flow of transportation and supply upon which Japan's vital war industry depends will be cut, as will the counter-supply of his forces to the south. A half-million men will be cut off without hope of support and with ultimate destruction at the leisure of the allies a certainty. In broad strategic conception the defensive line of the Japanese, which extends along the coast of Asia from the Japan Islands through Formosa, the Philippines, the East Indies to Singapore and Burma, will be pierced in the center, permitting an envelopment to the south and to the north. Either flank will be vulnerable and can be rolled up at will."

All my reports from that time on presaged the imminent collapse of Japan. . . .

Had my views been requested with reference to Yalta I would most emphatically have recommended against bringing the Soviet into the Pacific War at that late date. To have made vital concessions for such a purpose would have seemed to me fantastic.[8]

An official historian of the Army, Louis Morton, wrote an article for a magazine (*The Reporter,* April 7, 1955) disputing General MacArthur's statement, and categorically stating that MacArthur was willing to make some concessions to Stalin. Major General Courtney Whitney, MacArthur's aide and his biographer, issued statements flatly denying the assertions of both Senator Lehman and Mr. Morton.

Others entered the fray, and newspapermen asked to see the Army documents. Instead of making these available at this time—ten years after Yalta—

---

8. *New York Times,* March 24, 1955.

the Army upgraded the documents to a "confidential" category. The San Francisco *Examiner* protested editorially:

> The sudden decision of the Army to deny the press access to documents relating to the controversy that has arisen on the view of General MacArthur about the need and extent of Soviet help against Japan in World War II was unaccountably capricious.
>
> Whatever factors entered into it, the net result is that it is against the right of the American people to know.[9]

General Emmett O'Donnell testified at the Senate Committee hearings on June 25, 1951:

> ... I should say, we were in a position to enforce a period of peace in this world for at least 50 or 100 years by simply telling Mr. Stalin and his Russian hordes that we are not going home until you go home, and if you don't go home, we are going to take you home. And we were in a position to do that, just as surely as I am sitting here today.[10]

It seems that General O'Donnell was not the mysterious adviser.

On September 20, 1945, Major General Curtis LeMay stated to the Associated Press:

> The atomic bomb had nothing to do with the end of the war. . . .
>
> The war would have been over in two weeks without the Russians coming in and without the atomic bomb.[11]

There was present at this interview General Barney Giles, who was engaged in the action against Japan, and who agreed with General LeMay. It is clear they could not have advised Mr. Roosevelt to make the sacrifices in the Far Eastern Agreement.

In an address to Congress on October 5, 1945, Admiral Chester Nimitz said:

> The atomic bomb did not win the war against Japan. The Japanese had, in fact, already sued for peace before the atomic age was announced to the world with the destruction of Hiroshima and before the Russian entry into the war.[12]

---

9. San Francisco *Examiner* [April 7, 1955–ed.]
10. Senate Hearings, 1951, *Military Situation in the Far East,* Part 4, p. 3105.
11. *New York Herald Tribune,* September 20, 1945.
12. *New York Times,* October 6, 1945.

He reemphasized this in an Associated Press interview in Washington the following day, saying that he was convinced the end of the war would have been the same without the atomic bomb *or the entry of Russia into the war.*

He seems eliminated as an adviser to sign the Far Eastern Agreement.

At a Senatorial inquiry, Senator H. Alexander Smith asked General Marshall, then Secretary of State:

> I would like to ask you if you were familiar with this so-called secret agreement [Yalta] with regard to China?

> **Secretary Marshall.** I did not know the factors of it at the time.[13]

Senator Knowland asked General Marshall:

> ... Were you familiar at Yalta with the Manchurian provisions of giving Dairen and the rights on the Manchurian railroad and Port Arthur to the Soviet Union?

> **Secretary Marshall.** I don't think I was, sir.

> **Senator Knowland.** You were not. Was that made in the political—

> **Secretary Marshal.** Yes.

> **Senator Knowland.** ... Committee?

> **Secretary Marshall.** Those were entirely separate from the military.

> **Senator Knowland.** They were separate from the military?

> **Secretary Marshall.** Yes, sir.[14]

The following is from Eisenhower's *Crusade in Europe.*

> Another item on which I ventured to advise President Truman involved the Soviets' intention to enter the Japanese war. I told him that since reports indicated the imminence of Japan's collapse I deprecated the Red Army's engaging in that war. I foresaw certain difficulties arising out of such participation and suggested that, at the very least, we ought not to put ourselves in the position of requesting or begging for Soviet aid. It was my personal opinion that no power on earth could keep the Red Army out of that war unless victory came before they could get in. However, I did not then foresee the future relentless struggle born in ideological antagonisms, or the paralysis

---

13. Senate Hearings, 1951, Part 1, p. 696.
14. Ibid., pp. 564–565.

of international co-operation because of that struggle. I merely feared serious administrative complications and possible revival of old Russian claims and purposes in the Far East that might prove very embarrassing to our own country.[15]

The British Attitude at Yalta on the Far Eastern Agreement

From a statement by Secretary of State Stettinius, it would seem that the British were opposed to the Far Eastern concessions to Stalin. Stettinius states that on February 1, 1945—four days before Yalta—at a meeting of Eden and Stettinius together with their advisers, Eden's remarks are reported as follows:

> ... In his [Eden's] view if the Russians decided to enter the war against Japan they would take the decision because they considered it in their interests that the Japanese war should not be successfully finished by the U.S. and Great Britain alone. There was therefore no need for us to offer a high price for their participation, and if we were prepared to agree to their territorial demands in the Far East we should see to it that we obtained a good return in respect of the points on which we required concessions from them.[16]

Stettinius further states:

> I was advised by one of my friends in the British Government that Eden had tried to keep the Prime Minister [Churchill] from signing the agreement since he had not been present at the principal discussions. ... Churchill, however, had declared that the whole position of the British Empire in the Far East might be at stake. He was going to sign. ...[17]

The Atomic Bomb at Yalta

The question was raised as to whether Mr. Roosevelt had knowledge of the atomic bomb before Yalta and therefore had further reasons for not signing the concessions in the Far Eastern Agreement.

At the Senate hearings in 1951 Secretary of State Dean Acheson stated:

---

15. General Dwight D. Eisenhower, *Crusade in Europe* [Doubleday & Company, Inc., Garden City, N.Y.: 1948], p. [441–] 442.

16. [U.S. Department of State,] *Foreign Relations of the United States,* [*Diplomatic Papers,*] *The Conferences at Malta and Yalta, 1945* [United States Government Printing Office, Washington: 1955], p. 501.

17. E. R. Stettinius, Jr., *Roosevelt and the Russians,* p. 94.

Now, first of all, the Yalta agreements . . . at the time these agreements were entered into at Yalta, we did not know whether we had an atomic bomb or not. That was not proved until some months later, that we had one, and it was not used until considerably later.[18]

Senator Bourke B. Hickenlooper, on June 25, 1951, sent the following telegram to General Leslie R. Groves, head of the wartime atomic project:

It has been stated that you and then Secretary of War Stimson informed President Roosevelt at the White House just before he left for the Yalta Conference to the effect that it was a 99 percent certainty that the A-bomb would be successful. Also that you told him the first bombs would probably be ready in August 1945 and that the bombs would be extremely powerful. Can you confirm the above wire to me.[19]

General Groves replied:

The statement reported in your telegram of today reference information given to President Roosevelt is correct.[20]

Senator Hickenlooper also inserted into the record of the hearings a telegram from Colonel William Considine of the Atomic Bomb project to the effect that Secretary of State Stettinius had been notified before the Yalta Conference that the bomb would work.[21]

The Yalta Papers record a memorandum which Groves wrote to Chief of Staff General Marshall on December 30, 1944, six weeks before Yalta. The opening paragraph read:

It is now reasonably certain that our operation plans should be based on the gun type bomb, which, it is estimated, will produce the equivalent of a ten thousand ton TNT explosion. The first bomb, without previous full scale test which we do not believe will be necessary, should be ready about 1 August 1945. . . .[22]

As convincing as the information may have been that the United States had a weapon with which to end the war with Japan, it cannot be rightly

---

18. Senate Hearings, 1951. See Part 3, p. 1845 for Acheson's statement; see also, Part 5, pp. 3328–3342 for a statement by W. Averell Harriman.

19. Ibid., Part 4, p. 3119.

20. Ibid.

21. Ibid., p. 3120.

22. *Foreign Relations of the United States,* [*Diplomatic Papers,*] *The Conferences at Malta and Yalta, 1945,* p. 383.

concluded that Mr. Roosevelt could have been so certain as to have accepted it as a basis of national policy.

The Final Press Statement of the Yalta Conference

At the end of the Yalta Conference, a communiqué was issued to the press which concluded with the following paragraphs:

Unity for Peace as for War

Our meeting here in the Crimea has reaffirmed our common determination to maintain and strengthen in the peace to come that unity of purpose and of action which has made victory possible and certain for the United Nations in this war. We believe that this is a sacred obligation which our Governments owe to our peoples and to all the peoples of the world.

Only with the continuing and growing cooperation and understanding among our three countries and among all the peace-loving nations can the highest aspiration of humanity be realized—a secure and lasting peace which will, in the words of the Atlantic Charter, "afford assurance that all the men in all the lands may live out their lives in freedom from fear and want."

Victory in this war and the establishment of the proposed international organization will provide the greatest opportunity in all history to create in the years to come the essential conditions of such a peace.

Winston S. Churchill
Franklin D. Roosevelt
J. Stalin

February 11, 1945[23]

---

23. *New York Times*, February 23, 1945.

CHAPTER 71

Acclaim of the Yalta Agreements

WHEN THE DECLARATION on Liberated Europe and the press statements upon its principles appeared in the American press on February 14, 1945, I had a moment of exultation. Perhaps at last we were on the threshold of restoring free men. I made a short statement of approval to the press. But it had an "if" reservation at the end:

> If the agreement's promises and ideals which are expressed shall be carried out, it will open a great hope to the world.[1]

There were bursts of paeans of acclaim from the Administration officials. Senator Alben W. Barkley, Democratic leader of the Senate, sent a publicized cable to President Roosevelt:

> Accept my sincere felicitations upon the historic joint statement released today. I had it read in the Senate and it made a profound impression.[2]

Justice James F. Byrnes, who was an important member of the delegation at Yalta, said:

> Every American should be proud of the role played by the President, especially in the discussion of economic and political problems. . . . I was tremendously impressed by the comradeship and genuine affection showed by the three leaders.[3]

Senator Elbert Thomas, Chairman of the Senate Military Affairs Committee, said:

---

1. *New York Times,* February 13, 1945.
2. Ibid. [*Editor's note:* This quotation is not in the source cited. Probably Hoover read the remark in another newspaper.]
3. Ibid., February 14, 1945.

Mark this day down as one of the great days of world history.[4]

Senator Warren Austin said:

It's the answer to a prayer.[5]

Senator Scott Lucas said:

[The U.S.] can well be proud of the President and our other representatives who helped mark out the plans and programs at this conference.[6]

These eulogists cannot be blamed too much. They did not know of the time-bombs to world peace and free men planted at Yalta.

Soon after the return of the delegations from Yalta came speeches by Churchill of 11,000 words (about three hours) on February 27, 1945, and by Roosevelt of 7000 words (about two hours) on March 1, 1945. Both speeches contained much on their travels in strange parts. Both found the actions at Yalta to be very good. Both emphasized the great unity they had obtained, and reaffirmed their utmost confidence in Stalin. Both speeches were much concerned with directing the public mind to the forthcoming San Francisco Conference, which was to formulate a charter assuring a glorious and lasting peace. Neither of them disclosed the Far Eastern Agreement.

Churchill's address was a masterly eulogy of the Yalta Declaration on liberated Europe, with its promises of unfettered elections, democratic representation, etc. He painted a glorious future for Poland:

A most sovereign declaration has been made by Marshal Stalin and the Soviet Union that the sovereign independence of Poland is to be maintained, and this decision is now joined in by Great Britain and the United States. . . .

But he seemed a little bothered in his description of the "Operation Freedom Rescue," saying:

How will this declaration be carried out? How will phrases like "Free and unfettered elections on the basis of universal suffrage and secret ballot" be interpreted?

Will the new government be properly constituted, with a fair representation of the Polish people as far as can be made practicable at the moment and as soon as possible? Will the elections be free and unfettered? Will candidates

4. [*Editor's note:* Hoover left this footnote blank.]
5. [*Editor's note:* Hoover left this footnote blank.]
6. [*Editor's note:* Hoover left this footnote blank. As with the quotations linked to footnotes 4 and 5, Hoover probably read Senator Lucas's remark in a contemporary newspaper account.]

of all democratic parties be able to present themselves to the electors and conduct their campaigns?

What are democratic parties? People always take different views on that. Even in our own country there have been from time to time feeble efforts by one party or the other to claim that they are the true democratic party and the rest are either Bolsheviks or Tory landlords.

What are democratic parties? Obviously that is capable of being settled. Will the elections be what we should say was free and fair in this country, making some allowance for the great disorder and confusion which prevail[?–ed.] . . .

But he quickly dissolved these doubts:

These are questions upon which we have the clearest views in accordance with the principles of the declaration on liberated Europe to which all three Governments have subscribed. It is on that basis that the Moscow commission of three was intended to work, and it is on that basis that it has already begun to work.

The impression that I brought back from the Crimea and from all my other contacts is that Marshal Stalin and the other Soviet leaders wish to live in honorable friendship and democracy with the Western democracies. I also feel that no Government stands more to its obligations than the Russian Soviet Government.[7]

Mr. Churchill's mind seemed oblivious to the Soviet's previous violations of about fifty treaties within the previous seven years, to say nothing of the violations of the Atlantic Charter and the garrote of fifteen countries. He did not question the Soviet annexation of Eastern Poland or the already established Communist ministries of eight countries, the dates of whose demise I have listed at the time that Yalta convened. See page [463–ed.].

Mr. Roosevelt's Address

In his report to the American people on March 1, 1945, Mr. Roosevelt also found that the Yalta Conference was a great triumph:

. . . the Crimean conference was a successful effort by the three leading nations to find a common ground for peace. It spells . . . the end of the system

---

7. *New York Times*, February 28, 1945. Some minor changes occur in [Winston S.] Churchill, *Victory* [*War Speeches by the Right Hon. Winston S. Churchill*, compiled by Charles Eade] [Little, Brown and Company, Boston: 1946], pp. 71, 74.

of unilateral action and exclusive alliances and spheres of influence and balances of power and all the other expedients that have been tried for centuries—and have failed.[8]

This statement concerning the end of "unilateral action," "spheres of influence," and "other expedients," omitted the annexation of seven peoples and the creation of eight Communist puppet governments. As to Poland, Mr. Roosevelt said:

It is well known that the people east of the Curzon line are predominantly White Russian and Ukrainian. . . . And the people west of the line are predominantly Polish. . . .

I am convinced that the agreement on Poland, under the circumstances, is the most hopeful agreement possible for a free, independent and prosperous Polish state.[9]

Mr. Churchill submitted the "Yalta Declaration" to the House of Commons to be ratified, as ratification of such agreements is required under British constitutional practice. He did not, however, submit the Far Eastern secret agreement, which he also had signed. Nor did the Poles receive any comfort from the fact that 6,000,000 of their countrymen were annexed by Russia at this time.

The press release of Mr. Roosevelt's speech of March 1 contains the following passage:

I am well aware of the constitutional fact—as are all of the United Nations— that this charter must be approved by two-thirds of the Senate of the United States—*as will some of the other arrangements made at Yalta.*[10]

It is obvious that any United Nations charter to maintain peace would need ratification by Congress. The real point here is the expression "as will some of the other arrangements"—did Mr. Roosevelt include the secret Far Eastern Agreement?

Secretary Stettinius revealed the method by which it was proposed at Yalta to avoid troubling the Senate as to "other arrangements" saying:

The President told the Conference that the amendments he was proposing were necessary for American constitutional reasons. He suggested,

---

8. *New York Times*, March 2, 1945.
9. Ibid. See also [Samuel I. Rosenman, comp.,] *The Public Papers and Addresses of Franklin D. Roosevelt*, 1944–45 [volume] [Harper & Brothers Publishers, New York: 1950], pp. 570–586.
10. *New York Times*, March 2, 1945. Italics mine.

therefore, that instead of the first words, "The three powers," he would like to substitute, "The three Heads of Government consider." In the second sentence he proposed eliminating the words "three powers," and in the last sentence, the word "feel" instead of "agree" should be used. These changes transformed the statement on boundaries from a governmental commitment to an expression of *views* in which Roosevelt concurred.[11]

In any event, the secret Far Eastern Agreement was never submitted for ratification by the Senate.

Mr. Roosevelt, in this speech, again stated that no secret agreement had been made at Tehran, saying:

... No political arrangements were made [at Tehran] and none was attempted.[12]

In this address after Yalta, he said:

Quite naturally, this conference concerned itself only with the European war and with the political problems of Europe, and not with the Pacific war.[13]

The secret Far Eastern Agreement apparently was not a matter of war, and in any event was not disclosed until long after.

Both Mr. Churchill and Mr. Roosevelt in these speeches repeatedly assured the world that freedom, liberty, and democracy were on the march, and that there would be lasting peace.

The secret Far Eastern Agreement among all agreements of history, was one of the most fateful to mankind. From it came the downfall of free China to the Communists.

To make this clear, I will later give a detailed record, in Volume III of this memoir, of the step-by-step fall of China into the Communist pit.[14]

---

11. [Edward R.] Stettinius, [Jr.], *Roosevelt and the Russians* [Doubleday & Company, Inc., Garden City, N.Y.: 1949], pp. 270–271. Italics mine.

12. *New York Times*, March 2, 1945; *Congressional Record*, 79th Congress, 1st Session, Vol. 91, Part 2, March 1, 1945, p. 1619.

13. *New York Times*, March 2, 1945; *Congressional Record*, 79th Congress, 1st Session, Vol. 91, Part 2, March 1, 1945, p. 1622.

14. [*Editor's note:* In one of his final corrections, Hoover deleted the words "in Volume III of" from this sentence. I have restored them here for clarity. See his "case history" of China in Volume III.]

An Epitaph for the Yalta Conference

In 1946, after many of these agreements with Stalin had become public, the London *Economist* gave a succinct interpretation of this subject:

> Having abandoned principle for what they thought was policy, the Western Powers are now left with neither principle nor policy. . . .
>
> . . . we have no right to denounce Communists for betrayal of values which have never been theirs. . . .[15]

And I may say that the secret Far Eastern Agreement with Stalin was the Gotterdammerung of international honor.

---

15. London *Economist*, July 27, 1946.

The March of Conferences

The Rise, Decline and Fall
of the Atlantic Charter

CHAPTER 72

The Rise

IN ANY EXAMINATION of the long trail which led the American people to the cold war with the Communists, it is essential to examine in some detail the rise and fall of the Atlantic Charter. I have delayed the review of its career until its fate became clear at Yalta.

If the spirit of the Atlantic Charter had kept a diary of its brief and tenuous four years existence in a turbulent world, it might have recorded:

"I was born on a battleship in mid-Atlantic August 14, 1941.

"Peals of bells announced my coming upon the earth.

"For a while I enjoyed great esteem and I was regarded as a beacon of hope in a distraught world.

"I was confirmed at St. James['s–ed.] Palace by fifteen nations.

"I was again confirmed at Washington in the presence of twenty-six nations.

"Although Soviet Russia was not present at my birth, she adopted me in half a dozen ceremonies.

"I died at Tehran in December, 1943, when I was still the hope of great masses of suffering people.

"My death was not announced. My remains were preserved in the embalming fluid of propaganda.

"I haunted every conference where Roosevelt, Churchill and Stalin met.

"At Yalta my script was rewritten lest it embarrass the Russian and British empires.

"Finally, only the clank of my chains was heard in the conference halls."

The record of the Atlantic Charter, and the attitude of the Allied leaders toward it, comprise an important chapter in world history. The words of the Atlantic Charter glowed like beacons to the dominated peoples:

... [We] seek no aggrandizement, territorial or other;

... [We] desire to see no territorial changes that do not accord with the freely expressed wishes of the peoples concerned;

... [We] respect the right of all people to choose the form of government under which they will live ... sovereign rights and self-government restored to those who have been forcibly deprived of them.[1]

The confirmations of the Charter deserve more detail. On September 24, 1941, at St. James['s–ed.] Palace in London, the Charter was affirmed by fifteen governments including Russia and Britain.

On January 1, 1942, an agreement of unity against Germany was signed and the Charter reaffirmed by twenty-six Allied governments, and later, by twenty-one additional countries. The United States, Britain, and Russia were among these signatories.

Fourteen nations including Britain and Russia signed lend-lease agreements with the United States which again affirmed their acceptance of the Charter. For example, the text with Russia included the following:

... whereas the Governments of the United States of America and the Union of Soviet Socialist Republics, as signatories of the Declaration by United Nations of January 1, 1942, have subscribed to a common program of purposes and principles embodied in the Joint Declaration, known as the Atlantic Charter, made on August 14, 1941, by the President of the United States of America and the Prime Minister of the United Kingdom of Great Britain and Northern Ireland, the basic principles of which were adhered to by the Government of the Union of Soviet Socialist Republics on September 24, 1941...[2]

In order that the importance of the Charter as a world force may be appreciated, I record some of the public confirmations made over the years from 1942 to 1945 by President Roosevelt, Prime Minister Churchill, Marshal Stalin, and their authorized officials.

On February 23, 1942, Mr. Roosevelt re-affirmed the United States['s–ed.] fidelity to the Charter, and expanded its application to all the world saying:

We of the United Nations are agreed on certain broad principles in the kind of peace we seek. The Atlantic Charter applies not only to the parts of the world

---

1. *Review of the United Nations Charter, A Collection of Documents,* Senate Document No. 87, 83rd Congress, 2nd Session (1954), pp. 37–38.

2. E[dward] R. Stettinius, [Jr.,] *Lend-Lease* (New York: The Macmillan Co., 1944) p. 340.

that border the Atlantic but to the whole world; disarmament of aggressors, self-determination of nations and peoples, and . . . freedom of speech, freedom of religion, freedom from want, and freedom from fear.[3]

On July 3, Attorney General Biddle stated in a broadcast to the peoples of Polish descent:

The framework of peace already has been drawn. It is proclaimed in the Atlantic Charter and endorsed by the United Nations.[4]

On the first birthday of the Charter, August 14, 1942, Mr. Roosevelt stated in a message to Prime Minister Churchill:

Now, these [Allied] Nations . . . [have–ed.] formed a great union of humanity, dedicated to the realization of that common program of purposes and principles set forth in the Atlantic Charter. . . .[5]

On September 3, Mr. Roosevelt said:

. . . In the concept of the four freedoms, in the basic principles of the Atlantic Charter, we have set for ourselves high goals, unlimited objectives.[6]

At a press conference on October 27, 1942, Mr. Roosevelt affirmed that Germany, Japan and all enemies were to have the benefit of the Charter if they accepted and acted upon its principles. He stated:

. . . If you look back in the record, you will find that I, twice last spring, and Mr. Hull on one or two occasions, have already made it perfectly clear that we believed that the Atlantic Charter applied to all humanity. I think that's a matter of record.[7]

On November 14, Assistant Secretary of State Berle confirmed this idea in a public address directed to the Italians:

The United Nations have made a pledge to Italy, as to the entire world. It was drawn on a warship in the Atlantic by President Roosevelt in consultation with Prime Minister Churchill. . . .

Pledge was thus given not only to the victors but also to the vanquished.

---

3. Robert [E.] Sherwood, *Roosevelt and Hopkins* [Harper & Brothers, New York: 1948], p. 507.
4. *New York Times*, July 4, 1942. [*Editor's note*: Biddle's quotation does not appear in this source. Probably Hoover read the remark in another newspaper.]
5. Ibid., August 15, 1942.
6. Ibid., September 4, 1942.
7. [Samuel I. Rosenman, comp.,] *The Public Papers and Addresses of Franklin D. Roosevelt* (1942). [volume] [Harper & Brothers Publishers, New York: 1950], p. 437.

No American seeks to destroy or impair the nationhood of Italy. . . .
This pledge does not contemplate a punitive peace: the aim is justice, not
revenge.[8]

Britain and Prime Minister Churchill During 1942

Prime Minister Churchill's enthusiasm for the Charter seems to have started
to fade about three months after the United States entered the war. On
March 7, 1942, he urged President Roosevelt to agree that the Soviet Union
should have the Baltic States and part of Finland. Roosevelt did not agree at
that time.[9]

Marshal Stalin in 1942

The Soviet Union affirmed the Charter at the meeting of the United Nations
in Washington on January 1, 1942.

Molotov, on May 26, 1942, signed a pact with the British, providing for mutual assistance. In it, both Russia and Britain affirmed the Charter, saying:

> Desiring . . . to give expression to their intention to collaborate closely with
> one another as well as with the other United Nations at the peace settlement
> and during the ensuing period of reconstruction on basis of the principles
> enunciated in the declaration made Aug. 14, 1941 . . . to which the Govern-
> ment of the Union of Socialist Soviet Republics has adhered. . . .[10]

Marshal Stalin was in tune with the drums of freedom. On November 6,
1942, he stated publicly, in effect, the principles of the Charter, saying:

> The program of action of the Anglo-Soviet-American coalition is:
>   Abolition of racial exclusiveness, equality of nations, and integrity of their
> territories, liberation of enslaved nations and restoration of their sovereign
> rights, the right of every nation to arrange its affairs as it wishes, economic

---

8. *Department of State Bulletin*, VII, [No. 177, November 14, 1942,] p. 927.

9. Winston Churchill, *The Hinge of Fate* [Houghton Mifflin Company, Boston: 1950],
pp. 326–327.

10. *New York Times*, [June 12, 1942.] [*Editor's note:* Hoover's footnote gives the erroneous date
of May 27, 1942, but there was no mention of the Anglo-Soviet treaty in the *New York Times* on that
day. The British government, in fact, did not announce the treaty until June 11, 1942. In the passage
quoted in the text, I have corrected several typographical and transcription errors found in Hoover's
manuscript. The passage now reads as printed in the *New York Times* on June 12, 1942.]

aid to nations that have suffered and assistance to them in attaining their material welfare, restoration of democratic liberties. . . .[11]

British Attitude in 1942

On October 3, 1942, Walter Nash, New Zealand's Minister to the United States, addressing the Foreign Policy Association in New York, raised a question of doubt, saying:

> We have got to determine whether we mean what Mr. Churchill and Mr. Roosevelt set forth in the world charter they wrote in the Atlantic. If they didn't mean that, they will have humbugged 70 percent of the people of the world.[12]

President Roosevelt in 1943

On January 1, 1943, Mr. Roosevelt said:

> One year ago twenty-six nations signed at Washington the declaration by the United Nations. . . . these nations, bound together by the universal ideals of the Atlantic Charter, signed an act of faith that military aggression, treaty violation and calculated savagery should be remorselessly overwhelmed by their combined might and the sacred principles of life, liberty and the pursuit of happiness be restored as cherished ideals of mankind.[13]

On February 12, he said:

> It is one of our war aims, as expressed in the Atlantic Charter, that the conquered populations of today, the overrun countries, shall again become the masters of their destiny. There must be no doubt anywhere that it is the unalterable purpose of the United Nations to restore to conquered peoples their sacred rights. . . .
>
> For the right of self-determination included in the Atlantic Charter does not carry with it the right of any government anywhere in the world to commit wholesale murder or the right to make slaves of its own people or of any other peoples in the world.[14]

---

11. Ibid., November 7, 1942.
12. Ibid., November 1, 1942.
13. Ibid., January 2, 1943.
14. Ibid., February 13, 1943.

On July 13, he said:

One of our war aims, as set forth in the Atlantic Charter, is to restore the mastery of their destinies to the peoples now under the invaders' yoke. There must be no doubt, anywhere, of the unalterable determination of the United Nations to restore to the oppressed peoples their full and sacred rights.[15]

On July 28, he said:

In every country conquered by the Fascists and the Nazis or the Japanese militarists, the people have been reduced to the status of slaves or chattels.

It is our determination to restore these conquered peoples to the dignity of human beings, masters of their own fate, entitled to freedom of speech, freedom of religion, freedom from want and freedom from fear.[16]

On August 14, 1943, he said:

Today, on the second anniversary of the signing of the Atlantic Charter, I would cite particularly two of its purposes and principles. . . .

First—Respect for the right of all peoples to choose the form of government under which they will live. When the Atlantic Charter was first signed, there were those who said that this was impossible of achievement. And yet, today, as the forces of liberation march on, the right of self-determination is becoming once more a living reality. . . .

. . . We fight on the side of the United Nations, each and every one of whom subscribed to the purposes and principles of the Atlantic Charter.[17]

On August 25, 1943, he said:

I am everlastingly angry only at those who assert vociferously that the Four Freedoms and the Atlantic Charter are nonsense because they are unattainable. If they had lived a century and a half ago they would have sneered and said that the Declaration of Independence was utter piffle. If they had lived nearly a thousand years ago they would have laughed uproariously at the ideals of the Magna Charta. And if they had lived several thousand years ago they would have derided Moses when he came from the mountain with the Ten Commandments.[18]

---

15. Ibid., July 14, 1943.
16. Ibid., July 29, 1943.
17. Ibid., August 15, 1943.
18. *New York Sun*, August 25, 1943.

In a letter to Congress in August, 1943, transmitting quarterly lend-lease reports, Mr. Roosevelt again implied that the Charter would be extended to enemy states:

> The people of Axis-controlled areas may be assured that when they agree to unconditional surrender they will not be trading Axis despotism for ruin under the United Nations. The goal of the United Nations is to permit liberated peoples to create a free political life of their own choosing and to attain economic security. These are two of the great objectives of the Atlantic Charter.[19]

The United States publicly affirmed the Atlantic Charter at the First Moscow Conference, on November 1, 1943.

On November 23, 1943, five days before the Tehran Conference met, Assistant Secretary of State Adolph Berle stated publicly that the Atlantic Charter was of world-wide application. He said:

> The liberated countries undoubtedly will wish to rebuild their social structures when the enemy is expelled. They may wish to modify and change those structures. But this is a choice for them to make, and not for us. Our obligation was set forth in the Atlantic Charter which contains a declaration that nations have the right to live under governments of their own choosing.[20]

The United States affirmed the Atlantic Charter again at the Tehran Conference in December, 1943.

Statements from Britain in 1943

On March 17, 1943, a member of the House of Commons asked whether the Prime Minister still adhered to the principles of the Atlantic Charter. Churchill answered:

> Yes, of course.[21]

On June 30, in an address at the Guildhall, London, speaking on the affinities of the English-speaking peoples, Churchill said:

---

19. *New York Times*, August 26, 1943.
20. *Department of State Bulletin*, Vol. IX, No. 231, Nov. 27, 1943 [p. 386].
21. [Winston S.] Churchill, *Onwards to Victory* [Little, Brown and Company, Boston: 1944], p. 80.

. . . If they walk, or if need be march, together in harmony and in accordance with the moral and political conceptions . . . which are frequently referred to in the Atlantic Charter, all will be well. . . .[22]

On July 14, 1943 in the House of Commons, a member asked whether the Atlantic Charter, which had not been ratified by the United States Senate, had any binding force on the United States or Great Britain.
Churchill answered:

The so-called Atlantic Charter, indeed, the well-called Atlantic Charter, was not a treaty requiring ratification or any formal endorsement of a constitutional character on the other side of the Atlantic. It was a statement of certain broad views and principles which are our common guide in our forward march.[23]

Britain affirmed the Charter at the Moscow Conference of Foreign Ministers on November 1, 1943, and Mr. Churchill was a signatory of the Atlantic Charter declaration at Tehran on December 1, 1943.

Russian Affirmations in 1943

At the celebration on the creation of the Soviet Union on February 22, Stalin stated in his order of the day:

The Red Army is an army defending the peace and friendship between the peoples of all countries.

It was not created for the purpose of conquest of foreign countries, but to defend the frontiers of Soviet land. The Red Army has always respected the rights and independence of all peoples.[24]

In its declaration of November 1, 1943, the Moscow Conference of Foreign Ministers reaffirmed the Charter:

The governments of the United States of America, the United Kingdom, the Soviet Union and China:

United in their determination, in accordance with the declaration by the United Nations of Jan. 1, 1942. . . .[25]

---

22. Ibid., p. 162.
23. Ibid., p. 212.
24. *New York Times*, February 23, 1943.
25. Ibid., November 2, 1943.

On November 6, 1943, twenty-one days before Tehran, Stalin again joined heartily in advocating the independence and freedom of peoples, saying in an address before the Supreme Soviet of the U.S.S.R.:

... Together with our allies, we must, first, free countries subjected by the Fascist invaders and give assistance for the establishment of national states which were dismembered by the Fascist oppressors. The peoples of France, Belgium, Yugoslavia, Czecho-Slovakia, Poland, Greece and other countries under the Fascist yoke must recover full rights of freedom and independence.

The liberated countries of Europe must be given full right and freedom to decide for themselves their form of state....

... Economic, political and cultural collaboration of the peoples of Europe must be created and based on mutual trust and assistance, with the object of restoring what has been destroyed....

... The day is not far off when we will liberate from the enemy completely the Ukraine, and the Byelo-Russia, Leningrad and Kalinin regions, *when we will liberate from the invaders the people of Crimea and Lithuania, Latvia, Estonia, Moldavia and the Carelo [sic]—Finnish Republic.*[26]

On December 1, 1943, at the Tehran Conference, Stalin again affirmed the Atlantic Charter in the declaration on Iran, saying in part:

The Governments of the United States, the U.S.S.R., and the United Kingdom ... count upon the participation of Iran, together with all other peace-loving nations, in the establishment of international peace ... in accordance with the principles of the Atlantic Charter, to which all four Governments have subscribed.[27]

On November 6, 1944, a year after Tehran, without mentioning the Charter by name, Stalin gave forth more words in affirmation of freedom:

... the peoples of the Soviet Union respect the rights and independence of the peoples of countries abroad, and have always displayed their readiness to live in peace and friendship with neighboring states.

In this should be seen the basis of the developing and strengthening ties between our states and all the freedom-loving countries....

---

26. *New York Herald Tribune,* November 7, 1943. Italics mine.
27. [U.S. Department of State,] *Foreign Relations of the United States,* [*Diplomatic Papers, The*] *Conferences at Cairo and Tehran, 1943* [United States Government Printing Office, Washington: 1961], p. 647.

The ideology of the equal rights of all races and nations, which is established in our country, has won a complete victory over the ideology of bestial nationalism and the racial hatred of Hitlerites.[28]

At the Yalta Conference in February, 1945, Messrs. Roosevelt, Churchill, and Stalin again reaffirmed their fidelity to the Charter in a public statement released to the press.[29]

The Totals

Thus it may be seen that Mr. Roosevelt voiced his fidelities to the Charter well over twenty times between 1941 and 1945. Mr. Churchill and other British officials affirmed the Charter at least ten times; and Marshal Stalin and his Ministers at least eleven times.

Communist fidelity to the Charter should not have been expected by anyone familiar with Lenin's gospels and Stalin's oft-pledged adherence to them,[30] or by anyone familiar with the scores of Communist violations of solemn treaties.[31]

Moreover, anyone familiar with Stalin's views on international obligations must have remembered his statement of 1931:

> ... Who, save hopeless bureaucrats, can rely on paper documents alone? Who, besides archive rats, does not understand that a party and its leaders must be tested first of all by their *deeds* and not only by their declarations? ...[32]

---

28. *New York Times*, November 7, 1944.

29. [U.S. Department of State,] *Foreign Relations of the United States,* [*Diplomatic Papers,*] *The Conferences at Malta and Yalta, 1945* [United States Government Printing Office, Washington: 1955], pp. 968ff.

30. See Section I of this Memoir.

31. See Section III of this Memoir. [*Editor's note:* See pp. 158–59.]

32. Joseph Stalin, *Selected Writings* [International Publishers, New York: 1942], "Some Questions Concerning the History of Bolshevism," p. 230.

CHAPTER 73

The Step-by-Step Retreat from the Charter

DESPITE THE AFFIRMATIONS of the Charter by President Roosevelt, Prime Minister Churchill, and Marshal Stalin at the Tehran Conference, this was the spot where the Atlantic Charter died. At that Conference the two secret agreements deprived fifteen peoples of the independence and freedoms promised in the Charter.

After the death of the Charter, its Western authors were bothered by several ghosts. One of the spectres which haunted them was the assurance that the Charter would be applicable to the enemy. Prime Minister Churchill undertook to lay this one to rest in an address to the House of Commons on February 22, 1944, three months after Tehran.

He said:

> ... There will be ... no question of the Atlantic Charter applying to Germany as a matter of right and barring territorial transferences or adjustments in enemy countries. No such arguments will be admitted by us as were used by Germany after the last war, saying that they surrendered in consequence of President Wilson's fourteen points. Unconditional surrender means that the victors have a free hand. . . .[1]

On March 22, 1944, an Associated Press dispatch from London stated:

> Prime Minister Churchill told Commons today that there would be "renewed consultation between the principal Allies" on the application of the Atlantic Charter under the changing phases of the war. . . .
>
> His reference to the Atlantic Charter—on which he only last week refused to schedule an open debate in Commons—arose when Member

---

1. [Winston S.] Churchill, *The Dawn of Liberation* [Little, Brown and Company, Boston: 1945], p. 26.

Daniel Lipson asked for a clarifying statement in "view of the doubts which existed as to what territories the principles of the Atlantic Charter were to apply."

"It is evident that as the changing phases of the war succeed one another, some further clarifications will be required of the position under the document which has become honorably known as the Atlantic Charter," Mr. Churchill replied, "and that this must be a subject for renewed consultation between the principal Allies."

"I am not prepared to embark on this subject at question time today further than to state that the Atlantic Charter stands as a declaration of the spirit and purpose in which its signatories are waging this war—not without success—and that it implied no pact or bargain with our enemies," Mr. Churchill said.

Mr. Lipson asked: "May we take it that it means that the support of the Government to the principles of the Atlantic Charter remains as strong today as when the document was drawn up?"

... Mr. Churchill replied, "but it implies no contradiction of the question that I do not wish to add to what I have said."[2]

On March 28, 1944, Mr. Churchill was challenged in the House of Commons to amplify his remarks of March 22 about the need for inter-Allied revision of the Atlantic Charter. A member asked whether:

> ... in the further clarification of the Atlantic Charter in discussions with the President of the U.S.A., he will press for the reaffirmation in the interest of a more enduring peace, that the guiding principle respecting the future transference or resettlement of peoples will not be military conquest or aggression, but moral right and democratic choice and for a more specific declaration as to how post-war economic reconstruction is to be implemented to the benefit of the peoples of all nations.[3]

The Prime Minister refused to add to his statement of March 22, but when pressed, he said:

> I am always thinking about it, but there are others to be considered as well as His Majesty's Government. . . .

---

2. *New York Sun,* March 22, 1944.

3. Gt. Brit. Parliament. House of Commons. *Parliamentary Debates.* [5th ser., vol. 398.] March 30, 1944, pp. 1551–1552. Also see *New York Herald Tribune,* March 31, 1944.

I do not want to say much about it at the present time; I think it might lead us into more difficulties. As I have said, the Atlantic Charter and its principles remain our dominant aim and purpose.[4]

At the Yalta Conference, when considering the Declaration on Liberated Europe, Churchill announced that the Charter was not binding on the British. Secretary Stettinius reports:

The Prime Minister declared that he did not disagree with the President's proposed Declaration as long as it was clearly understood that the reference to the Atlantic Charter did not apply to the British Empire. He declared that he had already made it plain in the House of Commons that, as far as the British Empire was concerned, the principles of the Atlantic Charter already applied. The Prime Minister, a short time after the drafting of the Atlantic Charter, had told the House of Commons: "At the Atlantic meeting, we had in mind, primarily, the restoration of the sovereignty, self-government and national life of the States and nations of Europe now under the Nazi yoke, and the principles governing any alterations in the territorial boundaries which may have to be made. So that is quite a separate problem from the progressive evolution of self-governing institutions in the regions and peoples which owe allegiance to the British Crown."[5]

Mr. Churchill was not alone in trying to lay the ghost of the Charter to rest. President Roosevelt also had troubles with the ghost of the Charter.

Secretary of State Hull tried his hand at dissipating the idea that the Charter was a commitment. On April 9, 1944, in a nation-wide broadcast, he said:

... The charter is an expression of fundamental objectives. ...

It charts the course. ...[6]

On December 19, 1944, a year after the Tehran Conference, a reporter raised questions as to the Atlantic Charter at a Presidential press conference where, according to the *Christian Science Monitor,* the following conversation took place:

---

4. Gt. Brit. Parliament. House of Commons. *Parliamentary Debates.* Official report (Hansard) 5th ser., v. 398, 1944, March 30th, p. 1552.

5. E[dward] R. Stettinius, Jr., *Roosevelt and the Russians* [Doubleday & Company, Inc., Garden City, N.Y.: 1949], pp. 244–245.

6. From the text of Secretary Hull's Address on the Foreign Policy of the United States, reprinted in the *New York Times,* April 10, 1944.

Q. Did Mr. Churchill ever sign the Atlantic Charter?

A. Mr. Roosevelt said nobody ever signed the Atlantic Charter.

Q. Where is it?

A. The President then launched into his discursive discussion of how the Atlantic Charter came into being. He explained that it was not a formal document, but rather was scribbled on pieces of paper, some in Mr. Churchill's handwriting, some in his own, some by Sumner Welles, and that it was then given in assembled form to the radio operators on the Augusta and the Prince of Wales to be dispatched to the United States and British Governments and then released to the newspapers. He said that there just isn't any original copy of the Atlantic Charter as such, at least he didn't have one. The nearest thing one could get to such an original copy would be the assembled parts of it which were given to the radio operators.

Q. Is it not true that all the United Nations, including Britain and Russia have accepted formally the obligations of that Atlantic Charter which are a part of the declaration of Washington?

A. The President said definitely yes; that all have signed the declaration of Washington of Jan. 1, 1942.

Q. The statement issued to the press at that time said that the Atlantic Charter was signed by yourself and by the British Prime Minister. Is that literally not true?

A. Mr. Roosevelt repeated that there was not a formal document; that some of it was in Mr. Churchill's handwriting and some in his own.

Q. I understand that, sir. But the caption on the release said it was a statement signed by yourself and the Prime Minister.

A. The President said he thought they would probably find some documents and signatures. . . .

Q. As I recall, the message that went to Congress said that it was a statement signed by you and Mr. Churchill.

A. It was signed in substance, he replied. There is no formal complete document signed by us both. It was a memorandum to the press there and to the radio people. . . .[7]

---

7. *The Christian Science Monitor*, December 20, 1944, p. 7. In [Samuel I. Rosenman, comp,] *The Public Papers and Addresses of Franklin D. Roosevelt*, 1944–[4]5 [volume], which was published six years later, an edited account of this press conference is given (pp. 436–440).

The facts were that the text of the Charter was issued by the State Department as a document on August 14, 1941, and signed "Roosevelt and Churchill." It was officially transmitted to the Congress with these two signatures by the President on August 21, 1941. The President mentioned the "signing" on August 14, 1943, in a proclamation marking the second anniversary of the Charter. The Government Office of War Information distributed 244,000 large copies, printed in beautiful type, to schools, libraries, and other places to be hung alongside the Declaration of Independence. This print carried the names of Roosevelt and Churchill on the bottom.[8]

The press became indignant and sarcastic. A paragraph from the *New York Sun* of December 21, 1944, said:

> Now that funeral services have been read in several languages over the principles enunciated by the charter, it may seem to the President an appropriate time to break the news to the American public that this great document, which at one time threatened the place of both Magna Charta and the Ten Commandments, never was a real document signed in binding fashion. But it will seem to many Americans that again they have been treated by their President as if they were children and not very bright children at that.[9]

On December 22, the storm of demands to know if this was a real obligation of the Allied nations had risen to such heights that the President at a press conference on that date said:

> ... that the objectives of the Atlantic Charter were "just as valid today as when they were pronounced in 1941."[10]

On January 6, 1945, Mr. Roosevelt made an address to the Congress in which he portrayed the Atlantic Charter as a useful ideal but with difficulties:

> It is true that the statement of principles in the Atlantic Charter does not provide rules of easy application to each and every one of this war-torn world's tangled situations. But it is a good and useful thing ... to have principles toward which we can aim. ....
>
> I should not be frank if I did not admit concern about many situations— the Greek and Polish for example. But those situations are not as easy or as simple to deal with as some spokesmen ... would have us to believe. ....

---

8. See "Declaration by United Nations," [in World Peace Foundation,] *Documents on American Foreign Relations*, IV, [July] 1941–[June] 1942, p. 203.

9. *New York Sun*, December 21, 1944.

10. *New York Herald Tribune*, December 23, 1944.

We and our allies have declared that it is our purpose to respect the right of all peoples to choose the form of government under which they will live and to see sovereign rights and self-government restored to those who have been forcibly deprived of them. But with internal dissension, with many citizens of liberated countries still prisoners . . . it is difficult to guess the kind of self-government the people really want.

. . . we and our allies have a duty, which we cannot ignore, to use our influence to the end that no temporary or provisional authorities . . . block the eventual exercise of the people's rights freely to choose the government and institutions under which, as free men, they are to live.[11]

Finally the storm reached the Congress where, on January 10, 1945, Senator Arthur Vandenberg remarked:

I am sure that the President did not anticipate the shocking results of his recent almost jocular, and even cynical, dismissal of the Atlantic Charter. . . . It jarred America to its very hearthstones. It seemed to make a mere pretense out of what has been an inspiringly accepted fact. It seemed almost to sanction alien contempts. . . . even Mr. Churchill's memory about the Charter was proving to be admittedly fickle . . . the President's statement was utterly devastating in its impact. [. . . –ed.] These basic pledges cannot be dismissed as a mere nautical nimbus. They march with our armies. They fly with our eagles. They sleep with our honored dead. The first requisite of honest candor, Mr. President, I respectfully suggest, is to relight this torch.

The Senator, continuing, said:

We shall not reverse [these trends] . . . by our silence upon the issues [. . . –ed.] nor [. . . –ed.] shall we reverse them merely by a generalized restatement of the high aspirations revoiced in the recent Presidential message. . . .

[. . . –ed.] I hold the deep belief that honest candor, devoid of prejudice or ire, is our greatest hope and our greatest necessity; and that the Government of the United States, above all others, is called at long last to exercise this honest candor not only with its allies but also with its own faithful people.

[. . . –ed.] It cannot be denied that our government has not spoken out. . . . It cannot be denied, as a result, that too often a grave melancholy settles upon some sectors of our people. It cannot be denied that citizens, in increasing numbers, are crying, "What are we fighting for?" It cannot be denied that our

---

11. *New York Times,* January 7, 1945.

silence—at least our public and official silence—has multiplied confusion at home and abroad . . . and already hangs like a cloud. [. . . –ed.] So I venture to repeat, with all the earnestness at my command, that a new rule of honest candor in Washington—as a substitute for mystifying silence or for classical generalities—honest candor on the high plane of great ideals—is the greatest contribution we can make to the realities of "unity" at this moment when enlightened civilization is our common stake.

. . . Perhaps our allies will plead that their actions are not unilateral; that our President, as Bevin said, has initiated this or that at one of the famous Big Three conferences, that our President, as Churchill said, has been [kept–ed.] constantly "aware of everything that has happened"; in other words, that by our silence we have acquiesced. But that hypothesis would only make a bad matter worse. It would be the final indictment of our silence—the final obituary for open covenants. We, of course, accept no conception . . . that our [only–ed.] role in this global tragedy is to fight and die and pay. . . .[12]

The Senator had no effect.

The Ghost Comes to Yalta

On February 4, 1945, two weeks after Senator Vandenburg's speech, President Roosevelt, Prime Minister Churchill, and Marshal Stalin met at Yalta. They were accompanied by large staffs. But the ghost of the Atlantic Charter came also—and it was attended by the ghosts of fifteen peoples who by now were part of Communist Russia.

In a public statement entitled "Declaration of [on–ed.] Liberated Europe" issued at the conclusion of the conference, the views of the principals were set forth:

By this declaration we reaffirm our faith in the principles of the Atlantic Charter. . . .[13]

---

12. *Congressional Record,* [vol. 91] January 10, 1945, pp. 164–167. [*Editor's note:* These quotations from Senator Vandenberg's speech are out of order. The first quoted paragraph (which Hoover originally and incorrectly rendered as two paragraphs) is printed on page 166. Paragraphs 2, 3, and 4 appear, in the order shown, on page 165. But paragraph 5 appears *before* paragraph 4 on page 165 in the speech as printed in the *Congressional Record.* It is not known why Hoover altered the sequence of these passages.]

13. [U.S. Department of State,] *Foreign Relations of the United States, Diplomatic Papers, The Conferences at Malta and Yalta, 1945* [United States Government Printing Office, Washington: 1955], p. 972.

However, as shown in Chapter [65–*ed.*], this ghost was a great embarrassment to both the Prime Minister and the Marshal. With the tacit consent of Mr. Roosevelt, they actually amended the text of the previous four years by appending the phrase "by the aggressor nations." Thus, the Charter would apply only to those peoples who were deprived of their rights by the Axis Powers.

In further emphasis Churchill announced at Yalta that the Charter did not apply to the holdings of the British Empire.

Was the Atlantic Charter Legally Binding on Governments?

It can be said that the Charter was never ratified by the United States Senate; that the words "they desire" or "they believe" at the head of its paragraphs marked it as merely a statement of hope for good manners among friends. But it was solemnly affirmed by scores of governments. It had been reaffirmed many times by Stalin, Roosevelt, and Churchill. It had been approved hundreds of times in orations by officials of the United States and Britain. It was the faith and hope of fifteen peoples who lost their independence and personal freedom at Tehran and the free peoples who lost their freedom at the signing of the Far Eastern Agreement.

Charles Prince, writing in *The American Journal of International Law* (July, 1945) says:

> Thus these formal diplomatic instruments have unquestionably given the Charter the status of recognized international law and of a *bona fide* legal instrument.[14]

A question will rise from every paragraph of the history of World War II. All legalisms aside, was not the Atlantic Charter a sacred *moral* obligation on all nations which had so often reaffirmed it? Whatever arguments may be raised as to its being legally binding, there is a higher court where there can be no questions. Hundreds of millions of people placed their faith in it; millions died with its promises in their hearts.

As to the controversies regarding the date of the death of the Charter, it is clear that it should have a stone over its grave marked:

> "Died December 1, 1943, at Tehran, Iran."

---

14. *American Journal of International Law*, Volume 39, Number 3, July, 1945, p. 478.

And it is also clear that President Roosevelt, Prime Minister Churchill, and Marshal Stalin jointly presided over the funeral when they made the two secret agreements at Tehran.

The din of propaganda had led the American people to believe in the Charter as the emancipation proclamation of mankind. The shock to our people of the long-delayed discovery of their betrayal by the Communists (and others) did much to contribute to the makings of the cold war.

President Harry S. Truman (*left*) and Herbert Hoover confer about European food problems. The White House, Washington, D.C., March 1, 1946.

Herbert Hoover and his diplomat friend, Hugh Gibson, disembarking
from their military transport plane (the "Faithful Cow") during
their international food relief survey mission, Spring 1946.

Pope Pius XII and Herbert Hoover discuss European food problems. Vatican City, March 23, 1946.

Herbert Hoover visits Polish war orphans. Warsaw, Poland, April 2, 1946.

Herbert Hoover and associates visit the devastated "Old City" of Warsaw, Poland. April 2, 1946.

Herbert Hoover visits the ruins of the Warsaw Ghetto. April 1946.

Facing page: Herbert Hoover and Mahatma Gandhi after a conference on India's food problems. New Delhi, India, April 23, 1946.

General Douglas MacArthur and Herbert Hoover in Tokyo, Japan. May 7, 1946.

The First Days of the Truman Administration

CHAPTER 74

The United States Has a New President

FRANKLIN D. ROOSEVELT passed away on April 12, 1945. Vice President Harry S. Truman was sworn in as President on the same day.

With the change in Presidents, there came a departure from the Roosevelt policies that amounted almost to a revolution. Many of these changes resulted naturally from the different setting in American life of these two men.

Mr. Roosevelt was born June 30, 1882, of a wealthy and socially prominent New York family. He was educated in exclusive private schools and graduated from Harvard University. He studied law at Columbia University and was admitted to the bar. He entered political life when twenty-eight years of age by election as a New York State Senator in 1910. He served as Assistant Secretary of the Navy during the First World War, was defeated as a candidate for the Vice Presidency in 1920, was elected Governor of New York in 1928, and was elected President of the United States in 1932.

Harry S. Truman was born on May 8, 1884, in the village of Lamar, Missouri. He was two years younger than Mr. Roosevelt. He was educated in the public schools, mostly at Independence, Missouri. He began to earn his own living at seventeen years of age at minor employments and working on the family farm. In 1917 he enlisted in the Army in the First World War, rising to the rank of captain.

He entered political life twelve years later than Mr. Roosevelt, when he was elected as "County Judge" in 1922. The duties as "County Judge" in Missouri were more administrative than judicial. He was elected to the United States Senate in 1934, reelected in 1940, and elected Vice President in 1944. He succeeded to the presidency on the death of Mr. Roosevelt, and was reelected President in 1948.

While both men were members of the Democratic Party, their outlook on American life was fundamentally different. All of his life, Mr. Roosevelt was associated with members of society with a capital "S." Mr. Truman's life for fifty years prior to his election as Senator was associated with the plain people.

One of the contrasts of the two men was Mr. Roosevelt's adamant opposition to relief of the women and children of the German-occupied small democracies during the whole Second World War. Mr. Truman, on the other hand, voted in the Senate that such relief should be given, and soon after becoming President approved and supported relief measures which I had proposed. If the two men be measured on the ideological scale, it can be said that Mr. Truman was considerably to the "right" of Mr. Roosevelt, as witness his opposition to Communism as compared to Mr. Roosevelt's tolerance of it. Also, Mr. Roosevelt was more sympathetic to government in business in competition with private enterprise than was Mr. Truman.

Upon assuming the Presidency, Mr. Truman at once announced it was his purpose to carry out his predecessor's policies. Citizens generally do not take such pronouncements too seriously, as this is the usual announcement of Presidents who succeed to that office within their own party.

President Truman quickly replaced most of Mr. Roosevelt's Cabinet, either because of their resignations or by his design. Postmaster General Frank G. Walker resigned on May 2, 1945—within three weeks. Mr. Truman accepted the resignations of Secretary of Agriculture Claude R. Wickard, Attorney General Francis Biddle, the Secretary of Labor Frances Perkins on May 23, 1945—within six weeks. On June 27, 1945, he accepted the resignation of Secretary of State Edward R. Stettinius, Jr., and replaced him with former Supreme Court Justice James F. Byrnes. Secretary of War Henry L. Stimson resigned September 18, 1945, and Secretary of Interior Harold L. Ickes resigned on February 13, 1946. Their separations were not, however, on an ideological theory. Three of them could be claimed as having been on the conservative side of center, and three to the left.

Mr. Truman came to the Presidency with his Administration involved in two wars. With Germany, he was bound by Mr. Roosevelt's alliance with Britain and Communist Russia. In the war with Japan, he had no aid from Russia and only minor assistance from Britain.

The military situation in the Pacific was that General MacArthur had paralyzed the initiative of the Japanese, and they were soon making signals for peace. In Europe, all the enemy countries had surrendered except Germany, and the German armies had retreated to within their own borders. The Germans, under the hammer blows of the American and British troops commanded by General Eisenhower, and the Russian troops, were on their way to defeat. The surrender took place within a month after Mr. Truman became President.

President Truman made no change in the war command, retaining General George C. Marshall as Chief of Staff, General Dwight D. Eisenhower as Commander in Chief of the European Theater, General Douglas MacArthur as Commander in the Pacific, General H. A. Arnold as Commanding General of the Army Air Force, Admiral Ernest J. King as Commander in Chief of the United States Fleet, Admiral Chester Nimitz as Commander in Chief of the United States Pacific Fleet, and Admiral William D. Leahy as his personal Chief of Staff.

When Mr. Truman came to the White House, he was amply equipped in politics and in national domestic questions from his service as Senator and Vice President. He was well informed on constitutional questions and the structure of the government. He was aware of the military progress of the war from the daily press reports.

But Mr. Truman had little opportunity to know of Mr. Roosevelt's foreign policies and commitments. For instance, he had not been informed of the secret Far Eastern Agreement and other commitments at Yalta.

He had inherited an undermining, disloyal and traitorous group of American Communists and fellow travelers, who had infiltrated most of the agencies of the government during the Roosevelt Administration.[1] Conspicuous among those to be later proved as supplying information to the Communists were Alger Hiss in the State Department; Harry Dexter White in the Treasury Department; Klaus Fuchs, an important physicist in the atom bomb laboratories at Los Alamos; and Lauchlin Currie, personal adviser to the President, with his offices in the White House.

---

1. I have given an account of this Communist infiltration in Section I.

CHAPTER 75

Keeping the Secret Far Eastern Agreement a Secret

IT WOULD APPEAR that there was a determined effort among the former Roosevelt officials whom President Truman had inherited to keep the Far Eastern Agreement from the American public. At what point Mr. Truman became aware of this agreement is not clear. The agreement itself was not originally kept in the State Department but was "deposited in the President's personal safe" at the White House.[1] In the chapters on Yalta I have mentioned Secretary of State Stettinius' statement that he had not been informed as to the contents of that agreement. Stettinius' successor, James F. Byrnes, who was also at Yalta, wrote:

> I did not know of this agreement, but the reason is understandable. At that time I was not Secretary of State. Mr. Stettinius was Secretary.[2]

When Did Mr. Truman Learn of the Agreement?

If Secretaries Stettinius and Byrnes were ignorant of the agreement, it is likely that President Truman was not immediately informed of this vital commitment. By the end of May 1945, six weeks after his inauguration, his suspicions might have been aroused by the cable from Harry Hopkins from Moscow relating to the Far Eastern Agreement:

> ... [Stalin] repeated his statement made at Yalta that the Russian people must have a good reason for going to war [with Japan] and that depended on China's willingness to agree to the proposals made at Yalta.

---

1. Edward R. Stettinius, Jr., *Roosevelt and the Russians* (Doubleday & Company, Inc., Garden City: New York: 1949), p. 94.
2. James F. Byrnes, *Speaking Frankly* (Harper & Brothers Publishers, New York: 1947), p. 42.

. . . he stated that he was willing to take these proposals up directly with Soong. . . . He wants to see Soong not later than July 1 and expects us to take the matter up at the same time with Chiang Kai-shek. . . .[3]

Mr. Truman may have learned of the secret agreement a month after Hopkins' message when, on June 15, 1945, the State Department directed our Ambassador to China, Major General Patrick J. Hurley, to communicate it to Generalissimo Chiang Kai-shek.

When Did the American People Learn of the Agreement?

Suspicion that some sort of an agreement had been entered into was evidenced six months later, on August 9, 1945, when American newspapers indicated Russia's price for her participation:

> What will Russia expect out of the war? First and foremost . . . the southern part of Sakhalin ceded to Japan at the end of the war of 1905. Second, an end to Japanese exploitation of Siberian fishing rights. Third, a return of the Chinese Eastern Railway, built by Czarist Russia, to some kind of Sino-Russian control. Fourth, some sort of special rights in Port Arthur, again in arrangement with China.[4]

The public could have had more suspicions of some secret commitment from the *New York Times* report of a press conference of Secretary Byrnes on September 4, 1945, seven months after Yalta, when the Secretary was obviously still confused as to that commitment:

> Secretary of State Byrnes revealed tonight before his departure for the Foreign Ministers Council Meeting in London that the United States had tacitly agreed to Soviet possession of Sakhalin Island and Soviet sovereignty over the Kurile Islands in the Pacific.
>
> Mr. Byrnes said in answer to press conference questions that the matter had been first broached to this government at the Yalta conference, when it was "discussed" with the United States delegation as an informal plan, but that no "agreement" had been reached or even attempted. . . .
>
> He wanted it clearly understood that the United States had made no commitment on the matter of the Kuriles. . . .[5]

---

3. [Robert E.] Sherwood, *Roosevelt and Hopkins* [Harper & Brothers, New York: 1948], p. 902.
4. *New York Herald Tribune,* August 9, 1945.
5. *New York Times,* September 5, 1945.

In a press conference on January 29, 1946, nearly a year after Yalta, Secretary Byrnes stated:

> ... that even though he was at the Yalta Conference, Mr. Roosevelt had kept the agreement secret even from him. ...
>
> He was questioned closely today about the long secrecy preserved by Mr. Roosevelt, and said that the late President had kept the American copy of the agreement in the White House with no copy in the State Department archives. He said he did not know whether former Secretary of State Stettinius had known of the agreement.

(Stettinius must have given the instructions to disclose it to Chiang Kai-shek seven months before, on June 15, 1945.)

> Mr. Byrnes said he found out about it soon after the Japanese surrender [August 14, 1945] when some question concerning it came up and he asked Charles E. Bohlen, State Department Russian expert, who had served as interpreter for Mr. Roosevelt at Yalta.
>
> He told questioners that he did not know when President Truman learned about the agreement, but that Mr. Truman had said nothing to indicate that he had any knowledge of it before he [Mr. Byrnes] spoke to the President about it.[6]

It is improbable that Mr. Truman was informed of the two great commitments at Tehran as the gift of those fifteen peoples to Russia had been made eighteen months before he became President, and, as shown in Chapter 58, all of them had been taken over by the Communists before he became President.

---

6. *Washington Star,* January 29, 1946.

CHAPTER 76

I Am Asked for Advice
by President Truman

MR. JAMES A. FARLEY suggested to President Truman that I should be called in for advice. Mr. Farley informed me that the President wanted to see me at once. I called on the President in Washington on May 28, 1945. As to this meeting, Mr. Truman says in his book:

> The food situation in Europe gave me increasing cause for concern. The Department of Agriculture's experts came up with an estimate that continental Europe alone, not including the British Isles, would need twelve million tons of food during the next year to prevent large-scale starvation. Production for 1946, they calculated, would be five to ten percent below that for 1945, the lowest since prewar days. Our own farm yields were less promising for this year than they had been since the war began. I thought it might be desirable and useful to consult with former President Herbert Hoover on this situation. I invited him to visit with me and give me the benefit of his rich experience in the field of food relief. When he came, I had a most pleasant and satisfactory meeting with him. He helped me to review the world food-distribution problem, which he knew from one end to the other. The former President was pleased to be able to make a personal contribution to the settlement of the aftermath of the war.[1]

In my interview with Mr. Truman, we covered several subjects, the most important being a statement from me that I believed that an early surrender could be had from Japan. I based this belief upon the Emperor's shift from the militarists' Ministry to a civilian Ministry under "Elder Statesman" Kantaro Suzuki.

---

1. *Memoirs by Harry S. Truman,* Volume One: *Year of Decisions* (Doubleday & Company, Inc., Garden City, N.Y.: 1955), pp. 309–310.

Suzuki had been opposed to war with the "Anglo Saxons." He had narrowly escaped from an attempt by an extreme army group to assassinate him. The injuries he received had kept him in bed for many years.

Suzuki's new cabinet included Shigenori Togo (not to be confused with General Tojo) as Foreign Minister. Togo had tried to make peace with the Anglo-Saxons in 1941.[2] It seemed to me that Japan was signaling for peace.[3]

I suggested to the President that he put up a *ballon d'essai* saying we had no wish to disturb the Imperial House since the Emperor was the spiritual as well as the secular head of the nation, but otherwise the terms could be tough. I said that whether the Japanese kept the Emperor or not made not an atom of difference to the American people as obviously we could completely demilitarize the Japanese. I urged that since Russia was not in the war with Japan, we had complete freedom of action. Mr. Truman asked that I write out the sentences he might include in a speech which had been announced for the 31st of May. I did so. As nearly as I can remember, these sentences were:

> All of our enemies except Japan have surrendered. We want peace with Japan. We have no intention or desire to destroy the position of the Emperor. We will not relax other demands.

The President asked that I send him a memorandum concerning my views as to Japan. On May 30 I sent the memorandum in which I reviewed the events in Japan and the demands we would naturally make of demilitariza-

---

2. See Chapter [39–*ed.*].

3. Brigadier General Bonner Fellers confirmed Suzuki's attitude in an article in the July 1947 issue of *Foreign Service* (p. 11), saying: ". . . Tough, grizzly, 77 years old Kantaro Suzuki—so avowedly a pacifist that he was shot four times and left for dead in the uprising of the so-called 'young militarists' in 1936—was suddenly, on April 7 [1945], appointed prime minister by the Emperor. Hirohito believed that appointment of such a well-known opponent of the militarists would be regarded by the Allies as a clear signal that Japan desired peace. . . . To Hirohito's and Suzuki's amazement, no offer to negotiate came from the Allies. . . ."

General Fellers' statements are corroborated by Prime Minister Konoye's diary which reveals that Konoye was summoned by the Emperor on February 14, 1945. He informed the Emperor that defeat was certain but that, if the war were ended promptly, they would be able to save the Imperial system. Meetings between Japanese officials and the Soviet Ambassador in Tokyo began in February 1945, but no progress was made because the Russians were demanding settlement of special terms for themselves first. (Asahi-Shimbun edition of the *Konoye Papers*, p. 24.)

Matsudaira, Keeper of the Privy Seal, testified before the Tokyo trials court that the Emperor, on June 22, 1945, again convened the Supreme Council and ordered consideration of new measures to end the war. ([*Record of Proceedings of the*] *International Military Tribunal for the Far East* [Tokyo, 1946–1948], pp. 35,607–35,610.) [*Editor's note:* Hoover's citation here is partially incorrect. The witness who gave this testimony was not Yasumasa Matsudaira, the private secretary to the Keeper of the Privy Seal. It was Hisatsune Sakomizu, Chief Secretary of the Japanese Cabinet from April 7 to August 17, 1945.]

tion, disarmament, the dissolution of the militarist caste, the restoration of Japanese-occupied territory to China and the reparations to China. I included the following statement:

> ... the Allies have no desire to destroy either the Japanese people or their government, or to interfere ... in the Japanese way of life ... it is our desire that the Japanese build up their prosperity and their contributions to the civilized world.[4]

Joseph C. Grew, then Under Secretary of State, was an old friend and he knew of my proposal. He called upon President Truman on May 28 at 12:35 P.M. (two hours after my call). Grew states in his book that he recommended to the President that in his forthcoming speech he make a statement which would indicate the preservation of the Imperial House.[5] Grew states that the next day (May 29), at the President's suggestion, he submitted a memorandum to this effect before a meeting in the Pentagon at which Secretaries Stimson and Forrestal, General Marshall, Eugene Dooman, Samuel Rosenman, and Elmer Davis were present.

Mr. Grew says that General Marshall, Mr. Forrestal and Mr. Stimson supported him, but it was decided that for unrevealed military reasons it was inadvisable for the President to make such a statement at that time.[6]

Mr. Dooman, later on, testifying before a Senate subcommittee said the proposal was vigorously opposed by Owen Lattimore, Dean Acheson, and Archibald MacLeish.[7]

---

4. I may add here that in discussion with General MacArthur years later he requested that I send him a copy of my recommendations to President Truman of May 29, 1945. The General wrote me:

2 December 1960

Dear Mr. President:

Thank you so much for sending me a copy of your memorandum to President Truman of 30 May 1945. It was a wise and statesmanlike document, and had it been put into effect would have obviated the slaughter at Hiroshima and Nagasaki in addition to much of the destruction on the island of Honshu by our bomber attacks. That the Japanese would have accepted it and gladly I have no doubt. . . . Again, my thanks for sending me this valuable information.

Very faithfully,
s/ Douglas MacArthur

5. Joseph C. Grew, *Turbulent Era* [Houghton Mifflin Company, Boston: 1952], Vol. II, pp. 1423 et seq.
6. Ibid., p. 1434.
7. United States Senate Hearings, Subcommittee to Investigate the Internal Security Act and Other Internal Security Laws of the Committee on the Judiciary, 83d Congress, First Session, *Institute of Pacific Relations*, September 1951, Part 3, pp. 728–730.

Secretary Forrestal in his diary, as of June 19, records a State-War-Navy Meeting just before President Truman went to Potsdam in which the Japanese surrender terms discussed were:

> ... Grew's proposal ... that something be done in the very near future to indicate to the Japanese what kind of surrender terms would be imposed upon them and particularly to indicate to them that they would be allowed to retain their own form of government and religious institutions while at the same time making it clear that we propose to eradicate completely all traces of Japanese militarism. Both Stimson and Grew most emphatically asserted that this move ought to be done, and that if it were to be effective at all it must be done before any attack was made upon the homeland of Japan. . . .[8]

Secretary Forrestal adds:

> Stimson and Grew further pointed out that Leahy, King and Nimitz were all in favor of some such approach being made to the Japanese. . . .[9]

Secretary Forrestal states further in his diary that Mr. Stimson's impression was that the President was in accord but felt such a pronouncement might slow up General Marshall's preparations for the invasion of the Japanese mainland, if that became necessary.

On July 2, 1945, Secretary Stimson presented to President Truman a long memorandum on the stiff Japanese peace terms which included the sentence:

> ... I personally think that if in saying this we should add that we do not exclude a constitutional monarchy under her present dynasty, it would substantially add to the chances of acceptance.[10]

However, this opportunity for immediate peace was lost by confusion among the President's advisors.

---

8. [Walter Millis, ed.,] *The Forrestal Diaries* [The Viking Press, New York: 1951], p. 69.

9. Ibid., p. 70.

10. [Henry L.] Stimson and [McGeorge] Bundy, *On Active Service in Peace and War* (Harper and Brothers, New York: 1948), p. 623.

CHAPTER 77

The Preservation of Lasting Peace

Ambassador Hugh Gibson and I Explain
Some Experiences in Making Peace

In June 1942, former Ambassador Hugh Gibson and I published a book, *The Problems of Lasting Peace.* I have delayed summarizing our proposals set forth in this book until after discussing the principles and methods and action of Messrs. Roosevelt, Churchill, and Stalin.

Mr. Gibson and I were excluded by Mr. Roosevelt from any public service during the war. Naturally we had hoped that our experience of over thirty-three years in foreign relations might be of some service to the American people.

In view of this, we concluded that a statement based on our world experience in this field and some recommendations might be helpful. We labored unremittingly for several months to prepare a book. In it we presented the consequences and lessons of attempts to make and preserve peace over centuries. We examined human experience in the treatment of defeated peoples; the elimination of militarism; and the social and economic foundation of peace.

We submitted the text of the book to some fifty public leaders who highly approved it and also made useful suggestions.

The publisher estimated that 5,000 copies would be sold, and printed that initial number. Over 65,000 copies have been distributed. The book was reprinted by the Book of the Month Club, summarized by *Reader's Digest* and *Omnibook,* and syndicated in the press. In various forms, either in condensation or in full, it reached from eight to ten million reprints. It was extensively and favorably reviewed by practically every American journal. Many British publications gave it their approval.

Mr. Gibson and I not only presented our views in this book, but we stated them in other publications and addresses. Some paragraphs from these statements of ours are appropriate here, so that the reader of some twenty years later may look over the world scene and assess the validity of our recommendations. The reader at the same time should include in his reading an address of mine made a year prior to publication of the book,[1] in which I declared my opposition to American alliance with Soviet Russia as certain to spread Communism over the world.

As an indication of the ideas expressed in our book of 1942 and in an article prepared for *This Week Magazine*, I reproduce certain paragraphs. It will be seen from this memoir that Messrs. Churchill, Roosevelt, and Stalin proposed the dismemberment of enemy countries. The view of Mr. Gibson and myself was:

> There are those who propose to dismember defeated peoples into a multitude of states. That simply will not work, for the yearnings of racial solidarity are forces that will ultimately defeat any such idea. The history of periodically dismembered Germany is of intrigue and wars for unification that have disturbed the whole world. If we were defeated and our states separated, would we not conspire until we were united again?[2]

The Allied leaders proposed stupendous reparations. We said:

> Our experience is that indemnities such as Versailles imposed cannot be collected over a long term of years. There must be a terminal toward which the defeated peoples can look forward or they will constantly conspire.
>
> The defeated countries after this victory can pay some indemnities, but if we are not to create anew the cesspools of world infection we must not attempt to hold them in bondage. That is not only vengeance—it is a delusion.[3]

On punishment of enemy leaders, we were in agreement with Allied leaders:

> ... The leaders of the nations who brought this situation upon the world must be made to realize the enormity of their acts. There can be no moral distinction and there should be no legal distinction between such men and common criminals conspiring to murder. Too long has it been assumed that

---

1. See Chapter [34–*ed.*], Section [IX–*ed.*].
2. "History's Greatest Murder Trial" (jointly with Hugh Gibson—*This Week Magazine,* August 29, 1943), p. [5].
3. Ibid.

there is something sacred about the heads of state who project or provoke war and wholesale murder.[4]

But Allied leaders proposed to bring punishment to the people of enemy countries. We said:

A positive distinction must be made between imposing legal punishment for crime and the problem of what to do with enemy peoples. There should be no question of indiscriminate and wholesale punishment of whole nations, for that merely lays the foundation for future conflicts. . . .

This first lesson is sound defeat. Defeat itself is the greatest humiliation that can come to a nation. Moreover defeat will bring revolution, with all its internal violences; and revolution also is punishment.

But if we are not to have the periodic rise of aggressive, military action in these nations, impelled by humiliation, hate and pride, we have to do something more than give them a spanking.[5]

Certainly, experience shows that no nation can be punished as a whole and at the same time leave any hope of lasting peace. This endless treadmill of punishment must be stopped in the world if there is to be real peace. Victory with vengeance is ultimate defeat in the modern world.

We can have peace or we can have revenge, but we cannot have both.[6]

On demilitarization, we were in agreement with the Allied leaders. We said:

Germany, Japan and Italy all have a long-established warrior caste. This caste likes war, it lives by war, it eulogizes war, and it wants to dominate and exploit other nations. Through class traditions, through sons succeeding fathers as officers, through general staffs whose business it is to plan further wars, the military caste in each of these countries is a menace to the world. These warrior castes must be broken up. One of the failures of Versailles was that Germany was allowed to keep an army of 100,000 men and a small navy. Even the privates in these organizations were potential officers. Their generals and their staffs sat plotting war again.

There is only one answer to that: complete disarmament of the defeated nations. The cry that there must be an army to preserve internal order can be

---

4. [Herbert Hoover and Hugh Gibson], *The Problems of Lasting Peace* [Doubleday, Doran and Company, Inc., Garden City, N.Y.: 1942], pp. 246–247 (first printing).

5. "History's Greatest Murder Trial" (jointly with Hugh Gibson), pp. [4–5].

6. *The Problems of Lasting Peace*, p. 248.

answered by a constabulary in which no man who ever held an officer's commission may serve. And if its arms are limited to those necessary to deal with unarmed citizens, they will have little with which to practice.[7]

Certain leaders proposed to change the thinking and beliefs of the enemy peoples.

As to this we said:

There are those who think to re-educate the German, Japanese and Italian youth by forcing United Nations teachers into control of their schools. There are obvious difficulties—ideologies cannot be imposed either by foreign teachers or machine guns. Change must come from within the hearts of the peoples themselves.[8]

... Wrong ideas cannot be cured by war or by treaty. They are matters of mind and spirit. The lasting acceptance of any governing idea lies deep in the mores of races and in their intellectual processes. Liberty does not come like manna from heaven; it must be cultivated from rocky soil with infinite patience and great human toil. ...[9]

And we added this generalization on peacemaking with the enemy:

One of the greatest difficulties the world will have to meet when victory comes is the inevitable and universal emotional state. The hideous brutalities of the Axis powers will leave an ineradicable hate in millions of this generation [of Allied peoples]. We cannot expect a growth of brotherhood in those who have suffered. Famine and poverty will have enveloped the whole world because of the Axis. Hate, revenge will be the natural emotions of all the peoples of the United Nations.

Unless the forces of fear, hate and revenge between peoples and nations can be turned aside, the world will again enter upon the ceaseless treadmill of war. By statesmanship at the end of this war, that hate, fear and revenge may ultimately decrease and die.

The enemy must be made to realize war does not pay. But if we want lasting peace, we must realize that nations cannot be held in chains. In the end there can be no trustworthy security except by giving the decent elements in ... [enemy] people a chance to cooperate in the work of peace.[10]

---

7. "History's Greatest Murder Trial" (jointly with Hugh Gibson), p. [5].
8. Ibid.
9. *The Problems of Lasting Peace*, p. 203.
10. "History's Greatest Murder Trial" (jointly with Hugh Gibson), p. [5].

In a public address on April 17, 1945, I stated:

The great purpose of America in this war is lasting peace. That is all that we can possibly get from this dreadful sacrifice of life and the awful burdens upon our children. If the world will cooperate to give our children this boon, their tears will not be less but their labor over years to come will be brightened with confidence and their future lighted with hope.

We must not fail now.[11]

---

11. [Herbert Hoover,] *Addresses Upon the American Road, 1941–1945* [D. Van Nostrand Company, Inc., New York: 1946], p. 136. [*Editor's note:* In his final penciled corrections in early 1964, Hoover deleted what had been his concluding paragraph in this chapter:

"The reader may be reminded that these proposals and cautions, based on our world-wide experience, were issued months before such vital conferences as Tehran and Yalta. Should the reader survey the world scene today in the light of our recommendations, he might come to conclusions highly complimentary to Mr. Gibson and myself."]

CHAPTER 78

The Conference to Draw a Charter for the Preservation of Lasting Peace

AT THE TEHRAN CONFERENCE of December, 1943, it was agreed that a preliminary conference of representatives of the United States, the United Kingdom, the Soviet Union, and China should be convened to prepare a draft for the creation of a world organization to preserve peace.

The conference for this purpose assembled at a private residence in Washington, called Dumbarton Oaks, from August 21 to October 7, 1944,—about six months before Mr. Truman became President.

The proposals of the conference closely followed the pattern of Woodrow Wilson's League of Nations. Like the League, there was to be (1) *an assembly* of all nations; (2) *a council,* now called the Security Council, and as in the case of the League, the council was to comprise permanent membership of the great powers—now the United States, the British Commonwealth, the Soviet Union, and the Republic of China—and three representatives of the smaller nations to be elected by the Assembly; (3) methods of arbitration, conciliation, and a world court, similar to those of the League of Nations; (4) and provisions, like those of the League, for economic sanctions and military actions against an "aggressor." The Dumbarton Oaks proposal went a step further than the League as it proposed a permanent General Staff and a right to call quotas of military force from the members.

It was provided that the permanent members on the Security Council should each have a veto, but this issue was left open for further negotiations. Even this idea was not far from the provision in the League which required unanimity of the Council if force was to be used.

The Dumbarton Oaks proposal was issued with a blare of trumpets on October 9, 1944, four months prior to the Yalta Conference.

I supported the main lines of the proposal in the press but stated that there were (a) no provisions for review of onerous or wrongful or obsolete treaties;

(b) no adequate provision for regional organization; (c) no provision against dangers in the veto power; and (d) no definition of aggression.[1] I felt this plan was mostly an organization to settle quarrels among small nations but did not face the real dangers of world wars from quarrels among great nations.

The United Nations Charter Conference at San Francisco
April 25 to June 26, 1945

At the Yalta Conference in February 1945, the recommendations of the Dumbarton Oaks Conference were approved and the following declaration was given to the press:

> We are resolved upon the earliest possible establishment with our allies of a general international organization to maintain peace and security. We believe that this is essential, both to prevent aggression and to remove the political, economic and social causes of war through the close and continuing collaboration of all peace-loving peoples.
>
> The foundations were laid at Dumbarton Oaks. On the important question of voting procedure, however, agreement was not there reached. The present conference has been able to resolve this difficulty.
>
> We have agreed that a Conference of United Nations should be called to meet at San Francisco in the United States on April 25th, 1945, to prepare the charter of such an organization, along the lines proposed in the informal conversations at Dumbarton Oaks.
>
> The Government of China and the Provisional Government of France will be immediately consulted and invited to sponsor invitations to the Conference jointly with the Governments of the United States, Great Britain and the Union of Soviet Socialist Republics. As soon as the consultation with China and France has been completed, the text of the proposals on voting procedure will be made public.[2]

This conference of the United Nations met in San Francisco in April, 1945, to draft a charter. Secretary of State Stettinius was Chairman of the United States Delegation and Alger Hiss acted as its Secretary General.[3]

---

1. Herbert Hoover, *Addresses Upon the American Road, 1941–1945* [D. Van Nostrand Company, Inc., New York: 1946], pp. 111–136.

2. [U.S. Department of State,] *Foreign Relations of the United States, Diplomatic Papers, The Conferences at Malta and Yalta, 1945* (United States Government Printing Office, Washington: 1955), p. 971.

3. See Chapter [4–*ed.*] on *Infiltration of American Communists Into the Federal Government.*

The Charter comprised about 20,000 words, and like Dumbarton Oaks, the central ideas were again those from the mind of Woodrow Wilson—except in one particular, which I mention later.[4] The Charter was more verbose and less clearly stated than the Covenant of the League. The United Nations Charter was signed on June 25, 1945, two months after Mr. Truman became President.

I made an analysis of the Charter in a national broadcast soon after it was published. The essential parts of my statement were:

> I have received a multitude of requests from members of Congress, the press and individuals for my views upon the San Francisco Charter. . . .
>
> The San Francisco Charter is better than the Dumbarton Oaks version. . . . It should be ratified by the Senate promptly.
>
> The American people should be under no illusions that the Charter assures lasting peace. The Charter at best consists only of an expression of desire and machinery to advance peace. The problem of enduring peace is far wider than the Charter. The foundations of peace must also be laid in the economic and political settlements among nations by which this war is to be liquidated. The nature of these settlements will have more to do with lasting peace than the Charter. The Charter could not preserve a bad peace.
>
> The major strength of the Charter . . . [can be stated as follows: It has] a noble preamble and . . . it provides for continuous meetings of the nations where peace problems can be discussed. It stimulates the methods of peaceful settlement of controversies. It re-establishes the World Court and provides trusteeship for dependent countries. It provides for a limited action to prevent military aggression. It sets up machinery for promotion of social and economic welfare.
>
> There are many weaknesses in the Charter. There is no positive Bill of Rights for nations and men, but only a mere suggestion that they should be promoted. They are not expressed in the tones of the American Bill of Rights. The Charter does not recover the principles of the Atlantic Charter which were whittled away at Tehran and . . . Yalta. The political, moral and spiritual standards of conduct of nations and of men are thus insufficiently defined for the tests by which the conduct of nations should be judged by the Security Council. While the Security Council has the power to stop military aggression among small nations, yet this is not assured among the great nations, because of the veto power. The Charter fails to define aggression even

---

4. Herbert Hoover, *The Ordeal of Woodrow Wilson* [McGraw-Hill Book Company, Inc., New York: 1958], pp. 181–183.

in the admirable terms settled by the Soviet Government for inclusion in its treaties of eleven years ago. And it does not even mention the new disintegrating forms of aggression of one nation upon another through propaganda and fifth columns. The Regional Organization, the methods of review of out-moded treaties, and the lack of commitment to relative reduction of armies and navies leave much to be desired. Most of these vital questions are referred to in terms of hope or permission, not in terms of positive undertakings or agreements. . . . these weaknesses point the direction in which there should be amendment over the years to come.

I pointed out in detail what the minimum declaration of individual and national rights should have been. I said there was far less liberty in the world than when the Atlantic Charter was promulgated. I expressed great concern that there was no provision in the Charter by which states annexed by Russia or transformed into puppet governments could secure restoration of their liberties or independence through the Charter, and said:

> . . . there will be no peace unless these rights be applied to those peoples who have been deprived of them during this war or who have not yet attained them. This is more important today than ever before, because liberty and freedom have shrunk in great areas as a result of this war.[5]

The United Nations organization differed in one essential from the League of Nations. This difference is apparent in the words of President Wilson when he spoke at the Versailles Conference. He said:

> . . . Only free peoples can hold their purpose and their honor steady to a common end and prefer the interests of mankind to any narrow interest of their own.
>
> A steadfast concert for peace can never be maintained except by a partnership of democratic nations. No autocratic government could be trusted to keep faith within it or observe its covenants. It must be a league of honor. . . .[6]

---

5. *Addresses Upon the American Road, 1941–1945*, pp. 137–143.
6. Herbert Hoover, *The Ordeal of Woodrow Wilson*, pp. 302–3.
In 1955 the Committee on the Judiciary of the United States Senate published a list of over sixty violations by the Soviet Government of treaties and agreements.
Up to 1962 the record shows over 100 vetoes by Soviet Russia in the United Nations Security Council, many of which have resulted in violence which otherwise would have been avoided.

The March of Conferences

The Potsdam Conference and After

CHAPTER 79

The Awakening of Prime Minister Churchill to the Betrayal of Freedom

THE MANY PROBLEMS which had arisen after Yalta made another three-nation conference imperative. Mr. Churchill originally proposed it on May 11, 1945, and President Truman agreed to join him in approaching Marshal Stalin, which they did through the British and American Ambassadors in Moscow. Stalin informed the Ambassadors that he would attend a meeting about the fifteenth of July in Berlin (actually Potsdam).

Mr. Truman sent the former United States Ambassador to Russia—Joseph E. Davies—to London to convey a message to Mr. Churchill that at the coming Potsdam Conference, Mr. Truman should first see Marshal Stalin alone. There are three different versions of this meeting between Mr. Churchill and Mr. Davies which took place on May 26, 1945. One is given in Mr. Churchill's memoirs, one is in a report of Admiral Leahy from Mr. Davies' statements to him, and another is that of President Truman.

Mr. Churchill's Version

Mr. Churchill expressed indignation to Mr. Davies at the suggestion that Mr. Truman should meet with Mr. Stalin somewhere in Europe before he saw Mr. Churchill.

The Prime Minister states in *Triumph and Tragedy* that:

> In order that there should be no misconception I drafted a formal minute which I gave to Mr. Davies . . . [:–ed.]
>
> . . . The Prime Minister received with some surprise the suggestion conveyed by Mr. Davies that a meeting between President Truman and Premier Stalin should take place at some agreed point, and that the representatives of His Majesty's Government should be invited to join a few days later. *It*

must be understood that the representatives of His Majesty's Government would not be able to attend any meeting except as equal partners from its opening. This would be undoubtedly regrettable. The Prime Minister does not see that there is any need to raise an issue so wounding to Britain, to the British Empire and Commonwealth of Nations....[1]

Also, Mr. Churchill was now becoming disturbed over the consequences of the agreements which he and Mr. Roosevelt had made with Stalin at Tehran and Yalta. He states that he informed Davies:

It must be remembered that Britain and the United States are united at this time upon the same ideologies, namely, freedom.... The Soviet Government have a different philosophy, namely, Communism, and use to the full the methods of police government, which they are applying in every State which has fallen a victim to their liberating arms....

... The freedom, independence, and sovereignty of Poland ... [have] now become a matter of honour with the nation and Empire.... The rights of Czechoslovakia are very dear to the hearts of the British people. The position of the Magyars in Hungary has been maintained over many centuries and many misfortunes, and must ever be regarded as a precious European entity. Its submergence in the Russian flood could not fail to be either the source of future conflicts or the scene of national obliteration horrifying to every generous heart. Austria, with its culture and its historic capital of Vienna, ought to be a free centre for the life and progress of Europe.

... Yugoslavia is at present dominated by the Communist-trained leader Tito.... Rumania and Bulgaria ... have a right to live....[2]

Mr. Davies' Version

The Davies' account of this conference, as quoted by Admiral Leahy,[3] confirmed Mr. Churchill's rejection of President Truman's request to meet Stalin alone. As to Churchill's troubled mind, Davies said:

He [Churchill] was ... bitter toward Tito, and ... considered him thoroughly unreliable and under the domination of Moscow. Churchill complained

---

1. [Winston S.] Churchill, *Triumph and Tragedy* [Houghton Mifflin Company, Boston: 1953], pp. 577–578.

2. Ibid., pp. 579–580. Also see Chapter 58 [of *Freedom Betrayed*–ed.].

3. [William D.] Leahy, *I Was There* [Whittlesey House, McGraw-Hill Book Company, Inc., New York: 1950], pp. 378–379.

harshly of the Soviet unilateral tactics throughout the Balkans—particularly in Bulgaria and Rumania. . . .[4]

Leahy also quotes Davies (who had been one of the pro-Russian group in the Roosevelt Administration) as having replied to Churchill:

I said that frankly, as I had listened to him inveigh so violently against the threat of Soviet domination and the spread of Communism in Europe, and disclose such a lack of confidence in the professions of good faith in Soviet leadership, I had wondered whether he, the Prime Minister, was now willing to declare to the world that he and Britain had made a mistake in not supporting Hitler, for as I understood him, he was now expressing the doctrine which Hitler and Goebbels had been proclaiming and reiterating for the past four years in an effort to break up allied unity. . . .[5]

Leahy continues:

However, Churchill told Davies in the end that he would not oppose American policy toward Russia (although he was willing to take the risk of a much "tougher" attitude). . . .[6]

This is the first indication in the official record that Churchill had some realization of the betrayal of freedom at Tehran and Yalta.

President Truman's Version

With regard to Ambassador Davies' private talks with Prime Minister Churchill from May 26 to May 29, President Truman states in his *Memoirs*:

. . . on May 31 I had a cable from Churchill referring to his talks with Davies, but raising a puzzling question.

Churchill said that he was hoping I would soon be able to let him know the date "of the meeting of 'the three.'" The Prime Minister said his talks with Davies were agreeable, as he would report to me on his return. Then Churchill made the surprising statement that he would not be prepared to attend a meeting which was a continuation of a conference between myself and Stalin and that "the three" should meet simultaneously and on equal terms.

---

4. Ibid., p. 378.
5. Ibid., pp. 378–379.
6. Ibid., p. 380.

I had at no time proposed seeing Stalin alone at any separate conference. What I was anxious to do was to get Stalin and Churchill and myself at the same table and maintain the unity we had during the war. Unity was even more necessary to keep peace. I had even rejected the idea of meeting Churchill alone. Churchill intimated through regular channels that he would like to see me before we had a meeting with Stalin. He considered coming over to Washington and the two of us going back together. In my judgment that would have been a serious mistake at a time when we were trying to settle things with Stalin. Stalin was always fearful that the British and ourselves would gang up on him. We did not want that. We wanted world peace, and we needed the three powers working together to get it. Of course, since I was not personally acquainted with either Stalin or Churchill, I had intended that when we arrived at our meeting place I would have an opportunity to see each separately. In this way I would become better acquainted with them and be able to size them up, and they too would get a chance to size me up.[7]

However, the conference at Potsdam of all three at once was agreed.

---

7. *Memoirs* by Harry S. Truman, Volume One, *Year of Decisions*, p. 260. Doubleday & Company, Inc., New York, 1956. [*Editor's note:* In his manuscript, Hoover omitted the footnote number in the text. I have supplied it here.]

CHAPTER 80

Organization of the Potsdam Conference

THE POTSDAM CONFERENCE began on July 17, 1945, and ended sixteen days later, on August 2.

The principals at the conference were originally President Truman, Marshal Stalin, and Prime Minister Churchill. The British Conservative Party was defeated in the British elections in the midst of the conference. Churchill was then replaced, after eight days, by Prime Minister Clement R. Attlee, leader of the British Labor Party.[1]

---

1. The staffs of the principals were:

The American Staff: The Secretary of State, James F. Byrnes; Fleet Admiral William D. Leahy, U.S.N., Chief of Staff to the Commander in Chief of the Army and Navy; Joseph E. Davies, Special Ambassador; Edwin W. Pauley, Special Ambassador; Ambassador Robert D. Murphy, Political Advisor to the Commander in Chief, United States Forces of Occupation in Germany; W. Averell Harriman, Ambassador to the U.S.S.R.; General of the Army George C. Marshall, Chief of Staff, United States Army; Fleet Admiral Ernest J. King, U.S.N., Chief of Naval Operations and Commander in Chief, U.S. Fleet; General of the Army Henry H. Arnold, Commanding General, Army Air Forces; General Brehon B. Somervell, Commanding General, Army Service Forces; Vice Admiral Emory S. Land, War Shipping Administrator; William L. Clayton, Assistant Secretary of State; James C. Dunn, Assistant Secretary of State; Ben Cohen, Special Assistant to the Secretary of State; H. Freeman Matthews, Director of European Affairs; Charles E. Bohlen, Assistant to the Secretary of State; Major General John R. Deane, U.S.A., Commanding General, United States Military Mission to the Soviet Union; Emile Despres, Adviser on German Economic Affairs, Office of the Assistant Secretary of State for Economic Affairs; Rear Admiral Howard A. Flanigan, U.S.N., member of the Joint Military Transportation Committee, Joint Chiefs of Staff, and of the Combined Military Transportation Committee, Combined Chiefs of Staff; James Forrestal, Secretary of the Navy; Lieutenant General John E. Hull, U.S.A., Assistant Chief of Staff, Operations Division, War Department General Staff; Arthur Bliss Lane, Appointed Ambassador to Poland; J. Howard Marshall, General Counsel, United States Delegation, Allied Commission on Reparations; John J. McCloy, Assistant Secretary of War; Henry L. Stimson, Secretary of War; Charles W. Yost, Executive Secretary, Central Secretariat, Department of State, Secretary General of the United States Delegation; and other advisers.

The British staff: The Secretary of State for Foreign Affairs, Anthony Eden, M.P., he was later succeeded by Ernest Bevin, M.P.; Lord Leathers, Minister of War Transport; Sir Alexander Cadogan, Permanent Under Secretary of State for Foreign Affairs; Sir Archibald Clark Kerr, H. M. Ambassador at Moscow; Sir Walter Monckton, Head of the U.K. Delegation to Moscow Reparations

Six of the American civilian staff—Byrnes, Marshall, King, Leahy, Harriman, and Bohlen—had been present at Yalta. It may be noted that Harry Hopkins, Alger Hiss, and Lauchlin Currie were not included.

Six of the British staff had been present at Yalta.

Practically all the principal members of the Russian delegation had been present at both Tehran and Yalta.

Other Delegations

Various nations other than the United States, Britain, and Russia sent delegations to the conference. Russia did not permit her seven annexed states to send delegations. The Russian delegates controlled the delegations from eight of her satellite states.

The Military Situation at the Time of the Potsdam Conference

The fighting in Europe was over.

General MacArthur had brought the war with Japan near an end. The Japanese had lost two-thirds of their fighting ships. The remaining navy was in refuge in harbors blockaded by the American Navy; the movement of merchant ships was paralyzed. Their armies in China were isolated from the mainland of

---

Commission; Sir William Strang, Political Adviser to the Commander-in-Chief, British Zone in Germany; Sir Edward Bridges, Secretary of the Cabinet; Field Marshal Sir Alan Brooke, Chief of the Imperial General Staff; Marshal of the Royal Air Force Sir Charles Portal, Chief of the Air Staff; Admiral of the Fleet Sir Andrew Cunningham, First Sea Lord; General Sir Hastings Ismay, Chief of Staff to the Minister of Defence; Field Marshal Sir Harold Alexander, Supreme Allied Commander, Mediterranean Theatre; Field Marshal Sir Henry Maitland Wilson, Head of the British Joint Staff Mission at Washington; and other advisers.

The Russian staff: People's Commissar for Foreign Affairs, V. M. Molotov; Admiral of the Fleet N. G. Kuznetsov, People's Commissar, the Naval Fleet of the U.S.S.R.; Army General A. I. Antonov, Chief of Staff of the Red Army; A. Ya. Vyshinski, Deputy People's Commissar for Foreign Affairs; S. I. Kavtaradze, Assistant People's Commissar for Foreign Affairs; I. M. Maisky, Assistant People's Commissar for Foreign Affairs; Admiral S. G. Kucherov, Chief of Staff of the Naval Fleet; F. T. Gusev, Ambassador of the Soviet Union in Great Britain; A. A. Gromyko, Ambassador of the Soviet Union in the United States of America; K. V. Novikov, Member of the Collegium of the Commissariat for Foreign Affairs, Director of the Second European Division; S. K. Tsarapkin, Member of the Collegium of the Commissariat for Foreign Affairs; A. A. Lavrishchev, Director of the Division of Balkan Countries, Commissariat for Foreign Affairs; A. A. Sobolev, Chief of the Political Section of the Soviet Military Administration in Germany; M. Z. Saburov, Assistant to the Chief of the Soviet Military Administration in Germany; S. A. Golunsky, Expert Consultant of the Commissariat for Foreign Affairs; and also political, military, and technical assistants. ([U.S. Department of State,] *Foreign Relations of the United States,* [*Diplomatic Papers, The*] *Conference of Berlin (*[The] *Potsdam* [*Conference*]), *1945*) [United States Government Printing Office: Washington, 1960], [Vol. II,] pp. XLIII, XLIV, XLV, XLVI.

Japan. Their troops in the South Seas were unable to secure overseas supplies. Many were starving.

The Japanese air fleet was being steadily destroyed. Cities on the mainland were under constant air bombardment; many of the wooden sections of Japan's cities were aflame. The Japanese were repeatedly signaling for peace.

The Potsdam Declarations

During the course of the Potsdam Conference the protocols, agreements, declarations, and their annexes amounted to over 15,000 words or to about _____ [sic–ed.] pages of this printed text. I therefore confine quotations here to those which had subsequent important influence on the allied world and to the spread of Communism.

The Potsdam declaration embraced the same double meaning of the words "democratic," "equal rights," and "elective principles." They occur at least fifteen times in the declarations and agreements. At least one moral shock was avoided at the conference by omitting any mention of the Atlantic Charter and the Four Freedoms.

The Declaration of the Duties of the Council of Foreign Ministers

This Council had been considered at Yalta. It was now agreed that the membership should comprise officials from Britain, the United States, Soviet Russia, China, and France. The Council was directed to prepare peace treaties with Italy, Bulgaria, Finland, Hungary, and Rumania.

The Council's activities were restricted by an agreement which read:

> The establishment of the Council of Foreign Ministers for the specific purposes named in the text will be without prejudice to the agreement of the Crimea [Yalta] Conference that there should be periodic consultation among the Foreign Secretaries of the United States, the Union of Soviet Socialist Republics and the United Kingdom.[2]

---

2. *Foreign Relations of the United States,* [*Diplomatic Papers, The*] *Conference of Berlin* ([*The*] *Potsdam* [*Conference*]) *1945,* [Vol.] II, p. 1501.

CHAPTER 81

Potsdam Action as to
Germany and Poland

THE AGREEMENTS AND DECLARATIONS in respect to Germany comprised about four thousand words. Later, I shall give some appraisal of their effects. But I should mention here that the Russians had already converted their agreed occupation zone of East Germany into a satellite Communist state.

At Mr. Truman's request I visited Germany in April, 1946, on food matters. Again on January 5, 1947, the President requested me to go to Germany with an adequate staff and report to him on the effect of American and Allied policies. The details of this journey are covered in "The Case History of Germany."[1]

It is sufficient to say here that no economist intent upon restoring a peaceful world, or upon securing reparations from its only source—continued Germany productivity—sat in the Potsdam Conference. This, with the high state of emotions in the peoples of the Allied countries rising from their hardships and the loss of their loves ones, set the spirit of the Allies at Potsdam—vengeance.

Potsdam Action as to Poland

At this conference the Communist government of West Poland, under President Boleslaw Bierut, was recognized as representing Poland. All that the exiled democratic Polish government in London received during the Conference was an abrupt dismissal from the scene by these words:

We have taken note with pleasure of the agreement reached among representative Poles from Poland and abroad which has made possible the formation,

---

1. [*Editor's note:* This "case study" is included in Volume III, Section IV, under the title, "Vengeance Comes to Germany."]

in accordance with the decisions reached at the Crimea conference, of a Polish Provisional Government of National Unity recognized by the three Powers. The establishment of diplomatic relations with the Polish Provisional Government has resulted in the withdrawal of their recognition from the former Polish Government in London, which no longer exists.[2]

There was no exultation by the Poles throughout the world over this decision.

I give a more detailed discussion of the conference actions regarding Poland in later chapters, entitled "A Step-by-Step History of Poland."[3]

The annexation of East Poland by the Soviet Union was thus confirmed. The boundaries of West Poland set deep in Germany were also approved. These arrangements involved the movement of about 6,000,000 Poles from East Poland and about the same number of Germans from this area.

2. [Arthur Bliss] Lane, *I Saw Poland Betrayed* [The Bobbs-Merrill Company, Indianapolis and New York, 1948], p. 128.

3. [*Editor's note:* See Volume III.]

CHAPTER 82

Action as to Japan

PRIOR TO THE POTSDAM CONFERENCE in July, 1945, the Japanese were repeatedly signaling for peace. A review of these Japanese peace efforts sheds light on the actual situation at this fateful conference.

Early in February, 1945, Mr. Roosevelt received a long dispatch[1] from General MacArthur, outlining terms of peace that could be made with Japan. These terms amounted to unconditional surrender, except for maintaining the position of the Emperor and strongly urging that no concessions be made to Russia.

In March, 1945, a month after Yalta, the Swedish Minister to Japan was requested by Japanese Foreign Minister Shigemitsu to enlist his government to mediate peace for Japan. Nothing came from it and its only importance was the indication of Japan's determination to make peace.[2]

I have recited in Chapter [76–ed.] that in April 1945, the Emperor substituted a group of civilian anti-militarists for the militarist ministry. Admiral Kantaro Suzuki, who had a long record of friendliness toward the United States, was made Prime Minister. Suzuki's new cabinet included Shigenori Togo (not to be confused with General Tojo) as Foreign Minister who was also an anti-militarist and had opposed Japan's joining the war in 1941.[3]

In July, 1945, again in the hope for peace, the Japanese ministry proposed to send Prince Konoye to Moscow. Japan naturally needed a neutral nation as intermediary and felt that ostensibly she still enjoyed neutral relations with

---

1. This dispatch has never been disclosed. A summary appeared in the *Chicago Tribune* of August 18, 1945, and I have confirmed from General MacArthur that the *Tribune* account was generally correct.

2. [*Record of Proceedings of the*] *International Military Tribunal for the Far East* [Tokyo: 1946–1948], [Widar] Bagge [affidavit], pp. 34561–64. See also [Robert J. C.] Butow, *Japan's Decision to Surrender* [Stanford University Press, Stanford, California: 1954], pp. 54, 55, 56.

3. *Foreign Service*, July, 1947.

the Soviet Union.[4] On July 13th the Russians were notified of the Konoye mission.[5] Moscow replied on July 18, refusing his mission.[6] Again on July 21st the Japanese ministry urged their Ambassador to Moscow to propose that Konoye visit Moscow, this time flatly stating that his mission was to seek the good offices of the Soviet to end the war. This message was delivered to the Russians on July 25.[7] No reply was given.

Also during July Foreign Minister Togo was exchanging urgent messages by cable with the Japanese Ambassador in Moscow, Naotake Sato. These messages were all intercepted and deciphered in Washington, and they conveyed a strong desire to end the war short of unconditional surrender.[8]

Thus before the ultimatum issued at the Potsdam Conference on July 26th, there had been six months of peace feelers by the Japanese, and nearly two weeks before, the positive proposal of Japan to Russia of which Truman, Byrnes and Stimson had full information from intercepted telegrams.

The importance of this is to show (a) that at least Secretary Byrnes was informed of these proposals before he reached Potsdam and (b) that it might be surmised that Marshal Stalin was not interested in ending the Allied war with Japan until he had collected the great Chinese provinces given him under the secret Yalta Far Eastern Agreement of the previous February.

All of these peace feelers had one stipulation in common, the preservation of the Japanese Imperial House. Secretary Stimson had long favored this condition to the Japanese. In a long memorandum to President Truman on July 2nd concerning Japan's peace terms and warnings to her, he included the sentence:

> ... [if–ed.] we should add that we do not exclude a constitutional monarchy under her present dynasty, it would ... add to the chances of acceptance.[9]

Secretary Byrnes states[10] that the Stimson memorandum was used as the basis for the ultimatum. However his strong recommendation that the

---

4. Butow, *Japan's Decision to Surrender*, pp. 87, 88.

5. [U.S. Department of State,] *Foreign Relations of the United States, [Diplomatic Papers, The] Conference of Berlin ([The] Potsdam [Conference]) 1945* [United States Government Printing Office, Washington: 1960] (hereafter referred to as *Potsdam Papers*), Vol. I, p. 879.

6. *Potsdam Papers*, Vol. II, p. 1251. See also p. 1262.

7. Ibid., p. 1257. See also p. 1262.

8. Butow, *Japan's Decision to Surrender*, p. 130. See also [Walter Millis, ed.,] *The Forrestal Diaries* [The Viking Press, New York: 1951], p. 76.

9. [Henry L.] Stimson and [McGeorge] Bundy, *On Active Service [in Peace and War]* [Harper & Brothers, New York: 1948], p. 623.

10. [James F.] Byrnes, *Speaking Frankly* [Harper & Brothers Publishers, New York: 1947], p. 206.

constitutional monarchy be maintained was not included in the ultimatum.[11] Recommendations to the same effect by Secretary Forrestal, Under Secretary of State Grew, and myself which I have related in Chapter [76–*ed.*] were also ignored.

The following is the ultimatum issued to Japan at the Potsdam Conference on July 26, 1945:

(1) We, the President of the United States, the President of the National Government of the Republic of China and the Prime Minister of Great Britain, representing the hundreds of millions of our countrymen, have conferred and agree that Japan shall be given an opportunity to end this war.

(2) The prodigious land, sea and air forces of the United States, the British Empire and of China, many times reinforced by their armies and air fleets from the west are poised to strike the final blows upon Japan. This military power is sustained and inspired by the determination of all the Allied nations to prosecute the war against Japan until she ceases to resist.

(3) The result of the futile and senseless German resistance to the might of the aroused free peoples of the world stands forth in awful clarity as an example to the people of Japan. The might that now converges on Japan is immeasurably greater than that which, when applied to the resisting Nazis, necessarily laid waste to the lands, the industry and the method of life of the whole German people. The full application of our military power, backed by our resolve, *will* mean the inevitable and complete destruction of the Japanese armed forces and just as inevitably the utter devastation of the Japanese homeland.

(4) The time has come for Japan to decide whether she will continue to be controlled by those self-willed milita[r]istic advisers whose unintelligent calculations have brought the Empire of Japan to the threshold of annihilation, or whether she will follow the path of reason.

(5) Following are our terms. We will not deviate from them. There are no alternatives. We shall brook no delay.

---

11. The postwar records show the Japanese leaders were thrown into complete confusion by this ultimatum. (A full account is given in Butow, *Japan's Decision to Surrender.*)

Following the receipt of the ultimatum, the Japanese ministry and their Elder Statesmen were in almost continuous session, often with the Emperor. At one moment they again requested Stalin, through his Tokyo Ambassador, to act as an intermediary to modify the demand as to the Emperor. The Russian Ambassador refused to accept or forward the message.

(6) There must be eliminated for all time the authority and influence of those who have deceived and misled the people of Japan into embarking on world conquest, for we insist that a new order of peace, security and justice will be impossible until irresponsible militarism is driven from the world.

(7) Until such a new order is established *and* until there is convincing proof that Japan's war-marking power is destroyed, points in Japanese territory to be designated by the Allies shall be occupied to secure the achievement of the basic objectives we are here setting forth.

(8) The terms of the Cairo Declaration shall be carried out and Japanese sovereignty shall be limited to the islands of Honshu, Hokkaido, Kyushu, Shikoku and such minor islands as we determine.

(9) The Japanese military forces, after being completely disarmed, shall be permitted to return to their homes with the opportunity to lead peaceful and productive lives.

(10) We do not intend that the Japanese shall be enslaved as a race or destroyed as [a] nation, but stern justice shall be meted out to all war criminals, including those who have visited cruelties upon our prisoners. The Japanese government shall remove all obstacles to the revival and strength[en]ing of democratic tendencies among the Japanese people. Freedom of speech, of religion, and of thought, as well as respect for the fundamental human rights shall be established.

(11) Japan shall be permitted to maintain such industries as will sustain her economy and permit the exaction of just reparations in kind, but not those industries which would enable her to re-arm for war. To this end, access to, as distinguished from control of raw materials shall be permitted. Eventual Japanese participation in world trade relations shall be permitted.

(12) The occupying forces of the Allies shall be withdrawn from Japan as soon as these objectives have been accomplished and there has been established in accordance with the freely expressed will of the Japanese people a peacefully inclined and responsible government.

(13) We call upon the Government of Japan to proclaim now the unconditional surrender of all Japanese armed forces, and to provide proper and adequate assurances of their good faith in such action. The alternative for Japan is prompt and utter destruction.[12]

---

12. *Foreign Relations of the United States*, [*Diplomatic Papers, The*] *Conference of Berlin* ([*The*] *Potsdam* [*Conference*]) *1945*, [Vol.] II, pp. 1474–76. This ultimatum was later agreed to by Stalin.

Sometime between July 30th and the departure of the Americans from Potsdam on August 2nd, the decision was made to drop the atomic bomb on Japan. Despite all the evidence that the surrender of Japan was inevitable, the first atomic bomb was dropped on Hiroshima on August 6, 1945, and on August 9, the second bomb was dropped on Nagasaki. Both Secretary Stimson and General Marshall recommended this action.

The holocaust was described later on by the United States Strategic Bombing Survey, as follows:

> Most of the industrial workers had already reported to work, but many workers were enroute and nearly all the school children and some industrial employees were at work in the open on the program of building removal to provide firebreaks and disperse valuables to the country. . . . Because of the lack of warning and the populace's indifference to small groups of planes, the explosion came as an almost complete surprise, and the people had not taken shelter. Many were caught in the open, and most of the rest in flimsily constructed homes or commercial establishments. . . .
>
> At Nagasaki, three days later, the city was scarcely more prepared, though vague references to the Hiroshima disaster had appeared in the newspapers of 8 August.[13]

On August 8th the Russians declared war on Japan.

On August 10th the Japanese accepted all the terms of the Potsdam ultimatum on condition that the Imperial House be preserved. Their statement said in part:

> The Japanese Government are ready to accept the terms enumerated in the joint declaration which was issued at Potsdam on July 26th, 1945, by the heads of the Governments of the United States, Great Britain, and China, and later subscribed by the Soviet Government, *with the understanding that the said declaration does not comprise any demand which prejudices the prerogatives of his Majesty as a Sovereign Ruler. . . .*[14]

Admiral Leahy records:

> I attended a conference at the White House [August 10th] with the Secretaries of State, War, and Navy which the President called at 9 A.M., to discuss [the surrender]. . . .

---

13. [United States Strategic Bombing Survey,] *The Effects of Atomic Bombs on Hiroshima and Nagasaki* [United States Government Printing Office, Washington: 1946], p. 3.

14. U.S. Department of State *Bulletin*, XIII, p. 205.

... I had no feelings about little Hirohito [the Emperor], but was convinced that it would be necessary to use him in effecting the surrender.

Some of those around the President wanted to demand his execution. If they had prevailed, we might still be at war with Japan. ...

... Obviously the one point to be cleared up was the status of the Emperor of Japan. ...[15]

The American reply to the Japanese dispatch of the 10th stated:

With regard to the Japanese Government's message accepting the terms of the Potsdam Proclamation but containing the statement, "with the understanding that the said declaration does not comprise any demand which prejudices the prerogatives of His Majesty as a sovereign ruler," our position is as follows:

From the moment of surrender the authority of the Emperor and the said Japanese Government to rule the state shall be subject to the Supreme Commander of the Allied Powers who will take such steps as he deems proper to effectuate the surrender terms.[16]

Whether the American dispatch of August 10th was a concession or only a delegation of power to the "Supreme Commander" is not clear. But General Douglas MacArthur, the "Supreme Commander," at once upon Japanese surrender, announced the preservation of the dynasty with religious and certain secular authority.

Many Americans well feel that had this assurance been offered to the Japanese people three months before Potsdam, thousands of American lives would have been saved. The bombs which killed thousands of women and children and noncombatant men would not have been dropped.

15. [William D.] Leahy, *I Was There* [Whittlesey House, McGraw-Hill Book Company, Inc., New York: 1950], pp. 434–435.

16. U.S. *Department of State Bulletin*, XIII [No. 320, August 12, 1945], p. 206.

CHAPTER 83

Aftermath of Dropping the Atomic Bomb on Japan

THE USE OF THE ATOMIC BOMB on Japan has continued to stir the American conscience as well as the conscience of thinking people elsewhere in the world. Attempts have been made to justify the use of this terrible weapon. However, American military men and statesmen have repeatedly stated that its use was not necessary to bring the war to an end. Quotes from some of these statements follow.

On August 29, 1945, the Associated Press reported:

Secretary of State . . . Byrnes challenged today Japan's argument that the atomic bomb had knocked her out of the war.

He cited what he called Russian proof that the Japanese knew that they were beaten before the first atomic bomb was dropped on Hiroshima. Foreign Commissar Vyacheslaff M. Molotoff informed the Americans and British at the Berlin [Potsdam] Conference, Mr. Byrnes said, that the Japanese had asked to send a delegation to Moscow to seek Russian mediation for the end of the war—an act that Mr. Byrnes interpreted as proof of the enemy's recognition of defeat.[1]

On September 20, 1945, Major General Curtis LeMay, who directed the air attacks on Japan, stated to the Associated Press:

The atomic bomb had nothing to do with the end of the war. . . . The war would have been over in two weeks without the Russians coming in and without the atomic bomb.[2]

---

1. *New York Times,* August 30, 1945.
2. *New York Herald Tribune,* September 20, 1945.

There were present at this interview two American Generals who were engaged in the action against Japan—General Barney Giles and Brigadier General Emmett O'Donnell—both of whom agreed with General LeMay.[3]

In an Associated Press interview in Washington on October 5, 1945, Admiral Chester Nimitz said he was convinced that the end of the war would have been the same without the atomic bomb or the entry of Russia into the war. He reemphasized this in an address to Congress the same day, saying:

> The atomic bomb did not win the war against Japan. The Japanese had, in fact, already sued for peace before the atomic age was announced to the world with the destruction of Hiroshima and before the Russian entry into the war.
>
> In saying that the atomic bomb played no decisive part, from a purely military standpoint, in the defeat of Japan this is no effort to minimize the awful power of this new weapon. . . .[4]

In an address to the National Geographic Society on January 25, 1946, Admiral Nimitz again said:

> The atomic bomb merely hastened a process already reaching an inevitable conclusion. . . .[5]

Admiral William D. Leahy, in his book, says:

> . . . It is my opinion that the use of this barbarous weapon at Hiroshima and Nagasaki was of no material assistance in our war against Japan. The Japanese were already defeated and ready to surrender because of the effective sea blockade and the successful bombing with conventional weapons.
>
> It was my reaction that the scientists and others wanted to make this test because of the vast sums that had been spent on the project. . . .[6]

---

3. [*Editor's note:* According to a note in Box 64 of Hoover's papers relating to the Magnum Opus, he wished to include in Chapter 83 a statement by General Dwight D. Eisenhower in opposition to the American decision to drop the atomic bomb on Japan. In an interview in *Newsweek* (November 11, 1963), Eisenhower declared that he had opposed dropping the bomb for two reasons: "First, the Japanese were ready to surrender and it wasn't necessary to hit them with that awful thing. Second, I hated to see our country to be the first to use such a weapon."

Pursuant to Hoover's instructions, a member of his staff inserted a copy of Eisenhower's remarks in a folder of changes in the manuscript that Hoover wanted to make. Hoover did not live to incorporate the quotation in the text of his Magnum Opus, but in recognition of his clear intent, I record it here.]

4. *New York Times*, October 6, 1945. [*Editor's note:* Hoover's manuscript misquoted Nimitz slightly. I have corrected these evident transcription errors so that the quotation appears here as printed in the *New York Times* on October 6, 1945.]

5. Ibid., January 26, 1946. [*Editor's note:* Nimitz's remark does not appear in this source. Probably Hoover read the statement in another newspaper.]

6. [William D.] Leahy, *I Was There* [Whittlesey House, McGraw-Hill Book Company, Inc., New York: 1950], p. 441.

It is desirable for the record also to call attention to the observations on the dropping of the bomb by other leaders of the time. Lord Hankey, a member of the British War Cabinet, states:

> ... the Leaders of the Western Allies decided at Potsdam in July, 1945, to resort to the ultimate expedient of the atomic bomb. It was a strange and risky decision. They knew that the bomb was the most cruel and deadly weapon that had ever been produced, and that its effects would fall indiscriminately on civilian and military targets. They knew that Japan had already approached Russia with a view to peace discussions. They knew that Russia was on the point of declaring war on Japan. Yet in this fatuous fight for a phrase, they would not pause to seek some more normal means of obtaining the terms they needed, nor would they wait to learn the effect of the Russian declaration of war.
>
> There is no published evidence to show that they even inquired whether the use of the bomb was consistent with international law. . . .
>
> . . . If the enemy had solved the atomic problem and used the bomb first, its employment would have been included in the allied list of war crimes, and those who took the decision or who prepared and used the bomb, would have been condemned and hanged.[7]

Mr. Hanson Baldwin, one of our great military students and a man of conscience, summarized the thoughts of many when he said:

> The utilization of the atomic bomb against a prostrate and defeated Japan in the closing days of the war exemplifies—even more graphically than any of the mistakes previously recounted—the narrow, astigmatic concentration of our planners upon one goal, and one alone: victory.
>
> Nowhere in all of Mr. Stimson's forceful and eloquent apologia for the leveling of Hiroshima and Nagasaki is there any evidence of an ulterior vision; indeed, the entire effort of his famous Harper's article, reprinted and rearranged in his book, *On Active Service* is focused on proving that the bomb hastened the end of the war. But at what cost![8]

---

7. The Right Honorable Lord Hankey, *Politics, Trials and Errors* [Henry Regnery Company, Chicago: 1950], pp. 46–47.

8. February, 1947, *Harper's Magazine*. [*Editor's note:* Hoover's citation here actually refers to Henry L. Stimson's article, "The Decision to Use the Atomic Bomb," which appeared in *Harper's Magazine*, 194 (February 1947): 97–107. For Hanson W. Baldwin's critical comments (quoted in Hoover's text) see Hanson W. Baldwin, *Great Mistakes of the War* (Harper & Brothers, New York: 1950), pp. 88–89.]

CHAPTER 84

An Era of Vacillation in Relations with the Communists

When the march of conferences had ceased at Potsdam, the Truman administration was faced not only with the commitments made at Potsdam, but also with those made by Mr. Roosevelt. Many of Mr. Roosevelt's undertakings had not been disclosed to the American people and certainly Mr. Truman had not been taken into Mr. Roosevelt's confidence.

To go no further back than Yalta, Mr. Truman was not aware of the secret Far Eastern agreement and its obligation upon the United States to force Chiang Kai-shek to sign his approval of the huge concessions from China to Russia.

[There ensued a period of about two years after the war during which the President was groping with these entanglements. At times in this period he apparently still had some confidence in Communist Russia's fidelity to their commitments. Also, statesmen in the Western Democracies were slow to realize what had already been taken under control of the Kremlin.][1] Mr. Churchill showed evidence of awakening in his statement to former Ambassador Joseph Davies.[2] Two weeks after Potsdam, when he was no longer in office, he said in a speech to the House of Commons (August 16, 1945):

> ... Sparse and guarded accounts of what has happened and is happening have filtered through, but it is not impossible that tragedy on a prodigious

---

1. [*Editor's note:* Early in 1964 Hoover decided to delete the bracketed sentences in this paragraph, possibly because they could be construed as critical of Harry Truman, with whom he had been quite friendly. I have elected to keep these sentences because 1) they are of historical and biographical interest, and 2) without them, the remainder of the paragraph makes little sense.]

2. See page [551ff *–ed.*].

scale is unfolding itself behind the iron curtain which at the moment divides Europe in twain. . . .[3]

President Truman, in an address on August 9, 1945, a few days after his return from Potsdam, gave evidence of some anxiety because he repeated Secretary Hull's declaration (November, 1943) that there would be no more "spheres of influences," saying:

> . . . These nations [Rumania, Bulgaria, Hungary] are not to be spheres of influence. . . . They now are governed by Allied control commissions composed of representatives of the three governments which met at Yalta and Berlin. . . .[4]

Secretary of State James Byrnes showed signs of awakening when he returned from a meeting of the Foreign Ministers in London, in September, 1945. He related in his book, *All in One Lifetime,* that it became apparent that it was impossible to reach agreement for carrying out what I have called the "freedom rescue" agreed at Yalta. Therefore, Dr. Wang Shih Chieh, the Chinese representative, who was presiding on October 2, formally adjourned the conferences at Byrnes' suggestion.[5]

Upon his return home, on October 5,[6] Byrnes made an address in which

---

3. [Winston S.] Churchill, *Victory* [*War Speeches by the Right Hon. Winston S. Churchill,* compiled by Charles Eade] [Little Brown and Company, Boston: 1946,] p. 299. [*Editor's note:* Churchill was referring to reports of the "expulsion and exodus" of Germans from formerly German lands now within the redrawn boundaries of "the new Poland."]

4. *New York Herald Tribune,* August 10, 1945.

5. James F. Byrnes, *All in One Lifetime* (Harper & Brothers, New York: 1948), p. 317.

6. For the convenience of the reader I give the list of Foreign Ministers Conferences 1945–1949:

1. The first meeting of Foreign Ministers Byrnes, Molotov, and Bevin at London from September 11th to October 2nd (1945).
2. The second meeting of Foreign Ministers Byrnes, Molotov, and Bevin at Moscow from December 16th to December 27th (1945).
3. The meeting of Foreign Ministers Byrnes, Molotov, Bevin, and Bidault at Paris from April 25th to July 12th (1946).
4. The 21 nation "Peace Conference" held in Paris from July 29th to October 15th (1946). An extension of this conference was held in New York from November 4th to December 12th (1946).
5. The meeting of Foreign Ministers Marshall, Bidault, Vishinsky, and Bevin at Moscow from March 10th to April 24th (1947).
6. The meeting of Foreign Ministers Bevin, Bidault, Molotov and Marshall at London, from November 25th to December 15th (1947).
7. The meeting of Foreign Ministers Acheson, Bevin, Schuman and Vishinsky eighteen months later at Paris, from May 23rd to June 20th (1949).
8. The meeting of Foreign Ministers Acheson, Bevin, Schuman, and Vishinsky at New York, from September 26th to October 6th (1949).

he stated that the session had "closed in a stalemate."[7] In his book Byrnes was somewhat more explicit. He described the Russian habit of getting some package from every conference with Americans:

> Now, at London, Mr. Molotov saw no chance of taking home any packages. He could not understand why we would not accept his interpretation that "friendship" between our governments required that we let the Soviets establish complete suzerainty over the Balkan states. As far as I was concerned, Christmas was over—it was now January 1, and we had many bills to pay. Instead of issuing more I.O.Us, I wanted to collect some we held. One of these I felt was the Yalta pledge on the treatment of the liberated states.[8]

Byrnes, however, retreated somewhat by saying:

> The American Government shares the desire of the Soviet Union to have governments friendly to the Soviet Union in eastern and central Europe.[9]

On October 27, President Truman made another address in which he, in effect, revived the Atlantic Charter:

> The foreign policy of the United States is based firmly on fundamental principles of righteousness and justice. In carrying out those principles we shall firmly adhere to what we believe to be right; and we shall not give our approval to any compromise with evil. . . .
>
> Let me restate the fundamentals of that foreign policy of the United States:
>
> . . . We shall approve no territorial changes in any friendly part of the world unless they accord with the freely expressed wishes of the people concerned.
>
> . . . We believe that all peoples who are prepared for self-government should be permitted to choose their own form of government by their own freely expressed choice, without interference from any foreign source. . . .
>
> . . . By the combined and cooperative action of our war allies, we shall help the defeated enemy states establish peaceful democratic governments of their own free choice. . . .

In 1946 top level conferences were held by General George C. Marshall [and] Chiang Kai-shek with the Communist leaders of China.

7. *New York Times*, October 6, 1945.

8. James F. Byrnes, *Speaking Frankly* (Harper & Brothers Publishers, New York: 1947), p. 105.

9. *New York Times*, October 6, 1945.

... We shall refuse to recognize any government imposed upon any nation by the force of any foreign power.

But Mr. Truman put an anchor to windward by adding (no doubt meaning 15 nations annexed or dominated by Russia):

... In some cases it may be impossible to prevent forceful imposition of such a government. But the United States will not recognize any such government.[10]

On October 31, Secretary Byrnes made another address. He seemed to have retreated from "firmness" and to approve the Communist grip on the fifteen nations, saying:

Far from opposing, we have sympathized with, for example, the effort of the Soviet Union to draw into closer and more friendly association with her Central and Eastern European neighbors. We are fully aware of her special security interests in those countries, and we have recognized those interests in the arrangements made for the occupation and control of the former enemy States.[11]

On November 14, 1945 Under Secretary of State Dean Acheson made an address at Madison Square; he stated he approved the Tehran agreement by which the Communists got the nine satellite states:

... Never in the past has there been any place on the globe where the vital interests of the American and Russian peoples have clashed or even been antagonistic—and there is no objective reason to suppose that there should now, or in the future, ever be such a place. ... We understand and agree with them that to have friendly governments along her borders is essential both for the security of the Soviet Union and for the peace of the world.[12]

In December of 1945, Secretary Byrnes attended the second meeting of the Foreign Ministers in Moscow. He agreed to recognize the governments of Rumania, Bulgaria, and Hungary without even the prior application of the Yalta "Operation Freedom Rescue" which called for "free elections, of governments responsive to the will of the people. ..." Byrnes went even further and

---

10. *Public Papers of the Presidents of the United States, Harry S. Truman, 1945* [volume] (United States Government Printing Office, Washington: 1961), pp. 433–434.

11. *New York Times*, November 1, 1945.

12. Ibid., November 15, 1945.

agreed to limit the "other liberal elements" to only two in the ministries of the satellites.

On December 30, 1945, after his return from this conference, he stated:

Now I do not consider this solution ideal. . . .

It must be recognized that the Soviet government has a very real interest in the character of these states . . . It is . . . to be expected that the withdrawal of Soviet troops from these countries may depend upon the Soviet government's confidence in the peaceful character of these governments.[13]

In a radio address in December, 1945, Byrnes said:

Referring to the fact that since the London Conference we had found it possible to recognize the governments of Austria and Hungary, I emphasized that there was still a wide divergence between our viewpoint and Russia's over Rumania and Bulgaria. "Our objections . . . have been not only to the exclusion of important democratic groups from these governments, but to the oppressive way in which they exercise their powers. Until now our objections have been little heeded by those governments or by the Soviet government." I then spoke of the tripartite commission of ambassadors which would proceed immediately to advise the King on broadening the basis of representation in the Rumanian government. I stressed that we would recognize the Rumanian government only when our government decided that adequate safeguards had been taken for free elections and for freedom of speech, of the press, religion and of association. Attention was also called to the pledge of the Soviet government to advise the new Bulgarian government to take similar action. These agreements, I said, did not go as far as I should have liked, but were a great improvement over the generalities of Yalta and Potsdam. As time soon proved, they were so good from our point of view that the Soviets proceeded to ignore or to violate them.[14]

The American public reception of the work of this Moscow Conference of Foreign Ministers was not one of unlimited delight. *The New York World-Telegram*, on December 29, stated:

If Secretary of State Byrnes is really as jubilant about the Big Three Moscow agreement as he has been saying . . . he will be surprised when he arrives in Washington today. . . .

---

13. Ibid., December 31, 1945.
14. Byrnes, *All in One Lifetime*, p. 344.

... he has agreed to scrap America's nonrecognition policy toward Russia's undemocratic puppet governments in the Balkans. This is in trade for the meaningless inclusion of two members of unrepresented parties in the Romanian and in the Bulgarian cabinets, where they will have no power; and for an indefinite pledge of a free election in Romania, though not in Bulgaria—the kind of pledge broken by the Red Yugoslav regime now recognized by Mr. Byrnes.

The Secretary of State should tell the public what he gained ... by this underwriting of Russian dictatorship in eastern Europe.

Human Events commented:

The opinion that Secretary Byrnes made his "Munich-in-Moscow" ... is gaining wider currency. . . .[15]

That President Truman and Secretary Byrnes had not been in tune as to Byrnes' policies toward the Communists came to light in 1952. Byrnes at that time made some unfriendly remarks about Mr. Truman's policies. Whereupon, Mr. Truman produced a letter addressed to Byrnes in January, 1946, in which the President complained about Byrnes' concessions to the Communists at the December, 1945, meeting of Foreign Ministers in Moscow, and said he had been kept entirely in the dark regarding what Byrnes was doing. Byrnes denied ever receiving such a letter and implied that Mr. Truman was not telling the truth.[16]

Mr. Truman Reverses American Policies in Dealing with Communism in Europe

In an address to Congress on March 12, 1947, Mr. Truman outlined a foreign policy to combat communism throughout the world. He asked for $400,000,000 with which to bolster Greece and Turkey as a start. He stated:

We shall not realize our objectives, however, unless we are willing to help free peoples to maintain their free institutions and their national integrity. . . . This is no more than a frank recognition that totalitarian regimes imposed on free peoples, by direct or indirect aggression, undermine the foundations of international peace and hence the security of the United States. . . .

---

15. *Human Events,* Vol. III, No. 2, January 9, 1946.

16. The memorandum is printed in William Hillman's *Mr. President* [Farrar, Straus and Young, New York: 1952], pp. 21–22 [23]; and Byrnes' reply appears in *Collier's,* April 26, 1952.

... it must be the policy of the United States to support free peoples who are resisting attempted subjugation by armed minorities or by outside pressures.[17]

Legislation authorizing this aid to Greece was passed by Congress.

This was indeed a courageous act directed to stop the Communist flood over Europe. However, it was not completely consistent with American policies in Asia where at this same time great pressures were being exerted by Washington on Chiang Kai-shek to form a coalition with Mao Tse-tung's Communists.

---

17. The *Congressional Record* [vol. 93 (March 12, 1947): 1981.]

CHAPTER 85

I Make an Appraisal of
Communist Progress as of 1946

IN EARLY MARCH, 1946, eight months after Potsdam, President Truman requested me to undertake the co-ordination of the nations of the world to meet the greatest famine in human history.

To effect this co-ordination, it was necessary for me to visit 39 countries. This offered a unique opportunity for me to appraise the progress of Communism since my previous journey and appraisal in 1938.

For this purpose I assembled an experienced staff, and we undertook a journey by plane around the world.[1] The members of this mission of 1946 comprised:

Former Ambassador Hugh Gibson—35 years of career Foreign Service, including Assistant Secretary of State, Minister or Ambassador to Poland, Belgium, Brazil, and Ambassador-at-Large in Europe. From 1918 to 1921 he had served in the relief of the famine, the aftermath of World War I.

Dr. Dennis A. FitzGerald—who had been Director of the Office of Requirements and Allocations, Department of Agriculture, and was U.S. Executive Officer of the Combined Food Board.

Frank E. Mason—a long-time foreign correspondent in Europe and former President of International News Service, as well as former American Military Attaché in Berlin.

Hallam Tuck, Perrin Galpin, Maurice Pate—all of whom had served in the relief of the First World War famine and later in various government departments.

---

1. A full account of this mission is given in Herbert Hoover, *An American Epic*, Volume IV [Henry Regnery Company, Chicago: 1964]. [*Editor's note:* Hoover visited 38 countries during his famine relief mission in 1946. Afterward, he delivered his final report on this mission in a speech in Ottawa, Canada. This probably explains his reference in the text above to having visited 39 countries as part of his "co-ordination" effort.]

On our investigation of the Latin American nations, Dr. Julius Klein substituted for Mr. Tuck. Dr. Klein had served as Commercial Attaché in many of these countries, and later as Under-Secretary of Commerce.

A most able private secretary, Hugo Meier, accompanied us on this mission.

The members of the mission spoke many languages, and we had a host of friends among foreign officials from whom cooperation came freely.

On this mission we traveled 51,000 miles by plane. We visited London, Paris, Rome, Geneva, Prague, Warsaw, Helsinki, Riga, Stockholm, Oslo, Brussels, The Hague, Copenhagen, Berlin, Munich, Hamburg, Vienna, Belgrade, Athens, Cairo, Baghdad, Karachi, New Delhi, Bombay, Mysore, Bangkok, Manila, Shanghai, Nanking, Seoul, Tokyo, Honolulu, Mexico City, Panama, Bogota, Quito, Lima, Santiago, Buenos Aires, Montevideo, Rio de Janeiro, Caracas, Havana, and Ottawa.

On this journey to 39 countries we met with kings, presidents, ministers of foreign affairs, cabinet officers and military officials. While our major interest was relief of the famine, all on our staff were concerned about the forces moving in the world and their impact upon our country—especially the spread of Communism.

Invariably, with the exception of the Communist countries, the authorities in every country insisted upon discussion of the Communist danger which had greatly increased with the war. They talked frankly about Communist infiltration and conspiracies in their own as well as neighboring countries. The official American representatives overseas also raised the subject.[2]

We, of course, could not interfere with the functions of our State Department, but we made detailed notes on Communist progress. Upon our return, I concluded that the best way to present this disheartening information would be to use statistical tables. The tables would summarize Communist expansion in different categories by showing a population and square miles of the countries involved.

---

2. In Volume IV, *An American Epic*, I have prepared a detailed account of these many interviews, the mass of information which we collected, and the measures adopted which saved the world from a gigantic loss of lives by starvation. I have included in that volume parts of this chapter.

European Peoples' Annexation by Russia

The European areas annexed by the Soviet Union as a result of the Tehran agreements (November 28–December 1, 1943)[3] were:

	Square Miles	Inhabitants
Finnish Provinces	17,600	450,000
East Poland (Polish Provinces)	69,900	11,800,000
Bessarabia	17,100	3,200,000
Bukovina	2,300	500,000
Estonia	18,300	1,122,000
Latvia	25,400	1,951,000
Lithuania	21,500	2,957,000
Konigsberg area	5,400	1,187,000
Areas annexed from Czechoslovakia	4,900	731,000
TOTAL	182,400	23,898,000

European Peoples Transformed into Communist States

Under the Tehran agreements the following countries or peoples in Europe had been provided by Stalin with Communist presidents, Communist ministries of from about eight members upward, and, at most, two representatives of the "other liberal elements":

	Square Miles	Inhabitants
East Germany	42,900	18,807,000
Albania	11,100	1,186,000
Bulgaria	42,800	7,160,000
Czechoslovakia	49,300	12,463,000
Hungary	35,900	9,224,000
West Poland	120,400	24,500,000
Rumania	91,600	16,007,000
Yugoslavia	95,600	16,339,000
To enumerate the full extent of the Communist spread, we should add Russia itself with	8,600,000	190,000,000
TOTAL (estimate)	9,089,600	295,686,000

Countries in Asia Annexed to Russia

Under the Secret Far Eastern Agreement and other commitments, the following areas in Asia were now controlled by the Kremlin:

---

3. United States Department of State, Historical Office. *Foreign Relations of the United States, Diplomatic Papers, The Conferences at Cairo and Tehran, 1943.* [United States] Government Printing Office, [Washington:] 1961, pp. 463–471.

	Square Miles	Inhabitants
The North China Communist	849,420	100,000,000
Government of Mao Tse-tung		
and Manchuria	503,000	43,234,000
Mongolia	625,900	2,000,000
North Korea	48,500	9,100,000
South Sakhalin	13,900	415,000
Kurile Islands	3,900	18,000
Tannu Tuva	64,000	65,000
TOTAL	2,459,200	114,832,000
	[2,108,620–ed.]	[154,832,000–ed.][4]

The grand total of peoples under Communist rule was therefore about 434,416,000 [474,416,000–ed.] and about 11,731,200 [11,380,000–ed.] square miles. In 1939 before the war, there was one Communist country. By 1946 there were 23 nations or parts of nations dominated by Communism.

Moreover, the progress of Communism in the world after the Second World War was not limited to the areas which had actually been made Communistic. There were eleven countries which emerged from the war with Communists in their ministries, and with organized Communist political parties:

	Square Miles	Inhabitants
France (Europe only)	212,700	42,519,000
Belgium (Europe only)	11,800	8,388,500
Italy (Europe only)	116,200	45,646,000
Austria	32,400	265,300
Chile	286,300	5,191,000
Mexico	764,000	22,776,000
Venezuela	352,200	4,189,000
Peru	482,300	6,208,000
Guatemala	45,450	3,706,250
Bolivia	537,800	3,787,800
Iran	628,000	10,000,000 (estimated)
TOTAL	3,469,150	152,676,300
		[152,676,850–ed.][5]

The spread of Communism did not end at the time of this journey in 1946. To these Communist dominations we must at this writing add:

---

4. United States Congress, House Committee on Foreign Affairs, *World War II International Agreements and Understandings* [*Entered Into During Secret Conferences Concerning Other Peoples*] [83d Congress, 1st Session] (GPO) [United States Government Printing Office], March 12, 1953, p. 1.

5. The countries in this group gradually eliminated the Communists from their ministries. To this extent the march of Communism was pushed back, but active Communist parties and Communist conspiracies still continued without ceasing.

	Square Miles	Inhabitants
Cuba	44,000	6,743,000
New Guinea	151,000	730,000
China	3,746,453	601,938,035
Indonesia	735,865	92,600,000
TOTAL	4,677,318	702,011,035

Some of Africa's new nations, Ghana and Guinea, for example, show the effects of Communist influence in their governments.

On my return from this journey, on August 12, 1946, I replied to a press question with the following statement:

My blunt answer to the request for an appraisal of the world situation and our policies in relation to it are [sic–ed.] as follows:

... The dominant note in the world a year after World War I was hope and confidence; today it is fear and frustration. One year after the first World War we had signed peace; today there is no peace.

... there is universal desire in all nations except Russia to make ... peace.... Russia is obstructing to gain time for the elimination of all non-Communist elements behind the Iron Curtain and Manchuria, and thus the consolidation and practical absorption of those areas. Her invigorated fifth columns in every country add to the confusion....

... Far from freedom having expanded from this war it has shrunk to far fewer nations than a quarter of a century ago. In addition there are at least 15,000,000 people in concentration or forced-labor camps who are slaves in every sense of the word.

... The dismemberment of the German state and the attempt to reduce the German people to a level of perpetual poverty (if continued) will ... break into another ... explosion.

... Our own country has suffered great depletion of reserves and equipment. We are burdened with fabulous debt....

... In all this unhappy situation, necessity requires that the United States should observe three major policies.

... In the economic field we must now conserve our resources, improve our equipment and reduce our spending. We must end our role of Santa Claus.... we should announce that our economic relation with other nations is a two-way street—and balanced traffic at that.

... Our military are today spending large sums to improve the bomb.... It is nonsense to think we can ... give away the blueprints.

We should be willing to agree that it will never be used except in defense of free men. That trust we should keep, but until the world returns to keeping agreements and peaceful action—keep our powder dry.

... appeasement must cease. To hold up the moral banners of the world we should at all times assert the principles of the Atlantic Charter for which we fought the war and to which all other nations pledged themselves to us.[6]

My friends will forgive me if I recall some paragraphs of a nationally broadcast address (June 29, 1941), made when Mr. Roosevelt had set up a tacit alliance to join Russia in the war:

Momentous events have happened which greatly change the shape of things. They must be incorporated in American thinking. There is the war between Hitler and Stalin. . . .

. . . there are certain courses of practical statesmanship; there are certain eternal principles to which we must adhere. There are certain consequences to America and civilization which we must ever keep before our eyes.

In the last seven days that call to sacrifice American boys for an ideal has been made as a sounding brass and a tinkling cymbal. For now we find ourselves promising aid to Stalin and his militant Communist conspiracy against the whole democratic ideals of the world.[7]

. . . it makes the whole argument of our joining the war to bring the four freedoms to mankind a gargantuan jest. . . .

We know also Hitler's hideous record of brutality, of aggression and as a destroyer of democracies. Truly, Poland, Norway, Holland, Belgium, Denmark, France and the others are dreadful monuments. But I am talking of Stalin at this moment. . . .

If we go further and join the war and we win, then we have won for Stalin the grip of communism on Russia, the enslavement of nations, and more opportunity for it to extend in the world. . . .

Practical statesmanship leads in the same path as moral statesmanship. These two dictators—Stalin and Hitler—are in deadly combat. One of these two hideous ideologists will disappear in this fratricidal war. In any even both will be weakened.

Statesmanship demands that the United States stand aside in watchful waiting, armed to the teeth, while these men exhaust themselves.

Then the most powerful and potent nation in the world can talk to mankind with a voice that will be heard. If we get involved in this struggle we, too, will be exhausted and feeble. . . .[8]

---

6. Herbert Hoover, *Addresses Upon the American Road, 1945–48*. [D. Van Nostrand Company, Inc., New York: 1949] [pp. 20–21].

7. Mr. Roosevelt had made an appeal for sacrifice to spread his four freedoms.

8. [*Editor's note:* The preceding three paragraphs did not appear either in Hoover's original printed version, released to the press before his speech, or in the version he delivered on national

Again I say, if we join the war and Stalin wins, we have aided him to impose more communism on Europe and the world. At least we could not with such a bedfellow say to our sons that by making the supreme sacrifice, they are restoring freedom to the world. War alongside Stalin to impose freedom is more than a travesty. It is a tragedy. . . .

The day will come when these nations are sufficiently exhausted to listen to the military, economic and moral powers of the United States. And with these reserves unexhausted, at that moment, and that moment only, can the United States promote a just and permanent peace. . . .

Here in America today is the only remaining sanctuary of freedom, the last oasis of civilization and the last reserve of moral and economic strength. If we are wise, these values can be made to serve all mankind.

My countrymen, we have marched into the twilight of a world war. Should we not stop here and build our defense while we can still see? Shall we stumble on into the night of chaos?[9]

We not only stumbled, we fell.

---

radio on June 29, 1941. See note 9.]

9. Herbert Hoover, *40 Key Questions about Our Foreign Policy* [The Updegraff Press, Ltd., Scarsdale, New York: 1952], pp. 1–7. See also Herbert Hoover, *Addresses upon the American Road, 1940–1941* [Charles Scribner's Sons, New York: 1941] pp. 87–102. . . . [*Editor's note:* There are differences between the two printed versions of the June 29, 1941 speech cited here. For Hoover's explanation of these discrepancies, see page 231 of *Freedom Betrayed.*

Neither of these texts fully matches what Hoover said on that occasion. A National Broadcasting Company recording of his address, as he delivered it on the radio, is in the Recorded Sound Reference Center, Library of Congress, Washington, D.C. This oral version generally followed his original text (printed some months later in *Addresses . . . 1940–1941*), but with a number of mostly minor, last minute additions and modifications. The oral version did not, however, contain several notable passages that he included in the version of this speech that he published in *40 Key Questions* (and that appear on pp. 7, 233, and 581–82 of *Freedom Betrayed*). Perhaps the most striking of these passages were the paragraphs mentioned in the preceding footnote.

Why these textual variations? In chapter 7 of an early draft of the Magnum Opus in 1949 (Herbert C. Hoover Papers, Box 100, Hoover Institution Archives), Hoover stated that he did not have time during his 1941 broadcast to read certain additional passages "from the original manuscripts." He then incorporated some of these into the version of his 1941 speech that he printed in 1952. Some years later, in vol. 4 of *An American Epic* (Henry Regnery Company, Chicago: 1964), p. 298, he erroneously asserted that he had *delivered* what he called this "revised" version, which included these additional passages. The recording of his speech at the Library of Congress establishes that he did not utter these passages on the air.

Nevertheless, Hoover evidently came to believe that his "revised" version of his June 29, 1941 address was the correct one, and it is this later (and partially undelivered) version that he has quoted here and elsewhere in *Freedom Betrayed*.]

The living room of Herbert Hoover's suite in the Waldorf-Astoria Hotel
in New York City. (Hoover's writing desk is on the right.)

Herbert Hoover at work in his Waldorf-Astoria
apartment in New York City, August 3, 1962
(one week before his 88th birthday).

My Attitude toward Japan

That Japans ~~action~~ to aggression towards China violated every code ~~and~~ moral code and every international agreement needs no explanation. ~~However~~ ~~the further~~ Since ~~any~~ I dealt with it in 1932 her Militarists had expanded their ideas into the realm of "Asia for the Asiatics" with Japan in leadership. All this was unpalatable enough to ~~decent~~ decent ~~nations~~ and was threatened the white mans interests in the east. I never believed she could ~~over the years~~ succeed ~~over~~

Above and following 5 pages: Excerpt from an early draft chapter of the Magnum Opus (November 1944). Hoover wrote his first drafts entirely by hand.

the years because seventy millions of ~~egotists personally dzyadaus~~ hated egotists could not for long dominate one billion people. The question in my mind was two fold - First whether America should go on a crusade to correct this wrong at all but second and much more imediate whether we should undertake it in view of the ~~treats~~ dangers from Europe and this invite war on two fronts. Without resolving the first question ~~it so~~ the latter ~~seemed~~ was to me the utmost folly.

If the job had to be done it
should await the end of the
war in Europe when the
~~other~~ white races could be
mobilized for action against
her instead of America carrying
the entire burden and pulling
the British Russian ~~and~~ Dutch
and French chestnuts out of the
fire at an enormous cost
in American lives and
resources — It was ~~obviously~~ obvious
that Japan would not attack us
unless provoked into it as
~~a that~~ a rat driven into
a corner —

~~The~~ Roosevelt however undertook a series of provocative actions beginning early in 1940 and continued with increasing violence until both national pride and national desperation lead them ~~to the ~~~~~~~~~ to Pearl Harbor.

~~It is my belief that~~

I believe ~~history will~~ the verdict of history will show that either Roosevelt was wholly ignorant of Japanese psychology ~~and that ~~~~~~~~ and thought he could force her ~~to submission~~ with economic sanctions or that ~~he~~ despaired of getting the American people into the war ~~which ~~~~~~~~~~

~~~~~~~~~~

on the European ~~front~~
he determined to provoke
~~war~~ ~~us~~ war with Japan as
the method of entry —

Roosevelt ~~either believed or~~ the
apparently never understood the
import or violence of "Economic
sanctions" and played with them
like the toys on his desk — or as
I have said deliberately used them
to provoke war. ~~He acted~~
~~He~~ ~~move procedure of~~ ~~alternatively~~ permitting
Japan to drain ~~our the~~ the scrap steel
and oil which we badly needed for
our own preparedness in a dangerous
world ~~when~~ to stopping of which war
not an economic sanction and
at the same time
~~partial without~~ imposing economic
embarrassments on Japan shows

would indicate a confused mind
engaged playing with power politics.

On February 1st 1939 told I stated
in a full solemn words broadcast,

MY ATTITUDE TOWARD JAPAN

That Japan's aggression toward China violated every
moral code and every international agreement needs no explanation.   Since I dealt with it in 1932, their militarists
had expanded, their ideas into the realm of "Asia for the
Asiatics," with Japan in leadership.   All this was unpalatable
enough to decent nations and also was threatening to the white
man's interests in the East.   I never believed Japan could
succeed over the years because seventy millions of hated egotists
could not for long dominate one billion people.   The question
in my mind was twofold: First, whether America should go on
a crusade to correct this wrong at all, but second- and much
more immediate - whether we should undertake it in view of
the dangers from Europe and thus invite war on two fronts.
Without resolving the first question, the latter was to me the
utmost folly.   If the job had to be done, it should await
the end of the war in Europe when the other white races could
be mobilized for action against Japan instead of America's
carrying the entire burden and pulling the British, Russian,
Dutch and French chestnuts out of the fire at an enormous cost
in American lives and resources.   It was obvious that Japan
would not attack us unless provoked into it as a rat driven
into a corner.

A typewritten copy of the
handwritten draft "My Attitude
toward Japan" shown in preceding
photos (November 26, 1944).

-2-

Roosevelt, however, undertook a series of provocative actions, beginning early in 1940 and continuing
with increasing violence until both national pride and
national desperation led them to Pearl Harbor.   I believe
that the verdict of history will show that either Roosevelt
was wholly ignorant of Japanses psychology and thought he
could force Japan to submission with economic sanctions or
that despaired of getting the American people into the world
war on the European front, he was determined to provoke war
with Japan as the method of entry.

Roosevelt apparently never understood the impact
or violenceof "economic sanctions" and played with them like
the toys on his desk - or as I have said, deliberately
used them to provoke war.   He permitted Japan to drain
the scrap steel and oil which we badly needed for our
own preparedness in a dangerous world though the stopping
of which was not an economic sanction, and at the same time
he imposed economic embarrassments on Japan, all of which
would indicate a confused mind playing with power politics.

On February 1, 1939, in a nation-wide broadcast
I stated:

VOLUME III

Case Histories

EDITOR'S INTRODUCTION

As late as September 1961, Herbert Hoover planned to devote a section of the second volume of his Magnum Opus to a series of "case histories" of five countries that had fallen into ruin (or outright Communism) after World War II: China, Poland, Germany, Korea, and Japan. He subsequently decided to include these "tragic case histories" in a separate, third volume of the Magnum Opus.

Hoover seems to have quickly dropped Japan from his list. On the other four studies, however, he labored doggedly, in every instance producing more than one draft. Although not entirely free of rough edges by the time he stopped working on them, they had reached a sufficiently advanced state to merit publication. Accordingly, all four components of Hoover's projected third volume are printed here. They are presented in the order he intended. (See Appendix, Document 24.)

With the inclusion of these four case studies, Hoover's Magnum Opus assumes the shape he ultimately envisaged.

A Step-by-Step History of Poland

EDITOR'S NOTE: Hoover worked extensively on this case study in 1961 and completed it by early 1963, after at least seven drafts and revisions or "editions." On March 20, 1963 he sent a photocopied, typewritten copy (identified as the "Z" edition) to W. Glenn Campbell, the director of the Hoover Institution on War, Revolution and Peace. Hoover did not consider even this draft to be final; he hoped that one of Campbell's resident scholars—a Polish émigré—would read it and offer corrections.

So far as is known, Hoover did no further work on this edition of the manuscript, which may therefore be taken as his "last say" on the subject of Poland for the Magnum Opus. The "Z" text, as sent by him to Campbell, is accordingly the text printed here. The photocopied typescript is in the Herbert C. Hoover Papers, Box 102, in the Hoover Institution Archives.

For editing purposes I have treated Hoover's essay on Poland as an undivided entity. In the footnotes, therefore, full citations of sources are supplied only the first time and are not repeated in subsequent chapters.

PREFACE

MANY OF THE GREAT TRAGEDIES of history came to the world during the Second World War. Among them was the plunge of Poland into the Communist pit. Its narrative illuminates step-by-step the whole process of Communist conspiracy and aggression abetted by the weaknesses, the evasions, and the appeasement of Stalin by the leaders of the Western Democracies.

Over the years I had gained some familiarity with Poland and its problems. During the Czarist days, I crossed Poland by railway several times on journeys to and from Czarist Russia. They were depressing impressions unrelieved by the crops and verdure of the summer seasons. They were impressions of bleak plains, squalid homes, and drab cities.

In those times I knew none of the Polish leaders. But in 1917, a friendship began with Ignace Jan Paderewski which lasted for twenty-four years until his passing in 1941.

That year Paderewski came to Washington seeking President Wilson's aid for the independence of Poland. He came to see me and was my frequent guest.

He was one of the great geniuses of the twentieth century. He was not only the greatest musician of his time. He was a statesman and a surpassing orator in four languages.[1] He had been the leader in the cause of Polish freedom

---

1. My first glimpse of Paderewski was years before in 1893 or 1894. Two of my classmates and I at Stanford University, in order to augment our income, had organized a sort of entertainment enterprise. We sought out professional musicians, lecturers, and other notables visiting the West Coast, for whose appearances we could sell tickets to the faculty and our fellow students. We agreed upon a fee and usually made a profit as the University furnished free the assembly room, light, and heat. Upon learning of the impending visit to the West Coast of the great musician, we settled with his manager on a fee of $1500 and a date several weeks ahead. Unfortunately, our date turned out to be a University holiday and we had no hope of collecting the $1500 through the sale of tickets. Our collective assets were about one-tenth of this sum. We finally decided that the only thing to do was to

over many years before the First World War. He had financed his Committee for the Independence of Poland from his own earnings. It was Paderewski's coming to Washington that greatly stimulated President Wilson's interest in Poland's fight for her independence.

During the Peace Conference at Versailles in 1918–19, I was appointed by the Allied Powers to administer the relief and reconstruction of Europe. The relief of Poland during these conferences was a considerable task. It involved the delivery, mostly from the United States, of 419,162 tons of supplies at a cost of $134,191,223. Under the mandate of the Supreme Council I also had the job of reorganizing and administering the Polish coal mines, the railways, and waterways.

During the Peace Conference, Paderewski and his principal aide, Roman Dmowski, frequently requested my views on their problems.

After the signing of the peace, I directed the American Relief Administration until the harvest of 1923, when again the United States Government gave some assistance to this American voluntary charity, bringing to Poland an additional 331,757 tons of food and clothing and providing for the rehabilitation of about 1,973,000 debilitated children at a cost of $82,427,267.[2]

In August 1919, Prime Minister Paderewski appealed to President Wilson to come to Poland to confer with the Polish Cabinet on Poland's many problems and to make some addresses to lift the morale of the Polish people. The President could not go, but he requested me to do so.

I visited Warsaw,[3] Cracow, Lemberg, and other cities, making addresses which Mr. Paderewski translated. One of my speeches to several thousand

---

have a meeting with Paderewski's manager the moment he arrived in California and try to negotiate a settlement. We were in this meeting in the Palace Hotel with our $150 when Paderewski walked into the room and inquired what was going on. We explained our problem and said that we might possibly raise some more from the profits of future bookings. The manager had inquired into the details of our enterprise. He asked whether we had an office and a bank account. We confessed that our head office was on the pavement and that our meetings were held between classes. Paderewski laughed and proposed that we suspend the engagement until some future occasion when he was in the West. One of our members suggested we might not be able to do that as we might then have dissolved, and again offered our $150. Paderewski laughed again and said we would postpone that also. I recalled this episode to him when as Prime Minister I met him at the Peace Conference. He chuckled again.

2. These operations are given in detail in Herbert Hoover, *An American Epic* (Henry Regnery Company, Chicago: 1960, 1961, 1964), Vols. II, III, IV.

3. In Warsaw a most poignant reception was given me by the children. Some 50,000 of them had been brought in from the soup kitchens by the trainloads. They were organized into a march in front of an old race course grandstand. Ranging from five to fifteen years, often clad in rags and tatters, each carried a paper banner of American and Polish colors. Some brought banners with inscriptions addressed to me. They came by for hours—chattering, laughing, squealing, trying vainly to look sober and to maintain some sort of marching order. General Henri, the head of the French Military

Poles, only a few dozen of whom could understand English, lasted about ten minutes. After the Prime Minister had translated for about forty-five minutes I asked my Polish aide what he was talking about. The aide replied, "He is making a real speech." I also had several sessions with the Cabinet members and was able to secure for them additional American experts to those we had supplied during the Armistice period for their various government departments.

Nineteen years later, on a journey to appraise the rising danger of a second world war, I visited Poland as a guest of the Polish Government. At that time I had extended conferences with all of the principal Polish officials and with their industrial, professional, and labor leaders.[4]

In August 1939, Hitler and Stalin had formed their alliance and on September 1 [Germany–ed.] invaded Poland. The Second World War had begun. The Polish Government escaped to London under Prime Minister Wladyslaw Sikorski. He requested me to organize relief for his country. My old colleagues and I did so, but after about one year, during which about $6,000,000 was raised and supplies had been shipped, our work was stopped by the British blockade.

During the years until 1945 there were numerous occasions on which the Polish Ambassadors in Washington sought my views, Ambassador Jan Ciechanowski being the principal one among them.

In 1946, during the world-wide famine which followed the Second World War, President Truman had requested me to coordinate the nations of the world to meet the greatest famine in all history. I visited the then Communist Poland on this mission.

With this background I could not fail to have some understanding of the history of Poland, of its problems and its sufferings, and a great sympathy for this courageous and able people.[5]

Mission, stood near me with tears streaming down his face until, overcome with emotion, he left the stand. In parting, he said to me: "There has never been a review of honor in all history which I would prefer for myself to that which has been given you today."

4. An account of this visit is given in chapter [8–ed.] Section [II–ed.] of this Memoir.

5. The documented information on the fall of Poland is extraordinarily complete. The publications of the British, French and American Foreign Offices indicate no consequential suppressions. The documents of the German Foreign Office are available. The speeches and autobiographies and biographies of the leading participants are great in number and most revealing. In addition to this documentation, the Hoover Institution on War, Revolution and Peace at Stanford University is the depository of many unpublished documents, including the diary and papers of Hugh Gibson, former Ambassador to Poland, and the complete files of many of the Polish Legations after the Second World War.

CHAPTER A

The Resurrection of the Polish Nation

THIS MEMOIR IS CONCERNED chiefly with Poland during the Second World War and its aftermath, but for clarity to the reader it is desirable to reach briefly into the immediate past.

Prior to the Allied victory over the Central Powers in 1918, Poland for [more than–ed.] a hundred years had been partitioned between Russia, Germany and Austria. After America joined the war in 1917, President Wilson made his great call for lasting peace in his "Fourteen Points" and subsequent addresses. Prominent among his demands was the re-unification of Poland and the restoration of her independence.[1]

With the Allied victory in 1918, General Josef Pilsudski, a Polish officer in the Austrian army, brought together the Poles who were serving in the armies of Russia, Austria and Germany, and with them established a military government with himself as "chief of state." Pilsudski unwillingly consented to the Allied demands that Paderewski be the Prime Minister.

Paderewski at once called a constitutional convention and from it established a constitutional government in the parliamentary form. A score of political parties arose in Parliament representing the different pre-war partition states, ideological groups, together with representatives of landlords, peasants and labor. A majority party government was impossible, but Paderewski held these diverse elements together for a time by the fire of his patriotism and his magnificent oratory. After a year in office he received an adverse vote from Parliament, and on December 7, 1919, true to his democratic principles, he resigned as Premier. He left Poland, never revisited his country, and again resumed his profession as the greatest musician of his time.

---

1. For a full account of President Wilson's intervention on behalf of Poland, see [Herbert Hoover,] *The Ordeal of Woodrow Wilson* (McGraw-Hill Company, New York: 1958), p. 22.

Upon Paderewski's defeat, General Pilsudski established himself dictator. After Pilsudski's death in May 1936 [1935–*ed.*], the government of Poland was conducted by his "colonels" as a modified Fascist state, but with little restriction upon economic freedom.

Under the stimulating sunlight of independence and economic freedom, Poland during the twenty years from 1919 to 1939 made amazing economic and social progress. Her contributions to literature, art, and music spread over the earth.[2]

Related to Poland's background was the yielding by the British and the French to Hitler's demands at Munich on September 30, 1938 for the annexation of the Sudeten Germans from Czechoslovakia, a part of the agreement being a joint guarantee with Hitler of Czech independence. On March 15, 1939 Hitler violated this agreement and invaded Czechoslovakia. The Western Democracies took no action except verbal protests.

On March 21, 1939, Hitler demanded of Poland the return of Danzig to Germany and the reduction in the size of the Polish Corridor through Germany to the Baltic, which had been set at the Treaty of Versailles in 1919.

On March 25, 1939, the Polish Government replied, denying Hitler's claims and refusing any consequential concessions. Three days later the Prime Minister of Poland warned the German Ambassador in Warsaw against any German action involving Danzig.[3]

Six days later, on March 31, 1939, alarmed at Hitler's expanding aggressions, Prime Minister Chamberlain suddenly announced in the House of Commons that Great Britain would support Poland against Germany, saying:

> ... I now have to inform the House that during that period, in the event of any action which clearly threatened Polish independence, and which the Polish Government accordingly considered it vital to resist with their national forces, His Majesty's Government would feel themselves bound at once to lend the Polish Government all support in their power. They have given the Polish Government an assurance to this effect.

---

2. See chapter [8–*ed.*] of this memoir for my appraisal of Poland in 1938.

3. [Republic of] Poland, Ministerstwo spraw zagranicznych [Ministère des Affaires Étrangères], *Les relations polonc-allemandes et polono-soviétiques au cours de la période 1933–1939*, Flammarion, Paris: 1940, pp. 86–95; [Republic of Poland, Ministry of Foreign Affairs,] *Polish White Book* (London, 1940), pp. 56 ff.

I may add that the French Government have authorized me to make it plain that they stand in the same position in this matter as does His Majesty's Government.[4]

Chamberlain added that his government had urged the Poles to settle their differences with Germany by direct negotiations, and that he saw no occasion for threats. There was a momentary spasm of rejoicing in Britain and France that appeasement of Hitler was ended.

The practicability of militarily making good on the guarantees soon arose in the House of Commons by a question from Lloyd George. Churchill pointed up Lloyd George's question in a speech in the House of Commons on May 19, saying:

> ... His Majesty's Government have given a guarantee to Poland. I was as-tounded when I heard them give this guarantee. I support it, but I was astounded by it, because nothing that had happened before led one to sup-pose that such a step would be taken.... the question posed by [Mr. Lloyd George] ten days ago, and repeated today has not been answered. The ques-tion was whether the General Staff was consulted before this guarantee was given as to whether it was safe and practical to give it, and whether there were any means of implementing it. The whole country knows that the question has been asked, and it has not been answered....[5]

With the announcement of Hitler's demands on Poland, and the British-French guarantees of her independence, ominous lightning at once flashed from every capital in the world.

President Roosevelt Takes a Hand

President Roosevelt had on January 4, 1939 announced what amounted to a revolution in American foreign policy. He proposed action by the United States "stronger than words and less than war" on activities of foreign nations with which he disagreed.

The President at once took action under this new policy with respect to Hitler's demand of March 21, 1939 on Poland.[6]

---

4. Great Britain, Parliament, House of Commons, *Parliamentary Debates*, Official Report (Han-sard), 5th ser., v. 345, Cols. 2415ff.

5. *Poland in the British Parliament, 1939–1945*, Vol. 1, p. 76, Joseph Pilsudski Institute of America [for Research in the Modern History of Poland], compiled by Waclaw Jedrzejewicz, Director, New York, 1946.

6. chapter 19, Section IV [of *Freedom Betrayed*].

On March 24, 1939, Lord Halifax records a conversation with Ambassador to Britain Joseph P. Kennedy, in which Mr. Kennedy asked "whether His Majesty's Government and France really meant business."[7] He urged firmness.

The German Ambassador [Chargé d'Affaires–*ed.*] in London had earlier confirmed Kennedy's activities by informing his government on March 20 that:

> . . . Kennedy, the United States Ambassador here, is playing a leading part. He is said to be in personal contact with the Missions of all the States involved, and to be attempting to encourage them to adopt a firm attitude by promising that the United States . . . would support them by all means ("short of war").[8]

Further American activities were disclosed after the Germans had invaded Poland in September 1939 and seized the Polish Foreign Office records. The Germans released a mass of documents which certainly indicated that the American Ambassador to France, William C. Bullitt, who could act only on Mr. Roosevelt's authority, had made a profusion of oral assurances to officials of Poland and France which they could only interpret as a promise of assistance of some kind of force from the United States. These statements by Bullitt were contained in numerous dispatches from Polish Ambassadors abroad to their Foreign Ministers [Ministry?–*ed.*] in Warsaw.[9]

When published, these documents were denounced as fabrications by Ambassador Bullitt, by Count Jerzy Potocki, the Polish Ambassador to Washington, and by our State Department. But subsequently the Polish Ambassador informed me that the documents were genuine and that he had denied their authenticity at the request of the State Department.

However, more convincing than these denials, the files of the Polish Embassy in Washington were given to the Hoover Institution at Stanford University. A new translation showed only minor differences from the German publications. There were many of these documents—too long to reproduce here. A typical paragraph in one of Polish Ambassador Potocki's dispatches

---

7. [Great Britain, Foreign Office,] *Documents on British Foreign Policy,* [*1919–1939,*] 3rd Series, Vol. IV, [His Majesty's Stationery Office, London: 1951,] p. 499.

8. [U.S. Department of State,] *Documents on German Foreign Policy, 1918–1945,* Series D, Vol. VI, *The Last Months of Peace, March–August 1939* [United States Government Printing Office, Washington: 1956], p. 51.

9. For comment by German officials in the United States, see [U.S. Department of State,] *Documents on German Foreign Policy,* [*1918–1945,*] Series D, Vol. IX, [*The War Years, March 19–June 22, 1940*] (United States Government Printing Office, Washington: 1956), pp. 45, 48, 225, 281, 624.

to the Polish Foreign Office, dated January 16, 1939, nearly two months before the guarantees, reads:

> From the conversation with Bullitt I obtained the impression that he received from President Roosevelt a clear definition of the United States' attitude in the present European crisis which he will be presenting to the Quai d'Orsay and using in his conversations with European statesmen. The contents of these directions as outlined by Bullitt in his half an hour conversation with me, included the following: 1) the activation under President Roosevelt's direction of the [American] foreign policy which in an unequivocal and sharp manner condemns the totalitarian states. 2) the war preparations of the United States on land, sea and air, which will proceed in an accelerated tempo and will cost the colossal sum of $1,250,000,000. 3) the definite opinion of the President that France and Britain should abandon all policy of compromise with the totalitarian countries and should not enter into any discussion with them which might be directed towards any territorial changes. 4) a moral assurance that the United States is abandoning the policy of isolation and is ready, in case of war, to participate actively on the side of Great Britain and France, placing all its resources, financial and in raw materials, at their disposal.[10]

Another of the documents, a dispatch from Polish Ambassador Juljusz Lukasiewicz in Paris addressed to the Polish Foreign Office in Warsaw, dated February 1, 1939, two months before the guarantees, states:

> . . . In case of war, the participation of the United States in this war on the side of France and Britain is foreseen in advance—of course, a certain time after its outbreak. As Ambassador Bullitt puts it: "If a war breaks out, we probably would not participate in it at the beginning, but we would finish it." . . . For the time being I should like to refrain from formulating my own opinion of Ambassador Bullitt's statements. . . . One thing, however, seems to be certain, namely, that President Roosevelt's policy in the immediate future will tend to support France's resistance, to stay the German-Italian pressure and to weaken Britain's tendencies towards a compromise [over Poland].[11]

---

10. [Germany, Auswärtiges Amt,] *The German White Paper* ([Howell, Soskin and Company,] New York, 1940), Document No. 7, pp. 32–33. (Translation by the German Foreign Office). [*Editor's note:* The English translation of this document, as quoted in the text, differs somewhat from the translation as it appears in the source cited by Hoover in this footnote. Evidently he had a variant translation from an unknown source. The differences in phraseology do not appear to be material as to meaning.]

11. Ibid., Document No. 9, pp. 43–45. (Translation by the German Foreign Office). [*Editor's note:* See the editor's note in the preceding footnote. It applies to note 11 as well.]

The documentation of our State Department on these matters is as yet un-disclosed. But about this time Mr. Roosevelt told several visitors at the White House that he was having difficulty keeping Chamberlain's back stiff. This was [later–*ed.*] confirmed to me by Ambassador Kennedy, who said that he was instructed to "put a poker up Chamberlain's back and to make him stand up."

A further confirmation is a passage from the diaries of James Forrestal, then Under Secretary of the Navy, as follows:

> . . . I asked him [Kennedy] about his conversations with Roosevelt and Nev-ille Chamberlain from 1938 on. He said Chamberlain's position in 1939 was that England had nothing with which to fight and that she could not risk going to war with Hitler. Kennedy's view: That Hitler would have fought Rus-sia without any later conflict with England if it had not been for Bullitt's . . . urging on Roosevelt in the summer of 1939 that the Germans must be faced down about Poland; neither the French nor the British would have made Po-land a cause of war if it had not been for the constant needling from Washing-ton. Bullitt, he said, kept telling Roosevelt that the Germans wouldn't fight, Kennedy that they would, and that they would overrun Europe. . . . In his telephone conversation with Roosevelt in the summer of 1939 the President kept telling him to put some iron up Chamberlain's backside. Kennedy's re-sponse always was that putting iron up his backside did no good unless the British had some iron with which to fight, and they did not. . . .
>
> What Kennedy told me in this conversation jibes substantially with the remarks Clarence Dillon had made to me already, to the general effect that Roosevelt had asked him in some manner to communicate privately with the British to the end that Chamberlain should have greater firmness in his deal-ings with Germany. Dillon told me that at Roosevelt's request he had talked with Lord Lothian in the same general sense as Kennedy reported Roosevelt having urged him to do with Chamberlain. Lothian presumably was to com-municate to Chamberlain the gist of his conversation with Dillon.[12]
>
> (Forrestal was slightly wrong in his dates as the Polish guarantee was at the end of March 1939, not in "the summer of 1939.")

Although Mr. Roosevelt had not at this time entered into any actual agree-ment to join the war on the side of Britain and France, in its least dimensions the President's venture into "action more than words" would give confidence

---

12. *The Forrestal Diaries*, Walter Millis, ed. (The Viking Press, New York: 1951), pp. 121–122. [*Edi-tor's note:* The date of Forrestal's diary entry and conversation with Joseph P. Kennedy was December 27, 1945. Hoover's phraseology in the text may give the impression that Forrestal was Under Secretary of the Navy in 1939. This is incorrect. Forrestal was not appointed to that position until mid-1940.]

to Chamberlain and Daladier of some kind of realistic American aid. In European terms, "aid" meant anything from supplies to troops.

Within a week after they had announced their guarantee to Poland, the British sought an alliance with Stalin.[13] The French negotiated separately as, presumably, they had a more favorable relationship with Stalin than with the British because of their military alliance with Russia.[14] One of the unanswered questions of history is, why did not the British and French seek this alliance prior to the making of the guarantee? One of the certainties of international relations was that Stalin then automatically became the master of the situation by the sale of his favor to the highest bidder.

Stalin's asking price for an alliance with the Allies gradually emerged from Prime Minister Chamberlain's statements before the House of Commons on May 10, May 19, and June 7, 1939.[15] Stalin's price was the annexation of Finland, Estonia, Latvia, Lithuania, East Poland, Bessarabia, and Bukovina, which had been a part of Russia prior to the First World War. The Baltic States, anxiously watching the negotiations, themselves confirmed part of the price by their public protests.

Churchill, Lloyd George, and Eden continued their violent attacks on Prime Minister Chamberlain. On May 19, 1939, Churchill, in the House of Commons, demanded that the Russian terms be accepted.[16] In this he was supported by Lloyd George and Eden.

With Prime Minister Chamberlain's moral scruples against selling the freedom of peoples, he had nothing to offer Stalin except the assurance that, by an alliance with them, he would be more safe from attack by Hitler. On August 11, the last of the British and French missions which had been sent to Russia returned empty-handed.

Hitler also became a bidder for Stalin's favor, despite all of his long denunciations of Communism and his *idée fixe* of destroying the Communist government of Russia, and despite his determination to secure German territorial expansion at Russia's expense. These negotiations were carried on by Molotov and the German Ambassador to Moscow, Count Frederich von der Schulenburg. Hitler waxed hot and cold. His hesitation apparently was partly due to his uncertainty as to whether the Allies would fight.[17]

---

13. The details of these negotiations can be found in [Great Britain, Foreign Office,] *Documents on British Foreign Policy*, 3rd Series, Vols. V and VI [His Majesty's Stationery Office, London: 1952 and 1953]. Therefore I do not give the authority for each incident discussed.

14. *Documents on British Foreign Policy*, 3rd Series, Vol. V, p. 273.

15. See *Poland in the British Parliament, 1939–1945*, Vol. I, pp. 54–58, 62–89, 95–98.

16. Ibid, pp. 71–78.

17. Paul Schmidt, *Hitler's Interpreter* [The Macmillan Company, New York: 1951], p. 132.

Suddenly, on August 14, Hitler seemingly became alarmed at the Allied attitudes, and instructed von Schulenburg to push negotiations with Stalin, giving him elaborate instructions.[18] Although the negotiations were proceeding, Hitler wanted greater haste, and on August 20 sent a personal telegram to Stalin accepting the Russian terms and suggesting that von Ribbentrop go to Moscow at once.[19]

On August 21, a press announcement from Moscow stated that a non-aggression pact was to be signed by von Ribbentrop and Molotov. By a secret protocol Hitler had agreed to Stalin's re-annexation of the seven pre-First World War Russian states (which included eastern Poland)—and their independence of the previous twenty-one years was to be snuffed out. Also, a joint invasion and division of Poland was agreed upon and Hitler was to have a free hand in the conquest of Europe.[20]

---

18. For further evidence of Hitler's vacillations see [U.S. Department of State,] *Nazi-Soviet Relations*, [*1939–1941*] [U.S. Government Printing Office, Washington: 1948], pp. 15, 60, 66, 67ff.

19. On August 22, two days after his acceptance of the Russian terms, Hitler made a ferocious speech to his military commanders regarding his intentions. Thanks to the German habit of taking shorthand notes, we have this record of his speech:

"Our strength is in our quickness and our brutality. Ghengis Khan had millions of women and children killed by his own will and with a gay heart. History sees only in him a great state builder. What weak Western European civilization thinks about me does not matter. . . . I have sent to the East only my 'Death's Head Units' with the order to kill without pity or mercy all men, women, and children of Polish race or language. Only in such a way will we win the vital space that we need. Who still talks nowadays of the extermination of the Armenians?

". . . Poland will be depopulated and colonized with Germans. My pact with Poland was only meant to stall for time. And besides, gentlemen, in Russia will happen just what I have practiced with Poland. After Stalin's death (he is seriously ill), we shall crush the Soviet Union. . . .

"The occasion is favorable now as it has never been. I have only one fear and that is that Chamberlain or such another dirty swine comes to me with propositions or a change of mind. He will be thrown downstairs. . . .

"No, for this it is too late. The invasion and the extermination of Poland begins on Saturday morning. I will have a few companies in Polish uniform attack in Upper Silesia or in the Protectorate. Whether the world believes it doesn't mean a damn to me. The world believes only in success.

"Glory and honor are beckoning to you. . . . Be hard. Be without mercy. Act quicker and more brutally than the others. The citizens of Western Europe must quiver in horror. That is the most human warfare for it scares them off. . . ." ([Office of United States Chief of Counsel for Prosecution of Axis Criminality,] *Nazi Conspiracy and Aggression* [United States Government Printing Office, Washington: 1946], Volume VII, pp. 753–754).

20. The actual signed document became public when the Allies seized the German Foreign Office documents at the German surrender in May, 1945. I saw the original in Berlin in April 1946. A month later, at the Nurnberg trials, it was offered in evidence by the Germans but on Russian objection it was disallowed. However, on October 19 it was published in London. In 1948 the American Government officially released it.

In the midst of the bidding for alliances with Stalin, the British, anxious to avoid war, attempted to reach an understanding directly with Hitler. During May, June and July (1939) there had been a number of meetings of second-string British and German officials in which they tried to work out some accord.

On August 22, Chamberlain addressed a letter directly to Hitler. The Prime Minister (probably at this moment unaware of the terms of the Stalin-Hitler alliance) proposed a truce, a simple guarantee of independence to Poland by all the powers, a settlement of German claims, and of German wishes for colonial outlets. He continued:

> ... At this moment I confess I can see no other way to avoid a catastrophe that will involve Europe in war. . . .[21]

Hitler's reply on August 23 (the day he signed the pact with Stalin) was scarcely encouraging.

Chamberlain and Daladier had every right to righteous indignation. In a speech to the House of Commons, August 24, 1939, Chamberlain said:

> ... today we find ourselves confronted with the imminent peril of war. . . .
>
> ... I do not attempt to conceal from the House that that announcement [the Hitler-Stalin pact–ed.] came to the Government as a surprise. . . .
>
> ... discussions [between British and French emissaries and the Soviet government–ed.] were actually in progress and had proceeded on a basis of mutual trust when this bombshell was flung down. It, to say the least of it, was highly disturbing to learn that while these conversations were proceeding on that basis, the Soviet Government were secretly negotiating a pact with Germany. . . .[22]

On August 25, Hitler, either in his usual pursuit of perfidy or out of fear of Allied attack, sent for the British Ambassador in Berlin, Sir Nevile Henderson, and indicated that he would be satisfied by the annexation of Danzig and a settlement of the Polish Corridor question. He declared he did not want war

---

The probable explanation of the Soviet objection at Nurnberg is that the Russians, having joined at Nurnberg in establishing *ex post facto* Nazi crimes by which aggression became punishable by death, did not wish so obvious a conviction of themselves to be placed on record.

21. [Great Britain, Foreign Office,] *The British War Blue Book* [Farrar & Rinehart, New York: 1939], p. 127. See [U.S. Department of State,] *Documents on German Foreign Policy, 1918–1945*, Series D, 1937–1945, Vol. VII, *The Last Days of Peace, [August 9–September 3,] 1939* (United States Government Printing Office, Washington: 1956), p. 216.

22. [Great Britain, Parliament,] House of Commons, *Parliamentary Debates*, Vol. 351, Cols. 3ff.

with Britain. His demand for restoration of the ex-German colonies was not too emphatic; he suggested negotiation of that issue.[23]

On the same day a mutual assistance agreement was signed by Poland and Britain. The text of this treaty was not published in London until six years later—April 5, 1945.[24]

The French Ambassador in Berlin handed Hitler a letter from Prime Minister Daladier dated August 26, 1939. Both Chamberlain and Daladier sought to stay Hitler's hand by notifying him that they would fight if Poland were invaded.[25] Hitler then postponed his attack.[26]

On August 28, the British replied to Hitler's proposals. They accepted the idea of negotiating British-German colonial questions, urged direct settlement between Germany and Poland as a necessary preliminary step, and indicated that British interest in that matter was only to assure the independence of the Polish state, implying that they were no longer interested in the limited problems of Danzig and the Corridor.

On August 29, Hitler handed the British Ambassador in Berlin a long but generally amiable note, stating that the Germans would put their conditions in writing to the Poles.

On August 30, the British replied accepting Hitler's proposals regarding Poland.[27] The Poles consented to negotiate on the questions of the Corridor and Danzig, subject to the condition that no troops cross their borders pending the negotiation.

On August 31, German Foreign Minister von Ribbentrop told the British Ambassador in Berlin that Germany had asked the Polish government to send an authorized negotiator to Berlin at once. The Polish government instructed their Ambassador in Berlin to contact von Ribbentrop, which he did. Von Ribbentrop later stated that the terms he was prepared to offer the Poles included the provisions that Danzig go to the Reich, and that a plebiscite be held in the Corridor for its division, with communications guaranteed for both Poles and Germans across the Corridor, exchange of minority nationals,

---

23. *Poland in the British Parliament*, Vol. I, pp. 182–183.

24. See *Polish White Book*, pp. 100–102; *New York Times*, April 6, 1945.

25. Schmidt, *Hitler's Interpreter*, pp. 141–145. Also see International Military Trials, Nurnberg, *Nazi Conspiracy and Aggression*, Vol. VIII, pp. 529–530. [*Editor's note:* See note 19 for the full citation.]

26. This is confirmed from the captured German documents after the war. See *Nazi Conspiracy and Aggression*, Vol. VIII, pp. 534, 535–536. Goering, in his testimony at Nurnberg, stated [p. 534–*ed.*] "... the Fuehrer called me on the telephone and told me that he had stopped the planned invasion of Poland. I asked him then whether this was just temporary or for good. He said, "No, I will have to see whether we can eliminate British intervention." So then I asked him, "Do you think that it will be any different within four or five days?"

27. *The British War Blue Book*, Doc. 89, p. 184f.

and a suggestion that the British would consider colonial questions with Hitler. If these terms were accepted the armies were to be demobilized.

According to von Ribbentrop, when the Polish Ambassador came to him, the Ambassador was without authority to sign and therefore the "negotiator did not arrive," although the Germans waited "two days in vain."

Prime Minister Chamberlain, on September 1, made a speech in the House of Commons bearing on Hitler's treachery in their last moment negotiations for a settlement with him, saying:

> ... To begin with let me say that the text of these proposals has never been communicated by Germany to Poland at all. ...
>
> ... Germany claims to treat Poland as in the wrong because she had not by Wednesday night entered upon discussions with Germany about a set of proposals of which she had never heard.
>
> ... [that night at 9:15 P.M.] Herr von Ribbentrop produced a lengthy document which he read out in German aloud, at top speed. Naturally, after this reading our Ambassador asked for a copy of the document, but the reply was that it was now too late, as the Polish representative had not arrived in Berlin by midnight. ...[28]

In addressing the French Chamber of Deputies the next day, Premier Daladier reported that Hitler had agreed on August 31 to hold direct negotiations with Poland; that at one o'clock that afternoon the Polish Ambassador to Germany, M. Lipski, had requested a meeting with von Ribbentrop, but he was not received until 7:45 P.M. Von Ribbentrop refused to give him the German proposals on the pretext that the Ambassador did not have power to direct negotiations.

Daladier continued:

> At 9 P.M. the German wireless was communicating the nature and the full extent of these claims; it added that Poland had rejected them. That is a lie. That is a lie, since Poland did not even know them.
>
> And at dawn on September 1 the Führer gave his troops the order to attack. Never was aggression more unmistakable and less warranted. ...[29]

On September 1 Hitler invaded Poland, and Stalin followed a few days later. The combined German and Russian armies completed the conquest of

---

28. James W. Gantenbein, [ed.,] *Documentary Background of World War II, 1931 to 1941* (Columbia University Press, New York: 1948), pp. 404–405.

29. Ibid., p. 528.

Poland in less than a month. The Polish military machine of 600,000 men proved to be made of brave men with inferior equipment and incompetent generals. It is doubtful if the Germans and Russians lost more than 30,000 men in the invasion.

Stalin promptly deported some 250,000 military captives to Siberian work camps. He also deported 1,500,000 Polish civilians to Siberia.[30] Hitler seized several hundred thousand military prisoners and civilians for his work camps, and began the systematic extermination of the great Jewish community in Poland.

General Wladyslaw Anders, in his book, *An Army In Exile,* states:

> I tried to assess the real figure of Polish citizens deported in 1939–41, but it was extremely difficult to do so. I questioned the Soviet authorities. Eventually I was directed to Fiedotov, an N.K.V.D. general who was in charge of this matter, and I had a few conversations with him. He told me in a most confidential manner that the number of Poles deported to Russia amounted to 475,000. It turned out, however, that this figure did not include all those arrested while crossing the frontier or soldiers taken prisoner in 1939. All people arrested on account of their political activities, or Ukrainians, White Russians and Jews, indeed all Polish citizens belonging to racial minorities, were considered to be Soviet citizens. After many months of research and enquiries among our people, who were pouring from thousands of prisons and concentration camps spread all over Russia, we were able to put the number at 1,500,000 to 1,600,000 people. Statistics obtained afterwards from Poland confirmed these figures. But unfortunately it was clear that most of these poor people were no longer alive. God only knows how many of them were murdered, and how many died under the terrible conditions of the prisons and forced labour camps.[31]

The Polish Ministry retreated from Poland and established itself as a Government in Exile in Paris on September 30, 1939, and later in London, with General Wladyslaw Sikorski as Prime Minister. The Polish Ministry had escaped through Rumania, carrying with them the gold reserve of their National Bank of some $40,000,000 but the burden was too great and they were compelled to leave about $3,000,000 in Bucharest.

---

30. Stanislaw Mikolajczyk, *The Rape of Poland* (McGraw Hill Book Company, Inc., New York: 1948), p. 14. See also Lt. General W[ladyslaw] Anders, *Hitler's Defeat in Russia* (Henry Regnery Company, Chicago: 1953).

31. Wladyslaw Anders, *An Army in Exile* ([Macmillan & Co., Ltd., London:] 1949), p. 69.

Many Polish civilians escaped through Rumania and Hungary and were organized by their exiled government into an army to assist the Allies. The Poles in Poland, supported by the exiled Polish government, organized a vigorous underground to keep up opposition to the German and Russian invaders.

In October 1939, General Sikorski requested me to again organize relief for the people of Poland. I set up the Commission for Polish Relief from among my colleagues of the First World War under the leadership of Chauncey McCormick and Maurice Pate. We succeeded in delivering about six million dollars worth of supplies, financed by a million-dollar grant from the Polish Government in Exile and a large response from the American people. The Polish Government in Exile also assigned to us the gold left at Bucharest.[32] We carried on substantial relief in Poland until Mr. Churchill imposed a blockade on German-held areas, which ultimately brought our work to an end.[33]

Stalin lost little time in occupying Estonia and Latvia. On a pretext of mutual assistance, within sixty days he placed Communist garrisons in their cities, and in June 1940 he finally took over their governments. In the same month, also under the guise of mutual assistance, he seized Bessarabia and Bukovina from Rumania.

---

32. The Bank of Rumania in Bucharest refused to hand over the $3,000,000 to us. We garnisheed the balances of that bank here in New York and received a favorable judgment from the Court, but the war intervened and we were unable to collect the judgment. The action was compromised after the war by our receiving an amount to cover the Commission's outstanding liabilities.
33. The details of this effort appear in *An American Epic*, Volume IV.

CHAPTER B

Hope Comes to the Polish People Again

IN JUNE 1941, Hitler violated his alliance with Stalin and attacked Russia. In the course of this attack the Germans invaded and occupied all of Poland. Communist Russia, seeking every military support against Hitler, now turned to the creation of an army from her Polish military prisoners and civilians then in Siberia. As a first step, on July 30, 1941, Prime Minister Sikorski, with the aid of the British, signed a treaty with Russia providing for the establishment of diplomatic relations between Russia and Poland. The Poles construed this treaty to mean the abandonment of any annexations by Russia as one of its provisions stated:

> The Government of the Union of Soviet Socialist Republics recognizes the Soviet-German treaties of 1939 as to territorial changes in Poland as having lost their validity. The Polish Government declares that Poland is not bound by any Agreement with any third Power which is directed against the U.S.S.R.[1]

Prime Minister Churchill and Foreign Secretary Anthony Eden were present at the signing. Eden emphasized the non-annexation provision by saying in a formal note to the Polish Exiled Government the same day:

> ... I also desire to assure you that His Majesty's Government do not recognize any territorial changes which have been effected in Poland since August, 1939.[2]

---

1. *Poland in the British Parliament, 1939–1945*, Vol. I, pp. 471–472.
2. Ibid., p. 473.

On August 1, 1941 our State Department declared that the Russian-Polish agreement was in line with the American policy of non-recognition of territory taken by conquest.[3]

Also on August 1, Prime Minister Sikorski stated in a speech that the pact of July 30 had definitely restored the independence of Poland. However, the Soviet press at once announced that Sikorski's interpretation of the pact was not necessarily correct.

On August 12, the Russians issued an amnesty to all Polish prisoners—both military and civilian. Two days later detailed arrangements for the new Polish army in Russia were completed. General Wladyslaw Anders, now released from a Moscow prison, was placed in command. The exiled Polish Government in London announced that at this time 181,000 Polish prisoners of war were in Siberian prison camps, including about 10,000 officers and some 1,400,000 Polish civilians.

Great Assurances Come to Poland

On August 14, 1941, President Roosevelt and Prime Minister Churchill, on a battleship off Newfoundland, promulgated the Atlantic Charter. The Charter was patterned upon the "Fourteen Points" of Woodrow Wilson, which twenty-three years before had sounded the call for the freedom of Poland. The Charter stated:

> ... their countries seek no aggrandizement, territorial or other;
> ... they desire to see no territorial changes that do not accord with the freely expressed wishes of the peoples concerned;
> ... they respect the right of all peoples to choose the form of government under which they will live; and they wish to see sovereign rights and self-government restored to those who have been forcibly deprived of them. ...

To the despairing Poles here was an assurance from America and Britain of the restoration of their independence and freedoms.

On September 4, 1941, Mr. Roosevelt signed a further assurance to Poland by a declaration making the Exiled Polish Government eligible for Lend-Lease supplies and again giving the reassurance of the Atlantic Charter. It said:

> ... the gallant resistance of the forces of the Government of Poland is vital to the defense of the United States. ... this action demonstrated our intention

---

3. *New York Times,* August 1, 1941. See also [William L.] Langer and [S. Everett] Gleason, *The Undeclared War* [Harper & Brothers Publishers, New York: 1953], p. 556.

to give material support to the fighting determination of the Polish people to establish once again the independence of which they were so inhumanly deprived.[4]

At a meeting at St. James['s–*ed.*] Palace in London on September 24, 1941, the Atlantic Charter was reaffirmed by representatives of Britain and Russia. Ambassador Ciechanowski reported:

> ... representatives of all the Allies took part in it. . . . the Soviet Union was represented by Mr. Maisky, its Ambassador to the Court of St. James's, and by Mr. Bogomolov, Soviet Ambassador to Poland. . . .
>
> Ambassador Maisky in an inspiring speech declared, on behalf of the Soviet Union, that it "was, and is, guided in its foreign policy by the principle of self-determination of nations.
>
> "Accordingly," he continued, "the Soviet Union defends the right of every nation to the independence and territorial integrity of its country, and its right to establish such a social order and to choose such a form of government as it deems opportune and necessary for the better promotion of its economic and cultural prosperity."
>
> Maisky went on denouncing "all and any attempts of aggressive Powers to impose their will upon other peoples," and stressed the fact that the Soviet Union has been and still is "striving for a radical solution of the problem of safeguarding freedom-loving peoples against all the dangers they encounter from aggressors."

After which Maisky solemnly declared the acceptance of, and adherence to, the Atlantic Charter in the following words:

> *"In accordance with a policy inspired by the above principles . . . the Soviet Government proclaims its agreement with the fundamental principles of the declaration of Mr. Roosevelt, President of the United States, and of Mr. Churchill, Prime Minister of Great Britain—principles which are so important in the present international circumstances."*

Mr. Eden then put the following resolution. . . .

> *The Governments of Belgium, Czechoslovakia, Greece, Luxembourg, the Netherlands, Norway, Poland, Union of Soviet Socialist Republics, and Yugoslavia, and the representatives of General de Gaulle, leader of free Frenchmen,*

---

4. Jan Ciechanowski, *Defeat in Victory* (New York: Doubleday & Company, Inc., 1947), p. 55.

Having taken note of the Declaration recently drawn up by the President of the United States and by the Prime Minister, Mr. Churchill. . . .

Now make known their adherence to the common principles of policy set forth in that Declaration and their intention to cooperate to the best of their ability in giving effect to them.

Through this conveniently forgotten document . . . at that meeting at St. James's Palace, Soviet Russia's formal adherence to the Atlantic Charter was officially declared.[5]

In the midst of these great hopes, the Poles received a jolt to their interpretation of the Treaty of July 30, 1941—a month old. An official Soviet note handed to the Polish Ambassador to Russia on December 1st questioned the Polish citizenship of a large number of civilians who had been deported to Siberia, saying:

> . . . in accordance with the decree of the Presidium of the Supreme Council of the USSR . . . all citizens of the western districts of the Ukrainian and White Ruthenian SSR . . . acquired the citizenship of the USSR. . . . The Soviet Government's readiness to recognize as Polish citizens persons of Polish origin . . . gives evidence of good will and compliance on the part of the Soviet Government, but can in no case serve as a basis for an analogous recognition of the Polish citizenship of persons of other origin, in particular, those of Ukrainian, White Ruthenian, or Jewish origin, since the question of the frontiers between the USSR and Poland has not been settled and is subject to settlement in the future. . . .

Ambassador Ciechanowski observes:

> In this way the specific Soviet interpretation of the clauses of the Atlantic Charter, in which it was clearly stated that the United Nations would seek no territorial aggrandizement, had been officially defined.[6]

On December 1, 1941, Prime Minister Sikorski went to Moscow where he joined with General Anders in smoothing out various frictions over the new Polish army and the released civilian prisoners. General Anders had been able to find only about 40,000 Polish military prisoners, and he had difficulties in securing supplies and arms from the Russians. He asked for information on

---

5. Ibid., pp. 50–51. [*Editor's note:* Italics Ciechanowski's.]
6. Ibid., p. 80.

the thousands of Polish officers who had been taken prisoners. Stalin stated that they must have escaped from Siberia to Chinese Manchuria.[7]

Sikorski proposed that the Polish civilian prisoners should be evacuated to Iran, where the Allied governments had agreed to look after them. The Russians refused.[8] Nevertheless, Sikorski and Stalin signed a joint declaration on December 4, apparently settling their difficulties. The key paragraphs were:

> ... Implementing the Treaty concluded on July 30, 1941, both Governments will render each other during the war full military assistance, and troops of the Republic of Poland located on the territory of the Soviet Union will wage war against the German brigands shoulder to shoulder with Soviet troops.
>
> In peace-time their mutual relations will be based on good neighborly collaboration, friendship and reciprocal honest fulfillment of the obligations they have taken upon themselves.[9]

Three days after this agreement, on December 7, the United States, attacked by the Japanese at Pearl Harbor, entered the war. Soon thereafter both the United States and Soviet Russia gave recognition to the Exiled Polish Government.

---

7. Ibid., pp. 65–69.

8. [Republic of Poland, Embassy in Washington,] *Polish-Soviet Relations, 1918–1943* [Washington: 1943]. See also unpublished documents cited by Langer and Gleason, *The Undeclared War,* pp. 821–823.

9. *New York Times,* December 6, 1941; Stanislaw Mikolajczyk, *The Rape of Poland,* p. 261.

CHAPTER C

Reaffirmation of the Atlantic Charter

ON JANUARY 1, 1942, twenty-six United Nations—including the exiled Polish Government, Communist Russia, Britain, and the United States—met in Washington, reaffirmed their devotion to the Atlantic Charter, and agreed upon common action during the war, saying:

The Governments signatory hereto,

Having subscribed to a common program of purposes and principles embodied in the Joint Declaration of the President of the United States of America and the Prime Minister of the United Kingdom of Great Britain and Northern Ireland dated August 14, 1941, known as the Atlantic Charter,

Being convinced that complete victory over their enemies is essential to defend life, liberty, independence, and religious freedom, and to preserve human rights and justice in their own lands as well as in other lands, and that they are now engaged in a common struggle against savage and brutal forces seeking to subjugate the world, Declare:

(1) Each Government pledges itself to employ its full resources, military or economic, against those members of the Tri-partite Pact and its adherents with which such Government is at war.

(2) Each Government pledges itself to cooperate with the Governments signatory hereto and not to make a separate armistice or peace with the enemies.

The foregoing declaration may be adhered to by other Nations which are, or which may be, rendering material assistance and contributions in the struggle for victory over Hitlerism.

The Communists Again Begin Demands for Polish Territory

In January 1942 the British Foreign Minister, Anthony Eden, visited Moscow. The Polish Ambassador in Washington, Jan Ciechanowski, recorded:

> Mr. Eden's visit coincided with the first definite successes of the Soviet winter counteroffensive. I was informed that at the very moment when, in Washington, Mr. Churchill was signing the Declaration of the United Nations embodying the Atlantic Charter, Mr. Eden in Moscow was faced with the proposal of signing a Soviet-British-American treaty which, among other items, was to grant to Soviet Russia the territories of Finland acquired by force in the Russo-Finnish war of 1940, the entire territories of the three Baltic States, almost half of Poland, and the Rumanian provinces of Bukowina and Bessarabia.[1]

On February 25, 1942, Ambassador Ciechanowski and the Polish Minister of Foreign Affairs, Edward Raczynski, with these anxieties, called on President Roosevelt. The President gave them strong assurances, saying that:

> ... the British Government, through Churchill, had entirely co-ordinated its views with the American Government on the fundamental principle that that two governments would not agree to any territorial or political changes during the war.
>
> The President admitted, however, that, about two weeks before, the British Government had once more approached the American Government on the subject of the Baltic States.
>
> The President was frankly critical of this wavering attitude of the British Government. ...[2]

Ciechanowski notes

Our apprehensions ... were again revived when we were informed that the demands which Stalin had presented to Mr. Eden had not been finally rejected by the British Government. On the contrary, London was trying to persuade Washington to agree to participate in the conclusion of a tripartite agreement which would recognize Soviet territorial demands.[3]

---

1. Jan Ciechanowski, *Defeat in Victory*, p. 92.
2. Ibid., p. 95.
3. Ibid.

The Polish Ambassador was further disturbed when ten days later on March 7, 1942, at a meeting with the Acting Minister of Foreign Affairs of Poland, Edward Raczynski, and Lord Halifax:

> ... Lord Halifax ... brought forth a series of arguments in favor of acceptance of Moscow's claims. ...[4]

The apprehensions of the Polish Ambassador were quickly confirmed. The same day, Prime Minister Churchill addressed a cable to President Roosevelt, saying:

> ... The increasing gravity of the war has led me to feel that the principles of the Atlantic Charter ought not to be construed so as to deny Russia the frontiers she occupied when Germany attacked her. ...

He added:

> ... This was the basis on which Russia acceded to the Charter. ... I hope therefore that you will be able to give us a free hand to sign the treaty which Stalin desires as soon as possible. ...[5]

In spite of Mr. Churchill's statement, I can find no record that the Russians placed a limitation on their approval of the Atlantic Charter either when they affirmed it at St. James['s–ed.] Palace in September 1941, or at the ratification meeting of the United Nations in January 1942 in Washington.

Also on March 7, 1942, President Roosevelt wrote a memorandum to Sumner Welles in which he said:

> I think Sikorski should be definitely discouraged on this proposition. This is no time to talk about the post-war position of small nations, and it would cause serious trouble with Russia.[6]

The Polish Ambassador Ciechanowski records a conversation six days later on March 13, 1942, with the American Ambassador in London, John G. Winant, in which Winant commented:

> ... one should not forget that the Baltic States had been given their independence contrary to the will of Russia. Tsarist Russia had held these territories.

---

4. Ibid., p. 97.

5. Winston Churchill, *The Hinge of Fate* [Houghton Mifflin Company, Boston: 1950], p. 327.

6. [Elliott Roosevelt, ed.,] *F.D.R., His Personal Letters, 1928–1945*, Vol. II [Duell, Sloan and Pearce, New York: 1950], p. 1290.

As regards Poland, Stalin claimed territories only up to the Curzon Line, and his leading concern was Russia's security.[7]

Apparently, not wholly confident in the three specific ratifications of the Atlantic Charter by the Russians, General Sikorski, at a meeting with President Roosevelt on March 24, 1942, expressed fears as to the policies of Stalin and the Communists. Ambassador Ciechanowski's record of his interview was:

> [The President said] . . . emphatically that the United States Government was determined not to depart from its declared position of not admitting the settlement of any territorial issues in time of war. He said that at present the Soviet Government limited its demands to Estonia, Lithuania, and Latvia. However, should the Allies yield to pressure on this issue, it was certain that Russia would put forward further demands for territory of other countries: of Bukowina, Bessarabia, and Finland, possibly even Norway.
>
> "I want you to understand, General," said the President, "that the American Government has not forgotten the Atlantic Charter. As soon as Germany is defeated and disarmed, any threat to Russia from the Baltic will have vanished and the Soviet argument, based on anxiety for Russia's security, will become futile. I want you to know that I made this position quite clear to Stalin through Litvinov, and told him that it was too early to sit down to enjoy a cake before it was baked. I have received no answer from Stalin."
>
> When Sikorski drew the President's attention to the fact that it would not be sufficient for the United States to refuse its agreement to Moscow's claims because one had to reckon with the pressure of Moscow on London for an Anglo-Soviet treaty embodying these claims, President Roosevelt assured Sikorski that he was very strongly opposing the conclusion of any such treaty and that he intended to use all his influence to persuade the British Government to refrain from concluding a treaty on these lines.
>
> He felt confident that he would succeed in preventing the signing of such a treaty. In the President's opinion, Britain's conciliatory attitude was based on the fear that Russia might make some arrangement with the Germans, as she had in 1939. . . .[8]

On July 1, 1942, the Poles were given a special assurance of the benefits of the Atlantic Charter in a Lend-Lease agreement:

---

7. Ciechanowski, *Defeat in Victory*, p. 97.
8. Ibid., p. 100.

... whereas the Governments of the United States and Poland, as signatories of the Declaration by United Nations of January 2, 1942 ... [embracing] the purposes and principles ... known as the Atlantic Charter;

And whereas ... the defense of Poland against aggression is vital to the defense of the United States ... ;

... the United States ... will ... supply defense articles. ...[9]

On July 3, Attorney General Biddle stated in a broadcast to the people of Polish descent:

The framework of peace already has been drawn. It is proclaimed in the Atlantic Charter and endorsed by the United Nations.[10]

On the first birthday of the Atlantic Charter, August 14, 1942, Mr. Roosevelt said:

Now ... all the countries of the earth have ... formed a great union of humanity, dedicated to the realization of that common program of purposes and principles set forth in the Atlantic Charter. ...[11]

At this time, the Office of War Information, an official organ of the American government, was carrying propaganda by radio broadcasts, some of which was even directed to the people of Poland, favoring the Russian claims. Ambassador Ciechanowski protested, saying:

... some of the new war agencies actively conducted what could only be termed pro-Soviet propaganda.

So-called American propaganda broadcasts to occupied Poland were outstanding proofs of this tendency. Notorious pro-Soviet propagandists and obscure foreign communists and fellow travelers were entrusted with these broadcasts.

I protested repeatedly against the pro-Soviet character of such propaganda. ...

When I finally appealed to the Secretary of State ... protesting against the character of the OWI broadcasts to Poland, I was told that the State De-

---

9. *Department of State Bulletin*, [vol. 7,] July 4, 1942, [pp. 577–778.] [*Editor's note:* The quotation in Hoover's original manuscript contains several transcription errors. I have corrected these.]

10. *New York Times*, July 4, 1942. [*Editor's note:* Biddle's quotation does not appear in this source. Probably Hoover read this remark in another newspaper.]

11. *New York Times*, August 15, 1942.

partment was aware of these facts but could not control this agency, which boasted that it received its directives straight from the White House.[12]

General Sikorski again visited Washington in December, 1942. The Polish Ambassador records that at this time:

General Sikorski told the President that he was contemplating a second visit to Stalin to discuss all the accumulated difficulties. . . . He . . . added that he regarded one condition as essential to the success of this venture; namely, that he should have the full support of the President and that Stalin should be made aware of it.[13]

Sikorski asked for a letter from Roosevelt to Stalin which Roosevelt agreed to give. Ciechanowski states:

The general, naturally, was anxious that the wording of the letter should be as clear and unequivocal as possible and that the respect of Poland's territorial status should be specifically mentioned. The President pointed out that he could not go into "such detail, on account of the declared American policy of not discussing territorial issues during the war."[14]

---

12. Jan Ciechanowski, *Defeat in Victory,* pp. 130–131.
13. Ibid., p. 132.
14. Ibid.

CHAPTER D

Great Shocks Come to the Polish Leaders

THE POLISH AMBASSADOR on Washington records his last conversation with Sikorski (on January 10, 1943) at which time they reviewed Sikorski's visit:

> . . . Sikorski regretfully admitted that . . . for the first time he was beset by the fear that American policy was beginning to drift in the direction of appeasement of Soviet Russia. . . .[1]

Mr. Ciechanowski, nineteen days later, after an interview with Under Secretary Welles on January 29, 1943, records:

> . . . [Welles'] words showed me that American policy in relation to the USSR had reached a turning point. He had disclosed to me that appeasement was becoming the keynote of American policy toward the Soviets.[2]

Six days later, on February 5, Welles told the Polish Ambassador that he had made a very detailed report to the President. He said that:

> . . . The President considered the situation "so delicate and difficult" that he had asked Mr. Welles to impress upon me [Ciechanowski] that, in the circumstances, the Polish Government should not press him for immediate intervention. . . .
>
> In the meantime he told Mr. Welles to request me to tell General Sikorski and the Polish Government to "keep their shirt on."[3]

---

1. Ciechanowski, *Defeat in Victory*, p. 134.
2. Ibid., p. 141.
3. Ibid., p. 142.

The Ambassador notes that simultaneously there were increasing pressures by the Russians for partition of Poland, saying:

> The Soviet press and the bulletins of the Soviet Embassy in Washington began to publish numerous articles tending to show that the only just and fair boundary between Poland and the Soviet Union was the so-called Curzon Line.
>
> Thus, Soviet Russia was getting ready to carry out the annexation of nearly half of Poland. At the same time the Soviet Government was laying the foundations for the imposition upon Poland of a puppet government, completely subservient to Moscow, supported by an allegedly Polish armed force commanded by Red Army officers.[4]

This "Curzon Line" was never a recognized boundary. It was a compromise proposed by Lord Curzon and rejected at Versailles in 1919. It was proposed again when the Soviet armies invaded Poland in 1920. The Poles defeated the Russians in that war and restored their boundaries.

Eleven days later, on February 16, 1943, the Polish Ambassador was again received by Mr. Roosevelt. Of this interview Ciechanowski records:

> I . . . asked the President if he would allow me to be quite frank with him on this very serious occasion. . . . I told him that I believed American diplomacy had hitherto only superficially admitted the deep difference between Western and Soviet mentality. . . . It struck me that it had always been waiting for Stalin's further demands, and only then tried to find a way out, finally giving in to him in most matters. . . .
>
> I told the President . . . the territorial appetites of Russia . . . would [not] be satisfied even if the Western Powers were to agree to the annexation of the Baltic States, of part of Poland, of Bessarabia, and Bukowina. [Russian possession prior to the First World War.]
>
> . . . If no definitely negative attitude were encountered by Soviet Russia at this time, when her need of Allied assistance was so great and she was still so dependent on Allied support in war matériel and on a second front, what could one later interpose . . . ?
>
> The President . . . asked me whether I had definite suggestions to make.
>
> I replied . . .

---

4. Ibid., p. 150.

First, that for once an energetic joint American-British intervention be attempted in support of Poland, that it should be . . . sufficiently clear to convince Stalin that this time the United States and Britain were solemnly warning him that they would never agree to any violation of the fundamental principles . . . which the Soviets had accepted when they signed the Declaration of the United Nations [includes the Atlantic Charter].

Second, I thought it had become urgent for the President, and possibly also for Mr. Churchill, publicly to restate the principles of the Atlantic Charter and their unswerving determination to refuse to recognize any territorial changes brought about by force or threat of force during the war.

The President . . . replied that he . . . would like me to discuss them in greater detail with Sumner Welles.

I talked the matter over on the following day with Mr. Welles. . . .

One thing became clear in my mind, and I warned General Sikorski accordingly. We could not expect substantial support on the part of an American government which was pursuing a policy of appeasement of Russia. . . .[5]

At this stage, the Polish Ambassador observes:

. . . it was becoming painfully evident that there was little chance that this moral leadership would ever materialize.

. . . I feared that considerations of a political nature . . . would finally influence his [Roosevelt's] policy and direct it into channels of deals and compromise.

. . . I was becoming aware that official American policy, gradually but surely evolving into appeasement of Russia, had the support of White House circles and, at intervals, appeared to be directly inspired by them.[6]

On February 19, 1943, an article appeared in one of the official Soviet magazines assuming the Russian annexation of East Poland. On the 25th, the exiled Polish Government in London addressed a formal note to the Soviet Government, reciting the July 1941 agreement and repudiating any such contention. The Russians replied on March 2, again invoking the Curzon Line.

General Anders records that eight days later on March 10, General Sikorski protested to President Roosevelt, saying:

---

5. Ibid., pp. 144, 145, 147.
6. Ibid., pp. 147, 148, 151; R[oman] Umiastowski, *Poland, Russia and Great Britain* ([Hollis & Carter,] London: 1946), pp. 113ff.

"... My Government and myself wish to make it quite clear to you in what a terrible position we are placed by the latest Russian pronouncements. They ask us to fight side by side with Russia, while at the same time this very country is raising claims for half of our territory and one-third of our nation, and in her Note of the 16th of January reverts to the Ribbentrop-Molotov line". . . . Sikorski again appealed for action by Roosevelt.[7]

But at the same time, the Polish Ambassador notes that at a meeting with the British Ambassador in Washington:

Lord Halifax . . . asked me whether the acceptance by Poland of the Curzon Line as a border between Poland and the Soviets would really be such a hardship. . . . Lord Halifax did not think that any decisive steps could be taken to prevent Russia from pursuing her present policy.[8]

The next day, on March 11, 1943, British Foreign Secretary Eden arrived in Washington. Sherwood records Hopkins' notes of a dinner conversation with Roosevelt, Eden and himself on March 14:

... I [Hopkins] asked him [Eden] what he thought Russia's demands at the Peace Table would be. Eden said he thought they first would demand that the Baltic States be absorbed as states in the USSR. . . .

The President said he realized that we might have to agree to this, but if we did, then we should use it as a bargaining instrument in getting other concessions from Russia.

... Eden said he thought that Russia would demand very little territory of Poland, possibly up to the "Curzon Line." ... he believed that Stalin wanted a strong Poland, providing the right kind of people were running it and that (Russian) policy at the Peace Table would depend on this.

The President said it would be difficult to work out geographical boundaries on this basis because, while there might be a liberal government in Poland at the time of the Peace Conference, they might well be thrown out within a year.[9]

Sherwood also records Hopkins' notes of a meeting between Soviet Ambassador Litvinov and himself in Washington two days later on March 16:

7. W. Anders, *An Army in Exile*, p. 138.
8. [Ciechanowski,] *Defeat in Victory*, p. 155.
9. [Robert E.] Sherwood, *Roosevelt and Hopkins* [Harper & Brothers, New York: 1948], p. 709.

I . . . asked him [Litvinov] what he believed the Russian demands at the Peace Table would be. He said that they, of course, would want the Baltic States; that Russia considered them now part of the U.S.S.R.; that they had always been historically part of Russia, apart from the fact that they were essential to them for security reasons.

Litvinov said he thought Russia had no desire to occupy all of Finland . . . but . . . would insist on moving the line about to a point where the Russian armies were at the end of the Finnish War. . . .

He said he thought Russia would agree to Poland having East Prussia but that Russia would insist on what he called "her territorial rights" on the Polish frontier. . . .

He said he assumed that everybody would agree that Russia should have Bessarabia.[10]

That the Baltic States had always belonged to Russia omits four hundred years of history when they were a part of Finland—prior to about 1817, and about twenty-five years after 1917 when Estonian, Latvian, and Lithuanian independence was recognized by Soviet Russia after the Communists had been defeated in an attack upon these nations.

The Katyn Forest Massacre

On April 12, 1943 the Germans (then in occupation of Poland) announced that they had discovered the mass graves of thousands of Polish officers in the Katyn Forests in East Poland [western Russia–ed.]. The Germans declared that the Russians were responsible for the massacre.

The Polish Government in London requested an investigation by the International Red Cross since it was a function of that body to inquire into the mistreatment of war prisoners. The Russians professed great indignation at the Polish request. They refused to agree to the neutral inquiry and on April 26th, broke off relations with the Exiled Polish Government in London.[11]

The Germans appointed a commission composed entirely of medical authorities from the outstanding medical universities in Europe. Among these were Dr. Speelers of the University of Ghent, Dr. Tramsen of the Danish Institute of Medicine, Dr. Saxen of Helsinki University, Dr. de Burlet of the University of Groningen, and some 12 other medical authorities. The report

---

10. Ibid., p. 713.
11. Bronislaw Kuznierz, *Stalin and the Poles* (Hollis and Carter, London: 1949), p. 114.

made by this Commission on April 30, 1943 gave detailed evidence that the massacre had been carried out by the Russians.[12]

Secretary Hull states in his memoirs that Churchill and Roosevelt at once protested to Stalin over his break with the Exiled Polish Government in London, and that in Roosevelt's cable to Churchill,

> ... the President approved everything the Prime Minister had said to Stalin, particularly his statement that we would not recognize another Polish Government set up in the Soviet Union or anywhere else. ...
>
> The President's cable noted with gratification that Churchill did not mention the underlying territorial dispute between the Poles and the Russians, since attempts to solve it would not add to the unity of the United Nations at this time. ...[13]

Stalin, in the meantime, assuming the annexation of East Poland, was preparing a Communist government for West Poland immediately after the Germans retreated. Secretary Hull wrote:

> On April 28 [1943] the Union of Polish Patriots in the U.S.S.R., an organization of Polish Communists encouraged by the Soviet Government and cherishing ambitions toward ruling in postwar Poland, came to the fore with a declaration against the Polish Government in London. Here appeared the beginnings of a second Polish Government under the influence of Moscow.[14]

---

12. In 1952, about nine years later, a special Congressional committee, headed by Congressman Ray J. Madden of Indiana, endeavored to discover the full facts. Among the witnesses called were Arthur Bliss Lane, former Ambassador to Poland; George H. Earle, former Minister to Bulgaria and Turkey; Lt. Col. John H. Van Vliet, Jr., and Polish ex-Premier Stanislaw Mikolajczyk. Col. Van Vliet, a former prisoner of the Germans, had personally witnessed the exhuming of the bodies in one of the Katyn graves, and had later reported on it in full to the War Department. This report had been labeled "Top Secret." Then it "disappeared." The Congressional committee was unable to obtain it. Earle had reported similar facts disclosed by a Bulgarian witness and had been told by Mr. Roosevelt not to publish them as this might offend the Russians.

The Congressional committee interviewed 81 witnesses, took 300 depositions and statements, and received 183 exhibits. Its unanimous report declared that:

"The Soviet NKVD committed the massacre of thousands of Polish Army officers in the Katyn forest near Smolensk, Russia, not later than the spring of 1940."

[Editor's note: See New York Times, July 3, 1952 and December 22, 1952. Hoover's reference is to an investigation by a select committee of the House of Representatives of the mass murder of thousands of Polish officers near Smolensk, Russia in 1940. The committee's interim report (House Report No. 2430) was issued on July 2, 1952 and its final report (House Report No. 2505) on December 22, 1952.]

13. The Memoirs of Cordell Hull [The Macmillan Company, New York: 1948], Vol. II, pp. 1268–1269.

14. Ibid., p. 1268.

The "Union of Polish Patriots" held a meeting in Moscow on June 8, 1943, proclaiming itself the real representative of the Polish people. The announced members of the "Union" all had Communist records. Some of them were convicted felons, expelled from Poland before the war.

On July 4, 1943, General Sikorski was killed in an airplane accident and was succeeded by Stanislaw Mikolajczyk as Prime Minister of the Exiled Polish Government. The new Prime Minister records:

> Appeasement of Russia grew by the hour both in London and Washington. . . .
>
> We turned from Churchill to Roosevelt, then back to Churchill. They both were uniformly sympathetic but continued to impose silence upon us, as they were reluctant to inject anything into their relations with Stalin that might displease him. . . .
>
> We had thereafter to reckon with the Roosevelt administration's definite appeasement of Russia. . . .[15]

On July 28, 1943, the Polish Ambassador in Washington again saw Mr. Roosevelt. He reports that the President said:

> ". . . I presume that he [Stalin] will . . . insist on his demands for some rectification of the eastern boundaries of Poland. . . ."
>
> The President paused, as if waiting for my answer, and I voiced the opinion that only a firm attitude on the part of the United States could stop Stalin's territorial demands. . . .
>
> "Well, yes, but we cannot afford a war with Russia," said the President.
>
> "I can only repeat, Mr. President," I replied, "what I told you before on this subject. Soviet Russia will try to make you believe that she is ready for anything in order to achieve her territorial aims. But, in reality, she is bluffing, because she cannot afford a war with Great Britain and the United States. . . ."[16]

A conference of the three Foreign Ministers of Britain, United States, and Russia was announced to meet in Moscow in October, 1943. Prime Minister Mikolajczyk became active in London to insure that the Foreign Ministers would defend Poland. However, Mr. Churchill's instructions to Eden of October 11 could hardly have been reassuring to the Polish Prime Minister. They were:

---

15. Mikolajczyk, *The Rape of Poland,* pp. 25–26.
16. Ciechanowski, *Defeat in Victory,* p. 186.

We reaffirm the principles of the Atlantic Charter, noting that Russia's accession thereto is based upon the frontiers of June 22, 1941.[17] We also take note of the historic frontiers of Russia before the two wars of aggression waged by Germany in 1914 and 1939.[18]

These boundaries of the Russian Empire before the First World War implied the annexation of a large part of Poland to Communist Russia, together with Finland, Estonia, Latvia, Lithuania, Bessarabia, and Bukovina.

A memorable meeting between Secretary of State Hull and Ambassador Ciechanowski took place on October 6, 1943 to discuss the action which should be taken on the Polish question at this forthcoming Moscow Conference.

The essential parts of Ciechanowski's account of this interview are:

> I told Mr. Hull that never in the course of our three years' acquaintance had I called on him at so crucial a time and on such important and urgent matters.
>
> Soon the Soviet armies would enter Polish territory ... a precedent was about to be created which would set a most important pattern for the future. . . .
>
> . . . here Mr. Hull defined his attitude in words which I have always remembered:
>
> "The Polish Government," he said, "is entitled to act the part of host to the Soviets when they come into Poland. This is both just and logical and requires, as your government rightly maintains, the re-establishment of direct relations between the Soviet and Polish governments."
>
> . . . he [Mr. Hull] assured me that "he was decided to defend the cause of Poland as he would defend the cause of his own country."
>
> On the following day I heard that, in taking leave of Secretary of Commerce Jesse Jones, when the latter asked him what had finally determined him to undertake so difficult and dangerous a mission at his age, Mr. Hull had replied that, in the final analysis, the situation created by the problem of Poland had determined his decision. He said he felt that he "had to defend it to the end."[19]

Hull gives his views when he left for Moscow as follows:

---

17. There never was such a reservation by Russia as explained above.
18. [Winston S.] Churchill, *Closing the Ring* [Houghton Mifflin Company, Boston: 1951], p. 283.
19. Ciechanowski, *Defeat in Victory*, pp. 215, 217, 221.

... The future of Poland was naturally of keen interest to us. At the end of the last war, the United States Government had taken an active part in setting up a free and independent Poland, which was one of Wilson's Fourteen Points. ...

As I left for the capital of the U.S.S.R. I had made no promises to do more than urge the Soviet Government, with all the earnestness possible, to agree to a restoration of diplomatic relations with Poland.[20]

Prime Minister Mikolajczyk got no satisfaction out of the Moscow Conference.[21]

Ciechanowski's account of a conversation with Hull on his return in November 1943 is:

... Mr. Hull said that he wanted to give me a frank and accurate account of his views on the Moscow conference. ...

With regard to ... admitting the Polish authorities to take over the administration of Poland as it became liberated from German occupation, Mr. Hull had come to the conclusion that it was premature to raise this point in Moscow. ...

He asked me what I thought of the comprehensive picture of the Moscow conference he had drawn for me.

I replied that I had to admit that his very interesting description had by no means allayed my fears. We expected the entry of the Soviet troops on Polish territory in the near future. If this happened in the present circumstances, and if the Soviet armies brought with them communist Polish Quislings, it was certain that Soviet Russia intended to create accomplished facts in Poland.[22]

The Foreign Ministers' Conference arranged a meeting of Roosevelt, Churchill and Stalin to take place a month later at Tehran, Iran.

Keeping the Poles Happy

Before leaving the period prior to the Tehran Conference of November 1943, it is desirable to review some of the political action designed to keep the Polish soldiers in the Allied armies, and the American voters of Polish descent happy.

---

20. *The Memoirs of Cordell Hull*, Vol. II, pp. 1266, 1273.
21. Mikolajczyk, *The Rape of Poland*, p. 45.
22. Ciechanowski, *Defeat in Victory*, pp. 234, 236, 237–238.

On May 3, 1943, President Roosevelt expressed the admiration and gratitude of the American people for the valiant sacrifices of the Polish contingent in the Allied armies.

Two months later Mr. Churchill, no less eloquent in his pledges to Poland than Mr. Roosevelt, on June 30 said:

> We strove long, too long, for peace, and suffered thereby; but from the moment when we gave our guarantee that we would not stand by idly and see Poland trampled down by Nazi violence, we have never looked back, never flagged, never doubted, never flinched. We were sure of our duty. . . .
>
> . . . We expect no reward and we will accept no compromise. It is on that footing that we wish to be judged, first in our own consciences and afterwards by posterity.[23]

A week later, on July 8, 1943, Churchill told Mikolajczyk in a conversation:

> I will fight for the freedom of Poland. I will fight for a strong and independent Poland, and I'll never cease fighting for it.[24]

The next day, July 9, 1943, President Roosevelt, in reply to a Fourth of July message of congratulation, said to the new Prime Minister Mikolajczyk:

> The Polish people may be certain that their sufferings and unceasing contribution to our common cause will not be forgotten when the hour of liberation strikes.[25]

In a eulogy of General Sikorski, who had died in an airplane accident the day before, Churchill said on July 14:

> His efforts and your sacrifices shall not be in vain. Be worthy of his example. Prepare yourselves to die for Poland—for many of you to whom I speak must die, [as many of us must die, and–ed.] as he died, for his country and the common cause. In the farewell to your dead leader let us mingle renewed loyalties. We shall not forget him. I shall not forget you. . . .[26]

Two weeks later, July 28, 1943, the Polish Ambassador presented Jan Karski, an official in the Polish underground, to Mr. Roosevelt, who said:

---

23. [Winston S.] Churchill, *Onwards to Victory* [Little, Brown and Company, 1944], p. 159.
24. Mikolajczyk, *The Rape of Poland*, p. 41.
25. *New York Times*, July 10, 1943.
26. Churchill, *Onwards to Victory*, pp. 174–175. [*Editor's note:* Hoover's reference in the text to General Sikorski's death "the day before"—i.e., July 13, 1943—is inaccurate. Sikorski died on July 4, 1943. The bracketed words in the quotation were omitted by Hoover, probably inadvertently. I have reinserted them as shown.]

Tell the Polish Underground authorities . . . that their indomitable attitude has been duly appreciated. Tell them that they will never have cause to regret their brave decision to reject any collaboration with the enemy, and that Poland will live to reap the reward of her heroism and sacrifice.[27]

Again, on August 31, in a published exchange of telegrams with President Wladyslaw Raczkiewicz of the Exiled Polish Government in London, President Roosevelt said:

The whole world will recall again the gallant and defiant stand made by the heroic Polish nation. . . . The daring and heroic exploits of the Polish forces [and others] . . . will assure . . . the liberation of all the peoples. . . .[28]

---

27. Ciechanowski, *Defeat in Victory,* p. 190.

28. *New York Times,* September 1, 1943. [*Editor's note:* This quotation does not appear in the source cited. Hoover may have been quoting another newspaper account of this episode.]

CHAPTER E

Doom Comes to Free Poland

THE FOLLOWING STATEMENT by Prime Minster Mikolajczyk concerning the Tehran conference and subsequent events is of importance in any account of Poland. He states:

Still hopeful of intercepting Churchill and Roosevelt before they met Stalin, I wired them at their Cairo meeting with Generalissimo Chiang Kai-shek late in November, 1943. Eden, replying for Churchill, said the meeting with Stalin was still uncertain as to both time and place, as was the very participation of Stalin in the talks....

Roosevelt replied ... that he still looked forward to seeing me in Washington in January, 1944. He asked me to rest assured that he had made an extensive study of the Polish situation and was fully prepared to present our case at the meeting with Stalin.

... my first information as to what had taken place at Teheran concerning Poland specifically came from Eden....

Eden reported that Stalin had expressed anger at the "insufficient cooperation" of the Polish underground with the Red Army and was extremely critical of the Polish government.[... –ed.]

"I share the Prime Minister's view that Stalin will not try to annihilate Poland or incorporate it into the Soviet Union," Eden said. "But it is obvious that Stalin's demands center around the establishment of the Curzon line as the future boundary between his country and Poland. Naturally, we agreed to nothing in this respect. We were not empowered to do so either by the British government or by your own."

My reply was that I could see no possibility of settling frontier questions now and that I was going forward with my plans to visit Roosevelt.

Eden shook his head. It was imperative, he said, that I first speak with Churchill when the Prime Minister returned. . . .

A few days later I received a message from Roosevelt stating that Churchill had wired him, asking that as a "personal favor" my proposed meeting at the White House be postponed. "I agreed," Roosevelt concluded.[1]

The actualities of Tehran were that Prime Minister Churchill and Marshal Stalin agreed to the Curzon line as the eastern boundary of Poland, and that all three—Churchill, Stalin, and Roosevelt—agreed to Russia's having a border of friendly states. The significance of this agreement was that East Poland was annexed to Russia and that West Poland would become a puppet Communist state.[2]

Mr. Roosevelt on his return to Washington twice publicly denied that he had made any secret agreements at Tehran. Two accounts of his statements made to Stalin substantiate this denial. One version is recorded by Charles Bohlen, the interpreter, and the other by Harry Hopkins. They confirm each other.

Mr. Bohlen states:

THE PRESIDENT said he had asked Marshal Stalin to come to see him as he wished to discuss a matter briefly and frankly. He said it referred to internal American politics.

He said that we had an election in 1944 and that while personally he did not wish to run again, if the war was still in progress, he might have to.

He added that there were in the United States from six to seven million Americans of Polish extraction, and as a practical man, he did not wish to lose their vote. He said personally he agreed with the views of Marshal Stalin as to the necessity of the restoration of a Polish state but would like to see the Eastern border moved further to the west and the Western border moved even to the River Oder. He hoped, however, that the Marshal would understand that for political reasons outlined above, he could not participate in any decision here in Tehran or even next winter on this subject and that he could not publicly take part in any such arrangement at the present time.

MARSHAL STALIN replied that now the President explained, he had understood.[3]

---

1. Stanislaw Mikolajczyk, *The Rape of Poland*, pp. 46–49.

2. I give the details of this conference in Section [XIII–*ed.*] of [Volume II–*ed.*].

3. *The Cairo-Tehran Papers* published by the State Department, p. 594. [*Editor's note:* That is, U.S. Department of State, *Foreign Relations of the United States, Diplomatic Papers, The Conferences at Cairo and Tehran, 1943* (United States Government Printing Office, Washington: 1961).]

Harry Hopkins' account of this conversation, as given by Sherwood, was as follows:

> During the afternoon, Roosevelt had a private talk with Stalin and Molotov for the purposes of putting them in possession of certain essential facts concerning American politics. . . .
>
> Roosevelt felt it necessary to explain to Stalin that there were six or seven million Americans of Polish extraction, and others of Lithuanian, Latvian and Estonian origin who had the same rights and the same votes as anyone else and whose opinions must be respected. Stalin said that he understood this, but he subsequently suggested that some "propaganda work" should be done among these people.[4]

As a matter of fact, two understandings were entered into at Tehran as to Poland of which there is no specific record: The first was the Russian annexation of Poland up to the so-called Curzon line; the second, that Russia should have a border of friendly states. At Tehran, Churchill agreed with Stalin as to the annexation. As to the agreement about border states: its immediate confirmation was the prompt action by the Russian government with no protest from either Mr. Roosevelt or Mr. Churchill.

1944

On January 5, 1944, a month after Tehran, the Polish Government in Exile issued an energetic protest at what had taken place.

Their officials appealed to President Roosevelt and Prime Minister Churchill on January 16.[5]

The persistent Mikolajczyk met with Prime Minister Churchill five days later on January 20, 1944. He reports his statement to Mr. Churchill as follows:

> . . . Poland cannot emerge from this war diminished. You are asking for an intolerable concession. . . .
>
> . . . let me tell you that this will be a test case. It will compromise an Allied nation grossly and unjustly, and it will not bring peace to Europe.
>
> Don't you see, Mr. Prime Minister . . . that the Soviet Union's aim is not only to take the eastern half of our country but to take all of Poland—all of Europe? We have tried so diligently to keep the unity of the Allies, to

---

4. Sherwood, *Roosevelt and Hopkins*, p. 796.
5. Stanislaw Mikolajczyk, *The Rape of Poland*, p. 273.

cooperate. But do you realize that since the Red Army entered Poland it has been disarming and arresting the very members of the Polish underground who helped the Russians capture each point?[6]

On February 1, President Roosevelt replied to Mikolajczyk's appeal, saying that the

> ... United States Government would in principle be prepared to assist in helping the Polish Government freely to reach a settlement of its territorial problems through the offer of good offices to the Polish and to the Soviet Governments to facilitate direct discussions between them ...[7]

The Soviets had earlier indicated that their Government was "not in a position to enter into official negotiations with a government with which diplomatic relations have been severed."[8]

On February 7, 1944, two months after Tehran, a Polish-American Congressman from Buffalo, Joseph Mruk, addressed a letter to Mr. Roosevelt in which he said:

> If Russia, whose armies are now pushing the Nazis back across Poland, is permitted to hold eastern Poland after this war, as is the announced plan of Stalin—so far as our purpose of fighting for the freedoms of all peoples has been proclaimed, in the Atlantic Charter and in every other declaration of our nation's leaders—this war will have been lost by us of the United States. ... that is, lost idealistically and morally—even before we have been able finally to win it militarily.
>
> I was greatly pleased when you assured the Congress in your annual message this week that there were no secret commitments made in the recent conference at Cairo and Teheran. ...
>
> Do you think, Mr. President, that the Atlantic Charter can still be saved from the world's great heap of well-intentioned "scraps of paper"? ... I know that all the people of the United States will be glad for a frank and realistic clarification by you, Mr. President.[9]

On February 12, 1944, sixty days after Tehran, Stalin in Moscow reorganized his "Union of Polish Patriots" government for West Poland into the "National Council of Poland." It was comprised wholly of Polish Communists. (I

---

6. Ibid., p. 52.
7. Ibid., p. 277.
8. Jan Ciechanowski, *Defeat in Victory*, p. 262.
9. *New York Times*, February 20, 1944.

may state here that five months later this "Council" was transformed into the "Polish Committee of National Liberation," consisting mostly of the same members.)

On February 20, Mr. Roosevelt replied to Mruk, stating that the issue was one between the Russians and the Poles. He added:

> ... [The United States] will not rest in its efforts to free all victims of aggression and to establish a just and enduring peace based on the sovereign equality of all peace-loving States, large and small.[10]

On February 22, 1944, Mr. Churchill made a speech in the House of Commons stating that the British Government had never guaranteed "any particular frontier line to Poland," and that although he had "an intense sympathy with the Poles," he also had "sympathy with the Russian standpoint."[11]

Ambassador Ciechanowski, who was in London at this time, states as to Churchill's speech:

> Naturally Mr. Churchill's speech was received as a deadly blow by the Polish people in Poland and abroad, and particularly by our armed forces fighting alongside the British. . . .[12]

It appears that Mr. Churchill now tried to secure some modifications as to Poland from Stalin, but Stalin, on March 23, 1944, replied with a savage refusal.[13]

On March 25, 1944, Mikolajczyk addressed a personal letter to Mr. Roosevelt. It is too long for full reproduction here, but I repeat some paragraphs which are poignant and prophetic:

> I am sure that you will agree at this time, when the whole future of mankind is involved, that it is imperative to face reality in a spirit of sincerity and truth, on which alone the future of international relations and durable peace can be founded.
>
> I am firmly convinced that Nazi totalitarianism . . . shall be destroyed. But will not Poland and later Europe be overwhelmed against their will by a new wave of Communist totalitarianism? Can the nations condemned to the rule of such a new totalitarianism agree to accept its tyranny?

---

10. Ibid.

11. [Winston S.] Churchill, *The Dawn of Liberation* [Little, Brown and Company, Boston: 1945], p. 25.

12. Ciechanowski, *Defeat in Victory*, p. 275.

13. [William D.] Leahy, *I Was There* [McGraw-Hill Book Company, Inc., New York: 1950], pp. 232–234.

Never, as far as Poland is concerned.

. . . The activities of Communist agencies brought about disunity and fear of chaos, for these agencies have endeavored in every country to achieve supremacy, less for the purpose of strengthening the struggle against the Germans than for that of establishing communism in the countries concerned.

The concealment of truth on which this situation is based is more detrimental to the Polish nation than to others. . . . History will reveal . . . the methods used by Russia in her dealings and her intentions as regards my country. We have refrained from publishing such facts, although this is clearly against our interests, because we were anxious to reach an understanding with the USSR and to safeguard the unity of the Allies. Our reticence is . . . exploited by Russia. . . . Thus, the Polish government . . . is deprived of the elementary right of defense of its national interests and the right of the weaker to appeal for help to the stronger in the name of the principles and ideals enunciated by you, Mr. President, in the Atlantic Charter, the Four Freedoms, and many other statements that have won the respect and approval of the entire world. [. . . –ed.]

Mr. President, your name is revered by every Pole. The Polish nation looks upon you as the champion of the principles that you have proclaimed. . . .

Our people fighting in Poland's underground army have lost everything. They lay no value on life. . . . while being threatened with the loss of their last hope of freedom and by the prospect of another enslavement. They have faith in you, Mr. President. . . .[14]

Mr. Roosevelt made a non-committal acknowledgement of this letter on April 3.

Mikolajczyk, in a speech on May 3, again rejected the annexation of East Poland and the proposed Communist puppet government for West Poland. Once more he attempted to revive the spirit of the Atlantic Charter.

On the same day Mr. Roosevelt sent a comforting telegram to the President of the Exiled Polish Government in London, saying:

. . . I take great pleasure in sending to the Polish people through you my greetings and best wishes. . . . It is fitting to recall . . . that it was Poland who first defied the Nazi hordes. Their continued resistance . . . is an inspiration to all. The relentless struggle . . . by the United Nations will hasten . . . the liberation of all freedom-loving peoples.[15]

---

14. Mikolajczyk, *The Rape of Poland*, pp. 278ff.
15. *New York Times*, May 4, 1944.

Churchill made a further statement on May 24 in the House of Commons. He indicated that the Poles must accept the Curzon Line annexation determined for them at Tehran and settle their other troubles by direct negotiation with the Soviet Government.[16]

Mikolajczyk arrived in Washington on June 6, 1944. The Polish Prime Minister and the Polish Ambassador had four conversations with Mr. Roosevelt. They made a memorandum of these conversations and a copy was furnished to the President in confirmation of their negotiations. I also have a copy. It says, after reciting various items:

> In the above mentioned conversations the President explained that in this political year he did not see his way to approach Marshal Stalin with definite suggestions for a final solution of the Polish-Soviet conflict. Moreover, the President indicated that the policy of the U.S. Government was contrary to the settlement of territorial problems before the end of the war. The President said that at the Tehran Conference he had made it clear that he held the view that the Polish-Soviet conflict should not be settled on the basis of the so-called Curzon Line.[17]

Mr. Roosevelt urged the Polish Prime Minister Mikolajczyk to go to Moscow and discuss these questions with Marshal Stalin. According to the Prime Minister's account, Mr. Roosevelt also said:

> "I haven't acted on the Polish question because this is an election year. . . . You as a democrat understand such things. . . . You know, I mentioned the matter of our forthcoming American elections to Stalin, and he just couldn't comprehend what I was talking about. . . .
>
> ". . . you Poles must find an understanding with Russia. On your own, you'd have no chance to beat Russia, and let me tell you now, the British and Americans have no intention of fighting Russia.
>
> "But don't worry . . . Stalin doesn't intend to take freedom from Poland. He wouldn't dare do that because he knows that the United States government stands solidly behind you. I will see to it that Poland does not come out of this war injured."[18]

Mikolajczyk protested that there was every indication that Poland was going to be injured and asked for a written statement supporting the Polish

16. Churchill, *The Dawn of Liberation*, p. 124.
17. A copy of this memorandum was given to me by Jan Ciechanowski.
18. Mikolajczyk, *The Rape of Poland*, pp. 59–60.

position if he did not go to Moscow. Roosevelt refused but did send a message to Stalin, recommending that he see Mikolajczyk.[19] (Stalin replied suggesting that the Ministers in the Exiled Polish Government in London negotiate in Moscow with representatives of his Communist Provisional Polish Government.)

The President, in his June 7 conversation with Mikolajczyk said:

Poland will again arise strong and independent.[20]

However, Mr. Roosevelt again stressed the necessity of Mikolajczyk's being realistic in making some concessions. He said:

When a thing becomes unavoidable, one should adapt oneself to it.[21]

He repeated that the Prime Minister, being himself a politician, would understand "the political year."[22]

At Mikolajczyk's request, Mr. Roosevelt gave him a message for the Poles which was issued to the press on June 17:

. . . The forces of liberation are on the march to certain victory and the establishment of a peace based upon the principles of freedom, democracy, mutual understanding and security for all liberty-loving people. . . .[23]

On July 25, 1944, the Germans having retreated from East Poland, Stalin ceremoniously installed "The Committee of Liberation" at Lublin to administer the "Liberated parts of Poland west of the Curzon Line."[24]

---

19. *The Memoirs of Cordell Hull,* Vol. II, pp. 1445–1446.
20. Ciechanowski, *Defeat in Victory,* p. 291.
21. Ibid, p. 293.
22. Ibid, p. 294.
23. *New York Times,* June 18, 1944.
24. Ciechanowski, *Defeat in Victory,* pp. 319–320.

CHAPTER F

At Russian Request the Polish Underground Rises against the Germans

AFTER LONG CONVERSATIONS with Hull, Churchill and Eden, Premier Mikolajczyk flew to Moscow in accord with Churchill's and Roosevelt's urging to attempt negotiations with the Russians.[1] But an incident of Communist treachery now arose to overshadow the meeting.

At the end of July, 1944, the Russian armies had arrived just across the river from Warsaw and their guns sounded hope of at least freedom from the Germans. At this moment Moscow radioed (July 29 and 30) appeals to the Polish underground to rise against the Germans.[2] Our subsequent Ambassador to Poland, Arthur Bliss Lane, after investigating the facts, confirms these messages saying:

> On July 29, at 8:15 P.M., his [General Bor's] radio picked up a broadcast from Moscow . . . in the Polish language. . . . the broadcast was a direct appeal to Poles inside German-occupied Poland to rise to arms immediately. . . .
>
> . . . London monitored a similar appeal, broadcast by the Moscow radio. This was addressed not only to all the people of Poland but specifically to the inhabitants of Warsaw, and urged them to assist the Red Army to cross the Vistula and enter Warsaw.[3]

---

1. Jan Ciechanowski, *Defeat in Victory*, p. 319.

2. A detailed account of this insurrection and the Russian attitude was published by General [Tadeusz] Bor-Komorowski in his book, *The Secret Army* ([Victor Gollancz Ltd.,] London: 1951) pp. 199–396, specifically p. 212.

3. [Arthur Bliss] Lane, *I Saw Poland Betrayed* [The Bobbs-Merrill Company, Indianapolis and New York: 1948], p. 43.

Two years later during my visit to Warsaw in March-April 1946, two separate Poles of distinction who had participated in the uprising stated to me that they themselves had listened to this Russian broadcast and acted upon it. I went over the fighting ground to assure myself that there was no consequential obstruction to Russian entry into the insurrectionist-held area.

Churchill, as shown by his speeches, had urged the Poles to undertake this action as had also the American "Strategic Services."[4]

Promptly on August 1, the Polish underground army came into the open under the leadership of General Bor (General Tadeusz Bor-Komorowski). General Bor's forces seized a large part of Warsaw from the Germans. The Russians, instead of marching into Warsaw (to which there was now a complete opening), halted their forces outside the city directly across the Vistula.

Mikolajczyk was in Moscow. He states that he at once urged Stalin to "bring immediate aid to our men in their pitifully unequal battles with the Germans." Stalin's reply was:

> But you're not taking into consideration the agreement that has been reached between the Soviet Union and the Lublin Committee. . . .
>
> I cannot trust the Poles. . . . They suspect me of wanting to occupy Poland again. They're making a lot of trouble for me.[5]

On August 4, Churchill telegraphed Stalin that the British were about to send supplies to General Bor by air. Stalin replied on the 5th that he had no confidence in the uprising or their military ability.[6]

Mikolajczyk also records that when he appealed to Stalin to aid the underground uprising, Stalin said:

> You must realize this . . . that nothing can be done for Poland if you do not recognize the Curzon line. . . .

Mikolajczyk states:

> I protested that this was a direct violation of the Atlantic Charter, whose principles the USSR had accepted, and of existing Polish-Soviet pacts. After hearing me out, Stalin shrugged and said:
>
> "Maybe we can make some changes in the Curzon line that will be of benefit to Poland. But first you must reach an agreement with the Lublin Poles. Hereafter I intend to deal with only one Polish government, not two."
>
> . . . I could see as he talked that he was determined that all Polish resistance, as exemplified by the Polish Home Army, [General Bor and his army were not Communists] would perish.

---

4. T. Komorowski, *The Secret Army,* p. 88ff.
5. Mikolajczyk, *The Rape of Poland,* pp. 72–73.
6. [Winston S.] Churchill, *Triumph and Tragedy* [Houghton Mifflin Company, Boston: 1953], pp. 130–131.

I met with the Lublin Poles on August 6 in the fruitless hope that I might appeal to whatever Polish blood was left in their veins to secure their support for the Home Army and the future democracy of our native land.

They were a motley bunch. But Molotov had met them at the airport with a great show of ceremony. *Pravda,* which still had not mentioned our own presence in Moscow, ran long articles in praise of them. . . .[7]

Mikolajczyk relates at length his appeals and conversations with the Lublin Communist delegation. Among them was Bierut, who was later to be Communist President of Poland. Mikolajczyk says:

On August 7, 1944, I met Bierut. He is an old-line Communist. . . .

"Our relations with the USSR are more important than frontiers," he told me. Then he made me an offer. If I would return to Warsaw in agreement with the Lublin group and recognize him as president, he would appoint me prime minister of a Communist-controlled Polish government. He also offered to give minor cabinet posts in that government to three other independent party leaders. It would be an eighteen-member government, fourteen of which would be Communists or their agents.

"I cannot even discuss this with you," I told him. ". . . What you're asking me to do is to sell out the Polish people. You're asking me to become a swine. . . ."

Bierut looked me over with hostility. "If you want to go to Poland as a friend in complete agreement with us, we will accept you," he said. "If you attempt to go as Prime Minister of the Polish government that is no longer recognized by the USSR, we'll arrest you."

"I have no business here," I said, getting up. "All I want now is to get back to London and report to my government what I have seen and heard in Moscow."

At the door, however, I turned once again to him, unable to resist the fading hope that aid somehow might reach Warsaw.

"I beg of you two things," I said. "Help Warsaw—and stop the Soviet arrests of the Home Army [in the area east of Warsaw] that is helping to liberate our country."

He made no answer.

I saw . . . Stalin once more before I left Moscow. . . .

. . . he was less hospitable than before, assuming that such a thing is possible.

---

7. Mikolajczyk, *The Rape of Poland,* pp. 74–75.

"Can you give me your word of honor," he asked, "that there is fighting going on in Warsaw? The Lublin Poles tell me there is no fighting at all."

"I can give you my word of honor that there is a fight there," I told him. "It is a desperate fight. I beg of you—who are in the strategic position—to give us aid."

He made a negative motion. "I had two of my communications officers dropped into Warsaw after I saw you the other day," he said. "The Germans killed both of them when they attempted to land by parachute."

This was a lie. . . . Both men landed successfully and made their way to the [Bor] headquarters. . . . They eventually sent a number of messages to Moscow. . . . I was able to hand to Stalin a message from a Red Army officer then in contact with the Home Army—Colonel Kalugin. It had been sent to London by Bor-Komorowski's radio for retransmission to Moscow. . . . [This message said that he was in contact with General Bor and urged that the Russians support him.]

Stalin read the message solemnly. "I don't know this man Kalugin," he said. "I'll inquire about him. And I'll still do my best to help Warsaw. . . ."[8]

On August 10, 1944, the Polish Prime Minister returned to London to lay the situation before his colleagues and to implore help from the British and Americans for the insurrectionists in Warsaw.

On August 13 the British and American armies began to fly supplies from the Italian front, 800 miles away, dropping them into Warsaw by parachutes. Secretary Hull relates that next day Mr. Roosevelt cabled Stalin (August 14) asking landings for a shuttle service on Soviet army air fields a few miles outside Warsaw. Stalin refused, saying that the Warsaw uprising was a "purely adventurist affair" and that the Soviet Government would not lend its hand to it.[9] The Lublin Communist government denounced General Bor as a traitor who would be court-martialed when the Red Army took Warsaw.

Mikolajczyk telegraphed Stalin on August 16, from London, reminding him that the uprising had taken place at his (Stalin's) request and appealing again for support. On the same day Stalin telegraphed Churchill that the Red Army had dropped some arms; that a liaison officer in the city had been killed by the Germans; and stated that he would have nothing to do with the uprising.[10]

---

8. Ibid., pp. 76ff. [*Editor's note:* The word within brackets are Hoover's.]
9. *The Memoirs of Cordell Hull*, Vol. II, pp. 1445–1446.
10. Churchill, *Triumph and Tragedy*, p. 134.

Secretary Hull again cabled Ambassador Harriman in Moscow to urge help for Warsaw and once more asked for landings for American planes. The Kremlin refused.

On August 20, at Mr. Churchill's urging, a joint appeal by himself and Mr. Roosevelt was sent to Stalin. The appeal urged action by the Russians to aid General Bor and again asked for facilities for a shuttle service.[11]

Stalin replied on the 22nd charging the Warsaw leaders with being criminals and deriding their military importance.

On August 24 Mr. Roosevelt wrote Mikolajczyk sympathetically, in response to an appeal for aid to Warsaw, but added:

> . . . I feel . . . that these unfortunate developments should not deter you from presenting reasonable proposals to the Polish Committee of National Liberation [the Communist Government in Lublin]. . . .[12]

It must be borne in mind that the dealings with the Lublin Government referred to the puppet West Poland, not Russian-annexed East Poland.

On August 25, Mr. Churchill telegraphed Mr. Roosevelt, proposing the text of an eloquent and forceful joint appeal to Stalin for landing fields for shuttle service from the West. Next day Roosevelt refused to join and suggested that Churchill go it alone.[13]

General Wladyslaw Anders, Commander of the Polish armies on the Western Front, reports an interview with Churchill on August 26. After discussing aid to the Warsaw uprising, Anders quotes:

> . . . Prime Minister Churchill (deeply moved): "You should trust Great Britain, who will never abandon you—never. I know the Germans and Russians are destroying your best elements, particularly the intellectuals. I deeply sympathise with you. But be confident, we will not desert you and Poland will be happy."[14]

The Germans began a general assault on the Warsaw defenders in the latter days of August, and on September 3, General Bor reported that he had to withdraw from parts of the city.

On September 4 Mr. Churchill again telegraphed Mr. Roosevelt, giving the text of a telegram sent from the British War Cabinet to Stalin, reciting

---

11. Ibid., p. 136.

12. Mikolajczyk, *The Rape of Poland*, p. 287.

13. Churchill, *Triumph and Tragedy*, pp. 139–141.

14. Anders, *An Army in Exile*, pp. 209–212. [*Editor's note:* The quotation appears on p. 211.]

adverse public opinion and urging Mr. Roosevelt's support. The next day Mr. Roosevelt replied that he had been informed:

> ... that the fighting Poles have departed from Warsaw and that the Germans are now in full control.[15]

This was obviously not the fact, since later on (September 18), 104 heavy bombers were sent out from London to Poland. They were loaded with supplies which they dropped on the embattled Warsaw.

On September 29, Mikolajczyk sent a telegram to Stalin through the British Embassy in Moscow, the important paragraph being:

> ... the defenders of Warsaw have reached the limit of endurance. ... Warsaw can hold out only for several days more. At this extreme hour of need I appeal to you, Marshal, to issue orders for immediate operations, which would relieve the garrison of Warsaw and result in the liberation of the capital. ...[16]

The Poles fought on until October 3 when, exhausted of men, food and ammunition, they gave up. Some 15,000 Poles [i.e., Polish resistance fighters– ed.]had died—the best blood of Poland.

Ambassador Lane's comment on the Warsaw uprising was:

> ... in two essential respects the cold-blooded, premeditated crime against Poland, conceived by the Soviet Government with the aid of its puppets, had succeeded:
>
> (1) The Polish Government in London had been discredited;
> (2) The Polish Home [Underground] Army had been broken, so that no leadership remained there to dispute the authority of the Lublin gang.
>
> The incredible betrayal was complete. What did it matter to its perpetrators if a great city had been laid waste and two hundred fifty thousand of its people slaughtered? Had not their [the Russian] objectives been attained?[17]

Immediately after the uprising had been quelled, the Germans began a ghastly systematic destruction of Warsaw. They were apparently determined to establish a symbol that would intimidate uprisings in other German-occupied cities of Europe. They employed three armored demolition divisions in this destruction. These troops systematically drilled holes with

---

15. Churchill, *Triumph and Tragedy,* p. 143.
16. Mikolajczyk, *The Rape of Poland,* p. 86.
17. Lane, *I Saw Poland Betrayed,* pp. 53–54.

air-compressors, and blasted with dynamite, the foundations of [word un-clear–*ed.*] buildings in miles and miles of streets. They added bombs from the air. In the end they had destroyed 90 percent of the whole city. The remaining 10 percent was mostly the buildings they themselves occupied. Hundreds of thousands of people were killed and 1,000,000 more were with-out shelter or driven into the countryside.[18]

About 250,000 Jews had been buried in the Ghetto by artillery and bombs.

In the meantime, the Polish question had been raised again in the House of Commons and Prime Minister Churchill on September 28, after much elo-quence on the British devotion to the Poles, stated:

> Territorial changes on the frontiers of Poland there will have to be. Russia has a right to our support in this matter, because it is the Russian armies which alone can deliver Poland from the German talons; and after all the Russian people have suffered at the hands of Germany, they are entitled to safe frontiers and to have a friendly neighbour on their Western flank. . . . I have fervent hopes that M. Mikolajczyk . . . may shortly resume those impor-tant conversations in Moscow which were interrupted some months ago.[19]

---

18. I visited the destroyed Warsaw in 1946 and received this description of the city from those who had witnessed. I was given an eye-witness account of the destruction of the ghetto where these 250,000 had been butchered. [*Editor's note*: Hoover appeared to be conflating the Germans' destruc-tion of the Warsaw Ghetto in 1943, following a Jewish revolt, with the Germans' destruction of the rest of the city after the separate uprising (largely by non-Jewish Poles) in 1944.]

19. Winston Churchill, *The Dawn of Liberation*, pp. 251–252.

CHAPTER G

A Death Scene in Integrity

In mid-October, two weeks after the end of the Warsaw uprising, Mr. Churchill arranged for another conference in Moscow. This time the conferees included Churchill, Eden, Stalin, Molotov, Mikolajczyk, the Polish Minister of Foreign Affairs, the Chairman of the Communist Provisional Government at Lublin, and the American Ambassador, Averell Harriman.

The official communiqué released jointly by the Russians, the British and the Americans October 20 stated in part:

> ... Important progress was made towards a solution of the Polish question. . . .
>
> These discussions have notably narrowed differences and dispelled misconceptions. . . .[1]

The record scarcely supports this assertion. The most important discussions took place on October 13, seven days before this communiqué, with all the gentlemen mentioned present, together with two other of the London Polish officials—Foreign Minister Tadeusz Romer and Professor Stanislaw Grabski.[2]

The official shorthand account of this conference shows that the Polish Prime Minister stated the Polish opposition to partition of Poland by which one part would be annexed by Russia and the other made a Communist state. Stalin allowed no compromise on either issue. Churchill supported Stalin.[3]

Mikolajczyk's account of the Conference states that Molotov said:

---

1. Mikolajczyk, *The Rape of Poland,* pp. 100–101.
2. I give Mikolajczyk's account of this conference. Churchill's account in his book, *The Dawn of Liberation,* generally confirms Mikolajczyk, but in less emotional terms, as he was not a Pole.
3. [From?–*ed.*] the Hoover Institution on War, Revolution and Peace at Stanford University.

"But all this was settled at Teheran!" . . . He looked from Churchill to Harriman, who were silent. I asked for details of Teheran. And then he added, still with his [Molotov's] eyes on Churchill and the American Ambassador:

"If your memories fail you, let me recall the facts to you. We all agreed at Teheran that the Curzon line must divide Poland. You will recall that President Roosevelt agreed to this solution and strongly endorsed the line. And then we agreed that it would be best not to issue any public declaration about our agreement."

Mikolajczyk continues:

Shocked, and remembering the earnest assurances I had personally had from Roosevelt at the White House, I looked at Churchill and Harriman, silently begging them to call this damnable deal a lie. Harriman looked down at the rug. Churchill looked straight back to me.

"I confirm this," he said quietly.

In a subsequent meeting:

I reminded him [Churchill–ed.] again of the Atlantic Charter and other pacts that directly or indirectly pledged sovereign rights to Poland.

"I shall tell Parliament that I have agreed with Stalin," Churchill declared flatly. "Our relations with Russia are much better than they have ever been. I mean to keep them that way."

". . . We are not going to wreck the peace of Europe. In your obstinacy you do not see what is at stake. . . . We shall tell the world how unreasonable you are. . . ."

"I am not a person whose patriotism is diluted to the point where I would give away half my country," I answered.

Churchill shook his finger at me. "Unless you accept the frontier, you're out of business forever!" he cried. "The Russians will sweep through your country, and your people will be liquidated. You're on the verge of annihilation. We'll become sick and tired of you if you continue arguing."

Eden smoothed matters for a moment, but Churchill came back strongly.

"If you accept the Curzon line, the United States will take a great interest in the rehabilitation of Poland and may grant you a big loan, possibly without interest. We would help, too, but we shall be poor after this war. You are *bound* to accept the decision of the great Powers."

I reminded him of his gloriously worded speeches early in the war, speeches that decried the taking of territory by force, and I spoke of the better treatment the Allies were according such turncoat Axis enemies as Italy and Rumania. He dismissed this argument.

"You're no government," Churchill said. "You're a callous people who want to wreck Europe. I shall leave you to your own troubles. . . . You have only your miserable, petty, selfish interests in mind.

"I will now call on the other Poles. This Lublin government may function very well. It will be the government, that is certain. . . ."

I resented everything he said and told him so. . . .

I was furious at the man and could not conceal it.

"Mr. Churchill," I said, "I once asked you for permission to parachute into Poland and rejoin the underground, which is at this very hour fighting the Germans. You refused to grant me that permission. Now I ask it again."

"Why?" he said, surprised.

"Because I prefer to die, fighting for the independence of my country, than to be hanged later by the Russians in full view of your British ambassador!" [. . . –ed.]

I asked to see Stalin alone before I left Moscow. I still hoped I might appeal to him to relent in his demands.

"Poles will bless your name forever if you make a generous gesture here and now," I told Stalin. . . .

"I cannot and will not do this," Stalin said.

I had long since found that it was useless to quote previous promises and pledges, so I quoted Lenin to him. Lenin had denounced the partition of Poland by czarist Russia. Stalin brushed this aside.

"Poland is fortunate that I am not asking for more. . . ."[4]

After this Moscow conference, Mikolajczyk addressed a letter to Ambassador Harriman, reciting Molotov's statement that all had been settled at Tehran, and asking for an explanation. Harriman replied that he would take the question up with President Roosevelt.

On October 27, Mikolajczyk cabled to President Roosevelt, calling attention to Molotov's statement about the Tehran decision and demanding to know the truth.[5] Ambassador Ciechanowski relates that, in an interview with a leading State Department official as to this message, the official stated that:

---

4. Mikolajczyk, *The Rape of Poland*, pp. 92–100. An account of the conference based on the shorthand note made at the conference is also given by Ciechanowski, *Defeat in Victory*, pp. 328–335.

This narrative by Mikolajczyk is confirmed by the shorthand note, in the Hoover Institution at Stanford University.

5. Mikolajczyk, *The Rape of Poland*, p. 289.

... He thought the President would certainly wish to intervene, but regarded it as most unfortunate that the necessity for his intervention had arisen a few days before the date of the [Presidential] elections.[6]

Ambassador Ciechanowski further records that:

Except for a brief message which I received from the President through the State Department that he had read Mikolajczyk's appeal and would reply as soon as he could, the American Government took no action.[7]

Mr. Roosevelt's reply came after the Presidential election.[8]

On October 27 Churchill tried to press the spectre back into its Tehranian grave in an address to Parliament. By implication, he once more denied that the British guarantees of integrity of Poland in March, 1939, applied to the whole of that country. He recited the negotiations in Moscow and recommended that the Polish Prime Minister again return to Moscow and settle with Stalin.[9]

On November 1 Mikolajczyk again attempted to secure British support against Stalin's activities. The British Government declined his proposal by letter on November 2.[10]

Despite all this the Polish Prime Minister stuck to his simple statement that no Polish official could sign away forty per cent of his country or submit the remainder to a Communist government.

Seldom in history has there been such indomitable moral courage as that of Stanislaw Mikolajczyk in those days.

6. Ciechanowski, *Defeat in Victory*, p. 340.
7. Ibid., pp. 340–341.
8. Mikolajczyk, *The Rape of Poland*, pp. 103–104.
9. Churchill, *The Dawn of Liberation*, pp. 283–294.
10. Mikolajczyk, *The Rape of Poland*, pp. 102–103.

CHAPTER H

The Polish Leaders Fight On

ON JANUARY 1, 1945, Prime Minister Arciszewski of the Exiled Polish Government in London, together with Mr. Mikolajczyk, broadcast vigorous protests against the annexation and the imposition of the Communist puppet government upon the remains of Poland. On January 5, the Russians countered by formally recognizing the Communist Government with Boleslaw Bierut as President.

Prime Minister Arciszewski, on January 19, again broadcast a protest to Stalin against the puppet government.[1]

On January 22, with a view toward the announced Yalta Conference, he appealed to Mr. Roosevelt again, recalling the promises to Poland. His statement deserves to be preserved for history as one of the most eloquent human appeals for freedom.[2]

The Polish Ambassador in Washington now endeavored to see the President but was unable to do so.[3] He communicated to State Department officials a vast amount of detailed and authentic information upon the conduct of the Communist-puppet government. The sum of it was that in collaboration with the Red Army a systematic liquidation of all the democratic leaders of the underground, together with all other leaders opposed to Communism, was taking place by shooting, summary execution and deportation. The arrests, executions and deportations were estimated at 100,000 in Galicia alone.

At the same time an appeal from a leading Catholic Bishop in Poland to the Catholic authorities in the United States was sent to Mr. Roosevelt. The Bishop said:

---

1. [*Editor's note:* Hoover left this footnote blank. See *New York Times,* January 20, 1945.]
2. [*Editor's note:* Hoover left this footnote blank.]
3. Ciechanowski, *Defeat in Victory,* pp. 357, 365.

In the name of God, the Lord, in the name of Justice and humanity, I implore you to appeal to all Catholics and to your Government authorities. . . . Christianity in Poland is being utterly and cynically exterminated by the Bolshevists.[4]

He gave details as to the deportation of 417 priests into Russia, the closing of churches and the execution of 12 professors of Lublin University.

Such was the situation in Poland when the Yalta Conference met in February, 1945.

---

4. A copy of this appeal is filed in the Hoover Institution on War, Revolution and Peace at Stanford, California.

CHAPTER I

The Death of Hope for a Free Poland

THE CONFERENCE AT YALTA, attended by President Roosevelt, Prime Minister Churchill, and Marshal Stalin, convened on February 4, 1945. On February 6, Mr. Roosevelt sent a letter to Stalin in which the President stated:

> ... I am determined that there shall be no breach between ourselves and the Soviet Union. Surely there is a way to reconcile our differences. ...
>
> I hope I do not have to assure you that the United States will never lend its support in any way to any provisional government in Poland that would be inimical to your interests.[1]

This would seem to be a green light to Stalin on the road into Poland. I give an extensive account of the Yalta Conference in another part of this memoir. However, a review of some of its actions relating to the fall of Poland into the Communist pit is pertinent here. Specifically affecting Poland were the "Declaration on Liberated Europe" and "a declaration as to Poland." These agreements provided a sort of "Freedom Rescue" operation applied to all the fifteen former independent states.

The following is that portion of the text concerning Poland.

> A new situation has been created in Poland as a result of her complete liberation by the Red Army. This calls for the establishment of a Polish Provisional Government which can be more broadly based than was possible before the recent liberation of western Poland. The Provisional Government which is now functioning in Poland should therefore be reorganised on a broader democratic basis with the inclusion of democratic leaders from Poland it-

---

1. [U.S.S.R., Ministry of Foreign Affairs,] *Stalin's Correspondence with Churchill, Attlee, Roosevelt, and Truman, 1941–1945,* [Lawrence & Wishart, London: 1958,] Vol. II, pp. 188–189.

self and from Poles abroad. This new government should then be called the Polish Provisional Government of National Unity.

M. Molotoff, Mr. Harriman and Sir A. Clark Kerr are authorized as a Commission to consult in the first instance in Moscow with members of the present Provisional Government and with other Polish democratic leaders from within Poland and from abroad, with a view to the reorganization of the present Government along the above lines. This Polish Provisional Government of National Unity shall be pledged to the holding of free and unfettered elections as soon as possible on the basis of universal suffrage and secret ballot. In these elections all democratic and anti-Nazi parties shall have the right to take part and to put forward candidates.

When a Polish Provisional Government of National Unity has been properly formed in conformity with the above, the Government of the U.S.S.R., which now maintains diplomatic relations with the present Provisional Government of Poland, and the Government of the United Kingdom and the Government of the United States of America will establish diplomatic relations with the new Polish Provisional Government of National Unity and will exchange Ambassadors, by whose reports the respective Governments will be kept informed about the situation in Poland.

The three Heads of Government consider that the Eastern frontier of Poland should follow the Curzon Line, with digressions from it in some regions of five to eight kilometers in favor of Poland. They recognise that Poland must receive substantial accessions of territory in the North and West. They feel that the opinion of the new Polish Provisional Government of National Unity should be sought in due course on the extent of these accessions and that the final delimitation of the Western frontier of Poland should thereafter await the peace conference.[2]

In summary, the Declaration provided as to Poland:

1. That independence and self-government would be established.
2. That the principles of freedom in the Atlantic Charter would be applied.
3. That there would be revision of the provisional Communist-controlled governments already established so as to make them more broadly representative of all "democratic elements."
4. That there would be free elections.
5. That diplomatic recognition would be extended to Poland only when these four requirements were met.

---

2. *New York Times*, February 13, 1945.

The free election machinery for Poland did not include eastern Poland, comprising between six and seven million Poles, who had already been annexed by Stalin.

Discussing the election provisions for West Poland, Ambassador Lane later observed:

> ... no provision was made for the supervision of the elections by the three Allies. It was merely provided that the ambassadors to be appointed would inform their respective governments about the situation in Poland. And how could elections be free as long as Red Army forces and the NKVD remained to enforce the will of the Kremlin?[3]

This declaration omits the essential facts that East Poland had been annexed to Russia, and that West Poland was already fitted with a Communist government.

The Polish Exiled Government in London naturally exploded at the whole Yalta agreement. On February 13, 1945, it declared:

> ... decisions of the three-Power conference were prepared and taken not only without participation and authorization of the Polish Government but also without their knowledge.
>
> The method adopted in the case of Poland is a contradiction of the elementary principles binding the Allies and constitutes a violation of the letter and the spirit of the Atlantic Charter and the right of every nation to defend its own interests.
>
> The Polish Government declares that the decision of the Three-Power conference concerning Poland cannot be recognized by the Polish Government and cannot bind the Polish nation.
>
> The Polish Government will consider the severance of the eastern half of the territory of Poland through the imposition of a Polish-Soviet frontier following along the so-called Curzon Line as the fifth partition of Poland now accomplished by her allies.
>
> The intention of the three Powers to create a "Provisional Polish Government of National Unity" by enlarging the foreign-appointed Lublin Committee with persons vaguely described as "democratic leaders from Poland itself and Poles abroad" can only legalize Soviet inference in Polish internal affairs.[4]

---

3. Lane, *I Saw Poland Betrayed*, p. 81.
4. *New York Times*, February 14, 1945.

On February 15 Prime Minister Arciszewski announced that the Exiled Polish Government in London, representing democratic Poland, would not retire despite the Yalta agreement.

On February 20 General Wladyslaw Anders, Commander of Polish armies still fighting and dying on allied fronts, arrived in London to protest the Yalta settlements.

Anders prophesied:

> ... the elections will be faked. ... Do not forget that Russia is a Communist country, and that the Communist idea is mastery of the whole world. ... they will never permit Poland to become independent. ... [5]

Some of the statements issued by American citizens following the Yalta declarations deserve to be preserved as indicating the shock to the free nations.

Paul Super, for twenty-five years a leading American resident in Poland, said:

> ... never in a hundred years have the American people had an act committed in their name of which they have so much reason to be ashamed. As an American of long American ancestry, and proud of his country, I protest against the acceptance of this Polish arrangement by our Senate.
>
> For those who know what is happening in Poland, and who love truth and justice and righteousness and humanity, these are very sad and heavy days indeed, days of pain and sorrow, of tragedy and alarm.
>
> I have spent nearly half a century trying to serve the cause of Christ in the world. To me, the fate of Poland today marks the twilight of Christianity in eastern Europe. In all those lands its sun is setting; the night will be very dark; and who knows how far the darkness will extend? [6]

A petition to the Senate in March, 1945, a month after Yalta, signed by 8,000 Americans of Polish descent representing fifty Polish organizations stated:

> We hold that the proposed endorsement by the American and British Governments of the partition of Poland by Russia and of the intended withdrawal of American and British recognition from the legal constitutional Government of Poland in Exile, in favor of an augmented puppet set up by Russia

---

5. Anders, *An Army in Exile*, pp. 259–260. [*Editor's note:* This quotation, as it appears in Hoover's manuscript, contains several transcription errors. I have corrected these here.]

6. Copy in the Hoover Institution on War, Revolution and Peace, Stanford University, California.

constitutes an immoral compromise of principle for expediency. We believe that the liquidations, concentration camps and exile to which Polish citizens were subjected ... again since the entry of the Russian troops into Poland make the holding of genuinely representative free elections in Poland almost an impossibility.

We hold that the United States, born with the aid and sympathy of lovers of liberty of the entire world, cannot endorse ... Russian aggression without losing America's most precious heritage and safeguard—the faith of all freedom loving peoples of the world in our integrity. We cannot deny the principles of our Declaration of Independence to the equally freedom-loving Poland without jeopardizing our moral leadership. ...[7]

A committee of the Polish Catholic Union stated:

The Yalta Conference regressed from the democratic principles for which our sons are fighting and dying on all fronts. ...

... The Poles ... cannot accept such a settlement of the Polish question. ... We feel strongly also that the frightful injustice committed by this new partition of Poland ... will remain a blot on the conscience of the present generation if we approve of this wrong.[8]

---

7. Copy in the Hoover Institution on War, Revolution and Peace, Stanford University, California.

8. Copy in the Hoover Institution on War, Revolution and Peace, Stanford University, California.

CHAPTER J

The Burial Services of Poland's Freedom

In accord with the Big Three agreement at Yalta that

> ... The Provisional Government now functioning in Poland should ... be reorganized on a broader democratic basis with the inclusion of democratic leaders from Poland itself and from Poles abroad. ....[1]

the British and American Ambassadors at Moscow, together with Commissar of Foreign Affairs, V. M. Molotov, met to agree upon the personnel of the Polish Ministry.

In early March 1945 Moscow offered safe conduct to a group of sixteen of the leaders of the democratic Polish underground to journey to Russia to negotiate the setting up of a new government. They were to represent democratic elements in Poland in the conference to be called in Moscow. The sixteen Polish leaders vanished completely on March 27. Inquiries of Moscow by the British and American Governments evoked only Soviet denials and evasions as to their whereabouts.

Prime Minister Churchill recites long communications between himself and President Roosevelt regarding Poland beginning March 10, 1945. In a telegram to Mr. Roosevelt on March 27, he stated:

> Surely we must not be manoeuvered into becoming parties to imposing on Poland—and on how much more of Eastern Europe—the Russian version of democracy? ... There seems to be only one possible alternative to confessing our total failure. That alternative is to stand by our interpretation of the Yalta Declaration. But I am convinced it is no use trying to argue this any

---

1. [U.S. Department of State,] *Foreign Relations of the United States,* [*Diplomatic Papers,*] *The Conferences at Malta and Yalta, 1945* [U.S. Government Printing Office, Washington: 1955], p. 973.

further with Molotov. In view of this, is it not the moment now for a message from us both on Poland to Stalin? . . .²

On April 1, Churchill protested strongly and at great length to Stalin over Molotov's actions in setting up the Provisional Government. In this message, he said:

> . . . If our efforts to reach an agreement about Poland are to be doomed to failure I shall be bound to confess the fact to Parliament. . . .³

On April 7, 1945, Stalin replied to Churchill, blaming the British and American Ambassadors who were members of a Moscow committee. He complained, among other things, that they wanted to have Mikolajczyk, to whom he objected, sit in the Moscow consultations.

On April 5, Ambassador to Poland, Arthur Bliss Lane, still in Washington, addressed a memorandum to Secretary of State Stettinius proposing that the situation in Poland be made public, and adding:

> . . . the passage of time will enable the Soviet authorities to organize Poland through the NKVD—both politically and administratively—in such a manner as to render the term "free and unfettered elections," should they ever be held, a farce. . . .⁴

When President Roosevelt passed away (April 12, 1945), the whole Polish tragedy faced President Truman.

Four days later on April 16 the Soviet Foreign Office informed Mr. Truman that the Russians were making a pact of "mutual assistance" (in reality a military alliance) with "the Provisional Government."⁵ The next day the State Department told Moscow it "was very much disturbed." On the 21st Moscow replied that the deed was done.⁶ On the 22nd, Stalin, in a new speech, hailed this treaty as a great precedent of things to come.⁷

On April 22, 1945, Molotov arrived in Washington en route to the United Nations Conference in San Francisco.

Eleven days after Mr. Truman became President (April 23), he called a meeting of the "men of Yalta"—General Marshall, Admiral King, Secretary

---

2. Churchill, *Triumph and Tragedy*, pp. 432–433.

3. Ibid., p. 437.

4. Lane, *I Saw Poland Betrayed*, p. 86.

5. Ibid., p. 100.

6. Ibid., p. [100–] 101.

7. Joseph Stalin, *The Great Patriotic War of the Soviet Union* ([International Publishers,] New York: 1945), p. 154.

Stettinius, Ambassador Harriman, Admiral Leahy and others. He also asked Secretary Stimson to attend.[8]

Leahy states that:

> The consensus of opinion among the group . . . was that the time had arrived to take a strong American attitude toward the Soviet Union and that no particular harm could be done to our war prospects if Russia should slow down or even stop its war effort in Europe and Asia. . . .[9]

The same day, President Truman, Bohlen, Harriman, and Leahy met with Molotov. Leahy[10] states that the President raised questions as to the Provisional Government of Poland. Molotov charged that the British and Americans had mis-interpreted the Yalta Declaration and the former agreements, insisting that the proper interpretation was that Russia should control the membership of the Ministry in order to maintain "a friendly border state."[11]

Six weeks after taking office, on May 23, 1945, President Truman sent Harry Hopkins to Moscow. His mission was to smooth out the differences that had arisen regarding Poland and the other puppet states; to bring about a new tripartite conference, and to intercede for the sixteen shanghaied Polish leaders. It turned out that twelve of these men had been condemned to imprisonment, for periods ranging from four months to ten years. The convicted had "confessed." (What they had been convicted of has never been made clear.) Subsequent to their release, they revealed the truth about their "confessions" and the tortures to which they had been subjected.[12]

Robert Sherwood gives a long account of Hopkins' mission and Hopkins' record of Stalin's statements.

He reported that Stalin said the British wanted a Polish Government unfriendly to Russia:

> . . . [they] wanted to revive the system of cordon sanitaire on the Soviet borders.[13]

---

8. Leahy, *I Was There*, p. 351.
9. Ibid.
10. Ibid.
11. Ibid., p. 352.
12. Lane, *I Saw Poland Betrayed*, pp. 116–118. When these 16 Polish leaders were invited to confer with a representative of the Soviet high command their safe-conduct was explicitly guaranteed by Colonel Piminov of the NKVD. Their "trial" was timed to coincide with the conference a few blocks away. The staging of this "trial" made the London Poles who had come to negotiate fear that unless they accepted the Russian terms in these negotiations, the 16 Polish patriots would be executed.
13. Sherwood, *Roosevelt and Hopkins*, pp. 888–890.

Hopkins stated to Stalin that:

> ... the United States would desire a Poland friendly to the Soviet Union and in fact desired to see friendly countries all along the Soviet borders.

In a later meeting, Stalin told Hopkins:

> ... that any talk of an intention to Sovietize Poland was stupid. ... the Soviet system was not exportable. ...
>
> ... there were eighteen or twenty ministries in the present Polish Government and that four or five of these portfolios could be given representatives of other Polish groups taken from the list submitted by Great Britain and the United States. ... Of course they would have to be friendly to the USSR. ... He added that Mikolajczyk had been suggested. ... .[14]

When Ambassador Lane heard of Hopkins' visit to Moscow he was worried lest Hopkins commit the United States to a compromise on the Polish question. Lane secured an interview with President Truman on June 4. He states:

> I outlined to the President ... my apprehensions. ... As earnestly as was in my power, I expressed my feeling that we should under no condition appease the Soviet Government by agreeing to its proposal on the composition of the Polish Government. ... .[15]

The result of all this was that on June 27, 1945, a "new" Polish Ministry was installed at Warsaw. It consisted of twenty-one members. Of these, 14 were Lublin Communists plus two local Communists. Of the others, two were extreme Socialists and two were from the Peasant's Party, including Mikolajczyk.

This Government was at once recognized by the American and British Governments through the exchange of Ambassadors.[16] Thus, even the Yalta "Operation Freedom Rescue" No. 3, of no recognition until after "free and unfettered elections," was abandoned by the United States before "Freedom Rescue" No. 2 (free elections) was carried out.

Poland at the Potsdam Conference

Poland came up for consideration at the Potsdam Conference which convened on July 17, 1945. At this conference President Truman represented the

---

14. Ibid., pp. 890, 900, [901–*ed.*]. [*Editor's note:* Hoover's quotation in the text contains a few minor transcription errors, which I have corrected.]

15. Lane, *I Saw Poland Betrayed,* pp. 114–115.

16. Ciechanowski, *Defeat in Victory,* pp. 385–397.

United States, Churchill represented Great Britain until defeated in a general election on July 26, when Clement Attlee replaced him, and Stalin represented the U.S.S.R.

The Exiled Polish Government in London was refused a hearing. The Communist-dominated Provisional Government was recognized as representing Poland.

A declaration regarding Poland was issued by the conference, which provided some detailed regulation of the property rights of Poles. The following general statement was included:

> The three Powers are anxious to assist the Polish Provisional Government in facilitating the return to Poland as soon as practicable of all Poles abroad who wish to go, including members of the Polish Armed Forces and the Merchant Marine. They expect that those Poles who return home shall be accorded personal and property rights on the same basis as all Polish citizens.
>
> The three Powers note that the Polish Provisional Government in accordance with the decisions of the Crimea [Yalta] Conference has agreed to the holding of free and unfettered elections as soon as possible on the basis of universal suffrage and secret ballot in which all democratic and anti-Nazi parties shall have the right to take part and to put forward candidates, and that representatives of the Allied press shall enjoy full freedom to report to the world upon developments in Poland before and during the elections.[17]

The conference determined a provisional western boundary of Poland, pending the Peace Treaty (which became its official boundary).

The net effect of these boundaries was:

a. Confirmation of the annexation of Eastern Poland to the Soviet Union.
b. Transfer of a large segment of Germany to West Poland.
c. Ratification of the Communist Government of West Poland.

One consequence was the movement of six million Poles from the Soviet annexed area to the area assigned Poland from Germany and the expulsion of about six million Germans into the already truncated Germany.

---

17. [U.S. Department of State,] *Foreign Relations of the United States,* [*Diplomatic Papers,* *The*] *Conference of Berlin (*[*The*] *Potsdam* [*Conference*]*), 1945* [United States Government Printing Office, Washington: 1960,] Vol. II, p. 1508.

CHAPTER K

Poland in the Communist Pit

IN FEBRUARY, 1946, President Truman requested me to undertake the coordination of world food supplies to overcome the greatest famine in all history—the inevitable aftermath of the Second World War.

On that mission I visited Poland in March, 1946. Among the members of my mission were Hugh Gibson, who had been American Ambassador to Poland, and Maurice Pate, who had served in the relief of Poland after the First World War and as the President of the Commission for Polish Relief, which was set up September 25, 1939.

We noted that the population of Poland was diminished by the war, and as a result of Tehran and Yalta, from about 35,000,000 to 23,000,000. This 12,000,000 decrease was partly due to the Russian annexation of East Poland; partly to the death in battle and air raids and the execution of about 3,000,000 Jews by the Germans; and the transport of 1,400,000 Poles by the Russians to slave camps in Siberia—few of whom ever returned. We were able to confirm that some 6,000,000 Poles were expelled from the Russian-annexed area and some 6,000,000 Germans were driven from the Polish-annexed German area.

We found from the press reports and many eye witnesses that both of these human migrations were pitiable beyond any power to describe. Neither group was allowed to take more of their belongings than they could carry on their own backs or the backs of their children, or in an occasional wheelbarrow or baby carriage. Hundreds of thousands streamed the roads, the veritable picture of exhaustion and despair—a sodden heart-broken, dispirited horde. Thousands died by the roadsides. Thousands of fleeing Polish and German women were raped and the men were plundered by the Russian soldiers of occupation.

At the time of our mission, in 1946, there were 1,100,000 orphans or half-orphans in Poland. An organization of devoted Polish women was picking up daily over 1,000 abandoned or homeless children from the streets and highways and placing them in some sort of homes.

Ambassador Lane gave me the following estimate of political situation in Poland:

No such an election as provided at Yalta is now possible for Poland is a puppet Communist state with terror in action. . . . A Russian army of 300,000 men is camped and living off the people; about 50,000 Russian secret police, partly in Polish uniform, infest the country; wholesale arrests are going on daily; over 120,000 non-Communist Poles are in concentration camps. They are being tried without witnesses, counsel or jury, and sent to liquidation or Siberia. The police are under the direction of the Minister of Security, Radkiewicz, a Soviet citizen who scarcely speaks Polish. His budget is nine times that of the Food Ministry. All industry has been nationalized and collective farming is being pushed. Mikolajczyk's Peasant Party is the only semblance of opposition left. However, it is being steadily destroyed by disappearance of its leaders and the government's recognition of a fake Communist Peasant's Party.

Former Prime Minister Mikolajczyk of the Exiled Polish Government was serving as one of the two "liberal representatives" in an otherwise Communist Ministry.

Mikolajczyk sought a meeting with me which the Ambassador arranged, and my note of his statement, made immediately after this meeting and subsequently checked by him is:

In spite of having been betrayed and lied to over years I joined in the Russian puppet government at American and British insistence that I must represent and defend the democratic elements. I did so with a faint hope that America especially might keep its promise in order to cover up its previous betrayals of the Poles. I am fighting alone for the ideals of Western civilization. I receive no support from the Western Powers. When I joined this gang I had hoped I would be supported, but I will not last long. There will be no "free and unfettered" election. The Communists have offered 20% of the representation in a Parliament for the peasant's Party if I would agree to their fraud of a "one ticket election." I have refused and my leaders are being executed or deported daily.

Even if the allies were to insist today on a free and unfettered election it is now months too late. The puppet government has created a police state in which no free will can be expressed. The Communists would not get 15% of the Poles [in the election] even now, if it was not for the terror. In another 6 months of terror and systematic liquidation of every democratic spirit, the Polish people are sunk for a generation. All members of the former underground which fought the Germans for 4 years, all members of the Warsaw insurrection against the Germans, all the non-Communist intelligentsia are now interdicted and being searched out. The arrests average over 2,000 a day.

My Warsaw newspaper with a one-time circulation of 250,000 has been cut down to 12,000 "for lack of paper" and any criticism and unpalatable foreign news is censored out. In the meantime, the number of Communist journals daily, weekly and monthly have increased to over 300. The non-Communist journals permitted are two small monthlies, two small weeklies and a daily. They are allowed to print under strict censorship just as a part of the general fraud. The opposition, including myself, will be suffered for a while as a "front" so as to secure food and money from the Western Powers.

I asked Mikolajczyk if the American government could do anything to restore its assurances of the Atlantic Charter and "rescue freedoms" in the Yalta Declarations. He replied:

Poland should never have been lied to and finally crucified at Teheran. America has surrendered to Russia so long that the Communists are now entrenched.

You will be told there is smoldering revolt in Poland. The spirit is already gone. It would be a massacre. If America would hold to its undertaking by real protest and by withdrawal of its Ambassador, it might keep hope alive in some of the Polish people—and as long as hope lives, there is a chance. Some day, I, too, will disappear. You can prolong my life by making it clear that the food supply would stop if I left the Ministry.

He gave Hugh Gibson tender messages for his family who were still in England.

Mikolajczyk's statements were confirmed by the British Ambassador, the Chief of the Associated Press and some few remaining Polish friends of my colleagues, Gibson and Pate. The extent of the terror was evidenced by the messages sent Gibson and Pate by old friends that they must see them in secret lest they be arrested for talking to Americans.

The era of terror has many confirmations. A report submitted officially to our military authorities by a lieutenant colonel of the United States Army, attached to General Eisenhower's headquarters at Frankfort-on-the-Main, said:

> The liberation of Poland by Russian Armies brought with it pillage, loot, rape, mass arrests, executions and deportations. The first phase of this—the inexpert handling—died down, only to be replaced by the dreaded systematic NKVD (Russian Gestapo) methods. Now only leaders of every category are arrested and executed. . . . The Russians are moving all machinery and rolling stock eastward. Farm tractors and farm horses are confiscated and moved to Russia. . . . Poland contains a very large Russian army. But the worst factor of this army of "liberation" is that large elements of it are being demobilized in Poland and the individuals given Polish citizenship, creating for the future either a troublemaking minority or flooding the country with NKVD members.
>
> . . . There is no self-rule anywhere, even in villages and small towns. All officials are appointed by the government, who regardless of political party affiliation must take oath of loyalty to the government and to Russia. The actual ruler of Poland is the Soviet ambassador sitting in Warsaw.[1]

Other observers gave similar reports.[2]

The arrogance of the Russian and Polish Communist governments toward the United States was well illustrated by the arrest of American citizens and refusal by Polish officers to allow the American Embassy any contact with them. American Ambassador Lane records[3] that by February 1946 there were eighty-four of them. He was not allowed to make contact with them and so far as he knew they were never heard of again.

President Bierut at this time tried to get Ambassador Lane recalled by the United States. I telegraphed Secretary of State Byrnes the whole story and nothing happened to Lane.

---

1. See the report of a Congressional subcommittee in the *Congressional Record,* July 24, 1946. [*Editor's note:* See remarks of Rep. Daniel Flood in the *Congressional Record* 92 (July 24, 1946): 9932–9936. Rep. Flood read into the *Record* (at p. 9933) the document quoted here by Hoover. Flood also quoted a report on conditions in Poland by a subcommittee of the House Committee on Foreign Affairs.]

2. See the column of Ivan H. Peterman, *Philadelphia Inquirer,* July 22, 1946; the column of Homer Bigart, *New York Herald Tribune,* July 22, 1946.

3. Lane, *I Saw Poland Betrayed,* p. 197.

The promised "free and unfettered" election of the Polish parliament was, after some postponements, set for November, 1946, but it was postponed again until January 19, 1947.

After the election, the Communist ministry announced an overwhelming majority of the votes in their favor. The American press and the American Embassy in Warsaw were caustic enough in their comment on the whole affair. Ambassador Lane states:

> When [after the Parliament convened in February, 1947] Mikolajczyk arose to protest the elections, Marshall Kowalski banged the gavel, calling him out of order, while the Communist members booed vociferously.
>
> Zulawski, in an impassioned speech . . . attacked the police-state methods which had been used in the pre-election days. He was allowed to continue, but part of his remarks were expunged from the . . . [Parliamentary] record. On the next day he objected to the excision, but no mention of his criticism was permitted in the minutes.[4]

Ambassador Lane resigned on January 23, 1947, after a long career of distinguished diplomatic service, in protest at the betrayal of Poland.

Mikolajczyk, having been warned that he was about to be arrested, evaded the police by leaving Warsaw in the night of October 20, 1947. After narrow escapes from his pursuers, ten days later he reached the British Zone in Germany.

The last effective voice of protest ended when Mikolajczyk departed from Poland. It was the departure of one of the world's heroes.

---

4. Ibid., p. 296.

CHAPTER L

Poland and the Presidential Campaign of 1944[1]

As an incident in the campaign I may relate that six weeks before the election, I received an invitation to meet on September 18, 1944, in Chicago with a dozen of the leaders of the Polish-American associations and editors of the prominent Polish press to advise them upon the action they should take to protect Poland. Mr. Chauncey McCormick, who had been Chairman of our Polish Relief Committee, accompanied me to the meeting.

In reply to their question I stated that, in my opinion, Poland had only one chance left to save herself from the annexation and a Communist puppet government in the remainder of Poland. That chance was for the Americans of Polish descent publicly to demand definite pledges from Mr. Roosevelt and from Mr. Dewey, the Republican candidate for President that, if elected, they would support the Mikolajczyk stand. I added that they should insist on specific commitments. Some of the leaders present asked what the wording of these demands should be. I wrote out the following propositions which I said they should publicly present to both candidates and ask that they be confirmed without quibbles:

1. Poland must be reconstituted a free nation under a government chosen by an immediate election of her people—free from all foreign dictation.
2. The proposed boundaries will not only place millions of Poles under foreign domination but will destroy the self-contained

---

1. [*Editor's note:* In an earlier manuscript version of his case history, Hoover placed this chapter after what is now chapter G. But in his final version, published here, he moved this chapter to the end, where I leave it in deference to his intent. Why he decided to print the chapter out of chronological order is unknown.]

economy of Poland, and will render her dependent on other nations for food. She must not be deprived of her great agricultural areas.

3. We ask both Presidential candidates to affirm in no uncertain terms that the United States will use her overwhelming moral strength to assure these proposals.[2]

An association, "The Polish-American Congress," under the presidency of Charles Rozmarek of Chicago, had in the previous May prepared a memorial to the President, and appointed a committee to visit him and present it. The Committee, after five months of waiting, was now invited to the White House on October 11. They expressed their views, concluding with this request from Mr. Rozmarek:

In view of the attitude of Soviet Russia to the Polish Government, we ask for your assurance, Mr. President, that you will insist that neither an alien nor a puppet system of government shall be imposed upon Poland nor that any part of her population will ever be disposed of or transferred against the really freely expressed will of the Polish people.[3]

Mr. Roosevelt's statement to the Committee at this time, began:

I am glad of the opportunity I have had to talk about the present position of Poland in the war and about the future of Poland. You and I are all agreed that Poland must be reconstituted as a great nation. There can be no question about that. . . .[4]

Ambassador Lane says of this exchange between the President and the Committee:

An interesting feature of the interview was that a large map of Poland, with the prewar boundaries as laid down by the Treaty of Riga in 1921, had been placed, before the delegation entered, in the room in which the President received his visitors. As is evident from photographs taken of the scene, the Curzon Line is not emphasized on this map. Whether or not Mr. Roosevelt was aware of the implication, the Polish-American community interpreted

---

2. A copy is contained in a letter which I wrote to Mr. McCormick on September 22, 1944. [*Editor's note:* A copy of this letter and enclosure are in the Herbert Hoover Papers, Post-Presidential Individual File, Herbert Hoover Presidential Library, West Branch, Iowa.]

3. *New York Times*, October 12, 1944.

4. Ibid., October 12, 1944.

the reproduction of the map as indicating the President's approval of the restoration of Polish territory east of the Curzon Line. . . .[5]

On the strength of their faith in the President the Polish-American delegation was able to persuade their organization to pass a resolution supporting Mr. Roosevelt for re-election. The gist of the resolution was:

Whereas, Franklin Roosevelt . . . by proclamation of the Atlantic Charter, the Four Freedoms . . . "has given sufficient proof and assurance of his friendship for the Polish Nation and that he will adequately protect the integrity and the rights of Poland" . . . we unanimously proclaim and express our faith and confidence in . . . Franklin Roosevelt.[6]

On October 28, a few days before the election, after an introduction by Mayor Kelly, President Roosevelt received the Polish leaders in his private car in Chicago. Mr. Rozmarek issued another statement supporting the President, which was published by the Foreign Language Division of the Democratic National Committee as follows:

Poland as the test case of the validity of the Atlantic Charter must be reconstituted after this war undiminished in area, strong and truly independent.

During the visit of the Polish-American Congress delegation to the White House on Oct. 11 and during my conversation with the President on Oct. 28 in Chicago he assured me that he will carry out the pledges of the Democratic party platform with regard to our foreign policy and that he will see to it that Poland is treated justly at the peace conferences.

Because I am convinced of his sincerity I shall vote for him on Nov. 7 for President of the United States of America.[7]

The Presidential vote on November 7 showed that Mr. Roosevelt had carried the districts of large Polish descent.

Ambassador Lane recounts that a week after the election (on November 14), Mr. Rozmarek wrote to Mr. Roosevelt reminding him of pre-election promises and saying:

Americans of Polish stock . . . firmly believe that . . . you will not allow our trusted ally, Poland, to be deprived of one half of her ancient lands, nor do

---

5. Lane, *I Saw Poland Betrayed*, p. 60.
6. *New York Times*, October 20, 1944. [*Editor's note:* This citation is incorrect. The quotation in the text does not appear in the source cited. Hoover may have found the quotation in another newspaper.]
7. Ibid., October 29, 1944.

they believe that you will allow a foreign-sponsored puppet government to be forced upon Poland against the will of her people. Freedom is a god-given right, and the thirteen million inhabitants of the centuries-old Polish lands to the east, which are now being coveted by a powerful neighbor, never renounced their right to be free.[8]

It is illuminating at this point to review the background of events in the Polish situation during this period of late October and early November.

With the increasing pressures on Mikolajczyk to negotiate with Stalin on the basis of acceding to Stalin's demands as to the eastern Polish boundaries, culminating in Mr. Churchill's speech of October 27 to Parliament, Mikolajczyk had wired President Roosevelt to remind him of his support promised at their previous meeting in Washington. His message reads in part:

> I think I have shown how diligently I have tried to reach a Polish-Russian agreement and how I wish to serve the cause of the Allies and the future peace. I think you appreciate, too, how terrible would be the injury to the Polish nation if, after all the losses it has suffered in this war, it would then be forced to suffer the loss of one-half its territory....
>
> Before I make my final decision, I would like to know your attitude.... I still cannot believe what Molotov revealed about the secret decisions made by the Big Three at Teheran, in view of the assurances that you gave me at our last meeting....[9]

The response to this plea is described by Ambassador Ciechanowski:

> The President's letter, dated [November 17,] thirteen days after his re-election, entirely omitted the points raised by Mikolajczyk, and, by implication, appeared to encourage the Polish Government to make the territorial concessions demanded by Stalin....[10]

On November 24, 1944 Mikolajczyk resigned as Prime Minister and was succeeded by Tomasz Arciszewski.

On November 29, a committee of Polish citizens, named the "Coordinating Committee of American-Polish Associations" issued a bitter public protest against the proposed settlements for Poland, saying "pressure is being exercised to bring about the formation of a Polish Cabinet in London amenable

---

8. Lane, *I Saw Poland Betrayed*, p. 62.
9. Mikolajczyk, *The Rape of Poland*, p. 289.
10. Ciechanowski, *Defeat in Victory*, p. 341.

to Russian demands . . ."[11] It protested the forcing of the Polish Government to accept dismemberment of Poland and to adopt a Communist government in western Poland as directly in conflict with both the Atlantic Charter and with a list of treaties which they cited. The protests complained of the equivocation of the American Administration—a "Pontius Pilate attitude," and asserted that the Administration had repudiated promises which they had made before the election.

Ambassador Lane states that:

> Mr. Rozmarek expressed the opinion that had the Yalta Conference been held before the presidential elections of 1944, Mr. Roosevelt would not have been re-elected, because of the votes of Americans linked by blood to those nations which had been "sold down the river."[12]

On December 15, Prime Minister Churchill again addressed the House of Commons. He reiterated his statement of the previous February, when he had disclosed the Tehran commitment to the partition of Poland. He recounted his urging the Exiled Polish Government in London to negotiate with Stalin and the Communist Government in Lublin. Mr. Churchill blamed the Exiled Polish Government in London roundly. He threatened and betrayed them. He painted a gorgeous picture of the advantages to Poland of the compensations in Germany territory and promised full expulsion of Germans from that territory. He did not mention that this expanded area was to have a Communist puppet government.[13]

On December 16, 1944, the new Prime Minister of the Polish Exiled Government in London insisted that "formal Allied guarantees for the reestablishment of the Polish State" must be given before his government could "undertake the discussion of the frontier problem."[14]

On December 27, Stalin sent a long telegram to Mr. Roosevelt charging terrorist activities by the London Polish Exiled Government against the Lublin regime, eulogizing the "democratic" character of the latter and proposing that it be recognized by the Allies as the "Provisional Government of Poland." Roosevelt replied urging that the whole matter be held in abeyance until the forthcoming conference at Yalta.[15]

---

11. Press release of the Committee, November 29 [28–ed.], 1944. [Editor's note: See New York Times, November 29, 1944, for a brief account.]
12. Lane, I Saw Poland Betrayed, p. 62.
13. Churchill, The Dawn of Liberation, pp. 372–385.
14. New York Times, December 17, 1944.
15. Arthur Bliss Lane, I Saw Poland Betrayed, pp. 73–74.

SECTION II

The Decline and Fall of Free China—a Case History

Editor's note: In a draft of this case study that he completed in the summer of 1961, Hoover made his intention clear. The first paragraph of his introduction began: "The purpose of these chapters is to demonstrate the step-by-step American policies which lead [*sic*] to the downfall of Free China to the Communists and also to show the stupidity of the free nations in their participation in China's affairs."

Hoover continued to tinker with this manuscript until, in mid-May 1963, one of his secretaries completed typing a new version. It was at least the sixth edition or draft. But his purpose never wavered, and the May 1963 version appears to have been his last. It forms the text reproduced here. The typescript manuscript is in the Herbert C. Hoover Papers, Box 83, envelope C-3, Hoover Institution Archives.

For editing purposes I have treated this case study as a single essay. In the footnotes, full citations of sources are not repeated in subsequent chapters.

INTRODUCTION

IN ORDER TO MAKE CLEAR the extent of this disaster to mankind, it is necessary to reach back into the forces which sapped away the vitality of a great civilization.

As I have related in Chapters [11–*ed.*] of this memoir, they included a century and a half of encroachment of foreign powers on the sovereignty of China; the infiltration of Russian Communists beginning in 1920 (which by 1945 had grown, under the leadership of Mao Tse-tung, as the Communist Republic of North China, with an army of ____ and ____ people); the long struggle of Chiang Kai-shek to preserve the Kuomintang (?); the annexation of parts of North China by the Japanese in 1905 (which with occasional interruptions by other powers had in 1945 led to the military occupation by the Japanese of all North and Central China, including the whole Chinese Pacific Seaboard); the retreat of the Chinese Government to Chungking in Szechwan Province; the struggle of the Chungking Government of Chiang Kai-shek to secure American and British military aid to loosen this Japanese stranglehold by combined attacks upon the Japanese armies in Burma.

And into this maze comes further confusion by the American cabal stating that Mao Tse-tung was a righteous agrarian liberal, and Chiang Kai-shek a wicked reactionary and that the remedy was to force Chiang to accept Mao's representatives in his Cabinet.

All of this requires many chapters in this Memoir for discovery of truth. But with this explanation, we may return to the effect of the Yalta Conference on China itself. And for convenience of the reader, we may reproduce the secret Far Eastern Agreement, signed by President Roosevelt, Prime Minister Churchill and Marshall Stalin at Yalta on February 11, 1945. It marked the beginning of the end of Free China.

That agreement was:

The leaders of the three Great Powers—the Soviet Union, the United States of America and Great Britain—have agreed that in two or three months after Germany has surrendered and the war in Europe has terminated the Soviet Union shall enter into the war against Japan on the side of the Allies on condition that:

1. The *status quo* in Outer-Mongolia (The Mongolian People's Republic) shall be preserved;
2. The former rights of Russia violated by the treacherous attack of Japan in 1904 shall be restored, viz:
   (a) the southern part of Sakhalin as well as all the islands adjacent to it shall be returned to the Soviet Union,
   (b) the commercial port of Dairen shall be internationalized, the preeminent interests of the Soviet Union in this port being safeguarded and the lease of Port Arthur as a naval base of the USSR restored,
   (c) the Chinese-Eastern Railroad and the South-Manchurian Railroad which provides an outlet to Dairen shall be jointly operated by the establishment of a joint Soviet-Chinese Company it being understood that the preeminent interests of the Soviet-Union shall be safeguarded and that China shall retain full sovereignty in Manchuria;
3. The Kuril islands shall be handed over to the Soviet Union.

It is understood, that the agreement concerning Outer-Mongolia and the ports and railroads referred to above will require concurrence of Generalissimo Chiang Kai-shek. The President will take measures in order to obtain this concurrence on advice from Marshal Stalin.

The Heads of the three Great Powers have agreed that these claims of the Soviet Union shall be unquestionably fulfilled after Japan has been defeated.

For its part the Soviet Union expresses its readiness to conclude with the National Government of China a pact of friendship and alliance between the USSR and China in order to render assistance to China with its armed forces for the purpose of liberating China from the Japanese yoke.

J. STALIN
FRANKLIN D. ROOSEVELT
WINSTON S. CHURCHILL[1]

February 11, 1945

---

1. [U.S. Department of State,] *Foreign Relations of the United States,* [*Diplomatic Papers,*] *The Conferences at Malta and Yalta, 1945* [United States Government Printing Office, Washington: 1955], p. 984.

Keeping the Far Eastern Agreement Secret
from Chiang Kai-shek

There was a determined effort among President Truman's inherited officials to keep the Far Eastern agreement secret. It soon appears that President Truman was not aware of this agreement for some months.

The agreement itself was not kept in the State Department but was "deposited in the President's personal safe" at the White House.[2]

Secretary of State Stettinius states that he had not been informed at Yalta as to the contents of the agreement. He states that when he made an inquiry about it to President Roosevelt he was brushed off with the remark that it was a military matter.[3]

His successor, James F. Byrnes, who was also at Yalta, states:

> I did not know of this agreement, but the reason is understandable. At that time I was not Secretary of State. Mr. Stettinius was Secretary.[4]

For the reader's convenience, I again list some of the Americans present at Yalta when this agreement was made (in addition, there were also present some ninety-two American political, military and technical advisers as well as interpreters and security guards):

Charles E. Bohlen, Assistant to the Secretary of State
James F. Byrnes, Director, Office of War Mobilization and Reconversion
W. Averell Harriman, Ambassador to the Soviet Union
Alger Hiss, Deputy Director, Office of Special Political Affairs, Department of State
Harry L. Hopkins, Special Assistant to the President
Fleet Admiral Ernest J. King, U.S.N., Commander-in-Chief, United States Fleet, and Chief of Naval Operations
Major General Laurence S. Kuter, Assistant Chief of Staff for Plans, United States Army Air Forces. At the Malta and Yalta Conferences, he represented General of the Army Henry H. Arnold, who was ill.
Vice Admiral Emory S. Land, U.S.N. (retired), War Shipping Administrator, Chairman of the United States Maritime Commission, and United States member of the Combined Shipping Adjustment Board
Fleet Admiral William D. Leahy, U.S.N., Chief of Staff to the Commander-in-Chief of the United States Army and Navy
General George C. Marshall, Chief of Staff, United States Army
H. Freeman Matthews, Director, Office of European Affairs, Department of State
Lieutenant General Brehon B. Somervell, Commanding General, Army Supply Services, United States Army
Edward R. Stettinius, Jr., Secretary of State.

(*Foreign Relations of the United States,* [*Diplomatic Papers,*] *The Conferences at Malta and Yalta,* *1945,* pp. xxv–xxxviii)

2. Edward R. Stettinius, Jr., *Roosevelt and the Russians* [Doubleday & Company, Inc., Garden City, N.Y.: 1949], p. 94.

3. Ibid., p. 92.

4. James F. Byrnes, *Speaking Frankly* [Harper & Brothers Publishers, New York: 1947], p. 42; Robert Sherwood, in his book *Roosevelt and Hopkins* [Harper & Brothers Publishers, New York: 1948], p. 835.

Secretary Byrnes obviously was not aware of all the stipulations of the Far Eastern Agreement—not even as late as seven months after Yalta. A press conference on September 4, 1945, was reported in the *New York Times* as follows:

> Secretary of State Byrnes revealed tonight before his departure for the Foreign Ministers Council Meeting in London that the United States had tacitly agreed to Soviet possession of Sakhalin Island and Soviet sovereignty over the Kurile Islands in the Pacific.
>
> Mr. Byrnes said, in answer to press conference questions, that the matter had been first broached to this Government at the Yalta Conference when it was "discussed" with the U.S. Delegation as an informal plan, but that no "agreement" had been reached or even attempted. . . .
>
> He wanted it clearly understood that the U.S. had made no commitment on the matter of the Kuriles. . . .[5]

It was not clear when President Truman became aware of the secret Far Eastern Agreement. It would seem certain he knew of it within four months after Yalta when, on June 15, 1945, it was presented to Chiang by Ambassador Hurley on instructions from Washington. Obviously Chiang Kai-shek did not know that Manchuria, Mongolia and other important Chinese territories had been, in effect, transferred to the Communists as shown by General Wedemeyer, who was present. He states:

> . . . these [Yalta] agreements had been made concerning his [Chiang's] territory without consultation with either himself or his representatives—it hurt him deeply.
>
> . . . He just was silent for about a minute. . . . He could not believe that what he had heard was accurate. . . . And it was repeated to him. And then he just said that he was terribly disappointed, or words to that effect.[6]

Secretary Acheson Claims That Chiang Liked the Agreement

At a Senate inquiry in June 1951, the following exchange took place:

Senator SPARKMAN. Did . . . [Chiang Kai-shek] ever make any protests against . . . [the Far Eastern Agreement]?

---

5. *New York Times,* September 5 (?), 1945. [*Editor's note:* Hoover's question mark suggests that he had not rechecked his source. The date of his citation is correct.]

6. [U.S. Congress, Senate,] *Military Situation in the Far East, Hearings before the Committee on Armed Services and the Committee on Foreign Relations, United States Senate* [82nd Congress, 1st Session], Part 3, June 1951, p. 2417.

Secretary ACHESON. I don't think so. . . . he thought that the treaties which were worked out as a result of this Yalta agreement, treaties which were worked out between China and Russia, were very helpful to China.[7]

Secretary Acheson also stated:

I should also like to point out that at the time the Chinese entered into this treaty with the Russians, a few months after Yalta, that is in August, 1945, they regarded the arrangements which they made with the Russians on the basis of Yalta as very satisfactory.

Such statements were expressed by the Generalissimo, Chiang Kai-shek, and by the Chinese Foreign Minister. In fact, in 1947 the Chinese Foreign Minister expressed grave apprehension that the Soviet Union might cancel the treaty with China of 1945, in which China had conferred these rights to the bases in Port Arthur, the interests in Dairen, and the interest in the railway.[8]

General [Patrick J.–*ed.*] Hurley told the Committee:

I believe that the verdict of history on the Yalta agreement will mark it as both immoral and cowardly.

Secretary Acheson, in his recent testimony, attempts to set up a defense against the charge that we betrayed our ally by saying that China really liked the fact that we betrayed it in secret at Yalta—Chinese property that we gave Russia in secret—Chinese property—and kept that agreement secret from the Chinese—that the State Department had betrayed China and that the Chinese people liked the betrayal.

That defense by Secretary Acheson is absurd. I was there at the time and I know that it is not true.[9]

Disclosure of the Secret Agreement to the Public

The full text of the Far Eastern Agreement was not given to the American people until February 11, 1946—a year after Yalta—when it was issued in a press release from the State Department.

---

7. Ibid., p. 1924.
8. Ibid., p. 1846 [testimony of Dean Acheson–*ed.*]
9. Ibid., Part 4 [June 1951], p. 2841 [testimony of Patrick J. Hurley–*ed.*].

As an indication of the storm which arose, I quote some sentences from an editorial which appeared in *The New York World Telegram* of February 12, 1946:

> If there was ever a more sordid deal by the United States than the needless bribery of Russia to enter the Jap war, we can't recall it. Now that the text of the agreement by Messrs. Roosevelt, Churchill and Stalin at Yalta has been made public, it turns out to be even worse than feared.
>
> It violated assurances by the President and State Department that no secret political agreements had been or would be made.
>
> In giving the Kuriles and South Sakhalin to Russia, it violated the first and second pledges of the Atlantic Charter against territorial aggrandizement and the United Nations declaration. It violated the Cairo agreement which said Japan would be expelled from territories taken by violence and greed—which does not cover the Kuriles. . . .
>
> This was also a denial of the United States Constitution and the Senate's treaty powers.
>
> Besides giving Russia the Jap territory, the pact invaded the sovereign rights of our Chinese ally. . . . Since none of this could be delivered without the consent of Chiang Kai-shek, the President agreed to "take measures in order to obtain this concurrence on advice from Marshal Stalin." So the later Chinese-Russian treaty, making good on the Big Three deal, was under this duress.
>
> The whole deal was dishonest, because it gave to Russia territory and privileges which the United States and Britain did not possess and over which they had no sole disposal authority.
>
> The deal was stupid, because no bribe was needed. . . . We could lick Japan without her help—and . . . did anyway.
>
> . . . Roosevelt and Churchill . . . undermined an orderly and just peace structure. And Premier Stalin has tipped his hand to America, that he is playing a game in the Pacific of grab and ruthless power.

Columnist George E. Sokolsky had learned the details of the entire Yalta agreement from Chinese sources. On February 21, 1946, in the *New York Sun,* he wrote:

> It is a curiosity of the disorganization and confusion of government that the Secretary of State should have sought to convey to the American people that he was not aware of the facts of Yalta. . . .

A Sample of Communist Diplomacy

On April 15, 1945, on his way from Washington to China, Ambassador Hurley visited Moscow for a conference with Marshal Stalin and Foreign Minister Molotov. They again stated their indifference to the Mao Tse-tung Communist Government in China and their solicitude for Chiang Kai-shek's Government. The Yalta secret Far Eastern Agreement had not yet been seen by Chiang Kai-shek.

Ambassador Hurley's report of this conference, dated April 17, said, in part:

> ... I stated with frankness that I had been instrumental in instituting conferences and negotiations between the Chinese Communist Party and the Chinese Government. I then presented in brief form an outline of the negotiations, of the progress which had been made. . . . I continued that the National Government and the Chinese Communist Party are both strongly anti-Japanese and that the purpose of both is to drive the Japanese from China. Beyond question there are issues between the Chinese Communist Party and the Chinese Government, but both are pursuing the same principal objective, namely, the defeat of Japan and the creating of a free, democratic and united government in China. . . . I informed him that President Roosevelt had authorized me to discuss this subject with Prime Minister Churchill and that the complete concurrence of Prime Minister Churchill and Foreign Secretary Eden had been obtained in the policy of endorsement of Chinese aspirations to establish for herself a united, free, and democratic government. . . . Stalin stated frankly that the Soviet Government would support the policy. . . . He spoke favorably of Chiang Kai-shek and said that while there had been corruption among certain officials of the National Government of China, he knew that Chiang Kai-shek was 'selfless', a 'patriot' and that the Soviet in times past had befriended him. . . . [The Marshal] wished us to know that we would have his complete support in immediate action for the unification of the armed forces of China with full recognition of the National Government under the leadership of Chiang Kai-shek. . . .[10]

There were American officials in Moscow who understood the real Soviet objectives. Ambassador Harriman, who was present during the Hurley

---

10. *China White Paper*, pp. 94–96. [*Editor's note:* The *China White Paper* was the informal, popular name for U.S. Department of State Publication 3573: *United States Relations With China, With Special Reference to the Period 1944–1949* (Washington: 1949). In his footnotes Hoover usually cited this source by its informal title, but at times he used the formal title.]

conference and who was aware of the secret agreement, presented his views to the State Department in Washington. The State Department's memorandum of April 19, reported that:

> ... Mr. Harriman was certain that Marshal Stalin would not cooperate indefinitely with Chiang Kai-shek and that if and when Russia entered the conflict in the Far East he would make full use of and would support the Chinese Communists even to the extent of setting up a puppet government in Manchuria and possibly of [in–*ed.*] North China. . . .[11]

The utter foolery of Stalin's and Molotov's statements to Ambassador Hurley was made clear by George Kennan, our able Chargé d'Affaires in Moscow, who sent a cable to Ambassador Harriman on April 23:

> ... it caused me some concern to see this report [of Hurley] go forward. I refer specifically to the statements which were attributed to Stalin. [. . . –*ed.*]
>
> ... to the Russians words mean different things than they do to us. [. . . –*ed.*]
>
> ... I am persuaded that in the future Soviet policy respecting China will continue what it has been . . . the achievement of maximum power with minimum responsibility. . . .

He then outlined with prophetic sense the objectives of Russia in the Far East:

> It would be tragic if our natural anxiety for the support of the Soviet Union at this juncture, coupled with Stalin's use of words which mean all things to all people and his cautious affability, were to lead us into an undue reliance on Soviet aid or even Soviet acquiescence in the achievement of our long term objectives in China.[12]

On that same day, Secretary Stettinius sent a warning to Ambassador Hurley:

> ... The U.S.S.R. is at present preoccupied in Europe and the basis for her position in Asia following the war is not yet affected by the Communist-Kuomintang issue to an appreciable degree. In view of these circumstances I can well appreciate the logic of Marshal Stalin's readiness to defer to our leadership and to support American efforts directed toward military and

---

11. Ibid., pp. 97–98.
12. Ibid., pp. 96–97.

political unification which could scarcely fail to be acceptable to the U.S.S.R. If and when the Soviet Union begins to participate actively in the Far Eastern theater . . . it would be . . . logical, I believe, to expect the U.S.S.R. to . . . revise its policy in accordance with its best interests. Consequently I believe that it is of the utmost importance that when informing Generalissimo Chiang Kai-shek of the statements made by Marshal Stalin you take special pains to convey to him the general thought expressed in the preceding paragraph in order that the urgency of the situation may be fully realized by him.[13]

Three months later Ambassador Hurley woke up. He now reported:

We are convinced that the influence of the Soviet will control the action of the Chinese Communist Party. The Chinese Communists do not believe that Stalin has agreed or will agree to support the National Government of China under the leadership of Chiang Kai-shek. The Chinese Communists still fully expect the Soviet to support the Chinese Communists against the National Government. . . .[14]

Stalin Demands and Gets His Pound of Flesh—and More—from China

Chiang Kai-shek had not yet been informed of the secret Far Eastern Agreement when Stalin began to demand his pound of flesh under the agreement.

On May 29, 1945, two weeks before Chiang was informed of the agreement, Harry Hopkins cabled President Truman from Moscow:

. . . [Stalin] repeated his statement made at Yalta that the Russian people must have a good reason for going to war [with Japan] and that depended on China's willingness to agree to the proposals made at Yalta.

. . . He wants to see Soong not later than July 1 and expects us to take the matter up at the same time with Chiang Kai-shek. . . .[15]

I may well recall the last three paragraphs of the secret Far Eastern Agreement which now came into action:

It is understood, that the agreement concerning Outer-Mongolia and the ports and railroads referred to above will require concurrence of Generalissimo

---

13. [*Editor's note:* Hoover's manuscript contains no citation for this quotation. It is found in ibid., p. 98.]

14. Ibid., p. 99.

15. Sherwood, *Roosevelt and Hopkins,* p. 902.

Chiang Kai-shek. The President will take measures in order to obtain this concurrence on advice from Marshal Stalin.

The Heads of the three Great Powers have agreed that these claims of the Soviet Union shall be unquestionably fulfilled after Japan has been defeated.

For its part the Soviet Union expresses its readiness to conclude with the National Government of China a pact of friendship and alliance between the USSR and China in order to render assistance to China with its armed forces for the purpose of liberating China from the Japanese yoke.[16]

Chiang at this time was dependent upon the United States for its very national existence as the war with Japan was still on and most of China was occupied by the Japanese. Chiang could do no other than respond to the American pressures for him to satisfy Moscow.

It was arranged that Foreign Minister T. V. Soong of China should go to Moscow early in July 1945 to negotiate these agreements. Stalin made demands even far beyond the terms of the Agreement and Soong returned to Chungking for instructions.

And later, General Wedemeyer wrote:

> However, rather than make a public protest, Chiang and his government went along with the U.S., by sending T. V. Soong and Wang Shi-Chieh to sign the Sino-Soviet Treaty of August, 1945, which sanctioned the concessions to Russia that we had made at China's expense. No doubt he expected that we would at least give him the necessary backing to insure that Moscow would honor its pledge in this treaty [the secret agreement] "to render to China moral support and aid in military supplies and other material resources, *such support and aid to be given entirely* to the Nationalist Government as the recognized Government of China."[17]

On July 19, Ambassador Hurley described how Chiang appealed to President Truman:

> ... in Chungking, the Soviet Ambassador called on the Generalissimo to speed up the process of transforming the Yalta Secret Agreement into a Sino-Soviet Treaty. ... He [Chiang] had not been consulted when his country was bound by a secret diplomatic deal between the United States, Great Britain

---

16. *Foreign Relations of the United States, Diplomatic Papers, The Conferences at Malta and Yalta, 1945,* p. 984.

17. General Albert C. Wedemeyer, *Wedemeyer Reports!* [Henry Holt & Company, New York: 1958], p. 347. [*Editor's note:* italics Wedemeyer's.]

and the Soviet Union, whereby his country was forced to concede certain rights within China which were an undeniable infringement of Chinese sovereignty to the Soviet Union; he had, in good faith, sacrificed his pride as head of state and entered into negotiations with the Russians only to find that their interpretation of the Yalta Agreement went far beyond what he had been led to believe would be expected; he had then made the fullest contributions to peace and cooperation by accepting the Soviet version of the Agreement. The Generalissimo felt that his repeated concessions were deserving of some appreciation from the American Government, and he hoped that he might be able to invoke the aid of America against further Soviet encroachment. He asked President Truman to urge Stalin to accept the Chinese concessions as the most reasonable that could be expected of weary China, and not to insist upon the impossible.[18]

From Potsdam, President Truman replied bluntly:

> I asked that you carry out the Yalta agreement but I had not asked that you make any concession in excess of that agreement. If you and Generalissimo Stalin differ as to the correct interpretation of the Yalta agreement, I hope you will arrange for Soong to return to Moscow and continue your efforts to reach complete understanding.[19]

The Japanese surrendered on August 10 [August 14–ed.]. Russia had performed no service for the bribe to enter the war in the Pacific. The only remaining bait to Chiang to ratify the Agreement was the hope of Russian support against the Chinese Communists. It may be wondered why, with their already expressed knowledge, Stettinius, Harriman and Hurley did not instruct Chiang and Soong to stop the whole business, at least when Stalin enlarged his demands beyond the secret agreement. They only mildly advised Soong to stiffen up.

Soong went back to Moscow and on August 14, signed a treaty of "friendship" between Nationalist China and the Soviet Union.

This "treaty of friendship" between Russia and Chiang confirmed the diseased Atlantic Charter for the ninth time by Russia. It proclaimed mutual respect for one another's sovereignty and territory. They agreed not to interfere in one another's internal affairs. The Soviet assured support for the Chiang

---

18. Don Lohbeck, *Patrick J. Hurley* [Henry Regnery Company, Chicago: 1956], p. 400.

19. [U.S. Department of State,] *Foreign Relations of the United States,* [*Diplomatic Papers,*] *The Conference of Berlin* [(*The Potsdam Conference*),] *1945* [United States Government Printing Office, Washington: 1960], Volume II, p. 1241.

Kai-shek government. The treaty conveyed over 600,000 square miles of Outer Mongolia for outright annexation to Russia.

Attached to the treaty were a number of subsidiary agreements going even beyond the secret Yalta agreement.

The provisions regarding Manchuria allowed the Russian camel's head in the tent. The whole camel quickly followed. The treaty provided that Russia was to have a half interest in the Manchurian railways. The railways were to be under joint management, but the managing director was to be Russian, who was to appoint all important officials, with the Chinese having the "right" to suggest candidates to these posts. A further agreement provided a joint naval base at Port Arthur under a commission of three Russians and two Chinese, with a Russian chairman. The civil administration in the town of Port Arthur was to be Chinese. Its members were to be:

> ... appointed and dismissed by the Chinese Government in agreement with the Soviet military command.
>
> The proposals which the Soviet military commander in that area may address to the Chinese civil administration in order to safeguard security and defence will be fulfilled by the said administration. . . .
>
> The Government of the U.S.S.R. have the right to maintain in region mentioned . . . their army, navy and air force and to determine their location. . . .
>
> The present agreement is concluded for thirty years. . . .[20]

Yet another agreement provided that Dairen, the major Manchurian port, was to be a "free port" while the "Administration . . . shall belong to China." Yet

> ... The harbor-master shall be a Russian national, and the deputy harbor-master shall be a Chinese national. . . .
>
> ... Goods entering the free port from abroad for through transit to Soviet territory on the Chinese Eastern and South Manchurian Railways and goods coming from Soviet territory on the said railways into the free port for export shall be free from customs duties. Such goods shall be transported in sealed cars.
>
> Goods entering China from the free port shall pay the Chinese import duties, and goods going out of other parts of China into the free port shall pay the Chinese export duties as long as they continue to be collected.
>
> The term of this Agreement shall be thirty years. [. . . –ed.][21]

---

20. *China White Paper,* pp. 590–591.
21. Ibid., p. 589.

Still further agreements set up the details of establishment of a Chinese civil administration replacing Russian occupation troops in Manchuria; an acknowledgement of Chinese sovereignty over Sinkiang and Manchuria under the Chiang Kai-shek government—but an acknowledgement of Soviet sovereignty over Outer Mongolia.

All this was part of the price paid by China for the Yalta betrayal. The leading Chungking Chinese journal referred to it as a "stain" and stated that the Chinese authorities had yielded to American pressures.

The whole transaction was a violation of the Cairo Declaration of two years before (December 1, 1943). In fact, it was an abandonment of the justification for our quarrel with Japan. After the burial of a multitude of American boys and vast treasure, instead of restoring Manchuria to China we, in fact, gave it to Russia.

General Wedemeyer's comment of [sic–ed.] this treaty is:

> . . . It was by now all too clear that the Soviet Government had no more intention of honoring the Sino-Russian Treaty of August, 1945, than its pledges and agreements in Europe. The Kremlin was not only denying the Chinese Nationalist forces access to Manchuria, but it had also supplied the Chinese Communist Party with surrendered Japanese arms and equipment, and was backing them with its powerful apparatus in America and elsewhere in the world. . . .[22]

Six months later in Shanghai, Soong personally described this treaty to me as due to American perfidy.

At the very time Soong was negotiating this treaty with Stalin, the Russians were engaged in wholesale plunder of Manchuria.

A report of the Pauley Reparations Commission[23] on these actions presents an appalling record. They stated that before the war the Japanese assets in Manchuria amounted to over $11 billion. The Russians removed all of the essential parts of the industrial plants, plundered the banks of about $3 million

---

22. General Albert C. Wedemeyer, *Wedemeyer Reports!*, p. 348.

23. November 12, 1946 [December 13, 1946–ed.]. [*Editor's note:* Edwin W. Pauley was President Truman's adviser on reparations and the U.S. representative on the Allied Reparations Commission. His report, released on December 13, 1946, scathingly criticized the Soviet Union's depredations of Manchuria's industrial plant after the Soviets' seizure of this Chinese territory from the Japanese army at the end of World War II. Hurley estimated that the Russians' removal of industrial machinery and other confiscatory acts in Manchuria caused at least two billion dollars in damage. See *New York Times*, December 14, 1946. Hoover's account in the text draws upon Hurley's report. But Hoover mistakenly claimed that the Russians issued 10 billion dollars in currency in Manchuria. According to Hurley, the Russians issued 10 billion yuan (Chinese currency) during their occupation of Manchuria.]

of bullion, and issued $10 billion of currency which was used, among other things, to buy the 2,000,000 tons of surplus soya beans.

The Stilwell Coalition Idea Comes Up Again

In a telegram to Ambassador Hurley two months after Yalta (April 23, 1945), Secretary Stettinius again raised the policy of coalition between Chiang Kai-shek's Nationalist Government and Mao Tse-tung's North China Communist Republic, saying:

> ... Please impress upon Generalissimo Chiang Kai-shek the necessity for early military and political unification in order not only to bring about the successful conclusion of the Japanese war but also to establish a basis upon which relations between China and the Soviet Union may eventually become one of mutual respect and permanent friendship.[24]

On May 7, 1945, the State Department sent another message to General Hurley, the import of which threatened withdrawal of American support from Chiang if he did not agree to a coalition with the Communists.[25]

A constant theme of the Stilwell-State Department cabal was that Mao Tse-tung's Communists were merely agrarian liberals and Chiang Kai-shek's nationalists were wicked reactionaries.

Ample information as to the falsity of the "agrarian liberal" character of Mao's Communist government was in the files of the State Department.

John C. Caldwell, who had been in charge of American radio propaganda in China, stated:

> When Mr. Acheson says that no officers in the Department of State have ever written off the Chinese Communists as agrarian reformers he is simply not telling the truth. All through 1944 and 1945 every one of us in the Department of State was subjected to indoctrination as to the fact that the Chinese Communists were not real Communists and that if we were patient long enough we would find a modus vivendi with far eastern communism.[26]

A report from the Military Intelligence Division of the War Department entitled "The Chinese Communist Movement" was prepared for the Assistant Chief of Staff, G-2, on July 5, 1945. The conclusions of this report were:

---

24. *China White Paper,* p. 98.

25. [Herbert] Feis, *The China Tangle* [Princeton University Press, Princeton, N.J.: 1953], p. 292.

26. Cited by John T. Flynn, *While You Slept* [The Devin-Adair Company, New York: 1951], pp. 40–41.

... (1) The "democracy" of the Chinese Communists is Soviet democracy. (2) The Chinese Communist movement is part of the international Communist movement, sponsored and guided by Moscow. (3) There is reason to believe that Soviet Russia plans to create Russian-dominated areas in Manchuria, Korea and probably North China. (4) A strong and stable China cannot exist without the natural resources of Manchuria and north China....

This report pointed out further, and precisely, that the "coalition government" was sponsored by the Communists:

... The Communists.... have boycotted the National Assembly and insist that the coalition government is the only solution of the interparty problem in China....

... the coalition government, were it to be established without the Communists being committed to a specific demarcation of their areas, would only serve the interests of the Communists....[27]

If a policy of a coalition of the Communists into Chiang Kai-shek's government had ever been arguable as a military necessity against the Japanese before their defeat in August 1945, it had not an atom of warrant after their surrender.

Now Mao became a greater menace, because the Soviet authorities either gave him, or allowed him to take, a large part of the Japanese arms and munitions from the surrendered Japanese armies. Also, Stalin supplied Mao with his no-longer useful American Lend-Lease materials.

However, Ambassador Hurley was pressed by the Administration into further action. He visited Yenan and brought Mao to visit Chiang (August 28, 1945). Nothing came of these negotiations. The war was over and Mao knew his next job was to take over China by force with the support of Moscow.

It is desirable to enter in this record those who were the original American officials directly or indirectly involved in the pressure upon Chiang Kai-shek to form a coalition government with Mao Tse-tung's Communists. As shown by quotations of them in this memoir, they include:

President Roosevelt
General George C. Marshall
Vice President Henry Wallace

---

27. *Military Situation in the Far East, Hearings* ... , June 1951, Part 3, pp. 2268ff. At this Hearing, General Marshall seemed ignorant, but Secretary of State Acheson had been aware of it.

Secretary of State Cordell Hull
Secretary of State Dean Acheson
Ambassador to China Clarence E. Gauss
Ambassador to China John L. Stuart
General Joseph Stilwell, Military Adviser to Chiang.

The State Department employees in China were:

Owen D. Lattimore
John Davies
Raymond Ludden
Edwin C. Carter
John S. Service
John Emerson
John Carter Vincent.

The State Department employees in Washington included:

E. F. Larsen
Alger Hiss.

President Roosevelt's Administrative Assistant, Laughlin Currie was most active. There should be included many American Communists in the Roosevelt Administration (see Chapter 4, Section I).

The motivation of the members of this group varied. The best that can be said for most of them is that they had no comprehension of the purposes and methods of Russian Communism in its determination to destroy free men everywhere.[28] Among them were men devoted to what they called "liberalism." There were many absolutely ignorant of the forces moving in Asia. And there were men later proved to be traitors to the United States.

The Washington Administration pressures on Chiang Kai-shek to incorporate the Communists in his cabinet were intensified after Yalta, despite the daily examples of the Communist methods in the Eastern European Satellite States.

Chiang steadfastly refused to be drawn into this trap. Two weeks after Yalta, Chiang made the following statement:

I have long held the conviction that the solution of the Communist question must be through political means. The Government has labored to make the settlement a political one. As the public is not well informed on our recent

---

28. See Chapter [1–*ed.*], Section I.

efforts to reach a settlement with the Communists, time has come for me to clarify the atmosphere.

. . . negotiations with the Communists have been a perennial problem for many years. It has been our unvarying experience that no sooner is a demand met than fresh ones are raised. The latest demand of the Communists is that the Government should forthwith liquidate the Kuomintang rule, and surrender all powers to a coalition of various parties. The position of the Government is that it is ready to admit other parties, including the Communists as well as non-partisan leaders, to participate in the Government, without, however, relinquishment by the Kuomintang of its power of ultimate decision and final responsibility until the convocation of the People's Congress. We have even offered to include the Communists and other parties in an organ to be established along the lines of what is known abroad as a "war cabinet." To go beyond this . . . would create insurmountable practical difficulties for the country.[29]

Such were the backgrounds at the time Chiang Kai-shek and the Government of Free China were informed of the secret Far Eastern Agreement.

President Truman succeeded to office on April 12, 1945, two months after the signing of the secret Far Eastern Agreement. And as stated previously (see page 6),[30] he probably knew nothing of it until three or four months after his succession to the Presidency.

Moreover, I do not believe that President Truman could have possibly been informed of the full situation in respect to China either politically or militarily. He had never been in the Far East. During his first months in office, he was confronted with the changing of his principal officials, the continued wars with Germany and Japan, the Potsdam Conference and the Conference of the United Nations to preserve lasting peace, and many other urgent matters.

Nor do I believe that Mr. Truman was properly informed that in China the fundamental issue of free men versus Communism was being fought out.[31]

The surrender of Japan on August 14, 1945, left Nationalist China in a sea of misery. After twenty years of continuous war with the Communists, and about fourteen years of war with the Japanese, the people were unbelievably

---

29. *China White Paper*, p. 83.

30. [*Editor's note:* Hoover's reference is to page 6 of his manuscript. See p. 672 above.]

31. Mr. Truman gave the first step on defining this issue in the public statement he issued in respect to Greece, [two–*ed.*] years after he became President, on [March 12, 1947–*ed.*], when he said: [*Editor's note:* Hoover did not complete this footnote. He appeared to be alluding to President Truman's address to a joint session of Congress on March 12, 1947, in which the President asked for assistance to Greece and Turkey to counter a dire Communist threat.]

impoverished. Millions were actually starving. Chiang's armies were said to number 3,000,000 but they had received little armament from the United States during the war beyond that swallowed up in Stilwell's Burma follies. The very demobilization of part of this army added to the economic difficulties and the problems of preventing brigandage and pillage.

Chiang's immediate problem was the military occupation of as much as possible of North China and Manchuria ahead of Mao Tse-tung and the Russians. The American Government gave some help in transporting his troops, and 50,000 marines were landed at northern coastal areas to hold strategic points. But the problem of returning the 3,000,000 surrendered Japanese to Japan soon absorbed the Americans, and Chiang's armies were not properly supported to meet the new danger.

The pressures upon him to accept Mao's Communist representatives in the government of Free China rapidly took on even greater vigor.[32]

A directive was issued on November 10, 1945, to General Wedemeyer, Chiang's military adviser, from the Joint Chiefs of Staff. It threatened to cut off American aid to China. The important paragraph was:

> ... American military aid to China will cease immediately if evidence compels the United States Government to believe that any Chinese troops receiving such aid are using it to support any government which the United States cannot accept, to conduct civil war, or for aggressive or coercive purposes. ...[33]

On November 26, 1945, Ambassador General Patrick Hurley resigned with caustic references to the cabal saying:

> ... The professional foreign service men sided with the Chinese Communist armed party. ... Our professional diplomats continuously advised the Communists that my efforts in preventing the collapse of the National Government did not represent the policy of the United States. These same professionals openly advised the Communist armed party to decline unification

---

32. I give such parts of the huge documentation of these pressures from the *China White Paper* (officially entitled *United States Relations with China,* a Department of State publication, based on the files of the Department of State, published in 1949), as are especially pertinent to this subject. Further evidence from participants in the various activities is added. The most important books quoted herein by participants, or about them, are: General Albert C. Wedemeyer's *Wedemeyer Reports!;* Prime Minister Winston Churchill's *The Grand Alliance;* Joseph C. Grew's *Turbulent Era;* Fleet Admiral William D. Leahy's *I Was There;* Don Lohbeck's *Patrick J. Hurley.*

33. *Military Situation in the Far East, Hearings before the Committee on Armed Services and the Committee on Foreign Relations, United States Senate,* Part 1, May 1951, p. 555.

of the Chinese Communist Army with the National Army unless the Chinese Communists were given control. . . .

I requested the relief of the career men who were opposing the American policy in the Chinese Theater of War. These professional diplomats were returned to Washington and placed in the Chinese and Far Eastern Divisions of the State Department as my supervisors. . . .

. . . a considerable section of our State Department is endeavoring to support Communism generally as well as specifically in China. . . .[34]

On December 9, 1945, a memorandum from Secretary of State Byrnes to the War Department, reads:

The President and the Secretary of State are both anxious that the unification of China by peaceful democratic methods be achieved as soon as possible.

At a public hearing before the Foreign Relations Committee of the Senate on December 7, the Secretary of State said:

"During the war the immediate goal of the United States in China was to promote a military union of the several political factions in order to bring their combined power to bear upon our common enemy, Japan. Our longer-range goal, then as now, and a goal of at least equal importance, is the development of a strong, united, and democratic China.

"To achieve this longer-range goal, it is essential that the Central Government of China as well as the various dissident elements approach the settlement of their differences with a genuine willingness to compromise. We believe, as we have long believed and consistently demonstrated, that the government of Generalissimo Chiang Kai-shek affords the most satisfactory base for a developing democracy. But we also believe that it must be broadened to include the representatives of those large and well organized groups who are now without any voice in the government of China.

". . . To the extent that our influence is a factor, success will depend upon our capacity to exercise that influence . . . in such a way as to encourage concessions by the Central Government, by the so-called Communists, and by the other factions."

The President has asked General Marshall to go to China as his Special Representative for the purpose of bringing to bear . . . the influence of the United States for the achievement of the ends set forth above. Specifically, General Marshall shall endeavor to influence the Chinese Government to

---

34. Don Lohbeck, *Patrick J. Hurley,* pp. 430–431.

call a national conference of representatives of the major political elements to bring about the unification of China and, concurrently, effect a cessation of hostilities.[35]

On December 15, President Truman issued a most important public statement on [the–*ed.*] United States' policies toward China. It could not have been composed from his own knowledge of the situation and must be attributed to the cabal. He said:

[The Government of the United States believes it essential–*ed.*]

. . . That a cessation of hostilities be arranged between the armies of the National Government and the Chinese Communists. . . .

. . . That a national conference of representatives of major political elements be arranged to develop an early solution to the present internal strife—a solution which will bring about the unification of China.

This statement then cited the various agreements and actions bearing on the immediate postwar readjustments, and continued:

. . . United States support will not extend to United States military intervention to influence the course of any Chinese internal strife.

. . . This[36] is the purpose of the maintenance for the time being of United States military and naval forces in China.

The United States is cognizant that the present National Government of China is a "one-party government" and believes that peace, unity and democratic reform in China will be furthered if the basis of this Government is broadened to include other political elements in the country. Hence, the United States strongly advocates that the national conference of representatives of major political elements in the country agree upon arrangements which would give those elements a fair and effective representation in the Chinese National Government. It is recognized that this would require modification of the one-party "political tutelage" established as an interim arrangement in the progress of the nation toward democracy. . . .

The existence of autonomous armies such as that of the Communist army is inconsistent with, and actually makes impossible, political unity in China. With the institution of a broadly representative government, autonomous

---

35. *China White Paper,* pp. [606–607. *Editor's note:* Hoover's original page citation was partly in error and has been corrected.]

36. [*Editor's note:* The preceding sentence, omitted by Hoover, reads: "The maintenance of peace in the Pacific may be jeopardized, if not frustrated, unless Japanese influence in China is wholly removed and unless China takes her place as a unified, democratic and peaceful nation."]

armies should be eliminated as such and all armed forces in China integrated effectively into the Chinese National Army.[37]

After stating that the Chinese must themselves work out these problems, the President offered economic aid to the Nationalist Government if these purposes were eventuated.[38]

On November 27, 1945, the President appointed General George C. Marshall, Army Chief of Staff, as Ambassador to China to succeed Major General Hurley.

In his letter of instructions to General Marshall of December 15, 1945, President Truman stated:

> ... Secretary Byrnes and I are both anxious that the unification of China by peaceful, democratic methods be achieved as soon as possible. It is my desire that you, as my Special Representative, bring to bear in an appropriate and practicable manner the influence of the United States to this end.
>
> Specifically, I desire that you endeavor to persuade the Chinese Government to call a national conference of representatives of the major political elements to bring about the unification of China and, concurrently, to effect a cessation of hostilities, particularly in north China.
>
> It is my understanding that there is now in session in Chungking a Peoples' Consultative Council made up of representatives of the various political elements, including the Chinese Communists. The meeting of this Council should furnish you with a convenient opportunity for discussions with the various political leaders. . . .
>
> In your conversations with Chiang Kai-shek and other Chinese leaders you are authorized to speak with the utmost frankness. Particularly, you may state, in connection with the Chinese desire for credits, technical assistance in the economic field, and military assistance (I have in mind the proposed U.S. military advisory group which I have approved in principle), that a China disunited and torn by civil strife could not be considered realistically as a proper place for American assistance along the lines enumerated. . . .[39]

Later, at a Senate investigation on May 10, 1951, which tried to determine who prepared the instructions to General Marshall, the following exchange took place:

---

37. *China White Paper,* pp. 607–609.
38. Ibid.
39. *Military Situation in the Far East* . . . , Part 5, August, 1951, pp. 3183–3184.

Senator Smith: Do you recall who had a hand in the preparation of the directives that sent you to China?

Secretary Marshall: At that time, Senator—Mr. Byrnes was Secretary of State, and I presume he had a hand in it; Mr. Acheson was Under Secretary of State, and I presume he had a hand in it; John Carter Vincent was the head of the China group in the State Department—certainly, he had a hand in it. I do not know what others did.[40]

On June 4, 1951, Secretary Acheson gave to the Committee his version of the preparation of the directives in which he showed that Marshall himself had a hand in the drafting, along with Carter Vincent, and Secretary Byrnes.[41] Secretary Byrnes states that:

The Sunday before I left for Moscow, Under Secretary Acheson, General Marshall and members of his staff met in my office. By the end of the morning's discussion, we had agreed upon the statement of policy that subsequently was approved by the President and released to the public on December 15 [1945]. Thereafter the President made no change in that policy except upon the recommendation of General Marshall or with his approval.[42]

---

40. Ibid., Part 1, May, 1951, p. 459.
41. Ibid., Part 3, June, 1951, p. 1848.
42. James F. Byrnes, *Speaking Frankly* (New York, Harper & Brothers Publishers: 1947), p. 226.

[CHAPTER 1-*ED.*]

1946

GENERAL GEORGE C. MARSHALL arrived in Shanghai, China, on December 20, 1945.

General Wedemeyer states that on the day of his arrival in Shanghai,

... General Marshall phoned to ask me to come to his suite at the hotel. He was unpacking his effects while we discussed plans for his first call on the Generalissimo. He showed me a copy of his directive from the President, which required him to bring the Nationalists and the Communists together in a coalition government. I told General Marshall that he would never be able to effect a working arrangement between the Communists and Nationalists, since the Nationalists, who still had most of the power, were determined not to relinquish one iota of it, while the Communists for their part were equally determined to seize all power, with the aid of the Soviet Union.

General Marshall reacted angrily and said: "I am going to accomplish my mission and you are going to help me." ...

... Even during dinner he continued to show his displeasure. . . .[1]

If any confirmation of General Wedemeyer's statement to General Marshall be necessary, it can be found in his testimony before a Senate Committee in June 1951:

... I [Wedemeyer] told him [Marshall] very frankly that in my judgment he could not accomplish that mission.

His mission was one that I thought was just like mixing oil and water. . . .

My observations further indicated at that time that the Communists had a little power, and they were determined to have all of it—all of it.[2]

---

1. *Wedemeyer Reports!*, p. 363.
2. *Military Situation in the Far East . . .* , Part 3, June, 1951, p. 2305.

Again testifying before the Senate Judiciary Committee in September 1951, General Wedemeyer was asked:

> Did you ever express disagreement with General Marshall on the advisability of forming a coalition government in China?
>
> **General WEDEMEYER:** Yes, sir. When General Marshall first came out and showed me his directive I told him I did not believe it was possible of accomplishment. . . . you cannot coalesce Communists with people who desire individual freedom. It just is not going to work. People who have a spiritual belief, people who respect the dignity of the individual, they are just antithetical to the views or philosophies of Marxism.[3]

Quickly upon his arrival in China, General Marshall, on January 10, 1945, negotiated a cease-fire agreement, effective January 13, with General Chang Chun representing President Chiang Kai-shek, and General Chou En-lai representing Mao Tse-tung.

In summary, their announcement of this agreement stated:

(a) All hostilities will cease immediately.

(b) Except in certain specific cases, all movements of forces in China will cease. There also may be the movements necessary for demobilization, redisposition, supply, administration and local security.

(c) Destruction of and interference with all lines of communications will cease. . . .

(d) An Executive Headquarters will be established immediately in Peiping for the purposes of carrying out the agreements for cessation of hostilities. . . .[4]

Somewhere along the line General Marshall abandoned the Stilwell coalition idea of Communist members in Chiang's Cabinet. He set up a conference of representatives of various groups to strengthen the cease-fire and to draft a basic plan of unified government in Parliamentary form and a fixed Executive Committee.

The membership comprised many academic persons representing the minor groups who were seeking some form of "liberalism and democracy." But

---

3. [U.S. Congress, Senate, Committee on the Judiciary,] *Institute of Pacific Relations, Hearings before the Subcommittee to Investigate the Administration of the Internal Security Act . . . [of the] Committee on the Judiciary, United States Senate,* [82nd Congress, 1st Session,] September, 1951, Part 3, p. 835.

4. *China White Paper,* pp. 609–610.

it also contained representatives of the two powerful groups, the Communists and the Nationalists. The Conference was called the Political Consultative Conference—the P.C.C. The Conference issued many documents and set up an Executive Committee to carry their decisions forward.

General Marshall, representing the Government of the United States, was able to exert great pressures. But the underlying division of Communism versus free men was far more powerful than Marshall. Although the Conference is referred to many times in subsequent negotiations between the two great factions, they, in reality, ignored its writings except for propaganda purposes.

In the meantime the secret Far Eastern Agreement became public on February 11, 1946. It was an immense gain for the Mao Tse-tung Communists and an immense weakening of the Chiang Kai-shek Nationalists. On February 14, 1946, the *New York World Telegram* editorial said:

> If there was ever a more sordid deal by the United States than the needless bribery of Russia to enter the Jap war, we can't recall it. Now that the text of the agreement by Messrs. Roosevelt, Churchill and Stalin at Yalta has been made public, it turns out to be even worse than feared.
>
> It violated assurances by the President and State Department that no secret political agreements had been or would be made.
>
> In giving the Kuriles and South Sakhalien [Sakhalin–*ed.*] to Russia, it violated the first and second pledges of the Atlantic Charter against territorial aggrandizement and the United Nations declaration. It violated the Cairo agreement which said Japan would be expelled from territories taken by violence and greed—which does not cover the Kuriles. . . .
>
> This was also a denial of the United States Constitution and the Senate's treaty powers.
>
> Besides giving Russia the Jap territory, the pact invaded the sovereign rights of our Chinese ally . . . Since none of this could be delivered without the consent of Chiang Kai-shek, the President agreed to "take measures in order to obtain this concurrence on advice from Marshal Stalin." So the later Chinese-Russian treaty, making good on the Big Three deal, was under this duress.
>
> The whole deal was dishonest, because it gave to Russia territory and privileges which the United States and Britain did not possess and over which they had no sole disposal authority.
>
> The deal was stupid, because no bribe was needed. . . . We could lick Japan without her help—and . . . did anyway.

... Roosevelt and Churchill ... undermined an orderly and just peace structure. And Premier Stalin has tipped his hand to America, that he is playing a game in the Pacific of grab and ruthless power.

Columnist George E. Sokolsky had learned of the entire Yalta agreement from Chinese sources. On February 21, 1946, in the *New York Sun,* he wrote:

It is a curiosity of the disorganization and confusion of government that the Secretary of State should have sought to convey to the American people that he was not aware of the facts of Yalta. . . .

Secretary of War Robert Patterson arrived in China shortly before the New Year—1946. General Wedemeyer comments as follows with regard to this mission:

... the Secretary had said he had been instructed to ask me if I would be willing to serve as Ambassador to China to replace Hurley. Marshall replied that he thought I should accept, adding that he had learned in the few weeks he had been in China that both the Nationalists and the Communists respected me, so that he thought I could help his very difficult mission. . . . [I replied that I wanted to help, and if he wanted me to, I would accept the post,] but that I would first have to return to the States because I needed an operation. . . . Marshall radioed to the President, telling him to disregard my negative reply to Secretary of War Patterson and asking that I be appointed as Ambassador to China.

In April, 1946, I . . . left for the States. . . .

Although General Marshall had recommended my appointment as Ambassador to China, I felt certain that his concept of what American policy should be was not mine. As with Pat Hurley the year before, I knew that there was no possibility of an accommodation between the Nationalists and the Chinese Communists controlled by the Kremlin. I acceded to General Marshall's desire because I still hoped that I might help him to realize the danger to America of the Communist menace in China.[5]

General Wedemeyer states:

... Early in July [1946] I was asked by Under Secretary of State, Dean Acheson to come to his office in the State Department. He showed me a

---

5. General Albert C. Wedemeyer, *Wedemeyer Reports!,* pp. 364–365. [*Editor's note:* The bracketed words in the first paragraph of this quotation are Wedemeyer's. Hoover omitted them. I have restored them for clarity.]

radiogram from General Marshall to the President stating that the news concerning Wedemeyer's appointment as Ambassador to China had leaked and was causing him considerable embarrassment in his delicate negotiations with the Communists. They had protested my appointment on the ground that I would not be impartial as between them and the Nationalists, since I had been closely associated with the Generalissimo during the war years, and because I had taken prompt steps to insure that the Nationalist armies were moved to key positions in North China immediately after the war.

Dean Acheson said that he was sorry, but my appointment as Ambassador must be cancelled. I replied that I had not wanted to be Ambassador in the first place and had agreed to accept the appointment only at the urgent request of General Marshall. But, I told Acheson, I did not like the idea that the Communists had the power to determine who might be appointed to positions of responsibility within the United States Government. . . . Acheson paid no attention. . . .[6]

I Make Some Personal Observations

Early in March 1946, I had been delegated by President Truman to coordinate the nations of the world to relieve the greatest famine in all history, which followed in the wake of World War II. Our mission arrived in Shanghai on May 1, 1946. Former Ambassador Hugh Gibson, a member of my mission, and I were brought up to date on the Communist progress in China by Monnet[t–ed.] B. Davis, the American Consul General, and by General Alvan C. Gillem and his intelligence staff, who were serving under General Wedemeyer.

Both Consul General Davis and General Gillem informed us that the "cease-fire" agreement had paralyzed military action by Chiang Kai-shek and that it had been beneficial to Mao Tse-tung. Chiang Kai-shek had loyally ceased all military action but Mao was continuing guerilla warfare. They cited such action a few days before, not far from Shanghai. They also stated that the agreement had further benefited the Communists who needed time to train a new army of over a million men which could be provided with arms from the Russians. The Russians had acquired arms from two sources: the surrender of the Japanese armies and the United States lend-lease which had been sent to Russia. Thus their army would have completely modern equipment while Chiang Kai-shek['s–ed.] forces were fighting with equipment greatly worn by his years of fighting both the Japanese and the Communists.

---

6. Ibid., pp. 366–367.

On May 3, 1946, Mr. Gibson and I went to Nanking to confer with President Chiang Kai-shek and with General Marshall on famine problems.

In our discussions with General Marshall on the idea of a unified government, we were astonished at his utter lack of understanding or appreciation of the fundamental forces with which he was dealing. He told Gibson and me that Chiang Kai-shek and Mao Tse-tung headed "only political parties like our Republicans and Democrats and that they ought to battle out their differences, not with bullets but by ballots in democratic fashion." I hazarded the suggestion that the difference was infinitely deeper than he assumed, and that Mao Tse-tung's government was part of the great Communist conspiracy to spread Communism throughout the world. Marshall repeated the old slogans originated by the Stilwell anti-Chiang cabal, that Chiang was a reactionary and Mao an agrarian liberal. He told us that Chiang had no support among the people, and that Mao was becoming increasingly popular.

Hugh Gibson's diary contains the following item with regard to this meeting:

> The General went into executive session with us and told us something of his troubles in bringing peace to warring China. He is filled with the subject but I had rather the feeling that he is a country boy from Leesburg, Va., who has got out of his depth.[7]

On our visit to Nanking, I discussed these questions with President Chiang Kai-shek. Chiang had a simple but very direct mind. He described the degradation of human freedom incarnate in Communism. He recalled that every Communist coalition setup in the European satellite states had in the end become Communist states.

The *Chicago Daily News,* on May 6, 1946, revealed that just nine days after Marshall's cease-fire order, an agreement had been entered into between Mao and Moscow by which 5,000 Russians were to train the Mao Tse-tung armies in the use of their newly acquired Japanese and American lend-lease arms which had been furnished to Mao Tse-tung.

In June 1946, hearings were held by the House Foreign Affairs Committee on a China Aid bill. The bill included provisions for reorganizing, arming and training ten divisions of Chinese *Communist* troops. As the war had been over for ten months, it is difficult to see what contribution to peace this new army could make. Instead, it would clearly advance the Communist conquest of

---

7. In the [Hugh Gibson Papers,] Hoover Institution on War, Revolution and Peace, at Stanford University. [*Editor's note:* Gibson's diary entry was May 3, 1946.]

free China. General Marshall supported the bill in a cable from China to the committee, dated June 18, 1946, saying:

> The assistance to Chinese ground forces authorized in the bill would be carried out in accordance with the program of reorganization and integration of National government and Chinese Communist armies. . . .[8]

Under Secretary of State Dean Acheson testified in favor of the bill:

> The Communist leaders have asked and *General Marshall has agreed,* that their integration with the other forces be preceded by a brief period of United States training, and by the supply of minimum quantities of equipment.[9]

Congresswoman Edith Nourse Rogers, a member of the Committee, asked Secretary Acheson:

> Is there any way we could have an agreement with China—and remember we are talking about training and military equipment for the Chinese communist forces—is there any way we could have an agreement with China whereby she would not use our arms against us?[10]

Secretary Acheson replied:

> Well, I suppose we have that in the United Nations Charter. . . . if anyone wished to employ force against us I am sure we would veto that. . . . I think we can rest assured that the Chinese will not do that. . . . I am sure that we do not need to worry.[11]

In 1951, Mrs. Rogers stated that at the time of the hearings she had sought to find out who had written the bill. Secretary of War Robert P. Patterson, who was also testifying, said that he believed it was prepared "In the State, War and Navy Coordinating Committee; by the three Departments."[12]

Mrs. Rogers said:

> Mr. Speaker, my Congressional Directory for June 1946, the time of these hearings were in progress, fails to list a State, War and Navy Coordinating Committee. It does list a State Department Coordinating Committee with Dean Acheson as chairman. Among its members were Alger Hiss and John

---

8. *Congressional Record,* Vol. 97, part 4, p. 5386.
9. Ibid. [Italics Hoover's.]
10. Ibid., p. 5387.
11. Ibid.
12. [*Editor's note:* Hoover left this footnote blank. The information cited in his text may be found in ibid., p. 5385.]

Carter Vincent. Mr. Hiss also is listed as Director of the Office of Special Political Affairs. Mr. Vincent is listed as Director of the Office of Far Eastern Affairs. Both positions, as you know, had an important bearing on the matter before the committee at that time. I think my question, which was never answered, was pertinent then and that it is pertinent today in the light of the tragedy we are undergoing now in Korea.[13]

Mr. Acheson, in a New York speech on June 28, 1946, said:

Too much stress cannot be laid on the hope of this Government that our economic assistance be carried out in China through the medium of a government fully representative of all important Chinese political elements, including the Chinese Communists.[14]

Further Pressures on Chiang to Accept a Communist Coalition

These pressures from American sources were even more insistent during the last half of 1946. The record will not be complete without quotations from the documents from both Washington and from Chiang Kai-shek.

On July 1, 1946, Chiang Kai-shek sent the following notice to President Truman, in respect to General Marshall's "cease hostilities" order of the previous January:

Our Government has been extremely patient, disregarding the great injustice done to itself and conceded time and again, for the purpose of obtaining peace. But up to date, no successful solution is being reached on any problem. Now, for sake of urging the Communist Party to repent itself, so as to reach basis for reaching agreement and establishing peace and unity, the following stipulations are made: If Communist troops do not attack our forces, then our troops will not attack the Communist Forces. Should the Communist troops advance against our forces, then our troops, for sake of self defense, protecting lives and properties of the people, and to keep local law and order will concentrate their strength and counter attack them, —so as to do the duties of us Soldiers. This order is being distributed and strict compliance by all units is requested. Also date of receipt of this order will be reported.[15]

---

13. Ibid.

14. *New York Times,* June 29, 1946. [*Editor's note:* In his manuscript Hoover inadvertently omitted a few words in this quotation. It now reads as it appeared in the *New York Times.*]

15. *China White Paper,* p. 648. [*Editor's note:* Chiang Kai-shek's "notice" was actually a message addressed to his military commanders, not President Truman. Presumably the President and the State Department soon became aware of it.]

On August 10, 1946, President Truman sent a message to Chiang[16] of strong insistence upon the coalition. In this message, the President stated:

I have followed closely the situation in China since I sent General Marshall to you as my Special Envoy. It is with profound regret that I am forced to the conclusion that his efforts have seemingly proved unavailing.

. . . While it is the continued hope of the United States that an influential and democratic China can still be achieved under your leadership, I would be less than honest if I did not point out that latest developments have forced me to the conclusion that the selfish interests of extremist elements, both in the Kuomintang and the Communist Party, are obstructing the aspirations of the people of China.

A far sighted step toward the achievement of national unity and democracy was acclaimed in the United States when the agreements were reached on January 31st by the Political Consultative Conference. Disappointment over failure to implement the agreements of the PCC by concrete measures is becoming an important factor in the American outlook with regard to China. . . .

The President complained of certain incidents in treatment of a faction called "liberals" and criticized the Nationalist Government:

American faith in the peaceful and democratic aspirations of the Chinese people has not been destroyed by recent events, but has been shaken. . . .

He then continued with a threat:

It cannot be expected that American opinion will continue its generous attitude towards your nation unless convincing proof is shortly forthcoming that genuine progress is being made toward a peaceful settlement of China's internal problems. Furthermore, it will be necessary for me to redefine and explain the position of the United States to the people of America.

I earnestly hope that in the near future I may receive some encouraging word from you which will facilitate the achievement or our mutually declared aims.[17]

On August 13, 1946, Chiang, in effect, replied to President Truman's dispatch by a lengthy public statement addressed to "My fellow countrymen." It was transmitted to the State Department.

---

16. Ibid., [p.] 652.
17. Ibid.

Chiang first listed the substantial reforms in govern-[ment?–*ed.*] he had accomplished, and the improvements being effected to ameliorate living conditions of the people:

.... During the past year the government has moved from Chungking to Nanking. Wartime legislation restricting civil liberties has been removed or amended. The National army is being reorganized according to schedule; thousands of officers are being retired from active service. Universities in the interior are moving back to their original campuses. Ruined and broken cities and towns are being repaired, damaged dykes rebuilt.

In areas not occupied or affected by the Communists the main communications systems . . . have been restored. Relief is being given to the famine areas. Systems of election and assembly are being extended in the various provinces and districts. Bumper crops are reported throughout the country this year which give hope of alleviating the famine that followed the war. The taxation system has been improved. Since March the rate of banknote issues has decreased steadily and there was no new issue during July. . . .

This much we have accomplished through hardship and industry during the past year. . . .

Chiang then described the situation created by the Communists and his efforts to reach a settlement with them:

When the war ended, the government decided on a policy of "national unity" and "political democracy". . . . We knew that the Communist Party was not an ordinary party with a democratic system. It is a party with an independent military force, and independent administrative system. It taxes the people within its areas and remains outside the realm of the National Government.

However, the [Nationalist] government exerted much effort hoping that the Communists would give up their military occupation of territory and change into a peaceful, law-abiding political party and follow the democratic road to reconstruction. We must not permit another state to operate within a state; nor permit a private army to operate independent of a national army. This is the main obstacle in the settlement of the present situation and is also the minimum demand the government has to put before the Communist Party for the interest of the country and the people.

During the past year the government took the first step to open negotiations with the Communist representatives. Then, at the Political Consultative Conference in which all political elements were represented, five agreements were reached. Through the assistance of General Marshall an agreement was signed for ending all hostilities and for the restoration of communications. A plan for reorganization of the National army and integration of the Communist armies into the National army was also reached. . . .

Chiang also made clear the tactics which the Communists were following:

Unfortunately, during the past seven months the Communists have taken advantage of the situation [cease fire] to expand their areas of occupation. They have increased their demands. They have refused to respect the decisions of the Executive Headquarters, in which the government, the Communists, and the Americans are represented and which was created to implement the agreements. They have continued to disrupt peace by their actions. . . .

Chiang, after describing the military reorganization, then stated six new major policies: a national assembly to be called, a draft constitution to be prepared, the assembly to include representatives of all parties, and the Nationalist government to abide by the truce agreement and give protection and security to the people and their properties.

He reviewed the Communist obstructions, conspiracies and violations of agreements:

In looking over the past year, if we had not suffered domestic strife, if a political party [the Communist Party] with armed forces had not insisted on expanding its territory, our country would be in a high and respected place, our people would have peace and prosperity.

If the Communists had carried out the three agreements reached since last January to cease hostilities, restore communications, and integrate their armies, and if they had, according to schedule, appointed representatives to participate in the National Government and attend the National Assembly, we could by now have instituted constitutional government. . . . The people of Northern Kiangsu, Hopei, and Shantung would not have had to go through again the sufferings of battle and floods. . . .

He stated his demands of the Communists:

Today our one important demand is that the Communist party change its policy of seizing power by military force and transform into a peaceful party. We want them to help us win the peace in China.

We must put down rebellions, and make China a peaceful, democratic, unified, and strong country. . . .

I will not change my determination to establish a peaceful, unified, and democratic country. . . .[18]

On August 28, 1946, the Chinese Ambassador in Washington, Wellington Koo, transmitted a letter from President Chiang Kai-shek to President Truman, which stated:

. . . The desire for peace has to be mutual, therefore, it means the Communists must give up their policy to seize political power through the use of armed force, to overthrow the government and to install a totalitarian regime such as those with which Eastern Europe is now being engulfed.

The minimum requirement for the preservation of peace in our country is the abandonment of such a policy. The Communists attacked and captured Changchun in Manchuria and attacked and captured Tehchow in Shantung after the conclusion of the January agreement. In June, during the cease-fire period, they attacked Tatung and Taiyuan in Shansi and Hsuchow in northern Kiangsu. They have opened a wide offensive on the Lunghai railway in the last few days, with Hsuchow and Kaifeng as their objectives.

Mistakes have also been made by some subordinates on the government side, of course, but compared to the flagrant violations on the part of the Communists, they are minor in scale. We deal sternly with the offender whenever any mistake occurs on our Government side.

In my V-J Day message on August 14, I announced the firm policy of the government to broaden speedily the basis of the Government by the inclusion of all parties and non-partisans, amounting to the effectuation of the program of peaceful reconstruction adopted on January 13 by the political consultation conference. It is my sincere hope that our views will be accepted by the Chinese Communist party. On its part, the Government will do the utmost in the shortest possible time to make peace and democracy a reality in this country.

. . . . I am depending on your continued support in the realization of our goal.

Chiang Kai-shek[19]

On August 31, President Truman sent the following reply to President Chiang Kai-shek:

---

18. Ibid., pp. 649–651.
19. Ibid., p. 653.

Your message was transmitted to me by letter on August 28 by the Chinese Ambassador Dr. Koo. I note with gratification your references to General Marshall. The strenuous efforts, indicated in the concluding paragraphs of your message, being made to effect the settlement of the internal problems now confronting you are greatly welcomed by me. It is earnestly hoped by me that a satisfactory political solution can soon be reached to bring about a cessation of hostilities, thereby making it possible for the great and urgent task of reconstruction to be continued by you and the Chinese people. With reference to the final paragraph of my policy statement of 15 December 1945, I hope it will be feasible for the United States to plan for assisting China in its industrial economy and the rehabilitation of its agrarian reforms. This can be rendered feasible, I believe, through the prompt removal of the threat of wide spread Civil War in China.[20]

On October 1, 1946, General Marshall addressed a letter to Chiang Kai-shek in which he expressed criticism of both the Nationalists and the Communists:

Since our conversation of Monday morning, September 30, and General Yu Ta Wei's call on me the same afternoon, I have carefully considered all the factors involved in the present status of negotiations and military operations. I have also taken into consideration the later developments;

(1) The Communist announcement of yesterday stating their refusal to nominate delegates to the National Assembly unless certain PCC conditions are met and the announcement of the [Chiang Kai-shek] government Central News Agency regarding the operations against Kalgan;

(2) The informal suggestions . . . of Doctor T. V. Soong for a series of actions as conditions precedent to a cessation of hostilities which he mentioned to Doctor Stuart this morning, and

(3) The memorandum from General Chou En-lai [the Communist representative] to me . . . which was handed to me by Mr. Tung Pi Wu today.

I am not in agreement either with the present course of the [Nationalist] Government in regard to this critical situation or with that of the Communist Party. I disagree with the evident Government policy of settling the

---

20. Ibid., p. 654.

fundamental differences involved by force, that is by utilizing a general offensive campaign to force compliance with the Government point of view or demands. I recognize the vital necessity of safeguarding the security of the Government, but I think the present procedure has past [*sic–ed.*] well beyond that point.

On the part of the Communist Party, I deplore actions and statements which provide a basis for the contention on the part of many in the [Nationalist] Government that the Communist's proposals can not be accepted in good faith, that it is not the intention of that Party to cooperate in a genuine manner in a reorganization of the Government, but rather to disrupt the Government and seize power for their own purposes.

I will not refer to the circumstances connected with the ineffective negotiations since last March. I wish merely to state that unless a basis for agreement is found to terminate the fighting without further delays of proposals and counterproposals, I will recommend to the President that I be recalled and that the United States Government terminate its efforts of mediation.[21]

On October 2, 1946, Chiang Kai-shek replied to General Marshall, again pointing out the violation of agreements by the Communists, but making some more concessions:

Your Excellency's letter dated October 1, 1946. . . . The Government is more eager than any other party for an early cessation of hostilities, but past experience shows that the Chinese Communist Party has been in the habit of taking advantage of negotiations to obtain respite and regroup their troops in order to launch fresh attacks on Government troops who have been abiding by truce agreements (attached is a list of important evidences of Communist troops attacking Government troops during the truce periods), and that conflicts only ceased temporarily but flared up again after a short interval. Therefore effective means should be devised to assure that cease fire is permanent and not temporary. . . .

With a view to saving time and showing its utmost sincerity, the Government hereby, with all frankness, expresses its maximum concessions in regard to the solution of the present problem:

(1) The Chinese Communist Party has been incessantly urging the reorganization of the National Government. This hinges on the distribution of the membership of the State Council. The Government

---

21. Ibid., pp. 662–663.

originally agreed that the Chinese Communist Party be allocated eight seats and the Democratic League, four, with a total of twelve. The Chinese Communist Party, on the other hand, requested ten for themselves and four for the Democratic League with a total of fourteen. Now the Government makes a fresh concession by taking the mean and offering one seat for the independents to be recommended by the Chinese Communist Party and agreed upon by the Government, so that, added to the original twelve, it makes a total of thirteen seats. But the Communist Party should without delay produce the list of their candidates for the State Council as well as the list of their delegates to the National Assembly. This reassignment of seats should be decided by the proposed group of five to be confirmed by the Steering Committee of PCC.

(2) For immediate implementation of the program for reorganization of the army, the location of the eighteen Communist divisions should be immediately determined and the Communist troops should enter those assigned places according to agreed dates. The above should be decided by the Committee of Three and carried out under the supervision of the Executive Headquarters.

If the Communist Party has the sincerity for achieving peace and co-operating with the Government, and is willing to solve immediately the above-mentioned two problems, a cease fire order should be issued by both sides, when agreement has been reached thereon.

Kindly forward the above to the Communist Party and let me know your esteemed opinion about it.

Chiang Kai-shek[22]

General Marshall continued to conduct various negotiations on these points and various letters and memoranda were passed. The net result was that on October 6 [9–ed.], 1946, Communist General Chou En-lai addressed General Marshall at length. The gist was that he:

1. Complained of some Nationalist military operations.
2. Refused to accept Chiang's proposal in regard to the number of seats the Communists would have in the State Council.
3. Rejected Chiang's proposal of a National Assembly to formulate a new constitution until a draft had been agreed upon.

---

22. Ibid., pp. 663–664.

4. Suggested changes in Chiang's proposed army reorganization plan.
5. Raised various questions, including release of political prisoners and lifting of bans on Communist newspapers, magazines, news agencies and bookstores in the Nationalist areas.[23]

On October 10, the 35th anniversary of the overthrow of the Manchu dynasty, President Chiang Kai-shek delivered an address at Nanking.

The address, after discussion of the origin and aims of the revolution, again urged the Communists to join in a National Assembly in which the Communists should be represented, and that they should cease invasion of Nationalist China, saying:

... We all know that the minimum requirements for national unification are the integration of military command and the unity of administrative decrees. To achieve integration of military command, we must carry out the nationalization of all the troops and thus establish a national army. To attain administrative unity, we must have decrees and regulations enforced throughout the country and eliminate regional domination. If and when in a nation there are two opposing armies and local governments assuming the proportions of regional domination, that nation no longer is a unified nation. . . .

... To attain political democratization, we must convoke the National Assembly and broaden the basis of the Government, thereby enabling the Government to return its rein to the people and the citizens to have actual exercise of their political power. . . .

Today the Government requests the various parties to participate in the National Government and to attend the National Assembly.

Today the Government asks the Chinese Communist Party to abandon its plot to achieve regional domination and disintegration of the country by military force and to participate along with all other parties in the National Government and National Assembly. . . .

Another thing I wish especially to bring to the attention of my fellow countrymen today is the question of the cessation of armed conflicts. This has been the consistent wish of the Government. . . .

Seeking permanent peace I, for one, during the last three months, have advanced certain proposals for consideration and acceptance by the Communists, but these were all rejected. . . .

Now the Chinese Communists have rejected the two proposals concerning the reorganization of the National Government and the implementation

---

23. [*Editor's note*: Ibid., pp. 667–669. Hoover did not provide this citation in his text.]

of the basis for army reorganization and the integration of the Communist troops into the National Army. They have also turned down the truce proposals from General Marshall and Ambassador Stuart. . . .

In short, in dealing with the Chinese Communists the Government will under no circumstances whatsoever abandon its expectancy of frank and sincere negotiations if only the Chinese Communist Party will place national interest and the people's welfare above everything else. . . .[24]

On October 16, endeavoring to find a method for unity that should be satisfactory to the American demands, Chiang issued a proposal for a Constitutional Convention to be held on November 12. On November 8, he announced that the Communists refused to send delegates to the convention.

However, on that date, Chiang, in Nanking, called a meeting of the National Assembly to create a constitution. He addressed the delegates who had assembled, reviewing his efforts to secure the cooperation of the Communists, and said:

On October 16th, I made public a statement regarding the policy of the Government, with a series of proposals as a basis for the termination of hostilities. I had hoped that this would evoke a response from the Communist Party leading to a final and complete cessation of war. Today, on the eve of the meeting of the National Assembly, I wish to reassert the consistent policy of the Government to promote internal peace and national unity. . . . As a further evidence of the sincere desire of the Government to achieve a lasting peace and political stability for the country, orders have been issued for all Government troops in China proper and the Northeast to cease firing except as may be necessary to defend their present positions.

. . . the National Assembly was to have been convened on May 5th, 1946. However, the Communist Party and other parties declined to submit the list of their delegates. Later, on July 4th, an announcement was made by the Government to the effect that the National Assembly would be convened on November 12th, thus leaving a period of four months for discussions and preparations by all parties concerned. . . . However, legally elected delegates to the National Assembly have already arrived in Nanking and any further postponement of the Assembly would serve not only to intensify political and military instability with the consequent sufferings of the people, but would deny the only legal step by which the Government can return political

---

24. Ibid., pp. [671–672–*ed.* Hoover's original page citation was partly in error.]

power to the people. Therefore, it is the decision of the Government that the Assembly be formally convened on November 12th as scheduled. . . .

In the meeting of the National Assembly, the Government will reserve quotas of the delegates for the Communists as well as for the other parties in the hope that they will participate in meetings of the committees to discuss the immediate implementation of the measures for the cessation of hostilities, the disposition of troops, the restoration of communications and the reorganization and integration of armies as proposed in my statement of October 16.

It is hoped that an agreement for the reorganization of the State Council will be reached and the Council formally established. The reorganization of the Executive Yuan cannot be effected before the adjournment of the present National Assembly. As such reorganization involved a drastic change in the administration of the Government, it must be approached with careful deliberation.[25]

Drafts of a proposed Constitution were submitted.

President Chiang again addressed the delegation to the National Assembly on November 15. The address was mostly a repetition of what he had said before.

Chou En-lai, speaking for the Communists, on November 16, 1946, at Nanking, criticized the National Assembly then in session. He complained of insufficient representation in the Assembly, and that the Communists had not agreed upon the date of the convention, saying:

This unilateral National Assembly is now afoot to adopt a so-called "constitution," in order to "legalize" dictatorship, to "legalize" civil war, to "legalize" split, and to "legalize" the selling-out of the interests of the Nation and the people. Should that come to pass, the Chinese people shall fall headlong into the deep precipice of immense suffering. We, Chinese Communists, therefore adamantly refuse to recognize this National Assembly.[26]

On December 18, President Truman, apparently ignoring all of Chiang's proposal for a convention that would include the Communists, made a statement on Chinese policies. The essential paragraphs were:

Last December I made a statement of this Government's views regarding China. We believed then and do now that a united and democratic China

---

25. Ibid., pp. [677–678–*ed*. Hoover's original page citation was incorrect.]
26. Ibid., pp. 683, 685.

is of the utmost importance to world peace, that a broadening of the base of the National Government to make it representative of the Chinese people will further China's progress toward this goal. . . . It was made clear at Moscow last year that these views are shared by our Allies, Great Britain and the Soviet Union. On December 27th, Mr. Byrnes, Mr. Molotov and Mr. Bevin issued a statement which said, in part:

"The three Foreign Secretaries exchanged views with regard to the situation in China. They were in agreement as to the need for a unified and democratic China under the National Government for broad participation by democratic elements in all branches of the National Government, and for a cessation of civil strife. They affirmed their adherence to the policy of noninterference in the internal affairs of China."[27]

The President then referred to the appointment of General Marshall and its purpose, and reviewed the history of United States relations with China since the defeat of the Japanese. He spoke of the progress made by General Marshall:

. . . With all parties availing themselves of his impartial advice, agreement for a country-wide truce was reached and announced on January 10th. A feature of this agreement was the establishment of a unique organization, the Executive Headquarters in Peiping. It was realized that due to poor communications and the bitter feelings on local fronts, generalized orders to cease fire and withdraw might have little chance of being carried out unless some authoritative executive agency, trusted by both sides, could function in any local situation.

The Headquarters operated under the leaders of three commissioners— one American who served as chairman, one Chinese Government representative, and one representative of the Chinese Communist Party. Mr. Walter S. Robertson, Chargé d'Affaires of the American Embassy in China, served as chairman until his return to this country in the fall. . . .

Events moved forward with equal promise on the political front. On January 10th, 1946, the Political Consultative Conference began its sessions with representatives of the Kuomintang or Government Party, the Communist Party and several minor political parties participating. Within three weeks of direct discussion these groups had come to a series of statesmanlike agreements on outstanding political and military problems. The agreements provided for an interim government of a coalition type with representation of all

---

27. Ibid., p. 689.

parties, for revision of the Draft Constitution along democratic lines prior to its discussion and adoption by a National Assembly and for reduction of the Government and Communist armies and their eventual amalgamation into a small modernized truly national army responsible to a civilian government.

Mr. Truman continued:

In March, General Marshall returned to this country. He reported on the important step the Chinese had made toward peace and unity in arriving at these agreements. He also pointed out that these agreements could not be satisfactorily implemented and given substance unless China's economic disintegration were checked and particularly unless the transportation system could be put in working order. Political unity could not be built on economic chaos. This Government had already authorized certain minor credits to the Chinese Government in an effort to meet emergency rehabilitation needs as it was doing for other war devastated countries throughout the world. A total of approximately $66,000,000 was involved in six specific projects, chiefly for the purchase of raw cotton, and for ships and railroad repair material. But these emergency measures were inadequate. Following the important forward step made by the Chinese in the agreements as reported by General Marshall, the Export-Import Bank earmarked a total of $500,000,000 for possible additional credits on a project by project basis to Chinese Government agencies and private enterprises. Agreement to extend actual credits for such projects would obviously have to be based upon this Government's policy as announced December 15, 1945. So far, this $500,000,000 remains earmarked, but unexpended.[28]

(The American government policies, announced on December 15, 1945, were that Chiang should take Communist representatives into his cabinet.)

This loan never materialized. The President, ignoring Chiang's proposals for a constitutional convention and the creation of a general assembly, noted that the negotiations were broken off by the Communists, saying:

It is a matter of deep regret that China has not yet been able to achieve unity by peaceful methods. Because he knows how serious the problem is, and how important it is to reach a solution, General Marshall has remained at his post even though active negotiations have been broken off by the Communist Party. We are ready to help China as she moves toward peace and genuine democratic government.

---

28. Ibid., pp. 690–691.

The views expressed a year ago by this Government are valid today [the taking of Communists into Chiang's cabinet]. The plan for political unification agreed to last February is sound. The plan for military unification of last February has been made difficult of implementation by the progress of the fighting since last April, but the general principles involved are fundamentally sound.

China is a sovereign nation. We recognize that fact and we recognize the National Government of China. We continue to hope that the Government will find a peaceful solution. We are pledged not to interfere in the internal affairs of China. Our position is clear. While avoiding involvement in their civil strife, we will persevere with our policy of helping the Chinese people to bring about peace and economic recovery in their country.[29]

The above account of General Marshall's activities did not appear to confirm this "hands off" idea.

With all my respect for President Truman and the difficulties with which he was confronted, my contention is that at the end of 1946 he had no more grasp of the fundamental problems in China than did General Marshall.

---

29. Ibid., p. 694.

[CHAPTER 2-*ED.*]

1947

ON JANUARY 7, 1947, General Marshall was nominated Secretary of State. He was confirmed by the Senate on the eighth, and on the same day, he issued a statement from Nanking prior to leaving for Washington. He said:

... On the side of the National Government, which is in effect the Kuomintang, there is a dominant group of reactionaries who have been opposed, in my opinion, to almost every effort I have made to influence the formation of a genuine coalition government. This has usually been under the cover of political or party action, but since the Party was the Government, this action, though subtle or indirect, has been devastating in its effect. They were quite frank in publicly stating their belief that cooperation by the Chinese Communist Party in the government was inconceivable and that only a policy of force could definitely settle the issue. This group includes military as well as political leaders.

On the side of the Chinese Communist Party there are, I believe, liberals as well as radicals, though this view is vigorously opposed by many who believe that the Chinese Communist Party discipline is too rigidly enforced to admit of such differences of viewpoint. Nevertheless, it has appeared to me that there is a definite liberal group among the Communists, especially of young men who have turned to the Communists in disgust at the corruption evident in the local governments—men who would put the interest of the Chinese people above ruthless measures to establish a Communist ideology in the immediate future. The dyed-in-the-wool Communists do not hesitate at the most drastic measures to gain their end as, for instance, the destruction of communications in order to wreck the economy of China and produce a situation that would facilitate the overthrow or collapse of the

Government, without any regard to the immediate suffering of the people involved. . . .[1]

During a Senate hearing, the following colloquy occurred:

Secretary MARSHALL. . . . our Government exercised its influence toward the establishment . . . of a people's government which [would] include the Communist regime.

Senator KNOWLAND. . . . We did not suggest to the Government of Greece that they make a settlement by taking Communists into a coalition government.

Secretary MARSHALL. No; I am quite certain that we did not.[2]

As a result of the Senate Hearings, the following joint statement was made by eight Senators:

The only conclusion that we can draw from this story is that the Secretary of State abandoned the use of his critical faculties and judgment when it came to any evidence which supported the Communist viewpoint.[3]

The evidence before the Committee proves two things: First, Chiang was under constant pressure by the State Department to take Communists into his Ministry; and second, Chiang refused to allow them to come in. General Wedemeyer's comment was[:–*ed.*]

I was appalled when General Marshall, on his departure from China in January, 1947, to become Secretary of State, washed his hands of the conflict between the Western-oriented Nationalists and the Soviet-backed Communists, as if it were no concern of ours. Subsequently as Secretary of State he seems to have failed to appreciate the ambiguity of his policy when he recommended that $400,000,000 be given to Greece to keep the Communists out of power, while continuing to deny military or economic aid to our Chinese ally unless and until Chiang Kai-shek should agree to take the Communists in.[4]

---

1. *United States Relations with China* . . . , p. 687. [*Editor's note:* This volume is the *China White Paper,* previously cited.]

2. *Military Situation in the Far East, Hearings before the Committee on Armed Services and the Committee on Foreign Relations, United States Senate,* Part 1, May 1951, p. 557.

3. Ibid., Part [5], [August] 1951, p. 3599. [*Editor's note:* Hoover's original page citation was erroneous and has been corrected. The senators' reference was to Secretary of State Dean Acheson.]

4. General Albert Wedemeyer, *Wedemeyer Reports!,* p. 378.

General Marshall would seem to have failed to understand the nature and aims of communism in general and of the Chinese Communists in particular. . . .[5]

On February 1, 1947, Mao Tse-tung's Communist government of North China commented on Chiang Kai-shek's proposal for a national assembly:

... Until China has a really democratic national parliament, all important internal and diplomatic affairs which would be passed by a parliament in democratic countries should pass through this Conference or obtain agreement of major political parties and groups before they can be regarded as effective.[6]

Chiang Kai-shek, on April 18, said:

The reorganization of the State Council, which takes effect Monday is another step in the transition from Kuomintang tutelage to constitutional government in China. It gives representation on the nation's highest policy making body to minor parties and to independent. . . .

If the Chinese Communist Party abandons its policy of seizing power by force and cooperates to achieve the unity of the nation, it still has the opportunity to join the government and participate in the work of national reconstruction. For the sake of China's suffering people, it is hoped that the Communists will change their present attitude of open rebellion.[7]

John Stuart, the United States Ambassador in China, wrote to Secretary Marshall on April 19:

It is too early to assess with any accuracy the eventual effect of State Council reorganization. . . .

The Embassy's initial impression, however, is that the caliber and standing of Kuomintang appointees indicates real effort to place in positions of power and responsibility the most capable and modern figures of the Party. It is indeed promising that in the case of Kuomintang appointees there is a notable exclusion of persons closely affiliated with the CC-Clique. A possible exception to this is the appointment of Wu Chung-hsin sometime governor of Sinkiang province.[8]

---

5. Ibid., p. 376.
6. *United States Relations with China*, p. 719.
7. Ibid., p. 739, 740.
8. Ibid., pp. 744–745.

In an address on April 23, 1947, Chiang Kai-shek said:

My fellow countrymen, four months have passed since the promulgation of the Constitution of the Republic of China. The Kuomintang is now in the process of concluding its political tutelage. It has broadened the basis of the Government. . . .

The next eight months will be a period of transition from political tutelage to constitutional democracy. . . .

. . . Ever since V-J day, the Government has, with the greatest zeal and patience, been seeking a political solution of the Chinese Communist problem. During the past year, on instructions of the President, I have time and again participated in the negotiations for peaceful unification. Unfortunately, the situation has deteriorated so that today the Chinese Communists are in an all-out armed rebellion against the state, thus slamming the door for further negotiations and nullifying all past efforts toward peace. . . .

. . . The Government will, in accordance with the constitution and the new administrative policies, safeguard all civil freedoms and rights according to law. At the same time, it is my hope that all the people of the country will fully respect the divinity of the law, enhance their law abiding spirit, and realize their responsibility towards the state. In so doing, freedom and law will go hand in hand, thus ensuring the successful development of a constitutional democracy in China. . . .[9]

The same day, the Chinese Minister of Information stated:

I am happy to be able to announce that one party rule in China has come to an end today. The Kuomintang has fulfilled its promise of handing over the political power to the people and carrying out its program for establishing constitutional government after the tutelage period. . . .[10]

---

9. Ibid., pp. 742–743.

10. Ibid., p. [741–ed.]. [*Editor's note:* Hoover's original page citation was incorrect. At this point in Hoover's manuscript, following the quotation cited in note 10, the following paragraph, written by Hoover, appears by itself on a separate page:

On April 5, 1947, Ambassador Stuart sent a dispatch to Secretary Marshall. He related the proceedings of the Third Plenary Session of the Kuomintang. He complained of ". . . the most fanatically anti-Communist group in China . . ." in Chiang's government.

At the end of this brief paragraph Hoover placed the footnote number "10a" and cited as his source *United States Relations with China,* p. 735.

On the margin of this page someone—not Hoover—wrote: "Insert where?" Hoover evidently never answered this query. His paragraph seems to have been intended to bolster his contention that key American government officials were excessively critical of Chiang Kai-shek's anti-Communist supporters and insufficiently critical of the Chinese Communists.]

The details of Communist activities were given by President Chiang Kai-shek in a radio broadcast on July 7. After a recitation of Communist army attacks in various places in North China, he said:

Fellow-countrymen, we must realize that, in thus engaging in armed rebellion, the Communists aim to disintegrate all of China and our whole nation. They seek total elimination of our national spirit and hereditary virtues, eternal enslavement of our race, and the complete deprivation of the basic human attributes of independence and freedom. . . .

The activities of the Communist rebels in the past year or so were centered in the destruction of communication lines, industrial and mining plants and the already-depleted farms. . . . If we do not discern the treacherous plots of the Communists, and if we are not determined to quell their rebellion, not only will the people's livelihood be impoverished, but the whole country will be disintegrated.

It was the pre-determined policy of the Chinese Communists to rebel against the Government after the conclusion of the war. After V-J Day, they openly launched the so-called "join-the-army movement," "social struggles," and "people's liquidation," in the rebel areas. They looted what food and clothing they could find in order to conserve their rebellious strength. Not even the old men and women or the children are spared from their terrorism and wantonness. Youngsters in rebel areas must either follow their dictates or perish, and burial alive or torture are meted out if the slightest opposition is shown. If a man escapes from rebel control, his whole family is executed. Thousands upon thousands of our compatriots in rebel areas have become sacrifices to the Communists, who have opposed the Government and menaced the people. . . .

Fellow-countrymen, there are two ways before us and we must immediately choose between them. The first is to vacillate before the ravages and devastation of the Communists and our whole people will perish. The other is to face the facts realistically, put down the rebellious elements and salvage our nation as well as ourselves. . . .

. . . we must exert our utmost to effect administrative reforms. We have committed ourselves to a dual political program: to quell the Communist rebellion and introduce governmental reforms. Admittedly many defects exist in our administration. Weaknesses can also be found in our way of life. Immediately after the conclusion of the eight-year war, the Communist rebellion began, thus, we have been given no time to put our house in order.

Our material resources, already drained by the war, are practically exhausted. The defects and weaknesses in the Government and in our way of life, which first made their appearance in the war, have now become more apparent. The sufferings of the people have immeasurably increased. Unless drastic reforms are introduced, China may not be able to exist in the family of nations. Therefore, political, educational, economic and social reforms, which should be made, shall not be delayed until the conclusion of the suppression campaign, but will be initiated right away. . . .[11]

General Wedemeyer's Mission

General Wedemeyer states that General Marshall sent for him and:

. . . told me that he had been discussing the Far Eastern situation with the President and other members of the Cabinet, and it had been decided that an objective survey should be made of conditions in China and Korea as a basis for future policy. He wanted me to undertake this mission and assured me that this would be only a temporary assignment requiring no more than two or three months.

I asked Marshall exactly what he expected me to uncover that was not already available in many State and War Department reports, or which the Embassy staff could not obtain. Marshall then admitted that pressures in Congress (from Congressman Walter Judd, Senator Styles Bridges, and others) and from other sources accusing the Administration of pursuing a negative policy in China were compelling a reappraisal of U.S. policy. . . .

When Marshall told me I could write my own directive for my mission to China. . . . I agreed to go, under the impression that I had been appointed not simply to give a superficially "new look" to our China policy but to provide the basis for a fundamental change. . . .[12]

General Wedemeyer describes his investigation:

I did not, of course, confine my observations, interviews, and discussions to Nanking; but traveled extensively north, east, and south, visiting Mukden in Manchuria, Peiping, Tientsin, Formosa, Shanghai, and Canton. Everywhere I discussed the situation and ascertained the views of a multitude of Chinese

---

11. Ibid., pp. 749–755.
12. General Albert Wedemeyer, *Wedemeyer Reports!*, p. 382 [to p. 383–ed.].

and foreigners, including Americans. I consulted Chinese of various political persuasions as well as government officials and military leaders. After several weeks of travel I went to Nanking to prepare for my return to the States and to start writing my report.[13]

General Wedemeyer's Report

General Wedemeyer submitted his report to President Truman and Secretary of State Marshall on September 19, 1947. The report contained a strong statement of facts and his conclusion. Some of the paragraphs in General Wedemeyer's report were:

> ... [The] goals and the lofty aims of freedom-loving peoples are jeopardized ... by [Communist] forces as sinister as those that operated in Europe and Asia during the ten years leading to World War II. The pattern is familiar—employment of subversive agents; infiltration tactics; incitement of disorder and chaos to disrupt normal economy and thereby to undermine popular confidence in government and leaders; seizure of authority without reference to the will of the people—all the techniques skillfully designed and ruthlessly implemented in order to create favorable conditions for the imposition of totalitarian ideologies. . . .[14]

In his conclusion to the major part of the report, he stated:

> The Communists have the tactical initiative in the overall military situation. The Nationalist position in Manchuria is precarious, and in Shantung and Hopei Provinces strongly disputed. Continued deterioration of the situation may result in the early establishment of a Soviet satellite government in Manchuria and ultimately in the evolution of a Communist-dominated China.[15]

In a special appendix attached to the report, General Wedemeyer further elaborated on the situation in China:

> Soviet aims in the Far East are diametrically opposed to and jeopardize United States interests in China in that their aims envisage progressive expansion of Soviet control and dominant influence. Realization of their aims in China would threaten United States strategic security. Time works to advantage of the Soviet Union.

---

13. Ibid., p. 387.
14. *United States Relations with China*, p. 766.
15. Ibid., p. 773.

The Soviet Union, in achieving her aims, is being actively assisted by the Chinese Communist Party, which, by its actions and propaganda, is proven to be a tool of Soviet foreign policy. . . .[16]

What Happened to the Wedemeyer Report

General Wedemeyer had a premonitory sign as to the Washington Administration views of his report. He states:

> After I had submitted my report to the President, I temporarily occupied an office in the State Department. . . . the then Chief of the Far Eastern Division, Mr. Walton Butterworth, visited me several times. But on only one occasion did we consider the findings on which my report was based, and Mr. Butterworth then told me that the Secretary of State wanted me to delete certain specific portions. I told him that I could not agree to do this. He then suggested that the Secretary might be angry if I did not accede to his wishes, because he wanted to publish my report but could not do so unless certain statements were removed. . . .
>
> I then explained to Butterworth that considerable research, analysis, and thought had gone into the preparation of the report. If the sections he indicated were deleted, the continuity of thought and, in fact, the very heart of the report would be removed. . . .
>
> . . . I believed it was not yet too late to remedy the unfortunate consequence of our former China policy, which had been formulated on the basis of illusions and myths about communism which had already been discarded in our policy toward Greece and Europe in general.[17]

But the premonitory signs quickly became more real. The following order was issued by General Marshall:

Department of State
Washington
September 25, 1947

MEMORANDUM FOR MR. CONNELLY

The following letter from Secretary Marshall to the President was dictated to me this morning over the secret telephone:

---

16. Ibid., Appendix "D" to the Wedemeyer Report to the President, pp. 813–814.
17. General Albert C. Wedemeyer, *Wedemeyer Reports!*, pp. 396–7, 395.

"Dear Mr. President:

"I understand General Wedemeyer is presenting his report to you at noon today. It seems to me mandatory that we treat Wedemeyer's report strictly top secret and that no indication of its contents be divulged to the public. This will allow us time to review our policy in the light of the report, giving due consideration to it in balance with our policies in other parts of the world.

"If you agree, I suggest Wedemeyer be informed by you accordingly.

"If questioned by the press, you might state that a summary of the report cannot be issued until careful consideration has been given it by the various Departments of the Government concerned.

Faithfully yours,
G. C. MARSHALL."

I agree HST   C. H. Humelsine
                                                     Executive Secretary[18]

General Marshall, in a hearing before the Senate Foreign Relations Committee, stated:

I personally suppressed it [the Wedemeyer Report]. . . . It seemed very unwise to give it publicity.[19]

The Wedemeyer Report was held secret from the American people for two years.[20]

General Wedemeyer's observation on this suppression was:

Not that I was ever again consulted, nor my report discussed. It was simply buried until in the course of time it was exhumed by Senate Committee investigators alarmed at the imminent loss of China to the Communists. . . .[21]

---

18. General Albert C. Wedemeyer, *Wedemeyer Reports!*, p. 446. [*Editor's note:* The words "I agree HST" were handwritten by President Truman.]

19. *New York Times,* September 30, 1950.

20. All references to Korea were deleted by the State Department before publication in 1949 and some deletions remained even after the Korea report was revealed in May 1951.

21. General Albert C. Wedemeyer, *Wedemeyer Reports!*, p. 398.

1948

THE WASHINGTON PRESSURES upon Chiang Kai-shek and the Nationalist Government to take representatives of Mao Tse-tung's Communists into his government was [*sic–ed.*] unceasing in 1948.

Also, the American Ambassador in China, John Stuart, flooded the Washington Administration during the whole period with criticisms of Chiang, of his attempts to build a constitutional government, and of his reforms generally. The Ambassador also increasingly expressed to Washington his pessimism about the future of China.[1]

The Congress enacted two "China Aid" bills simultaneously on April 3, 1948. The first of them provided economic aid and food relief from the raging famine—and was enacted upon President Truman's recommendation. It appropriated $338,000,000 to be available to the end of 1949.

The second bill provided $125,000,000 for military aid. The preamble to the bills was an expression of Congressional recognition of both the Chinese Communist threat to the world and a confirmation of the correctness of Chiang's attitude on Communism. The preamble stated:

> . . . recognizing that disruption following in the wake of war is not contained by national frontiers, the Congress finds that the existing situation in China endangers the establishment of a lasting peace, the general welfare and national interest of the United States. . . . It is the sense of the Congress that the further evolution in China of Principles of individual liberty, free institutions, and genuine independence rests largely upon the continuing development of a strong and democratic national government. . . .[2]

---

1. Examples may be found in the *China White Paper,* pp. 872–901. See also pp. 901–919 for a series of summaries during 1948 by the American Embassy in Nanking to the Department of State.

2. *China White Paper,* p. 991.

... it is declared to be the policy of the people of the United States to encourage the Republic of China [the Nationalist Government] and its people
to exert sustained common efforts which will speedily achieve the internal
peace and economic stability in China. . . . It is further declared to be the
policy of the people of the United States to encourage the Republic of China
in its efforts to maintain the genuine independence and the administrative
integrity of China, and to sustain and strengthen principles of individual liberty and free institutions in China through a program of assistance based on
self-help and cooperation. . . .[3]

For some reasons, the military aids to Chiang Kai-shek were slowed down.
The records show that arrangements with the Chinese Ambassador in Washington were not completed until August 6, or nearly four months after the
appropriation was authorized. During the last four months of 1948, shipments
at a value of $60,958,791 were made. The balance, valued at $64,041,209, was
not made until 1949.[4]

It is difficult to justify these delays on the grounds of productive capacity.
During the Second World War, we were able to turn out an average of roughly
$3,000,000,000 in supplies every eleven months. Therefore, the Chinese com-
plaints of delay in delivery would seem to be amply justified.

With regard to continued pressure, General Wedemeyer says:

... March 10, 1948, Secretary of State Marshall "replied in the affirmative" to a
question whether President Truman's December 15, 1945, statement demanding that the Communists should be included in the Chinese government was
still our policy. And on March 11, 1948, President Truman at his press conference replied to questions concerning the inclusion of the Chinese Communists in the Chinese Government by saying that his December 15, 1945,
statement of policy regarding this as the *sine qua non* of American aid and
support, "still stood."[5]

The following is a report of President Truman's press conference of
March 11, 1948:

... questions were put to the President . . . concerning the inclusion of Chinese Communists in the Chinese Government. The President was specifically
asked whether he still supported the statement he had made on December 15,

---

3. Ibid., p. 992.
4. Ibid., pp. [1052–1053. Hoover's original page citation was incorrect–*ed.*]
5. General Albert C. Wedemeyer, *Wedemeyer Reports!,* [p. 378. Hoover's original page citation
was incorrect.–*ed.*]

1945. The President replied that this statement still stood. In answer to further questions, he explained that it was not the policy of the United States to urge the National Government of China to take Communists into the Government, but that the policy of the United States, which had further been carried out by General Marshall on his mission to China, was to assist the Chiang Kai-shek Government to meet the situation with which it was confronted. He expressed his hope that the Chinese liberals would be taken into the Government, but stated that "we did not want any Communists in the Government of China or anywhere else if we could help it."[6]

This last sentence appears to be a retreat from previous policies, especially that expressed on December 15, 1945.

General Wedemeyer says:

> ... Political, military, and economic position of Central [Nationalist] Government has continued to deteriorate within recent months in accordance with previous expectations. Currently, the cumulative effect of the absence of substantial financial and military assistance expected from the Wedemeyer Mission and renewed Communist military activity are intensifying the Chinese tendency to panic in times of crisis.[7]

On March 31, 1948, Ambassador John Leighton Stuart wrote to Secretary Marshall:

> The Chinese people do not want to become Communists yet they see the tide of Communism running irresistibly onward. In midst of this chaos and inaction the Generalissimo stands out as the only moral force capable of action. . . .[8]

Five months later, on August 10, the Ambassador, opposing coalition, stated:

> Even though at present some form of coalition seems most likely we believe that from the standpoint of the United States it would be most undesirable. We say this because the history of coalitions including Communists demonstrates all too clearly Communist ability by political means to take over complete control of the government and in the process to acquire some kind

---

6. *China White Paper*, pp. 272–273.
7. General Albert C. Wedemeyer, *Wedemeyer Reports!*, p. 399. [*Editor's note*: Hoover's attribution here is inaccurate. Wedemeyer did not write these words; he was quoting a report by the U.S. Ambassador to China, John Leighton Stuart, to the State Department on September 20, 1947.]
8. *China White Paper*, p. 845.

of international recognition. We question whether a Communist government can in the foreseeable future come to full power in all China by means other than coalition. We would recommend therefore that American efforts be designed to prevent the formation of a coalition government and our best means to that end is continued and, if possible, increased support to the present government. . . .[9]

This was, of course, a complete negation of Secretary Marshall's policies. On November 6, 1948, Dr. T. S. Tsiang, the Chinese delegate to the United Nations, visited Secretary Marshall in Paris. Secretary Marshall reported the meeting to Under Secretary Lovett as follows:

Dr. T. S. Tsiang, Chinese delegate to the United Nations, called on me this morning with a message from Foreign Minister Dr. Wang.

(1) Would the United States agree to the appointment of United States officers in actual command of the Chinese army units under the pretense of acting as advisers [as in Greece]?

(2) Would the United States appoint an officer of high rank to head the special mission, primarily for advice and planning on an emergency situation?

(3) Will the United States expedite the supply of munitions?

(4) What was the thought as to the advisability of Chinese appeal to the United Nations because of Soviet training and equipping of Japanese military and also the Koreans?

I explained the efforts regarding the supply of munitions and stated I would request you to press for urgent action. I did not offer encouragement beyond present efforts.

I said I would refer the requests under (2) and (3) to Washington without making any comment to reference (1).

I remarked regarding (2) that the proposition inherently involved great difficulties if favorably considered; that if the individual did not know China it would require months for him to grasp understanding of the possibilities of the situation, and it would therefore be a very serious matter for the United States to send an officer to almost certain failure.

Regarding (4) I said I would have to consult my colleagues of the United States delegation to develop various possibilities; that offhand I thought it

---

9. Ibid., pp. 886–887.

an inadvisable procedure and discussed possible Soviet moves to take advantage rather than to counter such a move. Dr. Tsiang told me the proposition had been put to him three times and each time he had recommended against such action.

MARSHALL[10]

Again, on November 8, 1948, Secretary Marshall sent the following message to Under Secretary Lovett, from Paris:

Your report of November 6 shows why the visit of a high-ranking United States officer to China would be undesirable and unproductive. Even if the record of the repeated failure of the Chinese Government in the past to accept U.S. advice did not exist, it would be foolhardy for the United States, at this state of disintegration of the Chinese Government authority in civil as well as the military sphere, to embark upon such a quixotic venture. We are doing everything possible to expedite the shipment of military matériel under the $125 million grants. The pattern of defections and other accompaniments of the fall of Tsinan, Chinchow and the Manchurian debacle, although Chinese Government troops had adequate arms, indicate the will to fight is lacking. With respect to the Chinese Government appeal to the United Nations regarding Soviet treaty violations, this is a matter for Chinese decision, but could not be expected to change the internal situation in China.

You are authorized to inform the Foreign Minister that the National Military Establishment is making every effort to expedite the shipments of military materiel under the $125 million grants. You should point out to him the inherent difficulties involved in an attempt on the part of a foreign official to advise the Chinese Government regarding its courses of action even in the unlikely event such official could be completely conversant with all the complexities of the situation, and the even greater difficulties for a foreign official not familiar with China. You should state that it is not believed that the inspection visit of a high-ranking U.S. officer would or could offer the solution to China's problems. With respect to the Chinese Government appeal to the United Nations, you should reply in the sense of the final sentence of the preceding paragraph.[11]

On November 9, 1948, President Chiang Kai-shek, in a message to President Truman, summarized his situation and needs:

---

10. Ibid., p. 887.
11. Ibid., pp. 887–888.

I have the honor to acknowledge receipt of Your Excellency's reply dated October 16, 1948,[12] for which I am deeply grateful.

The Communist forces in Central China are now within striking distance of Shanghai and Nanking. If we fail to stem the tide, China may be lost to the cause of democracy. I am therefore compelled to send to your Excellency again direct and urgent appeal.

The general deterioration of the military situation in China may be attributed to a number of factors. But the most fundamental is the non-observance by the Soviet Government of the Sino-Soviet Treaty of Friendship and Alliance, which as Your Excellency will doubtless recall, the Chinese Government signed as a result of the well-intentioned advice from the United States Government [the Yalta Far Eastern secret Agreement and the August 1945 Treaties]. I need hardly point out that, but for persistent Soviet aid, the Chinese Communists would not have been able to occupy Manchuria and develop into such a menace.

As a co-defender of democracy against the onrush and infiltration of Communism through the world, I appeal to you for speedy and increased military assistance and for a firm statement of American policy in support of the cause for which my Government is fighting. Such a statement would serve to bolster up the morale of the armed forces and the civilian population and would strengthen the Government's position in the momentous battle now unfolding in North and Central China.

My Government would be most happy to receive from you as soon as possible, a high-ranking military officer who will work out in consultation with my Government a concrete scheme of military assistance, including the participation of American military advisers in the direction of operations.

As the situation demands your Excellency's full sympathy and quick decision, I shall appreciate an early reply.

Chiang Kai-shek[13]

In a letter written by President Truman to the Generalissimo on November 12, 1948, Mr. Truman says:

... As I stated in my letter of October 16, 1948, everything possible is being done to expedite the procurement and shipment to China of the weapons and ammunition being obtained in this country under the China Aid Program. I am again emphasizing to the appropriate officials the urgency of your

---

12. We have been unable to find this dispatch in the United States government publications.
13. *China White Paper*, pp. 888–889.

needs and the necessity of prompt action. In this connection, I have just been informed that one shipment of arms and ammunition sailed from Guam on November 4 and another from Japan on November 7 en route to China. I have also been informed that a further shipment of ammunition sailed from the West Coast of the United States on November 9 and is scheduled to reach China about November 24.

A message of November 9 from the Secretary of State to Ambassador Stuart, containing Secretary Marshall's reply to a request from the Chinese Foreign Minister for military aid and the visit of a high-ranking United States officer to China, apparently crossed Your Excellency's message in transmission. The Secretary authorized Ambassador Stuart to inform the Foreign Minister that the United States National Military Establishment was making every effort to expedite shipments of military materiel purchased in this country under the China Aid Act. He also authorized Ambassador Stuart to point out the inherent difficulties involved in an attempt on the part of a newly appointed foreign official to advise the Chinese Government regarding its courses of action in the present dilemma, even if such an official would be completely conversant with all the numerous complexities of the situation, and to point out the even greater difficulties for a foreign official not familiar with China.

However, Major General Barr, Director of the Joint United States Military Advisory Group in China, is conversant with the current situation and his advice has always been available to you.

Your attention may have been called to my public statement on March 11, 1948, in which I stated that the United States maintained friendly relations with the Chinese Government and was trying to assist the recognized Government of China [to–ed.] maintain peace. I also stated that I did not desire Communists in the Chinese Government. Secretary Marshall stated publicly on March 10, 1948, that the Communists were now in open rebellion against the Chinese Government and that the inclusion of the Communists in the Government was a matter for the Chinese Government to decide, not for the United States Government to dictate. I believe that these statements and the action of my Government in extending assistance to the Chinese Government under the China Aid Act of 1948 have made the position of the United States Government clear.

You will understand the desire of the United States Government to support the cause of peace and democracy throughout the world. It is this desire that has led this Government to extend assistance to many countries in their efforts to promote sound economies and stable conditions without which the peoples of the world cannot expect to have peace and the principles of democracy cannot grow. It was with that hope that the United States Government has extended assistance in various forms to the Chinese Government. I am most sympathetic with the difficulties confronting the Chinese Government and people at this time and wish to assure Your Excellency that my Government will continue to exert every effort to expedite the implementation of the program of aid for China which has been authorized by the Congress with my approval.[14]

Reviewing the deterioration of the Nationalist military situation, 1947–1949, Secretary of State Dean Acheson, in his testimony on June 4, 1951, before the United States Senate Hearings on the *Military Situation in the Far East,* said:

In mid-November, 1948, General Barr, who was the head of the military mission to China, reported to the Department of the Army:

"I am convinced that the military situation has deteriorated to the point where only the active participation of United States troops could effect a remedy. No battle has been lost since my arrival due to lack of ammunition or equipment. Their military debacles, in my opinion, can all be attributed to the world's worst leadership and many other morale-destroying factors that led to a complete loss of the will to fight."

In summarizing United States efforts in China, Secretary Acheson reiterated:

The military collapse of the Chinese Government had, for the most part, been the consequence of inept political and military leadership, and a lack of the will to fight on the part of its armies, rather than inadequate military supplies.[15]

General Wedemeyer says:

Dean Acheson was either misinformed or was deliberately misleading Congress when he cited "our military observers on the spot" as the authority for his statement that the Chinese Nationalist forces had lost no battles against the Communists for lack of arms or ammunition. Thanks to the State Department, American military observers had not been permitted to enter combat

14. Ibid., pp. 889–890.
15. *Military Situation in the Far East, Hearings before the Committee on Armed Services and the Committee on Foreign Relations, United States Senate* [82nd Congress, 1st Session], Part 3, pp. 1856–1857.

areas and therefore could not render firsthand reports of that nature. A civilian engineer representing the J. C. White Company of New York was present in the Soochow area during the fighting and told me personally that the Nationalists fought tenaciously against the Communists. He saw thousands of wounded and dead, both Communists and Nationalists. The latter withdrew only as the ammunition supply was exhausted.[16]

General Wedemeyer further stated that:

The U.S. Administration's refusal to give Chiang Kai-shek the military advice he had long requested was perhaps even more helpful to the Communists than General Marshall's 1946 embargo on arms and ammunition to China, and the failure of the Administration to implement the China Aid Act of April, 1948, which provided $128,000,000 worth of arms aid to China that was not delivered until the end of that year when it was too late to stop the Communists.[17]

16. Albert C. Wedemeyer, *Wedemeyer Reports!*, p. 401.
17. Ibid., p. 400.

[CHAPTER 4-*ED.*]

The End of Free China—1949

ON MARCH 12 [15–*ed.*], 1949, Secretary of State Acheson, in reply to a query from Senator Tom Connally, Chairman of the Senate Foreign Relations Committee, explained his views about extending further aid to China:

> ... the economic and military position of the Chinese Government has deteriorated to the point where the Chinese Communists hold almost all important areas of China from Manchuria to the Yangtze River and have the military capability of expanding their control to the populous areas of the Yangtze Valley and of eventually dominating south China. The National Government does not have the military capability of maintaining a foothold in south China against a determined Communist advance.... There is no evidence that the furnishing of additional military material would alter the pattern of current developments in China. There is, however, ample evidence that the Chinese people are weary of hostilities and that there is an overwhelming desire for peace at any price. To furnish solely military material and advice would only prolong hostilities and the suffering of the Chinese people and would arouse in them deep resentment against the United States. Yet, to furnish the military means for bringing about a reversal of the present deterioration and for providing some prospect of successful military resistance would require the use of an unpredictably large American armed force in actual combat, a course of action which would represent direct United States involvement in China's fratricidal warfare and would be contrary to our traditional policy toward China and the interests of this country.
>
> In these circumstances, the extension of as much as $1.5 billion of credits to the Chinese Government, as proposed by the Bill, would embark this Government on an undertaking the eventual cost of which would be

unpredictable but of great magnitude, and the outcome of which would almost surely be catastrophic.[1]

On June 30, 1949, Mao Tse-tung gave a radio broadcast of exaltation over their certainty of victory.[2]

The cabal who had exalted him as an agrarian liberal or urged Chiang Kai-shek to accept Mao's representatives in his cabinet should read some of the passages from this speech:

> Internationally, we belong to the antiimperialist front, headed by the USSR, and we can only look for genuine friendly aid from that front, and not from the imperialist front.
>
> "You are dictatorial." Yes, dear gentlemen, you are right and we are really that way. . . . The experiences of several decades amassed by the Chinese people tell us to carry out the people's democratic dictatorship, that is, the right of reactionaries to voice their opinion must be deprived, and only the people are allowed to have the right of voicing their opinion. . . .
>
> The democratic system is to be carried out within the ranks of the people, giving them freedom of speech, assembly, and association. The right to vote is given only to the people and not to the reactionaries. These two aspects, namely democracy among the people and dictatorships over the reactionaries, combine to form the people's dictatorship.
>
> . . . Our present task is to strengthen the people's State apparatus, which refers mainly to the People's Army, People's Police, and People's Court, for national defense and protection of the people's interests, and with this as condition, to enable China to advance steadily, under the leadership of the working class and the Communist Party, from an agricultural to an industrial country, and from a new democratic to a socialist and Communist society, to eliminate classes and to realize world Communism. The Army, police and court of the State are instruments for classes to oppress classes. To the hostile classes, the State apparatus is the instrument of oppression. It is violent, and not "benevolent." "You are not benevolent." Just so. We decidedly do not adopt a benevolent rule toward the reactionary acts of the reactionaries and the reactionary classes. . . .
>
> Chu Hsi, a philosopher of the Sung Dynasty, wrote many books and made many speeches about which we have forgotten, but there is one sentence we

---

1. *China White Paper,* pp. 1053–1054.
2. Ibid., [pp. 720–729–*ed.*].

have not forgotten, and this is: "Do to others what others do unto you." This is what we do. That is, do to imperialism and its lackeys, the Chiang Kai-shek reactionary clique, what they do to others. Simply this and nothing more. . . ."[3]

The Communist Triumph

In 1949, the Nationalist Government's armies, destitute of supplies, gradually disintegrated; Mao Tse-tung's forces equipped with Japanese and Lend Lease arms drove the Nationalist Government from the China mainland to the island of Formosa. The Nationalist withdrawal was completed on December 8, 1949.

In a Senate inquiry on the debacle, this exchange took place:

Senator CONNALLY. General Wedemeyer . . . Don't you agree that we did about all we could to keep the Nationalist regime in power with the possible exception of sending our troops into China?

General WEDEMEYER. No sir; I do not, sir.

. . . we Americans did not give China all the aid that we might have given. . . . it is moral aid that is more important, in my judgment, than the material aid. . . .

I do not think the people of China felt that their traditional friends, the Americans, were supporting Chiang Kai-shek.

. . . I feel if we had gone out there with economic advisers and with military advisers and a limited amount of equipment, intelligently used, that we could have stopped the advance of communism in China.[4]

With the collapse of Free China, over one-third of the people in the world were now dominated from Moscow.

---

3. Ibid., pp. 725, 726, 727.
4. *Military Situation in the Far East, Hearings before the Committee on Armed Services and the Committee on Foreign Relations, United States Senate,* June, 1951, part 3, pp. 2393–2394. [*Editor's note:* Hoover's citation was partially inaccurate. I have corrected it.]

Conclusion

Any student of the record of the responsibility for the downfall of China to the Communists must take into consideration:

(a) The betrayal of Chiang Kai-shek by the repudiation of military aid promised at Cairo Conference in November 1943 and repudiated at Tehran a few days later and at the Second Cairo Conference in January of 1944.

(b) The disintegration of China by the Far Eastern Agreement of Yalta in February 1945.

(c) The attempts to compel Chiang Kai-shek to accept representation of Mao Tse-tung's Communist government in his Cabinet by a cabal of American officers beginning in 1942 and continuing during the years 1947–1948. Chiang alone was defending freedom in China during these years while his prestige and his steadfast opposition to Communism were being undermined.

SECTION III

The Case History of Korea

EDITOR'S NOTE: In 1962 and early 1963, amid his other labors on the Magnum Opus, Hoover drafted and revised a case history on the fate of Korea after World War II. On March 6, 1963, one of his staff finished typing a clean copy of the "Z" edition. On March 21 a photocopy of it was marked "Returned from Xerox 3/21/63."

Hoover was not yet satisfied with his narrative. Sometime after March 21, he edited a copy of the March 6 version. He then returned it to a member of his staff for "correction," additional "research," and "clean up."

So far as is known, Hoover worked no further on this manuscript. No later variant has been found; accordingly, this amended text is the one reproduced here.

Like his case study of Germany elsewhere in this volume, the final version of Hoover's Korea essay contains handwritten changes (made with a dull pencil) that are difficult to decipher. Hoover's misspellings and frequent failure to cross his t's make the task even harder. Moreover, in part of Chapter 4 he scribbled several sheets of revisions for insertion into the text; it is not certain where these were to go. Nevertheless, by scrutinizing their content, one can determine where most of them plausibly belong. I have indicated my decision in these cases in brackets and footnotes. Throughout the text, where individual words are illegible I have so indicated in brackets.

As with the other studies printed in Volume III, for editing purposes I have treated this case history as a single unit. In the footnotes, initial citations of sources are given in full but are not repeated when a source is cited again.

The "Case History of Korea" file, including the post-March 1963 version printed here, and its antecedents, is in the Herbert C. Hoover Papers, Box 80, Envelope 3, Hoover Institution Archives.

INTRODUCTION

THE HISTORY OF KOREA is largely one of conflicts between China on the west and Japan on the east of this 600 miles of a peninsula extending south from Manchuria. Neither the Yellow Sea to the west or the Sea of Japan have afforded them much protection as they have never been a [illegible word—ed.] people. In fact the Koreans, being a race without aggressive or military instincts, their independence has been most uncertain.

Recorded history of Korea reaches back for over 2,000 years. It was united into a kingdom in 669 A.D. For centuries, Korean allegiance was mostly to China. But in 1895, in a war between Japan and China, the victorious Japanese exacted a declaration of Korean independence from China. Ten years later, in 1905, in the Russo-Japanese War, the victorious Japanese occupied Korea militarily, and in 1910 formally annexed it. Japan's possession of Korea ended with her defeat in the Second World War, in August, 1945.

I first visited Korea in 1910 [1909–ed.], to advise some Japanese industrialists on engineering matters. The Korean people at that time were in the most disheartening condition that I had witnessed in any part of Asia. There was little law and order. The masses were underfed, under-clothed, under-housed and under-equipped. There was no sanitation, and filth and squalor enveloped the whole countryside. The roads were hardly passable, and there were scant communication or educational facilities. Scarcely a tree broke the dismal landscape. Thieves and bandits seemed to be unrestrained.

During the thirty-five years of Japanese control, the life of the Korean people was revolutionized. Beginning with this most unpromising human material, the Japanese established order, built harbors, railways, roads and communications, good public buildings, and greatly improved housing. They established sanitation and taught better methods of agriculture. They built immense fertilizer factories in North Korea which lifted the people's food supplies to reasonable levels. They reforested the bleak hills. They established a general system of education and the development of skills. Even the dusty, drab and filthy clothing had been replaced with clean bright colors.

The Koreans, compared to the Japanese, were poor at administration and business. Whether for this reason or by deliberate action, the Japanese filled all major economic and governmental positions. Thus, in 1948 when they finally achieved self-government, the Koreans were little prepared for it.

CHAPTER 1

Korea—1943 to 1945

Korea at the Cairo Conference—November, 1943

The international future of Korea after the Second World War was discussed at the First Cairo Conference of November, 1943,[1] by President Roosevelt, Prime Minister Churchill and Generalissimo Chiang Kai-shek. Stalin did not attend the Cairo Conference, but a communiqué issued by the conference on December 1, 1943, signed by Roosevelt, Chiang Kai-shek and Churchill, stated:

> . . . The aforesaid three great powers, mindful of the enslavement of the people of Korea, are determined that in due course Korea shall become free and independent. . . .[2]

Korea at the Tehran Conference
November 27–December 2, 1943

The minutes of a meeting on November 30 at the Tehran Conference, recorded by Mr. Charles Bohlen, the official interpreter, state:

> . . . The Prime Minister asked Marshal Stalin whether he had read the proposed communiqué on the Far East of the Cairo conference.
> Marshal Stalin replied that he had and that although he could make no commitments he thoroughly approved the communiqué and all its contents. He said it was right that Korea should be independent, and that Manchuria, Formosa and the Pescadores Islands should be returned to China. . . .[3]

---

1. [U.S. Department of State,] *Foreign Relations of the United States,* [*Diplomatic Papers, The*] *Conferences at Cairo and Tehran, 1943* [U.S. Government Printing Office, Washington: 1961], pp. 257, 325, 334.

2. Ibid., p. 449.

3. Ibid., p. 566.

Korea at the Yalta Conference
February, 1945

According to Secretary of State Byrnes, President Roosevelt and Marshal Stalin had agreed informally at Yalta that Korea should win its independence, and that if a transition period were necessary a trusteeship should be established.[4] President Roosevelt proposed that there be a trusteeship for Korea for possibly twenty to thirty years. Marshal Stalin stated "the shorter, the better," but generally approved.[5]

Korea in Subsequent Meetings

On May 15, 1945, at a meeting of President Truman; the Acting Secretary of State, Ambassador Harriman; and Mr. Bohlen, it was pointed out that no official agreement was reached at Yalta as to trusteeship for Korea.[6]

At a conference in the Kremlin on May 28, 1945, at which Ambassador Harriman, Harry Hopkins, Marshal Stalin and Mr. Molotov were present,[7] the Korean trusteeship was again discussed and agreement reached that China should be included in the trusteeship, together with Great Britain, the United States, and the Soviet Union.

It can be concluded that Allied policies as to Korea, prior to the Japanese surrender on August 10, 1945, were:

1. There should be a trusteeship for Korea of all four major powers.
2. Ultimate independence was declared or implied.

---

4. James F. Byrnes, *Speaking Frankly* (Harper & Brothers Publishers, New York and London: 1947), p. 221.

5. [U.S. Department of State,] *Foreign Relations of the United States,* [*Diplomatic Papers,*] *The Conferences at Malta and Yalta, 1945* [U.S. Government Printing Office, Washington: 1955], p. 770.

6. [U.S. Department of State,] *Foreign Relations of the United States,* [*Diplomatic Papers, The*] *Conference of Berlin* ([*The*] *Potsdam* [*Conference*]), [Vol. I,] p. 14.

7. Ibid., p. 47.

CHAPTER 2

[Korea in 1945 and 1946–*ed.*][1]

Korea Divided at the Thirty-Eighth Parallel

On August 10, 1945 [July 26, 1945–*ed.*], the Japanese were served with the ultimatum from the Potsdam Conference, and after the atomic bomb was dropped on Hiroshima and Nagasaki, they surrendered on August 14.

On August 12, two days before the Japanese surrendered, Korea was invaded by Russian forces from the north. The immediate purpose of the military occupation was to accept the capitulation of the Japanese army. The nearest American forces were in Okinawa and the Philippines, and from there they invaded South Korea on September 8.

The military authorities had agreed, on August 11, 1945, on the thirty-eighth parallel as the administrative line between the American and Russian armies. Much mystery has surrounded the settlement upon the thirty-eighth parallel. Sumner Welles, in his book, *Seven Decisions That Shaped History*, says:

> . . . Some subordinate officers in the Pentagon hastily recommended that the Russians accept the Japanese surrender north of the 38th parallel in Korea, while the American troops would accept it south of that line. I am told that this line was fixed because it seemed "convenient." Certainly it was fixed by officials with no knowledge of what they were doing, and without consulting any responsible members of the Administration who might have had some regard for the political and economic considerations which the decision so lamentably ignores.[2]

But according to the testimony of Brig. General T. S. Timberman, chief of the Operations Group, Plans and Operations Division, U.S. Army:

---

1. [*Editor's note:* Hoover did not provide a title for Chapter 2. I have inserted one that is consistent with the titles of his other chapters.]

2. Sumner Welles, *Seven Decisions that Shaped History* (Harper & Brothers Publishers, New York: 1950), p. 167.

That decision was taken in the State-War-Navy Committee here in Washington and it was approved by the President. So the State Department did have a voice in this drawing of the thirty-eighth parallel. . . .[3]

This dividing line separated the rich agricultural south from the industrial north. Most of the good coal, minerals, water power, industries, and most of the fertilizer plants were north of the line. There were some factories in the south but their power sources and raw materials came from the north. The decision placed about 9,000,000 of the population under Communist occupation and about 20,000,000 under American occupation.

At a Moscow conference of Foreign Ministers, three months after the military division, in December 1945, the following declaration was agreed upon as to Korea:

1. With a view to the re-establishment of Korea as an independent state, the creation of conditions for developing the country on democratic principles and the earliest possible liquidation of the disastrous results of the protracted Japanese domination in Korea, there shall be set up a provisional Korean democratic government which shall take all the necessary steps for developing the industry, transport and the agriculture of Korea and the national culture of the Korean people.

2. In order to assist the formation of a provisional Korean government and with a view to the preliminary elaboration of the appropriate measures, there shall be established a joint commission consisting of representatives of the United States command in southern Korea and the Soviet command in northern Korea. In preparing their proposals the commission shall consult with Korean democratic parties and social organizations. The recommendations worked out by the commission shall be presented for the consideration of the governments of the Union of Soviet Socialists Republics, China, the United Kingdom and the United States prior to final decision by the two governments represented on the joint commission.

3. It shall be the task of the joint commission, with the participation of the provisional Korean democratic government and of the Korean democratic organizations, to work out measures also

---

3. *Background Information on Korea*, Report of the [House] Committee on Foreign Affairs (United States Government Printing Office, Washington: 1950), p. 3. (81st Congress, during consideration of H.R. 5330.) [*Editor's note:* This was House Report No. 2495, pursuant to H. Res. 206. This document was printed in the 81st Congress, 2nd Session.]

for helping and assisting (trusteeship) the political economic
and social progress of the Korean people, the development of
democratic self-government and the establishment of the national
independence of Korea.

The proposals of the joint commission shall be submitted,
following consultation with the provisional Korean government,
for the joint consideration of the governments of the United States,
Union of Soviet Socialist Republics, United Kingdom and China
for the working out of an agreement concerning a four-power
trusteeship of Korea for a period of up to five years.

4. For the consideration of urgent problems affecting both southern
and northern Korea and for the elaboration of measures
establishing permanent coordination in administrative-economic
matters between the United States command in Southern Korea
and the Soviet command in northern Korea, a conference of the
representatives of the United States and Soviet commands in Korea
shall be convened within a period of two weeks.[4]

Korea in 1946

It quickly became evident that the Communists had no intention of withdrawing from North Korea. They confirmed their regime by an "election" on
a single-slate ballot in the fall of 1946.

By appointment of President Truman, I visited South Korea in May, 1946,
to revise the food needs prior to the harvest of 1946. I found the Russians were
creating a disastrous situation in South Korean agriculture. The productivity
in South Korea is dependent for thirty-five per cent of its yield upon fertilizers. The Russians refused any supplies from the great Japanese-built fertilizer
plant in northern Korea. With this impoverishment of the crops, our mission
had need to recommend that 110,000 tons of grain be shipped at once from
the United States to carry the Koreans during the three months until the harvest of 1947. I reported that either we must build fertilizer plants or feed the
Koreans forever.

I also found that the industries of South Korea after eighteen months were
producing about twenty per cent of their normal capacity. Unemployment
was widespread, increased by thousands of repatriates from China and Japan,

---

4. *New York Times,* December 28, 1945.

and escapees from the north. At this time, 1600 North Koreans were migrating daily to South Korea.

General John R. Hodge, the American Military Governor, a most capable officer, operated under a Congressional enactment which provided him with funds and authority specifically limited to "combating disease and unrest." There was no provision of funds for reconstruction of the demoralized and war-torn economy.

At this time the American Military Government was also plagued by the Communists, who had organized cells in South Korea for overthrow of the Government. They had infected some of the privates in the American army, who upon discovery by our army were sent home.

CHAPTER 3

Korea in 1947, 1948 and 1949

Attempts to Unify Korea

General George C. Marshall was appointed Secretary of State by President Truman on January 7, 1947. But the General had never fully understood the basis or purpose of Communism, as was demonstrated amply in his actions in Korea as well as China. He thought Communists could be mixed in the government of a free people and that they could remain free. He made an earnest effort to find a solution of the Korean question on this line.

On August 13, 1947, the General wrote the Russian Foreign Minister, V. M. Molotov, that "there cannot be further delay," and called for a report by August 21 on the status of the dead-locked Joint United States-Soviet Commission talks in Korea.[1] One week later on August 28, 1947, the General proposed to the Soviet Union that the four powers meet at Washington to consider the Korean question. The Russians rejected his proposal.

In July, 1947, Lieutenant General Albert C. Wedemeyer had been directed by President Truman, on General Marshall's recommendation, to review on the ground and report on the whole situation in China and Korea, with recommendations. On completing his mission, General Wedemeyer submitted his report to President Truman on September 19, 1947.[2]

The significant portions of the Wedemeyer report as to Korea were:

A Soviet dominated Korea would constitute a serious political and psychological threat to Manchuria, North China, Japan and hence to the United States' strategic interests in the Far East. It is therefore to the best interest of the United States to insure the permanent military neutralization of Korea.

---

1. *New York Times*, August 14, 1947.
2. The Wedemeyer Report and its suppression is more fully described in the section on *The Case History of China.*

Neutralization can only be assured by its occupation until its future independence as a buffer state is assured. . . .

The long term purpose of military aid to Korea should be to enable South Korea, and later all Korea, to engage in a holding operation against the progressive expansion of militaristic communism. . . .

The North Korean People's Army constitutes a potential military threat to South Korea, since there is strong possibility that the Soviets will withdraw their [Russian] occupation forces and thus induce our own withdrawal.

This probably will take place just as soon as they can be sure that the North Korean puppet government and its armed forces, which they have created, are strong enough and sufficiently well indoctrinated to be relied upon to carry out Soviet objectives without the actual presence of Soviet troops. . . .

The withdrawal of American military forces from Korea would, in turn, result in the occupation of South Korea either by Soviet troops, or, as seems more likely, by the Korean military units trained under Soviet auspices in North Korea. . . . It would probably have serious repercussions in Japan and would more easily permit the infiltration of Communist agents into that country; and it would gain for the Soviet Union prestige in Asia which would be particularly important in the peripheral areas bordering the Soviet Union, thus creating opportunities for further Soviet expansion among nations in close proximity to the Soviet Union.[3]

Not only were the General's recommendations rejected, but his report was suppressed. His recommendations, which could have created some opposition to this march of Communism in Asia, were not revealed to the American people for three years.

[In 1951–ed.] Secretary Acheson was asked in a Senate investigation why the Korean section of the Wedemeyer Report was not made public. Acheson answered:

---

3. *New York Times*, May 2, 1951. [*Editor's note:* Of the five paragraphs quoted here by Hoover, only the third and fourth appear in the source he cites. The other three paragraphs are *not* found in the text of Wedemeyer's 1947 report on Korea as printed verbatim (with deletions) in the *New York Times*, May 2, 1951, p. 8. Nor are they found in the seemingly unexpurgated version printed in Albert C. Wedemeyer, *Wedemeyer Reports!* (Henry Holt & Company, New York: 1958), pp. 461–479. Just where Herbert Hoover found these additional purported passages is unknown.

Incidentally, a separate story in the *New York Times* on May 2, 1951, p. 9, quotes two passages from Wedemeyer's 1947 report that do not appear in the verbatim text printed that same day on the adjacent page of the newspaper. These two passages bear some resemblance to the first paragraph quoted by Hoover.]

It was not made public because of certain observations in it which we believed would not lead to harmonious relations in certain quarters. When we made it available to this [Congressional] committee some few passages of that sort were eliminated from it; otherwise the committee now has it.[4]

Enter the United Nations

On September 17, 1947, Secretary of State Marshall requested the General Assembly of the United Nations to place the Korean question on its agenda to establish an independent government. On November 14, the Assembly voted for the holding of a free election in Korea, under the observation of a United Nations Commission.

On September 27, 1947, Russia proposed the evacuation of Soviet and United States occupation forces by January, 1948. The United States maintained that evacuation should follow the establishment of a national government. On November 14, 1947, the United Nations assembly created a commission to hold Korean elections by the end of March, 1948, and to aid in the establishment of an independent government.[5]

Korea in 1948

The first formal session of this United Nations Commission was held in Seoul on January 12, 1948. The commission drafted letters to General Hodge and to General Shtikov,[6] requesting free access to all areas in Korea and the cooperation of the two commanding generals in holding the elections in their respective zones. General Hodge replied, affirming full support for their proposals. The letter to Shtikov, and all United Nations subsequent communications to him, went unacknowledged. However, on February 19 [26–*ed.*], 1948, the Assembly authorized their Commission by a vote of 31 to 2, with 11 abstentions, to observe elections "in all areas in Korea accessible to it."[7]

---

4. [U.S. Congress, Senate,] *Military Situation in the Far East* [*Hearings Before the Committee on Armed Services and the Committee on Foreign Relations*, 82nd Congress, 1st Session, 1951] (MacArthur Hearings), Part 3, p. 1987.

5. *New York Times*, November 15, 1947.

6. General Terentyi Shtikov, the Russian Ambassador, served in a dual capacity. He represented the Russian Foreign Office, but was attached to the Soviet Far East Military Command. His title was Ambassador, but he was Colonel General in the Soviet Army. (*U.S. News & World Report*, September 8, 1950).

7. [*Editor's note:* Hoover did not fill in this footnote. On February 26, 1948 the United Nations Little Assembly called upon the Korea Commission to hold elections in Korea and set up a na-

On May 10, 1948, South Korea held its first election. The people elected a Constituent Assembly which was to draft a constitution and elect a president. The elected members met in Seoul on May 22, agreed to hold their first formal organizational meeting on May 28 [27–*ed.*], and that day General Hodge published the text of a letter he had written to Syngman Rhee, outlining the basis for an orderly transition of authority, and containing the following sentence:

> The policy of the United States has always been that Korea shall be a *united* independent nation under democratic government free of foreign domination.[8]

On May 31, the Constituent Assembly elected Mr. Syngman Rhee chairman, and on July 19, 1948, with the constitution adopted, Mr. Rhee was elected the first president of the independent Republic of Korea.

Many simple-minded Koreans believed that with self-government their long dreamed of prosperity was assured. But the problems of the new republic were heartbreaking. Their mines, factories, farms, forests and fisheries lacked repairs, equipment and technicians. There was a shortage of everything needed for economic recovery. Korean political leaders had little background of tradition or experience to serve as guides and personal conduct.

The Policies of the State Department as to Korea—1949

On July 17, 1949, Owen Lattimore of the State Department stated that:

> The thing to do, therefore, is to let South Korea fall—but not to let it look as though we pushed it.[9]

Lattimore was not the only Russian sympathizer who had contact with the State Department.[10] I give an extended account of the Communist infiltration into the Federal Government in Chapter 4 of this memoir.

---

tional government there. The vote was 31 to 12, with eleven abstentions. *New York Times,* February 27, 1948.]

8. Robert T. Oliver, *Syngman Rhee, The Man Behind the Myth* (Dodd Mead and Company, New York: 1954), p. 262.

9. Sunday *Compass,* New York, July 17, 1949.

10. Adolf Berle, former Assistant Secretary of State, testified under oath: "In the fall of 1944 there was a difference of opinion in the State Department. . . . I was pressing for a pretty clean show-down [with the Russians] then when our position was strongest.

"The opposite group in the State Department was largely the men—Mr. Acheson's group, of course, with Mr. Hiss as his principal assistant. . . . I got trimmed in that fight, and, as a result, went to Brazil and that ended my diplomatic career." Later, he referred to the Acheson group as the pro-Russian clique. (*Congressional Record,* October 20, 1950, pp. A7573–74. Testified under oath before the Un-American Activities Committee August 30, 1948). [*Editor's note:* Hoover's quotation is

John M. Ohly, Acting Director of the United States Mutual Defense Assistance, admitted that the policy of the United Nations [States–*ed.*]National Security Council, laid down in March, 1949, had been to give the Republic of Korea "just enough arms to maintain internal security but not enough to cope with the army trained and equipped by the Russians in the north."

Mr. Ohly was asked by a Congressional Committee whether at any time they had "prepared any plans for the order, the procurement, and the shipment to Korea of any arms and ammunition to resist aggression from Northern Korea?"

Ohly replied:

I think the answer to that is no.[11]

Having set up a Communist puppet government, and trained a completely equipped army, the Russian troops left North Korea in January, 1949.

Although the new South Korean legislature, in a resolution of November 20, 1948, urged that United States troops be kept in South Korea until the security forces of the Republic became capable of maintaining national independence, the United States Department of the Army announced on June 30, 1949, that 50,000 United States troops had been quietly withdrawn from Korea, with no protests from the State Department.[12] All the American forces who remained as of July 1 were some 500 officers and men, comprising a mission to train [the–*ed.*] Korean army. They left the South Korean Army some munitions and materiel. That this equipment was light arms, adequate for maintaining internal order but inadequate to resist invasion, seems clear from subsequent events.

Of the $10,500,000 specifically earmarked for Korea in the Military Assistance Bill signed by the President on October 28, 1949, only $200 in signal wire had been delivered when the war began eight months later, on June 25, 1950.[13]

---

correct, but his citation is not. There is no reference to Berle's testimony in the *Congressional Record* at the pages cited. Berle did testify before a Congressional committee on August 30, 1948. The passage quoted here is found in U.S. Congress, House of Representatives, Committee on Un-American Activities, *Hearings Regarding Communist Espionage in the United States Government,* 80th Congress, 2nd Session (United States Government Printing Office, Washington, 1948), p. 1296. See also *New York Times,* September 1, 1948, p. 1.]

11. *Newsweek,* July 10, 1950, p. 26. [*Editor's note:* I have corrected two transcription errors.]

12. *Washington Post,* July 1, 1949.

13. *Congressional Record,* [Vol. 96,] June 28, 1950, p. 9321. [*Editor's note:* This citation is to a speech by Senator Robert A. Taft. The senator mentioned the $200 expenditure but did not refer specifically to signal wire. Hoover probably learned of this from the *Newsweek* article cited in note 11. Hoover may have wished to move this sentence in the text to the next chapter. But his precise intent is uncertain, and I have therefore left the sentence in place.]

CHAPTER 4[1]

1950

ON JANUARY 12, 1950, Secretary of State Dean Acheson, in an address before the National Press Club in Washington, [stated–*ed.*] that Korea lay outside the United States defense perimeter in Asia. He said[:–*ed.*]

> ... it is a mistake, I think, in considering Pacific and Far East problems to become obsessed with military considerations.

He warned against "foolish adventures" in the Far East, and declared that this nation's

> ... defensive perimeter runs along the Aleutians to Japan and then goes to the Ryukyus (Okinawa) ... and to the Philippines. So far as the military security of other areas in the Pacific is concerned, it must be clear that no person can guarantee these areas against military attack.[2]

It was clear that the United States was not to employ its military forces in maintaining the independence of the excluded areas, mainly Korea and the Chinese government in Formosa. However, this area, being members of the United Nations, were entitled to protection from aggression by that Organization.[3]

---

1. [*Editor's note:* Hoover's penciled markings suggest that he may have wanted to include the opening passages of Chapter 4 with Chapter 3. But he did not renumber the footnotes in Chapter 4, and the breaking point, if any, is unclear. I have therefore let the March 6, 1963 version stand.]

2. New York *Herald Tribune*, January 12, 1950.

3. [*Editor's note:* This handwritten paragraph, labeled "A," was written in an empty space at the bottom of page 20 of Hoover's marked-up copy of his March 6, 1963 draft. I have supplied a few commas for clarity. This paragraph seems to have been intended for insertion in the text, immediately following the block quotation by Dean Acheson. It is not known whether Hoover meant this insert to replace the next paragraph in the March 6, 1963 version of the text. I have retained that paragraph.]

Such a perimeter excluded South Korea, and was widely interpreted in the foreign world and domestic press as drawing a line of American defense of the Far East with South Korea excluded.

The danger to South Korea was underlined by frequent Communist raids across the thirty-eighth parallel. Intelligence reports from the north indicated beyond any doubt a large enemy buildup. Despite earnest and persistent requests by President Rhee and his Minister of National Defense, no provision had been made for naval support, fighting planes, artillery or other requirements for heavy fighting.

The United Nations and The Communist Aggression against South Korea

On May 10, 1950, the Korean Defense Minister informed the United Nations Commission that Communist troops were moving southward in force toward the thirty-eighth parallel, and "that there was imminent danger of invasion from the North." He reported a Northern Korean Communist Army of 183,000 men with 173 tanks, including 25,000 Koreans who had previously fought with the Chinese Communist Army, and said that "against such overwhelming odds, courage alone would not go far."[4]

The first North Korean Communist troops crossed the thirty-eighth parallel at 4:00 A.M. on Sunday morning, June 25, 1950. The South Koreans resisted heroically, but the North Korean armies rapidly swept over South Korea, occupying Seoul and pushing southward toward Pusan.

The Security Council of the United Nations, the same day at 5:45 P.M. under American leadership passed a resolution that this armed attack constituted a breach of the peace, and demanded the immediate cessation of hostilities. They called upon "the authorities of North Korea to withdraw forthwith their armed forces to the 38th Parallel," and requested "all members to render every assistance to the United Nations in the execution of this resolution."[5]

---

4. *Korean: Second Failure in Asia*, C. Clyde Mitchell (Public Affairs Institute, Washington: 1951), p. 36.

5. In spite of their decision to resist aggression, the contributions of the United Nations did not represent very effective collective security in action. On July 10, Senator Alexander Wiley, member of the Senate Foreign Relations Committee, urged the United Nations to redouble its efforts to mobilize allied ground troops to support American forces in Korea, saying: "If the present situation continues the American people will get to feel that the United Nations is willing to fight to the last American.

"We appreciate the moral help of half a hundred countries. We appreciate the handful of destroyers or cruisers or planes which they have turned over to us. But we are not going to let them think that they have fulfilled their commitments by these half-hearted measures. . . . once again it would be

There was no opposition by the Russians to this resolution, probably because their representative was absent in protest over the presence of the representative of the China Formosa Government.[6]

On June 27, President Truman announced that pursuant to the Security Council's call to the United Nations:

> ... I have ordered United States air and sea forces to give the Korean Government troops cover and support.[7]

Mr. Truman notes in his *Memoirs* that[:–*ed.*]

> A few days earlier I had approved a proposal prepared jointly by the Departments of State and Defense to introduce in the U.N. a resolution creating a unified command in Korea, asking us to name a commander and authorizing the use of the blue U.N. flag in Korea. This resolution was approved by the

---

Uncle Sam who alone would be giving lives of his youngsters on the field of battle while the rest of the world sat in the grandstands cheering" (*Congressional Record*, [Vol. 96,] July 10, 1950, p. 9738).

The following was the "fighting Allied men team in Korea:

Australia—two infantry battalions, which were part of the British Commonwealth Division, naval forces, a fighter squadron.

Belgium—one infantry battalion.

Canada—a reinforced infantry brigade including artillery and tank forces, all part of the British Commonwealth Division, naval forces and a squadron of transport aircraft.

Colombia—an infantry battalion and a naval frigate.

Ethiopia—one infantry battalion.

France—one reinforced infantry battalion.

Greece—one infantry battalion and transport aircraft.

Luxembourg—one infantry company.

Netherlands—one infantry battalion and naval forces.

New Zealand—a regiment of artillery, part of the British Commonwealth Division.

Philippines—one infantry battalion and one company of tanks.

Thailand—one infantry battalion, combat naval forces, air and naval transports.

Turkey—one infantry brigade.

Union of South Africa—one fighter squadron.

United Kingdom—three infantry brigades, one tank brigade, one and a half artillery regiments, one and a half combat engineer regiments and supporting ground forces, all part of the British Commonwealth Division, and the Far Eastern Fleet and units of the Royal Air Force.

"In addition there were medical units from five nations—Denmark, India, Italy, Norway and Sweden." (Mark W. Clark, *From the Danube to the Yalu* [New York: Harper & Brothers Publishers, 1954], pp. 222–23.)

6. [*Editor's note:* At this juncture in the manuscript, Hoover apparently wished to add something marked "A," but it is not clear what this was. The insert A that is cited in note 3 does not seem pertinent.]

7. *Memoirs by Harry S. Truman*, Volume Two: *Years of Trial and Hope* [Doubleday & Company, Inc., Garden City, N.Y.: 1956], p. 339.

Security Council on July 7, and on the following day I named General Mac-
Arthur to the post of U.N. commander.[8]

The United States contributed to the Korean War 450,000 men at a given
time, but more than a million men were rotated through Korea. Fifteen nations of the sixty members of the United Nations contributed less than
45,000 men.[9]

General Mark Clark, later on in Command of the United States Forces in
the Far East, in his book, *From the Danube to the Yalu,* described the United
Nations forces in Korea:

> I doubt that the great aggressor of our time, the Soviet Union, was impressed
> very much by the contributions made in Korea by United Nations members
> other than the United States. . . .
>
> In blunt language the United Nations numerical contribution to the war
> in Korea was piddling in light of the strength of the free world. Of the fifty-
> three nations who endorsed the decision for United Nations action against
> the aggressor in Korea, only fifteen other than the United States provided
> ground, air or sea combat forces. . . .
>
> . . . I could not help thinking in comparative terms. The great United Na-
> tions Organization was made up of so many peoples. It occupied such mag-
> nificent quarters in New York City. It held so many meetings on so many
> subjects. . . . Against this picture of grandeur I saw the tiny contribution
> made by these people to the first test of free world determination to stop
> aggression. . . .[10]

---

8. Ibid., p. 347.

9. *Review of the United Nations Charter,* Hearings before a Subcommittee of the Committee on
Foreign Relations, United States Senate, [83rd Congress, 2nd Session,] January 18 and March 3, 1954,
p. 14. [*Editor's note:* A penciled mark on Hoover's manuscript suggests that he may have wanted to
move this sentence elsewhere, possibly to footnote 5. Since his intent is uncertain, I have left this
sentence in place.

At this point in Hoover's marked-up copy of his March 6, 1963 draft, a problem arises: The next
several pages of his typescript (as found in his papers) appear to be out of order. For instance, page
23 is followed immediately by page 27; page 30 is followed at once by pages 25 and 26; and so forth.
Interspersed among these rearranged, typed pages are several sheets containing Hoover's handwritten revisions, with no definitive indication of where they were to be inserted.

It is not clear how much of this reshuffling may have been deliberate and how much accidental.
I have therefore reverted to the original page order of the March 6, 1963 draft (on which Hoover had
been working) and have inserted his handwritten emendations where they seem most logically to fit.
In one instance, I have simply quoted a problematic insertion in a footnote.]

10. Mark W. Clark, *From the Danube to the Yalu,* pp. 220–221.

On July 31, 1950, General MacArthur flew from Tokyo to Formosa, inspecting the Nationalist troops and equipment. Upon his return to Tokyo he issued a statement, including:

> My visit to Formosa has been primarily for the purpose of making a short reconnaissance of the potentiality of its defenses against possible attack. The policy has been enunciated that this island . . . is not under present circumstances subject to military invasion. It is my responsibility and firm purpose to enforce this decision. . . . Arrangements have been completed for effective coordination between the American forces under my command and those of the Chinese Government, the better to meet any attack which a hostile force might be foolish enough to attempt. Such an attack would, in my opinion, stand little chance of success.[11]

Ten days later, General MacArthur issued a further statement with regard to his trip to Formosa:

> [1.–ed.] . . . trip was formally arranged and coordinated beforehand with all branches of the American and Chinese governments.
>
> [2.–ed.] It was limited entirely to military matters, as I stated in my public release after the visit, and dealt solely with the problems of preventing military violence to Formosa, as directed by the President—the implementation of which directive is my responsibility. It had no connection with political affairs. [. . . –ed.]
>
> [3.–ed.] The subject of the future of the Chinese Government, of developments on the Chinese mainland, or anything else outside of the scope of my own military responsibility was not discussed or even mentioned.
>
> [4.–ed.] Full reports on the results of the visit were promptly made to Washington. [. . . –ed.]
>
> This visit has been maliciously misrepresented to the public by those who invariably in the past have propagandized a policy of defeatism and appeasement in the Pacific. . . .[12]

On August 26, 1950, the General, in response to an invitation from the commander-in-chief of the Veterans of Foreign Wars, sent the National Commander, Clyde A. Lewis, a message on Formosa's military importance to the

---

11. Maj. Gen. Courtney Whitney, *MacArthur—His Rendezvous with History* (Alfred A. Knopf, New York: 1956), p. 372 [–p. 373–ed.].

12. Ibid., p. 375.

United States, to be read at their annual convention in Chicago on August 27. The statement had not been cleared with the White House or State or Defense Departments. When President Truman saw an advance copy obtained from the press, he instructed Secretary of Defense Louis Johnson to have General MacArthur withdraw it. General MacArthur and the VFW announced withdrawals August 27, but the statement was already in print in *U.S. News & World Report*'s issue for the next day. Mr. Truman sent General MacArthur a message on August 29 praising his military leadership in Korea, incorporating a United Nations policy statement for his guidance, which implied (1) a rebuke to him for not having cleared his Formosa statement with White House and (2) a warning not to concern himself with foreign policy decisions.

After heavy fighting and many casualties, on September 26, 1950, General MacArthur, mostly with American troops, announced the recapture of Seoul, capital of South Korea. Three weeks later, on October 20, his troops advanced into North Korea and captured Pyongyang, the Communist capital, and were advancing toward the Manchurian border. The North Korean Communist armies had been decisively defeated.

The Chinese Communists Intervene

On October 26, 1950, the Chinese Communist government intervened, their troops crossing the Yalu River from Manchuria. General MacArthur at once announced that "an entirely new war"[13] had started. On November 26, the Chinese opened a massive offensive against United Nations troops in North Korea, forcing General MacArthur's slender armies to retreat toward the thirty-eighth parallel.

The Chinese government claimed that the hundreds of thousands of Chinese troops which plunged into the war were volunteers. The Washington Administration maintained this fiction, as President Truman announced that "under no conditions"[14] would the war be expanded into China.[15] General

---

13. Ibid., p. 421.

14. *Memoirs by Harry S. Truman*, [Vol. II,] *Years of Trial and Hope*, p. 360.

15. [*Editor's note*: One of Hoover's handwritten revisions of Chapter 4 consists of the following passage, which he may have intended to substitute for the first sentence or two of the paragraph in the text.

The Chinese Communist Government at Peking announced that these Chinese troops were mere volunteers and refused to accept any responsibility for them. [Illegible word–ed.] they crossed over the Yalu bridge from Manchuria and were armed with artillery, tanks and a large air force.

Since Hoover's intent was ambiguous, I have let the original wording stand.]

MacArthur declared that, forbidden to bomb the Yalu River bridges on which the enemy was crossing, or to bomb the bases from which their planes were coming—he was forced to fight under handicaps without precedent in military history.[16]

At once the United Nations and the civilian leadership in the governments [illegible word–*ed.*] in [their?–*ed.*] saving South Korea from aggression were thrown into confusion. Not one of them wanted or intended to be drawn into the gigantic quicksand of a full fledged war with Communist China.

It is not the purpose of this memoir to follow the mass of consultations [and–*ed.*] meetings where the separate members of the United Nations [were–*ed.*] [trying?–*ed.*] to save the face of the United Nations and still avoid meeting the Communist Chinese attack for what it was. That was the war by one powerful nation with [illegible word–*ed.*] forces which would and did shatter the feeble United Nations.

It is sufficient to say that if the [illegible word–*ed.*] of unity and independence in Korea it meant an all out war.

Conflict between General MacArthur and President Truman was inevitable.

General Mark Clark who later succeeded General MacArthur expressed the military point of view in his book.

General Mark Clark stated in his book:

> . . . it was inconceivable to me, as I am sure it was to General MacArthur, that we did not announce to the world that if these Chinese troops were not withdrawn immediately we would consider ourselves officially at war with Red China and would hurl our air might at their most vital installations, wherever they were located, in any part of China. It was beyond my comprehension that we would countenance a situation in which Chinese soldiers killed American youths in organized, formal warfare and yet we would fail to use all the power at our command to protect those Americans.[17]

---

16. [*Editor's note:* Of the next six paragraphs in the text, the first four and the sixth are handwritten additions by Hoover to his March 6, 1963 draft. The fifth paragraph, containing the quotation by General Mark Clark, he extracted from that draft. These six paragraphs appear to go together in the sequence shown. They also seem to replace pp. 28 and 29 of the March 6 draft; these pages are missing from the folder containing Hoover's revisions. I have therefore omitted these two pages, which discuss the Truman administration's failure to allow General MacArthur's forces to conduct "hot pursuit" of enemy aircraft into Manchuria.]

17. Mark W. Clark, *From The Danube to the Yalu*, p. 315. [*Editor's note:* Hoover's revisions for Chapter 4 include the following handwritten squib: "General MacArthur was not without support of great military leaders. General Mark Clark who succeeded General MacArthur." It is not

President Truman [unquestionably?–*ed.*] expressed the point of view of the major civilian leaders of all the United Nations that we were not going [to–*ed.*] expand the war in Korea to a war with Communist China. Moreover, his experience in the proportions of United Nations burdens in the defense of South Korea would scarcely carry [conviction?–*ed.*] that there would be many [illegible words–*ed.*] [other?–*ed.*] nations if a call had been made to this purpose.

The Wake Island Meeting

On October 12, 1950, General Marshall (who had succeeded Louis Johnson as Secretary of Defense) cabled General MacArthur that President Truman would like to meet him at Wake Island in the Pacific for an important conference.

President Truman was accompanied by:

Admiral Arthur Radford, Commander of the Pacific Fleet
Army Secretary Frank Pace
Press Secretary Charles Ross
U.N. Ambassador Philip Jessup
Joint Chiefs' Chairman Omar Bradley
State Department Far Eastern Chief Dean Rusk
Special Adviser Averell Harriman, and other Truman aides and aides'
    aides, including Major General Harry Vaughan.

General MacArthur joined the meeting on October 15, 1950, accompanied by:

Major General Courtney Whitney
Colonel Laurence E. Bunker
Lieutenant Colonel Storey.[18]

---

clear where Hoover planned to insert these words—most likely near the Clark quotation used in Hoover's text.]

18. [*Editor's note:* The sketchiness of Hoover's account of the meeting at Wake Island leads one to suspect that he planned further revision and amplification of his case history of Korea. But as mentioned above, no later draft has been found.]

CHAPTER 5

Korea in 1951

The Dismissal of General MacArthur

On January 17 [19–*ed.*], 1951, after Red China for the second time in a month rejected a United Nations demand for a cease-fire in Korea, the House of Representatives passed a resolution asking that the United Nations "immediately act and declare Chinese Communist authorities an aggressor in Korea." On January 20, the United States initiated a United Nations resolution to condemn Communist China as an aggressor and pave the way for sanctions. On January 23, the Senate called on the United Nations to "immediately declare Communist China an aggressor in Korea."

The *Washington Daily News,* on January 24, reported the result of these efforts:

> When the American resolution seeking to brand the Chinese Communists as aggressors in Korea was side-tracked by a 27-to-23 vote in the 60–member United Nations political committee the United States suffered its worst defeat in the UN's 5-year history.
>
> This humiliating situation invites President Truman's personal attention, for it shows the extent to which our bargaining power has been traded away for nothing through the State Department's political ineptitude.
>
> The defeat was sustained at the hands of the British, supported by India, France, Canada, the Asian-Arab bloc, and the Scandinavian countries—nations for the most part, presumed to be our friends.
>
> The Russians took no part in the proceedings, because Britain and India were carrying the ball for them. . . .
>
> After all of the proud boasts about the united front against communism, and all the billions we have contributed to this build-up, the only nations voting with us on an issue directly involving Communist aggression were the

Latin-American bloc, Greece, Turkey, and the Philippines—not one of them a member of the North Atlantic alliance.[1]

After two weeks of much bitter discussion, and by applying pressure and making concessions, the United States finally won its fight to brand the Chinese as aggressors. The resolution was passed, 44–7, by the General Assembly's Political and Security Committee on January 30, and it was referred to the Collective Measures Committee to study the application of sanctions.[2] The condemnation was made February 1, 1951.

As former Secretary of Defense Louis A. Johnson said at the Senate hearings, (June 14, 1951,) apropos our decision to oppose aggression in Korea:

> . . . that if you let this one happen, others would happen in more rapid order; that the whole world looked to the majesty of strength of the United States to see what we were going to do about this picture.
>
> . . . it looks to me now as though it was a testing ground for the Charter. . . .[3]

At the MacArthur hearings on June 6, 1951, Senator Saltonstall read a February 13, 1951, Joint Chiefs of Staff report:

> During the course of the discussion it became apparent to the Joint Chiefs of Staff that the Department of State would prefer not to express political objectives with respect to Korea until military capabilities there were established. On the other hand, the consensus of the opinions of the Joint Chiefs of Staff was that a political decision was required before there could be suitable determination of military courses of action.[4]

and a March 15 report:

> [. . . The Joint Chiefs of Staff held an informal conference with representatives of the Department of State and among other things discussed the Korean situation.] It appeared to be generally agreed that at some future meeting an agreement should be reached on the objectives in Korea. It was suggested that the Secretary of State talk to the Secretary of Defense and the Chairman of the Joint Chiefs of Staff. If this question was not settled

---

1. *Washington Daily News,* January 24, 1951.
2. *New York Times,* January 31, 1951.
3. *Military Situation in the Far East,* Part 4, p. 2585.
4. Ibid., [Part 3,] p. 2031.

before the next meeting, the question would be discussed at the Joint Chiefs of Staff-State Department meeting on that date.[5]

On June 6, 1951, before a joint meeting of the Senate Committee on Armed Services and the Committee on Foreign Relations, Secretary Acheson testified:

> I think there was understanding about the policy; but . . . some of the nations associated with us did not think that there should be military decisions to advance beyond the thirty-eighth parallel until the political decision to do so had been taken by the United Nations. . . .[6]

General Mark Clark had this to say as to experience with the State Department while he was still in Europe:

> Gradually as I watched the Russians make important gains at our expense in Europe, an uneasy, frightening suspicion entered my mind. . . .
>
> These were things I knew from my own experience when the Alger Hiss case broke.
>
> The nagging fear was that perhaps Communists had wormed their way so deeply into our government on both the working and planning levels that they were able to exercise an inordinate degree of power in shaping the course of America in the dangerous postwar era.[7]

On March 18 [8–ed.], 1951, former Speaker of the House Joseph W. Martin, Jr., sent a letter, inviting General MacArthur's views with regard to America's position in Asia:[8]

> In the current discussions on foreign policy and overall strategy many of us have been distressed that, although the European aspects have been heavily emphasized, we have been without the views of yourself as Commander in Chief of the Far Eastern Command.
>
> I think it is imperative to the security of our Nation and for the safety of the world that policies of the United States embrace the broadest possible strategy and that in our earnest desire to protect Europe we do not weaken our position in Asia.

---

5. Ibid. [*Editor's note:* The first sentence in this quotation does not appear on the page Hoover cited. I have therefore placed it within brackets.]

6. Ibid.

7. Mark W. Clark, *From the Danube to the Yalu*, p. 11.

8. *Congressional Record,* [Vol. 97,] April 13, 1951, p. 3831. [*Editor's note:* Hoover's original page citation was erroneous. I have corrected it.]

Enclosed is a copy of an address I delivered in Brooklyn, N.Y., February 12, stressing this vital point and suggesting that the forces of Generalissimo Chiang Kai-shek on Formosa might be employed in the opening of a Second Asiatic front to relieve the pressure on our forces in Korea.

I have since repeated the essence of this thesis in other speeches, and intend to do so again on March 21, when I will be on a radio hook-up.

I would deem it a great help if I could have your views on this point, either on a confidential basis or otherwise. Your admirers are legion, and the respect you command is enormous. May success be yours in the gigantic undertaking which you direct.

General MacArthur replied to Congressman Martin on March 20, 1951.[9]

I am most grateful for your note of the 8th forwarding me a copy of your address of February 12. The latter I have read with much interest, and find that with the passage of years you have certainly lost none of your old-time punch.

My views and recommendations with respect to the situation created by Red China's entry into war against us in Korea have been submitted to Washington in most complete detail. Generally these views are well known and clearly understood, as they follow the conventional pattern of meeting force with maximum counter-force as we have never failed to do in the past. Your view with respect to the utilization of the Chinese forces on Formosa is in conflict with neither logic nor with tradition.

It seems strangely difficult for some to realize that here in Asia is where the Communist conspirators have elected to make their play for global conquest, and that we have joined the issue thus raised on the battlefield; that here we fight Europe's war with arms while the diplomats there still fight it with words; that if we lose the war to communism in Asia the fall of Europe is inevitable, win it and Europe most probably would avoid war and yet preserve freedom. As you pointed out, we must win. There is no substitute for victory.

On March 24, 1951, General MacArthur stated that

. . . Within the area of my authority as military commander . . . I stand ready at any time to confer in the field with the commander in chief of the enemy forces in an earnest effort to find any military means whereby the realization

9. Ibid.

of the political objectives of the United Nations in Korea ... might be accomplished without further bloodshed.[10]

The State Department subsequently issued a statement that

... the political issues which General MacArthur has stated are beyond his responsibility as a field commander, are being dealt with in the UN and by intergovernmental consultations. ...[11]

On April 11, 1951, President Truman stated:

... I have concluded that General of the Army Douglas MacArthur is unable to give his whole-hearted support to the policies of the United States Government and of the United Nations in matters pertaining to his official duties. ...[12]

Many Americans felt deeply that an opportunity should be given to the public to express their appreciation for General MacArthur's services over the long years. He had performed a major part in the First World War as the Commander of an American army division. He, undoubtedly, was the greatest military leader of the Second World War. By his victory over Japan, and his statesmanship after the war he had restored Japan to a high place of cooperation among free nations.

I took part with some of his friends in organizing a public reception for him upon his arrival in San Francisco on April 17, 1951, which proved to be the greatest homecoming of any American in our history.

General MacArthur was invited to address the Congress on April 19. His address will long remain in American history. In it there was not one word reflecting upon the administration or bitterness over his treatment.

Some passages were:

I do not stand here as advocate for any partisan cause, for the issues are fundamental and reach quite beyond the realm of partisan consideration. They must be resolved on the highest plane of national interest if our course is to prove sound and our future protected. ... I address you with neither rancor nor bitterness in the fading twilight of life with but one purpose in mind—to serve my country.

---

10. *Military Situation in the Far East,* p. 3573.

11. Ibid.

12. *Memoirs by Harry S. Truman,* Volume II, p. 449. [*Editor's note:* Truman was referring here to his sensational dismissal of General MacArthur from his military command on April 11, 1951.]

The issues are global and so interlocked that to consider the problems of one sector oblivious to those of another is but to court disaster for the whole. . . .

The Communist threat is a global one. Its successful advance in one sector threatens the destruction of every other sector. You cannot appease or otherwise surrender to communism in Asia without simultaneously undermining our efforts to halt its advance in Europe. . . .

. . . the Asian peoples covet the right to shape their own free destiny. [. . . –ed.]

Of more direct and immediate bearing upon our national security are the changes wrought in the strategic potential of the Pacific Ocean in the course of the past war. . . .

We control it to the shores of Asia by a chain of islands extending in an arc from the Aleutians to the Marianas held by us and our free allies.

From this island chain we can dominate with sea and air power every Asiatic port from Vladivostok to Singapore and prevent any hostile movement into the Pacific. . . .

The holding of this littoral defense line in the western Pacific is entirely dependent upon holding all segments thereof, for any major breach of that line by an unfriendly power would render vulnerable to determined attack every other major segment. This is a military estimate as to which I have yet to find a military leader who will take exception. [. . . –ed.]

The Japanese people since the war have undergone the greatest reformation recorded in modern history. With a commendable will, eagerness to learn, and marked capacity to understand, they have, from the ashes left in war's wake, erected in Japan an edifice dedicated to the primacy of individual liberty and personal dignity . . . a truly representative government, committed to the advance of political morality, freedom of economic enterprise, and social justice. Politically, economically, and socially Japan is now abreast of many free nations of the earth and will not again fail the universal trust. . . .

. . . While I was not consulted prior to the President's decision to intervene in the support of the Republic of Korea, that decision, from a military standpoint, proved a sound one [. . . –ed.] as we hurled back the invaders and decimated his forces. Our victory was complete and our objectives within reach when Red China intervened with numerically superior ground forces. This created a new war and an entirely new situation—a situation not contemplated when our forces were committed against the North Korean invaders—a situation which called for new decisions in the diplomatic sphere to permit the realistic adjustment of military strategy. Such decisions have not been forthcoming.

While no man in his right mind would advocate sending our ground forces into continental China and such was never given a thought, the new situation did urgently demand a drastic revision of strategic planning if our political aim was to defeat this new enemy as we had defeated the old.

Apart from the military need as I saw it to neutralize the sanctuary protection given the enemy north of the Yalu, I felt that military necessity in the conduct of the war made necessary:

1. The intensification of our economic blockade against China;
2. The imposition of a naval blockade against the China coast;
3. Removal of restrictions on air reconnaissance of China's coastal areas and of Manchuria;
4. Removal of restrictions on the forces of the Republic of China on Formosa with logistical support to contribute to their effective operation against the common enemy.

For entertaining these views, all professionally designed to support our forces committed to Korea and bring hostilities to an end with the least possible delay and at a saving of countless American and Allied lives, I have been severely criticized. . . . the above views have been fully shared in the past by practically every military leader concerned with the Korean campaign, including our own Joint Chiefs of Staff.

I called for reinforcements, but was informed that reinforcements were not available. I made clear that if not permitted to destroy the build-up bases north of the Yalu; if not permitted to utilize the friendly Chinese force of some 600,000 men on Formosa; if not permitted to blockade the China coast to prevent the Chinese Reds from getting succor from without; and if there were to be no hope of major reinforcements, the position of the command from the military standpoint forbade victory. . . .

But once war is forced upon us, there is no other alternative than to apply every available means to bring it to a swift end. War's very object is victory—not prolonged indecision. In war, indeed, there can be no substitute for victory. . . .

I am closing my 52 years of military service. When I joined the Army even before the turn of the century, it was the fulfillment of all my boyish hopes and dreams. The world has turned over many times since I took the oath on the plain at West Point, and the hopes and dreams have long since vanished. But I still remember the refrain of one of the most popular barrack ballads of that day which proclaimed most proudly that—"Old soldiers never die; they just fade away."

And like the old soldier of that ballad, I now close my military career and just fade away—an old soldier who tried to do his duty as God gave him the light to see that duty.

Good-by.[13]

The Aftermath

The events in Korea launched a joint investigation by the Senate Armed Services Committee and the Senate Foreign Relations Committee. The two committees commenced hearings on May 3 and continued until June 27. Over 2,000,000 words of testimony were taken from the thirteen witnesses who appeared. In addition to the oral testimony, numerous statements and communications were received and made a part of the testimony.

The Joint Chiefs of Staff were unanimous in their statements that General MacArthur had not violated any military directives during the progress of the Korean campaign.

The New Command

Lieutenant General Matthew B. Ridgway, who had commanded the U.S. Eighth Army in Korea since December 26, 1950, replaced MacArthur in all his posts. On April 28, 1952, President Truman appointed him to replace General Eisenhower in Europe, and General Mark W. Clark was appointed Ridgway's successor as United Nations Supreme Commander in Korea and Commander of the United States forces in the Far East.

The war in Korea is well described by General Clark:

Politically I was guided by the basic terms of my mission, which was defensive. I was given neither the authority nor the military resources to achieve victory.[14]

General Clark bombed the Suiho electric power plant in North Korea. After the bombing, General Clark received a blast of criticism from the British press, to which he replied:

---

13. *Congressional Record*, [Vol. 97,] April 19, 1951, pp. 4123–4125. [*Editor's note:* In Hoover's manuscript the quoted passage contains a few typographical and transcription errors, which I have corrected. The original page citation is also inaccurate; I have corrected that as well.]

14. Mark W. Clark, *From the Danube to the Yalu*, p. 69.

The Suiho hydro-electric plant produces electric power which, transmitted to Manchuria, is used in war industries—industries whose end products are used against men of our own forces who are fighting the battle of the free world against communist aggression.

As a commander, I would be remiss in my duty if I did not employ all means at my disposal to save lives and minimize casualties among the men serving under me. Until a just and honorable armistice definitely is assured, therefore, I will continue to authorize attacks on enemy targets in North Korea, the destruction of which will save the lives of our men and reduce the power of a vicious enemy to continue his treacherous aggression.[15]

Like General MacArthur, General Clark sought to get Washington's permission to use the Nationalist Chinese troops that Chiang Kai-shek had offered the United Nations. Of this proposal, Clark said:

My recommendation for the use of Chiang's troops was never answered by Washington.[16]

The fighting was brought to a halt in Korea by direction [of–ed.] General [President–ed.] Eisenhower by the truce signed on July 27, 1953.

Of this armistice, General Clark wrote:

The Armistice was obtained and I signed it. But I would be less than truthful if I failed to record that I put my signature on that document with a heavy heart. I was grateful that the killing was ended for a time at least. But I had grave misgivings that some day my countrymen would be forced to pay a far higher price in blood than it would have cost if the decision had been made to defeat the Communists in Korea.[17]

The End Result

The futile Korean war cost the lives of 33,629 Americans, with an additional 103,308 causalities. The United States alone spent $18,000,000,000.[18] The costs will go on and on as part of our national debt.

Since the armistice, the government of South Korea has been too feeble to protect itself. It has been a military, economic and charitable burden on the American people down to this writing in 1963.

---

15. Ibid., p. 74.
16. Ibid., p. 71.
17. Ibid., pp. 317–318.
18. *World Book Encyclopaedia*, Field Enterprises Educational Corporation, Chicago, 1961.

About all that can be said of the whole United States Korean activity is

(a) The [independence?–*ed.*] of South Korea is set up and maintained
     by American military support;
(b) The Koreans do not have the [qualities?–*ed.*] to hold it for
     themselves;
(c) The test of the United Nations to assemble military strength for
     any major action is a feeble hope;
(d) It may keep peace among little nations.

SECTION IV

Vengeance Comes to Germany

Editor's note: "Vengeance Comes to Germany" is the title Hoover ultimately gave to his "case history" of postwar Germany. The essay is an account of Germany's economic prostration (as he observed it) in 1946 and 1947 and of his attempt to rescue the defeated enemy country from "economic slavery" wrought by the "follies" of Allied occupation policy. As will be seen, Hoover was severely critical of the so-called Morgenthau Plan of 1944–45 (named after President Roosevelt's Secretary of the Treasury, Henry Morgenthau Jr.), which called for the permanent "pastoralization" (deindustrialization) of Germany, so that a strong, militaristic Germany could never rise again. Hoover fought this policy (which had been implemented in a modified form in 1945) on both humanitarian and economic grounds. His battle was one of the subjects of the final volume (1964) of his multivolume *An American Epic*, wherein he condemned the Morgenthau Plan as "a program of vengeance" (p. 244).

Early in 1962 Hoover composed the first drafts of a chapter on postwar Germany's ordeal for inclusion in Volume II of *Freedom Betrayed*. Later in the year he renamed the chapter "Vengeance Comes to Germany." On November 30, 1962, he returned a previously typed copy of this version, more than fifty pages long, to his staff, along with a fresh batch of penciled revisions scrawled on its pages. On the cover of the folder he instructed: "Clean up send to Xerox" (for photocopying). This apparently was never done; no later version of this manuscript has been found. The marked-up November 30, 1962, draft seems, then, to reflect Hoover's final handiwork on this study, which he soon decided to move to the third volume of the Magnum Opus.

A few of Hoover's handwritten revisions and interlineations have proven impossible to decipher with certainty. But most of them are reasonably plain, and I have duly incorporated them, as he intended, into his November 30, 1962, draft. Thus altered, it is the text reproduced here. Where Hoover's words or intent are unclear, I have so indicated in brackets.

The "Case History of Germany" file, including the essay at hand and earlier drafts, is in the Herbert C. Hoover Papers, Box 80, Hoover Institution Archives.

CHAPTER A

RATHER THAN ATTEMPTING a case history of the decline and fall of Germany I have thought an account of what happens to a defeated aggressor nation is of more historic usefulness.

In the Introduction to these memoirs I have stated my contacts with Germany, German leaders and German problems extending over forty years, including two wars of aggression against us and their aftermaths.

The people of the Allies suffered immeasurably from these attacks. Every morning thousands of wives and mothers received notice of fathers or sons that had died or notices that they were in hospital from wounds. These people emerged from the wars with huge national debts and taxes; their economies were ruined and there was huge unemployment. Their countries had the burden of widows and orphans and millions who suffered life-long injuries.

After both wars the emotions of the Allied peoples demanded that their statesmen assure revenge, punishment, dismemberment, annexation of their foreign possessions and gigantic reparations. No Allied statesman could continue in office who did not impose these demands.

The blunt fact, however, was that here was a race of great genius, of centuries as one of the great military, commercial and intellectual powers of the world. No penalties or restraints by the victors could hold them for long, and further the restoration of their productivity was essential to the recovery of the victors.

The penalties and limitations to be imposed upon Germany after the Second World War could be catalogued about as follows:[1]

---

1. [*Editor's note:* I have left Hoover's catalogue numbering below as he composed it. Hence the repetition in two places.]

(1) Dismemberment;

(2) The truncated section to be divided into four zones of occupation; one each under the Russians, British, French, and Americans;

(2) Demobilization of her armed forces and extinction of her General Staff;

(3) Trial and hanging of military and civilian leadership or their long imprisonment;

(4) Removal or destruction of all munition production plants;

(5) Division of a large part of peacetime production plants among the Allies;

(6) Reduction of [important–*ed.*] production to specific levels to reduce her to a "pastoral economy";

(7) [illegible words–*ed.*]

(8) The wiping out of the Nazi spirit by the reorganization of the educational system and condemnation of members of the Nazi party to common labor;

(9) A reparations commission to be set up initially in Moscow;

(10) A control commission of Allied representatives to be set up in Berlin;

(11) A total reparations of twenty billion dollars—one half to Russia;

(12) Liquid assets in stocks of supplies or precious metals to be [divided?–*ed.*] at once;

(12) German prisoners in various Allied countries to be used for reconstruction labor in those countries;

(13) Nazi officials to be forever removed from public service;

(14) Reorganization of the judicial system;

(15) Restoration of "local self-government on democratic principles";

(16) "Democratic political parties and public discussion shall be allowed and encouraged";

(17) Germany to be a single economic unit with common policies as to industrial production; agriculture; wages, prices and rationing; currency, banking and taxation and customs; transportation and communications;

(18) "Measures shall be promptly taken" to repair transport, enlarge coal production and agricultural production, and to repair housing and essential utilities;

(19) A naval commission to divide war and merchant vessels among the three governments and a larger part of the captured submarines was to be sunk;

(20) For the time being no central government shall be established but "certain essential central administrative departments, headed by State secretaries" to act under the direction of the Control Council;

(21) Trade unions to be permitted, subject to military security;

(22) Free speech, religion and press to be allowed subject to Allied control.

Added to these Potsdam restrictions and requirements was an Executive order approved by President Roosevelt on _____ April 1945 which became known as Joint Chiefs of Staff Directive 1067[:–ed.][2]

4. Basic Objectives of Military Government in Germany:

a. It should be brought home to the Germans that Germany's ruthless warfare and the fanatical Nazi resistance have destroyed the German economy and made chaos and suffering inevitable and that the Germans cannot escape responsibility for what they have brought upon themselves.

b. Germany will not be occupied for the purpose of liberation but as a defeated enemy nation. Your aim is not oppression but to occupy Germany for the purpose of realizing certain important Allied objectives. In the conduct of your occupation and administration you should be just but firm and aloof. You will strongly discourage fraternization with the German officials and population.

---

2. [*Editor's note:* Hoover's statement here is not completely accurate. His reference is to Joint Chiefs of Staff Directive 1067 (JCS 1067), a set of instructions prepared for General Dwight D. Eisenhower and the U.S. Army to use in governing Germany after the Hitler regime collapsed. First circulated in draft form in September 1944, JCS 1067 became the center of months of revisionary efforts and bureaucratic infighting in Washington between advocates of a punitive peace and dismantling of Germany heavy industry (led by Secretary of the Treasury Henry Morgenthau Jr.) and those who favored a more flexible, less Carthaginian approach to the postwar Germany economy.

President Roosevelt never signed JCS 1067. He did, however, approve a compromise interagency memorandum on March 23, 1945 that became the basis for the final revision of JCS 1067. Roosevelt died before the interagency committee known as IPCOG (Informal Policy Committee on Germany) finished drafting the revised directive. As completed by IPCOG in late April, and amended at the Joint Chiefs of Staff's request in May, the document was approved by President Harry S. Truman on May 10, 1945 and dispatched to General Eisenhower in Europe.

This comprehensive and controversial policy document became the overarching directive for the United States Army's military government in Germany for the next two years. Technically identified as IPCOG 1/4 or JCS 1067/8, it is usually cited simply as JCS 1067. The version quoted by Hoover is the April 26, 1945 draft (JCS 1067/6) which does not contain the amendments obtained in May 1945 by the Joint Chiefs of Staff. Curiously, the April 1945 draft was the one officially released by the U.S. State Department later in 1945 and most often reprinted ever since.]

c. The principal Allied objective is to prevent Germany from ever again becoming a threat to the peace of the world. Essential steps in the accomplishment of this objective are the elimination of Nazism and militarism in all their forms, the immediate apprehension of war criminals for punishment, the industrial disarmament and demilitarization of Germany, with continuing control over Germany's capacity to make war, and the preparation for an eventual reconstruction of German political life on a democratic basis.

d. Other Allied objectives are to enforce the program of reparations and restitution, to provide relief for the benefit of countries devastated by Nazi aggression, and to ensure that prisoners of war and displaced persons of the United Nations are cared for and repatriated.

5. Economic Controls:

a. As a member of the Control Council and as zone commander, you will be guided by the principle that controls upon the German economy may be imposed to the extent that such controls may be necessary to achieve the objectives enumerated in paragraph 4 above and also as they may be essential to protect the safety and meet the needs of the occupying forces and assure the production and maintenance of goods and services required to prevent starvation or such disease and unrest as would endanger these forces. No action will be taken in execution of the reparations program or otherwise which would tend to support basic living conditions in Germany or in your zone on a higher level than that existing in any one of the neighboring United Nations.

b. In the imposition and maintenance of such controls as may be prescribed by you or the Control Council, German authorities will to the fullest extent practicable be ordered to proclaim and assume administration of such controls. Thus it should be brought home to the German people that the responsibility for the administration of such controls and for any break-downs in those controls will rest with themselves and German authorities.[3]

---

3. [*Editor's note:* In his handwritten corrections and instructions for his staff, Hoover wrote (just after his reference to JCS 1067): "Get paragraphs 4 and 5 referred to later and start with them." I have accordingly inserted these two sections from JCS 1067 here.

In his markup of a printed copy of these passages, Hoover deleted the title of paragraph 4, the numbers 4 and 5, and the subdivision indicators (a, b, etc.) in each of these sections. I have reinstated these deleted items.

A control commission was set up with detailed powers to destroy any "war potential" production; to control all research activities; etc.

Some of the provisions were of great economic potency, for instance [:–ed.]

Part II. Economic

General Objectives and Methods of Control

16. . . . . Except as may be necessary to carry out these objectives, you will take no steps (a) looking toward the economic rehabilitation of Germany, or (b) designed to maintain or strengthen the German economy. . . .

German Standard of Living

21. [. . . –ed.] You will take all practicable economic and police measures to assure that German resources are fully utilized and consumption held to the minimum in order that imports may be strictly limited. . . .

[30. In order to disarm Germany, the Control Council should–ed.]
. . .

b. prevent the production of merchant ships, synthetic rubber and oil, aluminum and magnesium and any other products and equipment on which you will subsequently receive instructions;

c. seize and safeguard all facilities used in the production of any of the items mentioned in this paragraph and dispose of them as follows:
   (1) remove all those required for reparation;
   (2) destroy all those not transferred for reparation if they are especially adapted to the production of the items specified in this paragraph and are not of a type generally used in industries permitted to the Germans (cases of doubt to be resolved in favor of destruction); . . . .

32. Pending final Allied agreements on reparation and on control or elimination of German industries that can be utilized for war production, the Control Council should

---

Hoover also underlined in pencil the first sentence in section 4b and the last sentence in section 5b. It is not known why he did this. Possibly he wanted to italicize them for emphasis.]

a. prohibit and prevent production of iron and steel, chemicals, non-ferrous metals (excluding aluminum and magnesium), machine tools, radio and electrical equipment, automotive vehicles, heavy machinery and important parts thereof, except for the purposes stated in paragraphs 4 and 5 of this directive;

b. prohibit and prevent rehabilitation of plant and equipment in such industries except for the purposes stated in paragraphs 4 and 5 of this directive; and [. . . . −ed.]

33. The Control Council should adopt a policy permitting [. . . −ed.] the production of light consumer goods, provided that such conversion does not prejudice the subsequent removal of plant and equipment on reparation account and does not require any imports beyond those necessary for the purposes specified in paragraphs 4 and 5 of this directive. [. . . −ed.]

[38. . . . −ed.] Prevention or restraint of inflation shall not constitute an additional ground for the importation of supplies, nor shall it constitute an additional ground for limiting removal, destruction or curtailment of productive facilities in fulfillment of the program for reparation, demilitarization and industrial disarmament. [. . . −ed.]

40. The Control Council should establish centralized control over all trade in goods and services with foreign countries. Pending agreement in the Control Council you will impose appropriate controls in your own zone. [. . . −ed.]

Part III. Financial

45. [. . . −ed.]

a. United States forces and other Allied forces will use Allied Military marks and Reichsmark currency or coins in their possession. Allied Military marks and Reichsmark currency and coin now in circulation in Germany will be legal tender without distinction and will be interchangeable at the rate of 1 Allied Military mark for 1 Reichsmark. Reichskreditkassenscheine and other German military currency will not be legal tender in Germany. [. . . −ed.]

49. All foreign exchange transactions, including those arising out of exports and imports, shall be controlled [. . . . −ed.]

[The Control Council should–*ed.*]

   c. Establish effective controls with respect to all foreign exchange transactions, including:
>   (1) Transactions as to property between persons inside Germany and persons outside Germany;
>   (2) Transactions involving obligations owed by or become due from any person in Germany to any person outside Germany; and[4]

No economist sat in those councils, since he would have insisted that the German economy was interlocked with that of all Europe; that the recovery of all the Continent, and even that of the United States, was dependent upon Germany's restored productivity. No engineer sat in those councils, as he would have insisted that the removal of plants to an allied country was a foolish idea. Industrial plants are not simply tools; they comprise the buildings, the complicated systems for [electricity–*ed.*], the water and air connections buried in walls, and floors. Even if the Allies had had the original blueprints, these plants were of no value except for this second hand and often obsolete [illegible words–*ed.*]

The after-war problems of the United States, Britain, and all free countries were further complicated by the Soviet determination to communize their zone as a part of their determination to spread Communism over the world. And Communist activities were made easier since their zone of occupation contained the major breadbasket and much of the industry of Germany.

Rather than include in this chapter the detailed consequences of all the twenty-two restrictions imposed on Germany, I will illustrate it from a personal examination of my own upon the spot.

---

4. [*Editor's note:* Hoover's partial copy of JCS 1067 ends here in mid-sentence. The full, revised text of JCS 1067, as of April 26, 1945 (the text quoted here) can be found in *Department of State Bulletin*, 13 (October 21, 1945): 596–607 and in U.S. Department of State, *Foreign Relations of the United States: Diplomatic Papers, 1945*, vol. 3 (United States Government Printing Office, Washington: 1968), pp. 485–503. The Joint Chiefs of Staff's proposed amendments to this draft (which were accepted and added to the final version approved by President Truman) are in ibid., p. 510.]

CHAPTER B

IN MARCH, 1946, at President Truman's request, I undertook to coordinate the food supplies of all the nations of the world to meet the greatest famine of all history—the inevitable consequence of the Second World War.

While I was en route to Germany, General Lucius D. Clay, our Commander of the American zone, was so troubled over [illegible word–*ed.*] food questions that he could not await my arrival a few days later in Berlin but came to Brussels to meet me on April 6. He informed me that the food supply had been reduced to such a low level in the American, British, and French zone that the Germans were at the point of mass starvation; moreover, that the Allied policies had produced immense unemployment and destitution in all directions.

General Clay and I were in agreement that sheer humanity to the vast majorities of the German people who had no part in Hitler's Nazi conspiracy demanded relief from the Allied powers. And General Clay gave to me other reasons than pure humanity: the occupying forces were endangered from infectious diseases which would result if food was not forthcoming. Riots and mass killing were inevitable.

Our mission already had much information as to German food supply and no one could doubt General Clay.

The British and French themselves were short of food and could not supply their zones. Under the Morgenthau plan to pastoralize Germany and its reduction of the "levels of industrial production" the Germans could not produce industrial exports with which to buy imports. Upon our arrival in Berlin all of the Allied officials confirmed General Clay's statements. At once I and my colleagues recommended that the United States undertake monthly shipments until the following harvest in 1917 [1947–*ed.*].

And we were to learn more of the situation upon our arrival in Berlin. The Allied military officials in the three zones were in confidence indignant over the follies imposed by civilian authorities. They gave me some samples:

By the taking of even old cargo ships for reparations, the prohibition of German shipbuilding, and the destruction of shipyards, the Americans and British were compelled to divert their own scarce merchant ships to transport German supplies, with consequent losses in their own foreign trade.

Germany, before the war, had developed a huge synthetic nitrogen production for fertilizers not only for German farmers but for all Europe. The part of these plants for manufacture of explosives could easily have been destroyed and their production of fertilizers could have been continued. At the end of the war, Germany had a capacity of about 700,000 tons of nitrates. These plants, except for a production capacity of about 200,000 tons, were destroyed.

Thus the food production of Germany and all Europe was diminished. A ridiculous consequence was that as a part of keeping the Germans alive, the United States was compelled to ship hundreds of millions of dollars worth of nitrate fertilizers to Germany and all the Allies at the expense of American taxpayers.

The Germans had developed a large production of petroleum products synthetically from coal. These plants were totally destroyed as a part of "disarmament." The United States was compelled to ship tens of millions of dollars worth of petroleum products to keep the railways and the industrial wheels moving which were essential for the armies of occupation.

My rough estimate of the burden on the American people was [the–*ed.*] spending [of–*ed.*] between one and two billions a year to keep the Germans alive.

One result of the condemnation of members of the Nazi party, when applied to the Western zone, was that competent organization and operations were deprived of skills and trained professors. The Russians did not follow this practice. Thus these skills and professors flocked to Russia and the Russian zone. Our State Department refused our universities their applications to bring German scientists to the United States. The consequence was the German scientists carried the knowledge of missiles to Russia.

I Go to Germany Again in 1947

As these burdens on the American people showed no signs of lessening, in January 1947 President Truman requested me to return to Germany again and make complete investigation and reports on the policies in the three Allied zones with recommendations. There were two of these reports: the first on food and other supply requirements, and the second upon the economic policies which imposed these huge drains on American taxpayers. I can do no better than to include here the important sections of those reports with interpolations for clarity in brackets.

February 26, 1947

The President
The White House
Washington, D.C.

Dear Mr. President:

I have now completed the Economic Mission to Germany and Austria, which I undertook at your request. . . .

In this examination of food questions in the combined zones, I have had the invaluable service of Mr. Dennis A. FitzGerald in food questions and that of Dr. Wm. H. Sebrell, Jr. in nutritional and health questions, together with the able assistance in other economic questions of Mr. Hugh Gibson, Mr. Louis Lochner, Mr. Frank Mason, and Dr. Gustav Stolper. I have received the full cooperation of Generals McNarney, Clay and Draper, Colonel Hester and their able staff, as well as General Robertson, Sir Cecil Weir and Mr. T. F. Griffin and their able staff on the British side.

My thanks are also due to the devoted service of Mr. Tracy S. Voorhees, Special Assistant to the Secretary of War, and to the Air Transport Command for their cooperation and skill.

Faithfully,
HERBERT HOOVER

Introduction to the Report[1]

At the time of her surrender, Germany had exhausted all of her reserves and most of her stocks of consumer goods and raw materials. We now know that, driven back into her own borders, she would have blown up in chaos within a short time without further military action.

---

1. [*Editor's note:* This document was entitled "Report No. 1—German Agriculture and Food Requirements." It was released to the press on February 28, 1947. The complete text may be found in Herbert Hoover, *Addresses Upon the American Road, 1945–1948* (D. Van Nostrand Company, Inc., New York: 1949), pp. 270–285.]

Promptly after the surrender, her liquid resources from which she could have been provided with supplies were seized and divided as reparations. The population thus became largely dependent for its life upon the armies of occupation.

It is hardly necessary to repeat that parts of Germany were annexed to Poland and Russia and that the shrunken territory was divided into four military occupation zones between the Russians, French, British and Americans. The American and British Zones have now been administratively combined . . . and this report relates to that area only. [. . . –ed.]

[The French supplied their zone partly from American shipments on credit which added further to American burdens. The Russians in their zone had the breadbasket of Germany and therefore had no important food problems.][2] The population of the combined [American and British][3] zones in 1939 was about 34,200,000. The Germans expelled from the Russian and Polish annexations together with those from Czechoslovakia, Hungary, and Austria, have raised the population in the American and British Zones to about 41,700,000. It is estimated that an additional 1,000,000 will come into this area by December 1947. There are also about 400,000 British and American military and civil personnel. Thus, the two zones will have to accommodate about 43,000,000 people, bringing the population approximately 9,000,000 above that in 1939. [Prior to the war.]

The skilled manpower and the ratio of working males in the population have been greatly affected by the war. For the whole of Germany, it is estimated that 5,700,000 were killed or permanently injured. It is also estimated that over 3,000,000 prisoners of war are [still] held in work camps in Russia; 750,000 in France; 400,000 in Britain; and 40,000 in Belgium. The detention of large numbers of skilled Sudeten German workmen in Czechoslovakia bears on this problem.

As applied to the American and British Zones, this represents a present subtraction of over 6,000,000 of the most vital and most skilled workers in the population. Likewise, the 90,000 Nazis held in concentration camps and the 1,900,000 others under sanctions by which they can only engage in manual labor naturally comprise a considerable part of the former technical and administrative skill of the country, and the restrictions upon them, however necessary, add to administrative and industrial problems.

---

2. [*Editor's note:* The bracketed sentences are Hoover's interpolation into the text. He bracketed them himself. Unless otherwise indicated, all brackets in this extended quotation are Hoover's.]

3. [*Editor's note:* Hoover silently added these words, evidently for clarity. Brackets here supplied by the editor.]

One consequence of these distortions is that in the age groups between 20 and 40 there are 6 men to 10 women, and in the age group between 40 and 60, about 7 men to 10 women. Thus, there are in these groups between 6 and 7 million more women than men. The results upon productive power are bad enough, but the consequences to morals are appalling.

Housing

The housing situation in the two zones is the worst that modern civilization has ever seen. About 25 per cent of the urban housing was destroyed by the war. Therefore, 25 per cent of the urban population must find roofs from among the remaining 75 per cent, in addition to all the destitute "expellees" and other groups brought in. There has been little repair of damaged houses, due to lack of materials and transportation. The result of all this is that multitudes are living in rubble and basements. The average space among tens of millions is equivalent to between three and four people to a 12′ × 12′ room. Nor is the overcrowding confined to urban areas, for the "expellees" have been settled into every farm house. One consequence is the rapid spread of tuberculosis and other potentially communicable diseases.

Coal

The shortage of coal is, next to food, the most serious immediate bottleneck to both living and the revival of exports to pay for food. The Ruhr, which is now almost the sole coal supply of the Anglo-American Zones, is, due to lack of skilled men and physical vitality in labor, producing only 230,000 tons per day, as against a former 450,000 tons per day. Of the present production, a considerable amount must [under agreements] be exported to surrounding nations which are also suffering. The shortage leaves the two zones without sufficient coal for transport, household and other dominant services, with little upon which to start exports in the industry.

The coal famine all over Western Europe and the unprecedented severity of the winter have produced everywhere the most acute suffering. As an example . . . no household coal has been issued in Hamburg since October. Other German cities have been but little better off.

Agricultural Production

It must be borne in mind that about 25 per cent of the German pre-war food production came from the areas taken over by Russia and Poland. . . . Some millions of tons formerly flowed into the American and British Zones from these areas. These sources now contribute nothing.

The British and American armies and civilians are entirely fed from home. The large Russian army is fed upon their zone.

Due to a lack of fertilizers, good seed, farm implements and skilled labor, the 1946 agricultural production in the American and British Zones was about 65 per cent of pre-war. A generalized appraisal indicates that in the American Zone the harvest of 1946 yielded a supply, beyond the needs of the farmers (self-suppliers) equal to about 1,100 calories per day for the "non-self suppliers." The similar supply in the British Zone was about 900 calories per day average to the "non-self suppliers." These amounts contrast with 3,000 calories of the pre-war normal German consumption.

With the efforts being made to improve agricultural production, there is an expected small increase from the harvest of 1947, especially in potatoes (if better seed is provided in time). The steps which I recommend, however, should show greater production from the 1948 harvest.

Food [Distribution–*ed.*][4]

This terrible winter, with frozen canals and impeded railway traffic, has rendered it impossible to maintain even the present low basis of rationing in many localities. The coal shortage and the consequent lack of heat, even for cooking, has added a multitude of hardships. The conclusions in this report as to the food situation are, however, not based upon the effect of this temporary dislocation, but upon the basic conditions, to which the winter has added many difficulties.

From the food point of view, the population of the combined [British and American] zones has been divided as below, based upon the German census undertaken last autumn. The table must not be regarded as precise for the different groups, as the Berlin Sector was not distributed on the same basis as others. It is, however, accurate enough for food computation purposes.

"*Self-Suppliers,*" i.e. farmers and their families 7,640,000
"*Non-self suppliers,*" i.e. urban population:
    Prospective and nursing mothers 660,000
    Children 0–6 years of age .3,070,000
    Children 6–15 years of age. 4,495,000

---

4. [*Editor's note:* For unknown reasons, Hoover silently omitted this word, which had been part of the caption in his original report.]

Adolescents, 15–20 years of age 2,100,000

"Normal Consumers," 20 years up 17,910,000

Moderate hard workers 2,500,000

Heavy workers 1,910,000

Extra heavy workers 720,000

Displaced persons 680,000   34,045,000

　　Total population, two zones 41,685,000

The base ration is 1,550 calories per person per day to the "normal consumer" group, with priorities and supplements, as the situation requires or permits, for other groups. For instance, milk and fats are given in priority to nursing mothers and children up to six years of age; more food, including more meat, is given in supplement to hard workers, etc.

This basic ration for the "normal consumer" compares with the minimum temporary maintenance food intake recommended for "normal consumers" by eminent nutritionists, as follows:

	Present German	Recommended Minimum	Percent Deficiency
Carbohydrates	283 grams	335 grams	16%
Fats	24 grams	45 grams	47%
Protein	52 grams	65 grams	20%
Calories	1,550	2,000	24%

Thus with the deficiency in quantity and in fats, protein and other nutrients, the 1,550 ration is wholly incapable of supporting health of the groups, which do not have supplements.

[Nutritional Condition of the Population–*ed.*][5]

The nutritional condition of the above different groups, irrespective of the immediate consequences of the hard winter, are:

(A) The 7,640,000 self-suppliers are, naturally, in good condition.

(B) The supplements and priorities in special foods given to 3,730,000 prospective and nursing mothers, and children under six years of age, appear to be enough to keep them in good condition.

---

5. [*Editor's note:* For unknown reasons Hoover silently omitted this caption, which had appeared in his original report.]

(C) Over half of the 6,595,000 children and adolescents, especially in the lower-income groups, are in a deplorable condition. Their situation is better in limited localities where school feeding has been undertaken but outside these limits stunted growth and delayed development is widespread. In some areas famine edema (actual starvation) is appearing in the children. A study of groups of boys between the ages of 9 and 16 years showed 5.5 lbs. under minimum standard weights, with girls 5.1 lbs. below such standard. Other groups studied showed even worse conditions.

(D) A considerable part of the "normal consumer" group of 17,910,000 is likewise in deplorable condition.

This group comprises the light physical workers and is in large majority women and many are aged. . . . a large part of the group shows a steady loss of weight, vitality and ability to work. A study in the British Zone shows urban adult males over 19 pounds and females nearly 5 pounds under proper weight. A study in the American Zone showed from 5 to 20 pounds under proper weight. Famine edema is showing in thousands of cases, stated to be 10,000 in Hamburg alone. In persons over 70, in three months last autumn the increase was 40 per cent.

(E) While the workers' rations, due to supplements, are perhaps high enough in themselves, yet the universal tendency is for the worker to share his supplement with his wife and children, and therefore it does not have its full effect in supplying energy for the worker himself.

(F) The 680,000 Displaced Persons are about one-third in the British Zone and two-thirds in the United States Zone. In the British Zone they receive the German ration only. In the United States Zone they receive supplements which amount to 700 calories per day, so there can be no doubt as to their adequate supply in that area. In fact, the American ration is above the "normal ration" of the other nations on the Continent, except the former neutrals.

A New Program

The Anglo-American bi-zonal agreement of last autumn calls for an increase of rations by 250 calories per day at some undetermined date. Such an increase is highly desirable. However, the world shortage in cereals, evidenced by the early reduction of bread rations in several other [European] nations, renders such an increase impossible until after the harvest of 1947. Such a program also implies increased import supplies which, in terms of grain, would add 1,260,000 tons and $136,000,000 annually to costs, above the already huge burden upon the taxpayers of our two nations.

As the present base of 1,550 calories for "normal consumers" is not enough to maintain health in many children or health and working energy in many adults, I propose a different program.[6] This new approach is to repair the weakest spots in the nutritional situation. I believe that this method will accomplish the major purpose of the proposed general increase in ration as nearly as can be accomplished within the limits of available supplies and finances for the remainder of the fiscal year 1946–1947.

In many ways, I believe it is a better program, and if this method proves a successful remedy during the next few months, it may modify the necessity of so large an increase in imports in the fiscal year 1947–1948 as has been proposed under the bi-zonal agreement.

There are two groups to which this repair of weakness should be given quickly:

First are the children over six years of age and the adolescents. The number of this group who are undernourished is estimated to be about 3,500,000 or more than 50 per cent. To cover this group and assure that the food reaches the child, the British in their zone, aided by the Swedish and other charities, are giving a small ration in certain schools. There is no systematic school feeding in the American Zone. A system of soup kitchens to provide a hot meal of appropriate body-building foods (meats, fats, milk, etc.) of at least 650 calories daily is imperative for the children in the worst areas of the combined zones, if a future Germany of wholesome character is to be created.

In order to start this system at once, I recommend using the Army surplus 10–in–1 rations, now enroute, and certain excess stocks not adapted to Army feeding and now in control of the American Occupation Forces. These resources can form the major base of this system for a considerable period. This is the more possible as it is proposed to slaughter during 1947 over 5,000,000 head of cattle, hogs and sheep in order to lessen the animal consumption of ground crops, and a portion of these meats and fats can be applied to this program. These various supplies, together with some minor cereal allotments, should carry the program for six months.

The second group demanding immediate relief is the "normal consumer" group of about 17,910,000 persons, now receiving 1,550 calories per day. I

---

6. [*Editor's note:* Here Hoover in 1962 wished to start a new paragraph. I have returned to the format in the document he was quoting.]

strongly recommend several lines of action. (a) A certain portion of them should be advanced to the group of moderate heavy workers and receive the supplement applicable to that category. (b) An emergency supply of cereals should be allotted to the German welfare organizations with which to provide a supplement to families in need and [to] the soup kitchens. (c) I recommend that the aged in the "normal consumers" group and others where medically certified, be issued tickets upon the soup kitchens for the meal of 450[7] calories per day during the school week, to be consumed either at these kitchens or taken home. These supplemental measures will substantially improve, and will at least carry over, the most needy part of this group.

By aid to the children and adolescents, some pressure will be removed from the "normal consumer" group, who naturally tend to cut their own food to help their children.

In support of the above program for children and "normal rations," I have included in the recommended deficiency appropriation an emergency supply of 65,000 tons of cereals. These measures as I have said, are in substitution for the great increase otherwise necessary to import for the proposed program of a lift in the whole ration system by 250 calories.

I described the need for imports of potatoes and potato seed, as the seed potatoes had hitherto come from Poland and the Russian zone.

I then dealt with the necessary imports of raw materials with which to create exports in payment for supplies and gave the full estimates of appropriations to cover all deficits in materials and food.

[For][8] the six months January 1st to July 1st, 1947, in which are included the supplies already shipped for this period:

Cereals (wheat equivalent) 2,505,000 tons. $288,000,000
Other foods, 720,000 tons 54,000,000
Fertilizers. 17,500,000
Seeds. 12,500,000
Petroleum products (civil population) 12,000,000
 Total $384,000,000

The British, for understandable reasons, were unable to take their share of the load and the whole was to fall upon the United States. I urged that the

---

7. [Editor's note: 350 in the original source. Why Hoover altered the number in 1962 is unknown.]

8. [Editor's note: The original source reads: "The following is the estimated cost for both zones: for" etc.]

Congress give priority to these appropriations or greater costs would arise from other causes. I then recommended the following appropriations for food supply during the fiscal year July 1947 to July 1948.

Cereals (in terms of wheat) for 1,550 calorie level,
2,785,000 tons...$278,500,000
Cereals for "normal consumers" emergency
supplemental feeding, 192,000 tons.........................19,200,000
Child feeding program (includes special foods),
130,000 tons 35,000,000
Other foods, 450,000 tons 75,000,000
Fertilizers (available) 45,000,000
Seeds 27,000,000
Petroleum products for civil population.......................25,000,000
$504,706,000
Cost of ration increase to 1,800 calories   [*sic–ed.*]
on or about October, 1947   62,300,000
Total $567,000,000

.... [*–ed.*]

[Further Savings to the Taxpayer that Can Be Made][9]

[*4.–ed.*] The Potsdam Declaration results in Germany having no consequential overseas shipping. If we could effect some temporary operation by German crews of, say, seventy-five Liberty ships, now laid up, to transport food and raw materials, all of the expense could be paid by the Germans in marks, except for fuel, and thus save a very large amount of dollars otherwise coming from the American and British taxpayers. This would probably amount to $40,000,000 per annum.

[*5.–ed.*] A further saving of possibly several million dollars could be made for the taxpayers if the large American Army return equipment, now being transported at high ocean rates, were sent home on the return voyages of these Liberty ships.

[*6.–ed.*] There are food surpluses in the control of other nations than ourselves and the British. They comprise possible increased catches of fish

---

9. [*Editor's note:* I have reinstated this caption, which Hoover had deleted, for clarity.]

in Norway, Sweden and Denmark, which otherwise are little likely to find a market, and some surpluses possible from the South American States. It would seem to me that some supplies could well be furnished by these nations, being repaid as indicated below, pari passu with the British and ourselves.

[7.–ed.] The Germans lost a considerable part of their deep sea fishing fleet.... The fishing grounds in the Baltic and North Seas are being limited against German fishing. As there are ample supplies of fish in these seas, it seems a pity that with this food available, British and American taxpayers are called upon to furnish food in substitution for fish the Germans could catch for themselves.

Fish is particularly needed, as the present diet is sadly lacking in protein content.

[8.–ed.] A still further saving to British and American taxpayers is possible if maximum expedition could be made of exports of German manufacture. The Joint Export-Import Agency is doing its best, but such exports are hampered by the lack of coal for manufacture; by [the] Trading-with-the-Enemy Acts, and restrictions on communication together with limitations on dealings between buyers and sellers [and the spirit of the Morgenthau Plan]. The restoration of trade is inevitable, and every day's delay in removing these barriers is simply adding to the burden of our taxpayers for relief that could otherwise be paid for in goods. No one can say that in her utterly shattered state, Germany is a present economic[10] menace to the world.

Should there be such good fortune as to realize all these possibilities, we could not only increase the food supply to health levels but also lessen the joint costs by $150,000,000 during the fiscal year 1947–1948....

I then made some minor recommendations which would reduce appropriations.

Conclusion of the First Report

It may come as a great shock to American taxpayers that, having won the war over Germany, we are now faced for some years with large expenditures for

---

10. [*Editor's note:* In his 1963 revision, Hoover crossed out "economic" and inserted "military." This was not his original wording in 1947, of course. I have left the original phrasing intact.]

relief for these people. Indeed, it is something new in human history for the conqueror to undertake.

Whatever the policies might have been that would have avoided this expense, we now are faced with it. And we are faced with it until the export industries of Germany can be sufficiently revived to pay for their food. . . . [11]

Entirely aside from any humanitarian feelings for this mass of people, if we want peace; if we want to preserve the safety and health of our Army of Occupation; if we want to save the expense of even larger military forces to preserve order; if we want to reduce the size and expense of our Army of Occupation—I can see no other course but to meet the burdens I have here outlined.

Our determination is to establish such a regime in Germany as will prevent forever again the rise of militarism and aggression within these people. But those who believe in vengeance and the punishment of a great mass of Germans not concerned in the Nazi conspiracy can now have no misgivings for all of them—in food, warmth and shelter—have been sunk to the lowest level known in a hundred years of Western history.

If Western Civilization is to survive in Europe, it must also survive in Germany. And it must be built into a cooperative member of that civilization. That indeed is the hope of any lasting peace.

After all, our flag flies over these people. That flag means something besides military power.

I hoped that future German students of this period would remember that the whole world was then involved in the greatest famine in all history. Therefore, these drastic recommendations of the barest subsistence were no part of "vengeance" on Germany.

---

11. [*Editor's note:* For unknown reasons Hoover in 1963 omitted the following sentence: "The first necessity for such a revival is sufficient food upon which to maintain vitality to work."]

CHAPTER C

Shortly after my presentation to President Truman of the report given in the preceding chapter, he, through his secretary, requested my views on the aspects of the German situation beyond the food problems.

I suppressed my emotions as to the enormous lack of statesmanship in relation to Germany and to the follies that were taking place. It was my belief that my greatest service would be a presentation of the cold realities and the imperative need for reversal of the economic policies of the previous twenty-six months.

I completed this report[1] and presented it to Mr. Truman on March 18, 1947. It was as follows:

March 18, 1947

Dear Mr. President:

I am sending you herewith my conclusions upon the problems of reviving German industry and thus exports with which to relieve American and British taxpayers from their burden in preventing starvation in Germany. These problems also involve economic stability and peace in Europe.

Whatever may have been our policies in the past, I am convinced that the time has come to face the realities that have developed. The mission you assigned to me would be less than performed if I did not state the stark situation and make such recommendations as seem to me necessary. . . .

---

1. [*Editor's note:* The full title is "Report No. 3. The Necessary Steps for Promotion of German Exports, So As to Relieve American Taxpayers of the Burdens of Relief and for Economic Recovery of Europe." It is printed in Hoover, *Addresses Upon the American Road, 1945–1948*, pp. 84–97.]

Introduction

Inquiry into the [American][2] economic policies in Germany which would relieve financial support from the United States was one of the subjects assigned to my mission to that country. Aside from a mass of information and statistical material secured on this journey, I have been familiar with German economic problems over many years, including my experience before and after World War I. In view of the gravity of the crisis which confronts the world, it would be an ill service if I did not state my conclusions fully and frankly.

These conclusions are not the product of sentiment nor of feeling toward a nation which has brought such misery upon the whole earth. They are not given in condonement of the enormity of her crimes. They are the result of a desire to see the world look forward, get into production and establish a lasting peace. They are based upon the stern necessities of a world involved in the most dangerous economic crisis in all history.

At the present time the taxpayers of the United States and Britain are contributing nearly $600,000,000 a year to prevent starvation of the Germans in the American and British zones alone. The drain is likely to be even greater after peace unless the policies now in action are changed. Therefore, entirely aside from any humanitarian and political aspects, policies which will restore productivity in Germany and exports with which to buy their food and relieve this drain upon us are of primary importance.

But our economic interest is far wider than this. We desperately need recovery in all of Europe. We need it not only for economic reasons but as the first necessity to peace. The United States, through loans, lend-lease, surplus supplies, and relief, in the last two years [since the German surrender], has spent, or pledged itself to spend, over fifteen billions of dollars in support of civilians in foreign countries. Even we do not have the resources for, nor can our taxpayers bear, a continuation of burdens at such a rate.

There is only one path to recovery in Europe. That is production. The whole economy of Europe is interlinked with German economy through the exchange of raw materials and manufactured goods. The productivity of Europe cannot be restored without the restoration of Germany as a contributor to that productivity.

---

2. [*Editor's note:* Unless otherwise indicated, all brackets in this extended quotation are Hoover's.]

[Some Assumptions][3]

In order to offer constructive conclusions as to economic policies which will relieve the American taxpayer and will promote economic recovery in Europe, I make six assumptions, which I believe will be accepted by sensible people. They necessarily include certain political aspects which underlie all these economic problems.

First. I assume that we wish to establish a unified federal state in Germany, embracing mainly the present American, British, Russian and French military occupation zones, with economic unity and free trade between those[4] states. I shall refer to this area as the "New Germany."

Second. I assume that our objective must be to clear German life of the Nazi conspirators and to punish those who have contributed to this conspiracy, which murdered millions of people in cold blood and brought this appalling disaster upon the world.

Third. I assume that we will not make the major mistake of Versailles, but will complete absolute disarmament of the Germans so that they shall not be able again to engage in aggressions; that this disarmament will embrace destruction of all military arms, fortifications and direct arms factories, with certain control of industry; that the Germans will have *no* army, *no* navy, and *no* air forces, retaining only a constabulary in which no Nazi or previous army officer may be employed; that this disarmament must be continued for a generation or two, until Germany has lost the "know-how" of war and the descent of militarism through birth.

Fourth. I assume that these requirements must be safeguarded by international guarantees and effective police service by the nations.

Fifth. I assume, in our own interest and that of Europe, that we wish to restore the productivity of the continent, that we wish to revive personal freedom, honest elections and generally to reconstruct the German people into a peace-loving nation cooperating in the recovery of Western civilization.

Sixth. I assume that the United States will not join in such guarantees and policing unless the treaty with Germany is so concluded that it contributes to the restoration of productivity and lasting peace in Europe and promptly relieves us of drains upon our taxpayers.

---

3. [*Editor's note:* In his 1962 draft essay, Hoover omitted this caption, which had appeared in the document being quoted.]

4. [*Editor's note:* In 1962 Hoover inserted the word "those" in place of "the" in the original source.]

[The German Economic Problems][5]

The German economic problems have two aspects:

First, the long-view, broad economic policies toward the New Germany which alone can produce the reconstruction of Europe and peace.

Second, our immediate problems in the joint Anglo-American military zones during the interregnum pending peace.

I therefore divide this discussion into these two parts.

[Part I][6]

The Long View Economic Problem

The long-view economic problems involved in the peace with the New Germany and its aftermaths are greatly affected by war destruction, the boundary settlements for the New Germany, the plant removals for reparations, and the policies with respect to "war potential" of industry.

These effects may be summarized:

1. There was considerable destruction of non-war industry from the air and otherwise during the war. The loss to peaceful productivity has not been determined, but it is considerable.

2. The proposed annexations to Poland and Russia, and the possible annexations of the Saar Basin by France, will take from Germany, as compared to 1936,* about 25% of her food supply, about 30% of her bituminous coal and about 20% of her manufacturing capacity.

3. The population of Germany in 1936 was about 68,000,000. The population of the New Germany by 1949 will be about 71,000,000, due to the expulsion of Germans from the Polish and Russian annexations, from Czechoslovakia, Hungary, Austria, Yugoslavia, Roumania and the return of prisoners into this area.

4. The Allied economic policies toward Germany are of two categories: the first involves world safety, and the second, reparations for wrong done:

---

5. [*Editor's note:* This caption appears in the original source. Hoover deleted the caption in his 1962 essay.]

6. [*Editor's note:* Hoover omitted these words (which appear in the 1947 document) from his 1962 essay.]

* I have adopted 1936 as a basis for economic comparisons because it was a full year before German industry was distorted by her annexations and her most intensive armament activity.

a. There has necessarily been, or will be, a demolition of all arms plants as part of disarmament. This destruction, however, has included some plants which might have been converted to peaceable production.

b. Reparations have been provided by assignment for removal to the different allies of certain percentages of "usable and complete industrial equipment." What proportion of Germany's peaceable productive plant has been, or is, in the course of removal in the French and Russian zones is not known. Certainly they have been very large from the Russian zone. The total for all Germany amounts to an important segment of its peaceful productivity. These removals include a large amount of "light industry" (producing mostly consumers' goods) as well as "heavy industry" (producing mostly capital goods). The removal of plants from the American and British zones has been halted because of the refusal of Russia and France to cooperate in inter-zonal economic unity as provided for at Potsdam.

5. In addition to the above course of action, there have been general policies of destruction or limitation of possible peaceful productivity under the headings of "pastoral state" and "war potential." The original of these policies apparently expressed on September 15, 1944, at Quebec, aimed at:

"converting Germany into a country principally agricultural and pastoral,"

and included,

"the industries of the Ruhr and the Saar would therefore be put out of action, closed down. . . . "

This idea of a "pastoral state" partially survived in JCS Order 1067 of April, 1945 for the American zone. It was not accepted by the British. The "pastoral state" concept was not entirely absent in the Potsdam Declaration. It was partially ameliorated or its name changed for another concept, the "level of industry," developed by the agreement of March 26, 1946, and signed by Russia, Britain, France and the United States. This agreement was a compromise between the drastic terms proposed by Russia and France and the more liberal terms proposed by the other two nations.

One major theme of this "level of industry" concept is to destroy Germany's "war potential." Under this concept certain industries are to be blown up or prohibited, others are to be limited as to production. The emphasis was placed upon the limitation of "heavy industry" with the view that Germany could export enough goods from "light industry" to buy her food and necessary raw materials.

The absolute destruction or prohibition includes ocean-going ships, shipbuilding, aircraft, ball bearings, aluminum, magnesium, beryllium, vanadium and radio-transmitting equipment, together with synthetic oil, ammonia and rubber. Some of these provisions may be essential to disarmament. Such exceptions are not included in the discussion which follows.

Beyond these prohibitions, however, the "level of industry" concept provides elaborate restrictions, mostly on heavy industry. The following items are illustrative:

Iron and steel production to be reduced from 19 million tons (as in 1936) to a capacity of 7.5 million tons, with a maximum production of 5.8 million tons and only the "older plants" to be used.

Heavy machinery production to be . . . . .31% of 1938
Light machinery production to be . . . . 50% of 1938
Machine tools to be . . . . 38% of 1938
Electrical machinery to be . . . . from 30% to 50% of 1938
Agricultural implements to be. . . . . .70% of 1936
Automobiles to be . . . . 10% of 1936
Trucks to be . . . . .67% of 1936
Basic chemicals, including nitrogen, calcium carbide,
    sulphuric acid, chlorine and alkali to be .40% of 1936
Cement to be . . . . 65% of 1936
Electric power produced to be . . . . .60% of 1936
No new locomotives until 1949.
Some "light industries" were also to be limited:
Textiles to be . . . . 77% of 1936
Paper to be . . . . 65% of 1936
Boots and shoes to be . . . . .70% of 1936
Precision instruments and optics to be. . . . . .70% of 1936
Miscellaneous chemicals to be . . . . .70% of 1936
Pharmaceuticals to be . . . . .80% of 1936
Dyestuffs (export) to be . . . . 58% of 1936

The Consequences to Food Supply

We may first examine what has happened, and what will happen, to the German food supply under all the circumstances of annexation and industrial controls.

Germany in 1936 was, by most intensive cultivation, able to produce about 85% of her food supply. This 85% has now been reduced by 25% through the Russian and Polish annexations, or is down to about 64% because even a larger population is to be concentrated in the New Germany.

Her production, however, was greatly dependent upon intensive use of fertilizers. The New Germany will require at least 500,000 metric tons of nitrogen and 650,000 tons of phosphoric anhydride, she having sufficient potash.

Under the level of industry agreement, the domestic production of nitrogen eventually would be reduced to under 200,000 tons; the production of phosphoric anhydride, would be reduced to about 200,000 tons. . . .

From these figures it is obvious that a great discrepancy exists between minimum agricultural needs and the possible fertilizer production under the "level of industry" plan. If we persist in these policies, unless there are large imports of fertilizer, Germany's food production is likely to drop under 60% of her requirements even with an austere diet.

New Germany, if there is to be a will to work, to maintain order and to aspire to peace, must have an average food supply of at least 2600 calories per person per day, with adequate fats and protein content. (The British average being 2800–2900 calories at present and pre-war Germany about 3000 calories.)

Taking the above limitations into consideration and based upon actual experience in the American and British zones, and extending that experience with adaptations to the Russian and French zones, the indications are that New Germany would need, at present prices, to import over $1,250,000,000 annually [a minimum] in food and animal feed alone.

At the end of the war Germany had a very large nitrogen capacity. Despite losses from war destruction, its potential production was still about 700,000 tons per annum. This capacity, if it had been preserved, would have supplied not only her own needs but large exports to neighboring countries as well. Fertilizers are now sorely needed all over Europe for crop restoration. Therefore, through the fertilizer reduction Germany not only loses in her own food production but her export potential to pay for food, and the crops elsewhere in Europe are reduced.

Consequences of "Level of Industry" upon "Heavy Industry"

The effect of the agreed "level of industry" is stated in American official reports that "The 'heavy industry' products for which Germany was noted will virtually disappear from her exports."

I have exhaustively examined the production and exports of Germany over some years in the light of this "level of industry" and they amply confirm this statement. What the result may be is indicated by the fact that her exports during peace from now-restricted "heavy industries" comprised between 60% and 70% of the total German exports. In 1936, for instance, a generally prosperous year, they amounted to about $1,900,000,000 out of a total of about $2,700,000,000, both figures converted into present prices. Under the "level of industry" most of this 60–70% is to be abolished, and Germany must pay for most of her imports from exports of "light industry."

Germany must not alone import food and animal feed, but also reduced amounts of copper, lead, zinc, iron ore, leather, cotton, wool, and other raw materials. Due to the prohibitions, she must import all of her oil and rubber, and considerable nitrogen for fertilizers.

It is indeed a cynical fact that today we are supplying Germany with oil and nitrogen at the expense of the American and British taxpayer, at a rate of $70,000,000. . . .[7]

Consequences Upon Light Industry

As I have said, the assumption is that exports from the German "light industry," from coal and native raw materials, such as potash, can pay for her imports of food and other necessities. There are two reasons for believing this assumption to be completely invalid.

Had there been no loss of "light industry" plants by annexation, had there been no destruction of them by war, had there been no removals for reparations, they could not have produced enough exports to pay the food bill alone. And the situation is made doubly impossible by the restrictions now imposed on what "light industry" is left, as, for instance, on textiles.

If Germany is to buy food and the necessary imports of raw materials for the "light industry," she would require not only complete restoration to pre-war level in "light industry" but a much larger equipment than she had even before the war.

Then Germany, with the expansion of these industries, would be in a competitive field of consumers' goods with all the rest of the world whose "light industries" have been little damaged by war.

---

7. [*Editor's note:* The omitted passage reads: "per annum, which, except for the 'level of industry' and the Russian refusal of zonal cooperation, Germany could have produced herself." Why Hoover deleted these words is unclear.]

Some Economic Illusions

There are several illusions in all this "war potential" attitude.

a. There is the illusion that the New Germany left after the annexations can be reduced to a "pastoral state." It cannot be done unless we exterminate or move 25,000,000 people out of it. . . .

b. There is an illusion in "war potential." Almost every industry on earth is a "war potential" in modern war. . . . If Germany be disarmed in the way I have assumed above, there must be a control commission to see that they do not have any army or any navy.[8] And two score of intelligent men, as part of that commission, could see that there is no arms production and that no industry is manufacturing or storing materials for evil purposes. Moreover, industry is not likely to waste its substance, either by storing or manufacturing for war, when there is no army or navy to use it.

   The question here is not "level of industry." The real question is whether the Allied nations will stick to their abolition of militarism itself in Germany. If they do that, there is little danger from "war potential" in industry.

c. Another illusion is that the "light industry" in Germany can be expanded to a point where she will be able to pay for her imports. In my view, it cannot be done for years, and even then it is doubtful in the face of competition with the "light industries" of other parts of the world.

d. The over-all illusion is that Germany can ever become self-supporting under the "levels of industry" plan within the borders envisioned at present for New Germany.

e. A still further illusion is that Europe as a whole can recover without the economic recovery of Germany.

[Consequences to Europe Generally][9]

Thus there is still a wider aspect of this "level of industry"—the needs of the rest of Europe. Germany had been for a century one of the great European

---

8. [*Editor's note:* For unknown reasons Hoover altered the order of the first three sentences in section b in his 1962 essay draft. I have restored them to the order in which they appeared in the quoted source.]

9. [*Editor's note:* This caption was in the original source. I have restored it here.]

centers of production of capital goods—"heavy industry," which I may repeat are construction materials, factory equipment, railway equipment, electrical and heavy machinery. The other nations of Europe are in desperate need of such goods for reconstruction from war damage. Moreover, a considerable part of the European equipment on these lines is German-made, and today, they cannot even get replacements and spare parts, in consequence of which their productivity [also][10] lags.

From the standpoint of other nations, the expansion of "light industry" to a point of self-support for Germany will, by competition, injure these industries in the rest of Europe. On the other hand, the products of "heavy industry" is Europe's first necessity for recovery.

It must not be overlooked that Germany was a market for every nation in Europe and such a reduction of her economy will tend to demoralize the industries and employment in those countries. For instance, Germany was the market for over half the exports of Turkey and over one-third those of Greece. In consequence, their loss of this market contributes to increase the relief [those countries] seek from us now.

Another illustration is the proposed limits on steel. Large and efficient steel and iron plants, undamaged or only partly damaged, are standing idle in Germany. Formerly the Germans imported millions of tons of iron ore from France and Sweden. These mines, under the "level of industry," must remain idle until a new steel industry is built elsewhere. That will require years and an amount of capital that is not in sight. In the meantime, Europe needs steel for reconstruction as she never did before.

To indicate the anxiety of surrounding states a memorandum of the Netherlands Government of January 1947, in presenting the absolute necessity to the surrounding nations that a productive economic state be created in Germany, said: "The provisions of the plan for reparations and the level of German economy of March 1946 require to be revised . . . it is inadvisable to lay down maximum quota for production of German industries including the iron and steel industries."

The sum of all this is: Germany, under the "level of industry" concept, unless she is to be allowed to starve, will be a drain on the taxpayers of other nations for years and years to come. In the meantime, if her light industries were built to become self-supporting, she would become an economic

---

10. [*Editor's note:* In 1962 Hoover inserted the word "also." I have added the brackets.]

menace to Europe; if her heavy industries are allowed to function, she has an ability to export and would become an asset in Europe's recovery. To persist in the present policies will create, sooner or later, a cesspool of unemployment or pauper labor in the center of Europe which is bound to infect her neighbors.

We can keep Germany in these economic chains but it will also keep Europe in rags.

A New Economic Policy

Therefore, I suggest that we adopt at once a new economic concept in peace with New Germany.

(1) We should free German industry, subject to a control commission, which will see that she does no evil in industry, just as we see that she does not move into militarism through armies and navies.

The difference between this concept and the "level of industry" concept is the saving of several hundred millions of dollars a year to the American and British taxpayers. It is the difference between the regeneration and a further degeneration of Europe.

(2) The removal and destruction of plants (except direct arms plants) should stop.

(3) A further obstacle to building Germany as an essential unit of European economy arises from the Russian Government's acquiring a large part of the key operating industries in their zone [and their confiscation by the Communist government]. Germany in peace must be free from ownership of industry by a foreign government. Such ownership can thwart every action of control or of up-building by joint action of other nations. German industry must be operated by Germans if any international control is to work, if she is to recover production and is to serve all nations equally.

(4) There can be no separation or different regime of the Ruhr or Rhineland from the [American and British Zones in] New Germany. That is the heart of her industrial economy. Any control commission can dictate the destination of coal or other exports from that area and even such control would not be needed after the era of scarcity passes from Europe.

[Part II][11]

The Interregnum Before Peace

How long it may be before there is such a constructive peace with Germany, no one can tell. It may be long delayed. In the meantime, we are faced with the feeding of the people in the Anglo-American zones on a level just above starvation until we can develop enough export goods from these zones so that the Germans may pay for their food. I have said, American and British taxpayers are called upon for about $600,000,000 a year for relief.

We have an admirable staff in Military Government of Germany under Generals Clay and Draper but their administration is constantly frustrated in building up the needed exports to pay for food and minimum raw material imports. A large part of these delays is due to the following:

a. The Russians and the French have failed to carry out the provisions of the Potsdam agreement for economic unity in the four zones. The Russian zone ordinarily produces a surplus of food but that surplus is used elsewhere, thus increasing the burden of imports on the Anglo-American zones. Both the Russian and French zones are producing industrial commodities which would relieve necessities in the Anglo-American zones and could contribute to exports with which to pay for food. The net effect is that the United States and Britain through relief are paying Russian and French reparations.

b. The inability to determine what specific plants are to be the victims of "level of industry," or destruction or the removal for reparations, produces stagnation because the Germans do not know where to begin work.

c. There is lack of working capital with which to import raw materials for such industries as are allowed to function.

d. An inflated currency and no adequate banking system hampers all forward movements in such industry as is left.

e. While de-Nazification and de-cartelization are necessary and important, certain phases of them limit recovery. They are so involved as not to warrant description here.

---

11. [*Editor's note:* Hoover omitted these words (which appear in the 1947 document) from his 1962 essay.]

Conclusion as to the Bi-Zonal Administration

If, however, we cannot get a quick and sound peace on the lines I have recounted, the Anglo-American zones should abandon the destruction of plants, the transfer of plants for reparations and the "level of industry" concept, and start every plant, "heavy" as well as "light," which can produce non-arms goods. This will relieve far more rapidly great costs to our taxpayers; it will do infinitely more for Europe than American loans and charity.

Indeed the Congressional Committee on Postwar Economic Policy urged, on December 30, 1946, that the "levels of industry" be ignored wherever they conflict with exports so that there may be earlier recovery and payment for food.

The violation by Russia and France of the agreement for economic unification of the four zones of military occupation and the additional burdens this imposed upon us in consequence certainly warrant our ignoring all agreements for "level of industry," transfer and destruction of non-arms plants.

If this interregnum is to endure for long, we could build a self-sustaining economic community out of the Anglo-American zones alone. This could be only a temporary expedient, not a final solution. Building a lasting peace in Europe should be our objective.

President Truman had the courage against strong political opposition to eventually reverse the whole economic system in the American Zone, and with British cooperation reestablished economic freedom in the new state of Western Germany. That part of Germany not only rose in prosperity but gave strength to the rising prosperity in all Europe. She is taking a full part in the cause of human freedom.[12]

---

12. At the invitation of Chancellor Adenauer I visited Germany in 1954. The Germans wished to express their appreciation for my services in preventing starvation and advocating sane economic policies. They arranged great demonstrations in various cities. And they requested me to make three public addresses on the dangers of Communism.

CHAPTER D

And Freedom Comes Also

ASIDE FROM THE REVERSAL of economic slavery, other important free-doms came to Germany.

The food programs which I initiated were at once put into action, as indicated by extracts from the following letters from General Lucius D. Clay and Secretary of War Robert Patterson:

7 March 1947

My dear Mr. Hoover:

. . . Authority has been received from the Secretary of War to implement the program recommended by you in your report to President Truman. We shall put this program into effect at the earliest practicable date.

I am deeply grateful to you for your sympathetic understanding of our problems here in Germany. If adequate funds are appropriated to meet our minimum needs it will be largely through your understanding and help.

Sincerely yours,
Lucius D. Clay

7 April 1947

Dear Mr. Hoover:

Thank you for your letter of 3 March and the printed copy of your report which the War Department had furnished us by radio.

We are ready to move into the child feeding program in the next few days. . . .

If it were not for your report, I know that we would face disaster in the months ahead. As it is, I believe we shall pull through with an appreciable economic revival and without substantial loss to communist penetration and influence.

Also, we can sense even now the improvement in American thinking and feeling toward the German problems which has come about from your report. In the long run, that may be even more valuable to us than the appropriation; although this latter need was so urgent from our viewpoint as to overshadow the former. . . .

No one else could have accomplished for us what you did. We are grateful, not only because we were honored by your visit, but also because your report has made possible the accomplishment of America's real objective in Germany.

Respectfully yours,
Lucius D. Clay

April 16, 1947

Dear Mr. Hoover:

I have been advised by General Clay's headquarters that the child feeding program for the occupied German Zone will become effective about the middle of this month, and it appears that we may expect good cooperation in its implementation from all concerned.

General Keating, Deputy Military Governor of AMGUS, advised me that, at a recent conference sponsored by the German Executive Committee for Food and Agriculture to complete arrangements for the program in line with your recommendations, the following was requested.

"The conference members requested that Mr. Hoover and the US/UK Governments be informed of the appreciation and gratitude that is felt for their support of a special child-feeding program for German children. German participating agencies state program promises to be extremely popular and beneficial."

I should like to add again my gratitude to the above message.

Sincerely yours,
Robert P. Patterson
Secretary of War

A report from the Military Government on June 19, 1947 stated:

The child feeding program (Hoover Program) is now in successful operation. By the 23rd of June 3,550,000 children will be receiving the extra meal. . . . The importance of this program cannot be over-estimated both from its nutritional value to the children and its public relations value between Military Government and the German people.

The numbers fed were rapidly expanded. I received thousands of touching letters from the children and their parents in all parts of Germany as the service was put on under my name.

In the middle of May 1947, there was a sudden and unexpected minor crisis in German food. The hard winter had prevented early planting of vegetables and there was some miscalculation of stocks. But the whole amounted to about two weeks food and was remedied by quick imports. As it attracted reams in the sensational press, I issued, on May 15, a statement of explanation of the incident to take some of the heat off General Clay and the Military Administration. I reviewed the temporary causes and freed the Military Government from blame. Secretary Patterson referred to this in a letter to me of June 13, 1947:

> Dear Mr. Hoover:
>
> I wish to express, both officially as Secretary of War and for myself personally, my deep sense of gratitude to you for the most recent great service which you have rendered to us in your courageous and vigorous support of our requested appropriation for Fiscal Year 1947 for Government and Relief in Occupied Areas. If we obtain this appropriation in full or without a very large cut, it will be due in principal part to your action. . . .
>
> Now in your recent testimony and press statement, supporting so effectively our request for the funds necessary to carry this work on through the next fiscal year, you have done everything that one man can do, and more than any other man living would be able to do, in giving aid to the War Department toward the successful discharge of this responsibility.

A Campaign for Clothing

On my return from Europe in March 1947, I took up in several directions the problem of clothing the destitute in Germany and Austria. I first set up the American Friends Service Committee in the job of collecting unused piece goods from manufacturers. I then arranged for the War Department and the War Assets Administration to assign a very large quantity of used Army and Navy clothing for these purposes. I also secured withdrawal of much of such material which had been classified for sale by the War Assets Administration. The sales were not covering the costs of selling in any event. We shipped enormous amounts of this material, which otherwise would have been a loss.

I also interested the Girl Scouts in a program of sending layettes for babies to all countries in need. They did a magnificent job. A typical statement of mine for their use was as follows:

June 20, 1947

Tens of millions of children in Europe are underclad. There is nothing that should so appeal to the children of America as for each of them to prepare and send them a garment. There are no enemies among children.

As a final word on Germany, I include here a letter from Louis Lochner who accompanied me on the mission to Germany dated September 30, 1959—twelve and a half years after our mission—written from Essen, Germany:

Dear Chief:

My wife and I have just returned from a series of visits to friends and relatives which took us as far eastward as Hannover. Already upon our arrival two weeks ago in Essen, the heart of German industrial production, we had been struck by something, the confirmation of which came so frequently during our trip, that I feel justified to present it to you as a conclusion:

There is so marked a difference in the stature of the young German women and men in their late teens or early twenties as compared with that of their parents that the fact is inescapable that there must be some connection between the towering figures of the youngsters and the food on which they were raised. In other words, the post-war Hoover Child Feeding Program of 1947 and the years following has paid off in a manner that perhaps even you—certainly we, who were members of your team on The President's Economic Mission—could not envisage.

At first, I confess, I was merely bewildered and could not figure things out. I merely *saw* what seemed like a miracle. I had sat at the feet of Dr. David Starr Jordan and heard him as a biologist state before audience after audience how the French population of his day was on an average two inches smaller than that of the days of Napoleon—all because the best and the bravest had become soldiers and were killed, leaving the procreation of the next generation to the weak, infirm and unstable, with a resulting deterioration of the race.

Suddenly it dawned on me that there must be some cardinal difference between what happened to the youth of the post-Napoleonic period of France and the post-Nazi period of Germany. How come, I wondered, that a totally defeated nation, compelled by Hitler to produce "cannons instead of butter," could raise such strapping youngsters as we now see constantly? It dawned on me:

Mr. Hoover came to prostrate Germany—and for that matter, to all Europe—just in time to reverse the process and make "butter instead of cannons" a reality.

To reassure myself that I, who am by no means an expert on nutritional and biological questions, am not totally wrong, I have asked husky, healthy teenagers and young people in their early twenties wherever I had an opportunity, whether they had been recipients in the early years of the "Hoover-*Speisung*," and all replied enthusiastically in the affirmative. I have asked their elders as to whether in their opinion the juvenile feeding program and the astounding height and apparent well-being of their offspring might be due to the "Hoover-*Speisung*." Again the reply was "most definitely so."

This is but one of your humble disciples' unscientific opinion, but I thought it might interest you to know that one of our happiest and most impressive experiences in Germany thus far has been this realization of the undreamed-of efficacy of the measures for the rehabilitation of Germany which you brought about. . . .

With warmest personal regards, I am,

Always faithfully yours,

(Louis P. Lochner)

P.S. The name and address of the gentleman in question follow:

Dr. Walter Latzke, Bundesarchiv, Frankfurt

Berliner Strasse 22

Frankfort, Germany

Who is the Victor in Modern War

A philosopher might well speculate on which side is the victor in modern war.

The Allies were victorious in both the First and Second World War against Germany. They imposed drastic peace terms, and the defeated Germans signed them. By these terms they, in each case, rid themselves of dictatorship. They were financially prostrate. Inflation and bankruptcy followed. They, thereby, practically rid themselves of all government obligations at home and abroad, all consequential private, commercial and industrial debts after each war. It was a huge gift to all the lender world. It enabled expansion and renovation of productive equipment which gave them advantages in world trade.

During and after the Second World War their industrial and housing equipment was greatly destroyed or removed. They simply sold securities to the Western powers and with their assets and their own rehabilitated currency they built new production plants which were more efficient than those in the victor countries.

While the victors struggled against high governmental debts and taxes, the Germans freed themselves not only from these but worried little about their widows, orphans or persons permanently injured.

The plight of destitution aroused the compassion of the victor and he poured his taxpayers' money into their relief.

In sum, victory came to the vanquished.

A Selection of Documents
Pertaining to *Freedom Betrayed*

EDITORIAL NOTE
ON THE APPENDIX

HOOVER'S MAGNUM OPUS in its final form, *Freedom Betrayed,* did not contain an Appendix. But it seems appropriate to include one as an aid to understanding the genesis, development, purposes, and significance of this monumental tome.

The papers directly relating to Herbert Hoover's Magnum Opus in the Hoover Institution Archives and the Herbert Hoover Presidential Library comprise, in toto, more than 200 archival boxes, occupying almost 100 linear feet of shelf space. In these files (as well as his other papers and those of certain of his associates) innumerable historical nuggets can be found pertaining to this project: correspondence, memoranda of conversations, drafts and redrafts of chapters, and other primary source materials. From this trove, I have selected a few items that seem especially illuminating. They are assembled in chronological order.

Herbert Hoover to William R. Castle Jr.

December 8, 1941

WITHIN HOURS OF the Japanese attack on Pearl Harbor, the seeds of Hoover's Magnum Opus were sown. Already at work on early drafts of his memoirs, Hoover saw the need to "preserve every record and every recollection" bearing upon the war that had just begun between the United States of America and the Empire of Japan. He asked his close friend William R. Castle Jr., who had served as Hoover's undersecretary of state, to collect as much documentation on this subject as possible.

A few weeks later, in his diary for March 5, 1942, Castle recorded that Hoover himself was busily collecting "documents of all kinds" pertaining to the negotiations leading up to Pearl Harbor, with a view to writing a history of this episode (or having someone else write it) after the war.

A microfilm copy of the William R. Castle diary is in the Herbert Hoover Presidential Library, West Branch, Iowa. Hoover's letter of December 8, 1941, printed here, is in the Herbert Hoover Papers, Post-Presidential Individual File, in the same repository.

The Waldorf Astoria
New York, New York
December 8, 1941

My dear Bill:

Your letter in the Herald-Tribune coming at this unlucky moment brings up a question in my mind.

You and I know that this continuous putting pins in rattlesnakes finally got this country bitten. We also know that if Japan had been allowed to go on without these trade restrictions and provocations, she would have collapsed from internal economic reasons alone within a couple of years. We also know the processes by which this debacle has been brought about.

Sometime the proper account of this will be of vast importance. And I am anxious that you preserve every record and every recollection that bears on the whole question and get as much documentary support for it as you can.

Yours faithfully,

H. H.

Mr. William R. Castle
2200 S Street
Washington, D.C.

Herbert Hoover to General Robert E. Wood

December 17, 1941

IN 1919 HERBERT HOOVER founded a "War Collection" of documents relating to the First World War and its aftermath. Soon renamed the Hoover War Library, it was located at his alma mater, Stanford University. Eventually it became known as the Hoover Institution on War, Revolution and Peace.

When the United States entered the Second World War, Hoover moved quickly to make his "War Library" an indispensable repository of documentation on the new global conflict. His prescience would prove a blessing to generations of scholars.

One example of his never-ending quest for historical source material was his appeal, printed here, to the chairman of the America First Committee, which, like Hoover, had fiercely opposed American entry into World War II. Hoover's pitch, in this instance, was successful. The America First Committee's papers are housed today in the Hoover Institution Archives.

Hoover's file copy of this letter is in the Post-Presidential Individual File of his papers at the Herbert Hoover Presidential Library.

The Waldorf Astoria
New York, New York
December 17, 1941

My dear General:

Our fight is over for the present. I just want to tell you how much I appreciate your fine efforts and to let you know that I feel you made a grand fight. We were right—and time will so demonstrate it. Of course, in the meantime, we have only one course to pursue and that is to win the war.

I believe it is important for history that the files of the America First Committee should be preserved. The War Library[1] at Stanford University has

---

1. [*Editor's note:* Now the Hoover Institution on War, Revolution and Peace.]

facilities for just that sort of thing. I am wondering if the America First Committee could not take the trouble to arrange these files in permanent order and ship them to the War Library at Stanford. They would thus be accessible or non-accessible to students, as you might wish. Sometime your movement is going to loom large in the history of the country and it is very important that these records be among the material that is preserved. It is to the War Library at Stanford to which sooner or later all history students of importance must come.

As you can probably appreciate the War Library is always short of funds. If your organization should have any residue of money, the Library could use this for cataloguing and putting the records in order.

Yours faithfully,

General Robert E. Wood
Sears, Roebuck & Co.
Arlington and Homan
Chicago, Illinois

"Going to War With the Yellow Races"

February 19, 1942

LESS THAN TWO MONTHS after Pearl Harbor, Hoover was already at work on a history of the antecedents of the war in the Pacific. This project soon became subsumed in his broader historical investigations leading to the Magnum Opus.

The excerpt reproduced here is in the Arthur Kemp Papers, Box 4, Envelope 39, Hoover Institution Archives.

2/19/42

Going to War With the Yellow Races

The titanic war between the yellow and white races is now a reality. And under the blundering leadership of the United States we, with 130,000,000 people, are left practically alone to carry on that war against ten times our number of Asiatics. By our policies we have created a war of white civilization and Asiatic civilization in which we are paying for the hates which come from violences, the arrogance and exploitation of Asia by the European nations during the last two hundred years.

And we are the one white nation which has sought fair dealing and decency between white and yellow races. Due to the follies of our policies in the last two years we have dug this abyss for millions of American lives.

Instead of adhering to pacific policies based upon moral standards which we pursued for 150 years up to 1936 we suddenly shifted and sought by aggressive provocation, by threats, by bluff, by making war through economic sanctions to dominate Asia and dictate who should and who should not rule among them. Asiatic civilization, 3,000 years old, bound by many ties of common religion and stirred by long hates to the white man, has now found a military leadership in Japan which at Hong Kong, Manilla [*sic–ed.*], Singapore and Burma has punctured the myth of white man's superiority. The white man has "lost face" all over Asia. And the Japanese are not only mobilizing Asia against the white man, but of deeper significance, are creating a renaissance and a solidarity in Asiatic civilization itself against the West.

It never was America's business to dictate the government of Asia. No such suggestion was ever made by America until Mr. Roosevelt came into office.

The first step in that course was the demagogic claim that Chiang Kai-Shek's government in China was a "democracy" fighting for "democracy" in Asia. That we must support our brother democracy against military dictatorship. That was never true in the remotest light. Chiang Kai-Shek was the war lord leader of a military oligarchy based upon a secret society, the Kao Ming Ting. There was never an election in China; there was never a representative government in any Western concept. There was never the remotest "freedom" of the Western variety. Beyond this was the claim by the Roosevelt administration that it was our duty to put down aggression everywhere. Asia puts down its own aggressions if given time. It has been doing it for 3,000 years. In any event, this is not the mission of the United States. The moment we departed from the pacific method of holding standards of international conduct by moral presentation alone we builded a catastrophe for all mankind. For we wakened the dragon. And under the cheers of Europe we took it on ourselves alone.

At what date Mr. Roosevelt reversed our life long American policies is not clear. It is not clear at precisely what date he thought "power politics" and "war of nerves" would frighten the Japanese from their course. But it was somewhere in 1937–38. It is not clear precisely at what date he took the next step of resolving upon economic sanctions under the same blind belief that he could thereby bluff and destroy Japan's strength and resolution. It is certain that he thought all these steps would somewhere somehow make him the dictator of Asiatic life. It was successively stronger bluee. And it was rank aggression successively by diplomatic, then provocative, then power politics, then economic sanctions of killing people by starvation and unemployment and finally farcical surprise when the Japanese turned and blew up Pearl Harbor. That it was bluff and that it was founded on ignorance of Japanese character, of the Asiatic forces he was dealing with, is proved by the fact that we were not prepared in a military way to make good on his bluffs. At the last moment, having given an ultimatum that meant war on November 26, 1941, he did not even send out proper alarms to our outposts. Then Mr. Roosevelt was aggrieved and surprised that these people would make war and do it under their own rules, not his.

We shall now review the march of events, of forces in action. I have elsewhere reviewed the incidents of 1931–32.[1]

---

1. [*Editor's note:* Hoover's original final sentence was: "But first we will review the events of 1931–32 when we met the same situation and adhered to our proper functions in international life." The final sentence now in the text was inserted in his own handwriting.]

Memorandum of Conversation with Charles G. Dawes

March 6, 1942

DURING AND AFTER World War II, Hoover regularly welcomed notable visitors to his home in the Waldorf Astoria Towers in New York City—men like Bernard Baruch, James A. Farley, Patrick Hurley, Joseph P. Kennedy, and Colonel Truman Smith. From these and many other well-connected informants, he learned much about the inner workings of the war effort. What he learned did not increase his confidence in the wisdom, competence, or integrity of President Franklin D. Roosevelt. Such briefings and conversations only whetted Hoover's determination to set the historical record straight: a powerful motive for the herculean memoir he soon undertook.

After a tête-à-tête with a distinguished guest, Hoover would routinely prepare a memorandum of this conversation for his files. A number of these are preserved in his papers relating to the Magnum Opus. An example is the one reproduced here. It is found in the Herbert C. Hoover Papers, Box 90, "Data for Reference 1942" folder, Hoover Institution Archives.

MARCH 6, 1942. General Charles G. Dawes called. The General had spent some days in Washington, mostly visiting with General Pershing.[1] He told Hugh Gibson and me that Pershing told him of a visit of Pershing's to the White House where Pershing had urged the President to appoint a General of the Armies; relegate the General Staff to its proper advisory and research functions and away from administrative functions as at present; and then leave all the military strategy to the Army in cooperation with the Navy. The President had replied that he (Roosevelt) knew more of the great strategy of war than anyone in the Army "including you, General."

---

1. [*Editor's note:* John J. Pershing.]

Dawes says Roosevelt is constantly telling friends that he sat in all the strategy councils representing the Navy in the last war and that Daniels[2] was merely a figurehead. (As a matter of fact, I was there; Daniels sat in the War Council[3] where I also sat, and I never heard Roosevelt's name mentioned. He was regarded merely as a playboy attachment to the Navy.)[4]

2. [*Editor's note:* Josephus Daniels, Secretary of the Navy, 1913–1921.]
3. [*Editor's note:* President Woodrow Wilson's informal War Cabinet, created early in 1918. Herbert Hoover, as U.S. Food Administrator, had been a member of this advisory group.]
4. [*Editor's note:* Franklin Roosevelt had served under Josephus Daniels as Assistant Secretary of the Navy, 1913–1921.]

Hoover's Attitude toward
Various Belligerent Powers
November 1944

BY LATE 1944, the volume of Hoover's memoirs that ultimately became *Freedom Betrayed* was underway. In November of that year—while the war was still on—he scribbled some pages candidly stating his attitude toward some of the belligerent powers. Excerpts from these early drafts, dated November 25 and 26, 1944, are reproduced here.

These documents are found in the Magnum Opus Materials, Box 3, Folder 1: "Magnum Opus: 1932–44, Vol. V, Chapt. 1, 1944" at the Herbert Hoover Presidential Library.

11/25/44

My Attitude toward German Natzism [*sic–ed.*]

I fully realized the dangers which were arising in Germany—in fact before most Americans and British and French leaders took real cognizance to it.

Speaking after my return from Europe in March 1938 I gave many warnings as to the import of rising forces in Germany. At this time I said—[1]

11/25/44

My Attitude toward Communist Russia

I considered, and I still consider, Communist Russia no less a, or possibly a greater, menace to free men than Nazi Germany. The Germans were not as

---

1. [*Editor's note:* Hoover stopped here in his holograph draft. He was probably referring to his speeches in New York and San Francisco on March 31 and April 8, 1938. The are printed in his *Addresses Upon the American Road, 1933–1938* (Charles Scribner's Sons, New York: 1938), pp. 309–334.]

efficient in their missionary work of penetrating other nations and creating destruction from within.

I need not repeat the review of Communism in Europe which I have set out in "my explorations," or in the address upon my return. My concern here is with the relation of the United States to Russia and its works.

. . . . .

I did not think it proper to continue public criticism of Russia after an entry into active war. Nevertheless, I am certain that the American people will rue the day they ever supplied them an ounze [sic–ed.] of Lend Lease. That is unless we abandon every purpose for which we undertook the Second American Crusade.

Done 11/26/44

My Attitude toward Great Britain

My beliefs and sympathies naturally extended to Britain. They just naturally from a thousand years of breeding ruthlessly put the interests of their Empire ahead of everybody every time. But despite all the irritants to an American they are the only nation in the world that can be depended upon to keep agreements and usually to keep the peace. I considered that they had made a ghastly mistake in reversing their policies and [word unclear–ed.] Poland, that they got themselves into the war. I certainly objected to their manipulation of the United States into the war by power politics and propaganda.

It seemed to me the best answer to the British and our domestic propagandists was not only to expose propaganda as such but to expose the ability of Britain to defend itself. I confess I had great anxieties during the Battle of Britain but neither before or after was there any doubt in my mind. In other words our joining the war was never necessary in order to save Britain.

. . . . .

11/26/44

My Attitude toward Japan

That Japan's aggression toward China violated every moral code and every international agreement needs no explanation. Since I dealt with it in 1932, their militarists had expanded their ideas into the realm of "Asia for the Asiatics," with Japan in leadership. All this was unpalatable enough to decent nations and also was threatening to the white man's interests in the East. I never believed Japan could succeed over the years because seventy millions of hated egotists could not for long dominate one billion people. The question in my mind was twofold: First, whether America should go on a crusade to correct this wrong at all, but second—and much more immediate—whether we should undertake it in view of the dangers from Europe and thus invite war on two fronts. Without resolving the first question, the latter was to me the utmost folly. If the job had to be done, it should await the end of the war in Europe when the other white races could be mobilized for action against Japan instead of America's carrying the entire burden and pulling the British, Russian, Dutch and French chestnuts out of the fire at an enormous cost in American lives and resources. It was obvious that Japan would not attack us unless provoked into it as a rat driven into a corner.

Roosevelt, however, undertook a series of provocative actions, beginning early in 1940 and continuing with increasing violence until both national pride and national desperation led them to Pearl Harbor. I believe that the verdict of history will show that either Roosevelt was wholly ignorant of Japanese psychology and thought he could force Japan to submission with economic sanctions or that despaired of getting the American people into the world war on the European front, he was determined to provoke war with Japan as the method of entry.

Roosevelt apparently never understood the impact or violence of "economic sanctions" and played with them like the toys on his desk—or as I have said, deliberately used them to provoke war. He permitted Japan to drain the scrap steel and oil which we badly needed for our own preparedness in a dangerous world though the stopping of which was not an economic sanction, and at the same time he imposed economic embarrassments on Japan, all of which would indicate a confused mind playing with power politics.

On February 1, 1939, in a nation-wide broadcast I stated:[2]

---

2. [*Editor's note:* Hoover's draft stopped at this point. For the text of his radio broadcast of February 1, 1939, see his *Further Addresses upon the American Road, 1938–1940* (Charles Scribner's Sons, New York: 1940), pp. 93–103.]

"Twelve Years 1932–1944"

December 13, 1944

In November 1944 Hoover began work on a chapter of his memoirs devoted to his interpretation of the coming of World War II. It was a kind of précis of what evolved into *Freedom Betrayed*.

As usual, Hoover rewrote and rewrote his chapter. By December 13, 1944, he had produced several drafts. The introductory paragraphs of the last one are reproduced here. The full document and its antecedent versions are in the Magnum Opus Materials, Box 5, Folder 3: "Magnum Opus: 1932–44, vol. 5 (2)," Herbert Hoover Presidential Library.

12/13/44

Twelve Years 1932–1944

Not until the inner history of the events leading up to our entry into World War II are brought into the daylight can the final history of how we got into it be written. And if I live long enough I propose to write that history. I possess much material and information which cannot be properly disclosed at this time. It is my purpose here only to state my attitude, the reasons for it and the events which influenced it. That I abundantly stated to the American people at the time.

My position was very simple. I was convinced during my visit to Europe in early 1938 that an explosion on the continent was probable. I believed then, and the events since have confirmed, that German national socialism would inevitably clash with the Russian communism and that western civilization would be tragically impaired unless the democracies stayed out. I believed then, and it is clear now, that it was only if the western democracies interfered with the German purpose to expand eastward that the democracies would be attacked by Hitler. I believed that Stalin would promote conflict between the democracies and Hitler as a method of weakening them both; while if western democracies kept hands off, the hideous despotisms of both Hitler and Stalin would be weakened by mutual destruction.

When the western European democracies determined to stop Germany and war became inevitable I believed then—and still believe—that not only America but civilization itself would be infinitely better off and a lasting peace in the world would be far more assured if we kept out of their wars.

A Conversation with Joseph P. Kennedy

May 15, 1945

ONE OF HOOVER'S SOURCES for his historical investigations was Joseph P. Kennedy (father of John F. Kennedy), who served as President Roosevelt's ambassador to Great Britain between 1938 and 1940. Although publicly loyal to Roosevelt in the 1940 presidential campaign, Kennedy profoundly disagreed with FDR's foreign policy—a divergence that soon led the ambassador to Hoover's door.

During World War II, Hoover and Kennedy met approximately twenty times. Hoover's account of one of these conversations is reproduced here. It adumbrated themes that Hoover soon developed in his Magnum Opus.

This memorandum is filed in the Herbert C. Hoover Papers, Box 90, "Data for Reference 1945: January–July 1st" envelope, Hoover Institution Archives.

The Waldorf Astoria Towers
New York, New York
May 15, 1945

Joseph P. Kennedy called me this morning.

Kennedy agreed with me entirely that it is urgent that we make peace with Japan and he thinks it should be done as soon as possible if it can be done upon terms of the restoration of China and disarmament of Japan for at least 30 to 40 years. We ought to allow Japan to keep Formosa and Korea to save her [illegible word–*ed.*] face and to recover her economic life.

Kennedy then discussed the book which he has been engaged in writing on his official experiences as Ambassador to Great Britain. He told me had some 900 dispatches which he could not print without the consent of the American Government. He is hoping that the time would come when he could print these and is going to prepare the book and put it away until that time comes. He said the book would put an entirely different color on the process of how America got into the war and would prove the betrayal of the American people by Franklin D. Roosevelt.

Kennedy said that after the Germans had occupied Prague and the great cry of appeasement had sprung up in the world and after the Germans had pressed their demands for Danzig and a passage through the Corridor, that Roosevelt and Bullitt[1] were the major factors in the British making their guarantees to Poland and becoming involved in the war. Kennedy said that Bullitt, under instructions from Roosevelt, was constantly urging the Poles *not* to make terms with the Germans and that he Kennedy, under instructions from Roosevelt, was constantly urging the British to make guarantees to the Poles. Kennedy said he had received a cable from Roosevelt to "put a poker up Chamberlain's back and to make him stand up." Kennedy saw Chamberlain on numerous occasions, urging him in Roosevelt's name to do all this with the implication that the United States would give the British support. He said that after Chamberlain had given these guarantees, Chamberlain told him (Kennedy) that he hoped the Americans and the Jews would now be satisfied but that he (Chamberlain) felt that he had signed the doom of civilization.

Kennedy claimed that he was constantly urging Roosevelt not to be engaged in this question, but his urgings were to no avail. Kennedy said that if it had not been for Roosevelt the British would not have made this the most gigantic blunder in history.

Kennedy agreed with me that the Germans were a land people, that they had given up the possibility of sea conquests, that they had built up a land army for expansion purposes, that they knew they could not spread out to the West and that they had determined to expand into the Balkan States and Russia. Chamberlain knew this and Kennedy said that Chamberlain's whole idea, despite Roosevelt's promises, was to keep hands off and to let these two dictators fight it out between themselves.

Kennedy told me of other instances of urgings and promises made by Roosevelt. He said that when the Ghormley Commission went to England in mid-1940, it was for the purposes of preparing joint military action, and yet through that entire election campaign Roosevelt was promising the American people that he would never go to war.

Kennedy told me that he thought Roosevelt was in communication with Churchill, who was the leader of the opposition to Chamberlain, before Chamberlain was thrown out of office and that afterwards, before Chamberlain died, he Chamberlain had written to Kennedy [a] nine-page letter in his

---

1. [*Editor's note:* William C. Bullitt, the U.S. ambassador to France (1936–1940).]

own hand saying that his original policies and Kennedy's like views, had they been adopted, would have saved the world.

Kennedy told me that in the campaign[2] Roosevelt had sent for him to come back, told him that he did not propose to get the country into the war at all. Kennedy said that he believed Roosevelt and went out and made a speech in Roosevelt's support. When Kennedy realized that these promises had no meaning, he went out and made two speeches denouncing Roosevelt and his proposals to get into the war.

---

2. [*Editor's note:* The presidential election campaign of 1940.]

Hoover's "12 Theses"

February 11, 1946

FOR NEARLY A DECADE, Hoover's principal research assistant was a young, conservative economist, Arthur Kemp. In a memorandum dated February 11, 1946, Hoover directed Kemp to examine and copyedit an early version of the Magnum Opus. In his instructions Hoover succinctly laid out the "twelve theses" that drove his historical revisionism.

This memorandum is filed in the Arthur Kemp Papers, Box 37, Envelope 12, Hoover Institution Archives.

2/11/46

1. Go over all Mss coming from the printer—1938 on—correct grammar, diction, vocabulary by pencil notes on margin.
2. Look up any doubtful points and where actual short quotations would be better than assertions. Look them up.
3. Bear in mind the 12 theses:
   a. War between Russia and Germany was inevitable.
   b. Hitler's attack on Western Democracies was only to brush them out of his way.
   c. There would have been no involvement of Western Democracies had they not gotten in his (Hitler's) way by guaranteeing Poland (March, 1939).
   d. Without prior agreement with Stalin this constituted the greatest blunder of British diplomatic history.
   e. There was no sincerity on either side in the Stalin-Hitler alliance of August, 1939.
   f. The United States or the Western Hemisphere were never in danger of invasion by Hitler.
   g. [This entry is missing in Hoover's typescript–*ed.*]

h. This was even less so when Hitler determined to attack Stalin.
i. Roosevelt, knowing this about November, 1940, had no remote warranty for putting the United States in war to "save Britain" and/or saving the United States from invasion.
j. The use of the Navy for undeclared war on Germany was unconstitutional.
k. There were secret military agreements with Britain probably as early as January, 1940.
l. The Japanese war was deliberately provoked. Read up the books and magazines of the period for any light pro and con on these theses. Have the girls copy out such passages as bear importantly on the subject.

4. A large question arises on the constitutionality of undeclared war, executive agreements, joint statements and "declarations." Please read up and extract anything you can find on the subject.

Hoover's Conversations with General Douglas MacArthur

May 4, 5, and 6, 1946

IN MAY 1946, while on a global famine relief mission for President Harry Truman, Hoover conferred with General Douglas MacArthur in Tokyo. At this time MacArthur was the supreme commander of the Allied Powers in occupied Japan. Hoover's account of these conversations is printed here. Of special interest is Hoover's blunt assertion that World War II in the Pacific ("the whole Japanese war") had resulted from "a madman's desire to get into war"—a stinging allusion to President Franklin D. Roosevelt. This memorandum underscored two of Hoover's revisionist contentions in his Magnum Opus: (1) that the United States could have avoided war with Japan in 1941 and (2) that the United States could have defeated Japan in 1945 without dropping the atomic bomb.

Although this document was written in the form of a diary, the wording of the final paragraph suggests that the memo was prepared sometime afterward. Whatever the precise date, the document provides a valuable window into Hoover's mind as he prepared the earliest drafts of his Magnum Opus.

The document is filed in "Famine Emergency Committee: General—Diaries, Herbert Hoover Diaries—Round the World Trip," Post-Presidential Subject File, Herbert Hoover Papers, Herbert Hoover Presidential Library.

Japan

May 4, 5, 6, 1946.

Tokyo.

I talked with General Douglas MacArthur alone for three hours on the evening of May 4th, for one hour on the evening of May 5th, and for one hour on the morning of the 6th.

MacArthur was bitter about Roosevelt's starvation of supplies to him at a time when the whole fate of the South Pacific and the Allies in Asia was at

stake. He received only 3½ tons of equipment and supplies per man as compared to 14 tons per man sent to North Africa. He said that Roosevelt had
shown his vindictiveness in many ways. He alone of the major commanders
had not been called into group consultations. The White House columnists
were always smearing him (which I can confirm—Roosevelt had called him
his "McClelland,"[1] his "problem child"). Finally, when he was called into the
Honolulu consultation, he was not at first permitted to see Roosevelt alone.
The Rosemans[2] and the Navy people ganged up on him with their plan of a
northern route of attack under naval direction. Finally, MacArthur openly demanded to see Roosevelt alone for ten minutes. He then told Roosevelt that
if he wanted to show progress in the Pacific War before his election (1944),
it could only be done by island-hopping to the Philippines on the southern
route. He guaranteed to show great progress and even to land in the Philippines before November 1944, if his plans were carried out. He interested, and
finally secured Roosevelt's approval. All during this conversation Roseman
was constantly sticking his head in through the door. Roosevelt wholly turned
down the Navy plan much to Nimitz's astonishment. MacArthur says that
Nimitz[3] never forgave him. MacArthur said that Roosevelt's whole interest
was in the political possibilities for himself, and said that his arguments as to
the superior strategic weights had no effect.

MacArthur said he told Roosevelt that peace could be made with the Japanese any time after the Philippines were taken as the Jap military gang would
know that with their supporting legs cut off they were beaten. He said that
Roosevelt, however, was determined that he should not command in the final
movement on Japan—that was his sop to Nimitz. The comparative high Navy
losses at Okinawa and [word missing–ed.] influenced Truman, plus public
opinion.

I told MacArthur of my memorandum of mid-May 1945 to Truman, that
peace could be had with Japan by which our major objectives would be accomplished. MacArthur said that was correct and that we would have avoided
all of the losses, the Atomic bomb, and the entry of Russia into Manchuria.

I said that the whole Japanese war was a madman's desire to get into war.
He agreed and also agreed that the financial sanctions in July 1941 were not

---

1. [*Editor's note:* That is, General George McClellan, the Union general in the Civil War who so
vexed President Lincoln.]

2. [*Editor's note:* Evidently Samuel I. Rosenman, President Roosevelt's aide and speechwriter.]

3. [*Editor's note:* Admiral Chester W. Nimitz, commander-in-chief of the U.S. Pacific Fleet from
1941 to 1945.]

only provocative but that Japan was bound to fight even if it were suicide unless they could be removed, as the sanctions carried every penalty of war except killing and destruction, and that no nation of dignity would take them for long. He said that Roosevelt could have made peace with Konoye[4] in September 1941 and could have obtained all of the American objectives in the Pacific and the freedom of China and probably Manchuria. He said Konoye was authorized by the Emperor to agree to complete withdrawal.

MacArthur said that Pauley,[5] the F.E.C., and the vindictive "liberals" were attempting to destroy Japan. He became even emotional upon their reports and attitudes. He cited the Potsdam Agreement as being in spirit entirely contrary to a constructive program. He said that if Japan were allowed to recover her peace-time economy, to reconstruct her industries that the Japanese might pay reparations but that they could not do so otherwise. That all that was needed was to destroy munition works, disarm the Japanese, and to keep a commission there to watch, and to have an airfield on some island an hour away. He said that there should be no restraints on the Japanese heavy or light industry of any kind; he said that they could no nothing toward recovery now because of the threats to remove the plants.

MacArthur said that he thought the chances were 2000 to one against Marshall's[6] succeeding in China, and gave me a long detailed account of Russian obstruction in his dealings with the Soviets. He said that they were steadily propagandizing the Japs; that they were conducting Communist schools among their Japanese prisoners and infiltrating them into Japan.

He said that if the Japanese standard of living were lowered and heavy indemnities imposed upon them that they [sic–ed.] Japanese would go Communist, both to get free and to secure Russian protection. He said we could make an ideological dam in the Pacific out of Japan as against the Asiatic tide of Communism.

He said that Russia would make a puppet state out of Manchuria unless we stopped such action quickly. He did not think the United States should do it by military means. Generally MacArthur was pessimistic on the whole consequences of the war in the Pacific.

---

4. [*Editor's note:* Prince Fumimaro Konoye (Konoe), prime minister of Japan between July 22, 1940 and mid-October 1941.]

5. [*Editor's note:* Ambassador Edwin A. Pauley was President Harry Truman's appointee to lead the American delegation to the Allied Reparations Commission, which dealt with German reparations after World War II. In 1945 and 1946 Pauley led U.S. reparations missions concerning Japan and Japanese assets in Soviet-occupied Korea and Manchuria.]

6. [*Editor's note:* General George C. Marshall, then in China on a mission to reconcile the Chinese Nationalists and Communists and establish a unified Chinese government.]

I mentioned to MacArthur the many suggestions at home that he should become a Presidential candidate in 1948. I said I believed he could be elected. He said he wanted none of it, and I concluded that was the case.

I said that there was great moral and political degeneration at home, a growing feeling of frustration, a wealth of extravagance, gambling, etc. That some time after the 1946 elections, if he were to come home to receive the appreciation of the American people and if he would make three speeches, one on moral questions, one of government, and one on our foreign relations, he might prove to be the John-the-Baptist that America needed. He said he would do it if I sent word to him that the time was right.

MacArthur spoke feelingly of our relations in 1930–1932; of Roosevelt's first friction with him for his defense of my policies of preparedness; of his bitter break when Roosevelt insisted upon reducing my preparedness program.

He had been afraid I would not support a food program for the Japanese and was grateful because I lifted the minimums (1000 calories) asked for by his staff. They were indeed too low for existence but had been made in despair that no more could be obtained.

I talked with a dozen of MacArthur's staff on questions of Asia, Japanese economics, the war and peace. The main theme in their minds was the threat of Russia. So great was this that one of our leading air commanders, then on a visit to Japan, asked me in all seriousness if I thought that war would come before ninety days, as his air organization was all shot to pieces by demobilization, but he hoped to have things somewhat straightened out by that time. I said No, that the Russians would start no wars until the harvests were in. (This was May and northern hemisphere harvests would be in in August and September.)

Hoover Memorandum to Arthur Kemp
n.d.

IN THE EARLY YEARS of his work on the Magnum Opus, Hoover often referred to it as the "War Book." In the following undated memorandum (probably written in the mid-1940s), Hoover again revealed the didactic thrust of his projected volume.

This document is filed in "'War Book' (Freedom Betrayed): Herbert Hoover Holograph Material," Arthur Kemp Papers, Herbert Hoover Presidential Library.

Dear Arthur—

Will you please look over the latter part of 1938 (War Book). We have built up the case of Hitler's malevolent eye on Stalin. We need to build up the cases of

Stalin's Malevolent eye on Hitler

    "   "   "   " Democracies

(by short quotations) and we need to strengthen the quotations of Lenin & Stalin on the now binding [nonbinding?–*ed.*] character of communist international contracts—likewise Hitler's gospel on this subject (if he was so unwise as to express himself)

I attach some material you may have already gathered and some things in a speech of Mrs. Luce.[1]

H.

---

1. [*Editor's note:* Probably Clare Booth Luce.]

Hoover's Visit to Germany, 1938

1947

IN HIS MANY successive editions of the Magnum Opus, Hoover invariably included a lengthy account of his trip to Europe in early 1938, when he conferred with leading figures in a dozen nations. The final version of his account is printed in Volume I of *Freedom Betrayed*. But earlier drafts of the Magnum Opus contain significantly longer versions, including "An Examination of Europe," which he completed in early 1947. As set in printer's page proofs in 1947, this essay is fully 75 pages long.

More detailed than the abridged version printed in Volume I, the 1947 draft is an intriguing primary source in its own right. Of particular interest are the eight pages describing Hoover's visit to Nazi Germany in March 1938 and his encounter with Adolf Hitler. These pages are printed in toto here.

"An Examination of Europe" was part of the "1938" section of Hoover's "War Book." The 1947 page proof version is in the Herbert C. Hoover Papers, Box 3, "M.O. 6" envelope, Hoover Institution Archives. A note on the envelope indicates that the page proofs of "M.O. 6" were returned to Hoover from the printer in March and July 1947.

1938

*An Examination of Europe**

After leaving the White House and during the next few years, I received many invitations from governments and institutions to visit Europe. The smaller democracies especially wished for an opportunity to show some appreciation of my services during and after the war.* I had no desire to receive such

---

* This account was written soon after my return from ample notes of conversations and observations. I have left the text as written at that time. Where the word "War" is used it necessarily refers to World War I. While some of the conclusions may have seemed faulty during the early World War II years they have been astonishingly vindicated with time.

attentions, and to visit Europe under such circumstances held out no attractions. But the steady growth of totalitarianism and the drift toward war did interest me profoundly. I concluded that some inquiry on the ground might yield some message of importance to the American people. I resolved to take advantage of these invitations and the opportunity they gave me to discuss the situation with many European leaders and informed laymen.

I received invitations from the Governments of Belgium, Austria, Hungary, Poland, Czechoslovakia, Lithuania, Estonia, Latvia, Finland, and Sweden and I should need pass through other nations enroute. The journey did not seem to meet with Mr. Roosevelt's approval, for the Polish Ambassador in Washington informed me that the Administration had sought to prevent the extension of the Polish invitation. Our State Department, however, could not dare refuse my request for the usual diplomatic passport. I received no invitation from the British, French, Italian or Russian Governments, although I had been of some service to their peoples.

With Perrin Galpin and Paul Smith as secretaries I sailed on the George Washington from New York on February 9, 1938, directly to Le Havre. . . .

. . . . . .

Germany

We motored from Prague, staying overnight at Carlsbad, arriving at Berlin the evening of the seventh of March, by way of a number of German Government housing projects which I wanted to see. I had not expected to meet any German officials but hoped to get some feeling of what was going on from Americans and some of my old personal friends among the Germans—chiefly former officials, engineers and professional men. In the morning, however, a high Nazi, Captain Fritz Wiedemann, called at the Adlon, placing a German army officer and two automobiles at our disposal, and informed me that Chancellor Hitler invited me to call at 12 o'clock with the American Ambassador. I was not enthusiastic as I had long since formed a great prejudice against the whole Nazi faith and its disciples for destroying every foundation of free men. The American Ambassador, Hugh Wilson, however, felt there was no escape; in fact he was delighted, as he had never seen Hitler except in parades. His relations were confined to the Foreign Office officials.

We were supposed to be with Hitler for a few moments of a formal call, but he kept us for considerably over the hour. He was aware I had been looking over some of Germany's new housing projects and gave me a very interesting and lucid statement of their experience and conclusions. The latter were, generally, that purchasable detached houses, no matter how small, with gardens and rapid transit were the only satisfactory solution—socially and economically. We ranged over many other economic and social subjects.

My definite impressions were that he was forceful, highly intelligent, had a remarkable and accurate memory, a wide range of information and a capacity for lucid exposition. All this was contrary to my preconceptions based on belittling books—most of which tried to make him out a dummy in front of some group of unknown geniuses. I was soon convinced that this was the boss himself. My adverse reactions were, however, confirmed by minor items which are perhaps unfair weights in judgment. From his clothing and hairdo he was obviously a great deal of an exhibitionist. He seemed to have trigger spots in his mind which set him off when touched, like a man in furious anger. The conversation touched on Communism whereupon he exploded and orated. I silently agreed with his conclusions so did not mind. A moment later the discussion spread to democracy, and he began to explode again whereupon I remarked that I could not be expected to agree as I was one of those myself. The subject was dropped and we went on to some less controversial topics.

Later we went to lunch at the American Ambassador's with a number of high German officials and Americans. I sat next to Count Von Neurath who, until recently, had been the German Minister of Foreign Affairs. A few chairs down was an Under-Secretary of State, Paul Schmidt, who had checked the interpretation at the Hitler interview. This gentleman proceeded in undertones to give Von Neurath an amusing account of the minor clash between these two "high priests" of rival faiths. I noticed two American newspaper correspondents at the opposite side of the table, listening intently. They hardly waited to be civil in their excuses for departure. I did not at the moment know what their haste was about. But they had smelled from the Schmidt-Von Neurath conversation that a fight had taken place between myself and Hitler at the morning interview and proceeded to telegraph such a story to the American press. They next thing I knew Schmidt came to see me, much perturbed, told me of the dispatches that had been sent especially to the Hearst Press, and asked me to make the statement that my impressions of Hitler had been most favorable. Schmidt's anxiety was, of course, for himself. I could not assist him. He later squared himself by giving the impression that the story was manufactured by Paul Smith, one of my secretaries—who was not present at the meeting at all.

The "Carl Schurz Foundation" gave a dinner and reception in the evening. I learned later that this was undoubtedly a fake "association" conducted solely to entertain visiting Americans. Dr. Hjalmar Schacht presided and told me the University of Berlin would like to confer an honorary degree upon me out of recognition of my services in feeding the German people after the Armistice and for my aid during the Bruening regime. I got out of that politely by not being able to be in Berlin on the appointed day. I wanted nothing from Nazis.

Field Marshal Hermann Goering had sent word he would like to see me. The American Ambassador was all for it, for he had never seen the No. 2 Nazi either, except in parades. We went to lunch at his hunting lodge, "Karin Hall," some distance outside Berlin. Its only relation to a shooting lodge was the imitation shingles on the roof. It was an immense structure, with rooms as large as a Waldorf dining room crammed with hundreds of thousands of dollars in furniture, paintings and art generally, including two or three busts of Napoleon. Goering came from an impecunious military family and had never legitimately enjoyed more than a general's salary. But this is ahead of my story. When our cars entered the courtyard we were stopped by a sentry for no apparent reason. In a few moments there emerged from a side door twelve or sixteen men dressed as huntsmen and armed with French horns. They played the Huntsman's Call from Siegfried the most beautifully I have ever heard it. I knew we were certainly in a Wagnerian atmosphere. This being over we pulled up at the entrance and the atmosphere changed again.

Many years ago I saw a play on the American stage called "The Beggar on Horseback." Its chief impression on my memory was twelve butlers, each with twelve footmen. They were all present here. Perhaps part of those we met were secret service men in livery to prevent visitors doing bodily harm to our host. In any event some of them were always within reach. After some general conversation, Goering asked me into his study where he had a memorandum list of questions, no doubt prepared by some functionary. He was now the head of the German Economic Council—the central body busy managing German industry.

He stated that all Germans appreciated the help I had given to Germany during the famine after the last war. And he remarked emphatically that they would never be caught like that again, as they had developed German agriculture to the point where they were practically self-supporting within their own boundaries. I did not believe it. The questions he had in hand mostly related to the general economic situation in the world. In one of them he inquired as to the progress of simplification in American industrial processes initiated under my direction as Secretary of Commerce which he said they were introducing into Germany. I mentioned that the adoption of such technical standards was necessarily slow because it must be voluntary among manufacturers and others. He replied that "national socialism" has no bothers like that. "If I am given a rationalization (the German term for our word simplification) in the morning, it is in effect by noon." With a prelude that he had been informed of my large engineering practice in Russia before the last war, he asked many questions as to their mineral resources. I restricted my information to facts already well known.

I asked him questions concerning progress upon the now gigantic Hermann Goering Iron Works which were being built to treat low-grade Austrian iron ores. I asked particularly about the magnetic processes which I had heard they were using. He told me they were a great success and that it would take about 18 months to complete the works.

He attempted to get into a discussion of American foreign relations, implying that my ideas would no doubt differ from Roosevelt's. I ended these questions by the remark that he would not want any German traveling abroad to take an attitude on foreign relations different from his government's. He laughed. He pushed a button and an illuminated map of Europe appeared on the wall with different brilliant colors for the different countries. He pointed to Czechoslovakia and said, "What does the shape of that country remind you of?" Nothing occurred to me apropos so he continued. "That is a spearhead. It is a spearhead plunged into the German body."

We went out to lunch with a number of young people, each of us attended by at least one butler and a footman. In the middle of the table was a life-sized bust of a lady wearing a string of pearls. Curiosity probably drew my eye to it in contemplation of whether it was brass or gold. Goering noted this and remarked, "My first wife. It's pure gold." His second wife, Emmy, was somewhere in the house.

My net impressions of him were that he was far more agreeable than Hitler; probably had a clever mind; was utterly ruthless, utterly selfish and probably utterly cruel.

During my stay in Berlin I had a great number of callers. They included in addition to Dr. Schacht, former head of the Reichsbank whom I had met in various negotiations in former years; Dr. Bruno Bruhn, former chief engineer of the Krupp Works; Dr. Lewald, former Minister of the Interior in World War I; Dr. Smitz, Food Administrator of Germany after the war; Dr. Schmitz, head of I. G. Farben; and a number of other unofficial old personal friends, together with American newspaper correspondents. The Reich Minister of Education called and invited me to inspect their various youth movements as he learned I had made some inquiries in respect to them. I did not inspect, but he gave me a full and enthusiastic description of the Government disciplines that began at seven years of age and extended in various stages for about fifteen years thereafter, including their separation of children "gifted in mind" from those "gifted in hand" and the special training of each. He believed they had the formula for developing genius for government and the professions. I did not ask where character came in or the basic freedom of men to choose their own jobs in life.

I noticed that when two or more of my German visitors were in the room together they all talked in banalities. Where there was only one he spoke softly, and answered social and economic questions fairly frankly—although only two of them offered any criticism of the Nazis. Dr. Bruhn and Herr Lewald, each whispered to me that Germany was en route to destruction. I had dealt with Lewald in connection with Belgian Relief during the first World War.

My greatest illumination on German economic life in these conversations came from an old personal friend who was a paper manufacturer married to a fine American lady whom I had known before her marriage. Without a word of criticism he described exactly how National Socialism worked in his business, employing 2,000 men. It had denuded him of real control; it had reduced his income to the extent that he had given up his seashore cottage and his Berlin house and was living in a three-room apartment. That did not seem to bother him so much as the fact that he had no free will or free judgment left in the conduct of his business and, above all, that Nazi controls had reduced both him and his workmen to a sort of peonage. Wages and promotions were fixed by the government; men could not leave their jobs without government approval and every youth was compelled to follow the calling chosen for him.

Germany had long had a most able bureaucracy of non-policy-making officials who really carried on the routine housekeeping of government. They had weathered the World War, the postwar revolution and now had mostly weathered the Nazi revolution. I had dealt with them over food supply, transport and other matters during Belgian relief and the relief of Germany and German children after the Armistice in 1918. They were most cooperative after the war and several—some now retired because of age—called to express their appreciation. They told me about great improvements in German agriculture by which Germany should never be reduced to the 1918–1919 situation again.

I, of course, talked at great length to some of my old friends among the American correspondents, particularly Louis Lochner of the Associated Press, and the American professional men in Berlin. The able American Military Attaché, Colonel Truman Smith, gave me a comprehensive account of the arming of Germany. He said that his own and Colonel Lindbergh's investigation indicated they were manufacturing military planes at the rate of 48,000 per annum. His conclusion was that it would take 18 months more to complete their military program up to an initial launching of 2,000,000 men on a battle front. Our Commercial Attaché, Mr. Miller, one of our old force, gave me a good summary of their industrial program and economic methods in foreign trade which also would seem to require about 18 months for full speed. Something seemed to revolve around 18 months.

One of my inquiries from such sources as I could properly ask was how has Hitler managed to get away with the violations of the Versailles Treaty, re-armament, the occupation of the Ruhr, and other actions without trouble? The invariable answer was "the British are glad to have a military power in Central Europe as a check upon Communist Russia." Nevertheless, I found an almost uncontrollable hate of the British—a survival of World War I.[1]

The Nazi regime with its destruction of personal liberty, its materialistic and militaristic aspects have been fully described elsewhere. My feeling was that no such system could last but that it might cause a world disturbance even if it did not lead to war and would require years to burn itself out. I was convinced it was a structure that would ultimately destroy itself from within. My impressions of Germany are perhaps indicated by the great lift of spirit that came over me the moment we passed over the frontier into Poland. One experienced a sort of indescribable oppression and dread while in Germany. Here was a nation preparing for some aggressive purpose, certainly it was not a system founded on peace. The great theme was "living-space" (*Lebensraum*) for an expanding population. The Nazis were going to expand Germany by peace if possible—by force if necessary. Their fanatical racialism was certainly directed to embracing all Germans in Europe into the German State. If their expansion went beyond that, the only really valuable area was the Balkans and Russia. I was convinced they had no desire for war with the democracies; they saw who [no?–*ed.*] profit in it; they were a land people with land armies; they could not cross the sea, and to occupy France, Belgium or the other already overcrowded European countries afforded no opportunity for expansion of German population. To reach Russia, they must crush Czechoslovakia, Poland or Roumania or obtain a permanent right of way over them. The sum of my view was that an explosion was coming; that they would sooner or later move eastward.

---

1. [*Editor's note:* Although Hoover stated at the outset that he wrote this account soon after his return from Europe in March 1938, he must have written (or at least revised) some of it later, after World War II began in September 1939. Hence his explicit reference here to World War I.]

"A Review of 1941 and Its Four Times Lost Statesmanship"

1947

HOOVER INITIALLY ARRANGED his "War Book" in the form of a chronicle: a chapter for the events of 1939, a chapter for the events of 1940, and so on. Some of these chapters exceeded 100 pages when set in page proofs.

In the document here, taken from the fourth (or possibly fifth) "edition" of his chapter for the year 1941, Hoover condemned the "lost statesmanship" of Franklin Roosevelt in that fateful year. These pages comprise the final section of a 240-page chapter. Hoover evidently composed them in early 1947; the complete chapter was returned to him by the printer in page proof format between March and July of that year.

The full document (including the excerpt reproduced here) is found in the Herbert C. Hoover Papers, Box 3, "M.O. 7" envelope, Hoover Institution Archives.

A Review of 1941 and Its Four Times Lost Statesmanship

It is worth a moment's pause at the end of 1941 to summarize the entire year in the light of statesmanship which should have protected the interests of the American people. And I use this term "interests of the American people" in its widest sense, not alone in the losses to our country, but also in the recovery of civilization and the making of real peace in the world. At four critical times during the year Roosevelt had the choice of roads where the right turn would have led in this direction.

The First Wrong Turning

The first wrong turn was at the end of 1940, or the opening of 1941, when Roosevelt turned away from "Fathers, mothers, I promise . . ." and determined upon an undeclared war on Germany. Statesmanship dictated that Lend-Lease should be limited to a simple grant in aid or a loan to the British with which to purchase ample American supplies and ships—if they were necessary these could have properly included light naval craft for convoy purposes.

Instead, under the guise of keeping out of war he demanded powers in the Lend-Lease Act which with his unique interpretation of his powers as Commander-in-Chief enabled him to launch undeclared war without the approval of the American people or the Congress.

The misrepresentations as to the purpose of his Lend-Lease Act and its disguise of war were disheartening enough. But the representation that it was necessary to save the British Empire from Hitler and to establish freedom throughout the world was even more stupendous violation of the truth.

Even accepting the premise that the independence and safety of the British Empire was an essential to the safety of the United States, the Western Hemisphere and civilization, the dangers at that time did not require any such action.

Any review of the military situation in the world at the time Lend-Lease was passed, as it must have been known to Roosevelt, would show:

(1) Hitler had abandoned, months before, any idea (if he ever had it) of trying an invasion across the 25 miles of the English Channel in the face of the British Navy.

(2) Hitler had been defeated five months before, in his air blitz in the Battle of Britain.

(3) Hitler's consistent ambition, intention and preparation during eight years had been the conquest of Russia and Eastern Europe and the uprooting of the Communist vatican in Moscow. Roosevelt knew in December 1940 and more emphatically in March 1941 that Hitler had turned his military objectives to that purpose. His State Department in mid-January had even warned Russia it was coming. With this military shift it was certain there would be an exhausting war between these two dictatorships which would weaken Hitler's situation no matter what happened. The world stood a chance that these dictators would destroy each other. In any event it assured complete safety to Britain.

(4) At this time (March, 1941) the British had sunk or put out of action many major units of the Axis fleets, had built up their own strength until they had double the tonnage of major war vessels of the whole European Axis. They were, on Churchill's own statement, on their way to defeat of the German submarine

menace. The British had announced that they required no men, that they wanted only tools.

(5) With Hitler not being able even to cross the Channel the stories of invasion of the Western Hemisphere were preposterous lies. And the more so as the American fleet alone was greater than the strength of the Axis, plus "General Atlantic Ocean."

For all these evident reasons there was at that time no danger of defeat of Britain nor invasion of the United States. Yet Roosevelt drove to war.

The Second Wrong Turning

On June 22nd came Hitler's attack on Russia. Even if the ample evidence before Roosevelt prior to Lend-Lease of such a forth-coming attack be ignored, it was now a reality and all the reasons given above for staying out of war were now indisputable. Moreover, Britain, through relief of pressure by Hitler and the arrival of American supplies, was greatly strengthened in her air, naval, and military forces. As outlined above, they could have taken over the "patrol" or "convoy." They could have purchased American ships on credit. They knew they would never have to repay.

Roosevelt had been active for four months with his undeclared war on Germany. It was evident despite Roosevelt's every provocative act that Hitler was determined not to be maneuvered into overt acts which would inflame the American people into a declaration of war by our Congress. To have taken at this point this open road out of war would have saved a generation of human tears.

The Third Wrong Turning

The third wrong turning was the imposition of the economic sanctions in July. That was undeclared war upon Japan by which starvation and ruin stared her in the face and if continued would soon be war, for the simple reason that no people of dignity would run up a white flag under such provocation. It could effect no strategic purpose in the protection of the United States or China or even the British Empire.

The Fourth Wrong Turning

The fourth wrong turning was certainly the rejection of the Konoye[1] proposals of September and the Emperor's proposals of November. It has been claimed that these proposals were the result of the economic sanctions and other threats. This may be partially true but it must be remembered that Konoye had begun his negotiations two months before the sanctions and being thwarted by Matsuoka[2] (of which Roosevelt was advised) had got rid of this evil spirit before their imposition so that he could move freely forward toward peace.

It can never be forgotten that three times during 1941 Japan made overtures for peace negotiation. America never made one unless a futile proposal to the Emperor the day before Pearl Harbor could be called peace.

A peace could have been made in the Pacific that would have saved China from ravishment and would have protected the American Pacific flank and, if Roosevelt was still determined to carry on his undeclared war with Germany until it provoked reprisals, that Pacific protection was the only sane course. It would have limited our engagement in any case to the European theatre. As the result of this policy—an undeclared war upon Japan—we suffered the greatest military defeat in all our history with immeasurable consequences.

Thus four times, real statesmanship plainly pointed a road to peace. Instead, the previous twelve months were the period of the most gigantic intellectual dishonesties of all American history. The first was Roosevelt's promises to "Fathers, mothers, etc.";[3] the second, that Britain was in danger of invasion; third, that the United States was in danger of invasion; fourth, that the Lend-Lease law was not an outright war proposal.

As I said at the beginning, we can look at these actions by Roosevelt from two points of view. We can deify him as a great statesman, dragging and pushing an unwilling, obstinate people into the duty of another world crusade for freedom; or we can construe his actions as blundering statesmanship, an attempt to cover the failure of the New Deal, an effort to reelect himself to satisfy his consuming desire for power and as one overcome by war madness of egotism. In either construction it is certain that his steps were intellectually

---

1. [*Editor's note:* Prince Fumimaro Konoye (Konoe), the prime minister of Japan between July 22, 1940 and mid-October 1941.]

2. [*Editor's note:* Yosuke Matsuoka, foreign minister of Japan, July 1940–July 1941.]

3. [*Editor's note:* Hoover was referring to President Roosevelt's campaign pledge to Americans on October 30, 1940 that "Your boys are not going to be sent into any foreign wars."]

dishonest, his statements untruthful and his actions unconstitutional. The hideous consequences will unfold as this narrative proceeds.

However, once we were in the war there was but one way out—to win military victory.

During 1941 I had given my whole time in an effort to keep our country out of war and to correct the current abuses. I had spent less than a month at home. Aside from the five principal addresses delivered in different cities and nationally broadcast, which are reproduced in these memoirs, I had written and spoken to scores of smaller audiences and maintained constant contact with leaders of the opposition. My public expressions may seem lacking in attack on Roosevelt's Japanese policies. After his important action of imposing the economic sanctions on July 25th, I was aware that negotiations for settlement of all Pacific questions were in progress. I was anxious that no word of mine would embarrass these negotiations. I was kept informed of their progress by Colonel O'Laughlin[4] who was in daily contact with Ambassador Nomura. In drafting a speech for September 16 I included a strong paragraph on the urgency of accepting Konoye's proposal of a Pacific meeting, but I struck it out for the above reasons. I did include a prayerful paragraph in a speech on November 15th. It seemed so preposterous that we would get into war on that front that I underestimated the purposes of Roosevelt and his colleagues.

Public opinion was overwhelmingly against our being involved in the war up to the day of Pearl Harbor. I claim little credit for this as thousands of men and women also worked steadfastly to save our country. I have no regrets. We were right.

In the days after Pearl Harbor I went back to things I had written many years before regarding the spirit of the world at the original outbreak in 1914 and at the American entry into World War I in 1917.

America came into World War I 33 months after its outbreak. She came into World War II 27 months after it started. The processes in the months of lag were the same. The appeal to crusade for freedom, for independence of nations, for lasting peace; the same pictures of atrocities; the fanning of hate and, above all, the mass of lies in stimulation of fear of invasion—they were identical. But in World War II the people believed much less of it and they believed much more that they were being deliberately pushed into the war. They

---

4. [*Editor's note:* John Callan O'Laughlin (1873–1949), publisher of the *Army-Navy Journal* and a confidant of Hoover's. Between 1933 and 1949 O'Laughlin regularly wrote lengthy letters to Hoover on events in Washington. He was one of Hoover's principal "inside" sources on the news.]

dimly recognized they were being ground in the mills of power politics and the personal ambitions of men. The first World War had been conducted on the Allied side in the names of the peoples. This war was in the name of Stalin, Churchill and Roosevelt. At times the whole political and military scene seemed their personal property—as it was.

In the first World War our sons marched to war with flowers in their rifles; bands and cheering people were on every platform. There were no bands, no flowers, no cheers on the railway platforms to World War II. There was little singing of war ballads by soldiers or civilians except under the urging of paid conductors of propaganda. The station platforms were stages for grieving and tears. The promises, the speeches, the propaganda filled the air as in World War I, but this time the people received it grimly and with little believing.

"The Results of World War II to the United States"

and

"A Review of Franklin Roosevelt's Foreign Policies"

1947

HOOVER WROTE the document that follows no later than early 1947. It was returned to him from the printer in the form of page proofs between March and July of that year. The pages reproduced here are pp. 208–21 (the final pages) of the chapter in Hoover's "War Book" entitled "1946." The entire chapter is in the Herbert C. Hoover Papers, Box 3, "M.O. 7" envelope, Hoover Institution Archives.

Once again one notes the polemical fury of the early versions of the Magnum Opus.

The Results of World War II to the United States

Before I relate the consequences of the war to the United States, I may well recall my own advance statements of what these results would be. I am well aware that some people will dislike "I told you so," but as this is an autobiographical essay, it is pardonable.

As the result of my combined experience in World War I, as President, and my personal examination of Europe in 1938, I began then to warn our people of the dangers of Roosevelt's foreign policies and the consequences of our being involved in this war. In continuous speaking and writing for nearly four years, until Pearl Harbor (December 1941) I endeavored, by appeal to reason, to establish certain principles and conclusions. Any reading of those addresses and writings, which are given in full earlier in these memoirs, will show repeated public statements in various forms of the following specific arguments and prophecies. Some minor sections of these statements may be challenged but in major essence every one has proved true.

1. In 1938, I stated that there was danger of another explosion in Europe, but that this explosion was heading primarily toward war between the leaders of rival and aggressive militarized ideologies: Hitler with Fascism, and Stalin with Communism.

2. I stated that the Western European Democracies would be involved only if they interfered in this struggle; that if they kept out, the mutual exhaustion of the two great military states would leave the world safe for democracy for a long time.

3. When Mr. Roosevelt began to indulge in foreign power politics, I insisted that we should not sit in that game. I stated that the Government and the people of the United States were not fitted for such a role and that it would add only to world confusion. Moreover, such a role would provoke alliances against us or even attack upon us.

4. I stated that if we did not engage in power politics and if we were adequately armed, both for military and political reasons, there would be no attack upon us or upon the Western Hemisphere.

5. I said a call to our people for a second crusade to establish freedom of men and independence of nations in the world was misleading, and worse, it would fail just as the first crusade in 1917 had failed. I said freedom in the world would shrink, not expand, if we again pursued that course.

6. After the Western Democracies of Europe had interfered in Eastern Europe in 1939 and war came between them and Hitler, I insisted that Britain was in no danger of successful invasion and defeat.

7. While I favored generous financial and material aid to Britain within the limits of international and constitutional law, I insisted that the other provisions of the Lend-Lease Law were simply undeclared war and would provoke reprisals.

8. Even before Lend-Lease I repeatedly said that Roosevelt was conducting a provocative, undeclared war on Germany and Japan and it would inevitably involve us in reprisals which were the slippery roads to war.

9. After Hitler's attack upon Stalin in June 1941, I insisted that it was unlikely that Hitler could defeat Russia, that even if he did, the result would so weaken him that he would no longer be a menace to the Western Democracies.

10. I insisted that Britain from this time on was thus doubly secure from danger of defeat and that her victory was most probable without our engaging in the war.

11. After the German attack on Russia, I protested that if we entered this war we would find ourselves on the side of Stalin; that the Atlantic Charter and the Four Freedoms would become a Gargantuan jest; that the aftermaths of the war would be revolution and world-wide extension of communism, not democracy. I repeatedly said, "The Communists will be the beneficiaries."

12. I protested that cultivation of war in the Pacific while we were already in danger in the Atlantic was the height of military folly.

13. I pointed out that the consequences to the United States of our getting into war would be:
    a. That war would sacrifice hundreds of thousands of our youth and bring grief to thousands of homes.
    b. That war would exhaust our moral and physical resources, bring brutality, inflation and impoverishment, and lower the standards of living and morals of our people for a generation.
    c. That we could not wholly rid ourselves of this after the war, that regimentation is easy, de-regimentation is difficult. We would find ourselves with less of the "Four Freedoms" than ever before.
    d. That there would be less liberty in the world, not more.
    e. That in this situation we would be less effective in bringing peace to the world.
    f. That the American mission should be to stay out of the war, reserve and conserve our moral and material strength and build up our military strength, so that with this power we could effectively insist upon a real peace.

I am confident that history will confirm the validity of this position.

Human and Physical Destruction

The American loss in military action was 385,575 dead or missing, and 225,000 permanently incapacitated. And among these was the genius and talent that might have given great aid in building a greater America but which is now lost to all future generations.

The superiority of our men and equipment is indicated not only by victory but by the fact that they caused the death or permanent incapacity of upward

of 2,000,000 of the enemy military forces and upward of 600,000 civilians—
men, women, and children. They took more than 3,000,000 prisoners.

Economic Costs

In addition to our enormous burden of dependents from the First World
War, the nation must carry the life-long burden of the 650,000 wounded, the
1,000,000 discharged for disability and the host of widows and orphans from
World War II. It means more than five billion dollars a year for a generation to
pay direct charity payments at home, the service charges and interest, and the
higher costs because of the vast destruction of our natural resources.

We escaped battle destruction at home. Nevertheless, our economic losses
were of gigantic dimensions. For five years we suspended all construction
that did not contribute to the war. Our housing had been inadequate ever
since the New Deal. We emerged from the war short of 10,000,000 homes;
our previous housing was unrepaired and deteriorating.[1] We have insufficient
churches, schools, and business buildings. Our machine tools are older, deteriorated and out-moded. Our highways are inadequate. Our railways are run
down and unable to cope with peace-time traffic. Our communication system
is now inefficient. The "eyes have been pecked out" of our natural resources.
We shall need to buy raw materials from abroad for all time to replace this
depletion.

The industrial unrest from distorted economic forces has resulted in the
most disastrous and prolonged strikes in all our history. Workers, partly tired,
but also unwilling, have decreased their individual effort until our factories
are running at 20% less than pre-war efficiency.

Our public debt in bonds and inflated currency exceeds $300,000,000,000,
or more than our whole national wealth before the war. The economic damage is only partly represented by this debt. Already inflation is upon us with
prices 180 compared to 1939, 100 in 1930 and take-home wages 225 compared
to 100 the same year. We thus have devalued the purchasing power of the
dollar by almost one-half and the end is not yet. While workers and farmers have forced their equation in prices and wages, the savings of our people,
their mortgage investments, their insurance policies have, in reality, already
been half wiped out. The middle class which comprises 70% of our people,

---

1. [*Editor's note:* Hoover's uncorrected page proof at this point repeats a sentence, which I have
deleted.]

has taken the brunt. Teachers today receive one-half the purchasing power of truck drivers.

With the lower purchasing power of the dollar, our endowed hospitals, colleges, universities and scientific institutions have to compromise between inadequate salaries and reducing their facilities for healing the sick and educating the young.

Our federal peace-time budget will have to exceed twenty-seven billions per annum as compared with four billion dollars before Roosevelt. The taxes to support this budget are not only a deduction from our standard of living but are a drag on the initiative and enterprise of the people.

We have yet to meet the inevitable postwar depression, which in all the world's previous great war experience, will come in about ten years. From it we will again suffer vast unemployment and impoverishment.

Had we spent one third of $300,000,000,000 on improvement of American life, we could have rebuilt every one of our 30,000,000 homes, we could have built more and better churches, schools, colleges, hospitals, streets, highways, and parks; and we would still have more than enough to maintain a military establishment that would guard the Western Hemisphere against all corners and make us a potent force for peace.

Political Costs

We have a vast centralization of government which is well indicated by federal bureaucracy increased from 600,000 in 1932 to 2,400,000 one year after the war. This bureaucracy is not only a heavy tax burden but through governmental interference and competition it enervates the productivity of our people. There is not a thinking person in the country today who believes that we will be rid of the whole of this increase.

Moral Costs

The first of the moral and social costs of the war to America was the total failure of our second crusade for independence of nations and freedom of men. It is not alone the consequences of the failure of American promises in the Four Freedoms and the Atlantic Charter, made in honor to hundreds of millions of people, but through our exhaustion of resources, our gigantic debt, our huge taxes and an increase in embedded bureaucracy, we have lost some of the Four Freedoms ourselves.

Our people have been dreadfully brutalized by the war. It is the same after all wars, but never before to the extent of today. Who would have believed America, without public protest, would drop an atomic bomb on helpless civilians whose government had already offered surrender? But of more immediate evidence—crime has increased by 25%, divorces have risen by 20%, one marriage in every three ends in divorce, illegitimacy has increased by 15%. Our streets teem with the delinquency of teen-age girls. The number of our boys in jail is appalling. The exposure of corruption in government officials becomes a daily stench. The black markets represented a pronounced decadence in business honesty. The increase in gambling, horse-racing, night life and extravagance has extended far outside our big cities.

A Review of Franklin Roosevelt's Foreign Policies

The superficial and the misled will say we went to war for any or all of four major reasons: First, the Western Hemisphere, which meant us, was in acute danger of attack by the Nazis; second, that we had to save Britain from defeat by the Germans in order to protect ourselves and our own safety; third, that we were attacked by the Japanese without provocation; and fourth, that we were duty bound for idealistic reasons and our own safety to undertake a second crusade for world freedom from totalitarianism and dictators.

Neither Germany nor Japan wanted war with America. They never even had a plan to invade the Western Hemisphere. With reasonable preparedness on our part there was no combination of powers capable of such invasion.

Every disclosure shows that the Germans originally and at all times intended to attack Russia for plunder and destruction of communist opposition to their Nazis system. It will show Hitler's attack upon the Western European Democracies was solely due to their obstruction of his march east. It shows that Hitler made no consequential preparation for invading Britain across the Channel. It shows that within a month after the surrender of France and the defeat of the British at Dunkirk, Hitler ordered all ideas and possible preparation for land invasion across the Channel abandoned, because he could not pass the British Navy. It shows that his air blitz against Britain—"the Battle of Britain"—was defeated by Britain's own air force and her steadfastness long before we ever gave her substantial aid.

History shows that Hitler, within three or four months after his victories in the West, resolved to turn his armies against Russia. Hitler had based his war on rapid blitz. When he was stopped by the British at the Channel and by the

Russians under General Winter in November, 1941, he was faced with a long, exhausting war without adequate food, raw materials, or man power. He was subjected to sea blockade and incessant air attack from Britain.

From the day Hitler launched his attack on Russia he was destined either to defeat or exhaustion and was beyond harm to Britain or the United States. History shows that Roosevelt and Churchill knew of Hitler's impending attack on Russia six months before the attack and two months before Lend-Lease and its undeclared war.

Mr. Roosevelt Wanted War

The first proof is his incessant endeavor to create a war spirit in the American people. From 1939 to 1941 he never delivered an address on related subjects that he did not engage in stimulating hate, raising fear, and smearing every opponent of war. He not only stimulated these emotions but he encouraged every available propaganda agency, including his own officials, public committees and the British. The larger proof lies in the fact that with different steps and policies, he could have not only kept the country wholly out of war, but at different times when he was en route to war he could have, with different steps and policies because the world situation had so shifted, retraced the road from which he had already departed back onto the road toward peace. And he could have done this at no danger to his purported chief anxiety—the safety of Britain and the United States.

Those occasions of world shift were:

First. While the subject is as yet partly speculative, history may disclose that had it not been for the confidence of Britain and Poland and France in some assurances that America would join in the war, they never would have made the gigantic blunder of guaranteeing Poland and thus have temporarily diverted Hitler's lightening from Stalin to themselves and a war involving themselves.

Second. At the end of 1940, Britain had won the air Battle of England and Hitler had decided that he could not cross the Channel. This latter was evident from his failure to attempt it for six months after the defeat at Dunkirk. But of far more importance, Roosevelt knew from his own intelligence that Hitler was moving his troops to Eastern Europe for attack upon Russia. This development made the situation no major danger to Britain and to the United States.

Third. By the time the Congress began debate on Lend-Lease, Mr. Roosevelt knew that the situation was even better and he could have turned away from the undeclared war on Germany which he was preparing by this bill and could have confined it to simple aid to Britain by way of finances, munitions supplies and ships, which would have been no violation of international law.

Fourth. After the actual attack on Russia by Hitler in June 1941, no one could any longer doubt the safety of Britain and the United States. Roosevelt could have withdrawn his undeclared naval war on Germany and given Britain the supplies, munitions and ships for Britain's own use and for her to supply Russia if she wished.

Fifth. Even after Mr. Roosevelt's undeclared war on Japan through economic sanctions in July 1941 he could have made peace in the Pacific with the Japanese. In September, 1941, the Japanese made offers and concessions which both the American and British Ambassadors in Japan urged on Roosevelt. It should have been accepted, basically to preserve peace, but also to prevent war on two fronts. Here was his last opportunity to have taken a right road. Had these offers not been kept secret from the American people, they might have demanded acceptance.

Any objective review of the years from 1938 to 1941, with the cold light of history even so far exposed, will demonstrate clearly that it was Mr. Roosevelt who got the United States into the war. He deliberately provoked war upon us by the Japanese, and in so doing he did more injury to Britain in the loss of her possessions and supplies than Hitler could ever have done.

Why Did He Want War?

The natural question will arise as to why he wanted to take the United States into war.

As there was no need for the United States to go to war, it is at least a tenable view held by many responsible non-partisan journals, that Mr. Roosevelt wanted to cover up the failure of the New Deal and six years' attempt to restore employment to ten million idle workmen, to cover up the scandals of the New Deal, and for that purpose he entangled himself in world power politics as a diversion of public mind. His excursion into power politics and his constant raising of fear and emergency secured his re-election but it also appealed to his egotism and his further ambitions.

What Happened to Intellectual Honesty?

In [the–ed.] view of his supporters, he led, with transcendent genius, an obstinate and unwilling people to their national duty. In the view of his opponents, he led a people into an unnecessary and monstrous catastrophe by consuming egotism, by evil intrigue, by intellectual dishonesty, by lies and by violations of the Constitution. Either way, the steps he used were the same.

His intellectual dishonesty is represented by his scores of assurances over three years to the American people that he would never send her sons to war while he was driving to that end, his wholly unconstitutionally undeclared war upon Germany, his constant fanning of war psychosis of fear and hate by misstatement, his vicious attacks upon the non-interventionists, his mis-representation of the real purpose of Lend-Lease, his undeclared war upon Japan by economic sanctions that could only provoke attack by Japan, and his refusal to accept Konoye's proposals, his military alliance with the British and his undertakings to attack Portugal and Japan on Britain's behalf without any authority from Congress, his call to America to make its second crusade for the Four Freedoms which became the mockery of the world and the Atlantic Charter which was conceived in propaganda and became a betrayal of the American good faith. At Teheran both were secretly burned on the altar of appeasement of Stalin and 150 million people consigned to slavery and to fear by night as well as by day, and then Yalta, where Roosevelt sealed this sacrifice and secretly made more commitments while constantly denying all of these.

It is obvious that the American people and the Congress were overwhelm-ingly opposed to our becoming involved in the war right up to Pearl Harbor. This was clear, not only from informal polls of the people and of the Congress, but it is evidenced by the line Mr. Roosevelt followed of not only constantly reassuring that he would not send our sons to war but also by his necessity to dress every measure, whether it be armament, Lend-Lease, convoys, or eco-nomic sanctions, with the camouflage that it will keep us out of war. And all this despite the gigantic propaganda for war through his own speeches, the Administration, the British, and a host of war committees.

The time may come when the American people, in frustration and disgust, will hate the memory of every man who contributed to getting the United States into this war. The attempts to deify them are already failing.

The long view of history will pass some harsh judgments upon Franklin D. Roosevelt, even beyond these foreign policy mis-steps in statesmanship.

Our Situation in the World Today

The net result of intervention was to build up the greatest and most danger-ous dictatorship the world has ever seen. Wise statesmanship would have al-lowed Hitler and Stalin to exhaust each other and thereby not only assuring the freedom of western democracies from the menace which it now meets in every quarter of the world.[2]

With a weak Britain and with our appeasements, we stand alone against a greatly strengthened and most aggressive Russia. Aside from the fact that sixteen months after V-E Day, we have not settled peace with a single nation, we are compelled to rely upon the good will of this aggressive power to implement even the United Nations.

We are today totally unable to secure peace because we have exhausted ourselves economically and morally to build up Red Russia into the domination of both Europe and Asia.

Aside from our weakened position as to Europe and Asia, we have not improved our standing or respect in the Western Hemisphere.

By violation of our basic national principle not to interfere in the internal affairs of nations, we interfere in domestic politics of our neighbors. These actions have a smack of Stalin's puppet governments. These acts deserve condemnation as a form of imperialism and are being so condemned and feared by every Latin-American state.

We did attain a great role the universal Santa Claus, but we are now hated for every suggestion of restriction on our gifts.

I have little need to review the falsities of the Atlantic Charter, of Teheran and of Yalta. At these places every one of the "Four Freedoms" and every promise of the "Atlantic Charter" for which the American people believed they were fighting, were abandoned. The freedom of independent nations and even liberty and the lives of 150,000,000 people were sold down the river— secretly, for Roosevelt denied having entered into any commitments!

The Pied Piper's tunes of the Four Freedoms and the Atlantic Charter are no longer heard in the world.

But hundreds of millions of people have gone into the dark night of slavery because of his desertion of the promises which led them on. And there lies the greatest injury ever done to the soul and honor of America.

The sole redeeming part of the war was the unparalleled action of our men who fought it to victory.

We won the war by the skill of our military officers who had been trained long before Roosevelt came into power and by the abilities and genius of American industry.

---

2. [*Editor's note:* This sentence in Hoover's document is ungrammatical, but if one omits the words "and thereby not only," his meaning seems plain.]

We won it by the courage, the valor and the sacrifice of American men and women for their country. It has brought glory to our race and pride in our people. That glory cannot be dimmed by the statesmanship which misled them and failed to secure the purpose for which they fought.

From the point of view of myself and many others who had seen the sacrifices, the futilities and the failure of America's First Crusade to establish freedom in Europe, there was only one course for our country to pursue in the face of a renewed second World War. That was to stay out, to give Britain such assistance as we possessed in supplies and ships that she might defend herself, to arm ourselves and to wait until the inevitable exhaustion of the dictator nations. When that time arrived, we could, with our reserves of moral, economic and military strength, dictate a constructive peace and we could restore the wreck of civilization. We believed and rightly, that the exhaustion and frustration of the American people by participation in the war would render us impotent in the face of the ascent of evil forces inevitably to rise from the burning of civilization over two-thirds of the earth.

On the other hand, by preservation of the United States as a sanctuary of decency, freedom and civilization, we could again set Europe on the road of recuperation and progress. That these views are no afterthought is amply evident in my many addresses at this time.

The Hope of the Future

Despite the physical losses and the moral and political disaster to America, I, nevertheless, have faith that we will grow strong again; that the march of progress will be renewed. I shall not live to see that recovery. My confidence rests not upon American cities, on government, or on demagogic intellectuals, but on the millions of cottages throughout the land where men and women are still resolute in morals and freedom. In those hearts the spirit of America still lives. The boys and girls from those homes will some day throw off these disasters and frustrations and will recreate their America again.

A Footnote on Winston Churchill

May 10, 1949

As ONE OF the earliest, and most determinedly revisionist, historians of World War II, Hoover was obliged to take account of Winston S. Churchill's multivolume *Second World War,* published between 1948 and 1953. Hoover seems to have read this rival narrative carefully. He greatly admired its style but not its substance. In a footnote written in 1949 and intended for his Magnum Opus, Hoover lambasted Churchill's first volume, *The Gathering Storm.* The note made clear Hoover's own preference for the foreign policies of Churchill's predecessor as British prime minister: Neville Chamberlain.

The final typed version of this footnote, dated May 10, 1949, along with its antecedents, can be found in the Herbert C. Hoover Papers, Box 6, "M.O. 13" envelope, Hoover Institution Archives.

5/10/49

Churchill

One of the most difficult problems with which the objective historian will need deal is that of Winston Churchill's account of the origins and course of World War II in "The Gathering Storm." His position to command material, his brilliant style, his dramatic descriptions, carry confidence. But his personal prejudices, his constant rationalization after the events with a persistent evasion of facts and realities are much short of objective truth. He ignores his own published attitudes at the time of events and when it suits his purposes, he ignores the vital and fundamental forces of the time. These forces were:

First. Hitler was preparing a land war; his face was turned east for "Operation Lebensraum"; his attitudes toward the Western Democracies were a determination to brook no interference, even at the cost of preliminary war with them. Stalin's Red Imperialism represented an equally dynamic aggressive force. His primary fear was Hitler. His policies were predicated upon avoidance of war with Germany. But more potent was his intent to promote possible war between the Western Democracies and Hitler as the foundation for world domination by communism. Yet Churchill's actions and writings assume Hitler as the major enemy of democracy to the neglect of the other equally potent enemy.

Second. He ignores the policy of Britain, which no Englishman probably ever will admit, from 1934 to prior to the Polish Guarantee (March 26, 1939).[1] That policy was by acquiescence or otherwise to strengthen Germany as against Russia. It was the balance of power policy which the British had practiced for 300 years as their defense against domination from the Continent.

Churchill's book is a mass of bitter attacks upon Baldwin and Chamberlain who had kept him out of office for years, thus thwarting his political ambitions—a fact that accounts for much of his vindictiveness. His major contention is that their policies had no direction and gave England no adequate preparedness; that they were supine and unintelligent.

If they had not departed from their traditional "balance of power" policy with the Polish Guarantee of March 26, 1939, they would have kept the Western Democracies out of war, at least until the two satans were greatly exhausted by warring on each other. Chamberlain, driven by the attacks of Churchill and his friends, together with the loss of prestige from Hitler's betrayal in marching into Prague, committed the most gigantic blunder of trying to stop Hitler's march east by the Polish Guarantee, without having previously settled an alliance with Russia. Churchill supported this guarantee at the time, but in his book, ten years later, he spends much space on demonstrating its futility.

Subsequently he attacked the Prime Minister bitterly for not obtaining an alliance with Russia after the Polish Guarantee and elaborated upon it extensively in his book. In these attacks he ignores the price demanded by Russia of effectual domination of the Baltic States and Eastern Poland which no decent statesman could accept, but which Stalin secured from the Germans in August, 1939. Churchill, at the time, repeatedly demanded that Stalin's terms, whatever they were, should be accepted. He implies that Stalin was genuine and that Chamberlain was incompetent. In his book, despite all subsequent revelations, he dismisses the crux of this negotiation with a statement that these dispatches have never been published. Yet as Prime Minister later on, he

---

1. [*Editor's note:* March 31, 1939. For the text of Prime Minister Neville Chamberlain's announcement, see *New York Times*, April 1, 1939, p.3.]

must have known what they were and from collateral evidence it was obvious what the price was but Churchill does not mention it.

He says, "There can be no doubt even in the after light that Britain and France should have accepted the Russian offer" (p. 262). This sentence was written nine years after and the "after light" could well be the fact that Churchill, in the course of his statesmanship of the war, had joined in the surrender of all these independent democracies to Russian slavery. At the time, however, Chamberlain and his ministry seemed to think such a transaction was immoral.

However, the case against Churchill's book will not rest on my own observations. Others have exposed chapter after chapter.

A Search for Communist Influences in the Roosevelt Administration

November 24, 1949

IN THE WAKE of the sensational Alger Hiss espionage and perjury case of 1948–49, and other revelations of Soviet spying against the United States in the 1940s, Hoover became very interested in the scope and significance of communist infiltration of the United States government during the Roosevelt and Truman administrations. His letter of November 24, 1949, to the conservative newspaper columnist George Sokolsky, is particularly significant in this regard, for it seems to have led to a new component of the evolving Magnum Opus: exposure of nefarious, leftwing influences on American foreign policies after World War II, especially vis-à-vis China.

Eventually he had an assistant who compiled data for him on Communist and pro-Communist persons who had held jobs in the federal government during the Roosevelt and Truman years. Hoover used this database to write what became chapters 4 and 5 of *Freedom Betrayed*.

The document printed here is Hoover's carbon copy of his letter. It is filed in "Sokolsky, George," Post-Presidential Individual File, Herbert Hoover Papers, Herbert Hoover Presidential Library.

The Waldorf Astoria Towers

New York, New York

November 24, 1949

My dear George:

I want to get a list of the fellow-travelers and Communists (where known as such) in the Roosevelt Administration, separately for each year from 1933 to 1945.

I wonder if Mr. Matthews[1] or Mr. Sterling[2], or some similarly informed person would undertake such a job for me—for a remuneration? Do you know their whereabouts or possibilities?

Yours faithfully,

Mr. George Sokolsky
300 West End Avenue
New York, New York

---

1. [*Editor's note:* Probably J. B. Matthews, a former research director of the House Committee on Un-American Activities. Matthews maintained a massive file of documentation on Communist front organizations and the Americans who had joined these groups in the 1930s and 1940s. Much admired in countersubversive, anti-Communist circles, Matthews later served as a confidant of, and briefly as an aide to, Senator Joseph McCarthy.]

2. [*Editor's note:* Possibly Robert E. Stripling, chief investigator for the House Committee on Un-American Activities.]

"Mr. Winston Churchill"

n.d.

[circa 1950–1953–ed.]

As HOOVER CONTINUED work on his burgeoning Magnum Opus, he toyed for a time with the idea of creating a series of appendices. The document partially reproduced here, entitled "Mr. Winston Churchill," was probably written between 1950 and 1953 and designated around 1954 as Appendix 4. It consists of a brief appraisal of Churchill followed by a much enlarged and fortified version of the footnote printed on pp. 861–63 as Document 14.

In each of these documents Hoover displayed an antipathy toward Churchill that he toned down in the final drafts of *Freedom Betrayed*.

Hoover eventually abandoned the idea of including a set of appendices in his Magnum Opus. His extended commentary on Winston Churchill was therefore never used.

Document 16 is found in the Arthur Kemp Papers, Box 26, "Appendices 1–8" folder, Hoover Institution Archives.

. . . . .

I had occasion to become acquainted with Churchill in the First World War, and later with Baldwin and Chamberlain. Intellectual integrity was not Churchill's strong point; it was the outstanding quality of the other two. Churchill possessed a surpassing power of oratory and word pictures; the other two lacked both these qualities. Churchill's character was absolutely ruthless; the other two were men of scrupulous regard for the rights of others. Churchill was irresponsible in statement; while the other two statesmen were the soul of honest presentation. They were, therefore, no equal for Churchill in the arts of demagoguery. Churchill has imprinted on the world the notion that these two statesmen were inept, without courage, supine, and without direction in their policies.

Nor was Churchill the "Liberal" which he called himself. He had opposed the Wilson program of a democratized Europe at the time of Versailles.[1] Churchill of course, was opposed to Communism, but future historians must assess upon him some responsibility in bringing on the war between the Western Democracies and Hitler and, as such, being a powerful supporter of Stalin.

One of the most difficult problems with which the objective historian will need to deal is Winston Churchill's account of the origins of World War II in *The Gathering Storm*. His position to command material, his brilliant style, his dramatic descriptions, carry confidence. But his personal prejudices, his constant rationalization after the events with a persistent misstatement and evasion of facts and realities, are much short of objective truth. He ignores his own published attitudes at the time of events and, when it suits his purposes, he ignores the vital and fundamental forces of the time.

His book sparkles with two major obsessions:

First. That Hitler was the primary enemy of mankind and must be polished off before Stalin, rather than allowing the inevitable clash of these two Satans to weaken their power.

Second. His bitterness toward Baldwin and Chamberlain, who would not permit him in their ministries. His major contention is that their policies had no direction and gave England no adequate preparedness; that they were supine and unintelligent.

His bitter attacks on Chamberlain, together with the loss of prestige from Hitler's betrayal in marching into Prague, drove the Prime Minister into the most gigantic blunder of trying to stop Hitler's march east by the Polish Guarantee. If the British had not departed from their traditional "balance of power" policy with the Polish Guarantee of March 26, 1939,[2] they would have kept the Western Democracies out of war, at least until the two satans were greatly exhausted by warring on each other.

Churchill supported the Polish guarantee at the time but in his book, ten years later, he spends much space on demonstrating its futility.

Churchill elaborates extensively on his claims of Chamberlain's errors. In these attacks he ignores the price demanded by Russia of effectual domination

1. [*Editor's note:* Here Hoover placed the following footnote:
See Herbert Hoover, *America's First Crusade* (Charles Scribner's Sons, 1941). In 1946, in *The Gathering Storm,* he [Churchill–ed.] was to assert that the Wilson solution was "insane" and that there should have been the restoration of the monarchy in Germany and the resurrection of the Austrian Hungarian Empire, and the continuation of the British-Japanese military alliance. (Houghton, Mifflin Co., Boston, 1948).]

2. [*Editor's note:* March 31, 1939. See p. 862, note 1.]

of the Baltic States and Eastern Poland, which no decent statesman could accept, and which became clear long before the book was written, for the annexation had already taken place. In his book, despite all subsequent revelations, he dismisses the crux of the negotiation for an alliance with Stalin with a statement that these dispatches have never been published.

He says, "There can be no doubt even in the after light that Britain and France should have accepted the Russian offer" (page 262). This sentence was written nine years after and the "after light" could well be a cover for the fact that he, in the course of his statesmanship of the war, had joined in the surrender of all these independent democracies to Russian slavery. At the time, however, Chamberlain and his ministry seemed to consider such a transaction immoral.

However, the case against Churchill's book will not rest on my own observations. Others have exposed chapter after chapter.

Hanson W. Baldwin, in the *New York Times* of May 9th, 1948, with authentic records from both sides of the war, proves Churchill's statements false as to the relative military supplies and productive capacity of the Axis nations and the Democracies. After reciting the facts, Baldwin mildly remarks:

> "These conclusions are at sharp variance with some of Mr. Churchill's statements."

A staff study of the whole record from all sources by Major General C. F. Robinson was available to Mr. Churchill when his book was written which certainly invalidates pages of Mr. Churchill's dramatic description of the time.

Francis Nielson in the *American Journal of Economics and Sociology* of January 1949 (Vol. 8, No. 2, pp. 193–208), says:

> When I finished reading Winston Churchill's book, 'The Gathering Storm,' I was foolish enough to predict that no one at present would have the courage to point out the inaccuracies it contained. I was mistaken. In an article published in the *New York Times* of May 9, 1948, Hanson Baldwin reviewed a staff study made under the direction of Major General C. F. Robinson, entitled 'Foreign Logistical Organizations and Methods.' This report was prepared for the Secretary of the Army. Baldwin tells us that the facts of this survey take 'sharp issue with some of Winston Churchill's contentions.' [. . . –*ed.*]
>
> [. . . –*ed.*] There were books enough in circulation to edify a schoolboy of sixteen; and many of them published in England presented the facts that Churchill ignored from the beginning. . . .

There are so many passages in this work to which the industrious and well-informed student will take exception that it is difficult to know which one or two should be considered in a critique. But it is essential for the reader to remember that Churchill is not only a protagonist, but one who shows in his work that it was necessary for him to defend his actions. Therefore, many of his recordings should not be accepted as history but as the opinions of a man who has a personal case to present. . . .

As an example of how Mr. Churchill has gone to work to create an atmosphere of his own making, we may take the case of the pledge to Poland given in March, 1939. If the student will turn to the letters that he wrote to himself in 'Step by Step,' he will find the last four dated after the pledge was given. In the one entitled 'The Russian Counterpoise,' Churchill writes to himself as follows:

> . . . The preservation and integrity of Poland must be regarded as a cause commanding the regard of all the world. There is every reason to believe that the Polish nation intend to fight for life and freedom. They have a fine Army, of which now more than 1,000,000 men are mobilized. The Poles have always fought well, and an army which comprehends its cause is doubly strong. . . .

$$[\,\ldots-ed.]$$

The above is all we have from him before the war began about the pledge which many have believed did more to bring about the conflict than any other action taken up to that time. The statement he makes in the letter dated May 4, 1939, is so moderate that not a note of alarm is sounded in it. Writing in 'The Gathering Storm,' long after the event, he presents us with the following tirade:

> And now, when every one of these aids and advantages has been squandered and thrown away, Great Britain advances, leading France by the hand, to guarantee the integrity of Poland—of that very Poland which with hyena appetite had only six months before joined in the pillage and destruction of the Czechoslovak State. . . .

$$[\,\ldots-ed.]$$

It would be an almost interminable exercise for the most industrious budding historian to go through Mr. Churchill's works published since 1932 and present a comparative portrait of him as he was in thought and action before the war and as he appears in this volume. The mass of contradictions of attitude of mind is most bewildering—certainly beyond the understanding of what is called 'the intelligent reader.' . . .

Joseph P. Kennedy, American Ambassador to Britain in this period, knowing the facts intimately, after pointing out several deficiencies in Churchill's account, says (*New York Times,* Sept. 26, 1948):

> Other judgments in *The Gathering Storm* suffer from the same cavalier treatment of recorded facts. They are numerous. Churchill's misquotations of documents that are public make it difficult for one to rely on his quotations from documents that are not generally available. Other facts not yet made public may further bring into question Mr. Churchill's position as a raconteur of history. They will not, of course, derogate from the vividness of his style.

I have found it necessary to reject every fact, statement, and conclusion of Churchill which cannot be confirmed from other evidence, and to discard much of his text. However, no one can fail to admire the fire and drama of his presentation.

Hoover Assesses Franklin Roosevelt's Wartime Record

1953

BY THE SPRING of 1953, Hoover's Magnum Opus had grown to 1001 printed pages, set in page proofs ready for publication. The following passage appears in Chapter 88 (specifically, pp. 990–93) of this version, now entitled *Lost Statesmanship*. Once more, Hoover's relentless, prosecutorial fervor is striking.

This excerpt is found in the Herbert C. Hoover Papers, Box 11, "Box 11, M.O. 21" folder, Hoover Institution Archives.

WE WON THE MILITARY WAR by the skill of our military officers who had been trained long before Roosevelt came into power and by the abilities and genius of American industry. We won it by the courage, the valor and the sacrifice of American men and women for their country. It has brought glory to our race and pride in our people. That glory cannot be dimmed by the statesmanship which failed to secure the purpose for which they fought. They won the war, but our leaders lost the peace. And they did irreparable damage to the ideals and soul of America.

Excuses

The direct responsibility for Roosevelt's plunging the American people into war requires answer to the assertions of his associates in the adventure who naturally must justify his conduct. They make many claims.

First, the claim is made that we went to war to protect ourselves from Hitler and his Japanese and Italian dictator allies, including the Western Hemisphere.

Second, that for our own survival we had to save Britain from defeat and destruction.

Third, that we were attacked by the Japanese without provocation and could do nothing but defend ourselves.

The answers are simple:

As to the first assertion, neither Hitler, Mussolini, nor Tojo wanted war with the United States or to invade the Western Hemisphere; they tried to evade war with us even with the great provocation of undeclared war from Roosevelt. Their faces were not in our direction—that of Hitler was east, toward Russia; that of Tojo was west, toward Asia. Even had they designs upon the Western Hemisphere, the Atlantic Ocean of 3,000 miles and the Pacific Ocean of 6,000 miles were our impregnable moat. With our Navy, Army and Air Force to protect it, there was never a remote possibility of their landing and sustaining an army even in the remote parts of the Western Hemisphere. Beyond all this summation of military fact the post war records of those countries confirm this conclusion. Even assuming Hitler, Mussolini and Tojo had these notions, the day when Hitler attacked Stalin these monsters were destined to exhaust each other and any dream of conquest of the Western Hemisphere vanished.

Second. Britain, with even her narrow moat of only 25 miles of the English Channel, proved invulnerable from a German army crossing against her navy. Even Hitler at the height of his conquest realized this and required his generals to dismiss such notions. Britain was endangered of great physical injury from the air blitz during the "Battle of Britain," but with no assistance from the United States she, in 60 days, defeated even this assault. When the positive knowledge of Hitler's attack on Russia came to the American Government in mid-January, 1945 [1941–ed.], together with the actual attack in June, England was not only decisively assured against defeat, but victory itself loomed as the outcome. Whether Hitler won or lost, the Red Army with their allies, General Space, General Winter, General Long Communications, and General Scorched Earth, was destined to leave the Germans exhausted.

Third. Roosevelt's provocative acts against Japan included an alliance with Britain against her long months before Pearl Harbor. The statements of our leaders were constantly provocative. Roosevelt engaged for a year in increasing economic sanctions, finally culminating in complete sanctions in July, 1941, five months before Pearl Harbor. The sanctions were war on Japan with all war disasters to them except the shooting. He was repeatedly warned that no nation of dignity would submit to such a provocation—least of all, a nation in which hari-kiri in presence of failure was a part of its religion.

Fourth. His supporters attempt his defense by laying his failures to Stalin's wickedness and betrayals.

These excuses require but little analysis. It is to be supposed that a states-man of the stature capable of leading the American people would inform himself of the history, the beliefs, the policies, and the character of leaders with whom he chose to make partners. Over years before the war and on multitudes of occasions, Stalin had publicly proclaimed his fidelity to Lenin's teaching and himself confirmed that his purpose was to envelop the world in Communism; that agreements and treaties had no validity if they obstructed these processes. His character was indicated in headlines over years recount-ing the thousands of even his own colleagues whom he had put to death in order to further his own ambitions. Roosevelt knew within a month that Sta-lin had violated his agreement of recognition by the United States in 1933. He knew of Stalin's betrayal of the democracies of Western Europe by his alli-ance with Hitler in August, 1939. As to the sanctity of agreements, he could not have been ignorant of Stalin's violations on this occasion of over thirty non-aggression treaties with Poland, Finland, Estonia, Latvia, Lithuania and Rumania. Roosevelt himself had denounced these actions.

His defenders even put forward the thesis that had he lived he could have beguiled Stalin into ways of rectitude. But beguilement had already failed at Teheran and Yalta. The less defense of him as betrayed by Stalin and the effectiveness of his powers of beguilement, the better for his reputation in history.

What Impelled Roosevelt into These Policies?

It is of some importance to inquire what pressures led Roosevelt into these swamps of lost statesmanship. It is not my purpose here to analyze his char-acter except so far as it bears on these questions. In 1940 he was faced with the failure of the New Deal. At no time in the eight years of his administra-tion prior to the war did he have less than about the same 10,000,000 unem-ployed and 18,000,000 people on relief which existed when he was elected. He had abandoned all the normal processes of recovery for collectivist ac-tion. Every other country with a free economy except Canada and France had not only recovered but gone beyond their pre-depression production and employment levels within three years after he came to office. Canadian economy was dominated by the failure in the United States. France had not recovered because, under Blum, she had adopted the New Deal. The judg-ment of history will likely be that resort to foreign power politics was at this time with no further thought than to divert the public mind—a policy as old as Machiavelli.

A second force pressing him step by step to war was his own left-wing mentality and his left-wing officials in government. He was not a Communist. But his left-wing inclinations led him to incorporate in his administration many avowed socialists, fellow-travelers, and actual members of the Communist Party. They were a potent force in his administration and his elections for six years before and for four years after Stalin's 22 months of lapse into the alliance with Hitler.

A third force impelling him was his consuming ego that he was a master of military strategy. It led him to policies of military victory without regard to political consequences. This ego also pressed upon him the desire to become a "War President." In his interpretation it was war and not peace that made the presidents who stood out in American history. Again this ego drove him to seek for the first time in all our history to break the two-term tradition by an election for the third and fourth times. Peace, war and national peril were in turn to be his campaign issues. His third term was won on a promise of peace in a war-torn world:

> Mothers and fathers, I give you one more assurance. I have said this before, but I shall say it again and again: Your boys are not going to be sent into any foreign wars. . . .

His fourth term was won on Lincoln's war issue of not changing horses in the midst of the stream. He was aided by his misleading of the great block of Polish voters.

Finally in defense of his name, Mr. Roosevelt's supporters assert that he led with transcendant adroitness an obstinate and unwilling people to their national duty.

In the view of his opponents, and the record abundantly shows, he led a people into a monstrous catastrophe by a multitude of sequent intellectual dishonesties, consuming ambitions, lies, intrigue, and by violations of the Constitution he was sworn to defend.

"A Review of Lost Statesmanship— 19 Times in 7 Years"

1953

THESE ARE THE FINAL, climactic pages (994–1001) of the last chapter (89) of the 1953 version of Hoover's Magnum Opus, which for a time he entitled *Lost Statesmanship*. These pages were probably written very early in 1953, not long after the presidential election of 1952. In this chapter Hoover summed up, with remarkable candor and intensity, his revisionist indictment of the Roosevelt-Truman foreign policy record. "I was opposed to the war and every step of policies in it," he wrote. "I have no apologies, no regrets."

This document is in the Herbert C. Hoover Papers, Box 11, "Box 11, M.O. 21" folder, Hoover Institution Archives.

Chapter 89
A Review of Lost Statesmanship—19 Times in 7 Years

There are those who still defend Roosevelt and Truman by blaming Hitler and Stalin for all the calamities which have come upon the world. That they were malignant and malign figures in human history needs no demonstration.

Any review of American and British lost statesmanship in dealing with them, however, has no excuse in history. Without these gigantic errors these calamities could not have come to the Western world.

I shall list those major occasions here lest the reader, in this maze of actions, has forgotten who was responsible for what and when. I refer the reader to those chapters in this memoir where the facts and reasons for their conviction are given.

The World Economic Conference of 1933

First. The first time (of importance) that Roosevelt became lost in international statesmanship was his destruction of the 1933 World Economic

Conference. This Conference was arranged by British Prime Minister Mac-Donald and myself to take place in January, 1933. Owing to the election of Mr. Roosevelt it was postponed until June. At that time the world was just beginning to recover from the world-wide depression but was engaged in bitter currency wars and multiplying trade barriers. The preliminary work had been done by experts. Roosevelt called ten Prime Ministers to Washington with whom he agreed to restore the gold standard in international transactions. Suddenly during the Conference he repudiated ("the bombshell") these undertakings and the Conference cracked and died without accomplishment. His own Secretary of State Hull explicitly denounced this action as the roots of World War II.[1]

The Recognition of Communist Russia in 1933

Second. Roosevelt's second lost statesmanship was in recognition of Communist Russia in November, 1933. Four Presidents and five Secretaries of State—Democrats as well as Republicans—had (with knowledge of the whole purpose and methods of international Communism) refused such action. They knew and said the Communists would be able to penetrate the United States, carrying their germs of destruction of religious faith, freedom of men and independence of nations. They considered our recognition of Soviet Russia would give it prestige and force among other nations. All of Roosevelt's puerile agreements with them that they would not deal in their wickedness within our borders were on the record repudiated in less than forty-eight hours. A long train of Communists and fellow travelers were taken into the highest levels of administration, Fifth Column action spread over the country, with a long series of traitorous acts during his remaining twelve years in the Presidency.[2]

Munich

Third. I am not disposed to condemn the agreement at Munich in September 1938 for transfer of Sudeten Germans to the Reich because it was a hideous heritage from Versailles which made such action inevitable. However, by Munich Hitler opened the gates for consummation of his repeated

---

1. Cf. Chapter 1. [*Editor's note:* All footnotes in this document are Hoover's.]
2. Cf. Chapter 2.

determinations to invade Russia. Having gone that far in providing for the inevitable war between the dictators, the lost statesmanship was then trying to stop these monsters from mutual destruction.

The British-French Guarantee of Poland and Rumania in 1939

Fourth. The fourth abysmal loss of statesmanship was when the British and French guaranteed the independence of Poland and Rumania at the end of March, 1939. It was at this point that the European democracies reversed their previous policies of keeping hands off the inevitable war between Hitler and Stalin.

It was probably the greatest blunder in the whole history of European power diplomacy. Britain and France were helpless to save Poland from invasion. By this act, however, they threw the bodies of democracy between Hitler and Stalin. By their actions they not only protected Stalin from Hitler but they enabled him to sell his influence to the highest bidder. The Allies did bid but Stalin's price was annexation of defenseless people of the Baltic States and East Poland, a moral price which the Allies could not meet. Stalin got his price from Hitler.

Yet Hitler had no intention of abandoning his determination to expand in Southeast Europe and to destroy the Communist Vatican in Moscow. But now he must of necessity first neutralize the Western Democracies which he proceeded to do.

The long train of the hideous World War II started from the blunder of the Polish guarantees. Roosevelt had some part in these power politics but the record is yet too incomplete to establish how much. Churchill, not yet in the government, had contributed something by goading Chamberlain to desperate action after his appeasement at Munich.[3]

United States Undeclared War

Fifth. The fifth major blunder in statesmanship was when Roosevelt, in the winter of 1941, threw the United States into undeclared war with Germany and Japan in total violation of promises upon which he had been elected a few weeks before.[4]

---

3. Cf. Chapters 18, 19, 27.
4. Cf. Chapter 30.

Failure in Watchful Waiting

Sixth. In the weeks before Lend-Lease and its war powers were forced upon the American people, Roosevelt knew definitely of Hitler's determination to attack Russia, and he informed the Russians of it. He should have turned away from the undeclared war on Germany, confined Lend-Lease to simple aid to Britain by way of finances, to buy munitions, supplies and ships, thus keeping within international law. Statesmanship at that moment demanded imperiously a policy of watchful waiting.[5]

Alliance with Stalin

Seventh. Indeed the greatest loss of statesmanship in all American history was the tacit American alliance and support of Communist Russia when Hitler made his attack in June, 1941. Even the false theory that American military strength was needed to save Britain had now visibly vanished. By diversion of Nazi furies into the swamps of Russia, no one could any longer doubt the safety of Britain and all the Western world. These monstrous dictators were bound to exhaust themselves no matter who won. Even if Hitler won military victory, he would be enmeshed for years trying to hold these people in subjection. And he was bound even in victory to exhaust his military strength—and the Russians were bound to destroy any sources of supplies he might have hoped for. His own generals opposed his action.

American aid to Russia meant victory for Stalin and the spread of Communism over the world. Statesmanship again imperiously cried to keep out, be armed to the teeth and await their mutual exhaustion. When that day came there would have been an opportunity for the United States and Britain to use their strength to bring a real peace and security to the free world. No greater opportunity for lasting peace ever came to a President and he muffed it.[6]

The Economic Sanctions on Japan of July, 1941

Eighth. The eighth gigantic error in Roosevelt's statesmanship was the total economic sanctions on Japan one month later, at the end of July, 1941. The sanctions were war in every essence except shooting. Roosevelt had been

---

5. Cf. Chapter 32.
6. Cf. Chapter 33.

warned time and again by his own officials that such provocation would sooner or later bring reprisals of war.[7]

Refusal to Accept Konoye's Peace Proposals

Ninth. The ninth time statesmanship was wholly lost was Roosevelt's contemptuous refusal of Prime Minister Konoye's proposals for peace in the Pacific of September, 1941. The acceptance of these proposals was prayerfully urged by both the American and British Ambassadors in Japan. The terms Konoye proposed would have accomplished every American purpose except possibly the return of Manchuria[8]—and even this was thrown open to discussion. The cynic will recall that Roosevelt was willing to provoke a great war on his flank over this remote question and then gave Manchuria to Communist Russia.[9]

Refusal to Accept a 3 Months'
Stand-Still Agreement with Japan

Tenth. The tenth loss of statesmanship was the refusal to accept the proposals which his Ambassador informed him came from the Emperor of Japan for a three months' stand-still agreement in November, 1941. Our military officials strongly urged it on Roosevelt. Japan was then alarmed that Russia might defeat her ally, Hitler. Ninety days' delay would have taken all the starch out of Japan and kept war out of the Pacific. As the Stimson diary disclosed, Roosevelt and his officials were searching for a method to stimulate an overt act from the Japanese. Then Hull issued his foolish ultimatum and we were defeated at Pearl Harbor.

The train of losses and this Japanese victory in the Japanese occupation of all South Asia were incalculable. Further, with the loss of sea control, Hitler and Togo were able to destroy our shipping in sight of our own shores.[10]

The Demand for Unconditional Surrender

Eleventh. The eleventh gigantic error in Roosevelt's statesmanship was demand for "Unconditional Surrender" at Casablanca in January, 1943, where

---

7. Cf. Chapter 37.
8. It had already been ceded to Japan by China in the T'ang Ku agreement of May 31, 1933.
9. Cf. Chapter 38.
10. Cf. Chapters 38, 39.

without our military, or even Churchill's advice, he was seeking a headline. It played into the hands of every enemy militarist and propagandist; it prolonged the war with Germany, Japan and Italy. And in the end major concessions in surrender were given to both Japan and Italy. It held out no hope of peace to the Germans if they got rid of the Nazis. The war to the bitter end left no semblance of a structure in Germany upon which to build again.[11]

The Sacrifice of the Baltic States and East Poland at Moscow, October, 1943

Twelfth. The twelfth error of lost statesmanship was the sacrifice of free nations at the Foreign Ministers meeting at Moscow, in October, 1943. Here amid words of freedom and democracy not a word of protest was made against the known Russian intentions to annex the Baltic States, East Poland, East Finland, Bessarabia and Bukovina (which he had in his agreement with Hitler). This acquiescence marked the abandonment of the last word of the Four Freedoms and the Atlantic Charter.[12]

Teheran and Its Sacrifice of Seven More Nations

Thirteenth. The thirteenth and possibly one of the greatest of all confused wanderings in Roosevelt's and Churchill's statesmanship was at Teheran in December, 1943. Here was confirmation of the acquiescence at the Moscow Conference of the annexations; here was the acceptance of Stalin's doctrine of a periphery "of friendly border states"—the puppet Communist governments over seven nations. Fidelity to international morals and their own promises of independence of nations and free men demanded that Roosevelt and Churchill at Teheran stand firm against Stalin once and for all. There were by this time no such military perils of Stalin's making a separate peace that could justify these agreements, acquiescences and appeasements.[13]

Yalta—the Secret Agreements on the Downfall of Nations

Fourteenth. The fourteenth fatal loss of statesmanship was by Roosevelt and Churchill at Yalta in February, 1945. Not only were all Stalin's encroachments

---

11. Cf. Chapter 42.
12. Cf. Chapter 46.
13. Cf. Chapter 47.

on the independence of a dozen nations ratified, but with a long series of secret agreements other malign forces were set in motion which will continue
to plague the world with international dangers for generations. Knowing that
Stalin had already created Communist puppet governments over seven nations, Roosevelt and Churchill sought to camouflage their lost statesmanship with gadgets entitled "free and unfettered" elections, "representation of
all liberal elements." Even the strongest defender on military grounds of appeasement at Teheran could no longer defend it at Yalta. Here at least a stand
might have been made for decency and free mankind which would have left
America with cleaner hands and the moral respect of free men.[14]

Refusal of Japanese Peace Proposals of May–July, 1945

Fifteenth. The fifteenth time of lost statesmanship was in respect to Japan in
May, June and July, 1945. Truman refused to take notice of the Japanese white
flags. Truman was not obligated to Roosevelt's "Unconditional Surrender"
folly. It had been denounced by our own military leaders in Europe. Peace
could have been had with Japan with only one concession. That was the preservation of the Mikado who was the spiritual as well as secular head of the
state. His position was rooted in a thousand years of Japanese religious faith
and tradition. And we finally conceded this after hundreds of thousands of
human lives had been sacrificed.[15]

Potsdam

Sixteenth. The sixteenth time of blind statesmanship was Truman at Potsdam.
Power had now passed to inexperienced men on the democratic countries
and the Communists had their way at every consequential point. The whole
Potsdam agreement was a series of ratifications and amplifications of the previous surrenders to Stalin. Not only were all the Communist annexations and
puppets further cemented to Stalin but the provisions as to government in
Germany and Austria were so set as to send parts of these states into Stalin's
bosom. The result of reparations policies was to load the American taxpayers with billions of the cost for relief of idle Germans and stifle the recovery
of Germany and thus of Europe for years. The wickedness of slavery of war

---

14. Cf. Chapters 54, 55.
15. Cf. Chapter 61.

prisoners, the expelling of whole peoples from their homes was ratified and amplified from Yalta.

Beyond all this, against advice from leading men, the ultimatum was issued to Japan of unconditional surrender without the saving clause allowing them to retain the Mikado recommended by a score of experienced American voices. The Japanese, in reply, asked only for this concession, which was met with the atomic bomb—and then conceded in the end.[16]

Dropping the Atomic Bomb

Seventeenth. The seventeenth wandering of American statesmanship was Truman's immoral order to drop the atomic bomb on the Japanese. Not only had Japan been repeatedly suing for peace but it was the act of unparalleled brutality in all American history. It will forever weigh heavily on the American conscience.[17]

Giving China to Mao Tse-Tung

Eighteenth. The eighteenth series of steps in loss of statesmanship was by Truman, Marshall and Acheson in respect to China. Beginning with Roosevelt's insistence to Chiang Kai-shek of a Communist coalition government there followed Roosevelt's hideous secret agreement as to China at Yalta which gave Mongolia and, in effect, Manchuria to Russia. Truman sacrificed all China to the Communists by insistence of his left-wing advisors and his appointment of General Marshall to execute their will. He must be assessed with a gigantic loss of statesmanship in those policies which in the end made 450,000,000 Asiatic peoples a Communist puppet state under Moscow.[18]

The Dragon's Teeth of World War III

Nineteenth. From the Moscow, the Teheran, Yalta and the Potsdam Conferences, the policies as to China, the dragon's teeth of a third world war were sown in every quarter of the world and we were to see "the cold war" over years and finally the hideous war in Korea and the feeble North Atlantic Alliance with all its dangers of American defeat again.[19]

---

16. Cf. Chapters 61, 62.
17. Cf. Chapter 62.
18. Cf. Chapters 51, 82.
19. Cf. Chapters 82, 83, 84.

The End

I do not need end these volumes with more than a few sentences. I was opposed to the war and every step of policies in it. I have no apologies, no regrets.

I had warned the American people time and again against becoming involved. I stated repeatedly its only end would be to promote Communism over the earth; that we would impoverish the United States and the whole world. The situation of the world today is my vindication.

Despite these physical losses and these moral political disasters, and these international follies, Americans can have faith that we will grow strong again; that the march of progress will sometime be renewed. Despite the drift to collectivism, despite degeneration in government, despite the demagogic intellectuals, despite the corruption in our government and the moral corruptions of our people, we still hold to Christianity, we still have the old ingenuity in our scientific and industrial progress. We have 35 million children marching through our schools and 2,500,000 in our institutions of higher learning. Sometime these forces will triumph over the ills in American life. The promise of a greater America abides in the millions of cottages throughout the land, where men and women are still resolute in freedom. In their hearts the spirit of America still lives. The boys and girls from those homes will some day throw off these disasters and frustrations and will re-create their America again.

The election of a Republican Administration in 1952 is the sign of this turning.

Hoover to Arthur Kemp

May 1, 1954

AFTER REACHING A crescendo in early 1953, Hoover spent much of the next ten years revising, updating, and condensing his Magnum Opus. As the document at hand attests, he continued to seek the assistance of his long-time aide in the project, Professor Arthur Kemp, who was now teaching at Claremont Men's College in California.

Hoover's instructions to Kemp reflected two distinct impulses: (1) an ongoing passion for accuracy and the mining of every possible source of documentation; and (2) a newfound desire on Hoover's part to be (or at least appear to be) "more objective." Hence his uneasiness about his book's polemical title, and his willingness to reconsider and even suppress some of his "acid remarks" about Churchill and Roosevelt. This new sensitivity about fairness and objectivity presaged a gradual shift in the tone of the Magnum Opus in coming years.

Hoover's carbon copy of this document is in "Kemp, Arthur," Post-Presidential Individual File, Herbert Hoover Papers, Herbert Hoover Presidential Library.

The Waldorf Astoria Towers
New York, New York
May 1, 1954

Dear Art:

Mrs. Nickel[1] will give you the latest MSS. You will find it considerably improved. It now falls into two volumes, one before and one after Pearl Harbor.

I enclose a memo about the job.

You can occupy the spare office next to mine on the 11th floor of the Library. Mrs. McMullin[2] can do your typing, and Mrs. Nickel will find anything

---

1. [*Editor's note:* Hazel Lyman Nickel was on the staff of the Hoover Institution on War, Revolution and Peace.]

2. [*Editor's note:* Dare Stark McMullin, a long-time friend of Hoover (and a former secretary of Mrs. Hoover), worked at the Hoover Institution.]

you want from my files. I do not believe there is anything from this source that we do not have.

Yours faithfully,

Dr. Arthur Kemp
706 West 11th Street
Claremont, California

Enclosure

May 1, 1954

Memorandum

A. There are some few statements which are not authenticated by reference to their source. Some are marked. There are probably others. It is desirable to find the references and put them in.

B. We have never carefully examined the British publications, except those of Churchill, Lord Hankey, General Fuller, Chamberlain, and a few other British books. It is desirable to examine the British material in the Library for any other light. There may be publications of the British Foreign Office that are important. We have, of course, examined the Parliamentary speeches.

C. As you go along, please note pages where there are acid remarks about Churchill and Roosevelt. We may want to consider some of them again.

D. Please consider whether title different from "Lost Statesmanship" would not be more effective and more objective. For instance, *Memoirs of Hebert Hoover—Foreign Relations of the United States from 1933 to Pearl Harbor* (Volume I); and *Foreign Relations of the United States from Pearl Harbor until 1953* (Volume II).

E. You might look through the Library for anything on our relations with the Iron Curtain States, China, etc., that we might not have examined.

Preface to *Lost Statesmanship*

July 1, 1957

AS HOOVER REVISED and condensed *Lost Statesmanship* in the late 1950s, he continually rewrote his prefaces, forewords, and introductions—restating and clarifying his purposes and themes. The Preface that he compiled in mid-1957 sheds considerable light on his intentions and research methodology. It marks another stage in the evolution of the Magnum Opus from outspoken memoir to scholarly monograph. But Hoover's point of view, though becoming more understated, was never hidden.

This document is part of the July 1, 1957, page proof edition of *Lost Statesmanship*. It is filed in the Herbert C. Hoover Papers, Box 19, "M.O. 39" envelope, Hoover Institution Archives.

Preface

My interest in American foreign policy did not by any means cease with my departure from the White House on March 4, 1933. In the ensuing 20 years of the Roosevelt and Truman administrations, I continued to be concerned with their foreign policies—and the consequences.

Those turbulent two decades form the subject of these two volumes. In them the reader will find much material never before published anywhere.

I can approach the history of this period from 1933 to 1953 with a background different from that of historians compelled to rely only on documents, or limited in their official contacts.

In 20 years of practicing my profession as an engineer all over the globe before the First World War, I lived and worked in every major country involved in our foreign policies. I was not a tourist; my work required me to deal with the governments as well as the people of those nations.

Next, during the four years of the First World War, I was officially involved in our foreign policies toward 22 European countries.

Later, for 12 years as Secretary of Commerce and President, I had to deal directly with problems arising out of our relations with the rest of the world. As President-elect in 1928, I visited the major Latin-American countries on a good-will journey.

In 1938 I visited 14 countries in Europe to study the growth of ideologies, the dictatorships, the political pressures, threats of war and the military preparations.

In 1946, on an official mission to co-ordinate the efforts of the world to overcome that greatest of all famines, I covered 37 [38–*ed.*] countries in Asia, Europe, and Latin America. On this journey I talked with the Prime Minister and Foreign Minister of every country I visited.

In 1947, at the request of President Truman I made a report on the economic condition of Germany and Austria. At this time I also visited France, Italy and Britain where I again discussed the world situation with the Prime Ministers and their Foreign Ministers.

Over the years I became acquainted with many leaders of these nations, and enjoyed the friendship of many of them.

In writing this volume I have had available to me the world's greatest collection of documents and materials on foreign relations from the First World War to this date—the Library on War, Revolution and Peace at Stanford University. I began building up the Library in 1915, with the aid of governments and officials throughout the world. It now contains more than 20 million items, including official records, treaties, newspaper files, governmental and institutional documents, books, memoirs, and the statements of responsible leaders for nearly four decades. The Library has, in addition, the value of a staff expert in all principal languages.

Much of the material is unavailable elsewhere.

Beyond this, I have over the years had available much confidential information not accessible to others.

A Note on Current Histories of This Period

Most histories of the period from 1933 to 1953 have been written by members and supporters of the Roosevelt-Truman regimes. The State Department's voluminous publications of this era are chiefly remarkable for their suppression of essential documents and their slanting of published material. Some of the most dangerous intellectual dishonesties by historians are not to be found in their sins of commission but in their sins of omission of the whole truth.

Aside from the mountain of military memoirs, official publications and miscellaneous fractional material, the major American postwar studies of the Roosevelt-Truman foreign policies fall into two major groups: those of the apologists and those of the revisionists. The apologies are mostly from civilians who participated in these policies or from professional historians either associated with the Roosevelt and Truman administrations, or [who—ed.] later were supplied with records in support of the two regimes.[1] One of the amazing omissions of these pro-Roosevelt-Truman historians is practically no reference to the Communist infiltration into the Administrations and their activities. (See Chapter 12.) The oppositionist or revisionist histories are those of professional historians and writers whose interpretation of the facts

---

1. Apologists:

Thomas A. Bailey, *The Man in the Street* (New York, 1948).

Denis W. Brogan, *The Era of Franklin D. Roosevelt: A Chronicle of the New Deal and Global War* (New Haven, 1950).

James F. Byrnes, *Speaking Frankly* (Harper and Brothers, New York, 1947).

Winston S. Churchill, Speeches from 1938 to 1945, Nine volumes (New York and Boston, 1948–1946): *While England Slept; Step by Step; Blood, Sweat and Tears; The Unrelenting Struggle; The End of the Beginning; Onwards to Victory; The Dawn of Liberation; Victory; Secret Session Speeches.*

Winston S. Churchill, *The Second World War,* memoirs of 1940–1945, six volumes (Boston, 1948–1953): *The Gathering Storm; Their Finest Hour; The Grand Alliance; The Hinge of Fate; Closing the Ring; Triumph and Tragedy.*

Herbert Feis, *The Road to Pearl Harbor* (Princeton, 1950).

Herbert Feis, *The China Tangle* (Princeton, 1953).

John Gunther, *Roosevelt in Retrospect* (Harper and Brothers, New York, 1950).

Cordell Hull, *The Memoirs of Cordell Hull* (New York, 1948).

William L. Langer and S. Everett Gleason, *The Challenge to Isolation, 1937–1940* (New York, 1952).

William L. Langer and S. Everett Gleason, *The Undeclared War—1940–1941* (New York, 1953).

Walter Millis, *This is Pearl Harbor! The United States and Japan, 1941* (New York, 1947).

Allan Nevins, *The New Deal and World Affairs: A Chronicle of International Affairs, 1933–1945* (New Haven, 1950).

William Phillips, *Ventures in Diplomacy* (Boston, 1952).

Basil Rauch, *Roosevelt From Munich to Pearl Harbor* (New York, 1950).

Eleanor Roosevelt, *This I Remember* (New York, 1949).

Elliott Roosevelt, *As He Saw It* (New York, 1946).

Elliott Roosevelt, *F. D. R., His Personal Letters, 1928–1945,* two volumes. (New York, 1950).

Franklin D. Roosevelt, *Public Papers and Addresses,* edited by Samuel I. Rosenman, 14 volumes covering years 1928 to 1945. (Published by Random House, Macmillan Company, Harper & Brothers during years 1938 through 1950.)

Samuel I. Rosenman, *Working with Roosevelt* (New York, 1948).

Robert E. Sherwood, *Roosevelt and Hopkins* (New York, 1948).

E. R. Stettinius, Jr., *Roosevelt and the Russians* (Garden City, New York, 1949).

Sumner Welles, *Seven Decisions That Shaped History* (New York, 1951).

has led them to quite different conclusions.[2] It is indeed interesting to note the quantity of smearing and abuse heaped upon some of the latter, despite the fact that many are respected scholars of high repute.[3]

It is the duty of historians to build the murals which line the corridor of history but [by?–*ed.*] fitting mosaics piece by piece, colored in good or evil by the acts of men. False colors supplied by those who would obscure the truth may temporarily tint the surface of this grand mosaic, but they are worn off by the implacable disclosures of truth over the years.

However, the books written to support the Roosevelt-Truman wars, and likewise those written to expose or revise the policies of that era, furnish pieces of information which, placed in the mural of history, make quite a different picture than that imagined by the authors.

---

2. Oppositionists or Revisionists:

Hanson W. Baldwin, *Great Mistakes of the War* (New York, 1950).
Harry Elmer Barnes, *Perpetual War for Perpetual Peace* (Caldwell, Idaho, 1953).
Charles A. Beard, *American Foreign Policy in the Making* (New Haven, 1946).
Charles A. Beard, *President Roosevelt and the Coming of the War—1941* (New Haven, 1948).
William Henry Chamberlin, *America's Second Crusade* (Chicago, 1950).
Claire Lee Chennault, *Way of a Fighter* (New York, 1949).
Jan Ciechanowski, *Defeat in Victory* (New York, 1947).
George Creel, *Russia's Race for Asia* (New York, 1949).
Bonner Fellers, *Wings for Peace* (Chicago, 1953).
John T. Flynn, *The Roosevelt Myth* (New York, 1948).
John T. Flynn, *While You Slept* (New York, 1952).
John T. Flynn, *The Lattimore Story* (New York, 1953).
Benjamin Gitlow, *The Whole of Their Lives* (New York, 1948).
Russell Grenfell, *Main Fleet to Singapore* (New York, 1951).
Russell Grenfell, *Unconditional Hatred* (New York, 1953).
Joseph C. Grew, *Ten Years in Japan* (New York, 1944).
Joseph C. Grew, *Turbulent Era*—Vol. I and Vol. II (Boston; Cambridge, 1952).
Herbert Hoover, *Addresses On The American Road,* from 1933 to 1953, seven volumes,
     (Charles Scribner's Sons, D. Van Nostrand Inc., and Stanford University Press—
     publishers 1935 [1938–*ed.*] to 1953).
Herbert Hoover, *Memoirs*, Volume III (New York, 1952).
Arthur Bliss Lane, *I Saw Poland Betrayed* (New York, 1948).
Raymond Moley, *After Seven Years* (New York, 1939).
George Morgenstern, *Pearl Harbor* (New York, 1951).
Frederic R. Sanborn, *Design for War* (New York, 1951).
Charles C. Tansill, *Back Door to War* (Chicago, 1952).
Freda Utley, *Last Chance in China* (Indianapolis, New York, 1947).
Freda Utley, *The China Story* (Chicago, 1951).
Chester Wilmot, *The Struggle for Europe* (New York, 1952).

3. See, for example, Harry Elmer Barnes, *The Struggle Against the Historical Blackout* (privately published, 6th ed., 1952).

A Note on the Preparation of These Volumes

Aside from continuous and contemporaneous collection of material, I wrote parts of these memoirs soon after the events described. Instances of these were: the account of the World Economic Conference; the recognition of Russia; my journey to Europe in 1938; the Lend-Lease debate; the undeclared wars; the tacit alliance with Stalin, and the course of the war. In 1945 I assembled the parts of the manuscript which I had already so prepared, and from there on revised the manuscript every year, to include new disclosures. As originally written (at different intervals) this text would have comprised several volumes. Because of its length, however, I have condensed it into two volumes largely by eliminating documents since made available to the public.

In order to give the reader the evidence to support my statements and conclusions, I have included a considerable number of quotations. I have presented them at greater length than would otherwise be necessary so as to avoid any misinterpretation of their context which would change their import. The italics in all quotations are mine. The full text of all documents quoted may be found at the Hoover Library at Stanford University.

This is not a history of military events and actions. I review them briefly, however, where necessary to provide a background for the problems of statesmanship.

Much of the inner actions, forces and purposes of enemy countries during wartime, were revealed only after the war's end. They could not have been known at the time to America's leaders. Justice to them requires that such disclosures should not be used in the appraisal of their statesmanship at such moments. To make this distinction clear I have presented information disclosed *ex post facto* in footnotes, or, in one or two cases, in chapters so marked.

From the ample lessons of World War I, and its aftermaths, I opposed every step toward World War II and the foreign policies that flowed from it. I make no apologies, for every day since has confirmed my judgment. A host of other public men and women, and indeed the majority of the American people, were opposed to intervention in the war.

The reasons for our opposition should be made clearly a part of the public record. And this record should include the great difficulties under which we of the opposition labored. We were viciously attacked by the Roosevelt and Truman Administrations and their collaborators. Moreover, the character of the propaganda used by these Administrations should also be a part of the record.

But a more important purpose of these volumes is to remind our people of the consequences of war. The victors in modern war are in reality the vanquished.

If at times this narrative appears blunt in its conclusions, I hope the reader will keep in mind the results of 20 years of Roosevelt-Truman domination of America. Those policies made nearly half the world Communist, armed and bent on the destruction of all free men; made another one-third of the world Socialist, both seeking to infect American life. The cost to the American people has been 400,000 dead sons and nearly 800,000 more wounded; imposed on us the need to support 2,000,000 widows, orphans and disabled veterans; saddled us with more than $300 billion in Federal obligations; brought such taxation through the front door, as to every cottage, and such inflation through the back door, as to make a post-war income of $5,000 a year no greater in purchasing value than a prewar income of $2,000; undermined our savings for insurance and old age; and, in the end, brought us ten years of cold war with no peace and the end is not yet.[4]

---

4. [*Editor's note:* The remainder of the document is omitted. It deals mostly with footnote citation procedures.]

Franklin Roosevelt and Communist Infiltration into American Life

August 21, 1957

As DOCUMENT 15 (above) indicates, in the late 1940s Hoover became interested in communist penetration of the United States during Franklin Roosevelt's presidency. To Hoover, the proliferating communist cells—including espionage networks—in Washington were among the malignant "forces" shaping America's foreign policy during and after World War II.

Not long after he began collecting data on this subject, Hoover started to incorporate it into his Magnum Opus. In the early 1950s he wrote an entire chapter entitled "Communist Forces in Motion in the United States." It became chapter 12 of *Lost Statesmanship* (as he entitled his manuscript in 1950).

The document here is taken from the opening pages of chapter 12 as it stood in the summer of 1957. This chapter is the direct precursor of what became chapter 4 of *Freedom Betrayed*.

As readers who compare the two texts will notice, Hoover eventually omitted the critical passages about Franklin Roosevelt that are reproduced here. Why Hoover decided to do so is unknown. Most likely it was part of his drive to condense his huge manuscript and to soften its polemical character. But there is no doubt that he still believed the substance of his indictment of FDR.

The full document (34 pages in page proof form) is in the Herbert C. Hoover Papers, Box 20, "M.O. 41" envelope, Hoover Institution Archives. A notation on the first page indicates that page proofs were returned to Hoover from the printer on August 21, 1957.

Chapter 12
Communist Forces in Motion in the United States

Roosevelt's Attitudes Toward Communist Infiltration into American Life

Roosevelt ignored the whole Communist infiltration into his Administration. Much of it was to be exposed before his death. But of more importance, he ignored the whole international purpose of Communism and its morals in international relations. Its purposes and methods had been blatantly stated to the world ever since 1917 and its statements and books were widely distributed in the United States (See Chapter 6).

Roosevelt was not a Communist. His leanings toward Stalin and blindness to Communist activities arose partly from his own leftish leanings and partly from the usefulness of the Communists in support of his Administration politically throughout his 13 years in office (except the 22 months of the Hitler-Stalin alliance prior to June 1941[1]).

His leanings toward Stalin and the Communists began with the recognition of the Soviet Government immediately upon his taking office in 1933, which I have related in more detail in Chapter 2.

During 15 years prior to the recognition, Democratic and Republic Administrations alike had barred any relations with a country which had returned huge numbers of mankind to slavery and which was constantly conspiring against the welfare of other peoples. By "recognition" Roosevelt gave it certain respectability in the family of nations. But also of importance, by that act, he had opened the door to Communist penetration and conspiracies in the United States.

I have related that the "recognition" agreement signed by Roosevelt and the Soviet Commissar Litvinov provided that there should be no Soviet conspiracies or propaganda in the United States. Within forty-eight hours of the

---

1. Benjamin Gitlow, a repentant Communist high official, revealed details of a party line dictated from Moscow which gave support to Roosevelt from 1932 to 1938:

"... negotiations were proceeding ... between certain elements in the New Deal and representatives of the Communist party which had for their objective a basis on which the communists could throw their support to the New Deal.

"... The communists, under Comintern direction, were hammering out a people's front, American style. They knew what they were doing. ...

"The communists, from the fall of 1935 up to the end of World War II, played ball with everyone who would play ball with them. The honeymoon ... was interrupted only for the brief period of the Soviet-Nazi Pact...." (*The Whole of Their Lives* [Charles Scribner's Sons, New York: 1948], pp. 258–266.) [*Editor's note:* I have corrected several minor transcription errors.]

signing of this promise, Litvinov met with the American Communist leaders in New York and informed them this agreement did not bind the Communist International, of which their "apparatus" was a part. He told them:

> Don't worry about the letter. It is a scrap of paper which will soon be forgotten in the realities of Soviet-American relations.[2]

Moscow undertook four great conspiracies against the American people, the first being the activities of our Communist party in organizing public opinion; the second, their control of certain great labor unions; the third, their capture of otherwise harmless activities, such as the Institute of Pacific Relations; the fourth, and worst, being infiltration of their members and fellow travellers into high policy-making positions in Roosevelt's Administration and the fifth, infiltration into education.

Roosevelt could not have long remained ignorant of the prompt, wilful and complete violation of the recognition agreement and of the Soviet's evil intentions toward all the world, including the United States.

The violations of the recognition agreement dawned on Secretary Hull and on August 14, 1934, he made a protest to Moscow. Nothing came of it.[3]

William C. Bullitt had been appointed American Ambassador to Moscow on December 6, 1933. Bullitt was destined to become completely disillusioned about Soviet purposes.

On July 13, 1935 Litvinov informed Bullitt that he had made no agreement with Roosevelt covering activities of the 3rd International.[4]

On July 19, 1935 Bullitt reported to Roosevelt his conclusions as to the objectives of the Communists.[5]

> [... –ed.]Diplomatic relations with friendly states are not regarded by the Soviet Government as normal friendly relations but "armistice" relations ... [which] can not possibly be ended by a definitive peace but only by a renewal of battle. The Soviet Union genuinely desires peace on all fronts at the present time but this peace is looked upon merely as a happy respite in which future wars may be prepared. ...

---

2. Ibid., p. 265.

3. [U.S. Department of State,] *Foreign Relations [of the United States, Diplomatic Papers, The] Soviet Union, 1933–1939* [United States Government Printing Office, Washington: 1952], p. 132.

4. Ibid., p. 223.

5. Ibid., pp. 224–227.

... It is the primary object ... to maintain peace everywhere until the strength of the Soviet Union has been built up to such a point that it is entirely impregnable to attack and ready, if Stalin should desire, to intervene abroad.

... War in Europe is regarded as inevitable and ultimately desirable from the Communist point of view. ...

It is of course the heartiest hope of the Soviet Government that the United States will become involved in a war with Japan. ... To maintain peace for the present, to keep the nations of Europe divided, to foster enmity between Japan and the United States, and to gain blind devotion and obedience of the communists of all countries so they will act against their own governments at the behest of the Communist Pope in the Kremlin is the sum of Stalin's policy.

Few more accurate summations of Moscow's intentions have ever been made. But it apparently made no impression on Roosevelt.

In July, 1935 the Seventh Communist International Congress met in Moscow. It was attended by Soviet leaders, including Stalin. Several American Communists attended the meeting, and speeches were made by Browder, Darcy and other Americans. They made great claims of Communist expansion in the United States, boasting that the Communists had penetrated into 140 labor unions and had caused the Bonus March of 1932 and a seamen's strike at San Francisco.[6]

Bullitt sent Washington the details of this meeting on August 21, 1935. He stated that the proceedings were managed by the Kremlin and that they proved gross violations of the recognition agreement.[7]

Hull again protested to the Soviet Government on August 25, 1935 against the flagrant violation of Litvinov's pledge.[8] Moscow replied, denying any responsibility for the Communist International. After further fuss and fury, Hull let the matter die, issuing a side-stepping statement to the press on September 1, 1935.

Bullitt, returning to the United States obviously out of tune with Roosevelt's views on Russia, resigned and was replaced by Joseph E. Davies, a wealthy New Deal lawyer without foreign experience. To avoid any hardships at his Russian post he sent his great private yacht to Leningrad with extensive

---

6. Ibid., pp. 231–232.
7. Ibid., pp. 233–234.
8. Ibid., pp. 252–257.

food supplies. His appointment was obviously intended better to represent Roosevelt's attitudes. In fact, Davies became an extoller of Soviet virtues.[9]

Pending Davies' arrival in Moscow, Loy Henderson, as our Chargé d'Affaires there, advised Hull of the Soviet Government's aggressive military activities. He reported on January 16, 1936 that their military budget had increased from 8.2 billion rubles in 1935 to 14.8 billion rubles in 1936. This enabled them, according to Henderson, to have a standing army of 1,300,000 men.[10] On August 18, 1936, Henderson further advised Hull that the expanded Soviet Army would number 2,000,000 men.[11] Later, on October 31, 1938, the American Embassy, through Alexander Kirk, Chargé d'Affaires at the time, informed the State Department that the Soviet Union's further increase in armament was accelerating, particularly in air power and heavy industry.[12]

Davies, however, furthered Roosevelt's actions despite all this evidence. His own report indicates that in January, 1938, Roosevelt authorized him to explore the possibilities of a military liaison with the Soviet Union for the purpose of exchanging information about Japan and the Pacific area. When Davies discussed the matter with Stalin and Molotov they expressed willingness, and Colonel Philip R. Faymonville, military attaché at the American Embassy, was suggested as the American liaison officer.[13]

In a general summation of his views, Davies advised the State Department on June 6, 1938:

> ... there is no doubt of the present sincerity of this regime in its desire to maintain Peace. . . .
>
> There are no conflicts of physical interests between the United States and the U.S.S.R. There is nothing which either has which is desired by or could be taken by the other. . . .
>
> There is one situation, where a very serious issue might develop. That is the possible intrusion of the U.S.S.R. through the Comintern into the local affairs of the United States. Fortunately *that has been measurably eliminated by the agreement entered into between President Roosevelt and Commissar Litvinov in 1934/1933/ (sic)*. . . .

---

9. See Joseph E. Davies, *Mission to Moscow* [Simon & Schuster, New York: 1941]. [*Editor's note:* Part of Hoover's original citation was erroneous and has been corrected.]

10. *Foreign Relations . . . Soviet Union, 1933–1939*, pp. 285–287.

11. Ibid., p. 299.

12. Ibid., p. 592.

13. Ibid., pp. 596–7.

A common ground between the United States and the U.S.S.R., and one that will obtain for a long period of time, in my opinion, lies in the fact that both are sincere advocates of World Peace.

In my opinion, there is no danger from communism here, so far as the United States is concerned.[14] . . .

Davies should have awakened when Litvinov, on June 23, 1938—less than two weeks after Davies' dispatch—delivered a vigorous Marxist speech in which he said:

With the preservation of the capitalist system a long and enduring peace is impossible.[15]

It would seem that Roosevelt from all this five years of education, experience, might have realized both the treachery and aggressive character of the Communists. But he brushed it aside—and he brushed aside an even more malignant development.

The Communist Infiltration Into the American Government

At once after the Litvinov agreement the Communists undertook a gigantic infiltration into American life and government.[16]

---

14. Ibid., pp. 555ff. [*Editor's note:* The italics in the quotation are Hoover's.]
15. Ibid., p. 588.
16. [*Editor's note:* The remainder of this lengthy chapter is omitted. Much of its contents appear in Chapter 4 of *Freedom Betrayed,* printed in this book.]

Foreword to *The Ordeal of the American People*

June 5, 1961

IN 1961 HOOVER wrote yet another Foreword to yet another edition of his Magnum Opus, which now bore a new name (later discarded): *The Ordeal of the American People.* The opening paragraphs of this document are reproduced here.

This typescript document is dated 6/5/61 (probably by one of his secretaries, Loretta Camp). This was probably the date of the typing, which was most likely done a few days (at most) after Hoover wrote the Foreword by hand. The item is filed in the Herbert C. Hoover Papers, Box 33, "M.O. 64" envelope, Hoover Institution Archives.

6/5/61

The Ordeal of the American People

Foreword

After having fought the greatest foreign war in all our history, in which 405,000 American youths perished and 671,000 were wounded or permanently disabled—and in which our enemies were vanquished—yet we have no peace.

The jeopardy in which we find ourselves comes from only one source— the Communist giant which our own leaders helped to build.

During and since this war the Communists have expanded their control over peoples from about one-tenth to about one-third of mankind. They continue in conspiracies to overthrow by violence the government of all remaining free nations in the world. They daily menace us with the threat of wholesale slaughter by nuclear bombs. To defend ourselves, we must tax away our otherwise advancing economic security, comfort, and savings for old age.

We have increased our national debt by over $240,000,000.[1] The taxes for our defense reach into the front door of every cottage. The inflation of our currency reaches through the back door. Today an annual family income of $5,000 will buy less than an income of $2,000 in the days before we entered upon this era of trafficking with the Communists in 1933.

This memoir is a step-by-step record of how and by whom we have been plunged into this greatest calamity of our national life. Its purpose is to present for public judgment the actions and the men responsible for this calamity—and to record those who opposed their policies. This account is based upon their own statements, their commitments, agreements, disclosed in after years.

No attempt is made herein to offer a history of military events and moves. From time to time I review these briefly, but only to clarify the background of important political commitments and declarations. The fate of mankind in this century has been determined less by military developments than by the actions of civilian leaders.

---

1. [*Editor's note:* Hoover presumably meant $240,000,000,000.]

"The Communist Infiltration into the Federal Government"

Summer 1961

THESE ARE THE introductory paragraphs of what became chapter 4 of *Freedom Betrayed*. These paragraphs indicated, more concisely than the ultimate version, what was on Hoover's mind as he assiduously compiled evidence of communist penetration of the United States government.

This document is filed among working drafts of *The Ordeal of the American People*, Volume I, Section I, in the Herbert C. Hoover Papers, Box 36, "M.O. 69" envelope, Hoover Institution Archives. The drafts are from the period June-September 1961.

The Ordeal of the American People
Section I

The Infiltration of Communism in the United States
Chapter 4

The extent of the infiltration of American (or Naturalized) Communists into the Federal Government was no phantasy of emotional persons. This record will show that the names of these persons, pledged to the principles and methods enunciated from Moscow and to serving the purposes of the Soviet Government, had gained strategic positions in the White House, in the Armed Services, in every government department, and even on the staffs of some Congressional committees. They were sent on foreign missions to Russia, Germany, France, Italy, Britain, Latin America, China, and elsewhere. They became secretaries and advisers at important international conferences.

This Memoir will show that this infiltration had potent effects upon peace and war; it was influential in bringing great disasters upon the American people.

It is not likely that we shall ever accurately know the full extent of this infiltration into the government. Their discovery often came after they had been in the government for years.

Hoover Memorandum for His Staff

November 13, 1962

By LATE 1962 Hoover was eighty-eight years old, in declining health, and acutely aware that the Magnum Opus was not yet done. In this memorandum to his staff of six secretaries and one accountant, he gave instructions for organizing their "maximum energies" for completing the herculean task.

This document is also interesting for its evidence that the Magnum Opus was not the only project that was absorbing Hoover's time and effort. He was simultaneously at work on two other books: the final volume of *An American Epic* and a volume of essays entitled *Fishing for Fun and to Wash Your Soul.*

Hoover's holograph memorandum went through several typewritten revisions. The apparently final version here (along with its predecessors) is found in *"Freedom Betrayed* Manuscript: Memos to Staff . . . ," Loretta Camp Frey Papers, Herbert Hoover Presidential Library.

November 13, 1962

For The Staff

As things have turned out, we will need curtail my outside activities and turn our maximum energies to completing the books we have in the mill before starting anything new.

To do this, I have divided the staff work in the following fashion:

There will be three volumes of the Magnum Opus:

Volume I   —   *Up to Pearl Harbor*
Volume II   —   *The March of Conferences,* ending with the section
                         on *Potsdam and After*
Volume III — *The Case History of Poland*
                         The Case History of China
                         The Case History of Korea
                         The Case History of Germany

* * * *

The least advanced are Volume I and Volume II.

Miss Miller[1] and Mrs. Camp[2] will manage these two volumes, with Miss Scanlon[3] as their assistant.

* * * *

Generally, as sections of the Opus are cleaned up they should be Xeroxed, even if research is not all complete, so that we can have copies for all staff members—and so that the Opus can be sent to our critics, such as Hans Kaltenborn and Neil MacNeil. The incomplete research should be noted in the margins.

* * * *

Miss Dydo[4] will direct the completion and publication of Volume IV of *An American Epic,* after which she will help clean [up the *Magnum Opus* and later complete such Case Histories as she has already worked upon.][5]

Miss Yeager[6] will manage the distribution of *On Growing Up* and prepare Volume II for next Christmas, and see the Fishing Book through to publication and distribution. She will do the clean-up and further research on *The Case History of Korea.*

* * * *

Miss Dempsey[7] will take over the office and managerial chores. She will occupy the reception room, take care of appointments, visitors and mail. Miss

---

1. [*Editor's note:* Bernice Miller]
2. [*Editor's note:* Loretta Camp]
3. [*Editor's note:* Mary Lou Scanlon]
4. [*Editor's note:* Joan Dydo]
5. [*Editor's note:* The bracketed words are missing from this version of the memorandum. They are supplied from the penultimate draft.]
6. [*Editor's note:* Naomi Yeager]
7. [*Editor's note:* M. Elizabeth Dempsey]

Yeager and Miss Dydo will help when pressures become too great. Miss Dempsey will handle our relations with the Hoover Institution and West Branch Library, with help from Miss Miller and Mrs. Camp.

* * * *

Hugo Meier[8] will keep all the accounts and pay the bills certified to him by myself.

* * * *

As I must have a permanent night attendant who will occupy the spare bedroom during the night, it will be necessary to make the following changes in staff rooms:

Miss Dydo to move into the room with Miss Yeager; Miss Miller to use the spare bedroom in the daytime.

* * * *

In my situation, I would like and will need to have some one of the six secretaries every day in the week. We will maintain a five-day week. I have asked Miss Dempsey to canvass the situation with each member of the staff in order that there be the least inconvenience to anyone.

---

8. [*Editor's note:* Hoover's accountant]

Hoover to Clarence Budington Kelland

January 31, 1963

IN THIS LETTER to a good friend, Hoover alluded to the importance that the Magnum Opus held for him as he neared the end of his days.

This document (a carbon copy of Hoover's letter) is in "Kelland, Clarence B.," Post-Presidential Individual File, Herbert Hoover Papers, Herbert Hoover Presidential Library.

The Waldorf Astoria Towers
New York, New York
January 31, 1963

My dear Bud:

I am sorry not to see you before you vanish into Arizona!

I have taken a bad licking with a set-back thrown in. However, I am doing better now. But I am not allowed any more journeys away from New York. I do see people, play a limited amount of canasta, and above all, am trying to finish five more books before my time runs out.

The book on fishing will be out in May. The fourth and final volume of *An American Epic* is in the last stages of completion. But the big job of three volumes on who, when, and how we got into the Cold War has already had twenty years of work and requires two more. I hope to leave them as a sort of "will and testament" before I finally vanish. Neil McNeil, Hans Kaltenborn, and Frank Mason have looked at the partially completed MSS and are enthusiastic that they are great and needed books.

I hope that Arizona is good to you. The advice of my doctors might apply to you: "You can provide any climate in your present abode, so why go out in the cold and meet a dozen kind of bugs which wish to kill you!"

Affectionately,

Mr. Clarence Budington Kelland
Cove Neck Road
Glen Cove, Long Island, New York

Hoover to Lewis L. Strauss
March 15, 1963

TOWARD THE END of his labors on *Freedom Betrayed,* Hoover sent out copies of his "top secret" manuscrpt to a number of close friends for comment. Here is a representative example.

A photocopy of this letter is filed in "Hoover, Herbert: 1963," Name and Subject Series II, Lewis L. Strauss Papers, Herbert Hoover Presidential Library.

The Waldorf-Astoria Towers
New York 22, New York
March 15, 1963

Dear Lewis:

At one time, in a moment of over-generosity, you offered to read and criticize my top secret *Magnum Opus.*

I send you herewith Volume I. Don't bother with it if you have something better to do. In any event, to save labor, make any suggestions on the margins as you go along and send them to me for incorporation.

Affectionately,
Herbert

Admiral Lewis L. Strauss
Camelback Inn
Phoenix, Arizona

Hoover to Bernice Miller and Loretta Camp

n.d.

(circa June 10, 1963)

By MID-1963, Hoover, now nearly eighty-nine years old, had almost finished his Magnum Opus. In a handwritten memorandum to two senior members of his staff, he again revealed his anxiety to complete this, "the most important job of my remaining years."

The original document is marked "Rec'd 6/10/63" (presumably by Miller or Camp). It is filed in "'War Book' (*Freedom Betrayed*): Herbert Hoover Holograph Material," Arthur Kemp Papers, Herbert Hoover Presidential Library.

Miss Camp Desk

B. Miller

L. Camp

Manager's job on *Magnum Opus.*

I have finished my revision of edition Z + H. It must be cleaned up and some research work done. It is desirable that some of the staff be assigned to this job.

Who?

I am dreadfully anxious to again edit Volume II Magnum. I have not got too far to go and *this* is the *most important job of my remaining years.*[1] Please consider

a getting the mss in my hands for edition Z. I might be expedited by concentrating on certain sections as otherwise I am idle.

---

1. [*Editor's note:* The words italicized here were lightly underlined in Hoover's holograph memorandum. It is possible that someone other than Hoover underlined them.]

DOCUMENT 28

Hoover to His "Historical Staff"
n.d.
(June 1963)

TWO DAYS AFTER Hoover's "history helpers" received the memorandum printed as Document 27, they received another directive in his own hand. The original document is marked "Rec'd from AH 6/12/63." "AH" was almost certainly Hoover's son Allan.

This item is found in "'War Book' (Freedom Betrayed): Herbert Hoover Holograph Material," Arthur Kemp Papers, Herbert Hoover Presidential Library.

To my history helpers.

I think we might think over our program on Magnum Opus.

1. Obviously we wish to compile Vol I as soon as we can. Therefore we postpone all Vol III Case Histories because they can not be polished until Vol I and Vol II are completed.

What this means is that Joan and any others be assigned to Vol I and Volume II. I believe I have completed an edition of Vol II.

We are not going to submit Vol II to our friendly critics in order that our staff may not be delayed in work on Volume II.

My own impression is that Volume II does not require much work as I have stuck close to the documentation and our previous editing.

All this means that as quickly as staff can be free from Vol I they should get at Vol II with a reasonable hope of Volume II being xeroxed.

Please have a convention of our Historical Staff and give me your conclusions as to where we are and our next step.

About the Author

HERBERT HOOVER

(1874–1964)

President of the United States from 1929 to 1933. An internationally acclaimed humanitarian, he was the author of more than thirty books and founder of the Hoover Institution on War, Revolution and Peace.

About the Editor

GEORGE H. NASH

A historian, lecturer, and authority on the life of Herbert Hoover, his publications include three volumes of a definitive, scholarly biography of Hoover and the monograph *Herbert Hoover and Stanford University*. Nash is also the author of *The Conservative Intellectual Movement in America Since 1945* and *Reappraising the Right: The Past and Future of American Conservatism*. A graduate of Amherst College and holder of a PhD in history from Harvard University, he received the Richard M. Weaver Prize for Scholarly Letters in 2008. He lives in South Hadley, Massachusetts.

INDEX

at Yalta Conference, 464–65, 523–24
See also Russia's annexations
Attlee, Clement, 322, 555
atomic bomb
  Acheson on, 495–96
  Baldwin, H. W., against use of, 568
  Congress and, 360
  controversy over, lxix, 490, 493–94, 565–68, 567nn3–4, 832–33, 854
  effects of, 564
  Eisenhower against use of, 567n3
  Emperor of Japan and, 882
  Far Eastern Agreement and, 490, 493–94
  FDR for, 330–31
  at First Quebec Conference, 359–61
  Hankey against use of, 568
  Hoover on, 580–81, 832–33, 882
  Leahy against use of, 567
  Marshall and, 496
  Nimitz against use of, 567
  O'Donnell, E., against use of, 566–67
  research on, 330
  Second Washington Conference and, 330–31
  Sherwood on, 330
  Stimson and, 568, 568n8
  Truman's lost statesmanship and, 882
  war's end without, 490, 493–94, 832, 833
  at Yalta Conference, 495–97
Atomic Energy Commission
  American Communists in, 36–39, 41, 43
  Strauss on, 47
Austin, Warren, 499
Australia
  South Korea military aid from, 751n5
  for U.S.-Japan mediation, 295, 296
Austria, 71–72
Avenol, Joseph, 93
Avezzana, Baron, 24

Baerensprung, Horst, 41
Balamuth, Lewis, 36
balance of power, 93
  Britain for, 96, 862
  Churchill against, 862
  toward Hitler, 134
  Poland and, 133–34
  toward Stalin, 134–35
Baldwin, Hanson W.
  critical of atomic bomb's use against Japan, 568
  critical of *The Gathering Storm*, 868
  on Hitler against Stalin, 242–43

  on Unconditional Surrender policy, 343–44
Baldwin, Stanley
  Churchill against, 862, 866–67
  Churchill compared to, 866
Balkan States
  Churchill and, 182, 358–59, 428–30, 445–46
  Halifax and, 432
  at Second Moscow Conference, 445–46
  Stalin and, 145, 389, 428–30, 445–46
  See also specific countries
Baltic States
  Communist atrocities in, 420–21
  FDR's lost statesmanship related to, 880
  loss of independence, 145, 578
  See also specific countries
Barkley, Alben, 253, 255, 498
Barr, Major General, 727, 728
Barron, Bryton, 461
Baruch, Bernard, lvii, xciin60, ciin249, 820
Battle of Britain, xlv
  Churchill on, 164–65
  Hitler and, 845, 855, 872
  Hoover's view of, xlv, 823
Beaverbrook, Lord, 251, 346
Beck, Jozef, 128, 150
Belgium
  CRB for, xxxvii, xlvi, lxxi
  Hitler's attack on, 161
  Hoover visit to, 59–61
  hunger in, xcixn171
  South Korea military aid from, 751n5
  Treaty of Versailles and, 69n9
Benes, Eduard
  Czechoslovakia and, 73, 122, 421
  for democracy, 122
  with Stalin, 421, 421n7
Bentley, Elizabeth, 35–36, 39, 43
Berle, Adolf
  against Acheson, 748n10
  for Atlantic Charter, 509–10, 513
  against Hiss, 748n10
Berlin, Richard, lxxx, lxxxii
Berlin-Rome Axis, 66–67
Berlin-Rome-Tokyo Axis
  agreements among, 209, 209n5
  Hitler's breaking of, 145, 263
  Hoover on, 210
  Willkie on, 210
Berlin-Tokyo Axis, 145
Bess, Demaree, 415–16
Bessarabia, 145, 421, 462

Biddle, Francis
for Atlantic Charter, 508–9, 612, 612n10
Polish Americans and, 509, 509n4, 612, 612n10
Bierut, Wladyslaw, 558, 635
Blake, George, 45
Blum, Léon, 60, 62–63
Bohlen, Charles E., 377
on Tehran Conference, 392–93, 626
Bonnet, Georges, 62
Bonus March (1932), American Communist
Party and, 25–26, 895
Boris (king), 223–24
Bor-Komorowski, Tadeusz, 633–34, 636–37
Borodin, Michael, 90–91
Boxer movement, in China, 89
Brewster, Owen
on document suppression, 306
in Pearl Harbor Congressional investigation,
294
on Roberts Commission Report, 306–8
Bridges, Harry, 51
Britain
aid request from, 211
Atlantic Charter and, 368, 465, 524
for balance of power, 96, 862
Battle of Britain, xlv, 164–65, 845, 855, 872
blockade by, cn190, 602
against Communists, 95–96
declaration of war by, xxxii, 161
de-empiring of, 366, 366n1, 367–69, 370n13
on Far Eastern Agreement, 95
FDR's desire for war related to, 190, 195,
202–3, 855–56, 872
FDR's foreign policy of prewar aid to, 112n3,
112–14
France's evacuation by, 162
German negotiations over Poland and, 147,
147n18
Germany and, 843
Germany's attack on Russia and, 226, 235–36,
258, 846
Germany's postwar food and supplies and,
781–82, 785–86
Greece in sphere of influence of, 428–30
Greece's aid from, 180–82
Hitler's appeasement by, 96, 145–47, 147n18
Hitler's planned invasion of, 164, 164n1, 190,
195–96, 845, 855–56, 872
against Hoover food relief work, xlvii–xlix,
cn194, 163, 602
Hoover attitude toward, 823

Hoover predictions about, lii, 851, 852
Hoover visit to, 95–100
Italy's attacks on colonies of, 166
on Italy's conquest of Ethiopia, 70, 111
Leopold III on, 60
military aid to, 201–3
navy of, 195–96, 201–3, 298–99, 845–46
against NCFSD, xlix
Palestine and, 477–79
Poland Guarantee and, xxvi, 128–29, 862, 877
Poland policy change by, xxv–xxvii, xcn34
Poland's mutual assistance for, 146, 146n14,
599
propaganda by, in U.S., 200–203, 823
retreat of, in North Africa, 181
for Russian aid, 235–36
Russia's appeasement by, 617, 620, 625–29,
631, 862
shipping losses of, 165
South Korea military aid from, 751n5
Togo and, 282–83
Treaty of Versailles and, 69n9
in WW I, 99
WW II Cabinet Office records of, cxiiin430
See also Chamberlain, Neville; Churchill,
Winston; Lend-Lease Act; Lothian, Lord
British Chiefs of Staff Committee, 323, 323n2
British Informational Services, 201
British-Soviet alliance
Chamberlain, N., against, 141–42, 150–51, 862
Churchill for, lii, 141–42, 596, 862–63,
867–68
British-Soviet relations
accusations in, 95
trade agreements in, 96
Brooke, Alan F., 298–99, 387
Brothman, Abraham, 41
Browder, Earl R., 51, 84
Brown, Constantine, lix
Bruhn, Bruno, 841, 842
Bryant, Arthur, 334–35
Bukovina, 421, 462
Bulgaria
Communism for, 422–23, 463
diplomatic recognition of, 572–73
Nazi Germany and, 223–24
oil from, 474–75
in Russian sphere of influence, 412, 428–29
Yugoslavia and, 474
Bullitt, William C.
on American Communists, 84

Churchill, Winston (*continued*)
Clark, M. W., for, 388–89
against Communism, 235, 389–90
Davies, J. E. versus, 552–53
on cross-channel operation, 338
Deane on, 388
de-empiring and, 366n1, 368–69
against FDR., 455–56
FDR meetings with. *See specific conferences*
for Finland, 157
at First Quebec Conference, 358–59
German peace proposals for, xin217
on Germany's attack on Russia, 226, 235–36,
  856
hindsight of, 862–63, 867–70
on Hitler against Stalin, 861–62, 867–68
on Hitler's methods of conquest, 256
Hoover critical of, lxvi, lxxxii, 861–63,
  866–70
on Iceland, 248
on Japan, 265–66, 278–79, 279n44, 282–83, 289
Kennedy critical of, 870
Lend-Lease Act praised by, li
Mikolajczyk meetings with, 446, 627–28,
  641–42
missing cablegram from FDR to, 379
Morgenthau Plan and, 439
naval blockade and, xlvii–xlviii
optimism of, 263
orations of, 200
on Poland, 129, 446, 499–500, 623, 625–29,
  631, 640n2, 640–41, 651–52, 665
Poland Guarantee and, 867, 869, 877
on Poland's partition, 640n2, 640–41, 665
Potsdam Conference planning and, 551–52
prior knowledge of Germany's attack on Russia by, 856
propaganda from, 201–3
publishing of, lxvi, 551–52, 861
against Communism in Russia, 235
for a Russian alliance, lii, 142
Russia's annexations accepted by, 403–5,
  408, 416
on Russia's friendly border states, 408, 411–13
on second front, 327–28
at Second Moscow Conference, 444–47
at Second Quebec Conference, 390
Sherwood on, 455
and "soft underbelly" of Europe, 358–59,
  387–90, 456

against Stalin, 388
Stalin and, 320, 351–52, 388–89, 500, 552, 652,
  862
Tito and, 424–26, 429, 552
for TORCH, 333–34
on Turkey, 393
Unconditional Surrender policy and, 340–41,
  343
on U.S.-British alliance, 253
Warsaw uprising (1944) and, 634, 636–39
Yugoslavia and, 179–80, 412–13, 428, 447
See also The Gathering Storm
Ciano, Galeazzo, 66
on Germany's military aid to Finland, 157
Hitler remarks to, 142–43
on U.S. involvement in European affairs, 172
Ciechanowski, Jan, 321
Hoover meeting with, 657–58
on Maisky, 605
against pro-Soviet propaganda, 612–13
on Russia's annexations, 609–10, 664
on St. James's Palace meeting, 319–20, 605–6
against U.S. appeasement of Russia, 614–16,
  621
C.I.O. *See* Committee for Industrial
  Organization
Clark, Bennett C., 239
Clark, J. Reuben, 249
Clark, Mark W.
Chiang Kai-shek and, 766
on China, 756, 756n17
for Churchill's Balkan strategy, 388–89
criticism of, by British press, 765–66
Darlan cease-fire agreement with, 335
Hiss and, 760
on Korea Armistice, 766
Korean War and, 765–66
for Operation ANVIL, 387
on possible war with China, 756, 756n17
for TORCH, 333n1, 333–34
on United Nations, 753
on U.S. government, Communist infiltration
  of, 760
Clausen, Henry C., 303
Clay, Lucius D., 778
appreciation from, 804–5
Cobb, Irwin S., 249
Cohen, Morris U., 46
Colby, Bainbridge, 24
Cold War, lxxvii, lxxxvi

Atlantic Charter as backdrop of, 507
as result of FDR's lost statesmanship, 882
Cole, Albert, lxxx
Collectivism Comes to America (Hoover), lxi,
lxvi, lxvii, lxviii, lxx
purposes of, lxvi
See also The Crusade Years
Collier's, xlviii, lxvii, xcixn184
Colombia, 289n25, 751n5
Commission for Polish Relief (CPR), xxxvii,
xcvn95, 155–56
Poland's gold for, 602, 602n32
Sikorski for, 602
Commission for Relief in Belgium (CRB),
xxxvii, xlvi, lxxi
Commission on the Organization of the Execu-
tive Branch of the Government, lxx
See also Hoover Commission
Committee for Industrial Organization (CIO),
52–53
Committee of American Serbs, A, 426
Communism, 258, 502
in Asia, 578–79
against Baltic States, 420–21, 578
Bierut for, 635
for Bulgaria, 422–23, 463
capitalism and, 22, 450
Churchill against, 235, 389–90
dictatorship under, 14–15
education about, 8n4, 8–9
in Europe, 578–79
FDR's ignorance about, 32–33, 893
Finland against, 80
Finnish Relief Fund and, xxxvii
Germany postwar against, 803n12
Gitlow on, 893n1
global ambition of, 763
Hitler on, 66, 839
Hoover analysis of, 13–23
Hoover predictions about, 852
inevitability of, lvii–lviii, 21–22
for international and intergroup strife, 19–20
international relations, under, 15
labor unions and strikes and, 17–18
legislative bodies' subversion by, 18–19
MacArthur against, 761, 763
Marshall and, 745
New Deal and, li, 893n1
against peace, 20–23
planned economy related to, 104

in Poland, 74, 421, 587, 589, 601–2
poverty and, 95
principles and methods of, 14–23
religion and, 15
spread of, lxviii–lxix, 7, 22, 859, 878, 898
Tehran Conference and, 402–8, 578
trained revolutionaries for, 17
U.S.-Soviet alliance and, 581–82
violent methods of, 16–17
WW II beneficial to, 581–82
in Yugoslavia, 463
See also China; Russia; Stalin, Joseph
Communists, 84, 751
Bonus March and, 25–26, 895
Britain against, 95–96
Communist fronts, 48–53
Deane on, 449–50
Europe's Communist parties, 579
fascism and, 93, 98–99
around FDR, xcviiin137, 289n25, 289–90,
485, 874
as a foreign conspiracy in U.S., 209
Germany's attack on Russia related to, 178n6
gold production for, 83
government conspiracies by, 24–25, 25n2
in Greece, 429–30, 713
Hiss connections with, 42
Hoover Magnum Opus on, lxxvi–lxxvii,
cixn358, 822–23
against military preparedness, 178, 178n6
Poland's repression by, 657–58, 660
in South Korea, 744
See also American Communists; Chinese
Communists; Russia; U.S. Communist
infiltration; U.S. government, Communist
infiltration of; *specific Communists*
*Communist Manifesto (Manifest der Kommunis-
tischen Partei)* (Marx and Engels), 8n4, 13
Communist Republic of North China, 350, 669
See also Mao Tse-tung
Communist Russia, 822–23
Congress (U.S.)
atomic bomb and, 360
MacArthur's address to, 762–65
presidential power compared to, l–li, 212–15
See also specific members of Congress
Congressional hearings and investigations
about Acheson, 746–47
about China, 672–73, 682–83, 686, 689–91,
713, 720, 728, 732, 746–47

Treaty of Versailles and, 69n9, 92
Truman's lost statesmanship relating to, 881
war initiated by, 301–2
See also atomic bomb; economic sanctions
against Japan; Emperor; Grew, Joseph C.;
Konoye, Fumimaro; Pearl Harbor;
U.S.–Japan mediation; U.S.-Japan meeting
rejection
JCS 1067. *See* Joint Chiefs of Staff Directive 1067
Jews, 601
African resettlement for, xxx–xxxi, xciin60
in Communist fronts, 50
deaths of, 155, 639, 639n18, 656
Hoover radio speech about Nazi persecution
of, xxx
Kristallnacht and, xxx
Palestine and, 477–79
in Poland's uprising against Germany, 639,
639n18
Johnson, Louis, 178, 755, 757
on China's invasion of South Korea, 759
Johnson, Walter, 197, 197n17
Joint Chiefs of Staff Directive 1067 (JCS 1067),
773–77, 773n2
Jordan, David Starr, 807
Jordana y Souza, Francisco Gomez, 345

Kaltenborn, H. V., lix, lxxvii–lxxviii, cixn363,
cxin381
Kamin, Leon J., 38
K'ang Yu-wei, 89
Karakhan, Leo, 90–91
Karski, Jan, 623–24
Katyn Forest massacre, 618–19, 619n12
Kauffmann, Henrik de, 219
Kearny incident, 260
Keating, General, 805
Keefe, Frank B., 305–6
Kefauver, Estes, 240
Kelland, Clarence Budington, 249, 905–6
Kelly, Madeline (Madeline Kelly O'Donnell),
lxv–lxvi, cvn298
Kemp, Arthur, lx, lxx, lxxviii, cvin308
Hoover letter to, 884–85
Hoover memoranda to, 830–31, 836
role of, lxiii, lxvii, lxxiii–lxxiv, 830, 884–85
on volume III of Hoover's *Memoirs*, cvin308
War Book and, lxiii–lxiv
Kennan, George F., 310, 407–8
on Russia's China intentions, 676
Kennedy, Joseph P., lii, lix, 130–31, 593, 820, 827

book by, 827–28
on Bullitt, 828
Chamberlain meetings with, 828–29
on Churchill, 870
on FDR desire for war, 827–29
Forrestal on, 595, 595n12
on *The Gathering Storm*, 870
Hoover memorandum of conversation with,
827–29
presidential campaign (1940) and, 829
Kessel, Albrecht von, 344, 344n26
Khrushchev, Nikita S., 14, 21–23
Kienböck, Victor, 71–72
Kimmel, Husband E., 301–4
Pearl Harbor and, 307, 308–9
King, Ernest J., 220, 398
ABC-1 Agreement and, 217–18
against Far Eastern Agreement, 490–91
King, Mackenzie, 124, 203
Kirk, Alexander, 896
Kitty, Fred J., 39
Klein, Julius, ciin248, 577
Knowland, William F., 459–60, 494, 713
Knox, Frank, 178, 247
FDR and, 181–82
on German submarine encounters, 220, 249
on Japan's supposed military weakness, 295
Pearl Harbor and, 302–3
WW II and, 210
Konoye, Fumimaro, lxiv, lxix, 263
Emperor and, 267n11, 536n3
fall of, 277, 277n40
FDR's lost statesmanship relating to, 879
Grew for, 268–71, 275, 277, 279–80
for Japan's surrender, 560–61
Matsuoka against, 847
U.S.-Japan meeting rejection and, 264–76,
265n3, 267nn11–12, 834, 847, 879
Koo, Wellington, 702–3
Korea, 382–83, 391, 579, 736
at Cairo Conference, 739
Clark, M. W., for, 765–66
Congressional investigations about, 746–47,
759–62, 765
democracy for, 742–43
division of, 741–43
elections for, 747, 747n7
Hodge and elections in, 747–48
Hoover on history of, 737–38
Hoover visit to, 737
independence for, 739–40

Germany's planned attack on Russia under-
mines case for, 226
Hoover against, l-li, 215–16, 851
introduction of, in Congress, 212–13
Neutrality Act and, 214
passage of, 215–16
Poland and, 611–12
presidential power enhanced by, l-li, 212–15
Russia and, lii–liii, 451, 451n15, 823
as a war-promoting measure, l-li, 214–15,
249–50, 845, 851
Lenin, Nikolai, 8–9, 13, 16, 836
against capitalism, 19–20
on Communist fronts, 48–49
on dictatorship, 14–15
for international and intergroup strife, 19
for legislative bodies' subversion, 18
on religion, 15
terrorism of, 25n2
for war, 20
Leonard, Walter E., 79
Leopold III (king), 59–60
Lewald, Theodor, 65, 841, 842
Lewis, Clyde A., 754–55
Lewis, John L., 52
Liberty, xxix, 136
Lillick, Ira, cxn366
Lindbergh, Charles, xxxiii, lii, 199
Lindley, Ernest, 266
Lithuania, 145, 159, 462
Russia's brutality in, 420–21
Russia's treaties with broken, 159
Litvinov, Maxim, 20, 327
American Communists and, 894–95
against Anti-Comintern Pact, 67–68
deceptions of, 28–29, 83, 85, 893–94, 896–97
Molotov's replacement of, 141
against permanent peace with capitalism, 897
on Russia's annexations, 618
for Russia's diplomatic recognition by U.S.,
27–29, 893–94
Livingston, Walter R., lxxi, cviin329
Lochner, Louis, 65
on Hoover Child Feeding Program, 807–8
LoDolce, Carl G., 43
Logan Act, xlix
Long, Breckinridge, 225
lost statesmanship
Cold War a consequence of, 882
Mao Tse-tung's victory in China a result of,
882

See also FDR's lost statesmanship; Truman's
lost statesmanship
*Lost Statesmanship: The Ordeal of the American
People* (Hoover), lxxv, lxxvii, cixn362
on "gigantic errors" in Allied and American
diplomacy, lxix
as indictment of FDR/Truman diplomatic
follies, lxviii–lxix
Mason on, cxn376
new name for, lxxiii–lxxiv
preface to, 886–87
Lothian, Lord, 130, 200
China and, 184–85
on isolationism, 98–99
propaganda and, 201–2
Lovett, Robert A., 724–25
Lucas, Scott, 499
Lukasiewicz, Jules, 133, 594
Luxembourg, 751n5
Lyons, Eugene, lxxvi, cixn355
Lyttelton, Oliver, 310

MacArthur, Douglas, xv, lxiv, lxxx, lxxxiii, 173n1,
459
accomplishments of, 762
against Communism, 761, 763
on Communism's global threat, 763
Congress addressed by, 762–65
Congressional investigations about, 759
dismissal of, by Truman, 762n12, 762–65
against Far Eastern Agreement, 491–92
FDR against, 832–33, 833n1, 835
on Formosa, 754–55
Hoover meeting with, 832–35, 833nn1–3,
834nn4–6
Hoover memorandum concerning, 832–35,
833nn1–3, 834nn4–6
Japan and, 560, 560n1, 565, 763, 832–34,
833nn1–3, 834nn4–6
on Japan's postwar development, 763, 834
for Japan's surrender, 560, 560n1, 565
Korean War and, 752–57, 756nn16–17,
760–62, 764
Korean War military decisions by, 764
against Marshall, 834, 834n6
Martin, J. W., Jr., with, 760–61
military handicaps suffered by, in Korean
War, 755–56, 764
Nimitz against, 833
politics and, 761–62, 835
against Potsdam Agreement, 834

Poland (*continued*)
German-British negotiations over, 147, 147n18, 598–99
Germans expelled from, 472–73
Germany's conquest of, 155
Goering on invasion of, 146n17, 599n26
gold of, 601–2, 602n32
Harriman on, 473, 640–41
Hitler's pressure on, 128, 591–94, 599
Hitler's seizure of, xxv–xxvi, xxxii, 143n10, 147–48, 593, 597n19, 600–601, 603–4
Hull for, 621–22
independence for, 433–34, 552, 604
Lane on, 633, 638, 652, 657, 659–60
Lend-Lease Act and, 611–12
Lukasiewicz and, 133, 594
migrations within, 655–57
Mikolajczyk on, 620, 625–26, 657–58, 660
Molotov on, 640n2, 640–41
Moscow Conference about, 640–42
NKVD employed to repress, 648, 652, 653n12, 659
orphans of, 657
Paderewski and, 587n1, 587–89
partition of, 615–17, 640n2, 640–41, 649–50, 665
Pilsudski and, 590–91
political structure of, 74–75
population decrease in, 656
Potsdam Conference on, 558–59, 654–55
presidential campaign (1944) and, 661n1, 661–65, 662n2
propaganda against, 612–13
provisional government for, 465–66, 558–59, 652–53, 655
revision of boundaries of, 405–8
Ribbentrop and, 147–48
Rumania's gold from, 601–2, 602n32
Russia's invasion of, xxxii, 155, 600–602
Russia's partition of, 615–17
Russia's treaties with broken, 158
Second Moscow Conference on, 446
Stalin against, 652
Tehran Conference on, 405–8, 625–27
terrorism in, 656–59
treasury of, 601–2, 602n32
Union of Polish Patriots for, 619–20, 628–29
U.S. appeasement of Russia over, 614–16, 620–22, 625–32, 654–55, 664–65
Warsaw's children in, 588n3

West Poland, 408, 421, 446, 463, 467, 472–73, 558–59, 578, 655
Wilson, W., for, 590
See also Commission for Polish Relief; Mikolajczyk, Stanislaw; Molotov, Vyacheslav; Poland Guarantee; Potocki, Jerzy; Sikorski, Wladyslaw; Warsaw uprising (1944); Yalta Conference
Poland Guarantee
Britain and, xxvi, 862, 877
Chamberlain and, xxvi, 128–30, 862, 877
Churchill and, 867, 869, 877
FDR and, 129–33, 828, 856
as FDR's lost statesmanship, 877
Hitler versus Stalin and, 134, 877
Hoover's criticism of, xxvi, 862, 877
Japan related to, 134–35
Polish Americans
Biddle and, 509, 509n4, 612, 612n10
Dewey and, 661–62
FDR dishonesty with, 406–7, 662–64
for FDR reelection, 406–7, 661–63, 874
Hopkins on, 627
Lane on, 662–63
in presidential campaign (1944), 661–63
against Yalta Conference, 649–50
Polish Guarantee. *See* Poland Guarantee
Polish Relief Committee, 661
Political Action Committee (P.A.C.)
created by C.I.O, 52, 53
Hillman in, 52, 53
Pressman in, 52–53
Political Consultative Conference (P.C.C.)
Chiang Kai-shek and, 699–703
for China, 704–5
Chinese Communists against, 703
FDR for, 699
Kuomintang and, 709
Marshall and, 692–93, 703
Truman for, 699, 709–10
politics
Hoover political aspirations, xviii, xxxiv, xliii, lxxxixn6, xciiin81
Hoover political philosophy, xvii–xviii
MacArthur and, 761–62, 835
power politics, xxix–xxx, xlv, 851
U.S. WW II political costs, 854
war compared to, 833
See also specific countries
Ponger, Kurt, 43

postwar settlement
  leaders' punishment in, 540–41
  See also Germany postwar; Japan
Potocki, Jerzy
  on Bullitt, 132–33, 594
  dispatches from, 132–33, 593–94, 594n10
Potsdam Agreement
  Germany's postwar food and supplies affected by, 788
  MacArthur critical of, 834
  violations of, in occupied Germany, 802
Potsdam Conference, 318, 322
  Churchill versus Davies on, 551–52
  Council of Foreign Ministers and, 557
  Davies, J. P., versus Churchill on, 552–53
  on Japan, 560n1, 560–65, 562n11, 563n12
  Japan's surrender and, 561–63
  military situation at, 556–57
  organization of, 555n1, 555–56
  participants at, 555, 555n1
  on Poland, 558–59, 654–55
  Potsdam declarations, 557–65
  as Truman's lost statesmanship, 881–82
  Truman's version of plans for, 553–54
Potsdam Declaration. *See* Potsdam Agreement
Powell, Doris W., 39
Pratt, William V., 173n1
  on Hitler's purported U.S. invasion plans, 195–96
predictions (Hoover's)
  regarding anti-interventionism, 851–52
  about Atlantic Charter, 852
  about Britain, lii, 851, 852
  about Communism, 852
  about consequences of WW II for U.S., 852
  about freedom, 851, 883
  about Germany's attack on Russia, liii–liv, 851–52
  about Hitler, cin224
  about Hitler versus Stalin, 851
  about Lend-Lease Act, 851
  to O'Laughlin, liii
  about Russia, cin224
  about Stalin, li, 233, 676, 826
  about WW II, li, 825–26, 851–52
presidential campaign (1940)
  anti-interventionism during, 206–7
  Hoover participation in, xliii–xliv, 208–10
  Kennedy and, 829
  Republican national convention in, xliii–xliv

Stalin during, 207–8
presidential campaign (1944)
  Poland and, 661n1, 661–65, 662n2
  Polish Americans and, 661–63
presidential power, xxviii–xxix, xliv, 231
  amendments against, 213
  Atlantic Charter and, 251–54
  Congressional power compared to, l–li, 212–15
  declaration of war related to, l–li, 212–15, 231, 259, 845
  Far Eastern Agreement and, 693
  FDR and, 213, 248–49, 417–18
  FDR's undeclared war related to, 210, 217–20, 261, 844–46, 877
  Lend-Lease Act as enhancer of, l–li, 212–15
Pressman, Lee, 39, 52–53
Prince, Charles, 524
Problems of Lasting Peace, The (Hoover and Gibson), lvii, 539–43
Procopé, Hjalmar
  appeal from, 157
  Hoover discussion with, xxxviii, xcvn97
  proposal to Strauss from, xxxvii
propaganda
  from abroad, 199–203
  Atlantic Charter as, 251–52
  from Britain, 200–203, 823
  British Informational Services and, 201
  against Chiang Kai-shek, 669
  about Chinese Communists, 682
  from Churchill, 201–3
  Ciechanowski against, 612–13
  from Halifax, 200
  about Hitler's purported U.S. invasion plans, 190–97, 195n11
  Hoover warning against, 189
  Lothian and, 201–2
  organizations for, 197n17, 197–98
  against Poland, 612–13
  public opinion on WW II unaffected by, 204, 848–49
  revolutions and, 104–5
  truth compared to, 189–90, 201
  in WW I, 189
PSI. *See* Permanent Subcommittee on Investigations of the Committee on Government Operations
public opinion
  on Atlantic Charter, 252–53
  despite propaganda, 204, 848–49

in postwar studies of WW II, 888–89, 889nn2–3

See also Baldwin, Hanson W.; Chamberlin, William Henry; Ciechanowski, Jan; Creel, George; Fellers, Bonner; Gitlow, Benjamin; Grew, Joseph C.; Hoover, Herbert; Lane, Arthur Bliss; Morgenstern, George; Wilmot, Chester

revolutions, 16–17
  propaganda for, 104–5
Reynaud, Paul, 162
Rhee, Syngman, 748
Rhineland, 801
Ribbentrop, Joachim von, 597, 599–600
  for German-Soviet Pact, 142–45
  Molotov meeting with, 228n14
  Poland and, 147–48
Rich, Robert F., 240
Richardson, J. O.
  FDR meeting with, 288n23
  Leahy against, 307
Richey, Lawrence, xli, xcviin130
Rickard, Edgar, lxxixn6, cn200, ciiin268
  Magnum Opus and, lviii, lxii
Ridgway, Matthew B., 765
Riemer, Mortimer, 36, 40
Roberts, Owen J., 303
Roberts Commission Report, 306–8
Robertson, Walter S., 709
Robin Moor sinking, 256–57
Robinson, C. F., 868
Rockefeller, Nelson A., 249
Rogers, Edith Nourse, 697–98
Romer, Tadeusz, 640
Rommel, Erwin, 300, 334–35
Roosevelt, Eleanor
  Hoover's perceived snub of, xxxv–xxxvi, xcivn87
  Hoover's relief work (1940) and, xlvi
  quoted, xxxiv, xxxv, xciiin81
  relief offer from (1939), xxxiv–xxxvi
Roosevelt, Elliot, 368
Roosevelt, Franklin D. (FDR)
  against aggression, 171–72
  anti-isolationism of, 110n2
  Atlantic Charter and, 342, 508–9, 511–13, 516, 520–21, 609, 611–12, 613, 615–16, 628, 663
  for atomic bomb, 330–31
  background of, 529–30
  Chiang Kai-shek meeting with, 381–82, 409
  China on TARZAN, 398–400

Churchill aid request to, 219–20
Communists around, xcviiin137, 289n25, 289–90, 485, 874
confidence in Russia's postwar intentions, 433–34, 486–87
Currie with, 289–90
for de-empiring, 366n1, 366–70
Dies and, 32–33
diplomacy of, 414–15
dishonesty of, 406–7, 410–11, 501–2, 847–48, 857–58
Estonia and, 403, 406–7
Finland and, xl–xliii, xcvin119, 156–57
Finnish Relief Fund and, xl–xliii
German-Soviet Pact and, 149
Goering on, 841
"Great Design" of criticized, 415–18
Greece's promised aid from, 180, 181–82
Harriman and, 444–45, 447, 455
against Hitler, 171–72
on Hitler's purported U.S. invasion plans, 191–94
Hoover's avoidance of, xxxvi, xcivn92
Hoover offer of aid to, lvi–lvii, ciin249
Hoover radio speeches on, xxvii–xxviii, 113–14
Hoover relief work and, xxxiv-xxxvi, xxxix–xlii, xlvi–l, lvii, cn200
HUAC and, 32–33
Hull critical of, 876
ignorance of Communism, 32–33, 893
interventionist tendencies of, prewar, xxvii–xxx, xxxiii
IPCOG and, 773n2
on Japan, 294–96
JCS 1067 and, 773n2
Knox and, 181–82
Konoye's proposed meeting with, 264–76, 265n3, 267n11, 847–879
Lend-Lease Act proposed by, 211–12
against MacArthur, 832–33, 833n1, 835
Malta Conference, 455n3, 455–56
media criticism of Hoover allegedly instigated by, xlii, xcviiin136
Mikolajczyk and, 629–33, 642–43, 664
military preparedness assurance by, 173–74
military preparedness reduction by, 174–77
missing cablegram to Churchill from, 379
Molotov meeting with, 367, 368
Mothers and Fathers Speech by, 207–8, 210, 847, 847n3, 858, 874
against Mussolini, 171–72

Roosevelt, Franklin D. (FDR) (*continued*)

Schuschnigg, Kurt, 71
Second Cairo Conference, 373n1, 397n1
  Burma and, 398–99
  China at, 398–401
  information gaps about, 377
  Turkey and, 397
  See also Cairo-Tehran Conferences
Second Hoover Commission, lxx–lxxi
Second Moscow Conference, 317, 444–47
  Balkan States at, 445–46
  without FDR, 444–45
  on Poland, 446
  on Russia against Japan, 446–47
  Russian sphere of influence increased by,
    369–70
Second Quebec Conference, 317
  Churchill at, 390
  information on, 437–38
  Italy at, 441–43
  Morgenthau Plan at, 438–41, 441n12
  organization of, 437, 437n1
Second Washington Conference
  on atomic bomb, 330–31
  military situation at, 326
  participants at, 326, 326n1
  second front at, 327–30
  TORCH discussed at, 331–35, 333n1, 334n4
Second World War. *See* World War II
Second World War, The (Churchill), lxvi, 861
Secret Service protection request, xxxvi
Seeds of Treason (Toledano and Lasky), 485
Selzam, Edward C. W. von, 346
Senate (U.S.)
  on Atlantic Charter, 253
  Internal Security Subcommittee, 31, 31n4
  See also Congressional hearings and investiga-
    tions; *specific senators*
Service, John Stewart, 353, 684
Seven Decisions That Shaped History (Welles),
  741
Seventh Congress of the Communist Interna-
  tional, 18, 25
  U.S. Communist infiltration and, 84, 895
"Shall We Send Our Youth to War?" (Hoover),
  xxix–xxx, 136–37
Sheppard, Morris, 32
Sherwood, Robert E.
  on ABC-1 Agreement, 216
  on atomic bomb research, 330
  on Churchill against FDR, 455
  on Eden, 369

  on FDR, 351, 367–68, 406, 455, 486
  on FDR and Polish Americans, 406
  on FDR's confidence in Russia, 486
  on Germany's attack on Russia, 236–37
  on Harriman, 329
  Hiss and, 485
  on Molotov with FDR, 367, 368
  on second front, 327, 351
  on Stalin, 327, 329, 351, 486
  on Stalin's trusteeships from FDR, 351
  to Stimson, 236–37
  on Tehran Conference, 388
  on Unconditional Surrender policy, 340, 342
Shigemitsu, Mamoru, 560
Short, Walter C., 303–4
  Pearl Harbor and, 307, 308–9
Shtikov, Terentyi, 747, 747n6
Siberia, 393
Sikorski, Wladyslaw, 601, 604
  Atlantic Charter and, 611–16
  for CPR, 602
  death of, 623
  Stalin and, 606–7
  treaty with Russia signed by, 603, 604
Simivitch, Dusan, 179
Sino-Japanese treaty, 90
Sino-Soviet Treaty
  Hurley on, 678–79
  Russia's annexations after, 680
  Russia's violation of, 726
  Soong and, 678–79
  Wedemeyer on, 681
  from Yalta Conference, 678–80
SISS. *See* Subcommittee to Investigate the
  Administration of the Internal Security Act
  and other Internal Security Laws of the
  Committee on the Judiciary
Sixth World Congress of the Communist Inter-
  national, 17–18
Slovaks
  Czechoslovakia and, 73, 124–26
  independence of, 124–26
Smith, H. Alexander, 494
Smith, Paul, 57, 838
Smith, Truman, lii, lix, 65, 820
  on Germany's attack on Russia, 223–26
  on Germany's military buildup, 842–43
  predictions of, 223
Sobell, Morton, 44, 51
Sokolsky, George, lxv, lxxvi, 694
  against Far Eastern Agreement, 674

Truman, Harry S. (*continued*)
  background of, 529–30
  against Byrnes, 574–75
  Cabinet changes by, 530
  against Chiang Kai-shek, 699–700, 708–9
  Chiang Kai-shek and, 678–79, 699–702,
    725–28
  on China concessions to Russia, 679
  for China's democracy, 708–9
  for China's unification, 688n36, 688–89,
    708–11
  Chinese Communists and, 722–23, 727
  Far Eastern Agreement and, 532–33, 672, 685
  FDR compared to, 529–30
  FDR's foreign policy commitments not
    known by, 531, 534, 569
  Germany's postwar economic recovery and,
    803
  on Germany's attack on Russia, 239
  Hoover appraisal of, 529–31
  Hoover foreign policy advice for (1945),
    535–38, 537n4
  Hoover foreign policy advice for (1947),
    791–803
  Hoover postwar relief work for, 535, 576–77,
    577n2, 656–57, 695–96, 778–79
  Japan's surrender and, 561
  MacArthur's dismissal by, 762n12, 762–65
  MacArthur 's rebuke by, 755
  Magnum Opus and, lxxxiii
  Marshall and, 709–11, 719–20
  military situation facing, at outset of presi-
    dency, 530–31
  Molotov and, 653
  for P.C.C., 699, 709–10
  Potsdam Conference plans of, 553–54
  Russian policy of, 569–75
  for South Korea, 752–53
  for U.S.-Japan mediation, lvi
  at Wake Island Conference, 757
  Yalta Conference and, 652–53
Truman's lost statesmanship
  atomic bomb and, 882
  China and, 882
  cold war and third world war resulting from,
    882
  at Potsdam Conference, 881–82
  Japan and, 881
  Mao Tse-tung and, 882
Tsiang, T. S., 724–25
Turbulent Era (Grew), 268

Turkey
  Churchill on, 393
  Second Cairo Conference and, 397
  South Korea military aid from, 751n5
Turn of the Tide, The (Bryant), 334–35
Turner, Richmond K., 247
Twelve Years 1932–1944 (Hoover), lxi, 825–26

Ulmanis, Karlis
  background of, 76
  death of, 78n1
  democracy and, 78
  dictatorship of, 76–78, 78n1
Unconditional Surrender policy
  Baldwin, H. W., on, 343–44
  at Casablanca Conference, 340–41
  Churchill and, 340–41, 343
  Dulles on, 345–46
  FDR for, 340–43, 879–80
  as FDR's lost statesmanship, 879–80
  at First Quebec Conference, 342
  Germany postwar and, 880
  Hankey on, 340–41
  Hart against, 343–44
  Hopkins on, 340
  Kessel on, 344
  Leahy on, 341
  peace compared to, 344
  as political bankruptcy, 343
  public criticism of, 343–46
  Sherwood on, 340, 342
  Stalin on, 342
  at Tehran Conference, 342–43
  Wedemeyer against, 341–42
Union of Polish Patriots, 619–20, 628–29
Union of Soviet Socialist Republics (USSR).
    See Russia
Union of South Africa, 751n5
United Nations
  Acheson on, 760
  China's condemnation by, 758–59
  Clark, M. W., on, 753
  Communist infiltration of, 34n1, 37, 40
  Formosa and, 750
  Hiss and, 545
  Korea and, 747, 750–53, 751n5, 758–59, 760
  Korea's inadequate protection by, 751n5,
    751–52
  League of Nations compared to, 547, 547n6
  MacArthur for, 761–62
  Marshall on, 724–25

against North Korea, 751n5, 751–52
Stettinius for, 545
U.S. Korean War policy opposed in, 758–59
against war with China, 756–57
United Nations Charter
Atlantic Charter compared to, 546–47
China and, 697
Hoover's criticism of, 546–47
Russia's annexations and, 547
United Nations Commission, 747
United Nations Conferences, 315–16, 318,
545–47
United Nations Pact, 324–25
United Nations Relief and Rehabilitation Ad-
ministration (UNRRA), lvii, 442
United States (U.S.)
Europe's relation to, 60–61
"gigantic errors" of in foreign policy, lxix,
875–82
Hoover predictions about consequences of
war for, 852
as hope of the world, 104, 117–18, 177, 260,
860, 883
information suppression by government of,
402, 410–11, 411n5, 619n12
Mao Tse-tung and, 682–85, 686–89, 696–97
planned economy in, xxiii–xxiv
as redeemer nation and sanctuary, xxxi,
xxxiii, 234, 582, 860
Russia's appeasement by, 614–16, 620–22,
625–32, 654, 664–65, 859, 873
safety of, xxviii, xliv, xlv, lii, liii, 117, 190–94,
196, 258–60, 855, 872
South Korea, military manpower for, 753
South Korea, military withdrawal by, 746, 749
South Korea's support by, 766–67
war psychosis in (1941), li, liv
WW I entry into by, 848
WW II economic costs to, 787–88, 792, 802,
853–54, 898–99
WW II entry into by, 260–62, 848–49
WW II human losses by, 852
WW II moral costs to, 854–55
WW II political costs to, 854
WW II enemy prisoners taken by, 853
See also Hitler's purported U.S. invasion
plans; Polish Americans
UNRRA. See United Nations Relief and Reha-
bilitation Administration
U.S. See United States
U.S. aid

Chinese government without, 710
Germany's attack on Russia and, 230, 233
See also China Aid; specific countries
U.S. appeasement of Russia, 614–16, 620–22,
625–32, 654, 664–65, 859, 873
Ciechanowski against, 614–16, 621
over Poland, 614–16, 620–22, 625–32, 654–55,
664–65
Welles on, 614
U.S. army. See army (U.S.)
U.S. navy. See navy (U.S.)
U.S. Communist infiltration, lxxvi–lxxvii,
cixn358
Bonus March and, 25–26
Congressional investigations of, 30n3, 30–31,
31n4, 43n1
Dies on, 32n11, 32–33
fraudulent passports for, 31
Hull against, 894, 895
Russian Embassy support for, 32
after Russia's diplomatic recognition, 208–9,
893–95
Seventh Congress of the Communist International and, 84, 895
Soviet financing of, 31, 31n6
See also American Communists; American
Communist Party
U.S. government, Communist infiltration of,
lxv–lxvi, 31n4
in Army Signal Corps, 34n1
Bentley and, 35–36, 39, 43
cells for, 35–36
by Chambers, 35, 36, 37, 39, 45
Clark, M. W., on, 760
Congressional investigations of, 30n3, 30–31,
31n4, 34n1
court action on, 41–45
in Department of Agriculture, 35, 39–40,
42, 46
in education, 34n1, 37
espionage and, 32–36, 34n1, 37, 41–46
extent of, 46, 900–901
FDR attitude toward, 32–33, 353, 531, 874
Fifth Amendment and, 46–47
Finland and, xcviiin137
fronts for, 35
in GPO, 34n1
Hoover on, 34–47, 864–65, 892
interlocking subversion and, 34n1
in IPR, 34n1
job terminations and, 47, 748n10

White, W. A., against, 198
with "yellow races," 817–19
See also declaration of war; FDR desire for war; peace; World War I; World War II; *specific countries*
War Book (Hoover), xvi, xvii
arrangement of, 844
beginning of, lxi, lxii
development of, lxv
editions of, xvi, cixn362
Kemp's work on, lxiii–lxiv
new name for, lxviii
theses of, lxiii–lxiv, 830
as volume V of Hoover's memoirs, lxi, lxii
See also Lost Statesmanship; Magnum Opus
Ware, Harold, 35, 46
Warsaw uprising (1944)
Anders for, 637
Atlantic Charter related to, 634
Bierut in, 635
Bor-Komorowski for, 633–34, 636–37
Churchill and, 634, 636–39
deaths from, 637–38, 638n18
FDR and, 636–38
Germany's violence after, 638–39
Jews in, 639, 639n18
Lane on, 633, 638
Mikolajczyk for, 634–39
Stalin and, 633n3, 633–39, 639n18
Washington, George, 109
Washington Daily News, 758–59
Wavell, Archibald, 181, 182
Wedemeyer, Albert C., lxxx
Acheson and, 694–95, 728–29, 746–47
Butterworth and, 719
on China Aid, 723
China ambassadorial appointment canceled, 694–95
on China's fall to the Communists, 732
on Chinese Communists, 718–19
Connally and, 732
on FDR, 486
on Hitler's purported U.S. invasion plans, 196
on Japan's war declaration, 301–2
on Korea, 745–47, 746n3
on leak of U.S. Army war plans, 296n14
on Manchuria, 718
Marshall against, 691–92, 694–95, 719–20
Marshall and, 691, 713–14, 717
mission to China (1947), 717–20

Patterson and, 694
report by, on China, 717–20
report's suppression and, 719–20, 746–47
on Russia, 678
for second front, 327
on Sino-Soviet Treaty, 681
against TORCH, 333
against Unconditional Surrender policy, 341–42
Wedemeyer Reports! (Wedemeyer), 196, 301–2
Welles, Sumner
against aggression, 125, 130
on Germany's attack on Russia, 224n3, 224–25
Halifax and, xin217
Halifax meeting with, 282–83
against Hoover relief work, xlix, cn190
on Korea's division, 741
for Russian aid, 230
on U.S. appeasement of Russia, 614
on U.S.-British alliance, 253–54
Wells, H. G., 201
Western Hemisphere
ideological threats to, 115
military dangers to, 115–17
Weygand, Maxime, 162
Weyl, Nathaniel, 39, 40
Wheeler, George Shaw, 45
White, Frank C., 40
White, Harry Dexter, 440, 440n9, 531
White, William Allen, 197–98
White, William L., cxn380
Whitney, Courtney, 492
Wiedemann, Fritz, 838
Wilbur, Ray Lyman, xcn34, 249
Wiley, Alexander, 751n5
Willkie, Wendell, xliii–xliv, lvii, 431–32
anti-interventionism of, 207
on Berlin-Rome-Tokyo Axis, 210
Wilmot, Chester, 350, 366n1
Wilson, Hugh, 64, 838
Wilson, Woodrow
Atlantic Charter linked to, 252
Hoover book about, lxxi–lxxii, cviiin332
Hoover praise for, 139
for League of Nations, 93, 94
for Polish independence, 590
on Russia, 208
against Soviet Russia's diplomatic recognition, 24–25, 231–32
Winant, John G., 610–11